PIMLICO

366

THE PIMLICO ENCYCLOPEDIA OF
THE MIDDLE AGES

Norman F. Cantor is an internationally respected scholar of medieval history and the author of *Inventing the Middle Ages, The Civilization of the Middle Ages* and *Medieval Lives*. He is Professor of History, Sociology and Comparative Literature at New York University.

❖ *Contributing Editors* ❖

Half-title page: Seal of Henry Plantagenet. Title page: Coronation of Charlemagne.

THE PIMLICO ENCYCLOPEDIA OF
THE MIDDLE AGES

NORMAN F. CANTOR, GENERAL EDITOR

PIMLICO

Published by Pimlico 1999

2 4 6 8 10 9 7 5 3 1

Copyright © The Reference Works, 1999

Norman F. Cantor has asserted his right under the Copyright, Designs and
Patents Act 1988 to be identified as the general editor of this work.

First published in the United States of America in 1999 by Viking Penguin, a member of Penguin Putnam Inc.

First published in Great Britian by Pimlico 1999

Pimlico
Random House, 20 Vauxhall Bridge Road, London SW1V 2SA

Random House Australia (Pty) Limited, 20 Alfred Street, Milsons Point, Sydney, New South Wales 2061, Australia
Random House New Zealand Limited, 18 Poland Road, Glenfield, Auckland 10, New Zealand
Random House South Africa (Pty) Limited, Endulini, 5A Jubilee Road, Parktown 2193, South Africa
Random House UK Limited Reg. No. 954009

A CIP catalogue record for this book is available from the British Library

ISBN 0-7126-6407-6

This book is printed on acid-free paper.
Printed in the United States of America

Produced by The Reference Works
Harold Rabinowitz, Executive Editor
Ross Mandel, Managing Editor
Regan Park, Image Research

Writers
Linda Blum
Daniel A. David
George Milite
Andrew Milner
Charles Patterson
Jacob Segal
Ben Soskis
Veronica F. Towers

Copy Editors
Diane Lane-Root
Patricia Godfrey

Designed and Produced by
Bob Antler—Antler DesignWorks

Maps by Dana Elefant

For Art Resource—Daisy Hu

For Corbis-Bettmann—Norman Curry

Grateful Acknowledgments To
Eloise Jacobs-Brunner
Professor Michael T. Davis
Theodore Feder
Vincent Nichols
Leslie M. Pockell
Hugo Sarago
Professor Bonnie Wheeler

ABOUT THIS BOOK

The Middle Ages—a period covering roughly one thousand years of human history, from the fall of Rome to the dawning of the Italian Renaissance in the early sixteenth century—is an era under perpetual scrutiny and investigation. Concepts are constantly being reviewed and new insights revealed as new information is obtained and analyzed. This work reflects the most current information available on the medieval world. To assist readers in getting the full benefit of the text, a thoroughly detailed index is included. In addition to the regular alphabetical listing of subjects, the reader will find all article titles in bold type in the index; larger survey articles and entries on important subjects—many of which have been written by noted scholars—appear in red bold type.

Cross-references. Most articles contain the usual complement of cross-references; words in the text for which there are entries appear in small capitals. Many articles also have "signposts" at their conclusion (sample below). These direct the reader to other articles

See BERBERS, ISLAM, *and* ARAB *for North Africa ethnography; also* EGYPT, ABBASID DYNASTY, *and* FATIMID DYNASTY *for political background;* EXPLORATION *and* PORTUGAL *for more on exploration and geography.*

that may provide background information or carry the subject of the article forward in time or in detail. Readers will find that going through the encyclopedia from entry to entry using the signposts as their guide will provide a coherent presentation of a particular subject.

Sidebars. To enhance the exploration of this fascinating age, three types of sidebars have been incorporated into the text: **Illuminations,** which focus on writings from medieval sources; **Life in the Middle Ages,** which elaborates on some aspect of everyday life; and **Legend and Lore,** which details a product of the medieval imagination. Throughout the book, there are chronologies regarding the lives of important figures or milestones in particular fields of endeavor. Readers will find the entries organized with a uniformity that will allow easy access to information while providing an enjoyable reading experience.

Maps. There are also over 25 color maps, created specifically for this book, designed to give the reader a real sense of historical development and forgoing the blandness of the usual atlaslike approach to this era.

Scope. This work goes much further in its departure from the usual medieval reference text. Despite what students of medieval history are accustomed to reading, life did exist outside of Europe in the Middle Ages. Areas such as the West, Asia, and Africa were all home to a tremendous amount of activity during the Middle Ages. Their histories are covered in this encyclopedia. Similar attention is given to fields that are often overlooked: the sciences and medicine are covered in many entries, as well as in survey articles. Fields such as women in the Middle Ages and family life—both subjects of intense investigation in the last ten years alone—are covered in detail, with particular attention to how these subjects (and there are many others) have contributed to modern life. Every effort has been made in this work to illustrate, in word and image, the sometimes startling similarities between life today and life in the Middle Ages.

Consistency. In the course of assembling this reference work, the editors were often confronted with differences of approach and attitude—and sometimes even of fact—about many subjects. Often this was the simple result of this encyclopedia's being a collaborative effort, and two learned individuals are apt to have different yet justifiable views on many subjects. An attempt to present a coherent and consistent view of this turbulent period has been made, but the reader is forewarned that there are many controversies and mysteries surrounding much of medieval history.

Begin with the Introduction. The connection between the Middle Ages and our contemporary world has never been as clear as it is today. The fall of the Soviet Union, the denouement of the cold war, may be viewed as the closing chapter of the larger conflict that encompassed, in the broadest sense, the two world wars that occupied much of the twentieth century. Many commentators have recognized that current world history, and in particular current European history, seems to be as much or more an outgrowth of the geopolitics of the medieval period than of the four intervening centuries. This connection between our world and the world of the Middle Ages is the theme of Professor Cantor's introduction, "The Middle Ages: Discovery and Identity," which sets the stage for the work as a whole as well as describing the current state of medieval studies. Our advice to the reader, therefore, is to begin the journey into this fascinating era by reading the introduction.

Illumination from Hildegard of Bingen's Scivias *shows man as the center of the universe. The concept of the individual—with thoughts and emotions that mattered—emerged slowly during the Middle Ages.*

THE MIDDLE AGES:
DISCOVERY AND IDENTITY

Norman F. Cantor

"How obscure truth is, how deep it lies buried, how far from mortal sight it has plunged into the depths, how it will admit only a few, by how much work it is reached, how nearly no one ever succeeds, how it is dug out with difficulty and then only bit by bit."
—Andrew of St. Victor,
northern France, c. 1170

In 1984, the English translation of a novel (*The Name of the Rose*) written by an Italian professor of medieval literature, Umberto Eco, surprised the publishing world by becoming a phenomenal bestseller. The popularity of Eco's highly cerebral novel was no doubt due in part to its being cast in the form of a compelling murder mystery. The fourteenth-century setting and the context for the story illustrated one of the more dramatic conflicts within the medieval Church, namely, that between the papacy and the radical wing of the Franciscans (known as the Spirituals) over the nature of the Church and its role in society. When asked to explain his success, Eco modestly attributed it "to a period of renewed interest in the Middle Ages in Europe and America. The fact is," he went on to say, "everyone has his own ideas, usually corrupt, of the Middle Ages."

The parallels between our own age and certain periods of the Middle Ages fuel the many literary and cinematic efforts dealing with the era, demonstrating both the vibrancy and the relevance of those thousand years of human history—as well as how much misinformation abounds regarding that time. We who are witnessing the passage into a new millennium have been lulled by the unchanging map of the postwar period into forgetting the geopolitical consequences of human power struggles. We have been distracted by the glut of information from realizing that the same all-too-human categories of power, loyalty, identity, love, force, will, conquest, subservience, fear, intimidation, ecstasy—that all these forces at play during the medieval period are no less at play today. We dream that we are modern, but we are awakened from the fantasy by the shock of recognition as medieval feuds are being fought today in central Europe, and by the medieval garb worn by the counselors who flank the evil emperor in the *Star Wars* film trilogy.

But in order to recognize, one has to have at some time known, and this has been the job of historians, who today painfully append to Santayana's famous saying (about those forgetting the past being condemned to repeat it) the observation that one cannot forget a history one did not know in the first place.

Medieval Study Begins. By the middle of the nineteenth century it was evident to scholars, archivists, and not a few politicians that European libraries contained millions of documents surviving from the period of the Middle Ages, from about 400 to 1500 C.E. Few of these documents had been published; the majority had never even been read by modern historians. Most were written on parchment (mostly sheepskin) in a manuscript hand that, at least for the period from 800 to 1300, was easy to read since it resembled modern book print.

The Romantic movement of the early nineteenth century had given a positive view of the era that Italian Renaissance humanists around 1500 had disparagingly called the Middle Ages—an interregnum between the glorious peaks of ancient Rome and the classical revival of the fifteenth century. In western Europe, nationalist ideologies of the nineteenth century encouraged close study of the Middle Ages in western Europe because the modern European states were presumed to have had their foundations laid in the medieval world. Indeed, it was the subsidies provided by the governments of Germany, France, and England, successively, between 1840 and 1880 that initiated serious archival research and the publication of many medieval records. These government-sponsored publishing ventures led to the training of the first generation of professional medieval researchers and the systematizing of their techniques of examining and editing medieval records.

Until about 1930, the major focus in medieval research was on political and legal institutions, in accordance with nationalist assumptions and the goals of government patronage. This political and legal discovery of the medieval past was accompanied by the editing of literary texts—also inspired by the search for national origins in vernacular language and literature—and the painful beginnings of organizing the vast legacy of the medieval visual arts along the lines of a new discipline that combined literary history and art criticism.

In the quarter century after 1930, with some interruption during World War II, there was a broadening of interest in the medieval era toward new or renewed scrutiny of Christian spirituality and Church organization. The papacy and the Vatican library played a small role in this development, but some Catholic universities did join Protestant, Jewish, and secular historians in bringing into focus the religious sensibility of the Middle Ages in a way that made nineteenth-century enthusiasm for the Age of Faith appear naive and arbitrary.

After about 1955, vanguard work on the Middle Ages shifted toward a deeper social understanding—the family, the working class, women, childhood—and to the illumination of the "Other" of medieval times—heretics, Jews, and homosexuals. At the same time, literary scholars turned from just editing texts to interpreting them critically along the lines of currently fashionable schools of criticism, while art history matured into an immensely learned, resourceful, and affluent (if intellectually somewhat conservative) discipline.

This is where we are now in medieval studies at the dawn of the twenty-first century. A vast amount of factual data have been established and interpretive dimensions have been formulated. With the support of universities, learned foundations, the Catholic Church, and the old patron of medievalism, the national state, this process of discovery continues, although hampered by the shrinking of the pool of prospective medievalists, due mainly to the waning of Latin instruction in schools throughout the Western world.

Medieval Study Today. Current study of the Middle Ages encompasses broader geographical areas—with more work being done in the Americas and in the Far East and Africa—as well as broader historical concerns. No longer is a history of the Middle Ages simply a history of the kings and battles of Europe, and no longer do those very subjects exist unperturbed by developments elsewhere in the world, including in those strata of society that could not afford to have their exploits and foibles chronicled. Ironically, Europe emerges from this depth of study in bolder relief, with a more clearly defined character that endures into the modern era. Far from relegating Europe to a secondary subject, wider appreciation of the medieval world has fostered greater appreciation of what was special about medieval Europe.

At this point in time, what can we say about the identity of medieval Europe? What was this distinctive civilization, and in which cultural and social parameters did it operate? While many factors contributed to European medieval identity, I would focus on five as being of special importance: Gregorian reform and friar apocalypticism and eschatology; St. Louis's form of highly stylized and stable kingship; the medieval war against the Jews; aristocratic culture vented in vernacular romance; and middle-class sensibility expressed in gentrified English common law and Italian Renaissance humanism.

Gregorian Reform and Mendicant Eschatology. The reforms initiated by Pope Gregory VII and the Gregorian reformers, and by their successors in Christian militancy and apocalyptic eschatology, the Franciscan and Dominican friars in the thirteenth and fourteenth centuries, contributed greatly to formulating a European identity. In their conception, Europe was not just a place with a set of institutions and a cultural texture. It was in the process of becoming a holy society through the conversion—by force if necessary—of all its inhabitants to Christian faith and behavior. The Second Coming of Christ would thus be precipitated. This apocalyptic view of the Gregorians and the friars predicted that the world was entering its final stage—one of conversion and purification. The success of the holy men and women would mean the end of history and the return of Jesus to the golden throne of judgment.

European identity in this formulation becomes one of developing perfection through the elimination of bad people and sinful behavior, and the enshrinement of Europe as the City on the Hill ready for the return of the Lord. Perpetuated in Jesuit culture, and in the Calvinism of Geneva, Holland, England, Scotland, and Massachusetts, this identification of Europe as the holy society, secularized by the Enlightenment, took on great power in the modern revolutionary movements of both the left and the right. This idea of Europe's special quality was also used, never very convincingly, by British and French imperialism in the nineteenth and twentieth centuries.

Nor has this conviction played itself out. Europe can be seen as a spaceship hurtling through history carrying within it only the pure and moral, aiming for some glorious destination. How long will it be before the idea of European Union, born of the strategies of wily diplomats seeking to achieve a German-French rapprochement, and of bankers anxious to create a facade for agricultural and commercial neo-protectionism, returns to this volatile root of European identity? Europe the Good, Europe the Civilized, Europe, home of empowered saints—this idea will become active again, especially when Europe is faced by waves of non-European immigrants and by militant Islam at its doorstep.

St. Louis's Kingship. Louis IX's contribution to the shaping of European identity was in the kind of kingship he developed, which, because of his attractive personality and the power of his state, became the European model. It differed from the English monarchy, embattled by and enmeshed in constitutionalism and different also from the charismatic, activist Staufen German monarchy of Barbarossa and Frederick II, a reconstruction of primordial tribal leadership into messianic mania (so remarkably thereby anticipating Hitler).

The elevated image of St. Louis's French monarchy was that of the king in burnished armor, riding peaceably among the people, enforcing justice and assuring peace. Behind the golden visor, however, loomed the face of insatiable ambition and ruthless cruelty. Compared to his brother-in-law and nephew, Edward I, in England, St. Louis was far above his people. He may have condescended to allow regional assembly but it had no power outside of his will. Compared to the Staufens, St. Louis's was a quiet monarchy. Elaborate military expeditions were attempted far abroad; close to home, there was only the sly expansion of frontiers.

St. Louis's image became the ideal of European government in the later Middle Ages and permeated the very center of European identity—a society and culture ruled by admirable kings, quiet and forceful, secure and responsible, who occasionally resorted to the massive use of force and ruthless vengeance on resisters and questioners of unlimited power, enforcing thereby the dignity and estate of a monarchy with no earthly superior. This was the harbinger of the image of the European state, with its elegant rulers, its firm control, its elaborate councils, its chanceries and law courts, its benign face, and its capacity for occasional necessary terror.

This pattern was the result of 800 years of European political development. Of course, early medieval magic, Church sanction, feudal institutions, and Roman lawyers from the schools played their part, as well as intrinsic dynastic skills and family fortunes. But St. Louis brought all these components together and fused them into something new: European high statism that still exists and is central to European identity. Thus, neither radical democracy nor charismatic mania have endured for long in the European political arenas; the system always reconditions itself to the quiet high statism of St. Louis.

The War Against the Jews. Judeophobia (or anti-Semitism, to use the inadequate nineteenth-century, French-coined term redolent with the context of the Dreyfus affair) has its roots in three aspects of the ancient Mediterranean world: the struggle between Jewish Christianity and Pharisaic Judaism, reflected in the Christ-killing image of the Jews in the Gospel of Matthew; the four centuries of conflict, including intermittent street fighting, between the Gentile majority population of Alexandria, at first pagan and later also Christian, and the large Jewish minority in the metropolis; and fear of the Roman aristocracy in the first and second centuries C.E. toward the Empire's large Jewish minority (perhaps as much as 10 percent of the population) as well as resentment at Jewish rebellions—twice in Judea, once in Alexandria—that were not easily suppressed. All these factors flowed into the segregationist and repressive policy against the Jews in the Theodosian monarchy and the patristic view of the Jews held by St. Augustine and more negatively by Ambrose of Milan.

Faced with renewed Jewish freedom and prosperity in Muslim Spain, with the Carolingian protection of Jewish merchants and landlords whose economic services the Carolingians valued, and with the Judaizing adoptionist heresy in the Spanish March, Alcuin, mentor of Charlemagne, saw the Jews as an internal threat to the transformation of Carolingian lordship into the Christian Empire. Ninth-century bishops like Agobard of Lyons perpetuated this vision of the Jews as conflicting with the transformation of the Frankish empire into a distinctive Latin Christian society of Europe.

Identity results as much from negative discrimination as from positive assessments. Jews provided the negativity, the "Other," against which the identity of a Latin Christian Europe could be formulated. In the great wave of anti-Semitism that engulfed the Jews between 1050 and 1150, articulated by churchmen such as Cardinal Peter Damian, Abbot Gilbert Crispin of Westminster (speaking for his mentor, St. Anselm of Canterbury), St. Bernard of Clairvaux, and finally the propagators of the blood libel among the episcopal clergy of Lincoln around 1150, the transition inaugurated by Alcuin came to fruition: Europe would not tolerate Jewry. Europe was a Christian society, a Latin patristic civilization from which the Jews must be excised.

Given impetus by the Crusades, and sanctioned by the slow but steady withdrawal of protection of the Jews by royal governments as the developing Christian bourgeoisie made the Jews redundant as merchants and bankers, European identity through Judeophobia was forcefully defined by Bernard of Clairvaux around 1140.

The theme that the Jews intrinsically had no place in a European civilization committed to Latin Christianity found repeated affirmation in the period from 1890 to 1945, not only among the Nazis, but in French, Bavarian, and Polish Catholicism, and in the High Anglicanism of T. S. Eliot, who made this a central theme in his 1931 lecture tour of American campuses, addressing cheering throngs in football stadiums. (Stilled momentarily by the shock of recognition generated by the Holocaust, the anti-Semitic theme slowly and ominously seeped its way back into European public discourse.)

Aristocratic Culture. The stable and omnipotent monarchy of St. Louis provided for an aristocratic court in Paris, drawing upon the examples of Henry II of England, Eleanor of Aquitaine, and, more immediately, that of Frederick II in Sicily, which in turn imitated the elaborate literary and artistic presence of Arab potentates. Aristocratic culture in Europe became courtly; it became associated with, supported by, and in service to rich and powerful monarchies and remained so for the next five centuries. But what was distinctly European, and a powerful cultural and intellectual elaboration of the European mind, was the aristocratic culture that flourished between 1150 and 1250. This culture featured a high degree of family autonomy and bold choices in fostering the vernacular literature that received the patronage and encouragement of the higher nobility.

In the late thirteenth and fourteenth centuries the new universities encountered increasing internal conflict and then stultification because they lacked the mathematics and the institutional reward system to move on to what became the scientific revolution of 1600. Much more flexible were the vernacular romances. These stories in French and German—Chrétien's *Lancelot,* Wolfram's *Parzifal,* and the *Nibelungenlied*—showed a capacity for literary formulation of original psychological and sociological motifs not seen since the age of Augustus Caesar, far transcending the creative imagination and linguistic skill of the Latin schoolmen.

In distinct ways the vernacular romances contributed to the development of European identity. They legitimated private feeling and personal quests (of women as well as men), especially important when sensibility and behavior were being regularized by an ambitious Church hierarchy and an expanding monarchy. The romances established a channel of personal sensibility, autonomy, and artistic freedom within the suffocating colossus of Latin culture. This direction was of immense importance when we think of what Europe was to become. The vernacular romance saved Europe from becoming just another mandarin culture and valorized the exercise of transcendent imagination. In modern times, this intellectual freedom and exercise of creative imagination was to make Europe the envy of the world.

Middle-Class Sensibility. Other societies—Arabic, Chinese—developed thriving bourgeoisies as did Europe. Why, then, did Europe continue to thrive and expand after 1500, taking on the formation of the world capitalist commercial system in the sixteenth and seventeenth centuries, and culminating in republican democracy in the seventeenth and eighteenth centuries?

Two manifestations of late medieval middle-class culture are important in this regard. In England, the civil law of property, liability, contract, and debt between 1250 and 1350 became essentially separated from both royal power and ecclesiastical Latin culture. It was conducted by an autonomous bench and legal profession trained in their own London law schools. It functioned solely to serve the needs of the gentry and the merchant class and continued to operate with almost no impediment through war, civil war, intellectual conflict in the Latin schools, and the dynastic vicissitudes of monarchy.

Like St. Louis's style of monarchy, English common law provided stability and continuity, but these conditions were controlled and perpetuated from within the upper middle-class groups in English society. The stability, continuity, and high degree of personal autonomy within a relatively broad population base that distinguishes European capitalism was born in the English common law of the late Middle Ages.

The other manifestation of middle-class ethos that contributed to European identity was the neoclassicism of Petrarch and his successors among the Italian humanists. By directly connecting themselves and their world to Roman literature, politics, and lifestyle they falsified history, but ideologically took a great stride forward by portraying Europe as the reinvention of ancient Rome. This simplified view gave increased legitimacy to the secular side of European life. Further, the Italian humanists developed a secondary school classical curriculum that not only implemented their ideological program but also spread by the early sixteenth century all over Europe. It provided a common literate culture for the European elite—from Cracow to Edinburgh and Copenhagen to Rome—and a capacity for trans-European discourse that persists to the present day. This capacity, fostered by Renaissance humanism, is central to European identity.

An autonomous legal system and a classically based secondary school system were cultural facets that the English gentry and merchant class enjoyed by the sixteenth century. Not surprisingly, these denizens of an economically disadvantaged offshore island thought themselves quintessentially European—and still do today. Yet geography is destiny, and England, by virtue of its location, could not be the focal point for the continental European identity that emerged in the later Middle Ages. By developing a distinctive non-Roman legal system and by ideologically expressing anti-Roman juristic consciousness by 1450, the leaders of English society were moving toward a peculiar English identity that is distinct and separable from the general European model.

Henri Pirenne, the great Belgian medievalist, tried to locate the creative fulcrum of European identity in the Middle Ages in Flanders and northern France. With Brussels as the administrative center of the European Union, Pirenne's vision of European identity takes on a reinvigorated and updated form at century's end. Meanwhile, three German medievalists—Heinrich Mitteis, Percy Schramm, and Ernst Kantorowicz—and the English historian of medieval Germany Geoffrey Barraclough tried to locate the center of European identity further east, somewhere between Strasbourg and Berlin. They would be delighted by the events of 1989 that reunited Germany and restored it to its dominant position in Central and East Central Europe.

The politics of the twentieth century, scarcely less than the nineteenth, thus still affects the European perception and investigation of the Middle Ages. Some of this attitude has spilled over into the academic centers of medieval studies in the New World. But by and large, American medievalism has been inspired by two other desiderata. First, as Charles Homer Haskins and his disciple Joseph Strayer believed, the American republic's transition from an inchoate frontier society to a highly complex civilization parallels the medieval European experience. Second, American medievalists have searched for wellsprings of a romantic and idealistic consciousness that would inspire a vibrant counterculture against American capitalist materialism and technocracy. This quest, central to the first great American book on the Middle Ages by Henry Adams, written around 1905, remains a driving force in American medieval studies.

ABBADID DYNASTY

The kingdom founded by Abu al-Kasim Muhammad ibn Abbad in Andalusia, the rich province of southern SPAIN. Sensing the weakness of the UMAYYAD caliphate in Córdoba, ibn Abbad declared independence in 1023; he and his successors expanded the kingdom as the opportunity arose for the next 70 years. He began as a religious mayor and judge (*kadi*) of Seville, chief city of Andalusia—the kingdom is thus also known as the Kingdom of Seville. A poet not above using ruthless tactics against his enemies (he is said to have suffocated several of his adversaries in a steam bath), he established Seville as a center of Spanish Muslim culture.

By the time his son and successor, Abbad al-Mutadid, came to power after his death in 1042, the Umayyads had fallen. Al-Mutadid occupied Córdoba, but he concentrated on smaller prosperous principalities (*taifa*) that became available with the fall of the Umayyads. Hoping an alliance with the ALMORAVIDS would prevent the Christian RECONQUEST of Spain, al-Mutadid's allies deposed him in 1095, ending the Abbadid era and a golden age of Muslim culture.

ABBASID DYNASTY

The dynasty of Muslim caliphs that ruled much of the Muslim world from 750 to 1258. Descended from Abbas, paternal uncle of the prophet MUHAMMAD, the Abbasids opposed the UMAYYAD policy of discrimination against non-Arab Muslims; they worked in secret against the Umayyads for decades before the opportunity arose to depose the caliph, Marawan II, at the Battle of the Zab in 750. The Umayyads retained power only in SPAIN, establishing the CALIPHATE of Córdoba.

First under Abu al-Abbas (known as al-Saffah), proclaimed caliph in Kufa (in southern Iraq) in 750, and then under his brother and successor, Abu Ja'far al-Mansur, installed in 754 in BAGHDAD, the new capital, the power in the kingdom shifted to the religious leader, the imam. Although the Abbasids were originally Shi'ites, and their opposition stemmed from their theology, the Abbasid rulers eventually adopted the religious views of the Sunnite majority. (*See* ISLAM.)

The empire grew, reaching its pinnacle during the reign of HARUN AL-RASHID (786–809), during which it experienced a golden age of art and literature. While the acceptance of non-Arab Muslims into the social structure widened the appeal of the caliphate, it also put power into the hands of viziers not familiar or friendly to the caliph, which eroded his influence.

The authority of the Abbasid caliph was lessened by the establishment of the separate FATIMID caliphate in EGYPT in 969. By the time the SELJUK TURKS conquered the empire in 1055, the caliph exercised only spiritual authority over Muslims. The MONGOL conquest of Baghdad in 1258 finally ended the reign of the Abbasids.

Minaret of the Great Mosque of Samarra, Iraq, built 847 to 861 by al-Mutawakkil, a great patron of the sciences.

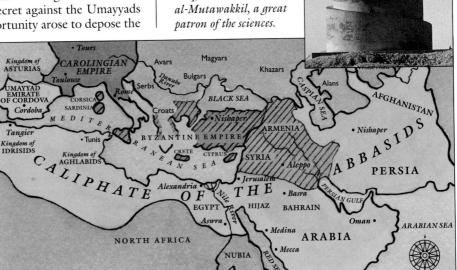

The Mediterranean World in 800 C.E.
The Roman Empire had given way to a world dominated by three major powers: Islam in the south, consisting largely of the Abbasids, with the Umayyads in Spain on the front lines; the Western Christian kingdoms, the largest of which being the Carolingian; and the Eastern Christian Byzantine, under constant attack from the south.

ABELARD, PETER

Though celebrated for his correspondence and long love affair with Héloïse, Peter Abelard (1079–1142) was an important medieval thinker who influenced the SCHOLASTIC movement and a stalwart advocate of independent and progressive thinking. Although he was condemned for his affair, his ideas—and his seemingly arrogant manner—were what drew the most criticism during his lifetime

Early Life. Peter Abelard was born into an aristocratic family in Le Pallet, a village in BRITTANY, in 1079. He showed himself to be an exceptional student early on, and he was sent to study in CHARTRES and then to PARIS to study with Anselm of Laon. He was quick and gifted, but he was also extraordinarily self-centered. He would often engage his teachers in debate that deteriorated into vituperative attacks. No one, least of all Abelard, questioned his superior intellect, but he had already collected a number of enemies by the time he fell in love with Héloïse in Paris.

After the affair with Héloïse was uncovered, Abelard retired to monastic life, first at a small Breton monastery and then at St.-Denis. He was bored and restless, and took comfort in writing. Abelard followed the Scholastic school, which sought to find ways in which philosophical and religious ideas could complement each other. He was hardly an opponent of the Church—"I do not wish to be a philosopher in order to contradict Paul," he said, "nor an ARISTOTLE in order to be cut off from Christ"—but he believed strongly in the importance of inquiry. His views on Church doctrine, particularly on the Trinity, were branded as HERESY, and he was summoned to a Church council in Soissons in 1121. He was found guilty, briefly imprisoned, and his works were burned.

Abelard and Héloïse (left), from Edward IV's royal manuscript, 1483.

Later Work. In 1122, Abelard obtained permission to establish the oratory in Le Paraclet near Paris. At Le Paraclet, he established a convent, which Héloïse joined in 1129, and wrote a series of essays, sermons, and hymns. His PHILOSOPHY stressed the importance of the individual—a personality with flaws as well as virtues.

His religious writings were still being questioned, however. St. BERNARD OF CLAIRVAUX, the influential CISTERCIAN monk, strongly condemned Abelard's works. Bernard was as formidable a personality as Abelard, and his condemnations led to Abelard's appearance once again before a council, this time at Sens, in 1141, where he was forced to recant and more of his works were burned.

The abbot of the monastery at Cluny, PETER THE VENERABLE, brokered a truce between Abelard and Bernard, and Abelard, by now quite ill, retired to Cluny. He died there in 1142.

ABELARD AND HELOISE

The story of Abelard (1079–1142) and Héloïse (1101–1164), one of the most famous romances in history, has often overshadowed the lovers' lives. The love affair has, over the centuries, inspired great works of prose and poetry, such as Alexander Pope's "Eloïsa to Abélard." Abelard was a noted scholar, key to the eventual founding of a UNIVERSITY in PARIS. Héloïse was abbess of the convent of Le Paraclet and instrumental in the establishment of several others. (*See* UNIVERSITIES.)

The Affair. Héloïse was the daughter and niece of church officials at the cathedral of NOTRE DAME in Paris. She was intelligent, though not as headstrong as Abelard. Because of her family's position, she was afforded better educational opportunities than many women of her time. (*See* WOMEN IN THE MIDDLE AGES.)

In 1120, Abelard, then teaching at Notre Dame, was hired to tutor the young Héloïse. Although the age difference between them was more than 20 years, the two fell in love. Given their respective positions, they felt compelled to keep their love secret; they eventually secretly married. Héloïse gave birth to a child in 1121; afterward, however, the relationship could no longer remain hidden. Héloïse's father, Fulbert, was so enraged that he sought revenge against the haughty Abelard, hiring two men to beat and castrate him. The

---

ILLUMINATIONS

Abelard's *History of My Calamities* is the finest medieval autobiography after Augustine's *Confessions*. In it, he delves into the idiosyncrasies of his personality and lays bare his faults.

But some of the most touching passages deal with his affair with Héloïse: "We were united first in the dwelling that sheltered our love, and then in the hearts that burned with it. Under the pretext of study we spent our hours in the happiness of love, and learning held out to us the secret opportunities that our passion craved. Our speech was more of love than of the books which lay open before us. Our kisses far outnumbered our reasoned words."

child born from their union was raised by Abelard's sister and eventually became a cathedral canon.

The Correspondence. Disgraced, Abelard sought refuge in the Benedictine monastery of St. Denis, and Héloïse entered the convent at nearby Argenteuil. They would soon both be in Le Paraclet, but during the time they were separated, the pair carried on a lively correspondence. Some believed Héloïse's letters had been authored by Abelard, using her as a literary device. Modern scholarship, however, views the letters as genuinely from Héloïse's pen.

Like Abelard, Héloïse died at age 63. The pair were buried together at Le Paraclet, but were reinterred at the Père Lachaise Cemetery in Paris in 1817.

ABU BAKR

T he first caliph (ruler) of ISLAM (b. 573), ruling from 632 until his death in 634. A wealthy merchant from Mecca, he became one of the prophet MUHAMMAD's early supporters; Muhammad was to marry his daughter, Aisha. He accompanied the prophet on the Hegira (Muhammad's flight from Mecca in 622 C.E.) and became his closest adviser.

Following Muhammad's death, Abu Bakr assumed control of Islam, brushing aside (or crushing by force) any dissension and creating a united Islam. This permitted him to spread Islam to every corner of Arabia, conquer Persia, and bring Islam to the brink of defeating BYZANTIUM and capturing Palestine, a mission fulfilled by his general, Khalid ibn al-Walid, known as the Sword of Allah. Before he died, Abu Bakr appointed a successor, Omar (I) ibn al-Khattab. He was buried in Medina next to Muhammad. (*See* ISLAM.)

ACCURSIUS

K nown as Accursius the Glossator (c. 1182–1260), an Italian jurist whose notes, or "glosses," on the Code and two other works by JUSTINIAN became the basis of medieval LAW. Born in FLORENCE, Accursius became a professor of law at Bologna, and he remained there until his death.

Accursius based his work on the work of earlier law theorists of Bologna, beginning with Irnerius and his student, GRATIAN, who composed the first code of canon law (laws regarding the administration of the Church and Church-controlled property), and the "Four Doctors"—Bulgarus, Martinus, Iacobus, and Hugo—all of whom took as their starting point the JUSTINIAN CODE. These works, though they accepted the authority of the Church, ironically, proscribed the power of both pope and king severely by setting down careful, rational rules for a wide variety of situations. BERNARD OF CLAIRVAUX was typical among ecclesiasts in decrying the fact that "the courts of Europe ring with the laws of Justinian and no longer with the laws of God." By the thirteenth century, the works of Accursius took on the aura of sacred texts, preventing the law from adjusting to new situations, leading to the decline of the teaching of law in ITALY. (*See* LAW.)

ADELAIDE, ST.

S aint Adelaide (931–999) was one of the most influential figures in medieval GERMANY. As the wife of OTTO I THE GREAT and regent for OTTO III, she devoted much of her time to strengthening the role of the German church in what became the HOLY ROMAN EMPIRE.

The daughter of Rudolf II of BURGUNDY, she was born in 931 and married the Italian king Lothair in 947. Lothair died in 950 and Adelaide was imprisoned by rival forces. She escaped and sought Otto's help in regaining her throne. He succeeded in September 951 and married Adelaide three months later.

As empress of the Holy Roman Empire, Adelaide deftly forged a stronger alliance with the Church. After Otto's death in 973, she influenced her son, Otto II, who before his death in 983 named her regent to Otto III. After Otto came of age in 994, Adelaide devoted her life to founding convents and monasteries. (*See* MONASTERIES AND MONASTICISM.)

ADELARD OF BATH

A delard (1090–1150) was an English cleric who served as an important bridge between the SCIENCE of Greco-Arabic culture and the Christian society of northwestern Europe.

Adelard traveled widely and was exposed to the science and culture of many areas from ENGLAND to Asia Minor. He translated many scientific works into LATIN, including an Arabic version of Euclid's *Elements,* which became a standard mathematics textbook in the West for centuries, and important mathematical works of al-Khwarizmi and Abu Ma'shar, making the best of Arab mathematics available to the rest of Europe. (*See* ARABIC LANGUAGE AND LITERATURE.)

Adelard is also credited with introducing to the Western world the astrolabe, an astronomical instrument developed from primitive Greek versions largely by Arab astronomers, for fixing the position of stars, telling time, and determining latitudes and altitudes.

ADHEMAR OF MONTEIL

A leader of the First CRUSADE. Adhémar (955–1098), bishop of Le Puy, was a friend of Pope URBAN II and was appointed in 1096 by the pope at the COUNCIL OF CLERMONT to serve as the pope's personal envoy to the crusaders. He traveled with the army of Raymond of Saint-Gilles, but was looked to as a leader by all the crusaders. As such, he often rallied the soldiers during difficult times and preached to them when their resolve waned.

Adhémar negotiated an alliance with the Byzantine emperor ALEXIUS COMNENUS, which resulted in the conquest of NICEA from the SELJUKS in 1095. He also kept the crusader armies unified under the leadership of BOHEMUND I during the siege of Antioch, resulting in the fall of the city and the establishment of the first crusader kingdom. He then rallied the crusaders for their final campaign, the conquest of Jerusalem, but he fell ill and died en route in 1098.

ADRIAN IV

A drian IV (c. 1100–1159), whose original name was Nicholas Breakspear, was the only Englishman ever to serve as pope. He reigned from 1154 to 1159, during a time when the Church and the HOLY ROMAN EMPIRE were vying for power; as with most popes of the period, he achieved only moderate success in keeping relations between these two powers peaceful and harmonious.

As a young man Breakspear joined a community of priests near AVIGNON, eventually assuming the position of abbot. A strong preacher and a shrewd leader with good administrative skills, he quickly rose through the ranks, becoming cardinal of Albano in 1149. In this capacity, he set about reorganizing the Church in Scandinavia. He was, more than anyone else, responsible for the establishment of the Catholic Church in NORWAY. (See CHRISTIANITY; PAPACY.)

His Papacy. In 1154, Breakspear was chosen to succeed Anastasius IV as pope and took the name Adrian IV. One of his first acts was to bring order to ROME, where citizens were fighting for independence. He placed the city under an interdict (prohibiting the entire region from partaking of Church sacraments). This so overwhelmed the city that the revolt collapsed.

Later, Adrian crowned FREDERICK I BARBAROSSA Holy Roman Emperor. At first the two were allies, but their relationship soon soured. The rest of Adrian's reign was focused on building papal strength and minimizing imperial power over the Church. Although an able administrator, Adrian could not reach a compromise with Frederick. Adrian died in 1159, and it would

be another 18 years before Frederick would make peace with the Church.

Adrian hired JOHN OF SALISBURY, an Englishman educated in PARIS, as one of his secretaries. In his book *The Papal History,* John offers an account of papal bureaucracy in Adrian's time, but highlights the importance of Adrian's pontificate. It depicts the era when canon lawyers and similar bureaucrats came to dominate papal administration and policy.

AELFRIC

A tenth-century English monk (c. 955–1010) considered the greatest prose writer of his time. Aelfric's works are basically instructional in nature, focusing mainly on religious teaching. He also wrote nonreligious works, however, including his *Latin Grammar,* which was used for generations. (In the seventeenth and eighteenth centuries he was known simply as "Grammaticus.")

Aelfric was born around 955 and served as a monk in Winchester and Cerne Abbas. He later became abbot of Eynsham, near Oxford, where he spent the rest of his life. Although his works were essentially teaching tools—such as his *Colloquy,* in which a teacher instructs novices in several occupations—the clarity of his prose and his stylistic expertise were exceptional for the period. (*See* MONASTERIES AND MONASTICISM.)

AETHELFLAED

T he oldest daughter of ALFRED THE GREAT, Aethelflaed (d. 918) ruled the semi-independent English province of Mercia. Her leadership earned her the name "Lady of the Mercians."

In about 886 she married ETHELRED, who went on to become alderman (nobleman) of Mercia. Together they organized the defense of Mercia against incursions by the Danes. When her husband fell ill and died in 911, Aethelflaed continued to govern Mercia by herself. During her rule she proved to be a woman of great political, diplomatic, and military skill. She successfully played the Danes, Scots, and Welsh off against each other, and, with her brother, Edward the Elder, king of WESSEX, she directed military expeditions against the Welsh and Danes.

She and Edward captured Derby, Leicester, and York and recovered all the Danish-held lands south of the Humber River. With Edward, she also constructed a series of fortresses against the Danes, including those at Runcorn, Stafford, and Warwick. After her death in 918, Mercia was fully incorporated by Edward into the kingdom of WESSEX. (*See* ENGLAND.)

AFRICA

The continent of Africa comprised a third of the known world for Europeans during the Middle Ages. Though the full size of the continent had been known by seafarers since antiquity, only the northern portion of the continent and northeastern rim bordering on the Mediterranean and Red Seas were inhabited. Occasional forays into the Sudan and the Sahara convinced many that the rest of the continent was uninhabitable. Serious EXPLORATION of the lower half of the continent did not take place until Portuguese explorers, encouraged by Prince HENRY THE NAVIGATOR and seeking to outflank the Moors in North Africa, fielded expeditions down the western coast of the continent in the late Middle Ages.

North Africa. Much of the history of the Middle Ages deals with the inhabitants and developments of North Africa (the Maghreb), particularly as it relates to the spread of ISLAM across the northern rim of the continent and into SPAIN. Most ancient civilizations gave way to societies based on Christian, Islamic, or BYZANTINE ideals. A notable exception was the Copts of EGYPT, who blended ancient Egyptian, Hellenistic, and Christian notions into a unique religious amalgam that had little trouble incorporating Islam following the Muslim conquest of Egypt in 641. The Copts remained a generally Christian sect whose fortunes followed the ebb and flow of Islamic society through the medieval period.

By the time Islamic civilization was established across North Africa in the late seventh century, vestiges of the societies created by the Romans; by the VANDALS, who ruled from their capital in Carthage; and by the Byzantines, who destroyed the Vandal kingdom in 534, made North Africa a hospitable area for culture and commerce. Under the UMAYYADS, North Africa enjoyed the benefits of a centralized administration and the support of the local populace, who saw ISLAM as heir to the glory of the Roman Empire. The BERBERS in the northwest and the Nubians in the south, both descendants from central African tribal stock, gladly accepted Islam and were important allies in Islam's military campaigns there.

Central Empires. Finding that their status as second-class Muslims (*dhimmis*) was not likely to change, conquered peoples remained cool toward their Islamic masters and sought independence whenever the op-

portunity arose. Thus, following the ABBASID revolution in 750, and again with the establishment of the FATIMID dynasty in the ninth century, and following such upheavals as the CRUSADES and the BLACK DEATH of 1348, independent principalities sprang up in the outer portions of the prevailing empire. The Empire of Ghana, for example, flourished in a semiprimitive state in the Niger River basin for seven centuries until destroyed by the ALMORAVIDS in 1076. The Empire of Mali, consisting of a confederation of Malinke tribes, dominated the banks of the Niger and spread to in-

Africa consists mainly of Egypt, surrounded by the Mediterranean, the Atlantic, and Arabian Sea, in a 12th-century atlas by Islamic geographer al-Idrisi.

clude all of the western Sudan, reaching its height during the reign of Sundiata, who died in 1255. The influences of these African cultures were felt in the artistic output of Islamic centers like Kairwan and Fez.

The opening of trade routes to the Far East and the brisk trade Europeans did in African salt, gold, and slaves slowly brought the deepest, most isolated portions of the continent to light and out of the Stone Age. The rise of the Kingdom of Gao in the fifteenth century, comprised of both Italian settlers and Nigerian tribespeople, marked the beginning of the first serious meeting of European and African cultures.

See BERBERS, ISLAM, and ARAB for North Africa ethnography; also EGYPT, ABBASID DYNASTY, and FATIMID DYNASTY for political background; EXPLORATION and PORTUGAL for more on exploration and geography.

At Agincourt, the victorious English used longbows, which they had seen used by Welsh warriors a century earlier. They were often as tall as a soldier and they required great strength to fire, but they could be fired rapidly by a solitary archer or by many in unison, producing a hail of arrows.

The crossbow, also used by the English at Agincourt (depicted in miniatures from Chronicles of Froissart*), was the principal weapon of the French. Requiring two stationary men and several minutes to load, it fired a bolt with enough force to pierce armor, but could rarely be fired twice by one soldier in a battle.*

AGINCOURT, BATTLE OF

The Battle of Agincourt, waged on October 25, 1415 (St. Crispin's Day) and immortalized in Shakespeare's play *Henry V*, saw a decisive British victory over FRANCE at the start of the second round of English conquests in the HUNDRED YEARS' WAR. English territorial gains in the fourteenth century had been undone by a French resurgence in the latter part of the century. In 1415, HENRY V reinitiated hostilities because of internal French disunion and the mental instability of the French king, Charles VI. The Battle of Agincourt marked the beginning of this campaign; it culminated in the Treaty of Troyes (May 21, 1420) in which Henry was made French regent and CHARLES VI's heir. *(See* HUNDRED YEARS' WAR.*)*

Henry invaded France with a large (10,500 strong), well-equipped and provisioned army in order to make good his claim on the French throne. He first attacked the Norman port city of Harfleur, which held out for five weeks, much longer than Henry had anticipated; it cost him 40 percent of his men, most through dysentery. Despite these setbacks, Henry chose to march his tired army 120 miles to the port city of Calais in extremely poor weather conditions. French occupation of the crossing over the river Somme forced the British army inland. When the French and English armies met at Agincourt, the latter was reduced to 6,000 exhausted men who were severely outnumbered by the French. The English had no choice, however, but to fight their way through the French to reach Calais.

The Battle. Henry's army consisted of some 900 unmounted men-at-arms in the center and 5,000 archers on the flanks. The British archers built protecting hedges of sharpened stakes in order to foil the French plan to disperse them with cavalry. The French army's first line consisted of 8,000 men-at-arms on foot and 1,600 cavalry. The second line was composed of 3,000 to 6,000 dismounted men-at-arms and 4,000 archers and crossbowmen. The third line consisted of the remainder of the 20,000 French fighters as cavalry. *(See* ARMS AND ARMOR; WEAPONRY.*)*

The French plan failed from the very start. The French cavalry on armored HORSES failed to break up the English archer lines, and the archers were able to launch devastating salvos into the French lines. The retreating French cavalry collided with the advance of the 8,000 men-at-arms in the first battle line. The confusion was complicated by the mud-soaked field; the charge had little energy when it met the English. Despite this, the French advance made an initial impression on the English lines, and the outcome of the battle could have been different had Henry been killed by the blow to the head he received. The armored French attack, however, soon bogged down in the mud. British archers engaged the French KNIGHTS in hand-to-hand combat with hatchets and swords. Unable to cope with this new unarmored opponent, many French were killed or taken prisoner.

The charge of the second French line did not change the momentum of the battle. The woods on either side of the battlefield made for a small area in which to fight. The French soldiers found themselves in dangerously close quarters, and their proximity to each other made it difficult to even use their weapons; fallen knights were unable to rise. Much of the immense French army thus never engaged. Their archers and crossbowmen had no effect on the battle whatever, and only a few hundred men from the third battle line entered the battle. The others prudently fled the field.

The Aftermath. The entire Battle of Agincourt lasted only one hour, but the defeat was total for the French. Six hundred nobles were killed, and one thousand captured—6,000 total dead. The English losses came to 300 men dead. The battle ended with an egregious act of violence by Henry V, who ordered that the French prisoners be killed lest they rebel. When the English men-at-arms refused this unchivalrous action, the prisoners were massacred by the British archers.

After the battle, the British reached Calais on October 28, 1415 and sailed to ENGLAND in November. The Agincourt campaign, in purely strategic terms, was more a raid in force than a systematic policy of conquest. The battle had, however, significant results. It confirmed Henry's genius at warfare, and solidified English support for him. The defeat intensified the French resolve to defeat the English, although the French were weary of battle; the loss of so many knights and noblemen crippled their war effort. Furthermore, the battle was another sign of the increasing importance of archery—both the longbow and the crossbow—and the continuing obsolescence of the mounted knight, marking the end of feudal warfare.

AGNES, EMPRESS

W ife of HENRY III, Holy Roman Emperor. Agnes (1024–1077) was born to William (V) the Pious, Duke of AQUITAINE, and Agnes of Aquitaine. Both mother and daughter had colorful lives. Both attained positions of power that they protected for their sons, underscoring the inability of women during the Middle Ages to lay claim to land, position, or power on their own outside of marriage.

Following the death of William, the elder Agnes married Geoffrey Martel of Anjou and convinced him to mount a campaign against Aquitaine, at the end of which she was left in power, ostensibly as regent until her son came of age. She remained in power, however, well past his majority; her reign ended in 1058, only by the combined efforts of Geoffrey and Agnes's (the elder) youngest son.

Agnes brokered the marriage of her only daughter, Agnes, to the Holy Roman Emperor, HENRY III. They were married November 1, 1043. Henry died in 1056 and Agnes served as regent for her minor son, HENRY IV. But, like her mother, Empress Agnes refused to relinquish the throne when her son came of age. She ruled until 1062, when she was ousted by two German bishops. She lived in ROME, a staunch supporter of POPE GREGORY VII, until her death in 1077.

AGRICULTURE

T he dependence of an empire on the production of FOOD—to feed its urbanized citizens, to finance its centralized bureaucracy, and, most of all, to support its army—has made the subject of agriculture of paramount importance to the fortunes of many a medieval kingdom. Three factors played important roles in the agricultural vitality of most areas: the availability of labor, the arability of available land, and the management of land and resources as provided by the prevailing authorities. In the absence of serious manufacturing, agriculture stood alongside international trading (and possibly military plunder) as the chief source of revenue and wealth during the Middle Ages. Agriculture developed along different lines in each of the three major geopolitical areas of the medieval world: BYZANTIUM, the Arab world, and western Europe.

Byzantium. The BYZANTINE Empire inherited many of the agricultural techniques developed by the Romans, although they were mainly suited to the fertile and relatively soft soils of southern ITALY. As the empire contracted in the wake of the Arab conquests, it found itself more dependent on the harder soils and shorter growing seasons of ANATOLIA and the Balkans. The Roman traditions, collected by the Byzantines in the tenth century in a series of works known as the *Geoponica*, gave the Byzantines a foundation on which to build, but several changes were necessary for successful agriculture in the harsher climates of the empire. Technologically, the swing plow of the Romans, which consisted of little more than a metal-tipped stick dragged over the light soil, gave way to the metal plow, typically pulled by oxen and capable of turning rockier, claylike earth. The Byzantines developed a number of tools, ancestors to the hoe, the sickle, and the rake. These made agriculture profitable in the areas of Asia Minor that were the seat of the empire, but which did not become vital to the empire's existence until it was deprived of its African and Italian holdings.

In its warmer dominions, Byzantium adopted the Roman practice of forming great estates to be administered by lords and worked by slaves or fiefs in a FEUDALISTIC manner. In the colder areas, however, where large estates were impractical and unprofitable, a free peasant class arose and developed an agrarian culture based on a combination of agriculture and animal husbandry. The integration of these two types of farming increased the fertility of the land by providing an adequate supply of fertilizing manure; it also promoted a sense of community, since most farmers required easements of their neighbors to take their herds to distant pastures for grazing. (*See* FEUDALISM.)

When the boundaries of Byzantium withdrew, the

ruling class attempted to institute a feudal system in ANATOLIA. They were met with severe resistance by the free peasant class, now essential for providing labor to an empire deprived of its sources of slaves. A compromise was reached in the Code of Agriculture promulgated by Emperor LEO III the Isaurian in 726, which recognized both the authority of the manor estates and the rights of a free peasantry. This code remained in force for eight centuries, providing an environment in which productivity could flourish. Byzantium benefited from its proximity to the East by both new crop options and new mechanical methods. This independence enjoyed by the peasants encouraged experimentation and invention. Thus, heartier crops than wheat, like rye, oats, and buckwheat, as well as fruits of Eastern origin, were cultivated successfully. Mills, windmills, and wheelbarrows were used as early as the fifth century in Anatolia—all brought from the East. (*See* BYZANTIUM.)

The Arab World. Among the Arabs, newly risen from nomadism, agriculture remained a secondary activity, usually carried out by the indentured class of conquered peoples. The Arab conquerors retained the herding elements of local agriculture, often pursuing it as a legacy from nomadic times and harking back to the caravans that provided great wealth and prestige to the Arabians of antiquity—but often sacrificing potentially rich cropland for less productive pasturing. Ironically, the establishment of the great caliphates in Muslim lands resulted in Arabs shunning the farmlands and settling in the cities, which accounts for the slow spread of ISLAM among the conquered peasantry.

England's open-field system. *Fields were divided into strips. The lord's land was interspersed with peasant land in order to ensure equal worker attention throughout the field.*

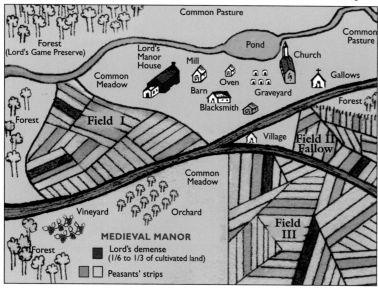

MEDIEVAL MANOR
- Lord's demesne (1/6 to 1/3 of cultivated land)
- Peasants' strips

Lacking practical experience on the land, and determined to leave farming in the hands of tenant farmers who were virtually slaves, the Arabs made little progress in agriculture, sorely mismanaging the soil and bringing little of the culture's scientific genius to bear. As a result, the lands under Arab control were exhausted by the eleventh century, leading to a general impoverishment of the Muslim empires. The only agricultural developments in Arab lands were irrigation techniques—in part because sophisticated ancient techniques were already in place and in part because the technology had direct applications to urban life and sanitation. Thus, Arabs invested heavily in the construction of underground conduits (*qanats*) that effectively irrigated wide areas, but which also discouraged the proper rotation of crops. (*See* FAMINE.)

Western Europe. Medieval agriculture in southwestern Europe appears to be an amalgam of Byzantine and Arab agricultural history, a blend of Arab technique and Byzantine structure. Sophisticated irrigation techniques and terracing typified the farms of Spain, southern France, and Italy; soil management consisted only of planting a wide variety of crops that taxed the soil in different ways. Durum wheat was introduced to the area by the Arabs, and forest lands, once cleared, became natural areas for citrus and grape growing. (*See* FOOD AND DRINK.)

The biggest problem faced by western Europe was the absence of labor, in large part due to the eradication of slavery by the ninth century. The south never adequately solved this problem, and crop yields were always lagging behind the needs of the populace—one of the factors that engendered the later interest of the Spanish, Portuguese, and Italians in their EXPLORATION across the seas.

A French calendar of 1460 by Pietro de Crescenzi, portraying medieval agricultural activities: (from upper left) shearing, pruning, planting (2), threshing, harvesting (2), reaping, hunting, animal husbandry (2), wine pressing, sowing.

In the north (GERMANY, northern FRANCE, and the British Isles), the climate and the land were wholly different from what the Romans and their heirs encountered: richer, but harder soil; shorter, rainier growing seasons; and sparse population with virtually no slave labor available. From uncertain origins developed the remarkable open-field system, in which the arable land of an estate was divided into three fields. One was allowed to lie fallow for one year, while one of the other two was planted in the spring (usually wheat or rye, requiring a longer growing season) and the third in the fall (oats, barley, and legumes). The field left fallow each year was rotated, so that it might recover and replenish itself for the next planting.

Perhaps most remarkable about this system was that it was practiced in a feudalistic society, so that vassals and tenants worked side by side, cultivating land that belonged to them individually alongside parcels owned by the manorial lord. The lord provided technological support by affording mills, the new wheel plow, oxen and smithy services, ovens, and the protec-

tion of his army. He maintained the forests as his private preserve, which stemmed the tide of deforestation that was to prove ecologically disastrous in the late Middle Ages. The high level of cooperation required to make this system work, however, and the communal cohesiveness it fostered, is one of the more remarkable aspects of medieval history, no doubt contributing to the rise of democratic institutions in the late medieval period, particularly in ENGLAND. (*See* FEUDALISM.)

The calamities that befell northern Europe in the fourteenth century—the BLACK DEATH, the VIKING invasions, and the failed PEASANTS' REVOLTS—left European agriculture in shambles at the close of the medieval period, causing many in Europe to turn their gaze to possibly more fertile lands across the seas.

Techniques and tools are discussed in FOREST LAW, HUNTING AND FOWLING, HORSES, WOOL TRADE, *and* MINING; *crop and estate management in* FAMINE, FEUDALISM, FOOD AND DRINK, *and* COMMERCE AND TRADE.

AISTULF

istulf (d. 756) became king of the LOMBARDS in 749, succeeding Liutprand, under whose reign the Lombard republic was at its most powerful, extending throughout much of central and northern ITALY. Aistulf continued Liutprand's project of territorial expansion, seizing RAVENNA in 751 and besieging ROME the following year. His aggression and anti-Roman policies frightened the PAPACY. Pope Zacharias was successful in gaining the support of the FRANKS in opposing him, as was Pope Stephen, who appealed to PÉPIN III the Short. Pépin, eager to expand his own territories, invaded Italy in 755, defeated Aistulf, and extracted from him a promise to return the lands he had seized. Aistulf soon recanted and attacked Rome again in 756. Once more, Pépin was called in by the pope, and again he defeated Aistulf, this time securing restitution by taking hostages and demanding a heavy tribute. At the Treaty of Pavia in 756, all of central ITALY was returned to the papacy, and Lombardy was made a Frank fiefdom. Aistulf died during this last campaign in 756. His defeat and the humbling of the Lombards paved the way for the CAROLINGIAN domination of Italy in the following decades.

AIX-LA-CHAPELLE (AACHEN)

Originally a Roman settlement known for its curative baths, Aix-la-Chapelle (Aachen in German, and called that in the HOLY ROMAN EMPIRE) became the capital of the CAROLINGIAN empire. In 765, King PÉPIN III built his palace there, which his son CHARLEMAGNE rebuilt and expanded.

Charlemagne's court moved locations several times, always resurfacing at one of his many magnificent palaces. However, he rebuilt his father's palace at Aix-la-Chapelle with the intention of making it his most important one, one he envisioned as a second ROME. Several parts of the palace were based on ancient Roman and BYZANTINE models and were named after Roman buildings. The royal chapel he built at the south end of the palace complex became the traditional site for the CORONATION of new kings. Attached to the chapel was the Palace School, a center of learning and art, headed by the Englishman ALCUIN. Charlemagne's son, LOUIS THE PIOUS, was crowned in Aachen in 813. After the Treaty of VERDUN divided the empire among Charlemagne's three grandsons, German kings were crowned there well into the 1500s.

Aix-la-Chapelle had religious as well as political significance as a place of pilgrimage after the Carolin-

The interior of the Palatine Chapel at Aix-la-Chapelle, built by Charlemagne and, since the days of Otto I, the coronation site of many Holy Roman emperors.

gians made it a center for the display of holy relics in the first half of the ninth century. Its reputation was further enhanced when FREDERICK I BARBAROSSA proclaimed Charlemagne a saint in 1165.

Later, after the city's walls were fortified, Aachen, as it came to be known, became a stabilizing force in the region between the Meuse and Rhine Rivers.

ALANS

An Iranian people who figured in the fifth-century destruction of the western Roman Empire. By the first century C.E., the Alans had emigrated to the steppes of southern RUSSIA. The conquests of another Asiatic people, the Huns, in the fourth and fifth centuries split the Alan people into two branches. One branch entered Europe, while the other remained on the steppes. The European branch, under the kings Goar and Respendial, invaded Gaul at the start of the fifth century.

The Alans entered a battle between the Germanic tribes of FRANKS and VANDALS, preserving the latter from destruction. The Alans became allies with two divisions of the Vandals (Siling and Asding) and jointly sacked many Gaulish cities. These tribes then moved into SPAIN. By 409, the Alans controlled the western sections of Iberia. However, the history of the organized European Alan people came to an end in 416, when they and the Siling Vandals were annihilated by the Germanic VISIGOTHS. The remnants of the Alan people were assimilated into the Asding Vandals and took part in their invasion of North AFRICA in 1430.

ALARIC I

King of the VISIGOTHS, Alaric (c. 370–410) was born to the prominent GOTH family of Balthi. He served in the Roman army as a commander under Theodosius I and believed his service would be repaid by his being made a senator after the emperor's death. The new emperor, Arcadius, feared Alaric's ambition and assigned him to a lowly post in the army, at which point Alaric accepted election as king of the Visigoths in 397. He attempted an invasion of the Balkans, but Arcadius, emperor of the eastern Roman Empire, bribed him, turning Alaric's attention westward, to Italy. There, on the northern shore of the Adriatic, he founded a Visigothic kingdom.

On August 24, 410, Alaric turned on ROME and invaded and occupied the city. This sent shock waves throughout the empire and marked the end of the ancient Roman Empire, although Alaric's intention was to leave Rome and attack North AFRICA. He died in 410, before he could mount his attack, and went down in history as the barbarian who caused the demise of the Roman Empire. (*See* BARBARIAN INVASIONS.)

Alaric seems, however, to have had great respect for Roman culture, showing clemency to Roman prisoners and preserving Roman buildings. Upon his death, Alaric's soldiers diverted the Busento River and buried him with full pomp in the river bed, then allowed the river to return to its original course.

ALBERT I

Holy Roman Emperor from 1298 to 1308. Albert (1255–1308) was born the eldest son of Rudolph I of HABSBURG and was given the duchies of AUSTRIA and Styria by his father in 1282. There he established a strong government, often in opposition to the interests of the nobility.

His Rise. Rudolph had declared that Albert should succeed him, but the princes, fearful of Albert's ambition and ability, chose Adolf of Nassau as the new emperor following Rudolf's death. Amid the ensuing

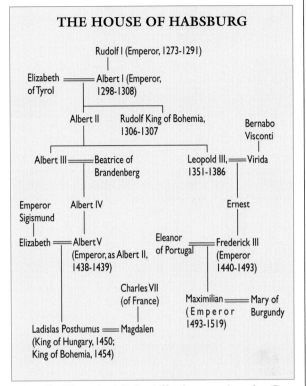

THE HOUSE OF HABSBURG

Rudolf I (Emperor, 1273-1291)

Elizabeth of Tyrol ═ Albert I (Emperor, 1298-1308)

Albert II — Rudolf King of Bohemia, 1306-1307 — Bernabo Visconti

Albert III ═ Beatrice of Brandenberg — Leopold III, 1351-1386 ═ Virida

Emperor Sigismund — Albert IV — Ernest

Elizabeth ═ Albert V (Emperor, as Albert II, 1438-1439) — Eleanor of Portugal ═ Frederick III (Emperor 1440-1493)

Charles VII (of France)

Maximilian (Emperor 1493-1519) ═ Mary of Burgundy

Ladislas Posthumus ═ Magdalen (King of Hungary, 1450; King of Bohemia, 1454)

turmoil, Albert had little difficulty wresting the German crown from Adolf. After his victory at the Battle of Göllheim in 1298, Albert declared himself king of the Romans and ruler of GERMANY and BOHEMIA.

Albert consistently imposed his will over the interests of the nobility and became an important force in European politics. He forged an alliance with PHILIP IV THE FAIR of FRANCE and supported him in his struggle against Pope BONIFACE VIII. He generally promoted commerce in his kingdom, abolishing the tolls on the Rhine collected by the Church since 1250.

In 1307, Albert suffered a humiliating defeat in his attempt to invade Thuringia. This, and the death of his son Rudolph that same year, weakened Albert's position and emboldened the Rhenish archbishops to revolt. The revolt was suppressed, but further unrest brewed in Swabia, and it was while he was en route to establish order there that he was murdered by his nephew, John Parricida, on May 1, 1308.

LEGEND AND LORE

William Tell

Albert's suppression of the Swiss cantons is also the background of the legend of William Tell. Refusing to obey the Austrian bailiff Gessler (installed by Albert) that homage be paid to a hat hung in the town square of Altdorf, William was forced to shoot an arrow at an apple placed on his son's head. He succeeds, but is arrested anyway. He escapes, and kills Gessler during an ambush, emerging a legendary hero of Swiss independence—although no evidence for the tale or William Tell exists.

ALBERT V (II) OF HABSBURG

Albert V (1397–1439) was duke of AUSTRIA and, for two years, king of BOHEMIA and HUNGARY as well as Holy Roman Emperor. He became child-ruler of Austria in 1404 on the death of his father, Albert IV. He continued his education until 1411, when he took power in his own name as Albert V. Supported by able advisers, Albert engaged the various problems that had arisen during his minority, the greatest of which being the Czech nationalistic Hussite movement that grew out of the religious heresy founded by JOHN HUSS. Albert joined with the Holy Roman Emperor, Sigismund, in the destruction of the Hussites. (*See* HABSBURG DYNASTY.)

In 1424, Albert married Sigismund's daughter and heiress, Elizabeth. He was subsequently designated Sigismund's successor. After the king's death in 1437, he was crowned king of HUNGARY and Bohemia. The Bohemians, however, with their Polish allies, resisted his rule, and Albert failed to control the region. In March of 1438, while fighting to assert his rule in Bohemia, Albert was elected king and ruler of the Holy Roman Empire, although it is believed that Albert did not pursue this position. The heart of his short rule was consumed in the defense of Hungary against the rising power of the Turkish OTTOMAN Empire. On October 27, 1439, Albert died of dysentery at Langendorf while in combat with the Turks.

ALBERTUS MAGNUS

Albertus Magnus (Albert the Great, also called Albert the German, c. 1200–1280), one of the most learned men of his time, was influential both as a scholar and as a religious figure. He was called "Magnus" and the "Universal Doctor" because of his vast learning. But he was also known in his later years as the "Bishop of the Boots" because of his habit of traveling extensively for the Church, always on foot. THOMAS AQUINAS was one of his pupils.

His Life. Albertus Magnus was born to a noble family (his proper name is actually Albert, Count von Bollstädt) around 1200, in the southern German town of Lauingen. He studied at the University of Padua and as a young man entered the DOMINICAN order of FRIARS. For the next several years he taught theology in GERMANY, but in 1241 he was sent to study at the University of PARIS. Upon completion of his studies, he lectured there intermittently from 1245 to 1254. During this time he was also busy establishing a Dominican center of learning in Cologne. (*See* SCHOLASTICISM.)

Miniature from De Natura Rerum *by Albertus Magnus, showing a thinker contemplating the planets. His travels opened his mind and sharpened his powers of observation.*

He was named religious superior of the German region of Teutonia, and in 1260 reluctantly became bishop of Regensburg. In 1262, he stepped down as bishop. He spent the rest of his life in Cologne, devoting himself to his studies until his death in 1280.

His Work. Albertus Magnus exerted great influence. Exposed to Greek PHILOSOPHY, as well as Arabic scholarship (increasingly, the works of Arab thinkers were being translated into Latin), he was the first western European to summarize the teachings of ARISTOTLE; his writings on the philosopher fill six volumes. As a Scholastic, he believed it possible to create a comprehensive and consistent belief system out of Aristotle's philosophy. His detractors, though, called him the "ape of Aristotle." He made many naturalistic observations in his travels and dabbled briefly (and skeptically) in ALCHEMY. He is credited with discovering the element arsenic, although there is evidence the discovery was made much earlier. His erudition raised suspicions among critics that he practiced sorcery, but his allegiance to the Church eventually sealed his reputation. He was canonized in 1931. (*See* PHILOSOPHY.)

ALBIGENSES

The Albigenses, also known as the Albigensians, were a group of heretics in southern FRANCE during the twelfth and thirteenth centuries. Members of the larger CATHAR movement, they were named after the French town of Albi, presumably where they first appeared. (In actuality, they seem to have originated north of Albi, in Toulouse.)

Most of what we know about the Albigenses comes from the writings of those who opposed them, since little Albigensian writing survives. Though small, the movement was influential, coming at a time when many people believed the Church to be corrupt. Albigenses were "antisacerdotal"(meaning, opposed to the priesthood), believing that clergymen were more interested in acquiring wealth and exerting political influence than in truly religious pursuits. A contemporaneous inquisitor describes them as opposed to the Eucharist, baptism, and the symbol of the cross, arguing that one ought not to adore or hold sacred the instrument of Jesus's death. They adopted an ascetic life and formed isolated communities of their own.

Between 1209 and 1244, a crusade to eradicate the group was waged by the northern French nobility, directed by popes from Lucius III to GREGORY IX. Innocent III charged the Dominicans with the mission of converting or eradicating the sect, and many horrific and indiscriminate massacres were led by SIMON OF MONTFORT. Only remnants of the sect survived the massacre at Montségur in 1244. (*See* HERESY.)

ALCANTARA, ORDER OF

A military order of crusading knights, one of a number of such organizations that played an important role in the Christian RECONQUEST of SPAIN from the Muslims. (The Muslims had invaded Spain in 711 and destroyed its Christian Visigothic kingdom by 716.) The military orders were feudal powers in their own right, often having land on the frontier. After the reconquest of Spain, the importance of the orders diminished. (*See* KNIGHTHOOD.)

The Order of Alcántara began in 1156 as the Order of Saint Julian, created by the brothers Suero and Gomez Fernández. The order received papal approval on December 29, 1177, and was reorganized in 1183, when its leader gained the title of "master" and the order was attached to the rules of St. BENEDICT. The order successfully conquered towns and fortresses in the south, expanding the territory of the Kingdom of León. In 1213, the king of León conquered the fortress at Alcántara. Originally, the town was given to the Order of CALATRAVA, but it was offered to the knights of Saint Julian if they would accept the lordship of the master of Calatrava.

The order was successful in its military encounters with the Moors. However, like other Spanish military orders, the history of the Order of Alcántara is dominated by many rivalries and internal conflicts. The Castilian kings were close to the order and King Ferdinand eventually appointed himself master of Alcántara in 1494. (*See* SPAIN; RECONQUEST.)

ALCHEMY

During the Middle Ages, a select group of people known as alchemists attempted to divine the secret properties of gold. Some goals of the alchemists were anything but theoretical: they sought the means of transmuting base metals into gold and creating medicinals that would bestow immortality upon their users. In order to plumb these secrets, alchemists believed they had to retain a purity of spirit in order to successfully interact with the purity of gold. No doubt certain alchemists considered the practice a SCIENCE, but it was widely viewed as a mystical art.

In Europe the basis for alchemy's methodology came from ARISTOTLE's theory that four natural elements, namely earth, air, fire, and water were the building blocks of everything in the natural world.

The Alchemist, *from an engraving by Vriese. Alchemy was a rich man's pursuit in the Middle Ages and frequently bespoke an eclectic mind and a curiosity about arcane arts.*

The correct blend of these elements could yield gold, which was thought to possess the perfect combination of these four elements. It was thought that if an "imperfect" metal, such as lead, could be transformed to retain the ideal balance of the elements, gold would be produced. In order to alter the properties of matter, alchemists would heat and disintegrate, liquefy and vaporize substances, in the process gaining practical experience that would ultimately form the foundation of the science of chemistry. (*See* SCIENCE.)

Alchemists hypothesized the existence of a substance called the "philosopher's stone" that was thought to have the power to transform base metals into gold, as well as restore youth and vitality. Finding the philosopher's stone became the primary focus of research and experimentation for many alchemists.

Alchemy was not a new art in the Middle Ages; it had been practiced by many ancient cultures before it was pursued by medieval society. One Arabic alchemist of note, Jabir ibn Hayyan, composed works on alchemy that cover the physical composition of certain metals and how to create elixirs through distillation. The eleventh-century Arab philosopher Ibn Sima proposed a theory that "impure" metals could never be transformed into gold until they were broken down into smaller components.

13th-century text in alchemy, precursor of modern chemistry.

Following the CRUSADES, Arabic texts on alchemy were translated into European languages, and alchemy gained popularity not only with the common populace and scientists, but with the Church as well. During the thirteenth century the Church accepted alchemy as a science and allowed THOMAS AQUINAS to study it. Noted scholars such as ALBERTUS MAGNUS and ROGER BACON wrote alchemical works. Yet, alchemists never lost sight of their objectives: the production of gold and the discovery of magical elixirs.

There were a few spurious success stories—such as one about Parisian Nicolas Flanel (1339–1418)—popularly believed during the late Middle Ages, which encouraged alchemists to continue working as well as attracting new initiates. In the fourteenth century, the Church condemned alchemy because of its association with ASTROLOGY. The study of alchemy continued, however, with some of its theories becoming accepted.

Alchemy is viewed today as the forerunner of chemistry. Some important discoveries made by alchemists were alcohol in the twelfth century and nitric acid, sulfuric acid, and hydrochloric acid, all known as mineral acids, discovered in the thirteenth century.

Occult aspects of alchemy are discussed in CABALA, HERESY, MAGIC AND FOLKLORE, *and* WITCHCRAFT AND SORCERY. *Scientific aspects are discussed in* HERBALS, MEDICINE, *and* SCIENCE. *Also see* BACON, ROGER.

ALCUIN OF YORK

Alcuin of York (c. 732–804) was an English theologian and educator, best known as the teacher of the Emperor CHARLEMAGNE and his family. He was an important educational reformer and a leading figure of the CAROLINGIAN renaissance. He also played a large role in the development of Roman Catholic worship in western Europe.

His Life. Born in Yorkshire, Alcuin was educated at the cathedral school of York and remained there as a teacher. York at that time was a center of religious learning, and the cathedral school was well known throughout Europe. He became the school's headmaster in 778. (*See* AIX-LA-CHAPELLE.)

While traveling in 781, he met Charlemagne in Italy. The emperor, impressed with Alcuin, asked him to head the imperial school he was forming in the German city of Aachen. Alcuin accepted the invitation. During his years as head of the Palace School in Aachen (Aix-la-Chapelle), Alcuin introduced many innovations. He was the foremost Latin scholar of his era and under his aegis, the Palace School became the center for collecting and copying the Latin classics. These manuscripts from Charlemagne's reign are, in many instances, the earliest surviving texts of the great writings of Roman antiquity. He encouraged study of the liberal arts, and blended religious study with secular study. The school gained a reputation for scholarship and was visited by many European scholars.

Influence. Alcuin's influence stemmed from his revision of the liturgy. He created an order in which votive masses are said during the week—an order still followed by the Church. He also revised such works as the Latin Vulgate and wrote a number of influential essays on religion and education. Among the indifferent poetry and persuasive prose that he produced, Alcuin wrote important works of political theory. He viewed Charlemagne as an anointed king of the Old Testament—a new King David. He urged the king to create a Christian empire and to give special attention to the needs and disciplines of the Church and its adherents.

In 796, Alcuin left Aachen to become abbot at St. Martin of Tours monastery, where he founded a scriptorium, in which monks made copies of the Bible and other texts. He died at Tours in 804.

ALDHELM, ST.

English churchman and scholar (639–709) who lived in WESSEX. Related to King Ine of Wessex, he studied at Malmesbury and at Canterbury under St. Adrian. He became master of the school at Malmesbury, where he was appointed abbot in 675. When Wessex was divided into two dioceses, Aldhelm became the first bishop of Sherborne, building the minster at Sherborne and churches at Frome, Corfe, Wareham, and Bradford-on-Avon. The church at Bradford-on-Avon, which still stands, is a good example of early medieval Saxon ARCHITECTURE.

Aldhelm's Latin writings were widely admired and imitated, and he was a skilled musician as well. He wrote his poems, hymns, songs, and ballads, not in LATIN, but in ANGLO-SAXON, so that ordinary people might understand them. Aldhelm's vernacular religious poems helped to spread CHRISTIANITY throughout Wessex. He died in 709 and was buried in Malmesbury. (*See* LATIN LANGUAGE AND LITERATURE.)

ALEXANDER III

Alexander III (1105–1181), pope from 1159 to 1181, spent much of his reign defending the power of the PAPACY. A scholarly and diplomatic man, he succeeded in strengthening the Church and forcing peace with his self-styled rival, the Holy Roman Emperor FREDERICK I BARBAROSSA.

Life. Born Rolando Bandinelli in Tuscany in 1105, the future pope studied theology and law and taught at the University of Bologna. His diplomatic skills and his shrewd judgment helped him rise in the Church under the reign of the popes Eugenius III and ADRIAN IV. Under Adrian IV, Bandinelli was named chief papal negotiator with Frederick Barbarossa. Bandinelli feared that Frederick was intent on dominating northern Italy at the expense of the independence of the papacy, and he expressed these fears publicly. When Adrian died in 1159, the cardinals chose Bandinelli as the new pope, Alexander III. However, Frederick refused to acknowledge their selection and instead supported Cardinal Octavian, who became the first "antipope," Victor IV.

Politics. Alexander was forced to flee ITALY in 1162, but he was able to broaden his base of power in FRANCE and ENGLAND. He returned to Italy in 1165, but was forced out again a year later. Over the next decade he used his diplomatic skills to build power; as his influence increased, Frederick's waned. By 1177, Frederick was ready to make peace and received a pardon from Alexander in the Peace of Venice, at a tearful ceremony. (*See* KINGSHIP.)

In 1179, Alexander led the Third LATERAN COUNCIL, which strove to unify the Church under the unquestioned authority of the pope. Alexander also inserted himself into some political disputes of the time: he helped Louis VII solidify his power in France by bestowing on him the title of "most Christian

Fresco depicting the pardoning of Frederick I Barbarossa by Pope Alexander III, painted by Spinello Aretino in the chapel of the Palazzo Publico in Sienna, Italy.

king," and attempted to broker a peace between HENRY II and THOMAS BECKET. When Henry had Becket killed, Alexander forced the king to serve his penance publicly. Alexander died on August 30, 1181, after a 22-year reign that saw the prestige of the papacy rise to new heights. (*See* PAPACY.)

ALEXANDER NEVSKY

Alexander Nevsky (c. 1220–1263) was a national hero of medieval RUSSIA, later canonized by the Russian Orthodox Church. Alexander was born to the family of YAROSLAV THE WISE and the line of Russian kings who fought the MONGOLS and the BYZANTINES. By his day, those battles were over, and Russia was paying tribute to the Mongols to ensure peace. Alexander faced a new challenge: invasion by the Swedish armies, who had the aid of the Teutonic Order of the Livonian Knights. On July 15, 1240, Alexander won a decisive battle against the Swedes on the Neva River (his namesake). He finally crushed the Swedish attempt to wrest northwestern Russia in a famous victory against the Livonians in the Battle on the Ice on frozen Lake Peipus and Lake Pskov on the border of Estonia on April 5, 1242.

Alexander added the principality of NOVGOROD to his Kingdom of Vladimir, and while he was unable to unite all the principalities of Russia—many were in the hands of his relatives who would not have cooperated—he was acknowledged to be the leader of the Russians. Soon after his death in 1263, he became a legendary hero of Russian independence. (*See* RUSSIA.)

ALEXIUS I COMNENUS

Alexius I Comnenus (1048–1118) was Byzantine emperor from 1078 until his death in 1118. He was the second member of the Comnenus family dynasty, which lasted until 1183. Alexius came to power when the Byzantine Empire was threatened with extinction after its army was destroyed at MANZIKERT, resulting in Asia Minor being lost to the SELJUK TURKS. Alexius was able to ward off various dangers to the empire such as the NORMAN invasion of the Balkans, the First Crusade, and the Patzinak drive to CONSTANTINOPLE. Although Alexius was successful in preventing further disaster, he failed to reverse the clear decline of the empire.

Career. Alexius was a prominent general under a number of emperors before his ascension. In 1078, he and his brother ISAAC rebelled against the Emperor Nicephorus Botaniates, who had himself forced Michael VII Ducas Parapinakes out of power. Alexius was faced immediately with the invasion of the Normans under ROBERT GUISCARD. Alexius was defeated a number of times, but Guiscard was compelled to return to Italy to defend his territory, at which point his Balkan conquests melted away. A second attempt by Guiscard to take the Byzantine throne failed when the Norman ruler died suddenly in 1085.

The second great threat to Alexius was the invasion of the Patzinak people, who, in league with the Turks, appeared ready to destroy BYZANTIUM. Alexius elicited the aid of the Cuman people, and at the battle of Levunium, the two forces virtually obliterated the Patzinaks. (*See* BYZANTIUM.)

Alexius used the turmoil of the First CRUSADE to expand his territory, but his last years were filled with palace intrigue. His wife, the Empress IRENE, and her daughter Anna conspired to have Anna's husband, Nicephorus Bryennius, named Alexius's successor instead of the emperor's eldest son, John. The plot failed, and John succeeded his father in 1118.

ALFONSO I

King of ARAGON and NAVARRE from 1104 to 1134, Alfonso I (c. 1073–1134) was also known as the Battler (*el Batallador*) for his brilliant military campaigns against the Moors in 1110 and his attempt to wrest the Kingdom of Castile from Urraca, his wife and heiress of the crown. By extending his kingdom southward to Andalusia, he established Aragon as a military power for the remainder of the Middle Ages. He was fatally wounded in battle at Fraga in 1134. (*See* SPAIN.)

ALFONSO V OF NAPLES

Also known as Alfonso the Magnanimous, Alfonso V (1396–1458) was one of the most famous men of his day due to his military exploits. Born in the court of Castile to Ferdinand I Antequera, who became king of ARAGON in 1412, he fled SPAIN following a failed marriage to his cousin, Maria, daughter of Henry III of Castile. He pursued a policy of expansion typical of the Aragonese. When asked in 1421 to help Queen Joan of NAPLES defend her kingdom against Louis III of Anjou, he entered the city as a liberator and settled a court there (where he lived with his mistress Lucrezia de Alagno).

Joan proved fickle, and Alfonso returned to Spain to help his family firm up their control—the mixture of Aragonese and Castilian blood embodied in the family was a constant irritant to both areas—and to raise an army for an invasion of Naples. When Joan and Louis died suddenly, Alfonso prepared to launch his attack in 1435, when he was surprisingly defeated and taken prisoner by the Genoese. He convinced his captors that his rule over Naples would keep the rival forces of VENICE, FLORENCE, and the PAPACY at bay, and he was allowed to take Naples in 1442.

Meanwhile, his family's fortunes in Spain deteriorated and his ancestral estates in Castile were lost in civil wars and uprisings. The focus of Alfonso's interests were clearly on Naples, and he established a court that supported many artists and writers (who gave him the name "Magnanimous") and in which art and literature flourished. Alfonso died on June 27, 1458, in Ovo Castle in Naples in the company of his mistress and his illegitimate son and heir, Ferrante.

ALFONSO VI THE BRAVE

The second son of Ferdinand I, king of León, Castile, and Galicia, Alfonso (c. 1040–1109) inherited León on his father's death in 1065. His brother Sancho II inherited Castile, and there ensued six years of struggle between the brothers for the other's kingdom. (A third brother, Garcia, inherited Galicia, but was arrested by Alfonso and died in prison.) Despite many military victories by Sancho's general, Rodrigo Díaz (EL CID), during which Alfonso sought refuge in Muslim Toledo, Alfonso, with the help of his sister Urraca (with whom he was rumored to have had an incestuous relationship), arranged for the assassination of Sancho in 1072 and united the kingdoms of León and Castile.

Alfonso was greatly influenced by his French wives, particularly CONSTANCE OF BURGUNDY. He in-

ALFONSO X THE WISE

Alfonso X, the Wise (left), depicted in a manuscript of one of his songs. (Note the musical notation at lower right.)

Alfonso X, (1221–1284) also called Alfonso the Wise (*el Sabio*), presided over a court that saw the flowering of Spanish culture and science in the Middle Ages. By the end of his reign, however, his frustrated pursuit of the title of Holy Roman Emperor and his indecision regarding his succession created turmoil that left the kingdoms of Castile and León in shambles. (*See* SPAIN.)

Life. Alfonso was born on November 23, 1221, in Castile, the son of King Ferdinand III and Beatrice of Swabia, niece of Holy Roman Emperor HENRY VI. Crowned king of Castile and León in 1252, he completed the conquest of Andalusia by 1265. He was preparing to invade Morocco when he began a fruitless campaign to be recognized as the Holy Roman Emperor. He actually managed to be elected to the post in 1267, but a papal veto prevented him from taking possession of the throne. Vast sums were spent bribing the Germans and the papal officers, to no avail. Finally, Alfonso gave up the quest in 1273, when Rudolf I, the first HABSBURG, ascended the throne.

The Court. Alfonso assembled outstanding scholars and artists in his court, ushering in a golden age of Spanish culture. Alfonso himself is said to have composed music and poetry; he supported the development of a refined Castilian Spanish that became the language of the educated in Spain. Drawing on the scientific talent of Muslim and Jewish astronomers, he sponsored the creation of carefully constructed guides to the heavens based on the Ptolemaic (Earth-centered) system that became known as the Alfonsine Tables. Completed c. 1272, they were used by scientists for centuries until supplanted by Copernicus.

Among the many literary and juridical undertakings of Alfonso's court were histories of Spain and of civilization (as of Creation), and the *Sietè Partidas,* a comprehensive code of law based on Roman law, but which also detailed manners and etiquette, as well as promoted a view of the king as an intermediary between God and humanity. Like many projects, however, the code was unfinished at Alfonso's death and was never fully implemented.

End of Reign. The end of Alfonso's reign was marked by a fierce rivalry between the children of his eldest son, Ferdinand, who had been killed during a Muslim invasion in 1275, and Alfonso's second son, Sancho. Alfonso's preference was unclear, giving each side encouragement and throwing the entire country into virtual civil war. At the time of his death in 1284, Alfonso, deposed by Castilian supporters of Sancho, sought the aid of the very Muslims he had warred against for three decades, but never regained control.

troduced the Cluniac monastic order to Spanish soil, CAROLINGIAN script, as well as many religious and artistic elements from the other side of the Pyrenees.

Toledo. Possibly as a result of his brief exile in Toledo, Alfonso was determined to establish his rule over the Muslim *taifa* kingdoms in the south. He waged a campaign to conquer Toledo, laying siege to the city in 1085. His recovery of an important city that had been in Muslim hands since the eighth century enhanced Alfonso's prestige and emboldened Christian kings throughout Europe. Alfonso, however, preferred to regard himself as the "emperor of all the Spains" and retain a tenuous control over Muslim Spain by exacting a high and burdensome tribute.

Soon the Muslims appealed to the ALMORAVIDS in North Africa, who invaded Spain and defeated Alfonso's army at Zallaqah on October 23, 1086. Alfonso rallied other Christian kings to mount a crusade against the Almoravids and even reconciled with his former adversary, Díaz. In spite of Díaz's talents, the Almoravids won battle after battle, until the final blow came at Uclés in 1108 with the death of Alfonso's only son and heir, Sancho. Yet, he arranged the marriage of his sister Urraca to an Aragonian, ALFONSO I, the Battler, so that the struggle against the Almoravids would continue. He died in Toledo in 1109.

ALFRED THE GREAT

The political and cultural achievements of Alfred (849–899) on behalf of ANGLO-SAXON ENGLAND, during his reign as king of WESSEX from 871 to 899, earned him the title of "the Great."

Early Years. Alfred was born in 849 in Wantage, the youngest son of King Aethelwulf of Wessex, who may have considered a career in the Church for his son, since the boy visited the pope in Rome in 853. Alfred is said to have suffered sorely from an unspecified ailment his entire life. (*See* ENGLAND.)

After Aethelwulf died in 858, his four sons took turns succeeding him. During the reign of Alfred's brother ETHELRED (866–871), the Danes attacked England in force, but were turned away by Alfred. However, Alfred and his troops were crushed when the Danes returned in 878, and he went into hiding briefly to regroup. He defeated the Danes later that same year at the Battle of Edington and signed the Treaty of Wedmore with the Danish king, Guthrum, dividing England along the road from LONDON to Chester. It established his rule of Wessex in the south, while extending his authority over the Danish-held territory in the north (known as the Danelaw).

Resurgence. He built a strong defense, incorporating forts, building a fleet of ships of his own design, and requiring military service for all free men. To further strengthen his position, Alfred married a member of the Mercian royal family, thus improving the alliance between Wessex and Mercia. During his rule, Alfred unified Wessex, annexed part of Mercia, and brought the princes of southern WALES under his authority. He fought off new Danish attacks in the 890s.

When he died on October 26, 899, he left Wessex stronger and its kingship better established.

Alfred's support for learning and vernacular Anglo-Saxon traditions played an important role in early English history. Like CHARLEMAGNE, he assembled scholars and established a court school to teach clergy and young people, and he promoted literacy among the nobility. Alfred learned Latin and translated several Latin works into Old English (Anglo-Saxon)— GREGORY the Great's *Pastoral Care*, BOETHIUS's *Consolation of Philosophy*, works by AUGUSTINE and Orosius, and possibly BEDE's *Ecclesiastical History*. Alfred's patronage stimulated the compilation of the *Anglo-Saxon Chronicle*. (*See* ANGLO-SAXONS.)

Alfred, first king of England (called "Great" only after the 17th century).

LIFE OF ALFRED THE GREAT	
849	Born the fourth son of Aethelwulf, King of Wessex, in Wantage, Oxon
869	Marries Aetheswitha of Gainas and Mercia. (They will have 6 children.)
871	Ethelred dies; Alfred succeeds his brother as king of Wessex.
878	Danish invasion of Wessex by the Great Army of Guthrum. Alfred hides on the Isle of Athelny. Victory at the Battle of Edington. Treaty of Wedmore.
886	Alfred recaptures London; recognized as king of all of Christian England. Asser becomes his Latin tutor.
890	Designs and builds ships to challenge Viking sea power.
891	Authorizes *Anglo-Saxon Chronicle*
899	Alfred dies.

ALHAMBRA

The Alhambra (from the Arabic for "red castle," the color of its outer walls) is a complex of buildings in the southern Spanish city of Granada. A palace for Muslim—and later Christian rulers—of SPAIN in the late Middle Ages. It is considered a masterpiece of ISLAMIC ART AND ARCHITECTURE.

Early History. The palace was begun around 1238 on the site of an old Muslim fort, the Alcazba, which defended the city in the ninth century. Built on a plateau overlooking the city, the palace was first expanded by Sultan Muhammad I El Ah-mar, and continued by his son, Muhammad II (who died in 1303), but much of the lavish development of the site is due to Yusuf I, who ruled to 1354, and Muhammad V, who added several important final features by 1391. A noteworthy element of the Alhambra is its extensive irrigation system that permitted the cultivation of beautiful gardens and imposing fountained courtyards. In contrast to the plain outer walls, the inner walls are lavishly decorated with arabesques and quotations from the KORAN and sacred Muslim texts.

Reconquest. Following the RECONQUEST of Spain by Christian rulers, the Alhambra was ransacked and defaced; CHARLES V destroyed some of the complex in 1527 and built a Renaissance-style castle in its place. In the nineteenth century, an effort was begun to restore the original structure and Islamic decoration. Today it is restored to the structure of the fourteenth century.

The Alhambra consists of three main sections: the citadel (fortress); the palace, for ceremonies; and a private residential area for the sultan and his family. These are built around two large courtyards: the Court of the Myrtles, at the center of which was a pool surrounded by trees; and the Court of the Lions (shown at right in a 13th-century engraving), named after the central fountain, which was supported by 12 marble lions and surrounded by a lavish garden.

Today, the Alhambra courtyards are bereft of vegetation. The irrigation of the complex has proven too difficult, which is a tribute to the advanced engineering techniques of medieval Islamic culture.

ALI IBN ABU TALIB

A li (c. 600–661) was the cousin of MUHAMMAD and fourth caliph and the first Shi'ite imam. He grew up in Muhammad's house and became a devoted follower of the Prophet at an early age. A tradition has him sleeping in Muhammad's bed the night of the Prophet's flight to Medina (the Hegira) in 622 to fool Muhammad's adversaries.

Ali married Muhammad's daughter, Fatima, and was considered by many a worthy successor of Muhammad, but he withdrew from public life after his mentor's death and reluctantly supported the first two caliphs. Ali believed the third caliph, Uthman, had betrayed Muhammad's teachings, however, and did not support him. After Uthman was assassinated in 656, Ali accepted the invitation of the assassins to become caliph, which angered Uthman's UMAYYAD supporters.

Ali was also opposed by Aisha, Muhammad's widow, who joined forces with Uthman's cousin Muawiya, now ruler of Syria. A war ensued between Ali, in control of Arabian and Umayyad forces of Muawiya in Syria, and Aisha in Iraq. Ali defeated Aisha in the Battle of the Camel (so called because Aisha led the troops atop a camel), but the battle with Muawiya was inconclusive (mainly because both sides strapped copies of the KORAN to their spears, making their opponents reluctant to fight). (*See* Islam.)

Ali was assassinated in 661; his followers became Shi'ites, a minority sect that believed the CALIPHATE ought to be occupied only by descendants of Ali.

ALMOHADS

A n Islamic religious movement that was founded around 1120 as a reaction to the corrupted Islamic values of the ALMORAVIDS.

Rise and Conquest. Founded by the BERBER chieftain Muhammad ibn Tumart, the Almohads (from the Arabic for "oneness of God") introduced reforms designed to counter the lax morality and libertine practices of the Almoravids. Ibn Tumart was declared Mahdi and launched a holy war against the Almoravids. He and his successor, Abd al-Mamun, expanded Almohad holdings; by 1145 all of the formerly Almoravid northwest AFRICA was in Almohad hands.

Muslims in SPAIN called upon the Almohads to help them withstand the RECONQUEST of Spain by the Christian north, but this resulted in the Almohads assuming control and installing a harsh Islamic regime. Forced conversions of Jews put an end to the golden age of Arabic-Judeo civilization in Andalusia, and the native Muslim populace remained inhospitable to Almohad austerity and fanaticism. (*See* ISLAM.)

At the end of the twelfth century, the Almohads, particularly under the leadership of Abu Yaakub Yussuf, showed remarkable military prowess in crushing a Jewish revolt in Granada in 1165, defeating the armies of Aragon and Castile, and conquering Madrid—all with only the half-hearted support of the indigenous Muslim population. The retreat of the Almoravids was slow, however, and was not complete until their last bastion, the Balearic Islands, was overrun in 1203.

Decline and Dissolution. Like the Almoravids before them, the Almohads discovered how difficult it is to administer a regime unpopular with its subjects. In spite of being poised to attack the Christian kingdom following their great victory at Alarcos in 1195, the constant attention that had to be paid to dissatisfied factions in Spain and North Africa eventually drained Almohad strength and resolve. The Christian north began its assault on the Almohads with a victory at Las Navas de Tolosa in 1212. The attempt to liberalize their principles in order to court favor from former "infidels" (even Jews were permitted to settle and thrive in Morocco during this period) was an example of too little, too late. The Christians, though divided, were still able to wrest Andalusia in the 1220s, then Seville, and by 1248, Granada, the Almohad stronghold in Spain. The Almohads were now relegated to the Maghreb, where they were still unpopular with most segments of society.

The next half-century saw local potentates across North Africa opportunistically revolting against their Almohad masters, who were busy enforcing Islamic strictures and defending borders from Gibraltar to Sinai. By 1290, only Morocco and Algeria remained firmly under Almohad rule, and even that ended with a revolt in 1296 and the creation of an independent Moroccan state. (*See* ISLAM.)

ALMORAVIDS

The BERBER dynasty that rose out of the Sahara, adopted ISLAM, ruled most of North AFRICA, and extended their empire to SPAIN, before falling to the ALMOHADS. Coming from nomadic stock, the Almoravids practiced an ascetic Islamic regimen until their conquests introduced them to the luxuries of power and urban life. They flourished for two centuries until vanquished and all but eradicated by the Almohads in 1148.

Beginnings. Consisting largely of the seminomadic Tuareg tribes who followed the teachings of the Muslim holy man Abdallah ibn Yasin, the Almoravids, already in control of the caravan trade routes that crisscrossed the Sahara, turned that control into political power by building a network of fortress mosques (*ribat*, after which the movement is named) that gave them unquestioned control of much of the Maghreb (North Africa). This grew from exacting tribute in the form of tolls for safe passage to dominion over Morocco, Algeria, and the last vestiges of the FATIMID Empire in the east. Their military innovations, including the use of terrifying drums and pinpoint archers, made them feared across the Mediterranean.

To Spain. The Almoravids were invited by the Spanish Muslims to help stem the mounting Christian RECONQUEST of Spain. Yusuf ibn Tashfin, after establishing a splendid capital in Marrakesh, embarked on a campaign of engaging the Christians while annexing more and more of Muslim Spain. Yusuf defeated ALFONSO VI of Castile in 1086 at Silaca, and the empire seemed at the time invincible. But a decadence born of the luxuries of urban life, and the weakness of Yusuf's heir, Ali, led to the quick collapse of the Almoravids, culminating in the conquest of Marrakesh in 1146 by an even more fanatical Islamic group, the Almohads. By 1148, the Almoravids had lost their last stronghold in Spain, and the desperate Muslims now turned to the new power, the Almohads, to protect them from the approaching Christians. (*See* SPAIN; RECONQUEST.)

ALP ARSLAN

Alp Arslan (c. 1030–1072) was the SELJUK sultan from 1063 to 1072. In his short reign, he launched the military campaign that marked the end of Byzantine supremacy in ANATOLIA and brought the Turks to the forefront.

Alp was the nephew of the Turkish sultan Toghrïl Beg and son of Chagrï Beg, ruler of the eastern province of Khurasan. Alp inherited his father's office in 1058, and with the help of his vizier, Nizam al-Mulk, took the sultanship in 1063 when Toghrïl died with no heir. Alp embarked on a campaign of expansion and, having come to the border of BYZANTIUM, was about to turn south and invade the FATIMID Empire in EGYPT when the Byzantines launched a preemptive attack. In the ensuing war, Alp destroyed the Byzantine army at MANZIKERT on August 16, 1071. The Byzantines would never recover. Alp was assassinated in November 1072, while attempting the conquest of Turkestan. (*See* SELJUK TURKS.)

AMBROSE, ST.

Saint Ambrose (339–397) served as bishop of MILAN in the fourth century and was one of the most important and influential clergymen of the early Middle Ages. He is remembered as the teacher of SAINT AUGUSTINE OF HIPPO, but he was also a prolific and eloquent writer and composer of evocative plainsong melodies.

Life. Ambrose was born in Treves (today part of Belgium) in 339, son of the prefect of Gaul. His father died when Ambrose was a boy. Raised by his mother and his sister, who was a nun, he rose to the position of governor of the Aemilia-Liguria region of ITALY while in his early thirties. He lived in Milan, where in 374 he was chosen as a compromise candidate to serve as the city's bishop. Ambrose was not then involved in Church affairs; he had not even been baptized. At first he refused the office, but he ultimately agreed, and held the position for the rest of his life.

Well-read in both Greek and Roman PHILOSOPHY, he drew from the works of pagans such as the Neoplatonist PLOTINUS for his sermons. His influence on Augustine began in 384, when the younger man came to Milan. Initially skeptical of the Church's teachings and its ability to combine the spiritual and the intellectual, Ambrose convinced Augustine that the two elements could in fact be intertwined in Christian thought.

Though he could be diplomatic, Ambrose was notoriously strict. He despised pagans and rejected pleas from the Roman senate for tolerance. His involvement in matters previously thought to be the concerns of government added a new dimension to the influence of the Church. He preached often on the duty of everyone, including the emperor, to the Church. It was said that the parents of young girls worried that his sermons on chastity would keep them from marrying. His most famous sermons are "On the Six Days of Creation" and "On the Goodness of Death." He also composed the hymns "Framer of the Earth and Sky" and "Maker of All Things, God Most High."

Ambrose died in Milan in 397. In addition to having been canonized, he was proclaimed one of the four doctors of the Latin Church.

ANATOLIA

At the beginning of the Middle Ages, Anatolia (modern day Turkey) was firmly part of the Byzantine Empire, the Romans having defeated the native Seleucids at the Battle of Magnesia in 190 B.C.E. The Romans drove native soldiers to the north, near the Black Sea, and east near the Euphrates. For centuries Anatolia was the eastern bulwark of the empire, and it became a major trading center between Europe and Asia. In the fourth century C.E., Byzantine Emperor CONSTANTINE allowed local governors to control Anatolia, and at the end of the fourth century he moved his empire's capital to CONSTANTINOPLE.

During the sixth century, however, cracks in Anatolia's strength began to emerge. Cities were bankrupted by both the plague and the high taxes Emperor JUSTINIAN I imposed. In the seventh century, Anatolia faced attacks from Persia, and later Muslim Arabs, who raided for the next two centuries. The Byzantines eventually regained control, but their defeat at the hands of the SELJUK TURKS at the BATTLE OF MANZIK-

ERT in 1071 spelled the end of Roman control. By the end of the century, Turks established rule in much of southern Anatolia. Eventually, the Osmanli Turks controlled the region, repelling several MONGOL invasions during the fourteenth century. In 1453 the empire fell victim to OTTOMAN TURKS. By 1500, Constantinople was in ruins, and the whole of Asia Minor was Turkish.

ANDREAS CAPELLANUS

Andreas Capellanus (flourished twelfth century) was a French writer best known for his *Book on the Art of Loving Nobly and the Reprobation of Dishonorable Love.* It is essentially a primer on the art of courtly love—the idealized, noble love outside the bounds of marriage that was so admired during medieval times. Andreas, also known as André le Chapelain, was attached to the court of Countess Marie de Champagne (daughter of Eleanor of AQUITAINE). Twentieth-century scholars are divided on the purpose of the work, with some believing it to be a satirical attack on freedom in heterosexual love.

Originally written in Latin, it was strongly influenced by the Roman poet Ovid. The book became highly popular and was translated into FRENCH in the thirteenth century. Because it covers the concept of courtly love so completely, it has served as a useful reference through the centuries for medieval scholars.

ANGELICO, FRA

Fra Angelico (c. 1400–1455), an Italian fresco painter and Dominican friar, is viewed as a transitional figure between the Middle Ages and the Renaissance.

Life. Born Guido di Pietro in a village near FLORENCE, he entered the Dominican monastery Santo Domenico at Fiesole about the year 1419, and took the name Fra (Brother) Giovanni. He soon earned the name Fra Angelico because of his placid demeanor and his tranquil angelic paintings.

Work. Fra Angelico painted in the GOTHIC style, marked by warm, elegant figures, gold backgrounds, and sweeping textile folds. He painted

Fra Angelico's fresco The Preaching of Saint Stephen, *in the Vatican's Nicholas Chapel, like much of Angelico's work shows a keen eye for architectural detail.*

throughout his life and left behind a large body of work, much of it frescoes (paint on plaster). Frescoes he created at the convent of Santo Marco in Florence are among the finest ever produced. In 1445, another highly praised series painted for the Chapel of the Sacrament in the Vatican was destroyed by fire. In 1447, he was summoned to Rome by Pope Nicholas V to paint frescoes for the pope's private chapel depicting the lives of Saints Stephen and Lawrence.

In 1449, he moved to Fiesole to serve as prior, and while there either painted or supervised the execution of a cycle of 35 paintings on the life of Christ. He returned to Rome in 1453 and lived his last years in the Dominican monastery, where he died on February 18, 1455. (*See* GOTHIC ART; PAINTING.)

ANGELS AND DEMONS

ngels, demons, and the ethereal realm played a large part in the medieval mind, though in ways that place that mentality apart from primitive demonology, classical mythology, or even the folk supersti-

tions that have persisted throughout history to the modern era.

The Classical Legacy. Angels and demons appear sparingly in the BIBLE, although their existence is accepted without question. They play important roles in the Old Testament and in the life of Christ. Their function is frequently as divine messengers (the word "angel" is derived from the Greek for messenger) and as part of the celestial retinue. In the KORAN, angels are regarded as inferior to humans and are ordered to prostrate themselves before people.

In the classical age of Greece and Rome, the distinction between the ethereal realm and the physical earthly realm was blurred as the gods were often depicted as having corporeal form and engaging in decidedly material acts. But the greatest difference between ancient and classical thinking was in the relationship between humans and spirits in the scheme of history. In antiquity, deities paid only glancing attention to human affairs, being engrossed largely in interdeistical matters. In the classical period, the affairs of humankind took on a more central place in the attitudes of the gods, who seemed to rise and fall in step with the fortunes of nations or heroes.

In the Middle Ages. Two factors shaped medieval attitudes toward the ethereal: First, the rise of CHRISTIANITY and ISLAM as politically powerful forces in history introduced a "bureaucracy" into the ethereal realm that mirrored the highly organized religious institutions. Thus, *The Celestial Hierarchy,* a work attributed (incorrectly, it was later determined) to Dionysius the Areopagite, a Syrian monk who flourished around 500 C.E., joined the same author's *Ecclesiastical Hierarchy* in providing a highly formalized structure to a universe that integrated the physical and the ethereal.

Nine levels of angels attended the Divine Throne, and a complex structure was theorized by Scholastic philosophers who delved into increasingly arcane matters such as the question of how many angels could fit on the head of a pin (actually a serious question regarding the physical attributes of spirits).

The second factor was the increasing difficulty human civilization encountered with the natural world as it spread through northern Europe and as the protective features of the Roman Empire were lost. War, famine, and pestilence brought out people's worst fears, which were played upon by mis-

A 15th-century view of the devil, often seen as embodying multiple personalities, mirroring the "demons" people sensed in themselves.

ANGEVINS

From the 800s, angels are depicted as winged. Above, a 13th-century depiction of angels and demons active in the Resurrection (top) and judgment of the dead.

Angevin (means "of Anjou" in French) is the name of two family dynasties that originated in FRANCE during the Middle Ages. One Angevin line ruled ENGLAND (the PLANTAGENETS), while the other ruled France.

The first Angevins came to power through Fulk, who became the count of Anjou in the 900s, and went on to rule parts of France and England. One of Fulk's descendants, FULK V, became king of Jerusalem in 1131, and one of his younger sons inherited the kingship as Baldwin III. Baldwin's descendants continued to rule Jerusalem until 1186, when that branch of the older Angevin house ended.

The Plantagenets. Fulk V's older son, Geoffrey IV (Plantagenet), inherited Anjou and along with it, the longtime feud the Angevins carried on with the dukes of Normandy, who ruled England following the NORMAN conquest. Geoffrey IV's marriage to Matilda, the daughter of King HENRY I of England, paved the way for the union of the ruling families of Norman England and Anjou. In 1154 the son of Geoffrey and Matilda, HENRY II, became the first Angevin (Plantagenet) king of England. His Angevin successors on the throne were RICHARD I, JOHN, HENRY III, Edward I, EDWARD II, EDWARD III, and RICHARD II.

The Angevins succeeded in holding on to the English throne until the last English Angevin king, Richard II, was deposed in 1399. After Richard II, the English branch of the Angevins split into the houses of Lancaster and York, and their feud over succession led to the WARS OF THE ROSES. There was also a Breton branch of Angevins, which began when a nephew of Richard I and John, Arthur I, became duke of BRITTANY in 1196. This line of Angevins ended when Anne of Brittany and her daughter married kings of France.

The French Angevins. The second great Angevin dynasty, which ruled over parts of France and for a time NAPLES, HUNGARY, POLAND, and Jerusalem, originated with Charles, the younger brother of King LOUIS IX of France, whom Louis made count of Anjou. By the early 1200s the Angevins had lost most of their lands to the French kings, but Charles, as the new count, expanded his holdings by marrying the daughter of the count of Provence. Then in 1266 the pope invested Charles with the kingdoms of NAPLES and SICILY. This papal support then allowed Charles to conquer Sicily and southern Italy by force. Although Charles was not able to retain all the territory he conquered (he lost Sicily in 1282), some of his descendants ruled Naples until 1435, while others were for a time kings of Hungary and Poland. This second Angevin dynasty died out in France in the 1480s, when the French king took over their lands.

sionaries who sought to convert the pagans and barbarian invaders of Europe. In this, the life and work of Pope GREGORY I THE GREAT set the tone for much of the Middle Ages. Gregory waged a campaign against pagan magic in the sixth century; his dark temperament and his recognition of the power of the fear of demons (fears that seemed to thrive better in the dank atmospheres of northern Europe than in the warm light of the Mediterranean) and of necromancy encouraged him to embrace both sides of the argument and promote spiritualism, even as he railed against paganism. This conflicted attitude was also prevalent in Jewish and Islamic circles, where mystical communities had little trouble finding adherents, and a rich literature arose (culminating in Judaism's *Zohar*, a product of thirteenth-century Spain).

By the end of the Middle Ages, even more rationalistic thinkers like SAINT THOMAS AQUINAS and DUNS SCOTUS accepted the existence of spirits and theorized about them. (*See* MAGIC AND FOLKLORE.)

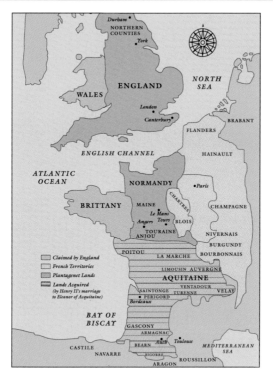

Norman and Angevin lands in France and England in the 12th century. The reward for uniting England and France was control of the important English Channel.

ANGLO-NORMAN FRENCH

A term used to describe the Norman inhabitants of FRANCE who considered themselves part of and connected to ENGLAND during the late Middle Ages, and their language. Although the Normans are said to have "conquered" England in 1066, the Normans had obtained a legitimate claim to the English throne more than 60 years earlier when England's ETHELRED THE UNREADY married Emma, daughter of the duke of NORMANDY, in 1002. Although England and Normandy were united for more than a century following the Battle of HASTINGS, the noble families who held sway in England and France created a precarious balance of power that fomented fierce rivalries and led to the HUNDRED YEARS' WAR. England lost Normandy in 1204, briefly regained it during the Hundred Years' War, but by 1450, Normandy was back under French control permanently.

Between Two Powers. The Normans, descended from the VIKINGS, were themselves newcomers to French soil, having settled in France in the tenth century. The birth of Ethelred's son, EDWARD THE CONFESSOR, gave the Normans a strong foothold in England. Edward, who became king in 1043, was at first strongly influenced by the English earls of WESSEX, Mercia, and Northumbria. Gradually, he began to develop stronger ties to the Normans. A number of Norman traders and clergymen settled in England over the next 20 years and quietly expanded their influence.

The Battle of Hastings. After WILLIAM I's crowning in 1047, Normandy became a strong, unified, important duchy. Following a dispute over the succession to the English throne, William launched an invasion of England and, on October 14, 1066, his forces dealt Harold's troops a crushing and decisive blow at the Battle of Hastings. William was crowned king, and his reign lasted until his death in 1087. He managed to rule both England and Normandy effectively, and he increased the holdings of both regions through a number of conquests.

In the centuries that followed, Normandy was involved in frequent disputes with the French province of Anjou as English monarchs continually tried to influence the succession in the ANGEVIN dynasty. In 1154, HENRY II, the son of Matilda and Geoffrey, became king of England, duke of Normandy, and count of Anjou, moving closer to unifying these kingdoms.

In 1204, the French King PHILIP II AUGUSTUS invaded Normandy and made it a French province. Political ties between England and Normandy were severed, although the two regions were still closely tied together through trade, history, and culture.

The Hundred Years' War. Over the next century, the rivalries between the English and the French escalated, resulting in the Hundred Years' War, which began in 1337. The war was more a series of sieges and battles punctuated by truces, but in 1417 England regained control of Normandy under the leadership of HENRY V. Normandy remained a part of England for the next three decades, during which time the English established the University of Caen. Henry formed an alliance with the French province of BURGUNDY in 1420, and for a time it seemed England would take control of most of France.

But the French were unwilling to give up. They mounted a number of sieges against the English. Battles such as that of Orléans in the late 1420s (led by JOAN OF ARC) provided victories that revitalized the French forces. Gradually, they forced the English out and reclaimed the provinces for France. In 1450, they succeeded in reclaiming Normandy permanently as a province of France. Within three years, England had abandoned its claims to its French holdings; the Hundred Years' War was officially ended.

See HUNDRED YEARS' WAR and entries on related personalities. Background material appears in NORMANS and ANGLO-SAXONS. Additional information may be found in ANGEVINS, ENGLAND, and FRANCE.

ANGLO-SAXON CHRONICLE

The Anglo-Saxon Chronicle is the name given to the collection of several English documents created and copied by Anglo-Saxon monks. The chronicle originated in the late 800s from the compilation of annals and tables of events made during the reign of ALFRED THE GREAT, when the decision was made to keep a continuous record to be updated on an annual basis. (*See* ENGLISH LANGUAGE.)

The work was thought to have been commissioned by King Alfred—there is no evidence that he was directly involved, but only encouraged its creation. After the original compilation of the chronicle, which begins with the start of the Christian era, monks in various monasteries added, subtracted, and continued the document, keeping it up to date. Much of the early material comes from BEDE, but from the wars between the SAXONS and Danes onward, most of the material is original and our sole source of information about the events described. Most of the chronicle consists of simple prose narrative, but several poems, such as "The Battle of Brunanburh," are also included.

The chronicle, which was kept up to date at the monastery at Peterborough until 1154, provides important information about the Norman Conquest and its effect on Anglo-Saxon ENGLAND. The chronicle's vivid account of the troubled reign of King Stephen is written in language that is clearly in the process of making the transition from Anglo-Saxon (Old English) to early Middle English.

ANGLO-SAXONS

The Roman withdrawal from their colonies in Britain in about 410 C.E. left a vacuum in leadership that opened the way for the Germanic invasions of the fifth and sixth centuries. These newcomers are now grouped under the heading Anglo-Saxons, from the tribal names of the Angles and Saxons, as first listed by the monk chronicler BEDE in the eighth century. However, they were, in fact, comprised of a number of tribes whose origins lay near the North Sea coast from the Elbe to the Rhine, in the Jutland Peninsula, and in southern Scandinavia.

Early Period. The original inhabitants of Britain were of Celtic stock, and literary sources such as the sixth century's *Ruin of Britain* by the English churchman Gildas and *The History of the English Church and People* by Bede, completed by 731, suggest that the first groups of continental warriors were invited to Britain by a Celtic king, Vortigern, in about 450, to

Barbarians—Saxons, Angles, and Jutes—depicted invading Britain by sea in the 5th-century Passion of St. Edmund.

fight as mercenaries against the northern PICTS and Scots. Unfortunately, these fierce Teutonic warriors eventually overcame the more peaceable native Britons. They either enslaved them or pushed them to the edges of the island, to WALES, Cornwall, and SCOTLAND. The legends of King ARTHUR, a native British leader who fought bravely against the Anglo-Saxon invaders, dates from this period of conflict.

Although the earliest arrivals in this new wave of settlers were warlords and their entourages, they were soon followed by clans of Germanic ploughmen who had been pushed ever farther west and north in this period of "folk wandering" by the vast shunting of peoples out of the Eurasian steppes and into Europe.

These pagan settlers brought with them a culture related to the Scandinavian, in which the kings were said to be directly descended from Woden, the supreme god of their religion. These rulers engendered fierce loyalty among their militant followers, called a *comitatus,* or war band. The warrior chief was chosen on the basis of his ability to fight, but eventually most kings were elected from the same powerful families, and dynasties, such as the House of WESSEX, developed and thrived as a result.

WARFARE and the raiding of neighboring territories were essential to these Germanic societies—it was only through seasonal pillaging that the chieftain, later king, could replenish the large amounts of wealth and land needed to reward, and thereby bind, his followers.

They had brought with them a large body of customary LAW, a rigid oral tradition of justice, based on a class hierarchy, in which vengeance and blood feud were valued. Each man's life had a fixed monetary value called "wergild" (man price), based on his class and status, to be paid to his kin if he were killed. Even after the conversion to CHRISTIANITY, beginning in 579 with the arrival of an envoy from Pope GREGORY I, the wergild retained its importance. Thus, a noble or "thane" was equated with a priest in terms of value.

Justice was administered in gatherings called "folkmoots," usually presided over by the ruler's representative, or "reeve." By the time areas became organized into shires, consisting of "hides" (60 to 120 acres), "hundreds," and "vills," the "shire reeve," or sheriff, had evolved into a hereditary position of power. The king's warrior companions of the invasion period had, by the eighth century, developed into the king's officials and the nobility.

Alfred's Reign. Society had rigidly stratified by the reign of ALFRED (871–899), the most famous English king, into royalty, the high nobility or earls, the low nobility or thanes, and the peasantry or "churls." Alfred's Kingdom of Wessex had achieved ultimate supremacy over the many smaller kingdoms that had previously developed throughout Britain, and over the interrelated royal families. Even the renewed Scandinavian incursions in the ninth century were eventually fought back, and the Scandinavian territory, the Danelaw, became a part of Wessex.

Archaeological evidence indicates that, even though the English migrated into a land crisscrossed by antique Roman roads and dotted with the remains of stone monuments and villas, they continued to build in wood and plaster. Their "burhs," or fortified residences, consisted of a single-story main hall used for meals, socializing, and sleeping quarters for retainers; detached buildings called "bowers" contained workrooms and bedrooms of the lord's family. These were surrounded by earthworks and a stockade. After 800 C.E., these buildings were often two-story stone structures with arches for support, as depicted in the BAYEUX TAPESTRY.

This was a society in which the position of WOMEN, to whom fell the tasks of baking, brewing, spinning, weaving, and related chores, was one of respect and importance. They had recognized legal rights, such as being able to hold land, swear oaths in lawsuits, release slaves, and bequeath property. Many of these rights were lost after the Norman Conquest.

TOWNS grew up around trading centers and meeting places, some going back as far as Roman times; some were developing at natural sites such as harbors, river fords, road junctions, and especially around the growing network of Benedictine monasteries, such as Lindisfarne, St. Albans, and Durham. The Church attained an importance second only to the kings and their close followers, and the clergy were drawn exclusively from the families of NOBLES.

Although the spread of Christianity reintroduced Latin into Britain as the language of the clergy and the educated upper classes, there was an extensive body of sophisticated vernacular literature based upon the Scandinavian and Germanic traditions of epic songs and poems. In these were celebrated the heroes of the past, the heathen gods, and memorable utterances of wise men. These last are known as gnomic poetry. Unfortunately, only fragments survive, often as parts of poems of Christian date, although the ancient pagan elements are only thinly disguised. The epic poem, BEOWULF, not only includes events and characters that must have existed in folk memory, but also gives a picture of upper-class daily life of the middle Anglo-Saxon period of about 750.

A listing of historic events can be found in the ANGLO-SAXON CHRONICLE, a compilation of annals in seven extant manuscripts, reaching from the very beginning of the common era to post-Conquest 1155. The chronicle combines older records, genealogies, world histories, and sometimes even fillers of scraps of poetry. It remains an invaluable source of centuries of history, written not in Latin, but in Old English.

Hastings. The last Anglo-Saxon king was of the Wessex line, EDWARD THE CONFESSOR, the builder of WESTMINSTER ABBEY. His death in January 1066 left no successor, and a struggle for the throne between several distantly related contenders ensued. The victor, established at the BATTLE OF HASTINGS in October 1066, was WILLIAM THE CONQUEROR of Normandy; the battle ended the Anglo-Saxon era.

ENGLAND by 1066 was a wealthy agricultural realm of 1 to 2 million people and therefore a prize for a foreign conqueror. Since the Anglo-Saxon nobility had never learned to fight on horseback, England was militarily backward and fell prey to colonial conquest.

 See BARBARIAN INVASIONS *and* WARFARE *for background on the period; see* ENGLAND *and* WESSEX *for material on Anglo-Saxon lands; also* ANGLO-SAXON CHRONICLE. *Also see* ALFRED THE GREAT, ANGLO-NORMAN FRENCH, *and* HASTINGS, BATTLE OF.

St. Anselm depicted (center) in the terra-cotta altarpiece by Della Robbia, in the Museo Dicesano, Emboli, Italy.

ANNA COMNENA

Anna Comnena (1083–c. 1155) was a member of the Comnenus royal family of the Byzantine Empire and the author of the *Alexiad*, a history of the reign of her father, ALEXIUS I. Anna was born two years after her father became Byzantine emperor. As an infant, she was betrothed to Alexius's presumed successor, Constantine Ducas, the son and grandson of emperors. Anna was educated for the role of empress; she was popular in the Byzantine capital of CONSTANTINOPLE, but her aspirations to be empress would not be satisfied.

Anna plotted against her brother, John, who had been selected by Alexius as his successor, and tried to make her husband, Nicephorus Bryennius, the emperor. The plot was discovered, and she was placed in a convent, where she began writing the *Alexiad*. Upon its completion, the *Alexiad* became a very important—perhaps the most important—documentation of Alexius's reign and of late eleventh- and early twelfth-century Byzantine history. (*See* BYZANTIUM.)

ANSELM, ST.

Archbishop of Canterbury from 1093 to 1109, St. Anselm (1033–1109) was one of the most original and insightful philosophers of the Middle Ages. (*See* PHILOSOPHY.)

Life. Born in Aosta, Lombardy, Anselm entered the monastic school of Bec in Normandy in 1059 and became a disciple of its head, Lanfranc. He succeeded his mentor as prior in 1063, and was appointed Archbishop of Canterbury in 1089. Clearly an independent thinker who believed in the supremacy of the Church over the monarch, his views were challenged by William II Rufus, and Anselm was forced into exile. The dispute was resolved in 1093 with a compromise that protected the king's interest; but the same sequence of conflict, exile, and resolution ensued following William's death in 1100, with HENRY I. The compromise was again reached in 1103.

Work. Anselm was one of the most creative Scholastic philosophers, adopting the motto *credo ut intelligam* ("I believe so that I may understand"), by which he meant that religion may be explained by reason, but only after faith had been accepted. His argument in the *Proslogion* for the existence of God, known as the ontological argument, argues that God must exist if He is conceived as a being with every perfection, which would include existence. It has been the subject of philosophic discussion up to the present day. Anselm's *Cur Deus Homo (Why God Became Man)* on the anthropomorphic verses in Genesis.

AQUINAS, ST. THOMAS

The work of Thomas Aquinas (c. 1225–1274) stands as the crowning achievement of medieval Scholastic philosophical theology. His work became so central that for centuries philosophers were categorized as either Thomists or Scotists (after his opponent, JOHN DUNS SCOTUS). By drawing on Aristotelian PHILOSOPHY as it came to him via Jewish and Arabic sources, he elevated the philosophic enterprise in the minds of the learned for centuries even after his arguments had lost their original authority.

Above, Aquinas conducting a class in a Dominican school. Although Aquinas wrote disparagingly of Jews and Muslims, he relied heavily on their intellectual output.

Life. Born in Aquino (Aquinas means "of Aquino"), near Naples, ITALY, Thomas entered the Dominican order in 1244 and was sent to PARIS to study with ALBERTUS MAGNUS. He spent his entire life teaching in Paris and later in Italy, where he died. His career was spent promoting the use of reason in religion and creating a curriculum for Dominican schools.

Work. Thomas was the preeminent thinker at the University of Paris in the thirteenth century, and he became the official philosopher of the Catholic Church in the sixteenth century. His greatest work is *Summa Theologica*, begun in 1264 and completed just prior to his death. In it, Aquinas argued that reason and science were compatible with revelation and faith. This was then a radical position for a Christian theologian, and he was condemned for it by the Bishop of Paris.

Thomas used reason to present a proof of God's existence (since there cannot be an infinity of causations, there must be an unmoved Prime Mover or First Cause) and to argue that the principles of ethics and the laws of the state must conform to the universal principles of reason. This position gained for him both passionate followers and bitter opponents, the latter including Duns Scotus and WILLIAM OF OCKHAM.

Aquinas also argued against another Parisian philosopher of his day, SUGER OF BRABANT, who claimed that reason and faith were separate and incompatible. This had been the view of the twelfth century Arab Aristotelian philosopher AVERROËS. Aquinas agreed instead with the Jewish philosopher MAIMONIDES that faith and reason could be reconciled.

The *Summa Theologica* and Augustine of Hippo's *The City of God* are regarded today as the two greatest works of medieval theology. (*See* SCHOLASTICISM.)

AQUITAINE

Aquitaine in southwestern FRANCE (sometimes also called Gascony or Guyenne) was a Frankish kingdom, a French and English duchy, and an English principality during the Middle Ages.

Julius Caesar's conquest of the Aquitani, an Iberian people of southwestern Gaul, brought the area under Roman rule and made it a province. By the time the VISIGOTHS occupied the region in the 400s, it had been completely Romanized. It retained its Latin culture after the Frankish ruler CLOVIS defeated the Visigoths in 507 and made it part of the Frankish kingdom. However, during the fierce strife among Clovis's successors, AQUITAINE escaped from Frankish control. After 670 the semi-independent native dukes of Aquitaine ruled until an Arab invasion in 718 forced them to seek protection from the Frankish ruler, CHARLES MARTEL, who defeated the Arabs in 732.

In 781, after CHARLEMAGNE subdued the local nobles, he turned Aquitaine into a kingdom for his son LOUIS I, who succeeded his father as emperor. After the death of Louis's son Pépin I, whom he had made ruler of Aquitaine, Louis added Aquitaine to the west Frankish kingdom which his youngest son, Charles the Bald, ruled after the TREATY OF VERDUN in 843. When a group of nobles made Pépin's young son, Pépin II, king, a struggle between Charles and the nobles broke out over control of Aquitaine. During this period both NORMAN and Muslim attacks on Aquitaine and civil strife within weakened CAROLINGIAN control. Charles's successors were forced to accept the hereditary rights of various noble families until royal control of Aquitaine became virtually nonexistent by the 900s.

After 973 the counts of Poitou held the title of duke of Aquitaine, even though it was not until later that they were able to expand their control beyond Poitou. During the 1000s the dukes of Aquitaine subdued their weaker neighbors, extending their rule over all of Aquitaine. By the early 1100s, the duchy's wealth, which included valuable salt mines and a thriving wine industry, centered in the city of Bordeaux, made it one of the leading states of Europe.

In 1137, when Duke William X of Aquitaine died without a son, his large duchy went to his 15-year-old daughter, ELEANOR. When she married the French dauphin, who soon became King Louis VII, her duchy fell under the control of the French crown. However, when their marriage ended with an annulment, the duchy reverted to her. Her subsequent marriage to Henry of Anjou and Normandy, who became King HENRY II of ENGLAND, linked Aquitaine to the English crown, although legally its ruler still owed homage to the French king. (*See* ELEANOR OF AQUITANE.)

In the early 1200s and 1300s, disputes between France and England were the source of repeated ruptures between the English dukes of Aquitaine and the kings of France. The French claim to Aquitaine was one of the causes of the HUNDRED YEARS' WAR (1337–1453). At the end of the first phase of the war after the signing of a treaty in 1360, King EDWARD III of England turned Aquitaine into a principality, which he then gave to his son, EDWARD THE BLACK PRINCE

Prince Edward set up a lavish court at Aquitaine, but the court was so expensive to operate that he had to impose heavy taxes on the principality's people. The ensuing revolt by the nobles of Aquitaine ended Edward's rule and the treaty as well, thereby contributing to the resumption of the Hundred Years' War.

Only at the end of the war in 1453 were the French able to capture Bordeaux and all English territory in France (except Calais). After the French recovered Aquitaine at the Battle of Libourne, it became the French province of Guienne. (*See* FRANCE.)

ARAB

The word "Arab" has several meanings in the context of medieval history. It refers first to the people who inhabited the Arabian peninsula and the outlying areas of the Middle East and their descendants. That last element is the source of the difficulty in defining the term adequately; the people from Arabia created empires that spanned the Western world, incorporating related peoples within their political and religious community and absorbing them from many far-flung areas with a cultural assimilation that even the Hellenistic Greeks would envy. This resulted in the distinctions between Arabs and non-Arabs becoming blurred in the process.

Pre-Islam. Before MUHAMMAD, the Arabs were still following their cultic origins, worshipping the descendant deities of Semitic antiquity. Only at the borders of Arab civilization were there influences of the "new" religions of Persia, Greece, and ROME. The advent of Muhammad radically influenced the Arab population by unifying them and bringing them under the authority of a religion that was related to those being pursued by their neighbors. There was one significant difference, however: from its very inception, ISLAM (the name of the new doctrine) was to be promoted and spread by armed conflict. By the time Muhammad died, the pattern of conversion by conquest had been set. The leader of the kingdom, the caliph, was also imbued with religious authority. All the conquests sponsored by Muhammad's successor, ABU BAKR, in the seventh century—be it Khalid ibn al-Walid's conquest of Iraq in 633, Omar ibn al-Khatib's victory over the Byzantines at the Yarmuk in 636, Saad ibn Abu Waqqas's conquest of Persia in 637, or the conquest of EGYPT by Omar ibn al-Aas in 642—were thus motivated not merely by territorial desires, but were "holy wars" (jihad) for the dissemination of the new religion.

This proved both advantageous and a hindrance. On the one hand, the soldiers fighting were driven with a fervor that made them effective militarily to a degree not seen since the heyday of the Roman legions. On the other, so pale a commitment was demanded from conquered peoples that a genuine conversion was simply unreasonable to expect, leaving the Arabs with only their own to administer their new territory. As the empire expanded, this became more difficult; power had to be shared with non-Arab Muslims, or with *dhimmis*—Christians and Jews who were tolerated as adherents of related religions, but who were discriminated against and never fully trusted.

ARABIC LANGUAGE AND LITERATURE

The spread of ISLAM led to the inevitable fragmenting of the empire into different dynasties, all operating in the context of a religious schism between the Shi'ites and the Sunnites. Each dynasty sought to prove its authenticity and its legitimacy by promoting Arabic language, literature, and culture in a central court that laid claim to being the seat of Arabic civilization, at least for a time. Thus, the UMAYYADS in Arabia, the FATIMIDS in Egypt, the ABBASIDS in North AFRICA, and all the smaller CALIPHATES from the Atlantic to the Indus, all experienced a "golden age" in which Arabic literature, art and music, science, and medicine received the support of the sovereign and flourished.

The transmission of knowledge from antiquity to the medieval Latin world often took a circuitous route through Judeo-Arabic translators.

Language. The importance of formulating religious doctrine (hadith) for a religion as far-flung as Islam created the need for a precise and highly literate language. Using the translation of ancient texts as a springboard, the Arabic writers, poets, historians, and liturgists created bodies of literature that reflected the interests and personalities of the court of their patronage. Thus, the very formal theological writings produced by the Umayyads were not likely to be created in the more artistically inclined Abbasid court; the highly imaginative tales spun in the *Thousand and One Nights* in the Abbasid environment, one that benefited from the liberalizing influences from BYZANTIUM and Persia, would have been dismissed back in the Umayyad palace as trivial. Similarly, the highly evocative music and poetry of the Abbasid

The same may be said regarding SCIENCE, though the Arab contribution to mathematics—the development of the decimal system and Arabic numeral notation—is so important that it is the cornerstone of modern mathematics. Mathematics may deservedly be considered an enterprise that Arab culture had reinvented and made wholly its own.

The background of Arab culture is discussed in ISLAM, KORAN, MUHAMMAD *and* CALIPHATE. *See also* LIBRARIES *for information on repositories of manuscripts; see also entries on* ISLAMIC ART AND ARCHITECTURE *and* JEWISH ART AND LITERATURE.

ARAGON

A small region of northeastern SPAIN, sandwiched between NAVARRE and Catalonia, Aragon became a dominant province in medieval Spanish history. A combination of events led to Aragon's rise in influence; ultimately, it became one of the cornerstones of the kingdom of modern Spain.

Aragon, situated in the Pyrenees, became an outpost for the VISIGOTHS in the south when they were forced north by Muslim conquests early in the eighth century. Without its own ruler, it fell under the influence of its neighbor Navarre, which had successfully resisted the Muslim forces. Aragon was for all intents and purposes a part of Navarre for some 200 years. During that time, its population steadily grew; by 922 a bishopric had been established there. But officially, Aragon was still nothing more than a county.

Rise. It was in the eleventh century that Aragon began its rise to prominence. In 1035, King Sancho (III) the Great of Navarre left Aragon to his son Ramiro. Ramiro's older brother succeeded Sancho, and Ramiro became the region's first ruler (although never actually king). Between 1035 and Ramiro's death in 1063, Aragon grew in area to more than six times its original size as Ramiro took control of frontier lands that were formerly part of Navarre.

Upon Ramiro's death, his son Sancho Ramirez succeeded. Aragon was then involved in a fierce battle with Muslims from the south. Interestingly, although French and Catalan forces joined the Aragonese in their battles, the Navarrones sometimes fought with the Muslims. When the king of Navarre died in 1076, Sancho Ramirez (who was his cousin) succeeded him. Aragon and Navarre became a single entity.

Eventually, the Muslim battles subsided, and Aragon became an important trading center for French and Muslim merchants. Pilgrims to the shrine

LEGEND AND LORE

The most famous work of Arabic literature is the *Thousand and One Nights,* collected over several centuries and committed to writing in the tenth century during the Abbasid reign. The stories are told within a frame story in which King Shahryar, having found his wife unfaithful, kills her and, hating all womankind, decides to marry a different wife each day, then kill her the next morning. The daughter of the king's vizier, Scheherazade, devises a plan that will save her life: she tells the king a story each night, leaving the ending for the next day, when she begins a new story. Her tales are so entertaining that the king falls in love with her and abandons his plan. Many of the tales are clearly of Asian origin; the most famous stories, "Ali Baba and the Forty Thieves" and "Aladdin and the Wonderful Lamp" are not found in any Arabic version of the collection. No Arabic version contains more than a few hundred tales, and the text contains many grammatical errors, all of which indicate that the collection was added to continually by storytellers and redactors over a period of several centuries. The collection did not become known to Europeans until Galland's 1704 French translation. The most celebrated English edition is Sir Richard Burton's 16-volume edition, completed in 1889.

composers of SPAIN contrasts starkly with the very logical and tightly knit philosophical masterpieces of Fatimid Egypt. In nearly every case, Arab cultural success was measured by the fidelity and creativity with which it took its Greek and Latin legacy, built on it, adapted it, and transformed it into a uniquely Arabic experience. It may be said that Arabic culture of the Middle Ages owes its flowering to being able to recognize and appreciate the vast body of knowledge and literature bequeathed to it by its Mediterranean neighbors.

of Saint James at Asturias-León traveled through Aragon as well. By the twelfth century, Aragon was a prosperous and powerful kingdom.

The Catalans. But renewed clashes with Muslims, coupled with threats from the nearby kingdom of Castile, began to take their toll on Aragon. King ALFONSO I, known as the Battler, expanded Aragon's western borders during several battles. When he died without an heir in 1134, his brother Ramiro, a monk, was persuaded to leave his order, accept the throne of Aragon, and marry a princess from AQUITAINE. In 1137 he and his wife had a daughter, who was immediately betrothed to Count Ramón Berenguer of Catalonia. Ramiro gave up the throne at this point, and Ramón became the ruler of what became known as the crown of Aragon, which was dominated by Catalonia.

The Navarrones refused to recognize the Catalan king and chose their own. But Catalonia brought a new prominence to Aragon, primarily in the form of the Mediterranean port city of BARCELONA. Now, land-locked Aragon would have access to still more trade. The Catalans, for their part, thought that the Aragonese would protect them from Muslim forces. Over the next 150 years, Aragonese forces captured the Muslim region of Valencia, and took control of SICILY, Sardinia, and Majorca. By the end of the thirteenth century, Aragon's influence spread throughout the Mediterranean to EGYPT. NAPLES was annexed in 1442. Navarre, which had broken away, was reunited with the kingdom in 1425.

Meanwhile, Castile was also gaining prominence. A marriage between Aragon's Alfonso IV and a Castilian princess in 1336 tied the two kingdoms together, but there were rivalries over the next several decades. Ultimately, the Castilian influence increased as more marriages between the two kingdoms took place. This was seen as a positive move by the Aragonese, who feared that the Catalans might try to exert greater influence over their kingdom. In 1410, when the Aragonese king died without an heir, nobles decided they had to act fast to maintain control over the kingdom. They chose to elect Ferdinand of Antequera, a Castilian prince, to the throne. He became Ferdinand I.

The marriage of Aragon's Ferdinand II to Princess Isabella of Castile in 1474 brought more unity between the two thrones; in 1479, the two kingdoms were joined. (Ferdinand and Isabella are best known today for their connection with the Italian explorer Christopher Columbus). The Aragon region remained relatively independent, with its own parliament and administration, until the eighteenth century; it was not until 1833 that Aragon ceased to exist officially as a separate administrative unit. (*See* SPAIN; EXPLORATION.)

ARCHITECTURE

T he architecture of the Middle Ages grew out of the architecture of the classical world. Yet, with the passage of time and with so many factors influencing the development of the art—developments in construction technology; new climatic and social pressures; and, most important, the development of very specific ideological and aesthetic values particular to each culture and epoch, to name a few— it is only reasonable to expect that the architectural forms that would develop would display the same diversity that was true in all other areas of society. Moreover, the significant dedication of resources required for the more ambitious architectural projects provided a good reason for the values represented by the finished product to be indicative of the culture that spawned the work. Thus, the architecture of each culture provides insight, possibly to an even greater extent than other art forms, into the views and values of the society in which the edifices were built.

One discerns five major periods or stylistic epochs in medieval architecture: early Christian, Byzantine, Islamic, ROMANESQUE, and GOTHIC. Elements of the architecture of the latter four of the above are dealt with in the relevant entries (BYZANTINE ART AND ARCHITECTURE, and so forth). The aim here is to view the discipline broadly by examining both the distinctive and the shared elements of each school.

Above, interior of the Great Mosque of Córdoba, built by Abderhamman I in the 8th century. Compare this closed and compartmentalized space with the interior of the Amiens Cathedral, left, a prime example of 13th-century French Gothic architecture.

Early Christian Architecture. Working closest to its classical origins, the early builders took the basic form of the Roman basilica and adapted it to the liturgical needs of the Church. Two structures that foreshadowed later developments were the basilicas of St. Peter and St. Paul in Rome, built in the form of a cross (as seen from above) not only for its symbolic significance, but also to provide separate areas for the altar, housed in the short top arm of the cross; the apse (from the Latin for vault); and the clergy, seated in the short arms of the cross (transept). The worshippers occupied the central hall, the nave, after the Latin for ship, from the metaphor of the church as a ship. The entrance was known as the galilee, symbolizing entry to the Holy Land from the north, or the narthex (vestibule), after the Latin for casket, symbolizing the entrance of the worshipper into the ethereal world of the afterlife.

This view of the church as a vessel, both symbolic and metaphysical, was to inform the development of early Christian architecture and carry on into the GOTHIC period. The same may be said of the introduction of bell towers: the strong nautical association of bells was instrumental in the design element becoming ubiquitous in church architecture.

In BYZANTIUM, architecture was marked by a diversity and complexity that represented the flowering of Roman premises. Architectural problems posed by increased cathedral size, such as those encountered in the construction of HAGIA SOPHIA (537 C.E.), were solved by designing more massive walls and using the support tension of vaults and the dome, forming the cupola (a vault-supported dome), which was to become an essential element of Islamic architecture.

Byzantine Architecture. The construction associated with JUSTINIAN I drew on classical styles and sought to accommodate the monastic orders that grew surrounding the church, while introducing a monumentlike quality to its structures. This approach allowed for easy transition into the creation of fortresses that Byzantium built in the many corners of the empire that were under virtually constant attack. The ornamentation of the walls of Byzantine churches shows clear Persian and Islamic influence, though the general isolation of the culture makes it difficult to say definitively in which direction the influence flowed. With the fall of Byzantium in 1453, the architectural style continued in the Balkan countries and Russia, where the Eastern Church wielded religious authority.

Islamic Architecture. In contrast to early CHRISTIANITY, Islam viewed its place of worship, the mosque—from *masjid*, literally "place of prostration"—as a miniature city on earth in which all the spiritual needs of the worshipper were met. Pilgrimage to the holy sites in Arabia was required as a show of religious fealty. But the design of the mosque is toward the here and now and to the practical day-to-day

The cathedral of Notre Dame in Paris, an example of 13th-century French Gothic architecture. Visible are the flying buttresses; the double bell towers, left; and the apse, right. The side entrances were decorated with rose windows to take advantage of the striking views from the banks of the Seine River. The cathedral is built on an island in the river.

observance. The requirement that the worshipper wash the hands and feet before prayer made it necessary to install baths and fountains nearby. The interior of the structure is divided into many compartments in which different religious functions may be taking place simultaneously. The bell towers of the church gave way to the tall minarets from which the muezzins announced the time of prayer to the faithful wherever they happened to be.

The influence of Persian and Byzantine design is clear in early Islamic architecture: the first mosque at Fufa in Iraq was probably built by local Persian craftsmen. The magnificent Dome of the Rock in Jerusalem (688–692) was constructed and decorated in all likelihood by Byzantine-trained masons and mosaicists. As late as the sixteenth century, one finds the continuing impact of prestigious non-Islamic models: the most outstanding example is the series of mosques in Istanbul and Edirne (c. 1500–1588), which were inspired by HAGIA SOPHIA. Palaces sometimes included mosques, but were distinguishable from religious structures. They were often vast complexes that in their grandest manifestations were composed of elaborate living quarters for the ruler; audience and reception halls, often domed; baths; military barracks; stables; and fountained gardens and parks. The most outstanding examples are the palace of Caliph Harun al-Rashid, built in BAGHDAD in the eighth century, and the ALHAMBRA, built near Granada, Spain, in the fifteenth century.

Romanesque Architecture. In the western Europe of the early Middle Ages, a reinvigoration of art and literature was initiated at the court of CHARLEMAGNE and continued into the tenth century in the court of OTTO I. Seeking to recreate the glory of Rome, this CAROLINGIAN RENAISSANCE spawned a new and distinctive set of architectural values. Charlemagne's palace and chapel complex at Aachen (AIX-LA-CHAPELLE) is an inventive amalgam of conscious Roman retrospection in planning, structural technology, decoration, Byzantine influences, and European innovation seen in the new emphasis on towers to create an impressive exterior silhouette. This combination of Roman, Byzantine, and European ideas coalesced into the Romanesque style that, in the main, is characterized by weighty structure, elaborate articulation, and a bold exploration of masonry vaulting techniques.

The cruciform plan dominated Romanesque religious architecture. In response to the rise in the cult of saints and the demand for an increased number of altars, the choir area developed in spatial complexity. Of enduring influence, a new type of choir was designed in which the apse containing the altar was enveloped by a semicircular aisle, or ambulatory. A series of chapels appeared in major pilgrimage churches such as Santiago de Compostela in Spain and Saint Sernin in Toulouse, France. The reintroduction of large-scale masonry vaulting, in the form of barrel and groin vaults, necessitated heavy piers, thick walls, and massive buttresses that limited interior illumination.

Gothic Architecture. The Gothic form represents, in the broadest sense, the evolution of the Romanesque informed by traditions inherited from early Christian building and enhanced by an aesthetic of spaciousness and light. This new architectural vision, composed of a structure of slim supports, pointed arches, and ribbed vaults that facilitated expansive windows, first emerged around Paris in the Ile de France in the 1130s and 1140s, most notably at the Abbey of St. Denis. Spreading through continental Europe and

MILESTONES OF MEDIEVAL ARCHITECTURE	
c. 500	Castle of Chinon, one of France's oldest, built on banks of Vienne.
532	Hagia Sophia, Constantinople.
762	Palaces of Baghdad begin the golden age of Islamic architecture.
805	Chapel at Aachen (Aix-la Chapelle) consecrated.
c. 1000	Massive Hindu temples in India; Far Eastern architectural style.
c. 1050	Arundel Castle, Sussex, England.
1063	Cathedral of Pisa, Italy, begun.
1078	Work begins on Tower of London.
1140	Abbey St. Denis, near Paris, inaugurates Gothic style.

England, the Gothic quest to realize tall, light-suffused structures was consummated in the thirteenth century at the cathedrals of CHARTRES, Bourges, Reims, and Amiens in France and the cathedral of Cologne in Germany. In the flamboyant Gothic style of France (such as Saint Maclou and Rouen) and the decorated Gothic (Wells Cathedral choir and Ely Cathedral octagon) and Perpendicular styles (King's College Chapel, Cambridge, and Henry VII Chapel at WESTMINSTER ABBEY) of England, architects of the fourteenth and fifteenth centuries pursued increasingly elaborate visual and decorative effects.

The enduring values of medieval culture are related in no small measure to the physical durability of the period's buildings, both sacred and profane, that have survived into the modern period. While in most other aesthetic areas human civilization has moved beyond the values of the Middle Ages, the continuing inspiration drawn from medieval cathedrals, castles, and all manner of structures is one reason medieval culture is still present—and is another indication of the way values can be embodied in brick, stone, and glass.

See BYZANTINE, ISLAMIC, ROMANESQUE, *and* GOTHIC ART AND ARCHITECTURE *for details on each style. See also* HAGIA SOPHIA, NOTRE-DAME, *and* WESTMINSTER ABBEY *on those structures. Also see* CATHEDRALS AND CHURCHES *and* CASTLES AND FORTIFICATIONS, *and* BRUNELLESCHI, FILIPPO.

ARISTOTLE, STUDY OF (IN THE MIDDLE AGES)

Aristotle was arguably the most influential philosopher of the Middle Ages—even though he had been dead since 322 B.C.E. Aristotle's logic appealed to many medieval thinkers, particularly his ideas on God and of human souls. But his PHILOSOPHY was often contrary to the religious doctrines of the Christians, Jews, and Muslims, which prompted many medieval philosophers to try to reconcile Aristotle's ideas with religious thought.

Aristotle relied on logic, analysis, and observation to discover what he thought were the universal truths about the world. This did not always mesh with the religious ideas of faith, but so intriguing was Aristotle's philosophy that scholars sought religious parallels and interpretations. Aristotle's vision of a "first mover" starting the chain of being substantiated medieval belief in the existence of God. His ethical theories of habitual behavior between extremes was consistent with medieval moral doctrine. But his argument for the eternity of matter and a collective, rather than individual, immortality represented difficult problems for medieval thinkers. (*See* PHILOSOPHY.)

Although neglected in antiquity, Aristotle was studied by the Byzantines as early as the fifth century. A translation of his work on logic into Latin was prepared by the scholar BOETHIUS in the sixth century. Arabic translations appeared in the ninth century, and Muslim scholars were influenced by his works. Jewish scholars such as the twelfth-century MAIMONIDES also studied Aristotle. Both ALBERTUS MAGNUS and THOMAS AQUINAS used Aristotelian ideas in their theology. Thomas Aquinas was the first medieval Christian philosopher to have access to the complete works of Aristotle in Latin, although some of them had been translated first into Arabic. (*See* AVERROËS.)

Aristotle's works were responsible for the development of SCHOLASTICISM in western Europe. By 1200, his major writings had become central to the curriculum of the philosophy schools of Paris and other universities. Among the best-known Scholastics influenced by Aristotle were PETER ABELARD, JOHN DUNS SCOTUS, and WILLIAM OF OCKHAM.

ARMENIA

Geographic locale at the crossroads between Eastern and Western cultures, situated southeast of the Black Sea, between the rivers Aras and Jura, with Byzantine Asia Minor to the west and Persia to the east. Armenia was a hot bed for international strife among several empires throughout the Middle Ages.

At the start of the Middle Ages, it was a Christian country divided between the Byzantine Empire and the Persians. The land prospered when left to its own religious and social way of life. Many political maneuverings were attempted to retain the independent spirit of Armenia, even to moving the head of their church away from the Christian Byzantine half of the country and closer to the pagan Persians.

The ARAB conquest of the Persians in 640 C.E. led to independent rule for the Christian leaders of Armenia, although the country was technically under Arab rule. Two hundred years later, a decline in the Abbasid caliphate opened the way for Armenians to control their own dynastic affairs. Thus, in the ninth century, Asot I was crowned king. The subsequent lineage of rulers, known as the Bagratids, brought about prosperity for the next 160 years.

Armenia was then to suffer a series of invasions during the late Middle Ages: Turkish sultans conquered it in the eleventh century; MONGOLS invaded in the thirteenth century; and finally, the OTTOMAN TURKS deposed the last king in 1375.

ARMS AND ARMOR

Personal armor—metal protective garments, shields, and helmets—was an important feature of medieval warfare. There is a false image in popular consciousness that links the medieval knight with full-body plate armor and lance. In fact, full-body armor developed only late in the Middle Ages as a reaction to the widespread use of the crossbow that penetrated older forms of armor. In medieval history, there is a development from earlier chain-mail armor (interlocked steel rings) to greater reliance on plate (sheets of metal) armor. Only in the fifteenth century did full-body plate armor appear. The use of armor, like other instruments of WARFARE, was connected to social class. The heaviest armor was restricted to the wealthiest landowners, while soldiers of lesser fortune had to use weaker armor. Since armor embodied social status, much energy was placed in the artfulness of its display.

Early Middle Ages. Plated armor disappeared at the beginning of the Middle Ages and then reemerged at the end of the medieval period. The BARBARIAN tribal people, who conquered the provinces of the western Roman Empire in the fifth century, wore heavy-metal plate armor tied by thongs or attached to a jacket. This type of armor soon fell out of use and was replaced by chain-mail armor, which provided protection from knives and swords; it was flexible and easy to wear. The length of the chain mail varied with place, although it often spanned the body from neck to knee. Early medieval warriors also fought with shield and helmet. Their shields were circular or oval, composed of wood, with reinforcing bronze or iron, and covered by leather. Helmets were iron or bronze with horn covering.

Late Middle Ages. By the end of the twelfth century, the protection afforded by armor increased. Newly developed chain-mail cloaks ("byrnies") were lengthened, and chain-mail mitts were introduced to cover hands. A padded undergarment or "acton" began to be worn beneath the byrnie to protect the wearer from ax blows. Armor protecting knees and more efficient helmets also came into wide use. Whereas earlier helmets had nasal guards, the new helmets covered the entire face with eye slits and breathing holes.

The development of armor led to a declining need for large shields. In the eleventh century, cavalry used long, almond-shaped shields that protected them from eye to knee. As armor got stronger, the almond-shaped shield fell into disuse and was replaced with a lighter, triangular shield. These shields were painted with bright colors identifying the partisanship of the knight, a necessary innovation since the face of the warrior was covered. In the thirteenth century, horses began to be covered with chain mail since archers often tried to defeat the knight by killing or disabling his horse.

In the fourteenth century, crossbow weaponry improved so much that arrows penetrated a mail coat and shattered wooden shields. Armor fashion changed to meet this new challenge. Iron plates linked together, such as those used by BARBARIAN tribes a thousand years earlier, were reintroduced. Another more common method of protection was lining the interior of surcoats with small rectangular metal plates.

The fifteenth century saw the last stage of armor development with the famous full-body suit of armor.

Left, knights fighting in battle could not move wearing heavy armor, so the hauberk was developed—a tunic made of chain mail that protected the knight but gave him flexibility. The headgear worn in battle was often custom designed for each individual knight. Above, several examples: top left, a casque; top right and bottom left, morions, which became virtually emblematic of the Spanish conquistadors; the rest are helmets with visors, all from a 15th-century Madrid manuscript.

In the full-body suit, the entire knight was secured behind plates of steel. This suit included a backplate and a skirt for the lower body. The central development was the solid breastplate. These had extended or puffed-out chest pieces to catch lances. Since shields were rarely used by knights with full suits of armor, the armor itself was used to break the opponent's lance. Helmets were made to fit the suit of armor, covering the entire head without allowing for open spaces. HORSES were also fitted with heavy armor because a dismounted knight could not regain his feet.

In the last years of the Middle Ages, the development of gunpowder would make armor superfluous. New technologies made war democratic; more individuals of lesser wealth could participate. However, heavy armor and the social stratification it represented did not disappear from medieval life. Armor was still used in TOURNAMENTS, as decorations, and as gifts, and military regalia is as important a status symbol in the modern era as it ever was in medieval times.

Material on implements may be found in CLOTHING AND COSTUME, WARFARE, *and* WEAPONRY. *The culture of the knight is discussed in* KNIGHTHOOD; *also see* CHIVALRY, FEUDALISM, HERALDRY *and* TOURNAMENTS.

ARPAD

A national hero who established Hungary's first ruling dynasty, Arpád (c. 850–907) was a Magyar chieftain, son of Almos, a prince of HUNGARY, who lived north of the Black Sea. In 895, he combined disparate elements of the tribe and led them across the northeastern section of the Carpathian Mountains. They settled in the ancient Roman province of Pannonia, an area now known as Hungary.

Hungary at that time was populated by SLAVS and other tribes congregated near the Danube River. Arpád's armies soundly defeated the Bulgarians at Alpar, a region between the Tisza and Danube. At the climax of the Magyar battles, the Magyars, according to Hungarian legend, ritualistically killed Almos so that his soul and spirit could enter Arpád, who could then become the leader of a united Hungary.

Arpád sent ambassadors to Louis the Child, the Frankish emperor, to receive formal recognition of the new land. When Louis refused recognition, Arpád sent armies to invade Bavaria in 901.

Arpád's moderately sized armies fought with bows and arrows on horseback. They called themselves the "scourge of God," and saw their battles as divinely inspired.

After Arpád's death in 907, he was succeeded by Solt, his son. The fact that Solt's reign was peaceful suggests that the dynasty was by then firmly established. The Arpád dynasty ruled Hungary until 1301.

A statue of Arpád in Budapest, erected nearly a thousand years after his death.

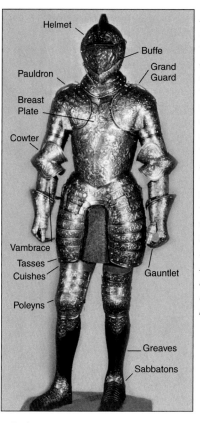

Helmet
Buffe
Grand Guard
Pauldron
Breast Plate
Cowter
Vambrace
Tasses
Cuishes
Gauntlet
Poleyns
Greaves
Sabbatons

Armor of the medieval knight. *Careful attention was paid to the design and suitability of every piece of equipment. Most pieces were custom made to fit one particular knight and required that the knight maintain a constant body weight. The suit was ventilated in the thigh area, which required the knight to raise himself slightly while mounted. Knights involved in jousting tried to take the lance full in the chest, hoping to break it. Armor could also deflect arrows, but the crossbow could pierce all but the heaviest plate.*

ARTEVELDE, JACQUES VAN

J acques van Artevelde (c. 1295–1345) was a merchant and a member of a wealthy commercial family in Ghent. He rose to political power as the leader of an alliance of Flemish towns during the HUNDRED YEARS' WAR. His motive for the formation of the alliance was economic. He organized the rich weaving centers of FLANDERS as a defensive alliance to protect the influx of English wool during wartime. Artevelde united all the towns of the NETHERLANDS under his war policy and eventually assumed near-dictatorial powers. While Artevelde provided great service to the idea of urban independence against feudal lords, his reign ended violently when a mob revolted.

An Alliance. Jacques entered political life when he realized that the threat of war between EDWARD III of ENGLAND and Philip VI of FRANCE might block the textile trade, the source of great wealth for the Flemish cities. At a public meeting in 1337, Artevelde advocated that Brabant, Holland, and Ghent unite in an armed neutrality in order to protect Flemish interests. Other towns joined the alliance, and Artevelde became the virtual dictator with the title of captain-general.

Among his successes were a commercial treaty with ENGLAND and foiling a military attempt by the count of Flanders to overthrow the new regime. The count was forced to sign a treaty at Bruges (June 21, 1338) that confirmed the alliance of Ghent, Bruges, and Ypres. Eventually the alliance included all of the Netherlands.

The original goal of neutrality, however, could not be sustained, and the alliance became England's explicit ally. Through Artevelde's competent administration and war policy, Ghent grew in wealth and importance on the European stage. Artevelde's success overturned the medieval social hierarchy: a merchant had become the diplomatic equal of kings.

Opposition. However, because of his success and tyrannical rule, Artevelde earned enemies. The opposition to his rule coalesced in 1345, when he proposed to take Flemish sovereignty from Louis, count of WALES, and give it to EDWARD THE BLACK PRINCE. The proposal caused a riot in Ghent, and Artevelde was captured and killed in 1345. After his death the count of Flanders resumed power. Forty years later, Artevelde's son Philip became governor of Ghent during a crisis and made an alliance with Bruges before being killed during a French invasion. The Artevelde family, despite its political defeats, remains a symbol of early Flemish independence; a statue of Artevelde was erected in Ghent in 1863.

ARTHUR, KING

Arthur was a legendary British king portrayed as head of the Knights of the Round Table of medieval romances, among the most popular romantic themes of all time. The Arthurian tales are also about Arthur's wife, Queen Guinevere; his close friend, Lancelot; his evil son, Mordred; and Merlin, the magician. The medieval writers who transmitted and elaborated on these legends wrote about the highest ideals of their age—honor, CHIVALRY, COURTLY LOVE, and religious quests.

The historical Arthur is buried in the mist of the Celtic past. It is believed he fought in the Battle of Mount Badon in 516, an important victory by the Celtic Britons over the Saxon invaders. However, the historian Gildas, who wrote about 540, described the Battle of Mount Badon without mentioning Arthur by name, describing the Briton who won the battle as Ambrosius Aurelianus. Writers in the late Middle Ages claimed that he was Arthur, but modern scholars are not convinced.

The Legend Born. The earliest apparent reference to Arthur as a mighty Celtic warrior is a brief passage in the Welsh poem *Gododdin*, written in the early

600s. The first clear mention of Arthur appears in the early 800s by a writer named Nennius. In his book, which described the history of the Britons, Arthur is described as a highly successful Celtic warrior who defeated the Saxons on twelve separate occasions. The *Annales Cambriae* in the 900s tells about Arthur leading the Welsh resistance against a Saxon advance that ended with Arthur's victory at the Battle of Mount Badon. These references testify to the fact that well before 1100 folktales about a hero called Arthur were circulating through WALES, Cornwall, BRITTANY, and other Celtic sections of Europe. At the same time, stories such as the tragic love story of TRISTAN AND ISOLDE and other tales of chivalry, which were not initially written down, spread through Europe as far as ITALY. Arthur was most likely a British (Welsh) chieftain who commanded a military force that played a major role in winning a decisive battle for the British against the invading Saxon forces in the early 500s.

The Legend Grows. The basic outline of the Arthurian legend as it emerged in the Middle Ages found literary expression in England. By 1100 King Arthur and his knights were regarded as historical figures. About 1135 GEOFFREY OF MONMOUTH wrote his highly popular *Historia Regum Britanniae* (*History of the Kings of Britain*), based on the folktales then in circulation. His Latin history, which depicted Arthur as a heroic king and described his reign in considerable detail, was soon adapted and translated into other languages. In 1155, a poet by the name of WACE wrote a version in Norman French called *Roman de Brut*, while Layamon wrote a version in Middle English a few years later.

The earliest literary romances based on the Arthurian legend were written in FRANCE, where the stories were spread by TROUBADOURS who traveled back and forth across the English Channel between Wales and Cornwall in Britain and BRITTANY in France. In the 1160s and 1170s, the French poet CHRÉTIEN DE TROYES wrote five major Arthurian works mixing history and legend. He and another French writer, Robert de Boron, added more romantic elements to the legend, such as the search for the Holy Grail, the sword in the stone, and the love affair be-

King Arthur (in Nuremberg's Beautiful Fountain) is no less a legendary figure in German folk culture.

Above, Galahad is introduced to the Knights of the Round Table by Merlin in a 14th-century Italian miniature. A sense of aristocratic community and brotherhood lie in the egalitarian imagery of the Round Table.

tween Lancelot and Guinevere. In the Holy Grail story, Arthur's knights search for the cup used by Christ at the Last Supper. This added religious theme increased the popularity of the Arthurian legend in the late Middle Ages. Chrétien also wrote a romance about Tristan and Isolde, now lost, which was added to the Arthurian literature that developed in both France and England among the French-speaking Norman nobility.

These French Arthurian romances were translated into many other languages. As early as the 1190s, German adaptations made their first appearance. WOLFRAM VON ESCHENBACH, a poet and knight, wrote *Parzival*, one of the best-known of the German Arthurian romances, while GOTTFRIED VON STRASSBURG wrote a celebrated version of the Tristan story.

The Middle English versions that followed Layamon's *Brut* added many of the features taken from the French romances. Two highly accomplished Arthurian classics written in England were *Sir Gawain and the Green Knight*, a long narrative poem in which the hero barely escapes beheading, and *Morte d'Arthur* (*The Death of Arthur*), written by Sir Thomas MALORY about 1470, a long prose version of Arthurian legend.

The literary form of Arthurian romances is discussed in ENGLISH LANGUAGE AND LITERATURE *and* MALORY, THOMAS. *See also* KNIGHTHOOD *and* CHIVALRY *for a cultural context; also* MAGIC AND FOLKLORE.

ARTILLERY

Artillery, the use of machinery to propel objects, was a common feature of warfare in the Middle Ages. Since battles between organized armies were rare, the ability to hold and conquer CASTLES was central to triumph or defeat. Early in the Middle Ages, artillery was limited to devices that hurled rocks at the walls of stone castles or other fortifications. However, in the early fourteenth century, with the introduction of gunpowder and cannons, a revolution occurred in the effectiveness of artillery which changed the nature of WARFARE.

Early Middle Ages. One form of early medieval artillery was the ballista, a technique inherited from Roman military art. This device resembled a huge crossbow that projected missiles by employing the principle of "torsion" or twisting. The ballista was used as early as 885 in the siege of PARIS by the VIKINGS. Another torsion-activated mechanism was the mangonel. First introduced during the Middle Ages, it employed a lobbing motion rather than the crossbow movement of the ballista. The mangonel had a limited range of about 200 yards. The development of another device, the trebuchet, in the twelfth century was a breakthrough in the science of artillery. Earlier artillery devices were unreliable; weather adversely changed the rope, and heavy use

Catapults were used since Roman times, but were perfected during the Middle Ages. Catapults were used to hurl stones, burning hay, and sacks of poison over walls.

would fatigue the spring used to create the torsion effect. The trebuchet, on the other hand, worked like a seesaw. The short end of the device was weighted by a large object with a spring on the long end that held the projectile. When firing, the long end was compressed and released. The trebuchet was reliable and considered the strongest artillery device before gunpowder. It could hurl objects 200 to 400 yards. One of its earliest uses was at Acre in 1191 by the crusaders.

A New Invention. Gunpowder was invented in Asia and brought to Europe by Muslim traders. It was first used in "sapping"—the placing of explosives beneath castle walls. Gunpowder was put to more efficient use with the introduction of cannons. The first European cannon was produced in 1320; its first recorded use was in 1324 in France. Another early use was by the Germans in ITALY in 1331. Cannons were in frequent use in siege warfare by the middle of the fourteenth century, although their primitive construction limited their worth. These cannons were simple devices with gunpowder poured into cylinders. The barrels of these weapons were often defective, disintegrating with the explosion. Larger guns solved this problem, but such guns created a dangerous recoil.

Late Middle Ages. Artillery was not a major force on the battlefield during the late Middle Ages. A monopoly of cannon use was no guarantee of victory even into the late fifteenth century because of its many deficiencies. Cannons, at that time, took a long time to be refired, lacked mobility, had limited range, and did not kill many enemies. Cannons were only used for an opening salvo and, due to their immobility, after the initial firing they were often captured by the advancing opponent. To prevent their capture, elaborate methods were undertaken to fortify the cannons.

Throughout the fourteenth and fifteenth centuries, technical improvements were made in cannon warfare. Newly developed wheeled guns were less likely to recoil. New methods of transport for large cannons were developed, allowing them to travel over water and on four-wheeled carts. Large cannons became more useful with the construction of special mounts for holding them during firing. However, large guns remained unwieldy; by the middle of the fifteenth century, they were out of favor, replaced by more mobile and faster-firing, small culverins.

The use of gunpowder changed the underlying dynamics of medieval warfare. Stone castles and fortifications had been difficult to capture because they could withstand ballistas and other stone-throwing devices, making long and costly starvation sieges necessary. The introduction of gunpowder gradually made fortresses less important and increased the frequency of pitched battles and hand-to-hand combat.

The significance of changes in artillery is evident in a number of wars. The quick French victory over the British at Bordeaux in the HUNDRED YEARS' WAR was due to the increasing use of artillery firepower. Artillery also played a role in the OTTOMAN TURK conquest of CONSTANTINOPLE (1453), a city that had withstood numerous sieges for centuries.

The development of artillery is further discussed in ARMS AND ARMOR, SCIENCE, *and* WEAPONRY. *More on the impact of artillery on warfare may be found in* CASTLES AND FORTIFICATIONS; TOWNS, VILLAGES, AND CITIES, *and* WARFARE.

Toward the end of the Middle Ages, the cannon was used as a means of breaking through fortifications. Above, a miniature from Campion des Dames, *15th century.*

ASSIZES OF JERUSALEM

The Assizes of Jerusalem was a set of laws, a compilation of legal procedures based on the customs and privileges of the European feudal kingdoms and applied to the Latin Kingdom of Jerusalem and other Latin crusader states of the East.

The foundation for the code was laid down during the twelfth century by the first king of Jerusalem, GODFREY DE BOUILLON. It was called the *Lettres du Sépulchre* and laid out, in detail, the duties of royal officials, the granting of fiefs, the proceedings of Justice, and trade regulation. The *Lettres du Sépulchre* were stored in the Holy Sepulchre in Jerusalem, but they disappeared after the invasion by SALADIN in 1187. But a similar code, written in French, was drawn up in Cyprus during the thirteenth century. The major contributors were Philippe de Navara, Geoffrey le Tor, James d'Ibelin and Jean d'Ibelin. (*See* CRUSADES.)

Bodies of legal work that emphasized the jurisdiction of feudal kings, nobles, and the common courts were combined with the Assizes of Jerusalem, creating a code that was perfectly adapted to the needs of the crusader states of the Middle East. (*See* LAW.)

The Assizes of Jerusalem consists of two parts. The first is the "letter to the king," which conveys the views of the nobility on the ruling parties of the crusader states, basically making up the laws of the kingdom and nobility. The second part of the Assizes deals with trade, townspeople, and the enactment and enforcement of laws by the legislative bodies.

As a result of the Assizes, Cyprus became the center of the practice of Latin law after the Europeans lost the Palestinian stronghold. The Assizes of Jerusalem was the legal glue that held together the remnants of European civilization in the East for 300 years.

ASTROLOGY

Astrology is a body of knowledge that claims to foretell the destinies of individuals and aspects of civilization through the observation of heavenly bodies such as stars, planets, comets, the sun, and the moon. Astrologers believed that these celestial bodies directly affect the designs and affairs of humans; by calculating the positions and motion of these objects, they claimed, one could divine an order emanating from above that dictates developments in human history.

Early History. Astrology has a long history in civilized societies. It was practiced by ancient civilizations in CHINA, EGYPT, India, and Greece, and gained wide public acceptance in medieval Europe. The basis for astrological thought was mainly Hellenic with some influence by Eastern astrological study. Before astrology became widespread in medieval society, it was shunned and condemned by the Church because of its pagan associations. Saint AUGUSTINE OF HIPPO played a major role in the decline of astrology in early medieval Europe by condemning the art in his work, *The City of God.*

The connection between astrology and astronomy was a strong one in the Middle Ages. Above, astrological interpretations of the constellations in a 9th-century manuscript.

Nonetheless, primitive forms of astrology persisted in medieval Europe. For example, the BAYEUX TAPESTRY (1077 C.E.) depicts a group of people observing Halley's comet, regarding the comet's flight as a harbinger of doom. People also attributed their health and the function of their bodily organs to the stars. During the eleventh century, astrology began to grow, but it was not until after the CRUSADES that the practice of astrology began to flourish.

The Crusades opened the door for astrological texts to be reintroduced in medieval Europe. Arabic works were being translated into Latin, and there was a resurgence in the study of Hellenic thought, which included the study of Hellenic astrological theorems.

The Greeks were the ones who developed the twelve constellations of the zodiac. Personal horoscopes were designed according to the date and time of one's birth. The study of astrology was maintained in the Muslim world. Even after the displacement of the diviner priests in Muslim religion, as a consequence of the preachings of MUHAMMAD, Muslims continued to observe and contemplate the stars throughout the Middle Ages in hopes of divining the future.

The Muslims carried the traditions of astrology into the late Middle Ages, giving rise to a culture of astrology in late medieval Europe. Astrology attracted intellectuals like ROGER BACON and ALBERTUS MAGNUS. Bacon attempted to interpret history using astrology, connecting the appearance of prophets and religion with certain conjunctions of planets. Indeed, many astronomers were known to dabble in astrological speculation. Although the art of astrology had very little scientific basis, the process of arriving at an insight or a prediction was as rigorous and calculated as a scientific experiment. The Church's attempt to brand astrology as a HERESY did not persuade the growing number of astrology followers.

In the late Middle Ages, pivotal human events were interpreted in astrological terms. The Black Death was said to have been caused by unfavorable planetary conjunctions. The HUNDRED YEARS' WAR provided an excellent opportunity for astrologers to make predictions, and to receive the good graces of the royalty. Astrology reached all echelons of the social order in medieval Europe: for the upper classes astrologers were given appointments at royal courts; common people indulged themselves in astrological insights as well. Even the use of MEDICINE and the practice of doctors were affected by astrological thought. Aside from bodily connections with the planets above, doctors would wait for the correct planetary or cosmic motion and conjunctions before starting surgery or administering treatment.

The quasi-scientific aspects of astrology are discussed in ALCHEMY, ASTRONOMY, *and* SCIENCE. *More on the impact of the discipline is to be found in* SCIENCE *and in* HERESY, WITCHCRAFT AND SORCERY, *and* MAGIC AND FOLKLORE. *Also see* BACON, ROGER.

ASTRONOMY

Astronomy—the study of celestial bodies—in the Middle Ages was based on the authority of the work of a Stoic Greek astronomer, Claudius Ptolemaeus, also known as Ptolemy, who summarized his findings in 142 C.E. in a work known as the *Almagest*. The Ptolemaic system, based on a vision of the universe in which Earth is at its center and all other bodies revolve around it (a "geocentric" view), which indeed was the view of ARISTOTLE, is not strictly correct. While Aristotle and his followers constructed ever more complicated systems that retained the Earth as the center of all motion, creating the retrograde motions (meaning changing directions) of the planets through complex interconnected spheres rotating in different directions, Ptolemy's system is more accurately an "epicentric" system, in which the retrograde motion is the result of heavenly bodies revolving around points that are themselves orbiting the Earth or points near the Earth. Thus, the breakthrough astronomical concept—that some bodies in the sky revolve around something other than the Earth—had already been made by the beginning of the Middle Ages. (See ARISTOTLE, STUDY OF.)

A much more serious problem posed by astronomical thinking, which troubled religious thinkers and cast a shadow over the entire enterprise, was reconciling the idea that the universe was created by God with the accepted reasoning of Aristotle that the universe must be eternal. Not until AQUINAS resolved the problem (basing his argument on an argument by MAIMONIDES) by concluding that, while Aristotle's view was logically correct, the world had in fact been created by God, who chose there to be a universe rather than nothing, did astronomy begin to emerge out of the shadows and separate itself from the pseudoscience of ASTROLOGY.

Several medieval thinkers grappled with the question of the Earth's motion, providing reasoning that Copernicus found useful in his revolutionary heliocentric theories of the midsixteenth century. For example, JOHN BURIDAN, though rejecting the idea of the Earth rotating, did believe that the Earth must be moving in order to adjust its center to the shifting of land mass by avalanches and river silt transport. If the Earth did not make these corrections, he reasoned, it would no longer be at the center of the universe.

(Almost no educated person in the Middle Ages believed the Earth to be anything but round. This was clearly proven by the fact that tall ships sailing toward the horizon disappear over that horizon with their masts still visible, returning to report the sea flat. Thus, legends regarding Columbus bravely proving the world round are just that: legends.)

A 13th-century astronomy lesson, from the Breviary of St. Louis. The center figure is using an astrolabe; an 11th-century Arabian model is shown at right. By sighting the sun or a reference star along the center bar (the alidade), one could tell time and make many astronomical measurements.

Another important astronomical thinker of the late Middle Ages was NICOLAS ORESME (1320–1382), Buridan's colleague at the University of Paris. Oresme noticed (as everyone had) that the Earth appears to be still and the sun, moon, and stars seem to revolve around the Earth, but he also noticed (remarked, but only parenthetically, by Ptolemy) that, just as sailors on ships passing each other at sea find it difficult to determine which one is moving and at what speed, the Earth rotating under a stationary sun has the same appearance as the sun revolving around the Earth. Oresme further noted how much simpler matters would be if the former were true instead of the latter.

An important reason why Oresme and other medieval thinkers had difficulty accepting the notion of a rotating Earth was Ptolemy's observation that arrows shot straight up into the air fall directly back to Earth, whereas if the Earth rotated, he argued, the arrow should swerve in the direction opposite to the Earth's motion. Oresme criticized this argument even as he championed it, suggesting that the air moving with the Earth might carry the arrow forward so that it appears to land on the same spot. This was probably as close as medieval science came to the kind of physical reasoning proposed by Galileo that resolved this puzzle; Oresme's perplexed tone provided an intellectual atmosphere that stimulated inquiry into these matters.

Meanwhile, striking celestial phenomena, such as comets and the aurora borealis, kept being interpreted as portents, and religious (or at least nonscientific) arguments kept being applied unproductively to physical questions: Are there other worlds? What powers the sun? How far does the universe extend, and what happens if one sticks one's hand beyond that? Careful measurements continued to be made and recorded in works like the thirteenth-century Alphonsine Tables, providing the raw data that would eventually support the new astronomy of Galileo and Copernicus.

See SCIENCE *and* ASTROLOGY *for more on the discipline;* CALENDARS, EXPLORATION, *and* EASTER, DATE OF *for applications. See also* AQUINAS, THOMAS; ARABIC LANGUAGE AND LITERATURE; *and* ORESME, NICHOLAS.

ATHENS, LATIN DUCHY OF

One of several Latin states created in Greece in the aftermath of the Fourth Crusade. After the fall of CONSTANTINOPLE, Byzantine domains were partitioned by the victors. In the region referred to as Romania—Greece and the Aegean—the Republic of VENICE was granted more territory than it could govern. The crusader states in Greece thus fell into several larger units: the possessions held directly by Venice; the Aegean islands held by Venetian citizens, but eventually ruled directly by Venice; the Peloponnese, called Morea, the ruler of which was the prince of Achaea; and the duchy of Athens, which included Thebes and territories to its north. Until the Latin states fell to the OTTOMANS, adventurers seized power, abetted or undermined by greater powers, such as the ANGEVINS, the French, and the Aragonese. Indeed, internecine conflicts in Greece often were extensions of those occupying the great Western powers. Achaea initially was the most prestigious of the states, but after its first 100 years, its glory dimmed and the luster of its brilliant Latin culture passed to the duchy of Athens. In the end, apart from some impressive

ruins, a long Latin occupation left little that endured.

In 1204, just months after the conquest of Constantinople, Athens fell to Boniface of Montferrat, king of Thessalonica. In 1205, Boniface gave Athens as a fief to the Burgundian lord Otho de la Roche, whose dynasty governed Attica, Boetia, and the Argolid for more than a century. In 1206, Pope INNOCENT III took the Athenian church under his protection; Greek bishops were asked to give their allegiance to ROME. When few did, Latin bishops replaced them. As with the population as a whole, a Latin hierarchy was grafted onto Greek roots.

Otho prospered and lavishly entertained the Latin emperor Henry in Athens in May 1209, and soon afterward assisted Geoffrey I (Villehardouin) of neighboring Morea in the conquest of Nauplia and Argos. A faithful if somewhat greedy devotee of the Church, Otho frequently labored under bans of excommunication, chiefly because of his raiding of the hospice and infirmary for pilgrims to the Holy Sepulchre in Jerusalem. An order of knights, the Hospitallers, was established to protect these institutions. The order became a large and powerful military entity under direct papal authority, rivaling the Templars.

In 1311, the duchy was taken over by the "Catalan Grand Company," a group of merchant-adventurers who traded extensively in the Mediterranean. They were eventually taken over by the very mercenaries hired to protect the trade routes, and by the late thirteenth century had developed into a respected military power. In 1330, Walter of Brienne, duke of Athens, hired the Catalans to fight in Thessaly. A dispute regarding their wages ended with the Catalans turning on Walter, then invading and conquering Athens.

Though the Catalans displayed a remarkable talent for commerce, the economic importance of Athens declined because of Turkish attacks, altered trade routes, and the Plague, which began in 1347. The Sicilian royal family nominally ruled Athens and Neopatras until 1377, when the Catalans became vassals of King Pedro IV of Aragon. Yet only two years later the Navarrese company under John of Urtubia conquered Thebes, setting the stage for the end of Catalan rule. Thebes was soon ceded to the Florentine Nerio Acciaiuoli, baron of Corinth, who in 1385, took Athens.

In May 1388 Catalan rule ended entirely when the Aragonese garrison surrendered the Acropolis. Ladislas, king of NAPLES, accorded Nerio Acciaiuoli the title of duke. Venice purchased Argos and Nauplia in 1388. After the death of Nerio Acciaiuoli in 1394, the Venetian republic assumed control of Athens. But then Antonio Acciaiuoli, a son of Nerio, seized Athens in 1402; in 1405, he compelled Venice to accept his rule. During the 33 years of enlightened rule, Antonio attracted to Athens many Florentine merchants and men of culture, as recorded by Ciriaco of Ancona. The Acciaiuoli dynasty lasted until June 1458, when the Ottoman Turks seized Athens from Franco Acciaiuoli. Sultan Mehmet II at first allowed the last Acciaiuoli to retire, but then in 1460 had him murdered, erasing all vestiges of the duchy of Athens.

ATTILA THE HUN

Gifted with acute cunning, Attila, king of the Huns (c. 406–453), was a terror of legendary proportions in the early Middle Ages. Early Christians called him the "scourge of God." He ruled the Huns for two decades in the fifth century, terrorizing much of the known world.

Little is known of his early life, except that he was born in 406, the nephew of Rua, king of the Huns, a MONGOL people who evaded Caesar's armies by settling north of the Danube. Rua was powerful enough to exact annual tribute from ROME. Rua died in 433, leaving his empire to Attila and his brother Bleda.

The brothers first negotiated with the Romans for them to ransom political prisoners the Huns were holding, to return Hun army deserters, and to pay the Huns 700 pounds of gold a year, all in return for the Huns refraining from attacking Roman territories. But in 441, the Huns launched the first of several attacks against the Roman Empire, marching from the east, through SICILY and Persia. The Romans turned back the Huns, but Attila and Bleda forced an increase of Rome's annual tribute to 2,000 pounds of gold.

Attila sought to expand the Hun empire to Europe and the Near East, but his brother harbored no such aspirations. Bleda was murdered in 444; many believed Attila was responsible. As sole Hun leader, Attila stepped up his assaults. Intent on attacking Rome, he got as far as CONSTANTINOPLE. He was able to negotiate for even more tribute from Rome.

No portraits of Attila survive, but contemporaries describe him as being a short, squat man with a giant head, broad shoulders, deep-set eyes and a scraggly beard. Attila was said to have had a charismatic personality; the Gothic historian Jordanes wrote that Attila "was a lover of war yet restrained in action, mighty in counsel, gracious to supplicants, and lenient to those once received under his protection." Through his Roman secretaries, Attila was kept abreast of international affairs. He understood the power of psychological warfare and allowed exaggerated stories of his terror to circulate and reach the ears of his enemies.

In 447 Attila attacked the Balkans, putting thousands into slavery and destroying the surrounding Danube area, including Sophia and Belgrade. The Huns' treaty with Constantinople called for Attila to regularly receive cattle and title. When the Turks fell behind in their payment in 448, the Huns crossed the Danube and took Phillipolis. The emperor relented and gave the Huns pasturing rights in Moesia.

In 451, the Huns enlisted the VANDALS and FRANKS and invaded Gaul, what is now FRANCE. When the armies stormed PARIS, a young girl named Genevieve begged Attila not to destroy the city. The Huns left Paris alone, and Genevieve became the city's patron saint. In Orléans, the invaders were halted by the VISIGOTHS and Romans (under leadership of Aetius, a former Hun hostage, and THEODORIC I), who halted them at the bloody Battle of the Catalaunian Plains, where Theodoric was killed and, by some accounts, each side suffered 165,000 casualties. Within a year the Huns invaded northern Italy, sacking Padua, Verona, and Milan. Attila intended to take Roman emperor Valentinian's sister Honoria as a wife, with much of Europe as a dowry. In Rome, Pope Leo the Great and two Roman senators met with Attila, and afterward the Huns retreated.

In 453, Attila took as one of his many wives Ildico (Hilda). On his wedding night, a blood vessel in his nose broke, and he bled to death. After Attila's death, the Hun empire quickly dissolved. Attila's sons lacked their father's determination and charisma, and fought mostly among themselves. (*See* BARBARIAN INVASIONS.)

AUGUSTINE OF CANTERBURY, ST.

Missionary and first archbishop of Canterbury, Augustine (d. 604) was the prior of St. Andrew's monastery in Rome. It was from this position in 596 that Pope GREGORY I THE GREAT selected him to lead a mission which would restore CHRISTIANITY throughout ENGLAND, where the recent ANGLO-SAXON invasions had left Christianity in a state of decline and paganism firmly entrenched as the Anglo-Saxons' religion of choice. Augustine interrupted his journey and stopped in Gaul, but at Gregory's urging, he resumed his journey.

Upon his arrival in Kent in 597, Augustine found himself well received by King Aethelbert and his wife, Bertha, who was already a Christian. The royal couple gave Augustine a house in Canterbury and allowed him to preach to their subjects. Augustine knew better than to ban paganism outright. Instead, he decided to incorporate many pagan aspects into the Church liturgy and use old pagan temples in the hope of gradually eliminating it. (*See* MISSIONS AND MISSIONARIES.)

By 601, Augustine had successfully converted the king and many of his people, and was given the archbishopric of Canterbury. His success made Canterbury the center of English Christianity and led to his being called the "Apostle of England."

AUGUSTINE OF HIPPO, ST.

More than 1,500 years after his death, Saint Augustine (354–430) is still considered one of CHRISTIANITY's most influential thinkers. He came of age at a time when the Christian church was still young and in a state of transition. His ideas, which he included in his numerous writings, helped shape the medieval Church and its later evolution into Roman Catholicism and Protestantism.

Life. Augustine was born in the Roman province of Numidia, on the north coast of AFRICA (modern-day Algeria), in 354. His father was a pagan, but his mother was a devout Christian, and the young Augustine grew up with a knowledge of essential Christian ideas. Possessed of a quick mind, his family sent him to Carthage to continue his studies. He became interested in PHILOSOPHY after reading Cicero, and for a brief time became a follower of Manichaeism, a religious philosophy that focused on the idea of dualism—the existence of good and evil forces with which humankind must struggle. (Du-

Augutine, surrounded by the Austin Friars, while beneath him is Aristotle brandishing a banner proclaiming the eternity of matter, a doctrine Augustine refuted.

alism was the focus of later sects, such as the CATHARS, labeled heretical by the Church.) During his early twenties Augustine lived as a philosopher-scholar and fathered an illegitimate son. At 28, he went to Milan, where he met ST. AMBROSE, then its bishop. Ambrose was the first Christian intellectual to make an impression on Augustine; until then he had seen Christianity as incompatible with philosophy.

In his early thirties Augustine had a mystical religious experience that led to his total conversion to Christianity; he was baptized by Ambrose. By 396 he had become bishop of Hippo (near modern Tunis), a position he held until his death. From his thirties on, he expounded his theories eloquently in his numerous sermons and writings, the most famous of which are his *Confessions* and his treatise *City of God*.

Work. Augustine's *Confessions*, written when he was 45, tell of his spiritual journey from a worldly life to one devoted to religious thought. His *City of God* presents a stirring defense of Christian faith and ideals. Other works discuss Augustine's ideas of God's grace as a means of human salvation. Many of Augustine's ideas show elements of earlier philosophies, such as Neoplatonism. His ideas on ethics, self-knowledge, and the role of free will in people's lives helped influence the Church's later teachings and were integral in shaping the monastic tradition. (*See* PHILOSOPHY.)

In defending Christianity, Augustine also strongly repudiated what he saw as heretical movements, including Manichaeism and other movements such as Pelagianism. His arguments were always carefully constructed, and he won over many disciples during his reign as bishop of Hippo. Some of his own disciples at times questioned his teachings, and his popularity waned toward the end of his life. But his works were solidly influential during the Middle Ages. The Scholastic movement, which strove to reconcile classical philosophy with religious ideas, owes much to his work. Such noted religious figures as BERNARD OF CLAIRVAUX, ALBERTUS MAGNUS, and THOMAS AQUINAS were greatly influenced by Augustine, as were later reformers such as John Calvin. During the early Middle Ages, Augustine was recognized as a Doctor of the Church, signifying his importance for Christian doctrine. (*See* AUSTIN FRIARS.)

AUSTIN FRIARS

The Austin, or Augustinian friars, are followers of the doctrines of ST. AUGUSTINE OF HIPPO. They are comprised of two separate groups, the Augustinian Canons and the Augustinian Hermits. The religious orders include separate branches for men and for women. (*See* MONASTERIES AND MONASTICISM.)

St. Augustine was active during the first 30 years of the fifth century, and is considered one of the key figures of Western theology. The Austin friars originated from those who followed Augustine's teachings after his death in 430. The Austin Hermits were the original Austin friars. (The Protestant reformer Martin Luther was originally an Austin Hermit.) They can trace their origins to the religious hermits who were forced out of northern AFRICA (where Augustine had lived) after the

A 15th-century miniature depicting Augustine's City of God. *The upper enclosure contains those who have been accepted into heaven; the lower contains those attempting to get in (or rebelling) through the seven Christian virtues.*

VANDALS invaded from Europe around 428. Eventually, they settled in central and northern Italy, where they established a number of monasteries.

Originally, as their name implies, the hermits lived in seclusion at these monasteries. In time, several orders of Austin Hermits emerged, each with a slightly different focus. In 1244, Pope Innocent IV established the various groups as one order, and 12 years later Pope Alexander IV called upon them to begin doing apostolic work in urban centers. In the sixteenth century a group of Austin hermits brought back the old ideas of solitary contemplation. They formed the Augustinian Recollects in SPAIN, and the movement quickly gained adherents. The order was established as a distinct province of the Augustinians in 1602. It was not until 1912 that they were recognized as an independent order.

The Austin Canons came into being in the middle of the eleventh century. The clerics who founded the Austin Canons agreed to give up whatever private property they had and live communally. The order grew rapidly and flourished in Europe until the Protestant Reformation was in full force. (*See* FRIARS.)

AUSTRIA

From humble roots as a German principality, Austria rose in power throughout the Middle Ages to become the centerpiece of the HOLY ROMAN EMPIRE.

The Early Middle Ages. In the fifth century, after the fall of the Roman empire, SLAV tribesmen invaded the area that would become Austria and penetrated as far as Styria, Carinthia, and eastern Tirol. In the following two centuries, the Slavs were conquered by the migrating Bavarians and AVARS, and with the support of Bavarian dukes, were converted to CHRISTIANITY. The Bavarians, under the political influence of the FRANKS, settled in the Danube Valley, while the Avars settled in the area east of Traun. By 700, the Bavarian dukes had become nearly independent from the Frankish kings; but, by the late eighth century, the Franks reasserted their sovereignty. In 788, CHARLEMAGNE defeated the Bavarian duke TASSILO III, subdued the hostile Avars, and assumed direct control of BAVARIA. In 800, he annexed the kingdom into his empire, establishing it as the Eastern March (*Ostmark*, in German; hence the Latinized Austria). Charlemagne encouraged German colonization, and the conversion of the Slavs, with the new archbishopric of Salzburg, was intensified.

The area prospered until the early tenth century, when it was devastated by the Magyar invaders. It was not until 955, with OTTO I's victory at the Lechfeld, that the Magyars were driven out of the territory and the march was reestablished. During Otto's reign, the march once again flourished, as the towns, especially Vienna, began to grow in prominence.

The Babenbergs. In 976, Otto made Leopold I of the Babenberg family margrave of Austria; the Babenbergs would rule there for the next 270 years, expanding eastward and northward, conducting wars against the Hungarians, Poles, and Moravians. In the eleventh and twelfth centuries, waves of Bavarian settlers contributed to the Germanization of the march, while German kings led several campaigns there.

Despite the efforts of German kings to limit their power, the Babenbergs were able to increase their influence in the region over the next century. The Babenberg Leopold III (later, the patron saint of Lower Austria) sided with the PAPACY against HENRY IV in the INVESTITURE CONTROVERSY. The family was also dragged into the HOHENSTAUFEN-Welf conflict in the twelfth century through family ties to the Hohenstaufen emperors. In an effort to end the conflict, in 1156, Emperor FREDERICK I BARBAROSSA separated the Austrian March from Bavaria, giving the latter to the Welf HENRY THE LION, and allowed the Babenberg

Henry II Jasomirgott to retain the former, elevating it to the status of a duchy. In return, the Babenbergs reaffirmed their support of the emperor. However, the creation of the Austrian duchy marked a crucial step in the movement toward Austria's political separation from GERMANY.

Henry Jasomirgott was succeeded by his son, Duke Leopold V, who in 1192 acquired the duchy of Styria. The union of Austria and Styria made the Babenbergs one of the wealthiest and most powerful families in Europe. The succession of Leopold's son, Leopold VI, inaugurated a Babenberg golden age in Austria, as cultural and economic life in the duchy flourished, and the court in Vienna became one of the grandest in Europe. (*See* NOBLES AND NOBILITY.)

Decline of the Babenbergs. With the death of Leopold V in 1194, however, the Babenberg fortune declined precipitously. Emperor FREDERICK II temporarily seized the duchy from Leopold's son, Frederick II (the Quarrelsome), who died in 1246 without an heir, thereby ending the Babenberg line. During the following years, both the emperor and the pope were involved in the redistribution of Babenberg territory. Eventually, Ottokar II of Bohemia seized the duchy. Having no legal right to the lands, he was challenged by Rudolf of HABSBURG. Rudolf gained the German crown in 1273, occupied the duchies, and defeated Ottokar in battle in 1278. Rudolf ascended to the imperial throne in 1282, a crucial year in Austria's history. He made his sons Albert and Rudolf II feudal lords of the duchies of Austria and Styria, respectively. This was the legal beginning of what would be 636 years of Habsburg rule of Austria.

The Habsburgs. However, after Rudolf's death in 1291, the Habsburgs were confronted with a series of frustrations. In 1291, the communities of Schwyz, Uri, and Unterwalden united against them as the Swiss Confederation; they won their independence by defeating an imperial force at Morgarten in 1315. Consequently, in the fourteenth century, the Habsburgs began attending their Austrian territories, as opposed to their Swiss domains, and even began calling themselves the House of Austria. In the following century, the Swiss chipped away at Habsburg territory; Zurich joined the confederation in 1351, Bern in 1353, Glarus in 1388, and by the midfifteenth century, the Austrians were almost driven out of the region. These losses were somewhat offset by the incorporation of Carinthia, Carniola, and Tirol into the Habsburg domains during the reigns of ALBERT II (1330–1358) and his son, Rudolf IV (1358–1365).

The Habsburg domains were split into two branches in 1379 between Rudolf IV's brothers Albert III and Leopold III. The Albertine line, which received most of Upper and Lower Austria, was extin-guished by 1457; it was the Leopoldine line that would restore the family to its past glory. The two branches were reunited under Leopold III's son, Frederick V, who seized the German crown in 1440 and became Emperor Frederick III in 1452. Frederick consolidated the Habsburg lands into what is roughly modern-day Austria. (*See* HABSBURG DYNASTY.)

Despite numerous setbacks, Frederick preserved an unyielding belief in his family's destiny. His motto, A.E.I.O.U., was taken to stand for *Austriae est imperare orbi universo* (Austria is destined to rule the world). He lived to see the first step of what seemed a fulfillment of that prophecy: his son MAXIMILIAN'S marriage to MARY OF BURGUNDY acquired for the family all the Burgundian territories in the Low Countries and vast estates in eastern FRANCE. Maximilian's son, Philip I, married Joan (the Mad), daughter of Ferdinand and Isabella, and secured for the family not only CASTILE and ARAGON, but also Spain's domains in NAPLES-SICILY, and her New World territories. Austria's newly won grandeur inspired another motto: "Others may fight wars, but fortunate Austria prefers marriage!" (*See* HOLY ROMAN EMPIRE.)

AVARS

T he Avars were, with the SLAVS, one of the two non-German groups occupying land in what is now AUSTRIA. They were a tribe of Altaic descent originating in Mongolia and Turkey that threatened CHINA from the north. During the fifth century, they migrated through Iran to the Russian steppes, and then to the base of the Volga River and Caspian Sea. The Bavarians sent missionaries to them several times. In 567, Avar King Bayan led an assault on the Gepids, a Germanic tribe allied with the Byzantine Empire, and the LOMBARDS at the Danube basin. A year later they invaded Dalmatia after Byzantine Emperor Justin II refused to pay them tribute. The Byzantines called a truce after three years, and Justin paid the Avars 80,000 pieces of silver in the treaty. In 581 they extracted 100,000 silver pieces from Emperor Maurice after capturing Sirmium on the river Sava. The Avars executed 12,000 Byzantine prisoners in 599. (*See* BARBARIAN INVASIONS.)

The Avars occupied the old Roman Pannonia, a Hungarian plain near the Danube and Tisza. HUNGARY became the Avars' homeland as they dominated the Balkans under Bayan's control, encouraging Slavs to migrate into the Balkans. Their empire stretched from the Baltic Sea to the Volga River.

In 601, Byzantine General Priscus beat back Bayan at the Tisza after having crossed the Danube. Yet the Avars continued their assault of the Byzantine during the early seventh century. Avar fighters dominated the south and west of the Danube in 603–604, and from 617 to 619 they reached the walls of CONSTANTINOPLE. Byzantine Emperor HERACLIUS paid a large tribute to keep the peace, but it was to no avail. The Avars joined forces with the Persians in an assault on Constantinople in 626, amassing a force of 80,000. The Avars invaded from the European side of the city and the Persians from the Asian side. The Byzantine armies, however, managed to drive the invaders out.

The Avars then directed their forces toward the FRANKS to the north, but were annihilated in 791 by CHARLEMAGNE, who annexed all the Avar territories. The Avars were then converted to CHRISTIANITY over the ensuing decade. With the growth of independent Slav and Bulgar states during this period, the Avars began to disappear as they were absorbed into the greater Hungarian population. (See HUNGARY.)

AVERROES

The Muslim philosopher Averroës (pronounced a-vair´-reez, 1126–1198), known as ibn Rushd in Islamic culture, was among the most influential thinkers of the Middle Ages. His work was valued both for its philosophical sophistication and for the fidelity with which he recorded Aristotelian teachings. He was also a world famous physician. (See ARAB and ARABIC LANGUAGE AND LITERATURE.)

Life. Born Abu al-Walid Muhammad ibn Rushd in Córdoba, SPAIN, in 1126, he became that city's *kadi* (religious leader) in 1171. In 1182, the ALMOHAD ruler, Abu Yaakub Yussuf, appointed him his personal physician and installed him in the royal court at Marrakesh. During this period he undertook the systematic study of the works of ARISTOTLE, writing commentaries on *De Anima* and the *Metaphysics,* which were translated into Latin and considered the most authoritative commentaries of Aristotle during the late Middle Ages. (See PHILOSOPHY; ARISTOTLE.)

During a brief period of persecution in 1195, Averroës was forced into exile and many of his works were condemned and burned. He was soon reinstated, however, and remained highly respected until his death in 1198. (*See* HERESY.)

Work. Averroës's approach was in stark contrast to that of AVICENNA, his forerunner and the other influential Islamic philosopher of the Middle Ages. While Avicenna accepted mysticism in philosophic thought, Averroës was a radical rationalist, his legacy from Aristotle. Averroës also wrote mathematical and naturalist treatises that show a keen power of observation and an aversion to mystical explanation.

The Averroists. The writings of Averroës were carefully studied (in Latin) at the University of PARIS in the 1250s. A number of scholars, most notably SIGER OF BRABANT, adapted his method and many tenets of his PHILOSOPHY. The centrality of the human intellect in Averroës was naturally attractive to the scholars, but it posed a threat to the authority of the Church. At the invitation of Pope Alexander IV, (St.) Albert the Great wrote a treatise attacking the Averroists in 1256. The following year, THOMAS AQUINAS included an attack on the group in his *Summa Contra Gentiles.* The Averroists became so powerful that in 1263, Pope URBAN IV condemned the group and banned the study of Averroës. A series of excommunications ensued until the school was all but eliminated from Paris by 1277. Averroës continued to exert his influence, however, as an underground movement that surfaced briefly in the teachings of the fourteenth-century Parisian scholar, John of Jandun, and the Italian school at Padua through the fifteenth century. (*See* PHILOSOPHY.)

AVICENNA

The philosopher and physician Avicenna (980–1037), known as Ibn Sina in Islamic culture, was an outstanding practitioner of both disciplines and his works were studied by Muslims, Christians, and Jews for centuries. They are, in fact, still used as a source on folk remedies in some parts of the world. (*See* MAGIC AND FOLKLORE.)

Life. Abu Ali al-Husayn ibn Sina was born in 980 in Buchara in Persia and came under the influence of both the philosopher-mystic AL-FARABI and the Ismaili preachers who visited his father's home. Avicenna became known as a healer at a young age and accepted an invitation to the court of the Buyid prince Sams al-Dawla in 1001 to be the prince's personal physician. It was here that he met al-Farabi. Avicenna spent about a decade in the court at Hamadan in western Persia, and then, after the death of the prince, he traveled to Isfahan, where he became a teacher and a physician. (See ARAB and ARABIC LANGUAGE AND LITERATURE.)

In 1037, while accompanying the ruler of Isfahan on a military expedition, Avicenna became violently ill and soon died. His mausoleum in Iran was rebuilt in the 1950s and is a shrine today.

Work. During the two periods of his life when he was not wandering—in Hamadan and in Isfahan—Avicenna produced a large body of work in virtually every field of human inquiry—nearly 300 works in all, ranging from brief medical papers to massive encyclopedias covering all of human knowledge. His most famous work is the majesterial *Kitab al-Shifa (Book of Heal-*

ing), five volumes comprising the largest encyclopedia produced by a single person during the Middle Ages.

Medicine. Two works by Avicenna have had a profound influence on the history of medicine. One is *al-Qanun fi attibb (The Canons of Medicine)*, a large compendium of diseases, diagnostic techniques, treatments, and drug therapies for nearly every ailment. *Al-Qanun* was translated into Latin and was the most authoritative work in medicine during most of the Middle Ages. The other work is a poem on the philosophy of healing, which once was memorized by medical students in Islamic lands as an introduction to the art of healing. (*See* MEDICINE AND CARE OF THE SICK.)

AVIGNON

City on the east bank of the lower Rhône River, it served as the seat of the PAPACY and hence the center of western Christendom from 1309 until 1377, and thereafter as the stronghold of the antipopes Clement VII and Benedict XIII. King Louis VIII of FRANCE destroyed Avignon in 1226 in retribution for its support of the ALBIGENSES. Avignon itself belonged to the king of NAPLES, a papal vassal, and was not formally purchased by the papacy until 1348. It remained a papal possession during the GREAT SCHISM, and for nearly another four centuries, until it was annexed to France in 1791.

The Papacy. Less vulnerable to attack than ROME, Avignon was chosen as the papal residence in 1309. It had become expedient for Pope CLEMENT V, who was French, both to avoid the turmoil and violence of ITALY, and to maintain close contact with the king of France, PHILIP IV, the Fair. Philip's machinations had brought down Pope BONIFACE VIII, and he continued to challenge papal authority, alternating threats with negotiation. Clement's successors constructed the battlement walls of the city (some three miles around) and the fortress like papal palace, a Gothic structure consisting of the architecturally austere Old Palace (1343–1342) and the more ornate New Palace (1342–1352), both richly furnished and decorated.

The money for these and other construction projects, for maintaining a splendid court that dispensed liberal patronage to artists and scholars, and for pursuing expensive policies such as Italian military campaigns, Asian missions, and the INQUISITION, was assumed to have come from sources beyond the papacy's tax and fee collections. (The system of centralized papal administration and finance was perfected in Avignon under Pope JOHN XXII. While in Avignon, the papacy was notorious for luxury and corruption.)

Although Avignon was not then actually on French soil (from which it was divided by the Rhône),

and each succeeding pope spoke of returning to Italy—Pope Urban V actually did so in 1367 but retreated to Avignon in 1370—the Avignon papacy was perceived to be in league with the kings of France, whose cooperation and influence were regarded as essential to papal interests. (See PAPACY; GREAT SCHISM)

Gregory XI returned the papacy to Rome in 1377 and died the following year. The cardinals chose his successor URBAN VI, but then repudiated him and elected CLEMENT VII, the first antipope, who took up residence in Avignon. This "Great Schism," as it was called, ended in 1417 when the cardinals at the Council of Constance acknowledged Martin V as pope and deposed both Clement's successor, Benedict XIII, and a third claimant, the "Pisan" Pope John XXIII. The papacy emerged from what the Italians called the Babylonian captivity with an even more centralized administration, an even greater reputation for corruption, and an ever more powerful College of Cardinals.

Avignon Today. The papal palace at Avignon still stands, stripped of its art and furniture in the nineteenth century, when it was used as a stable for the French cavalry. Today it is an art museum and theater.

AYYUBIDS

An Islamic dynasty that ruled EGYPT and Syria during the late twelfth and early thirteenth centuries. Originating from Kurdish tribes in Armenia, these fighters gained many victories against the crusaders while fighting for the Syrian warlord, Nur al-Din. In 1169, two of Nur's generals, SALADIN and his uncle, Shirku ibn Shadhi, defeated the FATIMID DYNASTY in Egypt and founded the Ayyubid dynasty, named after Saladin's father Ayyub ibn-Shadhi. In 1171, Saladin disbanded the Shi'ite Fatimid caliphate and pledged his loyalty to the Sunnite ABBASID caliphate. In 1174, following the death of Nur, Saladin took control of Syria. (*See* CRUSADES; ISLAM.)

Saladin extended his empire to Arabia and captured Jerusalem from the crusaders in 1187, though his defeat at Acre during the Third Crusade resulted in a truce with RICHARD I LION-HEART that put an end to expansion. Following Saladin's death in 1193, the Ayyubid throne went to Saladin's brother, al-Adil, whose line ruled until 1250. The elite MAMLUK regiment rebelled and took control in Egypt, and in 1260, the MONGOLS captured BAGHDAD and ended Ayyubid control of Syria. Yet, during their brief period of power, the Ayyubids unified Egypt and Syria, fostered a small golden age of art and literature, and turned Cairo from a Shi'ite capital to a center for Sunnite Islam. (*See* CALIPHATE; EGYPT; SALADIN.)

BACON, ROGER

Born in Ilchester, Somerset, ENGLAND, Roger Bacon (1214–1292) probably studied at Oxford in the late 1220s and during the 1230s, where he came under the influence of (but probably did not study directly with) the theologian and philosopher ROBERT GROSSETESTE. Bacon was impressed by Grosseteste's abilities as a translator of the BIBLE and Greek philosophical works, as well as by his knowledge of Greek and Arabic SCIENCE. Bacon believed that this made the Oxford scholar a better interpreter of ARISTOTLE and enabled him to correct Aristotle where necessary. Bacon lectured at the University of PARIS in the 1240s, being the first to lecture formally on Aristotle's work after it was condemned in 1231. (*See* SCIENCE.)

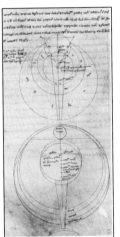

Bacon's analysis of the behavior of light inside the orb of the eye, from the Opus maius.

His Work. From 1247 to 1257, Bacon conducted scientific research, acquired many esoteric books (some on occult disciplines), wrote commentaries on several of Aristotle's books, and, as he put it, sought out "the friendship of the wise." In 1257 he entered the FRANCISCAN order and began a ten-year "exile from studies."

About 1264, Bacon offered to write a new work on philosophy for Cardinal Guy Le Gros Foulques. When the Cardinal was elected Pope Clement IV in 1265, Bacon received a papal order to send the work secretly and without seeking the approval of his FRANCISCAN superiors. The work, the *Opus maius (Major Work)* was a vast encyclopedia of the arts and sciences and all the disciplines taught in universities at that time. He also introduced a new science: the study of light, integrating all known Greek and Islamic knowledge on the eye, vision, perspective, and optics. There are intimations in his work of the possibility of a telescope, gunpowder, mechanical navigation, and even flight. He also sent a second work, *Opus minus (Minor Work)*, a treatise on ALCHEMY, but he withheld the *Opus tertium (Third Work)*, containing a spirited defense of the importance of scientific education in the development of the moral and religious personality.

Condemned. The wealth of new ideas in Bacon's writings and his failure to seek the approval of his superiors aroused Franciscan suspicions, and he was condemned in 1278. He was soon accused of sorcery and imprisoned briefly, but he seems to have returned to Oxford by 1280. He died there in 1292.

Bacon's views have often been characterized as a blend of the philosophies of AVICENNA and AUGUSTINE, but his main purpose was to defend Aristotle from what he regarded as the unscientific approach of neoplatonists like Richard Rufus of Cornwall.

BADR, BATTLE OF

A central battle in the early history of ISLAM and the life of MUHAMMAD. The Battle of Badr (624) was a decisive victory for Muhammad and his followers in Medina against the Quraysh ruling family of Mecca. It was the first of many victories for Muhammad culminating in the dominance of Islam over almost the entire Arabian peninsula. Perhaps more important, Badr became a legendary event in the annals of Islamic history that confirmed the Muslim belief that their victory was God's will, ensuring the solidarity of early adherents.

Muhammad first preached Islam in his native Mecca, an important center of trade, but persecution by the town's elite forced him to flee to Medina, where he had a small following. The youthful Islamic movement grew in Medina, and the Muslims supported themselves through raids on trading caravans from Mecca. One such caravan was met by a raiding party led by Muhammad at Badr, a small town near Medina.

The battle began in traditional Arabic fashion with a series of single combats between the leaders of the two parties that were won by leaders of the Medineans. In the battle that followed, the Meccans lost 45 to 70 men with only 15 losses for the Muslims. The victory produced needed resources for the previously impoverished Muslim community in Medina. The Islamic combatants at Badr wore their participation as a badge of honor, the first triumph in a string of victories that transformed the Arabs from a nomadic tribal people to the leaders of a world empire. (*See* ARAB.)

BAGHDAD

The city of Baghdad (from the Arabic for "Abode of Peace") was founded in 762 by al-Mansur, the second ABBASID caliph, who made it his capital. Situated on the Tigris near a canal to the Euphrates, the city was at the crossroads of trade routes between East and West, and fostered schools of PHILOSOPHY and SCIENCE that were vital to the growth of Arabic culture in Persia. (*See* ARAB *and* ARABIC LANGUAGE AND LITERATURE.)

Following the conquest by the SELJUK TURKS in 1055, Baghdad lost its importance as a center of trade and government and became the center of Sunnite Islam. In 1065, the Nizamiyah, a school that served as home of some of Islam's greatest scholars, was founded in the city, one of over 30 the community boasted by the end of the twelfth century.

The taking of the city by the MONGOL Hulagu in 1258 was devastating. The invaders killed the last caliph and 80,000 of his followers, and destroyed the elaborate canals and fountains that the traveler Benjamin of Tudela described as one of the wonders of the world. The city would not recover until modern times.

BALDWIN I

First king of the Frankish state of Jerusalem, Baldwin I (c. 1058–1118) is credited with transforming it from a weak ecclesiastical state into a feudal monarchy. He established the kingdom's territorial expanse and founded many of its administrative institutions. (*See* CRUSADES.)

His Life. Born in Boulogne, Baldwin was educated for the Church. In 1096 he embarked with his brother GODFREY OF BOUILLON on the First CRUSADE, but once in Cilicia, he moved eastward instead of accompanying Godfrey south into Syria. With a small group of knights, Baldwin proceeded to Edessa to aid its Armenian ruler, Thoros, but he soon took control himself (1097), thereby establishing the region's first Latin state, the county of Edessa. He secured his position by marrying an Armenian noble's daughter.

Baldwin succeeded his brother as "defender of the Holy Sepulchre" and was crowned king (Godfrey had declined) on Christmas Day, 1100. He managed to outmaneuver both the Latin patriarch of Jerusalem, Daimbert, and a secular rival, TANCRED, frustrating the former's claim to suzerainty in Jerusalem and Jaffa. Baldwin accepted control of Galilee from Tancred when the latter became regent of Antioch.

His Work. Baldwin pursued a vigorous military policy. By the end of his reign he held all of the port cities except Ascalon and Tyre, having enlisted Italian naval aid in return for commercial privileges. He withstood repeated attacks from EGYPT, built the great castle called Krak de Montreal in his honor, assisted Latin rulers to the north (as they in turn assisted him), and secured a truce with DAMASCUS. Baldwin sought to attract eastern Christians to his realm, and like his brother, accommodated Muslims and their commer-

cial activities to the economic benefit of the kingdom.

For pecuniary and political reasons, Baldwin repudiated his first wife in 1113 and married Adelaide, the mother of Count Roger II of Sicily. His first marriage had been childless; his second proved so also, and in 1116 he had it annulled. Baldwin died on April 2, 1118, after returning from an expedition in Egypt, and the crown devolved upon his chosen successor and cousin, Baldwin II of Le Bourg.

BALDWIN IV THE LEPER

Baldwin IV the Leper (c. 1161–1185), was king of Jerusalem (1174–1185) at the time SALADIN first threatened the Latin kingdom of Jerusalem. Baldwin, the son of Amalric I and Agnes of Courtenay, suffered from LEPROSY from his youth. He was educated by the historian William of Tyre, the chronicler of the Frankish principalities. Baldwin IV became king at age 13; for the first few years of his reign his cousin Raymond III, count of Tripoli, served as regent. Thereafter, Baldwin's health periodically necessitated the appointment of regents, contributing to the proliferation of political factions in the kingdom and intensifying the problem of succession.

Despite his age and ill health, Baldwin was a courageous and skilled warrior. He defeated the formidable SALADIN in battle when, after the latter assaulted Ascalon, Baldwin escaped entrapment in the city and was victorious in a pitched battle at Mont Gisard. A truce (1180) between the two held for two years, until it was wantonly violated by Reginald of Châtillon. Saladin again went on the offensive and completed the encirclement of Jerusalem with the fall of Aleppo in June 1183, making Baldwin's position critical. The following November, Baldwin named as his successor his five-year-old nephew, the son of his sister Sibylla and her first husband, William of Montferrat, appointing Raymond of Tripoli and his own maternal uncle, Jocelin II of Courtenay, the child's guardians.

Baldwin IV died of leprosy in March 1185, leaving a kingdom rendered dangerously vulnerable by internal discord. When his young nephew, who nominally ruled as Baldwin V, died only a year and a half after his uncle's death, the stage was set for the fall of Jerusalem.

BALL, JOHN

John Ball (d. 1381) was an English priest, social reformer, and itinerant preacher on behalf of equality and against privilege and social hierarchy. He played a major role in stirring up discontent and in leading the PEASANTS' REVOLT of 1381.

Ball was the only one of the leaders of the Peasants' revolt known for his outspokenness long before 1381. While serving as a priest in Essex, the bishop of London excommunicated him for his radical ideas in 1364. He then went to Kent where, according to one critic, "he preached many errors and scandals to the danger of his soul and to the manifest scandal of the Church." The archbishop of Canterbury repeatedly jailed him for his outspokenness as chaplain at St. James Church in Colchester where he preached to Sunday churchgoers revolutionary sermons that advocated common ownership of goods and an end to the feudal social hierarchy. (*See* PEASANTS' REVOLT.)

The imprisonments did little to instill in him greater respect for his ecclesiastical superiors. He was excommunicated again in 1376 and "tried and lawfully convicted by the clergy, who committed him to perpetual imprisonment" at Maidstone. He probably would have stayed there for the rest of his life had not WAT TYLER'S rebels released him in 1381. Ball joined Tyler at the head of his peasant force of 30,000 men. He was with them when they stormed the palace of JOHN OF GAUNT on the Thames and marched on LONDON on June 10, 1138. At Smithfield five days later, Tyler was killed. After the peasants were dispersed, Ball fled to the Midlands but was captured at Coventry.

Ball seemed to be a foolish fanatic to many, but others saw him as a prophet. The contemporary royal court historian JEAN FROISSART called the sermon Ball delivered at Blackheath "the most moving plea for social equality in the history of the English language." The authorities thought Ball was too dangerous to let live. He was brought before the king at St. Alban's, and on July 15, 1381, he was hanged, drawn, and quartered. (*See* SOCIAL CLASSES AND CLASS CONFLICT.)

BANKING

Banking emerged in medieval Europe in the latter part of the twelfth century as part of the transformation of trade and finance, generally known as the Commercial Revolution. Banks had existed in the Roman world (and continued to exist in the Byzantine world), but with the collapse of towns and international trade routes in the early Middle Ages, banking ceased to be a viable enterprise. From the fifth through the eleventh centuries, Europe had an economy predicated overwhelmingly on subsistence agriculture; the lords and peasants who made up the agrarian society had only a modicum of interest in merchants, and none at all in bankers. When banking returned to western Europe at the end of the twelfth century, first in ITALY, then in other parts of the western Mediterranean, and finally in selected towns in northern Europe, it did so as essentially a new departure in economic life. (*See* COMMERCE AND TRADE.)

Roles. While there was considerable variety in their form and function, medieval banks typically involved themselves in four endeavors: they acquired and managed deposits; they used the deposited money to invest in business ventures; they arranged for their depositors to transfer funds into and out of their accounts without using specie; and they extended credit to depositors, merchants judged to have favorable business prospects, and, in some instances, to the state. These functions developed in the first instance as offshoots of the business carried out by money changers; indeed, the word "bank" is derived from the tables (*banca* in Latin) set up by money changers in public market squares. In GENOA, FLORENCE, and perhaps a handful of other towns in northern ITALY, the money changers

A scene of commerce and trade going on alongside banking, from a 15th-century French manuscript. The three kinds of wares depicted—leather, which was a locally produced commodity and generally sold as manufactured goods; textiles, generally imported and sold as raw material; and metal smithing, where material was brought to the artisan for shaping or reworking into a desired form—all required the services of a banker. Payment for goods and services was frequently carried out solely on the books of the banker, who kept track (for a fee) of credits and debits of artisan and customer alike, giving the banker a great deal of power and prestige in the town.

accepted responsibility for safeguarding their clients' money in addition to changing it. In the warming commercial climate of the period, these early bankers realized that they could do more with the money than simply leave it in a chest, and their willingness to use the deposits as capital for investment set in motion an economic dynamic that is still unfolding.

Development. The success of these early bankers in investing deposited monies and in creating an institutional framework for financial transactions was predicated on several other simultaneous developments. One was the emergence in the Mediterranean world of public notaries who were familiar with the intricacies of Roman contractual law, newly rediscovered in the twelfth century. The notariate greatly improved the effectiveness of written contracts and inspired greater confidence that the terms stipulated in contracts would be honored. This had a direct bearing on the practice of banking. The earliest deposits with money changers were formally entered in the registers of the notaries, but as banking evolved, municipal authorities began to treat the banker's ledgers and journals as public records akin to the notary's registers, records that established formal rights and obligations between bankers and their depositors or debtors. Depositors could never be certain that their bank would not fail through imprudent investments, but, because of the formal status of the bank records, they could be reasonably confident that their banker would not be able to swindle them out of their money.

A second factor of considerable importance in the development of medieval banks was the rise of new methods of business organization in the twelfth and thirteenth centuries, notably in the formal composition of partnerships. One such arrangement was known as a *commenda*, a contractual partnership in which one of the parties took responsibility for seeking a profitable market for the partnership's goods, while the other party provided the working capital. These arrangements, formalized by the notaries, had three important consequences for banking. First of all, they created a climate in which people grew accustomed to the idea of placing their money in someone else's hands, which is what depositors had to be persuaded to do to keep bankers in business. Second, they provided the bankers with a way of using the money they acquired, without having to travel; bankers could stay at home and run their banks while still reaping the rewards of commercial enterprise. Third, they gave bankers a means to reward depositors without necessarily contravening the Church's ban on usury. A straightforward interest payment on deposited money was considered usurious—though it is fairly clear that bankers in some financial centers, such as VENICE, commonly ignored the Church's teaching—but if the return given to depositors could be treated as profit on an investment rather than as interest on a deposit, then all parties, including the Church, were satisfied with the arrangement.

Even with such loopholes, though, depositors were often happy to give their money to a banker without asking for any return beyond the principal. They did so because bankers could provide other useful services, such as the transfer of funds solely by entry in the bank's books, and the extension of temporary credit via overdraft. A mercer with a current account in a bank, for example, could pay a draper who sold him cloth by directing the banker to debit his account and to credit the draper's account, sometimes, perhaps, overdrawing the account (or, in effect, receiving a short-term loan). Similarly, the customers availing themselves of the mercer's wares could direct the banker to credit the mercer's account while debiting their own. Fairly early in their history, banks devised methods to make transfers between themselves in cases where debtor and creditor had accounts in different banks. (Basically, this is the same service banks provide today when they handle checks.) There are two main differences in this respect between medieval and modern banks: medieval bankers were unwilling to accept written orders for account transfers—transfers had to be made orally with both parties present—and they could not avail themselves of state-sponsored central banks to manage clearances. Though awkward by modern standards, the system of book transfer served the interests both of the holders of accounts and of the bankers reasonably well. Account holders did not need to deal as regularly with the inconveniences of coins (avoiding the risk of theft, for example, or the risk that coins had been clipped, sweated, counterfeited, debased, or corrupted in some other way), while the bankers secured a supply of capital for investment. Possession of a bank account may even have had a certain social cachet in the status-conscious world of the medieval town. (*See* COMMERCE AND TRADE; MONEY AND CURRENCY.)

Late Middle Ages. By the end of the thirteenth century, a number of Italian banks had established networks that extended to all of Europe's leading commercial centers, from Palermo to LONDON, and in

---

LIFE IN THE MIDDLE AGES

Liquidating the Templars

Banks sometimes found themselves embroiled in politics and accused of all manner of crimes by kings hoping to get their hands on the banks' assets. The Bank of the Knights Templar, begun by providing banking services for crusaders, had become immensely wealthy by serving as the bankers responsible for transporting monies collected by the Church throughout Europe to Rome. Philip the Fair, hoping to solve his financial woes, convened an inquisition in 1308 and charged the Templars with witchcraft. After a lurid trial, the head of the order was executed and the Templar bank in Paris was seized, bringing an end to the order.

some instances even to points beyond, such as Tunis. These international banks often grew out of mercantile enterprises, often entering the field of banking as extensions of their trading operations. As banks, the main interest of these international concerns was to arrange payments for merchants engaged in long-distance trade. From early in the fourteenth century, such payments were typically effected by means of a bill of exchange, a short document akin to a simple promissory note. A merchant who borrowed money in one place (FLORENCE, for example) in order to finance a trading expedition to another place (say, London) issued a note to the creditor specifying that the debt, contracted in the local currency (florins), would be repaid in the foreign one (English sterling). The recipient, or purchaser of the bill, forwarded the document to his branch manager in the country in which the debt was to be repaid, and the branch made arrangements with the seller of the bill, or his agent, for the repayment of the loan. Repayments abroad were ordinarily stipulated to be higher than the amount originally borrowed. (*See* TRAVEL AND TRANSPORTATION.)

This method of international transfer suited both parties involved in the transaction: the borrower acquired credit to underwrite a business venture, while the creditor made a profit that was technically derived from foreign exchange rather than from interest on a loan, and thus did not contravene the usury laws. The branch that received the money typically lent the repaid money out again by financing another bill of exchange drawn on the city where the original loan was made. In this way, the primary lending bank reacquired its capital along with a tidy profit.

Though ordinarily a boon to their bottom line, investments based on trading ventures frequently proved to be the Achilles' heel of medieval banking. Loans to defaulting governments accounted for the largest crashes of the period, but sour investments in commercial enterprises were the most frequent source of trouble. Failure and bankruptcy are recurring themes in the history of medieval banking; rarely did a bank stay in business for more than a few generations. Many of their problems were institutional: banks seldom had more than a few hundred depositors, and most accounts contained small amounts. Single tremors, such as the loss of a big account or the failure of a single commercial enterprise, could shake a bank to its foundations. In retrospect, though, one is surprised less by the frequency with which banks went out of business than by the willingness of individuals to place their money at the banker's disposal. The pessimist might explain this behavior by citing the lack of other forms of investment, but the optimist might do so by emphasizing the utility of the banker's services in an economy that was becoming increasingly sophisticated.

BANNOCKBURN, BATTLE OF

The Battle of Bannockburn (June 24, 1314) was a decisive victory by the Scots, led by their famous national leader ROBERT THE BRUCE, against the English, led by King EDWARD II. The victory overturned the English domination of SCOTLAND established by Edward's father, Edward I, and brought about an independent Scottish kingdom.

In 1310, Edward II launched a campaign to retake territory Robert of Bruce had taken since the death of his father three years earlier. In 1314, a large English army was sent to relieve a garrison at Stirling that was besieged by the Scots. Robert met the English force of 60,000 infantry, 20,000 archers, and 1,400 mixed cavalry with a smaller Scottish army. The Scots deployed themselves in an excellent tactical position with forest to the left, a marsh on the right, and in front a stream traversed by only one road.

Although the Scottish deployment was almost invincible, Edward II began with a frontal cavalry assault that was easily repulsed. A Scottish cavalry charge then broke up the English archer lines. These defeats demoralized the English army, which disintegrated entirely when a charge by Robert's camp followers was heard. The English, including Edward, fled and were killed by the thousands. Bannockburn was the greatest triumph ever of Scottish arms over the English, and the battle compelled Edward to accept Robert as king of Scotland. (*See* SCOTLAND; ROBERT I THE BRUCE.)

BARBARIAN INVASIONS OF EUROPE

The ancient Greeks thought that anyone who did not speak Greek was saying "ba-ba-ba," meaning nonsense. Hence the word barbarian for non-Greek-speaking foreigners—inferior people, it was thought, who lived primitively without the benefits of civilization centered on Athens. The Romans, heirs to Greek culture, adopted this concept, applying the term to inferior people principally congregated along the Rhine and Danube Rivers, invaders from the northeast and from the southeast who tried for centuries, but failed to break into the Mediterranean world that ROME ruled. Some individuals and small groups of barbarians made it peacefully across the Roman frontiers, especially the Rhine River; they were allowed to enter the Roman Empire in the west during its later centuries (250–400 C.E.) to become confederates or guest soldiers, armed and trained to help keep out their still-excluded barbarian kinsmen.

Beginnings. In 378 C.E. all of this began to change rapidly. The VISIGOTHS, who had been allowed to cross the Danube to settle as military buffers on the Roman side of the river, rebelled because they did not like the lands and other benefits offered to them. At the Battle of Adrianople that year, they defeated a Roman army and killed the emperor, Valens. By 406 the barbarian threat to Italy was so critical that the head of the Roman army, Stilicho, himself of barbarian lineage, pulled the Roman legions from the Rhine frontier to protect Rome. This drastic decision, combined with further incursions along the Danube, opened up western Europe and the Balkans to a series of barbarian invasions that did not cease until the late sixth century, and would begin again in the ninth and tenth centuries, this time involving incursions from the northwest by sea as well as from the east.

ST. AUGUSTINE OF HIPPO, when asked to explain the success of the barbarian invasions, replied that Providence had driven the pagans and heretical barbarians into the Roman Empire so that they could more easily be converted to Christianity. Besides, these painful events were only a cover for the real history of mankind—its march to the triumph of the Heavenly City, whose membership was known only to God until the Last Judgment. However, another Church father, ST. JEROME, busy in Jerusalem translating the Bible into what became the Latin Vulgate (or "popular" translation) regarded the barbarian invasions with

greater alarm. The Visigoths, who occupied Rome for a few weeks in 410, Jerome thought, were "vermin" who ought to be forthwith expunged.

Modern historians think the barbarian invasions were significant because their successor states to the Roman Empire were the beginnings of, or at least the forerunners of, the modern European states. The invasions also introduced new vernacular languages from which the German and English languages were developed. They also introduced distinctive ways of eating. Meals centered on beefsteaks replaced the Mediterranean diet of rice, oatmeal, and fish for those who could afford it. A fourth-century Roman historian tells us that the barbarians inspired fear by the multitude of cattle they drove in front of their migratory communities so they could have steak on the hoof.

The confusing, fragmentary, and meager accounts of the barbarian invasions by historians writing at the time have been supplemented in the twentieth century by information gathered from extensive archaeological digs. In the first era of the invasions, from the late fourth to the late sixth centuries, the invaders fell into two distinct ethnic groups—Scandinavians and MONGOLS—with the former constituting about 80 percent of them. (*See* NORWAY; SWEDEN; and DENMARK.)

Around 1000 B.C.E. large groups of Scandinavians from Norway and Denmark began to move south—

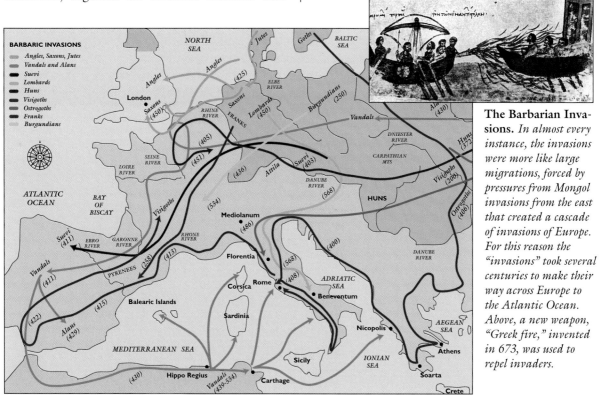

The Barbarian Invasions. *In almost every instance, the invasions were more like large migrations, forced by pressures from Mongol invasions from the east that created a cascade of invasions of Europe. For this reason the "invasions" took several centuries to make their way across Europe to the Atlantic Ocean. Above, a new weapon, "Greek fire," invented in 673, was used to repel invaders.*

BARBARIC INVASIONS
- Angles, Saxons, Jutes
- Vandals and Alans
- Suevi
- Lombards
- Huns
- Visigoths
- Ostrogoths
- Franks
- Burgundians

possibly in response to a climatically compromised food supply. By 300 C.E., they could even be found along the Danube. One group of the Scandinavian peoples was called Germani by the Roman historians, which became the general name for this cohort of Scandinavian invaders who went by such tribal names as GOTHS, FRANKS, and VANDALS. In English-speaking countries, the invaders from the north by way of the Rhine and Danube are still generally called Germans. The Germans usually referred to themselves as "Deutsch," Anglicized as Teutons, simply meaning "the people." (*See* GERMANY.)

Mongols. The Mongol peoples came from central Asia. After failing to penetrate CHINA and India, and probably in search of food, they moved westward and came around the Black Sea into the Danube basin. In the period 400–600 C.E. they were called Huns and AVARS. Unlike the Germans who fought—like the Romans—mainly on foot, the Mongols made heavy use of cavalry, which made them doubly fearsome and troublesome to the Romans.

Historians in recent decades have stressed that none of these barbarian groups were ethnically homogeneous. As they traveled they assimilated various peoples, forming communities called Franks or Huns. By 500 C.E., the Mongols had either been driven out by defending Roman armies or had been subjugated by the far more numerous Scandinavians or Germans and incorporated into the new post-Roman successor states and barbarian societies. For 150 years historians have debated whether the barbarians were at least as civilized as the lower classes of the Roman Empire, or were at a more primitive stage. Recent archeology has failed to clarify this issue. However, they rapidly adapted themselves to Roman provincial culture and to living on the great agricultural estates. By 600, as the barbarians had been converted to Catholic Christianity, intermarriage between barbarian chieftains and Roman aristocrats became common. Urban life was not a way of life the majority of barbarians took to; the cities withered and were eventually abandoned. By 700, the old Roman provincial aristocracy had blended into the leading barbarian families virtually everywhere; this combination spawned the medieval feudal lords. (*See* FEUDALISM.)

Vikings. The second wave of barbarian invasions occurred in the period from 850–1000. The VIKINGS (Norwegians and Danes) came from Scandinavia in their long ships, pushing up the river estuaries of western Europe, especially in northern France and the British Isles. They were pagan, violent, and fond of sacking monasteries for their ecclesiastical treasures. But by the mid-tenth century, they had settled down and formed feudal principalities, converting to the Church and skillfully drawing upon its human and material resources in building systems of government and LAW. They also became interested in long-distance trade, especially across RUSSIA from the north to the Black Sea along the river systems. A new Mongolian invader, the Magyars or Hungarians, had meanwhile pushed into what is now western Germany. They were defeated by the rising German emperors of the Ottonian (Saxon) dynasty and retreated to the Danube basin, where their descendants remain today.

Law. We can determine how barbarian societies functioned by examining their law codes (dealing almost exclusively with criminal law or peaceful alternatives to the blood feud) and from Germanic and Scandinavian epic poetry. The most important of such literary images are *Beowulf*, written in ENGLAND around 800 C.E., and the SAGAS OF ICELAND, the product of a thriving society of Norwegian immigrants, written in the thirteenth century. Both the *Beowulf* and Icelandic accounts portray a violent and unstable society, with constant fighting of one kind or another. *Beowulf* shows the importance of war leaders (chieftains, kings, lords) while the Icelandic works reveal a remarkable degree of popular government and law, through decision-making in local courts and councils. The English laws, "the dooms," also demonstrate this popular element at work. (*See* BEOWULF.)

The demography of the barbarian invasions is guesswork, but estimates can be made. The population of the western Roman Empire in 400 C.E. was about 50 million people. All the barbarians in the first wave of the late fourth to the late sixth centuries numbered no more than 1 million people. Barbarian armies fighting on Roman soil were never larger than 20,000, and usually fewer than 5,000 soldiers. Thus, the Roman Empire was not inundated by barbarians; it collapsed because of weak leadership, growing malaise about the benefits of Roman rule, and economic decline brought about by pandemics that thinned out the workforce and the army. Even then, strong leadership and careful management might have allowed the Empire to maximize its resources and keep out the barbarians, but it lacked the will and social intelligence to do so.

The second wave of barbarian invaders of western Europe in 850–1000 could not have numbered more than 300,000 people, against a western European population of possibly 8 million. The small numbers of invaders during this era explain why they were absorbed into European society more rapidly and with less disorder and destruction than before.

See the articles on VISIGOTHS, VIKINGS, *and* MONGOLS. *Background information appears in* WARFARE *and* CHRISTIANITY. *Additional information may be found in* AVARS, FRANKS, GOTHS, *and* VANDALS.

BARCELONA

A city on the northeast corner of the Iberian peninsula, on the Mediterranean Sea. First known as the Roman colony of Barcino, in the fifth century Barcelona was the center of the Germanic VISIGOTHIC kingdom. In 713, the ARABS conquered Barcelona, but failed to instill a lasting cultural or military influence. In 781, a Catalan group rebelled against the Arabs, and in 801, the FRANKS recaptured it for CHRISTIANITY. Barcelona then became an important outpost of the CAROLINGIAN Empire, until it gained independence under a native line of counts. Free Barcelona grew in size and wealth, mostly due to trade and agriculture. The counts of Barcelona extended their dominion to the south at the expense of the Muslims. They also traded with the Italian city-states of GENOA, PISA, and VENICE, thereby making Barcelona a center for trade in silks and spices from the Middle East and Asia. (*See* SPAIN.)

In 1137, the union of ARAGON and Catalonia led to further prosperity for Barcelona and the counts as it became the chief port and commercial center of Spain. Barcelona was the home of artisans and craftspeople, as well as a large number of Jewish merchants, who had a close relationship with the counts and the royal court. The city remained prosperous in the thirteenth and fourteenth centuries, but by the time of the INQUISITION in 1480, Barcelona's economy had begun to decline. The EXPULSION OF THE JEWS, the leading merchants of the city, as well as poor harvests and pirates in the area all contributed to the city's decline. However, more important, the kingdom of Castile in the west gained power, leading to a geographic shift in commerce from the eastern Mediterranean to the Atlantic Ocean, and ultimately to the New World.

BARON

A title identifying a noble or landed aristocrat. In the early Middle Ages, the term referred to a warrior or honored individual, who was a companion or counselor of a great lord or king. Over time, the title came to refer to a landed person who was part of the feudal system of superiors and inferiors. The title was more important in ENGLAND than in the continental feudal kingdoms. In England, the term was introduced after the Norman Conquest of the ANGLO-SAXON kingdom in 1066. English Barons were given land by the king in exchange for services, such as military duty and attendance at royal councils. The baronage of England was stratified by categories of lesser and greater, depending on the amount of land the baron owned. (*See* NOBLES AND NOBILITY.)

On the continent, the title baron had different meanings in different countries. In FRANCE, baronage evolved from the designation of a powerful man into a category of land owner. The amount of land needed to qualify for the baronage was indeterminate, unlike, for example, counts who had to own at least a county. Earlier in the feudal period, a continental baron usually held an important fief (or grant of land given by a higher lord). As time passed, barons identified feudal figures of lesser rank. By the fourteenth century, barons were usually inferior to a count and viscount.

BARTOLUS

A great legal commentator and jurist of the Middle Ages, Bartolus (c. 1313–1357) was born in Venatura, a small village in central ITALY. He entered the University of Perugia at the age of 14 and continued his studies at the University of Bologna, where he mastered Roman civil LAW. After serving as an assessor at Todi, Macerata, and PISA, successively, he began teaching at the University of Pisa in 1339, and at the University of Perugia in 1343.

Bartolus produced a vast and influential body of legal scholarship. His most important work is his extensive commentary on JUSTINIAN's *Corpus juris civilis*, in which he applied universal Roman civil law to address the reality of contemporary European practice. In his commentaries and in his many monographs on political, economic, and social issues, Bartolus arrived at innovative legal doctrines that shaped the development of medieval thought. Most significant of these are his discussion of the authority and limited autonomy of city-states, and the particular rights of citizens and corporate bodies. (*See* LAW AND LAW SCHOOLS.)

Bartolus died in 1357, widely regarded as one of Europe's most distinguished legal scholars. His doctrines were passed down under the name Bartolismo, and copies of his works appeared in libraries throughout Europe. After his death, his commentaries were considered so astute that they were often granted an authority equal to the JUSTINIAN CODE itself.

BASIL I THE MACEDONIAN

B asil I the Macedonian, (812–886), ruler of the Byzantine Empire from 867 to 886, founded the Macedonian dynasty that governed the empire until 1057. Under Basil and his successors, the Byzantine Empire, which had been on the defensive for hundreds of years, expanded in territory, grew wealthier, and became the greatest power in Europe. But though the Macedonian emperors ruled during the Byzantine "golden era," the dynasty came to an end shortly before the greatest disaster in Byzantine military history, the battle of MANZIKERT (1071), which began the long decline of the empire.

Rise to Power. Basil was uneducated and not of noble birth but he rose to power through resoluteness, shrewdness, and a complete absence of scruples. Basil's father was an Armenian peasant who settled in Macedonia. Basil's family was taken captive by the army of the famous Bulgarian tsar Krum. Basil escaped to CONSTANTINOPLE where a nobleman hired him as a stablehand. Basil's moment of opportunity came when he wrestled a Bulgarian in the presence of the emperor, Michael III. His victory lead to his employment by the emperor and a rapid rise through the imperial ranks, culminating in his appointment as chamberlain.

Basil and Michael became close friends. In order to further his own ambitions, Basil turned Michael against the caesar Bardas, Michael's uncle and the man responsible for Michael's becoming emperor. Basil personally murdered Bardas in the presence of the emperor and was subsequently made co-emperor. A sequence of murders followed (most important of which that of the minister Theocristus) ending in Basil's murder of Michael and his ascension to sole rule.

His Reign. Religious conflict occupied much of Basil's reign. He negotiated the dispute between rivals for the supremacy of the Church, the patriarchs Plotius and Ignatius, a rivalry which centered on the relationship between Constantinople and ROME. Plotius favored greater independence, while Ignatius was supported by Rome. Plotius was at first deprived of the patriarchy and exiled (867) by Basil. When Ignatius died in 877, Plotius was reinstated. By this time, the Greek church had become essentially independent of Rome. (*See* BYZANTIUM.)

An important religious triumph for Basil was the submission of the Bulgarian church to the authority of the Greek Orthodox Church in Constantinople rather than the Catholic Church in Rome. Basil also began making the confused Byzantine legal system understandable and resolving conflicts between the secular and religious codes. The code, called the *Basilica,* was completed by his son Leo. Basil also initiated a new form of BYZANTINE ARCHITECTURE with the building of the *Nea Ecclesia* or New Church in Constantinople.

In military matters Basil enjoyed minor successes on the Eastern borders of Asia Minor by pushing the boundary between the Arabic ABBASID caliphate and the Byzantine Empire eastward. Basil's military focus was in the west and in Italy. He regained the important Italian city of Bari, making the Byzantine Empire the most powerful state in south Italy. These Italian territories were reorganized into the administrative districts (known as themes) of Calabria and Lagoubardia. Cyprus was retaken from the Arabs but lost again after only seven years. The reconquest of Syracuse in Sicily by the Arabs was an important defeat and deterred Basil from a more general attack on the Arabs in the central Mediterranean. Significantly, Basil increased the prestige and power of the Byzantine navy. He also completed a terrible chapter in Byzantine history by pressing the war of religion against the Christian heretics, the Paulicians, slaughtering them and destroying their small state on the upper Euphrates .

Last Years. In some accounts, Basil lost his mind in his last years after the sudden death of his favorite son and chosen successor, Constantine. Basil lost none of his cruelty in his death, however. He was dragged off his horse by a stag while hunting. Before he died of a fever brought on by injuries, Basil beheaded the attendant who cut him loose in the mistaken belief that his rescue had really been an assassination attempt. On Basil's death, his son Leo VI ascended the throne.

BASIL II THE BULGAR SLAYER

Basil II Bulgaroktonus (the Bulgar Slayer; c. 958–1025) was the great-grandson of BASIL I and was the last emperor of the Macedonian dynasty. He took real power in 976 and ruled until his death. Basil was one of the most successful Byzantine emperors militarily. He brought to a victorious conclusion the long struggle between Byzantine and the Bulgar nation. He is also remembered for an act of brutality legendary even for his brutal age.

Basil become co-emperor with his brother Constantine at the age of two, while the empire was ruled in fact by his stepfathers Nicephorus Phocas and John Tzimisces. With the death of Tzimisces in 976, Basil and Constantine ascended to power, although real power belonged to the eunuch, Chamberlain Basil.

In 985, Basil forced Basil the Eunuch from power, and confiscated his vast wealth. Although finally in sole power—Constantine remained in the shadows—Basil's early rule was troubled. In 986, he was defeated in his first encounter with the Bulgarians and their czar, Samuel. In the following year, rebellious lords in ANATOLIA chose Phocas as their emperor. With the help of Prince Vladimir of Kiev, Phocas's troops were virtually eliminated. Phocas himself was set to engage Basil in hand-to-hand combat when the former fell dead. After defeating Phocas, Basil destroyed the power of the Anatolian aristocracy by confiscating their estates, reducing them to the status of the peasantry.

In 995 and 996 Basil waged successful campaigns in the East, defeating the Fatimids and annexing AR-MENIA. His most famous victories, however, took place in his war against BULGARIA. He defeated Samuel and, in 1014, captured some 14,000 Bulgars. Infuriated by their resistance, Basil proceeded to blind each prisoner, save one in a hundred who was left with one eye in order to guide the blind soldiers home. Samuel, upon seeing his men in this condition, is said to have died of a seizure two days later. Basil continued in power until his death in 1025. (*See* BYZANTIUM.)

BAVARIA

A duchy in the HOLY ROMAN EMPIRE situated in the southeast portion of GERMANY. By the late Middle Ages, Bavaria was bounded roughly by the Lech River on the west, by the king-dom of BOHEMIA to the northeast, and by the Salzburg and HABSBURG territories to the south and to the east.

Roman rule in the area fell in 488 with the Ger-manic invasions. Among these pagan invaders were the Baiuvarii, who migrated from northern Germany and modern Bohemia, and after whom the territory was named. In the next two centuries, the Germanic tribes settled along the Danube and mixed with the already established Celt and Roman populations. In the sev-enth and eighth centuries, they were christianized by Irish and Scottish monks.

The Franks. The Bavarian tribes were united in 560 under the Agilolfings, who ruled the region until the late eighth century. The Agilolfings recognized Frankish suzerainty, but functioned independently of their Frankish overlords. The FRANKS began to reassert their authority in the eighth century when PÉPIN THE SHORT demanded homage from the last Agilolfing ruler, Duke TASSILO III. CHARLEMAGNE repeated those demands, and in 787, eager to control the trade routes to ITALY within Bavaria, deposed Tassilo and annexed Bavaria into the CAROLINGIAN kingdom.

When the Carolingian empire was partitioned in 843, Bavaria was given to Charlemagne's youngest son, LOUIS THE PIOUS, and to his son, Louis the Ger-man, becoming the centerpiece of the East Frankish kingdom. In the following centuries, after the fall of the Carolingian dynasty and the invasion of the Hun-garians, Bavaria changed hands repeatedly. However, the Bavarian dukes managed throughout these turbu-lent years to increase their own power. By the begin-ning of the tenth century, they had earned the title of elector of German kings. The duchy also experienced great economic and demographic growth; new cities were established (such as Munich in 1158), and many of the great woodland areas were cleared.

The Guelphs. In the eleventh century, the duchy of Bavaria was given to the sons of the Salian emperors, who held the territory until 1061. In 1070, Bavaria then passed into the possession of the Welf dynasty, which was engaged in an extended feud with the HO-HENSTAUFEN DYNASTY. In a settlement between the Welf HENRY THE LION and the Babenberg duke Henry II Jasomirgott in 1156, the Hohenstaufen emperor FREDERICK I BARBAROSSA elevated AUSTRIA to the sta-tus of a duchy; he gave it to Henry II Jasomirgott, while Henry received the duchies of Bavaria and Sax-ony. However, after Henry came into conflict with the emperor over a breach of his feudal contract, Frederick stripped him of his duchies, and in 1180 gave Bavaria to Count Otto of Wittelsbach. The Wittelsbachs ruled Bavaria until 1918, bringing it great prosperity.

A Land Divided. Otto was succeeded in 1183 by his son Louis I, who took an active role in German pol-itics and increased his family's dominion to the east and north. Louis' son, Duke Otto II (1231–1255), continued Bavaria's expansion, and divided his king-dom among his three sons. This marked the beginning of a series of divisions and partitions of Bavaria that sig-nificantly weakened the power of the Wittelsbachs and undermined the family's efforts at consolidation. The dynastic feuds, which lasted for the next two and a half centuries, allowed neighboring countries to encroach on Bavarian territory, allowing other noble families within Bavaria to challenge the Wittelsbach's power.

Some of the splintering was reversed with the reign of Louis IV, duke of Upper Bavaria. Elected Ger-man king in 1314 and named emperor by the Roman people in 1328, he brought Bavaria to the height of its power. His court at Munich attracted some of the lead-ing artists and intellectual figures in all of Europe, such as WILLIAM OF OCKHAM. But after his death in 1347, Bavaria once again suffered partitions; by the end of the fourteenth century, it was divided into three rival duchies. However, some stability was maintained through the growing power of the Landtag, a repre-sentative assembly first organized at the beginning of the fourteenth century, and through the developing independence and prosperity of the towns.

Bavaria, although in a diminished state, began to move toward reunification under Albert IV, the Wise, duke of Munich, and became a single duchy once again under the rule of his son, William IV (1508–1550).

BAYEUX TAPESTRY

T he embroidery known as the Bayeux Tapestry is one of the most important documents of eleventh century history and art. Measuring 230 feet long by just under 20 inches wide, it depicts in more than 70 scenes the NORMAN Conquest of ENGLAND, concluding with the BATTLE OF HASTINGS and the death of England's KING HAROLD II GODWINSON. The Bayeux Tapestry is one of the oldest surviving records of the conquest.

Origins. Named for the French city in which it has spent nearly its entire existence, the Bayeux Tapestry dates to the end of the eleventh century. Exactly who embroidered the military chronicle is unclear. One popular legend attributes it to Matilda, wife of WILLIAM I THE CONQUEROR, but no evidence exists to support this. Some historians believe that it was commissioned by Odo, bishop of Bayeux and half-brother of William. Odo appears in the later scenes, as do several people known to be connected with him. Similarities between the Bayeux Tapestry and English works from the same period have led a number of scholars to conjecture that it was embroidered in England.

What It Depicts. The tapestry takes the form of a narrative that begins with King Harold's visit to the town of Bosham while on his way to Normandy (around 1064), and ends with Harold's forces fleeing Hastings in October 1066 after the king's death in battle. (The end of the tapestry is missing, so it may originally have included later events.)

Because the tapestry focuses on military rather than social events, it is most important to historians as a chronicle of military equipment and tactics used during the Norman Conquest. The decorative borders also provide insight into medieval treatment of fables. As a work of art, the tapestry is so richly detailed that it also provides a useful illustration of clothing, architecture, and ships common to the eleventh century.

Later History. The first reference to the Bayeux Tapestry dates to 1476, in a description of how it was used once a year to decorate the nave of the Bayeux cathedral. The antiquarian and scholar Bernard de Montfaucon made the first known complete reproduction of the tapestry in 1730. During the French Revolution the tapestry escaped destruction twice, and Napoleon exhibited it in Paris after he assumed power.

In 1804 the tapestry was placed in civil custody in Bayeux, where it remained for many years. It was removed in 1871 during the French-German War, and again during the Second World War. It currently resides in the former Bishop's Palace, known as the Museum of Queen Matilda's Tapestry—indicative of how seriously the Matilda legend is regarded by some. (See TAPESTRIES; HASTINGS; WILLIAM I THE CONQUEROR.)

BECKET, THOMAS

Thomas Becket (c. 1118–1170) was Archbishop of Canterbury during the reign of HENRY II. He had won favor with the king as his chancellor before Henry appointed him archbishop, but their quarrels grew in intensity, ending with the murder of Becket in his own cathedral.

Born in London to a middle-class Norman family, Thomas Becket was 24 when he entered the household of Theobald, archbishop of Canterbury. Theobald sent him to Bologna and Auxerre to study law. In 1154, after Becket was ordained a deacon, Theobald appointed him archdeacon of Canterbury.

Early Work. On the advice of Theobald, King Henry II chose Becket to be his chancellor. Theobald had hoped that Becket would represent the interests of the Church at court, but instead Becket quickly joined forces with Henry, becoming the king's close friend and advisor. His skill in administrative, financial, judicial, and diplomatic matters made Becket one of the most powerful and effective chancellors in medieval English history. He negotiated the marriage of Henry's son to the daughter of the French king and even took part in one of Henry's military campaigns in Toulouse in 1159.

Not surprisingly, when Theobald died in 1161, Henry appointed his friend to succeed Theobald as Archbishop of Canterbury, hoping he would help him

A battle scene in the Bayeux Tapestry. The Normans are depicted on horseback attacking the English from both sides. The English protect themselves behind interlocking shields as a single archer is seen in the middle. This section is about 5 feet wide.

curb Church power. As if already anticipating the conflict ahead, Becket hesitated to accept the position, but in 1162 Becket was ordained and consecrated archbishop of Canterbury. Not having completed his studies at the University of Paris, Beckett had to rely heavily on the humanist JOHN OF SALISBURY.

Opposition. Becket was clearly going to be as conscientious about his new responsibilities as he had been about being chancellor. One major conflict was over the issue of the control of Church courts. Henry wanted "criminous clerks"—clergy who were tried and convicted of secular crimes in Church courts—to be punished by secular authorities in accordance with the more severe English law. Becket vehemently opposed the king and was forced to flee to FRANCE when Henry enacted his plan in the Constitutions of Clarendon in 1164. In response, Henry had his son crowned by the archbishop of York in 1170, which resulted in a rift in the Church. The opposition to Becket was led by Gilbert Foliot, bishop of London, an aristocrat who detested Becket as a social upstart.

Assassination. While fuming at Becket's actions, Henry, at his court in Normandy, said he would love to be rid of the troublesome bishop, which four of his knights (rightly or wrongly) interpreted as a directive to assassinate Becket. They crossed the Channel and, on December 29, 1170, killed Becket in Canterbury Cathedral while he was conducting a service.

The murder shocked Europe and led to the canonization of Becket in 1173. Henry was forced to do public penance at Becket's tomb, and the judicial independence of the Church (or "benefit of clergy") was reinstated, helping to confirm the preeminence of Canterbury in English religious history.

BEDE THE VENERABLE

Bede (673–735) was the most illustrious scholar and teacher of medieval ENGLAND. His *Ecclesiastical History of the English People* (731) dramatizes the conversion of the English people to CHRISTIANITY and earned him the title "Father of English History." It is our primary source of knowledge about the early ANGLO-SAXONS. Renowned throughout Europe as a scholar, Bede never held an ecclesiastical office higher than priest; though called "the Venerable," he was canonized only in 1899.

Bede was born in 673 in Northumbria, near what became the paired monasteries of Wearmouth and Jarrow. He entered Wearmouth at age seven. He was placed under the tutelage of its founding abbot, Benedict Biscop, and later of Ceolfrid, abbot of Jarrow, both accomplished scholars. Ordained a deacon at age 18 and a priest at age 30, Bede spent his life at Wear-

mouth-Jarrow, which had rich cultural contacts with continental Europe and which Bede helped make a great center of learning. A dedicated teacher, Bede mastered Greek, Latin, mathematics, ASTRONOMY, and music. He wrote erudite commentaries on scriptures inspired by the Latin Fathers. (*See* LATIN.)

BEDFORD, JOHN, DUKE OF

John of Lancaster (1389–1435), duke of Bedford, was the son of King HENRY IV. After the death of his brother King HENRY V in 1422, he was designated protector of ENGLAND and regent of FRANCE. During the childhood of their nephew HENRY VI, who came to the throne of England at the age of nine months and soon thereafter was named king of France as well, John devoted his time to the affairs of France while his younger brother Humphrey, duke of Gloucester, performed his duties in England.

Bedford was a military leader of great skill and fortitude. John's initial successes also depended on his alliance with Philip the Good, duke of BURGUNDY, but that alliance wavered after JOAN OF ARC led the French to victories over the English. Bedford's role in Joan's trial and her execution during his administration harmed his later reputation.

The disruption of peace between Philip and King CHARLES VII of France was a major setback for English policy. It signified the end of English domination, and, in fact, its presence altogether, in France during the last stages of the HUNDRED YEARS' WAR.

BEGUINES

The Beguine movement, which lasted from the twelfth to the fourteenth centuries, was the only women's religious community totally under the control of WOMEN. Beguines did not take vows or become nuns; they modeled their lives after those of the apostles. Their guiding ideals were moral and spiritual purity and a simple, unadorned life.

The first Beguine communities appeared in Belgium late in the twelfth century; the movement soon spread to other parts of Europe. Many of the Beguines came from wealth and nobility, but they devoted their lives to serving others through simple charity. Some acted as nurses, others did sewing and embroidery, and others begged for alms. While some Beguines conducted their charitable acts from their own homes, many lived together in residences known as beguinages, which were sometimes grouped closely together to form a larger community. Some cities housed dozens of beguinages; there were more than 100 in Cologne, comprising some 15 percent of the city's adult female population.

The Beguines generated an extensive literature of piety and mysticism. Most important were the poems of Mechthild of Magdeburg (c. 1300). In recent decades, with the rise of women's studies and feminist theory, the Beguines have received a great deal of attention from historians. They can be regarded as forerunners of modern feminists. (*See* WOMEN.)

BELISARIUS

Belisarius (506–565) was one of the greatest generals in the history of the Byzantine Empire. He was close to JUSTINIAN I even before the latter became emperor. He became Justinian's bodyguard and was later made commander of the Eastern forces. After initial successes, he suffered defeat in Persia and was dismissed. When the Niké revolts erupted in CONSTANTINOPLE, however, Justinian reinstated him, and Belisarius successfully crushed the revolts through the slaughter of 40,000 persons.

His success continued. In 534 he defeated the VANDALS in AFRICA, regaining Carthage for the empire. He was then sent to ITALY against the OSTROGOTHS where he conquered ROME and RAVENNA, capturing the Ostrogoth king Vitiges. He was then sent to do battle with the Persians in Syria. He defeated them too, fortifying the empire's borders on the Euphrates. He then fought battles in Italy, SPAIN, and the Balkans, but his fortunes began to decline when he was accused of treason in 562. He was formally charged and his lands confiscated, although a year later he was exonerated.

BENEDICT OF NURSIA, ST.

Saint Benedict of Nursia (c. 480–c. 543) was a Christian abbot best known for the monastic order (the Benedictines) that bears his name.

Born in Nursia to an old Roman family, he was educated in ROME where he became disillusioned by what he saw as the city's licentiousness. He decided to devote himself to the ideals of monastic life, which had a strong BYZANTINE tradition but was virtually unknown in western Europe. For three years he lived a life of solitude in a cave on the outskirts of Rome. After that, he formed his own monastic group and monastery in the town of Monte Cassino.

His influence can be attributed to his book about

A 13th-century depiction of St. Benedict, shown reproaching Totila, the Ostrogoth general who drove the Byzantines out of Italy (after a fresco by Spinelli).

monastic life, *Regula sancti Benedicti* (*The Rule of St. Benedict*). The work outlined his views on monastic life and how monks could best serve both God and themselves. Many religious groups in Europe founded MONASTERIES based on this model, and for centuries the Benedictines were Europe's most prominent religious order. (*See* MONASTERIES AND MONASTICISM.)

BEOWULF

One of the most important poems in medieval literature and the first major poem to be written in the ENGLISH vernacular. Consisting of nearly 3,200 lines, it tells the story of the young warrior Beowulf and his victories over three monsters. The Germanic and Norse overtones, along with the strong Christian moral content, suggest that the work was written down in the late eighth century.

The Story. First, Beowulf is called to the court of the Danish king Hrothgar, whose castle has been under siege for 12 years and whose KNIGHTS are being killed every night by a monster named Grendel. Beowulf and Grendel engage in fierce battle; Beowulf rips off the monster's arm and Grendel bleeds to death as he returns to his lair. The next night, Grendel's mother seeks out Beowulf to avenge her son's death. Beowulf goes to her cave to await her, and destroys her with his magic sword. Beowulf's last fight comes 50 years later when he is called upon to slay a dragon that has terrorized his own people; both he and the dragon are killed during the battle. The poem ends with the gloomy prediction that catastrophes will strike Beowulf's people now that their hero has been lost.

BERBERS

The native inhabitants of northwestern AFRICA. The Berbers lived between EGYPT and the Atlantic and between the Mediterranean coast and the Niger River in an area considered part of the Roman Empire. After the fall of the western half of the Roman Empire in the fifth century, portions of their land were occupied by the Germanic VANDALS, only to be reconquered by BYZANTIUM (the successor state to the Eastern Roman Empire).

The Berbers were converted to ISLAM in the seventh century. By the start of the eighth century the entire Northern coast of Africa became part of the Arabic UMAYYAD Caliphate. Ironically ST. AUGUSTINE OF HIPPO, a man whose ideas were part of the foundation of the medieval Christian state, was himself a Berber. The Berbers would go on to become central actors in the ARAB conquest of the Spanish kingdom of the Germanic VISIGOTHS (711) and also in setting up the FATIMID DYNASTY in Egypt.

The Berbers often rebelled against Arab political and religious domination, and war between the two was endemic. While independent Berber dynasties were established twice (the ALMORAVIDS, from 1063 to 1147, and the ALMOHADS, from 1147 to 1269), Berber disunity meant they were usually on the defensive. Arab language and culture eventually came to dominate in North Africa, and today the Berber way of life continues only in remote areas of the African continent. (*See* AFRICA; ALMOHADS; ALMORAVIDS; ARAB.)

BERNARD OF CLAIRVAUX, ST.

Saint Bernard of Clairvaux (1090–1153) was one of the most influential religious figures of the twelfth century. Born to a noble French family, he became a CISTERCIAN monk and spent nearly 40 years as abbot of the monastery at Clairvaux in the Champagne region of FRANCE. There, he promoted simplicity in the monastic life, though he was a sophisticated writer and speaker who traveled frequently. He advised two popes and organized the Second Crusade at Pope Eugenius II's behest in 1146. Although the crusade failed, Bernard remained influential in Church affairs to his death. (*See* CRUSADES.)

Bernard affected medieval religious thought in three areas: the rise of the Marian cult; the intensification of a highly personal mysticsm; and exploring the meaning of friendship. He also contributed to the rise of anti-semitism in the twelfth century. His best known work is *On Loving God*. (*See* ABELARD, PETER.)

BEYEZID I YILDRIM

Beyezid I (1354–1402) was an Ottoman sultan whose string of military victories earned him the surname of Yildrim or "the Thunderbolt." He spread the rule of the once-minor Turkish OTTOMAN clan from a small corner of Asia Minor to the banks of the Euphrates and the upper Balkans. He defeated a large crusader army at Nicopolis (1396) and was positioned to destroy the millennium-old BYZANTINE Empire. However, Beyezid's reign ended in complete defeat when he was routed by TAMERLANE.

Rise to Power. Beyezid came to power in 1387 after his father, MURAD, was killed during the Battle of Kosovo against the Serbs. Beyezid then assumed command of the Ottoman army and defeated them. After his ascension, Beyezid began a tradition of the Ottoman elite consisting of imperial fratricide; he murdered his brother and possible rival, Yakud. The BATTLE OF KOSOVO was a significant victory for the Ottomans. Before the battle, the Serbs had been a growing power, ready to replace the decaying Byzantine Empire as the central Greek Orthodox power. After Kosovo, SERBIA became vassal to the Ottoman sultan and would not be independent for four hundred years.

Beyezid led an unbroken series of Ottoman conquests in the Balkans. In 1391 he made BOSNIA, Wallachia, and the shrunken Byzantine Empire part of the Ottoman domain. Beyezid's victory at Nicopolis over the last international crusade, in which much of the cream of European nobility was killed, put an end to European adventurism in the east. Another result of the battle was the annexation by the Ottomans of the once powerful Bulgarian kingdom.

In 1398, Beyezid besieged but failed to take CONSTANTINOPLE. Most historians believe, however, that Beyezid would have conquered the Byzantine Empire had he not been met by a greater warrior, the Turkish-Mongolian warlord, Tamerlane. Their armies met at Ankara in 1402. Beyezid's Tartar cavalry deserted him in the midst of combat and his forces fell quickly. At first, Tamerlane treated Beyezid as a fellow ruler, but he soon had the Ottoman sultan caged and humiliated. Beyezid died later that year, possibly a suicide.

BIBLE

The breadth and influence of the Bible throughout the world cannot be overstated. But during the Middle Ages, it was a way of life for virtually everyone in the Western world. By the fall of the Roman Empire, CHRISTIANITY had spread throughout Europe. Although there were fewer Jews than Christians, JUDAISM was firmly established as a religion as well. Many Muslims, too, studied the Bible; although the KORAN was—and still is—their holy book, they recognized both Moses and Christ as predecessors of MUHAMMAD.

The Bible served as a daily guide for many, even if they could not read it, because they worshiped regularly and heard recitations and sermons about the Bible's stories, prayers, and psalms. Still, as education

Bible were translated into numerous vernacular tongues. Often, religious artwork in churches (including statues, paintings, and STAINED GLASS windows) portrayed Biblical scenes. This gave illiterate people a sense that they were actively participating in the church service, and many still took pride in their knowledge of the Bible, even if they had never read it.

Since the Roman Church recognized only Latin as the language of the Bible, vernacular translations

Two Bible texts, five hundred years apart. At left, a 10th-century illuminated text in which Moses is depicted parting the Red Sea. At right, 15th-century Gutenberg and Furst Bible, in which illuminations would have been difficult to insert.

became more readily available, and as translations in vernacular tongues were published, the Bible's influence continued to grow. It is thus no accident that GUTENBERG's first printed book was the Bible.

Before Medieval Times. The Bible was initially made up of the 24 Jewish books of Scripture that consisted of the Torah (the first five books), the Prophets, and the Hagiographia ("writings"). Originally written in Hebrew, it was translated into the Semitic language of Aramaic and later into Greek, to accommodate Jews who no longer spoke or read Hebrew.

By the first century C.E., Christians were using a Greek translation of the Bible called the Septuagint. During the second century they added the Gospels, the letters of the apostle Paul, and other writings to create the New Testament (the original books of the Bible would henceforth be called the Old Testament).

New Translations. Most people, of course, did not speak or read Greek which led to the Bible being translated into various languages. In the East, Bibles appeared in Armenian, Syriac, Coptic, and Ethiopian. In the West, the Bible was translated into Latin. The official version of the Bible used during the Middle Ages was the Vulgate, a Latin translation compiled by ST. JEROME in the fourth century. But many people could not read Latin either, so selections from the

were slow in coming. With the invention of movable type, people began to demand authorized vernacular versions. Some biblical passages were printed in the vernacular, but it was not until the end of the fourteenth century that the Wyclif Bible appeared in ENGLAND, and the Hussite Bible in BOHEMIA. Neither version was approved by the Church; in fact it took the Protestant Reformation before vernacular Bibles were accepted.

Exegesis. Interpretation became increasingly important in medieval times. More scholars took part in biblical commentary in the Middle Ages than in any other period in history. Both Christians and Jews engaged in interpretation, or exegesis, devoting much time to debate the various meanings of different biblical passages. The desire to understand the Bible was the impetus for a great deal of scholarship and was in part responsible for the development of SCHOLASTICISM and the emergence of UNIVERSITIES in Europe.

See CHRISTIANITY *and* JUDAISM *for the role of the Bible in these religions. See* BRETHREN OF THE COMMON LIFE; GUTENBERG, JOHANNES; *and* MANUSCRIPT ILLUMINATION *for production of Bibles. Also see* WYCLIFFE, JOHN *for more on translation of the Bible.*

BLACK DEATH (PLAGUE)

By the account of the Piacentine chronicler, Gabrielle de' Mussis, the Black Death (or plague) spread throughout Asia in 1346, making its first contact with the West at the Genoese port of Caffa on the Black Sea. Here, the Tartar armies engaged in one of the earliest examples of biological warfare by lobbing Black Death corpses into the besieged city. The disease, carried by ship to Messina in SICILY and then GENOA, spread by sea and overland. It circumnavigated most of Europe and Asia Minor, striking Moscow in 1351 and decimating lands as far removed as GREENLAND. Its levels of mortality remain unknown, but estimates range from an eighth to over half of Europe. In places such as Pistoia, where hearth records survive, it appears to have killed as much as two-thirds of the population. By 1427, FLORENCE's population was only a third of what it had been at its peak in the early fourteenth century, and it did not regain its pre-Black Death population until the end of the nineteenth century. On the other hand, areas such as MILAN, parts of the Po valley, eastern Hainaut, parts of FLANDERS, and the regions of the Bernese Alps in SWITZERLAND were lightly grazed or not hit at all in 1348–1351. For some, the horror came later. A second wave of the plague struck Milan in 1361 and Douai (in 1400), but other areas may never have felt the full force of this epidemic during the later Middle Ages.

The Disease. Since Alexandre Yersin's discovery of the plague bacillus at Hong Kong in 1894, scientists and historians alike have assumed that this modern bubonic plague was the same as the ancient strikes of Justinian's plague in the sixth century and the Black Death and its subsequent epidemics from 1347 to 1720. For some time historians and epidemiologists have puzzled over the enigmas cast by this assumption. First, modern plagues depend on a slow and inefficient set of vectors involving rats that harbor the bacillus passing it on to rat fleas that then transmit the disease to humans only as a last resort, after killing off its local rodent populations. None of the sources, visual or literary, leave any signs of an epizootic of rodents preceding the human mortality—the drunken dance of dying rats, the "rat fall" from rafters, well known in African folklore and to inhabitants of other tropical zones even before scientists made the connections between rats, fleas, and bubonic plague in the early twentieth century. Second, even with the railroad and the steamship, the plague in the late nineteenth and early twentieth century spread at a rate of only eight to twelve miles a year, whereas the Black Death of 1348 spread at about that speed daily. Third, if the disease had been bubonic plague, how could it have inflicted such high mortalities in cold climates such as Greenland or NORWAY, where rat and flea densities are much lower than in tropical countries and are unable to survive the winter months? In answer to these puzzles, historians have surmised that the plague was principally pneumonic, spread directly from person to person. Yet such plagues were widespread during the winter months when people are huddled closely together; the peak mortalities from the Black Death and its late medieval followers came in the summer and largely dissipated by early October. And even pneumonic plague depends on a prior epizootic of rodents.

Image of a plague-afflicted couple, from the Toggenburg Bible, created around 1400. The buboes (boils) that were signs of the disease are visible.

Symptoms. The most striking connection between the medieval and modern plagues has been its most notable symptom—the carbuncles that formed in the lymph nodes. But such cutaneous necrosis are not unique to bubonic plague; the "sign" of plague, especially after 1348, was just as often freckles or skin blotches known as buboes in the arm pits and groin. Recently, other candidates have been proposed, such as anthrax and other varieties of yersinia bacteria, that do not depend on rats and fleas for its transmission to humans. But until successful DNA analysis of buried plague victims can be carried out, it will not be known for sure what this mysterious disease may have been, or if indeed it has a close present-day equivalent.

Causes and Consequences. Thirty years ago most historians saw the Black Death of 1348 as the inevitable consequence of overpopulation, poverty, and the unequal distribution of wealth throughout late-medieval Europe. Now, some historians are more inclined to argue that the plague was a fact of biology, an "exogenous variable" almost totally independent of the social conditions of the later Middle Ages. Indeed, the plague struck European populations not at their heights but in a period of slow decline; earlier European famines that struck closer to its heights of population and poverty did little to alter demographic and economic structures. However, once the Black Death spread, these historians have argued, it set Europe on a new path, breaking the "Malthusian deadlock" of the past, setting in motion a "new economic and demographic system" (D. Herlihy).

After an initial period of shock, the collapse of population liberated land for uses other than for the cultivation of grains and mills for uses other than grinding grain. By the fifteenth century, populations began to control their numbers through "preventive checks" such as delayed marriages and increased celibacy as opposed to the earlier "positive checks" of war, famine, and disease. Historians have gone even further, seeing the Black Death as the stimulus for labor-saving technology and the origins of industrialization, the growth of secular education and vernacular literatures, nationalism, distrust of the clergy, and the origins of the Reformation. Many of these arguments, however, have seemed circular to many.

Indeed, a comparison of the effects of plague on religion, economy, and society shows that all parts of the plague-stricken world did not develop along similar paths. Most striking is the difference between Asia Minor and those parts of Europe that were fast to restore their losses and to revive their economies. While the Near East was spared the initial political and psychological turmoil from outbursts of religious zeal, flagellant movements, and anti-Semitic pogroms, its economic and demographic recovery was much more protracted than Europe's. Nor did its losses stimulate new secular institutions for learning or the discovery of new labor-saving technology. Other variables than the Black Death alone and comparative analysis must be brought to bear to understand Europe's long-term developments in the latter Middle Ages and the early modern period both within Europe and between Europe and its wider world.

See MEDICINE AND CARE OF THE SICK *for more on responses to the Plague. Many geographical entries contain information on the Black Death. See also* TRAVEL AND TRANSPORTATION *for medieval travel patterns.*

The burial of a plague victim, a common sight during the Middle Ages, Sansepolcro, Italy. Some cities were so decimated, there were not enough survivors to bury the dead.

BLANCHE OF CASTILE

Blanche (1188–1252) was the daughter of King ALFONSO VIII of the kingdom of Castile in central SPAIN, wife of Louis VIII of FRANCE, and mother of LOUIS IX.

She was nearly 15 when she married Louis VIII in 1200. After Louis' death she served as regent during the minority of their son, Louis IX, who inherited the throne in 1226 at age 12. Blanche managed the government of France and advised her son until he came of age in 1234. She remained a strong influence on him until her death. Blanche proved to be a strong and capable ruler. While she was regent, she checked rebellious lords trying to exploit the youth of the new king. In 1230, she frustrated the attempt by her cousin, King HENRY III of ENGLAND, to regain lands in France once in possession of their grandfather, HENRY II.

Blanche became regent again in 1248 when Louis embarked on a CRUSADE to the Holy Land. During her son's absence, Blanche completed much of the work he had begun, including construction of the port of Aigues-Mortes in southern France. When she was brought news in 1250 that Louis had been captured, she was so outraged, she had the messengers hanged. She then made her son Alphonse co-regent with her.

BLONDEL DE NESLE

londel de Nesle was a TROUBADOUR, a poet and singer of the late twelfth century. A favorite of the legendary chivalrous figure, RICHARD I LION-HEART, king of ENGLAND. Like other troubadours, Blondel traveled from medieval court to medieval court, singing the praises of the feudal order. Blondel is known to have written twenty poems. Some of his work survives, with musical accompaniment, in the *Chansonnier Change*.

Blondel is most noted for the story which developed around his search for Richard. In 1192, on his return from the failed Third CRUSADE, the English king had been captured by Duke Leopold of AUSTRIA. The duke turned Richard over to HENRY IV, the Holy Roman Emperor, who held Richard until England had amassed a huge ransom. The legend, baseless in fact, has Blondel searching throughout Europe for the king. Finally, locating the castle where Richard was said to be held, Blondel sought to confirm the king's presence by singing a strophe of a song. Richard made his presence known by singing the next strophe. The significance of the story lies in the selfless loyalty of Blondel to his master, the king, part of the idealized structure of feudal life. Blondel's act repeated the submission of self to high ideals embodied in Richard's performance of his crusading duties.

BOCCACCIO, GIOVANNI

iovanni Boccaccio (1313–1375), a prolific writer, is today known chiefly for his masterpiece, the *Decameron.* Written as a series of tales, its clear and unpretentious narrative style makes the work easily ac-

Depiction of Boccaccio by Andrea del Castagno— painted nearly 50 years after the writer's death.

cessible even to modern readers. It influenced the work of later writers, including CHAUCER.

Early Life. Boccaccio was born in FLORENCE the son of a merchant. As a boy, he moved to NAPLES, where his father had him apprenticed in a BANKING establishment. The young Boccaccio had little interest in a career in business; instead, he was drawn to literature, and began writing poetry. At first his poems were standard medieval fare—celebrations of COURTLY LOVE and newer versions of old stories. But gradually he developed a unique voice.

His Work. His poems, written in Naples, include *La caccia di Diana,* ("Diana's Chase") which sings the praises of the women at the ANGEVIN court in NAPLES. He also wrote *Filostrato,* a poem that told the tale of TROILUS AND CRESSIDA. This poem would be the source of future works of Shakespeare and Chaucer.

Returning to Florence in 1340, he continued to write poetry. His *Elegy to My Lady of the Flame* is considered a precursor of the modern psychological novel. The BLACK DEATH began to ravage the region around 1348 and Boccaccio wrote evocative descriptions of the tragic circumstances. He also began the *Decameron.* The premise behind the book is a journey by seven women and three men escaping the plague in FLORENCE. To amuse themselves during their journey, they tell each other stories. The stories themselves, mostly about love and romance, are variations on earlier stories, but Boccaccio's fresh presentation brings to them a vibrancy they had not previously known.

In later years, Boccaccio continued to write poetry; he also wrote several reference works. He became a friend of the writer PETRARCH, and was the first to lecture on the works of DANTE. He died in 1375. (*See* LITERATURE.)

BOETHIUS

he philosopher Boethius (480–524) was in many ways a transitional figure. He came from a noble Roman family but was born at the end of the Roman Empire's long decline. His writings are influenced by both CHRISTIANITY and the philosophy of ARISTOTLE and Plato. Although he was not a scientist, his translations from Greek to Latin of scientific treatises gave medieval Europeans their most complete source of information about the sciences.

Life. Anicius Manlius Severinus Boethius was born in Rome about 480. He was distantly related to Olybrius, who from April to November, 472 reigned as puppet emperor of Rome. The last Roman emperor was deposed in 476. ITALY was ruled by the Germanic king ODOACER until he was overthrown by the Ostrogoths in 490. The Ostrogoth king, THEODORIC, pre-

Boethius depicted taking counsel from Dame Philosophy at left, from a miniature in Jean de Meung's 15th-century translation of On the Consolation of Philosophy.

served Roman law and traditions, and Boethius and his family were influential in government affairs and served in the royal court. Theodoric recognized in Boethius a capable and intelligent counselor, allowing him considerable influence. One of his duties was the reforming of Roman currency.

Translations. Boethius was one of the last Roman writers to understand Greek. He spent much of his time translating the works of Aristotle, as well as composing numerous commentaries on philosophy and SCIENCE. Until Arabic scientific writings were translated into Latin some 600 years later, the translations and commentaries of Boethius were regarded as Europe's most important scientific works.

But Boethius protested against what he saw as Ostrogothic abuses against Romans. Gradually, he lost favor with Theodoric, who had become increasingly suspicious of the Roman influence in his government. Eventually, Theodoric turned against his counselor and imprisoned him in 524.

Consolation. It was during his time in prison that Boethius produced his most important work, *On the Consolation of Philosophy*. Boethius was considered a strong proponent of Christian theology, especially during the Middle Ages, in part because of the *Consolation*. But while his writings show no animosity toward the Church, they show a stronger affinity for the ideas of the Greek philosophers.

He discusses the virtues of goodness and deplores evil, and he underscores the need for humanity to strive to follow God. Yet his views on free will are much more closely aligned with Aristotle than that of the Church. Readers of the *Consolation* have long been impressed that so calm and rational a work could have been written by a man in prison awaiting certain execution. (*See* PHILOSOPHY.)

Death of Boethius. After several months of confinement and torture, Boethius was executed without the benefit of a trial. Some theological tracts written in the early sixth century were erroneously attributed to Boethius to enhance their stature.

BOGOMILS

The Bogomils were members of a religious sect that at its peak held enormous influence over the Balkan countries. Founded in BULGARIA in the mid–tenth century by a priest named Bogomil, the sect relied heavily on the belief in dualism—that the universe was ruled jointly by the forces of good and evil. Evil, the Bogomils said, was represented by the material world; they thus lived extremely ascetic lives. They took neither meat nor wine, and they condemned marriage. They are regarded as successors of the Manicheans of later antiquity and forerunners of the ALBIGENSES of twelfth-century FRANCE and ITALY.

One of several such sects active throughout Europe, the Bogomils were considered heretics by the established Church. The Byzantines imprisoned and executed a number of Bogomils in the twelfth century. Later, the Roman Church set about converting them (under threat of exile). Ultimately, it was the OTTOMAN conquest, rather than the Church, that put an end to the sect. (*See* HERESY.)

BOHEMIA-MORAVIA

Bohemia got its name from the Celtic Boii tribe which first inhabited the land. By the start of the Middle Ages the land was inhabited by SLAV settlers who named themselves Czechs, after a legendary leader who had promised to deliver them there. (*See* GERMANY.)

With the help of Moravian tribes, the Czechs created the Samo state in the seventh century, which would eventually come under CHARLEMAGNE'S rule. The Slavs were subsequently joined by Frankish and other Germanic tribes, and would come to accept being governed by the FRANKS.

Magyar Invasion. Under assault from the Magyars in the late ninth century, the Bohemian nobility declared its allegiance to Arnulf, the East Frankish king, and to other Frankish leaders. Through the end of the twelfth century a symbiotic relationship existed between the Franks and Bohemia: the Franks supported Czech rulers and lands; the Czechs recognized the right of Frankish kings to lead and rule them. As a result of this relationship, in 1035 King Bretislav I accepted Bohemia as a fief from Emperor Conrad II.

In 1085, Bohemian's Duke Vratislav II refused to help Pope GREGORY VII encircle King HENRY V, out of loyalty to him. In gratitude, Henry crowned Vratislav king of the new Bohemian kingdom. His son and successor, Vratislav II, earned recognition for his claim to have a hereditary form of monarchy in Bohemia. Eventually, both the Byzantine emperor and Pope Innocent II confirmed these rights.

The military summit of Bohemian life occurred during the reign of Premysl Ottokar II (1253-78). He granted self-governing charters to his cities, which generated enormous sums of money, as did his silver mines at Kutna Hora. This power convinced him he could control other nations. In 1260 he conquered Syria, and nine years later captured Carinthia and Carniola. By 1270, he was the strongest ruler in all of central Europe, and he would then seek the imperial crown. The imperial electors disappointed him by electing Rudolf of Habsburg, a slight that led to a costly war. Premysl Ottokar II was killed in the Battle of Moravske Pole. His successors were all ineffectual, and internal battles dominated and weakened Bohemia. Only the intervention of the powerful nobility halted further deterioration. They persuaded Prince John of Luxembourg to marry the last surviving member of the Premysl family, Elizabeth.

Bohemia gradually returned to prominence under Charles IV, who established PRAGUE as the kingdom's major city, created central Europe's first university there, and attracted an artistic community to the area. In spite of Charles's popularity, his successor, Wenceslaus IV was removed when he attempted to expand the monarchy. The crown was given to SIGISMUND, king of HUNGARY. By the end of the fourteenth century, a balance of power was struck between the royal house and Bohemian nobility and incorporated into the legal system; it was to last into the modern era.

BOHEMUND I PRINCE OF ANTIOCH

An adventurer of Norman stock, Bohemund I (c. 1058–1111) was one of the most prominent leaders of the First CRUSADE who established a Latin state of Antioch that endured (albeit uneasily) for several decades, until Antioch returned to Byzantine control in 1137.

Early Years. Born around 1058 to ROBERT GUISCARD, an Italian mercenary who had received large duchies in the Balkans as payment for his services, Bohemund (christened Marc, but later named after a legendary giant, a name passed on to some of his descendants) was physically imposing and an able warrior. After his father's death in 1085, the major portion of the inheritance went to Roger Borsa, Bohemund's half brother, and it appeared a war would be fought by the brothers for control of the Balkans. Pope URBAN II intervened, settled the dispute, and by 1095 convinced Bohemund to take up the First Crusade.

On the March. Despite their bellicose past, the Byzantine emperor, ALEXIUS I, allowed Bohemund and his crusaders to pass through his lands in return for a promise of Byzantine sovereignty over some of the territory Bohemund would take from the Muslims. The early campaign was successful and included the conquest of Antioch in 1098 following a brutal nine-month siege. Claiming Alexius had forfeited his title when he failed to assist the crusaders in taking Antioch, Bohemund prepared to establish his own Latin kingdom there when he was taken captive in 1100 by Turks. He was ransomed in 1103 and, joining forces with BALDWIN I and Jocelin de Courtney, launched an attack against the Turks in the spring of 1104. The attack failed, and Bohemund retreated to FRANCE where he toured raising funds and collecting volunteers for a new crusade, this time against the Byzantines. He was hailed everywhere as a hero and was given the hand in marriage of Constance, daughter of King Philip I.

The attack against Alexius commenced in 1107 and went badly from the start. When Alexius offered Antioch and other cities to Bohemund under terms of vassalage in the Treaty of Devol in 1108, he accepted. News of the treaty earned Bohemund opprobrium in the West where he was seen as having forsaken the crusade for personal gain. He died in Canosa in 1111.

BONAVENTURE, ST.

Saint Bonaventure (c. 1221–1274) was a noted FRANCISCAN theologian whose writings and lectures were instrumental in guiding the direction of the order of St. Francis. He was known for his sharp mind and his masterful administrative skills.

Early Years. Bonaventure was born John of Fidanza around 1221 in central ITALY. As a child he became gravely ill but recovered. Convinced that his recovery was due to the intervention of ST. FRANCIS OF ASSISI, the young Bonaventure decided to study theology and become a Franciscan himself.

He attended the University of PARIS and then entered the Franciscan order, becoming a master of the Franciscan school in Paris around 1254. During this time he formulated his ideas about religion and wrote several books on theology and mysticism. Bonaventure strongly believed that to understand religion, one had to approach it not only spiritually and emotionally, but also logically. He was a strong supporter of such Franciscan doctrines as the vow of poverty. When some claimed that was contrary to Scripture, Bonaventure countered that a vow of poverty was the essence of humility, an integral element of CHRISTIANITY.

Bonaventure was named general of the Franciscan order in 1257. At the time, there were rivalries and disputes among its different factions. The Spirituals wanted to adhere more strictly to the teachings of Francis, while the Conventuals wanted a more moderate interpretation. Bonaventure himself believed strongly in the Franciscan vows—but he also recognized the practical need for moderation. Ultimately, Bonaventure's diplomatic skills helped unite the order.

He was not always so diplomatic, however—nor was he blindly genial. It was his decision shortly after becoming general to prohibit the philosopher ROGER BACON from publishing his works. Moreover, he was not above launching into spirited attacks against fellow Franciscans who were more moderate in their views, but who saw fit to criticize the Spirituals.

A pilgrimage in 1259 inspired him to write what would become his most famous work on mysticism, *The Mind's Road to God.* Bonaventure describes spiritual growth as a process that takes seven steps to achieve. He then wrote a biography of St. Francis, in which he relied in part on interviews with individuals who had known him (St. Francis had died in 1226).

In 1273 Bonaventure was named cardinal-bishop of Albano. He died in 1274 and was canonized just nine years later.

BONIFACE VIII

B oniface VIII (c. 1235–1303), pope from December 24, 1294, until October 11, 1303. His pontificate is regarded as a turning point in papal history, marking the ascendancy of the secular state over the PAPACY in temporal affairs. Boniface has been called the "last medieval pope."

His Life. Born in Anagni, ITALY, Benedetto Gaetani was trained in LAW at Bologna and in the later 1270s became a papal notary. Experienced in international diplomacy and a noted canonist, he was named cardinal deacon in 1281 and cardinal priest in 1291. After Pope CELESTINE V abdicated in December 1294 on his advice, he was quickly elected pope and promptly undid much of his predecessor's unwitting mischief. He moved the papacy from NAPLES back to ROME and was crowned there on January 23, 1295.

His Pontificate. Boniface was steeped in international affairs from the start of his pontificate, intervening most notably in the conflict between the kings of Naples and of ARAGON over SICILY and in the war between expansionist FRANCE and ENGLAND over English possession of Guienne and Gascony; the latter case stimulated the enmity of PHILIP IV, THE FAIR of FRANCE. Both France and ENGLAND taxed the clergy in order to underwrite their hostilities. Boniface sought to halt this practice by issuing the bull *Clericis laicos* in 1296, whereupon Philip took measures to assure that

the pope would not receive clerical taxes from France.

Compelled to retreat, Boniface acknowledged that the king of France (and others, by implication) could indeed tax the clergy for purposes of making war without prior papal approval. His hand was forced in part because of conflict in Italy with the powerful Colonna family; they at first supported him but then joined with the Franciscan Spirituals in attacking the validity of Celestine V's abdication and thus Boniface's legitimacy. He crushed the Colonnas temporarily, but their two excommunicated cardinals fled to Philip's court to sow further discord, thereby extending the personal battle between Philip and Boniface. Philip charged Boniface with HERESY (falsely) and called for his deposition, while Boniface attempted to excommunicate Philip.

This contest ended with Boniface being imprisoned, and although he was released shortly after his capture, the Humiliation of Anagni left him a broken man and he died shortly thereafter in 1303. Boniface's achievements as an administrator and a patron of learning (he had the Vatican Library catalogued and established the University of Rome) were eclipsed by the debacle of his final years. The conflict between papal and royal power was inevitable in the feudal milieu, but Boniface was ill equipped to face the crisis.

BONIFACE, ST.

B oniface (c. 675–754) was an English monk whose missionary work in GERMANY earned him the title, "Apostle of the Germans." Born Winfrid in Devonshire, he received his education in Exeter and then at the BENEDICTINE monastery at Nursling near Winchester.

In 715 he made his first missionary trip to Frisia to assist St. Willibrord, but unsettled conditions there forced him to return to ENGLAND. In 718, he went to ROME where Pope GREGORY II inspired his missionary zeal, bestowed on him the name of Boniface ("good works"), and sent him east of the Rhine River. While under the protection of Frankish kings, Boniface made many converts in Thuringia, Hesse, Franconia, and BAVARIA. Boniface was consecrated bishop to the Germans in 722 and metropolitan of Germany in 731. He created bishoprics for his English followers throughout Germany and founded monasteries at Reichenau (724) and Murbach (728). Later in his life he founded the abbey at Fulda in 744 and became its abbot. In his capacity as papal legate the following year he reformed the Frankish church, making Mainz the permanent center of his archbishopric in 747. Four years later, he consecrated PÉPIN THE SHORT king of the FRANKS.

Boniface arranged an alliance between the CAR-

OLINGIAN family and the PAPACY. Boniface's anointing of Pépin as king of the Franks set a precedent for medieval coronation ceremonies, perpetuated in England to the present day. (*See* CORONATION.)

Throughout his career in Germany Boniface remained in constant contact with the English church, which supplied him with missionaries and material support. In 754 Boniface set out for Frisia once again to gain converts, but he and 50 of his followers were set upon and martyred at Dokkum.

BOOK OF HOURS

A book of hours was a prayer book used by individuals of families in private homes. In structure they were somewhat similar to breviaries, the prayer books used by the clergy. Based on the ninth-century series of prayers and songs known as the "Hours of the Virgin" (their namesake), the "hours" were recited at eight specific hours each day. A book of hours was often the only book a family owned. As the number of literate individuals grew, so did the popularity of the books of hours. They began to include additional prayers, readings from the Gospels, and calendars of Church feasts and saint's days. However, wealthy families would have books of hours specifically prepared for them that included intricate designs and illustrations. (*See* MANUSCRIPT ILLUMINATION.)

The development of the printing press in the mid-fifteenth century meant that books could be produced more quickly and efficiently. However, wealthy families continued to commission hand-painted books and they remained symbols of status for many years.

BOOKS IN MANUSCRIPT

B ooks, it could be argued, attained their supreme beauty as physical works of art during the Middle Ages. Books were made entirely by hand—every binding stitch, every drawing, indeed, every letter. The craft of bookmaking required great skill and painstaking accuracy. Books were valued as much for their appearance as for their content.

Origins. The first bound books were produced in ancient ROME. By the early Middle Ages, all books were bound except for ceremonial manuscripts (such as sacred scrolls). Books had to be produced one at a time, and the process for doing so was a long one, requiring the work of several craftspeople. Early monasteries maintained active book production in rooms known as the scriptorium, in which monks would spend part of each day copying texts.

The Process. First, the pages needed to be mea-

A page from the Book of Hours of Catherine of Cleves, Netherlands, 1515, entitled "Piety: Lady Distributing Alms."

sured and cut. Most books were made of parchment (paper, a Chinese invention, was not widely used in the West until the thirteenth century). Pieces of parchment were stretched, smoothed, and then cut into sheets. The sheets would then be folded; each of which was called a *bifolium* to signify two leaves, or four pages. (The word folio is now used in book publishing to signify page numbering.) Each one would be numbered, and each page would be marked with ruled lines, which were used to guide the scribes doing the actual lettering. Sometimes teams of scribes would work on one book. They would do their lettering in dark ink, and the finished pages would be proofread. Then decorative opening letters would be added, or perhaps illustrations. Usually, these embellishments would be done by other specially trained artists.

For special illustrations known as illuminations, a special artist would be called in. The artist would hand paint each page and sketch in the design. Then the sketch would be filled in with different colored paints, and possibly gold leaf. Illumination was a particularly exacting process; for a large work, the process of illuminating a number of pages could take several years.

LIFE IN THE MIDDLE AGES

The Book Business

In the early Middle Ages, books were created in monasteries or by special commission and then were either kept as cherished possessions or traded with other monasteries for desired works. Jewish traders used books as a kind of currency, converting them into capital when reaching a foreign land.

By the 1300s, as the demand for books increased and surpassed the capacity of book producers in universities, commercial book production became increasingly profitable. Cities such as Florence, Rome, Milan, Paris, and London became centers for the trade and lay religious groups, such as the BRETHEREN OF THE COMMON LIFE produced books to support themselves. Workshops, where artisans produced illustrated books for wealthy clientele, were established by stationers like Vespasiano da Bisticci in Florence. As the workshops became more specialized, the craftspeople producing books formed guilds, creating standards and laying the foundations of the book industry.

BORGIA FAMILY

A powerful and notorious family, with roots in Valencia, that became prominent in fourteenth and fifteenth century ITALY. The family produced two popes, a saint, and many other political and Church leaders, but is best remembered for its depravity. Alfonso de Borgia (1378–1458) first established the family's prominence in Italy, serving as a respected jurist and diplomat in the Aragonese court. He became Pope Callistus III in 1455 and dedicated himself primarily to the organization of a CRUSADE to recapture CONSTANTINOPLE. While pope, he favored his nephew, Rodrigo Borgia (1431–1503); through those favors Rodrigo became one of the richest cardinals in Italy. Unlike his more austere uncle, Rodrigo was famous for his licentious lifestyle; nevertheless, he became pope in 1492 under the name Alexander VI. His term was marked by some diplomatic successes, including a papal alliance with the French, and by some perfunctory efforts at reform. But ultimately, though possessed of some piety, his aims were less than spiritual, consisting mainly of the aggrandizement of his family's power.

Alexander soon began showering his many (illegitimate) children with gifts and titles. His son Cesare (c. 1475–1507) became his chief political agent and soon surpassed him in infamy. Through assassinations, political marriages (often involving Alexander's daughter Lucrezia), and skillful duplicity, Alexander and Cesare began a bloody project to subject the papal states and central Italy to Borgia rule. Through these efforts Cesare became known for his ruthlessness and cunning. Machiavelli cited him as a model for *The Prince*. During the height of their power, in August of 1503, both Alexander and Cesare took ill; rumor had it that they drank poison intended for a guest. Alexander died, leaving his son without the financial and military support of the PAPACY. Cesare was soon stripped of most of his power, and died in battle in 1507.

The Borgia family produced various other figures of minor historical significance, including Saint Francis Borgia, a leading Jesuit, but none of them matched the exploits of Cesare or Rodrigo. The family virtually disappeared by the middle of the eighteenth century.

BOSNIA

B osnia is a rugged land in the central-western Balkan peninsula, distinguished by its deep valleys and steep mountains. The mountains provided Bosnia much of its economy during the thirteenth century, as MINING extracted minerals used in making cannons and firearms. It received its name from the Bosna River, which runs into the Sava River.

Early Middle Ages. Bosnia was settled in the sixth and seventh century by Slavic tribes ruled by the AVARS, who were taken over by the Croatians in the early 600s. In Bosnia's early history there was no central government; instead there were separate Bosnian districts called *zupas*, areas with distinct cultures and different rulers. The lack of a central government encouraged invasion from neighboring territories, and local rulers frequently shifted their alliances to the invaders.

Bosnia was part of SERBIA in the 900s, and following the death of Serbia's Prince Caslav, Bosnia fell under Croatian rule. In 1018, Emperor BASIL II beat BULGARIA and claimed Bosnia for the BYZANTINE Empire. Bosnia was under Byzantine rule for over eighty years until 1101, when Bosnia was annexed by HUNGARY. Bosnia's remote location made it difficult for Hungary to directly control it, so it allowed for local rulers, or "bans." Its remoteness also allowed for a variety of cultures in its *zupas*; significantly, not all of them had the same economic growth.

Late Middle Ages. Ban Kulin (reigned 1180–1204) granted asylum to heretics leaving neighboring Dalmatia. In the thirteenth century the Hungarians wanted to bring Bosnia in line with ROME, and in 1235 they received permission from the Vatican to mount a CRUSADE against the Bosnians. However, the Bosnians sided with their local leader, Ban Ninoslav. After six years the Hungarians were able to control only northern Bosnia. One of the northern territories was controlled by a local Bosnian noble, Ban Prijezda; the other was ruled by Stefan Dragutin, a former Serbian ruler and brother-in-law of the Hungarian king.

The Vatican attempted to reassert control in 1252 by placing the Hungarian archbishop in charge of the

Pope Alexander VI Borgia, kneeling in prayer. A late 15th-century painting by Bernardino Pinturicchio.

Bosnian Catholic Church, but the Bosnians responded by creating their own national church.

In 1318, Ban Prijezda's grandson Stjepan Kotromanic became the ban of a central Bosnian state, and, with the support of a struggling Hungarian government, he took control of Bosnia and oversaw its expansion into Hum (what is now called Hercegovina). He soon opened up Bosnia's silver and lead mines, which strengthened its economy. In 1347, he allowed Franciscans to settle in Bosnia and converted to Catholicism. By 1390, Bosnia had built no fewer than 35 Franciscan monasteries. While most of Kotromanic's successors would also be Catholic, the Bosnian Orthodox Church was still accepted and tolerated.

Kotromanic was succeeded in 1353 by his able nephew, Tvtrko, who improved the economy of Bosnia and kept the powerful Hungarians at bay until his death in 1391. Old rivalries resurfaced after Tvtkro's death; the Ottomans, originally mercenaries in Bosnian civil wars, took control of the area in 1426. They occupied Vrhbosna (today's Sarajevo) in 1451, and beheaded the last Bosnian king, Stefan Tomasevic, in 1481. During that period, most Bosnians converted to Islam. (*See* AVARS; HUNGARY; SERBIA.)

BOTTICELLI, SANDRO

S andro Botticelli (1445–1510), best known for his work "The Birth of Venus," was one of the early painters of the Italian Renaissance and is considered a transitional figure. He drew from late GOTHIC influences, which emphasized realism and vivid colors, but he tempered those influences with a softer, more expressive style.

Botticelli, born Alessandro di Mariano Filipeli in FLORENCE, was first trained as a goldsmith. He was later apprenticed to the painter Fra Filippo Lippi, and had his own studio by the time he was 25. Most of his early paintings had religious themes (not surprising, since many were commissioned by churches). Later, he contributed several paintings and frescoes to the Sistine Chapel in ROME.

In 1477, Botticelli began his "Primavera" (Allegory of Spring), which was painted for the villa of Lorenzo de MEDICI. "Primavera" and "The Birth of Venus" (painted in 1485, also for de Medici) show a shift away from the late GOTHIC style and toward his own technique. Throughout the 1480s and 1490s he executed frescoes and paintings for Florentine chapels and churches. In his later works, his style became more firmly rooted in the Renaissance. In fact, many critics have claimed that some of his later paintings, such as the "Mystic Nativity" (1501), have more in common with high Renaissance art than the early Renaissance.

Botticelli's celebrated painting The Annunciation *now in the Uffizi Museum, Florence, Italy.*

By the time of Botticelli's death in 1510, artists such as Michelangelo and Leonardo da Vinci were well established—and the Renaissance was the dominant influence of European art. (*See* ITALY.)

BOUVINES, BATTLE OF

T he Battle of Bouvines (July 27, 1214) was a decisive victory by the French king PHILIP II AUGUSTUS over the allied forces of King JOHN LACKLAND of ENGLAND and the Holy Roman Emperor Otto IV. It was the culminating event in the long struggle between the English ANGEVIN dynasty and Philip II in which the French king attempted to reassert his authority over the provinces in FRANCE that had belonged to the English crown. The victory at Bouvines made Philip the most powerful ruler in France, and France became the dominant country in thirteenth century Europe. (*See* FRANCE; WARFARE.)

The allied forces had a two-pronged strategy: King John would distract Philip in the west near Angers, and the imperial forces would simultaneously attack him in the north in Flanders. However, John was forced to retreat when his French vassals refused to fight. In the north, the Flanders allies of John and Otto lost a tactical advantage when they had to wait for the imperial forces, giving the French time to deploy after the action in the west. The final battle in Bouvines was a rare event in medieval WARFARE: a pitched battle between large armies. The two armies were nearly identical: cavalry formed their flanks, with infantry and mounted reserves in the middle. The French were triumphant on all three fronts, especially when the KNIGHTS on the wings joined the battle in the center.

BRACTON, HENRY OF

A practicing lawyer in ENGLAND, Henry of Bracton (d. 1268) worked as a justice throughout southwestern England. After 1245, he served as a royal judge on the King's Bench. Toward the end of his career he was on a commission authorized after the Montfort rebellion to hear the complaints of the disinherited.

Henry was one of the outstanding legal thinkers of his time. In the 1250s he wrote *De legibus et consuetudinbus Angliae* (On the laws and customs of England), a comprehensive philosophical treatise which became the most authoritative work on English law in the late Middle Ages. Although he used methods of analysis and classification derived from Roman law, his emphasis on case law and precedent was the essence of English common law. His belief that the king was under the law was expressed in his famous dictum: "The king himself ought not to be under man but under God and the law, because the law made the king." (*See* LAW.)

BRETHREN OF THE COMMON LIFE

A teaching order that was to influence elementary and secondary education throughout Europe for more than 400 years. Established in the fourteenth century with the help of a wealthy religious reformer, the order offered poor students the chance to study, to live harmoniously, and to support themselves by copying manuscripts.

Gerhard Groote, a wealthy man who renounced his wealth in the 1370s, became a religious reformer and teacher in the NETHERLANDS, stressing piety and simplicity of life. He donated his own home to be used to house poor women, preached against clerical abuses, and called for public repentance. Upon Groote's death in 1384, one of his students, Florenz Radewijns, formed the Brethren. The group was recognized as an order by Pope Gregory XI and spread rapidly throughout the Low Countries and GERMANY.

Eventually the Brethren branched out into three groups: the original Brethren Movement; the Sisters of the Common Life; and the Congregation of Windersheim. The Brethren and Sisters were not trained in theology and were therefore not recognized as monks or nuns. (They were thus a "lay" religious order.) The Congregation of Windershiem, however, was a full monastic order. (*See* BOOKS; LITERACY.)

With the invention of printing, the need for manuscript copyists dwindled, as did the influence of the Brethren. Their last house closed in 1811.

BRIDGET, ST.

N un who played a major role in the Christianization of IRELAND. Also known as St. Brigid or St. Bridget of Kildare (c. 453–525), she was born of humble Irish parents at Vinmeras near Kildare. Baptized by ST. PATRICK, she became a nun at an early age, and later founded the monastery at Kildare.

Little is known about her life, but her cult was very popular, second only to St. Patrick himself. The story of her life, written in Latin, was translated into Middle ENGLISH, Old FRENCH, and GERMAN. Popular devotion to her memory was widespread in ENGLAND and WALES as well as in Ireland up to the Reformation, as evidenced by the use of such names as Bridewell, McBride, Kilbride, and Kirkbride, as well as the many churches dedicated to her honor, including St. Bride's on Fleet Street in LONDON. St. Bridget died in c. 525, and she was buried with Saints Patrick and Columba in Ireland at Downpatrick; like them, she is considered a patron saint of Ireland. (*See* IRELAND; PATRICK, ST.)

BRITTANY

B rittany, a name given to FRANCE's northwestern peninsula, derives its name from the Celtic Bretons whom the ANGLO-SAXONS drove out of Britain about 500 C.E. When the Anglo-Saxons invaded Britain and drove the Celts westward to Cornwell and WALES, some of them fled even farther, escaping by sea to France where they joined mainland Celts. Named Brittany after the new Breton arrivals, the area remained basically independent of French control throughout the Middle Ages. (*See* FRANCE.)

Medieval Breton history is one of struggle for independence—first from the FRANKS up until the 800s; then from the dukes of NORMANDY and the counts of Anjou from the 900s to the 1100s; and finally from ENGLAND and France, who vied for the area from the 1200s on, fighting over it through the HUNDRED YEARS' WAR (1337–1453).

In 1196, Arthur I, an ANGEVIN, became the duke of Brittany, but after King JOHN LACKLAND of England had him murdered, the duchy passed to Arthur's brother-in-law, Peter I. The end of his line came during the War of the Breton Succession (1341–1365), which was part of the Hundred Years War. The dukes of Montfort, who gained control of Brittany as a result of the Breton war, tried to maintain Brittany's neutrality through the rest of the Hundred Years' War. In the late 1400s, France took control of Brittany after the rebellion of Duke Francis II against the French crown ended in failure. In 1532, King Francis I formally incorporated the duchy of Brittany into France.

BRUNELLESCHI, FILIPPO

An architect and sculptor, renowned as an innovator in the arts and in design during the late Middle Ages, Filippo Brunelleschi(1377–1446) was born in FLORENCE. Filippo showed an early inclination toward the arts and was apprenticed to a goldsmith. There he learned much about design and construction, even learning to build watch movements. His studies of the geometric rules of perspective, little understood at the time, led him to produce the first accurate renderings of perspective, upon which the work of later Renaissance artists was built. He studied sculpture and architecture with his close friend, the sculptor Donatello, and was one of the first in Tuscany to incorporate elements of the classical Greek and Roman styles in several building renovations in Florence.

In 1403, he was one of the invited entrants in the competition for the decoration of the east doors of the baptistery in Florence along with Donatello, LORENZO GHIBERTI, and others. His entry, on the Biblical theme of "The Sacrifice of Isaac," was a striking bronze relief which emulated classical models; it was much admired by the judges, although Ghiberti ultimately won.

After spending several years in Rome studying and drawing in detail the many antique Roman sculptures and buildings, he returned to Florence, where he was awarded the commission to supervise the construction of the Duomo of Santa Maria del Fiore's cupola. He worked mostly on this massive project until his death in 1446. The dome (known as the Duomo) was modeled on the ancient Pantheon in Rome, and was constructed without the use of side or center columns.

The Duomo still stands in Florence as a testament to this kindly and serene man, the premiere architect of his time. (*See* ARCHITECTURE.)

The Duomo, Florence, Italy, a Brunelleschi masterpiece.

BULGARIA

Bulgaria was formed from a combination of several different central Asian tribes. The word "Bulgar" itself is an ancient word meaning "mixture." These tribes began settling along the Black Sea during the fifth century in two groups—the western Kutriguri and the eastern Utiguri—as they inexorably moved towards the Danube River and the Byzantine Empire.

Early Middle Ages. In 551, the Kutriguri conquered Thrace and expanded both west, to the Adriatic, and south, to the Aegean Sea. Meanwhile, the Utiguri fell under control of the Byzantine Empire, and became a military buffer against oncoming Turkish tribes.

During the seventh century, the Khazars pushed the Bulgarians into Byzantine territory, and the Bulgarians began fighting the Byzantines. In 679, the Bulgarians crossed the Danube and founded a Balkan state. Byzantine Emperor Justinian II tried in vain to reestablish Byzantine control. In 710, a peace treaty recognized Bulgarian rule for three decades.

During the seventh and eighth centuries, the Bulgarians controlled the SLAVS with a strong military organization comprised of two tiers: the "boliades" or higher military status, and the lower "bagains." Gradually, the Bulgarians became a Slav ethnic group, learning the Slav language.

Khan Krum's reign in the early ninth century was

distinguished by military successes abroad and the codification of government at home. Krum's army captured Sofia in 809, and killed Byzantine Emperor Nicephorus I two years later. Krum's successor Omortag extended the Bulgarian state as far as Srem, having acquired more Slav territory.

Christianity. Bulgaria first resisted the new Christian religion; Khan Malamir rejected it outright. However, his successor, Boris, converted in 865 to improve Bulgaria's international reputation; he started a separate branch of the Church, so as to have total control of Church elders. He welcomed missionaries to translate Scripture into Slavic languages. When Boris's son Vladimir tried to banish CHRISTIANITY, Boris replaced him with his other son, Simeon.

During Simeon's legendary reign (893–927), he frequently fought the Byzantines, and acquired more territory; the Bulgarian state now stretched from the Adriatic to the Black Sea. Native Slav art and literature flourished, and the beginnings of codified Slav law began. Also, Simeon began an independent Serbian state. By the end of his reign he declared himself "Tsar of the Bulgarians and the Greeks." (*See* SERBIA; SLAVS.)

The first Bulgarian kingdom began to crumble from within during the reign of Simeon's son, Peter (927–969). The Byzantines delivered a crushing blow at the Battle of Balasitsa in 1004 in which 14,000 Bulgarian prisoners were blinded. (*See* BASIL II.)

Late Middle Ages. A second Bulgarian kingdom arose in 1187 under Ivan Asen, recognized by the Byzantines as tsar of the Bulgars and Vlachs. Bulgaria experienced a golden age of prosperity and culture during the reign of Ivan's son, Ivan Asen II (who ruled 1218–1241). After Ivan's death, however, Bulgaria was continually under attack, first by the Tartars; then by the Byzantines, who annexed Macedonia during the reign of Michael Asen (1248–1257); then by the Serbians, who defeated the Bulgarian king, Michael III Shishman, at Velbuzhd in 1330; and finally by the Turks, who took the capital, Turnovo, in 1394, after which, most Bulgarians migrated to Serbia and RUSSIA. (*See* RUSSIA; HUNGARY; NOVGOROD.)

BURGUNDY

In the Middle Ages, the name "Burgundy" applied to the Burgundian kingdom, also called the kingdom of Arles, formed out of two CAROLINGIAN successor states after the division of the empire in 843. The term also applied to a duchy and a county, later known as Franche-Comté, occupying the eastern frontiers of FRANCE.

The Burgundii, originally a Scandinavian people, migrated into the Roman Empire in the early fifth century, settling in the valleys of Sarne and Rhône Rivers in southeastern France. The region was Christianized by the Romans in the sixth century, and in 534, was conquered by the MEROVINGIAN FRANKS and absorbed into the Frankish empire. In the eighth century, the kingdom was conquered by CHARLES MARTEL, and became part of the Carolingian Empire. When the empire was partitioned in 843, the Burgundian lands were divided, so that the areas west of the Sarne went to Charles the Bald of France, while Charles's half-brother, Emperor Lothair, retained what would become the kingdom of Burgundy between the Sarne and the Jura.

Kingdom of Burgundy. Lothair left those territories to his youngest son Charles and granted him the title of king of Provence. Charles the Bald appointed his brother-in-law Boso the count of Vienne, and after Charles the Bald's death, Boso crowned himself king of Burgundy in 879. Meanwhile, in 888 Rudolf I laid claim to Upper Burgundy and also proclaimed himself king. The two kingdoms of Upper and Lower Burgundy remained separate until they were united by Rudolf's son, Rudolf II, who in 934, was able to come to terms with the successor to Boso's territories, Hugh of Provence. Rudolf renamed this enlarged kingdom, stretching from Basel to the Mediterranean and from the modern Italian-French border to the Sarne-Rhône, the kingdom of Arelate (after the city of Arles); by the twelfth century, the term "Burgundy" was reserved for the county and the duchy.

After Rudolf II there followed a series of weak monarchs on the Burgundian throne, and when Rudolf III died without an heir in 1032, the kingdom passed over to the German emperors. However, although the kingdom was incorporated into the HOLY ROMAN EMPIRE, the real power remained with the nobles. The HOHENSTAUFEN emperors attempted unsuccessfully to incorporate the county of Burgundy into their kingdom, just as FREDERICK I BARBAROSSA had failed to annex Provence: through CHARLES OF ANJOU's marriage to its heiress, it fell into CAPETIAN hands in 1245. France acquired bits of Burgundy throughout the thirteenth and fourteenth century despite German attempts to assert control over the area.

Duchy of Burgundy. Following the death of Charles the Bald, the major portion of the duchy was claimed by Boso, and upon Boso's death in 887, his son Richard took control of the territory. Richard's son and successor, Raoul, enlarged the duchy through his marriage to the daughter of Robert I of France, and his ascension to the French throne upon Robert's death in 923. The duchy eventually passed to Robert II, son of HUGH CAPET, in 1015, and Robert's son, Hugh, founded the CAPETIAN House of Burgundy in 1032, a dynasty that would rule the area until 1361.

For over three centuries, the Capetians ruled ably. The area experienced a period of economic prosperity and cultural ascendancy that saw an outpouring of excellent examples of ROMANESQUE and GOTHIC ARCHITECTURE and thriving monastic and reform movements, including those of the Orders of Cluny and the CISTERCIANS. The Capetian line ended in 1361 with the death of Phillip of Rouvres, and the duchy passed to the Valois king of France, John II.

BURIDAN, JEAN

The French scientist and philosopher Jean Buridan (1300–1358) was well known and highly regarded as a teacher and thinker, but of the many ideas he propounded, the one for which he is most famous probably came from another source. The simile of Buridan's Ass served as an illustration of Buridan's theories on free-will and determinism. According to the example, a hungry ass positioned between two identical haystacks, will, it is argued, starve to death because it cannot decide which stack to eat. A free choice must be based on a judgement that one choice is preferable. Whether this example comes from Buridan or from his critics who were ridiculing him (it appears nowhere in his surviving works), Buridan's contributions to philosophy and to science were far more substantive and far-reaching than this singular theory would suggest. (*See* PHILOSOPHY; SCIENCE.)

His Life. Jean Buridan was born around 1295, probably in Bethune, FRANCE. As with many scholars of the period, few details are known of his life. He was a student of WILLIAM OF OCKHAM, and later studied at the University of PARIS. He became a teacher at the University upon completion of his studies, then its rector for a year in 1328 and again in 1340. During his career, he published a number of works on mechanics, logic, and optics; his works were highly regarded, and a number were still being used in European universities as late as the seventeenth century. Some of Buridan's ideas on optics were particularly advanced. Toward the end of his life, he had criticized Ockham, which caused Ockham's followers to condemn Buridan's ideas, and after his death in 1358, his works were briefly on the Index of Forbidden Books. (*See* HERESY; WILLIAM OF OCKHAM.)

His Work. Buridan was generally in the Aristotelian camp in many matters, although he challenged some of Aristotle's ideas in physics. He believed, for example, unlike ARISTOTLE, that celestial objects move of their own accord and do not require the agency of angels or deities, clearly foreshadowing the concept of gravity to be explained by Newton some 300 years later. His "theory of impetus" may be viewed as an early statement of the law of inertia according to which an object in motion does not require continued force to remain in motion, also in opposition to Aristotle.

BYZANTINE ART AND ARCHITECTURE

Much of the art of the Byzantine Empire has been lost, but a sense of its grandeur can still be felt when examining what remains. Although a great deal of Byzantine artistic activity centered around the Church, secular art was also important, and the Byzantine capital of CONSTANTINOPLE was considered a major artistic center for many centuries. Byzantine art had a strong impact on the movement that would become the Italian Renaissance.

Major Influences. As with architecture and structural engineering, the Byzantines borrowed heavily from the Roman Empire. CONSTANTINE I, who founded Constantinople in 330 C.E., carefully laid out the city to include impressive public buildings, inspir-

The Katholikon, built in 1011 at Hosios Lukas in Greece, is a classic example of the so-called Middle Byzantine style of architecture of the Macedonian Renaissance, 843–1204.

ing houses of worship, and a magnificent palace. The emperor JUSTINIAN I, who ruled from 527 to 565, was a patron of the arts and a builder. He oversaw the construction of a number of new churches in Constantinople and commissioned the restoration of numerous public and religious buildings.

As the new capital of the Roman Empire, and later the seat of the EASTERN ORTHODOX CHURCH, Constantinople was home to stunning religious art and architecture. The famed HAGIA SOPHIA, which still stands, was built in the early sixth century. Typical of many churches, the interior was decorated with mosaics, tiles, MOSAICS, and precious metals. ICONS (the painted representations of religious figures) became

of many works of art by the Byzantines themselves.)

Byzantine figures differed from the earlier classical form: most figures faced front, with large eyes gazing outward to create a powerful impression on the viewer. Many of them were painted on a gold background, which produced an almost spiritual effect. The Byzantine contribution to sculpture is less noteworthy. Perhaps the most common form was relief carving, which was found primarily on miniature boxes, book covers, and other small decorative items.

Overall, Byzantine religious art was created under a strict set of rules that sacrificed creativity to care in form and composition, resulting in a more sophisticated—and more spiritual—style.

The Court of Empress Theodora, a mosaic on the wall of the Cathedral of San Vitale in Ravenna, Italy. The many thousands of pieces of colored and silvered glass used to make the mosaic gave the picture a luminescence not possible with paints, or even with metallic overlays. The durability of the materials used and the presumption that they would last virtually forever was part of the monumental element of the art form. The mosaics of San Vitale are noteworthy for the fineness of the mosaic and for being integrated seamlessly into the architecture.

common in Byzantine churches and flourished despite two efforts to eliminate them. In addition to mosaics, the Byzantines also painted frescoes in their churches.

Illuminated MANUSCRIPTS from the Byzantine period included copies of the Old Testament and other sacred works. The best known surviving manuscript is the Paris Psalter. Dating from the tenth century, it depicts the life of King David of Judea. Many of the illustrations in Byzantine manuscripts are icons; books that survive from the anti-icon movement known as the iconoclastic controversy of the eighth century have little illumination. (The episode also saw the destruction

The Secular Arts. Although the Church was the source of inspiration for much Byzantine art, secular artistic works also existed. Private homes were often decorated with intricate mosaics, paintings, and tiles. Small decorative items (utensils and small chests, for example) have survived; these were carefully decorated with precious metals, enameled glass, and ivory.

Books, both religious and secular, were also found in some Byzantine private homes; the larger homes may have had their own small LIBRARIES. One of the best known examples is the *Vienna dioscorides*, a medical and pharmacological text dating from 512.

The fall of Constantinople in 1453 marked the end of the Byzantine Empire, but the influence of its art was clearly felt in Russia through the seventeenth century, because the Eastern Orthodox Church had built a strong presence, and in the art of twelfth century Italian cities such as VENICE and Genoa. While much Byzantine art was destroyed in earthquakes and by misguided nineteenth century archeological excavation, examples of the forms survived in these areas.

Byzantine Architecture. Some of the world's most elaborate structures were created by the builders of the thousand-year Byzantine Empire. Originally drawing from Roman models, Byzantine architects developed their own unique and innovative styles. The influence of Constantinople, capital of the empire and seat of the Eastern Orthodox Church, helped spread Byzantine religious architecture beyond the empire's borders to RUSSIA and parts of Western Europe.

Early Designs. The earliest Byzantine designs date to the founding of Constantinople (the site of modern-day Istanbul) in 330 C.E. Constantine I, the city's founder and the first Roman emperor to allow Christianity to be legally practiced in the Roman Empire, imported architects and artisans from Rome to the site of his new city, which, not surprisingly, took on a distinctly Roman flavor. Grand public buildings, wide streets, bridges and aqueducts, and large open marketplaces were carefully laid out. Early in the fifth century construction began on a network of triple walls to surround the city (much of which survives).

Public buildings were characterized by brick or stone facades and richly designed marble interiors and mosaic floors. Houses of worship were also modeled after the Roman basilica—which had an oblong shape and large columns separating the nave from side aisles.

Beginnings of Change. Constantinople's proximity to Asia Minor and Syria exposed the city to a variety of non-European art and design styles, and as the Byzantine Empire rose in prominence, its architects became bolder and more experimental. This is most evident in the empire's religious structures. The basilica was not the only style for houses of worship in Rome. Smaller buildings, were round, square, or octagonal. Often, these buildings, known as "martyr's shrines," were topped with domes.

Byzantine architects blended the two styles together to create a new design that might combine a series of geometric shapes, which gave rise to the magnificent and complex churches for which the empire is known. St. John of the Studion, (now the Mosque of Imrahor) is the oldest surviving example of this design. Built in 463, it follows some of the precepts of the basilica, such as the requisite three aisles. But it is squarer than the typical basilica, and the decorations include bas-relief sculptures on the facade (Roman sculptures were typically high-relief). By the end of the century, this architectural style had become more distinctive—still squarer in shape and topped by domes. The most famous example by far is the Hagia Sophia, built by the emperor Justinian in the sixth century. Constructed in only five years, it is best known for its enormous dome, which, through the use of special supports known as pendentives, appears almost to float atop the structure.

Few examples of secular Byzantine architecture remain—the city walls of Constantinople and the city's network of underground cisterns for storing water are the best surviving examples. The walls were constructed of brick and stone and had 192 towers. They were so well-built that they protected Constantinople until the Turks invaded with cannons in 1453. The cisterns, which had columns and domed roofs, were likewise well-designed; some were functional until the end of the nineteenth century. Private homes are described in surviving writings as usually being elaborately designed, two-story structures.

Later Architecture. The rise of ISLAM beginning in the seventh century saw the decline of Byzantine architecture, though interiors became more elaborately decorated as the structures became simpler and less imposing. The Byzantine architectural tradition was carried on in Russia and in eastern Europe, where the Eastern Orthodox Church became a dominant force in Italy; the best known example of Byzantine architecture outside the empire is St. Mark's church in Venice. The conversion of many Byzantine churches into mosques would have a lasting influence on Islamic architecture for centuries after the Middle Ages.

BYZANTINE LITERATURE

Byzantine authors were keenly aware of continuing both a Greek literary tradition that went back to Homer and a Christian literary tradition that went back to the New Testament. This consciousness of being preceded by many great minds and pens was both inspiring and intimidating. Byzantine writers could hope to take their place in distinguished company, but might also despair of meeting such a high standard. Though by Byzantine times the ancient Greek language had evolved a long way in the direction of modern Greek, most Byzantine authors tried to write in the language of the first century C.E. at the latest, and ideally of the fifth century B.C.E. The literary tradition was particularly burdensome for poets, struggling to express themselves in a language unsuited to spontaneity and originality, and theologians, bound by the definitive formulations of the Greek Fathers of the fourth and fifth centuries. The Byzantine authors most likely to be inspired were historians, who might borrow their style from Thucydides, but could find fresh material in the events of Byzantine times.

While fifth-century Greek literature was far from decadent, that of the following period showed greater vigor, reflecting the economic and military recovery of the Byzantine Empire that peaked under the emperor JUSTINIAN I. In particular, the historian Procopius of Caesarea, blessed with a fine education, a dramatic subject in Justinian's wars, and an insider's knowledge as secretary to Justinian's general BELISARIUS, wrote elegantly and critically, although he had to reserve his harshest criticisms of the emperor for his furtive *Secret History*. Other significant historians of the time include John Malalas (c. 491–c. 578), who covered history from Adam and Eve to Justinian; he

Bejeweled cover of an early 13th-century Byzantine liturgical book, Venice, Italy.

wrote exceptionally well, in something resembling spoken Greek. There were also skillful poets, in particular Romanus the Melode, who wrote intricate hymns in New Testament Greek. The period had its accomplished theologians, hagiographers, orators, philosophers, and scientists as well, all forming a large and varied literary community.

In the late sixth and early seventh centuries, however, Byzantine literature declined in both volume and variety. The main reason was probably the empire's economic and military troubles of the time. After one last major poet, George of Pisidia, who celebrated the emperor HERACLIUS I's temporary RECONQUEST of EGYPT and Syria in 630, Byzantine literature languished for over a century. The persecution of most religious writers under iconoclasm made matters worse, though one authoritative anti-iconoclast theologian, John of Damascus, wrote in Greek while living in Arab-held Syria. Only in the late eighth century, when it became safe to write against iconoclasm, did Byzantine literature begin to recover. Among the anti-iconoclast tracts and saints' lives, the chronicle of Theophanes the Confessor (c. 752–818) is crucial for providing most of our knowledge of the two hundred years before its compilation in the early ninth century.

For years the Byzantines' main literary activity was recovering Greek literature of all sorts from before the Dark Age. The leading ninth-century figure in that process was Photius (c. 820–891), who compiled an account of his omnivorous reading known as the *Bib-*

liotheca (*Library*) before becoming patriarch of CON-STANTINOPLE. Several emperors became enthusiastic patrons of scholarship, especially CONSTANTINE VII in the tenth century, who commissioned various scholarly works, including a continuation of Theophanes' chronicle (*Theophanes Continuatus*). Among works of this date in which Byzantine scholars summed up literature in Greek from ancient times to their own are an encyclopedia, the *Suda* (*Palisade*), and a collection of poems, the *Palatine Anthology*. Since this rediscovery of the Greek past inhibited Byzantine writers more than ever, most of the period's considerable drop of epistolography, historiography, and hagiography is labored and unoriginal even by Byzantine standards.

Eventually the best-educated Byzantines gained more confidence and wrote with more creativity, reinvigorating history, poetry, and epistolography and reviving philosophy. Thus the eleventh-century polymath MICHAEL PSELLUS broke with the usual conventions of history in writing his *Chronographia,* a lively memoir of the emperors he had known.

By the twelfth century, a time of prosperity if not of military strength, Byzantine literature became more developed and diverse than it had been since the sixth century. The most famous poet of the period, Theodore Prodromus (d. c. 1166), composed elegant court poetry, exploited with other poets the new form of the romantic novel in verse, and was probably the same Prodromus who composed spirited satirical poems in vernacular Greek. At this time, if not earlier, an anonymous poet drew on traditional ballads to produce the *Digenis Akritas* (*Double-Blooded Frontiersman*), a delightful epic about a legendary, half-Arab Byzantine warrior. Among historians, ANNA COMNENA, daughter of the emperor ALEXIUS I, composed the *Alexiad*, a polished, admiring, but accurate account of her father's reign. Anna found a worthy successor in Nicetas Choniates, the sophisticated, humane historian of the decline of the empire up to its partial conquest by the Fourth Crusade in 1204.

That conquest, inevitably a blow to Byzantine self-assurance, began another period in which most Byzantine writers turned to research rather than to creative literature, although some did compose Greek versions of Western vernacular verse romances. Besides producing some wordy but noteworthy histories, like the memoirs of the former emperor John VI Cantacuzenus, Byzantine scholars particularly excelled at studying classical Greek literature and philosophy, which won Byzantine literature great fame in Renaissance ITALY. After the appearance of several contemporary descriptions of the fall of Constantinople in 1453, the disappearance of Byzantine secular education soon brought an end to Byzantine literature, most of which was read more in western than in eastern Europe.

BYZANTIUM

Byzantium was the name of an old Greek port on the Hellespont that the emperor CONSTANTINE THE GREAT transformed in 330 C.E. into CONSTANTINOPLE, the capital of the eastern, Greek-speaking part of the Roman Empire. Byzantium became synonymous with the East Roman or Byzantine Empire. In the fifth century the western, or Latin-speaking, empire was overrun by barbarian invaders and was replaced in western Europe by the Germanic successor states to the Roman Empire. Constantinople remained the capital of the Byzantine Empire until 1453 when it finally was taken by the OTTOMAN TURKS. Since the 1920s, Byzantium or Constantinople has been called Istanbul.

The Second Rome. Constantine founded a new eastern capital at Byzantium for two reasons, strategic and religious: to have a political and military center much closer than ROME to the crucial Balkan and Iranian frontiers; and because the first Christian emperor had discovered that many of the aristocratic families in Rome remained loyal to classical paganism. (They continued this rejection of CHRISTIANITY for another half-century.) Constantinople became "the second Rome," intended to be a more spiritually exalted, more orthodox bastion for the Greek-speaking world. After 395, Rome and Constantinople never again had the same ruler. Byzantium was a center of the Greek Christian faith, today called the Greek Orthodox Church. After Constantinople's fall to the Muslims in 1453, the seat of the Greek Church passed to Moscow—by 900, missionaries from Byzantium had converted the Russian people—and Moscow claimed to be "the third Rome," a claim that lapsed only with the Russian Revolution in 1917.

Byzantium had one of the largest natural harbors in the world. Its ethnically diverse population, comprising Jews, Balkan and Asiatic peoples, as well as direct descendants of the Greeks and Romans, numbered around three-quarters of a million by 1000 C.E., making it the largest city in the world west of China. It was the commercial entrepot between East and West, the market for the exchange of goods that brought oriental spices, perfumes, and jewels into Europe after these precious goods had been brought overland from east Asia or across the Mediterranean from EGYPT and beyond, through Arabia and the Indian Ocean. It was a city famed for its innumerable saints and churches, including the great cathedral of HAGIA SOPHIA (Holy Wisdom), built by the emperor JUSTINIAN I in the sixth century. (After 1453, Hagia Sophia became a Muslim mosque; it has been a dusty museum since the 1920s.)

The Byzantine gold coin, the bezant, was a prime currency for medieval international trade that has been found all the way from China to England, revealing the scope of Byzantium's commerce.

Government. As was the case in the Roman Empire, medieval Byzantium was governed by an authoritarian political system of despotism tempered by assassination. A dynasty gained the throne by blood and conquest, ruling by hereditary succession until it was overthrown, usually by an army revolt. The Byzan-

The Byzantine Empire. Above, the empire begins with the accession of Justinian in 527, centered on Constantinople and reaching as far as Gibraltar by his death in 565. The empire will undergo great changes in the ensuing centuries: Left, in the 9th century, the borders of the empire will shrink to encompass Anatolia and the Greek and Italian Mediterranean. By the 12th century, the western border extended up the Adriatic while the east collapsed before the emergent Ottoman sultanate.

tine emperor claimed to be the appointed of God, Christ's representative on earth for the good of mankind. The emperor alone could wear the imperial purple. He sat in a cavernous throne room on an elevated dais; to approach him, mere mortals crawled and grovelled before him (or sometimes her) on their hands and knees. He ruled the provinces through a sophisticated bureaucracy in Constantinople and military governors on the scene in the countryside. By medieval standards, heavy taxes were imposed on Byzantine subjects. The emperor benefited mostly from a customs tax on trade and a monopoly over certain industries. The royal family, officials, priests, and courtiers (among whom eunuchs were prominent) were a heavy burden upon society. The imperial army, like Rome's in late antiquity, was comprised mainly of mercenaries until the tenth century when the imperial treasury could no longer sustain such a military burden. The use of feudal contingents loyal to great lords came increasingly into use, weakening the emperor's power over the landed aristocracy. The emperor ruled the Greek Church with an iron hand, appointing the patriarch of Constantinople and other bishops and issuing dictates not only on Church administration, but on points of theology. These theologians on the throne stimulated resentment from dissenting devotional minorities ("heretics"); this intermittent religious conflict also weakened the emperor's power from time to time—theologians on the throne were considered public dangers. The Greek Christians were deeply committed to monastic saints and to the monasteries dedicated to these miracle workers and faith healers. They also put their trust into the religious icons that were housed and enshrined in the great abbeys—these icons too could become parts of the religiously based resistance to imperial power.

Religion. Until around 800, the Byzantine emperor laid claim to northern Italy. This brought about periodic tense or even conflicting relations with the Roman pope who made similar claims on the power to legislate on theology. At the Council of Calcedon in 451, the emperor tried to mollify the pope by endorsing the Western doctrinal view whereby Christ had two natures—both divine and human. Millions of Greek Christians, however, subscribed to the Monophysites faith (claiming a single divine nature for Christ).This religious tension weakened the efforts of Emperor Justinian I to restore the glory and territory of the Roman Empire. His conquests of Italy and North Africa were undone in the early seventh century by the Muslim ARABS and the German LOMBARDS. The emperor HERACLIUS I in the early seventh century fought a long and debilitating war with the Iranians, ending in a stalemate. This exhausted both sides, leaving the Middle East open to Arab conquest. By the

early eighth century the Byzantine state had shrunk to the size of modern Turkey and Greece; for a time even Constantinople was threatened by the Arabs. Heraclius persecuted both the Monophysites and the Jewish minorities, and these dissidents therefore looked with favor on the conquest by the Muslims, who did not interfere with religious beliefs.

For three-quarters of a century after about 750, Byzantium was consumed by its most divisive and critical religious dispute, the ICONOCLASTIC CONTROVERSY. A new dynasty from eastern Asia Minor, near the border with Islam, came to the throne and proceeded on a policy of destroying all the religious images the imperial government could find, much to the dismay of probably the majority of the population. The iconoclastic rulers were imitating the anti-representational Muslims and Jews in order to strengthen popular loyalty; that is one explanation for the policy. Another is that the emperors looked upon the monasteries as centers of political opposition and wanted to weaken the monastic hold upon society by removing their precious icons. By the second quarter of the ninth century, imperial policy had switched back toward supporting the "iconodules," the icon-worshippers, but not before vast amounts of late Roman and Byzantine Christian art—sculptures, paintings, and illuminated manuscripts, the rich artistic heritage of seven centuries—had been almost entirely destroyed. Fortunately there was an extensive library of early Greek illuminated manuscripts at a monastery in the Sinai Desert, so remote as to escape the predations of the iconoclasts. From the holdings of this remote depository, Kurt Weitzmann, the Princeton art historian, in the 1950s and 1960s, painfully reconstructed the contours of early Byzantine art. Among the leading artistic achievements of mankind, it survives now only in fragments. (*See* ICONS; BYZANTINE ART.)

Another great achievement of Byzantine culture was the codification of Roman law, the *Codex Justianus,* executed under the supervision of Justinian I in the sixth century. It was the last important Byzantine work to be written in Latin. As such, the JUSTINIAN CODE, as it is commonly called, became the textbook of the Roman law revival in western Europe in the twelfth century, thereby entering into the foundations of all the continental European legal systems to the present day. The Justinian Code perpetuated late Roman law in its procedures that focused on the domination of courtrooms by panels of impartial judges, on the maximal use of written briefs, and in its theory that civil law was a reflection of universal principles of reason enshrined within the laws of nature.

The military, bureaucratic, and legal hegemony of the emperor did not entirely eliminate an informal popular element in Byzantine political life. This was re-

The Court of Emperor Justinian, a magnificent mosaic on the wall of San Vitale in Ravenna, Italy. The church was completed in 547 and the two mosaics of Justinian and Theodora and their courts face each other on walls leading to the altar. (Justinian and Theodora are, in fact, making an offering toward the altar of the church, which is to Justinian's left and Theodora's right.)

flected not only in the monastic enclaves and their charismatic icons, but also in urban political communities organized around allegiance to factions in the circus games. Justinian was almost unseated by rioting among the Green and Blue sport factions in the circus.

The Crusades. In the tenth century under BASIL II of the Macedonian dynasty, there was both a revival of Byzantine neoclassical art (the Macedonian renaissance) and a political expansion of the frontiers of the empire, both in the eastern Mediterranean and in the Balkans against the Bulgars. At this time, at the end of the first Christian millennium, Byzantium reached its zenith in wealth and cultural innovation. But by the middle of the eleventh century with the invasion of the eastern Mediterranean by the fearsome SELJUK TURKS, the outward push against the Muslims was reversed. Byzantium entered into a half-millennium of desperate defensive posture, marked by dependency on the good will of the Roman pope and the French crusaders. The latter was summoned to the East to save Constantinople as well as to rescue the Holy Land. From the inception of the crusades, the western lords were almost as interested in taking the Golden City of Hellespont as in seizing and holding Jerusalem against the Muslims. As time wore on, the former became their primary goal, if only because it was deemed more attainable.

In 1204, Venetian fleets convinced French crusaders to divert their military enterprise to the conquest of Constantinople. The Latin kingdom of Constantinople endured until 1261. It had the blessing of the pope in the hope of reuniting the Greek and Latin churches, which after centuries of bad relations had experienced a formal schism in 1054. But the Latin kingdom of Constantinople had not healed the breach between the two branches of medieval Christianity; a Greek dynasty regained the Byzantine throne in 1261. Byzantium endured for another two centuries, but it was now a thing of shreds and patches, although still a center of philosophical and theological learning. Byzantium held on until it was finally overrun by the Ottoman Turks in 1453.

From one perspective, Byzantium was the savior of medieval Europe. Had it fallen to the Muslims in the eighth or ninth centuries, the Arabs could have moved on Europe from the Balkan back door and conquered the Latin world. By the eleventh century, Westerners, usually French or German, were ridiculing Byzantines as effete and decadent. But without Byzantium to guard the door, western European civilization might well have been nullified by the Muslims.

CABALA

The Cabala (also spelled Cabbala and Kabbalah, though these spellings usually denote a strictly Jewish context) is an elaborate mystical culture developed during the Middle Ages. Originating among the Provencal Jewry in FRANCE in the late twelfth century, it soon spread to SPAIN and ITALY, in part as a reaction to the teachings of MOSES MAIMONIDES. It focused on the belief that individuals could come to understand the mysteries of the Scriptures by interpreting words and letters in the Bible. Cabala (from the Hebrew for "tradition") began as a secretive culture whose studies were open only to those with a solid background in traditional Jewish learning. But it had a great deal of influence in Jewish thought, and many of its doctrines had a strong impact on the development of modern Judaism. It was also influential in Christian mystic and gnostic circles in which the study of the occult was encouraged.

Origins. A mystical element had existed in Judaism long before the development of the Cabala, and spirituality had always been an important part of Jewish life. But the considerable and extensive works of Maimonides in the twelfth century dismissed mysticism, and many Jews saw his views as too rational to leave room for spirituality. Although his books on Jewish law were highly regarded, his philosophic works were viewed as bordering on HERESY by many scholars of traditional JUDAISM. As a result, copies of his books were burned. (Surviving copies of Maimonides' philosophical works were not studied seriously by Jewish scholars until well into the modern era.)

At first, only those steeped in Jewish thought became Cabalists. But through their writings, the Cabalists exerted considerable influence in other quarters; many alchemists were familiar with Cabalist texts. The most important book from the Cabala is the *Sefer-ha-Zohar* (Book of Splendor). Much cabalistic thought was transmitted orally as well. Cabalist writings are filled with numerical calculations in which lessons are derived from the numerical equivalent of words and phrases, particularly those involving the name of God.

ILLUMINATIONS

The word "cabal", meaning a secretive group of individuals engaged in sinister activity, has the same root as Cabala. An incident in English history gave the word somewhat more currency, however (and accounts for its anomalous spelling). The five ministers of Charles II who in 1672 signed an alliance with France against Holland were Clifford, Arlington, Buckingham, Ashley, and Lauderdale —their initials spell out "cabal."

CADE, JACK

An Irish-born soldier in the English army, Jack Cade (d. 1450) fought in the final stage of the HUNDRED YEARS' WAR. In the summer of 1450, Cade became the leader of a revolt in Kent, eventually leading rebels into LONDON on July 4.

English people were angry at the effects of the seemingly endless and costly Hundred Years' War, which now the French were winning as they continued to drive the English back in northern FRANCE. The increased frequency of French raids on the English coast made a rebellious group charge that the king's advisers were incompetent, and that they should be replaced by "better" nobles, such as Richard, duke of York. During the revolt Cade claimed to be related to Richard, and in keeping with the claim that he was part of Richard's Mortimer lineage he called himself John Mortimer.

In May of 1450, Cade led his rabble toward ENGLAND from Kent, seizing and beheading Lord Saye, King Henry's treasurer. Cade was in turn seized, beheaded and quartered, and the rebellion was quickly quelled. Ten years later, however, when Richard of York's son, the future Edward IV, marched an army of agrarian rebels into London, the name and memory of Jack Cade was still fresh. (*See* PEASANTS' REVOLTS.)

CAESAROPAPISM

Caesaropapism was the dominant political ideology of the Byzantine Empire, the medieval successor state to the Eastern Roman Empire. The distinguishing characteristic of caesaropapism is the combination of secular and religious authority in the office of the emperor. The emperor is both caesar, the supreme secular authority, and pope, leader of the Christian Church. The emperor or, occasionally, the empress, had absolute power over the political state and the army, as well as the Church. The Byzantine Empire was therefore an autocracy, with a single figure holding unlimited power in all realms of life. Caesaropapism reinforced the conception of the Byzantine emperor as a universal ruler—king of all humankind—at the head of a cosmic "hierarchy," or system of superior and inferior, authorized by the Deity, in which a person has an unchangeable position in society.

Caesaropapism had its origins in the fourth century when the early Christian Church was split between warring factions, and each side sought greater authority than could be supported by simple armed might.

CALATRAVA, ORDER OF

n order founded in 1158 when monks from Fitero, SPAIN and allied knights fought with the Islamic BERBER kingdom of the ALMOHADS over the fortress town of Calatrava. The monks eventually returned to their abbey, but the knights remained and became an organized military order.

In 1164, Pope ALEXANDER III officially recognized the Order of Calatrava and attached it to the CISTERCIAN ORDER. The Calatrava, located in the Christian Iberian kingdom of Castile, gained power. By the fourteenth century, the order was responsible for 350 towns and 200,000 souls. As the RECONQUEST of Spain proceeded, the purpose of the order changed, and they became involved in the politics of Castile. By the late fifteenth century, it had become a political organization of nobles and, in 1482, the order was attached to the crown by Ferdinand and Isabella. (*See* SPAIN.)

CALENDARS

Calendars were used during the Middle Ages for both practical and religious purposes, it being just as important in most medieval minds to observe a religious holiday on the correct day as it was to plant a crop at the best time of year. Many holy days in the three major religions in the West (CHRISTIANITY, Judaism, and ISLAM) had to be carefully calculated, and families routinely observed personal holidays such as birthdays or death anniversaries.

Christians used the calendar of ancient ROME, known as the Julian calendar (after Julius Caesar, in whose reign it was fixed during the first century B.C.E.). The Julian is a solar calendar in that a year is measured by the sun and an arbitrary number of months are assigned an arbitrary number of days. Since the sun returns to its exact position in the noonday sky every 365.25 days, months will have varying numbers of

July: Harvest and Sheep Shearing, a magnificent page from the Très Riche Heures, *a 15th-century book of hours produced by the Limbourg brothers.*

days and an adjustment or "intercalation" (like adding a day during a leap year) will have to be made to bring the calendar into synchrony with the seasons. Jews and Muslims use a lunar calendar based on the moon going through its phases every 29.5 days. The Jewish year uses a leap month as an intercalatory device; the Muslim calendar does not, so the Muslim year aligns with the solar year every 19 years. In all cases, expertise in calculation and in astronomical measurement is necessary to determine festivals. (*See* EASTER, DATE OF.)

The New Year. What day of the year is to be determined as the first, an issue mainly of legal and record-keeping interest, was nevertheless one for which diverse practices abounded. The Roman civil year began on January 1, but the pagan associations of this practice gave rise to the "Christmas year" (*anno Domini,* or "year of our Lord"), in which the year began on Christmas day. This was formalized in calendric tables created by BEDE and was adopted by every western country except SPAIN.

From the ninth century onward, two systems became dominant: the so-called Pisan calendar, which was a modest adaptation of the Christmas year, used in Mediterranean countries and in most of the HOLY ROMAN EMPIRE; and the Easter cycle, according to which Easter (a highly movable holiday) was the first day of the year. Later, a set day, the day of the Annunciation, on March 25, was designated New Year's Day. This practice prevailed in ENGLAND, FRANCE, northern Europe, the NETHERLANDS, and parts of GERMANY.

Calendars were often elaborately decorated and prefaced or used in books of hours and breviaries, marking the many saints' days observed by a family or community. Tax collection was often coordinated with specific holidays, even if their date varied. For much of the West, the Julian calendar was replaced by the Gregorian calendar (named after its sponsor, Pope Gregory XIII) in 1582, although the Julian calendar continued in use in many parts of the world for some centuries after that date.

CALIPHATE

The main ruling institution in medieval ISLAM, roughly equivalent to the Western term "kingdom." The Islamic state is ruled by the caliph or "successor" who rules by virtue of a connection, by blood line or in some other way, with the prophet MUHAMMAD. This connection to the religious source of Islam emphasizes the religious role played by the caliph—he is custodian of both the body politic and the community's spirit. But in practice, the caliphs ruled as either kings or as heads of a bureaucracy. In most instances, military might prevailed and caliphs either established their military supremacy or became figureheads for the military power structure.

The First Caliphs. The first four caliphs were known as the *rashidun* ("righteous") and were particularly venerated throughout Islamic history. Beginning with ABU BAKR, Muhammad's immediate successor (632), these caliphs presumed to rule only as "first among equals" in Muhammad's absence. Omar ibn al-Khattab, who added the role of military leader, and Uthman ibn Affan, both Abu Bakr's successors, demanded a higher level of obedience from their subjects, which led inevitably to a schism. But the split came not only politically—as represented by the establishment of the two competing caliphates, the UMAYYADS and the ABBASIDS—but also religiously—as represented by the split of the people into the Sunnites and the Shi'ites. In both cases, caliphs surrounded themselves with religious scholars and holy men in an effort to uphold their claim on religious grounds.

A difficulty inevitably engendered by so close an association between politics and religion was the question a caliph's authority over non-Muslim subjects. Throughout the Middle Ages (and into the modern period), Islamic governments found it difficult to allow the secularization necessary for effective administration of a wide variety of peoples without compromising their claim of ordination. Attempts to distill out religious authority always seemed to undermine the caliph with his core supporters and weakened, usually mortally, his reign. The caliphs ruled to one degree or another for some 600 years, representing a constant threat and a formidable adversary of the Christian West, as well as the Byzantine and MONGOL East. When the last caliph was killed in 1258, the institution may have ended, but the empire it forged, its culture and values, was hardly shaken at all—testimony to the achievements of the caliphs in the Middle Ages.

See ISLAM *and related entries for background. Individual caliphates are described in* ABBA-DID, ABBASID, FATIMID, *and* UMAYYAD DY-NASTIES; *and entries on specific caliphs listed.*

CAPET, HUGH

Founder of a line of kings who ruled FRANCE for much of the Middle Ages. (His nickname "Capet" is from the Latin *capa*, meaning cape—in all likelihood derived from the cape of Saint Martin of Tours, a precious relic preserved in the basilica where Hugh Capet and his successors held the position of lay abbot.) The records for the reign of Hugh Capet are limited and often difficult to interpret. His piety, diplomatic skills, and political acumen are nonetheless clear. Although more able as a duke than a king, he succeeded in gaining the throne of France, cementing an alliance with the churches of the kingdom, and passing the crown to his son and heir.

Early Years. Hugh Capet (c. 938–996) was the son of Hugh the Great (d. 956), duke of the FRANKS, and of Hedwig, sister of Emperor OTTO I of GERMANY, and another of whose sisters was married to the CAROLINGIAN Louis IV, king of France. Hugh Capet and his father were descendants of Robert the Strong, marquis of BRITTANY (d. 866), whose oldest son Odo was king of France from 888 to 898 after the deposition of the Carolingian emperor Charles the Fat. Because of their descent from Robert, Hugh's line is known as the Robertian, although the name Capet (which gave the dynasty its name) was first applied to Hugh.

From the end of the ninth century to 987, the throne of France alternated between Carolingians and Robert the Strong's descendants and relatives. In 893, the Carolingian Charles the Simple was chosen king of France and ruled to 923, barely escaping replacement by Odo's brother Robert, who was pronounced king in 922, but was defeated by Charles the Simple. Robert's son Hugh the Great (Hugh Capet's father) in turn defeated Charles, but never became king himself. Instead, his brother-in-law Ralph (or Raoul), duke of BURGUNDY, succeeded Charles as king and ruled from 923 to 936, with Hugh the Great's support. In 936, after his brother-in-law's death, Hugh had the Carolingian Louis IV, son of Charles the Simple, recalled from exile in ENGLAND. Hugh the Great's title—"duke and leader of the FRANKS" (*dux et princeps Francorum*)—was the same accorded to CHARLES MARTEL and PÉPIN III THE SHORT. Hugh's power, however, was not as great as their's. By marrying his daughters to duke Frederick of Lorraine and duke Richard of Normandy, Hugh acquired important allies. The marriage of his son Otto to the daughter of the ruler of Burgundy won Burgundy for Otto (960–965) and then for Hugh's youngest son Odo-Henry. After Louis IV's death in 954 and the accession of his young son Lothair in 954, Hugh the Great effectively ruled France. Two years after Hugh died in 956, Hugh Capet succeeded his father as count of PARIS.

Since the young Hugh Capet, like his cousin King Lothair, was in his teens, political power rested in the hands of their mothers, both sisters of Otto I of Germany, who were advised by their brother Bruno, archbishop of Cologne. Lothair married Emma, stepdaughter of Otto I; in 979 Lothair had their son Louis crowned king. The Ottonians exercised considerable influence in Lothair's kingdom, with sympathetic ecclesiastics from Lorraine gaining the archbishoprics of Reims and Laon. Both would be instrumental in elevating Hugh Capet to the throne in 987.

The Throne. Before being invested in 960 with the title "duke of the Franks," Hugh Capet lost control of his father's lands, but he retained his powerful position as lay abbot of a number of monasteries, including Saint-Martin of Tours, Saint-Germain des Prés, and Saint-Denis. Before 970 he married Adelaide of Poitou. In 980, supported by Archbishop Adalbero of Reims, Hugh took advantage of hostilities between Lothair and Otto II, son and successor (973) of Otto I, to ally with Otto II. When Lothair died unexpectedly in March 986, and his son Louis V died in May 987, Adalbero engineered the election of Hugh Capet; he consecrated Hugh as king on July 3, 987. Following Lothair, Hugh had his son Robert crowned, again by Adalbero, that December 30.

Hugh's position was threatened by Charles of Lorraine, Lothair's brother, aided by Lothair's illegitimate son Arnulf, who in 989 had been elected Adalbero's successor as archbishop of Reims. But in 991, Bishop Adalbero of Laon, whom Charles of Lorraine had imprisoned in 988, regained his bishopric and betrayed Laon and Charles to Hugh Capet. Charles soon died, and his sons expired without heirs, clearing the way for Robertian-Capetian rule in France.

His Reign. The legitimacy of Hugh Capet's reign would be debated for centuries. Still, having disposed of the Carolingian threat, Hugh ruled circumspectly, cultivating an alliance with the ecclesiastics of the realm. Hugh relied on the sage counsel of GERBERT OF AURILLAC (c. 945–1003), who directed the cathedral school at Reims. In 991, Gerbert replaced the traitor Arnulf as archbishop of Reims with the support of Hugh and his son Robert over papal opposition and the protests of Adalbero of Laon. By the time Gerbert was obliged to retire to the court of Otto III, where he became the young ruler's tutor (subsequently becoming archbishop of RAVENNA, and in 999, Pope Sylvester II), Hugh Capet was no longer living. Struck by illness, Hugh died in November 996, having survived by several months one of his chief antagonists, Count Odo of Blois. He was buried at Saint-Denis, where his father and his great-uncle King Odo were interred. His son Robert, already crowned, became sole ruler of France. (*See* CAPETIAN DYNASTY.)

CAPETIAN DYNASTY

The Capetian dynasty, the third line of the kings of the FRANKS or French, takes its name from the surname of HUGH CAPET, who was elected king in 987 after the death without heirs of the last direct CAROLINGIAN, Louis V, in preference to Louis' uncle, Charles of Lorraine. The name Capet was also linked with Hugh Capet's father. The dynasty continues to the present day through the male line in the persons of the claimants to the throne of France, namely, the count of PARIS and the duke of Anjou and Cadix. Direct Capetian rule ended in 1328 with the death of Charles IV, son of PHILIP IV THE FAIR.

Because male inheritance was established as a principle of French royal succession after the death of Louis X in 1316, the throne passed in 1328 to Philip VI of Valois, son of Count Charles of Valois (1270–1325), younger brother of Philip the Fair.

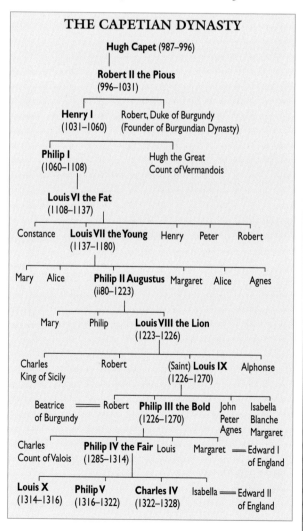

THE CAPETIAN DYNASTY

Hugh Capet (987–996)
|
Robert II the Pious (996–1031)
|
Henry I (1031–1060) — Robert, Duke of Burgundy (Founder of Burgundian Dynasty)

Philip I (1060–1108) — Hugh the Great, Count of Vermandois

Louis VI the Fat (1108–1137)

Constance — Louis VII the Young (1137–1180) — Henry — Peter — Robert

Mary — Alice — Philip II Augustus (ii80–1223) — Margaret — Alice — Agnes

Mary — Philip — Louis VIII the Lion (1223–1226)

Charles King of Sicily — Robert — (Saint) Louis IX (1226–1270) — Alphonse

Beatrice of Burgundy ═ Robert — Philip III the Bold (1226–1270) — John Peter Agnes — Isabella Blanche Margaret

Charles Count of Valois — Philip IV the Fair (1285–1314) — Louis — Margaret ═ Edward I of England

Louis X (1314–1316) — Philip V (1316–1322) — Charles IV (1322–1328) — Isabella ═ Edward II of England

When Charles VIII died in 1498 without a direct male heir, a descendant of Louis of Orléans, son of Charles V, ascended the throne as Louis XII. Since Louis XII also left no male heir, Francis I, son of Charles of Orléans, count of Angoulême, great-grandson of CHARLES V, gained the throne in 1515. Louis XII had made Francis count of Valois in February 1498; hence Francis's descendants often referred to themselves as Valois. After the death of Francis's third successive ruling grandson, HENRY III, in 1589, HENRY IV received the crown as the descendant of LOUIS IX's son, Robert of Clermont (1256-1317), duke of Bourbon through his wife. When he was tried and condemned in 1793, Louis XVI, Henry IV's direct descendant, was referred to as Louis Capet.

Early Years. Hugh Capet was not the first of his line to rule the Franks. He was the great-grandson of Robert the Strong of BRITTANY (died 866), whose sons Odo (reigned 888–898) and Robert (reigned 922–923) had been crowned kings. This line was known as the Robertian. King Robert's son, Hugh the Great, was the virtual ruler of France for much of the reign of the Carolingian king Louis IV (reigned 936–954) and for the first two years of that of his successor and son Lothair (reigned 954–986). Befitting his status, Hugh the Great was married to Hedwig, the sister of German Emperor OTTO I and Gerberga, wife of King Louis IV. Through his mother, Hugh Capet was thus the cousin of King Lothair and of his brother Charles of Lorraine, who failed to claim the throne of France after the death of Lothair's son Louis V in 987. Instead, Hugh Capet was chosen king. In 991 Charles of Lorraine was betrayed, imprisoned, and soon died.

The means Hugh Capet had used to ascend the throne were hardly admirable. The contemporary chronicler Adhémar of Chabannes suggested that the last two Carolingians had been poisoned. Still, Adhémar praised Hugh's dedication to the Church (especially Saint-Denis), and the piety of Hugh's son and successor Robert (972–1031). To strengthen his line's hold on the crown, Hugh had Robert consecrated as king in December 987, just six months after his own election. Such anticipatory succession by investing the eldest son into the kingship—a custom observed by the Carolingians and in Byzantium—would be practiced by the Capetians until the thirteenth century, when PHILIP AUGUSTUS's son Louis (reigned 1223–1226) became the first Capetian king to be crowned after his father's death.

Politics. The mystique the Carolingians and their advisors had created to justify Pépin's deposition of the last MEROVINGIAN ruler raised problems for the Capetians. The legend that Pope Stephen II had in 754 excommunicated any person daring to select a ruler from a line other than the Carolingian, elabo-

rated in the tenth century, was particularly troublesome. The Capetians' blood-ties to the Carolingians were not especially impressive; in any case, they were less concerned with justification than with ruling effectively. Aristocratic families linked to the Carolingians harbored both nostalgia and admiration for Carolingian traditions, which grew stronger as the power of the Capetians increased. Aspersions were cast on the Capetian line by noble houses seeking to rival and subvert it. By the eleventh century, a legend had developed in northern France presenting Hugh Capet's accession as a divine reward for rescuing the bodies of Saints Valéry and Riquier. His descendants, it was said, would hold the kingdom for seven generations. The story was adapted at the end of the twelfth century by André of Marchiennes, a chronicler working for Count Baldwin of Hainaut, for whom an irreproachable Carolingian ascendance had been found. Since Baldwin's daughter had married Philip Augustus, the chronicler said, the kingdom would be restored to Charlemagne's line when their son Louis became king. Though the story was unflattering to the Capetians, Louis IX (born 1215) accepted it. The tombs installed at the abbey church of Saint-Denis during his reign were arranged to depict the union of the Capetian line with those of the Merovingians and the Carolingians through Philip Augustus and Louis VIII. The vernacular history of the three royal lines of France, the *Grandes Chroniques* (The Great Chronicles), written at Saint-Denis in the late thirteenth century, also included the legend.

Earlier Capetians had fostered the development of connections with the two previous lines. The name "Louis" (a derivative of CLOVIS) entered the Capetian repertory when King Philip (whose name recalled Philip of Macedon) selected it for his first son. On his great seal Philip I had himself depicted on an antique throne, and on the seal of Louis VII (reigned 1137–1180) the throne resembles the royal seat of the Merovingian king Dagobert, which Abbot Suger had found at Saint-Denis. On their seals both Louis VII and Philip Augustus had themselves portrayed with the long hair of the Merovingians. Early-thirteenth-century histories proclaimed the existence of direct blood ties with the Carolingians through Adele of Champagne, mother of Philip Augustus, and through Hedwig, mother of Hugh Capet. King Philip the Fair rejected the seven-generation dispensation associated with the legend of Hugh Capet and the saints, and endorsed the genealogical link through Hedwig, featured in Latin historical compilations made at Saint-Denis. At King Philip's behest, the tombs at the abbey were rearranged to obliterate the distinction among the dynasties suggested by the earlier configuration. The seven-generation prophecy remained a popular legend; but after the canonization of Louis IX in 1297, the significance of descent from a saint eclipsed earlier concerns, particularly since exclusion of female royal succession rendered Hedwig's relevance to the question of Capetian legitimacy questionable.

Legacy. The Capetians exploited and created rituals as well as legends to solidify and expand their authority. One of the most important was the ceremony of consecration and CORONATION. Beginning with the anticipatory coronation of Philip, son of Louis VI, in 1129, the archbishopric of Reims was established as the site of this ceremony, thus implementing the privilege that Pope URBAN II granted to the archbishop of Reims in 1089. This prerogative was buttressed by the legend, recorded in the ninth century by Archbishop HINCMAR, that Reims possessed a vial of holy oil sent from heaven for Clovis's baptism by Saint Remi. The use of the chrism (consecrated oil) for a royal consecration is first recorded by Abbot SUGER of Saint-Denis, who wrote that in 1131 the future Louis VII was elevated to the kingship "by the unction of holy oil and the imposition of the kingdom's crown." In the thirteenth century, this chrism (believed to be miraculously replenished) and its container, the Holy Ampulla, were essential elements of the inaugural ceremony. The king's anointing with the holy chrism came to be linked with the power to heal, a power exercised through the ROYAL TOUCH from the time of King Robert II, the Pious (reigned 987–1031). Beginning with the coronation of Louis X in 1315, each new king made a post-coronation pilgrimage to the shrine at Corbeny dedicated to Saint Marcoul (who was associated with the curative power), and there first exercised the royal touch. Other important rituals that the Capetians promoted were the royal "entry" to an important city of the realm; the royal funeral, which gave expression to the notion that the dead king ruled until he was interred and that his justice (represented by the presidents of the Parliament of Paris) never died; and the *lit de justice* ("bed of justice"), occasions when the king visited and presided over the parliament.

In the thirteenth and fourteenth centuries the Capetians created institutions that were widely admired. Philip II Augustus expanded the kingdom by conquering Normandy and other ANGEVIN lands; he also established a chancery and fiscal mechanisms which enabled him to exploit the royal lands efficiently. Louis VIII instituted the use of *apanages* (endowments) to provide for younger sons (who also entered the Church). Louis IX elevated the prestige of the monarchy through his personal holiness and his crusading. Assisted by his brother Alphonse of Poitiers (1220-71), he succeeded in gaining control over the south of France (the Languedoc) after the ALBIGENSIAN Crusade. He and Alphonse used investigators to reform the activities of local royal officials. Louis fixed

the administration of justice in Paris and instituted the basic structure of a central Parisian court whose actions were recorded in registers that have been preserved in an almost unbroken series from the mid-thirteenth century to the French Revolution. Philip the Fair was responsible for establishing and organizing the Chamber of Accounts (*chambre des comptes*), which functioned as the realm's chief financial office until the end of the monarchy. Philip also convoked general assemblies on an unprecedented scale, establishing the practice of large-scale consultation of subjects to endorse royal policies and consent to taxation. The experiments he initiated for taxation influenced many later kings.

Many Capetians were patrons of architecture, literature, and learning. From Philip Augustus on, the Capetians encouraged the development of Paris and its university. They patronized the new style of architecture (later termed GOTHIC), which developed in and around the Paris region in the latter part of the twelfth century. Between 1241 and 1246 Louis IX had the Sainte-Chapelle constructed in Paris to house relics purchased from the exiled emperor Baldwin of Constantinople. By 1313 Philip the Fair had an imposing new royal palace built on the Île de la Cité, adjacent to the chapel. Charles V (reigned 1364–1380) rebuilt this palace as well as the Louvre.

See HUGH CAPET *and related biographical entries, especially* PHILIP II AUGUSTUS *and* PHILIP IV THE FAIR. *Important related articles are* CAROLINGIAN DYNASTY; MEROVINGIAN DYNASTY; FRANKS; *and* FRANCE.

CARMELITES

The Carmelites are one of the four mendicant orders of monks, (mendicant orders adhere to strict vows of poverty and support themselves by begging), founded around 1155 by a group of pilgrims and former crusaders near Mount Carmel, in Palestine. The founders hoped to emulate the life of the prophet Elijah, considered by early Christian historians as the creator of the monastic movement.

At first, the Carmelites were hermits, living in small huts in Palestine and adhering to strict vows of silence and seclusion. After several lost battles by crusaders threatened the Carmelites' lives, they decided to relocate to western Europe. Eventually they transformed themselves into mendicant FRIARS. (*See* MONASTERIES AND MONASTICISM.)

The first order of Carmelite nuns was founded in 1452; the most famous of these is Saint Teresa of Avila. Today, many of the Carmelites serve as teachers.

CARMINA BURANA

The Carmina Burana, or Songs of Beuren, are a series of medieval songs and plays dating from the thirteenth century. They take their name from the German monastery of Benediktbeuren, where they were discovered in 1803. In all, the collection contains about 300 songs and two religious plays.

The songs, written in Latin, German, French, and Greek, include a number that focus on religious themes. Many of the songs, however, extol the pleasures of drinking, gambling, and wandering—much like the songs of the wandering students called GO-LIARDS. In fact, the poetry of two well-known goliards, Hugh of Orléans and the Archpoet (from GERMANY), is included among the songs, as are poems by Ovid.

Although many of the songs contain musical marking, they have not been easy to decipher; scholars have reconstructed about 40 of the melodies. In 1937 the German composer Carl Orff created a clanging, modernistic musical setting for several of the songs, which won wide acclaim (especially in Nazi Germany.)

CAROLINGIAN DYNASTY

The Carolingian dynasty, the second line of kings of the FRANKS, came from the name "Charles" borne by CHARLES MARTEL, mayor of the palace of Austrasia who prepared the way for the replacement of the MEROVINGIAN line of kings by his descendants. His son Pépin was crowned and anointed as king of the Franks in 751 after the last Merovingian, Childeric III, was deposed. The eldest son of Pépin and his wife Bertha (died 783) was given his grandfather's name, Charles, and eventually became known as CHARLEMAGNE or Charles the Great. Charles's younger brother, Carloman (died 771), was given a variant of what had become a family name. Charles continued to be a favored name among the Carolingians, and its later adoption by members of the CAPETIAN DYNASTY revealed their desire to link themselves with the Carolingians. The ancestors of Charles Martel, known as the Pippinids and Arnulfings, were noble Austrasians, descended from Pépin I of Landen (died c. 640), mayor of the palace to the Merovingian king Clothar II, and Arnulf (died c. 645), who became bishop of Metz in 614 after fathering a son who married a daughter of Pépin I and produced a son, Pépin II (died 714), father of Charles Martel.

Early Years. The Carolingians mandated and supervised ecclesiastical reform, and the Church supported the monarchs. Abbot Fulrad of Saint-Denis was one of the emissaries of Pépin to Pope Zacharias (reigned 741–752), who sanctioned the deposition of the last Merovingian and the enthroning of Pépin in 751. The visit of Pope Stephen to FRANCE and Saint-Denis in 754 resulted in Frankish support of the PAPACY against the LOMBARDS and reciprocal papal support of Pépin. The pope also stimulated interest in and spread knowledge of the Roman liturgy, which Pépin, Charlemagne, and Charles the Bald promoted. Charlemagne and his son LOUIS THE PIOUS (emperor 814–840) also encouraged the observance of the Rule of Saint Benedict in monasteries they patronized.

A particularly important element in Carolingian rule was the ceremony of CORONATION (imposition of the crown) and consecration (anointing and blessing). The installation of Pépin as king in 751 witnessed the introduction of the ritual of anointing, a ceremony that was repeated in 754, when Pope Stephen II anointed Pépin and his family and blessed their rule. The rite was novel among the Franks, but it was part of the baptismal ceremony. It was described in the Old Testament and it was used by the VISIGOTHS and the Irish. It became a characteristic feature of Carolingian and then Capetian coronation ceremonies. Archbishop HINCMAR of Reims (c. 806–882) counselor of Emperor Charles the Bald, created a ceremony combining consecration and coronation. The rite Hincmar developed in 877 for the inauguration of Louis the Stammerer was adopted in France, Germany, and England.

Saint Denis. Abbot Hilduin of Saint-Denis (reigned 814–840) glorified both the Carolingians and the abbey he ruled, and elevated Saint Denis as the Carolingian dynasty's patron saint. Thus he added to his account of the saint's passion a commemoration of Pope Stephen's consecration of Pépin at Saint-Denis in 754, and also an account of the favors (including pallium and keys) the pope had bestowed on the abbey. Pope Stephen, he said, had been miraculously cured at Saint-Denis, and decreed that the Franks should never choose a ruler from any lineage other than the Carolingian. In the tenth century this legend was elaborated upon at the imperial monastery of Reichenau in the so-called *clausula*, in which Stephen's prohibition was issued under pain of excommunication.

Ties between the early Carolingian dynasty and the abbey of Saint-Denis were close. The first Carolingians—Charles Martel, Pépin and his wife Bertha (Bertrada), their son Carloman—were buried there. Almost a century passed before the next royal burial at the abbey, but the decision of Charles the Bald to be interred there was especially important for the abbey, since he was emperor (if only for two years) as well as king. Abbot Suger of Saint-Denis inaugurated elaborate anniversary services in Charles the Bald's honor in about 1140, and by 1223 a magnificent bronze tomb was erected in his honor, the first such funerary monument to be installed at Saint-Denis. The alliance between Saint-Denis and the Carolingians had reached its apogee under Charles the Bald. (Only two other minor Carolingians elected burial at Saint-Denis.)

The efforts made by Hilduin and later apologists to vindicate Carolingian right to the throne betray a certain uneasiness. The name Louis (a variant of CLOVIS) that Charlemagne bestowed on his third son recalled the first Merovingian Christian ruler, and through him the Merovingians' connections with the Trojans from whom they were believed to descend. Within fifty years of the Carolingian accession, supporters had discovered, (or possibly invented), a woman called Blitild, alleged daughter of one of the Merovingian kings named Clothar, who was said to have married Ausbertus, among whose saintly descendants was Bishop Arnulf of Metz, father of Pépin's great-grandfather.

The Carolingians developed and implemented a number of important governmental institutions. The most significant are the following: the palace, with trained staff and writing office (scriptorium, later called the chancery); officials known as MISSI DOMINICI (those dispatched by the lord) sent out as inspectors or ombudsmen; capitularies (collections of items or "chapters"—*capitula*) issued to transmit instructions from the ruler; oaths of fidelity linking all free men with their ruler; local courts and sworn inquests; counts and dukes who were more or less responsible to the ruler. Personal relationships counted for more than structures, and the functioning of both personal and governmental arrangements depended on the experience and genius of the ruler.

Charlemagne. Charlemagne's achievement in holding together the lands he ruled was impressive. His successors were less skilled and less fortunate. The VIKING invasions that disturbed the last years of his reign increased in frequency and severity. The custom of dividing the ruler's lands among his heirs was a source of continuing problems, and the situation was complicated by the struggles that periodically erupted over the title of emperor. Charlemagne was fortunate in having a single son who survived him. Louis the Pious, however, was too conscientious and spiritual-minded—and also too prolific—for his or his line's good. Made king of AQUITAINE IN 781 when he was three, he had acquired sufficient experience to govern by the time Charlemagne died in 814. He made a fatal error, however, in dividing his lands in 817 between the three sons he then had. Although doubtless intended to promote imperial unity when he died, his bequest created friction and jealousy among the sons, particularly given the ambitions of Louis's nephew Bernard (son of Charlemagne's son, Pépin of Aquitaine), whom Charlemagne had entrusted with governing Italy. The situation was complicated by the birth of Charles the Bald to Louis's second wife in 823. Dissension led to rebellion, and eventually to Louis's temporary abdication in 833.

After Louis died in 840, his three surviving sons, Lothair (795–855), king of Lotharingia and emperor, Louis the German (804–876), and Charles the Bald,

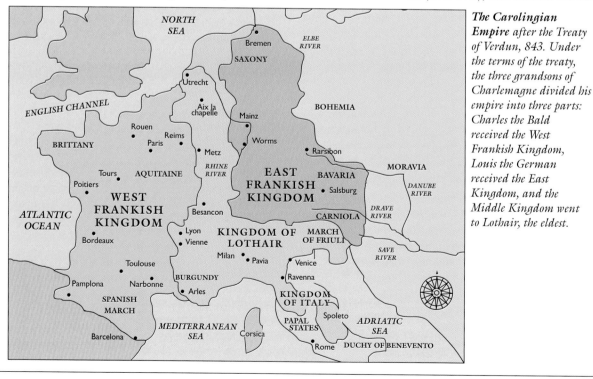

The Carolingian Empire after the Treaty of Verdun, 843. Under the terms of the treaty, the three grandsons of Charlemagne divided his empire into three parts: Charles the Bald received the West Frankish Kingdom, Louis the German received the East Kingdom, and the Middle Kingdom went to Lothair, the eldest.

divided the empire in accordance with the TREATY OF VERDUN of 843 following an agreement between Louis the German and Charles the Bald attested to in the oaths of Strasbourg of 842. The treaty eventually resulted in the separation of the German Empire from the western kingdom of the Franks, although Charles the Bald possessed the western realm, the imperial title, and Italy between 875 (after the death of Emperor Louis II, eldest son of Lothair I) and his death in 877. Louis the German's son Charles the Fat, king of the eastern Franks and emperor from 881 to 887, replaced Charles the Bald's grandson, Charles the Simple, as king of the western Franks between 884 and 887. During the century that elapsed between 887 and the accession of Hugh Capet in 987, the kingship of the western Franks alternated between descendants of Charles the Bald, increasingly less powerful and impressive, and members of the Robertian line, ancestors of Hugh Capet, who initiated what would be dubbed the Capetian dynasty. During the tumultuous tenth century, power and ability counted for more than royal Carolingian blood; later Capetians and their advisors expended much effort in attempting to justify Hugh Capet's displacement of the Carolingians.

Later Years. Despite the decline of the dynasty in the tenth century, the Carolingians left a rich cultural and political heritage. Art and intellectual activity flourished at the courts of Charlemagne and Charles the Bald, whose scholar-scribes developed the script known as the Caroline minuscule. This careful, beautifully articulated, and eminently legible script reflected the dedication of Charlemagne and his advisor ALCUIN to education and the cultural unification of the lands the emperor ruled. The script outlived the Carolingians and continued to be used well into the twelfth century. (*See* CAROLINGIAN RENAISSANCE.)

The early Carolingians, especially Charlemagne, Louis the Pious, and Charles the Bald encouraged the production of books. Classical as well as biblical and Christian texts were copied, and some manuscripts were beautifully illuminated. The Carolingians also encouraged fine metalwork, found in altarpieces, reliquaries, and book covers (which were also adorned with carved ivory, a skill that the Carolingians revived). The western empire that Charlemagne established is the Carolingians' most important political legacy. Charlemagne's own accomplishments, embellished by countless myths and legends, inspired later medieval emperors, such as FREDERICK II of HOHENSTAUFEN (reigned 1212–1250).

See FRANKS, MEROVINGIAN DYNASTY, *and* CAPETIAN DYNASTY *for background. For biographies, see* CHARLES MARTEL, CHARLEMAGNE; PÉPIN III; *and* LOUIS I THE PIOUS. *See also* CAROLINGIAN RENAISSANCE.

CAROLINGIAN RENAISSANCE

The term refers to the flowering of ART, ARCHITECTURE, and learning during the reign of CHARLEMAGNE and his successors from about 790 to 860. The renaissance was centered around the palace school of AIX-LA-CHAPELLE and the MONASTERIES at Tours, Metz, SAINT-DENIS, and near Reims. It tried to collect and revive the surviving remnants of the classical past by copying classical manuscripts and using classical models in art and in architecture, building vast basilicas, often intersected by large transepts.

The outstanding structure from the period is the Palatine Chapel in Palermo, which Pope LEO III dedicated in 805. The best preserved artistic achievements from the era are works of small dimensions such as manuscript illuminations, metalwork, and ivory carvings. The manuscripts owe much of their beauty to a new form of writing called Caroline minuscule, which greatly influenced medieval scripts and served as the model for the Roman type which was used when printing was invented in the 1400s.

The leading scholars of the Carolingian Renaissance were ALCUIN, a scholar and teacher from ENGLAND; the historian Peter the Deacon from Lombardy; the Visigothic poet, Theodulf, bishop of Orléans; and Einhard, who wrote a life of Charlemagne. The emphasis of the renaissance was on Roman heritage and Latin culture. It lasted through the 800s, as attested to by the works of HRABANUS MAURUS, Walafrid Strabo, John Eringena the Scot (even though he was from Ireland), and various artists and architects associated with cathedral schools and monasteries such as St. Gallen, Reichenau, Corbie, and Saint-Martin de Tours where Alcuin was abbot. (*See* ALCUIN; ARCHITECTURE.)

CASIMIR III THE GREAT

Casimir (1310–1370) was the last of POLAND'S Piast dynasty, which stretched over four centuries. During his nearly forty-year reign, he defined a distinct Polish state and government, earning the sobriquet "the Great."

Born the son of Wladyslaw I (the Short), Casimir inherited the throne at age 23. His father's reign was marked by inner dissension, but Casimir was more of a statesman; one of his successes was securing peace with BOHEMIA by surrendering control of East Pomerania and Silesia to the TEUTONIC KNIGHTS. In doing so he took Mazovia and Red Ruthenia, doubling the size of Poland. He again displayed his diplomatic skill in naming his nephew Louis of HUNGARY his heir, thus aligning Poland with rival Hungary. He also mediated disputes between Louis of Hungary and Holy Roman Emperor CHARLES IV.

In Poland, Casimir induced a birth of arts, education, and economic growth. During his reign the University of Cracow was established, which drew many of Europe's top intellects. He authorized the codification of law known as the Book of Teutonic Law (*Liber juris Teutonic*), a progressive system in which peasant rights (he was sometimes admiringly, sometimes derisively, known as king of the peasants), and Jewish merchants found great protection during his rule. As a result, the towns flourished and a great influx of Jews established Poland as a center of medieval Jewish civilization.

In 1370 Casimir died in a hunting accident, yet his code of law ensured an orderly transition of power, making his one of the few medieval monarchies where a ruler's death did not trigger a civil war or an invasion.

CASSIODORUS, FLAVIUS MAGNUS AURELIUS

Italian statesman, scholar, and educator. Cassiodorus was born around 487 C.E. into a prominent Calabrian senatorial family. He became involved in politics at an early age, serving as legal assessor to his father, as quaestor and secretary at ROME in 507, and as consul in 514. His talent and upbringing attracted the attention of the OSTROGOTH king THEODORIC, who in 526 employed Cassiodorus as the chief of his civil service (*magister officiorum*).

Cassiodorus was a skilled rhetorician, administrator, and public relations man; he served Theodoric briefly but well, justifying Theodoric's expropriation of Italian lands for his Ostrogothic army and composing works of propaganda for his reign, including a now lost *History of the Goths* (*De origine actibusque Getarum*), in which he hoped to provide the Goths with a heroic history that would impress a Roman population enamored with its own classical heritage. (In the history, he identified the GOTHS with the Scythians and Getes, ancient peoples of Greek mythology.)

Cassiodorus composed several other works while at the Ostrogothic court, most notably his *Variae Epistolae* (c. 537), a twelve-volume collection of official documents. After Theodoric's death in 526, Cassiodorus studied theology in CONSTANTINOPLE and Rome. In 544, he retired to his estate at Vivarium in southern Italy. He established two monasteries there where many classical works were copied and preserved, and he served as a scholar-patron of the schools until his death in c. 583 at the age of 93.

Cassiodorus was one of the first to conceive of the monastery as a center of both religious and classical learning. He composed a pedagogic manual in which he established the traditional division of the liberal arts curriculum into the *trivium* (three roads or disciplines) and the *quadrivium* (four), which together form the seven traditional liberal arts. This formulation was to influence education throughout the Middle Ages and reverberates in UNIVERSITIES to the present day.

CASTLES AND FORTIFICATIONS

The romantic image of medieval castles—all surrounded by moats and filled with lavish wealth, brave knights, and dignified nobles—is somewhat skewed. To be sure, many nobles had castles, surrounded by moats, and many castles' interiors were indeed sumptuously appointed. But this structure did not come into existence until the late Middle Ages. Castles evolved from relatively simple structures in response to the practical matter of protection from increasingly sophisticated weaponry.

Early Fortifications. Civilizations had devised means of protecting against invaders long before the medieval fortresses known as castles appeared. Fortifications were common in ancient Greece, ROME, and EGYPT, and in AFRICA and Mexico as well. The Great Wall of CHINA is a most noteworthy example.

The forerunners of the castle first appeared in Britain and Europe after the Fall of the Roman Empire. Relatively simple structures called burhs consisted of ditches and palisades (closely set fences of wooden stakes). Burhs were generally community efforts designed to protect the local citizenry. As FEUDALISM emerged and took hold throughout Europe, farmers and peasants fell under the control of local lords who maintained regional control. Power struggles and battles forced these lords to seek ways to protect their holdings (which usually included those peasants and farmers), and the construction of a fortified residence appealed to many. (The reason that surviving castles are usually located in relatively remote areas is that those in urban settings succumbed to development.)

The burh quickly gave way to the motte-and-bailey castle. These simple structures were effective means of protection until the twelfth century. These castles consisted of a mound (the "motte") on which a tower would be constructed, usually surrounded by a palisade. The motte, in turn, would be surrounded by a ditch (filled with water, or sometimes spikes), and the entire area would be surrounded by an earthen wall (the "bailey"). Some castles consisted of more than one motte, and a few even had more than one bailey.

Height was a key element in the placement of a motte-and-bailey castle. From the tower, soldiers could see enemy forces from a far enough distance that they could take precautions. The high walls were difficult to climb, and it was difficult to aim WEAPONS such as arrows with any real accuracy.

A Change in Construction. The motte-and-bailey castle served its purpose until the CRUSADES. European KNIGHTS returning from battle in the Middle East brought back Byzantine and Islamic military weapons that proved to be cruelly effective. Artillery weapons could hurl large rocks, along with pots full of a substance called Greek fire (whose composition is lost in antiquity) that burst into flame on impact. The wooden structure of the motte-and-bailey castle was no match for these weapons. (*See* WEAPONRY.)

Wood was now in shorter supply, too. Many ships had been built for the Crusades, and wood had also become a valuable trading commodity. Fortunately, the crusaders had come back with not only new weapon ideas, but new techniques for building castles out of stone. Stone castles were clearly more durable than wooden castles; they could withstand fire and heavy artillery, and they were more permanent.

Attackers rose to the challenge. They found that they could compromise castle walls through a process known as sapping—hollowing mines out underneath the walls, and then setting fires or lighting gunpowder in the mines. It was time-consuming, but the usual result was that a portion of wall would collapse from its own weight. In addition, enemy forces had devised new ladders and devices known as siege towers. These high wooden structures built on wheels could be rolled against castle walls, which the forces within could then easily scale. Often, attackers gained access to castles simply by forcing open wooden doors with huge battering rams. (*See* WARFARE.)

To discourage these attacks, castles were constructed with deep moats and drawbridges. Attackers could no longer sneak up on a castle. Some tried to fill moats with rocks and debris, thus creating a makeshift bridge. But the castle's inhabitants could retaliate by pouring hot oil or "Greek fire" on the would-be conquerors. The portcullis—a metal grate for castle entrances, operated by levers and pulleys—was developed to protect against enemy forces who forced their way through unprotected wooden doors with battering rams. (*See* ARCHITECTURE.)

Inside the Castle. Life inside a medieval castle was generally busy even during peaceful times. To get into the castle, a person would likely have to go through a gatehouse and cross a drawbridge. Inside the castle walls would be a self-contained community: stables, storerooms, an armory, a guardroom, living quarters, a kitchen, and a chapel. The donjon, or dungeon, was originally the name for the castle's tower. These towers (keeps) were used to house prisoners; later, the word "dungeon" came first to mean "prison" and later to denote underground prisons.

Medieval knights were often at war, but during peacetime they kept in shape by training for the next campaign in or near the castle. TOURNAMENTS became popular in Europe around the eleventh century; knights would participate in jousting matches, using axes or swords and lances. HUNTING was another popular pastime. Other forms of recreation were less violent, if not less hearty. Lavish feasts, often with musical accompaniment, were frequently prepared for residents and guests in the "great hall," the center of social life inside the castle.

Later History. Two factors led to the decline in castle construction in the late Middle Ages: the prohibitive cost, and the susceptibility of even the thickest castle walls to cannon fire. (*See* ARTILLERY.)

A 15th-century view of the Castle of Pierrefonds (from Dictionnaire d'Architecture *by Viollet-le-Duc) shows the typical features of a fortified castle—from the gate–drawbridge–porticullis entry to the loopholed windows for archers.*

The finest collection of surviving castles from the medieval period is to be found in the Loire Valley in northern FRANCE. There are also several remarkable medieval castles in WALES. Two crusader castles still stand at Acre in Israel and at Tyre in western Syria.

CATHARS

The Cathars, or Cathari, were members of a heretical Christian sect that took hold in the eleventh century and flourished in the eleventh and twelfth centuries throughout western Europe. As with most anti-Church movements during the Middle Ages, the Cathars were motivated by a disdain for what was perceived as a largely corrupt clergy. But they also promulgated beliefs beyond simply criticizing the established Christian church.

The Cathar movement grew out of several heretical movements from before the twelfth century, most notably the BOGOMIL movement of eastern Europe. Many of these groups believed in the concept of dualism (the equal division of the forces of good and evil in the world). All things spiritual, such as the soul, were good; all things material, including the human body, were evil.

Taking their name from the Greek *katharos* ("pure"), the new group began to establish itself in western Europe in the middle of the twelfth century. By the end of the century, the Cathar movement was flourishing in Flanders, GERMANY, FRANCE, and ITALY. In fact, they organized their own Church, with its own liturgy, doctrine, and clergy. Eventually there were 11 Cathar bishoprics, one in northern France, five in southern France, and the rest in Italy.

The Cathars, as believers in the impurity of the material world, claimed that the human soul must take as its aim the renewed communion with God, once it left the impure body in which it was encased. Cathars fasted frequently and were strict vegetarians. They shunned material possessions, and they were celibate. Many members of the nobility and the clergy joined the Cathar movement. In reality, there were two levels of Cathars—the "perfect" and the "believers." The perfect, who attained this state through an initiation ceremony called the *consolamentum*, were held to higher moral standards than the believers, who usually were from among the general population.

The Cathars also diverged from the established Church with regard to the sacraments, such as baptism and the Eucharist. Some questioned the veracity of the entire Old Testament. Jesus was regarded not as the Son of God but merely as an angel.

The Church worked vigorously to crush the Cathar movement, but it proved to be quite resilient.

Pope INNOCENT III launched the Albigensian crusade in 1209—a crusade that lasted 20 years. Pope GREGORY IX began a papal inquisition against the Cathars in 1233, imprisoning, torturing, and burning unrepentant Cathars at the stake. The movement was so popular, however, that it took generations to eradicate it. The last Cathar bishop was killed by the Inquisitors in 1321, yet there were remnants of the movement in Europe as late as the fifteenth century. (*See* ALBIGENSES *and* HERESY.)

CATHEDRALS AND CHURCHES

Any building used for Christian worship can be referred to as a church, and many of the earliest Christian places of worship were simply parts of domestic structures converted into churches. Even some pagan temples, such as the Pantheon in ROME, were converted into churches in the Middle Ages. But most medieval churches were built specifically for religious purposes, often on sites of previously pagan worship, simply because people were accustomed to gather there. In order for the mass to be performed, there had to be an altar, and from the end of the sixth century, every altar required a saint's relic in it in order to be consecrated.

Functions. Churches were built to serve basically two kinds of communities; religious and secular. The religious communities were those of monks and nuns living together under a rule, such as the Rule of St. Benedict (*See* BENEDICT OF NURSIA). Their monasteries were always built around a church, just as their lives were structured around church services.

The secular Church developed into a network of ecclesiastical units, ranging from local parishes to the dioceses overseen by bishops, and up to the pope in the West, and the patriarch in the East. Churches for the secular clergy included parish churches, noble or royal court churches, and cathedrals. The size and decorations of each church reflected the economic or political power of its community. Thus, parish churches tended to be small and simple, while the churches commissioned to serve a powerful noble or a king might be remarkably elaborate, as evidenced by CHARLEMAGNE's church at Aachen (*See* AIX-LA CHAPELLE), or Roger II's royal Cappella Palatina in Palermo.

A cathedral is defined as the home church of a bishop, the main place of worship of a diocese housing the bishop's throne, or "cathedra." A medieval cathedral was not necessarily larger or more ornate than a monastic church; in times and places where the monasteries held great power, their churches reflected that status (as, for example, Cluny Abbey in BURGUNDY).

By the twelfth and thirteenth centuries in Europe, when the secular clergy was overtaking the monasteries in power and wealth, the most impressive monuments were the cathedrals built by the bishops. (*See* GOTHIC ART AND ARCHITECTURE.)

In the Middle Ages, churches and cathedrals were considered to be more than just locations for religious rituals, more even than symbols of CHRISTIANITY or the power of the church. They were the "City of God," the Heavenly Jerusalem made sacred by the presence of the relics of saints, and by the perceived actual presence of God's grace. To enter a church was to take a step towards salvation, and the forms and decoration of the church—in STAINED GLASS, paint, and MOSAIC—furthered these larger symbolic meanings. No element of interior or exterior decoration was frivolous; they all added to the overall story being told to the faithful.

Church Types. Medieval churches can be divided into two types, basilican and central-plan. The basilican type dominated in western Europe, while the central-plan churches were more popular in the eastern Orthodox Byzantine Empire. Both types of church plans

grew out of the earliest churches built by CONSTANTINE I, the first Christian Roman emperor, in Rome, CONSTANTINOPLE, and Jerusalem, in the fourth century. These were, in turn, based on earlier architectural forms found in the pre-Christian Roman Empire.

By far the most widespread of the types, the basilican, is a rectangular building with an open center space, called the nave, flanked by side aisles separated from the nave by rows of columns. The roofs over the aisles are lower than the roof over the nave, where the colonnade supports a clerestory wall pierced by windows, which allow light into the central space. In its simplest form, a basilican church has a single, protruding semicircular apse at the far end of the nave. The altar is placed either in, or directly in front of, the apse, forming the focus for the religious rituals, the "liturgy." The entrance to the church is at the end opposite from the apse. An enclosed porch, the "narthex," is often placed before the entrance, with a courtyard in front of that. The earliest basilican churches were built with timber roofs. The earliest vaulted roofs appeared in the ROMANESQUE period.

During the early Christian period, before about 600 C.E., "occidented" churches were common—that is, with the apse facing west—but by the medieval period, most churches were "oriented," built with the apse facing east. The axis of the church carried symbolic meaning, and some occidented churches were built in the Middle Ages when the designers wished to evoke early Christian architecture.

Later Developments. Elaborations on the basic plan of basilicas continued throughout the Middle Ages, echoing an increasing complexity in the liturgy and in ways of worship, which made it necessary to divide the interior further, dedicating different areas to specific purposes. The widespread fascination with the cult of relics and the growing number of private masses and prayers for the dead led to a need for more altars. Multiple apses created private chapels; elaborate western towers and crypts added more altars and secluded spaces to worship. The interior was further expanded with the addition of an aisle running perpendicular to the nave, called a transept. By the GOTHIC period (1150–1550), it was placed in a position to create a cruciform building plan. Finally, the increase in pilgrim-

Above, the Cologne Cathedral, with the completed twin spires missing from many other Gothic cathedrals in Europe. At left, interior of the Laon Cathedral. Cathedrals were long-term projects that often took decades to build. The cathedral of Laon, for example, was begun in 1165 and not completed until 1200.

ages to view the saint's relics in each church necessitated a constant traffic flow. This was accomplished by extending the side aisles around the interior, creating the ambulatory. What also distinguished Gothic architecture (called the style of Paris in the twelfth and thirteenth centuries) was a raised clerestory from which light streamed through stained-glass windows onto the altar. The first such Gothic church, at St. Denis near Paris, was also distinguished by a rose window over the front doorway, symbolizing the Virgin Mary.

Some notable exceptions to the prevailing basilican planned church, such as the centrally planned Saint Mark's in Venice and Charlemagne's octagonal palace chapel at Aachen (Aix-la-Chapelle), may have been influenced by late antique models or by contemporary architecture in the Byzantine territories.

Churches and cathedrals in the Middle Ages were repositories of vast amounts of wealth—partly to ensure their salvation and partly as a show of power—reflected in their decoration and furnishings. The nobility poured riches into their local churches and commissioned lavish appointments such as stained-glass windows, gold fixtures, TAPESTRIES, and ornate vestments for the clergy.

See ARCHITECTURE *for a survey of styles. Specific schools are covered in* ROMANESQUE *and* GOTHIC ARCHITECTURE. *See entries on specific edifices:* CHARTRES; NOTRE DAME DE PARIS; SAINT-DENIS; *and* AIX-LA-CHAPELLE.

CATHERINE OF SIENA, ST.

C atherine of Siena (1347–1380) was an Italian mystic who became a patron saint of Italy (in 1939) and doctor of the Church (1970). She influenced Pope Gregory XI to hasten the end of the PAPACY's "Babylonian captivity" in AVIGNON.

She was born Caterina Benincasa in Siena and adopted severely ascetic practices early in life. Around 1364 she became a Dominican tertiary, taking vows but remaining secluded in her family's home until 1368, when a vision prompted her to begin an active apostolate. Her reputation as a saintly mystic soon attracted numerous followers. For them she composed a famed series of letters of spiritual instruction (dictated to "amanuenses"—scribes). Her rapid ascent to prominence was not without controversy. In 1374 she defended herself before a general chapter of the Dominican order in FLORENCE, which exonerated her and named Raymond of Capua her mentor.

In June of 1376 the city of Florence, then at war with the pope, sent Catherine to Avignon as an envoy to Gregory XI. She failed to secure peace but persuaded Gregory to return to ROME. Catherine had for some time been promoting a crusade, a project also favored by Gregory that depended on the pope's unchallenged control of Italy. When Gregory died in March 1378, there was no immediate prospect of peace. The election of Gregory's successor, URBAN VI, almost immediately precipitated the GREAT SCHISM, virtually ending any plan for a crusade. Catherine supported Urban's attempts to curtail corruption among the Church hierarchy, and from November 1378, she lived in Rome, working on Urban's behalf and writing her spiritual testament, the *Dialogue of Saint Catherine of Siena*. She died in Rome on April 29, 1380, and was canonized by Pope Pius II in 1461. Catherine of Siena is today regarded as one of the leading women writers of the Middle Ages. (*See* GREAT SCHISM.)

CAXTON, WILLIAM

P rinter of the first BOOKS in English to use GUTENBERG's printing press. Born around 1421, Caxton apprenticed with a mercer (fabric merchant) who taught him the intricacies of international commerce. By 1462, he had risen to the post of governor of the powerful trade association of English Merchant Adventurers in the Low Countries and had set up an office in Bruges. He began creating handwritten manuscripts as a sideline when he learned of the invention of the printing press by Johannes Gutenberg. He purchased a press in 1471 and joined forces with John Veldenen, a Cologne printer. The first book he published was his own translation from French of a history of the Trojan War, *Recuyell of the Historyes of Troye*, printed in 1474. In 1476 he moved to Westminster, where he published and sold books near Parliament. Among the 96 books he published until his death in 1491 are CHAUCER's *Canterbury Tales* and MALORY's *Morte d'Arthur*. He included his own critical analysis of the book, something a handwritten manuscript would never have contained, thus also making him the first English literary critic.

CELESTINE V

P ope from July 5 until December 13, 1294, and the first pope to abdicate. Pietro da Morrone was born in 1215 and, after a brief tenure as a Benedictine monk, became a hermit and preacher in the Abruzzi region of northern ITALY.

With a group of followers organized (with papal approval) as the Hermits of the Holy Spirit—the Celestine Order. When the College of Cardinals had been deadlocked for more than two years in their attempts to choose a successor to Nicholas IV (who died April 1292), he wrote to the cardinal of Ostia proclaiming that divine wrath would descend on the cardinals if they did not quickly elect a new pope.

The cardinals seized on the 80-year-old Pietro himself as the candidate. He was quickly elected and crowned Celestine V on August 29, 1294, despite the demurals of the cardinals of the Colonna family and his own disinclination. An unworldly ascetic with little education, Celestine was wholly unprepared for his pontifical duties and completely unskilled in administration. He spent his entire pontificate in the kingdom of NAPLES vulnerable to manipulation by Charles II of Naples and others. He did little beyond creating twelve new cardinals without informing the Curia, extending protection to the reformist FRANCISCAN Spirituals, and aggrandizing his own foundation. Celestine considered handing over his responsibilities to three cardinals in order to fast and pray during Advent, but instead abdicated, having been assured by Cardinal Benedetto Gaetani (who succeeded him as Pope Boniface VIII) that there were precedents for this step. Pietro was confined under house arrest (but not harshly) at a castle near Ferentino until his death on May 19, 1296; he was canonized on May 5, 1313.

CELTIC CHURCHES

Britain at the start of the Middle Ages was a largely abandoned Roman outpost and IRELAND had never been a part of the Roman Empire. Yet CHRISTIANITY took hold in the British Isles; what became known as the Celtic church flourished for several centuries. A number of missionaries spread Christianity throughout ENGLAND, SCOTLAND, WALES, and Ireland, and a strong monastic tradition developed in the region as well.

In England, Christianity was challenged by paganism and heathenism, but a number of Christian missionaries worked to convert the Angles, Saxons, and other English peoples. During the seventh century, ST. AUGUSTINE OF CANTERBURY, who established the archbishopric there, was able to convert the English region of Kent. Gradually, the people of regions such as East Anglia, Northumbria, and Essex were converted.

Celtic Christianity existed before the seventh century in a number of fairly remote places, such as the Scottish island of Iona (where ST. COLUMBA founded a religious community in 563) and along the rugged coasts of Scotland and Ireland.

Ireland, of course, traditionally claims that the fifth-century missionary ST. PATRICK brought Christianity to its shores. It is also likely that Ireland, which had trade with Rome, learned of Christianity in the course of its day-to-day commerce. The Irish Christians were influenced by British monasteries in England and Wales, and in the sixth century they began creating their own monasteries. Irish monks from such places of worship as Lindisfarne set about converting pagans in Scotland and northern England.

Celtic Christianity flourished in Ireland, and the Irish monks developed a reputation for scholarship. The Irish missionaries created extensive libraries and made beautiful illuminated manuscripts. The *Book of Durrow* dates from the late seventh century, and the famous BOOK OF KELLS dates from the late eighth century. By then, Christianity had taken root in much of England and Scotland. The last strongholds of paganism—Sussex and the Isle of Wight—were converted by the end of the seventh century. But much of the activity was Roman Christianity by now, and Celtic Christianity was slowly losing its influence. Part of the reason was that there was now better contact with Rome than there had been earlier. Differences between the Celtic and Roman Christians did not initially seem so marked, but there was controversy nonetheless. One issue—how the date of Easter Sunday was calculated—led to the Synod of Whitby in 664. Most Celtic Christians adopted the Roman formula, which led to the gradual acceptance of Roman Christianity in the region.

The Celtic cross, symbol of the Celtic Church, combines animistic symbols with Christian iconography.

In the relatively brief time the Celtic church held sway over British Christianity, it managed to have a significant impact. It was highly successful in converting non-Christians, and it encouraged scholarship while maintaining a sense of simplicity. Indeed, even as Roman influence became increasingly stronger, the Celtic influence never disappeared; today remnants of Celtic worship exist within the boundaries of Britain and Ireland. (*See* CELTIC LITERATURE; ST. PATRICK; ST. COLUMBA; *and* IRELAND.)

CELTIC LANGUAGE AND LITERATURE

More than 2,000 years ago the Celts inhabited much of northern Europe. A succession of invasions, first by the Romans and later by Germanic tribes, had pushed the Celts to the remotest reaches of western Europe by the Middle Ages. Notwithstanding their hardships, the Celtic people managed to retain their language and develop a literary and oral tradition that flourished for several centuries. (*See* CELTIC CHURCHES.)

Celtic Language. The languages of the Celts can be divided into two broad groups: the Brythonic (which includes Welsh, Cornish, and Breton) and the Gaelic, or Goidelic (which includes Manx, Irish, and Scots). Brythonic and Goidelic are also known as P-Celtic and Q-Celtic, respectively, because of a curious trait. Words derived from other languages would be spelled with a "p" in Brythonic and a "q" in Goidelic. The Indo-European word for horse, *epvos,* became *epos* in Brythonic, while to the Goidelic Celts the word was *eqous* (closer to the Latin *equus*).

Many Celts adopted Latin as a second language after the Roman invasions, especially after adopting CHRISTIANITY as their religion. But even after the German tribes crossed the North Sea in the fifth century and pushed the British Celts to IRELAND, SCOTLAND, and WALES, many refused to abandon their native tongue. (To this day, many people, particularly in Wales, are bilingual; speakers of Welsh can converse comfortably with speakers of Breton in the French region of Brittany.)

Celtic Literature. Both Brythonic and Goidelic literature exists from the Middle Ages, most of it from the later part of the period. This is not because the Celts lacked a literary tradition. Rather, it is because of their strong oral tradition of storytelling—particularly as practiced by the poets known as bards—that little appears to have been written down before the eleventh or twelfth centuries.

The bards were much more than mere wandering poets. They were specially trained is schools where they learned hundreds of poems and many styles of verse. Some bards trained for seven years. They would sing the poems they had learned, composing their own songs and verses to celebrate important events or to pay tribute to fallen leaders. Scholars believe that it is thanks to the bards of Wales and BRITTANY that the legendary stories of KING ARTHUR and his Knights of the Round Table survived in the Middle Ages.

The earliest written works in both Brythonic and Goidelic are Celtic names that appear in Latin inscriptions from the very early Middle Ages. Early Brythonic works from Wales date to the sixth century; the Welsh

An intricate monogram page from the Book of Kells. *The late 8th-century manuscript was produced on Iona and then deposited at the monastery of Kells in Ireland.*

wrote poems in praise of their leaders' bravery in the face of the ANGLO-SAXON invasions. One of the best known of these is the *Book of Aneirin* by the poet of the same name.

By the eleventh century, the Welsh had formed an independent nation, providing their bards with material and prestige. An outpouring of literature from this period includes the *Mabinogion,* a prose work that contains some material about King Arthur. The literary golden age ended when Wales became part of England in 1282. Meanwhile, Brythonic survived in France (where it became Breton) and in ENGLAND (where it became Cornish). Brittany's oral tradition helped spread the stories of King Arthur throughout Europe.

In Ireland, Goidelic tales were spread by oral tradition, though Irish monks maintained the practice of committing religious and secular tales and traditions to writing through the eleventh century. Goidelic also flourished in Scotland where bards were as popular as in Ireland. Many of the Scottish bards became hereditary poets for noble families, while others became historians and chroniclers. Toward the end of the Middle Ages, many of their poems were put to music.

CHALCEDON, COUNCIL OF

The Council of Chalcedon was one of the earliest ecumenical gatherings of the Christian Church. Convoked in 451 by the emperor Marcian, it took a number of important steps in establishing the Church as an organized institution.

This fourth ecumenical council was held in the maritime city of Chalcedon, located near CONSTANTINOPLE. It drew some 520 bishops and other Church representatives and was carefully documented. Although there had already been three councils, the Church was still relatively young and still in need of a fundamental administrative structure.

The council approved what would later be known as the Nicene Creed (which had been adopted at the COUNCIL OF NICAEA in 325), essentially an elaboration of the Apostles' Creed, which traditionally has been ascribed to the original Twelve Apostles; it is still part of many Christian services. It was also at this conclave that the divine nature of Jesus became an accepted doctrine of the Christian Church.

CHAMBERLAIN

The name in medieval western Europe for a royal officer responsible for domestic and financial affairs. The chamberlain was also often appointed to keep track of the finances of towns, cathedrals, and monasteries. The history of the word reflects a common medieval process by which a concept used for a merely private purpose developed into a public concept. In this case, a chamberlain was originally a servant or serf responsible for the care of the king's private room. The private office became public when chamberlains asserted responsibility for aspects of public finance, a change that occurred because the kingdom's treasury was often physically located in the king's chambers. (*See* TOWNS, VILLAGES, AND CITIES.)

The particular duties of chamberlains varied according to kingdom. The office of the chamberlain had the greatest power in the central European kingdom of BOHEMIA where its duties approached that of a minister of finance. In FRANCE, the chamberlain's duties were limited to the king's private estate. During ANGLO-SAXON dominance in ENGLAND (between the collapse of Roman rule and the Norman Conquest of 1066), the chamberlain was similarly responsible for the king's chambers and possessions. After the Norman Conquest, the chamberlain was responsible for the financing of war, while the newly created office of the EXCHEQUER handled peacetime finances. Eventu-

ally, the office became a purely ceremonial one, the main duty of which was to serve water to the king at the CORONATION ceremony and on feast days.

CHAMPAGNE, FAIRS OF

The fairs of Champagne were one of the original great fairs of the Middle Ages, and were a model for other fairs. In the twelfth century, the count Thibault began fairs in various towns of Champagne. They became popular with merchants as it was more convenient to travel rivers to Champagne than over northern land routes. Thibault's son Henry, who became count in 1152, continued his father's focus on Champagne, leading to 150 years of growth in the county. The fairs grew in size, sparking immigration into Champagne and expansion in the size of the towns and the local industries. However, in the fourteenth century, Champagne started to decay after it was incorporated into royal domains. In that century, the center of trade with the Mediterranean began to shift to the Atlantic coast, and the economy was undermined by the the disasters of the BLACK DEATH and the HUNDRED YEARS' WAR. By the fifteenth century, the county receded in importance. (*See* FAIRS.)

CHANSON DE GESTE

Epic medieval poems celebrating the exploits of legendary French heroes. Written in French instead of Latin, chansons de geste (plural) first appeared in the eleventh century and were widely popular. (*See* LITERATURE.)

The chansons were the artful creations of court poets and itinerant minstrel entertainers. The initial audience was the higher nobility, hence they included the heroic deeds of CHARLEMAGNE and other nobles. Although the people portrayed in the poems are often real, their deeds are frequently exaggerated in the interest of stressing heroic values and providing entertainment. Probably the best known is the *Chanson de Roland,* (*See* ROLAND), which recounts the heroic adventures and tragic death of Charlemagne's nephew. Another prominent chanson was the early twelfth-century *Raoul de Cambrai* which graphically describes the berserk behavior of a great lord after the emperor deprives him of his landed inheritance.

Originally simple in style, the chansons de geste became increasingly elaborate. While they dealt with valor and bravery, they also often included a comic element. Despite the exaggerations, they were considered by many to have true historical value by depicting the social life and cultural values of the nobility.

CHARLEMAGNE

Charles (742–814), who came to be known as the Great, or Charlemagne (*Karolus Magnus*), was the grandson of CHARLES MARTEL, and the eldest son of PÉPIN III THE SHORT (r. 751–768) and his wife Bertha. After Pépin secured the deposition of the last MEROVINGIAN king Childeric by enlisting the endorsement of Pope Zacharias, he was anointed king in 751. Three years later, in 754, when Pope Stephen II was forced into exile in FRANCE by the LOMBARDS, he reanointed Pépin and blessed and anointed his wife Bertha and their two sons, Charles and his younger brother Carloman. Pope Stephen also declared Pépin, Charles, and Carloman patricians.

His Reign. When Pépin died in 768, the Frankish lands were divided between Carloman and his brother Charles. In the three years before Carloman's death in 771, relations between him and Charles were strained. Their mother had Charles betrothed to the daughter of Desiderius, king of the Lombards, a step that dismayed the pope. After Carloman died, his widow and their sons took refuge with the Lombard king, whose daughter Charlemagne repudiated. Pope Stephen's visit to FRANCE resulted in Pépin's waging two campaigns against the Lombards, in 754 and 756. In 774, Charlemagne returned, decisively conquered the Lombards, capturing their king, as well as his brother, Carloman's widow, and their sons, who were never able to claim their father's lands. In ROME, Charlemagne confirmed the donation his father had made to the pope, which recognized the pope's rights to certain lands—

perhaps all Italy—as successor of the Roman emperors. The famous Donation of Constantine, in which the emperor Constantine promised the pope dominion over Rome and ITALY, may have been forged in the papal Curia to encourage Pépin and Charlemagne to vanquish the Lombards.

The determination and severity that Charlemagne exhibited in his pursuit of the Lombards characterized the other wars he fought. His favorite book was SAINT AUGUSTINE'S *City of God* and, like Augustine, he perceived the world as divided into the saved and the damned, the good and the bad. He battled the SAXONS for more than thirty years. At one point, having 4,000 free men killed to punish a revolt, he finally imposed conversion to Christianity as a condition of peace.

Conquests. In 778, Charlemagne led an army across the Pyrenees and obtained hostages from the SARACEN leaders there. On his return, the Basques ambushed and slaughtered the rearguard of his army, and ROLAND, lord of the Breton marshes, perished. This defeat was immortalized in the *Song of Roland,* composed by 1100, commemorating Roland's death.

In the next decade Charlemagne fought in BRITTANY and Italy. He was then forced to deal with rebellion in BAVARIA. In 787 he forced his cousin, Duke TASSILO, to surrender, enter his vassalage, and provide hostages, recalling the similar submission Tassilo had been forced to make to Pépin in 757. Tassilo foolishly rebelled again, attempting to enlist the AVARS as allies. An assembly of magnates condemned him to death in 788 (although in the end Charlemagne permitted him and his family to enter monasteries). By 796, Charle-

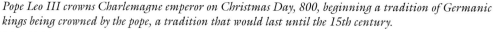

Pope Leo III crowns Charlemagne emperor on Christmas Day, 800, beginning a tradition of Germanic kings being crowned by the pope, a tradition that would last until the 15th century.

magne had conquered the AVARS and seized their fabulous treasure. For his lightening-swift campaigns, he drew on a force that comprised some 15,000 horsemen and a far greater number of foot soldiers.

In 800, Charlemagne received Pope LEO III after he had been attacked in Rome and had him restored to power. Having arrived in Rome in November, Charlemagne witnessed the pope's sworn denial of charges that had been brought against him. Then, on Christmas Day, in the basilica of Saint Peter, the pope crowned Charlemagne emperor of the Romans. Charlemagne's biographer EINHARD said that Charlemagne would never have entered the church had he known what was to happen. Charlemagne may indeed have regretted the impression of papal superiority the ceremony conveyed. Before his death, on September 13, 813, he himself crowned his son Louis as emperor Augustus, even though in 781, when Louis was three, he had had him crowned and anointed as king of AQUITAINE by Pope Adrian I. Whatever Charlemagne's misgivings, the imperial CORONATION transformed the conception of the office and its responsibilities. Its title identified him as "most serene, august, crowned by God, great and peace-loving emperor, governing the Roman empire by the mercy of God, king of the FRANKS and Lombards." Charlemagne saw his empire as a revival of the Roman, and he was saluted as a new CONSTANTINE or JUSTINIAN.

His military exploits continued. He waged war in Bohemia. Between 804 and 810, he fought the Danes, a struggle his successors would continue for a century and more. Before and after the imperial coronation he exchanged embassies with the Byzantine court, and with HARUN AL-RASHID of Persia, who offered him the fabled gift of an elephant.

Religious Reform. Inspired by the visit of Pope Stephen and his clerics to France, Charlemagne, following his father, encouraged monastic and liturgical reform. He aimed to achieve uniformity of observance throughout the kingdom, substituting Roman for Gallican usage. However ALCUIN of York and Amalarius of Metz, his liturgical advisors, acknowledged the necessity of tolerating and sometimes authorizing exceptions and variations. Charlemagne did not hesitate to become involved in and make pronouncements on doctrinal issues. At his command, Archbishop THEODULF of Orléans prepared the *Libri Carolini* to endorse the didactic and inspirational value of images while decrying their adoration, a position Charlemagne and Theodulf believed the Byzantine church endorsed. Under Charlemagne, the singing of royal lauds (*Laudes regie*) was introduced. The acclamations exalted the king and linked him, his family, and the army of the Franks with God, Christ, archangels, saints, and the Church.

Charlemagne had great admiration for learning; although he could not write, he knew Latin and understood Greek. He encouraged the fine, admirably clear script that came to be known as CAROLINGIAN miniscule. He encouraged scholars and attracted them to the court he established at Aachen (known also as AIX-LA-CHAPELLE). Dedicated to Frankish culture, he wore Frankish garb. He attempted to preserve Frankish sagas and reformed the law codes of the Franks to promote a juster and more cohesive society.

Charlemagne turned his attention to the problems of administering a large empire and devised several practices toward that end: the capitularies—detailed instructions—clarified the roles of government functionaries throughout the empire and made extensive use of MISSI DOMINICI (literally, "those sent out by the lord") to communicate with local officials. He also convened general assemblies and ecclesiastical synods.

Pope Stephen's blessing of Pépin and his family in 754 at Saint-Denis solidified the ties between the Carolingians and the abbey. Charles Martel had been buried there, and so too was Pépin. Charlemagne claimed credit for rebuilding the church, which was dedicated in 775. He had a porch constructed over the grave of his father and mother, which lay at the church's threshold because of Pépin's belief that bodies should not be buried within churches. Charlemagne expressed his own desire to be interred at Saint-Denis, although in the end he was buried with great magnificence in the splendid octagonal chapel he had constructed at Aachen. In 811, three years before he died, he drew up a will, endowing the 21 metropolitan sees of the realm, providing for his family and servants, and leaving enormous bequests to the poor. Saint Peter's in Rome was left a gold-and-silver table engraved with a map of Constantinople; the bishopric of RAVENNA was given a similar table with a map of Rome. In the will, Charlemagne raised the possibility of abdicating in favor of his son, but in fact he ruled until he died. He was succeeded by his only surviving son Louis, whom he instituted as his successor in 813. By then Charlemagne's other sons had died, thus preventing the division of the realm that would otherwise have taken place in 814, and which in fact, disastrously, occurred at the death of LOUIS I THE PIOUS in 840.

Legends regarding Charlemagne multiplied after his death. A twelfth-century Latin work, *History of Charlemagne and Roland,* mistakenly attributed to Turpin of Reims, was translated into the vernacular and was popular for several centuries.

See FRANKS; FRANCE; CHRISTIANITY; AIX-LA-CHAPELLE; MISSI DOMINICI; *and* EINHARD. *For additional information, see* PÉPIN III THE SHORT; ALCUIN; CAROLINGIAN DYNASTY; LOUIS I THE PIOUS; *and* CORONATION.

CHARLES I OF ANJOU

Charles I (1227–1285), king of NAPLES and SICILY for the last 20 years of his life, was the younger brother of King LOUIS IX of FRANCE and founder of the first ANGEVIN dynasty in NAPLES. Charles became the count of Anjou at age 20 as well as the ruler of Provence through marriage. He accompanied his brother Louis to EGYPT on a CRUSADE, which lasted from 1248 to 1250. (He accompanied Louis to Tunisia on a second crusade in 1270.)

Charles's rule over Provence allowed him to extend his influence into Piedmont. While a senator of ROME from 1265 to 1278, he supported the PAPACY in its war against the HOHENSTAUFENS over the Kingdom of NAPLES and SICILY. Pope Clement IV crowned Charles its king in 1266. Later that same year Charles defeated FREDERICK II's illegitimate son Manfred at the battle of Benevento. Two years later, he captured and killed Conradin, the last surviving member of the dynasty. As leader of the pro-papal GUELPH party, Charles exercised considerable political influence in ITALY, winning control over several cities in Tuscany, Lombardy, and Piedmont. Charles held the kingdom of Sicily as a papal fief, but his high-handedness in Italian politics eventually soured his relations with the pope. (*See* ANGEVIN; *and* HOHENSTAUFEN DYNASTY.)

Hoping to establish his own empire, Charles allied himself with the deposed Byzantine emperor BALDWIN II against Michael VIII. For years Charles waged military campaigns in the Balkans. He captured Corfu, Epirus, and Albania, but he was not able to hold on to Sicily. He alienated the people of Sicily with his oppressive taxes, transference of the capital from Palermo to Naples, and use of French officials to govern Sicily. His policies ignited the rebellion known as the SICILIAN VESPERS in 1282. Two years later the Sicilians succeeded in driving Charles from the island. Charles died in 1285 while making plans to repossess the island.

The war against the Sicilian rebels and Peter III of Aragon, whom the rebels chose as their king, continued under Charles's son and successor, Charles II.

CHARLES IV OF LUXEMBOURG

Charles (1316–1378) was Holy Roman Emperor (1355–1378), German king and king of BOHEMIA (1346–1378), who did much to bring about the golden age of Bohemia, making PRAGUE the cultural and political center of the HOLY ROMAN EMPIRE. Charles was a skilled diplomat, able to expand his dynastic holdings without engaging in needless WARFARE. He was also a generous patron of the arts and sciences, bringing some of the leading artists and thinkers of the time to his court, as well as a supporter of religious reform and lay pietism.

Born the eldest son of John of Luxembourg, the blind king of Bohemia, Charles was sent to the French court in 1323, where he married Blanche, the sister of Philip VI of France. While there, he also befriended the future pope, CLEMENT VI, who would be of great service in securing his future election to the German throne. Charles was summoned back to Luxembourg by his father in 1330 and given a number of important diplomatic and administrative positions. Tension arose between father and son due to Charles's obvious administrative superiority, but the two were eventually reconciled. In 1343, John, now almost completely blind, appointed Charles regent of his kingdom. The following year, Charles convinced Pope Clement to raise Prague to the status of an archbishopric, granting his Bohemian lands ecclesiastical independence.

In light of his accomplishments as regent, Charles became a candidate for the German crown and a leading opponent of the reign of Emperor Louis IV of Bavaria. The German princes rejected Louis in 1346; encouraged by Pope Clement, they elected Charles in his place. However, Charles was unable to accept the crown until 1347; Louis still maintained that he was the rightful king. When later that year Charles's father John was killed in the BATTLE OF CRÉCY, and Charles was wounded and nearly captured, his reputation suffered considerably. Charles was crowned in Bonn (as Charles IV), not in Aachen, because the latter, an imperial city, sided with Louis. However, Louis and Charles never confronted each other; Louis died in October 1347, and Charles was able to win over his supporters without violence, granting them privileges to towns in southern GERMANY.

At first, Charles was considered little more than a puppet of the pope, but soon showed himself a gifted and able monarch. Charles first turned his attention to his hereditary lands of Bohemia, although he was also recognized as the undisputed German king. He was crowned king of Bohemia in 1346 by the new archbishop in Prague, and immediately began to institute administrative reform, making Bohemia into a hereditary monarchy. He made Prague his capital, founding a university there in 1348 (the first in central Europe); he also oversaw the construction of numerous churches and monasteries. He encouraged Germans and other foreigners to settle in Prague, giving it a more imperial, cosmopolitan air. When Charles died in 1378, Prague was the largest city east of the Rhine with over 40,000 inhabitants. He also had increased the size of Bohemia, acquiring the territories of Lusatia, Silesia, Moravia, and the Upper Palatine.

In Germany, Charles encouraged the *Landfrieden*—the local peace associations—and signed territorial treaties with the HABSBURGS in AUSTRIA and the Arpads in HUNGARY. Charles also challenged the authority of the house of Wittelsbach, dukes of Bavaria and marquises of Brandenburg, and tried to check the power of the free cities in Germany. Charles's reign was not without its calamities, however; the BLACK DEATH devastated Germany and Charles was unable to prevent the violent anti-Semitic riots that followed.

Charles journeyed to ROME in 1354, and the next year, he was crowned emperor. He stayed in Rome for only one day, however, before returning to Prague, foregoing the enticement of Italian and papal politics. In 1356, Charles issued a new imperial constitution, the Golden Bull, which formalized the procedure for the election of the German king. The king would be elected by a majority vote of the College of Seven Electors: the archbishops of Mainz, Trier, and Cologne; the duke of Saxony; the margrave of Brandenburg; the count-palatine of the Rhine; and above them all, the king of Bohemia. These electors became almost independent rulers within their domains.

Charles' final project was ensuring the succession of his son Wenceslas to the German throne, achieved in 1378. Wenceslas did not inherit his father's sagacity or diplomatic skills, however, and his rule was marred by frequent rebellions of the Bohemian nobility. Charles's second son Sigismund became emperor in 1411, the last of the Luxemburg dynasty. Charles died in 1378 and was buried in Prague, the city that bore testament to his distinguished reign.

CHARLES V THE WISE

Charles (1337–1380), son of King John II the Good became the first French heir apparent to bear the title of dauphin after the area of Dauphiné was added to the royal domain in 1349. Charles became the kingdom's regent while he was still in his teens after the English captured his father at the Battle of Poitiers in 1356. As regent he dealt successfully with the revolt of the JACQUERIE and the popular uprising headed by Étienne Marcel, who armed PARIS against royal rule.

Charles entered into negotiations for the release of his father and was forced to agree to the treaty of Brétigny, which ceded large amounts of southwestern FRANCE to ENGLAND and demanded a ransom of three million gold crowns for the release of the king. After Charles became king in 1364, he cracked down on the marauding bands of discharged soldiers who had been ravaging the countryside and adopted a tougher stance toward the English. With the guidance and support of General BERTRAND DU GUESCLIN, Charles restored order in the French countryside and strengthened royal authority by assembling an army and a royal navy. He won back much of the land he and his father had been forced to cede to the English. He also reformed the coinage and instituted financial reforms that gave the crown greater fiscal authority.

Charles earned the title "the Wise" because he was a patron of the arts. He established the royal library and renovated the Louvre. During the last year of his life, he sided with Pope Clement VII against Pope URBAN VI at the beginning of the GREAT SCHISM. He died in 1380 and was succeeded by his son, Charles VI.

CHARLES VII OF FRANCE "LE BIEN-SERVI"

During the long reign (1422–1461) of King Charles VII of France (1403–1461) the French succeeded in ending the HUNDRED YEARS' WAR by driving the English out of FRANCE. Although the Treaty of Troyes prohibited Charles from assuming the throne, he assumed the royal title at the age of 19 after his father, the demented King Charles VI, died in 1422. Under John of Lancaster, duke of Bedford, who was acting as regent for King Henry VI, the English controlled northern France and AQUITAINE; Charles therefore, could lay claim only to France south of the Loire River. He had neither the will nor the resources to challenge English domination until the appearance of the charismatic French peasant girl, JOAN OF ARC. (*See* HUNDRED YEARS' WAR.)

Joan was the spark that ignited the French cause and turned Charles's career around. In 1429, she helped break the English siege of Orléans and then led a victorious march of French forces to Reims through territory previously held by the English. In 1430, with Joan of Arc standing nearby, Charles was crowned king in the Reims cathedral, the traditional site of French coronations. Afterward, when Joan was captured by the Burgundians and turned over to the English, Charles did little to help her (hence the note of irony in his sobriquet, "*le bien-servi*"—the Well-Served). She was tried and convicted of HERESY by a Church court in the English-held city of Rouen, then burned at the stake on May 30, 1431. (*See* JOAN OF ARC.)

In 1435, Charles made an alliance with the powerful duke of BURGUNDY, Philip the Good, a longtime ally of the English, which turned the tide. The French recaptured Paris in 1436, Cherbourg in 1450, driving the English out of Normandy. They finally defeated the English at Castillon in 1453. Charles's last years were marred by intrigues of his son, who succeeded him to the throne in 1498 as King LOUIS XI.

Charles the Bold, duke of Burgundy, on his throne, holding court, surrounded by his barons.

CHARLES THE BOLD

Charles (1433–1477) was the son and successor of Philip the Good and the last reigning duke of Burgundy (1467–77). He was count of Charolais and ruled BURGUNDY during his father's last illness. He opposed the growing power of the French king, LOUIS XI, and after his accession to the duchy in 1467, he allied himself with ENGLAND by marrying King EDWARD IV's sister.

Charles extended Burgundian rule as far as the Rhine River. Besides Burgundy, Charles ruled FLANDERS, Artois, Brabant, Holland, Luxembourg, Zeeland, and Friesland. By conquering the areas which linked his possessions, Charles became master of the Low Countries. His expanding power led to a confrontation with the Holy Roman emperor Frederick III, and the Swiss cantons worried that the expansion of Burgundian power would upset the balance of power in Europe. In 1477, Charles was killed in a battle against Lorraine and the Swiss outside Nancy. The once powerful state of Burgundy which he ruled ceased to exist after his heiress, Mary of Burgundy, lost some of her possessions to FRANCE and the rest to the HABSBURGS through her marriage to Maximilian.

CHARLES MARTEL

Charles Martel (c. 688–741) was the illegitimate son of Pepin II of Héristal, and mayor of the palace of the eastern portion of the MEROVINGIAN realm (Austrasia). His then-novel name, Charles, related to the English earl and German *Kerl*, signifying "staunch soldier," was passed on to many of his descendants. From him or his grandson, the Emperor Charles the Great (CHARLEMAGNE; reigned 771–814), it came to identify their dynasty, the CAROLINGIAN. His surname—derived from Old French for hammer—was bestowed upon him in the ninth century because of his military triumph over an invading Islamic army near Poitiers in 732. Never king, he exercised the office of mayor of the palace (*major domus*), which his forebears, the Arnulfings (so-called from their ancestor Saint Arnulf of Metz, who died c. 645) and Pippinids, had exercised. This office was the most important in the kingdom, and Charles's father expanded its importance, dominating the Merovingian puppet kings he served and extending his control over the kingdoms of Neustria and BURGUNDY.

Early Career. Pepin died in 714, but to succeed his father, Charles Martel had to overcome the threat posed by Pepin's widow Plectrud and her grandsons, since Charles Martel himself was the son of a wife or concubine of Pepin of Liège. By 718, aided by noble allies, Charles had triumphed, gaining not only his father's office, but also the treasure that Pepin II had amassed. In 719, he vanquished the Neustrians and their ally Odo of AQUITAINE. He retrieved the Merovingian Chilperic II (reigned 715–721), who had fled to join Odo in 717. Charles had to engage in continual struggles to maintain his power and was forced to tolerate the autonomy of various princes, secular and ecclesiastical. The extent to which he drew on the wealth of the Church to support the armies he raised is debated. He attacked and despoiled the lands of Bishop Eucherius of Orléans, and he was censured for this. It was, however, Charles's son and successor, Pepin, who in 741 seized most of the lands the bishop had controlled. Still, by the ninth century it was convenient to blame Charles Martel for all losses of Church property that had taken place since his day.

The Merovingian kings Chilperic II and his successor Theuderic IV (reigned 721–737) were mere figureheads, although they had talismanic utility when armies had to be raised. These armies were led by Charles Martel. He attacked the SAXONS, Alemans, and Bavarians. As a result of his campaigns, in 734 the pagan Frisians were said to be close to extinction. He erected fortresses and colonized border regions. He encouraged the missionary activity of the English Wynfrith (680–754), commissioned in 719 by Pope Gregory II (reigned 715–732) to bring Roman CHRISTIANITY to GERMANY and given the name Boniface. Charles Martel's most spectacular success was his victory near Poitiers in 732, where he triumphed over an invading Islamic army from SPAIN. Although in 721

Odo of Aquitaine had repulsed the ARABS before Toulouse, this victory was not decisive, and in 732 Odo appealed for Charles' aid. After his victory, Charles used his army not to pursue the Arabs, but to attack some unruly bishops, including Eucherius of Orléans. In later years, Charles himself became the plunderer of Aquitaine and Provence, especially after the death of Odo in 735. He razed cities and laid waste to the countryside in campaigns that recalled his conquest of Bavaria, Burgundy, and Saxony.

In 739, Pope Gregory III (reigned 731–41) sent an embassy to Charles to present him with gifts that included keys to the tomb of Saint Peter in hopes of gaining his aid in the papal conflict with the LOMBARDS. The Lombard king, Liutprand, had come to Charles's aid in Provence, however, and had made Charles's son Pepin his adoptive son-in-arms. Thus, although Charles sent an embassy to ROME, he does not seem to have responded positively to the pope's request. Within fifty years, however, Pepin and his son Charlemagne would accomplish the destruction of the Lombards, which the popes considered essential to their survival. (*See* LOMBARDS.)

Ruler of the Franks. In 737, the Merovingian king Theuderic died. From then until his death in 741, Charles Martel ruled alone, as chief (*princeps*) of the FRANKS, without a king. Realizing that the united kingdom he had created would be threatened after his death, he planned its division. He first decided to divide it between Carloman and Pepin, the sons borne by his first wife, Chrotrud. Shortly before his death, however, he decided to endow his son Grifo, the son of his second wife, a Bavarian, who also bore him a daughter Chiltrud. Because of this decision, the power Charles Martel had amassed was threatened with dissipation after his death. Grifo was imprisoned by his brothers, and his lands divided along lines that mingled Neustria and Austrasia. In hopes of legitimizing their rule, particularly after their sister married Duke Odilo of Bavaria, Carloman and Pepin revived the kingship, raising Childeric III, son of Chilperic II, to the throne in 743. In that year Carloman and Pepin conquered their brother-in-law Odilo, but Carloman abdicated in 747, retiring to a monastery in Italy, and Pepin freed Grifo, who fomented discord in Bavaria and in Italy. The installation of Odilo's son (Pepin's nephew) TASSILO as duke of Bavaria in 749 did not produce peace there. In 757, following a rebellion, Tassilo and the magnates of Bavaria were forced, in sign of subjection, to commend themselves to Pepin "in vassalage". Only when, in 751, Pepin secured Childeric's deposition and his own anointing as king, did Charles Martel's ambitions for his line begin to be realized. (*See* MEROVINGIAN DYNASTY; FRANKS.)

Charles Martel was especially devoted to the abbey of SAINT-DENIS, doubtless because the Merovingians had favored the Church. He had his sons educated at the abbey, and ordered his own burial there. Although other graves were marked at most by simple inscriptions, he was interred in a marble or alabaster sarcophagus, located north of the main altar. When the abbey's royal bodies were moved and reinterred under splendid new tombs in the 1260s, Charles Martel's was placed in the royal line of Merovingians and Carolingians south of the main altar. His effigy was adorned with a crown and the inscription *Karolus Martellus Rex* (King Charles Martel), thus elevating him to a rank he had never held, and distinguishing him from Count Hugh the Great of Paris (d. 956), buried beneath a flat stone identifying him simply as count of Paris and father of HUGH CAPET (reigned 987–996), founder of the CAPETIAN DYNASTY. (*See* CAPET, HUGH; CAPETIAN DYNASTY.)

Despite the honor paid to Charles Martel at Saint-Denis, his memory suffered. By the mid-ninth century, his tomb was said to have been opened by Abbot Fulrad (d. 784), and a hideous dragon supposedly emerged from a blackened, charred, and otherwise barren coffin, thus demonstrating Martel's damnation, incurred for despoiling the Church of its property. Later historians at Saint-Denis tried to palliate the legend by saying that he had taken Church lands only temporarily and had intended eventually to reimburse and further enrich the Church. (*See* SAINT-DENIS.)

CHARTRES, CATHEDRAL OF

T he cathedral at Chartres (southwest of Paris) is best known for its magnificent STAINED GLASS windows. Architecturally, it is one of the most important GOTHIC structures in Europe. The main portion of the cathedral was built in less than 30 years; typically cathedrals took over 100 years to build.

The cathedral (correctly called Notre Dame de Chartres) stands on the site of an older cathedral devastated by fire in 1194, leaving only the crypt, the base of the towers, and the western facade. The old cathedral had been built in the ROMANESQUE style, characterized by thick, heavy walls and small windows.

When work began on the new cathedral, the Gothic style (which was called the Style of Paris in the late twelfth century) was flourishing—a style that included high vaults supported by flying buttresses, and larger windows. (Large windows were particularly intriguing to architects, since the smaller Romanesque windows let in almost no light.) The stained-glass windows of the cathedral were donated by several GUILDS involved in the construction; they thus depict craftsmen at work on the building as well as biblical scenes.

CHAUCER, GEOFFREY

Not until Shakespeare did any English writer approach the fame and reputation of Geoffrey Chaucer (c. 1340–1400). Chaucer's masterpiece, the *Canterbury Tales*, remains one of the most well-known and widely studied works of medieval English literature. Chaucer appeared late in the Middle Ages, and his writings presaged the Renaissance. His works, particularly the *Canterbury Tales,* have influenced countless authors over the past 600 years.

Chaucer, from a manuscript of Thomas Hoccleve's poem De regimine.

Early Life. The details of Chaucer's early life are somewhat vague, but it is known that he was born in LONDON around 1340. His father, John Chaucer, was a successful London wine merchant. Long considered the language of the wine trade, it is likely that Chaucer first learned French (in which he was fluent) from his father. In 1357 he became a page in the household of Lionel, duke of Clarence. Soon afterward, he served in the army of EDWARD III against FRANCE in the HUNDRED YEARS' WAR. Captured by the French in 1360, Chaucer was held for ransom, which Edward paid. Upon his return, Chaucer remained a part of Edward's royal court. He met his future wife, Philippa Roet, who was a lady-in-waiting to Edward's wife and later the sister-in-law of Prince JOHN OF GAUNT. They married around 1366, and John of Gaunt became Chaucer's patron. By now Chaucer's position in the court was well established, and King Edward granted him an income for life.

ILLUMINATIONS

The Wife of Bath

Chaucer writes much about middle-class women, portraying them as autonomous, promiscuous, greedy, and difficult. His most memorable character is the often-married Wife of Bath. Her thoughts on the subject are captured in her prologue in *The Canterbury Tales:*

"Wedding's no sin, so far as I can learn. Better it is to marry than to burn...I know that Abraham was a holy man And Jacob too—I speak as best I can—Yet each of them, we know, had several brides, Like many another holy man besides. Show me a time or text where God disparages Or sets a prohibition upon marriages."

Travels and Writings. Chaucer spent the next several years traveling on diplomatic missions, many of them to France, where Chaucer read a great deal of French poetry. During trips to ITALY, he may have made the acquaintance of BOCCACCIO and PETRARCH, although there is no proof that he met either. But he was introduced to their writings, along with the works of DANTE—all of whom would influence his own work.

When Chaucer first began writing poetry he followed the French model, writing primarily about the pleasures of COURTLY LOVE. Later, he translated the famous French poem the *Roman de la Rose.*

Chaucer's first notable work was the *Book of the Duchess,* written around 1370 to honor John of Gaunt's wife, who had died in 1369. Although the French influence is still evident in this poem, it displayed an originality of form and content that helped establish Chaucer's reputation as a storyteller.

More original works followed: *The House of Fame* describes the joys of scholarship, and *The Parliament of Fowls* celebrates love (indirectly). Chaucer also continued to translate the works of others—notably, BOETHIUS's *On the Consolation of Philosophy.*

As a member of the artistic and literary entourage of his patron, John of Gaunt, duke of Lancaster, Chaucer carried out diplomatic assignments for the Crown and the Lancastrian family in France and Italy. Chaucer's wife was the sister of one of John of Gaunt's prominent mistresses, and she herself may have been the duke's mistress for a short time. Chaucer was once accused of rape in a judicial case brought by a young woman. As far as historians can establish, the case never came to trial, and the plaintiff was probably bought off.

In 1374, Chaucer was named customs controller for the port of London, which meant less travel and more time for writing. It was during this time that he wrote the masterful poem "Troilus and Criseyde," based on the tragic love story of the fictional Trojan war hero Troilus and the beautiful Cressida, who leaves Troy to join her father when he defects to the Greeks, and who later betrays Troilus's love. Other writers, notably Boccaccio, had written about this ill-fated pair (Chaucer may have used Boccaccio's story as a model), but Chaucer's treatment of the complexity of emotions between the lovers made his version noteworthy.

The Canterbury Tales. In the years following his wife's death in 1385, Chaucer composed his masterpiece, the *Canterbury Tales.* Based loosely on Boccaccio's *Decameron* and constructed in both prose and rhyming couplet, it describes a group on a religious pilgrimage who entertain each other by telling stories. The work presents a cross-section of medieval society (Boccaccio characters were all young and wealthy), and contains a healthy dose of satire. (*See* BOCCACCIO.)

Chaucer is buried in WESTMINSTER ABBEY.

CHILDREN'S CRUSADE

Whether there was an actual "Children's Crusade" during the Middle Ages remains unclear; the legend of this unusual occurrence dates from the thirteenth century. As with most legends, it is based somewhat on fact—but in all likelihood there was no great march across Europe of crusading youngsters.

According to the legend, a boy prophet led thousands of children from FRANCE and GERMANY to the Mediterranean, where he promised to part the sea as Moses had done, allowing the "crusade" to march to Jerusalem. The sea was not parted, of course, and there are different accounts of what happened to the would-be crusaders. One version has them gaining passage on merchant ships, but then being shipwrecked. Another has them being sold into slavery.

The legend is based on one of two movements that did occur around 1212. The first was a march, led by a German boy named Nicholas, of some 7,000 individuals from the Rhineland through the Alps, ultimately stopping at GENOA. From there, some went to France, while others went south into ITALY. But there was no crusade. The second movement was led by a boy named Stephen, who wanted to deliver a letter supposedly written by Jesus Christ to the French king. Starting north of PARIS, the boy attracted some 30,000 followers. The king dispersed the crowd when it arrived in Paris and ordered the people to return home. While there may have been some children in both movements, most historians now believe that the crusaders were drawn from the peasant class, and it was their simplicity and innocence that invited the comparison with children. (*See also* PETER THE HERMIT.)

CHINA

The dawn of the Middle ages coincided with the rise of the Second Chinese Empire, which attempted to bring stability and order to the often chaotic kingdom. Through a series of well-designed governmental and social structures, China developed an important presence in the Eurasian community, and cast its influence over much of the rest of the Western world.

Sui Dynasty. The Second Chinese Empire grew out of the remnants of the collapse of the northern Wei dynasty in the late 500s. In 577, the Pei Chou dynasty in northern China had conquered the northeastern dynasty in an attempt to reunify northern China. One of the nobles in the Pei Chou court, Wen Ti, seized the throne for himself in 578. Within a decade he had defeated the southern Ch'en capital on the Yangtze river, and reunited north and south China, thus beginning the Sui dynasty.

Wen Ti was a powerful but highly insecure monarch, given to violent fits and killing several of his aides. Savvily, he used religion as a way to unify and not divide, allowing Confucianism, Taoism, and a new religion—Buddhism—to flourish in his kingdom. He also unified his people by codifying a new legal code for the country combining elements of existing northern and southern laws.

Wen Ti revised the Chinese government structure. He established a civil service examination system to create a merit- and intelligence-based government, and to weaken the existing aristocracy. His administration consisted of three departments with just six ministries, cutting down on excess bureaucracy; his prefects controlled a small number of districts. Wen Ti also revised the census system, which changed the amount of taxes collected.

Militarily, Wen Ti strengthened Chinese defenses in the north, defending China from the eastern Turks, who then controlled Manchuria. Wen Ti sought to divide and conquer the MONGOL population.

Wen Ti's successor, Yang Ti, began his reign (604–617) by continuing most of his father's legal reforms. Having married into a southern royal family and having been an official in a southern province, he was, like Wen Ti, committed to bringing northern and southern China together. He continued the civil service testing, helping southern elites to enter Chinese politics. He built a second capital, Lo Yang, in the East to weaken powerful territories in the northwest.

Yang Ti's greatest legacy was China's canal system, which by 610, connected eastern Lo-yang to Chaing-tu and the Huai River. These canals were used in three battles with Manchuria, but they proved costly in time, money, and manpower.

Yang Ti had an active foreign policy, initiating diplomatic relations with Taiwan and JAPAN, and trade with Central Asia and the West. He attempted to weaken the dominant Turks in the northwest by supporting their opponents. He sued for peace with eastern Turks (many Chinese intermarried with eastern Mongols), but tensions increased in 612 when one of Yang Ti's aides tried to overthrow the Eastern Khanate.

The battles with Manchuria were costly, and the defeats added to internal unrest which Yang Ti unwisely ignored to focus on foreign problems. When he inspected the refortified Great Wall in 615, the Turks captured him. He escaped, however, and retreated to his southern capital in Chaing-tu. He would later be murdered by his own officials, whereupon a series of local leaders took unofficial control of China.

While the Sui dynasty lasted less than half a century, most historians credit it with bringing stability to China. In this regard, the Sui echoed the Han dynasty of the third century B.C.E, which was built upon the Ch'in dynasty.

T'ang Dynasty. The next dynasty in the Second Chinese Empire, the T'ang, ruled from 618–907. Modern historians attribute T'ang's duration to a better organized government over its conquered territories, based on a system of circulating officers. Its first emperor, Kao Tsu (618–626), had spent several years fighting for control with Wang Shih-ch'ung, a leader of what was left of the Sui dynasty. Kao Tsu wisely made sure that many of the aristocrats in his inner circle had blood ties to the Sui dynasty.

Compared to Sui governments, Kao Tsu's central government was smaller and less bureaucratic; where Wen Ti had six ministries, Kao Tsu had only two: the chancellory and the secretariat. Local government was granted some leeway in ruling provinces, but conformity to the central government was the standard.

Kao Tsu oversaw land allocations to taxpaying males who received a grant of land, part of which they could keep and part of which they were required to return to the government. Larger estates belonged only to specific royals and officials. Kao Tsu revised penal law, which every succeeding generation would rewrite. This adapted law would last through the nineteenth century, and would be adopted by Korea, Japan, and Vietnam. Upon Kao Tsu's death in 626, sons Chien-ch'eng and Li Shih-min fought for the throne. Li Shih-min murdered his brother and took over, taking the name T'ai Tsung (reigned 626–649).

His reign would later be called the "era of good government," as he was skillful enough to balance regional groups so that one would not dominate. More of an ethical than a forceful leader, T'ai Tsung frequently consulted with his Confucian advisers, and granted them the freedom to freely criticize him.

China remained dominant in the East. In 630 T'ai Tsung destroyed the eastern Turks after decades of defeat; he then attacked Tibet, wresting control of several provinces. By now, China was formally recognized by the Byzantine Empire, and it expanded trade with central Asia. Culture flourished and an indigenous

Above, Paradise of Amitabha *from Dun Huang, T'ang dynasty (10th century). Left, a vase from the Yuan period (14th century).*

drama and verse developed. The Chinese also embraced Buddhism on a larger scale; theologian Hsüan Tsung traveled to India and translated 75 key Buddhist texts into Chinese. In 643, China even exchanged ministers with India's ruling dynasty. But troubles with Korea remained. T'ai Tsung made two unsuccessful invasions in 645 and 647, and was preparing for a third invasion before his death.

The only disruption to the T'ang dynastic line led to one of the most infamous rulers in Chinese history. One of T'ai Tsung's concubines, later known as the Empress Wu, seized control after his death and drove many of his aides to death or suicide in the 650s. A conniving, ruthless leader (who resembled Russia's Catherine the Great), Wu used Buddhist scripture to justify her overthrowing the government by claiming that she was a direct descendant of the Buddha. Bizarre as her reign was, she had little long-term effect on China. She was deposed in 704.

Hsüan Tsung's reign (712–756) saw a flowering of Chinese culture and the development of an original national art. His leadership also saw military success over the Turks and Tibetans, although the Chinese would be defeated by the Arabs in 751, costing them Turkistan.

One of Hsüan Tsung's generals, An Lu-shan, revolted in 735, driving him out. An Lu-shan and his successors ruled until 763, as the central government was weakened in favor of local administration. Emperor Te Tsung (780–805) began tax reform to strengthen the central government, and his successors conquered many of the rebelling provinces, but in 907 northern invaders overthrew the T'ang dynasty.

Once again China was split along north-south lines, and for the next half-century was ruled by two different systems. Five dynasties ruled northern China, while ten kingdoms ruled southern and eastern China. One of the reasons for this dissension was the reassertion of Confucianism over Buddhism, which was now perceived as irrelevant next to modern philosophy and politics. The result of this split was the further decline of the aristocracy. Future Chinese rulers would come from more common backgrounds.

Sung Dynasty. The Sung dynasty began with General Chao Kuang-yin in 960. Humane towards his vanquished rulers, he concentrated his defenses in the capital. By replacing regional military leaders with central officers, the royal government now had more power than before.

During the Sung rule, cities became the hubs of economy and business. The rise of education created a new and upwardly mobile mercantile class. Trade now united eastern and coastal cities. In 1020, the first reference to a "floating magnet" or compass appears in Chinese literature. An efficient food system was implemented, remaining virtually unchanged into the twentieth century. A new type of rice imported from Vietnam became a staple of the Chinese diet.

Another area of development was philosophy, as Chinese writers composed commentaries on Confucian teaching. One Chinese philosopher, Zhi Xi, wrote an official creed emphasizing obedience of the weak to the strong, and the wife to the husband. This echoed the local government's subservience to the restored central government.

By 1127, however, the Ch'in tribe seized control of the north, forcing the Sung dynasty to retreat to the south, where for the next 150 years it ruled southern and eastern China as the southern Sung dynasty. Though the dynasty had moved, it continued to flourish, as trade brought in higher revenues and creativity boomed. The popular drama and the first novels were written to great acclaim during this time.

Yüan Dynasty. During the mid-1200s China again faced threats from the Mongols, who now occupied northern China. KUBLAI KHAN began assaults on the southern Sung, and by 1271 controlled the country. China was now under control of foreigners for the first time in its history. The Chinese did not accept rule from Turks, Armenians, and Russians. The Mongols did attempt to govern with Chinese bureaucrats, but the Chinese hated their native officials as well.

The central Mongol government established excellent road and water systems. The Grand Canal was renovated and, as a result, there was greater trade between China and Europe. As a result of this improved trade, the Chinese began adopting CHRISTIANITY. In 1245, the first Christian missionaries came to China. Italian explorer MARCO POLO arrived at Kublai Khan's home in 1275 with a letter from the pope and other Western religious artifacts. Khan made Polo an official emissary and, for the next two decades, Polo went out on fact-finding tours for the Mongols. Polo returned to Italy in 1295 with lavish tales of Chinese court splendor. These stories would form the basis of what Westerners thought of China for centuries to come. And many of China's technical advances, most notably gunpowder, were adopted throughout Europe.

Ming Dynasty. Upon Kublai Khan's death, the Mongol dynasty fell apart. There ensued a great internal struggle for control among his heirs. Flooding of the Huai and Huang river valleys in 1351 led to widespread rioting. A local rebel leader, Chu Yüan-chang, captured Nanking in 1356 and amassed enough territory by 1368 to declare himself Emperor Hung-wu of the new Ming dynasty.

The Ming dynasty was conservative, marked by a consolidation of central government power. Hung-wu callously oversaw two brutal purges, which killed literally tens of thousands of his officials. His son and successor, Emperor Chien-wen, gave greater power to his court secretaries. There was once again a resurgence of Confucianism. The naval voyages, which had once brought wealth and prestige to China ended, as time and money were increasingly devoted to fighting the Mongols to the north. In light of renewed Confucianism, territorial expansionism was perceived by Ming rulers as foreign to traditional Chinese ideals. Because of this turning inward, there grew among the Chinese the belief that their system of government, their society, was absolutely perfect, in no need of involvement from outsiders. Isolationism was an idea that did not last beyond the Middle Ages; by the sixteenth century the Japanese and Mongols began attacking.

One of China's strengths—its massive population—would ultimately prove to be a drawback. Historians now maintain that because there was never a shortage of manpower in China, the Chinese were never compelled to rush into the Industrial Revolution of the eighteenth and nineteenth centuries, as were their European counterparts. By the end of that revolution, China found itself behind the rest of the world.

CHIVALRY

A code of conduct for the feudal knight. A rigorous moral system, it organized the ethical meaning of the caste of KNIGHTHOOD. The values of chivalry—charity, benevolence, loyalty—sustained the moral self-understanding of the feudal elite; consequently, it also sustained the economic system which they dominated. The virtues of chivalry were praised in the myths of the Middle Ages, as in the English stories of ARTHUR of Camelot and the French CHANSONS DE GESTE (songs of heroic deeds), such as *La Chanson de ROLAND*. The ideals of chivalry were embodied in the literature of COURTLY LOVE, expressed in the songs of TROUBADOURS, of unattainable love between a knight and a married woman of the aristocracy. In its historical origins, chivalry was an important aspect of a broader cultural movement to moderate the violent tendencies of the early knights while maintain-

A duel over the honor of ladies. From Histoire de Gérard de Nevers, *a 15th-century manuscript, currently in the National Library of Paris.*

ing them as fierce opponents of non-Christians. The chivalric code also helped in the creation of crusading orders—military organizations of knights that played an important role in medieval history.

Knights as a distinct class of warrior emerged in the tenth century out of the early medieval cavalry, particularly in FRANCE during the CAROLINGIAN DYNASTY. In this early period, knights were usually petty landowners who held their land independently—that is, not as feudal grants from higher lords. At this early stage, knighthood was not a closed caste, which meant that entry did not depend on birth. These independent warriors took advantage of the chaotic situation in Europe and pursued their own enrichment through ruthless violence, with complete indifference to whatever local system of public order might exist. They were a threat to Church and peasant alike.

The code of chivalry was one effort of the European elite to control the warlike class of knights. The Catholic Church in particular responded to the suffering of the defenseless peasantry and, perhaps more importantly, to depredations against Church lands and personnel. Additionally, robbing the peasantry deprived the Church of a major source of rents and tithes. During the late tenth and early eleventh century, the Church sponsored the Peace of God and the Truce of God. The aim of theses arrangements was twofold. First, the Church endeavored to dissuade the knights attacking the peasantry. Second, the Church promoted the definition of knights as protectors of their "inferiors." Thus the knights were "Christianized" and made part of the feudal hierarchy in which each person had his or her place. The last step in controlling the knights was the First Crusade, in which knightly violence was directed towards the Islamic world.

The warrior code of chivalry spoke to both moral and martial virtues. The former are the Christian virtues embedded in the feudal moral universe of superiors and inferiors. The chivalrous knight should be generous, courageous, and faithful. Knights should take particular care with the weak, understood in feudal society as the sick, the oppressed, widows, and others. Loyalty was a central virtue since the feudal order was grounded in the faithfulness of each individual to the social hierarchy. The popularity of the ideals of chivalry led to the creation of the chivalric orders, which were to become power centers in the medieval world.

CHRETIEN DE TROYES

T he twelfth-century poet Chrétien de Troyes (c. 1135–1183) is considered one of the finest French medieval writers of courtly romance and the greatest French poet of his time. Four complete works and fragments of several others survive. Taking off from the stories of King ARTHUR, Queen Guinevere, Lancelot and other Knights of the Round Table, Chrétien created a complex world highlighting the psychology of heterosexual love—the impact of memory and struggle for domination between lovers as favorite themes. The rhymed verse is as subtle as the ideas in his poems. (*See* COURTLY LOVE.)

Chrétien was a university graduate who became a member of the court of Countess Marie de Champagne (the daughter of ELEANOR OF AQUITAINE) between 1170 and 1185. He was for a time a professional court entertainer, but he may eventually have been rewarded with a high ecclesiastical office.

CHRISTIANITY

T o say with the Victorians that the Middle Ages were "the Age of Faith" is not incorrect, but it is a pallid distillation of the social reality of Europe in medieval centuries. Christianity was centrally involved in all facets of medieval life. It shaped everything and was shaped by everything. Its grandeurs were medieval hallmarks and Christianity's limitations as a religious doctrine also proved both problematic and challenging for medieval society and culture.

Origins. The Christianity of medieval Europe had a five-fold derivation: from Judaism, Greek philosophy, the Mediterranean mystery religions, Roman institution building, and Germanic magic. Since the Christians of the Second century C.E., when the canon of the Christian BIBLE was established, were still interested in the conversion of JEWS, they adopted the Hebrew Bible as the Old Testament (the older truth now supplemented and improved upon by the New Testament). With the Hebrew bible came a sense of history as determined by divine Providence, a wrathful and judging God, a puritanical ethic, and a prophetic concern for social justice. From Greek, particularly Platonic philosophy, came the split between abstracted soul and body and the conviction that ideas count the most in seeking understanding of anything.

From the Mediterranean mystery religions came the vision of a dying, reborn god to whom humans may attach themselves through a ritual act and participate in the god's immortality. From the Roman heritage came a compulsive focus on organizational hierarchy, administrative control, and the virtuous exercise of power legitimized by law. From the Germanic culture came what Victorians pejoratively called superstition, and what anthropologists today call magic—the use of some physical act or material talisman for purposes of faith-healing and stimulating other moments of divine intervention.

Three Eras. Historians think they can identify three eras of medieval European Christianity: the age of the judging emperor-god, inspired by the Old Testament and Roman politics and law, from 300 to 1100 C.E.; the era of romantic spirituality, with focus on the Mother and Child and trend toward general feminization, inspired by the New Testament, from 1100 to 1350; and the closing, autumnal era from 1350 to 1500 of intense individualism combined with fascination with the body and the spiritual possibilities of material things.

It is the second era from 1100 to 1350 that has attracted the most attention in the twentieth century. The efflorescence of medieval spirituality stands out in Latin and vernacular literature and in ARCHITECTURE, sculpture, and PAINTING. There was a general drive to make Western Christianity an emotional faith meaningful to the common man as well as to the wealthy and educated. Modern scholars have devoted whole lifetimes to the motifs in the STAINED GLASS of the CHARTRES cathedral, the consciousness of individuality

The Fortress of Faith is besieged by heretics. Defenders include the pope, the bishops, the monks, and the doctors of the Church—in a 15th-century miniature.

in twelfth century romance, and the implications of this individuality on theology and piety. That era was marked by warm weather and, until around 1250, surplus food, inducing lower infant and child mortality and longer lives resulting in a population boom. People felt good about themselves and the beneficent deity enshrined in the Virgin Mary. The material context of theology and piety has not been given much attention in the enthusiastic writings about twelfth- and thirteenth-century Christianity. Nor has it been stressed very much that this highly emotional piety brought with it a sharp revival of the anti-Semitism that had its roots in the Roman Empire when Christians and Jews competed fiercely for converts.

The great intensification of Christianity in personal life and consciousness owed much to the functioning of the Latin Church as an evangelical, administrative, and wealthy institution. The first great step in the making of the medieval Church was the intensive missionary work among heathen Germans carried out between 500 and 800 C.E., with encouragement from the PAPACY and bishops, but largely effected by Benedictine and Irish monks who defined their own missionary goals. The second stage of Christian pacification of the countryside was the introduction everywhere of the parish priests, resident village clerics, between 800 and 1100. The landlords paid for the parish priests with grants of land. Such endowments were modest in size but absolutely necessary. Even if the parish clergy were themselves drawn heavily from the peasantry and their learning was slight, the offering of the sacraments, the hearing of confessions, and the functioning of the penitential system on the local level had an enormous impact on society. Whatever the great religious teachers might opine, it was the humble village cleric who carried the weight of medieval religiosity and integrated it into the daily life of ordinary people. Church historians have focused on the rise of a wealthy and activist papacy in the period 1050–1300 and the institutionalization of a measure (always exaggerated) of centralized control of the Church from Rome. But it was the parish priests who carried out this vast and cumbersome ecclesiastical edifice on their backs as did their peasant neighbors for the feudal system of economics and labor.

Later Middle Ages. In spite of its emotional impact and evangelical success, the medieval Church after 1100 could not satisfy the psychological needs of significant minorities within the population—not only Jews resisting the pressures towards conversion (although taken together probably twenty percent of medieval Jewry had joined the Church by 1500)—but also Christian separatist groups. The papacy, bishops, and university theologians called them heretics, people who subscribed to religious error. Since 1950, assiduous searching of archives has turned up much more information on the heretical communities than historians had earlier believed possible. At any given time between 1150 and 1500 anywhere between five and 25 percent of medieval Christians had separated themselves from the Catholics and formed their own religious communities. This situation prevailed both in urban enclaves and in the more distant and secluded rural villages.

The main heretical doctrines were antisacerdotalism, claiming that the ministration of the sacraments was only valid if performed by a saintly priest, recognized for his personal charisma rather than his institutional authority; and Catharism, a dualist belief in the perpetual struggle between the God of Light and the God of Darkness that harkens back to the Manichean (originally Iranian) doctrines of antiquity. But more than the doctrines, what gave currency and purchased devotion for the heretical communities was the personal comforting and caring they provided to middle-class and working-class people, that same kind of individuated counseling that had been a major reason for the conversion of pagans and Jews to the Church in antiquity. Whether the Latin Church after 1100 lacked the fiscal and human resources to countervail anomy and rebellions within the masses (it found such resources after the Council of Trent in the late sixteenth century but is similarly facing a crisis in pastoral care today), or whether the hierarchy and papacy were so mired in politics and materialism as not to be able to feed Christ's sheep, has been a matter of intense historical controversy for the past century.

Bishops had the best jobs in the medieval Church. Of aristocratic background or products of boot-strapping careers in royal or ecclesiastical administration or (rarely) of gained distinction for higher learning, the bishops ruled their sees with princely authority. Normally able to withstand the challenge of pope and king alike, the bishops enjoyed substantial incomes from their landed estates; some even attained the billionaire level. By 1200, the bishops generally were more concerned with artful building projects and support of the universities and in royal service than the condition and effectiveness of the parish clergy. But the rewards and prestige that accompany the patronage of the arts and letters and the building of monumental edifices seem greater at any time and place than the attention given to the moral and psychological well-being of the common man. The remarkable thing is the significant minority of bishops who tried hard to improve quotidian pastoral care. Historians today are much more interested in the patrons of the arts, the builders of GOTHIC cathedrals, and the aggressive politicians among the episcopate than in the handful of lonely idealists who held bishoprics.

The second best job in the medieval Church went to the holders of endowed cathedral "canonries," the priests who worked in cathedrals and who were assured of substantial incomes from endowed "prebendaries." They resembled the tenured professors of today; indeed it was from the wealthy cathedral canons that the idea of endowed and tenured professorships was derived. The third best job in the medieval Church was that of abbot or other senior officer in a wealthy old monastery with vast rural estates and inflating urban real estate. These were the institutional descendants of the Benedictine and Irish missionaries of the period 500 to 800. Before the rise of the UNIVERSITIES in the twelfth century, the MONASTERIES had also been centers of ART, LITERATURE, theology, and prolific writing of history books. Now, by 1250, social change had passed them by and they seemed to be highly vocal middle class critics, selfish communities interested principally in their diet and other comforts and contributing little to the world around them. Here again is a much-disputed topic among historians of the medieval Church. The kitchen records of the WESTMINSTER ABBEY in LONDON have been scrutinized, and show that around 1450, each monk consumed two pounds of red meat a day, plus untold amounts of fish and fowl. That the leftovers from the twice-daily gargantuan monastic meals were distributed to the poor at the abbey's gates does not diminish the force of the documented picture of fat and self-indulgent monks. The cloistered nuns, usually of wealthy families, were devoted assiduously not to food consumption, but to the raising of birds and the breeding of greyhounds.

In the fourteenth and fifteenth centuries, middle-class people were taking religious exercises and personal counseling more into their own hands. Private chapels called chantries, established cooperatively by families, became much more widespread. Service institutions providing physical and pastoral care, called confraternities (i.e., brotherhoods), became fashionable. Middle-class women joined the Beguines, non-monastic service organizations that exhibited strong feminist consciousness. The frequent taking of the sacrament of the mass—eating Jesus—became respectable and worthy behavior (the Church required taking the sacrament only once a year). Festivals and parades devoted to Corpus Christi (Christ's body) were much relished by urban populations. Faith healing acquired fanatical commitment and authenticity in a society virtually without medicines. This laicization of medieval Christianity used to be seen as a harbinger of the Protestant Reformation. More recently it has been viewed as demonstrations of the strength and innovative qualities of late medieval Christianity.

See BIBLE; PAPACY; PHILOSOPHY; *and* ANGELS AND DEMONS *for theological issues. See* CATHEDRALS AND CHURCHES; MONASTERIES AND MONASTICISM; *and* INQUISITION *for institutions. Also see* EASTERN ORTHODOX CHURCH; BYZANTIUM; *and* HOLY ROMAN EMPIRE. *Compare* JUDAISM; ISLAM.

CHRISTINE DE PISAN

Christine de Pisan (1364–1430) was an influential writer of the late Middle Ages, not only because of her talent, but because she was one of the few WOMEN writing at the time.

Born in VENICE around 1363, her father was a resident astrologer in the court of King CHARLES V of FRANCE—which gave her an opportunity to receive a solid education. She married in 1379, but became a widow with three children to support less than ten years later. She consoled herself with study and writing. Initially, she wrote poetry, but gradually she turned to prose. She wrote about religion and history—including a biography of King Charles—but in particular, she wrote about the role of women in medieval society. Christine authored a book on famous women of the past and attacked the *Roman de la Rose* for its negative depiction of women. She also praised the victory of JOAN OF ARC in a later poem.

Her writing was admired by many of her contemporaries. A number of her works

Christine de Pisan in a 15th-century Belgian miniature.

were translated into several languages during her lifetime. She died around 1429. Christine de Pisan is regarded as one of the two or three leading feminist writers of the Middle Ages. (*See* LITERATURE.)

CHRONICLES

The word "chronicle" dates from the fourteenth century and comes from the Greek *chronos* (time). Chronicles were the historical works of the Middle Ages, and many provide a detailed complete picture of medieval life.

Much of what appears in medieval chronicles focuses on events during the chronicler's lifetime, although stories of past events and even legends often got included. What made the chronicles particularly useful was that they often included eyewitness accounts of the events they covered.

Among the earliest chroniclers were ISIDORE OF SEVILLE, GREGORY OF TOURS, and the venerable BEDE. These writers produced histories of the VISIGOTHS, the French church, and the ANGLO-SAXONS, respectively. Later chroniclers included the monk Matthew of Paris, Geoffrey de Villehardouin, and JEAN FROISSART. Many chronicles were written by monks, in part because the Church saw history as the record of God's work. Writers who knew powerful Church leaders or nobles chronicled events surrounding their lives.

CHRYSOLORAS, MANUEL

Manuel Chrysoloras (c. 1355–1415) was a Byzantine humanist and diplomat who played a leading role in the spread of Greek literature to western Europe. Chrysoloras was born into an aristocratic family. As a young man, he studied at CONSTANTINOPLE with the famed professor Gemistus. Chrysoloras became a prominent professor himself and attracted many students to the university in Constantinople. In 1393, he traveled to ITALY on the order of the emperor. He was received with acclaim and taught in FLORENCE, Milan, and Pavia. He was then sent to ENGLAND, FRANCE, and SPAIN on diplomatic assignments from Constantinople. In 1415, at the request of pope Gregory XII, Chrysoloras went to the Council of Constance to represent the Greek Orthodox Church, but died suddenly on his arrival.

Chrysoloras's contribution to European culture stem from his important translations of Homer and Plato, and from his popularization of Greek culture, which greatly influenced young Italian humanists.

CID, EL (RODRIGO DIAZ)

El Cid, from the Spanish for "lord," was Rodrigo Diaz (c. 1043–1099), a Castilian military leader and folk hero. Rodrigo was born in the village of Vivar, six miles north of Burgos, the chief city of old Castile. On the death of his father in 1058, he was brought to the court of King Ferdinand I, where he was placed under the wardship of the king's eldest son, Sancho. When Sancho took the Castilian throne in 1065, he made the 22-year-old Rodrigo the commander and chief of the Castilian army. In 1067, Rodrigo (by now called El Cid) played an important part in Sancho's successful campaign against the Moorish kingdom of Saragossa.

With Ferdinand's death in 1065, his children began to struggle over the kingdom. The Cid helped Sancho win several decisive victories over Sancho's brother ALFONSO VI, concentrating on Alfonso's territories in León. However, when Sancho himself died in 1072 without a son, Alfonso was left as his only heir. By the laws of vassalage, Rodrigo's allegiance transferred to Alfonso. At first, Alfonso welcomed him, hoping to gain the support of the Castilian population. Although the Cid lost his position as *armiger regis* to his bitter enemy, Count Garcia Ordoñez, and his influence at the royal court declined, he remained loyal to Alfonso, even marrying his niece Jimena in 1074.

The Cid's position at the court remained uncertain, as he was considered the representative of those Castilians who resented serving under a Leónese king. Rodrigo also encouraged these suspicions through a number of unauthorized military expeditions: in 1079, he defeated the forces of Garcia Ordoñez; and in 1081, he led a raid into the Moorish kingdom of Toledo, which was under the king's protection. Convinced that Rodrigo was plotting against him, Alfonso exiled the Cid from the kingdoms of Castile and León.

The Cid first offered his services to two Christian princes. When they refused, he turned next to the Muslim king of Saragossa, al-Muqtadir, who gratefully accepted his offer. The Cid served al-Muqtadir and his heir, al-Musta'in II, for nearly a decade. During that time, he gained a valuable understanding of Hispano-Arabic politics, earned several important military victories, and added to his reputation as a leader who had never lost a battle. It was that reputation which led King Alfonso to recall Rodrigo, requesting his service in defending the kingdom against the Almoravid invasion in 1086. The Cid was willing to return, though he avoided direct battle. Alfonso's advisers suggested that this revealed Rodrigo's seditious intentions, and he was exiled for the second time in 1089.

After the second exile, Rodrigo turned his attention toward the conquest of the Moorish kingdom of Valencia. The Cid left the region to assist Alfonso yet again against the ALMORAVIDS in 1091 (he was forgiven quickly because of his military prowess). In the following year, during Rodrigo's absence, Valencia was captured by the Almoravid Ibn Yahhaf. Returning, the Cid began a 20-month siege of the city. The Almoravids sent huge forces in order to break the siege, but the Cid was able to beat them back in several miraculous battles. Valencia finally surrendered to the Cid in May 1094; he made a truce with Ibn Yahhaf, but then had him burned alive. Rodrigo ruled over the Christian and Muslim population of Valencia for the remaining four years of his life. Although he ruled in the name of Alfonso VI, in reality, he wielded complete power, and under his direction, the city was Christianized; the Great Mosque was turned into a church in 1096, and Jerome of Périgord was appointed bishop of a newly established see.

El Cid's last great military achievement occurred in 1097, during yet another Almoravid attempt to win back Valencia. At the Battle of Bairen, trapped and badly outnumbered, the Cid defeated the enemy decisively. Two years later, on July 10, 1099, Rodrigo Diaz, El Cid, died. The city was soon occupied by the Almoravids (1102), remaining in Muslim hands until 1238. The Cid's body was taken to his native Castile and buried in the monastery of San Pedro de Cardena, near Burgos, which quickly became a cult site.

Indeed, Rodrigo's life soon became the subject of a secular hagiography, as he was quickly elevated to the status of a Castilian national hero. The great twelfth-century Castilian epic poem, *El cantar de mio Cid* (*The Song of My Cid*) greatly contributed to the Cid's mythic identity; it is not considered a reliable historical document. The Cid's reputation suffered somewhat through other fictionalized versions of his life, and by the attacks of Arab historians and later Castilian writers; but for the most part, he remains an immensely revered figure in Castilian lore. (*See* SPAIN.)

CISTERCIAN ORDER

A monastic order in western Europe, established around the year 1120 by St. Stephen Harding at the French abbey of Citeaux (in Latin, *Cistercium*), after which it was named. The order spread rapidly throughout Europe and reached its greatest influence during the twelfth century under the leadership of ST. BERNARD OF CLAIRVAUX.

An ascetic order that established monasteries in remote locations, the Cistercians often wore white mantles to distinguish themselves from the black-garbed Benedictines, and became known as the White Monks. In 1145, a disciple of St. Bernard, Eugenius III, became pope. The Cistercians encouraged the formation of several chivalric orders such as the Templars and the Knights of Calatrava, all of whom adopted elements from the Cistercian constitution (the *Charta Caritatis*) created at its founding by Stephen Harding. The tension between the power and wealth amassed by the chivalric orders, who contributed generously to the Cistercians, and the order's asceticism, gave rise to an austere yet ornate Gothic style that permeated Cistercian art, architecture, and literature.

CLARENDON, CONSTITUTIONS OF

The Constitutions of Clarendon were a set of 16 articles issued by King HENRY II at a council meeting at Clarendon palace in January 1164. The articles defined the customs governing relations between Church and state. By issuing them, Henry tried to limit the power of the English church which had grown during the unruly days of King Stephen. Henry's claim was that the articles codified the practices that had been operative during the reign of his grandfather, Henry I.

The Constitutions placed a limit on clerical and papal authority in ENGLAND, with most articles dealing with the Church and its courts, and several contrary to canon law. Especially controversial were the two clauses forbidding appeals to ROME without royal consent and ordering clerics to be punished by secular courts after their conviction in Church courts (already a major point of contention between Henry and his archbishop of Canterbury, THOMAS BECKET).

At first Becket and the English clergy agreed somewhat reluctantly to the constitutions, but Pope ALEXANDER III soon condemned the constitutions in 1164. Becket then withdrew his support, an act that flamed the dispute between the king and Becket, ending with Becket's murder in 1170. Two years later Henry revoked the two contentious clauses at Avranches. The rest of the constitutions remained in effect, however, and effectively defined the relationship between Church and state in England.

CLEMENT V

Clement V (1260–1314), pope from June 5, 1305 until April 20, 1314, was the first pontiff to reside in AVIGNON. Born Bertrand de Got in the Bordelais region of FRANCE, he studied civil and canon law in Orléans and Bologna. He became bishop of Comminges in 1295, and was appointed archbishop of Bordeaux in 1299. Following the death of Benedict XI, Bertrand—a compromise candidate—was elected pope and crowned in Lyon on November 14, 1305. King PHILIP IV of France, who had a great deal of influence over the new pope, urged him to remain in France for political reasons and to avoid violent unrest in ITALY. Clement settled in Avignon which became the papal seat in 1309. This influence also led Clement to exonerate Philip IV and his ministers in Boniface's death and to convict Boniface of HERESY posthumously. Clement was unable to resist Philip's will in the latter's campaign against the Knights Templar. The Templars' coffers were largely appropriated by the French monarchy after Clement's Council of Vienne (1311) ended in the order's suppression in April 1313. Clement V's reign signaled a retreat in the temporal and spiritual power of the PAPACY.

CLEMENT VI

Pope Clement VI (1291–1352) reigned from 1342 to 1352. He had to contend with the devastation of the BLACK DEATH of 1347 and the unrest of the ongoing HUNDRED YEARS' WAR. He distinguished himself by his administrative skills and his fair-minded treatment of non-Christians.

Born Pierre Roger in FRANCE in 1291, he served first as a monk and later became a highly regarded theologian. He became archbishop of Sens in 1329 and Rouen in 1330. In 1338 he settled in AVIGNON as a cardinal before being elected pope in 1342.

One of his main goals upon becoming pope was to create the greatest court in all of Europe. He was able to do this by actually purchasing Avignon from Joan I, queen of NAPLES, and finishing the construction of a new papal palace, all financed by the surplus of money left by Benedict XII, his predecessor.

When the Black Death broke out in 1347, Clement offered assistance and land (for burial plots) to the sick and to the families of the dead. He also protected European Jews, whom many Christians blamed for the spread of the disease. He sheltered Jews at Avignon and throughout the PAPAL STATES, and excommunicated those who persecuted them.

CLERMONT, COUNCIL OF

Council in which Pope URBAN II, in 1095, delivered his call for the First Crusade. The meeting, held in the heart of the French kingdom, addressed many issues of Church administration, and confirmed the regulations of the Truce of God. (*See* PEACE OF GOD.) Urban was eager to find ways of regulating the bellicose knightly orders and seized the opportunity presented by a request made by the Byzantine emperor ALEXIUS I COMNENUS for aid in defending against the Muslims on his borders. In a rousing speech that marks a turning point in the history of the Middle Ages, Urban called for a crusade to recapture Jerusalem from the Muslims. Many who heard the speech were moved to take their vows to join the crusade right then and there, amid cries of *Deus volt* ("God wills it"), battle cry of the First Crusade.

CLOCKS

The clock as we know it today did not exist until after the Middle Ages, but its precursors made it possible for people to break the hours of the day into units of equal length. This was no small accomplishment. Although timekeeping devices had been in existence since ancient times, the "hour" was actually measured as one-twelfth of the total duration of daylight. The length of an hour thus varied according to season and latitude. The development of the first mechanical clocks made it possible to regulate time at night and regardless of geographical location.

Early attempts at keeping time included sundials, sand glasses, marked candles, and water clocks. Sundials, common today mainly as decorative garden objects, measured the shadow of the sun as it fell on the ground. (Astrolabes, which were like the more elaborate sundials, were used both to tell time and to calculate the position of stars for navigation). Sand glasses, precursors of the hourglass, marked off specific units of time by falling sand. Marked candles worked on the same principle: each section of the candle burned equaled one unit of time. The water clock, which originated in the Roman Empire, marked units of time by series of gears, weights, and axles that responded to a flow of water. As water filled a chamber of the clock, it would raise a floating object that would cause the weight to move and the axle to turn. Some water clocks, especially in Muslim lands, were quite elaborate; many had bells that sounded an "alarm" (most likely a call to prayer).

These clocks all had limited accuracy, and they were so large and cumbersome that they were found only in town squares or in churches. Most people still measured their days primarily by the number of hours in which there was sunlight. They rose at dawn, worked, finished at dusk, and went to bed at nightfall. There was no such thing as having a 3:15 appointment.

Although examples are found in tenth-century CHINA, practical mechanical clocks are first found in Europe toward the end of the thirteenth century. Most of the mechanical clocks were placed in churches, and they counted only the hours; the minute hand would not be developed for another two centuries.

ENGLAND was the first place in which mechanical clocks took hold. Early clocks were less than precise, but despite this, they often came equipped with bells and elaborate figurines called jacquemarts to help mark the hours. Mechanisms were large and often constructed by blacksmiths rather than clockmakers. By the end of the Middle Ages, clockmaking had become a far more exacting and prestigious skill, and clockmakers used their talents to design increasingly smaller, more accurate, and costly timepieces.

CLOTHING AND COSTUME

The popular notion that medieval clothing was simple compared to modern dress is contradicted by a wealth of evidence. The simple robes of the clergy and the coarse clothing of the peasants were plain enough, but the costumes of the nobility could be quite colorful, intricate, and richly designed. Moreover, as travel became more commonplace, styles of one region influenced other regions.

Early Styles. In Europe, the styles of the Roman Empire carried into the Middle Ages. Both Byzantine and western European dress was based primarily on the Roman tunic. In colder northern Europe, heavier clothes made of animal skins were more common, but the basic tunic style was still evident. Even early Muslims wore clothes copied from the Roman styles.

Eventually, as cultural changes took place, so did changes in regional costumes. Travel between Europe, the Near East, and the Far East meant more variety of material—particularly expensive silks. The wealthy and powerful often adorned themselves lavishly in colorful outfits with expensive jewels. But while the increase in travel exposed more people to the fashions of many different regions, distinct regional modes of dress still developed in many areas.

Regional Styles. In the Byzantine Empire, access to the riches of the East meant clothing decorated with silk, jewels, and fur. Wealthy Byzantines, particularly in the royal courts, had gems sewn into the hems of their gowns. Over several layers of tunics, the rulers would wear a long embroidered scarflike piece of clothing called a loros studded with precious stones. Crowns were made of gold and encrusted with pearls. On a more practical level, the Byzantines adopted leggings for men and long sleeves from their neighbors who lived in intemperate northern climes.

In the Islamic world, the ostentatious display of wealth through ornate clothes was frowned upon at first, but styles became more resplendent in later Islamic periods. Rich embroidery became quite fashionable, and for special occasions a Muslim might wear a robe of honor, embroidered with royal inscriptions and passages from Islamic holy books.

In western Europe, Roman and Germanic styles gradually gave way to the Eastern influences, which came about through the CRUSADES and through trade. Knights returning from Eastern lands brought back materials and fashions that were greatly admired, particularly by nobles. Such materials as damask (a decorated cloth from DAMASCUS), baldachin (a mixture of silk and gold made in BAGHDAD), and velvet became common materials attiring European nobility. Sleeves became more elaborate, and colors more vivid.

Knights, of course, wore heavy armor designed to withstand the blows of arrows or daggers when they prepared to go into battle. When soldiers went from Europe to Islamic territories to fight in the Crusades, they found that the blazing sun turned their chain-mail armor suits into ovens. The answer was a surcoat, a cloth vestlike garment worn over the armor to deflect the sun's rays. Religious dress tended to be simple—long, plain robes in somber colors. High-ranking clerics might wear ornate accessories, such as richly embroidered stoles.

Hats and head coverings were popular throughout the medieval world. Turbans, hoods, and brimmed hats were common, with certain styles more popular in different regions (such as the tall cone-shaped *qalansuwa* worn by Islamic men).

Restrictions. Peasants were usually less ornately attired than nobles, often because so-called sumptuary laws prohibited working-class people from wearing expensive clothing—even if they could have afforded it.

Foreigners were usually required to wear some sort of sign that they were from another country (often a cloth badge) unless their national dress was distinctive enough for others to place them. Non-Christians in Christian countries and non-Muslims in ARAB countries also had to wear some sort of identification. Jews, who had no home country, were required to wear some sort of symbolic apparel no matter where they lived. Sometimes this was by choice, as in the Byzantine Empire, where they wore the fringed garment known as *zizith*. But in other countries, Jews had to adapt local styles or otherwise wear some sort of identifying item of apparel. In ENGLAND and FRANCE, they were required to wear small yellow symbols on their clothing. The blunt-pointed cap called a *Judenhut* was also used as a symbol of one's Jewish faith. (*See* ARMS AND ARMOR; WOOL TRADE.)

At right, a lawyer dressed in courtroom attire, wearing poulaines on his feet. Above (from a miniature in Froissart's Chronicles), *the entrance of the royally attired Queen Isabeau of Bavaria into Paris. She is wearing a steeple hat, or henin, on her head, which first made its appearance in the 1420s.*

CLOVIS I

Clovis I (466–511) became king of the Salian FRANKS in 480 and went on to unite all the Franks under his rule. He was the founder of the royal MEROVINGIAN DYNASTY, which ruled all or most of FRANCE until the 740s. (The name "Merovingian" comes from a mythical ancestor of Clovis.) As a result of his conversion to Catholicism, he became a champion of the Roman Church against other Germanic tribes, who, as Arian Christians, were considered heretical by the Roman Church. At his death in 511, Clovis's kingdom covered most of Gaul and extended into southwestern GERMANY. Clovis is regarded as the founder of the French monarchy.

Early Life. Born the son of Childeric, Clovis was a tribal chieftain who, upon the death of his father, became one of several Frankish kings in northeastern Gaul and the Rhineland area of Germany. After he murdered several of his relatives and eliminated rival Frankish kings by treachery and brute force, Clovis became ruler of the Franks. In 486, his army defeated the Roman legions of Syagrius, the independent ruler of Romanized Christian Celts in Gaul, at Soissons, thus putting an end to Roman domination and establishing his uncontested control over northeastern Gaul. His conquest of the Thuringians further extended his kingdom. He strengthened his position with the Celts by marrying the Burgundian princess Clotilda in 493 and by having his children baptized as Catholic Christians.

Battles. His growth might have threatened the warlike Alemanni. In 496, while fighting the Alemanni, Clovis vowed to become Catholic himself if he was victorious. After Clovis defeated them, Saint Rémi, bishop of Reims, baptized Clovis, reportedly along with 3,000 of his followers. Clovis was soon recognized as the champion of the Catholic Christians against the VISIGOTHS, Burgundians, and other heretical Germanic Arian tribes.

Clovis won major battles against the Burgundians at Dijon in 500 and seven years later against the Visigoths, longtime enemies of the Franks in the Loire valley, under Alaric II at Vouille near Poitiers. In 508, the Byzantine emperor Anastasius welcomed him as an ally in hopes of enlisting his military assistance against the OSTROGOTHS, who ruled Italy. His conversion to Catholic CHRISTIANITY greatly increased his prestige in Europe; most of the other barbarian tribes were Arian.

In Clovis's enlarged, now mostly Celtic and Christian kingdom, the Church played a larger role and the influence of German paganism waned. Clovis won the support of the Gallic clergy and made PARIS his base of operations. As a Christian king, he gave gifts to churches and encouraged the spread of monasteries.

When Clovis extended his conquests into Germany, he foreshadowed the conquests of CHARLEMAGNE three centuries later. Shortly before his death he probably had the Frankish Salian Law (*Lex Salica*), combining both Roman and Germanic law, revised and committed to writing. At the time of his death his kingdom, which covered almost all of Gaul and southwestern Germany, was divided among his four sons—Theodoric I, Clodomir, Childebert I, Clothaire I—thus laying the foundation for the Merovingian dynasty of Frankish rulers who followed.

See entries on FRANKS; MEROVINGIAN DYNASTY; *and* FRANCE. *For additional information, see* CHRISTIANITY; CHARLEMAGNE; VISIGOTHS; ITALY; *and* GERMANY.

COEUR, JACQUES

Jacques Coeur (c. 1395–1456) was a rich trader who held numerous posts in the French government of CHARLES VII. His most significant accomplishment was a series of treaties that opened trade with the east.

Coeur was born at Bourges, the son of Pierre Coeur, a wealthy merchant. In his early years, he established a number of successful businesses with his brothers, and he became famous throughout Europe. In 1436, Coeur was first called to PARIS by Charles VII. He held a series of important posts including master of the mint, steward of the royal expenditure, and royal commissioner to the parliament of Languedoc. Coeur was particularly successful in his reform of the coinage system. Starting in 1445, Coeur's agents made a number of treaties between FRANCE and the crusading order the Knights of Rhodes and EGYPT, as well as other eastern states, providing France with markets in the east and adding greatly to the commercial wealth of the country.

Clovis I (left) and his wife Clotilda. Their marriage formed an alliance that allowed Clovis to rule Germany.

Coeur's wealth and power allowed him to establish virtual monopolies in BANKING and farming; he became the richest private person in France. His house at Bourges was one of the greatest structures of the medieval period. His power, however, aroused jealousy. He was arrested on false charges of murder, due to the allegation of a debtor; he was convicted by a commission composed of men who owed him money. Coeur's fortune was distributed, and he was imprisoned. He escaped after three years, making his way to ROME where he entered the service of the PAPACY, before dying on an expedition against the Turks.

COLUMBA, ST.

Saint Columba (521–597) was an Irish missionary to SCOTLAND. He was born at Gartran in Donegal, a prince of the O'Donnells, and trained as a monk under Finnian at Moville and Clonard. In IRELAND, he founded monastery schools at Derry, Durrow, and Kells. In 563, he and several companions sailed to Scotland to missionize the Scots. They landed at Iona and built a monastery from which they evangelized the Western Isles, the Highlands, and the northern Lowlands. By the time he died in 597, Columba and his associates had completely Christianized northern Scotland.

Columba was the scribe responsible for the psalter known as the *Cathach of Columba*, the earliest surviving example of Irish majuscule script. He ranks with Sts. PATRICK and BRIDGET as one of the three patron saints of Ireland. Tradition maintains that he is buried with them in Downpatrick. (*See* IRELAND, SCOTLAND.)

COLUMBAN, ST.

Columban (c. 543–615) was born in Leinster in IRELAND. He became a disciple of Comgall of Bangor. In 590, Columban set sail with 12 companions for the European mainland where he set up monasteries at Annegrey and Luxeuil according to Irish MONASTICISM. (*See* IRELAND; ST. PATRICK.)

He won the support of King Childebert II of AUSTRIA, but after the king's death, he came under attack by those who resented his criticism of the court and the clergy, his refusal to accept the Roman date of Easter, and to bless the illegitimate sons of Theodoric II. When summoned to appear at Chalon-sur-Saône, he refused to go. He was eventually expelled to SWITZERLAND where he joined his companion St. Gall. After Columban crossed the Alps into Lombardy, he founded a monastery at Bobbio, which later became famous for its learning and an extensive library.

Columban is the earliest Irish writer whose work—or at least much of it—has survived. The main sources of his life are his letters, a life written by a monk at Bobbio, and BEDE's *Ecclesiastical History*.

COMMERCE AND TRADE IN THE MIDDLE AGES

The history of medieval trade can be divided into two distinct periods: the early Middle Ages (from the fifth to the eleventh centuries) when trade was a relatively insignificant part of economic life; and the later and High Middle Ages (from the twelfth through the fifteenth centuries) when trade underwent a dramatic expansion and became a central feature of the economy. The transition between these two periods is commonly referred to as the Commercial Revolution, a revolution that encompassed the rise of TOWNS, the development of new techniques to facilitate trade, and a significant increase in Europe's wealth and economic dynamism.

Early Middle Ages. Even before the fifth century, the western half of the Roman world (encompassing most of western Europe) had become an impoverished area compared to the eastern half. ROME's last centuries had seen a steady drain of wealth, population, and state resources from the West to the East, a trend symbolized by the emperor CONSTANTINE's decision to build a new capital for the empire in the eastern city of CONSTANTINOPLE. In those troubled centuries, self-contained rural villas gradually replaced the towns as the principle units of production and consumption; western Europe's economy came to be predicated more on subsistence agriculture and less on trade. The shift towards a more agrarian society gained momentum with the violence and political turmoil accompanying the influx of Germanic tribes into the empire in the fifth and sixth centuries. Cities and towns faced a seemingly endless round of sieges and plundering raids, and they inevitably fell into a state of decay. By the eighth century, towns had virtually disappeared from western Europe, as had the regular use of money. Trade did not entirely die out, but, by early Roman standards or by later medieval standards—or by the standards of the contemporaneous Byzantine and Islamic worlds—it had become little more than a veneer on an economy that was overwhelmingly oriented toward subsistence farming. Periodic markets, few and far between, facilitated occasional exchanges of surplus rural produce. A cadre of itinerant merchants managed to carry a handful of luxury goods from the East to the monasteries and the halls of the warrior elite.

Prosperity. Europe's move away from the stark economic conditions of the early Middle Ages began in the eleventh century and slowly accelerated in the twelfth. Several developments came together to make this possible. Political and religious authorities finally achieved a measure of control over the endemic violence that had characterized the early Middle Ages, creating circumstances in which it was once more possible to vouchsafe the movement of merchandise and MONEY. For reasons that are still largely unknown, Europe's population began to increase after many centuries of decline and stagnation. Some of the hardier souls in this increased population gathered together into fledgling towns, particularly in northern ITALY and FLANDERS. The CRUSADES enhanced Europe's ability to move people and their possessions over long distances, while simultaneously exposing Europeans more directly to the consumer goods of the Middle East, creating a growing demand that Venetian and Genoese shippers and merchants eagerly exploited.

Along with these broader social developments went a series of changes in the methods used to conduct trade. As the volume of trade increased so did the merchants' sophistication in making international financial transactions. Written mandates for payment (letters of exchange) began to circulate as a substitute for the sacks of silver coins that had changed hands in early trading ventures. By the end of the twelfth century the first banks had appeared in the commercially advanced towns of northern ITALY; they quickly assumed a role in financing international trade. The most important change in business technique, though, involved the development of new methods of raising investment capital. Particularly significant in this regard was the adoption of formal partnerships and other types of business associations that encouraged investors to pool their capital as parts of a larger enterprise. The association known as a commenda, for example, consisted of an active partner, who managed the day-to-day interests of a trading enterprise, and a sleeping partner (or group of partners) who furnished capital for the enterprise, but did not have to commit time or energy to its management. Commenda contracts were drawn up by the newly forming class of public notaries. They were enforceable in a legal system that was becoming more sophisticated and more effective following the rediscovery of Roman law in the twelfth century. Well-suited for an economy with limited investment capital, they allowed trade to be carried out on a larger scale than could be achieved by individual merchants acting on their own; they spread the risks of engaging in trade more widely; most important of all, they encouraged people with modest savings and minimal commercial experience to play a role in the expansion of trade.

Fairs. These changes in technique were accompanied by a revamping of the geography of exchange. Over the course of the twelfth century, the counts of CHAMPAGNE took steps to improve the facilities and management of a number of hitherto sleepy fair sites in their county. By the end of the century, the FAIRS had become an international clearing house for trade between merchants from nearly all parts of Europe. These fairs, staggered to form a cycle lasting through virtually the entire year, were particularly favored by merchants from Europe's two most advanced economic regions, FLANDERS and northern Italy. They greatly expanded trade between northern and southern Europe. By the end of the thirteenth century, the fairs had passed their zenith, but by revealing the potential for profit inherent in trade between Europe's regions, the fairs encouraged merchants to go farther afield for longer times. By the end of the thirteenth century, a number of businesses, chiefly Italian, had arranged to settle permanent agents (or factors) in many of Europe's leading commercial hubs, often by setting up strings of partnerships. By increasing the stability and predictability of the international market, these networks of factors and managers helped to create an economic environment in which buyers and sellers would be more likely to find each other.

A 7th-century relief atop the entry to a grocer's shop shows the shopkeeper's scale being checked for accuracy.

Late Middle Ages. While these changes were occurring on the international stage, important developments were occurring in local and regional trade. All over Europe, surging populations and burgeoning urbanization created an insatiable demand for foodstuffs. In most towns, the victualing trades (bakers, butchers, fishmongers, and so on) mushroomed in the twelfth and thirteenth centuries. Petty purchases of provisions became a routine fact of life in the towns, while in the

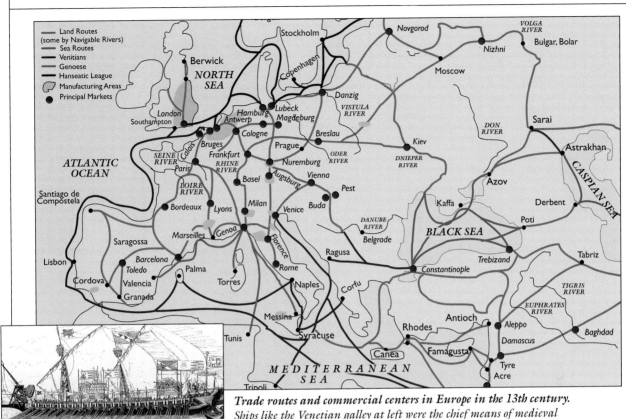

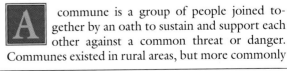

Trade routes and commercial centers in Europe in the 13th century.
Ships like the Venetian galley at left were the chief means of medieval
trade across politically hostile borders and impassable physical boundaries.

surrounding countryside, the farmers who could produce more than they needed for household sustenance were assured of a ready market for their surplus. Thousands of new rural market sites sprang up to facilitate the flow of goods between town and country. Some of these sites enjoyed so much success as trading venues that they developed into important towns in their own right. More commonly, though, they found themselves coalescing into regional trading systems organized around important towns, to which they sent grain and livestock, and from which they procured manufactured and imported goods. Trade was never as important in the countryside as it was in the towns, but much medieval trade was predicated on the willingness of farmers to take their goods to market.

The gradual convergence of regional and international trading networks allowed Europe to achieve a considerable degree of regional specialization. By CHAUCER's day, a prosperous Londoner might expect to wear a gown made from Flemish cloth, tinted with French dye, and trimmed with Russian fur. His or her shoes might be made from Spanish leather. Meals might include wine from Bordeaux, fish from Scandinavia, fish oil from ICELAND, apples from Normandy, salt from BRITTANY, sugar from SICILY, and spices

shipped from the Mediterranean by a Genoese merchant—all eaten on a table made from Irish boards set with Venetian glassware and silver mined near PRAGUE. The more fiscally astute Londoner may have fretted about the potential loss of the country's gold and silver coinage to pay for such goods—English kings certainly did—but such fears would have been assuaged by the almost limitless demand for English WOOL. By the end of the Middle Ages, trade had become an integral part of Europe's economy, and throughout Europe people were better off as a result.

See the articles on TOWNS, VILLAGES, AND CITIES; FAIRS; CHAMPAGNE, FAIRS OF; BANKING; MONEY AND CURRENCY; FLANDERS; ITALY, *and* WOOL TRADE. *Additional information can be found in* TRAVEL AND TRANSPORTATION; CRUSADES; *and* EXPLORATION.

COMMUNES

A commune is a group of people joined together by an oath to sustain and support each other against a common threat or danger. Communes existed in rural areas, but more commonly among urban people. The term "commune" became identified with city government and bourgeois society. Thus urban communes—self-governing entities that established their own laws and regulations—emerged in response to tight control of cities by feudal lords. Often, nobles would wield power over every aspect of city life. Merchants and artisans, seeking more freedom, especially in trade, joined together to further both their own interests and the interests of their city.

Beginnings. Not all of medieval Europe existed within the castle walls of nobles or the thatched cottages of peasants. Many people lived in cities and TOWNS; among the inhabitants were traveling merchants and skilled artisans. Each city and town came under the jurisdiction of a local feudal lord. With the fall of the Roman Empire, trade in the cities had dropped off, especially in western Europe. As a result, once-powerful urban centers had fallen into decline, with some disappearing completely. The growth of FEUDALISM further eroded the power of cities, as ruling nobles imposed restrictions on how their subjects could travel, how they could conduct their business affairs, and even when and whom they could marry.

The merchants and tradesmen who lived in these urban areas became increasingly frustrated by the imposition of what they considered arbitrary and onerous rules. Skilled artisans, guild members, and merchants banded together to re-establish their cities as self-sufficient urban centers that could make their own laws. These centers, the communes, initially appeared in the first half of the eleventh century in ITALY.

The citizens, or burghers, of a commune would swear an oath of allegiance to support the city, its inhabitants, and each other. The burghers were willing to accept the local nobles as overlords, but they were unwilling to let the nobles interfere in their day-to-day commercial activity. Nobles who refused to grant a certain degree of autonomy to the commune were sometimes faced with revolts, often successful.

Venice. One of the first and most successful communes was VENICE. Its location made it a vital link to overseas trade, and its natural protection in the form of sandbars and canals made it a difficult city to invade. MILAN and Pisa soon followed. Communes soon began to crop up in GERMANY, as well as modern-day Belgium and the NETHERLANDS.

In general, communes were more likely to form where the ruling parties were involved in conflicts. Disputes between Church leaders and local nobility made it difficult for nobles to rule in the cities. In contrast, areas whose rulers were strong (such as southern Italy, which was ruled by the NORMANS) saw no communes established for some time. When local nobles saw how lucrative communes could be for trade, they relaxed their opposition; many communes were in fact founded with the nobles' support. In FRANCE, entire new towns were planned on the commune model.

Commune Life. Communes did not cut themselves off from the local lords. In fact, they usually paid rent and taxes to the lords, who in return guaranteed protection and relative freedom. As communes became formidable political forces, a power structure developed within the commune and the more powerful members took control. Some communes placed themselves under the dictatorial rule of a podesta ("power holder") in hopes of maintaining order; others fell before the power of the local king.

The fourteenth century proved ruinous for many communes and for urban centers in general; plague and the exhaustion of natural resources made the crowded towns and cities virtual death traps. Communes had all but vanished north of the Alps by the end of the Middle Ages. In Italy, only the commune of VENICE survived; it retained its independence until the end of the eighteenth century. But for most, like FLORENCE, independence would soon become a forgotten memory or part of the city's legendary past.

See FEUDALISM *and* COMMERCE AND TRADE; TOWNS, VILLAGES, AND CITIES *for the social setting;* VENICE *and* FLORENCE *for the history of those communes;* NOBLE AND NOBILITY *and* SOCIAL CLASSES *for the social context.*

COMMYNES, PHILIPPE DE

 hilippe de Commynes (c. 1447–1511) was one of the most accomplished chroniclers of his time. His *Mémoires*, published after his death, mark him as a masterful storyteller with a keen eye for detail.

Philippe de Commynes.

Born in FLANDERS, the son of a knight and the godson of the duke of BURGUNDY, he grew up in a political atmosphere, and he displayed diplomatic skills as a young man. Eventually, this led him into the service of Kings LOUIS XI and XII. In this capacity he was able to travel to other countries as a representative. At one point, while on a diplomatic mission, he was briefly imprisoned, but eventually released. He died in FRANCE.

His position gave him a unique opportunity to witness the comings and goings of the different governments; his *Mémoires* give a detailed, if at times biased, picture of the royal courts.

CONRAD OF MARBURG

To say that Conrad of Marburg (1180–1232) was a religious zealot would be a considerable understatement. Chosen by Pope GREGORY IX as GERMANY's first papal inquisitor in 1231, he had already earned a reputation as a particularly brutal and cruel individual in the crusade against the ALBIGENSES nearly twenty years earlier.

Born in Marburg, Germany, Conrad managed throughout his life to secure positions of influence. Although he was not attached to any specific religious order, Pope INNOCENT III chose him to lead the crusade against the Albigenses, which involved a gruesome series of massacres. He joined the court of Louis IV, landgrave (count) of the German region of Thuringia and an ascetic, who brutalized his court and family. Louis died in 1227, but Conrad remained in power because he had become the confessor of Louis's wife, (St.) Elizabeth of HUNGARY. After Elizabeth's death in 1231, Conrad was chosen by Gregory IX to become the chief inquisitor of Germany.

Conrad, whose mission it was to root out HERESY and reform MONASTERIES, dealt with the clerics so severely that a group of German bishops pleaded with Pope Gregory to remove him. When Conrad declared Henry II of the Bendorf-Sayn region a heretic and traveled to Mainz to conduct a trial, he was met by a delegation of bishops and townspeople that declared Henry innocent. Conrad refused to back down and confirmed his intention to TORTURE Henry and bring him to trial. As Conrad rode away, the townspeople attacked and killed him.

CONSTANCE

Constance (1154–1198) was the daughter of King Roger II of SICILY, and heiress to the Sicilian crown. She married the future emperor HENRY VI in 1184, securing a temporary link between the Norman kings of ITALY and the HOHENSTAUFEN emperors of GERMANY. Constance was crowned as empress-consort with her husband in ROME in 1191. She had assumed the throne of Sicily two years before, but the Sicilians supported her nephew, Tancred of Lecce, and had rebelled against her rule. After Tancred's death in 1194, however, Constance assumed the throne of Sicily, unopposed.

When she was 41, an advanced age for childbirth in that era, Constance gave birth to her only child, Frederick; concerned that he be viewed as legitimate, she bore him in a public marketplace. After the death of Henry in 1197, Constance worked to ensure her son's succession to the throne. She died in 1198, and FREDERICK II (who would become one of the most powerful and controversial monarchs of the Middle Ages) was placed under the guardianship of Pope INNOCENT III. (*See* GERMANY; FREDERICK II.)

CONSTANTINE I THE GREAT

Constantine I the Great (c. 280–337) is considered the last great emperor of ROME, and although his reign (306–337) was before the Middle Ages, Constantine played an important transitional role in medieval history by his recognition of CHRISTIANITY as a legal religion and by creation of the city of CONSTANTINOPLE. The city was built to symbolize the triumph of Christianity and would become the center of Byzantine civilization and of Christianity for over 1,000 years.

Constantine was born in Nissus, a village in modern SERBIA.

A Byzantine mosaic in Hagia Sophia depicting Constantine the Great.

His father, Constantius, was a caesar, which, except for "augustus" was the highest title of the Roman Empire. In 305, Constantius became augustus, a title Constantine inherited when his father died a year later at York. After fighting a series of civil wars, defeating Galerius at the famous battle at Milvian Bridge outside Rome (312) and Licinius at Chrysopolis in (324), Constantine became sole ruler of the Roman Empire.

Constantine initiated important social and economic reforms that paved the way for medieval society. These reforms included transforming the ancient Roman legions into stationary regional armies with mobile reserves and reformed coinage to fight inflation. Constantine made offices and trades hereditary to ensure economic stability. Serfs and peasants, under the control of wealthy estate owners, were bound to the soil to ensure that the army would be well fed and to supply manpower for road maintenance.

Constantine began life as a pagan, but once in power he gradually adopted Christianity and became the protector of the Church. The reason for his conversion is a matter of controversy, but his political dispute with the pagan Licinius probably played a role in his decisions. In 325, Constantine tried to use imperial power to bring unity to the Church at the COUNCIL OF NICAEA. The council condemned the Arian HERESY and adopted the Nicene Creed. Although Constantine's death was followed by civil war, the order he established survived for over a hundred years.

CONSTANTINE VII

Constantine VII Porphyrogenitus (905–959) was the emperor of the Byzantine Empire from 912 until his death. Constantine's surname, "born to the purple," refers to his anointment as successor of his father Leo the Wise while an infant. Although Constantine became emperor in 912, his early rule was dominated by relatives; he assumed real power only in 944. He is best remembered for his patronage of the arts and his writings on Byzantine and Church history, and on military matters.

Although a generally successful ruler, Constantine's military policy met with mixed results. Ventures into Crete and southern ITALY failed, but an invasion of Thrace by the Magyars, an Asiatic tribal people inhabiting the upper Danube, was repelled. Constantine's real contribution to Byzantine power was improved diplomatic relations with a number of important states, including the Arabic caliphate of Córdoba, the HOLY ROMAN EMPIRE and, most important, the powerful Russian kingdom. Constantine was murdered in 959 by his son Romanus II.

CONSTANTINOPLE

In 330 C.E., Emperor Constantine moved the seat of his government from ROME to the ancient city of BYZANTIUM, renaming it and transforming the city into a bustling metropolis at the center of Roman culture. Constantine modeled his "New Rome" after the original: it was built on seven hills and many of its features mirrored Rome, down to the custom of giving its citizens a stipend of bread.

The city grew in size during the early Middle Ages; the wall around the city erected by Constantine was demolished, and a new one was built in 413 by Theodosius II which strengthened the city's defenses and doubled its size. Repeated attempts to conquer the city—by the Persians in 616, the AVARS in 626, and the

The second taking of Constantinople in 1204, after a fresco by Tintoretto in the Palace of the Doges in Venice, c.1540.

ARABS in 679, 672, and 717—failed because of this fortification. But the wall could not protect the city from internal strife caused by the mixing of eastern and western cultures and the rise of the city's Greek constituency. In the tenth century, especially during the reign of CONSTANTINE VII, the city experienced a cultural renaissance. In the eleventh century, the economy of the city blossomed under the leadership of Venetian traders who established their own quarter.

The Fourth Crusade conquered the city in 1204, subjecting it to three days of virtually genocidal destruction. What remained became the capital of the Latin empire of Constantinople, which lasted to 1261. The city never regained its former glory, and in 1453, it fell to the OTTOMAN TURKS, culminating nearly three centuries of attrition. (*See* CRUSADES.)

Four councils of Constantinople took place during the Middle Ages in which important matters of CHRISTIANITY were decided: the First Council of 381 issued the Nicene Creed that established belief in the Holy Trinity as Church doctrine; the Second Council in 553 ruled on the personhood of Christ as consisting of two natures (in opposition to the Nestorians); the Third Council in 680 asserted the dual natures and wills of Christ (in opposition to the Monothelites); and the Fourth Council in 869 (the only one rejected by the EASTERN ORTHODOX CHURCH) prohibited lay participation in Church elections and excommunicated Photius, patriarch of Constantinople.

CONVERSOS

Spanish term for converts, forced or voluntary, from JUDAISM to CHRISTIANITY, and their descendants. There is a tradition of conversion dating from late Roman SPAIN; many conversions of Spanish JEWS probably occurred during the reign of RECARED I, king of the VISIGOTHS (586–601) when he converted from Arianism to Catholicism, and during the reign of Sisebut, a seventh-century Gothic king. However, under Moorish rule in the eighth century, and the Christian rule in the eleventh and twelfth, the Jews in Spain managed to live and prosper with only occasional persecution. This relative tolerance lasted until the thirteenth century with the promulgation of anti-Jewish legislation, first initiated at the Fourth Lateran Council at Rome in 1215. The persecution of Spanish Jews reached its peak in the late fourteenth century, culminating in a massive riot and pogrom in 1391 that began in Seville and raged throughout Córdoba and into Castile, destroying the Jewish quarter of BARCELONA. Although religious fanaticism was the ostensible motivation for the riots, one contemporary observed, "all this was more out of a thirst for robbery than out of devotion." Those Jews not murdered were forced to accept baptism, resulting in a great wave of conversos entering Spanish society.

For the most part, in the next two centuries, these "new Christians" maintained the same social positions as before their conversions, working as merchants, moneylenders, tax collectors, doctors, and tailors. Many gained power and prestige, marrying into the ruling families of Spain. Other *converso* families entrusted their sons and daughters to religious orders that were avenues of power as well as demonstrations of faith. They became a large force in the Spanish clergy as well as a presence in the universities, earning distinction as scholars and writers.

A small minority of the conversos, however, were unable to adapt to Christian practice and secretly continued the performance of Jewish rituals. Suspicions of these "secret Judaizers" combined with jealousy over the prosperity and prominence of conversos in Spanish society led to renewed and increased persecution of conversos and Jews. Ultimately, these "new Christians," labeled *Marranos* by the old Christians—a pejorative term whose etymology is disputed—became even more mistrusted than the old Jews.

Resentment erupted in 1478 in the form of the INQUISITION, established by Ferdinand (who himself had a converso ancestor) and Isabella. Seeing the popularity of the persecution of crypto-Jews and of heretics within the masses, the Inquisition openly doubted the sincerity of the conversos and used any pretext—dining with Jews, wearing fine clothes on the Sabbath—to nullify their conversion. Partly with the support of the "new Christians" eager to prove themselves, the remaining Jews of Spain were expelled in 1492, followed by the Portuguese Jews in 1497.

Coming from affluent and well-educated families, the converted had an enormous impact on Iberian society; by the nineteenth century, as much as one third of Spanish nobility were at least partly descended from converso stock. (*See* INQUISITION; SPAIN; JEWS.)

CORONATION

Coronation was a central religious and political medieval ceremony in which new kings and popes were invested with their positions. Many elements of the coronation ceremony in the later Middle Ages had historical roots in the early Germanic kingdoms. With the Christianization of European society, the coronation of kings became a Christian event that symbolized the sacred character of KINGSHIP. The ascension of authority evolved into an elaborate ceremony with a diversity of ritual in the various medieval kingdoms. The central function of many of these ceremonies was the fusion of secular and religious authority. The coronation ceremony, therefore, was no mere formality, but the endowment of the new king with a quasi-religious sanctity.

The ceremony of coronation emerged out of Germanic rituals in which kings took power in the former provinces of the western Roman Empire in the fourth and fifth centuries. Newly crowned Germanic kings were carried on shields around the assembled three times by the leaders of the clan and then given the symbols of power: a spear and a diadem (band of silk or linen), which was bound around his head. Elements of these rituals can be seen in later medieval ceremonies such as the acclimation ritual in which the gathered subjects unanimously approved the king.

The coronation of an English king, presided over by a high-ranking official of the Catholic Church.

With the Christianization of these kingdoms, the coronation ceremony became more complex and took on Christian significance. The two central acts during coronations were religious in nature: the benediction, and the anointment with oil or oil and balsam. Anointment had specific biblical precedent and was therefore a clear attempt to endow the king with divine sanction. In ENGLAND and FRANCE, after the ceremony the king would retire to the church with the priests, offering bread and wine for his own communion, thereby imbuing the king with a priestly identity.

In the fourth century, coronation ceremonies initiated the rule of a new pope. Local bishops would lay their hands on newly elected popes in an act of consecration. By the seventh century, the new pope was invested or confirmed in office on election day, but the coronation ceremony took place on a later date in Saint Peter's cathedral. On that day, the pope was given his crown and received the adulation of the masses. In the late Middle Ages, coronation included the crowning of the pope with a tiara in front of St. Peter's, followed by a procession through ROME.

Germanic kings were crowned by the pope until the fifteenth century. This tradition began in the year 800 when the conquering Frankish (modern day FRANCE) King CHARLEMAGNE was crowned emperor by the pope on Christmas Day. Other religious figures took the pope's role in various kingdoms: the archbishop of Cologne in GERMANY; the archbishop of Canterbury in England; and the archbishop of Reims in France. Beginning in 1066, the English king was crowned at WESTMINSTER ABBEY where he took an oath proclaiming his duty to protect the laws and customs of the kingdom.

See KINGSHIP *for medieval theories on sovereignty;* CHRISTIANITY; PAPACY; *and* CHARLEMAGNE *for more on the involvement of the Church;* WESTMINSTER ABBEY *and* CHURCHES AND CATHEDRALS *for more on the ceremony.*

CORTES

The name given to the assemblies of nobles, clergy, and city representatives that began meeting in the kingdoms of Castile-León, PORTUGAL, ARAGON, and Catalonia in the thirteenth century. The development evolved from the early medieval practice of the *consilium*, debates and assemblies held in the *Curia regis,* in which the king consulted with his nobles and officials. As the regional TOWNS became more prominent in the political and economic affairs of the kingdom, their representatives were summoned to the court as well, and these new assemblies became known as *Cortes* (the plural expressing their greater size and importance).

Representatives of towns were called to the Curia as early as 1188 by Alphonse IX of León. By 1230, the kingdom Castile joined this cortes. The cortes of Aragon and Catalonia met soon afterward; the Portuguese Cortes first assembled in 1254. The power and character of these assemblies varied according to the designs of the presiding monarch and the unity of the regional nobility. The institution reached its peak in the fourteenth and fifteenth centuries, but in the next 200 years, civil wars and the rise of absolutism saw the Cortes wane in influence and power.

COSMETICS AND BEAUTY AIDS

People have embellished their physical appearance since antiquity, and this was no less true in the Middle Ages. Wealthier people had the fanciest cosmetics and perfumes at their disposal, but even the poor took pride in how they looked.

Makeup. Thick makeup was common among the women and men in ROME. The Byzantines continued the Roman fashion, and makeup was also popular in western Europe. Makeup was usually purchased from traveling merchants, but sometimes professional cosmetics makers would have shops in the larger towns.

People wore makeup to add (or subtract) color from their skin. Where a pale complexion was a sign of beauty, people wore white makeup or light colors over a white base. In other regions, rouged cheeks and eye shadow was common; ANGLO-SAXONS admired orange or rose-colored rouge. The "natural" look was popular in some areas, although there might be little natural about it; in late medieval ITALY, women often wore a flesh-colored base covered with a pinkish cover.

The ingredients that went into makeup were rarely pure and often toxic. Lead was a common ingredient in many face powders. Sometimes, heavy makeup caused people to break out in blemishes or spots on their faces. Healing substances were developed, but they would work only if the afflicted person refrained from using the cosmetics that had caused the problem.

Hair Care. Medieval men and women took great pride in their hair. Blond hair was especially admired. Many people tried to bleach or dye their hair, and those whose hair had turned white or grey sometimes used hair coloring formulas made from the ashes of vine stems and ash wood boiled in vinegar. Texture and style were also important. People washed their hair and treated it with olive oil to make it more supple. Bearded men would often wax their beards and wrap them in special "beard bags" while they slept.

Short hair was generally admired on men; the Church, in fact, frowned on facial hair as well as long tresses on men. Some men took great pains to appear carefully groomed, while others affected an unkempt appearance, sometimes requiring just as much work.

Women often did their hair up in elaborate styles. Braiding was quite common, as was curling. Women often ornamented their hair with jeweled hairpins, ribbons, or flowers. Undone hair on a woman was often a sign of illness or sorrow, but sometimes undone hair could take on erotic connotations. Women would shave or pluck their eyebrows; some, in a crude version of modern electrolysis, would use heated needles to destroy hair follicles. Medieval women often shaved their hairline to give them a higher forehead.

Head lice were a common affliction in medieval times, so people spent a fair amount of time delousing themselves or their intimates.

Cleanliness and Perfumes. People in the Middle Ages placed a high value on cleanliness. Bathing was common; it was more elaborate for the rich than for the peasantry, but most people bathed regularly. Public baths were common, especially in the larger towns. In some places, people recognized the curative powers of mineral waters and took medicinal baths.

Perfumes were popular in Europe and the Islamic world for the scents they created, not (as is mistakenly believed) to mask poor hygiene habits. As trade brought more spices and perfumes from eastern countries into Europe, perfume became more common, which led to their manufacture becoming more effective. The development of alcohol-based perfumes in the fourteenth century created a more durable and longer-lasting product.

Aniseed and mint were used to freshen and sweeten the breath. Teeth were cared for by spreading the medieval equivalent of toothpaste on pieces of cloth or the end of a twig, and brushed across the teeth. Many tooth-cleaning preparations contained calcium compounds; often, however, these were added to a tooth-decaying base of honey or sugar.

COURTLY LOVE

Courtly love was a major element of the LITERATURE of KNIGHTHOOD and CHIVALRY that emerged in the poetry and song of TROUBADOURS and poet-knights who rose to prominence in the twelfth century in southern FRANCE. Through the poetry of courtly love, the romantic ideal was introduced into European thought and spread to northern France, ITALY, GERMANY, ENGLAND, and SPAIN. TROUBADOURS departed from tradition by writing in provincial languages, rather than Latin, the lingua franca of the medieval elites. The troubadours sang of the love between a young knight and a lady married to a aristocratic lord. Courtly love was always adulterous, secretive, and unrealized. The ideal of courtly love was not normally identified with marital relationships.

A 12th-century depiction of courtly love in which a couple picnic and sing of their love for one another.

Courtly love presented a highly idealized image of love that contained elements common to all feudal relationships. The male lover assumed a subordinate role to his beloved; he was her "vassal" and therefore subject to her will. As in all feudal relationships, the value of loyalty was central. The knight dedicated himself entirely to the object of his desires; he would undertake any task and suffer any hardship. The image of women in courtly love, although extremely ambiguous, had an important impact on the place of WOMEN in medieval society.

Courtly love had a number of sources including the Roman poet Ovid's *Art of Love* as well as the Arabic *Ring of the Dove*, written in 1022. Two prominent sponsors of courtly love literature were ELEANOR OF AQUITAINE, wife of two kings, PHILIP I of France and HENRY I of England, and her daughter Marie de Champagne. A number of important works were written during Eleanor's reign: CHRÉTIAN DE TROYES' *Lancelot*, ANDREAS CAPELLANUS' *On the Art of Love*, and Guillaume de Lorri's *Roman de La Rose*.

The precise meaning of courtly love has been a subject of debate; like many familiar descriptive terms of the Middle Ages, the phrase is a product of nineteenth-century suppositions. Originally, historians took the Andreas Capellanus' description of a "court of love" literally where knights and ladies engaged in a mock trial of adulterers and other amorous matters. Early historians mistakenly thought that adultery was rampant and an accepted part of medieval courtly life.

Recent historical research has corrected this picture. Adultery in fact was a high crime in medieval society. A woman who betrayed her lordly husband would be expelled from society, and a knight who slept with his lord's wife was punished with castration. The adulterous love depicted in the songs of troubadours seems to have been mainly metaphorical. Unrequited courtly love may have reflected the frustration of young knights in finding a suitable wife, a necessary step in achieving adulthood.

Women appear in contradictory ways in the poetry of courtly love. On the one hand, the lady adored by the knight is idealized, but on the other she is depicted as somewhat nefarious. The knight is a "subject" to the lady, and his love sometimes appeared as an illness, making him pale and sickly. From another point of view, the lady is a subordinate element of the tale, merely a means for the knight's self-realization.

The heyday of courtly love lasted until the fourteenth century. It inspired a number of poets, including the Italians DANTE and PETRARCH, and CHAUCER in ENGLAND, all of whom refashioned the ideal of courtly love to fit their own imagination. (See LITERATURE, KNIGHTHOOD, CHIVALRY, TROUBADOURS.)

COURTRAI, BATTLE OF

Also known as the Battle of the Spurs (July 11, 1302); a great victory of Flemish infantry over French and Flemish knights led by Count Robert of Artois. The battle ended French ambitions of expansion into FLANDERS and was a significant victory for infantry during the feudal age. The defending Flemish forces were composed of pikemen militia, mostly of the burgher (city dweller) class, from the cities of Bruges, Ypres, and Courtrai, and a small group of knights. The decisive element of the battle was the excellent defensive terrain occupied by the Flemish militia, and the predictable inability of the French knights to think tactically about their situation. The militia positioned themselves near marshy land divided by canals and bridges; a deployment that made any advance extremely hazardous.

The French first attempted to dislodge their opponents through the use of crossbowmen and a charge by a small group of infantry. Even through the Flemish defenders did not move from their position, the main body of French and Flemish knights charged. The knights were repelled, and soon caught in the mud. No longer able to maneuver, the knights were surrounded by the militia who mercilessly slaughtered them with spear, cleaver, and flail. Robert was killed when he personally launched a second failed strike. This debacle lead to the death of 40 percent of the French knights. The battle was so named because of the 700 spurs taken from dead French knights and hung in an abbey. (*See* FRANCE; FLANDERS; WARFARE.)

CRECY, BATTLE OF

An important battle (August 26, 1346) in the early stages of the HUNDRED YEARS' WAR between ENGLAND and FRANCE in which the English king EDWARD III defeated PHILIP VI of France, a victory that opened the way to future English territorial gains in France. Crécy was also an important battle in the history of medieval WARFARE. The decisive impact of British archers undermined the long-standing superiority of the mounted knight, mirroring the decay of the feudal order. (*See* WARFARE.)

The Battle of Crécy was part of Edward's invasion of NORMANDY undertaken on July 11, 1346 in support of a rebellious Norman faction. Edward marched his 10,000 troops north from Normandy, and settled into a defensive position at Crécy on the coast of the English Channel in Picardy. Philip had wisely avoided battle against the tactically

The Battle of Crécy as depicted in Froissart's Chronicles. *Crécy was the first large engagement of the Hundred Years' War.*

superior English, but at Crécy his army numbered twice the English forces, and his nobles insisted on battle. The English deployment had three lines: the first line was composed of archers on the wings, the second line had archers in the center with dismounted men-at-arms on the flanks; and the third was a reserve of dismounted men-at-arms. The French deployed in two lines, with Italian crossbowmen at the front and knights in the second line.

The battle began with a duel between the English archers and the Genoese crossbowmen—mercenaries hired by Philip to counteract the British archers. The French lacked protection and were outshot by their British counterparts. The crossbowmen fled in disorder, and were trampled underfoot when their impatient knighted comrades charged. Confused and without support, the French knights were cut down by the English archers and men-at-arms. In the battle, 1,500 knights were killed, including the elite of the French nobility. (*See* HUNDRED YEARS' WAR; WEAPONRY.)

CRUSADES

Although CHRISTIANITY originally exhibited strong pacifist tendencies, following the accession of the first Christian Emperor CONSTANTINE I THE GREAT in 313 C.E., the Church blended this ethic with the Roman proclivity towards the legitimation of force and violence.

Use of Violence. In the early fifth century, the most prominent of the Latin Church Fathers, ST. AUGUSTINE OF HIPPO, justified the shedding of blood on behalf of Christ, citing Christ's words to his immediate disciples: "Compel them to come in." In the early Middle Ages, the use of force and violence to protect the Cross and defeat, convert, or obliterate pagans and other non-Christians was commonly justified by bishops, leading to such incidents as Emperor CHARLEMAGNE's massacre of heathen SAXONS at the end of the eighth century. *The Song of Roland*, the French nobility's favorite epic, written down around 1100, accepts religious war against Muslims in SPAIN as an inevitable and righteous course of action. Fully half of the poem is devoted to detailed accounts of war to the death between Christians and Muslims, who are depicted as satanic.

Only JEWS among non-Christians were put in a separate category with regard to being the object of Christian violence. In the opinion of most teachers and Church officials, the Jews were not to be physically attacked but segregated and disadvantaged until the Second Coming of Christ, who would deal with His ethnic kinsmen, the putative cause of His death.

Origins. In the 1070s and 1080s, four developments induced the Latin Church to organize a concerted attack upon its enemies, especially the hated and feared Muslims who were regarded as subscribing not to another religion but to a Christian HERESY, making them doubly loathsome. First, there was the beginning of the *Reconquista* of Muslim Spain by Spanish nobility who came out of their Pyrenees mountain redouts after four centuries and pushed down into the Castilian plain and the Aragonese and Portuguese coastal littorals. The Reconquista was not completed until 1492, but by the third decade of the thirteenth century three-quarters of the Iberian peninsula had been retaken for the Cross. The Gregorian Reform papacy enthusiastically endorsed the Iberian counterattack upon Islam. GREGORY VII would have widened the attack on ISLAM into the eastern Mediterranean if the pope were not already involved in a war with the German emperor. Second, the invasion of the Byzantine territories by a new Asiatic Muslim people, the SELJUK TURKS, and the consequent defeat and killing of the Byzantine Emperor, at the BATTLE OF MANZIKERT in 1071, impelled his successor ALEXIUS COMNENUS to appeal desperately for aid from Europe against the Muslim Turkish armies. Alexius was aware of the risks involved in this appeal for Western aid. The Norman nobility of southern ITALY were as much or more interested in invading the Byzantine Balkan territories as taking on the Turks, but Alexius took the risk of appealing to ROME for help. Third, the penetration of the eastern Mediterranean by the Turks had momentarily fractured the political stability of the Arab world and opened a glint of possibility that a Western invasion of the East to redeem Jerusalem from the Muslims had a chance of success. Fourth, the improving climate and greater food supply in northern Europe were increasing the number of landless younger sons among the French nobility, providing many recruits for an army devoted to battling the Crescent on behalf of the Cross and opening up conquest of rich eastern principalities.

First Crusade. It was the wily monastic Pope URBAN II who, in 1095, took advantage of this context and proclaimed what became the First Crusade at the Council of CLERMONT in France. Urban had another motive for proclaiming a crusade at this time. He hoped that all the important European kings would unite under the papal military banner and bring to an end the divisive controversy over Church-state relations that Urban II inherited from the Gregorian Reform PAPACY. Urban was to be disappointed. Not a single crowned head joined the First Crusade. Its leaders were all French or Norman Italian dukes and counts. Urban appointed a papal legate as nominal leader of the expedition.

A crowd of 5,000 lords, knights, priests, workers,

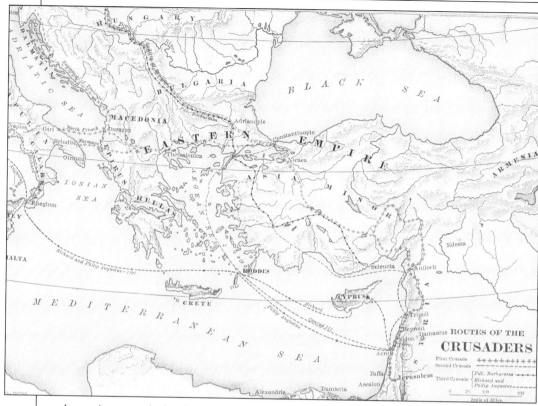

Failure. The five expeditions against the Muslims all ended in tragedy or farce. The Second Crusade of 1144, led by ST. BERNARD OF CLAIRVAUX, one of the most esteemed Catholic religious figures of his day, did succeed in recruiting two kings, and prostitutes took the Cross, believing that Urban had promised them plenary (full) indulgence for their sins if they joined. After first pillaging and massacring several Jewish urban communities in the Rhineland, this motley assemblage wandered through the Balkans towards CONSTANTINOPLE. Emperor Alexius I Comnenus quickly transported the army across the Hellespont to Asia Minor. After taking Antioch in Syria, the army took Jerusalem, killing many thousands of Arab and Jewish inhabitants.

Within two decades the Latin Kingdom of Jerusalem had been set up, comprising most of present-day Israel as well as a piece of Syria, with a rigid feudal hierarchy and a French aristocrat crowned as king. Muslim counterattack came quickly and steadily shrank the size of the crusading kingdom. In 1187, Jerusalem was retaken by the great Egyptian Arab warrior SALADIN. In 1291, the last Christian outpost, the massive port and fort of Acre surrendered to the ARABS, and the crusaders departed peacefully when it was clear they could expect no succor from Latin Europe. Europeans did not return in force to the Holy Land until 1917.

From the 1140s until 1270, there were five additional crusades from Latin Europe against the Muslims. One (the Fourth Crusade of 1204) ended by invading and taking Constantinople from the Byzantine Greeks and holding it until 1261.

Louis VII of FRANCE and Conrad III of GERMANY, but their armies were decimated in Turkey. The Third Crusade of 1190 was organized by Rome with much fanfare and was led by a stellar array: the kings of ENGLAND, France, and Germany. The monarchs ended up bickering with one another more than fighting the ARABS, and nothing was accomplished. Nor did a strange, largely peaceful expedition to the Holy Land carried out by the German emperor FREDERICK II in the 1230s—while he was at war with the Pope—have any consequences. The most serious and promising of the later crusades was the Fifth Crusade, a bold venture into the heartland of Arab power in Egypt by a large French army led by St. LOUIS IX of France. It resulted in a huge battle in the Nile Delta, St. Louis's defeat and capture by the Arabs, and his ransoming by his loyal people back home. In 1270, the now old and frail St. Louis launched a suicide expedition into Tunisia and achieved his goal of dying there as a Christian martyr. There was one further crusading expedition of sorts in the late fourteenth century, into the Muslim Balkans, resulting in yet another massacre of European knights.

Other Crusades. Meanwhile, the crusading idea was being applied within continental Europe. The PAPACY launched a crusade and seized the northern French nobility's land against the Albigensian (Catharist) heretics in southern France in the second decade of the thirteenth century. The invasion of southern Italy by the French in the 1250s was also legitimated by the papacy as a crusade. The invasion of Christian ARAGON by the French king Philip III in 1285, which had strictly political causes, was also urged on by the papacy. The French invaders were driven back, and this bitter defeat precipitated a falling-out between the papacy and its long-term ally, the French monarchy. In the late thirteenth century the German crusading order known as the TEUTONIC KNIGHTS launched an imperialist advance into eastern Europe under the guise of a crusade and the order's fierce armies penetrated as far as Lithuania over the next century and a half.

Europeans who clearly benefited from the Crusades were the Venetian, Genoese, and other Italian merchants, shipbuilders, and fleet-owners. They made a thriving business out of transporting and supplying the crusaders. It was the Venetians who turned the Fourth Crusade against Constantinople in 1204. French and German knights carved out territories during the Crusades in the Mediterranean or eastern Europe. The papacy gained prestige and visibility from the Cru-

A 14th-century Italian depiction of the siege of Jerusalem during the First Crusade, during which thousands were massacred.

sades, but Rome's use of the crusading ideal against heretics and political opponents yielded significant dismay and criticism. The origins of the northern Prussian (German) state lies in the crusading ventures of the Teutonic Knights. In the sixteenth century, the order was secularized and their lands passed to the rising HOHENZOLLERN DYNASTY of Brandenburg. Since 1945 most of these one-time German crusading territories have belonged to POLAND.

Results. The most important consequence of the Crusades was that they brought European nobility into close contact with Muslim Arabs and Turks. The Europeans discovered that the Muslims were not satans but intelligent, capable, and, after their fashion, devout people. Coupled with the Europeans' realization early on that fighting Arabs was a very dangerous if not mortal enterprise, this new familiarity slowly engendered a tolerance on the part of European Christians for the Muslim world. Beginning in France around 1140 and later extending to Christian Spain, schools of ARABIC LANGUAGE and Muslim thought were established in Latin countries. The greatest impact of the Crusades lies with the Iberian peoples. Spain and Portugal largely originated as crusading states, and they carried their devotional militancy into the conquest and settlement of Central and SOUTH AMERICA in the sixteenth century and beyond.

The appeal of fighting to save the Cross resonated deep into the ranks of European society. Going off on a crusade was always a dramatic career move for king, lord, and knight. But common people also yearned to be involved from time to time. This resulted in the Peasants' (or People's) Crusade preached by an itinerant evangelical PETER THE HERMIT. A crowd of farmers and artisans reached Constantinople in 1096 shortly before the First Crusade arrived there. The disdainful emperor readily transported this rabble to Asia Minor, where they were eliminated by the Turks. Similarly, in the early years of the thirteenth century, young vagrants from Italy and France formed the CHILDREN'S CRUSADE. Its members ended up either dead or enslaved by the Arabs.

See CHRISTIANITY; ISLAM; PAPACY; CONSTANTINOPLE; WARFARE; *and* HERESY. *For more on individuals, see* URBAN II, GREGORY VII, LOUIS IX, ST. BERNARD OF CLAIRVAUX, *and* SALADIN. *Also* PETER THE HERMIT *on the Peasants' Crusade.*

DAMASCUS

Situated between desert, mountains, and river regions, the ancient site of Damascus was, since antiquity, an important center of trade between east and west. The city was also situated on the frontier of several empires, and both benefited and suffered from this strategic placement. In 613, the city was conquered from the Byzantines by the Parthians, and then in 635, the city was taken by the ARABS who ended Western rule of the city. In 650, the caliph Muawiya made the city his capital and the city prospered under UMAYYAD control for the next century.

The city became world famous for its textile (damask being named for it) and metal crafts. Its wealth also attracted adventurers, however, and the city was coveted by Karmathian and Seljuk warlords through much of the Middle Ages.

In the early eighth century, Caliph Walid I seized the basilica of St. John the Baptist and converted it into a mosque. The resulting Great Mosque of Damascus is one of the Middle East's most impressive structures.

From the ninth century onward, Damascus was dominated by the ruling dynasty in EGYPT, even after 1076, when the city was briefly conquered by the SELJUK TURKS. In 1126, crusaders attacked the city, but they failed to establish a foothold strong enough to establish a kingdom.

In 1154, the city fell to Nureddin; he and his successor, SALADIN, made it their base in their ongoing war against the FRANKS. In 1260, the city was occupied by MONGOLS, but was soon liberated by the MAMLUKS. In 1401, TAMERLANE, seeking to avenge his Mongol predecessors, ravaged the city, burned it to the ground, and carried off many of the city's most capable artisans to Samarkand. The OTTOMAN TURKS took the city in 1516. They ruled it for 400 years until Anglo-Arab forces would march triumphantly into the city in 1918.

DANCE OF DEATH

A widespread concept in the late Middle Ages in Europe, rendered visually and allegorically, that Death was the ever-present equalizer of all mankind. (*See* MAGIC AND FOLKLORE.)

The representations in art, music, poetry, literature, and dramatic pageants usually depicted Death personified as a skeleton, either juxtaposed with living figures, or actually leading the living by the hand in a "danse macabre." The superstition was engendered by the prevailing religious hysteria marked by an obsession with penitence and the consequences of sin, which grew out of the strong feelings of mortality and helplessness in an age of the BLACK DEATH and the HUNDRED YEARS' WAR.

This theme of the inevitability of death appealed to writers and artists; it was utilized to remind people, from pope to prince to peasant, of their ultimate equality. The earliest representation is probably the series of paintings in the Cimietière des Innocents of Paris, dating from 1424.

DANDOLO, ENRICO

Enrico Dandolo (c. 1107–1205) was the most renowned member of a family of prosperous and powerful Venetian patricians who held important positions in VENICE from the eleventh to the fourteenth centuries. Elected doge in 1192 when he was 84, Dandolo was an able diplomat and administrator until his death. Under his rule the Venetian republic grew in power, although his own authority was somewhat limited by the restraints imposed by the Venetian mercantile oligarchy.

Dandolo is best known for his direction of Venice's participation in the Fourth Crusade. Under his supervision, Venice agreed to provide ships and supplies for the crusaders, on condition that it receive half the spoils of the conquest. When the crusaders were unable to pay the agreed sum, Dandolo, 94 years old and nearly blind at the time, agreed to waive the remaining payment if the crusaders would help Venice capture Zara, a powerful and rebellious port city on the Adriatic. Despite the angry protestations of the pope, the crusaders complied with Dandolo's demands and easily conquered Zara. Dandolo then managed to obtain the financial and military assistance of Alexius, the son of the deposed Byzantine emperor, and convinced the crusaders to lead an attack on CONSTANTINOPLE in order to place Alexius on the throne. However, the Greeks did not accept Alexius. In the ensuing struggle for the city, in which Dandolo played a surprisingly active role for a 94-year-old, much of Constantinople was destroyed by fire and pillaging.

The crusaders were ultimately victorious, and the Byzantine Empire was divided up among the various participating powers. Venice, greedy for territory under Dandolo's sway, took for itself many key ports of trade, including three-eighths of Constantinople. Dandolo died soon after the victory, unable to enjoy for long the satisfaction of his territorial ambitions.

DANTE ALIGHIERI

We can never know whether Dante (1265–1321) would be ranked with the world's great writers had he lived a more quiet life. But his political activism, coupled with his lifelong love for a woman who died when he was 25, inspired him to write what has been recognized for more than 700 years as one of the world's great works of literature. *The Divine Comedy*, written during the last decade of his life, allowed him—figuratively—to send his friends to Heaven, his enemies to Hell, and himself to his beloved Beatrice.

The Divine Comedy has inspired writers since GEOFFREY CHAUCER, although Dante was little read during the eighteenth century. A renewed interest in Dante and his work was spurred on early in the twentieth century by the author T. S. Eliot, who wrote a much-publicized essay on him in 1929 and referred frequently to the poet in his own works.

Early Life. Dante Alighieri was born in FLORENCE in 1265, during a time of political turmoil. The region had been torn apart by civil war between two rival factions, the GUELPHS, loyal to the PAPACY, and the GHIBELLINES, who supported the HOLY ROMAN EMPIRE. Dante and his family were Guelphs. The Ghibellines had taken over Florence before Dante was born, but the Guelphs had retaken the city by 1270.

Not much is known about his parents except that his mother died when he was five and his father died when he was 12. It is known that as a boy he was formally betrothed by his family to Gemma Donati, whom he married when he was 20. As a young man, Dante joined the Florentine forces as a citizen-soldier in battles against the cities of PISA and Arezzo.

Beatrice. During his twenties, Dante fell deeply in love with the woman who would remain his lifelong inspiration: Beatrice, the person who in his eyes most closely represented perfect Christian love on earth.

Who was Beatrice? She was most likely Beatrice (or Bice) Portinari, a year younger than Dante and married to a man named Simone de' Bardi. How well Dante knew her—if he knew her personally at all—is unclear. Dante was devastated when she died in 1290. It was around this time that Dante, to console himself, began his career as a writer.

La vita nuova (*New Life*), a series of 31 poems and 41 prose essays, were written between 1290 and 1294. In these works Dante celebrates Beatrice's perfection and the purity of his love for her. Later, Beatrice served as a central character in *The Divine Comedy*—apparently to fulfill a promise Dante made at the end of *vita nuova* "to say of her what has never been said of another woman."

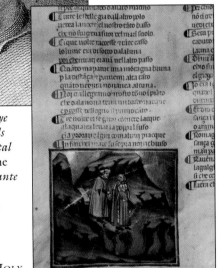

"All hope abandon, ye who enter here" reads the sign over the portal to hell in Dante's The Divine Comedy. *Dante (above) wrote his masterpiece while in exile because of his political activities.*

Political Activism. Dante was active in Florentine politics for several years beginning in 1295. He served as a city councilman and made diplomatic trips to other cities. Florence at the time was still controlled by the Guelphs, but by now they had split into two factions, the White Guelphs and the Black Guelphs.

In 1301, the leader of the Black Guelphs was banished from Florence and the White Guelphs assumed power. By now Dante, a White Guelph, had become an important political figure. Pope BONIFACE VIII supported the Black Guelphs and helped them regain control of Florence. Dante departed for ROME to plead before Boniface. But during his absence, the Black Guelphs returned to Florence and assumed power.

Dante was assessed a small fine, but he refused to pay it and as a result, his property was seized, and he was exiled permanently under threat of death. He never set foot in Florence again. After much travelling, Dante settled in RAVENNA; he died there in 1321.

The Masterpiece. Sometime after 1307, Dante began work on his masterpiece, *The Divine Comedy,* completing it shortly before his death. The work is comprised of three books—*Inferno, Purgatorio,* and *Paradiso*—in which the author is guided through Hell, Purgatory, and Heaven by the Roman poet Virgil, Beatrice, and ST. BERNARD OF CLAIRVAUX. Rich in symbolism and written in a flowing and elegant style, it established Dante as a master storyteller and one of the world's greatest writers.

DENMARK

The southernmost of the medieval Scandinavian kingdoms, so named for its location on the border (*mark*) between the CAROLINGIAN empire and German territory. The Danish kingdom consisted of the Jutland peninsula, Fünen, Zeeland, and other islands, and southern Sweden, which remained part of Denmark, except for a brief period, until 1658.

In the Middle Ages, Denmark gained its earliest notoriety in the early ninth century by resisting CHARLEMAGNE and the Frankish expansion. This began the building of a massive earthwork (the *Danevirke*), designed to protect the port of Hedeby.

Viking Era. During the VIKING era, Danes and Vikings from other parts of Scandinavia swept into western Europe to raid, explore, settle, and trade. The Danes were active as seafarers, traders, and colonizers, especially in ENGLAND and NORMANDY. King ALFRED and the later SAXON kings fought the Danes regularly.

Gorm the Old, the first king of Denmark who reigned in the mid-900s, established a powerful dynasty centered in Jutland. Gorm and his son Harald II Bluetooth, the first Christian king of Denmark, were the first Vikings to launch full-scale attacks beyond the Baltic and North Seas. (*See* ST. EDMUND.)

Harald's son, Sweyn I Forkbeard, conquered and ruled ENGLAND as its king from 986 to 1014. The Danes reached the height of their political power under Cnut I the Great, king of England (1016–1035). After 1019, Cnut was monarch of the united kingdoms of Denmark, NORWAY, and England, and was perhaps the greatest ANGLO-SAXON ruler in history. Shortly following his death in 1035, Denmark experienced a period of civil war as the empire slowly disintegrated.

In 1042 Cnut's nephew, Sweyn II Estridsen, an Anglo-Saxon earl, received Denmark as his share of his uncle's huge North Sea kingdom and ruled it until his death in 1074. During this period the Danes completed their conversion to CHRISTIAN-

St. Edmund captured by the Danes, tortured, and eventually executed for refusing to renounce his faith, 869.

ITY which had begun with the missionary work of St. Ansgar (801–865) and had intensified during the 900s. With the help of the archbishopric of Hamburg, Sweyn organized the Danish church into eight bishoprics. Pope GREGORY VII wrote Sweyn a series of letters complimenting him on his work. The Danish church was strengthened even more in 1103 when an archbishopric was established in Lund.

European interest in Denmark and the rest of Scandinavia increased after the mid-1000s. Adam of Bremen described in detail the missionary work of the German church in Denmark in his *History of the Bishops of the Church of Hamburg*. The most impressive Danish historian of the time, Saxo Grammaticus, wrote a massive history of the Danes to about 1185, *Gesta Danorum*, which scholars have compared to BEDE's epic *Ecclesiastical History of the English People*.

Following Sweyn's death, his five sons took turns ruling Denmark. After the last of the sons died in 1134, fierce dynastic feuds broke out between family members, eventually leading to the election of two kings, both of whom appealed to Holy Roman Emperor FREDERICK I BARBAROSSA. Frederick attempted to divide the kingdom between the two claimants, but family conflicts continued until one family member, WALDEMAR I, emerged as sole ruler.

The Waldemar Age. Waldemar I the Great (1157–1182) brought the civil strife to an end and established Denmark as the strongest Scandinavian state. Waldemar called on HENRY THE LION of Saxony and Albert the Bear of Brandenburg to help him subdue the WENDS and force them to accept Christianity. Waldemar became a vassal of the Holy Roman emperor Frederick I but later achieved independence from German control. Waldemar codified Danish laws and extended his kingdom through the conquest of Norwegian territory. His international prestige and influence increased after he married off three of his daughters to sons of Frederick I, Eric X of Sweden, and PHILIP II of France. Waldemar's son, Cnut VI, succeeded him and ruled Denmark until 1202.

The Waldemar age of Danish history (1157–1241), which includes the reigns of Waldemar I and his sons Cnut VI and Waldemar II (1202–1241), is regarded as the apex of Denmark's medieval history. The Danes extended their power to Estonia, the coast of Germany, and throughout the Baltic. Waldemar and his sons cooperated with the archbishops of Lund to enhance the power of both church and state, but after the reign of Waldemar II, the nobility revolted and the monarchy collapsed.

Royal rule enjoyed a brief revival under Waldemar IV in the mid-1300s. In 1397, his daughter Margaret, married to the king of Norway, established the Union of Kalmar, which united Denmark, Norway, and Sweden into a single confederation of Scandinavian kingdoms. The union prospered under Margaret and remained united until well beyond the Middle Ages.

DIETRICK OF BERN

Dietrick of Bern was a heroic but contradictory fictional figure in medieval south Germanic poetry. A thirteenth-century Icelandic author collected the stories into a coherent sequence and incorporated other heroic legends. Medieval chroniclers held that Dietrick was a poetic representation of THEODORIC THE GREAT, the fifth-century Ostrogothic ruler of ITALY. A number of historical anomalies in the legend contradict this association. For instance in the poems Dietrick is contemporaneous with the Hun king ATTILA and the Ostrogothic king Ermanarich, both of whom predated Theodoric. There are other elements in the poems, however, which suggest that the story of Dietrick is based on ambiguous historical memories of Theodoric. The central story of Dietrick concerns his exile and conflict with his uncle Ermanarich and his alliance with Attila. The fundamental moral of the legends depicts Dietrick as the good king opposed by Ermanarich, the archetypal tyrant.

DIMITRI DONSKOI

One of RUSSIA's first and most celebrated military heroes, Dimitri Donskoi (1350–1389) was prince of Moscow and grand prince of Vladimir from 1359 until his death.

He was born Dimitri Ivanovich and was enthroned when he was just nine at a time when LITHUANIA threatened Russia's western border and the GOLDEN HORDE exacted sizable annual tributes, creating tension in the realm. Dimitri was named prince in 1359, and the Tatar khan of the Golden Horde named him grand prince of Vladimir.

One of Dimitri's first official acts was to ask for a fortress of white stone, in the style of those his grandfather Ivan Daniolvich had built during his reign. The new walls were two to three meters thick, and some 60 meters outside the pre-existing ones. Dimitri saw the fortification of Russia's capital as a step toward the liberation of the country from authoritarian rule.

Upon Dimitri's elevation, members of the Golden Horde sent letters patent to Moscow's rivals, including Prince Michael of Tver. Dimitri invaded Tver in 1370 and reimposed Moscow's rule. After Michael received another letter patent from the grand duke of Lithuania in 1375, Dimitri's army defeated him, and Michael formally acknowledged Moscow's supremacy.

Dimitri was now confident enough to do battle with the Golden Horde itself. He prepared himself (and warned the Horde) by attacking Mongol incursions in neighboring principalities. Tatar Khan Mamai challenged Dimitri to a showdown on the Kulikovo plain alongside the Don River. When the Tatars' Lithuanian allies failed to show up, the MONGOLS were dispatched; some 200,000 on both sides were lost.

The result was a burst of Russian patriotism, a celebration of freedom from tyranny. Veterans of the battle were hailed all over Russia, and Dimitri was hailed as a hero. He adopted the surname Donskoi ("of the Don") and folktales of his exploits (such as the "Zadonschina") are part of Russian culture. To this day, the anniversary of the fight is celebrated in the autumn on "Dimitri's Saturday." Two years later, the Golden Horde did manage to depose Dimitri, but they permitted him to retain his title and even transfer it upon his death in 1389 to his son, Vasili I. (*See* RUSSIA; LITHUANIA; GOLDEN HORDE.)

DIPLOMACY

Only in fourteenth-century ITALY did the modern form of professionalized diplomacy emerge. Previously, medieval diplomats were mostly emissaries who were sent out on short missions for specific purposes. Despite their limitations, medieval diplomats, like their modern counterparts, fulfilled a number of functions, including the promotion of peace and the furthering of state interests.

The Byzantine Empire had the most active diplomacy of the Christian medieval states. In theory, the Byzantine emperor was the universal ruler of humankind, and therefore other rulers were his inferiors. In practice, however, the emperor did whatever was necessary—spying, blackmail, intimidation—to ensure the empire's continued existence. Emissaries were constantly employed to make peace treaties, pay tribute, and obtain the help of one neighbor against another. The Byzantines were particularly adept at gaining the support of tribal peoples, through bribes.

While the Byzantine Empire did not send out permanent ambassadors, it did have a professional corps of emissaries. Chosen from among the nobility, universities, bureaucracy, and Church, they were selected for their patriotism and language skills. The diplomatic agency—responsible for emissaries sent externally, as well as attending to emissaries sent to the Byzantine Empire from other kingdoms—was headed by the Logothete, who hosted receptions when the emperor was absent. (*See* KINGSHIP; BYZANTIUM.)

Diplomatic matters were more limited in the western Christian countries. Early diplomatic encounters were limited to meetings by military leaders and kings on neutral sites to settle disputes. As western kingdoms developed, diplomacy became more sophisticated. In most cases, monarchs chose emissaries from the nobility; nonnobles were sent when an insult was intended. In the Italian republics, emissaries were elected. Diplomacy was not popular among the nobility. Emissaries were not paid, and the voyages were long and hazardous. Monarchs were often forced to employ foreign nobles residing in their court as emissaries.

The modern diplomat originated in Italy. The various republics were in constant conflict, necessitating permanent ambassadors to construct alliances and counteralliances in order to gain an advantage or restore order. In the thirteenth and fourteenth centuries, Florence and the PAPAL STATES trained a corps of professional diplomats. But the real innovator in this field was the trading republic of VENICE, whose ambassadors were thoroughly trained and schooled in a strict code of ethics that restricted gifts and influence.

DOMESDAY BOOK

The Domesday (Doomsday) Book was the administrative masterwork of the Middle Ages. Originally called the *Book of the Day of Assessment*, it received its present (perhaps overly dramatic) name because its authority was considered beyond question—like Judgment Day, or Domesday.

Commissioned by WILLIAM THE CONQUEROR in 1085, the Domesday Book was meant to serve as a comprehensive record of all the properties of ENGLAND. Each locality was required to provide a complete accounting: landowners, their properties, their tenants, their livestock, and any natural resources such as water and timber. Information was gathered not only on who owned what as of the survey, but also the owners of record just before the NORMAN Conquest of 1066. Property values were then determined based on a formula that included current and pre-Norman ownership. (*See* CHRONICLES.)

To ensure that the information was accurate, the royal officials who conducted the survey would hold jury inquests at which they would ask local individuals to take sworn oaths. This allowed the book to be used to settle land disputes and to assess taxes.

DOMINIC, ST.

Dominic (1170–1221) was the founder of the Order of Friars Preachers, better known as the Dominicans. The order was founded to preach against HERESY, and the Dominicans soon became widely known as educators and theologians. Saint THOMAS AQUINAS was a Dominican.

Born in the Spanish town of Osma, Dominic became a priest and directed his efforts toward converting the French heretics known as CATHARS, strict ascetics who had rebelled against the Roman Church because they felt it had become materialistic and corrupt. Dominic joined forces with the bishop of his home town in 1206 to preach to the Cathars in southern FRANCE, but their mission failed.

Dominic decided that the only way to counter HERESY would be to create a preaching order that would reach out to those who could still be brought back into the Church. In 1216, with the permission of Pope Honorius III, Dominic founded his order.

The Dominicans traveled extensively; Dominic himself traveled all across Europe and was particularly successful in the university towns of Bologna and Paris, where he attracted many recruits. New members were sent to university to study theology. Dominic founded a number of convents for nuns who, like the monks, were charged with educating. Dominic died in 1221 and was buried in Bologna. He was canonized in 1234.

DU GUESCLIN, BERTRAND

Bertrand du Guesclin (c. 1320–1380) was the most famous French mercenary general in the HUNDRED YEARS' WAR. His tactical genius

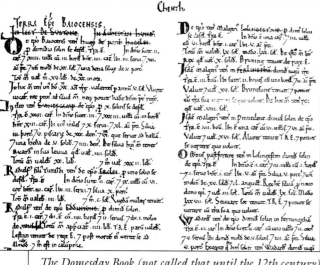

The Domesday Book (not called that until the 12th century) is an important source of English history.

helped the French king CHARLES V reverse his earlier defeats at the hands of the English. Du Guesclin fought in numerous engagements against England, in Castile for a contender for the throne, and against the "free companies" of unaffiliated soldiers that pillaged the countryside. He was held prisoner by the English on three separate occasions, each time ransomed by the French because of his great military value.

Du Guesclin was born in BRITTANY on the west coast of France. At an early age he fought for Charles of Blois, the French choice for ruler of the contested Breton duchy. He later served CHARLES V and was victorious over the NAVARRE allies of the English at Cocherel in May 1364. Du Guesclin's main tactical innovation was the insight that dismounted knights protected by pavises (large shields) could neutralize the British archers who hitherto had dominated the field of battle. This tactic was only partially successful at Auray. The French knights survived the English archers, but were defeated in hand-to-hand combat.

Du Guesclin fought many private campaigns. By 1369, he installed the French-backed Henry of Trastámara on the throne of Castile. In 1370, he was named Constable of France, and led the military strategy that produced the Treaty of Bruges (1375); it stripped the British of their French territories, except Calais and the southern province of Gascony. He died in battle in 1380, having achieved legendary status.

DUCAS DYNASTY

Rulers of the Byzantine Empire for a brief but crucial time (1059–1078) in the eleventh century. During a period of conflict between the provincial, militaristic aristocracy on the one hand and the Church and imperial bureaucracy on the other, the Ducas emperors represented the interests of the latter. During the four-year interlude between the rule of the two Ducas emperors, Constantine X Ducas Parapinakes and Michael VII Parapinakes, power was held briefly by Constantine's widow, Eudocia Macrembolitissa, and her husband, General Romanus IV Diogenes. The Byzantine army was decimated by ALP ARSLAN leading the SELJUK TURKS at the Battle of MANZIKERT (1071), and much of Asia Minor was lost.

Constantine X came to power in 1059 after illness forced the abdication of the successful emperor ISAAC I COMNENUS. Constantine, Isaac's finance minister, was a bureaucrat who spent much time reforming the administration. He limited the size of the army, cut pay, and did not keep up fortresses—inadvisable policies since the empire was increasingly threatened by the Seljuk Turks in the east, and the Patzinak and the Uze tribes in the north.

DUNS SCOTUS, JOHN

The Scottish Franciscan philosopher John Duns Scotus (c. 1266–1308) was one of the most influential thinkers of the medieval group known as the Schoolmen. The Schoolmen (whose ranks include ALBERTUS MAGNUS, THOMAS AQUINAS, and WILLIAM OF OCKHAM), tried over a period of four centuries to reconcile the teachings of respected philosophers with the teachings of the Church. Duns Scotus' writings reveal a man who was forward-thinking, yet traditional in his theology. His ideas on existence have influenced modern philosophers such as Heidegger and Peirce, and the poet Gerard Manley Hopkins.

Scottish theologian and philosopher Duns Scotus.

Early Life. Duns Scotus was born in SCOTLAND. Not much is known of his early life except that he entered the FRANCISCAN ORDER at Dumfries around 1278. He was sent to Oxford to study and became a Master of Theology in 1288. He studied ARISTOTLE and was influenced by several Arabic philosophers, notably AVICENNA. Ordained a priest in 1291, he studied and lectured at Oxford until 1302. He then accepted a chair (position) on the theology faculty at the UNIVERSITY OF PARIS. (*See* UNIVERSITIES.)

In 1303, Duns Scotus was forced to flee Paris when his support of Pope BONIFACE VIII against the French king PHILIP IV led to public protests. He returned the next year and remained in Paris until 1307, when he moved to the University of Cologne. He died in 1308 and was buried in the Franciscan church near Cologne Cathedral. Dun Scotus is known as the Subtle Doctor for his fine distinctions, and as the Marian Doctor for his defense of Immaculate Conception.

LIFE IN THE MIDDLE AGES

Any student asked to wear a dunce cap in class is actually in quite respectable intellectual company. During his lifetime, even those who disagreed with Duns Scotus recognized him as a learned and original thinker. After his death, he still had many followers, but his ideas eventually lost favor. By the sixteenth century, followers of his ideas, known as duns men or dunce men, were increasingly being ridiculed. The name "dunce" came to mean a foolish, ignorant, unlearned person.

EASTER, DATE OF

The process of establishing the day on which Easter falls was a complex one, based on a series of calculations involving the phases of the moon and astronomical cycles. After seven centuries, a formula (albeit with two versions) was finally adopted.

The COUNCIL OF NICAEA determined that Easter Sunday would fall on the first Sunday after the first full moon (the paschal moon) after the vernal equinox (the first day of spring). The paschal moon's appearance is calculated from a system that includes the use of "golden numbers" (fixed years based on the Metonic cycle, devised by the Greek astronomer Meton in 432). If the paschal moon falls on a Sunday, Easter falls on the following Sunday. Assuming that March 21 is recognized as the first day of spring, Easter Sunday can fall anywhere between March 22 and April 25.

Because the Byzantine Church used a different calculation, what is now the EASTERN ORTHODOX CHURCH usually celebrates Easter a week later than the Western Church. The two Easters can fall on the same day, and rarely, they can fall four or five weeks apart.

EASTERN ORTHODOX CHURCH

The distinction between the Eastern Orthodox and Roman Catholic Churches emerged slowly during the Middle Ages, and at first did not exist as such. The fourth ecumenical council at CHALCEDON in 451 grouped almost all the hundreds of bishoprics of the Roman Empire under the five great patriarchates of ROME, CONSTANTINOPLE, Alexandria, Antioch, and Jerusalem, in that order of precedence, enhancing the authority of the patriarchs of Constantinople and Jerusalem at the expense of those of Alexandria and Antioch. Partly in response to these changes in authority, large groups in the patriarchates of Alexandria and Antioch favored the doctrine condemned at Chalcedon, Monophysitism, which large majorities opposed in the patriarchates of Constantinople and Jerusalem.

Patriarchates. Yet the boundaries of the patriarchates did not correspond neatly to doctrinal, cultural, or political divisions. The patriarchate of Rome, headed by the pope as patriarch of the West, included not only the mostly Latin-speaking Western Roman Empire, but a portion of the largely Greek-speaking Eastern Roman Empire, with Greece itself. Although the cities of Alexandria, Antioch, and Jerusalem themselves were largely Greek in culture, most Christians in the patriarchate of Alexandria spoke Coptic and most in the other two patriarchates spoke Syriac; only in the patriarchate of Constantinople did a majority speak Greek. Outside the empire, the Christians of Ethiopia were subject to the patriarchate of Alexandria and those of Armenia and Iberia (Caucasian Georgia) to the patriarchate of Constantinople. When the Western Roman Empire disappeared, the Eastern Roman (Byzantine) Empire still ruled the eastern part of the Roman patriarchate along with the other four.

Monophysites. The Monophysite controversy plagued the Byzantine Empire for more than two centuries, even though most Monophysites' belief that Christ had a single nature which was both divine and human was barely distinguishable from the Orthodox Chalcedonian doctrine that Christ had separate divine and human natures. In 482, the patriarch of Constantinople, Acacius, approved the emperor Zeno's *Henoticon* (Act of Union), which was ambiguous enough in its wording to be acceptable to both Chalcedonians and Monophysites. But the *Henoticon* made possible an uneasy unity of the four eastern patriarchates only at the price of a rupture with the PAPACY known as the Acacian Schism, which ended in 519 with Constantinople's repudiation of the *Henoticon*.

The emperor JUSTINIAN I installed Chalcedonian patriarchs in Antioch and Alexandria, only to see Monophysites found schismatic churches of their own in Syria and Egypt. The emperor failed in his attempt to reconcile Monophysites by having the fifth ecumenical council at Constantinople (553) condemn some theological works that Monophysites considered heretical. Justinian's reconquest of North Africa and Italy brought much of the Western Church, including Rome, under Byzantine rule and subjected the popes to some imperial control. After Justinian's death and the empire's loss of much of Italy, the patriarch of Constantinople, John the Faster (582–595), claimed the title of ecumenical patriarch, which seemed to challenge papal primacy.

In 638, the emperor HERACLIUS and his patriarch of Constantinople, Sergius I, made a last attempt to compromise with Monophysites by proclaiming Monotheletism, the doctrine that Christ has two natures but one *will*. After some hesitation, however, the papacy repudiated this doctrine, and in any case the Arabs were already conquering Egypt and Syria, where most Monophysites lived. Since Monotheletism appealed to many Armenians, the emperors tolerated it as long as they still hoped to keep or regain Armenia, despite opposition from Byzantines led by the monk Maximus Confessor and the popes. Finally, the sixth ecumenical council at Constantinople condemned Monotheletism in 680. Under Arab rule, Egyptian and Syrian Christians remained divided among Monophysite and Chalcedonian patriarchates, the latter known as "Melkite" (Arabic for "of the emperor").

Eastern Church practices had long diverged somewhat from Western: for example, fasting was banned on Saturdays in Lent; a lifetime limit of three marriages even for those repeatedly widowed was imposed; and married men were allowed to become priests (although priests were forbidden to marry). The Quinisext Council ("fifth-sixth," completing the fifth and sixth ecumenical councils) held at Constantinople in 691–692 briefly tried to legislate some Eastern usages for the whole Church; a papal visit to Constantinople in 711 obtained toleration of the differences.

Iconoclasm. When the emperor LEO III imposed iconoclasm in 730, the patriarch of Constantinople, Germanus I, resigned in protest. The pope, still nominally a Byzantine subject, condemned iconoclasm the following year. In retaliation, Leo transferred the remaining Byzantine lands in Greece and southern Italy from papal jurisdiction to the patriarchate of Constantinople, which then corresponded almost exactly to the regions where Greek was spoken and, with the empire's loss of Rome, to the territory of the Byzantine Empire. The jurisdictional transfer lasted, even after the seventh ecumenical council at Nicaea (787) condemned iconoclasm and healed the schism.

The waning of iconoclasm, which almost all Byzantine monks had opposed, brought a resurgence of Byzantine monasticism led by Theodore, abbot of the Monastery of Studius in Constantinople. Theodore also mustered opposition to the reintroduction of iconoclasm in 815. Iconoclasm ended for good with the restoration of icons in 843 on the first Sunday of Lent, which the Eastern Church has commemorated ever since as the Sunday of Orthodoxy. Monks again enjoyed great prestige and often became bishops, like Methodius I, patriarch of Constantinople from 843.

Now relatively free from doctrinal controversies, the Byzantine Church responded promptly to appeals by partly Christian Moravia and pagan BULGARIA for Byzantine missionaries. The mission to Moravia of the monks Constantine-Cyril and Methodius introduced the Byzantine liturgy, which Constantine-Cyril translated into the contemporary Slavic language, Old Church Slavonic. His Slavonic liturgy was also adopted in Bulgaria, where the khan Boris accepted baptism in 865 under the name of Michael, taking the Byzantine emperor Michael III as his godfather. These Byzantine missions became an issue in a schism caused by the

A Byzantine mosaic of Christ from Hagia Sophia.

pope's refusal to recognize the patriarch of Constantinople, Photus, during which the papacy gained control of the Moravian and Bulgarian churches. But after a council at Constantinople resolved the Photian Schism in 870, the Constantinopolitan patriarchate regained jurisdiction over the Church in Bulgaria and sent a new mission requested by the Serbs.

The next major Byzantine missionary effort was to Russia, whose Prince Vladimir converted from paganism to Christianity in order to marry a Byzantine princess in 998. The Bulgarian, Serbian, and Russian churches followed Byzantine practice in matters from architecture to canon law, and used the liturgy of Constantine-Cyril and the Cyrillic alphabet adapted from a Slavonic alphabet that he had devised. The Bulgarian and Serbian churches obtained considerable autonomy, and the Bulgarians had their own patriarchate from 927 until the Byzantines conquered Bulgaria and abolished it. The head of the Russian church, the metropolitan of Kiev, was for centuries almost always a Byzantine prelate sent from Constantinople.

Schism. In 1054, a dispute between the patriarch of Constantinople, Michael I Cerularius, and legates from the pope provoked each side to excommunicate the other, causing another schism. The main issue was the patriarch's objection to Western and Armenian use of unleavened bread in the Eucharist instead of the leavened bread used by Byzantines, although both sides had tolerated this difference for centuries. Another issue raised as the schism persisted was the Western addition to the Nicene Creed specifying that the Holy Spirit proceeded both from the Father "and from the Son" (in Latin, *filioque*). Some Byzantine theologians, besides protesting the Western Church's altering the creed without an ecumenical council, deduced from the *filioque* that Western Christians must hold various heretical beliefs that they in fact did not.

The Bulgarians, Serbs, and Russians, and the Melkites of Egypt and Syria, followed the Byzantines into schism with the papacy. These Eastern Christians now can be conventionally called the Eastern Orthodox Church, and the Western Church is referred to as the Roman Catholic Church. Because each side considered the schism temporary, no such terms were used at the time. The spiritual headship of the Eastern Christians naturally fell to the Patriarch of Constantinople, especially because the other eastern patriarchs were mostly under Muslim rule. The peninsula of Mount Athos in northern Greece became a monastic center not only for the Greeks, but for Georgians, Bulgarians, Serbs, and Russians—all of whom established monasteries there. Tensions with the Western Church increased when the crusaders arrived in the eastern Mediterranean; disputes arose over such matters as the crusaders' replacing Melkite Eastern bishops with Western ones in the crusader states.

Fourth Crusade. The sack of Constantinople by the Fourth Crusade in 1204 so inflamed Byzantine opinion against Western Christians that reconciliation began to seem impossible. While the triumphant crusaders set up their own Latin patriarchate of Constantinople, which the Bulgarians and Serbs recognized for a time, the would-be Byzantine emperors at Nicaea established a patriarchate of Constantinople in exile that gained the allegiance of most Eastern Orthodox Christians. The patriarchs at Nicaea recognized a reestablished Bulgarian patriarchate, granted autonomy to the Serbian church (although it acquired its own patriarch only in 1346), and loosened Byzantine control over the Russian church, allowing Russians to alternate with Byzantines as metropolitans of Kiev.

After the Nicene emperor Michael VIII restored the Byzantine Empire by conquering Constantinople, he tried to forestall a crusade against him by ending the schism with the papacy. Michael and the Byzantine hierarchy agreed to a union with the Western Church at the Council of Lyon (1274), based on mutual toleration of the old differences over unleavened Eucharistic bread and the *filioque*. But most Byzantines and other Eastern Christians refused to accept the union, which lapsed at Michael's death in 1282.

Late Middle Ages. In the fourteenth century, a controversy arose in the Eastern Church over the growing popularity among monks of the mystical methods of prayer known as Hesychasm, considered heretical by some Byzantines. After the Byzantine

Church endorsed Hesychasm, a few of its opponents joined the Western Church. The idea of a reunion of the churches remained alive in Byzantium, particularly as a means of obtaining Western help against the advancing Turks, and eventually Emperor John VIII arranged a new union at the Council of FERRARA-FLORENCE (1438-39). Although the council accepted Hesychasm and led to the nearly successful Crusade of Varna, the union never won over most Eastern Christians; it lapsed when Constantinople fell to the Turks.

As the Turks conquered Byzantine, Bulgarian, and Serbian territory, the patriarchate of Constantinople continued to exercise authority over the Christians of Anatolia and the Balkans, as well as the Russians, the Georgians, and the Rumanians of Walachia and Moldavia, who joined the Eastern Orthodox Church in the fourteenth century. After the fall of the Byzantine Empire, the Ottoman sultans appointed their own patriarchs of Constantinople to head the Eastern Orthodox Church, to which a majority of Ottoman subjects by then belonged. The Ottomans suppressed the Bulgarian patriarchate when they took Bulgaria. After the Mongols conquered southern Russia, the Russian metropolitanate left Kiev; in 1328, it moved to Moscow. The Russian church claimed full autonomy from the patriarchate of Constantinople only in 1448, and the Russian metropolitan took the title of patriarch only in the sixteenth century.

Some modern historians have spoken of Byzantine "CAESAROPAPISM," meaning that the emperor exercised authority over the Byzantine Church similar to that of the pope in the West. Emperors did summon the first seven ecumenical councils, but they also summoned ecumenical councils that failed, like a council in 754 that endorsed iconoclasm. Although the emperors chose most Byzantine bishops, including patriarchs, emperors almost never prevailed in disputes with their hierarchy. Various emperors failed to overcome the Church's opposition to the *Henoticon*, Monotheletism, iconoclasm, and the church unions of Lyon and Ferrara-Florence. The Church repeatedly condemned the memories of emperors who had opposed its doctrines, and canonized churchmen who had opposed those emperors. By seldom interfering in purely political matters, the Byzantine Church, and the Eastern Orthodox Church that emerged from it, kept most of their authority in religious questions, and outlasted the Byzantine Empire itself.

See the articles on CHRISTIANITY; CAESAROPAPISM; PAPACY; CHALCEDON, COUNCIL OF; *and* BYZANTIUM *for background. For additional information see* ROME; CONSTANTINOPLE; JUSTINIAN I; HERACLIUS; ICONOCLASTIC CONTROVERSY; LEO III; *and* CRUSADES.

ECKHART, MEISTER

Meister Eckhart (c. 1260–c. 1327) was one of the most important mystics in the medieval world. A German who became a Dominican friar, he was influential as both a theologian and a teacher. In his later years, some of his postulations about religion were questioned by Church authorities—he was the first Dominican accused of HERESY—but his strikingly original ideas were to influence later religious figures, such as Martin Luther.

Born Johannes Eckhart in the town of Hochheim in what is now central GERMANY, he entered the Dominican order at the age of 15. He studied in Cologne and PARIS; one of his teachers may have been the famed Scholastic theologian ALBERTUS MAGNUS. Eckhart distinguished himself by his sharpness of mind, and he was named Dominican vicar of the German region of Thuringia in the 1290s. Later he taught and obtained his master's degree (hence the title "Meister") in Paris. He became leader of the Dominicans in Saxony in 1303 and vicar of BOHEMIA in 1306.

Eckhart wrote sermons and at least four treatises, the *Talks of Instruction, Book of Divine Consolation, The Nobleman,* and *On Detachment.* All of his works discussed the relationship between the soul and God. He wrote in both Latin and German, but his German works are considered more original and more influential. Eckhart, who derived his own inspiration from the Scholastics, the Greeks, the Neoplatonists, and the Arab world, believed that it was possible to attain a mystical union with God by purging the soul of desire. This could be accomplished, he explained, through prayer and meditation. Many of Eckhart's works were directed toward the BEGUINES, laywomen who devoted their lives to religion and charity.

From 1314 on, Eckhart preached in the Rhine valley, where he was also the prior of Strasbourg. In 1320, he was named a professor at the University of Cologne. (*See* HERESY; UNIVERSITIES.)

Around 1328, some of Eckhart's ideas were questioned by the Church. Part of this stemmed from the influence of the archbishop of Cologne (who was a Franciscan). Eckhart's contention that the distance between humankind and God could be bridged was deemed a heretical position, and a list of Eckhart's "errors" was compiled. He took his case to the papal court, then in AVIGNON, where he apparently retracted his controversial teachings. He died soon afterwards.

EDMUND, ST.

Edmund (841–869), king of East Anglia from 855 until his death. He was killed by invading Danes for his refusal to renounce his Christian faith. Defeated by the invaders near Hoxne in Suffolk, Edmund died on November 20, 869.

Graphic details of his death have survived in legend, according to which Edmund was tortured, shot to death with arrows, and then beheaded. Some accounts report that he was first buried in a wooden church at Hellesdon in Norfolk and then reburied at a site later, the shrine known as Bury St. Edmunds. The issuance of substantial amounts of coinage in Edmund's name by the late 800s suggests the emergence of a widespread popular cult centered around the martyred king. It was as a martyr to the faith that he was remembered in ENGLAND and Scandinavia. Bury St. Edmunds became an important medieval site for pilgrims.

15th-century depiction of St. Edmund in Hardwich House near Bury St. Edmund's.

EDWARD II (OF ENGLAND)

Edward II (1284–1327), son of EDWARD I and Eleanor of Castile, was king of ENGLAND from 1307 to 1327. After his father conquered WALES, young Edward became Prince of Wales in 1301, making him the first heir to the English throne to hold that title. He took part in the Scottish campaign prior to assuming the throne upon the death of his father in 1307.

Edward II's 20-year reign was marked by military defeats and domestic disorder. In 1314, Edward suffered a disastrous defeat in SCOTLAND, and ten years later was forced to give up control of AQUITAINE in FRANCE. Edward was constantly at odds with powerful BARONS over control of the government. Although Edward's marriage to Isabella of France produced an heir, EDWARD III, the royal couple became estranged as a result of the king's succession of affairs. His erratic behavior also aroused hostility towards him among the high nobility.

Edward's downfall began when Isabella went to France to negotiate with her brother, the French king PHILIP IV. There she met Roger Mortimer, an English nobleman living in exile. With him, she planned to overthrow Edward. In 1326, they invaded England and forced Edward to flee westward. After his capture, Edward was forced to abdicate in favor of his young son, Edward III. Edward was imprisoned in Berkeley Castle where he was murdered the following year.

EDWARD III

Edward (1312–1377) was crowned king of ENGLAND in 1327 at age 14 and reigned for half a century. His territorial ambitions in FRANCE was one cause of the HUNDRED YEARS' WAR. Early in his reign he enjoyed military successes, but disputes over succession plagued his final years.

His Reign. Young Edward came to the throne after his mother, Isabella, daughter of King PHILIP IV of France, and her lover, Roger Mortimer, forced King EDWARD II to abdicate and later had him murdered. Isabella and Mortimer were in control of government during the first years of Edward's reign. But after Edward took control in 1330, he had Mortimer executed and Isabella placed in a convent. In 1328, Edward married Philippa, daughter of the count of Hainault. They had twelve children, nine of whom survived, including EDWARD THE BLACK PRINCE and JOHN OF GAUNT, duke of Lancaster.

Military Career. Edward began his military career in SCOTLAND. In 1333, he and Edward Balliol defeated the Scottish king David II at the Battle of Halidon Hill and drove him into exile. The French alliance with the Scots, together with tensions over Gascony (AQUITAINE) and Edward's claim to the French throne through his mother Isabella, led to the outbreak of the HUNDRED YEARS' WAR in 1337. Edward defeated the French at CRÉCY in 1346 and went on to take Calais. In 1346, under the leadership of Edward's son, Edward the Black Prince, the English won another victory at Poitiers, which resulted in the capture of the French king John II. By 1360, Edward lost hope of ever conquering all of France and settled for undisputed title to the duchy of Aquitaine. Hostilities resumed, and this time England was pushed back by the forces led by the French king CHARLES V.

Edward III promoted the ideals of CHIVALRY, KNIGHTHOOD, and HERALDRY. In 1348, he founded the Order of the Garter to promote chivalry and made his son Edward one of its first members.

Final Years. Financial troubles marred the last years of Edward's reign. The BLACK DEATH and the expensive war with France forced Edward to rely more heavily on the English BARONS. Parliament thus became more important and was divided into two houses, the Lords and the Commons.

After Philippa died in 1369, Edward came under the influence of his mistress, Alice Perrers, who favored John of Gaunt as successor over Edward the Black Prince, Edward's eldest son. This conflict and the death of the Black Prince soured Edward's final years. Upon Edward's death in 1377, the crown passed to his grandson, RICHARD II, son of the Black Prince.

EDWARD IV

Edward IV (1442–1483), son of Richard, duke of York, and leader of the Yorkist party, was deeply involved in the WARS OF THE ROSES both before and after his rise to the throne in 1461.

During the 1450s when Henry VI's rule became increasingly ineffective. Edward's father Richard, a descendent of King EDWARD III, began advancing the claim of the house of York to the English throne. After the Lancastrians defeated Richard and Edward at Ludlow in 1459, father and son fled to IRELAND. When they returned the following year, Parliament acknowledged Richard as Henry's heir, but in the fighting that followed, the Lancastrians killed Richard at Wakefield.

Edward struck back, defeating the Lancastrians at Mortimer's Cross in 1461. Shortly afterwards he entered London and was proclaimed king. Later that year, the deposed Henry VI was forced into exile. However, when the earl of Warwick revolted against Edward's rule and sent Edward fleeing to Holland, Henry was restored to the throne. In 1471, Edward returned and killed Warwick in battle and then defeated the Lancastrians at Tewkesbury. After Henry's death in the Tower of LONDON later that year, Edward's position became more secure; except for his execution of his brother, George, duke of Clarence, for plotting against him, the remainder of his reign was peaceful.

Edward was a patron of the arts and built many magnificent churches. He also had a taste for luxury and pleasure. In addition to his wife, Elizabeth Woodville, with whom he had ten children, he also had several mistresses.(*See* ENGLAND; WARS OF THE ROSES.)

EDWARD THE BLACK PRINCE

Edward (1330–1376) was the oldest son of King EDWARD III of ENGLAND and Phillippa of Hainault. Although he died a year before his father's death and thus never became king, he upheld the ideal of CHIVALRY and was one of England's greatest commanders in the HUNDRED YEARS' WAR.

Born at Woodstock (he was known as Edward of Woodstock), Edward received major titles and positions from an early age. At the age of seven he became the duke of Cornwall (England's first), and the following year he received the title "Guardian of England" while his father was fighting in FRANCE. In 1347, at the age of 17 he became Prince of Wales and heir to the throne. In 1354, he became the fourteenth earl of Chester.

Military Life. Edward accompanied his father on his military campaigns and earned a reputation for valor and conduct befitting a chivalrous knight. He fought at the BATTLE OF CRÉCY in 1346 and at the siege of Orléans a year later. It was the French who dubbed him "the Black Prince," probably because he wore black armor at Crécy. The English did not use the name until the 1500s. (*See* CRÉCY, BATTLE OF.)

Prince Edward was also an enthusiastic and skilled participant in the TOURNAMENTS organized to celebrate the success of English battlefield victories. He was one of the first Knights of the Garter when King EDWARD III founded the order in 1348. In 1355, while serving as his father's lieutenant in Gascony, Prince Edward launched a series of raids against French positions which culminated in Edward's greatest victory at the Battle of Poitiers in 1356. Poitiers was a crushing defeat for the French that resulted in the capture of their king, John II. Legend has it that Edward chivalrously helped the defeated king out of his armor and then served him supper. Edward played a major role in the negotiations that led to the Treaty of Brétigny between England and France in 1360. Yet, Edward's treatment of peasants and the urban population was sometimes very harsh.

Later Years. In 1363, Edward became the ruler of the newly acquired AQUITAINE. With the the help of his wife, Joan of Kent, his cousin whom he married in 1361, he established a splendid court in Bordeaux. He tried unsuccessfully to help Pedro the Cruel recapture the throne of Castile in SPAIN, and encountered resistance from the nobles of Aquitaine when he tried to tax them to finance his military campaigns in Spain. In 1371, Edward was forced to return to England to recuperate from a disease he had contracted in Spain. He was successful in seeing to it that his son RICHARD II would succeed his father instead of his younger brother, JOHN OF GAUNT.

Tomb of Edward the Black Prince, son of Edward III, in the cathedral at Canterbury.

EDWARD THE CONFESSOR, ST.

Although Edward (c. 1003–1066), king of ENGLAND from 1042–1066, kept the kingdom in a state of relative peace, the later years of his reign were plagued by questions of succession. Edward, famous for his piety, was canonized in 1161. His most lasting contribution to English history was the building project that turned the Benedictine abbey in Westminster into the great religious and political center of the kingdom—WESTMINSTER ABBEY. Edward's death in 1066 precipitated the NORMAN Conquest that ended ANGLO-SAXON rule and ushered in a new period of English history.

As the son of King Ethelred II the Unready and Emma of Normandy, Edward was the direct descendant of the great Anglo-Saxon king ALFRED THE GREAT. Edward spent his early years being educated in a monastery in England. When the Danes invaded, Emma fled with her children to Normandy, and there Edward developed strong ties with the Normans. After Ethelred's death in 1016, Emma returned to England and married the new Danish king of England, Cnut the Great. Their son Hardecnut, Edward's younger half-brother, then succeeded his father as king. In 1041, Hardecnut brought Edward back to England. The following year, after the childless Hardecnut fell ill and died, Edward was proclaimed his successor and crowned king by the archbishop of Canterbury in the Canterbury cathedral on Easter Sunday.

Although Edward was in fact king, he was unable to assert his authority over the powerful earls of the kingdom, especially Godwin of WESSEX, who had been chief adviser to King Cnut and had been rewarded with great wealth and vast lands. Godwin's influence in the kingdom increased when Edward married his daughter in 1045. (*See* DENMARK.)

Edward appointed a Norman, Robert of Jumièges, as Archbishop of Canterbury in 1051, a move that created a rift with Godwin. When Godwin failed to support Edward's brother-in-law in a dispute with the citizens of Dover, Edward banished him and apparently promised William, duke of Normandy, that he would be his heir. Godwin returned to England in 1052. With the earls of Mercia and Northumbria, he forced Edward to name Stigand Archbishop of Canterbury in place of Robert. Edward withdrew from governance and concentrated on the building of Westminster Abbey. Shortly before his death in 1066, he named Godwin's son, Harold, his successor. News of the crowning of Harold spurred William of Normandy to invade England, culminating in his victory over Harold at the BATTLE OF HASTINGS.

EGYPT

The country on the eastern portion of North AFRICA, situated around the Nile River. At the dawn of the Middle Ages, Egypt was a prosperous province of the Byzantine Empire with a history that stretched into antiquity. More importantly, it served as the keeper of Greek culture through the schools and libraries of Alexandria. In spite of the compromising of the Alexandrian patriarchate by the Justinian reforms of the sixth century, resulting in the rise of alternative forms of CHRISTIANITY, (which the Church came to view as heresies), such as the Monophysites and the Monothelites, and the resurgent Coptic Church, Egypt retained its dignity. In fact, the insults from CONSTANTINOPLE made the Egyptian church receptive to conquest by ISLAM, which accounts for the ease of that very conquest in 640.

Islamic Rule. The persistence of Greek Christians, Jews, Copts, and Christian sects in the Islamic environment of the UMAYYAD and ABBASID caliphates is the clearest indication that the Islamic empires were welcome alternatives to the Byzantine; the Muslims for their part welcomed the contact they suddenly had with the great works and traditions of the Greek world. The result was a culture that was itself a great intellectual edifice, precisely because it was built on the foundations of Greek heritage. When the FATIMIDS established their empire in Egypt in 974, the land had both high culture and a political power base in which to thrive.

The tranquillity provided by the Fatimids and the prosperity their expansion ensured brought to Egypt and its new capital, Cairo, the glory of old. So firm was this foundation that challenges from the SELJUK TURKS in the eleventh century and the CRUSADES in the twelfth created hard times, but could not dislodge the Fatimid grip over the northeast corner of Africa.

After two centuries of decline, Egypt once again longed to be the center of an empire. Again a foreign conquest was looked upon with reserved approval in 1174, when SALADIN established the AYYUBID dynasty and united Egypt and Syria. The tension between these two nodes of power encouraged further crusader attempts to wrest Egypt from the Muslims, which in turn prompted the deployment of Mamluk mercenaries by the Ayyubids. Predictably, these protectors took control of Egypt in 1291, ruling the area until the sixteenth century with little interest in culture of any kind. (*See* AFRICA; AYYUBIDS; FATIMID DYNASTY; LIBRARIES; MAMLUKS.)

EINHARD

Einhard (c. 770–840) was a scholar and royal official at the courts of CHARLEMAGNE and his successor, LOUIS THE PIOUS. His biography of Charlemagne is one of the great literary and historiographical achievements of the early Middle Ages.

Einhard received his education at the monastic school of Fulda in central GERMANY, after which, while still in his early 20s, he joined Charlemagne's court at AIX-LA-CHAPELLE (Aachen). He taught at the palace school and eventually succeeded ALCUIN OF YORK as its director. After Charlemagne's death, Einhard became the personal secretary of Charlemagne's son and successor, Louis I, and tutored his oldest son, Lothair.

In 830, Einhard retired from royal service at the age of 60. During his retirement he wrote one of the greatest works of the period, *Vita Caroli Magni*. This *Life of Charles the Great* (Charlemagne) presented an account of all the major events of his reign as well as a detailed picture of court life and an intimate, if somewhat idealized, portrait of Charlemagne. (*See* CHARLEMAGNE; AIX-LA-CHAPELLE; ALCUIN OF YORK.)

ELEANOR OF AQUITAINE

Eleanor of AQUITAINE (c. 1122–1204) was one of the most remarkable women of the twelfth century. Extraordinarily long-lived and extraordinarily powerful, she was duchess of Aquitaine and queen, successively, of FRANCE and ENGLAND. She had ten children, three of whom (Henry, Richard, and

Tomb of Eleanor of Aquitaine, Fontevrault Abbey, France.

John) were crowned kings of England. One daughter (Matilda) married HENRY THE LION of BAVARIA and Saxony and was the mother of Emperor Otto of Brunswick; another (Eleanor) wed King ALFONSO VIII of Castile and had Blanche, the mother of LOUIS IX of France (Saint Louis); a third (Jeanne) was the wife of King William II of SICILY and, after his death, Count Raymond VI of Toulouse. Eleanor's achievements were considerable, but over time they have been obscured by the many legends that she has inspired.

Early Life. Eleanor was the eldest of two daughters of Duke William X of Aquitaine and his first wife Ainor, the daughter of Aimery, viscount of Châtellerault. His wife had been a mistress of Duke William IX of Aquitaine, Eleanor's grandfather, famed as a troubadour poet and "a vehement lover of women." In 1137, William X died on pilgrimage to SANTIAGO OF COMPOSTELLA, having left his lands and daughters under the protection of King Louis VI of France (r. 1108–1137). Thus Eleanor inherited the proudly independent duchy of Aquitaine, a disparate collection of territories stretching from Poitou in the north to Gascony in the south, and from the Atlantic Ocean to Quercy. King Louis decided to marry Eleanor to his eldest surviving son Louis VII (already crowned king in 1131). In late July 1137, Eleanor and Louis were married in Bordeaux; on August 8, a week after the death of Louis VI, they were crowned in Poitiers in a novel CORONATION ceremony (probably crafted by Abbot SUGER of Saint-Denis) emphasizing the union of France, BURGUNDY, and Aquitaine.

Queen of France. From 1137 to 1152, Eleanor was queen of France, and Louis VII, duke of Aquitaine. Eleanor bore Louis two daughters, the first in 1145, the second in 1149, after the couple returned from the failed crusade upon which they embarked in 1147. There were tensions in the marriage, and Eleanor raised the issue of their blood relationship, since as third cousins their union was banned by ecclesiastical law. In 1149, Pope Eugenius III had confirmed their marriage before the birth of their second child. Subsequently, however, Eleanor's unrest increased, perhaps after meeting Henry of Anjou. Henry, some ten years younger than Eleanor, was the son of Count Geoffrey of Anjou and Matilda of England, daughter of Henry I of England (r. 1100–1135) and claimant to the English throne. Matilda's right was disputed by her cousin Stephen, who in 1153 agreed that after his death the throne should pass to her son Henry. A year before, in 1152, Eleanor's marriage to Louis VII had been dissolved by a Church council because of their blood ties. Within two months she married Henry, who was soon acknowledged as duke of Aquitaine. Their first son William, born in August 1153, died in 1156, but another son was born in 1155.

Louis VII, angered by the marriage, continued to use the title duke of Aquitaine until peace was made between England and France in 1153.

Queen of England. In December 1154, Henry and Eleanor were crowned king and queen of England. During the next 19 years Eleanor bore Henry seven children. In 1168, following the birth of their last son John, Eleanor assumed active control of Aquitaine, leaving Henry to pursue his own interests, amatory and political, in England. Serious tactical errors, including the coronation of the young Henry and the murder of THOMAS BECKET in 1170 led to unrest in England and the rebellion of Henry and Eleanor's sons (abetted by their mother) against their father. Henry defused Eleanor's power by keeping her under close guard, but this did not deter his sons from conspiring against him before and after the death of the young Henry in 1184.

Later Career. Henry's death in July 1189, following the alliance of his sons Richard and John with King PHILIP II AUGUSTUS of France (r. 1180–1223), led to Eleanor's release and her exercise of governmental authority in England on behalf of her son Richard. While Richard was absent from England (on crusade and then imprisoned on his way home), Eleanor kept his troublesome brother John under control, governed England, and raised a huge ransom to gain Richard's release from Emperor HENRY VI. After Richard's return in 1194, Eleanor oversaw his reconciliation with John. She retired to the monastery of Fontevrault, which her family had supported and which had become a burial place for her line.

After Richard's death, Eleanor came out of retirement to defend John from a challenge for the throne by her grandson, Arthur of BRITTANY. She journeyed to Castile to arrange the marriage of her granddaughter Blanche to Philip Augustus' son Louis. She finally retired again to Fontevrault, where she died on March 31, 1204, three weeks after Philip Augustus had captured the castle of Château-Gaillard, built by Richard to protect NORMANDY. She did not live to see the French conquest of Normandy, Anjou, Maine, and much of northern Aquitaine, leaving the English possessions in France greatly diminished; they defended them until Bordeaux capitulated in 1453.

Eleanor seems to have been far less interested in art and literature than Henry II, whose court was a center of learning. Her reputation as a patron of troubadours or as an influence of Abbot Suger's new construction at Saint-Denis is purely mythical. Only the image of Eleanor in effigy at Fontevrault may bear some resemblance to her, although it is not an 80-year-old woman who is depicted. (*See* FRANCE; ENGLAND; AQUITAINE; WOMEN. *Also* RICHARD I LION-HEART; HENRY II; PHILIP II AUGUSTUS; *and* TROUBADOURS.)

ENGLAND

T he Middle Ages began in England with the collapse of Roman rule in the 400s and the invasion and eventual conquest of the island by Germanic tribes from the continent. In England, the ANGLO-SAXONS, as they came to be known, established eight separate kingdoms, each one ruled by an aristocracy of warriors headed by a king. To escape the Anglo-Saxon invasion, many native Celtic peoples fled west into Cornwell and WALES and north into SCOTLAND. The native British who came under Anglo-Saxon rule were forced to work as slaves and servants and adopted their conquerors' language and customs.

Anglo-Saxons. The Anglo-Saxon kingdoms included those set up by the East SAXONS (Essex) northeast of LONDON, by the West Saxons (WESSEX) west of London, by Saxons who went south to establish the kingdom of Sussex, and by Jutes and Frisians who set up Kent, the strongest of the early kingdoms. Other Anglo-Saxon tribes, who went farther north, established the kingdoms of East Anglia and Mercia.

The head of the most dominant kingdom of the time was called the *bretwalda* (British ruler), the first of whom was King Ethelbert of Kent. During the 600s, the title was given to the kings of Northumbria to the north, where learning and culture flourished at York. The rulers of the 700s were the kings of Mercia, the most noteworthy of whom was King Offa, who built a 200-mile defensive wall to mark the boundary between his subjects and the Welsh. His use of the title *rex Anglorum* suggests that the English were one people under a single ruler. Offa's success in uniting almost all of England made him well known on the continent where he and CHARLEMAGNE negotiated as equals. Upon Offa's death, Mercia weakened quickly. In 802, Wessex regained its independence. Under Egbert, Wessex became recognized by the other kingdoms, some of which joined it, as the dominant kingdom on the island. For the remainder of the Anglo-Saxon period, Wessex ruled southern England and dominated English politics.

Vikings. For more than 200 years after Egbert's death in 839, VIKINGS from DENMARK and NORWAY frequently raided and invaded England. After the Danes conquered Northumbria and East Anglia, the area became known as Danelaw. The Danes threatened Mercia and Wessex until King ALFRED THE GREAT of Wessex beat them back by establishing English supremacy on the seas. His successors recaptured the territory the Danes had conquered, including Danelaw.

In the eleventh century, a fresh wave of Danish raids and a full-scale invasion by the king of Denmark led to a period of Danish rule over England (1016–1042) under Cnut the Great and his two sons.

Their deaths without heirs paved the way for the restoration of the Anglo-Saxon rule of Wessex under EDWARD THE CONFESSOR.

The conversion of the Anglo-Saxons, initiated by the Roman church in the late 500s, spread CHRISTIANITY to the rulers of all the Anglo-Saxon kingdoms and their courts, and then eventually to the countryside as well. In the 600s, Celtic missionaries from Ireland and Wales joined the Romans in spreading the Christian religion, especially in the north. The Church under the leadership of its archbishoprics at Canterbury and York played an important role in the unification of England.

The Anglo-Saxons laid the foundation of local English government by the way they divided and ruled their territories. They divided their lands into hundreds and boroughs, administered by officials called reeves, which they then grouped into larger areas called shires, ruled by shire-reeves (which became "sheriffs"). This system of local government continued into the later medieval and modern periods.

Norman Invasion. The Norman Conquest marked a major turning point in English history. In 1066, French-speaking Normans—descendants of the Vikings who had earlier settled in northwestern France (Normandy)—invaded and conquered England, beginning several centuries of Norman-Angevin rule. The Normans ruled England until 1154, while their descendants, the ANGEVINS, ruled from 1154 to 1399. These two French-speaking dynasties developed new institutions that set England apart from Europe while at the same time bringing England into closer contact with European affairs.

When the last Anglo-Saxon ruler, Edward the Confessor, died without an heir, the English nobles offered the crown to Harold, earl of Wessex. However, William, duke of Normandy, contested the choice on the basis of an earlier promise he believed had been made by Edward and supported by the pope. William and his Norman army invaded England and defeated Harold, killing him at the BATTLE OF HASTINGS on October 14, 1066. Thus began a new era in English history that brought the feudal customs, laws, language, and culture of the Normans and ANGEVINS to England.

HENRY II was the first Angevin king of England (so called because of his title as count of Anjou in France). He and his son RICHARD I LION-HEART spent more time on the continent than in England.

The Norman Conquest and the Norman-Angevin era that followed turned England into a feudal society. Before 1066 Anglo-Saxon lords owned their lands, but in keeping with the feudal customs on the continent, William claimed all of England for himself and his family. He parceled out parts of it as fiefs to his supporters, who in turn granted portions to their followers as smaller fiefs. English bishoprics and abbeys also be-

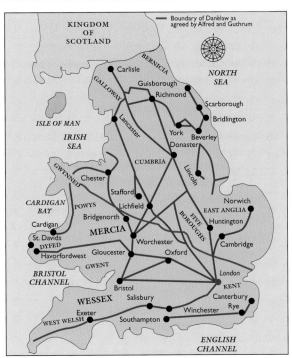

England in the 14th century. The Danelaw is the area north of the line running from London to Chester.

came fiefs. Eighty percent of the population were peasant workers. In the southwestern half of the country most were manorial serfs, tied perpetually to landed estates. After 1200, a rapid rise in population made serfdom expensive compared to the hiring of free labor; by 1340 serfdom had generally disappeared.

Although the Normans replaced English with Latin as the language of government, they preserved and developed the Anglo-Saxon governmental system. The unique feudal survey of England recorded in the DOMESDAY BOOK was the most extensive record of royal government up to that time. The legal and administrative records of the central and local governments after 1170 are by far the most extensive surviving records for the study of medieval government and society.

Late Middle Ages. Parliament began to emerge as a place to address legal questions and authorize taxation, although the full authority of Parliament was not firmly established until the late 1600s. Social upheavals such as the BLACK DEATH (1349) and the PEASANTS' REVOLT (1381) marked the late medieval period. One of the most important cultural developments in the late medieval period was the emergence of Middle English as the medium of national literary expression. After it survived the ascendancy of French and Latin under the Normans and Angevins, by 1450 English became the everyday language of the nobility as well as the common people. England is the only medieval European country for which we have reliable population statistics. At the time of the Domesday Book in 1086, it was 1.2 million people. In 1300, including the population of Wales, it was between five and six million, as a result of a tremendous demographic expansion in the thirteenth century, a time of peace and good weather. By 1400, the population had fallen to about three million, as a result first of famine (after bad weather and crop failure) and then the biomedical disaster of the Black Death of 1347–1348; it probably remained at that level in 1500.

The most important social development in late medieval England was the rise in prosperity and political influence of the gentry, the rural upper middle-class and the appearance of affluent peasants called yeomen. The most important intellectual development was the rise of Oxford University after 1200 as one of the two leading centers (along with Paris) of theology, philosophy and science in northern Europe.

Late medieval England was known as a land of intense piety, especially after the coming of the FRANCISCAN friars in 1230. LONDON, with a population of 100,000 in 1340, boasted over 200 churches. England was also the only country in Europe to develop a distinctive legal system (and not simply adapt the Roman legal system). In the late fourteenth century, it was also a country of exceptional poets, including CHAUCER, the author of *Piers Plowman* (thought to be WILLIAM LANGLAND), and the anonymous author of *Sir Gawain and the Green Knight*.

See ANGLO-SAXONS; ANGEVINS; VIKINGS; DENMARK; SAXONS; NORMANS; BATTLE OF HASTINGS; *and* CHRISTIANITY. *For individuals, see* EDWARD THE CONFESSOR; RICHARD I LION-HEART; WILLIAM I THE CONQUEROR; *and* HAROLD II GODWINSON. *For additional information, see* ENGLISH LANGUAGE AND LITERATURE; DOMESDAY BOOK; WOOL TRADE; BLACK DEATH; *and* PEASANTS' REVOLT.

ENGLISH LANGUAGE AND LITERATURE

Although the language we call English is spoken or understood almost everywhere in the world, its origins were not particularly auspicious. It began as the language of a small group of Germanic tribes, but thanks in part to its knack for blending and borrowing from other languages, it evolved over the course of several centuries, instead of simply dying out or being absorbed by another tongue. The sweeping works of medieval authors like CHAUCER and LANGLAND promoted English's importance in the later Middle Ages.

The English Language. English can be described as a language created by force. Celtic was the language of the British Isles. The Romans under Julius Caesar invaded and colonized Britain bringing LATIN with them, somewhat influencing the local tongue. For the most part, however, Latin remained the language of scholars and of the Church.

Early in the fifth century, Rome abandoned Britain. Soon afterward, Germanic tribes crossed the North Sea and launched invasions against the now-vulnerable Britons. The invaders pushed them to the "Celtic Fringe" (IRELAND, SCOTLAND, and WALES), and established themselves in ENGLAND. They developed a vernacular based on their Germanic languages, which became Anglo-Saxon, or "Old English."

Anglo-Saxon remained relatively unchanged until the Norman invasion of 1066. Norman FRENCH became the language of the nobility, the courts, and the schools. French essentially became a second vernacular in Britain. In time, the two languages blended together to form what was called Middle English. The Norman influence on the language remained strong until the English lost Normandy to the French in 1204. For a century afterward, French remained the language of the royal court in England; HENRY IV, whose reign began in 1399, was the first king for whom English was his native tongue. Gradually, the French influence lessened, and over the next three centuries English continued to evolve until it developed into a form we can generally recognize today. (*See* FRENCH LANGUAGE AND LITERATURE.)

English Literature. Latin was the preferred language for scholarly writing throughout Europe, but works in the vernacular played an important role in the lives of ordinary individuals. Many religious works were written or translated from Latin into English in order to reach as wide an audience as possible. (*See* LATIN LANGUAGE AND LITERATURE.)

The earliest important poem written in the English language is BEOWULF, written by an anonymous Anglo-Saxon. This epic, more than 3,000 lines long, recounts in Old English the adventures of a Germanic hero from Scandinavia. A number of other poems exist from the Anglo-Saxon period, but the names of most Anglo-Saxon poets have long since disappeared. Only one poem exists that can be attributed to an author— a short hymn by the seventh-century poet Caedmon, the "father of English poetry." As for prose works, many were translations of Latin texts, though many religious works were written initially in the vernacular. The ninth-century West Saxon king, ALFRED THE GREAT, was admired as a writer and translator.

Middle English literature included both popular works and religious writings. It was read by educated common people and by English nobles for whom French was a second language. The epic poem *Roman de Brut* by the priest Layamon (1189) chronicles the history of Britain up to the Anglo-Saxon invasions.

The late fourteenth century became known as the first golden age of English literature. Writing took a more worldly tone after the publication of the WYCLIFFE Bible, which was its first full English translation. Chaucer is the best-known writer of this period; other major writers include the anonymous author of *Pearl* and *Sir Gawain and the Green Knight,* and William Langland, author of *Piers Plowman*. The fifteenth-century printer WILLIAM CAXTON was the first to print books in English, important in disseminating English writing.

ETHELRED THE UNREADY

E thelred II (c. 968–1016) was the king of ENGLAND from 978–1016. He was the second son of King Edgar by his second wife Aethelfryth. Ethelred became king after the murder of his half-brother, King Edward the Martyr in 978.

Ethelred married Emma, daughter of Richard I, duke of Normandy, in order to consolidate his power with a Norman alliance. The ANGLO-SAXON CHRONICLE gave a harsh account of Ethelred's rule. According to the Anglo-Saxons he was "redless," which meant "ill counselled." The Victorians dubbed him "unready."

All was not bleak during his reign. The widespread use of vernacular literature, the efficiency of administrative and economic aspects of government, the development of a solid coinage and taxation system are all positive developments that took place during his reign. The invasions by the Danes, however, weakened his power, finally leading to the submission of northern England and LONDON to the Danish King Sweyn in 1013. Ethelred fled with his family to Normandy. The Danish king died in 1014, and Ethelred was reinstated.

Upon Ethelred's death in 1016, England was divided between Cnut the Great, son of Sweyn, and Ethelred's son Edmund II Ironside. When Edmund II died in 1016, Cnut married Ethelred's widow, Emma, and ascended to the kingship of England.

EXCHEQUER

T he office in medieval ENGLAND responsible for the country's finances. It took the name from the checkered cloth used to track financial accounts. The office was established by WILLIAM I THE CONQUEROR, after the Norman Conquest of Britain, as a central treasury. During the reign of Henry I in the twelfth century, the responsibilities of the office expanded to include the finances of the entire kingdom. It became a very efficient system for collecting and distributing resources, by far the most advanced national accounting system in medieval Europe. Some English kings tried unsuccessfully to bypass the Exchequer in order to avoid the controls imposed by Parliament. By the late fourteenth century, however, Parliament prevailed, and all finances were managed by the Exchequer. (*See* BANKING; MONEY AND CURRENCY.)

EXPLORATION

Exploration, a common feature of the ancient world, declined after the fall of the Roman Empire in the fifth century. While the ancient trade routes through CONSTANTINOPLE linking Europe with CHINA and India were still traveled by Italian traders, substantive knowledge and curiosity about China and India ebbed. Only the VIKINGS from Scandinavia continued the tradition of systematic exploration, colonization and conquest of unknown lands. Starting in the 700s, Swedish kings colonized the Baltic lands, then followed rivers into RUSSIA, venturing as far as south of the Caspian and Black Seas. Viking seafarers sailed into the Atlantic Ocean, reaching ICELAND in 850 and later establishing a colony in GREENLAND. The famous explorer Leif Ericsson "discovered" North America, which he called Vineland, when he sailed there in an attempt to reach Greenland.

The Crusades. The first explosion of exploration in Europe occurred after the First Crusade (1096). The crusaders developed a taste for goods from China and India, which had been brought to the Holy Land by Muslims. Subsequent travel to China and India was made easier by the conquests of the MONGOLS, who had imposed a peace on much of Asia and India. Early western European explorers include the FRANCISCANS Giovanni de Pain del Carpini and WILLIAM OF RUBRUQUIS. In the thirteenth century, del Carpini was sent east by Pope Innocent IV in order to enlist the MONGOLS against the Muslims. Del Carpini's travel account generated much interest in Europe. Sent to Mongolia by LOUIS IX of France, William de Rubruquis wrote a brilliant account of his travels.

Marco Polo. The most famous explorer of the Middle Ages was undoubtedly MARCO POLO and his family. The Venetian brothers Niccolo and Matteo Polo traveled to and from Peking between 1260 and 1269. In 1271, they returned to Asia with Niccolo's son Marco. Marco Polo's stay in the court of the Mongolian ruler, KUBLAI KHAN, lasted 24 years. Marco eventually wrote the *Books of Marvels*, an account of his

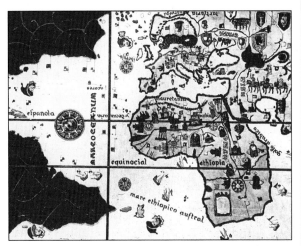

Map by Juan de la Cosa, Spanish navigator who sailed on the Santa Maria *with Columbus on his westward voyage.*

stay in the east. Another famous traveler was the fourteenth-century Muslim judge, Ibn Battuta, who wrote about his 27 years of travels in China and India.

These travel reports inspired a great curiosity and desire for trade, particularly in spices, with the East. The primary obstacle to expanding trade was the Muslim control of the land trade routes to China and India. Europeans sought new sea routes to Asia, initiating in 1414 the "age of discovery." The son of King John I of Portugal, Prince HENRY THE NAVIGATOR spent his life searching for a sea route to India and for the legendary and fictitious Christian African king Prester John. He sent many ships to the coast of AFRICA, improving mapmaking and maritime technology. By 1488, Bartolomeu Dias of PORTUGAL became the first European to round the southern tip of Africa. Perhaps the most significant Portuguese traveler was Vasco de Gama who left Portugal in 1497. He made his way through the Indian Ocean to Calcutta in India, thereby opening a trade route to India and, paving the way for a Portuguese empire in the far east.

Late Middle Ages. As the Middle Ages ended, Europeans made several famous discoveries. In 1492, Christopher Columbus was sent west to India by Isabella of Castile, discovering many parts of the Americas in his failed search. The Florentine Amerigo Vespucci reached SOUTH AMERICA; his name was given to the new continent by the German mapmaker Martin Waldseemüller. Other explorers include: Pedro Cabral, discoverer of Brazil; Magellan, who sailed past the southern tip of the Americas into the Pacific; John Cabot, who reached Newfoundland by 1497; Giovanni da Verrazano of Florence, who traveled to the Carolinas and to New York; and Jacques Cartier of France, discoverer of the sites of modern Quebec and Montreal. (*See* NORTH AMERICA; SOUTH AMERICA.)

FAIRS

Fairs were popular medieval gatherings of merchants that played an important role in the initiation of European modernization. The development of commerce, urbanization, and an increase in the power of political officials all had their place at these gatherings. Perhaps most important, fairs were central in overcoming the localism that was endemic to early medieval life. The end of the Roman era in the fifth century, and the consequent occupation of western Europe by Germanic tribes, had the effect of limiting much of the European population to their local communities. Fairs were international meetings, and therefore lead to a greater cosmopolitan sense. Fairs also fostered economic growth; local lords encouraged fairs by reducing taxes and tolls on days the fairs were active. They also offered protection for the merchants; guards were routinely posted on popular routes to their cities. (*See* COMMERCE AND TRADE.)

Early Fairs. In the Roman Empire, some cities had facilities for international fairs. However, these fairs declined as the fall of Rome led to a decay of a transportation infrastructure and an increase in danger to travelers. Commerce soon became limited to regional trade. Larger fairs began to flourish again when the Frankish kings gained power and established a greater sense of security. The earliest known fairs took place in the early seventh century at the Abbey SAINT–DENIS north of Paris. This fair, like others, featured agricultural transactions, such as grain, as well as vegetables, wool, leather, and animals. The fair at Saint–Denis became popular and attracted foreign traders, who brought popular dyes from Asia.

Expansion. The success of Saint–Denis led to the emergence of other fairs. In the eleventh and twelfth centuries, fairs occurred in important cities in FLANDERS, such as Bruges, Ypres, Lille, Torhout, and Messines. These fairs featured trade in wool, lead, copper, and tin from ENGLAND; Spanish iron; and French wine. Fairs also emerged in CHAMPAGNE, which became the central location for European commerce, credit, and currency exchange. Other French towns started fairs modeled on the ones in Champagne. Large international fairs took place in Lyons and Chalon, with smaller regional fairs occurring in Normandy, BRITTANY, and Languedoc.

These temporary fairs decreased in importance when permanent fairs were established in cities in Flanders and northern FRANCE. In the thirteenth century, Frankfurt was a popular location for merchants. A participant at the Frankfurt fairs could deal in goods from England, Scandinavia, RUSSIA, and Asia. In the fourteenth century, Leipzig also became a center of trade, where industrial products were exchanged for raw materials from the east. After the invention of the printing press, books became an important commodity at Leipzig. Temporary fairs, however, continued in areas without major cities. Fairs outside of Flanders and France took place in Pavia in northern ITALY, LONDON, and Skanor in SWEDEN. Fairs emerged in SPAIN as the RECONQUEST of Spain proceeded. (*See* CHAMPAGNE.)

The Foire (fair) du Lendi at Saint–Denis, at which merchants show their wares, miniature from the 14th–century Grandes Chroniques de France.

FAMILY LIFE

The social structure known as the family was as varied during the Middle Ages as it is today. One cannot therefore speak of the "typical" medieval family; family life depended on location, social status, religion, local laws and customs—virtually any external factor. Whether family members were close and loving or cold and distant was a matter of individual temperament, but in general members of medieval families were loyal and protective of one another. (*See* SOCIAL CLASSES AND CLASS CONFLICT.)

Different Regions. Families in Byzantine Europe, western Europe, and the Islamic countries had different structures but shared a number of traits. In general, the man was head of the house and supported the family; the woman ran the household and raised the children. Marriage was important in all cultures and regions; often they were arranged between sets of parents when the betrothed were still young children. Children were expected to learn useful skills, and would either be apprenticed or given further education. Those who chose to study usually became scholars, most likely clerics.

In the Byzantine Empire, families were often small—a nuclear family consisting of father, mother, and children. Among the nobility, it was more common to find extended families living together—on the theory that there was strength in numbers. The Byzantine father usually managed the family's finances, while the mother raised the children.

Islamic families evolved from the clans of pre-Islamic Arabia. As with the Byzantine family, the nuclear family was the core unit, but often grandparents, siblings, or cousins would become part of the family as well. The man was head of the house, and the woman raised the children. But under ISLAM, men and women were considered equal. WOMEN could own and inherit property and divorce their husbands. Husbands were encouraged to treat their wives with respect and kindness, and couples valued companionship as much as physical and material gratification.

In western Europe, the family unit was generally larger than in Byzantine or Islamic regions. Extended families often lived together. Moreover, medieval European households often included servants and workers. Wealthy Byzantine and Islamic households also included servants, but in Europe even families of more modest means might have servants. The man, once again, was head of the house, but the woman generally had more involvement in running the day-to-day activities of the household. Especially in a large household, the wife would have to manage the servants, keep supply inventories, and handle the family budget. In some cases, a widow may be expected to run her late husband's business affairs, even if he had been a guilded tradesman.

Rich and Poor. Not surprisingly, the wealthy lived more comfortably than the poor. Rich families had larger houses, more privacy, more servants, and better supplies than middle-class or merchant families. Peasant families simply worked all day and slept all night, only to repeat the process day after day. Usually crammed into one- or two-room cottages, they generally included only a father, a mother, and children.

Wealthy Islamic nobles might take more than one wife, though this was not as common a practice as is popularly believed. Byzantine nobles often placed great value on their extended families as important allies, especially in times of conflict with other nobles.

The closest to the middle class as we know it was probably the merchant class in western Europe. Often the husband, wife, their children, and several servants or assistants would live in a building that housed whatever shop they ran on the ground floor. Husbands and wives usually worked as partners in the business. Usually they apprenticed their children to the trade; in any event, the children helped with the business as they were growing up. Children who, for whatever reason, did not go into their parents' business were often apprenticed to another business.

Role of Children. Medieval scholars once believed that children were not particularly valued during the Middle Ages except as an economic commodity. What has been taken for coldness or indifference toward children was more likely a practical resignation to their future. Assuming that the child was born healthy (and often the mother died in childbirth), life expectancy was not high. Many children succumbed to disease. One reason farm families in particular had so many children was that they needed extra hands and knew that life expectancy was low.

Because children were needed to help out economically, they often had to grow up quite quickly. They might become apprentices at the age of seven, and during at least part of the Middle Ages, a boy reached full maturity at the age of 12. The children of the wealthy might be sent for schooling or special training at age seven or eight.

The idea that children were treated with indifference is probably exaggerated. More likely, children were allowed to be children—for a while. But because of the needs of their parents and their communities, childhoods were probably quite short.

 See AGRICULTURE *and* FEUDALISM *for more on communal life. Economic dynamics are discussed in* SERFS AND SERFDOM; NOBLES AND NOBILITY; *and* SLAVERY—*and extensively in* SOCIAL CLASSES AND CLASS CONFLICT. *See also* WOMEN *and* TOWNS, VILLAGES, AND CITIES.

FAMINE

In the agrarian societies that predominated during the Middle Ages, there were a limited number of options available for avoiding the famines that would periodically strike due to the normal variation of food production. One solution was to migrate to other areas, which often involved armed conflict, since inhabitants in the new areas were loath to allow strangers to work the land and strain their resources. The famines that occurred in the east Asian steppes during the early and middle periods of the Middle Ages were chief factors in causing the migrations and invasion of eastern peoples of Islamic, Byzantine, and western Europeans kingdoms. (*See* FOOD.)

Storage. Another solution involved storing food during times of plenty for periods of scarcity. But the techniques of food storage, particularly of grains, were not well developed, and generally required a sizable amount of capital to build storehouses and granaries. The wealthy in an area may have been able to afford these facilities, but the best the poor could do was borrow from the wealthy at usurious rates, which deepened the indenturedness and vassalage of the peasants. Not until the thirteenth century, and then mainly in the cities of the HANSEATIC LEAGUE in northern Europe, did governments undertake the systematic storage of food supplies for the general population.

Trade. A third solution was trade—to build an economy in which goods were created that could be sold to areas of better food production. Since adverse weather was likely to reduce food production over a wide area, only those cities and principalities that conducted trade over long distances could avail themselves of this solution. Coastal cities like VENICE and GENOA imported grain from as far away as RUSSIA; landlocked cities such as FLORENCE found such trading difficult. During times of extreme famine in Europe, Venice in particular controlled the price of grain through its massive imports, at times (in 1273 and again in 1380) using this control to defeat its military adversaries.

Cycles. There were three major periods of famine in Europe during the Middle Ages: the first in the first half of the sixth century, the second in the beginning of the tenth century, and the third in the fourteenth century. These cycles mirrored the climatic cycles of Europe, though they were also influenced by the political landscape. In these periods, travel, and thus trade, were restricted by war, invasion or the simple closing of borders, making the importation of food difficult.

By far the worst period of famine experienced in Europe was in the years 1315 to 1317, when unusually heavy rains devastated crops and created famine throughout the region. Reports from the period indicate that in many towns, over ten percent of the population died of starvation. In several German towns, soldiers were required to guard the gallows to prevent corpses from being cut down and eaten. The death rate climbed so high that many of the dead could not be buried, which led to the spread of disease, a factor in the outbreak of the BLACK DEATH later that century.

FARABI, AL-

The Muslim philosopher, Muhammad ibn Muhammad Abu-Nasr al-Farabi (c. 873–951) was born in Farab in central Asia. He probably came from a wealthy family because he was able to travel to BAGHDAD and study with two outstanding teachers—the logician Yuhanna ibn Haylan, and the grammarian Ibn al-Sarraj. (His later political philosophy also suggests an upper-class background.) After many years in relative obscurity in Baghdad, he travelled to Aleppo where he was received in the court of Saif al-Dawlah in 942. By the time of his death in 951, he was recognized as an important philosopher in the Arab world, and by the thirteenth century, throughout Europe (where he was called "Avennasar").

His Work. Al-Farabi was among the first of the Arab philosophers to recognize the importance of ARISTOTLE, and did much to revive interest in the Greek philosophers. He wrote many commentaries on Aristotle and, to a lesser degree, Plato, and produced a number of works that could be characterized as Neoplatonic (a blend of Plato and mysticism, the foremost proponent of which was the Egyptian-born Roman philosopher Plotinus). In his chief work, *Tahsil al-Sa'adah* (*The Attainment of Happiness*), al-Farabi describes a world that flows out of the mind of God, a world in which the human mind can find contentment only by being in harmony with creation.

Al-Farabi's most important contribution was his formulation of the role and qualities of the *imam*, the religious and political leader of the Islamic state, which he identified with the caliph. Taking his lead from Plato, al-Farabi saw the imam as a philosopher-king in whom every moral and intellectual perfection resided.

Al-Farabi influenced later Arab philosophers like AVICENNA and IBN RUSHD, and the Jewish philosopher MOSES MAIMONIDES. He was also medieval Islamic culture's foremost MUSIC historian.

FATIMID DYNASTY

The Fatimids, a Muslim Shi'ite dynasty, ruled from 909 to 1071. Their empire was centered in EGYPT. At their apex, they controlled virtually all of North AFRICA, Palestine, Syria, and SICILY.

Although the Fatimids reigned for less than two centuries, their radically fundamentalist approach to ISLAM gave the Shi'ite school a foundation and a voice within the ARAB world that it enjoys to the present day.

Origins. The Fatimids traced their origins to Fatima, the daughter of MUHAMMAD, and Ali, her husband and Muhammad's cousin, whom the Fatimids believed were the true heirs of the prophet's mission, thereby rejecting the claim of the ABBASID caliphs. The Fatimids began toward the very end of the ninth century when the Ismaili Shi'ite leader, Ubayd Allah, established an independent kingdom on the coast of Tunisia. Driven by religious fervor, and with the military support of the BERBERS, the Fatimids conquered EGYPT in 969 and established a capital in Cairo under the rule of Caliph al-Muizz. (*See* EGYPT.)

The Fatimids adopted two policies that proved very successful and helped drive out the Abbasids as it solidified their hold on northern AFRICA. First, they empowered families loyal to them to control large provinces until they were ready to expand. Thus, the Zirids controlled the Maghreb (central North Africa) until 1047, when the Fatimids were ready to expand. Second, they took a much more tolerant view of non-Muslims—*dhimmis*—which included the many JEWS and Christians who were important in Egyptian society. Regarding any avowal of loyalty by a non-believer to be worthless, the Fatimids did away with the pretenses that the Abbasids had required, which in turn allowed them to accept the talents and support of these minorities. (In fact, the Fatimids regarded their Sunnite coreligionists as only a bit more worthy of salvation, and hence respect, than Jews and Christians.) In this way, the Fatimids extended their domain east and west and became the predominant trade conduit between India and the Mediterranean.

Al-Muizz died in 975 and was succeeded by his son, al-Aziz, who, along with the entire line of Fatimid caliphs, launched several campaigns to conquer DAMASCUS. He took the city several times, but was never able to establish permanent rule.

The reign of Caliph al-Hakim (966–1021) was particularly vexing. Probably suffering from insanity, al-Hakim enacted harsh measures against the Sunnites and retreated from the tolerant attitudes of the others Fatimid caliphs toward Jews and Christians. Some believe his destruction of the Church of the Holy Sepulcher in Jerusalem instigated the First CRUSADE.

Decline. The empire declined steadily, beginning with the SELJUK conquests of 1071 and the Crusades. The Fatimids became dependent on the management skills of the viziers, whose power was greater than the caliph's. By the end of the twelfth century, Egypt was ripe for conquest. Following an aborted invasion by BALDWIN I, and the loss of Palestine to FULK V of Anjou, king of Jerusalem, in 1136, a crusader invasion led by Almaric I in 1171 deposed the last Fatimid caliph and established a Sunnite kingdom, which was unified with Syria by SALADIN in 1173.

FERRARA–FLORENCE, COUNCIL OF

The Council of Ferrara–Florence was an attempt by the Roman Catholic Church and the Greek Church to settle their doctrinal differences and reunite. Although the seven–year council did reach a reunion agreement, it never materialized.

Ferrara–Florence was a continuation of the Council of Basel, which had been convened some time earlier. Pope Eugenius IV moved the council to Ferrara in 1438. (The council moved to FLORENCE a year later when plague struck Ferrara.) The Greek delegation included the patriarch of CONSTANTINOPLE and the Byzantine emperor John VIII Palaeologus.

The points under discussion involved the doctrines of CHRISTIANITY—the definition of purgatory; the origin of the Holy Ghost (Holy Spirit). By 1445, after several years of debate, the problems seemed to have been worked out, though a final agreement was never drafted, and no reconciliation was reached.

At left, a Fatimid bronze griffin that shows the influence of ancient Egyptian style. Below, emblem of the Italian city-state of Ferrara.

FEUDALISM

Since the eighteenth century, historians have used the term "feudalism" (or "the feudal system") to designate the social, military, political, and sometimes economic relationships found in western medieval Europe (from the ninth century to C.E. 1500, with roots traced back to the fourth and fifth centuries). Originally devised as a construct encompassing certain specific features of medieval life, it has also been used as an abstract model or ideal type relevant not only to medieval Europe but also to other times and places. Although embodying phenomena associated with medieval Europe, "feudalism" in this sense denotes a general stage of social, political, and (for Karl Marx and Friedrich Engels and their followers) economic development. Whereas many people, including some scholars, still consider "the feudal system" and "feudalism" meaningful and useful terms, other similar constructs with even longer histories (such as "Oriental despotism") are now generally rejected as over-simplistic and misleading. Numerous scholars believe that this will eventually be the fate of the feudal constructs.

The construct that is termed "feudalism" in English was first devised by seventeenth-century French scholars, who called it "féodalité." The English term appeared in the late eighteenth century, some seventy years after "the feudal system" was conceived there. Before this, in the sixteenth century, French and English scholars had fashioned the concept of a unitary, simple feudal law, which they thought had been formulated and generally applied in the Middle Ages. Scholars seem to have developed the constructs "feudalism" and "feudal system" because they were searching for system and order in the history of human society. The constructs' appearance is closely related chronologically to the popularity of a style of scientific conceptualization linked with the Copernican system and the "system of the world" associated with Isaac Newton (1642–1727). Scholars believed that if the cosmos operated systematically, systems could surely be found to explain the working and development of human society. The historians and lawyers who created the feudal constructs were inspired by the *Libri Feudorum*, a twelfth- and thirteenth-century LOMBARD compilation, soon treated as an integral part of the Roman LAW, which set forth rules governing landed property called feuda or fiefs, and their holders, called vassi or vassals. This text molded the assumptions with which seventeenth- and eighteenth-century scholars manipulated the limited sources, chronicles, and charters that were available to them. Above all, scholars were influenced by contemporary tenurial and ceremonial conventions and institutions, which they assumed were survivals from the medieval past. Although the English PARLIAMENT abolished such tenures in 1660, they and their ceremonial trappings remained important in FRANCE until the Revolution. The historians and legal scholars used the constructs to describe in summary fashion mechanisms they believed functioned throughout western Europe from the ninth through the fifteenth centuries. The constructs were employed to fill the narrative void that existed between the Roman Empire's replacement by splintered barbarian kingdoms and the emergence of recognizable antecedents of contemporary European states in the thirteenth and fourteenth centuries. Until the Roman emperors moved the seat of their power to the East, the story of the past could be linked to the accomplishments of successive rulers, as it could be again when effective rulers reemerged some centuries later. CHARLEMAGNE and other powerful CAROLINGIANS were the exceptions that proved the rule,

King Philip of Valois offering charters to nobles, who then parceled out charters to the lower aristocracy.

although they were presented as "sowing the seeds" of feudalism's later development. (*See* CAROLINGIAN DYNASTY.)

Definition. The simplest, "classic" definition of feudalism focuses on "the fief" and "the vassal." The fief is defined as property, generally land, granted in return for military service. The vassal is defined as a person who renders service, generally military, in return for a fief. In this scheme, the vassal swears fidelity (or fealty) to the lord who grants the fief, and does homage to the lord, a ceremony culminating in a mutual kiss. The lord owes the vassal protection and respect. The vassal owes the lord counsel and aid, not only military, but also financial assistance when the

September harvesting at the feudal manor, Château du Saumur, from the Tres Riches Heures (Book of Hours) *du Duc de Berry.*

lord knights his eldest son, marries his eldest daughter, goes on crusade, or has to be ransomed. In the absence of centralized political authority, the lord exercises what earlier and later were public powers of justice and defense. Envisaged as practices with roots in institutions of late imperial and Carolingian times (commendation of clients, oaths of fidelity by free men, the grant of benefices or lands in connection with office), feudal institutions are seen as becoming widespread in the eleventh century, as being exploited by monarchs in the twelfth and thirteenth centuries, and as declining and becoming insignificant and archaic in the fourteenth and fifteenth (often labeled the era of "bastard feudalism" because of the prevalence of salaries and written contracts).

This schematic, legalistic definition of feudalism has never been universally accepted, and in the nineteenth and twentieth centuries elaborations of the "classic" definition have multiplied. In a popular, influential book published in 1939–1940, the French historian Marc Bloch defined European "feudalism" or "feudal society" as a society in which (1) peasants are subjected to lords, with the highest class specialized in WARFARE and linked by ties of obedience and protection in the form of vassalage; (2) military services are rendered in return for grants of land (in the form of fiefs) rather than money; (3) power is fragmented, and disorder dominates; yet in which (4) other forms of association, including the FAMILY and the state, survive. In a definition he proposed in 1965, Joseph R. Strayer emphasized the fragmentation of political authority, the private exercise of public power, and the use of private contracts to provide military force, but also declared that the systematization of "feudal institutions and customs" served as the basis for the creation of strong political units, the precursors of modern bureaucratic states. A recent terminological analysis delineates ten separate sets of connotations associated with "feudalism," ranging from those featuring ties of dependence, the holding of fiefs in return for service, the union of benefice (grants of land similar to fiefs) and vassalage, and the privatization of law and politics, through the exploitation of peasants by the lord (associated with Marx and Engels).

The Marxist approach to feudalism has been especially important in the twentieth century. Influenced by the writings of Adam Smith (1723–1790) and other eighteenth-century Scottish thinkers, Karl Marx (1818–1883) and Friedrich Engels (1820–1895) made the feudal mode of production, centered not on the fief but on lords' exploitation of dependent peasants, a stage of historical development, preceding capitalism, socialism, and communism. They thus linked feudalism with their revolutionary message, even though Marx presented no elaborated theory or description of a feudal mode of production. Nor did Marx and Engels attempt to prove that the stage had existed universally, and, for Asia, they hypothesized a specific Asiatic mode of production. Still, their presentation of a western feudal mode of production as a necessary antecedent of communism stimulated the search for feudal systems elsewhere, since unsophisticated Marxists viewed feudalism as a virtual guarantee of evolution through capitalism toward socialism and communism. With the disappearance of communism as a political system in most parts of the world, these ideas have lost much of their popularity. In future decades, as knowledge of medieval Europe increases, the other interpretations of "feudalism" and "the feudal system" seem destined to similar decline and eventual disappearance as satisfactory descriptive tools.

The non-Marxist definitions of "feudalism" raise many problems. Bloch's description is general and all-encompassing, a capsule delineation of all medieval European society. Strayer's definition does not refer to "fief" or "vassal." It is difficult to square either Bloch's or Strayer's approach with the development of strong monarchies in ENGLAND and France in the thirteenth and fourteenth centuries. It is also interesting that, like many other scholars, both Strayer and Bloch admitted that each historian's definition of the term is idiosyncratic, and that reliance on such terms cloaks the complexity of human life. (*See the* INTRODUCTION.)

As regards the "classic" definition of feudalism outlined above, its different components have come under increasing scrutiny and criticism. The concept of fief inherent in the legal definition has been shown to reflect the assumptions of later historians rather than the contemporary meanings of such words as feudum and fevum, which were used to refer to a variety of phenomena, including cattle and peasant landholdings. This is also true of vassal and the word vassus, which at various times was used to signify "slave," "boy," "freeman commended to a lord," and "retainer." Individuals who performed homage and swore fealty, and who served other people, were often simply called homines, or "men," and if vassus was sometimes used synonymously with miles ("knight") in the tenth century, the word rarely appeared thereafter. As to military service, historians now realize that soldiers were remunerated in a variety of fashions, and that mercenaries never entirely disappeared. The financial aid provided to lords was given by all who were subject to the lord's authority, not just by knightly dependents. In this case as in others, obligations imposed on one segment of society were often extended to others, a point that has been obscured by a tendency to compartmentalize and deal separately with the nobility and the peasantry (except insofar as the former is seen as the exploiter of the latter), and to treat both in separation from urban and religious communities. Throughout the Middle Ages courts of free men exercised judgment and provided mediation, often in cooperation with local ecclesiastical institutions, whose leaders were related to the secular aristocracy. As to land, freehold property (often designated as allodial) continued to exist throughout the Middle Ages, and the rights that property holders exercised over lands called feoda were not necessarily any less extensive than those exercised

LIFE IN THE MIDDLE AGES

The Kiss of Peace

The loyalty that a vassal owed to his lord was formalized into a ceremony known as "homage." The vassal would kneel in front of the lord, usually in a chapel or cathedral, with many other high-ranking nobles in attendance, and place his hands in the hands of the noble. He would then swear (often over the relics of a venerated saint) his loyalty to the lord, and that he would be his "man" (or, in Latin, *homo*), in return for the protection and benefits granted by the lord. The lord would then bestow a "fief" on the vassal in the form of land or a right, which was symbolized by a "kiss of peace," which the lord would give the vassal.

over lands called allodia. In eleventh-century Normandy, for example, property was rented, mortgaged, and transferred by sale, exchange, donation in alms, and as conditional gift, as well as in fief. The situation in contemporary BARCELONA and southern France was similar. Any standardization and regularization that took place occurred later, under the direction of increasingly powerful rulers, who recognized the usefulness of employing tenurial bonds to gain and solidify allegiances and to promote recognition of their own superiority. Under such rulers, the number and importance of lands held in fief, whose transfer was effected in ceremonies of homage and fealty, increased. This was, however, only one means rulers employed to buttress their power and authority. But it was advantageous enough to ensure its continuance after 1500. Despite the impression given by traditional accounts of fiefs and feudal ritual, such tenurial ties and ceremonial bonds remained important in France until the Revolution, although modern historians of the seventeenth and eighteenth centuries, interested in other topics, generally disregard this aspect of property holding.

Increasing tolerance for complexity, greater willingness to recognize gaps in human knowledge, and a growing realization of the part preconceived assumptions play in structuring understanding of the past are revolutionizing scholarly investigation of medieval Europe. The thirst for simplicity and system characteristic of the seventeenth and eighteenth centuries is nowhere better revealed than in that era's invention of "feudalism" and "the feudal system." Scholars now realize that these constructs in the end reveal more about the thinking processes, values, and assumptions of their seventeenth- and eighteenth-century inventors than about the society of the period they purport—and have too long been presumed—to describe.

For more on feudal relationships, see SERFS AND SERFDOM *and* NOBLES AND NOBILITY. *The structure of feudal society is discussed in* SOCIAL CLASSES AND CLASS CONFLICT. *For its practical implementation, see* AGRICULTURE. JAPAN *describes a Far Eastern feudal society.*

FIBONACCI, LEONARDO

 lso known as Leonardo of PISA (c. 1170– c. 1240), Fibonacci was an important Italian mathematician who was responsible for the introduction of Hindu-Arabic numerals to Europe.

Life. Fibonacci's father was a Pisan merchant who was sent to North AFRICA to manage Pisan interests. Leonardo joined his father and it was there that he came into contact with ARAB mathematicians and learned the system of Arabic numerals (which had actually come to the West from India). In 1202, he wrote *Liber abaci*, a book on the abacus, summarizing what he had learned from his Arab teachers, including the Arabic number system. A second work, on Euclid's geometry, was issued in 1220, which further enhanced his fame. He was invited to SICILY to join the court of FREDERICK II, an ardent patron of the sciences. It is known that he was a celebrated member of that court, but there is little documentation regarding his last years. He died around 1240, perhaps in Pisa.

Work. Despite the importance of Arabic numerals to the development of mathematics, Fibonacci's most important work in pure mathematics, *Liber quadratorum* (*Book of Square Numbers*) appeared in 1225. In it, Fibonacci introduced the concept of what French mathematician Edouard Lucas called in the nineteenth century the "Fibonacci sequence." This is the sequence of whole numbers created by adding the previous two numbers in the sequence; it begins 1, 1, 2, 3, 5, 8, 13, 21, 34, and so on. This sequence has been found to appear in nature with surprising regularity in the spirals of sunflower heads, pine cones, snail shells, and animal horns. (*See* SCIENCE.)

FINLAND

Finns, an Asiatic people who were mostly nomadic hunters and fishers, migrated into Finland from the south beginning in the first century C.E. Their language—called Finn-Ugrian—was not a Indo-European language; rather it was related to the language of the Hungarians. By the 700s, the Finns were settled solidly in their homeland, displacing the Lapps in southern and central Finland and driving them to the far north where they live today.

Beginning in the sixth century, the Finns were divided into three kingdoms. Out of these, one was dominant—the Suomi. Their kingdom encompassed the southern part of the country, and although they prospered greatly from their trading skills, they were not proficient in the art of politics. It was therefore not difficult for King Eric IX of SWEDEN to invade and conquer the Suomi kingdom in the mid-twelfth century. It was at this time that the Finns were converted to CHRISTIANITY, under the guidance of Archbishop Henry of Uppsala of Sweden in about 1152. Henry became the patron saint of Finland after he was martyred on a mission to Finland around 1160.

By 1293, the Swedes had conquered all of Finland. The Finns, however, were not enslaved by their conquerors. Sweden allowed the Finns to retain a good deal of their independence, and under the influence of the Swedes, the Finns achieved political and commercial success. Swedish language and culture quickly spread throughout the country and the political fortunes of Finland remained tied to the ebb and flow of Swedish history.

By the end of the Middle Ages, Finland had lost a good deal of its earlier independence and become a duchy within Sweden. However, the Finns retained some elements of self-government and a strong cultural and linguistic identity that served as the foundation for the later emergence of Finland as a nation.

FLANDERS

Flanders was an important region during the Middle Ages, from both a trade and strategic standpoint. Located between the Schelde River and the North Sea, it was a province of the state of BURGUNDY, covering the area that is now Belgium, Luxembourg, and the NETHERLANDS, as well as parts of GERMANY and FRANCE. The name "Flanders" is believed to mean "low land" and the countries that make up Flanders are referred to as the Low Countries.

Before the Middle Ages, Flanders was inhabited by Germanic tribes. The region was conquered by the FRANKS early in the sixth century, and it became the seat of the MEROVINGIAN kingdom (founded by the Frankish leader CLOVIS) around 506. The CAROLINGIANS seized Flanders in the mid-eighth century, and it became part of CHARLEMAGNE'S vast empire.

Expansion and Trade. Flanders came under the rule of Charles the Bald, a grandson of Charlemagne, in 843. He put his son-in-law, Baldwin I Iron-Arm, in charge of the region. Over the next 150 years, Baldwin and his successors gradually expanded the regions to the south and east. During this time, Flanders also became known as an important center for textiles. Earlier the regional economy had focused on AGRICULTURE, but gradually it became an international supplier of cloth. Its proximity to many waterways made it an easy trading partner, and it had especially good relations with ENGLAND (which supplied much of the wool needed to make the cloth.) Textile-producing towns such as Ypres and GHENT became important centers of trade, as did the seaport city of Brugge.

Because of its geography, Flanders developed into two distinct regions, each with its own language. The southern region was influenced by neighboring France, and its inhabitants, the Walloons, spoke a French dialect. The north came under German influence, and the language spoken evolved into modern Flemish and Dutch.

Military Value. Flanders continued to prosper until late in the twelfth century, when the French and Germans waged a series of battles for control of the region. By the early fourteenth century, Flanders came completely under French rule.

Trouble between the French and the English caused a rift between England and Flanders. Many Flemish merchants supported England, their chief source of wool. After the Flemish ruler Louis of Nevers supported FRANCE in the HUNDRED YEARS' WAR, England's EDWARD III placed an embargo on wool which led to Flanders' decline as a textile center. It was not until the latter part of the fourteenth century that Flanders rebounded, and by the reign of Philip the Good early in the fifteenth century, Flanders was restored to much of its former prominence.

As the Middle Ages drew to a close, Flanders became an important center for the arts, producing such masters as the van Eycks and van der Weyden. By the end of the Middle Ages, Flanders had become a part of the HABSBURG dynasty.

FLORENCE

At the outset of the Middle Ages Florence was under the control of neighboring rulers, but in the early 1100s it became an autonomous city-state. After centuries of relative obscurity, the city began to emerge as a major European economic and cultural center in the 1200s, thus living up to its name (from the Latin Florentia, meaning "flourishing town").

Emergence. Established as a Roman colony on the Arno River in Tuscany about 150 miles northwest of ROME, Florence entered the early medieval period that began with the fall of Rome in the 400s under the control of the GOTHS, BYZANTINES, and LOMBARDS, with both Florence and ITALY suffering severe economic decline. During its two centuries under Lombard rule which began in 570, the city barely survived on the food produced in the surrounding countryside.

After the CAROLINGIANS defeated the Lombards in 774, the FRANKS ruled Tuscany for a brief

Florence in 1480, as depicted in the Catena Map. The florin produced there became Europe's standard.

period. However, by the mid-800s, local Tuscan chieftains called margraves were in control of the region. That period saw the city's two most important developments: the rise of the COMMUNE (city government independent of the rule of surrounding feudal lords); and the intense struggle for power between the pope and emperor. (*See* COMMUNE; ITALY.)

By the time Countess MATILDA, ruler of Tuscany, died in 1115, the city's commune system was firmly in place, with consuls, elected by members of the commune, running the city. At first, membership in the commune was restricted to the city's noble families and city officials; merchants and workers were excluded. Gradually, however, these groups were admitted. By the late 1100s, the commune was the dominant political force in the city. In 1187 when the German king HENRY VI (to be crowned Holy Roman emperor four years later) granted Florence a charter, he was recognizing an already established political fact.

Divided City. During the 1200s, the populace divided into two parties—GUELPHS and GHIBELLINES—which fought for control of the city. In the power struggle between the empire and the PAPACY, the Guelphs supported the papacy, while the Ghibellines favored the imperial cause. In Florence their conflict was fueled by local issues and family feuds and often erupted into mob violence. The consular form of government gave way to the office of a city manager called a podesta, recruited from outside the city to assure his independence. (*See* GUELPH; and GHIBELLINES.)

By the end of the 1200s the Guelphs had triumphed over the Ghibellines and controlled the city, but they in turn divided into feuding factions called Blacks and Whites. When the Blacks won the support of the pope and his followers, the Whites were forced to seek support from Ghibellines in other towns and

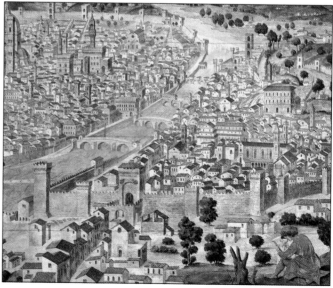

from neighboring monarchs. Henry VII of Luxembourg tried to conquer Tuscany for the Ghibellines, but his death in 1313 left Florence firmly in Guelph hands. The poet DANTE fell victim to the bitter feuding. Because he sided with the Whites, the Blacks banished him from his native city.

As the merchants and bankers of Florence amassed great wealth from the sale of silks, tapestries, and jewelry, commercial rivalries with other Italian cities, especially PISA, erupted into open warfare. One result of Florence's military expansion was the absorption of Arezzo, Pisa, Pistoia, and Volterra. The city's economic and political expansion was temporarily halted in 1348 when the BLACK DEATH killed more than half the city's population. (*See* BANKING.)

For a half century beginning in 1382, Florence regularly fought with Pisa and MILAN, sometimes enlisting VENICE as an ally. In 1427 Florence extended its direct rule to the western coast of Italy, a move that allowed it to operate a fleet of ships which competed with Genoa and Venice for Mediterranean trade.

The Medicis. In the 1400s, Florence came under the control of a banker named Cosimo de MEDICI, a wealthy patron of the arts with considerable political and diplomatic skills. After Cosimo's death in 1464, his son Piero succeeded him as the city's unofficial ruler, but he died five years later, leaving his 20-year-old son Lorenzo to lead the city. (*See* MEDICIS.)

Although Florence retained its republican structure, the Medici family ran the city. Under Lorenzo de Medici, who ruled the city from 1469 to 1492, Florence became the center of Renaissance art and culture. His death marked the end of the city's golden age, although it continued to flourish as Italy's premier Renaissance city. Florence was home to a long list of great artists, poets, and scholars. Dante, PETRARCH, GIOTTO, Michelangelo, Leonardo da Vinci, Raphael, Donatello, BOTTICELLI, Machiavelli, and Galileo all lived and worked in Florence.

In the late 1400s, the political life of the city became especially stormy. An uprising against the Medicis resulted in their expulsion from the city in 1494, and for the next four years the charismatic religious reformer Savonarola held sway. After the revolt against the Medicis ended in 1512, a new republic was established and lasted until the event that marked the end of the medieval period for all of Italy—the conquest of Italy by emperor Charles V.

FOLIOT, GILBERT

F oliot (c. 1110–1187) played an important role in English Church history, but is best remembered as THOMAS BECKET's opponent.

Born of noble NORMAN parents and trained at the aristocratic French Benedictine MONASTERY of Cluny, Foliot served as abbot of Gloucester and bishop of Hereford, and later of LONDON. He opposed Becket's election as archbishop of Canterbury in 1162. His elevation to the important bishopric of London in 1163 served as a counterbalance to Becket. Foliot administered Canterbury during Becket's exile in 1164–1170.

Foliot remained devoted to the ANGEVIN cause, negotiating with the PAPACY on King HENRY II's behalf and taking part in the coronation of Henry's young son in 1170. Foliot was in Normandy when knights loyal to King Henry murdered Becket in Canterbury cathedral in late December 1170. The papacy excommunicated Foliot in 1171 for his role in the feuding that led up to Becket's murder, but absolved him the following year. Foliot continued to play a leading role in the life of the English Church until his death in 1187. His letters are a major source of information about the Becket controversy.

FONTENOY, BATTLE OF

T he Battle of Fontenoy, fought in 841, is important in European history for its impact on the creation of the modern boundaries of western Europe. The battle led to the TREATY OF VERDUN, which partitioned off the empire created by CHARLEMAGNE, leader of the FRANKS.

The CAROLINGIAN Empire, as Charlemagne's territories were known, covered modern-day FRANCE, Belgium, the NETHERLANDS, SWITZERLAND, and parts of GERMANY and ITALY. Charlemagne created a strong empire that included some 400 divisions known as counties. Day-to-day matters were handled by the local counts, but ultimately they were responsible to Charlemagne, who convened them annually.

Charlemagne had planned to divide his empire among his three sons, but only one, LOUIS I THE PIOUS, survived him. It was Louis who indirectly (and inadvertently) set in motion the events that led to the Battle of Fontenoy. Under Frankish tradition, a ruler's lands were to be divided among his sons. Louis had three sons—Lothair, Pepin, and Louis (later called Louis the German). Because he wanted the empire remain strong and unified, Louis directed that upon his death the three sons would inherit their separate lands, but Lothair, the eldest, would have suzerainty (overlordship) of the other sons. This decree was compounded by the birth of a fourth son (by his second wife, Judith) who would be known as Charles the Bald. In 838, Pepin died, and Louis revised his plans; each son was to get a portion of the empire, but Lothair would not be allowed to exercise suzerainty.

Each of the three sons tried to win the support of various members of the nobility, but none emerged strong enough to stem off trouble when Louis died in 840. Lothair immediately declared that Louis's original decree was still in force and declared himself emperor. His brothers refused to acknowledge Lothair's position, and a civil war ensued. Charles and Louis fought Lothair for the next three years. But it was the Battle of Fontenoy that actually marked the turning point for Lothair. He never recovered from his defeat at Fontenoy, and eventually he was forced to capitulate to his brothers' demands.

Under the TREATY OF VERDUN, signed in 843, Lothair relinquished his claim and agreed to share the empire with his brothers as equals. Lothair's lands included BURGUNDY, the Low Countries (the Netherlands and Belgium), and the Italian holdings. Louis was given the eastern part of the empire (hence the nickname "German"). Charles the Bald was given the empire's westernmost lands. Lothair eventually partitioned his territory among his three sons, and then abdicated the throne to spend the remainder of his life as a monk. As these lands passed from generation to generation, they changed considerably, eventually emerging as France, Germany, Italy, Belgium, AUSTRIA, Switzerland, and Luxembourg.

FOOD AND DRINK

The month of January in the Très Riches Heures (Book of Hours) *of the Duke of Berry depicts a 15th-century nobleman's banquet and reveals the food itself to be quite simple, with heavy emphasis on baked goods and wines.*

T he production, processing, and consumption of foodstuffs was a primary preoccupation of the medieval population. In the earlier unsettled period, the production was strictly for the household; later, with the development of TOWNS and more stable settlements, there was the growth of markets and trade in foodstuffs. Throughout the period, the most important social activity was eating in the company of others; usually this was family, but often it was lord and retainers. The ability of the overlord to maintain power was partially dependent on his ability to provide food for his large retinue of family, retainers, and servants. In fact, the title "lord" is thought to be derived from the Old English "hlaford," or loaf, signifying bread-keeper.

Bread. The staple item of the medieval diet was some form of grain, usually made into bread; the poorest peasants would have eaten coarse, less desirable grains, such as oats, in the form of porridge or flat pancakes. The absence or presence of bread at a meal, and the degree of fineness of the flour, was indicative of social status and income. White bread was the most desirable because the wheat was ground fine and sieved for debris. Brown bread was made from rye or bran and was most widely consumed. The poorest quality was bread made from peas, beans or oats, called horse bread because it was commonly eaten by horses as well as by the poor. Bread occupied such an important place in the diet that towns enacted regulations to control its manufacture and sale by the bakers' GUILDS.

Dairy. Dairy products made up another important segment of the diet. Both sheep's and cow's milk were used to make butter and cheese, which were heavily salted to aid in preservation, and which permitted trade in these products over longer distances. The curds, whey, and buttermilk residues left from cheese-making were all consumed as accompaniments to bread. Most rural households and estates kept chickens or ducks, both for food and eggs.

Medieval Fare. Meat and fish were not regular fare for the poorer levels of society. Whereas in the earlier Middle Ages, wild game such as venison, boar, and hare were readily available for hunting in the forests of Europe, the spread of cultivated land and the encroachment of settlements eventually cut off access to these animals; only the nobility were allowed to hunt them. Mutton, beef, and pork (in descending order of popularity) were available to those who could afford them; professional butchers were often among the wealthiest burghers. (*See* HUNTING AND FOWLING.)

Fish and eel, salted or fresh, became a mainstay of the medieval diet, because of the Church's strong rules prohibiting meat at least one day (and initially three days) a week and during the entire Lenten period.

Most households had gardens to grow vegetables such as cabbage, leeks, onions, beans, and herbs. The cookery of northern Europe depended heavily on herbs for flavoring, as most spices were rare and expensive. (In the eastern Mediterranean and Islamic lands, food was heavily spiced, and the cuisine emphasized rice and vegetable oils.) Monasteries and the large estates of the nobility usually had orchards for fruits, olives, and nuts, and often incorporated vineyards.

Drink. Wine was the drink of choice for the nobility, the clergy, and the merchant class, and the trade in wine was one of the more important commercial enterprises. By the early fourteenth century, wine made up 30 percent of English imports from countries such as FRANCE and SPAIN. The rest of the population, however, seldom tasted wine. For them, ale, beer, and mead sufficed. The brewing of ale began as a domestic activity of women, but expanded with the population into a guild-organized commercial category.

There was a great variety of food available, and this fact is most evident in the literary descriptions of medieval feasts. Due to the pervasive influence of the Church, the calendar alternated constantly between fast and feast. Although great variations in menu planning were probably not possible for most peasants, the wealthiest classes and the clergy could indulge in splendid banquets.

These culinary celebrations varied in detail, but typically began with musicians playing while guests were seated at long tables in descending social order, with the host and most important figures, seated at a raised dais that placed them higher than the communal salt cellar (thus "above the salt".) The top of the first loaf was cut off by a servant and presented to the dais guests—hence the term "upper crust." The rest of the bread loaves were cut into thick slices to create plates, or trenchers, for each guest, who shared bowls and knives. Food was eaten with the fingers, so a pre-meal ceremony of pouring water over each guest's hands was performed. As the guests ate, holding the little finger extended in order to scoop up spices was considered a mark of good breeding.

Participants in a feast of the earlier Middle Ages, particularly in Germanic northern Europe, would have sat down to a meal heavy in fatty meats, but later a more refined and elaborate cuisine was offered. An artfully prepared array of dishes, including meat and game, fowl of every type (even crane and lark), and fish and shellfish, was served. Meats were roasted, fried, stewed, boiled, and made into pies, and flavored with countless herbs and costly spices. Fresh fruit and vegetables were boiled or preserved in pickling brine, or served with spices and honey. Sauces of various ingredients, including wine, cream, herbs, and vinegar, flavored many dishes.

For the upper levels of society, the medieval kitchen provided endless delights—even religious fast days didn't inconvenience unduly—but the poor remained grateful for their simple daily bread.

FOREST LAW

Forest law placed medieval legal restrictions on the control and use of the vast European forests. It was a central means by which the nobility sustained their rule; these laws symbolized the NOBLES' exploitative relationship with the peasantry. Forest law protected the privileges of the nobility to hunt in protected woodland and to take possession of timber. The peasants were thereby excluded from the use of forest products. With the decline of the feudal era, both the power of the nobility and the economic centrality of the forest waned, thereby removing the need for the forest law. (*See* NOBLES AND NOBILITY.)

In the chaotic period following the fall of ROME, there was little control over such activities as hunting, cutting wood, or clearing land. By the late seventh century, however, forest law began to take form, particularly in the new MEROVINGIAN Frankish (modern-day FRANCE) kingdom. The Merovingian rulers asserted their exclusive control over some forested areas. These laws were made stricter by the next Frankish dynasty, the CAROLINGIANS, who passed laws creating official royal forests with exclusive hunting rights. Since many peasants barely maintained subsistence, restrictions on their ability to hunt were a severe economic blow. After the Carolingian empire collapsed, separate French and

German kingdoms were founded, each of whose ruling monarchies instituted forest laws. Power over the forests passed over to local nobilities; by the thirteenth century, most forest law in GERMANY and France protected the rights of nobles not kings.

Forest law became a prominent aspect of British law after the NORMAN Conquest of 1066, WILLIAM I THE CONQUEROR protected those "beasts of the forests" that he particularly enjoyed hunting. He established "chases" where his barons could hunt wild animals, and "warrens," where barons could hunt animals besides "beasts of the fields." Over time the protected lands increased, including non-wooded areas such as villages and TOWNS, until the English protected areas covered almost one-fourth of the country.

The enforcement of the law varied from country to country. In ENGLAND, a large police and judicial apparatus was developed to maintain royal forests and enforce forest laws. A royal court called the forest eyre, moved throughout the country judging those accused of violating the forest law. Punishment for violation of the law could be severe. The guilty could incur such penalties as mutilation and even death for a third offense. However, these physical punishments were rare. More commonly, the offender was fined, with the fines becoming an important source of royal revenues.

In France and Germany, enforcement of the law was less systematic. The French king appointed a *maistres des forêts* (master of the forest) to judge violations of the law and other officials to supervise hunting and cutting of timber. In Germany, the royal lands were kept by a royal forester, while bailiffs were appointed by lords to enforce the forest law.

FOSCARI, FRANCESCO

Born to a prominent Venetian family, Francesco Foscari (c. 1373–1457) headed Venice's Council of Forty (1401) and Council of Ten (1405–1413) during the Republic's most aggressive efforts at territorial expansion. He served as Doge of VENICE (1423–1457), leading the city in a series of costly wars against the Milanese Republic. During Foscari's reign, VENICE won the Brescian and Bergamasque territories, the city of RAVENNA, and parts of Lombardy. But the years of war were extremely costly, ravaging northern ITALY until the Peace of Lodi ended the fighting in 1454.

After the Peace, the Venetian aristocracy, jealous of Foscari's power and angered by his failure to protect Venice's eastern territories from attacks by the Turks, charged the Doge with the murder of a Venetian admiral, and charged his son, Jacopo, with holding treasonous discussions with MILAN. Both charges were probably unfounded, though under TORTURE, Jacopo confessed and was excommunicated. Foscari, demoralized by these charges, was deposed by the Council of Ten from the position of Doge in October of 1457, ostensibly because of his severe old age. He died later that year, "listening to the tolling of the bell for the inauguration of his successor (de Sismondi)." His life and disappointments became the subject of a tragedy by Byron and an opera by Verdi.

FRANCE

For most of the Middle Ages the land known today as France was neither a distinct political entity nor a well-defined geographical area. The territorial boundaries of medieval France rarely coincided with those of modern France. For much of the Middle Ages, in fact, France was little more than the geographical setting for developments such as the rise of CISTERCIAN monasticism, NORMAN expansion, the theological flowering centered at the University of Paris, the AVIGNON PAPACY, the HUNDRED YEARS' WAR, and the Albigensian crusade.

Originally part of the Roman empire following Julius Caesar's conquest of the area called Gaul, the region was invaded and settled by Germanic tribes from central Europe, including the FRANKS, VISIGOTHS, and Burgundians. At the end of the fifth century, the Frankish ruler CLOVIS united the tribes of Gaul into a single kingdom and made PARIS its capital. His descendants—called the MEROVINGIAN DYNASTY—occupied the throne until the early eighth century.

France in the Middle Ages	
481	Clovis founds the Merovingian Dynasty.
768	Charlemagne crowned king of the Franks; beginning of Carolingians.
987	Hugh Capet begins Capetian Dynasty
1214	Victory of Philip II Augustus at Battle of Bouvines
1226–1270	Reign of Louis IX; major government reforms
1328–1589	Valois Dynasty rules France, beginning with Philip VI of Valois
1337–1453	Hundred Years' War
1348	Black Death strikes France
1378	The Great Schism
1429	Joan of Arc victorious at Orléans

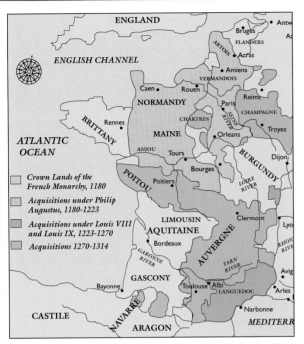

Growth of the French Monarchy. From modest beginnings in the 12th century, France grew with the acquisitions of Philip II Augustus from King John of England and with acquisitions by Kings Louis IX and Philip IV the Fair.

The next to control the kingdom was the CAROLINGIAN DYNASTY, whose greatest leader was CHARLEMAGNE (768–814). The Carolingian empire covered what today is France and GERMANY. The western part of Charlemagne's empire became the kingdom of France. However, it was surrounded by so many independent feudal counties and principalities, such as BURGUNDY, Normandy, BRITTANY, and AQUITAINE, it was a kingdom in name only.

The election of HUGH CAPET as king in 987 began the CAPETIAN DYNASTY which ruled France for much of the Middle Ages. However, the royal domain—known as the Ile-de-France—was small and weak, consisting of little more than the land surrounding the three major towns of PARIS, Orléans, and Laon. In the 1100s the Capetians took steps to strengthen the authority of the king in the Ile-de-France. Philip I, who reigned from 1060 to 1108, appointed local officials as administrators, while Louis VI (1108–1137) won the loyalty of townspeople by issuing charters to the TOWNS that increased their independence from local feudal lords. He also organized the royal court by increasing the responsibilities of household officers such as the chancellor, chamberlain, and seneschal.

Louis's son, PHILIP II AUGUSTUS, made a significant impact as king by centralizing the royal government and expanding the kingdom. His conquest of Normandy and other parts of the ANGEVIN empire in

1204 was a significant turning point for the French monarchy. Still, France continued to fall short of the level of royal centralization and financial management already achieved in ENGLAND and SPAIN.

What finally transformed the French monarchy at the end of the Middle Ages was the French victory under the Valois dynasty over the English in the Hundred Years' War (1337–1453). KING LOUIS XI, who ruled from 1461 to 1483, presided over France's recovery after the war and the integration of the territories returned from the English. He streamlined the administration of the kingdom, stabilized the currency and finances, and maintained a standing paid army. His kingdom, which extended farther than at any time since the Franks, began to resemble the modern French state that followed.

France was admired during the Middle Ages for its great cathedrals and MONASTERIES, the celebrity of its poets, the skill of its artists, and its three wine-growing regions—Bordeaux, Burgundy, and the Loire Valley—which continue to produce spectacular vintages.

See FRENCH LANGUAGE AND LITERATURE; HUNDRED YEARS' WAR; PARIS; FRANKS; *and entries on the* MEROVINGIAN, CAROLINGIAN, *and* CAPETIAN DYNASTIES. *See also* JOAN OF ARC; CHARLEMAGNE; PHILIP II AUGUSTUS; LOUIS IX; *and* PHILIP IV THE FAIR.

FRANCIS OF ASSISI, ST.

St. Francis of Assisi (1182–1226) was the founder of the FRANCISCAN ORDER and one of the most honored saints of the Middle Ages. He was born at Assisi, in central ITALY to Pietro di Bernardone, a rich cloth merchant. Francis attended school and learned to read and write, but he did not attend a university. Instead, he learned the family business and worked with his father until his early twenties.

Deciding to pursue knightly adventure, he joined the forces of Assisi in its war against Perugia. In 1202, Francis was captured and held prisoner for a year. Upon his release, Francis believed he had a mission; he abandoned his life of comfort and devoted himself to helping the poor. An example of his denouncement of wealth came when he sold some of his father's cloth and gave the proceeds to the poor instead of to his father. Francis's father became irate and had Francis thrown in prison. Francis severed his family ties and, in a shocking gesture, removed his clothing in front of a crowd and handed it to his father.

In 1208, Francis formed a small congregation at Assisi and by 1210, he had created a rule of living for his community called the *Regula primitiva* (Primitive

Rule) which was approved by Pope INNOCENT III. In 1212 Clare, a noblewoman from Assisi, asked to join Francis and his disciples. Francis helped her form a community of women who followed the ideas and practices of his newly established order.

During the next few years, thousands of people from all over joined the newly established FRANCISCAN order. Francis traveled extensively in an attempt to convert the Muslims in eastern Europe and EGYPT, preaching a "spiritual crusade." During his journey, he gave up administrative control of the order—he did not see himself as an able administrator—although he would remain the unquestioned spiritual leader of the order until his death in 1226. Pope GREGORY IX canonized him just two years after his death, and his disciples built a church to house his body and serve as a rallying point for the order.

FRANCISCANS

The Franciscan order was established in 1209 by ST. FRANCIS OF ASSISI. The order insisted on poverty for its followers, which was implemented in the order's *Regula primitiva* (Primitive Rule). The order began with Francis and a small number of disciples living in caves outside Assisi. The order's missionaries traveled to non-Christian regions in an attempt to gain converts and during the 1200s, it had over 1,400 convents. The spread of the order led to inevitable changes. While Francis and many of his followers maintained their vow of poverty, others found the rigors of the vow too difficult and impractical in allowing the order to establish monasteries.

Division of the Order. A new rule, the *Regula prima*, was created by Francis and his friend Elia da Cortona. Under the new rule, which had been approved by Pope Honorius III in 1223, neither the order itself nor any member of the order could own any kind of wealth. Property or a house could be given as a "gift" to the order provided it was still owned by the donor, so that at least technically, the rule was not being violated. Francis found the new rule discouraging and—believing himself unfit as an administrator—turned the administration of the order over to Cortona. Two factions soon emerged under Cortona's administration: the Conventuals, who sought compromise with the established Church; and the Spiritual

St. Francis depicted conversing with birds, from a 13th-century psalter.

Franciscans who maintained their vow of complete poverty. When Francis died in 1226, the order was on the verge of breaking in two, but was saved when ST. BONAVENTURA became its leader and allowed the two sides to coexist.

The Franciscans were renowned as university scholars. They taught PHILOSOPHY, the SCIENCES, and theology. Bonaventura, DUNS SCOTUS, and WILLIAM OF OCKHAM were at the center of this university development. Their names lent prestige to the order and fostered its growth.

Violent Disputes. However, the old dispute between the Conventuals and the Spirituals surfaced again at the beginning of the fourteenth century. The PAPACY in AVIGNON supported the Conventuals and Pope John XXIII condemned the Spirituals as heretics, burning four of their leaders at the stake. The Spirituals continued to spread the ideas of St. Francis and the order would eventually be split into many groups. The Observants, heirs to the Spiritual Franciscan philosophy of absolute poverty, were recognized by Pope Leo X in an attempt to end the disunity in the order once and for all. The Conventuals continued as a separate order, but the constant infighting drove the Franciscans to near extinction. The order would return reenergized and refocused with the discovery of the Americas as Franciscan friars assumed a new mission: the conversion of the New World's native population.

FRANKS

Pope URBAN II, while speaking at CLAREMONT in central FRANCE in 1095, cried out "O, Race of the Franks!" as he successfully inspired the assembled lords and knights to join the First CRUSADE against the Muslims. There was something about a Frenchman that seemed to give off a glint of heroism and piety. The Muslims who often enough, after the First Crusade, trounced the invading French crusaders over the next century, still spoke with respect and a bit of shudder about "the Franks." Love or hate them, admire or despise them, the Franks were the key people in early and even later European medieval history.

Emergence. Back in the time of the BARBARIAN INVASIONS of the Latin-speaking Roman empire, in the fifth century, there were two distinct groups that are referred to in the murky chronicles of the era as Franks. It was the group known as the Salian Franks that did the damage to the Roman Empire in Gaul and replaced Gaul with Frankland by the sixth century C.E. The Salian Franks came from quite far beyond the Rhine frontier between the Roman Empire and the German peoples—from about where the present-day city of Frankfurt is now located. In the eleventh century, the Salian dukes of Franconia, who stayed home rather than cross the Rhine into the Roman Empire, became emperors of GERMANY.

Salian Franks. Stacked up to the rear of the Germanic barbarian waves, the Salian Franks, unlike the frontliners, the GOTHS, were little affected by Roman culture, religion, and language when they entered Gaul from the north, via FLANDERS in the early fifth century. They followed the route southward that the German imperial armies of Kaiser Wilhelm II would follow in their surge toward Paris in 1914. But unlike the Kaiser's soldiers, the Franks took the old Roman city of PARIS and the northern part of Gaul, intersected and bound together by the mighty Seine and Loire Rivers. How deeply did this invasion by Salian Franks cut into the consciousness of French nationalist historians in the nineteenth century? They wrote books about the origins of the French race and this migration of the Salian Franks from Frankfurt to Flanders to Paris always sounded in their pages the opening tocsin of patriotic French history, communicated as far away as the French colonies of Algeria and Vietnam.

Recent historians and archaeologists with an aversion to nationalist sentiment rush to tell us that, like most of the Germanic peoples, the Salian Franks were not ethnically homogeneous—strictly speaking, not a race. As they moved forward, the Franks snapped up and included fragments from other Germanic peoples in their ranks. But they had a strong cohesiveness and extended family pride, a common language, and a common heathen religion as they settled in northern France by the middle of the fifth century. The Franks were unusual among the Germanic invaders in that they entered Gaul not as hunters and gatherers; they were an agricultural people from their first settling in Gaul. At first, they hated the Romans as oppressors and said nothing favorable about the old Empire in their law codes.

Clovis I. Between 481 and 511 the Franks were ruled by CLOVIS I, the first king of the MEROVINGIAN (so-called from a mythical ancestor, bold Merovich) dynasty. A great bad man, Clovis led the Frankish warriors on a series of forays into Gallo-Roman and Burgundian territory in the southeast and Visigothic territory in the Southwest. The VISIGOTHS, earlier German migrants into the empire, were decimated,

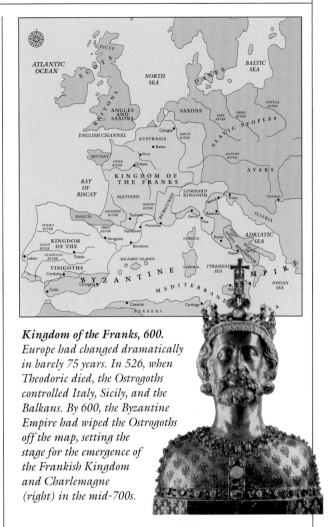

Kingdom of the Franks, 600.
Europe had changed dramatically in barely 75 years. In 526, when Theodoric died, the Ostrogoths controlled Italy, Sicily, and the Balkans. By 600, the Byzantine Empire had wiped the Ostrogoths off the map, setting the stage for the emergence of the Frankish Kingdom and Charlemagne (right) in the mid-700s.

subjugated, or driven over the Pyrenees into their Spanish bastion by Clovis. He was prepared to deal with the Gallo-Romans. After some fighting to mix his people by location and marriage with the Gallo-Roman nobility, with their vast estates, deep literary culture and Christian piety, Clovis and all his warriors accepted Christian baptism. The king was crowned by a churchman at the Cathedral of Reims, which remained the enthronement site of French monarchs for all time, to be devoutly visited by patriotic monarchists in the nineteenth century with reverential memory. The Visigoths were accidentally Arian heretics. Arianism was a feared and hated threat to the Catholic Church. Clovis's conversion made him and his warriors the bulwark of orthodox Latin Christendom, the light in the bishops' eyes.

The bishops rallied to the support of the Frankish monarchy with holiness and literacy and overlooked Clovis's boorish behavior as a necessary welcome instrument of divine providence. The Frankish monarchy did not take much advantage of ecclesiastical gifts and blessings. It allowed the Roman TAXATION system to disappear; the Frankish kings issued very few documents. They followed primitive and dysfunctional Germanic practice of dividing the crown among royal princes. The Merovingians spent most of their time in the two centuries after Clovis I hacking each other to pieces in squabbles over the throne.

The Carolingians. Finally, the bishops tired of Clovis's bestial progeny and in the eighth century shifted their allegiance to a great aristocratic family from the northwest, who became known as the CAROLINGIANS. In 754, the papal legate ST. BONIFACE used the sacramental instrument of anointment to raise the Carolingians in the person of PÉPIN III THE SHORT to the Parisian throne and send the last Merovingians off in an oxcart to deserved obscurity.

Frank means a freeman. The fifth and sixth century Franks were a people of free warriors of equal legal status. Only the royal families were special. But to obtain support, the Merovingian rulers handed out military (duke) and legal (count) offices in the provinces. By the seventh century, these titles had become patents of hereditary nobility. A great titled aristocracy emerged to lord it over the free warriors. Meanwhile as Frankish and slave-centered Gallo-Roman landlord classes merged, the less affluent Frankish families were driven into servile status, perpetually tied to the great estates as manorial peasants. From the ranks of the nobility came the bishops, abbots, and abbesses of the greater religious houses.

To be a Frank by 750 meant to be bold, fierce, and faithful to the Church, its sacraments, its saints, and its relics—a mixture of Germanic power and violence with Latin Christian tradition and LITERACY. Nineteenth century historians were right after all to see this as the civilizing mission of the French people. The Franks did not make good neighbors or generous lords, but they exhibited a military skill, personal courage, ambition, and greed that drove the forces of change in European history for a millennium.

In the first two centuries of Merovingian France, before clerical misogynist teachings and the intricacy of property law closed in, their women had a remarkable degree of freedom. Aristocratic Frankish ladies took bold leadership in the political turmoil of the time, not hesitating to spill blood for power and title, as commemorated in Wagner's operas of old Frankland.

Frankish Legacy. The Franks had a deep sense of historical continuity—pioneers in the heritage business. By 700, they had convinced themselves that the first bishop of Paris, allegedly in the late first century C.E., was a Greek churchman, Dionysus, or St. Denis, a disciple of St. Paul. St. Denis had been martyred, it was believed, by heathens on a hill on the right bank of the Seine—forever Montmartre. In a suburb of Paris, the monarchy endowed a monastery in St. Denis's memory. This became the royal monastery of France, where the crown and scepter were kept, although the actual CORONATION followed precedent in being consummated in Reims Cathedral. The squat early medieval Romanesque chapel at St.-Denis was rebuilt in the twelfth century into the first "GOTHIC" (Parisian style) church in Europe and is still standing.

We know about the history of the Franks to 600 C.E. from two unusual and prodigious sources. One was the late sixth century historical narrative composed by Bishop GREGORY OF TOURS, the last of the Gallo-Roman ecclesiastical magnates. He mixed admiration and horror at the behavior of the French kings and nobles, but running through his work is a sense that the Roman Empire was gone and a new world, violent and disorderly, was taking shape. There was no going back.

The other source for the early history of the Franks is a series of remarkable archaeological excavations undertaken in 1930s and 1940s, particularly in Frankish graveyards, reported skillfully by Edouard Salin in the 1950s, confirming Gregory's mixed assessment. It allows us to visualize the vigor and bad temper of the Franks, and the old Roman city of Paris, that the Latins proudly named after a Trojan hero, which became the political and religious center of a country and a civilization that was to draw the best in European life to itself like a magnet well into modern times.

 See FRANCE *and the entries on the* MEROVINGIAN *and* CAROLINGIAN DYNASTIES. *Also see* FRENCH LANGUAGE AND LITERATURE *and* CAROLINGIAN RENAISSANCE. *Biographical articles to consult are* CLOVIS I; CHARLEMAGNE; *and* GREGORY OF TOURS.

FREDERICK I BARBAROSSA

Frederick I Barbarossa (c. 1123–1190) was king of GERMANY and Holy Roman emperor for nearly 40 years during the twelfth century. His initial goal was to secure German dominance in Europe and restore the HOLY ROMAN EMPIRE to its former power. Later, he abandoned these goals and instead concentrated on unifying the German principalities—in which he had considerable success. He earned the name Barbarossa ("Redbeard") in recognition of his commanding presence.

Early Career. He was the son of Frederick II, duke of Swabia (a German duchy), and Judith, whose father was Henry the Proud, duke of BAVARIA. He succeeded his father as duke of Swabia in 1147. Germany was at this time disunified. Two rival royal families, the HOHENSTAUFENS and the Welfs, were on the verge of launching a German civil war. Frederick, related to both families, was viewed as a possible conciliator. In March 1152, he was elected king of Germany. As a means of restoring order, he granted a Welf rule over the duchy of Bavaria, while a Hohenstaufen was given control of the duchy of AUSTRIA.

Lofty Ambitions. Frederick's desire to bring back the former glory of the Holy Roman Empire included German dominance not only over Europe but over the PAPACY. He also planned to curtail the power of the various German princes and nobles. His first step was to force an alliance with Rome. He persuaded Pope Eugenius III to sign the Treaty of Constance in 1153, promising him protection from potential attackers (such as the NORMANS). Two years later, in accordance with the treaty's provisions, Frederick was crowned emperor by the new pope, ADRIAN IV.

It was not long before Frederick began to put his plans into motion. He launched a series of invasions against northern ITALY and SICILY. He alienated Pope Adrian's successor, ALEXANDER III. Alexander, widely respected for his knowledge of canon law, was not about to relinquish the Church's power to the emperor. In 1160, he excommunicated Frederick, who responded by recognizing two successive antipopes.

Golden reliquary of Frederick Barbarossa in Dome of Aachen.

Defeat and Success. Over the next 16 years, Frederick launched a half dozen Italian attacks. Despite a number of victories, he failed to make more than marginal headway, and after he lost the Battle of Legnano in 1176, he gave up his dreams of a renewed empire. He asked Alexander for forgiveness and pledged his loyalty; the pope forgave him publicly in VENICE in 1177.

Frederick devoted the remainder of his reign to creating a feudal system in Germany, allowing the nobles to retain their autonomy. In so doing, he actually went further toward unifying Germany than he had when he tried to centralize power. He modeled the German system on the French and English systems, and won much admiration from the German people.

He also became a strong supporter of the CRUSADES. Late in his reign he organized the Third Crusade, and in the summer of 1190, when in his late sixties, he accompanied his knights to Jerusalem. While crossing the Saleph river in Cilicia (what is now Turkey) in June of that year, Frederick drowned.

FREDERICK II

Nicknamed *stupor mundi* ("wonder of the world"), Frederick II (1194–1250) was one of the most enlightened and respected medieval monarchs. He was the grandson of FREDERICK I BARBAROSSA, and the son of Emperor HENRY VI and CONSTANCE of SICILY.

The Young King. After Henry's death in 1197, Frederick was crowned king of Sicily and brought to the island by his mother. She entrusted her son to the guardianship of Pope INNOCENT III, who also served as regent during Frederick's youth. Thus, although of German descent, Frederick considered himself an Italian and as he grew older became increasingly preoccupied with consolidating his power there, even if that meant disregarding his German territories.

During the early years of Frederick's minority, Frederick's uncle, Philip of Swabia, struggled with Otto of Brunswick for control of the German crown. Finally, with Philip's murder, Otto ascended to the throne. Frederick's minority was also marked by a chaotic struggle for control of Sicily by numerous powers, and the conflict there was not resolved until forces loyal to the regency conquered Palermo in 1206 in Frederick's name. Frederick entered his majority at age 14 in 1208, but his reign was not truly secured until Pope Innocent III arranged his marriage in 1209 to Constance of ARAGON, who brought with her much needed military and financial resources. With this support, Frederick was able to defeat the unruly local BARONS and subdue the island.

King of Germany. His position was again threatened in 1210 when Otto invaded the mainland territories and menaced Sicily. Otto withdrew, however, when he was excommunicated by Pope Innocent III and deposed by a council of German princes, who elected Frederick German king in his place. Before leaving for GERMANY to accept the crown, Frederick appointed his one-year-old son Henry king of Sicily.

Frederick had little trouble in subduing Germany, achieving a decisive victory over Otto with the assistance of French forces at the BATTLE OF BOUVINES in July, 1214. Following his victory, Frederick's election was then ratified by a large assembly of German princes. However, he was forced to make concessions before his kingship could receive the pope's affirmation. The most important concession was the Golden Bull of Eger, which recognized the privileges of the German princes and revised the laws concerning imperial elections. Frederick soon began consolidating his position in Germany and, in April 1220, secured the election to the German throne of his son Henry, which angered the PAPACY. (*See* KINGSHIP.)

Papal Relations. Frederick reconciled with the papacy by issuing laws against heresies and in support of the liberties of the Church. He also promised the pope that he would soon begin a crusade to the Holy Land, a vow which led to his imperial CORONATION at Rome by Pope Honorius II on November 22, 1220.

Frederick's relationship with the papacy soon soured, however, as he failed to make good on his promise of a crusade. He built a chain of fortresses across Italy and devoted himself to internal affairs. He instituted government reforms, established a new civil service, and in 1224 founded the University of Naples.

In an effort to revitalize Frederick's commitment to the crusade, in 1225 Pope Honorius arranged a marriage between Frederick and Isabella of Brienne, heiress to the kingdom of Jerusalem (his first wife, Constance, had died in 1222). Frederick soon declared himself king of Jerusalem and agreed to begin the crusade. As Frederick was finally set to depart, a terrible plague broke out among his troops and he was forced once again to postpone the voyage. Refusing to accept his excuses, the new Pope GREGORY IX excommunicated him. Unfazed, Frederick departed in June 1228, and with a small force sailed to Acre. He achieved a controversial diplomatic success by entering into a secret treaty with the Egyptian Sultan, al-Malik al-Kamel, obtaining the cities of Jerusalem, Bethlehem, and Nazareth (many of the terms were similar to those that had been rejected by the crusaders in 1221 at Damietta). Frederick had himself officially crowned king of Jerusalem in March 28, 1229, in the Church of the Holy Sepulchre. Most of the French population of the three cities, and many of the religious and military orders stationed there, rejected Frederick's rule. His entrance into Jerusalem was compared by his followers to that of Christ's on Palm Sunday—a comparison

The coronation of Frederick II by Honorius III, a miniature in Le Miroir Historial *by Vincent de Beauvais, a 15th-century history of the monarchs of Europe.*

Frederick did not discourage. Though his reputation grew with his victory in the Holy Land, his absence and the growing hostility of the papacy had encouraged uprisings in Italy by the newly revived Lombard League. With support from papal forces, the League had invaded the island of Sicily. Frederick returned and drove out the invaders, but did not invade the PAPAL STATES. He was rewarded for his restraint with the revocation of his excommunication ban.

Restoring Order. After his victory in Sicily, Frederick issued a new constitution, the *Liber Augustalis* of 1231, which ensured the centralization of the kingdom, codified administrative law, and moved to the establishment of an effective bureaucracy. Meanwhile, affairs in Germany, where Henry had ruled independently since 1228, began to deteriorate. Henry had attempted to enforce a strong imperial policy, but the ambitious and discontented nobility had rebelled and forced upon Henry a number of concessions recognizing their rights (later ratified by Frederick in 1232). Ultimately, Henry joined these nobles in an uprising against Frederick, and formed an alliance with the Lombard League. Frederick reacted swiftly, putting down the rebellion in 1234, dethroning his son, and sending him to prison in Sicily, where he remained until his death in 1242. After defeating the rebellious duke Frederick of Austria, the emperor placed another son on the throne, nine-year-old Conrad IV in 1237.

Frederick then turned his attention back to Italy.

He captured Mantua, and defeated the Milanese-led Lombard League at the Battle of Cortenuova in 1237. At this point Frederick was at the height of his power, but he made a major miscalculation in rejecting the Milanese peace offerings, demanding unconditional surrender instead. Frederick's intransigence encouraged and regalvanized the opposition, which continued to oppose his rule until his death in 1250. Frederick committed another diplomatic blunder by marrying his illegitimate son Enzio to a Sardinian princess and placing him on the throne of Sardinia. The papacy, already mistrustful of Frederick's intentions, claimed suzerainty over Sardinia, and became increasingly concerned that the Papal States would be surrounded by imperial domains. Pope Gregory again excommunicated the emperor in March 1239, and encouraged the Lombard League in its opposition of Frederick's rule. In response, Frederick intensified his military activities in northern Italy, raising funds by reorganizing the administration of imperial Italy.

War with the Papacy. In 1240, Frederick invaded the Papal States and threatened Rome. Only at the last moment did Pope Gregory, aided by the capture and imprisonment of a delegation of over 100 important prelates by a pro-imperial Venetian fleet, manage to gain the support of the Romans. But then Pope Gregory died in 1241, and Frederick retreated back into Sicily and began negotiations with the new pope, Innocent IV, in 1243. Though Innocent was under pressure to assume an anti-imperial attitude, the two men seemed close to an agreement when talks collapsed in 1244. For the last time, Frederick was deposed by the pope in 1245, and the battle between the two resumed. Pro-papal forces defamed Frederick as the anti-Christ, while those who pushed for papal reform hailed him almost as enthusiastically as when he entered Jerusalem. However, Frederick was unable to gain substantial support from the German princes.

Innocent escaped to Lyons where he called an ecclesiastic council to deal with the problem of Frederick's power. The excommunication was reaffirmed, and all oaths of obedience to Frederick's rule were revoked, over the protests of Frederick's representatives. In 1247, Frederick made plans to travel to Lyons in order to defend himself; but as he was about to leave, the key city of Parma fell to the Lombard League in February 1248. That setback set off a series of defeats in central Italy and Romagna, accompanied by other indignities, including the capture and imprisonment of Enzio by Bolognese forces in May 1249, and the suicide in prison of one of Frederick's most trusted counselors, Peter of Vigna, charged with treason.

End of Reign. The emperor's position was improving, with a number of military advances in northern Italy, when he took ill in late 1250. He died on

The Life of Frederick II	
1194	Frederick born to Henry VI and Constance of Sicily.
1198	Crowned in Sicily; placed under guardianship of Pope Innocent III.
1208	Marries Constance of Aragon.
1211	Supported by German princes in claim to throne; Otto IV deposed.
1222	Constance dies.
1225	Marries Isabella of Brienne
1226	Crowned by Honorius III; vows to embark on crusade.
1227	Frederick begins crusade; turns back, claiming epidemic on ships.
1228	Pope Gregory IX excommunicates Frederick for halting crusade.
1229 1230	Frederick resumes crusade; Gregory revokes excommunication.
1239	Gregory again excommunicates Frederick
1241	Gregory dies as Frederick attacks.
1250	Frederick dies of dysentery.

December 12, 1250, in his favorite palace in Apulia, and was buried in a cathedral in Palermo. Many in Europe refused to accept the news of his death; he was sighted, still alive, in various locations, and apocalyptic predictions circulated wildly of his imminent return to punish a guilty Church. Many of his supporters assumed that Frederick's legacy would live on with his heirs, but within 22 years they were all dead.

Frederick was a great and complicated man, hailed as the prototype of the Renaissance king, but he was a quintessential medieval figure, as capable of extreme cruelty and stubborn intolerance as of enlightened cosmopolitanism. His intelligence, however, is undisputed; he was one of the more learned men of his age, a sponsor of the arts and scholarship throughout his reign. His court was one of the most brilliant in all of Europe, a center of culture, poetry, natural sciences, and mathematics; he demonstrated his own talents with his meticulously researched treatise on falconry, *De arte venandi cum avibus* (*The Art of Falconry*). He stands as one of the great figures of the Middle Ages.

See PAPACY; PAPAL STATES; *and* CRUSADES *for background.* FREDERICK II *was an integral part of the history of* GERMANY; ITALY; *and* SICILY. *He also had a great influence on the medieval concept of* KINGSHIP. *See also the biographical entries indicated in the article.*

FRENCH LANGUAGE AND LITERATURE

The French language developed over a period of several centuries during the Middle Ages. From a series of dialects derived from LATIN, French ultimately became influential as the language of diplomats. A rich literary tradition also developed during this period, and some of the world's most beautiful poetry and prose was written in French.

French Language. French is one of several tongues derived from LATIN, or Romance languages. Before the Romans invaded FRANCE (then known as Gaul) in the first century B.C.E., its inhabitants spoke Celtic. The Romans brought Latin with them—but it was Vulgar (meaning common) Latin rather than the classical Latin of scholars. This colloquial form of Latin was the primary language in France until the Roman Empire began its decline in the fifth century. The waning of Roman influence, combined with invasions from neighboring tribes, the VISIGOTHS and the FRANKS, led to the formation of what is known as Old French.

Old French flourished from around the ninth to the fifteenth century. Numerous dialects were spoken, but they generally fell into one of two basic divisions: northern French, or *langue d'oil*, and southern French, or *langue d'oc*. ("Oil" and "oc" were their respective words for "yes.") Modern French is derived from Francien, a Parisian langue d'oil dialect.

Despite the many dialects, French became an increasingly important and well-respected language in Europe. The NORMAN invasion of Britain brought French to the English-speaking world; more modest invasions of other parts of Europe spread French still further. French knights who fought in the CRUSADES brought their language to the Middle East and Asia; French gained distinction as the language of diplomacy (a reputation it holds to this day). French became an increasingly diverse language as more people traveled; it also became more standardized. Finally, in 1539, King Francis I decreed that French would be the official language of the legal courts. This set the stage for modern French—a language whose uniformity today is regulated by the scholars of the Académie Française.

French Literature. Latin was the official written language in France throughout the Middle Ages, but manuscripts written in Old French began appearing in the ninth century. Authors wrote in either langue d'oil or langue d'oc; the earliest surviving work from the period, in langue d'oil, is the *Sequence de Ste. Eulalie*, chronicling a young saint's martyrdom.

Eventually, langue d'oil became the preferred language for narratives, while langue d'oc became the language of poetry. Narrative writing became popular around the eleventh century, mainly focusing on saints' lives or heroic epics known as *chansons de geste*. The most famous chanson de geste is the *Song of Roland*, composed about 1100. Many of these works were meant to be accompanied by song; their authors were often traveling entertainers called jongleurs.

In the twelfth century, romance became a popular literary theme in French works. Medieval romance authors strove to combine literary and poetic techniques

Left, Jean Froissart presenting his book to a king, possibly Edward III. At right, Queen Isabella greets her brother, Charles IV of France. From Froissart's Chroniques, *1412.*

with compelling stories; while many romances dealt with the idealized form of love known as COURTLY LOVE, others dealt with less savory topics such as betrayal. Stories based on the legend of KING ARTHUR were popular. Writers such as CHRÉTIEN DE TROYES and MARIE DE FRANCE helped popularize courtly love lyrics, which were often set to music and performed by traveling poets known as TROUBADOURS.

Thirteenth-century France produced the allegorical *Roman de la Rose*, a romance of over 23,000 lines. French prose also became increasingly important. Detailed historical works such as the *Grand Chronicles of France* and the *Life of St. Louis* appeared during this period, setting the stage for influential works by the historian JEAN FROISSART and the early feminist writer CHRISTINE DE PISAN.

Humor also played an increasingly important role in French works as authors wrote comedic and satirical pieces, and moralistic fables featuring Renard the Fox.

By the fourteenth century, poetry in clearly structured forms, including the ballade, the virelay, and the rondeau, had become popular. Courtly love was a common theme in these poems, but the poet Guillaume de Machaut broke new ground with his autobiographical poem, *True Story*. The play also became an important literary genre. Many plays had religious themes, but more secular topics were also popular. These were often presented as comedies or farces. Fifteenth-century French writers focused more on realistic themes and less on romantic ones; poems such as FRANÇOIS VILLON's *Le Grand Testament* offer a down-to-earth view of the poet's life.

FRIARS

As the Christian Church grew in influence, its leaders became more worldly than many Christians thought appropriate. By the twelfth century, many people rebelled against what they saw as the Church's hypocrisy regarding wealth. This led to the establishment early in the following century of new religious orders whose members were known as friars. Initially, these orders, known as mendicant (meaning, dependent on the charity of others), were made up wandering religious men who gained what little sustenance they needed through begging. Eventually, the orders modified their rules, and friars assumed a prominent place in medieval religious life.

Orders. The four main orders of friars are the FRANCISCAN (named after ST. FRANCIS OF ASSISI), the Dominican (named for ST. DOMINIC), the Augustinian, or AUSTIN (named for ST. AUGUSTINE), and the CARMELITE (named for Mount Carmel). Many famous theologians were friars—DUNS SCOTUS and WILLIAM OF OCKHAM were Franciscans; Martin Luther was an Augustinian; and ST. THOMAS AQUINAS was a Dominican. Although each order had its own philosophy, they all generally held the same basic concepts. Friars could own no material possessions other than the barest necessities, and they wandered from town to town preaching and converting people to CHRISTIANITY.

Periodically during the Middle Ages, people questioned the Church and created their own religious groups, such as the CATHARS, which the Church labeled as heretic. The friars were a reaction to these new groups, allowing the devoted to adhere to vows of poverty and simplicity without abandoning the Church. In fact, St. Dominic had begun his career preaching to heretical sects before forming his order.

Public Servants. Friars differed from monks in several ways. Monks devoted themselves to prayer and religious study in monasteries and usually did not minister to people. Friars, because they were itinerant, had many more dealings with the public, and eventually became involved in missionary and charitable work.

Eventually friars were allowed to use property supplied by the Church for shelter. These houses, called friaries, were technically owned by the pope, so the friars would not be property owners per se. The establishment of housing as a necessity for friars made it possible for women to become more active in the movement. Nuns attached to the friar orders resided in cloistered communities, divorced from the world and devoting themselves to prayer. Others became active in charity work, care of the sick, and teaching.

The friars reached out to the people, but the people did not always welcome them. Many, in fact, were openly disdainful of the friars' begging and regarded them more as vagrants. The role of friars gradually changed as friars and the nuns ministered to so many people. Friars became important scholars and educators and philosophers; many taught in the great universities of Europe. Today, the friars' orders are still active in education and charitable work.

FROISSART, JEAN

Jean (also Jehan) Froissart (c. 1333–c. 1410) was a French priest, poet, courtier, and one of the leading historians of the late Middle Ages. Born to a middle-class French family in Valenciennes, Froissart traveled to ENGLAND where he became a clerk in the court of Philippa of Hainault, the French wife of King EDWARD III of England. In 1365, he visited the court of King David II of SCOTLAND and the following year accompanied EDWARD THE BLACK PRINCE to Gascony in southwestern FRANCE where he chronicled Edward's campaign against CASTILE across the Spanish border. He also traveled widely in ITALY and the Low Countries where he made friends with the nobility. From 1373 to 1382 he was rector of Les Estinnes near Thun and in 1383, he became canon of Chimay in Hainault in FLANDERS.

His Work. Froissart's writings include light, charming poems about COURTLY LOVE (which influenced CHAUCER) and *Meliador*, a romance in verse about the adventures of an ideal knight. Froissart is best remembered for his *Chroniques* (*Chronicles*), a four-volume history of the major European countries from 1322 to 1400. Although his history relies on gossip and is often more stylish than accurate, it is an invaluable source of information about the events of the time and a notable literary achievement that captures the spirit of the age. (*See* CHRONICLES.)

FULK V

Fulk V (1092–1143) was king of Jerusalem (1131–1143), count of Anjou and Maine (1109–1143), and progenitor of England's ANGEVIN line of kings. Son of Fulk IV, count of Anjou, he took title to Maine by virtue of marriage to Arenburga of Maine; his son, Geoffrey PLANTAGENET, married Matilda, daughter of HENRY I of ENGLAND. Fulk's second marriage, to Melisande, daughter of King Baldwin II of Jerusalem, in 1129, led to his CORONATION as king of Jerusalem on Baldwin's death in 1131. On a first visit to Palestine in 1120, Fulk had befriended the Templars, and on his return to FRANCE he granted the order an annual subsidy.

Under Fulk, Jerusalem was relatively tranquil. Early in his reign, he put down a revolt led by Hugh of Le Puiset, his wife Melisande's lover (who at times virtually ruled the kingdom). A serious challenge came from the Seljuk atabeg 'Imad al-Din Zangi of Mosul, who in the 1130s was seeking to expand to the south his unified Muslim state. Zangi defeated Fulk near Ba'rin (Montferrand) in 1137, but Fulk later temporarily checked his progress by forming an alliance with the Muslim vizier of DAMASCUS. Fulk was also able to forestall the potential threat posed by John II Comnenus, the Byzantine emperor. Fulk is chiefly known for the construction of fortifications in Palestine, notably Ibelin and Gibelet near Ascalon and Belvoir at the head of the Jordan Valley.

FUR TRADE

Medieval commerce in a highly valued luxury item. RUSSIA was the central source of furs, which were traded to western Europe, the BYZANTINE Empire, and Asia. While they were a luxury, furs also came to represent the social positions of aristocrats and public officials. For some, furs had an almost magical quality. As an item of social status, a fur became more valuable if more pelts, or animal skins, were used. Famously full coats worn by King John of FRANCE were made from as many as 366 pelts; Marie of Savoy wore a coat made from 618 sable skins. Furs were used as ransom for captured royalty, as gifts between monarchs, and by state as signs of high rank.

Fur trading was a complicated process. First, furs were gathered by Russian and Lapp (from Lappland in contemporary Finland) peasants whose climate made farming impossible. These peasants captured, killed, and skinned the animals. The most prized skins for furs came from ermine, sable, weasel, squirrel, bear, beaver, mink, lynx, otter, polecat, marten, and fox. If those an-imals were not available, furs were taken from hare, rabbit, lamb, or wolf. The furs were then procured, through a combination of force or exchange, by a diverse group of tax-collectors, merchants, and raiders, who transported the furs to markets in eastern Europe. There the furs were bought by another group of merchants and brought to major markets in western and central Europe. A final group of merchants then had the furs made into garments to be sold in local markets throughout Europe.

The early history of the fur trade, from the eighth to the tenth centuries, was dominated by Scandinavian VIKINGS, who occupied the major sources of fur-production in Russia, the Baltic countries, and NORWAY. By the late ninth century, the Russian city of NOVGOROD became the hub of fur trading. This trade was often dominated by German merchants. When Novgorod was occupied by the Russian state of Muscovy in the fifteenth century, the fur trade came under the control of Moscow. The popularity of furs encouraged Russian colonization into Siberia in order to exploit the large supply found in that frigid region. Furs were also brought to the Byzantine Empire, central Asia, and the Middle East through the activities of Russian, Bulgarian, and Muslim merchants.

FURNITURE

Medieval homes were sparsely furnished by modern standards, but they were not necessarily uninviting. Furniture was designed to be practical and durable. Beauty was for many an important consideration, with many pieces quite lavishly appointed.

European Furniture. Furniture was considered a luxury, even among the wealthy and powerful. Peasant homes might contain little more than a bed and a few chests. Larger homes and castles might contain several beds and many chests, but they might not have more than three chairs (for master, wife, and one guest).

Part of this was practical. For the peasant, it often made more sense to spend his money on his livelihood (usually farming) than to invest in furniture, especially when most people saw little need for any but the most

---

LIFE IN THE MIDDLE AGES

Credenza

Many nobles were fearful that their rivals might try to eliminate them through more subtle means than armed attack. One method was poison. To ensure that no food was poisoned, it was placed on a side table and tasted by a servant before being given to the noble. If the servant survived, the food could be served with confidence—which in Italian is *credenza*. In time, the name was given to any such furnishing.

basic furnishings. For nobles, who often had more than one castle, furniture had to be portable so that it could travel with them from castle to castle.

Among the most practical pieces of furniture were chests and beds. Chests came in a variety of sizes and could hold anything from small trinkets to provisions and weapons. They could also double as seats or tables, and were easy to carry. Chests eventually evolved into cupboards and armoires, which typically held foodstuffs or clothing. Beds were probably the most important piece of furniture; all but the poorest homes had at least a cot or straw mattress. In the homes of the well-to-do, beds were often enormous—sometimes 11 feet long. They were often used as couches during the day, and then as beds for several people at night.

Dining tables were usually long and heavy, to accommodate many guests and great feasts. People sat on long benches; the head of the family and important guests might sit at a special raised table. Food was served from side tables called credences, or credenzas.

Colors and Fabric. Medieval homes were generally not at all dark and colorless, as is often depicted. Furniture was often decorated with colorful fabrics or painted designs. Fabric pillows and furniture coverings often depicted scenes from daily life and Biblical stories. Folding chairs called curule chairs were made with embroidered fabric seats.

TAPESTRIES—large carpetlike fabrics that were hung from walls—were often elaborately colored and decorated. They served not only as decorations, but also as insulation against drafts and against the cold stone walls of the castle. They often traveled with noble families along with the furniture; many were especially prized and often became heirlooms.

Bedclothes were likewise richly decorated. A bed might have a canopy that supported heavy curtains, as well as a colorful bedspread. These provided color and beauty, but they also protected against drafts and provided privacy.

Islamic Furniture. Medieval Muslim homes may have appeared more sparsely furnished than European homes, but in truth the furnishings were merely different. Muslim homes, for example, had fewer chairs because people sat on cushions or pillows, even when dining, placing their food on low tables. Chairs were elaborately decorated and reserved for ceremonial use.

Like Europeans, Muslims used chests for storage. They also built recesses into the walls of their homes for storage, and they had racks for hanging items.

One reason Muslim furniture was less substantial than European furniture is that Muslim culture was derived in part from the nomadic ARABS who traveled freely in the desert, so furnishings had to be even more portable. So strong was the nomadic influence, in fact, that Muslim furniture changed very little in design until the twentieth century.

Religious Furniture. Churches, unlike castles, were used year-round, so their furnishings could be more permanent. By the late Middle Ages, many churches were better furnished than most homes. Initially, worshippers stood at services; only a bishop had a chair, called a cathedra (from which the word "cathedral" is derived). Other clergy sat on benches or simple stools. By the thirteenth century, churches were installing benches for worshippers.

Choir stalls became common after the eleventh century. Choir benches had hinged seats with projections called misericords. When choir members stood,

The bedroom and living room of a 14th-century Seigneur. Beds were often built into the structure and placed so as to be near the fireplace. A room such as this might have been the primary living space for the noble family, with children's quarters nearby.

they could lift the seats and support themselves on the misericords. (*See* CATHEDRALS AND CHURCHES.)

As in private dwellings, churches made frequent use of colorful fabrics, often depicting biblical scenes. Banners, canopies, and carpets added to the awe of the church service and conveyed a sense of grandeur and power to those who worshiped. (*See* FAMILY LIFE; TAPESTRIES; ISLAMIC ART AND ARCHITECTURE; *and* CASTLES AND FORTIFICATIONS.)

GAISERIC

Gaiseric (390–477 C.E.) was king of the Germanic tribe of the VANDALS and the founder of the Vandal kingdom of North AFRICA, created during the period when provinces of the Western Roman Empire were conquered by various Germanic tribes. Gaiseric was ruthless and shrewd—qualities essential to the survival of a tribal people at that turbulent time. He ascended the throne in 428, at a time of great crisis for the Vandal people. They had occupied southern SPAIN but were under threat by a Roman army and Germanic VISIGOTHS. In 429, Gaiseric removed the Vandals from this precarious position by crossing the straits of Gibraltar.

The Vandals marched east from the western coast of AFRICA to the important Roman province of North Africa. In 430, they besieged the central Roman city of Hippo. After fourteen months, the Roman general Boniface fled Africa and Hippo was finally taken. Vandal conquests in North Africa continued until 435 when Gaiseric signed a treaty with Roman emperor Valentinian III. Under the terms of the treaty the Vandals kept their gains and Rome retained Carthage. However, Gaiseric abrogated the treaty in 439 and made the entire former Roman province into a Vandal kingdom, thereby commencing 30 years of war.

Gaiseric's reign in Africa was relatively benign, although he persecuted Christians. Gaiseric understood the tactical advantages of North Africa and quickly built a fleet of warships. The Vandals pillaged much of the western Mediterranean and added SICILY, Corsica, Sardinia, and the Balearic Islands to their kingdom. In 455, Gaiseric and the Vandals plundered Rome for fourteen days and stole much of the wealth of the city. He captured Empress Licinia Eudoxia (whom he gave in marriage to his eldest son, Huneric) and her daughters. In 460 and 468, Gaiseric defeated Roman attempts to recapture North Africa, becoming stronger with each victory. Upon Gaiseric's death in 477, the Vandals were strongly entrenched in Africa.

GALLA PLACIDIA

Galla Placidia (c. 390–450), daughter of the Roman emperor Theodosius the Great, ruled the western Roman Empire from 425 to 434 as regent to her son Valentinian III. In 410, Placidia was taken hostage by the VISIGOTHS after their sack of ROME. Four years later, her half-brother, the western Roman Emperor Honorius, agreed to the Visigothic demand that Placidia marry their king, Ataulf. In 416, Placidia was successfully ransomed after the death of Ataulf. On her return to RAVENNA, Placidia was again married against her will, this time to Constantius, an advisor to Honorius. Placidia fell out of Honorius's favor after the death of Constantius and was exiled to CONSTANTINOPLE, the capital of the eastern Roman Empire. She returned to Ravenna as regent. Galla Placidia's reign is chiefly remembered for her sponsorship of a number of famous churches, particularly the Mausoleum of Galla Placidia. Her reign ended when FLAVIUS AETIUS became Valentinian's main counselor.

GAMES AND PASTIMES

Although a commonly held picture of medieval society at play might be a jousting match followed by a huge and boisterous feast, in fact many pastimes and games were considerably more sedate and cerebral. Both had a purpose: highly physical games helped contestants develop fighting skills, while board games such as chess helped develop the mind.

Games in Europe. Children's games in medieval Europe were similar to games played by modern children, albeit somewhat rougher. Medieval children played variations of blind-man's bluff, leapfrog, and tug-of-war. Blind-man's bluff, and a variation known as "hot cockles," for example, consisted of players hitting the blindfolded player with knotted pieces of cloth until he or she could identify the attacker. These games were also popular with adults, for whom a favorite game was mumming, in which elaborate costumes were donned that made the wearer appear as if he were on horseback, and then TOURNAMENTS were reenacted.

Other popular games included ball games similar to tennis, handball, soccer, and bowling. (Balls were not made of rubber and did not bounce.) More rigorous activities were geared toward preparing the individual for using weapons during wartime. Fencing and archery were highly valued activities. Many European cities had schools of fencing and archery and awarded diplomas to students who excelled.

LIFE IN THE MIDDLE AGES

Gambling

Despite warnings from the Church, and bans on certain so-called "games of chance," they were immensely popular, and city dwellers frequently engaged in various dice games. In the early Middle Ages, gambling on the outcome of horse racing and tournaments was respectable. It was the association of gambling with drinking by the GOLIARDIC POETS that made gambling disreputable.

13th-century miniature of a French document depicting young lovers playing chess.

GENGHIS KHAN

S o wrote the Genghis, the great khan: "The greatest pleasure is to vanquish your enemies and chase them before you, to rob them of their wealth and see those dear to them bathed in tears, to ride their horses and clasp to your bosom their wives and daughters." Genghis Khan (c. 1162–1227) was the MONGOL leader during the thirteenth century whose empire stretched from the Aral Sea in Central Asia to CHINA'S Yellow Sea—it was said that it took two years to walk from one side of his empire to the other. MARCO POLO would write that Genghis "was a man of great worth and of great ability, and valor." GEOFFREY CHAUCER wrote "ther was nowher in no region so excellent a lord in alle thing."

Early Life. He was born Temüjin (or Temuchin, meaning "blacksmith"—and also the name of a rival chieftain his father had killed) in what is now Siberia. Legend has it he was born holding a blood clot in the shape of a stone in his right fist. His father, Yesukai, led the Bourchikom clan of the Yakka Mongols. When Temüjin was only nine, he was betrothed to 10-year-old Borte, daughter of Dei Sechen, and Yesukai took Temüjin to the eastern part of Mongolia to live and study under Dei Sechen. En route home, Yesukai was poisoned to death by members of the rival Tatar Mongol tribe. Temüjin, his mother Houlun, and his siblings fled and lived in hardship, which helped shape

For real tests of physical prowess, nothing matched the medieval tournament. Limited to knights, a typical tournament would include the joust (in which two armored knights on horseback would attack each other); the melee (like the joust except with groups instead of individuals); and the baston (in which knights would try to knock the crests off each others' helmets). Fencing and sword-fighting exhibitions were also popular at tournaments. Although only knights could participate in the tournament games, the tournaments were festive occasions that included parades, pageants, and other entertainments.

For those who preferred less physical pastimes, board and card games were popular. Board games were also considered essential training tools for future warriors. Chess and backgammon were the most prestigious board games, in part because they required a keen understanding of strategy. Chess, a "war" game, originated in India in the sixth century and spread westward to the Islamic world. Europeans discovered the game when soldiers brought it back upon their return from the CRUSADES. Card games came later, also from the East, and soon became a favorite pastime.

Many games involved flirtatious romance between men and women—such as apple-bobbing and the Maypole dance—or fanciful predictions of the future. "Ragman's roll" was a game in which players would pick a sealed parchment with a prediction out of a hat.

Games in Muslim Lands. Although many Muslims viewed game-playing as frivolous, a variety of games were nonetheless popular in the Islamic world. The only pastime that was specifically prohibited by the KORAN was gambling.

Children often amused themselves by playing on swings or see-saws; or they might play games similar to checkers or Chinese checkers. More active games involved running, jumping, or racing. As they entered adulthood, they might learn backgammon (which had been created in the Middle East) or chess. Mastering chess and backgammon was considered important for developing strategy skills for future military leaders.

The Mongols in the Middle Ages	
1196	Great tribes united under Temüjin; Crowned as Genghis Khan.
1215	Peking falls; Mongols conquer China—North China by 1235.
1216–1227	Mongol conquests extended to southwest Asia.
1227–	Genghis Khan dies; empire divided among his sons.
1230–1240	Ogödair leads Mongol troops, conquers Ukraine, Poland, Hungary.
1242	Ogödair dies. Batu establishes Golden Horde control of west.
1259–	Mongol Empire reaches peak under Kublai Khan.
1300–1377	Golden Horde wanes as many rulers convert to Islam.
1402	Tamerlane defeats Ottomans; captures Sultan Beyezid.
1405	Tamerlane dies; empire divided.
1502	Golden Horde ends rule in west.

Temüjin's leadership skills. Houlun told him, "You have no companions but your shadow."

Temüjin's half-brother Bekhter harassed Temüjin and his brothers as a child. At age 15, Temüjin shot an arrow into Bekhter, killing him—an incident ignored by biographers for many generations.

When he was a young man, members of the Tayichi'yud tribe kidnapped Temüjin so that he could not avenge his father's murder and inherit his title. They did not kill him, but instead made him wear a wooden collar as punishment. One night, Temüjin escaped the Tayichi'yud camp with the assistance of a woman who had been Yesukai's nursemaid.

Temüjin returned to claim the hand of Borte, and received a sizable dowry, which he gave to Toghril, leader of a Mongolian tribe, in return for Toghril's protection. When the Merkit tribe kidnapped and raped Borte, Toghril, with a young Mongol chieftain named Jamuka, helped Temüjin track the Merkits down and defeat them. Jamuka and Temüjin quickly became close friends, but a breach developed and they eventually became rivals.

In 1196, the Mongol tribe named Temüjin overlord of their tribe, over Jamuka. As overlord, Temüjin defeated the Tanguts in the Battle of the Carts, boiling 70 captured chieftains alive. In 1201, he defeated Jamuka with the assistance of Toghril. Then, Toghril and Temüjin led a successful assault against the Tatars. "Let us take advantage of our victory," he is to have said. "Let us kill all the males who are taller than the axles of our wagons. The rest we will divide among us as slaves." In 1204, he conquered his former allies, the Kereits, in central Mongolia. Later that year he defeated the Naiman in western Mongolia. By 1205, he had defeated all enemies. A year later, he was named Genghis Khan—"universal monarch," ruler of the universe—at

a congress of Mongol tribes at the Onon River.

Leader of the Mongols. Genghis, a man of great physical strength, intellect, and personal charisma, united disparate Mongol tribes to form the strongest army in the known world. Under his orders, all Mongol men between the ages of 14 and 70 were automatically enlisted in the army. Nearly every segment of Mongol life was designed around the military; even the annual winter food hunts were organized to prepare soldiers for combat. One historian would call the Mongols "a peasantry in the dress of an army." Placing a high value on loyalty, he allowed his most trusted generals free reign in the field. He assigned specific duties to each member of his horde. His armies attacked with large bodies of HORSES (no infantry) maneuvered by waving pennants.

Khan's soldiers were so mobile and effective, it was said, that in one day his army could destroy land 60 miles away, come home, and return the following day. He was often savage and sadistic toward his opponents. One opponent, Inalchuck, was taken to Khan's headquarters where molten silver was poured into his eyes and ears.

Yet in other areas, Genghis was progressive. He promoted religious tolerance to

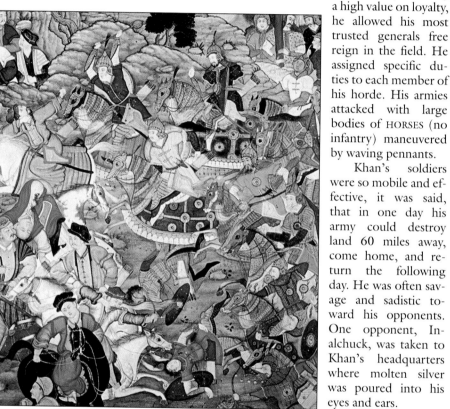

A 16th-century miniature from History of the Mongols, *created under the patronage of Akbar the Great, depicting Genghis Khan leading his Mongol troops in battle against the Khitai and Jurje tribes.*

those who lived under his domain—an almost unheard of freedom among leaders of the Middle Ages. He also made sure to set down just and fair laws ensuring peace in his domains. And he incorporated the wives and children of slain opponents into the Mongol tribe. One of his great accomplishments in bringing disparate tribes together was in building great roads, promoting commerce and trade.

The Battle for China. As khan, he sought to expand his empire into CHINA, some 600 miles south of Mongolia. His army quickly conquered the Xi Xia kingdom, making it a Mongol vassal. With military advisers Chepe Niyun, Muhuli, and Subuta Bahader, he fought the Chin empire in northern China from 1212 to 1214. Twice he attempted to break through the Great Wall of China but failed. In 1213, he finally breached the Wall in two places, and invaded with three armies. The Chin emperor offered his daughter to Khan in exchange for withdrawing. The princess became one of Khan's several wives, but Khan soon returned, capturing Peking in 1215, subjugating Chin territories, and conquering north China by 1235.

Conquests. Khan turned his attention to territories beyond the steppes of Southeast Asia. In 1218, he sent a caravan of 1500 camels to Khwarizmshah, ruler of lands near what is now Afghanistan, as a peace offering. Trade between the empires commenced. During this period, a Khwarizmshah's governor hijacked the caravan and killed all but one passenger, who returned to tell Khan. Khan responded by attacking Khwarizmshah's lands, systematically destroying its cities, which often surrendered without a fight. Skilled workers in these lands were shipped to Mongolia.

Khan's armies attacked Bokhara in February 1220, and neighboring Samarkand a month later. Samarkand's leader, Shah Muhammad, fled to the west and was unsuccessfully pursued by Khan's generals. He died (it seems of exhaustion) on an island in the Caspian Sea as Khan was laying siege to Khorezm, Muhammad's capital.

After these battles, Khan retired from active combat, and returned to Mongolia in 1225. But his soldiers continued their battles, fighting the Tangutans of China later that year. He had begun planning an invasion of the Tangutans when he died on August 25, 1227 at his summer home in the Ch'ing-shui, south of the Liu-p'an Mountains in Kansu. (*See* MONGOLS; WAR AND WARFARE; *and* CHINA.)

GENOA

Genoa, a medieval trading port on the northwestern coast of ITALY, was blessed with a natural harbor at the head of the deepest gulf of the Mediterranean, which allowed it to compete with PISA, VENICE, and other Italian cities for control of Mediterranean trade. Thanks to the CRUSADES and the special trading privileges it established in the eastern Mediterranean, Genoa achieved its greatest power and influence in the 1300s when it rivaled Venice as the premier center of an extensive trading network that extended from India to ENGLAND.

Beginnings. Before the Roman period Genoa had been little more than a large village, but under the Romans the city flourished as a vital link between Rome and northern Europe. After Germanic invaders sacked

the port in 642, it reverted back to being a small fishing village.

In the 930s, Muslim raids galvanized Genoese resistance. Genoa allied itself with the nearby Italian port of Pisa for self-defense, then launched raids against Muslim bases in Sardinia and Tunisia, which brought booty and power to northwestern Italy, and eventually drove the Muslims from Corsica and Sardinia.

By the 900s, Genoa had become a free commune under the government of consuls and its political influence spread to Elbe and Norman SICILY. Genoa developed into a formidable and ambitious maritime trading power, sailing east to EGYPT and Syria, west to Provence in FRANCE and Catalonia in SPAIN.

Trading Haven. The CRUSADES opened up new commercial opportunities in the eastern Mediterranean for Venice, Genoa, and other Italian ports. Genoa supplied many of the ships and equipment needed to transport European crusaders to the Holy Land. As a result of the First Crusade, Genoa obtained special trading privileges in Acre and established numerous trading colonies in the eastern Mediterranean, although these were usually little more than commercial beachheads around a seaport which allowed merchants to trade safely, free from interference from nearby authorities. (*See* COMMERCE AND TRADE.)

The trading system created by the Crusades led to Genoa's greatest period of prosperity, which continued even after the decline and eventual defeat of the crusader states. In the late 1200s, Genoa and Venice competed for trade with the revived BYZANTINE empire. Genoa set up trading posts and colonies on the coast of the Black Sea at the mouth of the Danube River and in Crimea, allowing the Genoese to link up with overland trading routes that reached the MONGOLS, India, and even CHINA. Genoese ships sailed westward to England, Morocco, and even reached the Canary Islands. Genoa's rivalry with Pisa over Sardinia, which led to a series of wars, ended with the Genoese victory in the naval battle of Meloria in 1284. By 1300, Genoa was one of the largest cities in Europe with a population approaching 100,000.

Genoa's policies in the East clashed with the ambitions of Venice, causing wars that finally ended with the Peace of Turin in 1381, a settlement favoring the Venetians. Genoa's further commercial and military expansion was financed by a group of powerful merchant-bankers, the Banco San Giorgio, in 1408.

Decline. In the latter part of the Middle Ages, Genoa's decline was brought on by ineffective government and factional strife between the GUELPHS and GHIBELLINES and between the nobility and the popular party. In 1339, Genoa elected its first doge (chief magistrate) for life, but that did not bring political stability. Rival factions called on foreign help, and from the late

1300s to the end of the Middle Ages, France and Milan took turns controlling the city. The city was further weakened by plagues—during the BLACK DEATH, the city's population fell to 50,000—and the HUNDRED YEARS' WAR. Genoa struggled to maintain itself by increasing its BANKING and currency exchange.

Following the fall of CONSTANTINOPLE in 1453, which dealt a fatal blow to Genoa's colonies in the east, the city's maritime interests turned westward to Spain and PORTUGAL to find new economic opportunities. One of the Genoese who went westward seeking new prospects was a mariner who was soon to become Genoa's most famous son—Christopher Columbus.

Genoa enjoyed a brief revival under the leadership of the admiral-statesman Andrea Doria, who wrote a new constitution for the city in 1528. After his death, however, Genoa came under Spanish, French, and Austrian control; its medieval age of glory was past. (*See* TRADE AND COMMERCE; ITALY; *and* VENICE.)

GEOFFREY OF MONMOUTH

Welsh writer Geoffrey of Monmouth (c. 1100–1154) was known for his monumental work *Historia Regum Britanniae* (*History of the Kings of Britain*). The history covers every British ruler from Brut, the legendary founder of the Britons, to Cadwallader, whose reign ended in 689. How much of the work is based on historical documentation and how much on Geoffrey's creative mind has remained an unanswered question for over 900 years.

Geoffrey studied and taught at Oxford and may have been a Benedictine monk. He was appointed bishop of St. Asaph in 1152. His *Historia Regum*, written in Latin and completed around 1136, includes a considerable amount of material on the legendary KING ARTHUR. It is not his writing of Arthur, however, that leads scholars to question Geoffrey's veracity, but his alleged sources. He claimed to have been given a "most ancient book in the British tongue" by the archdeacon of Oxford that contained valuable information. Unfortunately, this book, if it ever existed, is lost to history. Other documents he claims to have used are likewise nonexistent.

Scholars believe that Geoffrey's work was probably a combination of historical research, folk knowledge, and imagination. What made his work stand out was his lively writing style. His vivid descriptions of the King Arthur and his knights helped popularize the Round Table stories throughout Europe. After Geoffrey's death, the history was translated into several languages, including English and French.

GERARD OF CREMONA

Gerard (1114–1187) was the most celebrated and prolific translator of Greek and Arabic works into Latin. Born in Cremona in Lombardy, and schooled in ITALY, Gerard moved to Toledo, a century center of scholarship and scientific study. There he learned Arabic, and he began to study Ptolemy's *Almagest,* which was not available at the time in Latin. He began translating the work, and soon took on a systematic translation of many other major texts of SCIENCE and PHILOSOPHY. (*See* LATIN.)

Tradition generously attributes Gerard with over 80 translations while in Toledo, but it is possible that a number of helpers assisted him in his work. The group was almost definitely informal, more like an artist's studio than an official school. Among the Greek authors whose texts Gerard (or his assistants) translated from Arabic versions into Latin are Ptolemy, ARISTOTLE, Euclid, Archimedes, Apollonius of Perga, and Galen. He is also responsible for translating many original Arabic works, including books on medicine (most notably, AVICENNA's *Canon*), philosophy, mathematics, ASTRONOMY, ASTROLOGY, and geomancy.

GERBERT OF AURILLAC (POPE SYLVESTER II)

Gerbert (c. 945–1003) was born of humble parents in Auvergene and educated at the Benedictine MONASTERY of Aurillac. He later studied at Muslim schools in SPAIN where he learned mathematics and astronomy. A meeting in ROME with the German emperor OTTO I in 970 was a crucial encounter that influenced him to spend much of his later life in the service of the HOLY ROMAN EMPIRE.

In 972, Gerbert went to Reims to study and then eventually teach in the bishop's school. In 991, his fame as a teacher led to his election as archbishop of Reims. However, his election was nullified four years later when it was decided that his predecessor had been deposed illegally. In 997, he left FRANCE to serve in the court of OTTO III as the emperor's mentor. He accompanied Otto to Rome where the emperor prevailed upon Pope Gregory V to appoint Gerbert archbishop of RAVENNA in 998. The following year, Otto helped Gerbert ascend to the PAPACY, making him the first Frenchman to hold that office.

As Pope Sylvester II, Gerbert helped Christianize POLAND and HUNGARY, strengthened the Church in eastern Europe, and supported Otto's effort to restore the former glory of the Holy Roman Empire. As a scholar of international reputation he wrote about theology, MATHEMATICS, and the natural sciences, and he opposed simony (selling Church offices) and worked to strengthen clerical celibacy. His learning became legendary in the later Middle Ages; popular belief even credited him with the gift of sorcery. During his teaching career he advanced the study of logic and mathematics in northern Europe. He was also an avid collector of ancient manuscripts.

GERMAN LANGUAGE AND LITERATURE

Despite the facility with which the term is used, it is important to note that for most of the Middle Ages there was no standard German language. Rather, there existed in GERMANY a collection of regional dialects that gradually gave way to the dialect of High German. By the late Middle Ages, High German had become the primary literary language of Germany, although other dialects persisted orally and informed later German works.

The history of the German language is traditionally broken into three developmental stages: Old High German (700–1100), Middle High German (1100–1500), and New High German (1500–present). The works of Old High German, a designation comprising regional dialects such as Old-Saxon, Low Frankish, High German, Alemannic, and Bavarian, have little internal relation except for their chronological overlap. The first written records of these dialects come from the early eighth century, though there is evidence of an earlier oral culture rich in ballads and hymns that went unrecorded. In official usage, these dialects were almost entirely subservient to Latin, the language of Church, government, and scholarship. In fact, much of what we know of these early writings comes from translations of religious works from Latin, such as those by the Alemannic monk Notker Labeo and ISIDORE OF SEVILLE. The first known German book, created around 770, is a German-Latin glossary, and many Old High German dialects borrowed heavily from Latin vocabulary. It was not until the end of the Middle Ages that German would gain independence from Latin as the dominant language of learned society; even as late as 1570, seventy percent of all books printed in Germany were done so in Latin.

Old High German. Although Old High German was not frequently used as a literary language, some popular works were produced in the vernacular in the eighth and ninth centuries. The earliest heroic play recorded in the German language is the *Hildebrandslied* (c. 800), a grim account of a duel between a father and son. Another important work is *Otfrid von Weissenburgs Evangelienbuch* (c. 870), a life of Christ in over 7,000 lines of German rhyming verse.

Middle High German. The transition to Middle High German occurred in the late eleventh century with a gradual movement toward linguistic uniformity. The Middle High German poets still wrote in their own dialects, but in an effort to reach a wider audience they began avoiding awkward phrases and regional peculiarities. The Middle High German period is also marked by a dramatic increase in the number and range of texts produced.

The high point in the development of Middle High German, known as its classical period, began around 1200 and is associated with the rule of the HOHENSTAUFEN DYNASTY (though, in reality, the Hohenstaufen emperors preferred homage made in Latin, so many writers turned to regional lords willing to support their efforts in the vernacular). Although this period saw the continued production of religious texts, at this point some clergy wrote religious texts for a lay readership, which, despite the preachings of the Cluniac reform movement, began to address contemporary political and social issues.

German Literature. The most famous work of the period is a secular one, the nationalistic heroic epic of an anonymous Austrian poet, called the NIBELUNGENLIED (c. 1200–1210). Also extremely popular were the courtly epics, inspired by French chivalric literature, and influenced by contact with Provençal TROUBADOURS and French crusaders. Some of the most distinguished poets of the genre include WOLFRAM VON ESCHENBACH, famous for his epic Arthurian tale *Parzival*, and GOTTFRIED VON STRASSBURG, the author of *Tristan*. The phenomenon of the courtly epic marked a transition of literary spokesmanship from the cleric to the knight, and from the monastery to the secular court.

LEGEND AND LORE

The Niebelung

The Nibelungenlied (Song of the Nibelungs) is a thirteenth-century epic German poem, which was freely adapted by the composer and dramatist Richard Wagner in his *"Ring des Nibelungen"* operas. The poem was an important addition to German literature—not only for its structure, but for its scope and breadth. It is in some respects a feminist work, focusing on the bitter rivalry between two women of high nobility. The author of the Nibelungenlied is unknown, but the poem draws from Norse myths and stories. The version extant was written down at Passau in Austria between 1230 and 1260.

The poem tells the story of Siegfried, the son of Sigmund and Sieglind (king and queen of the Netherlands). His adventures include stealing the treasure of the Nibelungs, a race of dwarfs, his marriage to the princess Kriemhild, his assisting in the marriage of her brother Gunther to the queen Brunhild, and his eventual murder by the treacherous Hagen. After Siegfried's death, Kriemhild marries Etzel (Atilla the Hun) and sets about avenging the death of Siegfried. She entraps those responsible for the murder. She herself kills Hagen, and is then killed by the Ostrogothic knight Hildebrand.

Poetry. Another popular genre, especially in the southeast of Germany, was love poetry composed by the Minnesingers, the minstrel-noblemen. These semi-professional poets, travelling throughout Germany, AUSTRIA, and SWITZERLAND and performing their works in public settings, spawned a community of readers, many of whom were women. This community benefited from and contributed to the intertextuality of many of the works, rife with rivalries and references to other compositions and artists. The late eleventh and twelfth centuries also saw a wave of historical and polemical works, brought about by the INVESTITURE CONTROVERSY, as well as a series of legendary accounts of heroic and historical figures such as Alexander the Great, THEODORIC THE GREAT, and various CAROLINGIAN emperors.

By the middle of the thirteenth century, the epic form was on the decline, and uniformity of works gave way to greater regional variety. A new class of itinerant poets emerged, the *Sangspruch*, dedicated to moral instruction. Though prose did not replace verse as a narrative instrument until the sixteenth century, the end of the classical period also witnessed a surge of prose writing, especially in the theological and mystical work of MEISTER ECKHART and Mechthild of Magdeburg. These writers struggled to mold a German that could express the richness and subtleties of their private experiences and visions. They were aided by a sort of bilingualism, a symbiotic relationship between LATIN and Middle High German that allowed the latter to gain greater flexibility and texture. This more advanced prose style culminated in the work of the Bohemian Johannes von Tepl (c. 1370–1430), whose *Death and the Ploughman* and *The Laborer of Bohemia* marked the beginning of German Humanism.

Humanism. In the fourteenth century, the lull after the creative flurry of the classical period continued. Cities became the centers of literary life, especially Nuremburg, and writers turned their attention to urban themes. Cities also provided an arena for drama, as public theater, such as morality, passion, and satiric Shrovetide plays became increasingly popular. The fifteenth century also saw the growth of German Humanism, assisted by the advent of the printing press, as well as a renewed interest in chivalric ideals and literature, reflected in Emperor MAXIMILIAN's attempts to revive old chivalric legends. In the next century, with the beginning of the New High German period, an even more widely recognized standard German would emerge.

For more on German Humanism, see MAXIMILIAN I; *more on German prose, see* ECKHART, MEISTER; *further on German literature, see* WOLFRAM VON ESCHENBACH *and* GOTTFRIED VON STRASSBURG.

GERMANUS, ST.

Germanus (c. 378–448) was a churchman who held a civil office in Gaul before he was chosen bishop of Auxerre in 418. Germanus made two extended visits to Britain to combat the spread of the HERESY of Pelagianism. After Pope Celestine I sent him in 429, he defeated a heretic force at Verulamium. On that trip he was accompanied by the deacon Palladius, the first known missionary to IRELAND. In the 440s, Germanus returned to Britain and led a contingent of Britons to victory near Mold in WALES over a marauding party of PICTS and SAXONS. Since it was Easter, the battle cry of Germanus's forces was "Alleluia," and the victory was called the Alleluia Victory.

At Auxerre, he is believed to have had ST. PATRICK under his tutelage for 12 years before Patrick embarked on his mission to Ireland. Germanus died in 448 in RAVENNA, where he had gone to plead the cause of Armorican rebels to Emperor Valentinian III.

GERMANY

Germany's borders in central Europe expanded and contracted throughout the Middle Ages, though it was not until the ninth century that German lands achieved a distinct political identity. At the beginning of the Middle Ages, the western part of the country was populated by various Germanic tribes, while Slavic tribes settled the territory east of the Elbe River. By the sixth century, much of the country had fallen under the control of the FRANKS, who granted those tribes relative autonomy. In the eighth century, these semi-independent states were united under the rule of the CAROLINGIANS. PEPIN THE SHORT deposed the MEROVINGIAN rulers and, with the assistance of ST. BONIFACE, established religious unity throughout the country. Pepin's son, CHARLEMAGNE, made even more progress toward German unification in the pursuit of his vast European empire. He fought over fifty campaigns, and managed to annex Saxony (777), BAVARIA (792), and Lombardy (774), and captured the Carinthian and Austrian marches from the AVARS (798–799). But it was not until his kingdom was partitioned in 843, with the TREATY OF VERDUN, that Germany was recognized as a political entity, when Louis the German, Charlemagne's grandson, received the territories east of the Rhine. However, the vast territory, stretching from the North Sea to the Alps, and from the Rhine in the northeast to HUNGARY in the southwest, had little else to unify it besides Louis' sovereignty. Many of the earlier tribal divisions remained intact, and the chieftains retained much of their power.

When Louis the German died in 876, his domains

were divided between his three sons: Louis received Saxony, Carloman received Bavaria, and Charles III the Fat received Swabia. After the death of his brothers, Charles was once again able to rule over a united kingdom, the last Carolingian king to do so. After Charles was deposed in 887, and the Carolingian empire was divided, a period of civil war and devastating foreign invasions—VIKINGS from the north, ARABS from the south, and Magyars from the east—ravaged the country. In this time of social unrest and weak central authority, the German nobles further consolidated their power and the vast territory fractured along the old ducal and tribal divisions.

Otto I. From out of this turmoil emerged Henry, the powerful duke of Saxony, who managed to secure the support of the other ducal powers. He was able to pass on his entire kingdom, preserving its unity, to his second son, OTTO I, who became king in 929. Otto, one of the greatest rulers in German history, survived initial opposition, replacing hostile dukes with members of his own family. He was also able to gain the valuable support of the Church, which throughout his reign supplied him with much needed military and financial assistance. In return, Otto showered the bishops and abbots with secular offices and privileges. This alliance, though highly profitable during Otto I's reign, sowed the seeds of conflict for the future.

Otto's greatest military victory came over the Magyars in 955 at the BATTLE OF THE LECH. The victory halted the Magyar invasion, secured Germany's eastern borders and paved the way for Otto's imperial CORONATION in ROME in 962, establishing the tradition of German kings receiving the imperial crown from the pope in Rome.

When Otto I died in 973, his successors were faced with a series of revolts that began in Bavaria and quickly spread to Swabia, Lorraine, POLAND, and BOHEMIA. Eventually, many of these uprising were suppressed, and Germany continued expanding eastward: Poland became a protectorate and Bohemia a duchy. The short reign of the ambitious OTTO III, who died at 22 before he could execute his expansionist plans, was followed by that of Henry II, who concentrated on Germany itself and attempted to disentangle the empire from Italian conflicts. When he died without an heir in 1024, the crown passed to the Salian dynasty, which would rule until 1125.

Salian Dynasty. The Salian period was marked by increased tension between the king, the pope, and the regional princes, who considered the Frankish Salians untrustworthy foreigners. The most distinguished of the Salians, the deeply pious HENRY III, was forced to

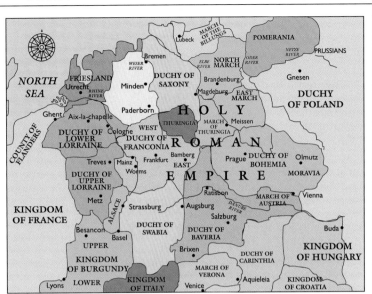

Germany in 1000. The Holy Roman Empire brought the duchies of central Europe together under one sovereign.

make a number of concessions to the princes and lay nobility. Toward the end of his reign, Henry's popularity waned and he left an inheritance of unrest to his son, HENRY IV, whose reign was disrupted by a Saxon-led civil war in 1074. Henry also became involved in a prolonged dispute with the Pope GREGORY VII that persisted after his death: the INVESTITURE CONTROVERSY that lasted from 1075 to 1122. The conflict weakened imperial authority, and encouraged separatist activities in Saxony and Swabia, including the election of anti-kings in 1076–1080.

These anarchic conditions continued for Henry's son, Henry V, who overthrew his father and gained the imperial crown in 1106. Preying upon the weakened monarchy, the German princes seized additional property and power, and convened a number of diets that led to the resolution of the Investiture Controversy at the CONCORDAT OF WORMS in 1122. The Salian period was also marked by the development and growth of cities throughout the realm, which set the stage for the commercial prosperity of the following century.

Hohenstaufen Dynasty. The next dynasty to rule Germany, the HOHENSTAUFENS, would restore confidence in the central authority, and preside over a period of prosperity unequaled in medieval German history. Depending heavily on the ministeriales, landed but unfree civil servants, the Hohenstaufens were able to check the power of the German nobility. In the latter half of the twelfth century, they oversaw the *Drang nach Osten,* Germany's eastward expansion into territories between the Elbe and the Oder Rivers.

The first Hohenstaufen, Conrad III, was succeeded as Holy Roman Emperor by FREDERICK I BAR-

BAROSSA in 1152. Frederick annexed Silesia and Pomerania, and expanded imperial domains in Swabia, Franconia, and Thuringia. He also carved out a large imperial domain in central ITALY, although he met resistance from the pope and the LOMBARD cities. Back in Germany, Frederick settled the long-standing feud between the Hohenstaufens and the Welf dynasty by granting Bavaria to the Welf leader HENRY THE LION, who controlled the duchy of Saxony. But Frederick grew displeased with Henry and in 1180, stripped him of his duchies and divided them among his supporters.

After Frederick's death in 1190, and after a series of disputed elections, the German princes rejected the Welf candidate Otto IV and elected the Hohenstaufen FREDERICK II in 1215. Frederick, one of the most enlightened rulers of the Middle Ages, became increasingly preoccupied with consolidating his power in Italy and SICILY, even ignoring his German territories. His absence allowed the German princes to regain strength and pursue autonomy; his reorganization of the imperial constitution also granted the princes additional privileges. Frederick came in conflict with the papacy because of his reluctance to fulfill his crusading pledge, and was excommunicated twice by the pope, who encouraged the GUELPH faction in Italy to rebel against his rule. He finally journeyed to the Holy Land in 1229, and was crowned king of Jerusalem. Frederick spent his final years trying to suppress numerous challengers to his rule in Germany, Italy and Sicily.

After Frederick II's death in 1250, the princes had a difficult time agreeing on suitable successors, and after a number of troubled reigns, the Hohenstaufen dynasty came to an end with Frederick II's grandson, Conrad, in 1268. This period of dynastic vacancy, called The Great Interregnum (1254–1273), was a time of great instability, and Germany lost much of its Italian and Sicilian lands to the French ANGEVINS. But it was also a time of progress, as the nearly independent dynastic states within Germany, as well the developing German cities, became more powerful and autonomous, and urban confederations formed, such as the League of Rhine and the Hanse.

The Habsburgs. The Interregnum ended with the election of the most powerful prince in southwestern Germany, Rudolf of Habsburg, in 1273. The rise of the HABSBURGS marks the final chapter of medieval German history. The Habsburgs, whose original hereditary domains were in modern-day SWITZERLAND, concentrated less on the ideal of empire and more on consolidating their own territorial power. With the rebellion and succession of the Swiss cantons (1291), the Habsburgs moved the center of the empire eastward, with its capital in Vienna. Rudolf acquired the duchies of Austria, Styria, Cariola, and Carinthia after defeating the Bohemians in 1278. In

1282, after his coronation, he invested his sons with the conquered lands, beginning 636 years of Habsburg rule in Austria.

The German princes, however, largely mistrusted the growing power of the Habsburgs. After Rudolf died, his son Albert assumed the German throne, but he was assassinated in 1308. The House of Luxembourg, which also ruled over Bohemia, contended with the Habsburgs for the German throne. After a series of confrontations between kings, anti-kings, popes, and antipopes, Louis the Bavarian, who received the imperial crown in 1328, was deposed in 1347 in favor of Charles IV of Luxembourg. Charles moved the center of the empire even farther east, spending much of his energy on his lands in Bohemia, and making PRAGUE one of the grandest cities in Europe. As a consequence, many of the western principalities, including the Low Countries, loosened their ties to Germany. After returning from his imperial coronation (unlike many of his predecessors, he only spent a day in Rome) in 1355, Charles issued the Golden Bull, which established a formalized procedure for the election of the German king through the seven-member College of Electors. These electors were granted near autonomy in their respective domains, which fragmented the German kingdom into semi-independent dynastic states.

After Charles's death in 1378, the Luxembourg dynasty was hotly contested by German nobles. At one point, three rival kings and three rival popes all claimed authority. After the death of SIGISMUND, the last of the Luxembourgs, the Habsburg ALBERT II took the German crown; a Habsburg would remain on the throne until 1806. Albert was succeeded by Frederick III, who reigned for 53 years, and was the last German king to be crowned in Rome. During his remarkably long reign, the empire lost much of its control over HUNGARY and Bohemia. Yet, the marriage of Frederick's son Maximilian to the heiress of BURGUNDY secured that duchy for the family. (The duchy was not easily integrated into the empire, however, and would one day bring the Germans into conflicts with the French.)

The Habsburgs continued their expansion through their fortuitous marriages; Maximilian's son Philip I married the daughter of Ferdinand and Isabella, inheriting Castile and ARAGON, as well as Spain's territories in the Low Countries, NAPLES, Burgundy, and the New World. But even as the Habsburg's territory expanded well beyond the borders of Germany, the nobles in the stem duchies, the Wittelsbach in Bavaria, the Wettins in Saxony, gained even more power. These princes also began to share their power with the estates—parliamentary representative assemblies which had first formed in the early fifteenth century—and with the urban magistrates, who came to prominence as the empire's approximately 80 cities became even more independent and economically viable in the late fifteenth century.

For more on individuals, see PÉPIN THE SHORT, CHARLEMAGNE, OTTO I, OTTO III, HENRY III, HENRY IV, HENRY THE LION, FREDERICK I BARBAROSSA, *and* FREDERICK II. *For information on dynasties, See* CAROLINGIAN, HOHENSTAUFEN, *and* HABSBURG.

GERSON, JEAN

Jean Gerson (1363–1429) was a French theologian and writer best known as a reformer who helped heal the GREAT SCHISM, the battle for the PAPACY that lasted nearly 40 years.

Gerson was born in FRANCE and studied at the University of PARIS. He became chancellor of the University in 1395, by which time what was known as the Great Schism was in full swing. Nearly 20 years earlier, the papal seat had been moved back to ROME after 70 years in AVIGNON. But rival forces in Rome and Avignon elected their own popes, and for years there were two separate papal seats, each with strong support. An attempt to get both popes to resign and replace them with one left Europe with not two but three popes.

Gerson was a key figure in arranging a church council to decide finally who was the legitimate pope. The Council of Constance finally ended the Great Schism. Avignon was no longer recognized as a papal seat, and a new pope was elected to serve in Rome. Gerson did much of the necessary maneuvering to gain approval from both sides of the issue.

In later years, Gerson pushed for Church reform. He wrote an eloquent defense of St. JOAN OF ARC, who, despite Gerson's efforts, would be burned as a heretic in 1431. Gerson's last years were spent in Lyons, where he died in 1429. Because of his leadership in higher education and Church reform and his deep learning and tolerant, humanistic attitude, Gerson is seen as one of the founders of the Renaissance in northern Europe.

GHAZALI, AL-

Abu Khamad al-Ghazali (1058–1111) was the great Islamic jurist, philosopher, and mystic who is considered the father of Sufism and Islamic philosophy's severest critic of rationalism.

Born in Khorasan in eastern Iran, he was recognized as ISLAM's most gifted scholar, and was appointed in 1091 by the SELJUK vizier Nizam al-Mulk as head of the Nizamiya, the law school he had founded in BAGHDAD. In 1095, al-Ghazali had a personal crisis in which he lost the power of speech, forcing him to resign his post. He became an ascetic and a mystic, or Sufi, wandering through the desert for the next 12 years, becoming a legendary figure in Islamic culture.

It was during this period that he wrote his major work, *The Revival of the Sciences of Religion,* a critique of Aristotelian rationalism and the manner in which it had been embraced by Islamic thinkers. The work gave legitimacy and a philosophic underpinning to mysticism in Islam that it enjoys to the present day. Another of his works refuting other philosophies was so clear in its exposition that it became a textbook for students studying the very philosophers being criticized.

In 1106, al-Ghazali resumed lecturing at the Nizamiya, the most renowned Islamic theologian of his day. He died five years later.

GHENT

Ghent, today a Belgian city of some 250,000, was one of the most important commercial centers of medieval Europe. Situated in the county of FLANDERS, a center of international trade, Ghent's proximity to the Schelde and Lys Rivers made it ideal for both import and export. It became a leader in the textile industry and was the leading producer of wool cloth in Europe in the thirteenth century.

The Schelde and Lys rivers flow into the North Sea, which made Ghent easily accessible to foes as well as friends. During the ninth century, Ghent was a frequent victim of NORMAN raids. Gradually, however, the city began to build itself up, and by the eleventh century, Ghent was a major market for cloth, which it made out of WOOL imported from nearby ENGLAND. Ghent earned a reputation for the high quality of its cloth and for the textile FAIR it held annually.

Rise of the Merchant Class. As textile merchants and manufacturers prospered, they established themselves as a political, social, and economic force. Local businessmen, both artisans and merchants, managed to gain both property rights and a fair degree of economic autonomy from the Flemish rulers. The city magistrates were chosen from among their ranks, and a hereditary system was established to maintain power in the textile makers' hands.

Other artisans in Ghent eventually established GUILDS to further their own economic interests, though they never became as powerful as the textile class, whose wealth and power were firmly entrenched. Still, everyone benefitted from Ghent's prosperity.

Decline. In the fourteenth century, a number of factors contributed to Ghent's decline. The most noteworthy event was the HUNDRED YEARS' WAR, the series of extended battles between FRANCE and ENGLAND between 1337 and 1453. Ghent, which relied on England for its most important raw material, wool, sided with the English. But the count of Flanders, Louis of Nevers, was solidly behind the French. England's king EDWARD III cut off the export of wool to Flanders, hoping to sway Louis through economic pressure. Edward's plan failed, and Ghent and several other towns actually went so far as to establish a military alliance with England.

There were other forces at work: England was no longer merely exporting wool; it had begun manufacturing its own cloth, and as its textile industries grew it had less need for Ghent. Moreover, other regions, such as Italy, had entered the textile market. Ghent, which had once had the wool cloth market virtually cornered, was now one of several competitors. By the end of the Middle Ages, its power and influence had declined considerably.

GHIBELLINES

The Ghibellines were one of the two main political factions (their opponents were the GUELPHS) that operated in GERMANY and ITALY in the late Middle Ages. The Ghibellines supported the HOLY ROMAN EMPIRE and the authority of the emperor, while the Guelphs supported the Church and the authority of the PAPACY. (*See* GUELPHS.)

Although today the names refer mostly to the papal and imperial parties that engaged in the long struggle for power which defined the political life of Italy for more than two centuries, the names originated in Germany in connection with the rivalry of two German princely houses—the Welfs or Guelphs, who were dukes of Saxony and BAVARIA, and the HOHENSTAUFEN (the name Ghibelline probably derives from Waiblingen, a Hohenstaufen castle). The rivalry of the two families, both with large holdings in Swabia, began with their rise to power during the reign of the Holy Roman Emperor HENRY IV, and intensified during the reigns of Henry the Proud and his son and successor, HENRY THE LION, and further with the election of Otto IV as Holy Roman Emperor.

The Guelph-Ghibelline conflict in Italy began during the reign of the Holy Roman Emperor FREDERICK I BARBAROSSA when he used force to reestablish imperial authority in northern Italy, a policy which divided Italians, with some of them supporting the papacy and others backing the empire.

Depiction of the Battle of Montaperti, 1260, between Ghibelline Siena and Guelph Florence.

The terms entered the vocabulary of Italian politics in FLORENCE in the 1240s to designate the supporters of Pope Innocent IV and the supporters of Emperor FREDERICK II. By the 1250s, the terms spread to northern Italy, the scene of virtual civil war, with the papal supporters on one side known as Guelphs and their opponents known as Ghibellines

The identity of the two parties shifted often, and at no time did either party clearly or consistently represent a political program or social class. In fact, by 1300 the names ceased to represent papal and imperial interests, but the ever-shifting political struggles between rival Italian families, factions, cities, and provinces. Noble families tended to have fixed party loyalties, but TOWNS and cities shifted with the political winds. VENICE managed to remain neutral, but other cities were generally defined by the party in the ascendancy. MILAN, FLORENCE, and GENOA tended to be Guelph, while Cremona, PISA, and Arezzo were usually Ghibelline. In Rome, the center of papal power, the Ghibellines nevertheless maintained a strong presence, represented by the Colonna family, the republicans, and other enemies of the papacy. (*See* GUELPH.)

GHIBERTI, LORENZO

Florentine sculptor (1378–1455) who led the way in bringing Classicist (i.e., Greek and Roman) elements to Italian sculpture. He imitated the ancient artists, but surpassed them in his technical and story-telling skills.

He began his training as a goldsmith under his father, casting small bronzes, carving reliefs in jewelry, and designing unique new settings for ancient coins and stones.

Giotto's fresco "Resurrection of Lazarus," in the Scrovegni Chapel in Padua, Italy.

In 1403, he won the competition to cast the Baptistery doors in FLORENCE, and he devoted 27 years to the project. He incorporated whole narratives from the Bible into each discrete panel. His figures and backgrounds were so natural and life-like (he often used real people as models, including himself) that his student Michelangelo Buonarotti said the doors were so beautiful they could be "the gates of paradise," by which name they are known. Though he was not well-educated, he wrote an influential book, the *Commentari,* in which he urged that all artists be literate and knowledgeable in history.

GIOTTO DI BONDONE

G iotto (1266–1337) was a painter and architect from FLORENCE, often called "the grandfather of Italian art" and considered to be one of the earliest and most accomplished practitioners of the new style of painting that incorporated classical (i.e., Greek and Roman) elements of art, which came to be known as the Renaissance. His use of naturalism in portraying figures, landscapes, and architecture was almost photographic in its verity, even without an understanding of perspective.

Even in his own lifetime, Giotto was respected as an innovator and a leader in creating a realistic art form, eschewing the prevailing highly formalized and stylized depictions of Byzantine and northern European modes. He exercised a poet's eye to create life-like stances, movement, and facial expressions in his works. His skills were widely praised by contemporary writers such as DANTE, PETRARCH, and BOCCACCIO (who wrote that Giotto's genius outshone his stout and conspicuously ugly appearance).

Among his works are the paintings of the "Life of Christ" in the Vatican Sacristy and the intricate MOSAIC of the apostles (the Navicella) over the portico of St. Peter's, both in ROME, and architectural design for the Campanile of Santa Maria del Fiore in Florence. His frescoes of the life of ST. FRANCIS in the Church of Santa Croce in Florence, humanized the saint, minimizing the mystical aspects of the popular lore surrounding him, and contributed to the image of St. Francis as a dynamic but very human religious leader.

GLASSMAKING

T he people of the Middle Ages were well aware of glassmaking prior to their era—it was a technology that traced its roots into the ancient world—and sought to advance it as an art and religious form as well as an everyday practicality.

The art of glassmaking continued to develop in the Byzantine Empire and the Muslim world, where glassmakers produced glass for windows (its most common use) and also for decorative art. In Asia minor and the Balkans, the art form advanced with the development of colored glass. The Italians were well-schooled in the art of glassmaking, having once been the center of the Roman Empire. (Actually, so-called Roman glass came from Phoenecia and was brought back by the Romans.) VENICE would distinguish itself and become the center of European glassmaking. Only in western and northern Europe did glassmaking lag behind. The quality of glass was poor, perhaps because

Europeans had a limited supply of soda, the salt compound needed for glass production (then available only in the Mediterranean). A suitable substitute was found in potash, a potassium compound produced from wood ash. With a healthy supply of wooded areas, the Europeans now had an easier time making glass. (Potash-produced glass tends to deteriorate; consequently, not much glass from that era survives.)

Progress in glassmaking throughout the medieval world came at the beginning of the twelfth century with the birth of ROMANESQUE architecture. This new form required much larger windows for churches. Not only did the quantity of glass production need to increase, but the quality as well; worshippers did not want big shoddy windows in their church. The solution came with the new technique of glassblowing. All the necessary materials were melted together in a furnace. When they had reached the proper temperature to become viscous, they were removed and placed on the end of a long stick. The glassmaker would then blow and spin the glass until the desired form was obtained. This method is chronicled in a series of writings on crafts by the priest Theophilus. Later in the twelfth century, another advance in the glassmaking industry took place as copper and iron were added to the usual mixture of materials to create STAINED GLASS. (*See* METAL PRODUCTION; *and* STAINED GLASS.)

GLOSSATORS

Medieval scholars often encountered difficulty when reading Roman legal texts. To ensure that scholars and students understood what they were reading, specially trained scholars would go through manuscripts and make explanatory annotations, or glosses. The scholars who added the glosses were thus called glossators.

Beginnings. Study of the LAW in the Middle Ages focused on its most practical aspects for several hundred years. Most students of law were trained in administration. They knew how to keep legal records and draw up contracts. Because society was structured more simply than it had been during Roman times, there was little need for more abstract training. By the eleventh century, however, medieval society was becoming more complex; cities and governments were developing, and people began to travel more. It soon became clear that legal training would have to expand.

With the establishment of the law school at the University of Bologna, the study of Roman law became popular. Often, however, students found the texts confusing and many terms unfamiliar.

The first glossators painstakingly reviewed manuscripts, identified problematic words or phrases, and wrote explanatory annotations under the word or in the margin. An early project of the glossators was the reconstruction of the original JUSTINIAN CODE by comparing existing manuscripts and making appropriate annotations.

Influence. Eventually, all the original Roman legal texts had been annotated, doing away with the need for glossators. One of the last glossators, a law professor at Bologna in the thirteenth century named Franciscus ACCURSIUS, compiled all available glosses in one reference work. The resulting compilation was called the *Glossae magna* (*Great Gloss*), and it proved a valuable work for years afterward.

Because Bologna was the center of legal study, the glossators' influence spread throughout Europe. Moreover, increased trade between countries necessitated some system of common law that could be applied across borders. Thus, though Roman law gave way to the development of laws in other countries, legal scholars found that the Roman texts were still valuable resources. By the fourteenth century, a new group of scholarly annotators called commentators were at work finding ways to incorporate important elements of Roman law into legal systems of the day. Ultimately, the work of the glossators was to influence European law well past the Middle Ages. (*See* LAW, SCHOOLS OF.)

GLYN DWR, OWAIN

Owain Glyn Dwr (also Owen Glendower; died c. 1415) was the last independent prince of WALES (1400-08). His sustained defiance of the English immortalized him as a Welsh national hero. A descendant of Welsh landowners, he was educated in LONDON at the Inns of Court and became a skilled soldier. In 1400, he led a rebellion of Welshmen against the English occupation of their borderlands. That same year he claimed descent from the princes of Powys in northern Wales and was proclaimed Prince of Wales. For the next two years, King HENRY IV tried unsuccessfully to defeat Glyn Dwr's swelling band of Welsh rebels. In 1404, the rebels captured two key English strongholds at Harlech and Aberystwyth. At the height of his power Glyn Dwr was widely regarded as the independent ruler of Wales.

In 1405, the tide began to turn when Prince Henry (later HENRY V) defeated the Welsh forces on the border and began the reconquest of Wales, which he completed in 1408. Glyn Dwr went into hiding, but the English captured his family. Glendower was never captured and it is believed he died some seven years later early in the reign of Henry V. He became the subject of many legends about his bravery and character.

GODFREY DE BOUILLON

n ideal Christian knight, Godfrey de Bouillon (1060–1100) was the first ruler of the crusader kingdom of Jerusalem and a prince of the HOLY ROMAN EMPIRE under HENRY IV.

He was born the son of Count Eustace II of Boulogne and the nephew of duke Godfrey II of Lower Lorraine. Godfrey was named heir to the duchy of Lower Lorraine in 1076 and received the duchy from Henry IV in 1082 as a reward for his service in battle against the SAXONS. Although he was a relatively important prince in the empire, his authority was weakened by the growing power of the counts. Though a pious man, Godfrey was not the best politician and was able to maintain control over only a small portion of his territory.

15th-century woodcut of Godfrey de Bouillon depicted wearing on his head "the instruments of the Lord's Passion"; namely, the whip and rods used by monks for self-flagellation.

In 1096, Godfrey became the undeclared leader of the First CRUSADE, replacing Raymond of Toulouse in 1099. Traveling with his brothers Eustace and Baldwin (later BALDWIN I), Godfrey and his army marched to the siege of Jerusalem in 1099 and together with troops of TANCRED OF HAUTEVILLE, captured the city. As the leader of the first troops entering the city, Godfrey was offered the crown; he declined, assuming the title Advocate of the Holy Sepulchre instead. After the majority of crusaders had returned home, Godfrey and Tancred successfully defended Jerusalem from attacks by Egyptian Muslims and neighboring coastal cities.

Godfrey wanted to implement a theocratic system of government in Jerusalem, but the volatile political and military conditions made this an unrealistic goal and further illustrated his political shortcomings. When Godfrey died in 1100, his brother Baldwin became the first king of the Latin kingdom of Jerusalem. (*See* CRUSADES.)

GOLDEN HORDE

he Golden Horde was an attempt by the MONGOLS to resurrect the glory days of GENGHIS KHAN'S reign. During its century-long dominance during the late Middle Ages, the Horde controlled much of RUSSIA and Central Asia.

The Horde was established by Genghis Khan's grandson Batu around 1236 during a Mongol invasion of Russia. Batu led his army from Turkistan into Russia, where he sacked and looted town after town, including Moscow, reaching POLAND and HUNGARY, and defeating Henry II, duke of Silesia.

Russian princes were forced to pay the Horde tribute, and Mongol troops were placed in Russian towns to enforce Horde laws, while the Horde established its capital in Saray on the lower Volga. The Golden Horde was named for Batu's golden encampment ("orda"), an immense tent that had the dimensions of a palace.

Batu died in 1255 and his brother and successor Berke converted the Horde to ISLAM, mostly out of contempt for Buddhist and Christian Mongols. His targets included his cousin, KUBLAI KHAN, and another cousin who was a Persian khan. The remainder of the thirteenth century was marked by Horde infighting. Berke's grandnephew, Nogai, deposed rivals to the throne, and was murdered. Ozbeg, who would rule the Horde from 1313 to 1341, made an effort to reassert Islam's primacy and his control of the Russian aristocracy. One of his most significant acts was granting Ivan Kalita a grand duchy for Moscow in 1328, a major step in Moscow's eventual growth as a European and world power. (*See* RUSSIA; MONGOLS.)

Ozbeg's death by assassination prompted another round of internal conflict. Toktamish, ruler of the White Horde, tried to regain control in 1378 and occupied Saray, but he was killed by TAMERLANE. The Horde continued breaking up into smaller factions despite Tamerlane's leadership. Local chiefs in LITHUANIA, Moldava, and Moscow became more independent. Finally, at the battle of Kulikovo in 1380, DIMITRI DONSKOI decisively beat the Horde.

The Horde further disintegrated in the fifteenth century, as the population shifted west to Kazan. By the 1430s, several separate Horde states had formed. The Horde did not officially come to an end until 1502 when the Crimean khan, who was a vassal of the OTTOMAN EMPIRE, conquered and destroyed Saray.

GOLIARDIC POETS

he importance of church support for literary activity fosters the impression that writers and poets of the Middle Ages were on the pious and conservative side. But one observer from the period writes of a group of student-poets who "roam from city to city, in Paris seeking the liberal arts, in Orléans classics, in Salerno medicine—but nowhere manners or morals." These were the goliards—the wandering scholars who today are best remembered for their poetry, which satirized the morals of those around them. Many poems in the collection known as *Carmina Burana* are believed to be of goliardic origin.

Origins. The goliards took their name from one Bishop Golias, a debauched priest who is featured in many of their poems (and who may never have existed). While many students and clerics wandered from university to university to satisfy their thirst for knowledge, the goliards, it seems, wandered simply to satisfy their thirst. They sought pleasure and adventure and delighted in drinking, loving freely, and gambling away what little money they had.

The goliards seem to have first appeared in France in the ninth century, but because they were wanderers, they soon made their way throughout Europe. Only a few goliardic poets are known by name: Pierre de Blois, Hugh Primas of Orléans, Gautier de Châtillon, and Phillipe the Chancellor. One of the best known goliards was known simply as the Archpoet.

Their Poetry. The goliardic tradition is one of irreverence and high spirits. Poems and songs, sometimes intricately crafted, celebrated good living—wine, food, love, and adventure. They poked fun at both Church and state; religious ceremonies were a frequent target, and many religious works were parodied. The concept of responsibility was utterly distasteful to the goliards. It is suspected, however, that many of these poets did not live quite so riotously as they claimed; the goliardic style may have been popular because it allowed writers a creative outlet for launching attacks against conventional beliefs.

Most of the goliardic poems were written in LATIN; some were written in FRENCH, GERMAN, and ENGLISH. Although little music remains with the goliardic manuscripts that currently exist, scholars believe that most goliardic poems were intended to be sung.

In addition to the poems in the *Carmina Burana*, the poems of the Archpoet, especially his *Confesio Goliae,* are noteworthy for their portrayal of the goliardic way of life and for their skillful construction.

Later Years. Although the goliardic movement flourished for several centuries, the church finally took stern measures against these wandering poets and in the thirteenth century took away religious privileges of any cleric who adopted or advocated the goliard's way of life. Faced with the stricter policy of the church, fewer and fewer scholars chose to wear the goliardic label. Eventually, the word "goliard" came to mean simply "minstrel."

GOTHIC ART AND ARCHITECTURE

The "Gothic Style" emerged in the mid-twelfth century in the Ile-de-France and remained generally confined to the countries north of the Alps. The term "Gothic" was not used by the actual artisans in the style, but was coined as a derisive epithet in the fifteenth century by Italian followers of the classical-revival Renaissance style. They considered the Gothic to be a crude and barbaric import of Visigothic tribes which had invaded ROME in the fifth century and destroyed the remains of classical culture there.

Criteria. It was only in the nineteenth century that the Gothic style was formally defined (by Eugene Emmanuel Viollet-le-Duc) as consisting of pointed arches, ribbed vaults, and flying buttresses. This definition has endured. It was also at this time that the term Gothic was extended to incorporate an entire time period, from the thirteenth to the fifteenth centuries.

Although earlier historians made much of separating Gothic from the ROMANESQUE style which preceded it, more recent scholarship suggests that such a sharp separation is misleading. The two styles, while different, often existed alongside each other, or in mixed elements. In Italy, where the Gothic was never truly accepted, use of the term at all is questionable.

It is in architectural forms that this style is most recognizable. However, at least two of the basic elements of the new style, groined vaults and pointed arches, were already being experimented with in some Romanesque buildings in ENGLAND and Normandy in the early twelfth century, and the third criterion, the flying buttress, was absent in the earlier Gothic structures. So it is perhaps more accurate to define the emerging style in terms of its overall attitude: a feeling of soaring height and space, and of shimmering light. This sense of weightlessness alone would set it apart from the ponderous, grounded Romanesque style.

Cathedrals and Churches. The pivotal moment in the development of the Gothic was the rebuilding of the royal abbey church of ST.-DENIS, near PARIS, beginning in 1140, under the guidance of Abbot SUGER. His innovative renovation, which opened up the dark church to faith-inspiring light, opened the way to more and more breathtakingly high and spacious churches. This veritable masonic and engineering contest for creating expansive, thinner walls, pierced with myriad windows, necessitated the invention of the exterior brace, the stone flying buttress. CHARTRES CATHEDRAL, begun in 1194, was a leader in this late, "High Gothic" aesthetic, and during the thirteenth century, at least 80 cathedrals and 500 abbey churches were built in the Gothic style, astonishing monuments to God's glory.

New Styles. From the late thirteenth century to the sixteenth century, due to the shifting currents between lay and clerical powers (as symbolized by the growing humanism movement) Gothic architecture split into the precious and overly-decorated Rayonnant Style of the Saint-Chapelle in Paris, and the more simplified Romanesque-like style of southern Europe.

The structural forms of the Gothic model are useful in discussing some types of art as well, such as architectural sculpture and metalwork, even some woodwork, because they reflected these forms. The figural arts are more problematic. The new figural style, which developed in FRANCE from the early thirteenth century, emphasized the physical presence, not only of religious figures, but also of worldly objects such as animals, buildings, and domestic paraphernalia. This new artistic vision reflected the awakening awareness of the individual and his journey through life, contrary to the early-medieval single-minded religiosity. Byzantine ICONS and the increasingly secular patronage of art were also influential in this turn towards worldly decorative arts. An example of this is the increasing inclusion of actual persons, usually art patrons, in paintings, STAINED GLASS windows, and MANUSCRIPT ILLUMINATIONS.

New Forms. Sculpture now became a discrete profession, and sculptors were recognized as craftsmen, distinct from other stone workers. Stone sculpture was used for tombs, church furnishings and decorations, and statues. Wood sculpture was used for cult figures, free-standing statues, liturgical objects, and altar pieces. Both stone and wood sculptures were often painted. At St.-Denis, there was an innovative use of sculpted figures as part of the architectural columns. The most striking difference between pre-Gothic and Gothic figural representation was the shift toward more life-like and less stylized depictions.

STAINED GLASS advanced technically by the late thirteenth century to where it was lightweight enough to be incorporated into vast expanses of windows. These windows not only allowed entry of the celestial light so important in the Gothic religious mystique, but also related elaborate picture-stories, from the Bible and legend, for the often illiterate congregation.

The elements of Gothic architecture, such as linear tracery and pointed arches, did not appear in portable objects and metalwork until the early fourteenth century, but then remained popular until the Renaissance. In this period, metalworkers developed a wider range of forms, most often used for religious objects such as altar furnishings (chalices, candelabra, tabernacles, censers) and reliquary boxes modeled after body parts.

Paris became a major center for ivory carving as trade expanded and ivory became more abundant. Larger works, such as statues, were carved, as well as combs, dice, beads, and buttons.

Luxury textiles in the Gothic period, especially TAPESTRIES, embroidery, and woven silks and velvets, were costly and highly prized possessions. Used in the court and church, and increasingly, by the emerging

The Gothic style permeated all design elements, from large structures to incidental adornment. Simone Martini's "Annunciation" displays the Gothic form in presentation.

bourgeoisie, the patterns for tapestries and embroidery were designed by highly skilled artists. England was the source of a particularly sought after type of embroidery called *Opus Anglicanum* (*English work*) produced between 1250 and 1350.

Ultimately, the Gothic style was eclipsed in most parts of Europe by the return to the classical motifs of the Renaissance.

 For more on Gothic art and architecture, see CHURCHES AND CATHEDRALS; SUGER; STAINED GLASS; MANUSCRIPT ILLUMINATION; TAPESTRIES; *and* CHARTRES CATHEDRAL. *For additional information on variations of Gothic art, see* ROMANESQUE.

GOTHS

The Goths were probably the largest of the Germanic tribes, and the most dedicated to perpetuating Roman government and Latin culture in the successor kingdoms to the Empire. The Goths in 500 C.E. controlled ITALY, the western half of FRANCE, and the Iberian peninsula. A little over two

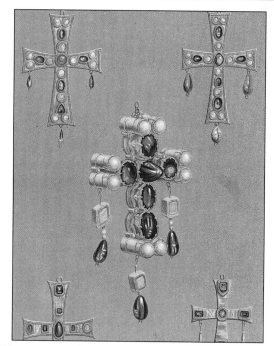

7th-century jeweled crosses of the Gothic kings, found at archeological digs at Guarrazar, in central Europe.

centuries later, however, there was almost nothing left of the Gothic kingdoms—only a handful of tiny principalities in the northern, mountainous regions of SPAIN.

The Goths were Scandinavians who moved south after 1000 B.C.E. and by 370 C.E. were located in the Danube basin facing the Balkan frontier of the Roman Empire. The Goths were divided into two groups: the VISIGOTHS, just over the Danube River from the Roman Empire, and behind them, farther from the Danube and the Roman Empire, the OSTROGOTHS. (Some historians translate Visigoths into West Goths and Ostrogoths into eastern Goths, but there is no secure basis for this derivation. They could just as easily have been named after some eponymous heroes.)

Visigoths. Both the Visigoths and Ostrogoths were Arian Christians. They had been converted to this heretical church in the middle of the fourth century by missionaries led by Ulfilas, dispatched from the eastern Mediterranean by the then temporarily flourishing separatist Arian church. The Arian church was eliminated within the empire by orthodox emperors in the 380s. Ulfilas translated parts of the Bible into the Gothic language, inventing a German alphabet. Early in the 370s the Huns, an Asiatic people from Mongolia, broke into the Balkans from the Caspian and Black Sea basins. Fighting mainly on horseback, (while the Goths, like the Romans, had only infantry armies) they crushed and subjugated the Ostrogoths. The terrified Visigoths, who had close commercial relations with the

Roman Empire, begged the emperor to be allowed to cross the Danube and settle in the Roman Balkans. In 376, the Visigoths were allowed to do so; there was an ample precedent for such permitted mass immigration, although never before had such a large group (between 100,000 and 250,000 people) entered the empire at one time. Within two years, the Visigoths were unhappy with their land settlement and felt exploited by Roman officials and merchants. They prepared for war. The Emperor Gratian attacked them before a key part of his army arrived and was defeated and killed at the Battle of Adrianople in 378, one of the important battles of history because it showed that a German army could beat the Romans.

Battle with Rome. A new emperor pacified the Visigoths, but after his death in 395 the Visigoths were again on the move, this time toward Italy, in order to force a more favorable land settlement on the imperial government. The head of the Roman army in Italy, a German of obscure background named Stilicho, considered the advancing Visigoths to be a grave threat and in 406 summoned his armies back from the Rhine frontier to protect Italy from them. A variety of German peoples now flooded into Gaul, Spain, and northern AFRICA. The Visigoths at this point chose the determined warrior and wily politician ALARIC as their king. When Stilicho was assassinated in 408 by Roman aristocrats in complicity with the emperor in Italy, the Roman defenses fell apart and Alaric advanced upon Rome and entered, holding the Eternal City for a few weeks in an effort to force a new settlement from the imperial government. (*See* VISIGOTHS.)

This Visigothic "sack of Rome" did little damage because the Visigoths admired Rome and its people, but it sent a shockwave through the Mediterranean world. For the first time in more than a millennium, Rome had fallen. Getting nowhere with the Roman government, perhaps because the Visigoths' commitment to Arianism made them appear hostile and untrustworthy, Alaric pulled his vast cortege from Rome and marched down to the bottom of Italy, preparing to invade Roman North Africa with its attractive grain-growing estates and salubrious cities. He died suddenly and his brother Autulf led the Visigoths back up the whole length of Italy and then into western Gaul and Spain. While passing by Rome, Autulf kidnapped and married the emperor's sister, who thoroughly enjoyed herself as a Gothic queen and played a significant role in the confused politics of the next two decades.

Finally in 418, the emperor had no choice but to recognize the Visigothic settlements in Gaul and Spain. From Gaul, the Visigoth kings and nobles were driven by the Catholic FRANKS in the early sixth century. In Spain, the Visigoths converted to CHRISTIANITY around 600; during the seventh century, their bishops pursued a policy of militant persecution against the sizable Jewish community in Iberia. In 711, the Jews welcomed and assisted a large army of Muslim ARABS who came across the Straits of Gibraltar from North Africa. The Arabs easily defeated the Visigothic kingdom. A handful of Goth nobility hid out in the Pyrenees until their descendants began a reconquest of CASTILE and ARAGON after 1070. Meanwhile, most of the Visigothic population in Iberia converted to Islam and Spain lost its Gothic identity.

Ostrogoths. The Hunnish Empire in the Balkans, in which the Ostrogoths lived as a subjugated people, disintegrated in the mid-fifth century after the death of ATTILA, and the Ostrogoths now began to cross the Danube into the BYZANTINE Empire. In the 480s, a scion of an old Ostrogothic noble family, THEODORIC, emerged as the king of the Ostrogoths, a position he held until his death in 526. Theodoric had spent several years in his youth in CONSTANTINOPLE and he greatly admired Roman culture and law. Trying to turn the Ostrogoths away from Constantinople, the emperor gave Theodoric authority to invade and conquer Italy from a motley crew of German warlords headed by ODOACER. Theodoric (later called The Great), a man of great intelligence and energy, set up his capital in the Byzantine city of RAVENNA in northeastern Italy. The king treated the pope with deference and in practice surrendered the city of Rome to the pontiff. For about two decades Theodoric ruled Italy as the emperor's representative and employed Roman aristocrats such as CASSIODORUS and BOETHIUS in his government. The Ostrogoths were awarded one-third of the landed estates in Italy and lived as a conquering army with Theodoric as their king; they did not assimilate into the general population. (*See* OSTROGOTHS.)

Byzantine Relations. The Goths remained Arians, which limited the loyalty that the pope and the Roman aristocracy could accord the Gothic king. Behind the king's back they began to negotiate with the Byzantine emperor for the restoration of imperial rule. Perhaps in retaliation against this treason, Theodoric in his later years entered into a more independent and aggressive policy, fashioning close relations with the Visigoths in Gaul and Spain. The king may possibly have had the creation of a Mediterranean Gothic empire in mind. Boethius, a distinguished philosopher, was put to death for treason and the pope was imprisoned by the king. Shortly after his death, the Byzantine emperor JUSTINIAN I launched an enormous effort to reconquer Italy, dispatching an army across the seas to North Africa and then up the length of Italy. The Ostrogoths resisted with great valor and skill. The result was the two-decade long Gothic War which devastated the Italian economy and contributed to a massive shrinking of Rome and other urban communities. By 570, the Gothic kingdom had disappeared. But in the seventh century a new German menace, the LOMBARDS, entered Italy from the north and seized most of the northern half of the peninsula—which was not reunited into one state until 1871.

The motto of Theodoric the Great's government was *civilitas,* which stood for Roman civilization. The motto was stamped on the royal coinage and Cassiodorus, a prolific writer, set to work producing a history of the Goths whom he identified in origin with an ancient people in the Crimea, the Scythians. Cassiodorus's propagandist historiography might have had some basis in fact, but it was all for naught. The future of the early medieval European Mediterranean lay with the Franks and the Arabs. (*See* THEODORIC.)

Ironically, the term Gothic lived on only in architectural style. The term was used by eighteenth-century Renaissance humanists to refer to the French cathedral style of the late twelfth and thirteenth centuries. Medieval people called the style of CHARTRES and NOTRE DAME cathedrals "the Style of Paris." Gothic architecture is a misnomer; even when the name Goth survived, it was for the wrong reason.

GOTTFRIED VON STRASSBURG

L ittle is known about the life of German poet Gottfried von Strassburg (flourished c. 1210). He was probably born toward the end of the twelfth century and his works of poetry reflect an extensive education and cultural background. He was probably a member of the lower nobility and lived in the Rhineland. His *Tristan and Isolde* is considered the definitive version of the Celtic legend of the two tragic lovers.

Different versions of the story have different endings: in some Tristan dies; in others, TRISTAN AND ISOLDE both die; in still others, Tristan falls in love with another Isolde but still ultimately dies. A version of the story is believed to have been written by the French writer CHRETIEN DE TROYES around 1170, but it has never been found. The ending is missing from Gottfried's version, written some time between 1200 and 1210 (and apparently based loosely on a twelfth century French version).

But his treatment of the subject matter makes his version stand out. Gottfried does not stick to the traditional Arthurian formula of courtly love that characterizes so many romantic stories of the period. Instead, he manages to focus more on artistic, religious, and intellectual interpretations of love—which adds a rather different perspective to the legend.

GRATIAN

G ratian (d. c. 1159) was a twelfth-century Italian monk who became known as the "father of canon law." His works were so influential that they were studied as part of the traditional body of canon (Church) law until the early twentieth century.

Born in Tuscany at the end of the eleventh century, Gratian became a Benedictine monk and a teacher and lecturer at the monastery of Saints Felix and Nabor in Bologna. Around 1140, he completed a systematic compilation of canon law, his *Concordia discordantium canonum*, also known as the *Decretum Gratiana*. This collection of some 4,000 texts on Church discipline was not the first such compilation, but two things made Gratian's work stand out. First, it was the most comprehensive compilation to date, covering events and documents up to 1139. Second, Gratian combined the legal and scholarly intricacies of canon law in a way not done previously. Gratian took his influence from the scholars of civil law in Bologna (by then recognized as the center of legal studies in Europe) and the theologians of FRANCE.

Gratian continued to write and teach until his death. His work remained the standard text of canon law in all UNIVERSITIES until the Church completed a formal codification of canon law in 1917.

GREAT SCHISM

T he Great Schism was the crisis of the PAPACY that split western Christendom from 1378 until 1417. Conflicting views of the nature of the papacy lay at the heart of the crisis, which was also bound up with national and internecine power struggles. At stake were papal legitimacy and independence as well as huge sums in papal revenues.

By the time Pope Gregory XI permanently returned the Curia to ROME, the institution was widely perceived as the tool of French power. Such sentiments led FLORENCE and its allies to raise a revolt in the PAPAL STATES, and although Gregory arrived in a state formally pacified, hostilities continued. Gregory died in March 1378 without concluding a peace. The conclave to elect his successor opened in an atmosphere of mob violence, with unruly crowds demanding an Italian pope of the predominantly French College of Cardinals. The sixteen cardinals prudently decided on an Italian, the archbishop of Bari, a veteran of the Curia. The new pope, URBAN VI, was duly crowned and formally presented to the six cardinals who had remained in AVIGNON and to the European heads of state.

Avignon. During the years in Avignon, the cardinals had come truly to function as princes of the Church; Urban refused to go to Avignon and also swiftly and unexpectedly served notice that he intended to assert the primacy of the pope and reform the Church, assailing luxury and corruption among the cardinals. So harsh and uncompromising was he that the cardinals (led by the French), casting doubt on his mental balance, soon deserted him and formally declared his election to have been coerced. In September, they chose a new pope—a relative of the French king, styled Clement VII. His election threw the Church into turmoil. Forced from ITALY, Clement took up residence in Avignon, and all of Europe then chose sides. Some took the opportunity to encroach on papal prerogatives and revenues.

Successors were chosen for Urban and Clement in turn, but not until the 1390s did it become politically as well as spiritually expedient to end the crisis. The French court then proposed the voluntary abdication of both popes, so that a candidate acceptable to all could be chosen; when Urban's successor Boniface IX and Clement's successor Benedict XIII declined to cooperate, the French sought to compel them by "subtraction of obedience." Aligning these European rulers of behind this policy took several years to accomplish.

Resolution. In 1408, the French made a last attempt to persuade Benedict and Gregory XII (latest of the Roman line) to abdicate; when this failed, they managed the merger of the two Colleges of Cardinals. This body summoned the COUNCIL OF PISA (March 1409). Invoking the theory of conciliarism, which set the authority of a general council of the Church above even that of the pope, the council chose a new, "Pisan" pope, Alexander V, and formally deposed the obdurate Benedict and Gregory. Yet Alexander's short reign (June 1409–May 1410) and the turpitude of his successor, (antipope) John XXIII left the Church with three popes instead of one, since each of the deposed popes retained some support. This clearly untenable situation was finally resolved at the COUNCIL OF CONSTANCE (1414–1417), which deposed the Avignon and Pisan popes, accepted the abdication of the Roman pope, and in November 1417, elected Pope Martin V, who finally could claim universal obedience.

The result of the schism was a weakened papacy. Conciliarism became official Church doctrine, much spiritual prestige was irretrievably lost, and the European powers retained many of the concessions they had gained over almost 40 years of disarray.

For more information on the Great Schism, see CHRISTIANITY; ROME; AVIGNON; FRANCE; FLORENCE; ITALY; PAPACY; PAPAL STATES; FREDERICK II; URBAN VI; *and* COUNCIL OF PISA.

GREENLAND

Greenland may have been known to the Greeks and later the Irish, but it was not colonized until Norsemen, mostly Icelanders under the leadership of Eric the Red, settled there about 982. Eric named it "Greenland" in order to make it sound more attractive to potential settlers. It was while sailing from NORWAY to Greenland in about 1000 that Leif Ericsson, son of Erik the Red, reached NORTH AMERICA after being blown off course. (*See* EXPLORATION.)

The Norse set up two main settlements on Greenland: an eastern settlement and western settlement in the vicinity of modern Godthaab. After the Norsemen brought CHRISTIANITY to Greenland and it was accepted at an early stage, the eastern settlement became the home of the cathedral at Gardar, an Augustinian monastery, a Benedictine nunnery, and a dozen parish churches, the ruins of some of which can still be seen today. By 1126, Greenland had its own bishopric and a population of about 3,000.

Although Greenland achieved self-rule and governed itself through its assembly, called an Althing, it had difficulty maintaining political stability. Thus, Greenland's self-rule ended in 1261 when the colony accepted Norwegian sovereignty. However, the colony floundered with shifting climatic conditions forcing the Eskimos south, threatening the Norse settlements.

By the 1300s and 1400s, Norway's interest in the colony waned. The western settlement collapsed completely in the mid-1300s, and communication with Norway became more intermittent. Although some survivors lingered on well into the late 1400s, they either died out or assimilated with the Eskimos. When the English explorers Martin Frobisher and John Davis came upon Greenland in the 1500s, they found no evidence of the colonists. (*See* NORWAY; DENMARK.)

The end of the Norse colonization of Greenland—one of the most impressive colonial efforts of the medieval period—was brought about by a combination of colder temperatures, Eskimo attacks, and Norwegian neglect. (*See* VIKINGS; SAGAS, ICELANDIC.)

GREGORIAN CHANT

Gregorian chant, also called plainsong or plainchant, was first sung in early medieval churches in western Europe. Although much of the MUSIC did not survive past the Middle Ages, some of it can still be heard today—for example as the liturgical music used in the Roman Catholic Church.

Legend has it that Gregorian chant was given (as divine inspiration from the Holy Spirit) to Pope GREGORY I THE GREAT during his reign in the late sixth century. It is characterized by marked simplicity—only one melodic line, unlike the richly polyphonic church music that emerged in the late Middle Ages.

In the early Middle Ages, the Church had five liturgies, or prescribed public worship ceremonies: the Ambrosian, Celtic, Gallican, Mozarabic, and Roman. Only the Ambrosian (which exists primarily in Milan) and Roman still exist. Gregorian chant was, and still is, used in the Roman Catholic mass, including the *Introit, Alleluia, Offertory, Kyrie Eleison, Gloria in Excelsis, Credo, Sanctus,* and *Agnus Dei.* It was also used in the liturgy of the Divine Office (continuous prayer services for nuns, monks, and clergy), which did not continue after the Middle Ages. Many of the chants are meant to be sung every day, but a number are reserved for specific days and services. (*See* CHURCHES.)

By the eleventh century, churchgoers were beginning to develop a taste for more varied music. Gradually, more complex melodies emerged, and by the end of the Middle Ages virtually all of the music being written for the church was polyphonic. (*See* MUSIC.)

GREGORY I THE GREAT

Saint Gregory I (540–604) was one of the most influential popes of the early Middle Ages. He earned a reputation as both a strong administrator and a prolific writer. Originally a monk, he devoted much of his time to promoting the monastic life.

Early Life. Born into a wealthy family in ROME, Gregory was given a classical education; he may have studied law as well. Upon completing his education he became a government official in Rome, but after a year he gave up his position to become a monk. Over the next several years, he founded six monasteries in SICILY on property belonging to his family; he also founded one in Rome. He became a deacon and was named papal ambassador to CONSTANTINOPLE by Pope Pelagius II. After seven years in Constantinople, he returned to his monastery in Rome.

The Papacy. In 590, Gregory was chosen as the new pope. ITALY had been ravaged by famine, floods, disease, and invasions from the neighboring LOMBARDS. Gregory spent much of his time helping the poor and dispossessed and preaching the importance of monasticism. He provided better educational opportunities for his clergy and sent monks (including Saint Augustine of Canterbury) to the British Isles to convert the ANGLO–SAXONS to CHRISTIANITY. He also initiated a peace with the Lombards. (*See* PAPACY.)

Gregory sent missionaries to heathen ENGLAND to forestall conversion by independent Irish missionaries and brought England into the Latin Church, an accomplishment memorialized in the tax sometimes

GREGORY VII

Pope Gregory I the Great, in a miniature from a 12th-century edition of his Moralia (Morals of the Book of Job).

levied on the English clergy in later centuries, called Peter's Pence. He gave the PAPACY a new-found dignity and visibility. His voluminous writings reveal a man who was an unusual combination of bureaucrat, pastoral leader, monastic devotee, and visionary.

His Legacy. Gregory was the most important pope before the eleventh century. He is regarded as the last of the Latin Church fathers and he profoundly shaped the penitential system of the Latin Church in the form that essentially survives—contrition, confession to a priest, decreeing of penance, and absolution. While remaining on peaceful if tense terms with the Byzantine emperor, he worked to establish an alliance with the French monarchy, a policy that was consummated in the eighth century. He made the Benedictine form of monasticism the preferred form of religious life in the Latin Church. He fostered the development of the Roman liturgy and its musical form that appropriately came to be called GREGORIAN CHANT.

Gregory's writings include the *Cura Pastoralis* (*Pastoral Care*), written for the clergy, and a book on Italian saints. He also compiled collections of sermons and commentaries on the Bible. He wrote letters constantly; nearly 900 survive.

P ope Gregory VII (1020–1085) is best known as the pope who excommunicated the German emperor HENRY IV. His strong stance against the emperor led to a symbolic victory for the Church that strengthened the PAPACY considerably during the twelfth and thirteenth centuries.

Originally named Hildebrand, Gregory was born in Tuscany around 1020. He went to ROME, where he became a monk and proceeded to serve six popes, beginning with Gregory VI. In 1073, Hildebrand was named pope and took the name of Gregory VII.

The Papacy. Gregory was a reformer, but he believed strongly that the pope, as head of the Church, deserved allegiance from heads of state, even kings and emperors. He outlined his strong belief in the supreme authority of the papacy in his *Dictatus papae* in 1075.

Gregory's trouble with Henry IV began when he complained to the emperor about his favored choice for bishop of Milan. Henry decided to punish the pope for his impertinence. He convened a council of German bishops who deposed Gregory. Gregory, in turn, excommunicated Henry and asked the German nobles to choose a new emperor. Henry decided to ask for the pope's forgiveness and traveled across the Alps in the winter of 1077 to Canossa, a small castle where Gregory was staying. Henry allegedly made penance by standing outside the castle door for three days before Gregory was forced, by the ecclesiastical practice of the day, to meet with him and grant his forgiveness. The German nobles, formerly Gregory's allies, now had no legal basis to oppose Henry. The pope had lost the upper hand in Germany and had lost face there in the process. Gregory attempted to mediate the disputes between Henry and the nobles, but Henry refused. Gregory then attempted to excommunicate Henry again, but the attempt was ineffective. In response, Henry invaded Italy, appointed Clement III antipope, and attacked Rome in 1081. When a third excommunication of Henry failed in 1084, Gregory was forced to flee Rome and seek refuge in Salerno, where he died the following year. (*See* INVESTITURE CONTROVERSY.)

A Revolutionary. Gregory VII is regarded as one of the three greatest popes of medieval Europe, along with GREGORY I and INNOCENT III. He was resented not only by the German royal family but also by most of the German bishops. His efforts at unification of the Church under a centralized papal power and his attempted demotion of kingship to a dependency on Rome was also questioned by many of the prominent clergy in FRANCE and ENGLAND. One of his closest associates, Cardinal PETER DAMIAN, called Gregory "the holy satan." Many learned and experienced bishops and abbots thought that even if Gregory's ideology was defensible in theory, his conflict with kings was dangerous to the well-being of the Church and the stability of society. That Gregory at times expressed sympathy for the poor against the rich and powerful raised concern among the nobility. Gregory's family had a close relationship with a rich family of Jewish converts in Rome and rumors spread that he himself was a Jewish convert and thus untrustworthy. There is no doubt that Gregory had the temperament and zeal of a revolutionary ideologue. His last words were, "I have loved truth and justice; therefore I die in exile."

Effects. Gregory's reform movement and his tempestuous pontifical reign had a marked impact on the medieval world. He greatly strengthened the papal administration and set up the system of papal legates in each country that still prevails. Borrowing ideas from another one of his close associates, Cardinal Humbert, he insisted that the election of the pope be vested exclusively in the College of Cardinals, where it remains today. He promoted a policy of clerical celibacy for the first time, claiming that priests and bishops were already married to the embodiment of the Holy Spirit in the Church, and set the Church on the road to creation of an unmarried priesthood and episcopate by 1500. Gregory authorized the beginning of the codification of the canon law, and it was he who conceived the idea of a crusade against the Muslims.

Gregory was an immensely complicated, combative, and idealistic leader. But his behavior also represented an effort to apply to the organization of the Church the consequences of two great cultural movements of the eleventh century: the New Piety, a much more intense and sentimental religious sensibility, and the New Learning, especially in the rediscovery of Roman law. Facing bitter opposition on all sides and the increasing materialism of European society, his effort to create an Augustinian City of God on earth was bound to fall well short of realization, making his accomplishments all the more amazing. He is one of the great, bold personages of European history, and the Catholic Church as it exists today is in many respects his monument. (*See* PAPACY; CHRISTIANITY.)

GREGORY IX

T he influential but volatile pope Gregory IX (c. 1145–1241) circulated the *Decretals,* the canon law code that remained an important church document until the early twentieth century. He was also the founder of the papal INQUISITION and a fierce foe of the Holy Roman Emperor FREDERICK II.

Born Ugo di Segni around 1170, he was a nephew of Pope INNOCENT III. He studied theology at the University of Paris and became a canon lawyer. He

served as a papal legate for Innocent and his successor, Honorius III. In March 1227, di Segni ascended to the PAPACY as Gregory IX. (*See* FREDERICK II; PAPACY.)

Gregory was sincere, but he was also quick-tempered and unyielding. Impatient with Frederick II's delays in carrying out the CRUSADES, and suspicious of his motives, Gregory excommunicated the emperor in September 1227. This led to a series of attacks, both verbal and military, throughout Gregory's reign. In 1231, Gregory formalized the investigation of alleged heretics by the Church, which officially marked the beginning of the Inquisition. (*See* INQUISITION.)

GREGORY OF TOURS, ST.

T he fame of Gregory of Tours (c. 538–594) rests not on his career as a bishop but on his chronicles of life in MEROVINGIAN FRANCE. His writings, particularly the *Historia Francorum,* provide a lively and often blunt view of the way nobles, the clergy, and ordinary individuals went about their lives at a time of social and political upheaval.

Early Life. Gregory, born Georgius Florentius, was born in the town of Avernus, in Gaul (present-day France). His aristocratic family included a number of bishops, one of whom was bishop of Tours. When this relative died in 573, Florentius assumed his position, taking the name "Gregory" to honor an uncle who had been bishop many years before.

Most of France at the time was ruled by the Merovingians, a Frankish dynasty that had captured the land a century earlier. Merovingian family disputes had split the region into three kingdoms, which often fought each other in the hopes of taking control of more land. Tours was a frequent target of such takeover attempts, and the city changed hands more than once during Gregory's tenure.

His Work. Gregory compiled a historical chronicle of life under the FRANKS. The result was his *Historia Francorum* (*The History of the Franks*), written in three parts between 575 and 591.

What makes the *Historia* stand out is not only its detail, but its engaging literary style. Gregory provided vivid descriptions of daily life, political turmoil, battles, culture, and education. Gregory wrote in Latin, and while his writing was lively, he was a notoriously poor grammarian. Latin requires strict adherence to certain rules in forming the parts of speech, and Gregory, despite his talents, never mastered these. He himself thought that his writing was below par and often tried to adorn it with lofty classical quotations. But Gregory had the ability to make events come alive through his writing—a skill that transcends form. Most historical chronicles of Gregory's time were dry and dull; they merely recorded dates and facts. But even when Gregory's grammar was questionable, his books were never boring. (*See* LATIN LANGUAGE.)

For all his sloppy grammar, Gregory paid close attention to historic detail. He mentions, for example, a battle between the Franks and the Scandinavians that had taken place in 520. This battle is mentioned in the epic English poem BEOWULF; it is the only corroborated historical event in the poem.

Gregory's other famous work is his book on the lives of the saints, which his mother encouraged him to write. Gregory's inspiration for the book came in part from the fact that Tours holds the remains of Saint Martin, a former bishop of Tours himself and a legendary worker of miracles. Gregory wrote about Saint Martin and a number of other saints, as well as several books of miracles. (*See* CHRONICLES.)

Gregory continued to write until his death in Tours in 594. His works served as the models for later writers throughout the Middle Ages. (*See* LITERATURE.)

GROOTE, GERHARD

Gerhard Groote (also known as Gerardus Magnus; 1340–1384) was the driving force behind the teaching order known as the BRETHREN OF THE COMMON LIFE. The Brethren were influential in elementary and secondary education throughout Europe for more than 400 years.

Born into a wealthy family in the Dutch town of Deventer, Groote studied theology in PARIS and later received money from the Cologne Cathedral in recognition of a diplomatic mission he made to AVIGNON (then the seat of the Catholic Church). He lived a life of ease, but in his thirties he underwent a spiritual conversion; he renounced worldly goods and devoted himself to meditation. He also helped the religious scholar Florentius Radewyns establish a residence for poor scholars, where they earned a living copying manuscripts. Out of this effort grew the Brethren, which was officially recognized as an order by Pope Gregory XI.

Groote later gained a large following as an activist preacher. He died of the BLACK DEATH in 1384.

GROSSETESTE, ROBERT

Robert Grosseteste (1168–1253) was a thirteenth–century English bishop who distinguished himself as a scholar and translator. Traditionally considered to have been the first chancellor of Oxford University, his writings cover theology, PHILOSOPHY, and SCIENCE.

Born in Suffolk, Grosseteste served in his youth as a clerk for the bishops of Lincoln and Hereford. He received a degree in theology from Cambridge University and began teaching at Oxford. He was named bishop of Lincoln in 1235 by king HENRY III, whom he served as a tutor, and remained there for the remainder of his life.

Grosseteste translated a number of important Greek texts into Latin, including several of Aristotle's works. He helped popularize ARISTOTLE but he was also influenced by Plato. He also wrote a number of works based on his own scientific observations and mathematical calculations; he conducted experiments in optics and is regarded as the founder of experimental science. (*See* SCIENCE IN THE MIDDLE AGES.)

In addition to his scholarship, he was also an active Church leader who worked to implement reforms during his tenure as bishop. Although not a member of the newly established FRANCISCAN ORDER in ENGLAND, he was closely associated with the FRIARS and served as their protector.

GUELPH

The term refers to the one of two parties in a struggle for power that pervaded Italian political life from around 1200 to the mid-1300s. The Guelphs (from the German "Welf") supported the Church and the authority of the pope; the GHIBELLINES supported the Holy Roman Emperor. At times, attempts were made to make the struggle an ideological or religious one: DANTE ALIGHERI and MARSILIUS OF PADUA argued that the emperor was the ideological savior of ITALY, while the Church accused its enemies of HERESY in an attempt to turn a political struggle into a religious one. Usually, the objective was simply political advantage, and the struggle between rival clans, cities, provinces, and seats of power.

The Guelph-Ghibelline conflict began during the reign of FREDERICK I BARBAROSSA when he attempted to restore imperial authority in northern Italy by force. The conflict reached its greatest intensity in FLORENCE as factions supporting FREDERICK II (Ghibellines) and Pope Innocent IV (Guelphs) in the 1240s fought one

LIFE IN THE MIDDLE AGES

From Welf and Waiblingen

The Guelph-Ghibelline conflict could also be seen as a struggle between two families of German emperors: the Welfs of Saxony, house of Otto IV, and the Hohenstaufens of Swabia.

The symbol of the Italian Guelphs was the eagle used in the coat of arms of the House of Saxony. As for "Ghibelline" it is derived from the name of the Hohenstaufen castle in Swabia, Waiblingen, which became the family and the party's battle cry.

another, sometimes in the streets. The issue was settled with the decisive victories of Guelph forces led by CHARLES OF ANJOU at Benevento in 1266 and of the ANGEVINS of NAPLES at Tagliacozzo in 1268. Yet, the terms remained in use for another century to describe conflicts between factions, rulers, and cities. Thus, Guelph MILAN battled Ghibelline Cremona for control of western Lombardy; Guelph Padua sought to maintain its independence from the Ghibelline lord Ezzelino da Romano; in Tuscany, Guelph FLORENCE vied with Ghibelline Siena and PISA. (*See* GHIBELLINE.)

The COMMUNES of Italy suffered from this conflict, creating tensions between and within cities that would have benefitted from a more cooperative environment. When power transferred from the emperor to the popular governments of the communes to the signori (despots who ruled the cities of northern Italy), the warfare between the greatest of the signori, the Visconti of Milan, and their opponents, the AVIGNON popes and Florence, was the fourteenth century version of the Guelph-Ghibelline conflict.

GUILDS

The corporations of artisans, craftsmen, merchants, and other professionals that furthered the interests of their members. The origin of the guilds goes back to Roman times when the state instituted standards for weights and measures and for the quality of work done by craftspeople. The government was particularly watchful of food merchants and providers, controlling those areas of commerce strictly in times of famine. In this period, guilds served mainly as representatives to the authorities. The practice continued into Byzantine times.

European Origins. In the eleventh and twelfth century, guilds formed in western Europe not as state-controlled groups, but as self-governing organizations. Their ostensible reason for forming was to ensure standards, but they also devoted much attention to restricting competition, particularly from foreign sources. (*See* COMMERCE AND TRADE.)

Guild members tended to congregate in specific areas of the town (to create a market; to avail themselves of support services; to keep an eye on one another), which made the guild responsible for civic life in their quarter or district. The guilds were thus important in the development of independent town government during the late Middle Ages.

The guilds established an apprentice system in which "masters" would train young people (usually from the family of members) in a trade in return for their free servitude. Guilds were generally of two kinds: aristocratic, for merchants, professionals (like lawyers and doctors), and certain highly-trained artisan (like goldsmiths and tanners); and plebeian, for other (mostly semi-skilled) craftspeople. The aristocratic guilds often sought political power and controlled many civic governments to the exclusion of the plebian guilds. This often led to open rebellion and rioting (like the English PEASANTS' REVOLT of 1381), prompting periodic changes in municipal constitutions aimed at curbing the power of the aristocratic guild, as in fourteenth century Europe—or else the seizure of power by tyrants like the signori in ITALY. Several monarchs felt threatened by the guilds (who were always in lock step with the wealthy nobility) and some, like FREDERICK II in 1219, tried unsuccessfully to ban guilds from his empire.

The biggest challenge to the guilds, however, was posed by the sudden collapse of Europe's economy and the feudalistic system, caused by the severe shortage of workers (and consumers) that resulted from the BLACK DEATH of the 1340s.

Social Aspects. Guilds became social and religious organizations, adopting patron saints, leading processions, and conducting festivals (which were also good for business). The guild-hall became a center of social activities in many towns and provided the social welfare services to its members and to traveling guild members of other towns. (*See* FAIRS; TOWNS.)

The guilds of Italy provided an assurance of standards and fairness. Above, a roster of guilds of Pisa with their respective emblems.

GUTENBERG, JOHANNES

Johannes Gutenberg (c.1400–1468) is often credited with having invented the printing press, but his real accomplishment was the development of a system of movable type cast in molds that made the mass printing of documents and books feasible and practical.

Early Life. Born in Mainz, GERMANY, Gutenberg's full name was Johannes Gensfleich zur Laden zur Gutenberg; he adopted as his last name the name of the house in which his family lived. In 1428 he moved to Strasbourg and became involved in the jewelry and metalwork business, but also in several lawsuits involving debts he had incurred developing his business of manufacturing "pilgrim badges,"

Top, a 16th-century engraving of Gutenberg. Above, the 42-line Mazarin Bible, produced by Gutenberg and Fust in Mainz between 1452 and 1456 on the printing press (right) Gutenberg had developed, originally to print classical works that were no longer being copied by hand.

artifacts purchased by pilgrims as mementos and proof of their journey.

Career. Gutenberg was reputed to be a highly skilled craftsman and goldsmith, which would have been important in his development of methods for casting soft lead into printing type. Gutenberg developed his system—a press adapted from one used by binders; a machine for creating type forms; and a formula for ink—in secret, since he had several creditors who would have either disapproved of his use of their funds, or confiscated his invention as payment.

Return to Mainz. Gutenberg returned to his home town sometime between 1444 and 1448, his

printing system having reached a considerable degree of refinement. He established a partnership with the financier Johann Fust for the purpose of printing an edition of the Bible. Fust grew impatient as Gutenberg experimented with inks and methods of recreating the illuminations that had adorned manuscripts. In 1455 Fust called his loan and confiscated Gutenberg's machinery and the first printings of the BIBLE—the famed 42-line Bible that was Gutenberg's masterpiece and his first publication.

Fust then joined forces with Gutenberg's skilled assistant Peter Schöffer (who had testified against him in court) to print (from type created by Gutenberg) the Psalter, a book of prayers with hundreds of ingeniously produced polychrome initial letters and designs that clearly bear the stamp of Gutenberg's genius. The book, however, the first to bear the name of the printer, lists Fust and Schöffer as its creators.

Later Years. Gutenberg's last years were spent trying to regain his leadership in printing, an effort that was made difficult by his failing eyesight (he may have even gone blind). Gutenberg printed other editions of the 42-line Bible, including a 36-line Bible printed in Bamberg, as well as other works, though many were either experimental or completed by other printers

using Gutenberg's equipment or his techniques. The archbishop of Mainz provided Gutenberg with a modest pension on which he lived until his death in 1468.

See BIBLE IN THE MIDDLE AGES; BOOKS; CHRISTIANITY; HANDWRITING, CALLIGRAPHY, AND WRITING TOOLS; *and* MANUSCRIPT ILLUMINATION. *Also* WILLIAM CAXTON; LITERATURE; LIBRARIES; *and* LITERACY.

GUY DE LUSIGNAN

Guy de Lusignan (1129–1194) was briefly the king of the Christian kingdom of Jerusalem and, after his loss of that crown, became king of Cyprus and began the long rule of the house of Lusignan over that island. In 1180, Guy married Sibylla, the widowed heiress of the kingdom of Jerusalem, and thereby became the next to line to the throne after Baldwin, the young son of Sibylla from her first marriage. In 1183, Guy de Lusignan became regent for Baldwin. His regency was marked by defeats at the hands of the Muslim leader SALADIN. While he was officially removed from the line of succession, Guy was still able to obtain the crown of Jerusalem in 1186, after the death of Baldwin. Guy's reign started to unravel after the death of his wife Sibylla when CONRAD OF MONTFERRAT married Isabella, Sibylla's sister, and claimed the throne. In 1192, Guy was forced from power, despite the initial support of RICHARD I LION-HEART, king of ENGLAND. Following that defeat, Guy bought the island of Cyprus from the crusading order the Templars and reigned as king of Cyprus for the last two years of his life.

GWYNEDD

A kingdom in northwestern WALES whose kings achieved preeminence in the early Middle Ages. It went on to become a focus of resistance against NORMAN and English rule.

As early as the 500s, Gwynedd—which included the island of Anglesey—had kings mentioned as more prominent than the other kings of Wales. Records suggest the kings of Gwynedd succeeded in making deep inroads into Britain in the 600s. A tombstone on Anglesey commemorated King Cadfan in the mid-700s as "the wisest and most renowned king of all." By the 800s, Gwynedd ruled the Welsh kingdoms of Powys and Ceredifion. (See WALES.)

After the Norman Conquest of ENGLAND, Gwynedd became the center of Welsh resistance to English and Norman rule. Although the border region and southern Wales were controlled by English lords, the princes of Gwynedd, especially Owain Gwynedd, achieved a fair degree of independence.

In the early 1200s, Llywelyn the Great solidified his authority in Wales (especially northern Wales) while paying homage to the English crown. The status of his grandson LLYWELYN AP GRUFFYD became even stronger when the treaty of Montgomery with the English (1267) affirmed his position as prince of Wales with feudal supremacy over "all the Welsh barons of Wales." During the reign of King EDWARD I, the Welsh struggle for independence slackened—particularly after the death of Llywelyn ap Gruffyd in 1283. Wales never again came as close to independence, although Welsh princes, especially OWAIN GLYN DWR continued to rebel against English rule. Welsh resistance ended in 1485 when Henry VII became king of England. (See ENGLAND; LLYWELYN AP GRUFFYD; OWAIN GLYN DWR.)

GYPSIES

The nomadic people known as the Gypsies had their origins in India, but by the late Middle Ages they had migrated and could be found throughout Europe. Because they were constantly on the move, Gypsies were hard to keep track of, but most seem to have congregated in southeastern Europe.

The word "gypsy" originates from a legend that the wanderers were originally Egyptian nobles who had been driven from their homeland by Muslim forces. Gypsies refer to themselves as Rom or Romani, from the Sanskrit word for man.

The Gypsies migrated from India to Persia, and from there to Greece, where they arrived early in the fourteenth century. They then made their way to the Balkan countries of eastern Europe, and gradually spread westward until eventually they could be found in Britain. They supported themselves by taking odd-jobs, usually as metalworkers. Many Gypsies entertained for money, some as musicians, others as fortune-tellers. Due to their apparent lack of roots and their connection to fortune-telling, Gypsies earned a reputation for possessing supernatural powers.

All of these factors served to instill in people a fear or dislike of Gypsies. Inhabitants of small European villages were leery of these itinerant people who set up temporary campsites and who seemed to have no desire to assimilate with those around them. Incidents of Gypsies committing theft and other crimes to maintain their way of life were exaggerated, giving rise to the canard that they were dishonest and untrustworthy. Many communities banned Gypsies from camping even briefly, ironically forcing them them to engage more in the behavior that so many found offensive.

At the same time, Gypsies were considered skilled craftspeople. Gypsy metalworkers were so highly regarded that people saved broken utensils in hopes that a Gypsy group would soon pass by. Gypsies also had a keen understanding of animals, and Gypsy livestock dealers were considered among the most knowledgeable in matters of animal husbandry.

Henry VIII threatened to expel Gypsies from England unless they became farmers, but the Gypsies bore the persecution and continued to live as they had.

HABSBURG DYNASTY

German dynasty that attained the imperial crown in 1273 and held it, as Holy Roman Emperors or emperors-elect, for much of the next six centuries (1438 to 1816, except for a five-year period in the eighteenth century). Their name comes from the family's seat, Habichtsburg (Hawk's Castle), which overlooks the Aare River in modern SWITZERLAND. The Habsburgs (also Hapsburg) ruled AUSTRIA from 1282 until the dissolution of the Austro-Hungarian empire in the early twentieth century. Thus they have also been called the House of Austria, though their territories extended far beyond Austria's borders.

Early History. In the late Middle Ages, the dynasty attempted to legitimate their imperial claims by tracing their ancestry back to Julius Caesar. The first historically documented member of the family, however, was Guntram the Rich, possibly the same Count Guntram who rebelled unsuccessfully against King OTTO I in 950. The family might thus be traced back further to the eighth-century dukes of Alsace. Guntram's son, Lanzelin, and grandson, Radbot, extended the family's estates in southern Alsace into Swabia. It was Radbot's brother (or brother-in-law) Werner who built the family castle in 1020; by the end of the century, the Habsburgs had gained more territories in Upper Alsace and northern Switzerland, and began using the Habsburg surname.

Rise to Power. Through faithful service to the kings of the HOHENSTAUFEN DYNASTY, the Habsburgs increased their influence and power in the twelfth century. The family was only temporarily weakened by the creation of a Habsburg-Laufenberg branch in 1232. By the middle of the century they were one of the most powerful families in Germany. Rudolf, son of Albert IV and godson of Emperor FREDERICK II, was the family's most prominent member. Rudolf acquired the territories of Turgau, Aargau, and Zurichgau, bought back most of the fiefdoms from the Laufenburg branch, and recovered for the family Fribourg, Laufen, and Grasburg, as well as the seignorial protectorate of St. Gall.

The German nobility elected Rudolf emperor in 1273, thereby ending the Great Interregnum. The election was disputed by Ottokar II of BOHEMIA, who had seized the throne in 1251; Rudolf defeated him in battle at Marchfield in 1278, sealing his claim to the duchies of Austria and Styria. Rudolf enfeoffed his sons Albert and Rudolf II in 1282 with the new duchies, by which he officially began 636 years of Habsburg rule in Austria. These new duchies became the future territorial foundation of the Habsburg dynasty.

This territorial expansion was partially offset by the gradual loss of much of the family's Swiss estates after Rudolf's death in 1291, hastened by the revolt of the forest cantons. The reign of Rudolf I's son, King ALBERT I, was opposed by the German princes, and he was murdered in 1308. Albert's son, Leopold, was defeated by the Swiss at Morgarten in 1315; his other son, Frederick the Fair, was defeated by Louis the Bavarian in 1322, forfeiting the German crown, which was not recaptured by the Habsburgs until 1438.

Relocation. During the early fourteenth century, the family was challenged by the powerful Swiss and Swabian dynasties, who were supported by the Luxembourg and Wittelsbach kings of Germany. By 1415, the Habsburgs had even lost the territory in Aargau which had originally given them their family name. In light of these disappointments, in the middle of the thirteenth century, the Habsburgs began to identify themselves only with their Austrian holdings, and moved their capital to Vienna. Failing to maintain the imperial crown, they extended their territories beyond the eastern Alps. Through marriages, inheritances, and annexations, the Habsburgs laid claim to Carinthia and Carniola in 1335, Tyrol in 1363, parts of Istria in 1374, Vorarlberg in 1376, and Trieste in 1382.

Internal Struggles. These newly acquired territories led to internal tensions after Albert I's death. Rudolf IV (1358–1365), known for his founding of the University of Vienna and his reconstruction of St. Stephen's Church, became head of the house and, convinced of his family's rightful place as Germany's royal dynasty, forged documents giving the Habsburgs the privilege to participate in the election of future German kings. At his death, his brothers Albert III and Leopold III agreed to divide the kingdom between them. From the Treaty of Neuberg (1379), Albert received Austria and the areas to the east, and Leopold inherited Carinthia and the territories to the west.

More dynastic squabbles followed in the fifteenth century, though most of the land eventually reverted back into the control of the Leopoldine Emperor Frederick III. The Albertine line of the family ended with the death of Albert III's grandson Ladislas Posthumus in 1457, who had served as king of HUNGARY and BOHEMIA. The Leopoldine line continued, however, and eventually restored the family to its past glory. Leopold III's son, Frederick V, was crowned Holy Roman Emperor in 1452 as Frederick III, the last emperor to be crowned in Rome. After him, a Habsburg remained on the imperial throne until Charles VI's accession in 1711.

Future Glory. One would not have guessed the future grandeur of the House, however, from the many disappointments of Frederick's reign. The Bohemian and Hungarian kingdoms were lost for nearly 70 years, and much of the Austrian domains were threatened by infighting and aggressive Hungarian neighbors. But Frederick seemed to have an uncanny sense of his family's destiny; he ratified the honorific "archduke of Austria" for the Habsburg family, and one of his mottos, "A.E.I.O.U.," was taken to stand for *Austriae est imperare orbi universo*—"Austria is destined to rule the world" (or *Alles Erdreich ist Osterreich untertan*—"The whole world is subject to Austria"). He also gave his name to the "Habsburg lip," a physiognomic prominence inherited by future Habsburg kings.

Frederick witnessed the beginning of the Habsburg revival in 1477 with the arranged marriage (one of the most significant in European history) of his son MAXIMILIAN to Mary of Burgundy. The marriage acquired for the family Burgundian territories in the Low Countries and vast estates in Eastern France. Thus, when Maximilian came to the imperial throne, he ruled over an extensive kingdom, which he expanded to include territories in eastern and western Germany, Italy, and Spain. That kingdom was again expanded when in 1496 Maximilian's son, Philip I married Joan (the Mad), who inherited Castile and Aragon from her parents, Isabella and Ferdinand. The marriage also secured for Philip Spain's domains in Naples-Sicily, and the vast territories in the New World that would soon be Spain's. (*See* ALBERT I.)

HAFIZ

Hafiz (c.1320–1390) was the pen name of Shams al-Din Muhammad, also known as Hafiz Shirazi after his native city, Shiraz, in modern Iran. He was the greatest master of the Persian *ghazal*, a lyric poem ten to thirty lines long, that combines rich imagery and intense emotion. Hafiz's collected poems, the *Diwan*, is one of the masterpieces of medieval poetry, and was to influence such important western writers as Goethe and Emerson.

Hafiz was born to a poor family and was orphaned at an early age, yet he received a thorough Islamic education ("hafiz" is, in fact, a title bestowed on Muslims who have memorized the entire KORAN). Very little is known of his life. He was supported by royal patrons: first Abu Ishaq Inju (1342–1352); then Shah Shuja' (1358–1384). But unlike other poets supported by a patron, Hafiz devoted little space in his poems to praising his benefactor and concentrated on the lyricism and emotional content instead. This may have caused him difficulties with his patrons, but the universal acclaim his poetry received ultimately ensured his high position in the royal court.

HAGIA SOPHIA

One of the most famous and enduring Byzantine structures, the Hagia Sophia is not only an impressive building but an engineering masterpiece. The building, which has housed Eastern Orthodox, Roman Catholic, and Muslim worshippers during its 1,500-year history, has outlasted two empires, withstood numerous battles, and survived a series of earthquakes.

Design and Construction. Located in CONSTANTINOPLE (now Istanbul), Hagia Sophia was designed by the architects Anthemius of Tralles and Isidorus of Miletus. The Roman emperor JUSTINIAN I commissioned the building on the site of a cathedral that had been destroyed during a revolt. Construction began in 532 and was finished by the end of 537—a remarkable achievement considering the structure's size.

Although it is often called the Church of St. Sophia, the term "Hagia Sophia" is actually Greek for "Holy Wisdom."

Justinian spared no expense on the new church. The interior of Hagia Sophia was sumptuously decorated with marble, MOSAIC, gold leaf, and precious metals. But its most impressive feature is the domed roof that rests atop the rectangular structure. The dome measures 100 by 106 feet and stands 184 feet high. Anthemius and Isidorus employed pendentives—spherical triangular members that fit into each corner of the building—to support the dome. The dome, with a ring of windows at its base to allow light from all angles, appears to float weightlessly. It is the second largest dome (the largest is atop the Pantheon in ROME) to survive from the Middle Ages.

Inside the building, columns of green marble separate the nave from the aisles, and many of the walls, arches, and vaults are covered in colored marble cut so that the veining of the slabs creates a pattern.

Later History. In 558, an earthquake damaged the structure. Repair and rebuilding began immediately; and was completed in 563.

Hagia Sophia served as an EASTERN ORTHODOX CHURCH until 1204, when it was converted into a Roman Catholic cathedral. In 1453, the OTTOMAN TURKS conquered Constantinople and transformed Hagia Sophia into a mosque. By then many of the original mosaics were gone, and the Ottomans covered the remaining ones. The most noteworthy addition by the Ottomans are the four minarets surrounding the building. During the 1840s, the Ottomans added a brownish-red stucco banding to the exterior.

After the Ottoman Empire was disbanded in 1918, the new secular Turkish government permitted the mosaics to be uncovered. Following an earthquake in 1935, the building was declared structurally unsound. Although it was closed to the public shortly thereafter and converted into a museum, some devout Muslims still manage to sneak inside to pray.

HANDWRITING, CALLIGRAPHY, AND WRITING TOOLS

During the Middle Ages, any written work, from the simplest letter to the most lavishly decorated BIBLE, was done by hand. The art of decorative handwriting, or calligraphy, flourished, and everyday script underwent many changes as more people became literate. (*See* LITERACY.)

Early Medieval Writing. Most writing in the early Middle Ages was done by scholars (usually clergy). Writing materials were generally in short supply and paper, made from the papyrus plant, became less readily available as Islamic conquests affected Mediterranean trade. Parchment, made from animal skins, became the most common writing surface in Europe, but it was not always easy to find. Often, scholars would erase the pages of entire books to retrieve the parchment for new writings. Faint remnants of the erased writing, known as palimpsest, have become important historical sources. (*See* KELLS, BOOK OF.)

Partly to save parchment, European handwriting underwent a major change with the development of lower-case letters, or minuscules. (Upper-case letters were known as majuscules.) Smaller letters meant that more words could be fit on a page. Use of majuscules was reserved for ceremonial books.

Scribes practiced intricate handwriting for works

requiring special decorations. Calligraphy was particularly important to Muslims, because ISLAM forbade the depiction of human or animal forms in religious works.

Later Developments. The increasing availability of paper made an enormous difference in the development of writing. The Chinese had long known how to make paper, and the skill was introduced into the Islamic world in the eighth century. BAGHDAD and DAMASCUS became major paper manufacturing centers; later, EGYPT and SPAIN produced paper. Europeans re-

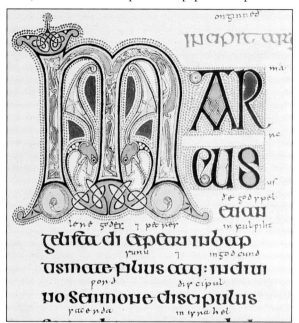

Opening page of the Book of Mark in the Lindisfarne Gospels, known as the Book of Durham, produced c. 698. In between the Latin text is a rough Anglo-Saxon translation.

lied less on parchment and more on paper, imported from Arab countries. Later, Europeans began to make their own paper. (*See* ARABIC LANGUAGE.)

As vernacular tongues replaced Latin in Europe, and as paper became readily available, more people began to write in everyday cursive rather than careful script. These early attempts at cursive writing planted the early seeds of modern western handwriting.

Writing implements were made from quills or reeds, and ink was made from lampblack, soot, tannin,

---

LEGEND AND LORE

The Great Calligrapher

Calligraphy, in addition to being a leading art form, took on spiritual and social significance in the Islamic world. Scribes who mastered Arabic script were deemed holy and held places of high stature in Islamic society. Allah was referred to as the Great Calligrapher. The reed pen was said to be one of his first creations, and his followers were portrayed as the pens with which Allah wrote history on the parchment of the world.

and other naturally available materials. Lead was also used (much as is used today in pencils). Calligraphers' pens, especially in Islamic lands, were themselves works of art, valued and cherished by their owners.

When the printing press was invented in the mid-fifteenth century, typefaces were designed based on decorative handwriting styles. In time, the styles once painstakingly crafted by calligraphers became standard typefaces, making them more readily available, but also spelling the end of calligraphy as a major art form. (*See* GUTENBERG, JOHANNES; CAXTON, WILLIAM.)

HANSEATIC LEAGUE

A late medieval association of northern German cities and towns, many of them communes. The league originated around 1250 and dominated trade in north GERMANY for hundreds of years. At its height, the league had 200 towns and membership varied considerably. Only 39 members, for example, were represented in the diet of 1447. As the cities of the League were dominated by merchant classes, its primary function was the promotion of trade and the trading interests of its members. The League dominated trade in a number of goods including grain, amber, timber, and furs.

The League was also a mutual defense partnership. The cities defended their political independence from the Germanic feudal aristocracy and the Scandinavian kings. The League also combated piracy and set commercial laws.

Early Years. In its early period, the League was governed at the local regional level. In 1356, a central diet began to meet regularly in order to frame general policy for the entire League. Lubeck was a major force in the league because it had been a founding member and the city had an advantageous location. Other important members were Visby, Wismar, Griefwald, Riga, Reval, and Danzig. The League was responsible for a number of important military triumphs, such as the defeat of the Danish king, Waldemar IV, a victory that lead to the Treaty of Straslund.

The strength of the League gained its members important trading privileges in major European cities. The merchants of the member towns had special offices or kontors, where they lived and traded—in LONDON, Bruges, NOVGOROD, and Berg in NORWAY.

Success. There were many reasons for the successes of the League. It dominated trade because of relatively better business practices and superior ships. The League exploited the weakness of the HOLY ROMAN EMPIRE, the central political entity in northern Europe, so that there was little organized opposition to the League's policies. The League could enforce its

will through the powerful weapon of the embargo, to which the neighboring Scandinavian kings were particularly vulnerable.

Decline. Trouble first arose for the League in the middle of the fourteenth century. The BLACK DEATH hurt commerce and dangers for shipping increased. Still, the League survived and remained strong. In the fifteenth century, competition from outside merchants began to undermine the trading power of the League. It declined, but continued to exist until 1669, when the last diet of the League met with but nine members. Ultimately, the medieval association of communes could not endure in the early modern world, now dominated by national monarchies. (*See* COMMERCE AND TRADE; GERMANY.)

One of the reasons for the success of the Hanseatic League was that merchants could rely on the support industries of transport and banking.

HAROLD II GODWINSON

H arold (1022–1066), earl of WESSEX and the most powerful lord in ENGLAND in his day, was the last ANGLO-SAXON king of England. He reigned briefly in 1066 before his defeat and death at the BATTLE OF HASTINGS.

Disputed Throne. Harold's election as king in January 1066, following the death of King EDWARD THE CONFESSOR, set the stage for the showdown that followed. On his deathbed Edward, who left no heirs, had named Harold as his successor, but William, duke of Normandy, claimed to be the rightful heir to the throne since he was Edward's cousin and claimed that Edward had designated him his successor years earlier.

Harold built fortifications along the English coast to defend against William's invasion, but in September the VIKINGS invaded northern England, forcing Harold to march his army north to fight the Viking threat. While Harold was winning a great victory against the Norwegian Viking king, Harald Hardrada, at Stamford Bridge in late September, William crossed the English Channel, landed unopposed on the English coast, and marched his army to Hastings.

After his victory, Harold marched his forces back south to Hastings, where the two armies clashed on October 14. The battle raged all day, but the repeated charges of the Norman cavalry and the arrows of the Norman archers gave William's troops the mobility and flexibility they needed to prevail over Harold's foot soldiers. Harold and his brothers were killed on the battlefield. Legends about Harold and the possibility that he survived the battle are evidence of his popularity.(*See* HASTINGS, BATTLE OF; ANGLO-SAXONS.)

HARUN AL-RASHID

The fifth ABBASID caliph, Harun (766–809) ruled the empire during its "golden age" from 786 to 809. In spite of the brilliance of his court in BAGHDAD, and the flowering of Islamic culture under his patronage, Harun's reign marked the turning point toward the decline of the Abbasids.

Early Life. The son of the third caliph, al-Mahdi, and a Yemenite slave girl, Harun was raised in the royal court in Baghdad, second in line to the throne after his older brother, Musa al-Hadi. Harun led two military expeditions against the Byzantines in 779 and 781 that brought the Abbasids to the shores of the Bosporos near CONSTANTINOPLE, in honor of which he was called *al-Rashid*—"one on the righteous path."

Musa became caliph upon the death of his father in 785, but died mysteriously the following year, the victim, it was rumored, of a plot by Harun's mother and his tutor, Yahya. Harun became the new caliph, but he turned over the administration of the empire to his sons and to Yahya's powerful family, the Barmecides. The Barmecides ruled effectively, encouraging the growth of industries, promoting trade with the East, and quelling the occasional rebellion in the outlying areas.

Great wealth flowed into the treasury of Baghdad and the court became the pleasure palace depicted in the *Thousand and One Nights* (in which a son of Yahya, Jaffar, appears as a character). Harun was a great patron of the arts and gave generously on his pilgrimages to Mecca, but the nightly reveling in the palace, his taking seven wives (three more than permitted by the KORAN), and his allowing graven images of animals and humans in the palace drove Muslims to repudiate Harun. After his death, the western provinces became virtually independent and the empire entered a long period of decline.

HASTINGS, BATTLE OF

The Battle of Hastings, fought on October 14, 1066, the decisive battle in the NORMAN conquest of ENGLAND, is the most famous battle in English history. The victory by WILLIAM I THE CONQUEROR brought an end to ANGLO-SAXON rule in England.

Claims to the Throne. The death of King EDWARD THE CONFESSOR, who left no heirs, in January 1066 set the stage for the showdown that followed. Among those who claimed the throne were the Anglo-Saxon earl HAROLD II GODWINSON and William, duke of Normandy. On his deathbed, Edward had named Harold as his successor and he was crowned shortly thereafter. However, William had reason to believe he was the rightful heir to the throne since he and Edward were cousins, and Edward may already have designated William as his successor years earlier. William also had the support of the pope and claimed that Harold had earlier sworn to support William's claim to the throne.

When news reached Normandy that Harold had been crowned king, William prepared to invade England. He spent months building up his army and constructing ships to transport them across the English Channel. In anticipation of the Norman invasion, Harold built fortifications along the English coast and waited. However, in September when the VIKINGS invaded northern England near York, Harold had to march his army north to fight off the threat. Harold's involvement in the north allowed William to cross the Channel in late September and land unopposed on the English coast. He then proceeded to march his forces to Hastings where they made camp.

After the Battle of Hastings, the relatives of the vanquished were permitted to carry their dead off the field of battle. Harold's body was taken to Waltham. William later established Battle Abbey (seen in the background) on the site.

A 14th-century depiction of the Battle of Hastings, showing the unlikely event of William's personally killing Harold; from the Decrees of the Kings of Anglo-Saxon and Norman England.

The battle raged all day, with the Anglo-Saxon troops at first holding their ground against Norman charges, using their shields to defend themselves against Norman thrusts and their battle-axes against Norman horses.

Between charges, the Norman archers fired volleys of arrows into the Anglo-Saxon ranks where the soldiers were packed closely together to withstand the Norman charges, and were thus easy targets. The repeated charges of the Norman cavalry, aided by the salvos of the archers, gave the Normans the additional mobility and flexibility necessary to prevail. During the course of the day Anglo-Saxon resistance gradually weakened until by late afternoon Harold and his brothers were dead and by evening the last of the Anglo-Saxon troops had fled.

William's victory at Hastings paved the way for his advance on LONDON, where his CORONATION in WESTMINSTER ABBEY on Christmas Day 1066 ushered in a dramatic new era of English history.

The Battle. After their victory over the Vikings in the north, Harold's army marched back to southern England, arriving at Hastings on October 13. The next day, the two armies clashed. The Anglo-Saxon army consisted of about 7,000 peasant foot soldiers wielding shields, swords, and battle-axes, while the Norman force, about the same size, consisted of archers and armored knights on horses. The Normans had an advantage over their opponents, who were weary from their 250-mile march to York and back.

See WAR AND WARFARE *and* ARMS AND ARMOR *for military background. See* WILLIAM I THE CONQUEROR, NORMANS, ANGLO-SAXONS, *and* HAROLD II GODWINSON *for the political content of the battle.*

HENRY I OF ENGLAND

Henry I (1068–1135), the third and youngest son of WILLIAM I THE CONQUEROR, outmaneuvered his older brothers to become king of ENGLAND in 1100 and ruled for 35 years.

William left Normandy to his oldest son, Robert II Curthose, and England to his next oldest son, William II Rufus (r. 1087–1100). He left Henry wealth, but no lands or power. Henry tried unsuccessfully to establish a base for himself in FRANCE. During the reign of William Rufus, Henry generally sided with him against their oldest brother Robert, but in 1100, William Rufus died; while William was hunting with Henry, a member of the hunting party, Walter Tirel (possibly acting under Henry's orders), shot an arrow that killed the king. Henry immediately went to Winchester and seized the royal treasury; three days later he had himself crowned king. Tirel was not punished for his faulty marksmanship but was instead given a reward. Henry's marriage soon afterward to Matilda of SCOTLAND, who was of ANGLO-SAXON royal heritage, helped him win the support of the English.

Robert, who also claimed William Rufus's crown, returned to Normandy from a crusade and invaded England in 1101. The brothers reached a peaceful agreement that allowed Henry to remain king of England, in return for giving up any claims to Normandy. Henry did not keep his promise, however. Four years later he invaded Normandy and defeated his brother in battle, thus uniting Normandy and England. He imprisoned his brother in a castle in England where he remained for the next 28 years. (*See* NORMANS.)

Henry married his daughter, also named Matilda, first to the Holy Roman Emperor, Henry V, then after his death to Geoffrey of Anjou. Henry, the oldest son of Matilda and Geoffrey, went on to become the future King HENRY II of England and founder of the PLANTAGENET royal dynasty that ruled England until 1485.

Henry is remembered for expanding and strengthening royal justice, integrating the Norman and Anglo-Saxon legal systems, and laying the foundation for more centralized royal rule. During Henry's reign, the system of itinerant justices sent out to preside over the shire courts was inaugurated. Also begun in his reign was the EXCHEQUER, the accounting division of the English Treasury which produced the Pipe Rolls, detailed fiscal records of the court.

HENRY II PLANTAGENET

Henry II (1133–1189), who ruled ENGLAND for 35 years, and created the ANGEVIN empire, which covered much of FRANCE and the

Seal of Henry II Plantagenet, 12th century. The sprig Henry wore in his helmet (from which "Plantagenet" may be derived) can be faintly seen.

British Isles. His success made him one of the most powerful of medieval English kings and European monarchs.

Early Life. Henry was born in France, the son of the count of Anjou, Geoffrey PLANTAGENET, and Matilda, the daughter of King HENRY I and granddaughter of WILLIAM I THE CONQUEROR. After Henry inherited the duchies of Anjou and Maine in western France from his father, he gained further control of the region by bringing Poitou and Touraine under his rule. His marriage to ELEANOR OF AQUITAINE in 1152 gave him control of that duchy's extensive territories in southwestern France.

After Henry's father died in 1135, Matilda's cousin Stephen seized the English throne, thus beginning a 20-year period of civil strife. In 1153, Henry invaded England and forced Stephen to accept the terms of the Treaty of Winchester, which made Henry Stephen's heir. Stephen's death the following year made Henry king of England at age 21.

His Reign. At the height of Henry's reign, his empire—called the Angevin empire after Anjou, the home of Henry's father—stretched from SCOTLAND to the Pyrenees, making Henry the most commanding figure in Europe. Since by birth and training he was French, he remained much more involved on the continent, rarely visiting England. (*See* ANGEVINS.)

Yet Henry accomplished much and left an impressive inheritance to his successor, RICHARD I LION HEART, and eventually to his youngest and favorite son, John. The peace England enjoyed was welcome after the turmoil of King Stephen's days, but he also made significant advances in the areas of law, finance, and administration, which laid the foundation for the future English state. Henry's most enduring legacy was his creation of royal courts to replace the local laws of private feudal jurisdictions. He established the courts with the help of such capable jurists as Ranulf de Glanvill, who toured the country and administered stronger criminal laws and a reformed land law. The new legal procedures instituted during his reign included the more extensive use of juries and writs.

Henry expanded his holdings in England as he had done in France. In 1157, he won back the northern counties of England from Scotland, and in 1171 he launched a military expedition in IRELAND, where he consolidated the holdings of an earlier English conquest. He was less successful, however, in his attempts to extend English royal authority in WALES.

Battle with Becket. Henry came into conflict with THOMAS BECKET, whom he appointed archbishop of Canterbury in 1162. The dispute, which was mostly over the issue of the jurisdiction of Church courts, became so heated that Becket fled to France where he remained for six years. The quarrel ended when Becket returned to England in 1170 and was murdered in his own cathedral by knights loyal to Henry. The murder aroused such indignation that Henry was forced to make peace with the PAPACY in 1172 and did public penance at Becket's shrine.

Henry had problems with his sons, which marred the last years of his reign. Encouraged and helped by Henry's rival, King PHILIP II AUGUSTUS of France, two of the brothers rose up in revolt against their father late in his reign. Depressed by his sons' treason, Henry died on July 6, 1189. (*See* BECKET, THOMAS.)

HENRY III OF ENGLAND

The long reign of Henry III (1207–1272) was marked by political ineptitude and incompetent foreign administration. Only the intervention of Henry's far more able son Edward I rescued ENGLAND from utter chaos.

Henry was crowned at age nine after the death of his father, King JOHN (LACKLAND), in 1216, but the kingdom was ruled by the regent, WILLIAM MARSHAL, Earl of Pembroke, while Henry was growing up. When Marshal died in 1219, Hubert de Burgh ruled until 1232, when Henry assumed the throne.

Troubled Reign. Henry's lack of real political and military experience now became apparent. He selected foreign advisers to guide him, aristocrats who did not have England's interests at heart and who were no more competent than he in administering a state. When Henry raised taxes to pay his debts to the PAPACY, the BARONS revolted and forced Henry to accept the PROVISIONS OF OXFORD in 1258, which placed real power in the hands of an English council of 15. Henry renounced the Provisions in 1261, which precipitated a civil war between the barons and the king.

The baronial forces were led by Henry's brother-in-law, SIMON DE MONTFORT (the Younger), who captured Henry in the battle of Lewes in 1264, but who was himself slain at Evesham the following year.

Order was restored when Henry's able eldest son, Edward I, took control of more and more of the government. He defeated the rebels in 1266, but nevertheless adopted many of the Provisions.

HENRY III OF GERMANY

The greatest emperor of the Salian dynasty, by the mid-eleventh century Henry III (1017–1056) was the undisputed political leader of Western society, nearly reaching the preeminence of CHARLEMAGNE or OTTO I. Henry combined zealous military temperament with administrative talent and a deeply felt piety.

Early Life. Henry was born the son of the first Salian king, Conrad II, and his wife, Gisela of Swabia. Unlike many of his royal predecessors, Henry was not rushed onto the throne in his youth. He may, in fact, have been the best-prepared crown prince of his era, educated by the finest scholars in the land, and allowed to mature during his father's reign. He first served as duke of BAVARIA and Swabia, and became German king after his father's death in 1039. Also unlike his predecessors, Henry did not meet with immediate unrest or opposition on his accession.

His Reign. Henry devoted much of his initial energy to resolving the violent rivalries among the German princes. He also continued his father's program of extending the family's territories into the east, ultimately controlling the duchies of Franconia, BAVARIA, Swabia, and Carinthia, and gaining sovereignty over BOHEMIA and MORAVIA. After his first wife, the sickly Gunhilda, died in 1038, Henry married Agnes, daughter of William V of AQUITAINE and Poitou in 1043. She bore him a son in 1050—the future Emperor Henry IV. The marriage secured peace in the west, and stretched Henry's domain into BURGUNDY and ITALY.

Coronation. To culminate his successes he sought imperial CORONATION. He traveled to ROME in 1046, but three rivals were vying for the PAPACY. Henry did not want the dispute to interfere with his coronation, nor did he want to provide Italy with an excuse to reject German supremacy. He called a synod at Sutri, which under his direction deposed the three rivals and in their stead elected a German, Suidger, bishop of Bamberg (Clement II). On the same day, December 25, the new pope crowned Henry emperor.

A deeply pious man who easily could have pursued a more contemplative life in a monastery, Henry considered himself the instrument of Christ on earth, endowed with a sacramental office that allowed him to invest ecclesiastics with the symbols of their authority. The deteriorated, debased condition of the papacy, spoiled by the excesses and interference of the Roman nobility, led Henry to embrace papal reform as well. He appointed three more popes during his reign (all of them German bishops), including Leo IX. Leo initiated the papal reform movement that culminated in the term of GREGORY VII, who opposed Henry's son Henry IV during the INVESTITURE CONTROVERSY.

Cluniac Reform. Henry shared with his wife Agnes a passionate devotion to ecclesiastical reform, particularly that of the Cluny school. Agnes's family, the house of Aquitaine, had founded Cluny in the early tenth century, but Henry's attachment to Cluniac reform was based more on ideological than on familial ties. His dedication reflected both the contemporary movement toward lay piety and his deeply felt belief in the importance of a theocratic rule. Henry promoted many ecclesiastics from Cluniac monasteries to bishoprics and to positions of secular power. Although he was criticized for his intervention into ecclesiastical matters, Henry brought about many important changes, moving to eradicate simony (the selling of ecclesiastical offices), founding the collegiate churches of Sts. Simon and Jude near Goslar, which served as a training ground for members of the German episcopate, and completing the cathedrals of Speyer, Mainz, and Worms.

A Golden Age. In 1043, Henry instituted a "Day of Indulgence" throughout his kingdom, in which he offered pardon to all those who had injured him, and encouraged others to do the same. Indeed, for a brief period of time, he brought a golden age to central Europe, in which the ducal feuding subsided and German culture was allowed to blossom. Henry introduced a new kind of royal soldier and administrator in the figure of the ministerialis, the serf-knight who was well-trained and well provided for, but not a freeman. The ministerialis played an important role in the Salian empire, and helped Henry defeat the invading Hungarian forces in 1045, which ultimately recognized his overlordship. Henry also used the ministerialis to garrison the castles he built all over northern GERMANY, as part of his project to join Saxony and Franconia, and to incorporate these lands permanently into German domains. Setting up his capital at the great fortress of Goslar in Saxony, Henry was able to subdue the Saxon nobles and bring a period of relative peace to the area.

However, Henry's good intentions and piety did not always translate into political success. He suffered frequent disappointments in internal politics, and had difficulty carrying out his ecclesiastical reforms in Germany because he lacked the support of the native clergy. Henry's reforms met foreign challenges as well, especially from the Scandinavian and Saxon churches. He met frequent opposition to his rule from German nobles, most persistently from Godfrey II, duke of Upper Lorraine, who led several unsuccessful rebellions. Henry was also threatened by the NORMANS and by Henry I of France, and in 1054–1055, a conspiracy to overthrow the emperor (masterminded by dukes Conrad of Bavaria and Welf III of Carinthia) was thwarted. The two dissidents fled to HUNGARY, however, and weakened Germany's influence there.

Decline. As Henry's reign continued, his power began to slip. Opponents within Germany protested that his policies favored the Church at the expense of the lay nobility. Others were angered over the heavy taxes he levied in order to support his ambitious military program and the costs of clerical reform. Forced to find additional sources of revenue, Henry began to foreclose on mortgages, confiscate properties, and seek credit payments. Instead of consolidating his power, Henry entrusted his inherited duchies to disloyal and incompetent officials. His vulnerability demonstrated, the earlier territorial gains were lost as neighboring states recovered lands in northeast Germany, Hungary, southern ITALY, and Lorraine.

Succession. Some speculate that the change in Henry's character might have been caused by his debilitated state of health. Henry became so ill that in 1045 he began to plan the succession. In September 1056, Henry fell sick in the imperial palace at Bodfeld near Goslar, and having assured the succession of his seven-year-old son, Henry IV, he died a month later. The trouble that was brewing during his reign, among the discontented prelates and dukes and the hostile papacy, he bequeathed to Henry, who would roil Europe with the INVESTITURE CONTROVERSY.

HENRY IV OF ENGLAND

Henry IV (1367–1413), who reigned as king of ENGLAND from 1399 to 1413, was a skilled warrior but not a very successful monarch. He spent most of his reign fighting his opponents and putting down rebellions. Although he left his son, HENRY V, an undisputed succession, he did not have the skill or patience to attend to matters of royal government and address the problem of financial stability that put his kingdom in great debt. (*See* ENGLAND.)

Henry was the oldest son of JOHN OF GAUNT and grandson of King EDWARD III. Born in Bolingbroke in Lincolnshire, he was called Henry Bolingbroke. At age ten he became earl of Derby, and three years later he married Mary de Bohun, co-heiress of the earldom of Hereford. In 1387, at age 20, Henry joined the opposition to King RICHARD II led by his uncle, Thomas of Woodstock, duke of Gloucester.

In 1390, Henry's love of adventure took him to LITHUANIA, where he fought with the TEUTONIC KNIGHTS. He also went to PRUSSIA and Cyprus and made a pilgrimage to Jerusalem. Upon his return to England he regained the favor of Richard and became duke of Hereford. The following year, after Henry quarreled with the duke of Norfolk and tried to fight a duel with him, Richard became increasingly suspicious of Henry and banished him for ten years.

In 1399 when Henry's father, JOHN OF GAUNT, died and Richard confiscated his vast holdings, the exiled Henry became the leader of the growing number of Richard's enemies. While the king was campaigning in IRELAND, Henry invaded, and when Richard returned from Ireland, he was forced to abdicate. In September, Parliament confirmed Henry's claim to the throne. Henry imprisoned Richard in Pontefract castle in Yorkshire, where he died the following year.

Insurrection. Although Richard left no heirs to contest the new royal house of Lancaster, Henry was immediately faced with insurrections. Supporters of Richard rebelled in early 1400, but Henry crushed their revolt easily and executed most of its leaders. Early in Henry's reign both the Welsh and Scots revolted. English forces defeated the Scots in 1402, but the Welsh continued their rebellion under OWAIN GLYN DWR until 1408. In 1405, there was a rebellion in northern England, which Henry put down. He executed its leaders, among them the archbishop of York, for which he earned widespread criticism. When Henry fell victim to a mysterious disease, possibly leprosy, in 1408, many of his subjects believed it was God's vengeance for the murder of the archbishop.

By the end of his reign, Henry relied increasingly on his son Prince Henry to battle his opponents; by 1410 the prince (later Henry V) was virtually ruling the kingdom for his father. In 1413, King Henry IV died in Westminster and was buried in the Canterbury cathedral. (*See* JOHN OF GAUNT; TEUTONIC KNIGHTS.)

HENRY V

Despite Henry V's (1387–1422) premature death at the age of 35 after having reigned for only nine years, his strong personality and military successes in FRANCE made him one of the most beloved kings of medieval ENGLAND.

Early Life. Henry was the son and heir of HENRY IV (Henry Bolingbroke) and was raised mainly by his uncle Henry Beaufort. In 1399, King RICHARD II knighted the 12-year-old Henry shortly before Henry IV overthrew Richard and made his son Prince of Wales—heir apparent to the English throne. From 1400 to 1408, young Henry received his military training under his father and Sir Henry Percy, who fought against the Welsh. In WALES, Henry himself led several campaigns against OWAIN GLYN DWR. In 1403, he was wounded fighting the Percys at Shrewsbury.

In 1409, Henry took an active role in the privy council and supported the Burgundians rather than the Armagnacs in France, putting him at odds with his father. When his followers made it no secret that they wanted young Henry to succeed immediately to the throne, Henry was dismissed from the council. Shortly after his dismissal, Henry's father died, leaving Henry V the throne at the age of 26.

His Reign. First, Henry dismissed his father's ministers and replaced them with his own, beginning with his uncle Henry Beaufort, whom he made lord chancellor. During his first two years as king, he spent much time and energy quelling political and religious revolts. A rebellion by the LOLLARDS, led by Sir John Oldcastle, resulted in a strong parliamentary condemnation of the sect; Lollard agitation continued until Henry's ruthless suppression of the sect and Oldcastle's execution in 1417. Henry showed toleration and skill in reconciling political factions created after Richard II's deposition and in dealing with the Percy family, which had rebelled against his father.

After these difficulties were overcome, Henry turned his attention to regaining the territories in France claimed by his NORMAN and ANGEVIN ancestors. After making a secret pact with the Burgundians, he made a series of demands that he knew the French could not possibly accept. That gave him a pretext to invade France and resume the HUNDRED YEARS' WAR.

Agincourt. In August 1415, Henry led a large invasion fleet to Normandy where he directed the successful siege of the port of Harfleur. After he announced his claim to the French throne, Henry marched his tired army across northern France toward Calais, meeting the French army at the village of AGINCOURT. Although the French greatly outnumbered the English, the military experience Henry had learned in Wales came to his rescue. His choice of terrain, the clever placement of his archers, and his great ability to inspire his troops produced a spectacular English victory in what is today regarded as one of the most glorious battles in English history. The battle lasted only three hours, but it left 6,000 French soldiers dead and brought French resistance to the brink of collapse, leaving Henry the virtual master of northern France.

Henry followed his Agincourt victory with further military and diplomatic successes. In 1416, Henry formed an alliance with the Holy Roman Emperor SIGISMUND and extended his accord with the Burgundians. The following year Henry threw his support to Martin V, whose election as the new pope finally brought the GREAT SCHISM to an end.

In 1417, Henry embarked on another expedition to France, where his skillful use of siege WARFARE led to the surrender of Rouen in 1419 and the capture of Normandy. In 1420, aided by his alliance with the Burgundians, Henry concluded the Treaty of Troyes with the French king, CHARLES VI. The treaty, which recognized Henry as Charles's heir and gave him Charles's daughter Catherine of Valois in marriage, marked the triumph of the English over the French. Since Charles was elderly, it seemed certain that Henry would shortly inherit the French throne. Henry continued his military campaign to consolidate his newly won territories and entered PARIS in late 1420.

Sudden Demise. The following year Henry returned with his wife Catherine to England where he made preparations for yet another military expedition despite strong opposition. Henry's third invasion of France produced a series of small victories before Henry fell ill and died in September 1422, less than two months before the death of the French king, which would have made him king of France in any case, as well as king of England.

During his short reign Henry proved himself a highly skilled administrator, statesman, and military commander, after abandoning the reckless ways of his wayward youth (probably somewhat exaggerated by Shakespeare). He succeeded in restoring civil order after the near anarchy of his father's reign, and his victories in France greatly increased English national pride. Despite his overriding interest in gaining control of lands in France, he also attended to Church matters, founding two royal monasteries and encouraging reform among the English Benedictines.

His reign was marked by relative peace and prosperity at home in contrast to the periods which came before and after him. He is remembered fondly as the first king of England after the Norman Conquest who was able to read and write the English language with facility. (*See* ENGLAND; AGINCOURT, BATTLE OF; RICHARD II; *and* CHARLES VI.)

The coronation of Henry VI (depicted as an aged king) at Westminster Abbey, from an English Psalter, 1470.

HENRY VI OF ENGLAND

Henry (1421–1471) became king of both ENGLAND and FRANCE during his infancy. Although he remained a king for most of the next 50 years of his life, he never was able to master the art of government and rule effectively. During his reign England lost the HUNDRED YEARS' WAR and withdrew permanently from France (except the port of Calais). In the final years of Henry's reign, power struggles divided England and led to the WARS OF THE ROSES.

The Young King. Henry, the only son of HENRY V of England and Catherine of Valois, was only nine months old when his father died and he became king of England. Two months later his grandfather, King CHARLES VI of France, also died, making him, according to the terms of the Treaty of Troyes, king of France as well. During his minority, authority in the two kingdoms rested with his uncles: John, the duke of Bedford, who served as protector in France; and Humphrey of Lancaster, duke of Gloucester, who ruled England through a council. At the age of seven, Henry was placed in the hands of Richard Beauchamp, earl of Warwick, who was responsible for his education.

Henry was literally a boy-king after being crowned king of England at Westminster in 1429 at the age of eight and king of France in PARIS three years later. Henry was an intelligent and pious child; he avoided virtually all contact with women before his marriage to Margaret of Anjou in 1445.

His Reign. He was a patron of the arts and learning, founding Eton College and King's College, Cambridge, but Henry despised the battlefield and was the first English king never to lead forces on the battlefield. He officially assumed his royal powers at the age of sixteen, but early on he showed himself to be indecisive and easily influenced. Prompted by his wife, he made the unpopular decision to surrender the English fief of Maine to CHARLES VII of France. At age 32, Henry suffered his first attack of mental illness—a problem he inherited from his grandfather, Charles VI of France.

During Henry's reign, the tide of the Hundred Years' War turned in favor of France when JOAN OF ARC led a French force that lifted the siege of Orléans in 1429 and the dauphin Charles was then crowned King Charles VII in Reims cathedral. Encouraged by his wife and his influential adviser, Henry Beaufort, bishop of Winchester, Henry opted for peace rather than more war in France. In the meantime, the inspired French kept pushing the English back, capturing Brittany in 1449, Normandy in 1450, and the historic English possession of Gascony (AQUITAINE) in 1453. The loss of all of England's former French territories except Calais caused widespread discontent, culminating in JACK CADE's rebellion in 1450.

Later Years. Henry spent the last part of his reign confronting various challenges to his authority. In 1453, Richard, duke of York and England's most powerful noble, served temporarily as protector of the realm while Henry was suffering from one of his bouts of insanity. When Henry recovered in late 1454 and returned to the throne, Richard claimed he was the rightful monarch and took up arms against the crown. Thus began the civil war between Henry's Lancastrians and Richard's Yorkists known as the Wars of the Roses.

In 1460, after Henry was captured at the battle of Northampton, he was forced to acknowledge Richard as rightful heir to the throne. However, later that same year, Richard was killed in battle and Henry escaped and rejoined his wife and his Lancastrian forces. The war ended in 1461 with the defeat of the Lancastrians and the crowning of Richard's son as King EDWARD IV. Henry and Margaret fled to Scotland, but later, when Henry was captured in northern England in 1465, he was sent to the Tower of London. He was restored to the throne briefly in 1470, but after Edward IV's victory at the battle of Tewkesbury, where Henry's only son and heir, Edward, prince of Wales, was killed, Henry was sent back to the Tower, where he was murdered on May 21, 1471. (*See* WARS OF THE ROSES.)

HENRY VI OF GERMANY

Henry VI of Germany (1165–1197), Holy Roman Emperor and son of FREDERICK I BARBAROSSA, is probably best known for having held the English king RICHARD I LION HEART for ransom. During his brief reign, however, he annexed the kingdom of SICILY, and he tried but failed to make the crown hereditary. (*See* SICILY; ITALY.)

From his youth, Henry was artistically inclined. He wrote poetry, some of which was set to music. But his interest in writing poems did not make him a docile ruler. His takeover of Sicily was part of a plan to expand the HOLY ROMAN EMPIRE, making ITALY its base.

Henry captured Richard and held him for ransom because Richard had supported Henry's cousin HENRY THE LION, ruler of BAVARIA and Saxony (and Richard's brother-in-law), when Henry had been deposed by Frederick I Barbarossa some years earlier. Richard was ransomed for a large sum, which was to be paid in annual installments. The first installment was made, and Richard was released. (*See* HOLY ROMAN EMPIRE.)

In 1197, Henry tried to convince Pope Celestine III to crown his son Frederick, but the pope refused. Shortly afterwards, while preparing to leave on the Fourth Crusade, Henry was taken ill and died. He was only 32, and with no succession plan in place, GERMANY became embroiled in a 15-year civil war.

HENRY THE LION

Henry the Lion (1129–1195), duke of Bavaria (as Henry XII, 1156–1180), Saxony (1142–1180), and Luneburg (1180–1185), was the dominant figure in German politics during the reign of Emperor FREDERICK I BARBAROSSA. His status in GERMANY was linked to his relationship with Frederick: when they were on good terms, Henry flourished, but the ultimate deterioration of their relationship paved the way for Henry's downfall.

Early Years. Henry was the only son of Henry the Proud, duke of Saxony and BAVARIA, and Gertrude, daughter of Emperor Lothair II. He was therefore heir to several powerful dynasties as well as to several dynastic conflicts. The marriage of Henry and Gertrude led to the HOHENSTAUFEN–Welf feud; Henry's father refused to recognize the Hohenstaufen Emperor Conrad III, who in retaliation, stripped Henry the Proud of Saxony and Bavaria. Henry the Lion spent much of his early years recovering the lands his father had lost to Conrad, regaining control of Saxony in 1142.

Henry's cousin, Frederick I Barbarossa of Hohenstaufen, became king of Germany in 1152, and in an attempt to end the feud, made peace with the rival Welf family. He granted Henry's territorial claims to Bavaria in 1154 in exchange for Henry's support; in September 1156, Henry took possession of the duchy of Bavaria, while AUSTRIA was elevated to a duchy and restored to the Babenbergs.

Military Career. In return for Frederick's favor, Henry was a loyal imperial supporter for the next 20 years, participating in Frederick's campaigns in ITALY and POLAND. Frederick and Henry managed to avoid conflict and maintain a firm relationship because Frederick concentrated much of his energy on Italy, while Henry built a strong territorial state within Saxony. Henry was one of the leading participants in the German *Drang nach Osten,* or eastward expansion, extending Saxony's borders into Slavic lands. He led multiple military campaigns against the SLAV tribes east of the Elbe, slaughtering much of their population and thoroughly Germanizing the rest by bringing with him hordes of German colonists. In 1160, Henry conquered the Obodrites, extending his power over Mecklenburg. He also founded the city of Munich (1157) and re-founded the city of Lubeck (1159), developing it into a commercial center.

Henry built an imposing castle in Brunswick as his personal residence in 1156, in front of which he erected a statue of a lion representing his family. But the lion threatened as many as it impressed, and Henry's growing power provoked the hostility of the Saxon nobility. In the 1160s, a coalition led by the margrave of Brandenburg and the archbishop of

Cologne nearly overthrew Henry's authority; Henry was saved only through Frederick's intervention.

Henry's power grew with his second marriage in 1162 to Matilda, the daughter of King HENRY II of England. The marriage laid the foundations for the future Welf–PLANTAGENET alliance and made Henry one of the most powerful princes in Europe. In 1172, Henry made a pilgrimage to the Holy Land, and was received in CONSTANTINOPLE with imperial fanfare.

Loss of Power. Henry's fortunes soon began to change, as the true emperor, probably wary of Henry's growing power, and with a rekindled interest in his German territories, became more willing to lend an ear to the complaints of rival Saxon princes. In 1176, Frederick asked for Henry's assistance against the LOMBARD cities in northern Italy. In return for his services, Henry asked for the rights to the imperial city of Goslar; Frederick denied his request, and later blamed the defeat of his imperial forces at Legnano on Henry's absence. A rift had appeared in the alliance.

After returning to Germany in 1180, Frederick charged Henry with failing to fulfill his feudal responsibilities, and summoned him to a feudal trial to be judged by other German princes. When Henry refused to heed the summons, Frederick stripped Henry of his two duchies of Bavaria and Saxony, as well as all of his imperial fiefs. Henry was able to hold out in northern Bavaria against Frederick, but finally submitted in 1181. He was allowed to keep his family's estates in Luneberg and Brunswick, but was exiled to the court of his father-in-law, Henry II. He returned to Saxony in 1185, and began to reassert his claim to his old lands. After refusing to participate in the Third Crusade, he was again banished to the English court in 1189. Returning to Germany for the last time after Frederick's death in 1190, Henry became involved in a conflict with Frederick's son and successor, HENRY VI. The two were reconciled in 1194, and Henry died the following year. His son, Otto of Brunswick, was considered the GUELPH candidate for the German crown after the death of Henry VI. (*See* FREDERICK I BARBAROSSA; HOHENSTAUFEN DYNASTY; *and* GERMANY.)

HENRY THE NAVIGATOR

Henry the Navigator (1394–1460) was a Portuguese prince who played a central role in the development of European EXPLORATION. Henry was the son of John I, who was the founder of the Avis dynasty that made PORTUGAL an important European power. Henry never left Portugal, but he spurred exploration through the funding of improved ship-building and the patronage of important explorers. Henry's most general goals were the exploration of the "western sea" and the traveling of the mysterious coast of AFRICA. Henry hoped to discover the legendary (but fictitious) Christian African king, Prester John, and find a new trading route to India and the Far East. Henry's exploits embodied the ambiguous nature of European exploration. He "discovered" new lands for Europe, and thereby opened the way for European imperialism, such as the Portuguese Empire which he helped found. (*See* EXPLORATION.)

The first explorers Henry sponsored traveled in the western seas, discovering the Canary Islands and the Azores, suggesting that Henry was searching for a western route to the Far East. In 1419, his attention shifted to the coastal area of Africa, known by the Muslim name of Guinea. One of Henry's explorers, Antam Gonçalves, reached the Guinean coast in 1441 and returned to Portugal with gold and slaves. Gonçalves's expedition increased the popularity of this enterprise and the number of volunteers. Explorers under the sponsorship of Henry discovered Senegal in 1445 and Sierra Leone the next year.

At first, the discoveries produced massive amounts of slaves. However, in 1455, Henry forbade the kidnapping of natives because slaving had produced conflicts with the Africans, leading on one occasion to the death of one of Henry's most important explorers. However, this injunction was not strictly enforced and in any case, explorers were allowed to purchase slaves from African kings. In 1455, the explorer Giogo Gomez traveled to Senegal and Gambia, and reached the Cape Verde Islands. Gomez failed in his ultimate goal of reaching India (he brought a translator just in case) but he did map these areas and the land south of the Cape Verde Islands better than prior explorers. Under the aegis of Henry, missionaries were brought to Gambia to Christianize the natives.

Henry's historical fame goes beyond the exploits of the explorers he sponsored. He was responsible for a number of improvements in seafaring that made further exploration possible.

Henry the Navigator; detail from the Polyptych of St. Vincent in Lisbon, Portugal.

Jewish and Muslim experts he employed advanced the science of mapmaking and schooled his sailors in navigation and instrumentation. Henry was also a patron of scholarship, sponsoring professorships at Lisbon in theology, mathematics, and MEDICINE, and providing living quarters for teachers and students.

Henry was also active in Portuguese politics and had an excellent reputation as a warrior. In 1447, he fought against his brother, Dom Pedro, who had risen in revolt against the Portuguese king. He also fought successfully in the Portuguese campaign in Morocco. Still, Henry is mostly remembered for the explorations he encouraged. While he died in 1460, forty years before the opening of sea routes to the Indies, Henry was instrumental in preparing the way to those discoveries.

HERACLIUS

Heraclius (575–642), emperor from 610–641, was a great tragic figure of BYZANTINE history. He preserved the empire from dissolution and reversed a series of military losses to Persia. But his military successes were overshadowed by the loss forever of much of the Asian empire to the Muslim ARABS.

Rise to Power. Heraclius was the son of a high military official and governor of the important province of AFRICA, who kept his province independent during the disastrous and murderous reign of the military usurper Phocas (who ruled as Emperor 602–610). In 610, Heraclius sailed to CONSTANTINOPLE with much of Asia in the hand of the Persians, and the AVARS triumphant in the Balkans. Heraclius took power without force and before having Phocas killed inquired of him, "And is it thus that you have governed your empire?" (Phocas is said to have replied, "Are you sure that you will be able to do better?")

Heraclius began the reorganization of the empire, most significantly through the introduction of *themes*, the military division of land designed to promote a base of agrarian-based soldiers. Military disasters, however, continued to afflict the empire and Heraclius considered withdrawing to Carthage. Byzantine fortunes changed beginning in 623 when Heraclius invaded the Persian homeland. Persia responded with an attack on Constantinople in league with the Avars. The counterattack failed and the longtime enemy of BYZANTIUM, Chosroes, was dethroned. Persia was forced to make a peace despite still holding much of the East.

Demise. Heraclius undertook a systematic persecution of Jews and the Monophysite Christian minority. His wars against the Persians exhausted the resources of the imperial treasury. When shortly before his death, the Arab Muslims invaded the Mediter-ranean world, the fiscal and military exhaustion of the Byzantine Empire stemming from the Persian wars, and the understandable dissidence of the Jewish and Christian minorities, greatly facilitated the rapid Muslim conquests. It was in 634 that the Arabs began their war of conquest, and by 636 Heraclius was completely defeated by the Arabs at the battle at Yarmuk river. Old and sick, his life's work in ruins, he had little choice but to abandon the East to his bitter enemies.

HERALDRY

Heraldry was a complex system of symbols and marks that adorned the armor of knights and functioned in identifying knights with family lines and feudal-social positions.

Emergence. Heraldry emerged in the twelfth century during the golden age of FEUDALISM out of necessity as the use of armor created a need to distinguish friend from foe. Out of this practical need, heraldry developed into an elaborate symbolic system representing social status. At first, heraldic symbols were set on the shield, an arrangement known as a shield of arms. Over time, various other elements in knightly protective garb, such as the helmet, were covered by adornments. The various symbols were organized together on the surcoat, or tunic, worn over armor. This arrangement gave birth to the expression "coat of arms." Heraldry as a symbol of lineage survived the waning of medieval WARFARE that gave it birth. (*See* CHIVALRY.)

The employment of banners by armies was commonplace during the Middle Ages before the emergence of heraldry. The VIKINGS used the symbol of a galley in full sail as a means of self-identification. A number of tribal peoples used animals as symbols: the Scots employed the lion; ANGLO-SAXONS had the horse; and the eagle was used by the armies of CHARLEMAGNE and other Germans. These primitive markings were eventually integrated into the heraldic system.

The development of armor, particularly a helmet that hid the face, increased the popularity of heraldry. During the Crusades, heraldry was used to distinguish between the various nationalities of Christians.

Functions. The functional aspects of heraldic markings were soon joined by ideological uses such as knightly warfare. War was the occasion for great deeds and the carrying out of feudal oaths, even though actual combat between armies of knights was a rarity. The use of heraldry made clear who was fighting whom, and therefore showed who was performing which heroic acts. The symbols became increasingly colorful and flamboyant to accentuate the social position of the warrior. Central to heraldry was the representation of family position, thereby reinforcing the hereditary nature of social power in the Middle Ages.

The use of heraldry originated in the aristocratic class and was used primarily by them. Since the majority of the NOBILITY were illiterate, the coats of arms were made into seals that aristocrats could use to stamp on documents. Since the aristocracy was the dominant class, their habits spread throughout the rest of the culture. Coats of arms grew in popularity and were used by other institutions and groups, such as clerics, heads of corporations, colleges, and towns. The emerging burgher class (city dwellers) also began to use heraldry.

In battle, heraldry was the monopoly of the knights, the ideological leaders of the armies. Foot soldiers, squires, and all the lesser figures of medieval battle were denied the use of the elaborate system of heraldry. Instead, they wore badges for identification and as a sign of loyalty to a king or family. These badges were chosen by social superiors. Two famous badges were worn by the great houses of ENGLAND: the white rose of the house of York and the red rose of the house of Lancaster. The civil conflict between these two families was thus known as the WARS OF THE ROSES.

History. The first heraldic marks developed from the need to identify individual knights. Markings were placed on the largest surface area available, such as on shields or the mounting of a crest on the helmet. The first recorded heraldry took place in 1127 with the investing of Geoffrey PLANTAGENET by his father King HENRY I of England. Henry gave Geoffrey a shield with figures of little gold lions. This shield was passed on to Geoffey's grandson, thus demonstrating that heraldry soon took on hereditary meaning. Early "shields of arms" had heraldic charges and were very simple, containing perhaps unadorned stripes or crosses. Soon, aristocrats grew impatient with abstract designs and replaced them with concrete symbols. King RICHARD I LION-HEART, the first English king known to use heraldry, used a shield with two lions facing each other. This arrangement was later changed to three golden lions on a red shield—the pattern which has remained the Royal Arms of England.

By the beginning of the thirteenth century, the continuous proliferation of heraldry meant that the arrangement of arms had to grow more sophisticated in order to ensure distinctiveness. Different types of shields-of-arms were combined to make new patterns.

Design. Heraldry employed two categories of colors: a dark "color" (red, blue, black, green, or purple) and a light "metal" (yellow representing gold and white representing silver). The contrasting colors created a highly visible motif that could be seen from the distance of the flight of an arrow. The background color of a design was called a field. The main design, such as an animal, was the charge. Often the color pattern was simple, such as the dark "color" red as the background and a "metal" yellow as the charge. The color arrangement became more complex with the increasing sophistication of heraldry. Like other aspects of heraldry, the function of color arrangement soon developed aesthetic and ideological

A presentation by the King at Arms to the Duc du Bourbon of the armorial bearings of the chevaliers (knights) who will be participating in the tournament. From a 15th-century manuscript. During the Middle Ages, heraldic design was considered a science.

meaning. The ordering of colors had to be strictly obeyed; a knight who mixed colors could be banned from TOURNAMENTS.

Other elements of battle equipment became adorned with heraldry. Banners with symbols were employed by commandants of field units so that the warriors could determine the disposal of forces on the field and which side was actually winning the battle. Banners containing coats of arms were used by French knights. English warriors used the popular symbol of the Cross of St. George. Markings on helmets were made to indicate the rank of the knight. By the beginning of the fourteenth century, knights wore "crests," which were places for markings on helmets. At first, crests were restricted to use in tournaments but over time they were used in battle and were eventually made an official part of the coat of arms. Mostly the crests remained on the helmet, but they were also borne on wreaths, crest cornets, and on a chapeau. In a complete gathering of the elements of heraldry on a tunic, called the armorial achievement, the helmet and crest were placed above the shield of arms. Other elements were added and arranged in a particular order on the arms. The complete arrangement included mottoes below and above the arms and crest, or compartment; a ground below the shield; and "supporters" or guardians of the arms, that took animal or human form and flanked the shield.

Rules and Regulations. The system of heraldry was officially enforced by officers of the arms called heralds and pursuivants. These officials made sure of the purity of coats of arms—whether they were duplicated or fraudulently worn. They also officiated at tournaments and the gatherings of knights before battle. The battle formation was drawn up according to the call of arms. National organizations were also formed in order to sustain heraldic standards. In 1484, for example, RICHARD III formed the Heralds' College of Arms, an organization that mediated disputes about coats of arms and determined what emblems could appear. The Scottish kingdom established the Lord Lyon King of Arms, who had judicial functions and arbitrated disputes about arms and titles.

Late Middle Ages. Heraldry survived despite changes in warfare. In the fourteenth century, full body armor became commonplace. This armor offered completed protection and so shields, the original location of heraldry, were no longer necessary. The introduction of gunpowder meant that armor itself was no longer functional. Despite these changes and the eventual demise of classical medieval warfare, the coats of arms and heraldry in general retained their popularity.

The coat of arms had become deeply embedded in the late medieval social structure. Heraldic marks indicated the history of the family, and were sometimes

Lords and barons exhibit their nobility by displaying their banners and coats of arms from the windows of the local herald's lodge, found throughout medieval Europe. From a 15th-century manuscript, Tournois du Roy René.

used as evidence in court cases concerning inheritances, marriages, property, and other family matters.

In England, the coats of arms were legal symbols, authorized by the king. In 1486, the first publication, the *Boke [Book] of St. Albans,* was published, which listed coats of arms. Coats of arms continued in family histories, tournaments, and ceremonies. With the end of the medieval system of privileges, heraldry was eventually voided of any legal standing. The coats of arms remain popular with various European families, although few coats can be authentically traced back to medieval times.

For military aspects of heraldry, see ARMS AND ARMOR *and* WARFARE IN THE MIDDLE AGES. *Also see* FEUDALISM *and* NOBLES AND NOBILITY *for information on society at the time of heraldry. See also* CHIVALRY; KNIGHTHOOD; TOURNAMENTS; GAMES; *and* SOCIAL CLASSES AND CLASS CONFLICT.

HERBALS

In medieval times people could not turn to the drugs or medical treatments taken for granted in much of the modern world. But they did have access to a remarkable variety of plants and herbs, many of which could effectively alleviate symptoms of common conditions. Experts on medicinal plants compiled their knowledge into books known as herbals.

The knowledge that certain plants and herbs could treat illness has existed for thousands of years. Colchicine, a substance that occurs naturally in the seeds of the autumn crocus, was known to the ancient Greeks as an effective treatment for gout. Many plants, in fact, have highly important medicinal qualities. Other plants were recognized for their value as beauty aids. Such plants as laurel, hyssop, and myrtle were used in the Middle Ages (as they often are today) to improve the appearance of the skin and hair.

Page from Rizzardo's medicinal herbal, popular well into the 17th century.

The information on which plants possess the right qualities, how to extract useful substances from the plants, and which ailments they treated most successfully was included in herbals. The earliest herbals date from antiquity, but one of the most influential was *The Herbal*, written by a first-century Greek physician Dioscorides. Part of his five-volume *De materia medica,* it provided detailed descriptions of many plants and their medicinal qualities and was considered authoritative until the 1600s.

The Byzantine and Arab cultures were particularly interested in the effects of herbs and other plants. Byzantine scholars used older Greek texts to get their information. Arab scholars translated the works of Dioscorides and other herbalists from Greek into Arabic. In Islam, plants held a place of special significance; the Koran represents plants as examples of God's power and grandeur, and plants are in abundance in Paradise. The ninth-century scholar al-Dinawari compiled a detailed listing of herbs and herb names.

Many of the herbals were designed to be not only instructive but beautiful as well. Surviving texts are often richly illustrated with pictures of different plants. (*See* MEDICINE AND CARE OF THE SICK.)

HERESY

Heresy means error in the faith. Those accused of heresy in the Middle Ages obviously did not consider themselves heretics; they saw themselves as true believers. The fourth century Church was angered by heresy in the Eastern-Greek speaking part (disputes about Christ's nature, Arianism) and additional Christological heresies (Monophysites, Nestorians) remained a cause of divisiveness in Byzantium in the sixth and seventh centuries.

In the Western Latin Church the main early heretical movement was Donatism (named after one of its leaders, a North African bishop) which envisioned a purified, sectarian Church, comprised exclusively of saints. The Donatists held that the ministration of the sacraments by an unworthy priest was invalid; the orthodox position, enunciated by St. Augustine, held that the priest acted as Christ's minister and the sacraments were valid irrespective of the priest's personal qualities. In western Europe in the early Middle Ages (before 1000) the Church had more pressing missionary and organizational problems than the pursuit of heresy. Denunciation of heretics began again in the eleventh century. The heretics were theologians who had strayed too far from the consensus doctrine; or the expanding urban middle class seeking a more personal religious experience than the clergy offered; or country people of modest means looking for the personal attention and communal care that membership in a sectarian group offered. By the middle of the twelfth century, an expanding and more urbanized population, class conflict, the growth of universities where the fine points of theology were examined and disputed, and possibly contact with heretical groups in the Byzantine Balkans, generated large scale heretical movements, particularly in FRANCE, western GERMANY, and northern ITALY.

The two main heretical groups were the WALDENSIANS (named after a French merchant) who revived ancient antisacredital Donatism, and the Cathars, or Albigensians,

The burning of heretics, 1208, by Philip Augustus. From 14th-century Chronique de St. Denis.

primarily in southern France, who held ideas similar to the ancient Manicheans, namely that there were two gods—one of light and goodness and the other of evil and darkness. In the first half of the thirteenth century, the PAPACY lauched an all-out war against heretics in the form of preaching and educating by new religious leaders, courts of INQUISITION licensed to use Roman law methods of TORTURE to ferret out the heretics, and a military crusade. The Church did not want to kill the heretics; it wanted them back in the orthodox faith. But heretics who resisted reentry to the Church or who recanted and then lapsed back into heresy were harshly treated, sometimes even burned at the stake. Yet, the number of heretics suffering that extreme penalty from 1100 to 1500 CE in all of western Europe could not have numbered more than 5000.

The Church's strenuous counterattack had only temporary and partial success. After 1150, at least five percent of western Europeans belonged to separatist heretical communities. (*See* CATHARS.)

HERMANN OF SALZA

Hermann of Salza (died 1239) was elected the leader of the German crusading order the TEUTONIC KNIGHTS, in 1209. He implemented its eastern European policy and in 1211, he helped bring about the German colonization of PRUSSIA by forcibly converting the pagan inhabitants of Prussia to CHRISTIANITY. In 1228, Hermann crusaded with Emperor FREDERICK II to recover Jerusalem, which eventually resulted in the negotiated acquisition of the Holy Land. While in Jerusalem, Hermann began building the castle of Montfort, which was to become the base for the Teutonic Knights in the crusader kingdom. He died before the project could be completed. (*See* CRUSADES; TEUTONIC KNIGHTS.)

HILDEGARD OF BINGEN, ST.

Hildegard of Bingen (1098–1179) was a German nun whose contributions to medieval MUSIC, LITERATURE, and SCIENCE made her one of the most influential figures of her time. She was canonized as a saint in the fifteenth century.

Early Life. Born in the Rhine Valley to a family of mid-ranking German nobility, she claimed to have experienced visions and auditory messages during her childhood spent under the tutelage of a famous woman hermit. Educated by Benedictine nuns in the convent of Disenberg, she became part of their com-

munity. Named prioress of the convent in 1136, she and a group of nuns from Disiboden left for a new convent in Bingen in 1147.

At Bingen. During her time as prioress, she grappled with the question of whether she should reveal her childhood visions or the elaborate later ones that came to her during what now appear to have been migraine headaches. The visions focus on complex cosmological constructions. Both her confessor, Godfrey, and the local archbishop encouraged her to write about her experiences. This she did, dictating the work to her secretary, Volmer. The work, called *Scivias* (*Know the Way*), quickly became popular and was praised by the pope, making Hildegard something of a celebrity. In later years, she became still more influential; she corresponded with important political and religious leaders, such as FREDERICK I BARBAROSSA and ST. BERNARD OF CLAIRVAUX. Her works were probably written first in German and then somewhat awkwardly translated into LATIN. (*See* LITERATURE; SCIENCE.)

Influence. Hildegard was an important figure in science as well as religion. Well-known as a healer during her lifetime, she conducted a number of experiments and wrote two medical books, *Physica* and *Causa et curae*. She lists a number of drugs and herbs used by physicians (listing their names in German, though the book is in Latin) in these works. The books were consulted by physicians well into the fifteenth century. Hildegard was a prolific composer of choral music, blending church styles with popular folksongs. Her compositions have become very popular in the late twentieth century. (*See* MUSIC.)

HINCMAR

Hincmar, archbishop of Rheims (c. 806–882), was one of the leading personages of the CAROLINGIAN era. Son of a noble Frankish family, he received his training as a child-oblate to Saint-Denis and was a student of Abbot Hilduin. He later became a member of the palace clergy at the court of LOUIS I THE PIOUS where he served until the death of Louis in 840.

He then moved on to serve Charles the Bald, who appointed him to the archbishopric of Reims, the largest and most important episcopal see in the West Frankish kingdom. Hincmar won Charles's favor by administering his archbishopric efficiently and supplying the kingdom with revenues raised from the Church's land and vassals for Charles's military campaigns. Hincmar's influence later declined when Charles increasingly relied on the advice of younger counselors.

Hincmar was a respected scholar and a prolific writer. He wrote a life of Saint Remigius, as well as numerous letters, episcopal statutes, and treatises on political and theological subjects such as kingship, royal consecration rites, and marriage. From 861 until his death, Hincmar continued the *Annals of Saint Bertin,* a chronicle rich with historical detail. He was killed while fleeing Rheims during the VIKING invasion.

HITTIN, BATTLE OF

The Battle at Hittin (also Hattin), waged on July 4, 1187, between the crusaders, led by GUY OF LUSIGNAN, and the Muslims, under SALADIN, saw the virtual destruction of the Christian forces and marked a turning point in the CRUSADES. In June, Saladin had amassed an army of 20,000 men and laid siege to the Christian-held city of Tiberias, the first step in Saladin's holy war against the crusader states of the Holy Land. Guy ignored the advice of his able commander, Raymond of Tripoli, and launched a quick counterattack that led his troops into the arid plains near the town of Hittin in Galilee. Saladin waited for the Christian troops to be driven by thirst to make for a nearby lake and attacked, annihilating Guy's troops and capturing him. Saladin released the king in exchange for a promise to refrain from coming to the aid of other crusader states; this paved the way for Saladin's successful campaigns against the crusader states of Jerusalem, Antioch, and Tripoli.

HOHENSTAUFEN DYNASTY

The Hohenstaufen dynasty, also called the Staufer dynasty, ruled the HOLY ROMAN EMPIRE for more than a century in the latter half of the Middle Ages. The founder of the dynasty was Count Frederick, builder of Staufen Castle in the Jura Mountains of Swabia (a German duchy). Frederick was named duke of Swabia by Emperor HENRY IV in 1079. The first Hohenstaufen to serve as Holy Roman Emperor was Conrad III, who reigned from 1138 to 1155. Except for the years between 1208 and 1212, the Hohenstaufens continued their rule until 1254.

Origins. Henry V, the last ruler of the Salian dynasty, died childless in 1125. His closest surviving relatives were two Hohenstaufen nephews, but the electorate chose to ignore blood right and chose instead Lothair of Supplingenburg, duke of Saxony. Lothair formed an important alliance with the influential Welf dynasty by marrying his daughter to the GUELPH Henry the Proud. As the Welfs gained power and leadership in BAVARIA, Saxony, and Swabia, it seemed that the Hohenstaufens would be eclipsed. But upon Lothair's death in 1137, the electorate decided that the Guelphs were too powerful and chose Conrad, one of Henry V's nephews, to succeed him.

As Conrad III, the emperor made the suppression of the Guelphs his political priority. Upon his death in 1152, his nephew, FREDERICK I BARBAROSSA, was chosen as his successor. Frederick was the son of Conrad's older brother Frederick, and Judith, a Welf princess. Frederick I Barbarossa began a secularizing movement that was to continue for the next century. It was he who added the word "holy" to the name of the empire, which was now officially known as the Holy Empire. This created a definite distinction between the crown and the Church. Earlier dynasties had chosen to use their relation with the Church as a source of strength, but the Hohenstaufens chose to focus on the secular foundations of their power. Frederick I Barbarossa had alienated the Church early in his reign, but eventually reconciled with Pope ALEXANDER III. Frederick's son and successor, HENRY VI, alienated the church when he annexed the kingdom of SICILY and tried to fashion an empire with ITALY as its base of power. The Church saw this as a direct threat, and refused to acknowledge Henry's son as his successor.

Dissension. Upon Henry's early death in 1197, the throne went to his brother Philip. A web of political intrigue, including PHILIP II of FRANCE, RICHARD I LION HEART of ENGLAND, and Pope INNOCENT III, conspired to create instability in the region, and GERMANY suffered through civil war for the next 15 years. Philip was replaced by Otto IV, a Welf, in 1208. Otto's reign, which lasted until 1214, was the only break in the Hohenstaufen rule.

The next ruler to be chosen was Henry VI's son, Frederick, who was crowned Frederick II in Aachen (AIX-LA-CHAPELLE), which had been CHARLEMAGNE's royal city. Frederick was a scholarly man who made education a top priority during his long reign. He founded the University of NAPLES and made Sicily a center of culture that attracted Christians, Jews, and Muslims. He commissioned the translation of numerous Arabic and Greek texts. Of his own writings, his book on falconry is still regarded as useful.

But Frederick's reign was not a smooth one. He ignored pledges to go on crusades; when he did go to the Holy Land, he signed a truce with the Muslim leader of EGYPT. He also married the heiress to the kingdom of Jerusalem and had himself crowned its king. Upon his return to Europe he suppressed enemies in northern Italy. His actions so angered the Church that he was excommunicated three times.

In 1245, the newly elected Pope Innocent IV called a special council to determine the fate of Frederick. The council urged not only excommunication but removal from his position. A noble from the German region of Thuringia, Henry Raspe, was named in his stead, but Frederick ignored the council's decrees. In the next five years many of Frederick's former supporters turned against him, and by the time of his death in 1250 he was a thoroughly weakened ruler.

Although Frederick was succeeded by his young son Conrad (who reigned as Conrad IV), his death marks the turning point in the political structure of the Holy Roman Empire. Conrad ruled for only four years, dying in 1254 at the early age of 26. This began the interregnum that resulted in a weaker, more loosely structured empire.

HOHENZOLLERN DYNASTY

The Hohenzollerns were a German dynasty and princely family who rose to power in the late Middle Ages, becoming electors of Brandenburg in 1415; in the late nineteenth century, they would become the ruling house of PRUSSIA and of imperial GERMANY.

The Hohenzollerns traced their origins back to the tenth-century dukes of Swabia, where they were lords of the castle of Zollern in the Black Forest region of southern Germany. The first recorded member of the family is Burchard I, the eleventh-century count of Zollern. In the next 200 years, the family's faithful service to the Hohenstaufen emperors brought them increased land and power. It was with Emperor FREDERICK I BARBAROSSA's support that the Hohenzollern built their castle on the Zollern mountain, from which they derived their family name. The first truly prominent member of the family was Frederick III, who served the duke of Swabia, Frederick of Hohenstaufen. In 1191, Frederick III married the heiress of the burgrave of Nuremberg, and became burgrave himself the following year as Frederick I. Frederick established his dynasty throughout Franconia, and before his death in 1204, split his acquired territories between his two sons, Conrad and Frederick IV.

In 1227, Frederick I's sons divided up the family inheritance, creating two branches of the family, the Franconian and the Swabian lines. Conrad received Nuremberg, starting the Franconian line, which became Protestant after the Reformation. His brother Frederick received the Swabian estates, beginning the Swabian line, which remained Roman Catholic. In the Middle Ages, the Franconian line was the more dominant of the two. Its members settled in Nuremberg and, during the Great Interregnum, gained political prominence. Frederick III (1220–1297), through his support of Rudolf of Habsburg, gained possession of Bayreuth for the family, and his descendants acquired Ansbach and Kulmbach. At the beginning of the fourteenth century, the Hohenzollerns were one of the most powerful families in Germany. In 1363, Frederick V was elevated to the status of an imperial prince, and throughout the century, the family continued to prosper through its strong relationship with the emperors of the Luxemburg dynasty.

In 1411, Emperor SIGISMUND rewarded Frederick VI, his trusted diplomatic adviser and count of Nuremberg, by appointing him margrave of Brandenburg. In 1415, Frederick was appointed an elector of German kings. The family held the position until 1918. They revived a stronger central government in Brandenburg in the intervening centuries.

Frederick VI's son, Albert Achilles, made Brandenburg the house's principal territorial holding, after the Franconian possessions were yielded to a junior line of the family. The Brandenburg Hohenzollerns acquired considerable territories in the sixteenth century, including the influential duchy of Prussia in 1525, which was added to their holdings in 1618.

HOLY ROMAN EMPIRE

The Holy Roman Empire officially lasted for just over a thousand years—from 800 to 1806—but it was not known by that name until 1254; none of its rulers ever held the title Holy Roman Emperor. In its last years it was nothing more than a shadow; the writer Voltaire quipped that the Holy Roman Empire was "neither holy, nor Roman, nor an empire." Yet it played an instrumental role in the development of western Europe. During the Middle Ages, it exercised considerable influence over both Church and secular politics.

Origins. The Holy Roman Empire can more accurately be called the Western Christian Empire. The events leading to the crowning of CHARLEMAGNE by

Pope LEO III were caused by a rift between the Roman and Byzantine Christians. Until the establishment of a Western empire, the PAPACY, despite its prestige, was subject to Byzantine rule. The LOMBARDS, who inhabited much of Italy and who were allied with the Byzantines, were a growing source of concern to the Roman church. When they threatened to annex ROME, Pope Stephen II appealed to the Byzantine emperor for help. When none was forthcoming (the Byzantines were fending off Muslim forces in the east), Stephen turned to the Frankish king Pépin III the Short. The FRANKS wrested control of northern and central Italy from the Lombards in 756, and Pépin donated the land that would make up the PAPAL STATES to Stephen, establishing important ties between the papacy and the FRANKS and giving the papacy a power base.

When Charlemagne ascended the Frankish throne, he made attempts to build ties between the Western Church and the Byzantines. He arranged for the marriage of his daughter to the son of the Byzantine empress IRENE. But the establishment of a separate Western empire was still a goal of the Church. On Christmas Day, 800, Charlemagne was crowned the first emperor of the Western Roman Empire by Pope Leo III in Rome. (He continued to refer to himself simply as king of the Franks.) Empress Irene refused to recognize the new empire, but she was to fall out of favor and would be deposed within two years.

In the ensuing years, the Byzantine Church was to split with the Roman Church—a split that exists to this day. The Byzantine Empire itself gradually declined after a resurgence of power and influence in the ninth century, partly because of Muslim forces and partly because of looting by returning crusader armies.

The title of emperor was not inherited. An electorate made up of various nobles elected the emperor. A father could arrange for his son to be elected emperor, but he could not guarantee what the electorate would do. By the time the power base of the empire had shifted to GERMANY, it was established that a German king would be elected emperor.

After Charlemagne. Charlemagne was considered the first ruler of the CAROLINGIAN DYNASTY. He reigned until his death in 814. His son, LOUIS I THE PIOUS, reigned until 840. Lothair, the oldest of his three sons, had been promised that he would have suzerainty of the empire, even though each of the three sons would get a portion of the lands. But Louis changed his mind shortly before his death. Lothair declared that Louis' original decree was still valid and declared himself emperor, but his brothers refused to acknowledge the decree. A civil war ensued, ending in Lothair's defeat and capitulation. He nonetheless maintained the title of emperor.

The holdings of the three brothers included BURGUNDY, the Low Countries, most of ITALY, Germany, FRANCE, and numerous duchies and principalities throughout the region. Over the next several centuries, political alliances determined who had control over which lands at any given time.

The Carolingian dynasty slowly died out. The Carolingian emperor Charles III (the Fat) was succeeded by Guy of Spoleto, the king of Italy in 891. During the next 30 years

The Holy Roman Empire.
The political divisions of Europe in the mid-12th century show the Holy Roman Empire stretching from the Baltic to the Mediterranean, with the First Crusade serving as Europe's great unifying factor. Above, the crown of the Holy Roman emperor, made for the coronation of Otto I in 962.

there would be three more Carolingian emperors, but a transformation was taking place that put the empire's power base into the hands of the German rulers.

German Dominance. The rise of German dominance in the empire begins with the House of Saxony, whose first ruler, the German king Henry I the Fowler, reigned from 919 to 936. He was succeeded by his son, Otto I (who was not officially crowned emperor until 962). Interestingly, Otto was the first emperor to be crowned "king of the Romans." His son, Otto II, adopted the title "Emperor Augustus of the Romans" in 982, a year before his death. The last Saxon emperor was Henry II, who died in 1024. His son, who reigned as Conrad II, founded the Salian dynasty, which would dominate the empire for the next century.

Conrad II was the first to refer to the region as the Roman Empire, in 1134 after the unification of Germany, Italy, and BURGUNDY. Conrad's son, Henry III, added BOHEMIA, Moravia, Lorraine, and other duchies to the empire. He also forced the king of HUNGARY to accept German rule. His goal was to create an empire modeled after that of Charlemagne, but Henry made some diplomatic errors. In trying to unify Church and state, he gave more power to the papacy. Even though he chose the popes who served during his reign, they were able to build power for themselves. Henry's blunders were exacerbated after his death by his widow Agnes, a pious but politically naive woman, who seems to have had a talent for taking every piece of bad advice proffered. Her mistakes created enormous political problems for her son, Henry IV, who challenged the authority of Pope ALEXANDER III. Henry found himself excommunicated and then ignored by the pope, who then called for the election of a new emperor. According to legend, Henry was forced to stand outside an Alpine castle for three days, barefoot in the snow, before Alexander would meet with him and forgive him. Although Henry remained in control of the empire, the power of the pope was proof of the moral and political authority of the Church.

The Hohenstaufens. The HOHENSTAUFEN (or Staufer) dynasty ruled the Holy Roman Empire for more than a century toward the end of the Middle Ages. The first Hohenstaufen to serve as Holy Roman Emperor was Conrad III, who reigned from 1138 to 1155. Conrad III concentrated on suppressing the powerful Welfs, who were serious rivals to the Hohenstaufens. His nephew, FREDERICK I BARBAROSSA, was chosen as his successor as a way of unifying the two rival forces; Frederick was the son of Conrad's older brother Frederick, and Judith, a Welf princess.

It was Frederick who added the word "holy" to the name of the empire, which now became known officially as the Holy Empire. Interestingly, he did this to create a distinction between the crown and the Church. Earlier dynasties had used their relations with the Church to strengthen their base, but Frederick and later Hohenstaufens chose to focus on the secular foundations of their power. Frederick I Barbarossa had alienated the Church early in his reign, but later reconciled with the pope. Henry VI, Frederick's son and successor, also alienated the Church when he annexed the kingdom of Sicily and tried to create an empire with Italy as its base of power. The Church refused to acknowledge Henry's son as his successor. Upon the succession of Henry's brother Philip in 1197, forces led by PHILIP II of France, RICHARD I LION HEART of England, and Pope INNOCENT III managed to foment a 15-year civil war in Germany. During this time, Otto IV, a Welf, served briefly as emperor—the only break in Hohenstaufen rule until it ended in 1254.

FREDERICK II, Henry VI's son, succeeded Otto in 1215. He was a tolerant, scholarly man who founded the University of Naples and made Sicily a center of culture that attracted Christians, Jews, and Muslims. But Frederick consistently "forgot" pledges to go on CRUSADES. He signed a truce with the Muslim leader of Egypt and married the heiress to the kingdom of Jerusalem, and then had himself crowned its king—all of which infuriated the Church. Frederick was excommunicated no fewer than three times.

A Shift in Power. Frederick's authority was badly eroded by the time he died in 1250. His son, Conrad, chosen as his successor, was young and inexperienced. He died only four years later. This marked not only the end of the Hohenstaufen dynasty, but a major change in the political structure of the Holy Roman Empire.

After Conrad's death, the throne was left vacant for 19 years, a period known as the Great Interregnum (although there were, in fact, two emperors during this time, Richard and ALFONSO X of Castile, but they had little power or influence). The electorate finally chose Count Rudolf of Habsburg as the new king of Germany and emperor. The title of emperor would be held by a Habsburg for more than 350 of the next 500 years, but the structure of western Europe had changed so much by the end of the Middle Ages that the Holy Roman Empire held little real power. MAXIMILIAN I, crowned emperor in 1493, was the first emperor not crowned by a pope; the last emperor to be crowned by a pope would be CHARLES V in 1530. The empire became less and less important; by the time Francis II of AUSTRIA resigned the position in 1806, it held little more than historic value.

For more on the empire, see CAROLINGIAN; HOHENSTAUFEN; *and* HABSBURG DYNASTY; LOMBARDS. *For primary individuals involved, see* CHARLEMAGNE; LOUIS I THE PIOUS; FREDERICK I BARBAROSSA; FREDERICK II; *and* ALEXANDER III.

HORSES

The horse was an integral and essential component of medieval existence. Horses were needed for TOURNAMENTS, for HUNTING, for pleasure, for travel, for transport and haulage, for agricultural work, and for war.

Early Uses. In the early Middle Ages, the horse was primarily a luxurious method of travel. By the eleventh century, however, horses had begun to share some of the burdens of the plow with oxen. In the twelfth century, horses began to play a more prominent role in the transport of goods; by the thirteenth century, horses were pulling carts, an important vehicle for road transport. Horses developed a social hierarchy as is reflected in the extensive vocabulary used to distinguish between types of horses according to purpose and quality. The noblest of horses was undoubtedly, the destrier, the medieval warhorse.

Horse training in the Middle Ages was a respected but arcane art that Europeans left largely to Moors and Gypsies.

New Breeds. The Islamic conquests of Iberia and SICILY brought desirable breeds to the West, where the indigenous breeds tended to be small ponies. The Moors introduced SPAIN to the Barb, the Turkmene, and the Arabian; they also used indigenous breeds, such as the Andalusian. This blend of breeds had a profound effect on the development of the warhorse in western Europe.

Quality horses were regularly imported from Spain, Lombardy, and the Low Countries for the purpose of breeding warhorses. The numbers of mounted infantry grew in the eighth and ninth centuries, and cavalry came to have a major role in medieval WARFARE. Developments in warfare practice demanded specific developments in the horse—mainly larger horses able to support armor and sustain blows—which had to be bred and maintained.

New Uses. In late ninth century, France's and England's programs of warhorse acquisition and breeding were undertaken and continued into the era of the HUNDRED YEARS' WAR. High-quality horses were imported from other countries; large horse-fairs emerged, serving to improve and distribute the animals. English and French kings imposed export restrictions in what became, in essence, a medieval arms race. The Great Horse of the late Middle Ages, which stood around 15 hands (5 feet) high, was a result of careful breeding and maintenance. It became recognized for its stamina, strength, and fierce temperament.

The attentive breeding of warhorses had an impact on the quality of horses used for other purposes. By the thirteenth century, horses had become affordable and available to all classes of medieval society. In ENGLAND, for example, where a mason might earn 4 pence a day, prices of horses ranged from 2 shillings, 6 pence (8 days wages) for a peasant work horse, to 3 pounds for a riding horse (180 days), to 100 pounds (6,000 days) or more for a destrier.

Because of changes in military tactics, the decline in breeding activity, the sale of many horses abroad, and the destruction of studs and stock in wars, there was a dire shortage of horses by the close of the fifteenth century, especially in England. The revival of conscientious horse breeding to meet new military demands had to wait until the sixteenth century and the reign of Henry VIII. (*See* WARFARE IN THE MIDDLE AGES; HUNDRED YEARS' WAR.)

HRABANUS MAURUS

The scholar Hrabanus Maurus (c. 780–856) was one of the most important teachers in GERMANY during the ninth century. A student of ALCUIN OF YORK, he was known during his lifetime as *Praeceptor Germaniae* (Teacher of Germany).

Hrabanus (the *h* is silent; he is thus also known as Rabanus) was born in Mainz, Germany. After his studies, he became a teacher at the royal palace in Aachen, where he won fame not only as a teacher but as a writer. His 22-volume *De rerum naturis* (*Concerning Natural Things*) and his overview on religious education, *De institutione clericorum* (*Concerning the Education of the Clergy*), were received with much praise. (*See* LITERACY; LITERATURE OF THE MIDDLE AGES.)

Hrabanus compiled information from a broad base and put it into a comprehensive and accessible encyclopedic form—an important educational tool that allowed students to read summaries of rare works they might otherwise never see. Hrabanus later served for many years as abbot of the monastery at Fulda, which he shaped into one of the leading schools in Europe.

HROTSWITHA VON GANDERSHEIM

Hrotswitha von Gandersheim (c. 935–c. 1000) was important not only as a poet, but as a driving force in reviving drama as an art form. Hrotswitha (also Rosvitha) rediscovered classical Greek and Roman drama, and added a new literary form of her own creation: plays in rhyming prose. She is also noteworthy as one of the earliest literary women of the Middle Ages.

Born in GERMANY to a noble family, she entered the Benedictine convent in Gandersheim, a center of learning in Saxony, as a young woman. While there, she received a thorough education. She was an eager student, reading the works of early Christian writers, as well as classical Roman literature, with a particular interest in the lives of the saints. She became an accomplished poet and eventually abbess of Gandersheim.

Hrotswitha adapted several comedies by the Roman dramatist Terence for use in the convent, replacing some of the pagan dialogue with more appropriate Christian themes, and managing to make them both entertaining and instructive. Her use of rhyming prose in her dramatic works was particularly innovative. Nevertheless, some have noted a strong sexually sadomasochistic undertone to her dramas.

Hrotswitha also wrote a number of sacred poems and at least two historical poems covering the reign of OTTO I, the first German emperor, and the history of Gandersheim from its founding to the tenth century.

HUNDRED YEARS' WAR

The Hundred Years' War was actually a series of wars fought by ENGLAND and FRANCE in the late Middle Ages. The wars, consisting mostly of sieges, raids, sea battles, a few land battles, and long periods of tense truce, lasted from 1337 to 1453. During most of the war's 116-year duration, the English had the upper hand with the main fighting and destruction taking place on French soil. During the last part of the conflict, however, the tide of battle turned, and the French went on to drive the English from all of France except the port city of Calais. The Hundred Years' War was part of a long and bitter rivalry between England and France that lasted from the eleventh to the nineteenth century.

Causes. The war arose from problems created by the French territories claimed by the NORMAN and ANGEVIN rulers of England who had large feudal holdings in France which they could not control successfully. A series of local tensions, commercial rivalries,

Miniature depicting the entry of Charles VII into Rouen in 1450, marking the end of the Hundred Years' War.

and dynastic disputes also contributed to the war, as did conflicts over territory in Gascony, piracy in the Channel, and the desire of the English to control FLANDERS, an important market for English wool.

The immediate cause of the war was the rivalry between EDWARD III of England and PHILIP VI of France. Edward resented Philip's support of SCOTLAND and his refusal to honor his pledge to return part of Guienne captured by Charles IV. In 1337, Edward proclaimed himself king of France, a title already held by Philip; the Hundred Years' War was underway.

The Wars. The war had four distinct phases. In the first phase (1337–1360) England, under the leadership of EDWARD III and his brilliant warrior son EDWARD THE BLACK PRINCE, held the advantage. They attacked the French through the Low Countries and defeated the French fleet in the Battle of Sluis. They then invaded France and won a decisive victory at CRÉCY in 1346. The English, using artillery for the first time, besieged Calais, which surrendered in 1347.

After a pause in the hostilities caused by the BLACK DEATH, the English invaded southern France. In 1356, they defeated the French at Poitiers where they captured King John II and many of France's most important knights. As a result of the Treaty of Brétigny (1360), the French recognized Edward as the ruler of AQUITAINE, and England received Calais and a huge ransom for the captured king.

The second phase of the war (1369–1395) began when the nobles of Gascony, heavily taxed by Edward the Black Prince, sought help from the French king, CHARLES V. The French won few major battles during this phase; instead, they let the English march around the countryside while they nipped away at their flanks and cut off their supplies. Weakened by troubles at home, the English withdrew to their coastal fortresses and let the French control the interior of the country.

Henry V. The third phase of the war (1415–1420) began when King HENRY V of England captured Harfleur and defeated France's best knights at AGINCOURT in 1415. During the next four years he conquered Normandy and advanced to the gates of PARIS. Charles VI sued for peace in 1420. He recognized Henry's right to rule the French lands he conquered and gave him his daughter in marriage. Most important of all, Charles recognized Henry as heir to the French throne, disinheriting his oldest son, the dauphin Charles. Henry seemed on the verge of uniting England and France, but two years later both he and Charles VI died. That left Henry VI of England, a nine-month-old baby, as heir to both thrones.

In the ensuing period of confusion, the dauphin Charles claimed the throne of France, but failed to rally the French to his side. The English and their Burgundian allies waged successful military campaigns. By 1429, only southern France acknowledged Charles as king. Total victory seemed within England's grasp.

Joan of Arc. The final phase of the war (1429–1453) began with the dramatic emergence of a French peasant girl, JOAN OF ARC. The teenager claimed to have heard "voices" that told her to lead an army to drive the English out of France. Even though Joan was an illiterate peasant girl, she was able to persuade Charles and his officers of her divine mission. In 1429, Joan led an army of several thousand French soldiers to Orléans where they defeated the English and lifted their siege. After the French regained Rheims, Joan saw the dauphin crowned CHARLES VII of France in Rheims cathedral. In 1430, the Burgundians captured Joan and turned her over to the English. She was tried for HERESY in Rouen and, on May 30, 1431, Joan, still in her teens, was burned at the stake.

Results. Joan of Arc had given Charles the momentum he needed; by 1451, he succeeded in driving the dispirited English out of all of France. In 1453, the English departed France, leaving only a small garrison to defend Calais. The war had strengthened the monarchy in both England and France at the expense of the nobility and the Church. LOUIS XI, who succeeded Charles VII, was able to rally the rising middle class of France and unify the country, and England turned to establishing its military power on the seas.

HUNGARY

Hungary was a relatively stable medieval kingdom on the plains of the Danube and Tisza rivers on fertile land rich in minerals. The kingdom originated in the settlement of the once nomadic Asiatic tribe of the Magyars. Hungary was strategically located between western Europe and the Byzantine Empire, and was thus often where East met West in battle. Yet Hungary generally retained its independence until the conquest of the entire region in the sixteenth century by the OTTOMAN TURKS.

Much of the land of medieval Hungary was part of the Roman Empire under the name Pannonia. After the fall of ROME, this territory was occupied by various tribal groups, including Germans, Huns, and AVARS. In the late ninth century, the Magyars, a Finno-Ugric tribe from beyond the Ural Mountains, gained control. The Magyars were a fierce raiding people who, during the reign of their legendary chief ARPÁD, unleashed great suffering throughout GERMANY and ITALY. Along with the Muslims and the VIKINGS, the Magyars contributed to both the development and the despair of Europe in the ninth and tenth centuries.

A New Kingdom. Magyar raids continued until 955, when the Holy Roman Emperor OTTO I THE GREAT defeated them at the famous battle of Lechfeld. The Magyars were transformed from raiding tribes into a typical medieval kingdom. The new Hungarian kingdom kept close ties with the Holy Roman Emperor. In 975, the first Hungarian ruler, Duke Géza, became a Christian. Around 1001, his son, Stephen I, was officially recognized as king by the PAPACY. During Stephen's reign, paganism was suppressed, administration was centralized, and non-Magyars were exploited; feudalistic institutions began to emerge.

After Stephen's death in 1038, Hungary fell into a period of civil war as families struggled to claim the throne. In spite of this, Hungary experienced periods of stability and growth during the reigns of King Ladislas I (1077–1095) and Coloman (1095–1116). These kings expanded the territory of Hungary into Croatia, BOSNIA, Transylvania, and Dalmatia; protected property and trade; and enforced CHRISTIANITY. The monarchy and nobility began to decline under the rule of the inept Stephen II (1116–1131). By this time, Hungary had become a battlefield for the rivalries of the HOLY ROMAN EMPIRE and the Byzantine Empire. The Byzantine emperor Manuel I Comnenus himself occupied the Hungarian throne and moved the country deeper into feudalism by granting land to the noble families. After Manuel's death in 1180, Hungary regained its independence from the Byzantine Empire, but the landed aristocracy retained their power.

Nobility. While Géza II (1141–1162) reasserted

royal authority, his son Andrew's ill-fated rule lead to a resurgence of the nobility. After Andrew's failed invasion of Galicia in 1221, the nobles forced him to sign the Golden Bull, sometimes called the Hungarian MAGNA CARTA. It limited the power of the monarch, established a parliament, guaranteed the right of *habeas corpus*, limited noble military obligations, and granted tax exemptions to the aristocracy.

During the thirteenth century, Hungary suffered, as did much of eastern and central Europe, from the MONGOL invasions. The Mongols ravaged the country, killing or enslaving half the population. But in 1241, following the death of the Great Khan, the Mongols retreated and Hungary was rebuilt. The aristocracy reclaimed their power, creating independent principalities, while the monarchy founded representative bodies to balance the nobility.

Expansion. In the fourteenth century, the new ANGEVIN royal family rose to power in 1308 when Charles Robert of Anjou took power as CHARLES I. He led a resurgence of monarchical authority that included the restoration of internal order and the limitation of the power of the nobility. Charles expanded Hungarian power into BOSNIA and a part of SERBIA. He also married the sister of the king of POLAND, which guaranteed that his son, Louis, would ascend the Polish throne. Under Louis I, Hungary's expansion continued, commerce and science advanced, and Hungary became one of Europe's most prosperous kingdoms.

However, the growth of Hungarian power mirrored the growth of the great enemy of central and eastern Christianity: the Ottoman Empire. Near the close of the reign of Louis (d. 1382), the Ottomans seized the southern buffer provinces in the Balkans. King SIGISMUND of Hungary, crowned in 1387, launched a crusade against the Turks, but his army was annihilated in 1396.

In the fifteenth century, Hungary was defeated by the Venetians and was preoccupied by an ongoing struggle with an heretical Christian sect, the Hussites. When the Ottomans gathered their forces again, Hungary's prospects appeared dim. However, in 1456, the Hungarian national hero, János HUNYADI, broke the Ottoman siege of Belgrade, giving the Hungarian kingdom a reprieve. But in 1526, the Turkish Sultan SULEYMAN I the Magnificent defeated the Hungarians at the Battle of Mohács, marking the end of the medieval Hungarian kingdom, and the division of Hungary between the Ottomans and AUSTRIA.

Above, the church of St. Stephen in Budapest, Hungary. Also above, an equestrian statue of Stephen I, king of Hungary. At left, Stephen in his later years depicted in a more ecclesiastical role. Stephen was largely responsible for Hungary's strong ties to the Catholic Church.

HUNTING AND FOWLING

Both hunting for wild game and fowling (hunting for birds) played an important role in medieval life. For the nobility, hunting served the dual purpose of recreation and training in the art of war. For peasants, who were severely limited as to when and what they could hunt, it served primarily as a means of securing additional FOOD. (*See* FUR TRADE.)

Hunting in Europe. There was no social class in Europe that did not hunt, but as feudal society became more established, noble families began to claim hunting and fowling as their exclusive right. Hunting became an increasingly popular pastime. It was a way for nobles to socialize; organized hunts often ended with feasts and celebrations. Perhaps more important, it was a way to hone one's fighting skills. Hunting and fowling gave men the chance to practice using such weapons as bows and arrows, spears, swords, and knives. It also allowed them to develop useful military skills, such as moving through forests undetected. Large game included the deer, boar, wolf, and bear; small game included the rabbit, hare, and fox.

In addition to using weapons, hunters trained falcons and hawks to seize and retrieve prey. Falconry and hawking, as these sports became known as, became favorites of the few women who hunted. Trained dogs also assisted hunters in subduing larger game.

Peasants, rarely allowed to hunt in what the nobles considered their private forests, were restricted to specified areas and animals. Whatever peasants caught was used for food; animal skins and furs were used for clothing. Anyone caught hunting in a restricted area faced severe penalties, sometimes even execution, particularly in Norman ENGLAND, where the royal forests were carefully administered on the king's behalf.

Hunting in the Islamic World. Before the spread of ISLAM, many ARABS hunted for food, often assisted by dogs. Islam introduced rules about the ritual killing of animals, so that as Islam spread, hunting became a much more complex activity.

As in Europe, hunting ultimately became the sport of nobility and power. Falconry and hawking were also popular. Many Muslims used birds of prey in conjunction with their dogs; for example, the dogs might chase birds out of thickets and the falcons and hawks would then attack them in the air. In the late seventh century, some Muslim hunters trained cheetahs to assist them in the hunt. Although Islamic peasants did not face such severe restrictions against hunting as their European

Departure for the hunt. A nobleman with bird, dog, and servant (but no weapon) prepares to leave for the hunt, a popular theme in 15th-century tapestries.

counterparts, hunting was such an expensive sport that most simply could not afford it. (*See* FOREST LAW.)

Hunting in Art and Literature. Hunting figured prominently in medieval LITERATURE and art. The heroes of romances were often depicted hunting, and hunting books were produced in large numbers in the thirteenth century. The hunt actually gained popularity as a metaphor for love. Courtship was presented as a "hunt" in which the hero (the hunter) pursues his love (the prey). Hunting scenes were common subjects in tapestries, illuminated MANUSCRIPTS, and STAINED GLASS. (*See* TAPESTRIES.)

HUNYADI, JANOS

J ános Hunyadi (c. 1387–1456) was a fifteenth-century Hungarian leader who was instrumental in repelling the OTTOMAN TURKS. The son of a knight, he rose to the rank of general in the Hungarian army and served as governor of the Hungarian kingdom for six years. (*See* HUNGARY.)

Hunyadi was born in Transylvania, in what is now Romania, around 1407. His father, Woyk, was a knight who had received Hunyad Castle (also in present-day Romania) from the king. This raised the family's standing, and young János entered the KNIGHTHOOD. He soon showed himself a natural leader, eventually earning a place of favor in the royal court. He married the daughter of a distinguished noble and military leader, and he accompanied the king and his troops on several trips to other countries. He was introduced to new military techniques in ITALY and BOHEMIA and adapted them to his own method of fighting. He scored a number of small but decisive victories against Ottoman forces, and was soon considered one of Hungary's best fighters.

During the civil war that followed King Albert I's death in 1439, Hunyadi supported the candidacy of Vladislav. When Vladislav I assumed the throne, he made Hunyadi governor of all of Transylvania, as well as captain of Belgrade, count of Timis, and head of all southern Hungarian border forces. Hunyadi became one of the first European commanders to employ a large-scale regular army instead of relying on mercenaries or untrained peasants.

In the fall of 1443, the infamous "Long Campaign" began. Hunyadi and some 30,000 troops attacked several Turkish strongholds in the Balkans, and pushed back the Ottoman threat significantly. By the beginning of February 1444, the Ottoman sultan Murad II acknowledged defeat and sued for peace. A ten-year truce was signed, but it was broken only a few months later when a Venetian fleet was dispatched to the Dardanelles to further weaken the Ottomans' European strongholds. The Ottoman forces staged a preemptive attack. Led by Hunyadi and the young Hungarian king Ulászló, the Hungarian troops fought bravely, but lost the battle. Ulászló was killed and Hunyadi was almost captured.

Hunyadi was still important and influential, and he was made Hungarian governor in 1446. He faced a setback in 1448 when his army was defeated by Ottoman forces in Kosovo, and his influence was diminished. Probably his greatest regret during these years was that he could not go to CONSTANTINOPLE to help fend off Ottoman forces in 1453.

In 1456, however, Hunyadi launched a campaign to save Belgrade, which had recently fallen to the Ottomans. He allowed both mercenaries and untrained peasants to fight with his regular army, and the battle, waged on July 22, was a decisive victory for Hunyadi—one that kept the Ottomans out of Hungary for another 70 years. Hunyadi did not live to see any of the fruits of his labor; he fell ill and soon died, a victim of an epidemic that had swept through his troops.

HUS, JAN

Jan Hus (also John Huss; c. 1373–1415) was a religious reformer branded a heretic and burned at the stake. His ideas on religion anticipated many elements of the Protestant Reformation. Hus was also a staunch defender of Bohemian nationalism, particularly in the University of PRAGUE and in the Prague municipal government, both dominated by Germans. He thus became a symbol of Bohemian (and later Czech) nationalism.

Early Life. Jan Hus was born in the small town of Husinec (which gave him his surname) to a poor family. He studied theology at the University of Prague, and was ordained a priest in 1400, receiving an appointment as preacher at the university's Bethlehem Chapel in 1402. Hus had a reputation for being a fiery speaker, and he preached in both LATIN and in the vernacular as the occasion demanded. The university had been founded in 1348 by CHARLES IV, but had difficulty attracting scholars, most of whom taught in GERMANY. To attract German academicians, the charter of the university was amended in 1378, giving each German professor three votes in UNIVERSITY affairs to the single vote granted Bohemians. Hus campaigned vigorously against this and in 1409, King Wenceslaus IV (1363–1419) decreed the statute be changed so that German faculty had the same power as Bohemian professors, causing a mass exodus of the Germans from the university. Hus was elected rector of the university that year, marking the height of his influence.

Criticisms of the Church. Hus was also interested in reforming the practices of the Church. Strongly influenced by the writings of the English reformer JOHN WYCLIFFE, and associating himself with the reform movement led by Jerome of Prague, Hus believed that the Church was subservient to the body of the faithful. He was critical of the sale of INDULGENCES, which brought him into conflict with the emperor (who received a portion from such sales), and he challenged the infallibility of the pope. While Hus was promoting the study of Wycliffe in the university, the Church was banning the English theologian's work, going so far as to order his works burned publicly in 1410. Hus's protests further strained his relationship with the Church; in 1411, he was excommunicated.

Jan Hus fought for broader understanding of the Bible and thus diminished authority of the Church. He was tried and executed as a heretic at Constance, in 1415.

By 1412, Hus was forced to flee Prague. It was while in hiding that he wrote *De ecclesia* (*On the Church*), in which he set forth his ideas. Though influenced by Wycliffe in arguing against papal authority, Hus did not promote a break with ROME. His vision emphasized the authority of the BIBLE, which he believed was to be the supreme authority, and he urged a return to the simple values of the old monastic religious orders.

The Council of Constance. In 1414, Hus was summoned to appear before the Council of Constance to defend his views. Hus agreed only after Emperor Sigismund guaranteed safe conduct. Upon his arrival, however, Hus was arrested and brought before the Council, where he was condemned as a heretic. Weeks of debate followed during which Hus kept silent. Finally condemned, on July 6, 1415, he was taken to the outskirts of the city and burned at the stake.

The Hussites. The death of Hus sent shock waves across BOHEMIA, fueled by impassioned letters Hus wrote while imprisoned and smuggled out, copied, and disseminated by his followers, who became known as Hussites. They were also known as the Utraquists (after *utraque specie*, or "two kinds") due to their practice of holding "Holy Suppers" in which bread and wine, symbolic of the body and blood of Christ, were served. In 1417, the University of Prague adopted the Utraquist practice and threatened to challenge Emperor Sigismund's claim to the crown of Bohemia if he forbade it. Sigismund sided with the pope and, in response to open revolt in the streets of Prague, proclaimed a crusade against the Hussites. Known as the Hussite Wars, a series of battles took place between 1419 and 1436 between the imperial forces, supported by the Church, and the Hussites.

Under the command of Jan Zizka and then Prokop the Great, Hussite forces were successful through the early 1430s, even establishing a stronghold on the shores of the Baltic Sea. But civil war erupted between the moderate Utraquists and the radical Taborites, from which both Zizka and Prokop had emerged. In 1434, the Taborites were beaten at the Battle of Lipani, ending the Hussite movement.

ICELAND

Before the 800s, Irish monks visited Iceland and a few Irish hermits lived there, but no permanent settlement ensued until Norsemen, mostly from NORWAY, began colonizing Iceland in the mid-800s.

Early Settlement. A Norse explorer discovered Iceland by accident after a fierce storm blew him off course as he was trying to sail to the Faeroe Islands. His discovery led to more exploratory voyages and finally to large-scale colonization. The settlers set up farms on those areas of the island capable of sustaining AGRICULTURE and pastoral farming. Many thousands of colonists came to the island in the late 800s and the early 900s. Most of the settlers came from Norway, but some came from DENMARK, SWEDEN, and Norse settlements in IRELAND, SCOTLAND, and the North Atlantic islands. Some of the settlers brought Irish and Scottish slaves with them. The main reason for the migration to Iceland was overpopulation at home and dissatisfaction with the oppressive policies of the Norwegian king Harold I Fairhair. By 930, more than 30,000 Scandinavians had settled in Iceland.

The Althing. Early settlers empowered local chieftains to govern small areas, but soon the increased population led to the formation of judicial assemblies. The most important of these assemblies—the Althing—was created in 930 at Thingvellir near Reykjavík as an island-wide general assembly which met each June for two weeks. The Lögrétta, the legislative body associated with the Althing, had 146 members and a "lawspeaker" whose job it was to recite the laws to the assembly from memory (Icelandic laws were written down about 1117).

After Iceland was divided into quarters in 963, the Althing created four so-called Quarter Courts whose members were selected from the island's 36 chieftaincies. The Fifth Court, which was added in the early 1000s, served as a court of appeals.

Although the Lögrétta adopted CHRISTIANITY about the year 1000, paganism persisted and the chieftains found a way to control the new Christian religion the way they had controlled the old pagan one: they built their own churches and became priests or hand-picked priests for their churches. After two new dioceses were created at Skalholt in 1056 and Holar in 1106, the Althing chose the bishops, who more often than not were the relatives of influential chieftains. The two bishops became members of the Althing. When a church tax was imposed in 1097, the chieftains collected it in their respective districts and were allowed to keep half of what they collected.

In the 1100s and 1200s, Old Norse literature achieved its greatest flowering in Iceland. Icelandic SAGAS, written by such Old Norse saga-writers as Snorri Sturluson (1179–1241), provided some the finest vernacular literature of the Middle Ages.

Iceland never became a strong trading country. Its main product was rough WOOL cloth, but it never produced enough of it to trade it for the grain it needed. Iceland's only steady trading partner was Norway, which strengthened its ties to Iceland in 1022.

Struggle for Control. In the 1200s, internal rivalries became so intense and the resistance of the chieftains to Church reform so stubborn that some of the islanders called on the Norwegian king Haakon IV for help. Sturluson tried to help the king establish control over the island, but he was not successful. However, Haakon did succeed in bringing the churches of Iceland under the authority of the Norwegian archdiocese of Trondheim. In 1262, the leading chieftains of Iceland agreed to a political union with Norway. In return for an annual tax, the king established tighter control over the island. After the union, however, the Norwegian crown imposed new laws and heavy taxes, and reduced the authority of the Althing and Lögrétta.

Norway and hence Iceland came under Danish rule in 1380. The Danes were even less concerned about the welfare of Icelanders than the Norwegians had been. By the end of the Middle Ages the island had succumbed to its fate as a colonial dependency. Founded in part to escape royal power, Iceland was now dependent on the united kingdom of Denmark and Norway. (*See also* SAGAS, ICELANDIC AND NORSE.)

ICONOCLASTIC CONTROVERSY

The Iconoclastic Controversy was a violent religious and political controversy that afflicted the Byzantine Empire. Excessive and superstitious practices in venerating holy images provoked a demand for the abolition of the images themselves. The controversy began in the early eighth century and continued until the middle of the ninth. The use of images (called ICONS in the east) of Christ, the Virgin, and the angels and saints as aids to devotion had grown up in the centuries after the Christianization of the Roman Empire. When some in the eastern empire protested against excesses in the veneration of images, the monks fiercely defended the practice. Thus the quarrel over images became entangled in one over the wealth and power of the monks. (*See* ICONS.)

ICONS

Icons, painted images of sacred figures or stories, have been a particularly important element of Eastern Orthodox Christianity since the early Middle Ages. Although at times they were condemned by leaders of the Byzantine Empire, icons have endured for hundreds of years, in part because they provided a visual frame of reference for churchgoers, many of whom were devout but not literate.

Early History. The early model for icons may have been the funereal portraits that were popular in the fourth century B.C.E., as well as later portraits of Roman emperors. Visual representation of religious figures was expressly prohibited by JUDAISM, ISLAM, and early CHRISTIANITY. But the Christians of the Byzantine Empire believed that, since God had appeared in human form as Jesus Christ, He and other Church symbols could be venerated in art works.

Iconostasis. One offshoot of iconic popularity in Byzantine churches is the iconostasis. Usually made of stone or wood, it separates the nave from the sanctuary, and the worshippers from the activities at the altar. A typical iconostasis has a door in the center, around which will be placed a number of the church's icons. Events such as the Incarnation, the Annunciation, and the Last Supper are always portrayed.

Iconic Composition. Artists who painted icons were expected to adhere to strict rules regarding their work. For example, figures in icons had to be presented as two-dimensional; the Byzantines felt that three-dimensional paintings were too realistic and would therefore fail to capture the true spiritual essence of their subject matter.

By the eighth century, the use and veneration of icons had spread throughout the Byzantine world. But in 726 and again in 815, Byzantine emperors decreed that icons were not religious symbols and ordered them destroyed. What became known as the ICONOCLASTIC CONTROVERSY centered on whether icons should be venerated, merely respected, or eliminated from the Church. The controversy ended in 843, but many priceless iconic treasures were destroyed during this period. Icons remain to the present day characteristic symbols of the EASTERN ORTHODOX CHURCH.

Origins. Iconoclasm began in 726 or 725 under Leo III. Historians have ascribed various motives to Leo, including a desire to make Christianity more palatable to Jews and Muslims (whose religion forbids the use of images); an attack on the monks, who favored the images; or sincere religious conviction. In 730 a council formally condemned the veneration of images. Those who continued to venerate images, called iconodules, suffered increased attacks under Leo's son Constantine V. He called a council in Constantinople, which he intended to be the seventh ecumenical council of the Christian Church. It confirmed the condemnation of images and made iconodules liable to punishment. The destruction of the icons increased, monks were persecuted, and their monasteries were expropriated. Constantine's son Leo IV was far less fervent in supporting iconoclasm, and under his successor, Irene, who was an iconodule, the seventh ecumenical council, Nicaea II, condemned iconoclasm in 787.

Rebirth. The second period of iconoclasm began in 815 during the reign of Leo V. The destruction of icons ensued, but the iconodules were able to unite and opposed iconoclasm more ably than in the first period. The policy abated somewhat with Leo's successor Michael II, but the last iconoclast emperor, Theophilus, was the most brutal of the second period. Resistant monks were subject to all sorts of TORTURE. Iconoclasm came to an end with the ascension to power of Theophilus's wife, Theodora, at his death in 842. A council was summoned, and March 843 marks the official date, celebrated still by the Greek Orthodox Church, of the end of iconoclasm.

15th-century Byzantine icon of the Trinity by Rublev, a favorite theme in Russian art.

Effects. Iconoclasm caused the destruction of many thousands of religious art works, some going back to the third and fourth centuries. Among these icons were some of the finest art works of all time. It is fortunate that the small monastery of St. Catherine's in the Sinai peninsula was too remote to be attacked by the iconoclasts, and its fabulous collection of illuminated manuscripts was thereby preserved. Based on this collection, the great twentieth-century art historian Kurt Weitzman patiently re-created early Byzantine iconology. His work revealed that the iconoclastic era obliterated many of the world's great art treasures.

INDULGENCES

In the early days of Christianity, grave sinners had to do public penance—show they were sorry by, for example, standing at the church door all through Lent. By the Middle Ages, reciting private prayers and other good works had replaced these public penances. But according to Catholic teaching, even after a sin is repented and forgiven in Confession, its effects, called the temporal punishment due to sin, remain on the soul of the sinner. Those who still had those effects on their souls when they died would have to be cleansed in Purgatory before they could enter heaven.

In the Middle Ages, a whole system of removing those effects, for both the living and the dead, arose. The Church declared certain good works to be equivalent to doing so many days of public penance in the manner of the early Church; one could thus gain a partial indulgence. Some works were even said to remit all the temporal punishment on a person's soul in a plenary, or full, indulgence. Two important sources of plenary indulgences were going to Rome during a jubilee year, first observed in 1300, and fighting in a Crusade against the Saracens.

Giving money to the poor, or to build a church, was one way of gaining indulgences. Unfortunately, from the thirteenth century on, it often seemed as if sinners were buying forgiveness by doing this. As the Church came to depend on the money so raised, many reformers deplored what was called the selling of indulgences. In 1517, a friar in eastern Germany, Martin Luther, made it a prime example of Roman corruption and its elimination a hallmark of his Reformation movement. The Church responded by doing away with the abuses, but the doctrine of indulgences itself remains part of Roman Catholic teaching today.

INNOCENT III

Innocent III (c. 1160–1216) is considered one of the three greatest medieval popes along with GREGORY I (died 604) and GREGORY VII (died 1085).

Innocent came from an aristocratic Italian family and was well-educated in both canon law and theology. He was elected at the earliest age of any pope, 37, because of the need for strong and decisive leadership in the Church. Innocent did not disappoint the cardinals who elected him; he was an extremely active pope and a highly controversial one as well. He attended vigorously to the growth of separatist, heretical churches, especially the CATHARS in southern FRANCE.

Pope Innocent III depicted presiding over the papal bull establishing the monastery of Sacro Speco in Subiaco, Italy.

Innocent blamed the proliferation of popular HERESY on the lack of discipline and commitment on the part of the clergy in southern France; he called them "dumb dogs who do not bark." His solution was threefold: the founding of two new religious orders of friars, the Dominicans and Franciscans, to preach against heresy, reinforce Catholic traditions in the universities, and work with and among the urban populations. His second course of action was to call upon the nobility of northern France to wage war against the Catharist heretics, which culminated in the Albigensian Crusade. Thirdly, he advocated attacking the heretics with the judicial power of the Church courts, resulting in the formation of the papal INQUISITION.

Much of Innocent's time was devoted to international politics. By the end of his pontificate, he had allied the papacy with the rising CAPETIAN DYNASTY, and secured the throne of SICILY and the title of emperor of GERMANY for FREDERICK II of HOHENSTAUFEN.

In 1215, at the Fourth LATERAN COUNCIL, Innocent confirmed four important policies. First, new religious orders and canonization of saints henceforth required papal license. Secondly, Jews were to be segregated and forced to wear a distinctive badge. Thirdly, the number of Church sacraments, previously floating between three and eleven, was set at seven. Fourthly, one of these sacraments was marriage. This decision had much impact on family life; divorce (annulment) could only be provided by the Church. Innocent also effected the first universal income tax on the clergy.

Innocent was a brilliant, aggressive, confident leader who brought the papacy to the pinnacle of power in European society and politics. He was criticized in his day for being too political and involving the papacy in many areas that seemed beyond the spiritual mandate of the Roman Church. (*See* PAPACY.)

INNS AND TAVERNS

U ntil around the eleventh century, most travelers relied on the hospitality of private homes or monasteries to provide food and lodging. The increase in travel, particularly by merchants, made it impractical to rely on private dwellings, but it gave rise to the concept of "commercial" hospitality in the form of inns and taverns. (*See* TRAVEL AND TRANSPORTATION.)

The type of lodgings a traveler could expect depended upon where he was going. In FRANCE and ITALY, a traveler could find inns or hostels in major cities, and smaller inns in outlying regions. In the ARAB countries, travelers could rest at a caravansary, which usually consisted of buildings surrounding a large courtyard. Less-traveled countries such as ENGLAND and SPAIN offered fewer—and more expensive—choices, although in England, travelers could get a drink, and sometimes a simple meal, at an ale house.

As travel increased, so did the number and quality of inns and taverns. Some enterprising individuals turned their homes into inns; others leased the inns from owners. Innkeepers eventually formed their own GUILD, which afforded a certain degree of quality control. Each room in these lodgings might hold several beds, and each bed in turn might hold several guests. Inns in university towns often rented rooms to students by the year. Inns usually had one or two paid employees besides the innkeeper.

Taverns also became more common, offering villagers, merchants, and students a place to eat and drink in simple but convivial surroundings. Already in the Middle Ages, merchants found taverns a convenient meeting place to conduct their business.

INQUISITION

T he general term used to denote the papal institution whose aim was identifying and eliminating HERESY. The word is derived from the inquest, a method used by royal officials to determine revenues owed to the king; the most famous inquest was the one conducted by WILLIAM I THE CONQUEROR in 1081–1087 that resulted in the compilation of the DOMESDAY BOOK. At first, the Inquisition was directed at Christian sects suspected of heresy, particularly the CATHARS and the ALBIGENSIANS. Finding that a body of doctrines was heretical was followed by threats of excommunication; until the twelfth century, personal intimidation was employed but not physical violence. When the institution was turned over to lay authorities and used to further political goals, methods such as incarceration, confiscation of property, flagellation, and TORTURE were used.

Origins. In the mid-1100s, uprisings by textile workers in FRANCE and FLANDERS were quelled by King Louis VII through the convening of inquiries in 1163 at the request of the archbishop of Reims. Those found guilty of heresy (the ringleaders of the unrest) were put to death. The effectiveness of these measures impressed Pope Lucius III, who was waging a losing war of words against the Albigensians and the Waldensians. In 1184, the pope and EMPEROR FREDERICK I BARBAROSSA created the Inquisition and put local bishops in charge of its administration. In the early thirteenth century, the pope enrolled the Dominicans and the Franciscans to administer the Inquisition, but in 1232, Frederick I insisted that state officials carry out verdicts of the Inquisitors by force.

Pope GREGORY IX looked at this development with mixed feelings. On the one hand, the orderly administration of the Inquisition by the new partnership of Church and state was effective, putting an end to the previous century's mob violence against suspected heretics, but it also gave the state control over what was fundamentally a Church proceeding. In 1231, the pope issued a bull, *Excommunicamus,* in which some rules were laid down regarding the conduct of the Inquisition. The tribunal proceedings would be firmly placed in the hands of the Church, and guidelines were set for the means by which their decisions could be carried out by the state. Gregory appointed two zealots, however, in the person of CONRAD OF MARBURG and Robert le Bougre, to conduct the Inquisition. The two proceeded to terrorize communities throughout GERMANY and FRANCE before Conrad was murdered in 1233, and Robert was suspended.

Changes in Policy. The decisive change came in 1252 when Pope Innocent IV, possibly to curb abuses by the lay enforcers of the Inquisitorial findings, issued the bull *Ad extirpanda* that permitted the use of torture and starvation to extract confessions from suspected heretics. Suspects who professed their innocence in spite of such measures were to be turned over to the civil authorities for execution, often by burning at the stake or by means even more horrible. It was then that the ceremony of condemnation took on the trappings of a state occasion. The public affirmation (*sermo generalis*) of the charges was a grandiose ceremony, the *auto-da-fé* (act of faith), at which the fate of the accused became almost secondary to the pomp of the procession and the public pronouncements. Frequently works of the accused (or documents purported to be such) were burned as part of the ceremony. The affair was grand theater, but the outcome was often gruesome as the proceedings gave religious sanction to society's most sadistic elements.

The auto-da-fé ceremony in Spain as depicted in a 17th-century engraving. The grand theater of the procession was viewed as both devotional and a way of relieving medieval tedium.

The Inquisition became an almost routine part of European life through the thirteenth century and was practiced with particular ferocity in the early fourteenth century against the KNIGHTS TEMPLAR and the Spiritual Franciscans. Through this period, the institution of the Inquisition applied only to Christians suspected of heresy (or who might be politically disenfranchised by such a charge); non-Christians were never targeted. In fact, the entire proceeding would not have made sense as a means of prosecuting non-Christians (against whom a panoply of other persecutorial devices were at hand). For this reason, historians have sometimes distinguished the European Inquisition of earlier centuries from the Spanish Inquisition, but the latter must still be looked upon as a blood relative of the former.

Spain. This changed when the Inquisition was reinstated with renewed vigor in SPAIN in the late fifteenth century. As Jews and Moors entered the upper echelons of Spanish society through the device of accepting baptism at least superficially, the nobility felt threatened. With the approval of Pope Sixtus IV, the Spanish aristocracy convinced the monarchs Ferdinand and Isabella to root out insincere converts—crypto-Jews (Marranos) and Moors (Moriscos), who practiced their faiths in secret while professing CHRISTIANITY—by reinstating the Inquisition. Research has shown that the actual number of such converts was very small and that the Inquisition was used by the crown to control the aristocracy and intimidate the non-Christian population. Under the leadership of the Dominican friar Tomás de Torquemada, who was the Grand Inquisitor from 1478 until his death in 1498, the Spanish Inquisition set up tribunals in many Spanish cities and proceeded to execute over 2,000 supposed heretics, many of them Jews accused of practicing Judaism in secret (on the basis of no more evidence than wearing fine clothing on Saturday). Torquemada, who had been the king and queen's confessor, engineered the expulsion of Jews from Spain in 1492 as part of the general policy of persecution and intimidation. The Inquisition had a devastating effect on Iberian Jewry, and echoes of the episode survived into the twentieth century. (The Inquisition did not officially end until 1908.)

The rise of Protestanism and the consolidation of nation states following the Middle Ages ended the effectiveness of the Inquisition, though the memory of the horrors committed under its banner persisted.

For information on the origins of the Inquisition, see FREDERICK I BARBAROSSA; ALBIGENSIANS; CATHARS; *and* GREGORY IX. *Also, see entries on* CHRISTIANITY; SPAIN; TORTURE; *and* HERESY.

INVESTITURE CONTROVERSY

The investiture controversy was a power struggle between the PAPACY and the HOLY ROMAN EMPIRE that lasted nearly half a century. It began in 1075, with a celebrated standoff between Pope GREGORY VII and the Holy Roman Emperor HENRY IV. It did not end until the CONCORDAT OF WORMS was signed in 1122. Even after this agreement was reached, later popes continued to assert their power against the empire, firmly establishing the doctrine of papal control over Church affairs.

Pope Against Emperor. In 1075, Gregory VII condemned the practice of lay investiture of bishops. He held that only the pope could invest bishops. Henry IV disagreed. Part of the issue was that Henry saw the pope not merely asserting the Church's position in religious affairs, but declaring its superior standing over the empire. Henry's charge was not entirely without merit; indeed, Gregory had stated quite clearly in his *Dictatus papae* (1075) that the Church should have more involvement in the day-to-day lives of the common people. All mortals, he said, owed allegiance to the pope, and the Church's opinion was the definitive one in all matters.

Soon after the pope's pronouncements, Henry voiced his support for a rival candidate for the bishopric of Milan over the pope's choice. The pope wrote to Henry to complain, and Henry declared the pope deposed. Not to be outdone, the pope declared Henry excommunicated and called for the German nobles (no friends of Henry in any case) to depose their emperor and choose a new one. Henry traveled across the Alps in the winter of 1077 to seek Gregory's forgiveness. According to legend, the pope made him wait barefoot in the snow for three days before allowing him into the castle where he was staying. Gregory granted his forgiveness to Henry, but the symbolic victory for the Church was substantial. Not only the PAPACY, but also the German aristocracy gained power at the emperor's expense. (*See* GREGORY VII.)

Settlement. Afterward, there were a series of compromises. In 1106, England's HENRY I abandoned the practice of investing prelates with spiritual office (that duty fell to the Church); in return, the Church allowed homage to the king to precede the prelates' consecration.

The Concordat of Worms, signed in 1122, seemed to strike a balance for both the Church and the emperor. Pope Calixtus II and Emperor Henry V reached a number of agreements; the emperor could be present at the election of prelates for example, but only in Germany (not in ITALY or BURGUNDY).

Later popes, including ALEXANDER III, INNOCENT III, Innocent IV, and BONIFACE VIII, raised new challenges to the empire. The Church increased its power and the Holy Roman Empire declined, but the new kingdoms that came out of the divided empire gained power as well. Ultimately, religious matters fell under the Church's jurisdiction, while political matters fell under the jurisdiction of the kings. (*See* PAPACY.)

IRELAND

Ireland escaped occupation by the Romans and ANGLO-SAXONS who controlled Britain before and during the early Middle Ages. It remained relatively untouched by foreign invasions until the VIKING raids that began in the late 700s.

The Golden Age. In the early Middle Ages, the Irish were organized into clans and tribes under the authority of five provincial kings who were nominally in service to the king of all Ireland at Tara. With literature and the arts held in high esteem, Ireland enjoyed a golden age of learning and culture. Each king and chieftain had his own poet (druid) who preserved his people's oral traditions.

The Christianization of much of Ireland by ST. PATRICK in the 400s produced a vibrant Celtic CHRISTIANITY, which sent scholars and missionaries to ENGLAND and Europe and attracted students from abroad to Irish monasteries. While all the arts flourished in Ireland, the Irish were most famous for their ILLUMINATED MANUSCRIPTS, the most notable example of which was the BOOK OF KELLS. (*See* CELTIC CHURCH.)

Viking Invasions. However, the Viking invasion in 795 began a new chapter in Irish history. The Vikings raided the Irish coastline where they eventually set up permanent bases, the first being at Dublin in 841. In reaction to the Viking incursions, the Irish set up larger and stronger political units. Some local Irish kings allied themselves with the neighboring Viking settlements and used their warriors as mercenaries.

In the wake of the Viking invasion, the idea of a single king gained acceptance and led to conflict between Irish chieftains for supremacy. Brian Borumha, who headed an obscure kingdom in western Ireland, subdued the south and the midlands by 1002. Feeling strong enough to proclaim himself "king of the Irish" in 1005, he then gained ascendancy over northern Ireland as well. He was soon faced with rebellion in Leinster; he subsequently died at the Battle of Clontarf. The submission of the other kings to Borumha marked a new chapter in Irish politics, which increasingly centered around the growing town of Dublin.

English Rule. To bring order to Ireland, Pope ADRIAN IV designated King HENRY II of ENGLAND overlord of Ireland. Henry invaded the island in 1171, then granted lordships and land to his followers around Dublin. Thereafter, the center of English authority became the area around Dublin called the Pale. The involvement of the English crown in Irish affairs was inconsistent, however. In 1394, after a period of neglect, King RICHARD II invaded Ireland to strengthen royal control, but he was not able to follow through on his initial success. Efforts to limit the use of Irish language, laws, and customs proved unsuccessful. In the late Middle Ages, Ireland experienced a Gaelic renaissance in the countryside outside the English-controlled areas of Dublin and other large towns.

IRENE, EMPRESS

The Empress Irene (c. 752–803) was the wife of Byzantine emperor Leo IV and became the first woman to rule the empire in her own name. An Athenian orphan, Irene married Leo IV in 768. When he died 12 years later, she was named regent for her ten-year-old son, Emperor Constantine VI. Irene soon took over as sole ruler and remained at the helm of the empire for ten years, continuing the rule of the ISAURIAN DYNASTY.

Irene's greatest success was the return of the icons to the churches as decreed by the Second Nicene Council in 787. However, she also met military defeat on the empire's eastern border and was forced to make a disadvantageous truce with the Arab caliphate. Irene's most notorious act was the blinding of her son. She feared (with some reason) that he was planning to take power for himself. Eventually, dissatisfaction with Irene's rule intensified in the face of repeated military debacles and her unpopular proposal to wed CHARLEMAGNE, king of the FRANKS. In 802, she was dethroned and forced to enter a convent. (*See* BYZANTIUM.)

ISAAC I COMNENUS

Isaac Comnenus (1005–1061) ruled the Byzantine Empire from 1057 to 1059. The son of Manuel Comnenus, an officer of BASIL II the Bulgar Slayer, Isaac and his brother were left in the care of the emperor who had them educated in a monastery. They eventually rose to prominence in the army. In 1057, already a successful general, Isaac allied with the military and the nobility to dethrone the emperor Michael VI Stratioticus and became emperor. His short rule was dominated by the ongoing struggle between two political forces: the bureaucracy and the Church in the Byzantine capital against the feudal aris-

tocracy in Asia Minor. Whereas Michael VI had represented the interests of the bureaucracy, Isaac I was a member of a great feudal family.

Isaac's primary concern as emperor was the restoration of the empire's fiscal health. He confiscated land illegally taken by the nobility, reduced salaries, and took certain revenues from the wealthier monasteries. Isaac conducted successful military campaigns in the Balkans against the Hungarians and Patzinaks (a primitive tribal people inhabiting southern RUSSIA). He successfully defended the eastern border of Asia Minor from the growing threat of the SELJUK TURKS. Isaac Comnenus ruled for only two years. In 1059, illness forced him to retire. Power once more shifted with the succession of Constantine X Ducas, his finance minister, and a loyal follower of the interests of the bureaucracy. Isaac retired to a monastery where he devoted himself to literary studies of the *Iliad* and other Homeric texts. (*See* BYZANTIUM.)

ISAURIAN DYNASTY

The Isaurian dynasty ruled the Byzantine Empire from the ascension of LEO III the Isaurian in 717 to the dethronement of IRENE in 802. It is considered successful because it saved CONSTANTINOPLE during the siege of 717–718, and it extended the *theme* (military province) organization of the empire. The Isaurian Empire also, however, initiated the destructive and cruel policy of iconoclasm. The dynasty was also marked by the novelty of a woman in sole control of the empire.

Rise to Power. Leo the Isaurian was a renowned general who came to power without a struggle after the murderous regime of the last Heraclian emperor Justinian and the brief rule of a civil servant named Anastasius. Leo ruled until his death in 740. He was followed by his son Constantine V Copronymous. Constantine's long rule ended in 755, when he was succeeded by his son Leo IV known as the Chazar (his mother was a Turkish princess). After Leo's five-year rule, the ten-year old Constantine VI came to power under the regency of his mother, IRENE. Irene took sole power in 797 when she had her son blinded, causing his death shortly thereafter. The dynasty came to an end when Irene was dethroned by her treasurer Nicephorus. (*See* IRENE, EMPRESS.)

Defending the Empire. Perhaps the most significant event of the dynasty occurred immediately after Leo III took power when the ARABS tried to complete their conquest of Byzantine with the siege of CONSTANTINOPLE. The Arab navy, however, failed in the crucial attempt to blockade the city. The Byzantine use of "Greek fire" was decisive in destroying Arab ships and demoralizing the enemy. The Arabs settled in for a long siege, but their provision supply dried up. The end of the siege occurred in 718 when the Bulgarians came to the aid of the Byzantine Empire, slaughtering 20,000 Arabs. In August of the same year, the caliph Omar recalled the army. By one account, of the 1,800 ships that started the siege, only five remained.

The Isaurians are credited with significant internal reforms. Leo III (c. 680–741) initiated legal reform in order to translate the Latin JUSTINIAN CODE into Greek and to reform the law to fit the many changes in the empire since the reign of JUSTINIAN I. This produced the Ecloga, as well as rural and military codes.

An important internal change during the Isaurian dynasty was the increase in SLAVS throughout the Balkans, most significantly in Greece. This was helped by the depopulation produced by the BLACK DEATH of 746–747, which led to problems for the Byzantine emperors' efforts to control the Balkans and Greece.

Iconoclasm. The Isaurian dynasty began the 100-year conflict regarding iconoclasm. Historians dispute the rationale for Leo III's banning the use of images in CHRISTIANITY. He was undoubtedly concerned with the growing wealth and prestige of the monasteries, a power that conflicted with that of the emperor. In addition, Leo probably hoped that iconoclasm would induce Byzantine JEWS and Muslims, who rejected image worship, to accept imperial rule. Leo's policies were intensified by his son Constantine V, who mercilessly rooted out iconodules, particularly in the ranks of the monks. He expropriated monasteries and exiled monks who refused to submit. The military was also used against common folk in the West who resisted iconoclasm. There was a relaxation of the policy with the advent of Leo IV, and Irene, an Athenian, which reimposed image-worshiping throughout the empire.

End of a Dynasty. The Isaurian dynasty came to an end with the troubled rule of Irene. Many elements of the empire resisted the rule of a woman. The Arabs gained territory in the East, and Irene was forced to accept a disadvantageous truce. These military failures as well as a rumored proposal to marry CHARLEMAGNE, recently crowned Roman Emperor of the West, led to general dissatisfaction and Irene's eventual downfall.

Historians credit the Isaurian dynasty with preserving the empire when it could have been defeated by Arab armies. The extension of the themes is also seen as a significant development for the future of the Byzantine Empire. On the other hand, there were defeats, such as Irene's losses in Asia Minor, as well as the permanent loss of the middle section of Italy. The introduction of iconoclasm only caused problems for the empire, hastening the schism between the Catholic and Orthodox churches, and causing tremendous suffering for both iconoclasts and iconodules.

ISIDORE OF SEVILLE, ST.

Isidore of Seville (560–636) was an archbishop, a theologian, an encyclopedist, and was considered by many contemporaries to be the most learned man of his age. He was probably born in Cartagena, but moved to Seville as a boy, where he was educated by his elder brother (Saint) Leander (c. 540–600), archbishop of Seville.

In 600, Isidore succeeded his brother as archbishop and held the episcopate for 37 years. During that time he presided over a number of important ecclesiastical councils and became involved in political life. He also worked toward the conversion of the JEWS and the VISIGOTHS (from Arianism), even though he espoused toleration and deplored forced conversions.

Isidore was one of the most prolific authors of his age; however, as a function of his celebrity, many works have been erroneously attributed to him. His most important work is the *Etymologiae*, a mammoth encyclopedia of almost 1,000 (hand-written) pages collecting nearly all the secular and religious knowledge available at the time. In creating the work, Isidore made use of classical and Christian texts, adapting and distilling from them what he considered their most essential points. The work relied heavily on etymologies, many of which are fanciful and absurd, and it is riddled with inaccuracies. Yet the *Etymologiae* was one of the most influential works of the Middle Ages. Almost 1,000 medieval editions of the work are still in existence.

Isidore was the author of numerous other works of note, including several on natural science, a history of the GOTHS, and several important religious works, most notably his *Sententiae*, a theological manual for the clergy, as well as liturgical and exegetical works. Although today Isidore is not considered a formidable scholar or a reliable historian, his writings had as much influence on medieval scholarship as did those of ST. AUGUSTINE (the only author with more surviving manuscripts from before 800) or Pope GREGORY I. He paved a bridge back to the classical past, for which he is honored as "last of the Western fathers of the Church." Isidore died in 636, and was canonized in 1598.

ILLUMINATIONS

Definitions as Instruction

Isidore may have proposed several of his more fanciful etymologies purely as a pedagogical device. Regarding the word *medicine*, for example—derived from the Latin for "cure" (something he almost certainly knew)—he writes: "It is thought that the word medicine is derived from the word *modo*, that is, in moderation, indicating that only a little medicine should be used. For nature is grieved by excess and rejoices in moderation. Thus, those who often drink herbal elixirs and imbibe great amounts of medicinal substances are continually suffering injury. For all immoderation causes not benefit, but harm."

ISLAM

Islam means submission to God (Allah). God's message to humanity, the religion of Islam insists, is communicated through God's "seal of the prophets," the last and most important prophet, MUHAMMAD. "There is no God but Allah, and Muhammad is his prophet." This is the fundamental tenet of Islam, which emerged in the seventh century in Saudi Arabia. It had become the dominant faith of the Mediterranean world and the Middle East by 800 C.E. In the subsequent six centuries, Islam spread to India, Indonesia, and other parts of East Asia. Today Islam embraces some 1.3 billion believers. Its only competitor as a world religion—a situation that already prevailed in 800 C.E.—is the Roman Catholic Church with some 1.1 billion members.

Muslims and Arabs. Since the holy book of Islam, the KORAN, was putatively dictated to Muhammad by the archangel Gabriel in Arabic, Muhammad's native language, and since Islam was spread in the seventh and eighth centuries by Arabic-speaking preachers (*mullahs*) and political leaders (caliphs, successors to the Prophet Muhammad), the terms "Muslim," a member of the Islamic faith, and "Arab" are frequently used interchangeably. But in the year 1000 C.E. in Arab-speaking and Muslim-dominated countries, there still remained significant minorities (perhaps 10 percent of the population) of mainly Greek Orthodox Christians. One such group, the Egyptian Copts, endures in substantial numbers to the present day. Furthermore in the Muslim, Arabic-speaking countries around 1000 C.E., there lived 1.5 million JEWS.

At least until the twelfth century the Islamic faith was highly tolerant of religious minorities and no effort at forced conversion was made by the Islamic political and religious leadership. Christians and Jews had to pay a special but not onerous poll (head) tax. Not being a Muslim made it difficult but not impossible to get a government job in an Islamic state. In fact, Christians and Jews generally prospered, economically and intellectually, and even politically, under Islamic rule .

Early Conquest. What Islam accomplished between 650 and 800 C.E. was to unite the warring peoples in the Arabian peninsula under a caliph. This united group invaded the Fertile Crescent of the Middle East, then under Byzantine rule. The Byzantine Greeks in CONSTANTINOPLE and the Iranians under the Sassanid dynasty had fought a long and debilitating war in the early seventh century that had severely weakened both states. This partly accounts for the rapid Arabic Muslim conquests in the area. By 720 C.E., the Arabs had driven the Byzantine Empire back into Asia Minor and part of the Balkans; they overran the Iranian kingdom; and by enlisting recently converted Mediterranean and Middle Eastern peoples for their Muslim armies, the Arabs then proceeded to conquer North Africa and nearly all of the Iberian Peninsula as well.

Dynasties. Until the middle of the eighth century this vast empire, from Iberia to Iran, was ruled from DAMASCUS, Syria, by caliphs of the UMAYYAD DYNASTY who traced their lineage back to lordly families in the Arabian peninsula in Muhammad's lifetime—but not by family lineage to the Prophet himself. When, in the latter half of the eighth century, the ABBASIDS, a native Persian dynasty, replaced the Umayyads in Iran, the great Umayyad Mediterranean empire fractured into smaller states, Umayyad rule surviving only in SPAIN.

European rendering of Muhammad on horseback, leading his followers (attended by the angel Gabriel) into Mecca.

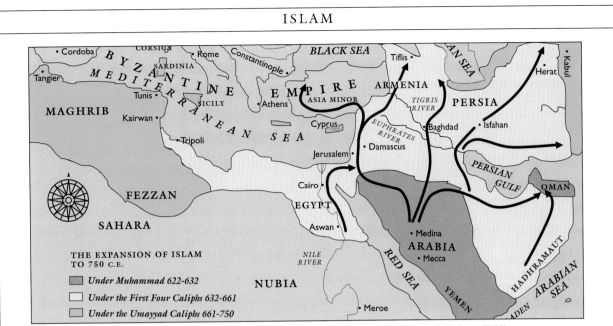

The Expansion of Islam from the career of Muhammad (622) until the Umayyad Caliphate (750).

Conversions. Henceforth, "Arab" stood for linguistic and cultural unity and Islamic religious dominance, but no longer simply for a political entity. What had happened in a century and a half was one of the great transformations of history. The Mediterranean world with its myriad of ancient cultures, languages, and religions was now under the rule of the Muslim Arabs, who emerged as the eventual political and economic successors to the Roman Empire. With little or no pressure from the Muslim mullahs and caliphs, at least 80 percent of the population of this vast land mass had converted to Islam by 1000 C.E. (*See* ARAB.)

In part, this was because Islam was a monotheistic religion with a puritan ethic like JUDAISM and CHRISTIANITY. But its reward system was simpler and more generous than either of the other two ancient Mediterranean religions. Islam promised Paradise (assured a heavenly reward) to all those of its members who followed the teachings of the Prophet without question; there was none of the agonizing complexity of St. Paul's and ST. AUGUSTINE's salvation theory. Judaism before 1200 C.E. did not offer individual immortality. Even after this article of faith was added to rabbinical dogma—by the great rabbi MAIMONIDES who lived in Muslim EGYPT—little emphasis was placed on it. Be conscientious, ethical, charitable, family-caring, attentive to daily prayers, avoid eating pork and drinking alcoholic beverages, Islam taught, and eternal life in Heaven will be your reward. Should one die fighting for Islam, then heavenly reward was automatic; in all, an appealing set of religious beliefs.

Division. In spite of these common doctrines, there was a big divide within the Islamic community, which had emerged by 1000 C.E. The Sunni majority gave leadership to mullahs and caliphs who perpetuated the kind of leadership offered by the original Umayyad lords within the Muslim world—scholars, preachers, and government officials who defended and propagated the faith. The Shi'ite minority, with its medieval center in Iran, accorded charismatic leadership to religious teachers who claimed direct descent from Muhammad's only child, his daughter FATIMA, and her husband Ali, who was martyred by the Umayyad lords. Sunni Islam was more tolerant, easier on minorities, more respectful of secular learning, and generally less militant and puritanical than the Shi'ites. In addition to these main groups—about 75 percent Sunnite and 20 percent Shi'ite—there were mystical groups called Sufis, who borrowed ideas from ancient Neoplatonism and extreme Greek Christianity.

Warfare. Intermittent warfare between Muslim and Greek Byzantine armies flared between the late seventh century and the fall of Constantinople to the Muslim OTTOMAN TURKS in 1453. In the West there were a series of conflicts between Latin Christian armies and Muslim Arabic-speaking peoples, especially in the frontier regions of Spain and southern Italy. From 1096 to 1240, Latin crusading armies periodically invaded the Islamic world in the eastern Mediterranean. Only the first of these Catholic expeditions, the First Crusade, was successful. A century later, the Muslims had regained Jerusalem. By 1290 they had driven the Latins—or "the FRANKS" as the Arabs called them and most of the crusaders for two centuries who were, in fact, French—from the Holy Land.

Around the year 1100 C.E., the Latin Christians hated "the Moors" (so-called because Muslim armies in Iberia used Moroccan mercenaries) as heretics as much as they feared their military skill, even though they envied the wealth and learning of Córdoba and other Arabic cities. After 1150, the Latin Christians established institutes of Islam and Arabic studies in FRANCE and then Spain. The Latin Christians became much more tolerant of Islam, which they now tended to regard as a separate legitimate if somewhat inferior religion, not as a dreaded HERESY. Recognition of the tremendous wealth, intellectual resources, and military and naval power of the Islamic world also encouraged tolerance of Islam by Catholic Europeans. In the sixteenth and seventeenth centuries, naval and military conflict on a grand scale between Latin Christians and Muslim Arabs and Turks resumed, ending only after a Turkish army was defeated at the gates of Vienna.

The two great and much-disputed questions of Islamic history are the life and personality of Muhammad and why the Islamic world began an economic and intellectual decline in the fourteenth century, which was not reversed until the twentieth century.

Muhammad. Much of the information on Muhammad as a person is derived from oral tradition and not any more reliable than the New Testament's life of Jesus. It appears that Muhammad came from a less affluent segment of a prominent family; that he became a business manager for a wealthy widow whom he married; that he was aware of the teachings of Judaism and possibly also those of Greek Christianity; and that after bitter conflicts with the prominent lordly families in Arabia, he asserted his leadership.

Decline. Why the Islamic world entered a period of decline after 1300 or 1350 is unclear. Excessive, autocratic, and self-indulgent political leadership; changes in international trade routes away from the Mediterranean; adverse climatic changes and diminution of the water table; intolerance on the part of the mullahs and caliphs for secular learning and natural science; pandemics—all these explanations have been offered with little consensus. Although mountains of documents from late medieval Islamic history survive, little study of these archives has yet been undertaken.

One thing is certain: the medieval Islamic world from before the fourteenth century, possibly up to 1650, was the site of one of the world's great civilizations. Its beautiful cities; its thriving international trade; its reservoir of learning, medicine, and SCIENCE; and its generally tolerant and congenial ambience made this multicultural, ethnically diverse, but generally religiously united society a very attractive place.

See ISLAM, RELIGIOUS PHILOSOPHY OF; MUHAMMAD; *and the entries on the* ABBASID, ALMOHAD, ALMORAVID *and* UMAYYAD DYNASTIES. *Also* ARABIC LANGUAGE AND LITERATURE; AFRICA; *and related material in* SCIENCE; MEDICINE; *and* LITERATURE.

ISLAM, RELIGIOUS PHILOSOPHY OF

T he Arabic word *Islam* means "submission to God" and designates a religion of uncompromising acceptance of the unity of God and the teachings of MUHAMMAD. This is expressed in the basic tenet of Islam: "There is no God save Allah, and Muhammad is His prophet." Islam differs from both Judaism and CHRISTIANITY in important ways, even though it is related to these religions and treats many religious and theological issues in similar terms.

Early History. The background against which Islam arose was the pagan bedouin culture of Arabia. The JEWS of the area were still recovering from the loss of their homeland in 135, and their Christian counterparts were fragmented and only loosely associated with churches in EGYPT and Mesopotamia. People of heightened spiritual awareness, *hanifs,* spoke of a search for a "high God," but there was little tradition on which to base a monotheistic religion in that region of the world at that time. This makes the career of Muhammad all the more remarkable. Although he based his preaching, first in his native city of Mecca, and then in neighboring Yathrib (later called Medina, "city of the Prophet"), on revelations, his teachings were a complete rejection of the paganism and the spiritual values he saw around him. In sober contemplation of his visions (Muhammad very reasonably wondered if he had not hallucinated or gone insane), he preached a unique, original, and consistent religion that has won millions of devout followers.

The teachings of Islam are contained most clearly in the Koran (also written as Qu'ran, meaning "recitation"), which contains messages received and transmitted by Muhammad during the twenty years of his ministry. The KORAN is the final work inspired by the book in heaven—called the "Mother of the Book"—that embodies the word of God. With the Koran, the emanation from the Mother of the Book is sealed, just as Muhammad is the seal of prophecy. In 114 chapters (*suras*), the Koran conveys the teachings of Muhammad in Arabic. Only the Arabic text is accepted for religious use; translations are viewed with suspicion.

Religion of Islam. As Islam spread, Muslims were faced with new situations which required guidance on matters not clearly covered in the Koran. The Muslim jurist ash-Shafi'i (who died about 820) identified four sources (or "roots") of Islamic law (the *shari'a*): The first and most important is the Koran, supreme authority over all else; the second is the *sunna* or practices of Muhammad handed down in an oral tradition, or *hadith*. If neither of the first two roots indicates a clear course of action, then one may resort to *ijma*, traditions of past Islamic communities. If the matter is still in doubt, then (and only then) may one resort to *qiyas*, or reason—arguing logically from what is known.

This order tells much about the Islamic attitude toward the place of humankind in the universe. In Islam, humanity has a benevolent relationship with God who created the universe as an act of loving kindness. God's goodness is manifested in His revelations to humanity through the Prophets; humankind acknowledges this relationship by obedience to God's will. Obedience, submission, and suppression of the boastful, self-assertive human ego are the life-long tasks of the Muslim; pride and self-reliance are the principal sins that lead people astray.

Much loving attention is paid to the hadith in an effort to discern the behavior prescribed by the Prophet. Early in the history of Islam, traditions were transmitted that were questionable, making it important to validate the transmitter of the hadith, the *isnad* ("list" of authorities). The most respected collections of such traditions are two works, one by Bukhari and the other by Muslim (they died in 870 and 875, respectively), which, along with four others, form the "sound" hadith, the basis of Sunni Islam and the core of Islamic law. Study of these works is the chief occupation in Islamic seminaries and the lifelong pursuit of the pious.

Page of the Koran, 13th century, with elaborate calligraphy, but with no figural representations.

Laws. Islamic laws and precepts are generally divided into two categories: *ibadat*, or religious duties owed to God, and *mu'amalat*, practical duties toward individuals and society—though there is no distinction between the two in Islam; they are of equal importance. Islamic law is concerned with tangible behavior and not with intentions and motivations. Proper actions are what count; the extolling of inner motivations and dispositions by both Judaism and Christianity is, from a Muslim point of view, haughty and vain, placing too much emphasis on the individual. Finally, Islamic law transcends human reason and understanding. God has lovingly sent His message to humanity for the purpose of guiding humankind to freedom and goodness; the intent of God is beyond understanding. Obedience requires acceptance and fulfillment of the law regardless of whether one understands it or not. The law applies to the individual, not to a community or group.

Thus, the individual is accountable only to God, not to a church or a clergy class. (Strictly speaking, there are no priests in Islam, only teachers. Prayers are not led by officiants; any mature Muslim can lead them.)

The Five Pillars. The five "pillars" upon which the religion of Islam rests are: the profession of faith (*shahada*); ritual prayer (*salat*); charity to the poor (*zakat*); fasting (*sawm*); and pilgrimage (*hajj*). To some, holy war (*jihad*) is the fifth pillar, and shahada is the foundation of the five pillars. Islamic law regulates many aspects of daily life, including the food a Muslim is permitted to eat, proper dress and etiquette, the slaughter and preparation of animals for food, and the rituals surrounding daily prayer and pilgrimages. The key to the shahada is the belief in the Oneness of God (known as the principle of *tawhid*). A Muslim is required by salat to direct prayer (*qibla*) toward Mecca six specific times a day in a series of recitations from the Koran with bowings and prostrations. The salat may be performed in any clean place, but on Friday Muslims gather in mosques for communal prayer. Fasting is observed during the lunar month of Ramadan, when Muslims abstain from food, drink, and sexual relations during daylight hours. After the month of Ramadan ends—and the month can be trying when it occurs during the summer (as it can, since the Muslim lunar calendar is not fixed and the months rotate through the seasons)—a festival of several days is observed throughout the Muslim world. Finally, the hajj is performed at the holy shrines of Mecca, particularly the Kaaba, the hills of Safa and Marwa, Mount Ararat, the plain of Muzdalifa, and the valley of Mina, all shrines associated with Muhammad.

The process of examining the roots to determine the law is called *ijtihad*, meaning "strenuous examination." In time, however, Sunni schools of law (*madhhabs*) arose and established norms of behavior throughout the Islamic world. There are three major schools emanating from Damascus, Medina, and Baghdad. Every Muslim is expected to adhere to the teachings of one school or another; the differences between them are, even in the eyes of Muslims, minor. Submission (*taqlid*) to the authority of one particular Muslim school is the basis of living as a Muslim.

Schools of Islam. The different schools of Islam have nearly as much to do with questions of political succession as with theology. But the natural inclination of the human mind to impose order on a body of knowledge (which Muslims regard with suspicion) led to the creation of a philosophical theology known as the *kalam* or "speech," meaning the speech of God.

The first controversy in Islamic theology was over how to reconcile the conflict between Divine Omnipotence and Omniscience and human free will. The position favorable to the Umayyads, developed by the Murji'a, was that all is preordained, so that the best indication that the Umayyads should rule is that they, in fact, did rule. The Khawarji countered that humans have the free will to sin or not to sin; by defying the authority of the Prophet (in the person of Ali), the Umayyads had violated the sunna and become sinners.

Out of this debate, a splinter group developed into a full-fledged school of theology that dealt with all manner of issues concerning the attributes of God. This group was known as the Mu'tazila, and while they were regarded by some Muslims as freethinkers and heretics, they were traditional and pious Muslims who had great influence on Jewish and Christian theology in the late Middle Ages. The Mu'tazila used the full literature of Greek logic and philosophy to analyze a host of theological problems. Their writings on logic are some of the most astute and mathematically sophisticated produced prior to the modern era (and in some views, ever produced). They were warmly supported by the early Abbasid caliphs, particularly al-Ma'mun.

The Mu'tazila taught that anthropomorphic (human-like) descriptions of God have to be interpreted allegorically, because the qualities of God (His "attributes") are identical with His essence and not something distinct from or added to it (as are qualities of ordinary objects). This led the Mu'tazilites to believe that people have free will (because God wills that they do) and that the Koran was "created" (as opposed to having pre-existed all of creation).

The Mu'tazila were never able to gain a large following in Islam, but their most significant contribution was the reaction they provoked. Beginning with Ahmad ibn Hanbal and continued most forcefully by Ash'ari (who died in 935), a reaction to the overly rational approach of the Mu'tazila led to the formation of an "orthodox" Islamic theology that insisted the Koran was the literal truth, viewed the attributes of God as real but unknowable, regarded human freedom as a momentary gift from God, and believed the Koran to be eternal and uncreated. Along with the writings of Maturidi (who died in 944), the writings of al-Ash'ari form the basics of orthodox Sunnism. Some of the most influential Islamic scholars, such as AL-GHAZALI, adopted al-Ash'ari's theological positions, while later

philosophers who did not, such as AL-FARABI and Ibn Sina, remained on the periphery of Islamic thought.

Another reaction to the dry reasoning of the Mu'tazila was represented by the schools of Islamic mysticism collectively known as Sufism. The Sufis exhibited many characteristics typical of religious mystics: asceticism; secret training; a concern with the afterlife and Judgement Day; rituals designed to heighten awareness or ecstatic experience of communion with God.

The Sufis, who studied and practiced in secret, did not anticipate conflict with orthodox Sunnism. But orthodox Muslims found much in Sufism that was problematic. They were accused of placing internal mental prayer above public, ritual prayer, giving intentions precedence over action. In addition, Sufi claims to have been Divinely inspired while in a trance challenged the notion that prophecy was over after Muhammad. In the face of persecution, Sufis devised handbooks that provided guidelines for religious practices that embodied the values they sought to achieve. These guidelines developed into different orders or communities where different practices could be observed as a means of achieving the religious ecstasy the Sufis sought. Each order was headed by a sheikh, who was master of the brethren, known as *faqir* or darvish (dervish). Each Sufi order had rituals (*dhikr*) peculiar to it, taught and practiced in its monastery (*ribat* or *khanqah*). Some orders preferred silent meditation; others, like the Mawlawis (the whirling dervishes) were famous for introducing ecstatic dance and music into their services; still others, like the Rifa'is (howling dervishes) were known to inflict wounds on themselves to make themselves cry out in painful ecstasy.

Another religious group that began out of political concerns was the Shi'ites. Shi'a ("party") is the general name for Islamic sects that recognized Ali as Muhammad's legitimate successor. Shi'ite leaders, called imams, never achieved power in the Islamic world (many were murdered by Sunni leaders or killed in battle), and the group itself split into three factions after the death of the sixth imam, Ja'far al-Sadiq, in 767. Shi'ites were united in believing that the only legitimate succession to the Prophet was from his own blood line, because only Muhammad's descendants are imbued with Divine insight that enables them to reveal the hidden sense (*batin*) of the Koran. "Whoever dies without knowing the true imam of his time," goes a Shi'ite proverb, "dies an unbeliever." Like the Sufis, the Shi'ites have had an enormous influence on Islamic religion right to the present day.

See MUHAMMAD; KORAN; ISLAM; *and* ISLAMIC ART AND ARCHITECTURE. *Teachings of individual Islamic thinkers are discussed in* AL-FARABI; AVICENNA; AL-GHAZALI; *and* AVERROËS. *See also* UMAYYAD *and* ALMOHADS.

ISLAMIC ART AND ARCHITECTURE

The art and architecture of the Islamic world developed rapidly as the Muslims extended their influence during the Middle Ages. At its peak, the Islamic Empire stretched from SPAIN to India. The rich mixture of diverse cultures, joined together by a common religion, allowed for the emergence of an artistic tradition that drew from regional influences to produce a distinctive style.

Throughout the Islamic world could be found definite similarities. All Muslims prayed in mosques, which were built according to a broadly standard design. Students went to Islamic schools called *madrasas*, also built on a standard plan featuring courtyards and small mosques. Traveling Muslims could stop at special lodging places called caravansaries, and those seeking religious retreat could go to small buildings called *zawiyyas*. But these structures featured regional embellishments. A number of decorative arts thrived throughout the medieval Islamic Empire. Each region, however, was generally known for its expertise with a particular art form, often predating the establishment of Islam.

Rise of the Mosque. The word "mosque" derives from the Arabic word *masjid* ("a place for prostration"). The first mosque, dating from the early 600s, was established by MUHAMMAD in Medina. It was a simple enclosed structure made of mud brick walls, which may have in fact originally been his home. The building remained intact in the years following Muhammad's death in 632; eventually it was expanded into a more elaborate structure.

The typical mosque contains an interior wall facing Mecca (so worshippers know which direction to face), a recessed area—a *mihrab*—where prayers were said, and the pulpit from which those prayers were given, the *mimbar*. Outside the mosque are towers known as minarets (usually at each corner of the building), from which worshippers are called to prayer.

Later mosques were often quite elaborate in design, both inside and out. High domes, vaulted ceilings, and courtyards were common. Interiors were lavishly decorated with tiles, MOSAICS, metalwork, and glass. The exteriors were often decorated with stucco, which was usually fashioned to form a pattern.

Regional Variations. In the early days of Islam, its art and architecture were primarily Iraqi and Syrian. As the religion spread, so did its contact with other peoples—and other art forms. By the second half of the Middle Ages, Islamic art and architecture followed a general pattern throughout the empire, but variations stemming from different cultural influences had a significant impact. In Iran, for example, mosques were built with domed halls called *eyvans* that opened onto courtyards. The Iranians also built a series of richly designed tombs, often cylindrical or octagonal in shape, also with high domes. In Iraq and Syria, calligraphy flourished, as did MANUSCRIPT ILLUMINATION. Syrian buildings were decorated with different colored stone and marble. (*See* ARCHITECTURE; ALHAMBRA.)

In Islamic EGYPT, buildings were given decorative ornamental facades. Decorative arts included linen textiles, jewelry making, and glassmaking. In SPAIN and North AFRICA, many mosques were built, as were palaces and a number of *zawiyyas*. Buildings were decorated with tiles and intricately carved woodwork. Turkish Muslims devoted most of their artistic energies to madrasas. Madrasas throughout the Islamic world had similar features

Entrance portal to the shrine of Imam Riza, the Mosque of Gawharshad, built in 1418, Mashhad, Iran.

(small classrooms surrounding a courtyard and a small mosque), but the Turkish buildings boasted particularly beautiful ceramics and splendidly decorated portals. The Turks were also well known for their rugs. Rug-making was an important art in Turkey, and Turkish rugs were coveted throughout Europe as well as the rest of the Islamic world.

Religious Restrictions. Islam expressly forbids the worship of likenesses of prophets or other religious figures. Because of this, neither human nor animal figures are used as religious decoration in houses of worship or religious texts. When the Muslim Turks conquered CONSTANTINOPLE in 1453, they converted many of the Byzantine churches into mosques—taking care to cover ICONS and other religious symbols.

But this prohibition does not preclude representations of figures in secular settings; Islamic palaces, for example, often had wall paintings and mosaics depicting humans and animals. Nor does it mean that religious texts were devoid of decoration. Religious texts such as the KORAN may have no human or animal figures, but they are nonetheless often lavishly decorated with colorful geometric patterns or vegetal (plant) designs. Calligraphy, the art of decorative handwriting, became an important and much-admired artistic skill throughout the Islamic Empire.

By the end of the Middle Ages, the Islamic states had largely been absorbed by the Ottoman Empire, which, as an Islamic dynasty, carried on the rich traditions of Islamic art and architecture. (*See* ISLAM; ISLAM, RELIGIOUS PHILOSOPHY OF; MOSAICS; KORAN; HANDWRITING; *and* MANUSCRIPT ILLUMINATION.)

ITALY

After the disappearance of the Roman emperor from Italy in the late fifth century, the destiny of the great peninsula depended mainly on two things: the capacity of the pope to exercise leadership in Italy; and the capability of the Italian cities in the north and south, including SICILY, to transform their material resources into political autonomy and cultural achievement. The pope exercised control over a band of territory running across the central part of Italy, including ROME, called the Patrimony of St. Peter, also known as the PAPAL STATES.

The Papacy. Over the centuries, the popes spent much time and resources in trying to keep an emperor from the north (CAROLINGIAN FRANCE and then GERMANY) from controlling northern or perhaps all of Italy, thereby subjugating the PAPACY. The issue came to a head in the period 1160 to 1250 when the papacy allied itself with the LOMBARD League of northern Ital-

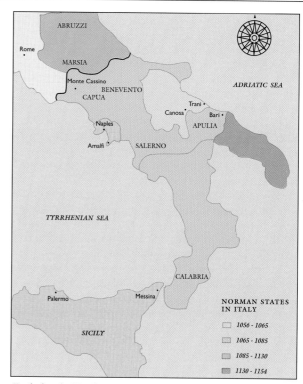

Italy in the Early 13th Century. The Italian peninsula was the meeting ground of forces that would determine the future of all of Europe in the coming centuries.

ian cities and heavily subsidized the League's armies against the HOHENSTAUFEN emperors FREDERICK I BARBAROSSA and FREDERICK II. The latter emperor posed a special threat by also being king of Sicily in inheritance from his mother. The papacy, by enormous exertion and expenditure, just managed to defeat the Hohenstaufens, but this venture left the papacy dependent on the French monarchy to which it had also allied and to which it had rashly proffered Sicily.

It was the northern Italian cities, especially the great ports of VENICE and GENOA, and the inland cities of MILAN, FLORENCE, and Siena, which derived their wealth from industry as well as trade, that now came to the forefront in Italian political and cultural life in the early fourteenth century as the papacy fell prey to the political hegemony of the French monarchy and long exile from Rome to AVIGNON. Sicily, after 1300, began its slow decline from agricultural and commercial prosperity to its modern renown for crime and poverty, probably because of mismanagement by a succession of French and Spanish regimes, possibly also owing to climatic deterioration.

Urban Culture. The fourteenth and fifteenth centuries were the golden age of the northern Italian cities, the scene of a thriving bourgeois elite who engaged in international trade from ENGLAND to India and CHINA; who developed modern credit and BANK-ING institutions; and who showed remarkable taste in their patronage of the visual arts and the adornment of the urban environment, both in public spaces and in private residences. From the time of the Florentine writer PETRARCH in the 1360s, a succession of human-ists celebrated the accomplishments of the northern Italian cities, and their capitalist autocracies, as the Re-naissance of the glory of classical Rome. They set up secondary schools to train the sons of the high bour-geoisie in classical LATIN, modern Italian, and the man-ners of courtly gentlemen.

Urban Politics. The northern Italian cities did not fare as well as republics on the political side. After decades of tumultuous conflicts between rival wealthy families, and social unrest on the part of the artisan class, by 1400, the cities had generally surrendered their republican quasi-democracy to the dictatorship of a podesta or, as he was called in Venice, the Doge. Be-cause of technical problems related to sewage and pub-lic health, the great Italian cities of the Renaissance never grew beyond 125,000 people. But in the fif-teenth century, those cities were the scene of artists, sculptors, architects, writers, publishers, and classical scholars whose capability and ingenuity has never been surpassed. The cities also generated the start of mod-ern high cuisine, using spices imported from East Asia. Transmitted to France in the sixteenth century by a Florentine princess who became a Parisian queen, in-novative northern Italian cooking also got French cui-sine started. The central parts of Florence and Venice look today much as they were in 1500 and no more salubrious urban environment has ever been devel-oped. In the early sixteenth century, most of the great cities lost their independence to invading armies of the HABSBURG Empire, but their wonderful art and lifestyle continued undiluted to the present day.

 See entries on VENICE; GENOA; MILAN; FLO-RENCE; *and* ROME. *Additional material in* PAPACY; PAPAL STATES; NORMANS; SICILY *and* SICILIAN VESPERS. *Italian writers in-clude* PETRARCH; BOCCACCIO; *and* DANTE.

IVAN III THE GREAT

Ivan III (1440–1505) was Russia's first grand duke of the House of Rurik, consolidating power during a 43-year reign, as MONGOL dominance of the region weakened.

Early Life. Ivan was born the son of Vasily II, grand prince of MOSCOW. Ivan's childhood coincided with civil turmoil in Moscow, as a result of tensions be-tween his father and his father's family, which sided with Moscow's enemy, NOVGOROD. When he was seven, Ivan was named co-grand prince and, in a peace offering, was betrothed to Maria of Tver, daughter of a NOVGOROD grand prince. As an adolescent, Ivan fought against the Tatars. In 1462, the 22-year-old Ivan succeeded his father. It was the first time that a Russian emperor was chosen without the confirmation of the khan of the GOLDEN HORDE, an early sign that Mongol control—the "Tatar yoke"—of what is now RUSSIA was slipping. (*See* MONGOLS; GOLDEN HORDE.)

Ivan's Reign. Early in Ivan's reign, the khanate of the Golden Horde tried to reassert its control, but Ivan's armies held off the Mongols. In 1471, Ivan de-feated Novgorod, which now became subject to the dukes of Moscow. Ivan refused to pay tribute to Grand Khan Ahmad five years later and subsequently defeated him. When the Tatars crossed the Don and threatened Moscow, Ivan ordered a tactical retreat, which halted the Mongol advance. Ivan tore up the charter subju-gating Moscow to the Mongols. Ahmad was murdered in 1481 after trying to reimpose the Tatar yoke.

Ivan's armies successfully quelled rebellion in Novgorod in 1478 and 1480, when Ivan declared himself prince of Novgorod. In 1484, his troops an-nexed the principality of Tver, a northern rival. As a re-sult, Ivan added the title of prince of Tver to the others he had already.

As grand duke, Ivan attempted to establish himself as the heir to the Byzantine Empire. He brought Eu-ropean art and culture to Russia, specifically bringing artists such as the painter Dionysus and the architect Marco Ruffo to Moscow to work. He also oversaw the rebuilding and expansion of the Kremlin; to this day, a bell tower and square at the Kremlin bear his name. In the royal court, Ivan began referring to himself as czar, a variation of "caesar." He adopted the Byzantine dou-ble-eagle crest as a Russian national symbol. Most sig-nificantly, after his first wife's death in 1472, Ivan married Zoë Paleologa, the niece of the last Byzantine emperor, Constantine XI. Yet leaders of the more es-tablished European states, including the HABSBURG and OTTOMAN empires, did not see Moscow as a wor-thy successor to Byzantium—a "third Rome"—and withheld recognition.

Rebellion. Ivan also had to deal with internal ten-sions. Two of his brothers openly rebelled against him, and his wife Zoë left the Kremlin in 1480, later plot-ting against him. Ivan had great difficulty choosing a successor. His only son by his first wife died in 1490, leaving his son by Zoë, Vasily (the eldest of nine), and his nephew, Dmitry. Dmitry was named crown prince in 1497, but the intrigues of Zoë and Vasily led to Dmitry's abrupt imprisonment in 1502. Ivan, having named Vasily his heir, died on October 27, 1505. (*See* RUSSIA *and* NOVGOROD.)

JACOB BEN MEIR

almudist Jacob ben Meir (1100–1171), known as Rabbeinu Tam ("Our master, par excellence") was the grandson of the Biblical and Talmudic commentator RASHI, and the younger brother of Rabbi Samuel ben Meir, another famous Talmudist. He was born in the town of Ramerupt in northern FRANCE, and was acknowledged as the greatest rabbinic scholar of the age. Communities throughout Europe sought his rulings on difficult matters. The academy he established became a center of European Jewish learning. (*See* JEWS; JUDAISM; RASHI.)

In 1146, when the Second CRUSADE passed through Ramerupt, a mob seized Rabbeinu Tam and attempted to crucify him. He escaped and moved to Troyes, Rashi's home town, where he remained until his death. Such incidents colored his legal opinions, and he usually urged JEWS to remain separate and aloof from their neighbors, which only hardened the barriers already existing between the Jewish and non-Jewish communities. However he also extended the rights of women and eliminated many superstitious customs that had been observed by Jews for centuries.

Rabbeinu Tam's commentary on the Talmud took the form of notes in which he questions (often vociferously) the interpretation of Rashi and then offers his own. These notes were collected mainly by Rabbeinu Tam's nephew and pupil, Rabbi Isaac Ben Samud of Dampierre, and presented as *Tosafot*, or "additions" to Rashi's work. The Tosafot were enlarged by the similar work of other rabbis of the period (the group collectively known as the Tosaphists) and became, along with Rashi, the basis of all future rabbinic analysis of the Talmud. Modern editions of the Talmud are invariably printed with the commentaries of Rashi and the Tosafot alongside the Talmudic text.

JACOPONE DA TODI

acopone da Todi (1230–1306) was a noted religious poet of the thirteenth century. Over the course of more than 30 years he wrote over 100 poems, including "*Donna del paradiso*," which describes Mary's sorrow at Christ's suffering. The Latin hymn *Stabat Mater Dolorosa*, which became part of the Roman Catholic liturgy in the eighteenth century, was probably composed by him as well.

Jacopone, whose original name was Jacopo Benedetti, was born to a noble family in the duchy of Spoleto. He studied law and made a comfortable living doing legal work. The sudden death of his young wife in 1268 led him to renounce his worldly life. He took a vow of poverty, devoting his life to God. In 1278, he became a lay brother of the FRANCISCAN friars.

The poetry and hymns of Jacopone are noteworthy for the strength of their spirituality. Most were written in Italian, although some (including *Stabat Mater Dolorosa*) were written in Latin and are among the great works of medieval liturgical literature. But he also wrote satires directed at Pope BONIFACE VIII, critical of what he believed was the pope's materialism. He was one of the signers of a manifesto in 1297 that declared the election of Boniface invalid. In 1298 Boniface excommunicated and imprisoned Jacopone, who remained imprisoned until the pope's death in 1303. (He continued to write poetry while in prison.) The new pope, Benedict XI, released him, and he retired to the monastery at Collazone, where he died in 1306.

JACQUERIE

he French uprising of 1358, one of the most violent peasant revolts of the Middle Ages. Although it lasted less than a month, the rebellion embroiled a large area outside PARIS and terrorized hundreds of noble families before it was put down with equal violence. (*See* PEASANTS' REVOLTS.)

The revolt was a response to the rising costs of war with other countries, notably ENGLAND. French nobles kept raising taxes on the peasantry to finance their battles. The peasantry's anger grew until it finally exploded in May 1358. A peasant group was organized by Guillaume Cale in St. Leu d'Esserent, north of Paris. (The name "Jacquerie" comes from the common practice of referring to all peasants as "Jacques.") The group grew quickly and spread throughout the region, brutally killing nobles, including women and children. In June, the nobles (aided, paradoxically, by the English) viciously crushed the Jacquerie, killing many who had not been involved in the rebellion.

JACQUES DE MOLAY

acques de Molay (c. 1243–1314) was the last grand master of the Templars. Born in eastern FRANCE, he joined the order about 1265, did military service in Syria, and was elected grand master about 1298. In 1307, he presented an impressive plan for a CRUSADE to Pope CLEMENT V. He also made known his opposition to a proposed union of the Templars and their longtime rivals the Hospitallers, thus, perhaps, sealing his own and his order's fate. Despite Clement's temporizings, in October 1307 King PHILIP IV of France, seeking to expropriate the Templars' wealth, arrested de Molay and the other Parisian Templars. A former member of the order testified that the Templars had for many decades been secret Muslims and sodomites. Appearing before the INQUISITION, de Molay, evidently after TORTURE, confessed to blasphemy but denied accusations of sodomy. He recanted before an investigative commission appointed by Clement. At a national council in May 1308, de Molay and his brethren were condemned. Their trial reopened, and they languished in prison for more than five years, during which time Clement was maneuvered into suppressing the Templars in March 1312.

On March 19, 1314, a commission of cardinals finally sentenced de Molay to life imprisonment. When de Molay again repudiated his confession, Philip seized the opportunity to have him burned at the stake as a heretic on an island in the Seine. (*See* KNIGHTS OF THE TEMPLE *and* KNIGHTS OF ST. JOHN.)

JAMES I

The most renowned king of ARAGON, James I (1208–1276) was born to King Peter II of Aragon and Mary of Montpellier. His father died at the hands of the crusaders, and James, five years old at the time, was left in the hands of the crusader leader SIMON DE MONTFORT. Released through the efforts of POPE INNOCENT III in April 1214, James was recognized as the sovereign of Aragon and CATALONIA and placed under the protection of the Templars at Monzon. (*See* SPAIN; ARAGON.)

Early Reign. James's uncle Count Sancho ruled during his minority, resigning in 1218 in the face of opposition from Aragonese, Montpellier, and Catalonian nobles. James matured during the rebellion and the private wars that followed Sancho's resignation, becoming a skilled and fearless fighter, and developing a keen sense of chivalric honor that remained with him throughout his life. James reached his majority in 1227 and, with the support of his BARONS, the Templars, and the pope, dedicated himself to the RECONQUEST of Christian territories from the Moors. He began with the Balearic Isles, capturing Majorca in 1229 and Ibiza in 1235, using the islands to defend the Catalan coast and as bases for commercial and territorial expansion. In 1233, James began the second stage of his reconquest, this time directed against the SARACEN rulers of the kingdom of Valencia. He captured Valencia in 1236. He spared many of the cities and allowed the defeated Moors to leave in peace.

Expanding Kingdom. By his second marriage to Yolande, daughter of Andrew II of HUNGARY (he had married Eleanor of CASTILE in 1221, but divorced her in 1229), James acquired territories in northern Europe, and produced several heirs to his kingdom. However, the partition of the kingdom between his sons Alfonso, Peter, and Ferdinand led to bitter contention. Alfonso claimed that James favored Peter, to whom he gave the kingdom of Catalonia, expanding its western limits and separating it from ARAGON. James's expansion in SPAIN was somewhat balanced by his disappointments in southern France; through the treaty of Corbeil (1258), James ceded all rights to territories in southern France except Montpellier (his maternal heritage) to King LOUIS IX of France, while Louis renounced his claims to territories of Catalonia. James then engaged his daughter Isabel to Philip, heir to the throne of France, to seal the exchange. James also initiated profitable diplomatic relations with North Africa. His son Peter married Constance of SICILY, preparing the way for Sicily's eventual incorporation into the Aragonese kingdom.

Balearic Islands. One of the more celebrated of James I's military campaigns was his conquest of the Balearic Islands, an archipelago in the western Mediterranean off the coast of Spain. On the pretext that Catalan merchants were being harassed by Moorish pirates based on the islands, James laid siege to Majorca, the largest island, in 1229 and captured it that December. He gave the islands to his youngest son, James, who ruled the Kingdom of Majorca and used it as base for periodic challenges to his brother's reign in Aragon. Majorca was to remain a thorn in the side of the rulers of Aragon until it was conquered in 1344.

Late Reign. James's final years, however, were not a fitting conclusion to his distinguished reign, which had included major advances in Catalan trade, the first assembly of the Aragon cortes, significant administrative advancements, and the compilation of a new maritime legal code. James led a CRUSADE to Jerusalem in 1269 (getting no further than France), and his last years saw a growing dissatisfaction among his barons over his military program. An uprising in Valencia led to a general Saracen rebellion in 1275, which James was in the process of quelling when he fell ill and died at Valencia on July 27, 1276. He was succeeded by his son Peter.

A gifted soldier and an able ruler, handsome and purportedly amorous, James inspired (though did not write) the *Book of Deeds*, which chronicled his impressive achievements. James was also responsible for the creation of a new maritime code that served as a model for other such systems, and he established the CORTES of Aragon, an assembly of clergy, nobility, and representatives of the cities and towns that advised him.

JAPAN

Japan is an island nation located in eastern Asia, between the Pacific to the east and the sea of Japan to the west. The group of four islands was brought together as an empire before the Middle Ages, and remained one up to the modern era. Although the country had an emperor, for much of its history the emperor was more a figurehead than an actual ruler of the people.

Early Middle Ages. In the late sixth and early seventh centuries, Prince Shotoku, acting as regent of Japan, constructed an aristocratic government that was modeled after the Chinese government. CHINA's influence extended beyond government to culture and religion as well. Works of art, architecture, and sculpture were influenced by Chinese culture. Only in language and literature were the Japanese able to preserve a unique style, despite the introduction of Chinese literature and language to the island.

Buddhism found its way into Japanese civilization both artistically and religiously, promoted by the governing body of Japan as a means to individual happiness and peace for the nation as a whole. Monasteries called *kokubun-ji* and nunneries called *kokubun-niji* were built.

With the advent of the aristocratic government in the early seventh century, Japan's imperial rule was weakened as political power was parceled out amongst its nobility. In the middle of the seventh century, imperial rule was restored and remained in place for another 500 years. During this time, a feudal system emerged. The aristocracy exempted the large landowners from taxes in return for military service. Peasants who worked for the landowners were organized into private armies.

Late Middle Ages. The middle of the twelfth century brought a time of civil war with the collapse of the Fujiwara regime. It was not until 1185 that order was restored with a new constitution. The chief commander of the army, the *shogun*, appointed by the emperor, was given military and political power, and held supremacy over the civil government. The shogunate system lasted for some 700 years.

As a result of the political infighting, a class of warriors emerged among the wealthy peasants—the *samurai*. They developed a strict code of ethics and behavior, and were instrumental in turning back the MONGOL invasions in the late thirteenth century.

In 1318, Daigo II, with samurai support, divided the shogunate into two courts, northern and southern. In 1392, however, Yoshimitsu of the Ashikaga house reunited the shogunate and restored military rule. His house ruled as a dynasty until the sixteenth century. (*See* CHINA; MONGOLS; EXPLORATION.)

JEROME, ST.

St. Jerome (c. 347–419), one of the most influential early Christians, is best known for the Vulgate, his translation into LATIN of the BIBLE, which would remain the standard Latin version for more than a thousand years. He was also a noted monastic leader and a classical and biblical scholar, for which he was declared a doctor of the Church.

Jerome was born in what is now Slovenia. His family was well off and sent him to school in ROME when he was around 12 years old. He was a gifted and eager student, especially of Latin and Latin literature.

Travels. Upon completion of his studies in Rome, around 366, Jerome was baptized a Christian. For the next 20 years he traveled extensively. He became interested in the monastic life after meeting a group of ascetics; in 375, he decided to live as a hermit for two years in the desertlike climate of the Greek city of Chalcis. Although lonely and unhappy, he made the best of his situation, writing extensively, studying Hebrew, and studying old manuscripts. He left the desert in 377; a year later, he was ordained a priest. He studied scripture, and began translating a number of Greek religious works into Latin. (*See* MONASTERIES.)

Rome. In 382, Jerome returned to Rome to serve as secretary to Pope Damasus. He continued translating Greek religious works into Latin, and became spiritual adviser to a group of noble Roman widows and virgins. He found Roman life increasingly unfulfilling and felt that the priests there had become too worldly. Making his feelings known did not win him many friends within the Church hierarchy. When Damasus died late in 384, Jerome decided to seek a more ascetic life in Bethlehem. He left Rome in the summer of 385. A widow he had advised accompanied him and they established a convent outside Jerusalem. Jerome would also build a monastery in the city itself where he lived for the remainder of his life.

Later Years. It was during these years that Jerome translated the Old Testament of the Bible into Latin. He used both Greek and Hebrew texts for this project, which he worked on between 391 and 406. He also wrote numerous commentaries on sections of the Bible (both the Old and the New

Ivory triptych illumination of St. Jerome translating the Gospel of John.

Testaments), and on many of the prophets. He wrote many other works, including a volume on Palestinian place names and another on the origins of Hebrew proper names in the Bible.

During those years Jerome corresponded with a number of friends and colleagues, including ST. AUGUSTINE. Jerome also wrote a number of original works, including several biographies of religious figures and numerous homilies.

His combination of scholarly knowledge, biblical scholarship, and ascetic beliefs made for a complex individual, but it was his complexity that caused Jerome to embark on so many different projects. As a result, his influence on medieval scholarship was particularly far-reaching. He remained an active scholar up until his death in Bethlehem. (*See* BIBLE.)

JEWISH ART IN THE MIDDLE AGES

Jewish art of the Middle Ages was molded by two restrictive forces: the biblical prohibition, the second of the Ten Commandments, against "graven" or sculptured images for the purpose of idol-worship (Exodus 20:4); and the frequent persecution of the Jews in both Christian and Muslim societies. The prohibition against graven images was often interpreted to mean that no artistic representation of any kind was permitted, though the Bible describes the Tabernacle and Solomon's Temple as adorned with elaborate images. The striking biblical scenes painted on the walls of the Dura Europus synagogue in Syria indicate that even in the mid-200s, when the paintings were created, artistic expression was a part of Jewish life. (*See* JEWS; JUDAISM.)

The pressures of anti-Jewish persecutions were to influence Jewish artistic values for centuries. Laws in both Christian and Muslim lands placed restrictions on the design and decoration of a synagogue; it could not outdo the local church or mosque. As people who might be forced to move at a moment's notice to a place with different artistic tastes, Jews learned that art was a risky investment. (*See* JEWS, EXPULSIONS OF.)

Synagogue Art. The MOSAIC floors of Byzantine synagogues like Bet-Alfa and Naarah show the rich use of both geometric and astrological designs and pictorial images; the overall design was no doubt influenced by similar designs in local churches. In fact, often the craftsmen who installed the mosaics in the synagogues were the very ones who had worked on the churches. In only two cases—Bet-Alfa and the neighboring synagogue of Bet-Shean—are the names of the Jewish folk artists known (Marrianos and his son Hanina).

"Hallelujah page" of the Prato (Spain) Haggadah, a brilliantly illuminated work of the early 14th century.

In medieval Christian Europe, synagogues were designed with a minimum of decoration. Literary sources mention ceremonial objects used in the synagogue service. Splendid artifacts (Torah scroll covers; ark curtains; chalices) were probably common, but nearly nothing has survived the ravages of time and persecution. Synagogues in SPAIN and in ARAB countries followed the patterns and designs of the nearby churches and mosques. Two beautiful surviving examples (both now churches) are in Toledo, Spain, the oldest dating back to the early 1200s.

Illuminated Manuscripts. The best examples of illuminated manuscripts were produced in the Islamic countries (EGYPT, Palestine, Yemen, and Persia) from the 800s onward, and in western European countries from the 1200s through the 1400s. The earliest dated Hebrew illuminated manuscript from the Islamic east is the Moshe ben Asher Codex from the Karaite synagogue of Cairo, containing the books of the Prophets. It is dated 894 and originated in Tiberias in Palestine. It is prefaced by a "carpet page"—an ornate and intricately designed page, adorned with symbols and micrography presenting the title and origin of the work. (*See* MANUSCRIPT ILLUMINATION.)

LIFE IN THE MIDDLE AGES

The Oldest Synagogue

The oldest surviving medieval European synagogue (called a *schule*, because it also housed a school) is in Worms, Germany, dating from 1175. The "double-nave" floorplan of two large halls intersecting was adapted from the monastic refectories and chapter houses of convents. In churches, the wings housed the choir, while in synagogues they served as the women's gallery. The style eventually became the standard for synagogue design throughout central and eastern Europe. The synagogue was destroyed by the Nazis in 1938, but was subsequently restored.

The works most frequently illuminated were codex Bibles; works used in synagogue or home observances, such as the *megillah* (the Book of Esther, read on Purim), the *mahzor* (a prayer book used on specific festivals), and the Passover Haggadah (recited at the Seder); and the ceremonial documents associated with marriage (such as the *ketubba*, or marriage contract).

In Islamic countries, some Hebrew illuminated manuscripts contained carpet pages; others had the first word or letter of the work enlarged and in a panel, surrounded by an arabesque design (a style still found in rabbinical works). Symbols, such as a stylized menorah or the Ark of the Covenant, were more likely to be shown than human or animal figures, which usually appeared only as micrographs or in silhouette.

The earliest illuminated Hebrew manuscripts in western Europe come from the Franco-German region (Ashkenaz), the oldest surviving being the Rashi commentary to the Bible, created in GERMANY, in 1233. The most significant manuscript illuminated in medieval Ashkenaz was the *mahzor*. Biblical scenes depicted figures in medieval dress, sometimes wearing the special garments required of Jews. Outstanding examples of illuminated manuscripts are the German Passover Haggadahs of the 1400s, many of which contain biblical scenes. Because of the qualms about the use of human forms on sacred works, artists drew people with the heads of animals or birds.

Virtually no illuminated Hebrew manuscripts survive from the Islamic phase of Spanish Jewish history, but the prevalence of Arabic designs in the works that survive from the Christian period beginning in the 1200s indicates that a tradition for such works existed earlier. In 1300, the center of such activity shifted to Italy, where, under the influence of Christian illumination, Hebrew legal codes, such as MAIMONIDES' Mishne Torah, and Hebrew translations of secular works, such as AVICENNA's medical works, were illuminated.

See JEWS IN THE MIDDLE AGES *and* JUDAISM *for background information. Compare with* ISLAMIC ART AND ARCHITECTURE. *See also* MAIMONIDES *and* MANUSCRIPT ILLUMINATION, *as well as* JEWS, EXPULSIONS OF.

JEWS IN THE MIDDLE AGES

E urope in the period from 500 to 1500 C.E. has traditionally been viewed as a dark, sad period in Jewish history, marked by oppression and violence at the hands of Christians and militant Muslims, alleviated only by a "golden age" (900–1150) in Muslim SPAIN under relatively benign rulers in Arabic Iberia. The reality of the fate of medieval Jewry is more complex and diverse than this traditional gloomy picture. (*See* SPAIN.)

In western Europe and also in pockets of central Europe, the Jews did very well in the era of the Great Migrations and the Germanic successor kingdoms to the Roman Empire, especially in the period between 700 and 1050 C.E. The Jews were under the protection of the most important and powerful political family of that era, the CAROLINGIANS, who loosely ruled FRANCE, much of western GERMANY, and some of northern ITALY in the eighth and ninth centuries. Jews were also under the patronage of the French aristocratic dynasty who ruled Normandy in the eleventh century, and after 1066, also ENGLAND. Such patronage and protection was extended by the French dynasties and lords because Jewish merchants and bankers offered facilities of long-distance and international COMMERCE and readily available large-scale loans to royalty and the aristocracy. (*See* COMMERCE.)

Even when bishops railed against the privileged economic and political status of the Jewish merchant and banking groups, the protection and patronage offered by kings and dukes nearly always continued. The Jews were especially helpful during the period of so-called Dark Age economics from 750 to 950, when there were tense and sometimes warlike conditions between the Christian and Arab worlds. Jewish mercantile families crossed the political frontiers and played an important role in keeping commercial channels open.

The Jews imported luxury items into Germanic Europe for the aristocracy from the southern and eastern Mediterranean shores and from lands as far away as India—spices, perfumes, silks, jewels. In return, Jewish merchants exported from Germanic Europe to the Arabic world—furs, swords, lumber, and, above all, slaves. Jews were the leaders in the robust white slave traffic from northern and central Europe to the Mediterranean during the early Middle Ages, as was proven conclusively in the 1940s—although it is blatantly evident in early medieval social records—by the Belgian scholar Charles Verlinden.

Out of this global economic situation emerged the structure of the Jewish communities in early medieval Europe, a structure that was in many ways perpetuated into the nineteenth century. The Jewish communities, numbering between a few hundred and a few thousand people in Germanic Europe, were dominated by a very small elite at the top of a dozen or so merchant families who over time—by 1000—had intermarried with a hereditary rabbinical elite. There was frequently a Jewish middle class of merchants in local trade and of successful artisans, comprising perhaps a quarter of the Jewish population. Bright adolescents from this middle class who distinguished themselves in rabbinical studies sometimes moved up the social scale by being absorbed into the upper classes through marriage to the daughters of wealthy merchants, thereby founding a new elite family.

Otherwise there was no significant social mobility in Jewish communities. The majority of the population—at least three quarters—were working class or lower middle class, working as laborers and craftsmen for the merchant capitalists. As such, they were subject to the rigorous legal and religious authority of the rabbinical elite, which intermarried with the merchant and banking magnates. This made for a turgid and suffocating society and culture.

These adverse conditions had little or nothing to do with Christian hostility or indifference to Jews. The early medieval world was one of family-based corporate communities. Even if a young Jew wanted to escape from the confines of the Jewish community by converting to CHRISTIANITY, he (rarely a she) would need a new corporate community and family to join. Even the monasteries were not an easy option. Early medieval MONASTERIES were highly selective, aristocratic brotherhoods that did not welcome rootless, impoverished strangers of any kind. The medieval world had no place for unconnected individuals.

That the small Jewish population of western Germanic Europe (two million at most) remained relatively static in the early Middle Ages indicates that there was loss through conversion, but not much.

In France, England, Germany, and northern Italy, from 1050 to 1200, there was a slow but steady dete-

Illumination from the 1351 edition of Mishne Torah, *the Jewish religious code written by Maimonides about 1180.*

rioration of the security and prosperity of the Jewish communities. In the following three centuries, the deterioration became acute, resulting in the impoverishment and exile of the Jews. By the early sixteenth century the majority of observant Jews from west European Christian lands (aside from Iberia) had sought refuge in POLAND. There the aristocracy found them useful for the same BANKING and credit skills that had endeared the Jews to western European magnates in the early Middle Ages. In Poland and the Ukraine, the Jews also co-opted estate management over servile peasants on behalf of the aristocracy. For their serf-driving services, the Jews were paid off with very profitable monopolies of liquor sales.

The main reason for the great decline in the status of the Jews in western Europe in the High Middle Ages was economic change. With urbanization and capitalist commercial expansion, there emerged ample Christian banking and mercantile families and corporations. By 1200, the old Jewish capitalist elite no longer had a useful function to serve in Christian society.

The Jewish capitalist elite hung on to its special protected status longest in England because there the mid-twelfth century monarchy drew a remarkable 20 percent if its income from taxing Jews (who still had enough wealth left over to support a handful of millionaire families). But after 1200, this vestige of early medieval society was rapidly eliminated.

In addition to economic change, the other main adverse factor affecting the Jews was the rise of a highly emotional, and at times militant, kind of Christianity. Now the traditionally hostile bishops received popular support when they railed against Jews and often exerted pressure or violence on Jews to obtain their conversion. Kings and lords, faced with this popular groundswell, could no longer protect Jews. Some kings, like the famous ST. LOUIS IX of France, were vehemently anti-Jewish. By the early fourteenth century, Jews were gone from England (not to return until 1653) and from most of France, except Alsace. (Many prominent modern French Jewish families are descended from that enclave).

In the fourteenth century, the Jews migrated into Germany, where the myriad of small principalities gave the Jews opportunity to find or buy occasional protection from a ruler. But the spread of the new militant Christianity into central Europe in the late Middle Ages and the social malaise of the BLACK DEATH of the mid-fourteenth century, for which Jews were often blamed, meant that the Jews in large numbers had to move to a more welcoming Poland after 1500, taking with them their German (Yiddish) dialect and their old elite–dominated communal structures.

The impression often given by Jewish historians of the rise of Christian hatred of the Jews in the High Middle Ages is that it was propagated by violent and greedy soldiers as crusaders, envious peasants, mad monks, mischievous bishops, and slow-witted monarchs. Though these kinds of people were involved, the most spiritual and creative minds of medieval Christianity—ST. ANSELM of Canterbury, ST. BERNARD OF CLAIRVAUX, ROBERT GROSSETESTE, GEOFFREY CHAUCER—were passionately committed to the same phobia. Anti-Semitism permeated not only the worst but also the best aspects of medieval Catholic spirituality, art, literature, and theory.

It is very likely that the Jewish population of western Europe increased rapidly in the twelfth and thirteenth centuries, along with escalation of the European population in general, due to benign climate and greatly improved food supply. But the actual Jewish population seems to have experienced only a modest net increase by 1200, indicating a substantial rate of Jewish conversion and departure from the Jewish communities—a conclusion suggested by anecdotal information. Western society after 1200 offered opportunities for individual advancement, so a Jewish convert was more likely to find that he (or she) could survive and even prosper in the expanding cities of the era. Moreover, the vast multiplication and expansion of Catholic religious orders, many of them new and seeking numbers, made access of Jewish converts to Christian religious orders much easier than in the early Middle Ages. By 1300, five percent of the Christian European population were members of the clergy. A bright literate young Jewish male (less often a female) could easily find a place within this burgeoning clerical population.

The outward migration of Jews into the surrounding populace was heightened by a cultural conflict within the Jewish community itself. From about 900 to 1100 C.E., there was a deepening of Halachic and Talmudic culture in western Europe, which drew upon the learning of the rabbinical schools in Iraq and Egypt. Such was the intellectual side manifested by the

rabbinical-merchant elite's strengthening control over the European Jewish communities. By the late twelfth century, as an expansion of philosophical and scientific thought was occurring in the ambient Muslim and Latin Christian worlds, the issue emerged of the extent to which rabbinical thought, long dominated by Talmudic legalistic learning, should participate in this classical Greek renaissance of the twelfth century.

MAIMONIDES and his followers campaigned vehemently for the melding of traditional Judaism with Aristotelian philosophy and science. After decades of disputes among the rabbinical elite, particularly in southern France and northern Spain, the followers of Maimonides lost out to the protagonists of the Kabbalah, a theosophical, astrological, and magical pastiche derived from ancient Hellenistic sources. This irrational, esoteric culture continued to dominate vanguard rabbinical thought into the late 1800s.

Whatever the merits or demerits of Kabbalistic culture, its triumph in France and Spain in the thirteenth and fourteenth centuries had disastrous consequences. It had the effect of driving Jewish intellectuals drawn by the rise of neo-classical philosophy and sciences away from the Jewish community and into the Catholic schools, universities, and religious orders committed to this secularizing culture.

The rise of militant anti-Semitism in the early thirteenth century in France was unquestionably exacerbated by the feeling of Church leaders that Jews were involved in the rise and spread of the dualist Manichean (Catharist, Albigensian) heresy, which by 1220 had gained the adherence of a quarter of the population of southern France. The Kabbalah was emerging in southern France at the same time as the Christian Manichean heresy; like Catharism, the Kabbalah drew heavily on first- and second-century Gnosticism. The Kabbalah had a tendency to theological dualism. It advertised an association of piety with sexual promiscuity, as did the Albigensians. And both the Kabbalists and Manicheans believed in the transmigration of souls. The Dominican friar–inquisitors sanctioned by the papacy against the Catharists were not insane when they turned their scrutiny and venom against Jews, although strictly speaking the Dominicans inquisitors had no mandate to do this.

It is also significant that in the first generation of Dominican inquisitors there were a number of Jewish converts. So the attack of the papal inquisition on the Jews in thirteenth-century France in part represented a split among the intellectuals of the Jewish community. The same internal culture conflict occurred in the days of the Spanish INQUISITION around 1500.

The Jewish golden age in Muslim Spain of 900–1150 was a product of the imagination of German Jewish scholars of the nineteenth and early twentieth centuries, seeking a sharp alternative to what they erroneously considered the unrelieved horror and distress of Jews in Christian lands. Jews were in fact second-class citizens, subject to special taxes in Muslim countries; Jewish ascendancy into Iberian Muslim government was an exceedingly rare occurrence.

Tenth- and eleventh-century Arab Iberia consisted of several principalities that practiced a loose centralized control in varying degrees. The Arab state was porous in its jurisdiction. The Arab elite was interested in collecting taxes and tribute from the subject Christian and Jewish populations. They had no other policy at the time toward either subject group. Under these circumstances, there was little incentive for Jews to convert to Islam, and the Jewish population increased. There was a steady infusion of wealth into the narrow elite of the Iberian Jewish communities from large-scale, long-distance commercial traffic; some of this prosperity trickled down to the Jewish masses. The learning and literary creativity of the Iberian Jews is much exaggerated. Maimonides did all his important writing in Egypt, and Judah Halevi's literary and philosophic output is charitably deemed second-rate. The finest of the Jewish writers, Solomon ibn Gabirol (c. 1022–c. 1070), wrote highly secular works powerfully influenced by Arabic forms and behavior patterns.

With the takeover of Muslim Spain by militant Islamic people from North Africa in the mid-twelfth century, the Sephardic Jewish position significantly deteriorated. Jews now found refuge in the expanding Christian states of northern and eastern Spain, especially Aragon and Catalonia.

In the thirteenth and fourteenth centuries, Jews played a much greater role in Christian Iberian governments, mainly in fiscal management, than they had ever played in Muslim principalities. The opportunity for Jewish participation in the rich Iberian scholastic Christian culture was, however, impeded by the rabbinical decision to depart from Maimonidean humanism in the direction of obscure Kabbalistic mysticism.

When in the closing years of the fourteenth century pressure was brought to bear in Spain by militant Christian groups and popular preachers for Jewish conversion, there was a crisis in the million members of the Iberian Jewish community. The intellectual, economic, and political advantages of conversion were overwhelming; the result was a massive Sephardic Jewish conversion to Christianity—at least half a million people. In the first three-quarters of the fifteenth century, Jewish converts or offspring of converts advanced to high positions in the Spanish Church and came to play highly visible roles in Christian spirituality and intellectual culture. What happened in 1492 was as much an onslaught by Jewish converts on the remaining minority of faithful Jews (probably 200,000) as an attack by an intransigent Church and a compliant monarchy.

The demographic importance of the famous expulsion of 1492 has also been greatly exaggerated. The traditional figure of 300,000 Jews departing—mostly at first to Portugal, and from there eventually to Holland and the Turkish Empire—cannot be sustained by modern research. The figure of voluntary exile lies at between an eighth to a third of that figure.

In 1492, there were already three-quarters of a million Jewish converts or descendants of converts to Iberian Catholicism. In that same year, at least 100,000 new converts were added—Jews who chose not to go into exile. As had been the case in France in the early thirteenth century, a significant number of Dominican friars and inquisitorial judges were Jewish converts. King Ferdinand of Aragon himself was partly Jewish. A leading modern scholar claims a quarter of the modern Spanish and Portuguese nobility were at least partly descended from Jewish converted families.

The dispute over the Marranos (converted Jews in medieval Spain) in the early sixteenth century, and the claim made by some militants that these converts were "crypto-Jews" was inspired by a bitter conflict within the Jewish convert community. The great majority of Jewish converts were sincere Christians; they hated and feared crypto-Jews, an acrimony that was no doubt heightened by Gentile jealousy over Jewish convert prominence in Iberian life.

Finally, the impact of the Spanish Inquisition on Iberian Jewry has been ridiculously exaggerated. In the whole history of Catholic inquisitions from early thirteenth-century France to early seventeenth-century Spain and Portugal, not more than 5,000 Jewish families suffered capital and less severe punishment at the hands of the Church courts.

Gentile intransigence and intolerance, the rigid Jewish hierarchical class structure, and the catastrophic decision of the late medieval rabbis to plunge into Kabbalistic obscurantism and exclude Maimonidean humanism resulted in Jewish self-segregation from European intellectual life until the nineteenth century. But it was not only the Jews who lost. Considering that Spain's leading humanist in the early sixteenth century, Juan Vives, was from a Jewish convert family as was the leading woman spiritual leader, Teresa of Avila, one can imagine the loss to European culture by the eastward migration of Jews from England, most of France, and large parts of Germany in the later Middle Ages into the cultural wasteland that was Poland and Ukraine at the end of the medieval period.

See JUDAISM; JEWS, EXPULSIONS OF; *and* INQUISITION. *Also,* JEWISH ART; BIBLE; MAIMONIDES; RASHI; *and* CRUSADES. *Jews play important roles in the histories of* ISLAM, CHRISTIANITY, *and* POLAND.

JEWS, EXPULSIONS OF

T he Jews of the Middle Ages lived in danger of persecution or expulsion nearly everywhere; Christians regarded their existence as a challenge to the authority of the New Testament, and Muslims saw their refusal to adopt ISLAM as insulting. As a despised and oppressed minority, they might still have managed in the various medieval societies were it not for the fact that their high level of learning and social organization allowed them to prosper as merchants. This made them convenient scapegoats for the lower classes and prime targets for rulers whenever funds were needed. (*See* JEWS; JUDAISM; CRUSADES.)

In the late Middle Ages, monarchs discovered that, with help from the clergy, they could incite the peasantry against the Jews and banish them, allowing the crown and the Church to seize Jewish property. Debts owed to Jews would be cancelled, and severe limits on what Jews could take with them would ensure a rich booty when Jewish homes were looted.

The first major expulsion took place in France in 1182. Desperate for funds, PHILIP II AUGUSTUS (then in his teens) confiscated Jewish property and forgave all debts owed to Jews if the debtors would pay 20 percent of the debt to the king. This made the young king very popular and solved his financial problems, but it also deprived the kingdom of some of its ablest merchant leaders. In 1198, a more mature Philip Augustus reversed himself and allowed the Jews to return, but a dangerous precedent had been set.

The next major expulsion involved the Jews of ENGLAND, who had entered the country following the NORMAN Conquest of 1066. For some 150 years, they prospered as merchants and bankers, in spite of being sapped through heavy taxation. In a final effort to realize a windfall, King EDWARD I tried an expulsion of Jews from Gascony, a French province under English control. When that proved profitable, he banished the Jews from England itself in 1290, an expulsion that lasted until the 1600s. The rhetoric of the king and the Church expressed pious intentions, but the real objective was to confiscate Jewish property and wealth.

In 1306, King PHILIP IV THE FAIR of FRANCE followed in his great-great-grandfather's footsteps and expelled the Jews once again from France. This time, he first arrested the Jews and confiscated their business records. Once the Jews were expelled, the king attempted to collect debts owed the Jews for himself. King Louis X readmitted the Jews into France in 1315, but only so that they could collect the pre-1306 debts not yet collected by the monarchy. The Jews were then expelled again in 1322. They were readmitted in 1359, only to be expelled finally in 1394.

The most devastating and unanticipated expulsion

Jewish Expulsions in the Middle Ages	
629	From the Frankish dominions by Dagobert.
875-6	From Sens.
1010-1012	From Limoges and from Mainz.
1099	From Jerusalem by crusaders.
1254	By Louis IX from his French Dominions.
1262	From Treves (again in 1418).
1290	From England.
1306	By Philip IV the Fair from France.
1420–1426	From Lyons, Austria, Cologne, and many Moravian towns.
1492–1498	From Spain, Lithuania, Portugal, Navarre, Nuremberg, and Ulm.

of Jews was the expulsion from Spain by King Ferdinand and Queen Isabella in 1492, together with the banishment from Portugal that the Spanish monarchs forced on a reluctant King Emanuel I in 1497. The Jews of Spain and Portugal were far more powerful, wealthier, and more entrenched than French or German Jews, and while they suffered the same problems of religious persecution and discrimination, the large number of Jewish converts to Christianity (the so-called New Christians) made total assimilation into Spanish society impossible. In order to confiscate Jewish wealth and prevent the return of New Christians to their ancestral faith, the Jews were expelled from the realm in one of the harshest episodes of medieval religious persecution. (*See* Spain; INQUISITION; JEWS).

JIHAD

T he term in Arabic for "holy war" (also *Gihad*) to be waged by Muslims against nonbelievers. The KORAN and the early caliphs taught that jihad was a supreme duty of Muslims; one who died in the course of a holy war was a martyr who would be able to enter Paradise immediately.

Initially, the precept of jihad was used to motivate Muslim soldiers to participate in wars of conquest. But as Islam spread across the Mediterranean world, the term took on a spiritual meaning: Jihad was the war each individual Muslim must wage against inner demons that led one astray from the true faith. Historically, the term has held both meanings for Muslims.

JOACHIM OF FIORE

The twelfth-century Italian mystic Joachim of Fiore (c. 1130–c. 1201) is best known today for the establishment of the monastic order of San Giovanni. But during his lifetime he was looked upon either as a great theologian and philosopher—some even thought he was a prophet—or as a heretic. Even present-day religious scholars are divided as to how to interpret some of his views.

Joachim was born in NAPLES and became a CISTERCIAN monk after a pilgrimage to the Holy Land convinced him to devote his life to religion. In 1177, he became abbot of the MONASTERY at Corazzo in SICILY. Around 1191, he abruptly left the monastery and took up residence in the mountains. The Cistercians labeled him a fugitive, but Joachim had won the approval of Pope Celestine III to form his own monastery in 1196. (*See* MONASTERIES.)

Joachim was fascinated with the idea of the Trinity (God as three beings—Father, Son, and Holy Spirit). For many years he had doubts about its existence. In fact, much of his work was initially based on the idea of "twos." His initial philosophy of history had been that history could be broken into twos just as the Bible could be broken into Old and New Testament. He expressed this idea in works such as his *Liber concordie novi et Veteris Testamenti* (*Book of Harmony of the New and Old Testaments*). (*See* CHRISTIANITY.)

According to his own record, he struggled over the doctrine of Trinity until one night he had a vision of a ten-stringed psaltery—a musical instrument that, coincidentally, is triangular in shape. Joachim saw this as clarification of the mystery through an actual visual symbol. He took this idea further and developed a Trinitarian philosophy of history. His contention was that history develops in three distinct ages that parallel those of the Father, the Son, and the Holy Spirit.

In works such as the *Psalterium decum chordarum* (*Psaltery of Ten Strings*) and *Expositio in Apocalypsim* (*Exposition of the Apocalypse*), he expounds on his theories about the Trinity. He attacked what was known as the doctrine of quaternity, which he attributed to Peter Lombard. Quaternity, which viewed God as a separate entity from the three Persons of the Trinity—thus becoming a fourth entity—was for Joachim a view that misconstrued the meaning of God. His philosophy became popular in the thirteenth century under the name "Joachinism."

In addition to being a writer of religious works, Joachim was a talented artist. One of the most famous examples of his work was discovered in 1937. (Most scholars have concluded that it is authentic.) Known as the *Liber figurarum* (*Book of Figures*), it includes drawings of his interpretations of paradise and eternity.

JOAN OF ARC, ST.

Joan of Arc (c. 1412–1431) is arguably the most famous teenager in history. The simple, devout peasant girl who led the French forces to victory against the English at Orléans provided the spark that roused French patriotic feeling and turned the tide in favor of FRANCE during the HUNDRED YEARS' WAR. After the Burgundian allies of the English captured her and an English-backed Church court condemned her, Joan was burned at the stake in Rouen as a heretic and witch.

Early Life. Although today her remarkable story is intertwined with legend, the facts of Joan's life reveal a remarkable personality possessed of single-minded courage, charismatic leadership, and utterly sincere devotion. Born into the peasant family of Jacques d'Arc in Domrémy in northwestern France, Joan at the age of about 12 began hearing the "voices" of her favorite saints—Margaret and Catherine—as well as that of the archangel Michael, the patron defender of France. She became convinced that she was destined to be the fulfillment of the prophecy that in France's darkest hour a young woman from Lorraine would save France.

A Divine Mission. In February 1429, Joan trav-

Charles VII returning a letter to Joan of Arc.

A 15th-century German tapestry depicting Joan of Arc arriving at the Château de Chinon in March of 1428. She is dressed in knight's armor and is being greeted by Charles.

was sentenced to be burned at the stake and was executed in the center of Rouen on May 30, 1431.

Verdict Reversed. In 1456—after the Hundred Years' War had been over for three years—a papal commission reversed the verdict of the Rouen court. However, it took several centuries for the Church to go further and declare her a saint. On May 9, 1920, in St. Peter's Square in Rome, the Church canonized Joan of Arc. It is an ironic ending to her story that Joan, who used to call on the saints so fervently for help, had herself now become one of them. (*See* HUNDRED YEARS' WAR; FRANCE; HERESY; CHARLES VII; WITCHCRAFT; WOMEN.)

eled to southern France where she obtained an audience with the dauphin Charles. She convinced him that she had a divine mission to lead the French troops to victory at Orléans and secure his coronation. Charles appointed a board of theologians to examine her. When they found she was sincere and not a heretic, Charles appointed her to lead a French force to Orléans, a city then under English siege. Joan, dressed in knight's armor, led the French to victory against the English, lifting the siege of Orléans. She led the French to victories along the Loire and accompanied the dauphin to Reims, where Charles was crowned king of France, with Joan dutifully at his side.

Trial. In 1430 after the Burgundians captured Joan at Compiègne, CHARLES VII made no attempt to ransom her. The English bought her from their Burgundian allies and brought her before a Church court in Rouen, presided over by Bishop Cauchon. She was tried for HERESY and witchcraft. The Church judges condemned her visions as worthless and her male dress as perverted. The full record of the trial, which still exists today, shows Joan's nobility of character and innocent defiance as she argued that her loyalty was to God alone. The record also reveals the lengths the English and their French accomplices went to condemn her and that her "confession" was extracted by torture.

At first Joan received a sentence of life imprisonment, but when she resumed wearing men's clothing (and it appeared she was winning over her captors), she

JOHN LACKLAND (KING JOHN OF ENGLAND)

King John of ENGLAND (1167–1216), fifth and youngest son of King HENRY II and his queen, ELEANOR OF AQUITAINE, was nicknamed John Lackland, because, unlike his brothers, he received no significant continental fiefs from his father. However, he later received scattered possessions in England and FRANCE, and the lordship of IRELAND.

His Reign. In 1199, he succeeded his brother RICHARD I to the throne and to the extensive ANGEVIN possessions in France. John's alleged failure to fulfill his feudal obligations to his overlord Philip II of France and his murder of Arthur of Brittany caused him to lose Normandy and Anjou to the French crown. Eventually, he lost all his French possessions except AQUITAINE and part of Poitou.

In England, John's quarrels with the Church over the appointment of STEPHEN LANGTON as Archbishop of Canterbury led to a bitter power struggle with Pope INNOCENT III. When John refused to accept Langton, Innocent installed him anyway and placed England under an interdict. John retaliated by confiscating Church property from the clergy who supported the interdict, but the pope retaliated by excommunicating John in 1209. Four years later he gave his approval to the French to invade England. John was forced to capitulate and accept a humiliating settlement in which he turned England over to the pope and received it back as a papal fief.

Magna Carta. Quarrels with his BARONS and towns, which resented his abuse of feudal customs and extortion of tax money, led to a domestic crisis that climaxed not long before John's death. In 1215, the English barons forced him to seal the MAGNA CARTA. Despite John's reputation for heavy-handedness—he had no intention of abiding by the Magna Carta—modern scholars give him credit for improving royal government, especially by making significant advances in the keeping of royal records. He died in 1216 during the unrest that followed his refusal to obey the Magna Carta's provisions. (*See* MAGNA CARTA.)

John was a capable administrator, but his weaknesses were serious. His manic-depressive tendencies would cause him to lapse into inaction at critical times: he was endlessly suspicious that the baronial class in England, particularly in the north, were disloyal, forcing them into confrontation with him; he seemed unable to keep his hands off the wives and fiancées of the high nobility; and he was simply overmatched in his encounters with PHILIP II AUGUSTUS of France.

JOHN OF GAUNT

ohn of Gaunt (1340–1399) was the fourth son of King EDWARD III of ENGLAND. Born in Ghent, he married Blanche, heiress of Lancaster in 1359. Through her, he became duke of Lancaster three years later. John's Lancaster holdings made him one of the richest and most influential nobles in the kingdom; he was the most visible of the wealthy members of European nobility of his day. Besides the duchy of Lancaster, he held extensive lands in western FRANCE and SPAIN. Close to a million people in three countries recognized him as their lord.

John fought in the HUNDRED YEARS' WAR with his brother EDWARD THE BLACK PRINCE, going with him to aid Peter the Cruel of Castile in 1367. After Blanche died, he married Peter's daughter and became involved with personal and dynastic interests in Castile. After the Black Prince took ill in France and was forced to return to England, John took command of the English forces and marched them from Calais to Bordeaux.

After the truce was signed in 1375, John returned to England where he became one of the most active and powerful political figures in the kingdom. After the Good Parliament of 1376 dislodged his party from power, he restored his friends to power by assembling a hand-picked Parliament in 1377. After the accession of his nephew RICHARD II in 1377, John continued to

be the most powerful figure in the government. His role in suppressing the PEASANTS' REVOLT in 1381 made him enemies among some parts of the population. As a result, his magnificent house in London was burned by rebelling peasants. In the late 1380s, he again became involved in the affairs of Castile.

In 1396, John married his mistress of many years, Catherine Swynford, thereby becoming the brother-in-law of the poet GEOFFREY CHAUCER, whose work he had long supported, and with whose wife the duke probably had an affair. John died in 1399, soon after King Richard exiled his eldest son, Henry Bolingbroke. He did not live to see his son's return to become King HENRY IV, the first member of the House of Lancaster to rule England.

John of Gaunt was an assiduous patron of writers, scholars, and artists. As one would expect, Geoffrey Chaucer was a member of the duke's entourage, but he also supported the radical Oxford theologian JOHN WYCLIFFE. This devotion to the arts and learning was continued by John's son Humphrey, duke of Gloucester, whose splendid library is today preserved in the Bodleian Library at Oxford University.

JOHN SCOT ERIGENA

ohn Scot Erigena, also John Scottus Eriugena (c. 810–c. 877), was a scholar and philosopher whose ideas presaged later medieval thought. Both western European mysticism and the Scholastic movement were influenced by his teachings.

Born in IRELAND (until the late Middle Ages, the term "Scot" was applied to people from Ireland as well as SCOTLAND), he went to France in the 840s and obtained a position as teacher in the court of Emperor Charles the Bald. During this time he translated a number of Neoplatonist Greek works into Latin, which influenced his thoughts on theology. He then wrote a number of original works, the most important of which was *De divisione naturae* (*On the Division of Nature*). In it, he sets forth a vision of nature united among its several divisions: nature includes God (nature that "creates, but is not created"); creative ideas (nature that "creates and is created"); the Universe (nature that "is created and does not create"); and the "First Cause" (the immanent God, or nature that "is not created and does not create"). He then proposes a theory of Creation and God's role in the world.

Erigena's writings covered many subjects in addition to religion; he commented on the arts and wrote a number of poems. His philosophical works influenced western European philosophers throughout the Middle Ages and beyond. (*See* PHILOSOPHY IN THE MIDDLE AGES; SCHOLASTICISM; *and* ARISTOTLE.)

JOHN XXII, POPE

John XXII (c. 1244–1334), pope from August 7, 1316 until December 4, 1334, the second pope to reside in AVIGNON and the chief architect of modern papal administration. Elected when he was over seventy, after two years of stalemate, he was expected to be nothing more than a caretaker of the office. Instead he proved to be a force to be reckoned with, one of the ablest administrators ever to hold the office and also one of the most controversial.

Rise to the Papacy. Jacques Duèse was born into a wealthy middle-class family in Cahors, Gascony. He studied civil and canon law in FRANCE and became bishop of Fréjus in 1300. After brief stints as chancellor to kings Charles II of Anjou and Robert of NAPLES, he was named in rapid succession bishop of Avignon, cardinal priest of San Vitale, and bishop of Porto (1313). He was enthroned on September 5, 1316. John moved decisively to shore up the financial and spiritual prestige of the curia, both notably decayed under his predecessor CLEMENT V and during the interval before his accession. John forbade the holding of more than two benefices (the Church equivalent of a fief, in which income would be received as a tax on land or a product), thereby proscribing abuses and greatly extending the pool of patronage under his control; he also arrogated unto himself the selection of bishops. He set the fiscal and judicial organization of the Church on their present course, doing more than any other medieval pontiff to centralize Church organization. John published the decretals of Clement V; his own decretals, published under the title *Extra-vagantes*, were a major addition to medieval canon law.

The Franciscans. John was at first allied with Michael of Cesena, general of the FRANCISCAN ORDER, in seeking to compel the radical "Spiritual" faction of the order to obey their general chapter and to relinquish some of their more extreme (as John saw it) practices and tenets, particularly their assertion that Franciscans ought to hold no property, individually or communally. But the decision of the order's general chapter of May 1322, approved by Michael, to adopt the Spirituals' position on absolute poverty drew John's condemnation. Summoned to account for his actions and detained in Avignon, Michael in May 1328 fled with theologians WILLIAM OF OCKHAM and Bonagratia of Bergamo to the court of the Holy Roman Emperor Louis IV of BAVARIA, John's declared enemy. (John had, a decade earlier, taken advantage of the inability of rival claimants Louis and Frederick of AUSTRIA to secure the imperial throne and imposed his own administration on the emperor's domains.) John had excommunicated Louis in 1324; he later (1329) excommunicated Michael and his two prominent sup-

porters. In January 1328, Louis had had himself crowned emperor in ROME and set about trying to depose John. In April 1328, Louis made a Spiritual friar Pope Nicholas V (the last imperial antipope). In February 1329, at an elaborate ceremony, he burned John in effigy. When Louis was forced to withdraw from Italy, however, Nicholas submitted to John in Avignon in July 1329, and he was pardoned.

Later Years. Toward the end of his pontificate, John enunciated the view (characterized by him as "personal") that not until the Last Judgment would saints fully share in the Beatific Vision of Christ in His full divinity, nor would sinners be condemned to hell, a question on which Church doctrine was not yet clear. Louis, William of Ockham, and John's other opponents pronounced these views heretical, as did theologians of the University of Paris in 1333. The wily John partially retracted them the day before he died. The charges of HERESY, and the protracted struggle with the Franciscans, left John with a besmirched reputation despite his considerable accomplishments.

JUDAISM

Judaism is the body of religious beliefs of the Jewish people. It includes beliefs about God, the universe, the world, and the history and destiny of the Jewish people. It also includes a code of behavior (Halakhah) extending from the most routine details of daily life to proper conduct in business to the conduct of nations at war. Judaism is considered the source from which two other major religions, CHRISTIANITY and ISLAM, sprang.

Judaism Before the Middle Ages. After nearly a thousand years in their own land—sometimes independent, but frequently living under foreign rule—the Jews found themselves during the first century without a home and without the center of their religious life, the Temple of Jerusalem, which was destroyed by the Romans in 70 C.E. When the Romans crushed the Bar Kokhba rebellion (132–135), they laid waste the land and took the few survivors into exile as slaves.

The destruction of the Temple might have meant the end of Judaism as an active religion, as was the case with many other vanquished ancient peoples. But the rabbis changed Judaism from a Temple-based religion to a religion based on beliefs and ideas. They composed a large body of religious thought and law, based on laws in the Bible and preached by the prophets and rabbis of the Temple period. From about 100 to about 600, they collected a library of these teachings: the Talmud. The way of life prescribed for every Jew (not just the Temple priests—the *kohanim*—and the rabbis) replaced the sacrifices of the Temple with prayer, to be recited by Jews three times a day. Every aspect of life was designed to show the presence of God, and the Jews' belief in Him. Synagogues, a minor institution in Temple times, became the focus of Jewish life; the study of the law, now known as the Torah, became the central activity of Jewish religious life.

Judaism in the Early Middle Ages. At the beginning of the Middle Ages, only two of the Babylonian academies, at Sura and Pumbedita, flourished. The head of an academy was known as a *gaon* ("pride" of Israel); the period from about 600 to 1000 is thus known as the Gaonic period. Jews throughout the world sent questions (*she'elot*) to the Gaon about Jewish law, and their answers (*teshuvoth*) were accepted by Jews everywhere. The Geonim—especially Sa'adiah ben Joseph (882–942), Gaon of Sura, known as Sa'adiah Gaon—were effective in preventing a Jewish sect, the Karaites, from gaining a foothold in Jewish life. The sect was founded in the second half of the 700s by Anan ben David, a disappointed candidate for "exilarch" (leader in exile) of Babylonian Jewry. Karaites preached that only the written law (*mikra*) was binding on Jews, and not the oral law (now in written form as the Talmud) as taught by the rabbis. The same dispute had arisen in the days of the Temple between the Sadducees and the Pharisees, but the Sadducees had the Temple behind them. The Karaites could only appeal to their interpretation of the written Bible.

The battle against the Karaites forced the rabbis to pay closer attention to the language of the Bible. It also stimulated rabbinical study of the ancient Greek philosophers, since the Karaites often appealed to the Greeks for "self-evident" truths. Finally, it prepared the rabbis for the more difficult and far more dangerous debates they would be forced into by Muslims and Christians a few centuries later.

Sa'adiah's masterpiece, *The Book of Beliefs and Opinions* (*Sefer Emunot ve-De'ot* in Hebrew, but written in Arabic to make it more accessible), began a tradition of rabbinic Jewish philosophy that was to remain active throughout the Middle Ages. For the first time, a rabbinic authority accepted the idea that truth, even the existence of God, could be arrived at through reason. Sa'adiah was greatly influenced by the Mu'tazilite school of Islamic theology, which created a special place for Kalam (Islamic) theology in Jewish thought for the next 250 years. After Sa'adiah, it became the task of rabbinic thinkers either to reconcile Judaism with PHILOSOPHY or to reject philosophy (ironically, by using philosophical arguments) in favor of scripture.

The defense of the use of philosophy in Jewish religious thought reached its greatest moment (perhaps for all time, but certainly in the Middle Ages) in MAIMONIDES' work, *Guide for the Perplexed* (*Moreh Nevuchim*). The most celebrated work rejecting philosophical rationalism was the *Kuzari*, as the book by the Spanish Hebrew poet Judah Halevi (c. 1075–1141), is known as. Halevi presents a fictitious debate in which the king of the Khazars puts questions to representatives of different religions, including a rabbi. In the course of rejecting philosophy and glorifying rabbinic Judaism, the rabbi sings the praises of the land of Israel. The work was immensely popular in the Middle Ages, especially among mystics, and is still studied as a forerunner of modern Zionist thought.

Other works that entered the fray were: *Mekor Hayyim* (*The Well of Life*, translated into Latin as *Fons vitae*, and closely studied by medieval Christians), a work of Neoplatonic philosophy by the Hebrew poet and liturgist, Solomon ibn Gabirol (died. c. 1057); *Hovot ha-Levavot* (*Duties of the Heart*) by the Spanish rabbi Bahya ben Joseph ibn Pakuda of Saragossa (flourished c. 1080), a summary of Neoplatonic Jewish philosophy, with the first systematic presentation of Jewish ethics, a work popular in traditionalist circles for centuries (and remains so today); *Ha-Emunah ha-Ramah* (*The Exalted Faith*), the first major work of Jewish Aristotelianism (and an inspiration to Maimonides), by the Spanish Talmudist Rabbi Abraham ben David Halevi ibn Daud (died c. 1180); and *Sefer ha-Ikkarim* (*Book of Principles*) by the Spanish rabbinic philosopher Joseph Albo (died c. 1444), in which philosophy and religion are reconciled.

In the midst of all this philosophical wrangling, the business of Jewish Talmudic legal analysis continued. New centers of learning (known as *yeshivot*) arose outside Babylonia, in the Tunisian city of al-Qayrawan and in Córdoba in Muslim Spain, all during the late 900s and mid-1000s. In Christian Europe, the Kalonymus family of Lucca established a yeshiva at Mainz, which soon produced the greatest rabbinic luminary of this period, Rabbi Gershom ben Judah, called *Me'or ha-Golah* (light of the exile). Rabbi Gershom issued sweeping decrees (*takkanot*), such as a ban on polygamy, accepted by all Ashkenazic (western European Germanic) Jews from his day to the present.

Judaism in the Late Middle Ages. The Gaonic period of Jewish learning came to an end with the passing, around 1038, of Hai Gaon, head of the academy of Pumbedita. The new generation of Talmudists, beginning with Rashi of Troyes (1040–1105) and continuing with rabbis known as Tosaphists (because their works were appended—*Tosafot*—to Rashi's commentary) analyzed the law with less authority than the Gaonim. Systematic codes of Jewish law (Halakhah) summarizing the Talmud topically were composed. For generations, creating a code of law was viewed as arrogant and sacrilegious. Several such works were accepted, however, including: the *Sefer ha-Halakhot* (*Book of Laws*), by the North African–born Spanish

LIFE IN THE MIDDLE AGES

The Sabbath Candles

A dispute between the Karaites and the rabbis was over whether there could be a light burning in a Jewish home on the Sabbath. The Karaites interpreted the biblical verse, "And a fire shall not burn in your home" literally and spent the Sabbath in darkness. But the rabbis interpreted the verse to mean that only kindling a fire was forbidden from Friday. Thus, lighting candles Friday at sunset and allowing them to burn into the night became a sign of allegiance to the rabbis, and Sabbath candles became an important Jewish custom right into modern times.

scholar Rabbi Isaac ben Jacob Alfasi (who died around 1103); Maimonides' *Mishneh Torah* (*Summary of the Torah*); and the *Sefer ha'(arba)-Turim* (*Book of Four Columns*), by Rabbi Jacob ben Asher (who died in 1340, and was known as the Tur, after his work), which organized Jewish law into four basic subjects or "columns."

Medieval Judaism drew to a close with the composition of what became the most authoritative code throughout the Jewish world, the *Shulkhan 'arukh* (*Prepared Table*), by the Spanish-born mystic of Safed, Rabbi Joseph Karo (1488–1575), who adopted the arrangement of the Tur, and used Alfasi, Maimonides, and the Tur as his guides in determining the law.

Two trends in Judaism that influenced Jewish life in the late Middle Ages were mysticism, known as kabbalah ("received" teaching), and the rise of very pious groups, or hasidim (separatists, because they separated themselves from the workaday world). Cabalists (as followers of Kabbalah are called) were found nearly everywhere in the Jewish world, but were most active in Provence in the 1100s and in Spain in the 1200s. The greatest work of the Spanish cabalists was the *Sefer ha-Zohar* (*Book of Splendor*), written in Spain in the 1280s, probably by Moses de León. In spite of its late origin, Jews deem the Zohar a sacred book.

The most important of the hasidic movements was the Hasidei Ashkenaz (the hasidim of the Germanic lands) that grew between 1100 and 1300. They emphasized the omnipresence of God and extolled love of God above fear of God. They believed that the greatest expression of love of God was to die a martyr's death *al kiddush ha-shem*—while sanctifying the Divine Name. Many of the martyrs to Christian inquisitors and crusaders were from this group. The piety, ethics, and heroic devotion of the Hasidei Ashkenaz was to have a lasting impact on European Jewry for many centuries.

See JEWS, JEWISH ART; JEWS, EXPULSIONS OF *for historical background. Compare with* BIBLE; CHRISTIANITY; ISLAM, RELIGIOUS PHILOSOPHY OF. *See also biographical entries on* MAIMONIDES; JACOB BEN MEIR; *and* RASHI.

JULIAN OF NORWICH

Julian of Norwich (c. 1342–c. 1417) was an English author and mystic whose book, *Revelations of Divine Love*, is one of the most important spiritual works of the Middle Ages. Based on visions she claimed to have had, it gained particular prominence in the nineteenth century.

Julian was born in Norwich and in 1373, while still a young woman, she became seriously ill. On May 8, it appeared that the end was near. As a priest held a crucifix near the dying Julian, she experienced visions of the crucified Christ. She saw 16 visions in all, and by May 13, she had recovered completely.

She recorded a version of what had happened to her shortly afterward, and then produced a longer version more than 20 years later. Neither version attracted much of an audience at the time, although the second version gained more attention than the first. *Revelations* described Julian's sorrow for sin, her joy at receiving God's love, and her views on the mysteries of faith. Her clear and simple prose shows her to have been a strong, intelligent, and perceptive individual.

Julian spent the last several years of her life as an anchorite (a religious recluse) at St. Julian's Church in Norwich. Little is known of her later life except that she died sometime after 1416. In the nineteenth century, a renewed interest in the Middle Ages and spirituality spurred a new interest in *Revelations*, and it became recognized as an extraordinary example of spiritual prose. Although Julian was never canonized, May 13 is unofficially celebrated as her feast day.

ILLUMINATIONS

Visions of a Hazelnut

At the end of a three-day fever, Julian had a vision that inspired her: "And in this He showed me something small, no bigger than a hazelnut, lying in the palm of my hand, and I perceived that it was as round as any ball. I looked at it and thought: What can this be? And I was given this answer: It is everything which is made. I was amazed that it could last, for I thought that it was so little that it could suddenly fall into nothing. And I was answered in my understanding: It lasts and always will, because God loves it; and thus everything has being through the love of God."

JUSTINIAN I

Justinian I (483–565) ruled the Byzantine Empire from 527 to 565. Justinian was called the Great because of his many conquests; the creation of the JUSTINIAN CODE—a codification of Roman LAW—and his public works. Byzantine artistic and architectural expression flourished during his reign, most notably in the construction of the cathedral HAGIA SOPHIA in CONSTANTINOPLE.

Justinian portrayed with his court in an early Byzantine mosaic on the walls of the Church of San Vitale, Ravenna, Italy.

Early Reign. Born in a Macedonian peasant village, Justinian joined the line of imperial succession when his uncle Justin became emperor in 518. In 525, he married the famous future Empress THEODORA and ascended to the throne in 527. Justinian saw himself as destined to reconquer the West and reunite the old Roman world as a Christian Empire. He was willing to sacrifice almost everything for his goals.

Justinian soon achieved military success. In a war from 533 to 548, under the leadership of General BELISARIUS, the Byzantines expelled the VANDALS from Carthage. In the devastating Ostrogothic Wars from 535 to 554, ITALY was reconquered from the OSTROGOTHS. Belisarius at first swept the Ostrogoths from Italy. However, under the leadership of Totila, much of the Byzantine gains were retaken. Belisarius was called back from Persia, but failed to reverse events. His replacement, Narses, finally ended Ostrogothic independence, defeating Totila at the Battle of Busta Gallorum. The war brought ruin to Italy, leaving its AGRICULTURE and COMMERCE in a state that took centuries to reverse.

These wars forced Justinian to impose massive taxes on the eastern half of the empire, which retarded economic growth and alienated much of the public from Constantinople. By his death, Byzantine finances were in terrible disarray. Justinian also tried unsuccessfully to diminish Persian dominance of Byzantine trade with the Far East.

Nika Riot. The most notorious event of Justinian's reign was the Nika riot of 532. The people of Constantinople had for a time been divided into Blue and Green factions, originally signifying support for different charioteers, but which had taken on class and political meaning. In the Nika riot, however, both parties found much common ground to unite them in opposition to Justinian. The revolt began in the Hippodrome, but soon spread to the entire city. Justinian and his advisers considered fleeing, but encouraged by Theodora, they successfully stamped out the rebellion by massacring over forty thousand people.

Justinian also believed strongly in religious unity and suppressed the remnants of paganism, including closing the famous school of PHILOSOPHY in Athens. He attempted to reconcile the dominant Orthodoxy with the minority sect of Monophysites (since Theodora was herself a Monophysite). Justinian pleased no one in his attempt at compromise. At the end of his life he favored another interpretation of the nature of Christ, *Aphthartocathartism*, for which he was labeled a heretic. He died childless, leaving a larger but weaker empire to his nephew Justin.

JUSTINIAN CODE

The Justinian Code (*Codex Justinianus*) was a consolidation and abridgement of Roman law written during the reign of JUSTINIAN I the Great. The code streamlined and clarified the thousand–year–old tradition of Roman law. A committee of jurists, under the guidance of Justinian's legal adviser Tribonian, undertook the enormous task of bringing order out of the chaos that had been Roman law. Though Justinian was fortunate to have brilliant legal minds working on this monumental task, his commitment to unification—of religion, of the empire, and of its laws—was the driving force responsible for seeing the project through to completion.

The Code consists of four parts: first came the Code proper—which included a compilation of all previous laws in a single volume. The committee was empowered to eliminate contradictions in any single law or between different laws. In 529, this Code was enacted in 12 books. All decrees not included were considered voided.

The second stage in the codification was the clarification of legal opinions of previous Roman jurists, which appeared in 534 as the Digest. The committee had to choose the most significant legal opinions (many were derived from the THEODOSIAN CODE of 438), improve the clarity of the writings, and make the opinions consistent with the new Code.

The third portion of the Code, instituted in 532, consisted of a textbook for law students called the Institutes. Much of this work is still studied as part of the law curriculum.

The final part of the Justinian Code, called the Novellae, consisted of decrees and laws issued by Justinian and collected by Tribonian, a process that continued until 545, the year of Tribonian's death. The four parts constitute the *Corpus Juris Civilus* (the Body of Civil Law), which served as the basis of civil law in medieval (and later modern) Europe.

See the entry on JUSTINIAN *and on* BYZANTIUM. *Also* BYZANTINE LITERATURE; LAW, SCHOOLS OF; *and* THEODOSIAN CODE. *For additional information, see* GLOSSATORS; BANKING; COMMERCE AND TRADE; *and*

KELLS, BOOK OF

One of the finest examples of the art of medieval manuscript design, the *Book of Kells* is a richly illustrated book of the four Gospels of the New Testament dating from about the ninth century. Both the calligraphy and the illustrations reflect the painstaking care with which manuscripts were created, entirely by hand.

The origin of the *Book of Kells* is unclear, but it was most likely written by monks from the Kells monastery, where it was kept from at least the eleventh to the early seventeenth century. Written in a decorative script known as Irish majuscule, the book includes many intricate decorations, drawings, and miniatures. Many of these are depictions of religious figures, but a number of abstract and fantastic animal forms appear amid the illustrations as well.

The *Book of Kells* was presented to Trinity College in Dublin in the mid-seventeenth century, where it remains today. (*See* IRELAND; CELTIC CHURCH; CELTIC LANGUAGE AND LITERATURE.)

The Book of Kells, *associated with St. Columba (late 6th century), but clearly produced a century later.*

spiritual truth. With her husband's support, she withdrew from her family and began a life devoted to this quest—a quest that included pilgrimages to Jerusalem, Rome, Santiago de Compostella in Spain, and Wilsnack in POLAND.

Although Kempe's husband may have accepted her mysticism, her neighbors and the local church were skeptical. Eventually she was imprisoned for what was considered bizarre behavior—she was given to fits of screaming while she was in a mystical trance—and tried for HERESY but found innocent. Sometime in the late 1420s, she began dictating her autobiography to two clerks. Over the course of several years (as many as six), the work developed into *The Book of Margery Kempe.*

Noted for its vivid descriptions and vigorous style, it recounts her travels, her visions, her temptations, her imprisonment and her trial. It is perhaps most noteworthy for its vivid depiction of a middle class feminist personality rather than its spirituality; it paints a picture of a very human individual struggling for guidance. (*See also* JULIAN OF NORWICH; WOMEN.)

KEMPE, MARGERY

Margery Kempe (c. 1373–c. 1439) was a medieval feminist writer and popular mystic whose fame rests on her memoir, *The Book of Margery Kempe.* Written in the early fifteenth century but not discovered until 1934, this chronicle of her pilgrimages and her search for spirituality is the earliest known autobiography written in English.

Kempe's early life was typical for WOMEN IN THE MIDDLE AGES and gave no sign of her later mysticism. she was born in Norfolk; her father, John Brunham, was mayor of the town of King's Lynn. Around 1393, she married John Kempe, by whom she bore 14 children. It was after a serious illness that she turned to religion, eagerly seeking what she hoped would be

KHWARIZMI, AL-

Muhammad ibn Musa al-Khwarizmi (c. 780–c. 850) was an Islamic mathematician and astronomer who wrote several important works introducing the Hindu-Arabic numeral system (and its critical device, the zero) that he had learned from Persian and Greek sources. His work on numerals, Kitab al-jabr, gave the world the term algebra. The mathematical term *algorithm* was derived from a Latin version of his name. A member of the court of Caliph al-Ma'amun in Baghdad, he is credited with inventing the astrolabe—one of several Arab scientists so honored—and with further refining the Sinhind, the Arabic version of the Ptolemaic astronomical system. (*See* ASTRONOMY; ARABIC LANGUAGE; SCIENCE.)

KINGSHIP

By far the most common political system of the Middle Ages was kingship, which is the vesting of authority in a single person, normally the eldest surviving son of a privileged dynasty. Medieval people did not invent this system; they inherited it from the later Roman Empire and from the Germanic societies that replaced the Roman Empire in western Europe.

Two Types of King. From the beginning of medieval political development in the sixth century there was a tension, even a conflict between two views of kingship. For the Germans, the basis of kingship was in part hereditary, that is, inherited succession. More important was election by the nobility, by the leaders of the community, the warriors and leading churchmen. Kingship for the Germanic societies of the Early Middle Ages (500–1000) was also functional—the king had to be an effective war leader, or at least choose good surrogates to defend the people and their territory. As a consequence, a child inheriting the throne might be passed over by the nobility for his more "throne-worthy" uncle. If there were no surviving sons in the royal dynasty, a woman could usually inherit if she had a suitable husband of high lineage and military capability.

On the other side was the kingship inherited from the Roman Empire. The king held a divinely ordained office and kingship therefore had a religious basis for his rule. Any consensual element in selecting the king and limiting his power, as by the old Roman senate, had lapsed by the fourth century. The king ruled absolutely; authority was in his arm and the law in his mouth. To oppose him was a sin as well as a grave personal risk. The royal dynasty ruled by inherited right, even if a king was ineffective, cruel, and foolish. However, if a rebellion overthrew and killed the king, and a new dynasty gained the throne, then it too ruled by divine right and persisted on the throne until it in turn was overthrown.

Anointment. The Germanic and Roman traditions of kingship persisted, overlapping and generating a certain amount of confusion and conflict at critical junctures. In the eighth century, the Church in FRANCE, with the warm approval of the PAPACY, introduced another theory of kingship. The king was

A procession of King René at Aix-la Chapelle, after a painting reputed to have been painted by King René himself.

anointed to the royal office in an elaborate CORONATION ceremony with the same holy oil by which a bishop was anointed at his installation. This anointment ceremony was given biblical precedent in the stories about Saul and David. Before a senior bishop anointed the king, the latter had to vow to be a protector of the Church and be good and just to the people; how seriously the crowned king took this oath naturally varied immensely in practice. The coronation and anointment ceremony first used in France in the 730s was imported into ENGLAND around 900, and with some later amendments in the monarch's oath to stress the consensual element in kingship (again, not necessarily meaningful in practice) it is used to the present day, as at the coronation of Elizabeth II in 1953.

Innovations. When the Gregorian Reform of the late eleventh century called into question this theocratic, or sacred, side of kingship—the papacy talking about kings in a purely functional manner and comparing them to swine herders—the monarchies of the twelfth and thirteenth centuries, without giving up the anointment ceremony, came to emphasize two other newer bases of kingship. One was derivation from Roman law and reflected the renewed study of the JUSTINIAN CODE in the universities. The king, it was claimed, held a supreme and unmitigated legal authority. The other innovation was to build up the bureaucratic machinery of government and express the king's authority in diurnal administrative effectiveness in taxation, legal operations, and peace-keeping. The populace, even the high nobility, now encountered the technique of government which used its long arms to hold down and exploit all groups in society.

Perhaps inevitably, vanguard ecclesiastical thinkers, and in the case of ENGLAND also some secular lawyers, developed liberal ideas aimed at limiting the claims and exercise of kingship. A king's actions that flouted justice lost their validity, it was held. The law vested in the people and its constitutional assemblies stood higher than the king. Bad and unlawful kings could be opposed and even—a very radical view—be justifiably assassinated. These disputes about the nature, functioning, and limits of kingship were an important legacy of the Middle Ages for the next three centuries. (*See* CORONATION; ROYAL TOUCH; FEUDALISM; HOLY ROMAN EMPIRE; *and* SOCIAL CLASSES.)

KNIGHTHOOD

The knight emerged during the late CAROLIN-GIAN empire of the ninth and tenth centuries as a separate social class in European society. They were above the peasantry but because of their generally poor and humble origins, they were also far below the nobility for whom they worked. This changed, however, when Church actions such as the CRUSADES and the creation of religious military orders gave the knights a great deal of prestige in European society. Knights became chivalrous Christian warriors, glorified in romantic tales such as the *Song of Roland*, *Tristan and Isolde*, and the KING ARTHUR legends. As their status grew, the knights acquired their own lands which blurred the class lines dividing knights and the nobility, creating one enlarged aristocracy.

Knights were originally obliged to serve their lords in times of battle. However, as various territories shifted possession, the obligations of knights decreased; they were no longer forced into battle. The knights could now pay their king or lord in lieu of service, an institution known as scutage. That money would be used to procure knights-for-hire—mercenaries who earned their livelihood through battle.

By the thirteenth century, a code of CHIVALRY or knightly behavior emerged. The code demanded courage, military prowess, virtue, service to God, and loyalty to a lord or king (though at times also to the lord's wife). A knight also had to be wealthy, as it was no easy task maintaining his position financially. Armor and arms were extraordinarily expensive; many would-be knights remained unknighted simply because they lacked sufficient funds.

In the late Middle Ages, the military role of the knight decreased substantially. Weapons and strategies became more elaborate—the use of the longbow and cannon made knights less important on the field of battle—and knights concentrated their energies on pageantry and elaborate tournaments. New, nonmilitary orders were formed, rewarding nobles and political supporters who had performed heroic deeds on the battlefield or service to the monarch or had lived exemplary chivalrous lives. (*See* CHIVALRY; WARFARE; *and* KNIGHTS OF THE TEMPLE.)

KNIGHTS OF ST. JOHN (HOSPITALLERS)

The Knights of St. John was a chivalric order originally organized before the First CRUSADE to protect a hospice and infirmary for pilgrims to the Holy Sepulcher in Jerusalem. Although its asso-ciation with the hospice continued and the scale of its almsgiving, unheard of in Europe, astounded contemporary observers, the Hospitallers soon became a large and powerful military entity under the direct authority of the pope. Like their rivals, the Templars, the Hospitallers rendered courageous military service in the Holy Land. Nevertheless, the order maintained its charitable activities to a greater extent than its rivals and did not involve itself as deeply in financial dealings. This may be why the order escaped the Templars' fate and, with a complex and fascinating history, has survived to the present time.

Malta. After the fall of Acre and the final destruction of the Latin Kingdom, the Hospitallers withdrew to Cyprus; in 1309, they established themselves on the island of RHODES and later, in 1530, on the island of Malta. They thus became known as the Knights of Rhodes and, more commonly, the Knights of Malta. Through the late medieval period until 1798, the Knights of Malta guarded the Mediterranean against pirates and Muslim forces. After Malta fell, first to Napoleon in 1798 and shortly thereafter to ENGLAND, the order survived as a charitable organization. Since 1961, it has been known formally as the Sovereign Military Hospitaller Order of St. John of Jerusalem, of Rhodes, and of Malta, with its headquarters in ROME.

Administration. The Hospitallers were organized in three ranks: priests, knights, and "serving brothers," living within convents, which were in turn organized in provinces under provincial masters, who reported to the order's master (called the grand master after 1430). Provincial masters were responsible for administration of the convents in their care and for conveying the province's donations to the order's headquarters. Masters at each level were appointed rather than elected by general chapters, but they generally took action only with the advice of the general chapters. Even the order's grandmaster was limited by the order's constitutions and statutes. Eventually, Hospitaller convents were also grouped in national units known as langues, or "tongues." All recruits had to be free born and meet health and financial requirements; most postulants made a gift to the order upon entering. The majority of recruits entered as sergeants; all took vows of poverty, chastity, and obedience, although for some, the vows were temporary. As in other orders, Hospitaller brethren (including the officers) residing in convents were expected to follow a modified monastic rule, with daily religious services, dormitory accommodation (at least in the early centuries), and meals taken in refectories. Dress was, at least theoretically, strictly regulated. The order also admitted women who lived in separate quarters.

Expansion. The pilgrims' hospital dedicated to St. John the Baptist had been founded around 1070 as

Krak de Chevaliers, the Hospitaller fortress in Lebanon in 1131, said to be impregnable until conquered by the Arabs.

part of a Benedictine monastery. Gerard de Martignes (later called Blessed Gerard) established the order's independence, which was formally recognized by Pope Paschal II in 1113. By then the Hospitallers held properties in France and Italy as well as in the Holy Land. Yet the order of the Knights of St. John did not fully take shape or acquire its military character until the accession of its second master, Raymond de Puy (died 1160), who replaced the Benedictine rule with an Augustinian one. The Hospitallers swiftly expanded their membership and activities, constructing hospitals and fortifications along important trade and travel routes in Europe, where they actively recruited, and in the Holy Land. By 1130, the order had assumed military duties. Granted the castle of Beit-Jibrin (Gibelin) near the southern border of the Kingdom of Jerusalem in 1137 by King FULK V, who was reluctant to commit his own troops to defend it, the Hospitallers became the first order to garrison a citadel, and came to control more land in the Latin Kingdom than any other order.

Politics. The Hospitallers came to exercise considerable political independence: they could not be compelled to supply troops to the king of Jerusalem. In Tripoli and Antioch they were empowered to make their own foreign policy with respect to the Muslims. In 1141, the formidable citadel Krak des Chevaliers in eastern Tripoli (now Lebanon) became the Hospitallers' headquarters, a gift of Raymond II of Tripoli. Other important Hospitaller strongholds included Margat in the north and Belvoir in Galilee. Many castles fell to SALADIN in the aftermath of the Battle of Hittin (1187) in Galilee, but Krak des Chevaliers and Margat remained in the hands of the Hospitallers until

1271 and 1285, respectively. Belvoir resisted for more than a year before falling. With Jerusalem lost, the Hospitallers operated from Margat and then Acre, where their headquarters remained until the final collapse of the Latin Kingdom in 1291.

Military Actions. The events of 1291 and ensuing failures to reestablish Latin power in the Holy Land recast the order's mission. Ten years after retreating to Limassol in Cyprus from Acre, the Hospitallers, seeking more independence, set about conquering the island of Rhodes (1306–1309). There they established a sovereign state, and in 1310, launched a crusade against ANATOLIA. In 1312, CLEMENT V awarded the Templar estates to the Hospitallers, continuing the papal policy of protecting the order. The Hospitallers' activities in the East now aimed at naval containment of the Muslims (and later the Ottomans). They harassed MAMLUK, Ottoman, and even Venetian shipping and derived substantial income from a well-orchestrated pirate operation called the corso.

Rhodes itself, though lightly garrisoned, did not come under sustained direct attack until 1480, when a determined Ottoman siege was successfully resisted. The advance of ISLAM nevertheless made the Hospitaller's position vulnerable. Once EGYPT fell to the Ottomans, Rhodes became impossible to defend. After another long siege, the knights abandoned Rhodes in January 1523. The order was settled on the island of Malta in 1530 by the Spanish emperor CHARLES V, by whose order the knights became vassals of the king of SICILY to whom they paid annual tribute consisting of a Maltese falcon—hence the origin of the fabled golden statuette. Thereafter the Knights of Malta, as the order was now called, continued the naval warfare that had been its military mission since 1309. Despite the loss of Tripoli and the enslavement of Goza's population in 1551, the Knights of Malta were able to resist another fierce Ottoman siege in 1565 under Grand Master Jean de la Vallette (a veteran of the Rhodes siege), and they sent galleys against the Ottomans in the crucial Battle of Lepanto in October 1571.

The Battle of Lepanto was a great psychological victory for Christian Europe, but it by no means destroyed Ottoman naval power. As of 1565, Malta was strongly fortified, and its cities were greatly expanded.

Although international in makeup and structure, the order had been predominantly French from the beginning. Ironically, the destruction of the Hospitaller regime on Malta came not from any Muslim state—by the eighteenth century, the Ottoman empire was in decline—but from France itself. Over the centuries on Malta, the order had become increasingly aristocratic, with knights far outnumbering clerics and sergeants; the monastic rule was relaxed. In 1792, the French Assembly nationalized the goods belonging to the order's three French provinces, cutting off critical revenues; in 1798, the grand master of Malta surrendered without resistance to Napoleon. This marked the end of the Hospitallers as a military or policing body. Fragmented, demoralized—even briefly hijacked by Czar Paul I of RUSSIA, who declared himself protector of the order and then had himself proclaimed grand master—the order finally established new headquarters in Rome and returned to its original mission. It has since made important contributions in charitable and medical relief for the sick and needy. (*See* KNIGHTHOOD *and* KNIGHTS OF THE TEMPLE.)

KNIGHTS OF THE TEMPLE (TEMPLARS)

A chivalric order founded in Palestine about 1119 to protect pilgrims traveling to the Holy Land. Organized by a small group of French knights led by Hughes de Payens, the order quickly expanded throughout the West. Its functions broadened to include reinforcement of the Christian military in the Holy Land, putting the Templars in the midst of the internal affairs of the Latin Kingdom of Jerusalem. By the 1140s, they were taking part in European military expeditions as well (soon supplemented by local military foundations such as the CALATRAVA in SPAIN). Their independence of royal or episcopal control, no less than their immense wealth, nevertheless secured them distrust among powerful factions in medieval society. Once their military service was rendered unnecessary by the fall of Acre to the Muslims in 1291, they became vulnerable to their enemies. They were eventually suppressed in 1312 by Pope CLEMENT V at the instigation of King PHILIP IV THE FAIR of France. (*See* CALATRAVA, ORDER OF.)

Origins. At first the Templars (so named because King Baldwin II of Jerusalem had given them quarters in the royal palace in Jerusalem, on the putative site of Solomon's Temple) followed the rule of the Augustinian canons. They took vows of poverty, chastity, and obedience, and swore allegiance to the patriarch of Jerusalem. Their rule was considerably augmented at the Council of Troyes (1128) and further amended in 1130 by the patriarch of Jerusalem, from whom, however, the Templars became independent in 1139. The uneasiness occasioned by the combination of monastic vows with a military function led BERNARD OF CLAIRVAUX (who had probably drawn up the 1129 rule provisions) to defend the order in his *De laude novae militiae* (*In Praise of the New Military*).

The order comprised four divisions: knights (of noble birth), sergeants (of nonnoble birth), chaplains, and servants. Only the chaplains (a small minority) were clerics; they did not take arms. Knights took perpetual vows; members of the other divisions might take temporary ones. Recruits had to meet certain standards of age, health, and social status and commonly made a gift to the order upon entering, implying that most had some financial means. Both the Templars and their great rivals the Hospitallers recruited throughout Western Christendom.

Military Force. Like other orders, the Templars fielded troops for various military campaigns. They also held a number of fortifications not only in the Levant, where their strongholds were refuges for travelers as well as strategic military installations, but also in Spain and the Baltic region. Their fighting skills were much respected by their adversaries; they displayed considerable courage and fortitude in battle, occasionally in the face of heavy losses, as at the BATTLE OF HITTIN (1187), and at La Forbie (1244). During the latter, the number of Templars killed (some 300) outnumbered those who survived by a factor of 10. They were better disciplined and more reliable than crusader contingents, and, since their vows and duties required a state of readiness for military activities, they could be mobilized more quickly.

Of the Templars' nonmilitary activities, which included almsgiving, their financial interests became most prominent, even notorious. Their castles served as places of safe deposit; they could arrange for the safe conveyance of funds, a service few other organizations or institutions were then equipped to provide. They lent money and performed functions later undertaken by banks. They were not unique among the orders in this respect, but none of the orders had such extensive money dealings. In the thirteenth century, for example, the Templars of Paris virtually functioned as the French royal treasury. The Templars lent large sums to European royalty, and individual nobles had ongoing accounts with the Templars, who would collect revenues and disburse sums on their clients' behalf. They collected taxes for secular and religious authorities. Their fabled wealth inspired envy and mistrust as well as the good will and patronage of the powerful.

The military orders in general declined in popularity over the thirteenth century. Despite the Templars' wealth, meeting their charitable and military obligations and maintaining the brethren became increasingly difficult. Critics contended that they (and the other orders as well) devoted less of their great resources to military purposes and were using force against fellow Christians. With the extinction of the Latin Kingdom, the military orders lost their traditional mission, although the Templars and Hospitallers (among others) retired to Cyprus, where they drafted various plans to retrieve the principalities and reestablish themselves in Palestine. In 1307, Templar Grand Master JACQUES DE MOLAY, on Pope CLEMENT V'S instructions, moved his order's headquarters to France.

Decline. While occasionally criticizing the orders and exacting some financial concessions from them, the papacy had generally been firm in their defense. Yet soon after the turn of the fourteenth century, the loss of Palestine exposed the Templars in particular to the machinations of King Philip IV the Fair in his largely successful financially motivated challenge to papal authority. The result was the end of the Templars.

The undoing of the Templars is a sordid episode in the history of the West. Jacques de Molay had resisted the merging of the Templars with the Hospitallers, a step proposed by some critics of the orders and taken up by Philip IV. With the connivance of Guillaume de Nogaret, Philip abruptly arrested all the Templars of Paris in October 1307 and charged them with HERESY on the basis of rumors that they conducted blasphemous initiation rites. Clement V protested the arrests but to no avail. Under torture, Jacques de Molay and others confessed to some of the charges, which gave Philip the justification he needed to order the arrest of all Templars in Europe and the seizing of all their assets. Local inquisitions followed, and the Templars were at the mercy of the political maneuvering of pope and king. Under duress, Clement finally summoned the Council of Vienne in 1311, at which he issued the bull *Vox in excelso*, dissolving the order on March 22, 1312. All the while Jacques de Molay and his associates remained in prison, awaiting their fate. A panel of cardinals sentenced them to life imprisonment, but they recanted their confessions. On learning this, Philip promptly had them burned at the stake in front of NOTRE DAME in March of 1314. The surviving Templars were left unharmed. Templar properties were conveyed to the Hospitallers or confiscated. Most historians take the dimmest view of Philip IV's motives; none of the charges against the Templars had any basis or received any notice before 1307, and it is generally believed that the charges were spurious.

See PHILIP IV THE FAIR *and* BANKING *for more on the fortunes of the Templars. Also see* KNIGHTHOOD; KNIGHTS OF ST. JOHN (HOSPITALLERS); CRUSADES; *and* WARFARE. Also biographies CLEMENT V *and* JACQUES DE MOLAY. *Also see* HERESY *and* TRAVEL.

KORAN

The holy book of ISLAM. Koran (also Qur'an) means recitation, reflecting its provenance: the sermons delivered by MUHAMMAD to the people of Mecca and Medina from 613 until his death in 632. Several oral traditions existed after Muhammad's death, but a definitive text was created under the direction of Caliph Uthman around 655. This led to the Kufan version in the late eighth century, which is accepted by Sunnite Islam, though Shi'ite Islam has contested the omission of the Prophet's teachings regarding Ali. (*See* ISLAM, RELIGIOUS PHILOSOPHY OF.)

After an opening prayer, the Koran consists of 114 chapters (suras) arranged by length from longest (about 700 lines) to shortest (just two lines). The style is roughly rhymed, with many subjects dealt with in the course of a single sura. The powerful and direct message is one reason the work has had so profound an influence. Though the Koran has been translated from its original Arabic into many languages, Muslims regard only the original as authoritative.

KOSOVO, BATTLE OF

The Battle at Kosovo Plaje in June 1389 cemented the domination of the Ottoman Empire in eastern Europe, and began nearly five centuries of Turkish control of SERBIA.

Kosovo became part of the Serbian state early in the ninth century, and was distinguished by the many churches in the region. Serbia was directly in the line of sight of Ottoman leader MURAD I during the 1300s, as he sought to expand his empire westward.

The Turks started attacking the Nis and the Hum in Serbia. Prince Lazar of Serbia led a coalition of Albanians, Serbs and Bosnians to fight the Turks in what is now YUGOSLAVIA. Before the battle, Murad was murdered by a Serb, but Murad's son and successor, Beyezid I, was able to lead the Turks to a resounding victory. During the battle, Lazar was wounded, captured, and executed. As a result, the Serbs were now vassals, obligated to pay tribute to the Ottomans, who then began to encircle the Byzantine Empire.

Nearly six decades later, from October 17 to 20, 1448, a second battle at Kosovo took place between Beyezid I's son, Murad II, and the Hungarian army (aided by German mercenaries) of JÁNOS HUNYADI. Once again, the Turks won easily. BOSNIA remained part of the Ottoman Empire until 1878 when the empire collapsed. Bosnian attempts at self-rule led to World War I, and the issue remains unresolved at the close of the twentieth century. (*See* BOSNIA.)

KUBLAI KHAN

GENGHIS KHAN'S last words, according to legend, were, "Listen to the words of the boy Kublai, they are wise; he will one day sit on my throne and he will bring you prosperity as I have done." Kublai Khan (1215–1294) indeed rose to become a worthy successor to his grandfather.

Family Ties. Kublai was born in the same year that Genghis overthrew Peking. When Kublai was 20, he was granted lands in CHINA. In 1253, his brother Mangu, then the khan, chose Kublai to lead a Mongol attack on the Sung dynasty of South China. Kublai outflanked the Chinese from the southwest by going through Tibet and coming down the upper valley of the Yangtze into Yunnan. Kublai conquered Shaanxi and Sichuan before capturing Dali, Yunnan's capital. He returned to northern China to build his brother's new capital, making it his summer residence. It would be known as Shangdu ("Upper Capital"), and later as Beijing (the city the poet Samuel Taylor Coleridge called Xanadu six centuries later).

The Great Khan. The MONGOLS reached the Tangking Delta in 1257, and within two years Mangu controlled all of northern Sichuan. In 1259, Mangu was killed. Kublai was summoned from the Yangtze, and at a congress of Mongol princes in Kaiping in April 1260, Kublai was elected the Great Khan, inheriting a region from the Black Sea to the Pacific—at the time the largest empire in history. Kublai set out to make major changes in the Mongolian way of life, beginning with moving the capital from Karakorum to Peking.

However, his brother Arigh Boke, at a second convention that same year in Karakorum (where Arigh had commanded troops during the Sung battles), was also named Great Khan. A civil war erupted lasting three years and at the end of which Arigh surrendered.

Kublai Khan resumed his war against the Sungs for three reasons: because his other brother Hulagu had conquered BAGHDAD; because Kublai's wife Chabi had encouraged him to devote his energies to defeating Arigh Boke; and, most important, because Kublai

Kublai Khan (left) was very hospitable to Marco Polo.

saw military victory as the way to change the Mongol economy to an agricultural one. His best general, Bayan ("of the Hundred Eyes"), crossed the Yangtze and captured Chinese cities in the Yangtze valley. The battles ended after nearly 15 years, with the fall of Canton in 1279. Kublai Khan was now the ruler of all China and was the first of a new dynasty, the Yuan.

His delegation of authority was astonishingly advanced for the era; Kublai surrounded himself with a court of advisers, both Chinese and Mongol. He also nationalized the currency and began regular mail service. Merchants found China a welcoming land. In 1271, MARCO POLO accompanied his father and uncle on a trip through central Asia and reached Khan's estate at Peking. Khan took an instant liking to Polo and sent him as his personal emissary throughout the empire.

Kublai also divided his people into four categories—Mongols, northern Chinese, southern Chinese, and foreigners—and imposed strict racial division, forbidding intermarriage between groups.

Expansion. Kublai continued his expansionism. He befriended Korea, which Mongu had conquered and which had been a tributary for the Mongols for decades; Kublai married off his daughter to the Korean grand prince. He made several overtures to JAPAN in the 1270s, sending naval expeditions. The last of these, however, was scattered by kamikaze typhoon winds in 1280. Later, the Japanese would rebuff formal delegations, and they executed several of Kublai's emissaries. Conquering Japan was one goal Kublai never realized.

Kublai attacked Cambodia and Annam, but even toppling the emperor of Annam in 1288 cost Kublai money and troops he could ill afford. Kublai's wife Chabi had died in 1281. She had been a trusted adviser and had pushed him into many military endeavors. Severely depressed after her death, Kublai had difficulties with both his staff and even with General Bayan. His hand-picked successor, Crown Prince Chen-chin, predeceased him, dying in 1285. Khan died on February 18, 1294, at the age of 78. (*See* GENGHIS KHAN; CHINA; MONGOLS; MARCO POLO; EXPLORATION.)

LANFRANC OF BEC

Lanfranc (c. 1010–1089) was a dominant figure in the theological and political life of Europe. After a distinguished career in Normandy as a priest, monk, and scholar, he went to ENGLAND following the NORMAN Conquest and served as archbishop of Canterbury under WILLIAM I THE CONQUEROR for the last two decades of his life.

Born in Pavia, Lanfranc received a strong legal as well as theological education in ITALY before leaving for FRANCE, where he established a reputation as an outstanding student and teacher. In 1042, at the age of 32, Lanfranc entered the newly reformed monastery of Bec where he served as prior for 18 years and flourished as an outstanding teacher of theology and scripture. Although Lanfranc's relationship with Duke William of Normandy was stormy at times, his stature was such that William chose him to be abbot of the great new monastery of Saint-Etienne at Caen. Four years after the Norman Conquest, William called on him again, this time to be archbishop of Canterbury.

Lanfranc was one of England's greatest archbishops, working well with King William and making lasting Church reforms. He asserted the primacy of Canterbury over the archbishopric of York. He also created fresh constitutions for his cathedral at Canterbury and encouraged the spread of the reformed Benedictine order he promoted in Normandy. Lanfranc sided with William in his dispute with Pope GREGORY VII over the issue of fealty to the PAPACY.

During William's absence from England, Lanfranc often served as regent; after William's death, Lanfranc helped ensure the succession of William's son, William Rufus, to the English throne. (William's eldest son became duke of Normandy.)

LANGLAND, WILLIAM

The poet William Langland (c. 1330–c. 1400) was born in the West Midlands near WALES and may have attended school at Great Malvern Priory. Although he did take minor orders, he never entered the priesthood. He spent most of his life in LONDON where he eked out a living by copying documents and singing masses.

His great poem, *The Vision of William Concerning Piers the Plowman* (more commonly known as *Piers Plowman*), is an allegory written in unrhymed alliterative verse. It consists of three dream visions about salvation that combine social satire with a vision of simple Christian life. Langland began the poem about 1362 and wrote at least two other versions. Today *Piers Plowman* is regarded as the greatest Middle English poem prior to CHAUCER'S *Canterbury Tales*. Langland may also be the author of *Richard the Redless*, a poem attacking the rule of King RICHARD II.

LANGTON, STEPHEN

Stephen Langton (c. 1165–1228) served as Archbishop of Canterbury early in the thirteenth century, but he is best known as one of the key players in the establishment of the MAGNA CARTA. This document was a milestone in English law and stands today as the foundation upon which the British Constitution is built. Though not controversial himself, Langton found himself squarely in the middle of a dispute between England's King John (JOHN LACKLAND) and Pope INNOCENT III. Largely because of his diplomatic skills, the dispute was settled, and the threat of serious unrest in Britain was averted.

Rise to Power. Langton was born in Lincolnshire and studied theology in PARIS, where he remained for a quarter century. In 1206, Innocent III sent for him to come to ROME, where he was named cardinal of St. Chrysogonus. But Innocent had other plans for him.

Hubert Walter, the previous Archbishop of Canterbury, had died in 1205, and a successor had not yet been chosen. Langton was the pope's choice, and the pope arranged for Langton to be elected to the post in Rome. He was consecrated in June 1207.

Disputes. This infuriated King John, who felt that he should have the power to choose the next man to be elected to the position; that right had been clearly outlined in the CONCORDAT OF WORMS nearly a century earlier. The pope, however, disagreed. John refused to accept Langton as the new archbishop. The pope in turn placed England under an interdict (ecclesiastical censure) and then excommunicated the king.

Upon finding that the French king PHILIP II AUGUSTUS was planning to invade ENGLAND, John needed the Church's support. Reluctantly, he accepted Langton as archbishop in July 1213. Though Langton came quickly to England and absolved the king, John's troubles were far from over. Disputes with BARONS who opposed the king were getting more heated. Langton supported the barons and encouraged them to remove John from the throne. But he was also actively involved in negotiations between the two sides, believing an agreement could be reached.

Magna Carta. By 1215, the barons were so incensed that they took up arms against John. This Langton opposed; he wanted to see any changes made peacefully. Serving as one of the king's commissioners in the spring of 1215, he helped draft the Magna Carta, which laid out broader powers and greater liberties for nobles, the Church, and the city of London (or, from John's perspective, less power for the king). John did not want to sign the Magna Carta, but he knew he had little choice; the document was signed at Runnymede in June.

Langton spent the remainder of his tenure as archbishop working to guarantee stronger rights for the Church. He died in England in 1228.

LATERAN COUNCILS

The Lateran Councils were a series of five ecumenical gatherings of leaders of the Roman Catholic Church held at the Lateran Palace in ROME between 1123 and 1517. These councils were instrumental in formulating Church administration, relations with political rulers, and reform measures.

The First Lateran Council, which was the ninth ecumenical council, was convoked in 1123, during the reign of Pope Calixtus II. Among the decrees issued: laymen could not dispose of Church property and clerics in the higher orders were forbidden to marry.

The Second Lateran Council, convoked in 1139, was instrumental in unifying the Church behind Pope Innocent II. The reformer Arnold of Brescia and his followers had strongly opposed the pope's power and a rival pope, Anacletus II, had been elected. Innocent was acknowledged to be the legitimate leader of the Church.

Pope ALEXANDER III convoked the Third Lateran Council (the eleventh ecumenical council) in 1179. In addition to accepting the Peace of Venice (marking the reconciliation of Alexander and FREDERICK I BARBAROSSA), the council decreed that popes be elected by a two–thirds majority of the College of Cardinals.

The Fourth Lateran Council was convoked in 1215 by Pope INNOCENT III. It took years of planning and was attended by more than 1,200 Church and political leaders. This council established many rules of Church administration, organization, and judicial procedures. Catholics were henceforth required to make confession and receive Holy Communion at least once a year, preferably during Easter. The Fourth Lateran Council, the most important such general assembly between the COUNCIL OF NICAEA in 325 and the Council of Trent around 1580, established the number of Church sacraments (seven), which included marriage. It advocated the ghettoization of Jews who had to wear a special insignia, such as a yellow patch or

star. It stipulated that new saints could not be recognized nor could new religious orders be authorized except by going through a rigorous process under close papal control.

The Fifth Lateran Council (eighteenth ecumenical), convoked by Pope Julius II from 1512 to 1517, initiated reforms and repudiated earlier decrees giving Church councils more power than the pope.

LATIN LANGUAGE AND LITERATURE

Latin was the language of the Roman Empire, but it remained influential throughout the Middle Ages. Over a period of several centuries, Latin developed into what are today known as the Romance languages—French, Italian, Spanish, Portuguese, Catalan, Provençal, and Romanian. Each language developed its own written form as well. But classical written Latin remained the language of scholars. Anyone who wished to study law, medicine, or theology required a solid command of Latin.

Origins. Latin is classified as an Indo-European language, as are German, Greek, Celtic, and Sanskrit. It developed into the language known today as classical Latin more than 3,000 years ago, eventually taking hold in Italy and western Europe (which would later become the heart of the Roman Empire).

As the Roman Empire grew, so did the number of people speaking Latin. The great Roman writers—Virgil, Ovid, Horace, Cicero—were read and studied widely. The works of many Greek writers were translated into Latin, as was the Bible.

Distinct Languages. Partly because the Roman Empire was so vast, people in different regions began to speak Latin a little differently. Some borrowed words from other languages; others just developed their own colloquial speech. Gradually, this "vulgar" Latin (meaning "common") became the spoken language, while classical Latin remained the language educated people read and wrote. Vulgar Latin was firmly entrenched by the fourth century.

Eventually, Vulgar Latin developed into forms so distinct that they each constituted a separate language. Gradually, these new tongues, such as French, Italian, and Spanish, developed written languages. Latin remained the language of scholarship, but even scholars spoke both Latin and a vernacular tongue; eventually no one learned Latin as their first language.

Classical Latin was taught according to a set of strict grammatical rules, as outlined by the fourth-century *Ars grammatica* of Aelius Donatus that comprised two volumes—*Ars major* and *Ars minor*—of which the latter was used as an elementary textbook during the Middle Ages, and the sixth-century *Institutiones grammaticae* of Priscian. (The phrase *"diminuere Prisciani caput"*—"to break Priscian's head"—meant for many centuries to ignore the rules of grammar.) The first dictionary of Latin, the *Elementarium doctrinae rudimentum,* was published in the eleventh century. One reason classical Latin has not changed since antiquity is that the rules of grammar are so carefully laid out. The verbal interaction that could possibly change the language no longer exists now that Latin is no longer spoken (referred to by some linguists as a "dead" language).

Most European literature was written in Latin until relatively late in the Middle Ages. As vernacular tongues became more prevalent, writers experimented with the new languages, and classical Latin works were translated. The invention of the printing press in the fifteenth century helped increase the number of books in Latin, but it also helped established the vernacular tongues as distinct languages, each with its own richness and character. (*See* LITERACY; LIBRARIES.)

LAW, SCHOOLS OF

Much of what forms the basis of law in the West had its beginnings in medieval times. As legal issues became increasingly complex, involving both secular and religious matters, scholars created schools that specialized in the study of law. In addition to providing students with a practical grounding, these schools also offered lectures on how to interpret the law. (*See* GLOSSATORS; COMMERCE AND TRADE.)

Beginnings. The university as we know it had its beginnings around the sixth century, and over the next few centuries became firmly established in Byzantine and Islamic lands (which had a relatively high literacy rate). The earliest schools of law were established in the Byzantine Empire during the sixth century. Two of the earliest were founded in Beirut and CONSTANTINOPLE (now Istanbul). These schools taught law based on the code developed by JUSTINIAN and laid out in his *Corpus Juris Civilis* (Body of Civil Law), and were primarily devoted to administrative training (in, for example, drafting legal documents). Depending on their training, graduates might become notaries or serve in judicial offices from clerk to judges.

To the east of the Byzantines, schools based on Islamic tradition were being established, where students would be given a firm grounding in legal interpretations based on the teachings of the KORAN. Islamic students studied in schools, or madrasas, that were funded both by the state and by private donations.

As medieval society became more complex, the

A 15th-century miniature depicting "how the plaintiff and the defendant take the final oath before the judge." From the Cérémonies des Gages de Bataille.

need arose not only to enact and enforce laws, but to interpret them. The influence of the Church, of the nobility, and the growing merchant class all contributed to a shift in the scope of law. Legal administration was no longer enough—legal scholarship became equally important.

Formal Legal Education. Legal education in Europe took its first major step away from the Byzantine model toward the end of the eleventh century when the University of Bologna (which still exists) was established in Italy. It was the first to provide legal training based on a formalized course of study, including the examination of Byzantine and Roman legal texts. It became one of the most prestigious institutions in the Western world, attracting students from all over Europe and becoming the standard for nearly all subsequent schools of law.

That an education system based on secular, rather than religious, studies originated in ITALY is not surprising. In much of Europe, scholars were usually clerics; so religion may be expected to play a prominent role in education. But in Italy, a tradition of lay scholarship dating back to the days of ancient Rome had continued into the Middle Ages. (By contrast, the Sorbonne, founded in France around the same time as Bologna, was originally a school of theology.)

European law schools did not ignore religion; students were generally required to study canon law for four to five years. But because Church administration, like society in general, was becoming more complex,

Church leaders often found need for lawyers who understood both canon and civil law. Thus, after completing their studies in Church law, students were required to study five to six years of civil law. A number of law schools were founded by nobles or Church leaders: Holy Roman Emperor FREDERICK II founded the law school of NAPLES in 1224; Pope GREGORY IX founded the University of Toulouse in 1229.

By the fourteenth century, legal education based on the Bologna model had taken firm root throughout Italy and France. These schools attracted students from all over Europe. Later, law schools would open in GERMANY and other parts of Europe.

English Schools. Around 1300, the legal profession in ENGLAND founded four residential schools called the Inns of Court (former residences that the legal profession took over to house its students) devoted to the training of barristers. The teachers at the Inns of Court assembled legal anthologies in case books called Year Books, using them as textbooks.

Islamic Schools. Because much of Islamic teaching is centered on the KORAN, the division between civil and religious law never occurred as it did in Europe. But different traditions of legal education developed within the Islamic community. The four most important were: Hanafi (dominant in the Middle East, Asia, and parts of India); Shafi (dominant in Africa); Maliki (dominant in the Maghreb and Spain); and Hanbali (dominant in Saudi Arabia). Islamic law was considered the most important subject of study in all schools, and law professors held the most prestige and power (the heads of most universities were also law professors). The study program could take as many as 20 years to complete. A student who had successfully completed his studies would be issued a license to teach and to issue legal opinions. (*See* ISLAM; UNIVERSITIES; JUSTINIAN CODE.)

LECH, BATTLE OF THE

rguably the most important battle of the tenth century, fought in 955 between the Magyars and a unified German force, led by King OTTO I. The battle was fought on the Lechfeld, the valley south of Augsburg, and freed GERMANY from the threat of future Hungarian invasion.

From the late ninth and early tenth centuries, the Magyars, a fierce nomadic tribe of western Siberian descent, ravaged Europe, reaching as far as FRANCE and ITALY. In 907, the Magyars achieved a decisive victory over the Bavarians. In 954, they invaded Germany, where they were met and assisted by the challengers to Otto's rule: his own, son Ludolf, and son-in-law Conrad. The Magyars went as far as the Lech River in BAVARIA before they were finally stopped and defeated in 955 by Otto's forces. The decisive victory put an end to the Hungarian invasion, allowing Otto to dedicate himself more fully to internal affairs and building a strong German kingdom. Indeed, the victory greatly increased Otto's prestige in Europe; it silenced the internal opposition to his rule, paving the way for his imperial coronation in 962.

After Lechfeld, the Magyars returned to Hungary, and their kingdom was reorganized by its Arpádian rulers. In 975, under Prince Geza, the Hungarians accepted Christianity. German settlers moved into the region and, in the following centuries, the once-nomadic people slowly became a part of civilized Europe. (*See* ARPÁD; GERMANY; HUNGARY; BAVARIA.)

LEO III, ST.

eo III (750–816) was pope from 795 to 816. He is best known as the pope who crowned CHARLEMAGNE, the first ruler of what would later become known as the HOLY ROMAN EMPIRE, in 800. Although his action established as a legal precedent the sole right of the pope to crown the emperor, it also created a solid division between the Holy Roman Empire and the Byzantine Empire.

Leo was chosen to succeed Pope Adrian I in December 795. However, this choice was not without opposition. Some members of the Roman aristocracy were so against his election that allegations of murder were made against him. Leo's handling of Charlemagne also drew the ire of the aristocracy. Adrian had tried to keep the Church out of the rivalry between the East and the West, in which Charlemagne, then king of the FRANKS, was trying to consolidate his power. But Leo almost immediately conferred recognition on Charlemagne as leader of the Romans, thus giving him immense power. (*See* FRANKS; CHARLEMAGNE.)

In 799, Leo was attacked by a group of enemies who had planned to blind him and cut out his tongue. The attack failed, and Leo fled to Charlemagne's court in Paderborn, across the Alps. He was safely escorted back to Rome, and his assailants were punished.

In 800, Leo was supposed to consecrate LOUIS I THE PIOUS as king of Rome. At the gathering for this consecration, on Christmas Day, Leo instead turned to Charlemagne and crowned him emperor. Not only did this act signify a shift in power away from the Byzantine Empire, it also allied the papacy with the West rather than the East. The coronation itself, however, had no legal standing at the time, and the Byzantines never recognized Charlemagne as emperor.

Leo died in 816, two years after the death of Charlemagne. (*See* HOLY ROMAN EMPIRE.)

LEPROSY

Leprosy, a debilitating and disfiguring affliction, has been feared and dreaded since biblical times. The bacterium that causes leprosy was discovered in the late nineteenth century; before then, particularly during medieval times, it was treated as a disease caused by moral uncleanliness.

During the Middle Ages, no one understood exactly how leprosy spread. Some thought that rich foods were to blame; others believed that unclean food was the culprit. The thirteenth-century FRANCISCAN monk Bartholomaeus Anglicus said it could develop from eating spicy foods. But all agreed that leprosy was contagious. Once a person became a leper, he or she would effectively be cut off from society.

Depending on where they lived, lepers were not allowed to drink from public wells or fountains, walk through markets, enter churches, or touch other people. In many communities, lepers wore distinctive hooded robes, and were obliged to ring a bell as they passed through a populated area. Deceased lepers could not even be buried with nonlepers.

In 1067, the Spanish soldier and hero EL CID founded the first hospital for lepers, or leprosarium. Over the next several centuries, leprosaria became an increasingly common, and humane, way to separate lepers from the general public. Living quarters in these special hospitals were clean and relatively comfortable; patients were provided with food and clothing. They were also given spiritual sustenance; some leprosaria included small chapels and adjacent cemeteries. Some historians believe that a significant number of medieval people called lepers were not actually suffering from the disease. They were just homely or annoyingly unpopular people who were removed from society on the pretext of being lepers. (*See* MEDICINE.)

By the fourteenth century, the number of new cases began to decline, due in part to widespread epidemics of the BLACK DEATH, which struck lepers before they could be diagnosed.

LIBRARIES

During the Middle Ages, when all books were still made entirely by hand, the expense of owning books was prohibitive for most individuals. Libraries, which had existed since antiquity, were originally repositories for religious and scholarly works, but library holdings became more varied as literacy spread. Because books were so highly prized, there were strict rules regarding when and where they could be read; communities saw libraries as important tools in the spreading and preservation of knowledge.

The home of a leper is placed under quarantine—in some cases in anticipation of its being demolished. Miniature from a 13th-century manuscript, Le Miroir Historial.

Early Libraries. The ancient Greeks, Romans, and Egyptians were the first to establish libraries for general or scholarly use. Wealthy individuals often had their own libraries; Cicero and Pliny, for example, were known to have private collections of books.

By far the largest library before the Middle Ages was the one in Alexandria, Egypt. It flourished for more than 200 years; at its peak, it housed 700,000 manuscripts. (*See* EGYPT; LITERACY.)

In CONSTANTINOPLE, after the establishment of the Byzantine Empire, a palace library was established. It was especially important during the reign of JUSTINIAN I, who availed himself of the ancient Roman texts to help formulate his famous legal code.

Islamic Libraries. Without question, some of the most important medieval libraries were established and maintained by the Muslims. In the centuries following the birth of ISLAM, scholarship, the arts, and sciences flourished in Arab lands. Not surprisingly, the Muslims placed a high value on books and libraries.

Muslims established public libraries in major cities such as DAMASCUS, BAGHDAD, and Cairo. At one point, Baghdad boasted no fewer than three dozen libraries, and the Cairo library housed 1.1 million manuscripts. Mosques often had their own libraries. As the Islamic Empire grew, so did the number of libraries. For many years, Islamic libraries were superior to the European libraries in the scope and quantity of their holdings. (*See* ARABIC LANGUAGE AND LITERATURE.)

The Muslims created some libraries on their own; others became theirs as part of the spoils of battle. As a result, Islamic libraries, such as those in SPAIN at Córdoba, Seville, and Toledo, contained many manuscripts in Latin and Greek that were used by scholars from across Europe.

European Libraries. Early libraries in medieval Europe were usually established in monasteries and convents. (Later, individual cathedrals would create their own libraries.) CHARLEMAGNE opened the palace library of Aachen, which was overseen by the scholar ALCUIN OF YORK, and which became a model for other collections. (*See* AIX-LA-CHAPELLE.)

Libraries were established in nearly all monasteries and convents because many monks and nuns were scholars who needed source material, and because many monasteries required a period of daily reading.

University libraries were established later in the Middle Ages. Often, these libraries were created with gifts from wealthy patrons. In Paris, Robert de Sorbonne founded the library of the University of Paris. Humphrey, duke of Gloucester, founded the library at Oxford University. Scholars would collect books and, if they could afford to, would create their own private libraries. PETRARCH became famous for his private library, and often traveled in search of rare manuscripts.

Jewish Libraries. For the JEWS, creating a library was a means of preserving their religious and cultural heritage, something they were unwilling to entrust to others. Jewish libraries were housed in synagogues, and they contained a variety of religious and scholarly works. Many of the works had been translated from Hebrew to Arabic and Latin, so they could also be used by both Muslim and Christian scholars.

Library Innovations. Medieval practices of cataloguing, protecting, and lending laid the groundwork for the way modern libraries operate. By the thirteenth century, individuals could arrange to borrow a book from a distant library—the medieval equivalent of the interlibrary loan. The idea of circulation itself took hold during the Middle Ages. Because books were so valuable, there were many restrictions on what could be borrowed, for how long, and by whom. Many libraries required users to handle manuscripts with gloves to avoid getting finger marks on the pages. Libraries in Holland and elsewhere chained books and manuscripts to the shelves to prevent theft.

The library at Córdoba, Spain, had a 44-volume catalogue of its holdings that users could browse through to find a book. Library employees were scholars and scribes, who worked at preserving manuscripts, cataloguing new books, and updating other records.

The Printing Press. The invention of the printing press in the fifteenth century meant that books could be mass-produced, resulting in enormous growth for libraries as new books could be acquired more quickly and less expensively. A library could even have two or more copies of the same book. Moreover, since the establishment of mass printing made more literature available to individuals, literacy rates rose and so did library use. Older libraries were able to grow, and new libraries could be built. In time, religious libraries became less important than large urban public libraries and university libraries. (*See* BOOKS.)

LITERACY

L iteracy—the ability to read and write at least one language—took a decided downturn in the early Middle Ages after the disintegration of the Roman Empire, which had held education (of the upper classes) in high regard, and because of the influx into Europe and the British Isles of illiterate Germanic tribes. (*See* LITERATURE; BOOKS.)

For most of the Middle Ages in Europe, from 500 to 1100, literacy was attained and promulgated entirely by the clerical members of the Catholic Church, who, mindful of their origins in the Roman Empire, preserved LATIN as a living language. Until at least the twelfth century, being literate meant knowing LATIN.

Byzantium. This was not the case in the Byzantine world, which had broken away from the empire centered in ROME in the fourth century, and reformed in CONSTANTINOPLE with a Greek-speaking constituency; the language of the Byzantine literate remained the vernacular Greek. There was thus less of a divide between the schooled and the unschooled than there was in the West. In BYZANTIUM, literate administrators and bureaucrats in both the royal court and the law courts stemmed as much from the laity as the clergy. Most wealthy families sent their children to schools, where the language of instruction was Greek.

The eastern Byzantine empire was also much less affected by the BARBARIAN INVASIONS of the fifth and sixth centuries, and the VIKING invasions of the ninth and tenth centuries. As a result, there was an almost unbroken literary tradition that was instrumental in preserving many valuable antique texts. Evidence for the ownership of books by members of society outside the clergy, including military men and women, attests to a fairly widespread literacy—at least among the upper classes—because books were too costly to own unless they could be read.

Monasteries. The situation was almost entirely different in the West. For at least 500 years, literacy was kept alive only in the MONASTERIES, where the monks built upon the techniques and traditions of letter forms, script, and phonics of the Roman system. They continued the reading methods of the Romans, which was to read aloud in groups. Even when studying alone, monastic readers murmured the words.

In the early Middle Ages, people were still accustomed to learn by hearing, reflecting the belief in the strength and endurance of oral and pictorial, not written, records. During this early period, knowledge (history, custom, law) was transmitted orally among the masses by poets and "law-speakers" and by clergymen in sermons; men with finely honed memories were greatly respected. In this society, an oath spoken in front of witnesses held far more weight than a written document. Still, to the majority of people who remained illiterate, the ability to understand and interpret abstract symbols gave an almost magical prestige to the literate clergy. Reading and writing were seen as gifts from God to the servants of God; the language of the Church was incomprehensible to the common man. For centuries, ideas were transmitted to the laity mostly orally or symbolically, in religious art.

By the tenth century, word separation and punctuation marks were introduced in order to guide the reader, who was encouraged to read silently. Study aids, such as glossaries, alphabetized dictionaries, and grammars appeared.

Writing Styles. The Roman cursive was overtaken by the elaborate, cumbersome book script, called uncial; it required each letter to be formed separately. This process was only somewhat relieved by the introduction of the Carolingian minuscule, but until the twelfth century, there was no informal script. Copying texts remained a lengthy and tedious process, forcing monks to concentrate on preserving only Christian texts, such as the BIBLE and patristic writings, with little or no original composition except for historical chronicles and saints' lives. (*See* HANDWRITING.)

Late Middle Ages. In the later twelfth century, the introduction of the Gothic cursive radically changed writing, at a time when the West was in the midst of a resurgence in learning, thanks in part to the century's relative peace, prosperity, and stability. Advances in travel and trade further facilitated the interchange of ideas and promoted literacy.

This renaissance of learning and literacy had its beginnings in the cathedral schools of northern Europe, such as CHARTRES, Paris, and Bologna, established by the bishops to provide educated administrators. These eventually became inadequate, and the university was born, where long-forgotten works could be translated into Latin and out of which emerged the distinctive figure of the scholar who devoted his full time to learning and the study of texts.

Illuminated page from the 14th-century work Rationale Divinorum Officiorum *by William Durand, depicting the robing of a bishop for his consecration.*

LITERATURE OF THE MIDDLE AGES

I n the 1860s, a Parisian Catholic priest, J.P. Migne, established a private publishing company to produce a series of books comprising all the Latin Church writings of the Middle Ages. Some 140 volumes eventually appeared under the series title *Patrologia Latina*. Each volume ran to some 800 double columned pages. Most of the volumes were not freshly edited from manuscripts. They were edited reprints of texts that had been published during the sixteenth and seventeenth centuries. (Migne's series, with clever promotion, actually turned a profit. *Patrologia Latina* can be found in every good academic library today, and most of the volumes are still in print. *See* LATIN.)

Early Publishing. The story of this phenomenal publishing success bears upon one's understanding the vast scope of the extant Latin writings of the Middle Ages, comprising theological and philosophical treatises; saints' lives (hagiography); chronicles and narrative histories; letters, devotional tracts, and sermons; poetry and drama; and liturgical expositions. Migne did not come close to publishing the whole corpus of medieval Latin writings. Perhaps three or four times the contents of the *Patrologia Latina* remained in unpublished manuscripts in his day. A substantial amount of such medieval Latin writing is located at European archives such as the Vatican Library, the Bibliothèque Nationale in PARIS, the British Library in LONDON, and Bodleian Library at Oxford and remains there, still unpublished, to this day. There are also vast archives of governmental and judicial records, which have less right to be placed under the rubric of literature than the kind of more didactic, formal, and Church-related material that Migne's entrepreneurship (and the hard work of the underpaid clerics he employed as editors) made available.

Quality Works. The astonishing fact is that however one defines literature—whether broadly to mean any writing of a formal, conscious, imaginative, persuasive, or forensic nature or more narrowly as imaginative or evocative of intellect and sensibility—the Latin literature of the Middle Ages vastly exceeds the surviving body of ancient classical Latin literature, and is in no way inferior in quality of mind or expression to the classical literature.

In addition, the medieval corpus includes the extensive bodies of vernacular medieval literature (French, English, Spanish, Italian, German, Icelandic) in which much of the most innovative and emotionally resonant literature of the Middle Ages came to be written after 1100 C.E. Added to this is the vast collection of Greek medieval Church writings (which the indefatigable Migne also published in a separate series, with parallel Latin translations) or the prolific imaginative and didactic writings, especially poetry, in medieval Arabic and Hebrew.

Given that before 1150 literacy was confined in Europe to clerics and a very narrow stratum of laity, and given the expense of producing written materials, the extensive output of medieval writers, even considering literature in its narrower definition, was prodigious and probably exceeded the output of the classical world. The European Middle Ages were one of the great literary epochs of mankind. It is only since 1950 that critical analysis—as distinct from simply textual editing and cataloging—has come to throw light on the main currents of ideas and genres and the subtle cross-currents of the medieval literary sensibility.

The survival rate of medieval literary manuscripts was greatly enhanced by western Europe's lack of paper from about 750 to 1450, and the consequent use of stretched and bleached animal skin (usually mature sheep but sometimes expensive lambskin or calfskin), called parchment or vellum, as the writing surface. Writing was done with a stylus pen or a paintbrush; the surface also lent itself to the application of paint for richly illuminated pages. There are thousands of such brilliantly illuminated manuscripts bound into codices (books) in the great European archives, as well as in the Morgan Library in New York City. It seems the skins of at least ten million mature sheep were dried, stretched, and bleached to make medieval manuscript parchment, after the importation of paper from EGYPT stopped in the eighth century, and before Europeans learned the chemical process of making paper from rags in the mid-fifteenth century.

Styles. All medieval Latin literature (and to a significantly lesser extent, vernacular) is heavily formulaic. It employs a collection of standard ways of describing people, events, locations, motivations, and behavioral patterns. These formulas are called tropes. Medieval

Milestones of Medieval Literature	
524	Boethius, *The Consolation of Philosophy*.
629	First appearance of the Koran.
731	Bede, *History of the English Church*.
893	Asser, *The Life of Alfred the Great*.
c. 985	*Beowulf* written (from oral sources).
c. 1120	*Rubaiyat* of Omar Khayyam.
c. 1170	Eilhart von Oberg, *Tristan und Isolde*.
c. 1275	*Grandes Chroniques de Saint-Denis*.
1321	Dante Alighieri dies.
c. 1385	*Sir Gawain and the Green Knight*.
c. 1387	Chaucer's *Canterbury Tales*.
c. 1400	Jean Froissart, *Chroniques*.
1455	Gutenberg prints the Mazarin Bible.
1475	William Caxton publishes in English.
1485	Thomas Malory, *Morte d'Arthur*.

literature, especially the Latin writings, are almost uniformly heavily typological or tropological. On this assessment, all major critics of medieval literature agree.

What is most interesting in medieval literature for many readers today is what occurs at the margin—the greater or lesser degree of massaging, manipulating, interpreting, or even departing from the tropes or formulas. But some critics see great cultural value in the tropological and formulaic nature of medieval literature itself, in the perpetuation over many centuries of a universe of discourse, a standardized body of ideas—heavily derived from classical literature and the early centuries of the Church—fashioning a comprehensive and broadly agreed-upon way of looking at writing about the world and humanity. This admiration of medieval tropes that some have called "the medieval synthesis" has been ideologically valued on the more conservative side of twentieth century thought.

The active and creative tension in medieval literature can therefore be seen as a tension between the tropes—the typological and formulaic discourse that dominated the Latin writings (and was still substantial in vernacular medieval literature)—and efforts to express personal feeling and individuated perceptions of God, the world, and human behavior. This situation can be said to exist in all literature; good writing of any time or place is the expression of a radical, angular or uncommon perception of standardized cultural and psychological and social facets. But the polarity and tension between trope, personal sensibility, and uncommon individuation is stronger in medieval literature than in modern literature because of the tidal wave of personal sensibility in literature since the advent of the Romantic movement around 1790.

Romanticism. The medieval literary complex had a similar movement after about 1150, which some critics have seen as inspired by the remarkable erotic strain in Arabic and Hebrew poetry written mainly in Spain. Others viewed it as completely indigenous Christian movements rising from economic, demographic, and literacy booms of the twelfth century in FRANCE, southern ENGLAND, western GERMANY, and northern ITALY. Medieval romanticism—working within the contents and yet against the boundaries of inherited literary forms—found its main expression in the efflorescence of Latin religious poetry, including hymns and confessional prose in the period between 1150 and 1280, especially within the genre of the Marian cult. This school of Latin poetry and prose is extremely sophisticated in its language. (Unfortunately, it can be read today by only a handful of scholars, and little of it has found good English translation.)

The other main expression of medieval romanticism, now easily accessible to Anglophone readers because of excellent translations, is found in the vernacular poetry of the twelfth and later centuries. This genre initially received great attention in the nineteenth century because of its identification as the founding texts of European national literatures, especially in Spain, France, and Germany between 1100 and 1220. (The canonized national texts for Italy date from 1300 and England from around 1390.)

Early twentieth century critics signaled the polarity between trope and sensibility in twelfth-century vernacular literature as the transition "from epic to romance." Nowadays, we would say that in two or three generations of writers, from about 1100 to about 1180, there was a transition from formulaic heroic narratives of the Spanish heroic epic *El Cid* and the French narrative *Song of Roland* to the astonishing psychological and social sensibility and individuated focusing found in the four surviving romance narratives of CHRÉTIEN DE TROYES (1180) and WOLFRAM VON ESCHENBACH'S *Parzival* (1210). For the next six decades, due to the repressive ecclesiastical and political authoritarian mechanisms of the thirteenth century, there was a hiatus in the medieval romantic movement only to burst forth again in the the thirteenth and fourteenth centuries. Among the finest achievements of the European literary imagination are DANTE'S *The New Life* and *The Divine Comedy* (1290–1310), the *Romance of the Rose* by Jean de Meun (1285), and the major works of GEOFFREY CHAUCER, particularly *Troilus and Cressida* and the *Canterbury Tales* from the late fourteenth century, as well as the anonymous English dirge *Pearl* (1370).

These poets wrote under aristocratic patronage, held government jobs, or lived on private means coming from gentry or merchant families. The audience they addressed were literate people of the nobility and upper middle class, who themselves had to be well-educated readers receptive to new shades of meaning within old genres and typological contexts. This social and cultural ambience in which the poets worked contributed to the highly disciplined nature of their works, and the care and subtlety by which they communicated their uncommon sensibilities.

See ARABIC, BYZANTINE; CELTIC; ENGLISH, FRENCH, GERMAN, JEWISH, *and* LATIN LANGUAGE AND LITERATURE. *See also subjects such as:* CHANSON DE GESTE; COURTLY LOVE; CHIVALRY; CHRONICLES; BOOKS; GOLIARDIC POETS; HERALDRY; SAGAS; *and* UNIVERSITIES.

LITHUANIA

L ithuania, a small country situated northwest of POLAND, was a latecomer to what might be called "Westernization." Isolated by its distance from most of Europe and its lack of important natural resources, it did not adopt CHRISTIANITY until the end of the fourteenth century.

Early Years. Originally settled by an eastern people known as the Balts, Lithuania generally kept to itself, although it frequently had to fight Poles, Prussians, and Russians. Beginning in the twelfth century. Lithuanian forces took over part of the SLAV territories (in present-day RUSSIA). A century later, Lithuania became the unwitting victim of an attack by the TEUTONIC KNIGHTS, a military group originally formed to fight in the CRUSADES. They attacked PRUSSIA at the behest of a German prince, and in the course of their battle they entered Lithuania, enlisting the aid of disenchanted Lithuanian princes in the hopes of building a power base.

In the thirteenth century, a warlord known as Mindaugas united Lithuania and helped create a Lithuanian "state." Mindaugas formed a number of alliances with his neighbors, and these alliances proved beneficial later. Eventually, Lithuania controlled most of the Slav territories.

Christianity. Lithuania remained a pagan country, worshipping the forces of nature rather than any deity. Although they allowed others (such as the Slavs) under their control to practice their religion, they seemed less than enthusiastic about conversion. Christian missionaries had not traveled into Lithuania, mainly because of its distance and isolation.

This began to change in the fourteenth century, when the Lithuanian ruler Gediminas (c. 1275–1341)

An Apron of Roses

The legend of St. Hedwig, or Queen Jadwiga, is cherished by Poles and Lithuanians, and has united those two countries for centuries. Jadwiga, daughter of the king of Hungary and Poland, was forced to marry the pagan Jogailo, grand duke of Poland when she was only nine. A devout Christian, Hedwig would smuggle food to the poor out the back door of the castle in her large apron. Jogailo learned of this and suspected his bride of providing arms or secrets to rebels, so he determined to catch her. One night, as she was leaving by a secret door, Jogailo sprang out of the bushes and demanded to see what was in Hedwig's apron. A miracle occurred, goes the legend, and the food she was carrying (which still would have earned her a death sentence) turned into a garland of roses. For this reason, St Hedwig is always depicted wearing an apron of roses.

asked the pope for help in ending the war with the Teutonic Knights (who had never left the region). Little help was forthcoming, but Gediminas's grandson Jogailo devised a plan to strengthen his country considerably. In 1385 he married Jadwiga, who was heiress to the Polish throne. Upon their marriage, Jogailo became king of Poland as well as Lithuania. Jadwiga was a Christian, and Jogailo converted to Christianity. It was not long before the rest of Lithuania followed suit.

The Teutonic Knights were finally defeated at the Battle of Grunwald in 1410, by a Polish-Lithuanian force under Jogailo and his cousin Vytautas, who had succeeded him in Lithuania when Jogailo became king of Poland. Lithuania remained tied to Poland for the rest of the Middle Ages and well into the eighteenth century.

LLYWELYN AP GRUFFYD THE LAST

Llywelyn (c. 1246–1282) was the last of the Welsh princes to rule an independent WALES. His resistance to English control lasted until King Edward I put an end to his rule and his life.

Llywelyn's fortunes depended on the relative strength of the English crown. In 1246 he succeeded his uncle David II as ruler of northern Wales, and the following year, with his brother Owain as co-ruler, he paid homage to King HENRY III of ENGLAND, surrendering to him a large piece of their territory. Later after overthrowing his brother, he launched a campaign to recover his lands and win the allegiance of other Welsh princes. By 1263, Llywelyn controlled most of Wales.

He allied himself with SIMON DE MONTFORT, earl of Leicester, and other English BARONS in their revolt against Henry III, and continued to gain strength even after Montfort's defeat. The Treaty of Montgomery in 1267 recognized Llywelyn as Prince of Wales. When Edward I became king in 1272, Llywelyn refused to pay him homage. After Edward invaded in 1276, Llywelyn had to give up all but a small part of northern Wales. When Llywelyn rebelled again in 1282, the English killed him in battle; his head was displayed on a pole in LONDON to show the fate reserved for those who defied the English crown. The Welsh mourned the death of their great leader and wrote many poems honoring his memory.

LLYWELYN AP IORWERTH THE GREAT

Llywelyn (1173–1240), grandson of Owain Gwynedd, was one of the ablest Welsh princes. In 1194, at the age of only 21, he seized control of North WALES from his uncle David I. Five years later he captured the border fortress of Mold from the English. At first he was on good terms with King JOHN LACKLAND, cementing his alliance with the English monarch by marrying his illegitimate daughter Joan in 1206. However, after King John attacked him in 1210, Llywelyn allied himself with the English BARONS opposed to John. In the MAGNA CARTA, which the barons pressured John to sign in 1215, the rights of Llywelyn and the Welsh were recognized. Llywelyn destroyed the NORMAN castles in southern Wales, and continued his fight for Welsh independence against the English. His support of bards and poets stimulated a Welsh literary renaissance.

LOLLARDS

The Lollards were a group of English advocates of Church reform whose ideas stemmed mainly from the teachings of JOHN WYCLIFFE. The movement grew in popularity, especially after 1387 when the GREAT SCHISM, which produced two and then three rival popes, further discredited the PAPACY. After 1400, the authorities persecuted the movement and drove it underground, but its ideas persisted into the 1500s and influenced the Reformation in England. (*See* BIBLE; CHRISTIANITY; PAPACY.)

Wycliffe. John Wycliffe, a priest who taught theology at Oxford University, held that the Bible was the only true authority for the Church: only souls in a true state of grace could be true members of the Church. Since nobody knew who these souls were, members of the clergy and even the pope were not necessarily among their number. Wycliffe taught and wrote pamphlets attacking the doctrines of transubstantiation (the transformation of bread and wine into the body and blood of Christ) and the sacraments. He also promoted the idea that the Bible (available only in Latin) should be translated into the vernacular so Christians could read it for themselves. Wycliffe was condemned and tried as a heretic several times. Protected by the royal family, he was finally allowed to retire into seclusion in Leicestershire where he translated the Bible into English. His followers became Lollards and disseminated his ideas. (*See* WYCLIFFE, JOHN.)

Increasingly, Church and secular authorities saw the Lollards as a threat to the established order because they were critical of the power and corruption of the Church and its enormous wealth. They also insisted on studying the Bible in Wycliffe's English version, which the Church condemned.

Early Lollard leaders had been Wycliffe's students at Oxford, but the movement soon began attracting people from the middle and lower classes as well. By the late 1300s, well-established groups of Lollards were scattered across ENGLAND. These "poor priests" traveled around the countryside spreading Lollard ideas and preaching against the established Church.

Beliefs. A manifesto of Lollard beliefs called *Conclusions,* presented to PARLIAMENT in 1395, summarized the movement's beliefs: condemnation of clerical celibacy, as well as transubstantiation and the sacraments, and support for priestly poverty and the translation of the Bible into English. Some Lollards went well beyond Wycliffe's teachings and embraced pacifism and free love. In 1401, after the English government issued the antiheretical statute *De heretico comburendo* and introduced the death penalty for HERESY, it denounced the Lollards as heretics and drove them underground, where itinerant preachers continued to propagate Lollard beliefs. The authorities arrested and convicted many Lollards and burned some of them at the stake. Lollards were involved in several revolts against the crown that Church and secular authorities cruelly suppressed. The best known of the rebellions was the one led by Sir John Oldcastle against King HENRY V in 1414. Henry crushed the rebellion. However, the movement survived at least in northern England until the sixteenth century and contributed to a weakening of the control of the English people by the Church, making England fertile ground for the ideas of the Protestant Reformation.

LOMBARDS

T he Lombards were a Germanic tribe that conquered much of ITALY in the sixth century. Italy had been the heart of the Roman Empire, but after the fall of the western empire, it had been conquered and reconquered a number of times. In 493, the German OSTROGOTHS established a prosperous kingdom. However, this kingdom was destroyed when the eastern Roman Empire (which survived the collapse of the west) retook Italy after the long Ostrogothic wars (535–554). The violent Lombard conquest of Italy, a land mostly ruined by Ostrogothic wars, established a kingdom that lasted for two centuries until the FRANKS, under CHARLEMAGNE, conquered northern Italy. The long rule of the Lombards left little behind; only the name of an Italian province.

Beginnings. The hitherto unimportant Lombards entered the stage of history in the middle of the sixth century when JUSTINIAN, emperor of the east, repaid them for attacking the Germanic Gepids with territory in HUNGARY and AUSTRIA. In 568, the Lombard king Albion led an invasion of Italy. The Lombards gained the fruits of the devastating Ostrogothic wars, and neither the ruling Byzantines nor the native Italians were able to resist. By 572, the Lombards had conquered the north of Italy and the central and southern provinces of Spoleto and Benevento. The Byzantines still occupied some land in northern central Italy, thus splitting the Lombard possessions into two parts: northern Italy, and southern Italy and SICILY. Eventually, the Byzantine provinces existed only in southern Italy, while an independent papal state continued to divide the Lombard provinces. (*See* ITALY; PAPAL STATES.)

Albion was murdered around 572, perhaps by his Gepid wife, whom he had forced to drink from the skull of her father. The Lombards experimented with a form of collective leadership, dividing up their territories into a numbers of localities under the leadership of a chief or "duke." It was a scheme that resulted in civil war and anarchy.

The Lombards introduced a rudimentary form of German law that was technically binding on all Italians. Non-Lombards, however, continued to follow traditional law and custom whenever possible. The apogee of the Lombard kingdom was the reign of King Liutprand (712–744), who reformed the law and expanded the kingdom. The Lombards during this period warred with the Franks, the Byzantine Empire, and the papacy.

Decline. The end of the Lombard kingdom began when the papacy made an alliance with the Franks. PÉPIN the Short defeated the Lombards (754–755) and gave RAVENNA and Pentapolis to the papacy. Charlemagne completed the complete destruction of the northern Lombard kingdom. The last Lombard king, Desiderius, was captured in 774. Charlemagne became king of the Franks and Lombards and was crowned emperor of the Romans by the pope in 800. Lombard principalities, greatly reduced in size, survived in central and southern Italy until the NORMAN conquests in eleventh-century Italy.

A 15th-century illumination of the city of London.

LONDON

During the Middle Ages, London became one of the great cities of Europe. Important as the first point at which the Thames River could be bridged, London remained an important center of politics, culture, commerce, and communications throughout the medieval period. In SAXON days, the city spread farther west along the river; during the reign of EDWARD THE CONFESSOR, the construction of the new WESTMINSTER ABBEY established Westminster as an important royal and ecclesiastical center. However, throughout the medieval period, the heart of London remained the old Roman city of Londinium and the bridge that spanned the Thames.

Post-Roman Development. After the Romans withdrew from Britain in the 400s, Saxons, Angles, and other Germanic tribes invaded the island and drove the Celtic and Roman peoples west and north. Although London was largely abandoned, it retained its importance as a trading center. The Christian missionaries who began arriving in Britain in the 500s used London as their base. The town served as an ANGLO-SAXON base and a source of tax revenues from goods shipped in and out of London until 871, when the VIKINGS attacked and occupied the town. After the Anglo-Saxon king ALFRED THE GREAT retook the city in 886, he turned London into an urban center from which to defend the rest of England. He gave land to bishops and leaders called aldermen and allowed them to collect tolls and dues. (*See* ALFRED THE GREAT.)

In the 900s, London became a major port as ships from FRANCE and FLANDERS brought goods to the city's docks. The increased COMMERCE stimulated the growth of basic institutions of city government. EDWARD THE CONFESSOR (king of England, 1042–1066) rebuilt the Benedictine abbey church and turned it into Westminster Abbey, which served as a royal palace as well as a center of government, making London the political and economic focal point of the kingdom.

Norman Period. The CORONATION of WILLIAM I THE CONQUEROR as king of England in Westminster Abbey on Christmas Day, 1066 increased the city's importance. By submitting rather than resisting the Norman invaders, London was granted a charter that allowed it to keep its laws and customs. Under the NORMANS the city grew and prospered. Many new buildings were constructed, including churches, hospitals, the Tower of London, and the famed stone bridge across the Thames. (*See* WILLIAM I THE CONQUEROR; NORMANS.)

London's wealth helped it win political concessions. King HENRY I granted the city the right to choose its own sheriffs and administer its own courts, and RICHARD I allowed the city to have a form of administration from which its corporation emerged. King JOHN LACKLAND was pressured to grant the city basic rights, spelled out in the MAGNA CARTA, including the right to elect a mayor each year, protection for city merchants, and free passage on the Thames.

In the late medieval period, London built new docks along the waterfront, filling up vacant spaces within the city with shops and houses, and spreading well beyond the original city walls. In 1348–1349 the BLACK DEATH wiped out a third of the city's population, but as the city recovered, people from the countryside came to the city looking for new opportunities. By the end of the Middle Ages, London's population was 150,000, making it England's largest city. (*See* WESTMINSTER ABBEY; PARLIAMENT.)

LOUIS I THE PIOUS

Louis I the Pious (778–840) ruled the Frankish empire from the death of his father CHARLEMAGNE in 814 until his own death in 840. Under Frankish law, Charlemagne's empire was to be divided among his three sons, but the deaths of his sons Pépin, king of Italy, in 810, and his second son, Charles, king of Franconia, a year later, left Louis, king of Aquitaine since 781, as Charlemagne's sole surviving son and successor. In 813, during the last year of Charlemagne's life, Louis ruled the empire as joint emperor with his father. When Louis ascended the throne as the sole ruler, he found himself beset by challenges from all sides, not the least being the constant and growing raids by the NORMANS.

His Reign. Throughout his reign, Louis supported court and Church reforms, especially the monastic reforms of his friend and adviser, St. Benedict of Aniane. To make it easier to benefit from Benedict's advice, Louis built a monastery for him close to the royal palace at Aachen. With Benedict's encouragement and help, Louis set out to establish his empire according to Christian principles. He ordered bishops to stop wearing military attire, expelled women of loose morals from the court, and arranged to have Charlemagne's daughters, once regarded as "doves" of the court, sent to nunneries.

Louis also tried to centralize the legal system, since the empire he inherited was a patchwork of different peoples, each with its own laws and traditions. His dream of presiding over an empire with one ruler, one people, and one law made only limited headway.

Church Reform. His greatest success came in the area of Church reform where the influence of his friend Benedict was greatest. Cathedral canons were required to live by the Rule of ST. BENEDICT OF NURSIA, which had to be committed to memory. He made other monastic regulations more uniform. For example, during Lent, monks had to fast on bread and water and their hoods were only allowed to be two cubits long.

The ancient Frankish law that at the death of a king, his kingdom had to be divided equally among his sons created a problem for Louis who had four sons— three by his first wife Hermingard and one by his second wife, Judith of Bavaria.

Succession. In 817—only three years after he assumed full power as emperor—he named his oldest son Lothair as his successor, assigning lesser kingdoms to his other two sons by Hermingard, Pépin and Louis. However, the very next year he remarried and Judith bore him another son, Charles. Louis then tried to rearrange the dynastic succession in favor of his new son, creating dynastic unrest for the rest of his reign. Louis was even deposed from the throne in 833 for two years, then barely held on until his death in 840. (*See* FRANKS; CHARLEMAGNE; BENEDICT OF NURSIA.)

A 15th-century illumination of Saint Louis setting out for the Crusades. Louis IX is credited with establishing the character of European polity for the next 800 years.

LOUIS IX, ST.

L ouis IX (1214–1270), king of FRANCE, is best remembered for the austerity and piety that made him a symbol of the ideal Christian ruler. He went on TWO CRUSADES, collected and preserved sacred relics from the Holy Land, and gave lavishly to the poor and needy from the royal treasury. His canonization 27 years after his death earned him the title of "Saint Louis."

Early Reign. Louis was the oldest son of Louis VIII and BLANCHE OF CASTILE. He became king in 1226 at the age of 12, but for the next eight years his mother ruled the kingdom as regent. During her son's minority, Blanche put down several revolts, the most serious of which was led by Peter I, duke of BRITTANY, who received support from Raymond VII of Toulouse and King HENRY III of ENGLAND. Blanche remained her son's chief adviser until her death in 1252. At age 20, Louis married Margaret, daughter of Raymond, count of Provence, and together they had 11 children. However, Margaret's influence on government never equaled that of Louis's mother.

Not only did Louis have a religious appearance (the chronicler Salimbene described him as "thin, slender, lean, and tall," having "an angelic countenance and a gracious person"), but from his youth he had a keen interest in holy relics. In 1239, he purchased at great cost from BALDWIN I, king of Jerusalem, what was purported to be a piece of Christ's crown of thorns. Two years later, he obtained a supposed piece of the "True Cross." In 1245–1248, Louis built the Sainte-Chapelle in Paris for his expanding collection of sacred relics. He was extremely generous to religious orders and the poor. He was also a source of frustration to his advisers, who tried to curb his generosity.

Crusades. In 1244, after barely surviving a serious illness, Louis vowed to go on a crusade to the Holy Land. Before he left, he appointed officials to root out local corruption and right any wrongs done to his subjects, and appointed his mother as regent. Louis left for the crusade from Aigues-Mortes in southern France in 1248, and spent the winter in CYPRUS. After he landed in EGYPT, he captured Damietta, intending to seize Cairo, a strategic city for any effective assault on Palestine, but the SARACENS defeated his army near El-Mansura and took him prisoner on April 6, 1250.

When news of the king's capture reached France, bands of peasants mobilized to rescue him in what came to be known as the "crusade of the shepherds." When the restless bands got out of hand and began wreaking havoc in France, Blanche suppressed them in June 1251. Several months after his capture, Louis agreed to surrender Damietta as the price of his ransom. Upon his release he went on to the Holy Land and spent four years fortifying the crusader strongholds in Syria.

Despite his military failure in Egypt, Louis returned to France with his reputation as a crusader greatly enhanced. Becoming an even more religiously austere figure, he eschewed the traditional regal garb of royal ermine and squirrel fur trimmings, dressing instead in plain woolen cloth and a black taffeta cape. In the spirit of charity and humility, Louis regularly washed the feet of the poor. According to his biographer and longtime friend, courtier Jean de Joinville, in the summer the king liked to go to the woods of Vincennes near PARIS to make himself available to any of his subjects who wanted to talk to him.

Later Reign. Louis took steps to make royal government more effective by issuing ordinances about the duties of provincial officials and the circulation of currency. His differentiation of the judicial and financial functions of the *curia regis* (royal court) greatly accelerated the process of government specialization.

Louis was not always generous and friendly. He could be harsh in his treatment of the bishops who asserted independence from the crown, and he intensely disliked Jews, seeing them as Christ-killers. (*See* JEWS, EXPULSIONS OF.)

Louis was also active in promoting European solidarity against the Muslim threat in the east. He settled a suzerainty dispute with ARAGON that eventually resulted in the Treaty of Corbeil in 1258 and then resolved his dispute with King Henry III over England's territorial claims in France, his envoys negotiating what came to be called the Treaty of Paris of 1259. The terms of the treaty called for Henry to abandon his claims to Normandy, Touraine, Maine, Anjou, and Poitou and to hold Gascony as a fief of the French crown. In return, Louis paid Henry a vast amount of money, and confirmed certain rights of Henry's in Perigueux, Limoges, and Cahors. The treaty succeeded in keeping the peace between the two kingdoms for the next 24 years.

In 1263, Henry called on Louis to arbitrate his dispute with a group of rebellious barons led by SIMON DE MONTFORT who were trying to curb Henry's power. At the Mise of Amiens in 1264 Louis ruled in Henry's favor, but Montfort and the other barons disregarded Louis' ruling that allowed Henry to rule as he wished.

Late in Louis's reign, after the Mamluks of Egypt began a new offensive against the Christian crusader states, Louis set off on another crusade. On the way, he attacked Muslim Tunis in North Africa; he died there of dysentery in 1270. His body was returned to France and buried at SAINT-DENIS. The efforts of Louis's son, Philip III, to have his father declared a saint succeeded; Pope BONIFACE VIII canonized him in 1297. (*See* CRUSADES; KINGSHIP; *and the* INTRODUCTION.)

LOUIS XI

L ouis XI (1423–1483) as king of FRANCE (1461–1483) helped France recover from the devastation and disorder caused by the HUNDRED YEARS' WAR. His diplomatic skills allowed him successfully to neutralize his foreign and domestic enemies and establish an efficient central administration.

The Dauphin. Born the son of CHARLES VII of France and Mary of Anjou, Louis at age 13 was given in marriage to Margaret, the daughter of James I of SCOTLAND. As dauphin, he was constantly in rebellion against his father. In 1440, he joined a coalition of French nobles supported by Philip the Good, duke of Burgundy. After Charles pardoned him, Louis conspired against his father's powerful mistress, Agnes Sorel. Charles then exiled Louis to the Dauphiné, which he allowed Louis to govern. When Louis continued to plot against his father, Charles forced him to flee to the court of Philip the Good. Louis returned in 1461 to take the crown after his father's death, which he may have hastened by poisoning him.

Embattled Ruler. As king, Louis broke with and was opposed by many of the nobles who had once been his allies. His brother Charles remained his principal opponent until his death in 1472. Louis spent much of his time forming alliances to neutralize threats from ENGLAND and BURGUNDY. When Charles of Maine died in 1481, Louis added his territories of Anjou, Maine, Bar, and Provence to the royal domain.

Later chroniclers had little good to say about Louis, concentrating on his intrigues and capacity for treachery that earned him the name of the "spider king." During his final years, Louis's fear of assassination caused him to live in virtual self-imprisonment near Tours. He died in 1483 and was succeeded by his son, Charles VIII.

LULL, RAYMOND

Raymond Lull (c 1235–c. 1316) was a Spanish missionary and scholar who spent much of his long life trying to convert non-Christians and reunifying the Roman and Byzantine churches. Legend has it that he was murdered in Algeria when he was in his 80s while trying to convert a community of Muslims.

His Life. Lull (also known as Ramón Lully) was born to a prosperous family on the island of Majorca. They were friendly with the nobility, and Lull eventually became the seneschal (property and financial manager) to King JAMES I of ARAGON. In 1263, he had what he believed to be a mystical religious experience that compelled him to leave the court and devote the rest of his life to missionary work. He spent several years studying theology, as well as Latin and Arabic. Then he set out to convert the Muslims. (*See* MISSIONS AND MISSIONARIES.)

His Religion. A second mystical experience about ten years later was the inspiration for his encyclopedic collection of works known as *Ars magna* (The Great Art). In this series of books, Lull discussed the importance of religious faith and proposed that all knowl-

Raymond Lull, depicted as an alchemist in a 14th-century engraving.

edge can be reduced to a small set of first principles. *Ars magna* influenced religious thought well past the Middle Ages.

The remainder of his life was spent traveling as a missionary throughout North Africa, the Middle East, and present-day Turkey. He also made numerous visits to the pope and to European rulers to seek aid for his work, which stressed teaching Arabic to missionaries.

In addition to his missionary activities, Lull was also a poet, who wrote most of his work in his native Catalan, inspiring other Catalan poets to compose in the vernacular. Lull is known today as a great Arabic scholar and a pioneer in the learned Christian study of the Muslim world. He authored a handbook on CHIVALRY that was disseminated and translated into several languages, including English (and published by WILLIAM CAXTON as *The Book of the Ordre of Chivalry*), which became a training manual for young knights. (*See* ALCHEMY; CHIVALRY; KNIGHTHOOD.)

LYDGATE, JOHN

The medieval writer John Lydgate (c. 1370–1449) was one of the most prolific poets of the English language. Influenced strongly by CHAUCER, he wrote more than 140,000 lines during his lifetime (including translations of other works). Although much of his work may not have been particularly brilliant, he wrote so much and became so well known that he was often compared favorably with such writers as Chaucer and Gower. (*See* LITERATURE.)

Lydgate was born in Suffolk and entered the Benedictine monastery of Bury St. Edmunds in 1385. He was ordained a priest; except for short periods of study and travel, he spent most of his life at Bury St. Edmunds, where he died.

At Bury St. Edmunds he began to write, and he soon established a reputation as a talented poet. Drawing on Chaucer's works in particular as a model, he composed a number of works that were well-received. Allegory and satire were common devices in his poems, which covered numerous topics. He gained the patronage of a number of wealthy nobles, who commissioned him to write poems for and about them. Among the authors he translated were BOCCACCIO, Deguileville, and Guido delle Colonne.

Although his early works showed promise, his later works became increasingly less interesting. His poems got longer and less creative. During his own lifetime his work remained popular, and it was routinely praised well into the seventeenth century. But among the huge number of poems that Lydgate produced, the prevailing modern opinion is that only a few can be considered as having literary merit.

MACBETH

Macbeth (died 1057), immortalized by William Shakespeare in his play of the same name, was king of SCOTLAND from 1040 to 1057. He succeeded his father as ruler of the province of Moray in northeastern Scotland about 1031 and then was a military commander for King Duncan I. In 1040, after killing Duncan in battle, Macbeth seized the throne. Macbeth may have had some royal lineage himself, but his claim to the crown came through his wife Gruoch, granddaughter of Kenneth III, overthrown by Duncan's ancestor, Malcolm II.

Macbeth was strongly supported by the people in the northern parts of Scotland who were opposed to ties with the ANGLO-SAXON English favored by King Duncan. In 1046, Siward, the earl of Northumbria in northern ENGLAND, invaded Scotland and put another king on the throne. However, Macbeth was able to win back his kingdom. By 1050 he was in full control of Scotland, aided by an understanding with the English king, EDWARD THE CONFESSOR.

In 1054, Siward invaded Scotland again, and after defeating Macbeth reclaimed southern Scotland for Duncan's son, Malcolm Canmore. Three years later, Malcolm killed Macbeth at the Battle of Lumphanan and succeeded to the Scottish throne as Malcolm III. William Shakespeare based his version of the Macbeth story on the accounts of Raphael Holinshed and Hector Boece. (*See* SCOTLAND.)

MACHAUT, GUILLAUME DE

Guillaume de Machaut (c. 1300–1377) was one of medieval FRANCE's most important poets and composers. Although he set many of his poems to music, his work was far above that of the TROUBADOURS and trouvères who wandered Europe singing and composing poetry. His work was, in fact, a significant influence not only on French writers, such as FROISSART and CHRISTINE DE PISAN, but also on English writers such as CHAUCER.

Machaut was born in France at the beginning of the fourteenth century. Few details are known about his life except that he managed to attract a number of influential patrons in western and central Europe. Among his supporters were the rulers of BURGUNDY, France, and BOHEMIA. Not surprisingly, many of his poems and songs are celebrations of his patrons, but he also wrote about medieval life. While he could write about the romanticized ideals of COURTLY LOVE, beauty, and CHIVALRY, he could also write devastatingly direct pieces on war, poverty, and epidemics.

What made Machaut's poetry and music stand out from that of his contemporaries was his intricate construction. Although he worked in the poetic forms common to his time—rondeaux, virelays, and ballades—his careful selection of words shows an uncommonly good ear for the sound of language as it is written. Similarly, his musical compositions display painstaking attention to rhythm, as well as a talent for mixing different melodies within the same work to create the complementary effect known as counterpoint.

Machaut's supportive patrons allowed him to live comfortably until his death in 1377.

MAGIC AND FOLKLORE

Medieval views on magic evolved from a continuing search for explanations of unnatural occurrences. The word *magic* comes from the Persian for "sorcerer," and magical forces were held responsible for many unexplained events. Folklore grew up around some of these events; people would recount stories of magical occurrences, which would be passed from generation to generation.

Religion played a significant role in daily life during the Middle Ages. People believed that, even with God in supreme control, both ANGELS AND DEMONS could interfere with people's lives. As a result, magic was taken seriously, even by religious leaders. Each region of the medieval world had a somewhat different interpretation of magic, reflected in its folklore.

Western Europe. Medieval Europeans believed in both angels and demons. They also believed that the heavenly bodies (sun, moon, planets, and stars) could control events. In this regard they were not entirely wrong, of course; weather and tides are affected by the sun and the moon, a fact known since antiquity.

Of more concern to them was magic that could either do great good or great harm. For example, ALCHEMY, whose practitioners were believed to have the ability to turn common metals into gold, was considered a benevolent, or white, magic. ASTROLOGY and divination also fell into this category. But black magic, including WITCHCRAFT AND SORCERY, was a source of fear for many individuals.

Spirits including fairies and nymphs were often believed to inhabit inanimate objects, such as rocks and trees; they could be either good or evil. From these concerns grew a series of beliefs and folk notions that were passed down from one generation to the next. Various behavioral patterns developed in which performing a certain act could portend either a good or a bad event. Herbs and flowers were often used to ward off evil spirits. Since "evil spirits" were often nothing more than diseases and since many plants have medicinal qualities, these "cures" were sometimes effective and became part of folk tradition.

Byzantine Magic. The Byzantines were extremely interested in astrology and divination. Many scholars devoted much of their time to writing about these disciplines. Astrology, which had its origins in ancient Greece, was popular with people of all backgrounds—much to the chagrin of astronomers (who had limited success condemning astrology).

Divination was taken quite seriously. People used a number of divining techniques; props included mirrors, sand, water, and special divining dishes. Dream interpretation was also a popular pursuit.

Herbs and plants were used for magical purposes, as were special charms and amulets. So popular was magic in the Byzantine world that the Church was often critical of how strongly people believed in it. Magic continued to flourish despite these efforts.

Jewish Magic and Folklore. The Talmud, the authoritative compendium of Jewish laws and rituals, appeared around 500. In addition to learned subjects, it contains many elements of folklore. Fables, myths, folk remedies, superstitions, and stories about supernatural beings are included alongside juridical discussions and analysis of the BIBLE and religious rituals.

Much Jewish folklore is based on the lore of lands in which the Jews settled. Since Jews had lived in Greece and ROME, as well as in Islamic lands, their folktales are often based on Arabic or ancient Greek tales. Even Indian folklore appears in Jewish tales; the Jews translated the Indian *Panchatantra* into Hebrew from Arabic (the Arabs having originally translated it from the Indian) in the twelfth century.

The popular medieval German *Sefer Hasidim* (Book of the Pious) contains Jewish folktales and accounts of evil spirits, demons, witches, and sorcerers—as well as advice on how to protect oneself from them.

Islamic Magic and Folklore. Muslims believed in spirits called jinni (from which the word "genie" is derived). Like the nymphs and fairies of Europe, jinni resided in inanimate objects. According to the teachings of the prophet MUHAMMAD, all magic was bad magic. But magic could be used to counter evil magic, such as wearing an amulet to ward off the "evil eye."

The richness of the ethereal realm in Islamic culture is evidenced by the popularity of such folktale collections as the *Thousand and One Nights*. (*See* ARABIC CULTURE; ALCHEMY; ASTROLOGY; WITCHCRAFT AND SORCERY; ANGELS AND DEMONS; *and* BIBLE.)

MAGNA CARTA

Regarded as the foundation of English constitutional law and liberties, the Magna Carta ("Great Charter") is one of the most well-known and important documents in English history. It is based on the medieval contractual idea that a feudal lord, such as a king, has certain obligations to his vassals—and that the vassals have, in turn, the right to force their lord to fulfill those obligations. The significance of the charter for the later development of English constitutional law was its assumption that the king, like those he ruled, was subject to the rule of law.

Origins. In 1215, JOHN LACKLAND put his seal on the Magna Carta at Runnymede by the Thames under extreme pressure from English BARONS. Unhappy with the king's heavy taxes and mismanagement of the kingdom, the barons under the leadership of STEPHEN LANGTON, Archbishop of Canterbury, presented the king with their list of feudal rights which was the result of many months of drafting and negotiations. There

Baronial coats of arms and royal seals surround the Magna Carta (here in facsimile) sealed by King John.

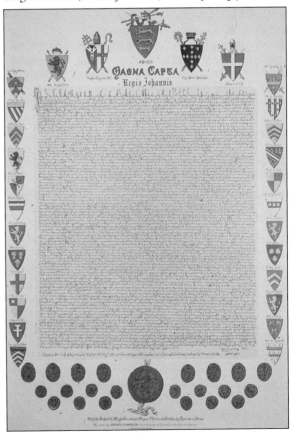

was precedent for such a document: HENRY I, in 1100, had issued a Coronation Charter of Baronial Liberties to strengthen his claim to the throne. What made the Magna Carta significant was the scope of its provisions, which covered five main areas: rights and liberties of the Church; financial obligations; royal courts and treasury; relationship between king and barons; and obligations of the king to his subjects.

The Charter. In the Magna Carta, John made concessions to just about every faction that had a complaint against him. He swore that "the English church shall be free and hold its rights entire and its liberties uninjured" and promised to respect the feudal rights and privileges of the NOBLES. He also guaranteed the city of LONDON that it "shall have all its ancient liberties and free customs." He accepted the fundamental principle of the rule of law that became enshrined in later constitutional documents when he agreed that "no freeman shall be taken or imprisoned . . . except by the legal judgment of his peers or by the law of the land" and guaranteed the right to trial within a reasonable time. He also agreed that "no scutage or aid [tax] shall be imposed in our kingdom except by the common council of our kingdom"—a provision that anticipated the necessity of parliamentary assent to TAXATION from the late thirteenth century forward.

The charter also contained a wide assortment of other matters, such as arrangements for peace with SCOTLAND and WALES and details over weights and measures, forest charters, and fishing rights. It enthusiastically endorsed the recent introduction of the grand jury into the common law.

The Magna Carta was an aristocratic document, to be sure, but it also assured rights of due process to the rural and urban middle classes, extending its rulings and spirit into English society as a whole. In its original form the charter had 63 clauses, but reissues of the charter in 1217, 1225, and later omitted certain clauses, most notably clause number 61, which sought to encumber the king with a council of 25 barons, four of whom were to serve as an executive committee.

Repeal and Reissue. Shortly after Runnymede, John appealed to Pope INNOCENT III to allow him to repudiate the Magna Carta on the grounds that it was forced upon him. The pope agreed; as an expert on Roman law, Innocent did not like the liberal political implications of the charter. He suspended Stephen Langton from his office as archbishop. Langton died in 1217, in ecclesiastical disgrace. John's repudiation of the Magna Carta precipitated an extensive baronial rebellion, but the king died in 1216 before much fighting occurred. The most respected of the barons, Earl William Marshal—who had been neutral in 1215—became regent for the young KING HENRY III. It was Marshal's government that issued the Magna Carta in its final and definitive form in 1225.

By the late Middle Ages, the Magna Carta was recognized as the supreme statute of the realm. In 1297, King Edward I was forced by the barons to reaffirm it as a symbolic gesture that he would follow the rule of law. In 1399, King RICHARD II's abdication and deposition was justified because he was deemed by PARLIAMENT to have violated the spirit of the Magna Carta. Under the strong Tudor monarchy of the sixteenth century, the document was virtually forgotten. It was invoked, however, in the seventeenth century during the conflicts between the Commons and the Stuarts. (*See* ENGLAND; JOHN LACKLAND; STEPHEN LANGTON; LAW, SCHOOLS OF; WILLIAM MARSHAL; PARLIAMENT.)

MAIMONIDES, MOSES

R abbi Moses ben Maimon (1135–1204), known as Rambam (an acronym of his name) and as Maimonides ("son of Maimon"), was the most prominent, and possibly the most controversial, rabbinic sage of the Middle Ages.

Born and educated (possibly by his father) in Córdoba, SPAIN, he and his family fled the ALMOHAD invasion of 1149 and the subsequent persecution of the JEWS. They settled in Fez, Morocco, which they were forced to flee in 1165. Maimonides, by now a celebrated physician, settled in Fustat (modern Cairo) in 1169 and became the chief physician to SALADIN.

Maimonides's reputation rests on three major works of monumental influence in the Jewish world (and of great influence in the non-Jewish world as well): his *Commentary on the Mishnah*, begun in Fez and completed shortly after his arrival in EGYPT, is a lucid and simple explication of the core document of the Talmud; his code of Jewish law, the *Mishnah Torah* (*Summary of the Law*), completed around 1178, is a novel attempt to formulate the laws of Judaism in concert with the strictest demands of logic and reason; and the *Moreh Nebuhim* (*Guide for the Perplexed*), written in Arabic, completed in 1190, grappled with difficult issues concerning the relationship of faith and reason. The book was translated into Hebrew and Latin, later studied by Christian philosophers such as ALBERTUS MAGNUS and THOMAS AQUINAS.

Maimonides also wrote epistles—responses to questions put to him by distant Jewish communities under intellectual (and physical) siege by Muslims, Christians, and especially the lures of rational intellectualism. His rulings, which today represent the liberal impulse in Judaism and for which he was sorely criticized and even ostracized, provided guidance and comfort to a beleaguered Jewry. Maimonides died in 1204, and, in accordance with his wishes, he was buried in Tiberias. (*See* JUDAISM; JEWS.)

MALORY, THOMAS

Sir Thomas Malory's (d. 1471) epic *Morte d'Arthur* (*Death of Arthur*) is one of the most important and enduring works of English literature. It tells the story of KING ARTHUR, Queen Guinevere, and the Knights of the Round Table. Filled with adventure and romance, it provides a vivid picture of the age of CHIVALRY.

In the more than 500 years since the work's first appearance, however, no one has been able to determine exactly who Sir Thomas Malory was. Two men of mid-fifteenth century England had this name—one, a courtly gentleman of good reputation, the other, a former mercenary.

Morte d'Arthur was completed around 1470 and printed by the English publisher, WILLIAM CAXTON, in 1485. The title is somewhat misleading, since it covers much more than King Arthur's death. Caxton's edition was divided into 21 books, but a different version of the manuscript, discovered in the 1930s, was divided into eight. Beginning with the early days of Arthur, it tells of his marriage to Guinevere, his creation of the Round Table, and the quest for the Holy Grail. It also recounts the deeds of such knights as Sir Lancelot and Sir Tristram, and describes other key players such as Merlin the magician. The story concludes with the disbanding of the Round Table, Arthur's death, and his soul's final voyage to Avalon, the mythical Celtic land of the dead.

Its simple and direct language and its detailed narrative has made *Morte d'Arthur* one of the most enduring literary works in the ENGLISH LANGUAGE, the subject of numerous stories, poems, and plays.

The Author. Some scholars believe Malory was an English knight; others say he was an adventurer. He was long believed to have been a Welshman. He himself notes that the book was written in the ninth year of King EDWARD IV's reign, which dates it at 1470. *Morte d'Arthur* may have been written while Malory was a prisoner, in part because a poem that accompanies the work asks for deliverance from prison. His claim that much of the work was translated from a "French book" has led some to surmise that he may have written it while being held prisoner by the French during the HUNDRED YEARS' WAR. Others believe he was imprisoned during the WARS OF THE ROSES.

A widely accepted opinion is that he was Thomas Malory of Newbold Revel, in Warwickshire. This Malory was born around 1393, knighted in the 1440s, briefly in PARLIAMENT, and imprisoned on several occasions between 1460 and 1470 for a variety of unspecified offenses. Upon his death in 1471, he was buried in the chapel of St. Francis, near Newgate, with no other works attributed to him. (*See* LITERATURE.)

MAMLUKS

The Mamluks (also Mamelukes, from the Arabic for slave) were dynastic rulers of EGYPT who began as bodyguards to the caliphs in the ninth century, becoming warrior slaves for their masters, the FATIMIDS in Egypt, and the ABBASIDS and AYYUBIDS in Syria and Arabia. The danger of arming slave hordes was driven home when the Mamluks, led by General Aybak, deposed the Fatimids in 1252, establishing a dynasty that lasted for 260 years.

Soldiers first and foremost (who fought mainly as cavalry), the Mamluks left the administration of their empire to Islamic functionaries as they sought only to expand their territory militarily. Their greatest leader, the sultan Baybars, solidified Mamluk control over the Syrian Ayyubids after repelling the MONGOLS at Ain Jalud in 1261. He went on to conquer the crusader principalities, and by 1291, his successor had conquered the last crusader stronghold at Acre.

The period from 1252 to 1382, known as the Bahri period, was marked by great wealth pouring into the kingdom, accompanied by a revival of Islamic culture and religion in a minor "golden age." Egypt became the hub of East-West trade; lavish palaces and seats of learning were built in Fustat (modern Cairo), BAGHDAD, Mecca, and Medina.

The Burji period from 1382 to 1517 marked a sharp decline for the Mamluks, brought on by the BLACK DEATH, but more by the crushing burden of the taxes required to support their military adventures, and the distance between them and their Arabian subjects. When the OTTOMAN TURKS invaded Syria in 1517, the Mamluks found themselves without local support; the Ottomans would rule Syria for the next 400 years.

MAMUN, AL-

Abu al-Abbas Abdallah al-Mamun (786–833), the son of HARUN AL-RASHID, was the seventh ABBASID caliph. Having won a civil war against his brother for the throne in 813, al-Mamun was never completely secure in his caliphate because of the tension between his liberal support of the arts and the intellectual Mutazilites, on the one hand, and the fundamentalist strain in ISLAM, on the other. He forced judges and officials to take an oath professing that, contrary to orthodox belief, the KORAN was created by God. Al-Mamun's *Bayt al-Hikmah* (*House of Wisdom*) in BAGHDAD attracted scholars, poets, translators, and philosophers from throughout the realm, creating one off the most scintillating courts in Islamic history. He died suddenly in 833, construed by fundamentalist Muslims as divine punishment.

MANDEVILLE, JOHN

J ohn Mandeville (1300–1372) was the author of *The Voyage and Travels of Sir John Mandeville* (usually referred to simply as *The Travels*), possibly the most popular book of the late Middle Ages. Mandeville undoubtedly invented much of his purported travels (especially his account of his sojourn in the Valley of the Devils and among the lost tribes of Israel), and borrowed material from other works.

However, his book was notable in that he linked the traditional imperative of pilgrimage to religious shrines with the emerging desire to explore for the purely secular reasons of discovery and material gain. Mandeville also articulated some novel opinions about the shape of the earth and its population.

Little is known of Mandeville's life; only that he was a traveling French knight. While *The Travels* was originally written in Norman

John Mandeville taking leave of Edward III before embark-ing on his adventures "beyond the Seas."

FRENCH, it was translated into many other languages, including ENGLISH and LATIN. Eventually, 300 complete manuscripts were in circulation.

The book is a remarkable source of what the medieval mind knew about the outside world as well as medieval speculation about exotic lands, such as Jerusalem, India, and CHINA. For example, Mandeville insisted that the world was round and argued that life existed everywhere on the globe—both unusual views for a person of Mandeville's time.

Mandeville's work (if not his reliability) inspired later explorers such as Christopher Columbus and the Englishman Walter Raleigh. (*See* EXPLORATION.)

MANFRED

M anfred (1232–1266), king of SICILY from 1258 until his death, and hero of the GHIBELLINE cause, was the illegitimate son of the HOHENSTAUFEN emperor, FREDERICK II. In 1250, when Frederick died, he left the empire to his natural son Conrad IV, appointing Manfred regent of Sicily. Conrad ruled Sicily under his half-brother's tutelage from 1252 until his death in 1254, at which time Manfred sought the Sicilian crown for himself. However, the PAPACY sought to keep the island out of Hohenstaufen control, and Manfred surrendered the kingdom to Pope Innocent IV, receiving the principality of Taranto in return. (*See* HOHENSTAUFEN DYNASTY.)

The succeeding pope, Alexander IV, then offered the Sicilian crown to Edmund, son of HENRY III of England, in April 1255. But Manfred had a change of heart; when papal troops entered the kingdom to enforce the ruling, Manfred successfully beat them back. When Conrad's son, Conradin, decided to remain in GERMANY, Manfred had himself crowned king of Sicily at Palermo on August 10, 1258.

While in office, Manfred pursued an aggressive foreign policy. He strengthened his Ghibelline ties by marrying his daughter, Constance, to the infant Peter III of ARAGON, who would eventually follow his stepfather to the throne. Meanwhile, in 1265, the new popes, URBAN IV and then Clement IV, offered the Sicilian crown to CHARLES OF ANJOU, who immediately set sail for ROME with French and papal forces. He defeated Manfred near Benevento in 1266 and received the crown soon after. Killed in battle, Manfred's death marked the end of Hohenstaufen rule in Italy.

MANSUR, AL-

A bu Jaf'far 'Abdullah al-Mansur (714–775) was the second ABBASID caliph, reigning from 754 to his death. Al-Mansur may be considered the true founder of the Abbasid CALIPHATE insofar as it was he who established its unique administrative and governing systems. The brother of Aby'l Abbas, founder of the dynasty and the first Abbasid caliph, al-Mansur spent the first years of his caliphate suppressing challenges from the UMAYYADS and Shi'ite Muslims; these suppressions became legendary for their cruelty. By 762, he had established his unchallenged rule everywhere in the Islamic world except in SPAIN, where the Umayyads retained an independent state under Abd al-Rahman. (*See* UMAYYAD DYNASTY.)

In 766, al-Mansur established BAGHDAD as the new capital of the empire, building it into a splendid cosmopolitan center. Al-Mansur was a harsh administrator who terrorized even his own supporters, but he was also a patron of the arts, especially of Arabic poets and scholars. Al-Mansur introduced many Persian practices into his governmental structure, which led to a strong Persian influence in the art and literature of the period. Al-Mansur died during a pilgrimage to Mecca in 775, possibly the victim of an assassination.

MANUSCRIPT ILLUMINATION

Illumination is the art of ornamenting a book's pages with pictures or designs. Books from the Middle Ages are more correctly called manuscripts (from the Latin for "writing by hand") because, until the invention of the printing press in the mid-fifteenth century, all books were created entirely by hand. Each book was a work of art, and each person involved in the process of creating a book had to possess not only skill, but enormous patience.

Illumination Process. Basic design elements, such as providing different colored inks for different letters, were handled by scribes. More elaborate details and illustrations required the service of a professional illuminator.

Although the illustrations would vary depending on the subject matter and the illuminator's skill, the mechanics of the process were straightforward. The illuminator would first apply a coat of paint to the area that was to be illustrated. The next step was to sketch in the outlines for illustrations; the outlines for other decorations and embellishments on the page would be sketched in as well. For the actual painting, the colors were added layer by layer until the desired effect had been obtained. White paint or gold leaf might be added to give a picture special highlights. Depending on the detail of the illustrations, it could take months or even years to complete an illumination. (*See* HANDWRITING.)

Christian Illuminations. The earliest illuminated manuscripts date from the early Christian and Byzantine periods (fourth to sixth centuries) and include Homer's *Iliad*, works by Virgil and Terence, and scientific texts. These texts were decorated with miniatures including a number of human and animal figures. Both the illustrations and the writing were carefully executed, but these early manuscripts were somewhat less sophisticated in style than later examples.

A brilliant example of an illuminated manuscript: the Battle of Poitiers (fought on September 19, 1356) highlights Jean Froissart's account of the battle in his Chronicles.

By the seventh century, the art of illumination began to come into its own. Byzantine manuscripts focused primarily on religious themes (although during the ICONOCLASTIC CONTROVERSY in the eighth and ninth centuries, no illuminated Byzantine books are believed to have been produced, and many were destroyed). Hundreds of motifs or artistic formulations in Byzantine manuscripts before 1100 were adapted into Latin (western European) illuminated manuscripts well into the fifteenth century. In the British Isles, particularly in IRELAND, monks were turning out magnificently designed and illustrated copies of the Gospels. These books, of which the most famous by far is the BOOK OF KELLS from the eighth century, had paintings of religious figures and also a fair number of abstract human and animal forms. The intricacy of the decorative work and the remarkable geometric patterns created by the monks (especially on the "carpet" pages, so called because they bear a close resemblance to the patterns found in oriental rugs) are especially impressive.

By the eighth century, French and German books were being illuminated in a style known as CAROLINGIAN (from the royal French family who were patrons of artists), which drew on earlier styles, but also produced art that in some cases looked more like nineteenth-century Impressionism than conventional medieval painting. The Ottonian style of illumination, popular in the tenth and eleventh centuries, elaborated on Carolingian artistry and was known for its lavish use of gold leaf in illuminations.

The ROMANESQUE style, which flourished in the eleventh and twelfth centuries, again focused on religious works, although by now the scope of those works was expanding. More people were able to read, and popular books included lives of the saints, missals, and psalters. Illumination of Romanesque books is characterized by two interesting embellishments. Grotesques—fanciful creatures such as dragons, half-human half-animal figures, dwarfs, and giants—were represented in illuminations. Opening initials of a chapter, some of which extended the entire length of the page adorned by portraits and other figures, were subject to particularly elaborate treatment.

In the thirteenth century, the GOTHIC style became prominent. Religious texts were still popular, but more secular works were being produced and illuminated. Depiction of the human face and figure became more naturalistic. Illuminations showing the lives of nobility also became popular; private prayer books, known as BOOKS OF HOURS, often featured portraits of the book's patron and his family.

Islamic Illumination. ISLAM forbids the representation of religious figures for veneration, and no Islamic religious texts ever depict humans or animals. But Islamic books from the Middle Ages were just as painstakingly constructed—and just as beautiful—as the illuminated manuscripts of Europe.

The medieval Islamic world was perhaps the most learned and scientifically advanced society of its time; far from producing only religious works, the Muslims produced books on MEDICINE, SCIENCE, and PHILOSOPHY. These works were often illuminated with designs and miniatures. The KORAN, Islam's sacred book, had no human or animal representations, but many editions of the Koran were embellished with splendidly intricate geometric designs and carpet pages.

Moreover, the art of calligraphy was so highly developed in the Islamic world that calligraphers were among the most respected Muslim artists. Copying the Koran was considered an act of piety, and many nobles and aristocrats became professional copyists.

Jewish Illuminations. Most of the illuminated Jewish manuscripts surviving today are religious texts. Jewish books were more likely to have been created by skilled individuals rather than copyists and illuminators working together. (See JEWS; JUDAISM.)

The manuscripts produced by the Jews were often elaborately decorated. Because Hebrew does not have capital letters, Jewish designers usually decorated the opening word of a section rather than just the first letter of the word. Like the Muslims, the Jews were prohibited from worshipping images, so there were no religious figures in their manuscripts. Medieval Jews in Islamic countries followed the Islamic custom of including no human or animal forms in their holy books, but in Christian countries, Jews often illuminated their religious books with human and animal forms—including human figures with animal or bird heads.

Jews used illuminated manuscripts as a kind of currency in international trading. Manuscripts of commentaries and rabbinic works could be converted into capital abroad and were usually safe from confiscation by pirates. Thus, many manuscripts were produced that had value for Jews in foreign lands.

Decline of Illumination. By the late fifteenth century, the printing press was making it possible to mass-produce books for the first time. Handwritten and hand-illustrated books had always been a luxury, but now books could be acquired by almost anyone.

However, the printing press did not immediately sound the death knell for illuminated manuscripts, though it significantly cut back the number produced. Because the printing press could not print in color, wealthy bibliophiles still sought hand-painted books well into the sixteenth century. (See GUTENBERG.)

Medieval illuminated manuscripts are now regarded among the greatest works of world art and fetch enormous prices on the art market. The majority are not in private hands but are in museums, particularly the British Library in London, the Bibliothèque Nationale in Paris, the Morgan Library of Art in New York, and the Getty Museum in Los Angeles. Possibly the finest collection of early medieval Byzantine manuscripts remains at St. Catherine's monastery in the Sinai Peninsula. (See BOOKS OF HOURS; ROMANESQUE; ISLAM; KORAN; BIBLE; JUDAISM; CHRISTIANITY.)

MANZIKERT, BATTLE OF

The Battle of Manzikert was a decisive victory for Turkish forces against the BYZANTINE Empire because it led to the Turkish conquest of nearly all of the area known as ANATOLIA.

At the time of the battle (1071), most of Anatolia was under Byzantine rule. Troops from the Turkish SELJUK dynasty, led by the sultan ALP ARSLAN, had begun to make some headway into parts of Anatolia, and the Byzantine emperor, Romanus IV Diogenes, decided to take action. He put together a sizeable army (60,000) to shore up the empire's eastern border, and led this army into Armenia (then held by the Turks).

Manzikert is a small town (now known as Malazgirt) in Turkey. It was near there that Romanus divided his army. One group went with him into Manzikert; another was dispatched to nearby Lake Van, with orders to secure a fortress at Akhlat.

Unfortunately for Romanus, Alp Arslan found out about the Byzantine plan and led his troops to Manzikert to confront the Byzantines. Romanus, realizing that he had too few men with him to have any hope of victory, quickly abandoned Manzikert and headed for Akhlat. On the way, he was confronted by some 100,000 Turkish troops. Crippled by the defection of some of his men (those of Turkish extraction) to the sultan's army, plus the retreat of one of his generals, Romanus and his followers nonetheless fought on. Eventually, he and his weakened army gave way. Romanus was taken prisoner but eventually released.

MARCO POLO

Marco Polo (1254–1324) was an Italian explorer who spent over 20 years in the service of KUBLAI KHAN, Mongolian ruler of CHINA. Polo recounted his many wondrous sights and observations in his memoirs, *The Book of Marvels,* one of the most famous documents of medieval history. Polo's name has become synonymous with travel and travel writing. His memoirs responded to the curiosity of Europeans about the invincible MONGOLS, who had invaded eastern Europe a century before.

Journey to China. Marco traveled to China in 1271 in the company of his father Nicolo and his uncle Maffeo. Niccolò and Maffeo had already made a trip east, returning in 1269, bearing messages for the khan from the pope, who was eager to enlist the MONGOLS as allies against the Muslims. They began the trip with two Dominican friars, but the friars had a change of heart when confronted with the 9,000-mile trip. So the three members of the Polo family made the long march alone, across territory that would not be seen by Westerners again until the mid-nineteenth century.

The khan was pleased to see the Polos again, and became especially friendly with the young Marco. Marco Polo soon became a roving ambassador, traveling to the ends of the huge empire (Mongolia, China, Burma, Vietnam, Malaysia, and the East and South Indies), reporting back to the khan. Kublai could apparently rely more on Marco than his own agents for reliable firsthand reports. Marco's notes and reports would become the basis of his memoirs. Polo's writing remained useful to travelers up to the twentieth century. He was best in recounting details about finances and trade, memorably describing the riches of Eastern ports and the khan's palaces.

In 1292, the three Polos escorted a Mongolian princess to Persia (modern-day Iran), where she was to become a queen. However, after the completion of that difficult two-year trip, they heard that Kublai Khan had died. Since the death of a Mongolian khan invariably led to civil war, the Polos knew they were in danger as the favorites of the late khan, so they returned to VENICE in 1295.

Return to Venice. On his return, Polo became well-known for his vivid stories of the East. In 1298, he commanded a galley in one of the many sea battles between Venice and GENOA. He was captured and spent a year in jail. However, this imprisonment was fortuitous in that he was jailed with a writer, Rusticello, with whom he collaborated on refashioning his notes and reports into *The Book of Marvels.* When released, Polo returned again to Venice and looked after his successful business. Little is known about the later stages of

Antonio Vereses fresco portrait of an elderly Marco Polo.

his life, other than he married and had three daughters. It is said that while on his deathbed, his friends suggested he change what they thought must be imaginary parts of *The Book of Marvels.* Polo replied that he had recounted only half of what he had seen. (*See* EXPLORATION; KUBLAI KHAN; CHINA.)

MARGARET OF DENMARK

Margaret (1353–1412), queen of DENMARK, NORWAY, and SWEDEN, ruled one of the largest empires in Europe. The daughter of Waldemar IV of Denmark, Margaret was ten years old when she married King Haakon VI of Norway, son of Magnus VII of Norway and Sweden. After Waldemar died in 1375, her son Olaf became king of Denmark with Margaret and Haakon serving as regents.

Margaret virtually ruled Denmark, while Haakon was involved in Norway. When Haakon died in 1380, Olaf assumed the Norwegian throne as Olaf V with Margaret serving as regent. Margaret continued to press Haakon's claim to the Swedish crown and groomed her son for that throne as well. However, Olaf died in 1387, leaving Margaret to rule Denmark and Norway. Meanwhile, she advanced her goal of ruling Sweden as well. In 1389, at a battle at Falkoping in Sweden, she defeated and captured her longtime rival, the king of Sweden, Albert of Mecklenburg. Margaret then succeeded in persuading the three diets (parliaments) of Denmark, Norway, and Sweden to accept her grandnephew, Eric of Pomerania, as king of the three kingdoms.

In 1397, Margaret united all three kingdoms under the terms of the Union of Kalmar with the coronation of Eric as king of Denmark, Norway, and Sweden. Sweden resisted Margaret, but surrendered in 1398. While Eric was the nominal ruler of the three kingdoms, Margaret ruled the empire until her death in 1412. During her rule, she incorporated into her empire many formally independent feudal estates, such as Gotland and much of Schleswig. Her strong and autocratic rule left many offices unfilled and reduced others to complete dependency. Her appointment of a disproportionate number of Danes to royal office stirred up resentment in Norway and Sweden. However, Margaret's rule remained unchallenged to the end of her reign. (*See* NORWAY; SWEDEN; DENMARK.)

MARGARET, MAID OF NORWAY

Margaret (1283–1290) was the daughter and only child of Eric II of NORWAY and Margaret, the daughter of Alexander III of SCOTLAND. The Norwegian infant girl was an unlikely candidate, but in 1284 the nobles of Scotland proclaimed King Alexander's granddaughter heiress to the Scottish throne. When Alexander died suddenly in 1286, three-year-old Margaret became queen of Scotland under a regency. King Edward I of ENGLAND arranged a marriage between his oldest son, Edward, and Margaret. The Scots agreed to the marriage in 1290 under the terms of the Treaty of Birgham, which declared that Scotland would remain independent.

Margaret was only seven years old when she set sail from Norway to Scotland to assume her crown. En route, however, she fell ill and died in Orkney, never having reached Scotland. The vacant throne was then claimed by both ROBERT I THE BRUCE and John Baliol. Their struggle over the succession opened the way for Edward to subdue Scotland, and in 1292, he declared his son John its next king.

MARIE DE FRANCE

Marie de France (died c. 1190) was one of the most talented writers of the Middle Ages. At a time when poets wrote anonymously, Marie boldly signed her works with her first name. Marie was born in FRANCE, but spent her adult life in ENGLAND in Norman aristocratic circles. She wrote more than 100 fables and a dozen short stories of adventure and COURTLY LOVE in verse called *lais*. She also wrote a long poem called *Espurgatoire* about a journey through purgatory, foreshadowing the purgatory section of DANTE's *Divine Comedy*. Marie was schooled in Latin, but she wrote in the Anglo-Norman vernacular. She is best known for her *lais*, some of which were based on Celtic myths and legends and included elements of Arthurian legend. (*See* FRENCH LANGUAGE.)

MARSHAL, WILLIAM

William Marshal (1146–1219), a famed English knight and political leader, was a central figure in three major wars: between the PLANTAGENET dynasty in ENGLAND and FRANCE; the English civil wars between HENRY II and his sons; and between the Plantagenet kings and rebellious barons. In the last years of his life, Marshal himself ruled ENGLAND as regent. He died a revered figure, called by some "the best knight who ever lived."

Early Life. Marshal was born into an Irish feudal family. His father, John Marshal, occupied the hereditary position of marshal to the king, responsible for the supervision of the palace, keeping track of military service performed by vassals to the kings, and various housekeeping matters. At the age of 13, William was sent to France to serve as squire to his father's cousin, the chamberlain of Normandy. As a young man in Normandy, William showed himself to be a talented knight; he was victorious in many TOURNAMENTS, displayed great military skill, and was schooled in the knightly code of CHIVALRY.

His Rise. William escaped what might have been a relatively obscure career with the help of his admirer ELEANOR OF AQUITAINE, wife of HENRY II, Marshal was made the military tutor of their eldest son, Henry (the Young), the 15-year-old crowned heir apparent to the English throne. Although Henry (the Young) died in 1183, William remained at court as he had become an indispensable military and political adviser. During the civil war between Henry II and his sons, William Marshal defeated the king's future successor, Richard, in one encounter, sparing the life of the prince who would soon be called "Lion-Heart."

When Richard became king on his father's death, William became his loyal servant and, in return, Richard made him one of the richest barons in England with the gifts of a rich wife and vast lands in England and Normandy. William fought for Richard against the king's archenemy, PHILIP II AUGUSTUS of France. When Richard departed for the Holy Land on the Fourth Crusade, William was made one of four "associate justiciars" who advised William de Longchamp, the temporary ruler of the kingdom. Problems mounted for the kingdom when Richard was captured and held for ransom on his way back from the failed crusade. William had to raise the enormous ransom and keep an eye on John, Richard's ambitious younger brother. (*See* PLANTAGENET; HENRY II.)

A Man of Loyalty. Richard was eventually freed, but died during a siege of a castle in France in 1199, disastrously leaving the kingdom to John. William valiantly defended the English domains in France for the new king against Philip II Augustus. Eventually, however, the Plantagenet empire in France collapsed, leading to a revolt by discontented barons against the incompetent John. William remained loyal to John, even though the king often distrusted and persecuted him. In 1216, the dying John, with half of England in the hands of the barons, made William the regent for his son, Henry. As regent, William restored the power of the Plantagenets in England. After the civil war, he endeavored to reconcile the warring factions and bring the kingdom's finances into some order. He died in 1219, a much-honored figure. After his death, his family hired a French poet to write his biography.

MARSILIUS OF PADUA

The Italian political philosopher Marsilius of Padua (also Marsiglio; 1280–c. 1343) is considered by many scholars to be a guiding influence in the Protestant Reformation and a key figure in the development of modern democracy. In particular, he paved the way for the concept of separation of Church and state.

Born in Padua, Marsilius went to FRANCE, where he briefly served as rector of the University of PARIS. After a stay in ITALY, he returned to Paris, where he wrote his most famous and influential work, *Defensor pacis* (*Defender of the Peace*), between 1320 and 1324.

In that work, which drew from Aristotelian philosophy, Marsilius outlined a concept for a secular state in which the Church hierarchy would have limited power. While the Church might hold authority in moral matters, the state was responsible for maintaining law and order and guaranteeing individuals a safe and peaceful existence. Highly disdainful of Church politics, he added that the Church's moral authority should be determined and carried out by a council of clergy and laity, not just Church officials.

Not surprisingly, these notions did not go over well with the established Church. At first, no one knew he was the author of *Defensor pacis*. When this was discovered in 1326, Marsilius was forced to flee Italy and

seek safe haven in the court of the king of the Romans, Louis IV the Bavarian. He was excommunicated in 1327, and then supported the election of the antipope Nicholas V in 1328. Marsilius spent the remainder of his life in Louis's court, conversing with another intellectual refugee, WILLIAM OF OCKHAM.

MARTINI, SIMONE

Simone Martini (c. 1283–1344) was a painter of the early Sienese school and a student of the earliest proponent of this style, Duccio di Buoninsegna, which incorporated rhythmic, expressive lines, sensuous color, and bold light. His first known work, the *Maesta* of 1315, depicting Siena's patroness, the Virgin Mary, in a huge fresco (almost 40 feet wide) for the Palazzo Publico, captures his fascination with courtly ideals and medieval CHIVALRY. His portrait of the warrior Guidoriccio da Fogliano (1328), commemorating a recent military victory, shows the mounted soldier as a heroic, romantic figure in realistic detail, but set against a mystical abstract landscape.

Detail, The Annunciation *triptych, 1333.*

In 1340, Martini was invited to AVIGNON by Pope Benedict XII, where he decorated several (now destroyed) chapels. Here he became friends with the poet PETRARCH, who immortalized the artist in a sonnet praising Martini's portrait of Petrarch's beloved Laura. Martini died in Avignon in 1344.

MARY OF BURGUNDY

Mary of Burgundy (1457–1482) was responsible in part for the HABSBURG DYNASTY's gaining control of the NETHERLANDS. Through her marriage to the archduke Maximilian (the future Holy Roman Emperor, MAXIMILIAN I), she helped establish the line that allowed the Habsburgs to annex additional lands to their imperial holdings.

Born in Brussels the daughter of CHARLES THE BOLD, duke of BURGUNDY, she was betrothed to Maximilian, son of the emperor Ferdinand III, in 1476. A year later, her father was killed in the Battle of Nancy, and the French king LOUIS XI invaded Burgundy soon afterward. The French tried to pressure Mary to marry the future Charles VIII, but she refused, marrying Maximilian instead in August 1477. At the time, Burgundy controlled much of the Netherlands

From this marriage came Philip the Handsome, who would wed Juana, or Joanna (called Joanna the Mad because she lost her mind after Philip's death at 28). Juana was the daughter of Ferdinand and Isabella of Castile (the same Ferdinand and Isabella who sponsored the voyages of Christopher Columbus), and the marriage linked SPAIN to the Habsburg empire. A series of deaths, births, and marriages eventually made CHARLES V, Mary and Maximilian's grandson, emperor of not only Spain, but the Netherlands as well. Mary was only 25 when she died in FLANDERS in the spring of 1482, the result of a hunting accident. (*See* HABSBURG DYNASTY; NETHERLANDS; BURGUNDY.)

MATILDA OF TUSCANY

Matilda (1046–1115) was one of the great independent women of the Middle Ages. She was the daughter of Margrave Boniface of CANOSSA and Beatrice of Lorraine. After Boniface's assassination in 1052, Beatrice married her cousin, Geoffrey of Lotharingia, and Matilda inherited the marches of Tuscany and Lombardy-Emilia. With Geoffrey's death in 1069, and Matilda's marriage to his son, Geoffrey the Hunchback, duke of Lorraine, she became countess of Tuscany, where she ruled with her mother from 1069 to 1076. The marriage to Geoffrey strengthened her antiimperial ties, although they divorced in 1071. (*See* WOMEN.)

Matilda was a loyal supporter of the GUELPH party, and a close friend and faithful ally of Pope GREGORY VII during the INVESTITURE CONTROVERSY. It was, in fact, at Matilda's castle at Canossa that HENRY IV, on a cold day in January 1077, made his barefoot penance to Gregory. With the ascension of the new pope, URBAN II, Matilda remained a vigorous opponent of Henry, who in 1081 deposed her from her margraviate. She continued to be at war with the emperor until his death in 1106, even, according to legend, donning armor herself and leading Guelph troops into battle. She further angered the emperor by encouraging his son Conrad to rebel against him, and by marrying the antiimperial Welf V of BAVARIA in 1089.

Under Gregory's influence, Matilda agreed that on her death, her rich allodial lands on both sides of the Alps should pass to the PAPACY, a vast donation of territory that represented nearly a fourth of ITALY. However, in 1111, after Matilda became reconciled to Henry's son and successor, Henry V, and her imperial titles were returned to her, she decided to make Henry her heir, without revoking her prior donation. She probably meant the gift as a move in resolving the investiture struggle, but rival claims to her land led to much contention between papal and imperial forces in the ensuing decades.

Matilda died on July 24, 1115, and was buried in a Mantuan monastery founded by her grandfather. Pious and devoted to the Church, she was held in such high regard that her body was transferred to St. Peter's in Rome on command of Pope Urban VIII.

MATTHIAS I HUNYADI

Matthias I Hunyadi (1443–1490) was king of HUNGARY for more than 30 years, during which he introduced a number of administrative, judicial, and military reforms. His efforts met with limited success, but he managed to keep Hungary from falling into the hands of the OTTOMANS to the east or the HABSBURGS to the west. (*See* HUNGARY.)

Matthias was born in Transylvania (present-day Romania), the son of the famous Hungarian leader JÁNOS HUNYADI. He was elected king of Hungary by a diet (council) in the twin cities of Buda and Pest just before his fifteenth birthday. He faced opposition from the start by local barons, the Holy Roman Emperor Frederick III, and the Polish ruling family. Matthias managed to hold the opposition in check, also keeping the Turks from taking territory through a series of defensive strategies.

During his reign, Matthias implemented numerous reforms of the finance and TAXATION system. This met with opposition from special interests previously exempt from taxes, but Matthias was able to build up a surplus of much-needed funds for military and administrative needs. He reorganized local government without taking power away from regional leaders, and he initiated a codification of Hungarian law. He maintained good, albeit tense, diplomatic relations with his neighbors. By his death in 1490, several countries had already set their sights on Hungary, which eventually came under Habsburg control.

MAXIMILIAN I OF HABSBURG

Maximilian I (1459–1519), Holy Roman Emperor for nearly 30 years, was instrumental in strengthening the role of the HABSBURG DYNASTY in western Europe. He fell short of his goal of revivifying the empire of CHARLEMAGNE, but he increased the empire's holdings and created a network of alliances that further solidified his position.

Expansion. Maximilian was born in AUSTRIA, the son of the emperor Frederick III and Eleanor of PORTUGAL. He showed an early interest in the arts that he would later express through extensive patronage. He also showed military prowess that would serve him in his efforts to expand his empire. In 1477, he married the duchess MARY OF BURGUNDY, thereby annexing the Burgundian holdings (including most of the NETHERLANDS) to the empire. This meant a series of battles with France, which had been busy fighting Burgundy. Maximilian fought off several French attacks and, hoping to surround France with his holdings and allies, negotiated several treaties, one of which called for his daughter, Margaret of Austria, to marry Charles VIII of France.

Portrait of Emperor Maximilian I, one of the Habsburgs' most able strategists, by Bernhard Strigel.

Maximilian then married duchess Anne of Brittany by proxy in 1490 (Mary had died eight years earlier). He hoped this would keep France from trying to invade BRITTANY. However, his marriage to Anne was annulled in 1491, and much to his surprise, Charles VIII then annulled his marriage to Margaret, and took Anne of Brittany to be his wife. Brittany was now annexed to France. (Maximilian married Bianca Maria Sforza of Milan in 1494.)

Strategist. At the same time, he was annexing parts of Austria that had once been Habsburg lands but had been seized by the Hungarians. Although he lost a 1490 election to the Hungarian throne, he arranged a treaty whereby HUNGARY and BOHEMIA would pass into Habsburg rule if the new king, Vladislav II, left no male heirs. In 1493, Maximilian and Charles executed the Treaty of Senlis, which recognized Burgundy and the Low Countries as Habsburg possessions. That same year, Frederick III died, and Maximilian became head of the House of Habsburg.

A year later, Charles annexed ITALY, which caused Maximilian to invade, but to little avail. He would continue to fight off and on in Italy for the remainder of his reign. His luck with Spain was much better. He betrothed his daughter Margaret to the Spanish crown prince, and his son Philip to Juana (or Joanna).

Over the next twenty years, Maximilian's skills as a strategist allowed him to annex additional lands, and he formed important alliances with numerous countries, including Russia and England. At home, he convened the Diet of WORMS in 1495, where he proposed a series of measures designed to strengthen the HOLY ROMAN EMPIRE by reforming the government structure. The various princes and nobles who made up the Imperial Chamber opposed these moves and even attempted to depose Maximilian, but his many alliances made him too powerful to overthrow.

Maximilian continued to reign until his death in 1519. He was succeeded by his grandson, Charles V. (*See* HABSBURG DYNASTY; HOLY ROMAN EMPIRE.)

MEDICI FAMILY

T he Medici family dominated the political, artistic, and intellectual spheres of Florentine life for more than a century during the late medieval and Renaissance periods. Their pervasive powers grew out of their prodigious political and social skills, and great collective charm, rather than from the military skill that was usually the requisite talent of the Italian city-state despots.

The leaders of the Medici clan shone in a place and era filled with luminaries, particularly in the fields of art and letters. One of the Medici family's most valuable contributions was their generous patronage of the emerging Renaissance neoclassical and humanist movements. Both the rise of the Medicis, however, and the flowering of the Renaissance arts owe much to the development of TOWNS and the merchant class and the secularizing influence they engendered.

Emergence. The first members of the clan to greatly influence Florentine life in the fifteenth century came from the Mugello farmland north of FLORENCE around 1200. By 1282, at least one family member, Ardingo de' Medici, had risen to the important position of prior (or *signore*), and leader of the merchant GUILD. In the next hundred years, 53 members of the Medici family are recorded as elected members of the *Signoria*, the city's highest magistracy.

It was with the emergence of Giovanni di Bicci de Medici (1360–1429) that the family began its rise to the pinnacles of Florentine power and respectability.

Giovanni amassed a huge fortune through his Medici bank, established in 1397. The bank's international transactions were facilitated by a network of branches throughout Italy, as well as in France, Flanders, and as far away as London. The family expanded into manufacturing and trade in fine textiles, spices, jewelry, silver, and other goods. By 1427, the Medici household was listed as the third wealthiest in a Florentine tax survey; the stage was set for the Medicis to enter Italian politics.

Rise to Prominence. The city of Florence, although constitutionally a republic, was, in reality, governed by powerful coalitions made up of the wealthiest families and their allies. In the time of Giovanni de Medici, the leading family was the Albizzi, headed by the prudent Maso, who tolerated the genteel rivalry of the Medici family. With the deaths of Maso degli Albizzi in 1417 and Giovanni de Medici in 1429 and the ascendancy of their sons Rinaldo degli Albizzi and Cosimo de Medici (1389–1464), the balance of power began to tip toward the Medicis. In 1433, a volatile and envious Rinaldo attempted to eliminate his arch-rival Cosimo by engineering a rigged *balía*, or commission of reform, with the intention of accusing Cosimo and his family of being the principal instigators of the recent devastating war with Lucca, and calling for his execution. This ploy backfired disastrously, as Cosimo was only sentenced to exile in VENICE. From his secure Venetian base, with his fortune intact, he simply arranged for a new *balía* stacked with his supporters, who promptly overturned the exile ruling. One year later, in October 1434, Cosimo returned to Florence to the acclaim of the townspeople, and to the position of supreme leadership that he and his clan were not to relinquish for almost a century.

Cosimo. The 30 years of Cosimo's stewardship were marked by his unique Medician style of governance, which entailed ruling from behind the scenes, maintaining a serene low profile in city politics, and not arrogantly flaunting his immense wealth. He utilized his expertise and influence as a banker to control his allies and rivals, by extending or withholding credit. He also profited enormously in prestige and wealth by being the chief lender to the city of Florence and to the papacy. A more far-reaching political coup attributed to Cosimo was the brokering of the Peace of Lodi of 1454, which at least superficially created a peaceful partitioning of formerly warring city-states, including MILAN, Venice, NAPLES, and Florence.

Cosimo was a generous and involved patron to the new humanist scholars (who had no means of support other than patronage) and to the talented artists of the return-to-classicism movement, most notably, the sculptor Donatello. He funded the search for forgotten Latin manuscripts in MONASTERIES and the translations of classical Greek literature. So enamored was he of written knowledge that he established the first public LIBRARY in western Europe, housing the 800 volumes collected by his protégé Nicolò Niccoli in a newly built wing of the monastery of San Marco. The founding of the Platonic Academy, a group of scholars dedicated to the study of the works of Plato under the leadership of the humanist philosopher Marsilio Ficino, was facilitated by the gift of a farm outside Florence and a lifetime allowance to Ficino.

Lorenzo. Cosimo's invalid son, Piero, adhered to his father's policy of discreet but shrewd management for his short tenure of five years as head of the Medici family. At his death in 1469, the leadership passed to his far more vital son, Lorenzo, later called the Magnificent. Lorenzo (1449–1492) stands out as the most visible and flamboyant of the Medicis, but he still retained power with the backing of the Florentine hierarchy. Still, Lorenzo barely escaped an assassination attempt in the Cathedral of Santa Maria del Fiore during Easter Mass, 1478, engineered by his most fervent rivals, the Pazzi family, with the support of Pope Sixtus IV. His brother Giuliano was not so lucky and was killed in front of the altar. The outcome once again favored the Medici; a vengeful mob hanged the conspirators from the upper floors of the town hall.

Lorenzo consolidated his considerable power by involving himself in foreign diplomacy, thus adeptly deflecting outside threats to Florence's independence. He also married into the nobility, specifically the baronial Orsini family of Rome.

Although he was highly educated, a poet, and well acquainted with the artists and scholars of his time, he invested less in artistic patronage than his grandfather. Nevertheless, his political finesse and personal charisma were attested to by Machiavelli, who dedicated *The Prince* to him.

Further Glory. By 1488, Lorenzo's influence extended as far as the PAPACY. Pope Innocent VIII ordained Lorenzo's thirteen-year-old son Giovanni as cardinal who later became Pope Leo X (reigned 1513–1521), the patron of Michelangelo.

After 1531, the family finally abandoned the pretense of being only private politically involved citizens. They declared themselves dukes of Florence, which in 1537 expanded into grand dukes of Tuscany. By the time of the death of the last Medici in 1743, the family had produced another pope, Clement VII, and Catherine de Medici, queen of France.

See ITALY; FLORENCE; VENICE; *and* HABSBURG DYNASTY *for background. Additional material may be found in* BANKING; MONEY AND CURRENCY; COMMERCE AND TRADE; PAPACY; PAPAL STATES. *Also* ROME *and* NAPLES.

MEDICINE AND CARE OF THE SICK

During the millennium before 1500, European medicine and health care became increasingly diversified and complex. This evolution proceeded along two main lines. On the one hand, health care developed an increasingly well defined and specialized institutional framework; on the other, the intellectual discipline of medicine grew ever more sophisticated. These two developments were closely related: the emergence of UNIVERSITIES as institutions of higher education facilitated the growth of a body of specialized written knowledge concerning both theoretical and practical medicine. The existence of such a body of knowledge allowed the physicians and surgeons who mastered it to claim formal licensing structures and a monopoly of medical practice in many European cities. For many of the same reasons, the later Middle Ages saw the emergence of early forms of health care practices and institutions fundamental to the modern medical order, including specialized medical hospitals, public health boards, and formal licensing procedures.

Health Care. But such developments, however important, should not mask the continuity of more traditional ideas and practices in the area of healing and health care. For one thing, most health care, including nursing, was the province of WOMEN—mothers, wives, daughters, female domestics—who were excluded by their sex from university study and from most medical GUILDS and colleges. For another, the overwhelming majority of Europeans did not live in cities, where the intellectual and institutional advances were concentrated, but in TOWNS and villages with little, if any, access to medicine of this sort; they turned instead to the services of local healers—men and women of acknowledged expertise. These men and women dispensed advice, remedies, and medical services that ranged from herbal prescriptions and surgical interventions to religious prayers and magical incantations—practices rarely seen as opposed to one another, let alone mutually exclusive. This eclectic approach to healing was not confined to the countryside, nor to the poorer classes; a wide variety of healers also flourished in the larger cities, serving not only immigrants and laborers but also members of the urban elite. Faced with a worrying health problem, a wealthy merchant or lawyer would probably first consult his family physician or a formally licensed surgeon.

But if he received no relief from them, he might well have recourse to a local cunningwoman, a faith healer, or simply a prayer to a favorite saint.

Early Treatments. The diversity of patient options and choices that characterized late medieval cities was less evident during the early Middle Ages. In the mid-fifth century, the western Roman Empire had disintegrated under the military pressure of the Germanic tribes, and during the period between the sixth and the mid-eleventh centuries, theoretically trained medical

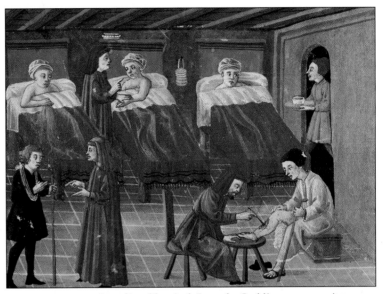

A medieval hospital, from the Gaddiano manuscript, Florence. While the necessary scientific underpinnings of medicine were still to come, many therapies were tried.

experts were few and far between. Learned medicine was based on a core of Roman and Greek texts; located in MONASTERIES, courts, and ecclesiastical schools, early medieval scholars and teachers studied and transmitted these texts to their students, often in the form of Latin translations, compilations, and summaries. If they composed original works, these were usually brief and practical in orientation. Most practitioners, however, adopted a much more eclectic approach; even the literate drew not only on the three classical naturalistic techniques of medication (mainly HERBALS), diet (controls of food, drink, exercise, and the like), and surgery (bleeding, for example, cautery, lancing, and setting bones) but also magical devices such as charms and invocation, and minor Christian rituals—a mix that had characterized much late Roman medicine as well.

Most patients received treatment at home, although a few may have had access to the services of monastic infirmaries or the urban hospices of SPAIN, ITALY, and southern Gaul; the latter were charitable institutions intended to aid the needy, such as destitute widows, orphans, travelers, and the aged.

Urban Expansion. Thus the medical system of the early Middle Ages was fluid and undifferentiated, and the boundaries between the different kinds of healers remained blurred and indistinct. This fluidity was related to the lack of specialized medical institutions. The bodies that trained or employed experts in healing—for example, hospices, monasteries, and courts—were not exclusively or even primarily medical in orientation; their medical functions were part of a much broader social and cultural life. This situation began to change in the late eleventh century, as part of more general social and economic developments and specifically the revival of a commercial economy and an urban civilization for the first time since the disintegration of the Roman Empire in the West. The growth of the population and its concentration in cities created an increasing demand for medical services, and the relative prosperity of urban society made that demand effective. The result was an expanding market for medical services of all sorts.

This expanding market coincided with a dramatic increase in the extent and sophistication of learned medicine. Whereas earlier medical writers made do with scraps of classical texts salvaged from the wreck of the early Middle Ages, eleventh-century scholars began to look to the eastern Mediterranean and the Middle East, and later to Islamic Spain, where Greek medical learning had been not only preserved but dramatically expanded. To be of use to Western scholars, these works had to be translated into Latin, the language of learning in western Christian Europe. Thus, the next 150 years saw an intensive translation campaign, concentrated on Latinizing the Arabic works both of Greek authorities like Galen and of important Arabic writers—Jews, Muslims, Persians, Christians—in the Islamic world. These works became the center of the medical curricula in the universities being founded with increasing frequency in western Europe, beginning in the late twelfth century.

Growth. These social, economic, and intellectual changes fueled two linked developments. The first was the growth of a more differentiated, stratified, and well-defined body of medical practitioners with clear, if variable, standards and procedures for training, licensing, and practice (the process often referred to as nascent professionalization). In part, this process resulted from a series of exclusionary moves, as particular groups were successively edged out of medical practice, at least in theory: Jews, Christian clerics, and empirical practitioners; the last was a group that included most women. (It is worth noting that repeated proscriptions of this sort were not necessarily wholly effective; despite a series of ecclesiastical decrees prohibiting the treatment of Christians by Jewish practi-

tioners, Jewish physicians and surgeons continued to be highly regarded.) At the same time, the remaining core of Christian, lay, largely male, and formally trained practitioners began to take on the shape of a more differentiated body of healers, organized in a clear social and economic hierarchy, with university-educated physicians at the top, formally trained general surgeons in the middle, and at the bottom, barbers and surgeons specialized in a single or a small number of procedures (bleeding, bone setting, hernia, or cataract surgery). To their number we may add apothecaries, who typically dispensed medical advice along with drugs. These officially recognized, full-time practitioners enjoyed a virtual monopoly in larger cities, guaranteed by the medical guilds and colleges to which they belonged or by the university faculties from which they held medical degrees. Midwives appear in urban records beginning in the thirteenth century, but were not officially licensed until the late fifteenth century—and then mainly in northern Europe.

Specialization. The appearance of medical guilds, colleges, and faculties formed part of the second main shift that characterized health care in the period after the middle of the eleventh century: the gradual emergence of specialized medical institutions. These included not only licensing and regulatory bodies, but also specialized bodies and organizations concerned with the health of the population as a whole. Of these, the most important were urban hospitals specialized in treating the impoverished, and public health boards. The hospitals, like their early medieval predecessors, were charitable foundations; the most impressive were large and highly organized, accommodating several hundred patients at a time. The public health boards were originally emergency magistracies established to deal with individual epidemics, but by the fifteenth century, a few cities were beginning to create permanent boards in response to the threat of plague.

These developments took place at dramatically different rates in different parts of Europe: earlier and more quickly in Italy and other Mediterranean regions, which were more highly urbanized and could draw on the remnants of Roman law and institutions; more slowly in northern GERMANY, northern FRANCE, and especially ENGLAND, where the medical order appeared relatively undeveloped well into the sixteenth century. Meanwhile, however, throughout Europe, casual healers and unlicensed practitioners continued their work in both urban and rural areas, largely undisturbed by the political struggles of the medical elites.

See UNIVERSITIES; WOMEN IN THE MIDDLE AGES; GUILDS; *and* HERBALS. *Care of the sick was an important function of* MONASTERIES. *See also* BLACK DEATH; LEPROSY; *and* FOOD AND DRINK *for more on specific health issues.*

MEROVINGIAN DYNASTY

The first line of kings who ruled the FRANKS was given the name Merovingian, a term in common use by the fourteenth century. The name is derived from the mythical ruler Meroveus, who (according to the seventh-century chronicler Fredegar) was conceived when the wife of the semi-legendary King Clodio encountered a monstrous Quinotaur. As for the Franks, the chronicle associates them (and their name) with Duke Francio, and Francio with Priam and those who fled from Troy, a connection developed in the eighth-century *Book of the History of the Franks* (*Liber historiae Francorum*). The sixth-century historian GREGORY OF TOURS was far more sober and less inclined to inventiveness. He reports Sulpicius Alexander's references to the Franks' leaders as "dukes" and "regales" as well as "kings," regretting Sulpicius's failure to give their names. Gregory notes that reliable sources designated Theudemer and Clodio as kings of the Franks, and he mentions Meroveus, father of Childeric (reigned 457–481), who was said by some to be descended from Clodio; the name was given to younger sons of King Chilperic I (561–584) and King Clothar II (584–629).

Childeric was the first Frankish king about whom Gregory of Tours could find substantial information. According to Gregory, he was best known for seducing his subjects' daughters and for marrying the king of Thuringia's wife, who bore him a son, CLOVIS I. Clovis, the first great king of the Franks, was 15 when he succeeded his father in 481. He ruled until 511.

Clovis. Clovis made the fortune of his line by converting to CHRISTIANITY, in 496 or 498. The reasons for his conversion are debated. According to Gregory of Tours, he was persuaded to do so by his Christian wife Clotild, granddaughter of King Gundioc of BURGUNDY, whose son, Clotild's father, had been killed by his own brother. Clovis married her in 493, and Gregory presents his subsequent conversion as a desperate measure, taken in hopes of preventing the total annihilation of his army by the Alemanni. Another source links the conversion to miracles that Clovis witnessed at the tomb of Saint Martin of Tours. Politics may well have influenced Clovis, since he was surely aware that the Catholic bishops persecuted by the Arian king of the VISIGOTHS would support the efforts of a Catholic ruler to conquer the king and win AQUITAINE. Clovis was already acquainted with Rémi, Bishop of Reims, who had written to salute him and offer counsel soon after Clovis's accession. It was Rémi who instructed Clovis in the faith and baptized him at Reims on Christmas night. Writing to congratulate Clovis, Bishop Avitus of Vienne alluded to the unction that the king had received, unction which in the ninth

THE MEROVINGIAN KINGS

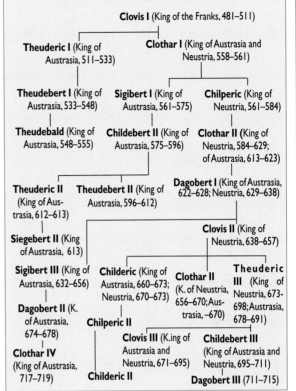

century HINCMAR of Reims would declare had been performed with chrism brought by a dove from heaven. This chrism and the Holy Ampulla, the vessel that held it, came to be indispensable artifacts of French coronations by the thirteenth century.

After his baptism, Clovis conquered Burgundy and then Aquitaine. Impressed by his victories, the Byzantine emperor Anastasius (reigned 491–518) sent him consular vestments, elevating him above other barbarian kings. Clovis made PARIS his capital and was acknowledged as king of Cologne. He is credited with overseeing the first compilation of the Salic Law, the laws of the Salian Franks. In 511, he presided over a council convoked to reform the Church in Gaul. He died soon afterward and was buried in what would later become the abbey church of Sainte-Geneviève, where a splendid marble tomb, now in the church of SAINT-DENIS, was erected in the thirteenth century.

The legend of Clovis inspired his successors and the French (leading to the splendid celebrations at Reims of both the fourteenth and fifteenth centenaries of his baptism, in 1896 and 1996). In the fourteenth century, he was credited with having exercised the curative power of the "royal touch" and with having miraculously received the three *fleurs de lis* that distinguished the French royal arms. The French battle cry *Ma joie Saint-Denis* was also linked to him. In the fifteenth century, he was venerated as a saint. A barbarian king noted for his treachery and violence, Clovis hardly merits his reputation. Still, he established important precedents for the future relations between rulers and the Church.

A Kingdom Divided. As Frankish custom mandated, on Clovis's death his enormous kingdom, which stretched from present-day GERMANY and Belgium to the Pyrenees, was divided among his four sons. Childebert ruled Paris (511–558) after his father's death. There he founded a basilica, later Saint-Germain-des-Prés, where he was buried. The church also received the bodies of his wife, his son Chilperic (d. 584) and Chilperic's wife Fredegund (d. c. 596), his grandson (Chilperic's and Fredegund's son) Clothar II (r. 584–629) and Clothar's wife Bertrud (d. 620), and three seventh-century Merovingians (Childeric II, r. 662–675, his wife Bilihild, and their son Dagobert). These Merovingian gravesites made Saint-Germain-des-Prés a rival of Saint-Denis. In the twelfth century, new monuments were installed to honor the royalty buried there, perhaps inspiring the royal tombs created at Saint-Denis in the thirteenth century.

Warfare among Clovis's sons disrupted the decades after his death, although the Franks succeeded in conquering Burgundy by 534 and in acquiring Provence by 536. Union of the Frankish kingdoms of Neustria, Austrasia, and Burgundy occurred only when a single heir survived, which happened in the case of Clovis's son Clothar I (between 558 and 561), Clothar's grandson and namesake Clothar II (between 623 and 629), and Clothar II's son Dagobert (between 629 and 638 or 639).

Dagobert (603 or 605–638 or 639) was the last great Merovingian ruler. He ruled Austrasia with his father from 622 and Neustria and Burgundy from 629, the year of his father's death. Dagobert was an effective military leader, and he took an interest in codifying the laws of the peoples he ruled. He was dedicated to the reform of the Church and promoted missionary activity. He was particularly devoted to the shrine of Saint-Denis north of Paris. He endowed the church and decorated it; his decision to be buried there rather than in Paris was the first step toward establishing Saint-Denis as a royal necropolis. His wife Nanthild was also interred there, as was their son Clovis II (died 657). An elaborate celebration of Dagobert's anniversary was instituted at the abbey in 1108, and an imposing tomb was erected to Dagobert and Nanthild south of the main altar in the thirteenth century, decorated with sculpted friezes illustrating the legendary salvation of Dagobert's soul by Saint Denis.

The Merovingians were great builders of churches and palaces, employing many skilled stonecutters and masons. Objects found in Merovingian tombs reveal the proficiency of their metalworkers, which exceeded that of the Romans. In the mid-fifth century, they developed the art of cloisonné enamel. Merovingian artisans produced fine glass and ivory, which was exported. Under the Merovingians, Jewish and Syrian merchants flourished, as did the slave trade.

The Merovingian rulers preserved the Germanic custom of wearing long hair and beards, and were called long-haired kings (*reges criniti*). Until the middle of the seventh century, they led their armies — composed of soldiers of many ethnic backgrounds, including Roman descendants—personally, though they also delegated authority to relatives and officials.

Decline. From the middle of the seventh century on, the authority and power of the Merovingian kings declined precipitously. They were regarded as "do-nothing kings" (*rois fainéants*), dominated by their powerful officials and the leading aristocratic families. According to EINHARD, CHARLEMAGNE'S biographer (and thus hardly unprejudiced), the mayors of the palace (*maiores domus*) possessed supreme authority. The king was a figurehead, a puppet, distinguished by his long hair and beard and by his throne.

This depiction may well be largely accurate, but the importance of the KINGSHIP was revealed after the death in 743 of CHARLES MARTEL, the Pippinid mayor of the palace. Since the death of the Merovingian king Theuderic IV (r. from 721) in 737, Charles Martel had ruled alone. The throne was vacant, but Charles did not attempt to claim it. Rather than imitating him and ruling autonomously and independently, however, the two sons who succeeded him as mayor of the palace (PÉPIN and Carloman) instituted another king, Childeric III (r. 743–51), son of Theuderic's predecessor, Chilperic II (r. 716–721). Pépin retained Chilperic after 747, when Carloman retired to become a monk. Only in 751, after consolidating his power through force and enlisting the support of Abbot Fulrad of Saint-Denis and Pope Zacharias (r. 741–752), did Pépin have Chilperic deposed.

Unlike his father, Pépin did not rule simply as mayor of the palace but rather replaced Chilperic as king and had himself anointed. The ceremony distinguished CAROLINGIAN from Merovingian kingship. More important, Pépin's decision to become king (and in 754 to provide for the royal succession of his sons) reveals how essential kingship was to the functioning of Frankish government, whatever the shortcomings of the last Merovingian rulers.

See CLOVIS I; FRANKS; FRANCE; CHARLES MARTEL; *and* PÉPIN. *The sequel to the Merovingians is in* CAROLINGIAN DYNASTY *and* CHARLEMAGNE. *The development of concepts of sovereignty is found in* KINGSHIP.

MILAN

Situated in the heart of the Po basin in northern ITALY, Milan was one of the dominant cities of the Roman Empire. However, the beginning of the Middle Ages saw it suffer repeated indignities: the city was sacked in 452 by ATTILA THE HUN and invaded by the OSTROGOTHS in 489. The city thrived as a center of intellectual life, but was heavily damaged by the Gothic Wars of the sixth century and destroyed by the GOTHS and Burgundians in 539. Milan next passed into Byzantine control (553–569), years marked by oppressive TAXATION, poverty, and famine, although the city maintained its political preeminence in Lombardy. When the LOMBARDS took the city in 569, much of the Milanese aristocracy left for GENOA. The Lombard reign began with ruinous civil wars, but under King Liutprand and his successor, King AISTULF, Milan was restored. When Milan passed on to Frankish rule with the victory of CHARLEMAGNE (774), the city began to prosper again.

War and Prosperity. It was through the fighting among Charlemagne's successors for ascendancy that the archbishops of Milan began to take on added political importance, first under Ansperto da Biassono in the late ninth century, and culminating in the rule of Aribert of Intimiano (1018–1045). Tensions over the authority of the archbishopric led to a populist rebellion against Aribert and the city's nobles in 1042; that uprising and the threat of imperial intervention led to the creation of the Milanese commune in 1045.

The early years of the commune were marked by a furious civil war between the nobles and high clergy and those who wanted to see the Church reformed, called pejoratively, *patarini*. The twelfth century saw some stability return to Milan, allowing for increased economic development and territorial expansion. Milan became involved in a series of battles with the other cities of Lombardy; it conquered Lodi in 1111, and, after nearly 10 years of struggle, destroyed Como in 1127. Responding to the protests of these other towns, FREDERICK I BARBAROSSA intervened, besieging Milan in 1158, and again in 1162. After nine months of the second siege, Milan surrendered. It quickly recovered from the defeat, joining the Lombard League in 1167 and, through the League's victories over imperial forces, secured rights for the commune. The peace brought on a century of enormous growth and prosperity for the city.

Visconti. The thirteenth century saw additional prosperity, but also greater infighting. When FREDERICK II defeated the Milanese forces at Cortenuova in 1237, the city turned in defense to Pagano della Torre, a member of a leading Milanese family. With the rise of della Torre, the struggles between the Milanese nobles and the populace intensified. Supported by the archbishop Ottone Visconti (1207–1295), the nobles backed the GHIBELLINE party, while della Torre and his family backed the GUELPH party, supported by the artisans, guild workers, and the growing bourgeoisie.

Visconti routed della Torre and his supporters at the Battle of Desio in January 1277, thus initiating more than a century and a half (1277–1447) of Visconti rule in Milan. They became *signori* and their administration replaced that of the commune with only occasional opposition. Under the Viscontis, industry blossomed—especially the prosperous silk trade—and Milan expanded its territorial dominion to include Bologna, Genoa, Verona, Padua, PISA, and Siena. The period also saw the development of the city itself, and the flourishing of the Milanese artistic community. (*See* ITALY; LOMBARDS; FREDERICK I BARBAROSSA.)

MILLENNIALISM

During the Middle Ages, the idea that the world would someday experience a millennium of peace and tranquillity became increasingly popular. Its origins were biblical, but it was not confined to CHRISTIANITY or even to religious circles.

The Book of Revelation in the New Testament states that Jesus Christ will return to earth for a reign of a thousand years. Early Christians interpreted these passages literally, but theologians of the early Middle Ages taught that Revelations should not be interpreted to mean this. Gradually, the expectation of Christ's return for a thousand years was dropped, but not the idea of a millennium of peace.

In the twelfth century, millennialism became popular again, although not quite in its original sense. The belief became widespread that a thousand years of peace would be brought about by a conquering hero who would unite humanity into one Christian kingdom. This concept was known as political millennialism. Others believed that there would be a period during which non-Christians would all be converted and the Church would be reformed—theological millennialism—an idea inspired by the writings of ST. JEROME, an early Church leader, and promoted by JOACHIM OF FIORE, a southern Italian abbot.

In the second half of the thirteenth century, "Joachist" millennialism was embraced by the radical minority of the FRANCISCAN ORDER. They used this apocalyptic theory of history to claim that the Antichrist had taken over the papal throne and that they, the radical Franciscans, were the vanguard of the Second Coming of Christ, who would overthrow him.

The idea of millennialism existed in Islamic countries as well. Muslims believed that a savior known as the Mahdi would come to earth and create peace and harmony. (*See* ISLAM, RELIGIOUS PHILOSOPHY OF.)

Natural disasters and plague epidemics were often looked at as temporary situations that would disappear with the coming of the millennium. Thus, millennialism served as a source of hope.

MINING

Mining is the process of extracting metals from the earth. While common in the classical (Greek and Roman) period, mining barely survived the Fall of Rome. By the tenth century, however, it had again become an important industry. Despite this resurgence, there was little improvement in the technology of mining during the Middle Ages. Further, the law governing mining was primitive throughout the early medieval period. Almost no legal restriction or control of mining land claims or operations existed. Only by the later feudal period did some system of regulation begin to emerge.

The casting of a bell in the presence of a bishop, who blesses it. Mined ore was seen as a blessing drawn from the earth like produce and water.

Decline. After the collapse of the Roman Empire and the emergence of the Germanic kingdoms in the fifth century, mining declined in most of Europe, although iron and tin mining survived in Britain, FRANCE, ITALY, and SPAIN. As a replacement for newly mined materials, important substances such as gold, silver, and lead were remolded and reused.

Rebirth. Starting in the ninth century, mining was revived, followed by a tenth-century expansion. A number of European regions became important mining centers: western Britain for tin and copper; central Spain for copper, silver, and lead; France for iron and zinc; and the Harz Mountains in Germany for silver, lead, and copper. In the later Middle Ages, Saxony in Germany emerged as the most important mining center. Saxon mines of silver and lead became training centers. BOHEMIA, Slovakia, the Balkans, and Scandinavia also contained important centers of mining.

The technology of mining remained primitive despite the expansion of the scope of this activity. In fact, medieval technique differed little from ancient Roman methods. Fire was used to crack rocks from which metals were removed. Then, tools not much improved since antiquity—picks, hammers, and chisels—were employed to break through the rock and earth and crush ores. (Gold was found by panning at rivers.) From the ores, pure metals were extracted by smelting, that is, the process by which heat melts the ore, leaving the desired substance.

The backwardness of medieval technology limited the regions in which mining could occur. Moving resources necessary for mining—either ores to forestry areas or flammable material for smelting to the mining areas—was financially prohibitive. Mining therefore had to be done near forests so that trees could be easily used for smelting. In much of medieval Europe, still heavily forested, this posed no problem. However, a dearth of trees retarded mining in Spain and England.

Laws. In the early Middle Ages, the concept of property in material embedded in the earth was not developed. Consequently, communities and groups mined as they wished without legal restrictions. However, with the development of FEUDALISM, the legal status of buried material was enfolded in feudal law—it became the property of lords and kings. The growth in mining led to increases in disputes and consequently the need to be able to adjudicate these disputes. Regulations for controlling mining were established, as well as special mining courts to interpret and enforce the new codes. (*See* LAW, SCHOOLS OF; FOREST LAW.)

MISSI DOMINICI

The royal officials whom Frankish kings and emperors employed to oversee their domains were called *missi dominici* ("envoys from the lord"). CHARLEMAGNE instituted the system when he sent envoys out into his realm to strengthen his control. He divided his kingdom into districts, each of which contained several counties, and sent two *missi*—one lay, one clerical—out to each district once a year. At the end of their inspection circuit, they reported directly back to Charlemagne. (*See* KINGSHIP.)

The main responsibility of these envoysi was to supervise the local counts and to hear complaints against them. Before they visited a district, they would write a letter announcing their visit and invite all the people in the district to come forward with their complaints. Generally, Charlemagne assigned the *missi* to districts where they held neither land nor title in order to reduce the possibility of corruption. He allowed only his most trusted envoys like Abbot Fardulf of SAINT-DENIS and Archbishop Arno of Salzburg to be *missi* in areas where they lived or officiated. Nonetheless, the practice of greeting the arriving envoy with gifts (and bribes) was widespread. By the late 800s, the system was already in decline, reflecting the deterioration of centralized government in the divided empire.

MISSIONS AND MISSIONARIES

The idea of spreading the word of God has been central to CHRISTIANITY since Jesus ordered his disciples to "preach to every creature." Missionary work, therefore, goes back to well before the Middle Ages, but it flourished in medieval Europe when Christianity became firmly rooted.

Early missionary activity in Europe was centered in the western regions and the British Isles. Christianity was introduced to FRANCE in the fourth century, and by the dawn of the Middle Ages, Britain and IRELAND were home to numerous MONASTERIES. Missionaries such as ST. PATRICK, St. Ninian, and ST. COLUMBA were among the most successful. Later missionaries who were successful in Britain returned to continental Europe especially SWITZERLAND and northern ITALY.

By the seventh century, ROME had taken an active role in missionary work. One of the earliest and most notable examples was in 596 when Pope GREGORY I sent the Roman monk AUGUSTINE to Britain to convert the ANGLO-SAXON tribes. Religious leaders initially concentrated their efforts on pagan tribal chieftains, for a highly practical reason: when these rulers accepted Christianity as their religion, their subjects almost immediately followed. Thus, converting one king could mean converting tens of thousands.

In the eighth century, missionary work focused on GERMANY and Scandinavia. ST. BONIFACE managed to make strong inroads among the Germans. In so doing, he also expanded the pope's influence in the region. Scandinavia proved to be particularly difficult for missionaries. So firmly entrenched were the Scandinavians' pagan beliefs and gods that it took nearly 500 years for Christianity to be accepted.

While Roman missionaries were spreading Christianity across western Europe, Byzantine missionaries were doing the same in eastern Europe. The last eastern Europeans to be converted were the SLAVS, a conversion that began in the ninth century and took nearly 400 years.

While Christianity was spreading, so was ISLAM. Although Islam did not have the same tradition of missionary work, it had taken hold quite solidly in the Middle Eastern countries and in northern Africa since the death of the prophet MUHAMMAD in 632. The only European country in which Islam ever gained any real ground during this time was Spain.

While some Christians wished to try to convert the Muslims, others saw them as enemies to be conquered. Thus, while active missionary work in the Middle East was only marginally successful, there were also CRUSADES in which Christian soldiers hoped to crush Islam and capture Muslim territories.

By the end of the Middle Ages, Christians had essentially given up trying to convert or conquer the Muslims. But they looked to other parts of the world to spread their faith, and Christian missionary work has continued actively to the present day. (*See* CHRISTIANITY; INQUISITION; ISLAM; HERESY.)

MONASTERIES AND MONASTICISM

Monasticism originated at the end of the third century C.E. in EGYPT and Syria, where religious men sought to worship God and withdrew from the affairs of secular society. St. Anthony (c. 250–355) sought the solitude of the desert and became the first Christian monk, counseling other hermits who sought to follow his example. Monasticism remained an Eastern institution for over two centuries; the West was then religiously less mature and unprepared for the physical and mental hardships that accompanied a life of asceticism.

Western Expansion. In the sixth century, monasticism made its way to the West. The early founders of Western (Catholic) monasticism included JEROME, AUGUSTINE OF HIPPO, Martin of Tours, and above all, BENEDICT OF NURSIA. Benedictine monasticism, which stressed the collective power of the congregation, became the dominant form of monasticism in the Church by the end of the eighth century. The Benedictine rule, established with the emergence of Monte Cassino, required its followers to lead a life of perfection and poverty, and to withdraw from secular society. Adherence to the Benedictine rule led

School for monks, c. 1450, where the regimen included "birching."

The Abbey of Monte Cassino, Italy, founded in 529 and the center of the Benedictine Order.

to salvation for not only the individual monk, but for Christian society at large. Byzantine monasticism stressed the individual's role within the monastic community. Though the Eastern Church adopted this approach, both shared the ascetic ideals of poverty and solitude.

New Orders. By the end of the eleventh century, new monastic orders (such as the CISTERCIANS and the Carthusians) appeared, and the Benedictine rule was drastically modified. However, an important change would take place in the thirteenth century with the foundation of the Mendicant orders (such as the Dominicans and Franciscans), which took vows of poverty and relied on begging for their livelihood, believing that the Church had become far too materialistic. They sought to awaken society to this fact by introducing FRIARS, who involved themselves in daily social life, especially in the UNIVERSITIES and large cities. In the later Middle Ages, new orders such as the Franciscan Observants and the BRETHREN OF THE COMMON LIFE emerged as a response to the Mendicant orders.

Medieval monasticism contributed significantly to the Church and to society. Medieval monks and friars converted a multitude of pagans, became involved in higher learning, distributed vast amounts of charity, and helped solidify the leadership of the PAPACY. But monasticism also ultimately failed to achieve its anti-materialistic ideals. The landed monasteries became an important cog in the feudal order, while their abbots often became involved in the medieval political world, seeking secular positions of power and prestige.

See CHRISTIANITY; FRIARS; JEROME; BENEDICT OF NURSIA; BRETHREN OF THE COMMON LIFE; *and* AUSTIN FRIARS. *Monasteries were important in providing* MEDICINE AND CARE OF THE SICK *and in housing* LIBRARIES.

MONEY AND CURRENCY IN THE MIDDLE AGES

The history of money in the Middle Ages is best described as a series of peaks and valleys. In the early Middle Ages (from the fifth through the eleventh centuries), the supply of money in circulation in western Europe was extremely limited. For the vast majority of the population the use of money was an irregular and often insignificant part of the struggle for survival. In the High Middle Ages (from the eleventh century through the middle of the fourteenth century), Europe experienced a change in the supply and use of money. First in the TOWNS and then in the countryside, a burgeoning supply of silver gave people of even modest status the opportunity to engage in monetized transactions; money became the measure of everything from alms for the poor to ransoms for kings and nobles captured in battle.

The flood of money gradually receded in the later Middle Ages, giving rise to a third major epoch in medieval monetary history, defined by what experts refer to as the "bullion famine." Money continued to serve as the yardstick for prices and wages in a relatively complex economy, but the actual number of coins in circulation fell precipitously because of a prolonged dearth of precious metals. There was never any question of a return to the barren "unmonetary" world of the early Middle Ages, but there was also little likelihood that the monetization of the economy would continue at the pace it had acquired in the High Middle Ages. The famine eased somewhat with the discovery of new silver mines in GERMANY in the 1460s, but the real cure for these monetary woes came only after Spanish ships found their way to the Americas.

Raw Materials. Each of these long-term cycles was the product of a complex interplay of forces, two of which were particularly important. The first was the availability of precious metals with which to mint coins. Only toward the end of the medieval period were Europeans willing to accept a truly fiduciary money, one that had a value and use unrelated to the intrinsic value of the gold or silver physically present in the coins. For most of the period, money was accepted as a medium of exchange solely because the metal that changed hands could, in a pinch, be melted down to yield a coveted substance. Consequently, the supply of money was directly linked to the fortunes of prospectors and miners. The monetary plenty of the High Middle Ages, for example, began with the discovery of silver in Saxony in the 1040s, but had its most pronounced impact after the 1160s, when major silver deposits were opened in eastern GERMANY, the Austrian Alps, and Tuscany. Similarly, the monetary dearth of the late Middle Ages can be ascribed to the failure in the fourteenth and fifteenth centuries to find new deposits to substitute for the older sites that had by then largely been depleted.

The second principal explanation for the vicissitudes in medieval monetary history is based on concurrent changes in social and economic life. Among other things, money is a medium of exchange. Its utility depends on the degree to which individuals engage in buying and selling goods and services. In the early Middle Ages, such buying and selling was not an integral part of economic life. Europe was then a sparsely populated continent with an economy oriented almost entirely toward simple pastoral and agrarian pursuits. Productivity levels were extremely low, and niches for specialized laborers were few and far between. Subsistence farming was nearly always the order of the day. Goods and services were more likely to circulate in a social economy of coercion than in a market economy predicated on monetary transaction.

The Rise of Commerce. While some of these traits persisted into the High Middle Ages and beyond, a fundamental restructuring of economic life occurred from the eleventh century on, one that is often dubbed the Commercial Revolution. Significant developments included the growth of towns; the forging of new trade routes (spectacularly symbolized by MARCO POLO'S travels in the late thirteenth century); the rise of specialized forms of manufacturing, notably in textile production; a new vigor in exploiting natural resources with an eye toward international markets; and the evolution of new business techniques designed to increase the volume and efficiency of capital available for investment. The economy's backbone was still agrarian, but its sinews and muscles were increasingly formed by towns and trade. Even agriculture found itself transformed in the new world of markets lubricated by money. In this new world, a significant majority of the population found itself regularly engaging in transactions based on money, as recipients of wages, as vendors of surplus wool or wheat, as patrons of bakers and tavern keepers, as payers or recipients of cash rents, as taxpayers, or in other roles predicated on the circulation of money.

Black Death. The relationship between general economic developments and the money supply in the later Middle Ages is not as clearly cut as it is in earlier periods. The evidence for a serious and prolonged shortage of currency is overwhelming. But while many historians also see the period as one of prolonged recession (sometimes called the Renaissance depression), they tend to blame Europe's woes on the ravages of the BLACK DEATH more than on the dearth of bullion. The vibrant world of Marco Polo gave way to a world in which plague relentlessly decimated the population, leaving deserted villages and decayed towns in its wake. The effects of the Black Death were, in fact, so

pronounced that it is difficult for historians to decipher how other circumstances, such as the shortage of money, influenced the economy. Some historians have suggested that the bullion famine was not a serious problem, arguing that while there were fewer and fewer coins in circulation there were also fewer and fewer people to spend them. Others suggest that monetary innovations—such as the growing use of base metal coinage with only a wash of silver ("black" money, as it was known at the time), and the increasingly sophisticated methods of making transfers and extending credit without cash used by bankers and merchants—overcame most of the problems associated with a shortage of specie in circulation. The dearth of bullion clearly did not erode money's importance as the standard of value in the economy, but it is probably going too far to suggest that it did not aggravate the problems associated with demographic collapse. Contemporary sources reveal a host of problems created by a shortage of ready money in the economy: mints were closed for decades; runs on banks became common; and chroniclers drew attention to the difficulty people had when paying taxes and rents or when trying to sell goods in the marketplace. Even given the medieval penchant for exaggeration, it seems reasonable to accept that the bullion famine was a serious problem that impeded social and economic life.

The kind of money actually used by medieval people varied widely from one place to another, and from one period to the next. Late Roman coinage was based principally on gold, and the early Germanic successor states sought to perpetuate Roman forms, albeit with waning ability. In the eighth century, the CAROLINGIANS reformed the currency, adopting silver as the principal medium for minting coins, and instituting the silver penny (known in Latin as *denarius*, whence *denier* in French, *denaro* in Italian, and *dinero* in Spanish, typically abbreviated as "d") as the basis of the circulating coinage. The Carolingians also devised an accounting system to deal with larger sums of money, in which 12 pennies constituted one shilling (*solidus*, or "s") and 20 shillings constituted one pound (*libra*, or "£"). This system became the basis of most European monetary systems throughout the medieval pe-

---

LIFE IN THE MIDDLE AGES

Counting and Accounting

Any sort of banking—in fact, any serious business—requires an accounting system. The double-entry accounting method common today was developed in Italy in the fourteenth century in Genoa and perfected in the 1420s by the Medicis, who took great pains to keep their accounting methods secret. In 1494, Luca Pacioli, an Italian mathematician and Franciscan monk, wrote the first treatise on accounting, which became the standard until revised by English bookkeeper Hugh Oldcastle in 1543.

riod, and, in some cases, beyond: ENGLAND adopted a decimal currency system only in 1971. The silver penny remained the basic coin in use until the thirteenth century, when it was supplemented by two new types of coin. One of these additions was a heavier silver coin known as the groat (*grossus denarius*, literally "thick penny"), worth a multiple number of pennies depending on time and place. When the groats began to circulate, the original silver pennies typically became "small pennies" and tended over time to contain less and less silver, circulating only as petty local coins. The second addition to the circulating coinage resulted from the issue of new gold coins. While there were many types issued, two were particularly successful on the international stage, the Florentine florin (introduced in 1252 and particularly prominent until the fifteenth century) and the Venetian ducat (introduced in 1284, and the successor of the florin as the leading coin for international trade). Thus, from the second half of the thirteenth century, Europeans typically dealt with three types of coins: small pennies used for petty day-to-day transactions; groats used for more substantial local or regional trade, or for such things as rent and tax payments; and florins or ducats, used primarily by merchants and states involved in international transactions. Those who handled groats on a regular basis probably considered themselves among the better sort of people in society, while those who handled gold undoubtedly saw themselves as members of society's elite.

 See COMMERCE AND TRADE; BANKING; FAIRS; GUILDS; *and* WOOL TRADE *for background. The career of the* MEDICI *is important, as is* FEUDALISM. *See also* TOWNS, VILLAGES, AND CITIES; SOCIAL CLASSES; *and* HORSES.

MONGOLS

The Mongols were once a nomadic people traveling the areas north and west of CHINA before uniting under the rule of GENGHIS KHAN in the late twelfth century. For the most part, the Mongols lived by herding sheep and HORSES and occasionally raiding a weaker tribe. The Mongols were religiously diverse, counting among their number followers of Buddhism, Nestorian Christianity, and Islam, but for the most part Mongols were a shamanistic people. The diversity among the Mongols carried over to the religious tolerance they showed to conquered peoples. The structure of a common Mongolian tribe had the priests as one class, along with warriors and chieftains making up the upper class, followed by a vast number of tribespeople.

Genghis Khan. At the beginning of the Middle Ages, the Mongols joined Turkish tribes in invading the Middle East and Europe. The Mongol tribes in the east would periodically attack China, and sometimes work for the emperor of China. In 1206, after uniting the Turkish and Mongolian tribes, Genghis Khan was elected supreme ruler in a great assembly. After reorganizing his army, he set out to conquer Asia. In the years 1211–1215, the Mongols seized Peking and all lands north of the Yellow River. Five years later, they swept across Persia, defeating the princes of RUSSIA.

Genghis Khan assembled a coherent code of Mongol customs, known as the Yassak. The Yassak was considered the law of the state, and it gave the great khan supreme authority over his subjects. He proved to be an able administrator of government as well as a great military leader. Genghis Khan imposed a uniform legal and administrative system that held together the extensive Mongol empire. His nomadic heritage also had an influence on the way he would conquer. He would lay waste the towns as his treasury began to fill up with booty from plunder.

Even after Genghis Khan's death in 1227, the Mongols continued their conquering ways. Under the leadership of Ogadai, Genghis Khan's third son, the Mongols attacked Russia in 1237. In 1240, Kiev was sacked. The Mongols marched on, invading HUNGARY and crossing the Danube River. But after Ogadai's death, the Mongols retreated, never to return.

Further Conquest. Genghis Khan's grandsons continued expanding the Mongol empire. Batu Khan invaded Russia successfully and founded the GOLDEN HORDE. Hulagu, another grandson of Genghis Khan, conquered Persia and Iraq causing the fall of the ABBASID caliphate in 1258. Hulagu continued through the Middle East, going as far as the borders of Syria and Palestine before being defeated by the MAMLUK Sultan of EGYPT. Upon learning of his brother Mangu's death, Hulagu returned to Karakorum, the Mongolian capital. Mangu's death splintered the unified Mongol empire into four main khanates: the Great khanate, Chaghatai khanate, the Golden Horde, and the Il-khanate. Yet, the Mongols would continue expanding a divided empire.

Kublai Khan. The empire as a whole reached its peak under KUBLAI KHAN. During his leadership, he conquered China, and extended his influence towards Indo-China, Korea, and JAPAN. Kublai encouraged relations with western Europe, permitting travelers to visit Mongolian lands. MARCO POLO, one such traveler, provided detailed accounts of the land, people, and customs, enlightening Europeans about the civilizations of east Asia. Kublai Khan also moved the capital of his Mongol territories from Karakorum to Peking, thus symbolizing a break from the other khanates. Although he never received full recognition as the great khan, he did receive support from his brother, Hulagu, in Persia. Both were in favor of claiming the title of supreme authority of conquered countries, even if it meant mixing with the ruling class it had just conquered. The third brother, Arigh Boke, was in defiance of Kublai Khan's philosophy. When Arigh Boke ascended to the position of great khan, he maintained Genghis Khan's ideology of conquest and rule: warriors were meant to conquer and fight, while exacting tribute from those the warriors protect, namely the farmers, denizens of cities, and caravan riders or traders. Kublai Khan eventually prevailed, holding Arigh Boke in honorable captivity until his death.

Kublai Khan's reign was peaceful and prosperous as the Mongols controlled the East-West trade routes, enhancing their economy. The dynasty Kublai Khan founded lasted until 1368, when the last emperor fell to the armies of the Ming dynasty. Kublai's dynasty fell easily, in part because Kublai had adopted Chinese administrative methods; the Chinese found themselves conquering a familiar system of government.

A 16th-century Mongol miniature shows Kublai Khan's armies laying siege to the fortress of O'chou on the Yang-tse-Kiang River in 1259.

Sometime at the end of the thirteenth century, the vast Mongolian empire started to divide. The khanate remained a nomadic state, but independent empires were founded in China, Persia, central Asia, and Russia. The dynasty in China formally accepted Chinese culture, while the khanates in Persia adopted ISLAM. Hordes would constantly fight among themselves in Turkestan, with the Golden Horde maintaining its supremacy until the fourteenth century.

Tamerlane. Toward the end of the fourteenth century, a new leader, TAMERLANE, rose to power. He attempted to restore the glory from the days of Genghis Khan. He seized the khan title of central Asia in 1370, organizing an army of Mongols and Turks to invade Persia. After his victory in Persia, he imposed his authority over the Golden Horde and raided India. Following his victory at Angora, he became lord of all the Mongol khanates.

Fall of the Empire. After Tamerlane's death, the Mongol empire declined. The Golden Horde, weakened by Tamerlane, was defeated by the Russian princes. The Golden Horde would soon split into various states, and the region it once governed ceased to

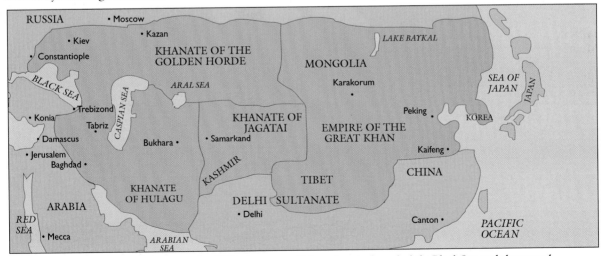

Mongol Empire in the 13th Century. By 1259, the extent of Mongol control reached the Black Sea and threatened Constantinople. Each of the khanates went on to expand and influence the history of the lands beyond its borders but never again with the same singular purpose of conquest as under Genghis Khan.

be a part of the Mongol empire. Kiev was reconquered by the grand dukes of LITHUANIA and China also regained its independence.

 See CHINA *for background. The lives of* GENGHIS KHAN, KUBLAI KHAN; *and* TAMERLANE *are covered in those entries. See also* GOLDEN HORDE; *and articles on* RUSSIA; BYZANTIUM; BARBARIAN INVASIONS.

MONTPELLIER

Originally a fief of the feudal lords of Toulouse, Montpellier is a city located in Languedoc, in southern FRANCE. After the fifth century, it was known as a trading city specializing in wines and the importation of spices. By the tenth century, the city had grown and become a financial and economic center. There was an attempted insurrection by the burghers of Montpellier against their lords in 1141, but it was squashed. As a result of the victory, the lords established a dynasty in Languedoc.

In the latter half of the twelfth century, the economy took an upward swing. Montpellier added to the commercial success of trade around the Mediterranean by establishing trade with the crusader Kingdom of Jerusalem. The kings of ARAGON inherited the city through marriage in 1204.

In 1220, the school of MEDICINE in Montpellier was recognized as a UNIVERSITY. It soon became one of the leading universities of medicine in Europe. Many of the university's professors of medicine were Jewish; indeed the Jews of Montpellier had played an important part in laying the groundwork for the establishment of the university. The kings of Majorca claimed Montpellier in 1276, and the city eventually became the capital of the kingdom of Majorca. In 1349, Montpellier was annexed by France.

MOSAIC

An art form in which small pieces of glass, semiprecious stone, marble, or other hard materials are laid into an adhesive such as mortar or plaster on a flat surface, forming a picture or a geometric or floral design. This technique, first used in the ancient world in Greece, ROME, and Crete, was refined and perfected in the early Christian period of the Middle Ages. Mosaics were used primar-

ily to decorate the walls, floors, and vaults of CHURCHES, shrines, and MONASTERIES; most notably, in the sixth-century cities of the Byzantine Empire, such as the HAGIA SOPHIA in CONSTANTINOPLE. (*See* CHURCHES AND CATHEDRALS.)

The Byzantine mosaic artists produced their intricate and usually large artwork through collaboration in workshops, where only the most skilled and senior craftsmen were capable of creating the faces and details of their religious subjects. The Byzantines also developed the art of mosaic portraiture; many high-ranking members of royalty were depicted in this medium.

Later, Byzantine expertise was exported to the Islamic world, where richly colored mosaics were ideal for decorating architecture with geometric patterns and sacred verses, in the abstract Islamic manner.

Over time, the size of the stone pieces, or tesserae, became smaller, and artists worked with ever-increasing degrees of refinement. By the early fourteenth century, portable ICONS of mosaic on wood panels, which rivaled paintings, and intricately embellished objects such as jewelry and altar decorations were being produced.

Between the eleventh and thirteenth centuries in Rome, VENICE, and the NORMAN kingdom of SICILY, Byzantine and Islamic artists produced spectacular mosaic-decorated churches and palaces, incorporating stylized depictions of Christ and the saints.

Mosaic art was eclipsed in the fourteenth century with the advent of frescoes. (*See* BYZANTINE ART AND ARCHITECTURE; ISLAMIC ART AND ARCHITECTURE.)

Apse mosaic on the inside of the dome of the Church of Santa Prassede in Rome. Depicted are Sts. Paschal, Pudentiana, and Paul receiving the blessing of Christ.

MUHAMMAD

Muhammad (also Mohammed; c. 570–632) was the founder of the Islamic religion and the inspiration for a culture and a series of empires that dominated a large portion of human civilization during the Middle Ages. ISLAM continues to play a pivotal role in much of the world, taking as its source the writings that constitute this man's teachings.

Early Life. Born Abu al-Qasim Muhammad ibn Abd Allah ibn al-Muttalib ibn Hashim in the city of Mecca on the Arabian peninsula, he was orphaned at an early age and spent his youth working on the caravans that transported both goods and ideas between BYZANTIUM, Arabia, and North Africa. In 595, he married a wealthy widow, Khadija, who provided him with a large income from trading. In 610, while on a retreat in the countryside, he had a profound religious experience. He described it as receiving a mission from the angel Gabriel on Mount Hira to be a prophet to his people. He acknowledged his debt to all previous prophets, from Adam to Abraham to Moses to Jesus, but claimed his prophesy was the summation and seal of all prophesy.

16th-century depiction of Muhammad rising to heaven on al-Buraq, his legendary donkey, guided by Gabriel and the angelic retinue. From a Nizami manuscript.

Flight. At first, Muhammad conveyed his message and his teachings to his family and to an inner circle, but as he criticized the merchants of Mecca, he attracted both adherents and enemies among the townspeople. In 619, his clan withdrew their protection, forcing him to flee in 622 to Yathrib (later called Medina—"city of the prophet"), another Arabian commercial center. That flight, known as the Hegira ("breaking away"), July 16, 622, marks a turning point in Muhammad's career and the beginning of the Islamic calendar.

Muhammad arrived in Medina on September 24. He was almost immediately successful in establishing a power base among nearly all classes, who regarded him as a powerful Meccan businessman of high standing. In Medina, Muhammad entered into several marriages with the powerful families, including with Aisha, the daughter of ABU BAKR, one of Muhammad's earliest and most devoted followers. Aisha was to become the favorite and most influential of Muhammad's wives.

War. In order to support his followers, and possibly to goad the Meccans, Muhammad led an attack on a Meccan caravan in 624, which led to the BATTLE OF BADR in which 300 fighters led by Muhammad defeated a much larger Meccan force. The victory was seen as a vindication of Muhammad's mission and cast a military light on Islam's entire future.

The ensuing war with Mecca did not go well at first, and Muhammad was even wounded in the early fighting at Uhud. At the suggestion of a Persian soldier, Muhammad defended Medina by digging trenches around the city. The unfamiliar method of WARFARE confounded the Meccans and saved the city.

Triumph. At this stage, Muhammad broke all ties with Judaism and Christianity, declaring Islam an independent religion. He sued for peace with Mecca and, following the Treaty of al-Hudaybiyah (628), marched triumphantly into Mecca leading 10,000 followers. Mecca became the religious capital of Islam and Medina its political capital. The Kaa'bah, a Meccan shrine housing the Black Stone, is a monument that, legend has it, was given by God to Adam upon his expulsion from Paradise. It became the most sacred place in Islam, replacing Jerusalem in 630 as the place Muslims must face while praying.

On June 8, 632, Muhammad complained of a severe headache and suddenly died. Two years earlier, he had dispatched an expedition to prepare for the invasion of Syria, sowing the seeds for the expansion of his religion and the creation of several empires. His teachings were collected after his death as the KORAN, the sacred text of Islam.

See ISLAM; ISLAM, RELIGIOUS PHILOSOPHY OF; KORAN; JIHAD; *and* ISLAMIC ART AND ARCHITECTURE. *Also see entries on* ABBASID; ABBADID; FATIMID; UMAYYAD DYNASTIES. *Also* ABU BAKR; BADR; *and biographical entries.*

MUSIC IN THE MIDDLE AGES

Of all the artistic accomplishments of the medieval world, music is the least accessible to us. Much of medieval music has been lost or was never written down. Examining what survives, we can only approximate how it sounded. Yet we do have evidence that music was important to the people of the Middle Ages, and in much the same way it is today. There was religious music and patriotic music, solemn and celebratory music, music to accompany poetry, and music for pure entertainment. Music was often structured according to class; the music enjoyed by nobles was different from what peasants sang or played; sacred music stood apart from secular melodies. But, given human nature, it is not unlikely that there existed songs and tunes that appealed to a wide range of individuals as well.

Early Thoughts. In Europe, music was originally counted as one of the Seven Liberal Arts, recognized in ancient Greece and ROME, but not categorized until the fifth century. Music was grouped with the *quadrivium,* which included arithmetic, geometry, and ASTRONOMY (as opposed to the *trivium,* which comprised grammar, rhetoric, and logic). Musical scholars of the early Middle Ages were more concerned with the mathematical structure of a melody than its sound or ease of performance. This sort of musical "harmony," they argued, reflected the harmony of the universe.

In the Islamic world, music was looked upon with suspicion. The prophet MUHAMMAD had disapproved of poetry, and since many tunes were written to accompany poems, clerics and scholars viewed it warily. Many Islamic scholars believed that music had no ennobling value but merely functioned as entertainment. There is little doubt that many individuals did in fact enjoy music for its own sake, at least privately. In public, carefully structured music did become an important element of religious worship.

Singing and Instruments. Obviously singing was the easiest—and least expensive—way to perform music. It is likely that people sang to themselves; many people also played musical instruments, which had been popular in the ancient world and became more complex in medieval times.

Initially, musical instruments were rare in medieval Europe. The Church frowned upon them, identifying them with paganism. Drums, horns, and simple stringed instruments were nonetheless played. As contact with the Middle East increased (both through trade and the CRUSADES), instruments from that region, such as the lute, made their way into Europe. From these instruments developed the flute, the recorder, the bagpipes, and the psaltery (a forerunner of the harpsichord and piano). Organs first made their appearance around the tenth century; initially they were operated by means of levers rather than keyboards. The organ, with its grand, sweeping sounds, became a significant component of church music.

Religious Music. Christians, Jews, and Muslims all used music in their religious services. Much of the written music that exists from the Middle Ages is sacred music—in Europe, the Christian liturgies were chanted as part of the service. The GREGORIAN CHANTS, so named because they were supposedly a divine gift from God to Pope GREGORY I, are the best known. The Gregorian chant of the Roman liturgy is still used today by the Roman Catholic Church.

Islamic sacred music included chants accompanying passages of the KORAN, as well as the call to prayer (five times daily, according to Islamic custom), songs praising Muhammad and ISLAM, songs honoring Muslim pilgrims, and hymns sung on religious holidays. One Muslim sect, the Melevi, combined music with a wild, spinning dance as a means of attaining spiritual completeness. (In the West, they became known as whirling dervishes.)

Jewish sacred music consisted of chants to which biblical passages and prayers had been set. The Jews, who also sang hymns, were often influenced by the cultures around them. It is likely that their sacred music was based in part on the sacred music of other religions, at least in its basic form.

Later in the Middle Ages, religious music became more complex, particularly in Europe. The introduction of choirs and musical instruments into services allowed for more variation. However, many of the original chants continued to play a role in services, as they do to this day.

Secular Music. One reason so much sacred music survives is that religious scholars could write the notations down. It was not until late in the Middle Ages that secular melodies were written down for posterity. As a result, even though the words to many songs are known to us, their actual tunes remain a mystery.

In Europe, music was enjoyed at all levels of society, but the nobility put particular emphasis on

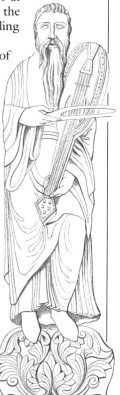

A 12th-century sculpture on the portico of the Abbey of St-Denis of a trouvère playing a violin.

its importance. Musicians were part of the royal court, and were expected to perform for everything from ceremonial occasions to banquets and dances. Even lesser nobles might include a musician as part of the household. Composers of the day often accepted the patronage of various NOBLES. Probably the best-known composer from medieval Europe was GUILLAUME DE MACHAUT, some of whose melodies have been preserved.

Minstrels, who sang and played musical instruments, might perform for the nobility, or they might wander from town to town to perform. Nobles were sometimes musicians themselves—the TROUBADOURS, trouvères, and minnesingers, for example. Often, these individuals wrote poetry that was then set to music. (Minstrels might write their own songs or play the songs of others.)

Enjoyment of music was not limited to the nobility, however. Peasants and townspeople were able to enjoy the music of the jongleurs, wandering singers who passed through towns performing music and sometimes acrobatic stunts. Because they traveled extensively, they were able to spread songs and melodies across wide regions. Jongleurs were also informal sources of information, spreading news across a kingdom as they traveled.

Students, too, enjoyed singing and playing music. The wandering scholars known as the GOLIARDS often wrote and sang irreverent songs praising drinking and gambling. The CARMINA BURANA, a set of some 300 songs dating from the thirteenth century, is the most famous example. The composers made musical notations on the songs of *carmina burana*, but they have been difficult to decipher, and only about 40 of the melodies have been reconstructed.

By around the twelfth century, it was becoming increasingly common for musical notation to be made as a matter of course. A new notation system, introduced by composers at the NOTRE DAME cathedral in Paris, preserved melodies and provided a sense of permanence to melodic compositions. Gradually, this notation spread from church music (for which it was developed) to secular music, so that by the fifteenth-century music was being written down on a fairly regular basis. Moreover, composers were now clearly indicating, for their instrumental pieces, precisely which instruments would be used in each piece.

Islamic secular music was more restricted, but because the Islamic world stretched from SPAIN to India, influences from different cultures affected musical of-

Music was often used as accompaniment to a story (not unlike the modern film score). Above, a minstrel plays as the Roman de Cleomadès *is recited to Blanche of Castile.*

ferings and tastes. The Islamic nobility, like its European counterpart, hired court musicians. Influences from Spain, AFRICA, and even CHINA meshed to create a variety of musical forms. Islamic music also influenced Europe. Morris dances, popular in western Europe (particularly in Britain), originated in northern Africa (where they were known as Moorish dances).

Later Developments. In the late Middle Ages, individual regions began to develop distinct musical styles (although influences from other countries were still evident). Musical notation continued to improve, and composers gained more recognition.

Musical instruments became increasingly complex, and secular music developed a firmer footing in society. As towns and cities became more prominent, music became an important part of civic ceremonies. Sacred music, too, became more varied. The late Middle Ages set the stage for the music of the Renaissance—but the simplicity of medieval music remained an important source of inspiration for later composers.

See UNIVERSITIES *for the role of music in higher learning. See* GREGORIAN CHANT; TROUBADORS; CARMINA BURANA; *and* GOLIARDIC POETS *for specific forms. Also see* GAMES AND PASTIMES; HERALDRY; SOCIAL CLASSES *for more on music in everyday life.*

NACHMANIDES, MOSES

Moses ben Nachman (c. 1195–1270), also known as Nachmanides (or Ramban, a Hebrew acronym of his name) was a leading rabbinic figure in northern SPAIN, comparable in learning and influence to MAIMONIDES, though he embraced Jewish mysticism (the Kabbala) in his works and was suspicious of Aristotelian rationalism.

Nachmanides was born in Gerona in Catalonia, educated there, and rose to the position of adviser to King James I of Aragon. In 1263, Nachmanides was forced to participate in a debate with Christian monks. His defense of his religion was so spirited and effective that he was threatened with death and eventually was forced to flee in 1267. He settled in Jerusalem, reviving the Jewish community there that had all but disappeared during the CRUSADES. The synagogue he founded in the Old City still stands. (*See* JUDAISM.)

NAPLES, KINGDOM OF

The Kingdom of Naples in the Middle Ages occupied the southern portion of the Italian peninsula, below the PAPAL STATES, and often included the isle of SICILY. By the mid-twelfth century, the NORMANS under Roger II had formed a state by consolidating territories previously held by the Byzantines, the LOMBARDS, and the Muslims. After the Norman reign, the kingdom passed into the control of the HOHENSTAUFEN DYNASTY. Under the Hohenstaufen rulers, most notably FREDERICK II, the kingdom blossomed, reaching a political, economic, and cultural peak, becoming a major commercial center, and drawing artists and scholars from all over Europe and Arab

The Stozzi Panel depicting the port of Naples, dated 1464. Note the fortifications protecting the harbor from piracy.

lands. However, after Frederick's death and through the efforts of Pope Clement IV, CHARLES I OF ANJOU was invested with the crown in 1266, after defeating Hohenstaufen forces at Benevento. Under ANGEVIN control, the capital of the kingdom was moved from Palermo to Naples, and Charles began several major building projects in the city, such as the construction of the Castel Nuovo. Like his predecessors, Charles also attracted many of the great figures of medieval art and thought to his court. However, heavy TAXATION and harsh rule led to the rebellion known as the SICILIAN VESPERS in 1282, and the island of Sicily was put into the control of the House of ARAGON and separated from the territories on the Italian mainland.

Battles. The division of the kingdom led to a century of wars between the Angevins and the Aragonese over the island; a temporary peace was achieved in 1302, with the Treaty of Caltabellotta, when Naples was recognized as a distinct political entity. It was not until 1373 that the Angevin Queen Joan I of Naples renounced her claim to Sicily. The nobility of Naples attempted to overthrow Angevin rule with unsuccessful rebellions in 1284, 1346–1347, 1378, and 1381. During those years, Naples grew in power and prestige. (*See* WARFARE.)

Under the rule of King Robert the Wise (1309–1343), the influence of the Neapolitan kingdom stretched as far as Greece and the Balkans. During these years, the court in Naples was one of the most splendid in Europe, attracting distinguished noblemen and artists. The city also developed profitable commercial ties to FLORENCE and Tuscany, and its industries grew in prominence. But the effort needed to maintain its military dominance and the lavish spending at the court taxed the resources of the kingdom too greatly; it had no local middle class on which to lean for support. During the unfortunate reign of Robert's daughter, Joan I (1343–1382), the kingdom fell into economic ruin and a violent civil war between Sicilian

Aragonese and Angevin claimants to the throne. These dynastic disputes began between Charles of Durazzo (later Charles III of Naples) and Louis of Anjou, and were continued by their heirs. Charles's descendants, Ladislas (1399–1414) and Joan II, defended the throne against their French rivals, despite the latter's receiving the support of the pope. Yet Joan II adopted as her heirs both claimants from the Houses of Aragon and Anjou, and thus the dynastic struggle continued.

Spanish Control. In 1442, the Sicilian Aragonese claimant, ALFONSO V, defeated René of Anjou, and was invested with Naples by the pope, beginning official Spanish rule. Alfonso began a reconstruction of the capital and encouraged scholarship in the kingdom. Sicily was united once again with the mainland, and the title "King of the two Sicilies" was inherited by Alfonso's heirs, Ferdinand I (1458–1494) and his son, Ferdinand II. The Angevin claim to the kingdom, with the death of René's nephew in 1486, passed to the French crown; in 1495, Charles VIII of France seized Naples briefly. Thus began the Italian wars between France and Spain over the territories; in 1503, the Kingdom of Naples fell into the autocratic and exploitative hands of the Spanish HABSBURG viceroys, where it remained for the next two centuries. (*See* ITALY; ANGEVINS; ARAGON; ALFONSO V.)

NAVARRE, KINGDOM OF

A kingdom in northeastern SPAIN, situated between the Pyrenees and the upper Ebro River, with its roots in the rebellion of the Basques and Ibero-Romanized people of the city of Pamplona and surroundings against the VISIGOTHS in the sixth century. The people of the region turned back ARAB invaders and CHARLEMAGNE's army in the eighth century, thus maintaining its independence.

Until the ninth century, the country was a disorganized confederation of clans, tribes, and townships. The lords of Pamplona finally united the clans and tribes, and Sancho I became the first king of Navarre.

Through a series of truces and marriages between surrounding states, Navarre retained its independence; Navarre reached the height of its power under Sancho III, becoming the leading Christian Spanish state.

After Sancho III's death in 1035, the dynasties of Navarre occupied the thrones of ARAGON and Castile. Castile was lost in dynastic wars, and Aragon became an independent kingdom. What was left of Navarre continued on, eventually losing contact with Muslim Spain. The kings of Aragon moved in to rule from 1076 to 1134. (*See* ARAGON; SPAIN.)

In 1234, Navarre was made a province of FRANCE, as the people annulled an attempt to make JAMES I of Aragon king. The crown was instead offered to Count Thibault of Champagne.

The heiress to the Navarre-Champagne province married King Charles IV of France. Navarre therefore became involved in the French dynastic conflicts that eventually led to its decline. Navarre regained some of its prestige under the leadership of Charles the Noble (r. 1387–1425). However, when his daughter married King John II of Aragon (r. 1406–1454), conflict again led to Navarre's decline.

NESTORIAN CONTROVERSY

N estorius was patriarch of CONSTANTINOPLE from 428 to 431, at which point he was condemned by the Church as a heretic because he believed that Christ was actually two persons—divine and human. Upon condemnation, Nestorius and his followers formed a new Christian sect, which today is known as the Persian, or Nestorian Church. Most of its members (numbering fewer than 200,000) live in Iraq, Syria, and Iran. At one time, however, the Nestorian Church reached as far as India, Mongolia, and CHINA.

Nestorius objected to calling the Virgin Mary *Theotokos* ("Mother of God"). Mary, he said, was a human who had given birth to the "human" Jesus. The "divine" Jesus, he added, was God Himself, who had no human mother. Saint Cyril, patriarch of Alexandria, vehemently opposed Nestorius's claim, believing that the human and divine characters of Christ were united. A special council was called in the city of Epheseus, near the Turkish city of Izmir. The council was presided over by Saint Cyril, so not surprisingly, it resulted in the condemnation of Nestorius.

Later, a group known as the Monophysites put forth the argument that the divine and human natures of Christ were identical. This was as offensive to many Christians as the Nestorian claim. The COUNCIL OF CHALCEDON, which met in 451, decreed that Christ had two natures in one person.

After the ARABS conquered Persia in the seventh century, the Nestorian Church was recognized as a separate, legally protected religious community. The church spread throughout Asia, becoming so strong in China that it came close to becoming the established religion. By the end of the tenth century, the Nestorian Church counted 15 metropolitan (ecclesiastical) provinces in the Persian caliphate and five abroad.

Nestorianism waned toward the end of the Middle Ages; in the sixteenth century many Nestorian groups joined the Roman Catholic Church and later the Syrian Jacobite Church.

NETHERLANDS

The Netherlands constitutes part of the region known in medieval times as the Low Countries—so called because much of it was close to sea level and thus subject to floods. (The universal image of Holland today is of a country protected by a series of dikes and dams—an image not entirely accurate.) It borders present-day BELGIUM, GERMANY, and the North Sea, which gave it a degree of strategic importance.

The Netherlands were originally inhabited by Celtic and Germanic tribes, who were considerably influenced by each others' cultures. (Modern Dutch is often described as a cross between German and English.) The Romans occupied the southern region in the centuries before the fall of their empire and made their mark on the culture as well. The northern region (north of the Rhine) was inhabited by the Frisians, who never came under Roman rule (the Romans did not expand beyond the Rhine).

In the sixth century, the region came under Frankish rule, in the form of the MEROVINGIAN and CAROLINGIAN dynasties. The Netherlands eventually became a series of small principalities, some secular in scope and others ecclesiastical. Most of the region was allied with German kings, except for FLANDERS, which was primarily under French control.

Important businesses in the Netherlands included trade, agriculture (and later livestock), and decorative arts. The region also produced a number of painters, sculptors, and scholars (both religious and secular.) The arts got a firm grounding in late medieval Holland and paved the way for masters such as the van Eycks and Rembrandt.

The various Netherlandic counties and the towns that sprang up within them had common economic and social characteristics, but each county was an independent entity. Eventually, however, the region came under the control of the duchy of BURGUNDY, which itself came under French control. This added a new unity to the region, but it also added problems, since BURGUNDY was an active participant in the wars between the French and the English. By the middle of the fifteenth century, Burgundy and FRANCE were locked in battle, but when the Burgundian duchess

Mary married MAXIMILIAN I of Germany (later Holy Roman Emperor), Burgundy came under the HABSBURG DYNASTY. France and Germany fought over the region but eventually it fell under Habsburg control. Maximilian was not particularly adept at dealing with the Low Countries, but his son Philip and his grandson Charles V did a much better job of administering the region. (*See* BURGUNDY; HABSBURG DYNASTY; MAXIMILIAN I; GERMANY.)

NICAEA, COUNCIL OF

The Council of Nicaea (325) was the first ecumenical council of the Christian Church. Constantine I the Great, the first Roman emperor to profess CHRISTIANITY, called the council in order to end the disunion caused by the emergence of Arianism. Arius, the founder of Arianism, broke with the orthodox interpretation of the divine Trinity in his teachings that the Son of God was divine but created and therefore inferior to God. Constantine hoped that the entire Christian world would feel bound by the conclusions of a universal council. The council, however, was not truly universal, since it was dominated by clergy from the eastern half of the Roman Empire.

The deliberations of the council were dominated by Constantine. Under his guidance, the council condemned Arius and officially named Arianism a HERESY. The orthodox Christian interpretation of the Trinity was written into the Nicene Creed. This creed held that God the Father and the Son were "consubstantial" (of one and the same substance or being) and co-eternal. This contradicted the Arian belief that the Son was created, not co-eternal, and that the two were "of like substance," not the "same substance." Despite this condemnation, the Arian heresy continued to split the Church for over 200 years. Other important council decisions included establishing the authority of the clergy and settling a dispute between the eastern and western Churches about the DATE OF EASTER.

16th-century fresco of the Council of Nicaea, in the Vatican Apostolic Library.

NICHOLAS II

During the short reign (1059–1061) of Pope Nicholas II (c. 980–1061), an orderly process of papal election was established that put power in the hands of the Church and eliminated imperial influence. Although his decree was challenged by the German court, it set a precedent that was later strengthened by the third LATERAN COUNCIL in 1179.

Nicholas was born Gerard of BURGUNDY in Lorraine. He moved up in the Church hierarchy and was bishop of FLORENCE when he was chosen in 1058 to succeed Pope Stephen IX (also known as Stephen X). He found a rival in the antipope Benedict X, but Benedict was expelled from his office in January 1059.

Although his reign as pope was brief, Nicholas enacted substantive reforms. The most important centered on how the pope was chosen. In April 1059, he issued a papal bull that established a formalized election process. The seven highest-ranking cardinals would be responsible for choosing a candidate, who would be voted on by the remaining cardinals.

Conspicuously absent from Nicholas's model was any imperial authority from the throne in GERMANY (then the seat of what was later called the HOLY ROMAN EMPIRE). The German court thus condemned the decree and circulated its own version. The German bishops declared the decree void in 1061, and Nicholas died soon afterward. But he set in motion a plan that was ultimately adopted, securing more power and independence for the Church.

NICHOLAS OF CUSA

The fifteenth-century German scholar Nicholas of Cusa (1401–1464) was primarily a philosopher, but his ideas and activities in the world of science showed the true level of his powers of perception. Many of his theories appear to have been the result more of intuition than of actual experimentation, but they were later confirmed by the scientific work of such pioneers as Copernicus and Galileo. (*See* ASTRONOMY.)

Born Nicholas Krebs in the town of Kues (Cusa), in the Rhineland, the son of a fisherman, he originally planned to pursue a career in law, which he studied at both Heidelberg and the University of Padua. He received his degree in 1423, but abandoned the law for the Church in 1430. He was made a cardinal in 1448.

His theological and philosophical views were influenced by the ideas of such scholars as WILLIAM OF OCKHAM and the Arabic philosopher AVERROËS. One of his theological beliefs was that God was an entity totally outside nature, and that direct communion with God was the only way for individuals to know and understand His divine will. He called this concept "learned unknowing."

Intuitive Science. Nicholas had excellent intuition in matters of SCIENCE. A book he wrote in 1440 explained his theory of the earth's movement around the sun. He espoused the then unpopular notion that the earth moved on its axis; his contemporaries truly believed that if the earth really did move, everyone would be falling off. But Nicholas claimed that space was infinite, not a place with an "up" or a "down" to fall into. He also believed that stars were other suns and that other worlds revolved around them the way the earth revolved around its sun. The experiments done by Copernicus, Galileo, Newton, and others proved Nicholas right. But while Nicholas believed in observation of phenomena, he did not conduct his own formal experiments. Some doubt thus persists whether Nicholas's writings actually had any influence on these later scientists; or if they were even known to them. (*See* SCIENCE IN THE MIDDLE AGES.)

Among Nicholas's other prescient theories was his belief that plants received sustenance not just from water and soil but from air as well.

Nicholas did make several practical contributions to our understanding of how the human body works. He was one of the first people to believe that pulse measurement could be used to help diagnose disease. He also developed the first concave eyeglasses for nearsightedness. Until Nicholas's time, only convex lenses were used, and only to correct farsightedness.

Nicholas spent most of his life recording his observations. Although many of his views were questionable in the eyes of the Church, he fortunately lived at a time when the Church was not launching its strongest or most damaging attacks. Eventually he settled in Lodi, Italy, where he died on August 11, 1464.

NITHARD

Nithard (c. 790–844), the son of CHARLEMAGNE'S daughter Bertha and her lover Angilbert (court chancellor and one of Charlemagne's favorites), became a learned historian. During the reign of LOUIS I THE PIOUS, he was actively involved in the political affairs of the empire. His political reputation preceded him and at the request of Charles the Bald he wrote the *History of the Quarrels Between the Sons of Louis the Pious*. This four-volume chronicle remains our main source of information about the wars and political intrigues of Louis's reign. In 843, Charles appointed Nithard lay abbot of Saint-Riquier, but he served only a few months before he was slain in battle. (*See* CAROLINGIAN DYNASTY.)

NOBLES AND NOBILITY

Nobles were the ruling class in the Middle Ages and the quality of nobility rationalized their rule. In economic terms, the power of the nobles rested in their control of the land and their capacity to exploit the labor of the overwhelming majority of the population: the free peasantry and the quasi-slaves, the SERFS. In ideological terms, nobles claimed the right to rule based on their "high birth," that is, their innate qualities inherited from a family line of nobles. Nobles were supposed to enact great deeds and perform service for their superiors. The power of the nobles declined with the rise of the urban merchant class. Mercantile wealth replaced landed wealth as the source of political power in Europe.

Medieval European nobility emerged in the early Middle Ages with the fall of the western Roman Empire. The leaders of the Germanic tribes that conquered the former provinces of the empire seized the estates of the Roman noble class. A new, mixed class of landed elites was produced by the intermarriage of the Germanic elite with the noble Roman families. This elite class supported the new kingdoms and supplied the expanding Church with bishops and abbots. A higher class of nobility was formed when some nobles with strong ties to kings were given additional land and privileges. The noble class became central to the administration of the new kingdoms. Family lines were established that lasted for centuries and dominated the political and social life of Europe.

Beginning in the eleventh century, a number of noble families (who suffered a low birthrate and a notoriously high rate of infant mortality, and who sent many of their members to war) terminated when no son or daughter was produced who could inherit the family land. Inheritance laws also led to estates becoming smaller, making it more difficult to support a noble lifestyle, essential in maintaining respect.

Some families survived these problems through gaining additional estates. This was done by merging with other families in marriage, gaining additional land from the king, placing some children in church positions (thereby voiding their claim on family land), or by clearing new land or founding villages.

A new class of nobles emerged in the twelfth century when independent warriors were given the noble title of knights. Granting land to these warriors, who had terrified the European elite, provided some measure of control. However, the knights, while noble, usually only had enough land to support their families, and family lines of knights were short as few children of knights rose to KNIGHTHOOD themselves.

In the late Middle Ages, the nobles suffered a decline in authority. Many entered the service of the monarchs in order to retain social status and power. But the loss of their land-based power signified the end of the era of nobles and the rule of nobility. (*See* BARONS; KNIGHTHOOD; FAMILY LIFE; SOCIAL CLASSES.)

NORMANS

Normans (also called Northmen or Norsemen) were Scandinavian VIKINGS who raided and then settled in northern FRANCE during the 900s. Although they abandoned piracy for COMMERCE and adopted the customs, religion, and language of the French, they did not give up their taste for adventure, enrichment, and expansion.

Early Expansion. Around 820, the Vikings had begun raiding the French coast and sailing up the Seine and other rivers to plunder the countryside. The raids ended in 911 when King Charles the Simple made a treaty with the Viking chief Rollo. The treaty gave Rollo and his followers a large tract of land around Rouen, soon to be called Normandy, in exchange for the Normans' protection of France from other raiders and their conversion to CHRISTIANITY. Rollo and his descendants, who became dukes of Normandy, gained considerable wealth from trade, rents collected from the Church, and raids on other regions. Significant Viking immigration until the mid-900s increased the population of the new Norman duchy.

During the reign of Duke Richard II (996–1026), social stability and intermarriage with the local population hastened Norman assimilation, while the Normans' acceptance of Christianity did much to spur the revival of the Church in Normandy. By the end of Richard's reign, the Normans had stopped speaking their original Scandinavian language in favor of the vernacular of the French inhabitants of the region.

Duke William. From the end of Richard's reign to about 1050, Normandy was torn by feuds and political strife between rival factions of the Norman ruling class. After Duke William came to power, he pacified the duchy and increased its power in northern France, paving the way for his conquest of ENGLAND.

Duke William (later known as WILLIAM I THE CONQUEROR), the illegitimate son of Robert I, was chosen as his father's successor after Robert died on a pilgrimage to the Holy Land, but for the next decade various members of the duke's family disregarded his claim as they struggled for power. In 1046–1047 William's cousin, Guy of Burgundy, sought to seize control of the duchy with the help of several Norman lords, but William defeated them with the assistance of the French king, Henry I. William enlarged his domain by gaining control of Maine to the south and BRITTANY to the west, and successfully defended his duchy against invading forces sent by the count of Anjou and the French king. William's marriage to Matilda, the daughter of the count of FLANDERS, strengthened his position in the east.

By the 1060s, William had unified Normandy and established his preeminence in northwestern France. When the half-Norman English king EDWARD THE CONFESSOR died childless in 1066, William was in a strong position to assert his claim to the throne. Edward, who was William's cousin, had invited William to England in 1051 and, according to William, promised to make him his heir. When King Edward died and the English earl Harold of Wessex (later HAROLD II GODWINSON) became king, an irate William invaded England in 1066.

On October 14, 1066, at the BATTLE OF HASTINGS, William defeated Harold's army. Ten weeks later, on Christmas Day, the Archbishop of Canterbury crowned William king of England in WESTMINSTER ABBEY. His CORONATION was the climax of the Norman Conquest, which changed forever the course of English history, culture, and language.

Mediterranean Adventures. In 1016, Norman adventurers sailed into the Mediterranean Sea and landed in southern ITALY. At first they helped local nobles in their rebellion against Byzantine rule, but soon more land-hungry Normans arrived and took over the land for themselves from the Greeks. The numerous sons of TANCRED DE HAUTEVILLE spearheaded the Norman penetration of southern Italy. One of them, William Iron Arm, became lord of Apulia in 1043. He was succeeded by his brothers Drogo and Humphrey, who defeated forces sent by Pope Leo IX attempting to enforce papal rights in southern Italy. In 1059, Pope Nicholas II granted Humphrey's brother and successor, ROBERT GUISCARD, the duchies of Apulia and Calabria, as well as the large island of SICILY, at the time under Muslim rule. After Robert completed the Norman conquest of southern Italy, his brother Roger I conquered Sicily. His son Roger II joined the island and the Norman territories of southern Italy to create the kingdom of Sicily. The Norman success against the Byzantines in southern Italy, which inspired them to want to penetrate further eastward, was a factor in the CRUSADES, in the early stages of which the Normans played a leading role. (*See* BATTLE OF HASTINGS; WILLIAM I THE CONQUEROR; ENGLISH LANGUAGE AND LITERATURE; ITALY; VIKINGS.)

The Norman States in Italy. Beginning with a small outpost in Lacadonia in 1056, the Norman holdings in Italy grew steadily until they dominated the southern peninsula.

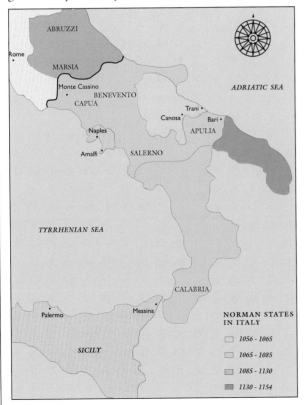

NORTH AMERICA

Before its discovery by Europeans, North America was populated by numerous indigenous tribes, who had lived on the continent for thousands of years. They were initially of Asian descent, and had migrated to North America during prehistoric times across the Bering Strait to Alaska. By the dawn of the Middle Ages they had formed into many distinct tribes across the continent.

Early Settlements. The first major city in pre-Columbian America was Teotihuácan, located 25 miles north of what is now Mexico City. It was founded by the Olmec tribe (c. 100 B.C.E.) and grew to a population as high as 100,000. The city was toppled around 600 C.E., in all likelihood by the northern Chichimec tribe. Most of these tribes were hunter-gatherers. Tribes in Middle America domesticated as many as 102 species of plants, most of them for food. They used long spears and an atlatl, or spear thrower. By the beginning of the Middle Ages, they had begun to use the bow and arrow.

The southwest section of North America was the most developed. The ancestors of the modern-day Pueblos were the Anasazi (Navajo for "ancient ones"), who settled in the American southwest at the beginning of the common era. They were farmers and weavers who established elaborate trade within their communities. Their legacies include their pottery and their stone dwellings or pueblos, some of which had as many as 1,200 rooms. By the end of the first millennium, however, climatic factors (both frosts and droughts) destroyed much of the Anasazi's agricultural system, and forced its members to slowly disband. By the mid-1300s, the Anasazis were extinct; their culture eventually was absorbed into the Mogollon tradition of what is now southern New Mexico.

The Aztecs. The late Middle Ages saw the rise of the mightiest native nation, the Aztecs. They emerged in the mid-1300s from the Mexica, a nomadic tribe in the Valley of Mexico. They sought their own land, but instead became warrior slaves to surrounding tribes. They fled their tormentors in 1322, settling in a wetland area near Lake Texcoco. Three years later they founded their capital, Tenochtitlán, after they saw an eagle atop a cactus—according to their patron god, Huitzilopochtli, this was an auspicious sign.

For the next two centuries, the Aztecs dominated most of central Mexico from the Gulf to the Pacific, developing a rich and sophisticated culture including ASTRONOMY, architecture, engineering, and metalwork. Some 50,000 people lived in Tenochtitlán alone, and about five million throughout the entire empire. The monarch was elected and the central government elected regional governors. Alongside their technical achievements, the Aztecs were also the greatest practitioners of human sacrifice in history.

When the Spanish made their invasion of Mexico in the early 1500s under Cortés, Aztec emperor Montezuma believed the Spanish were descendants of an Aztec god, and sought to curry favor with them with gifts. Most of the subjected people, however, were more than willing to join the invaders in overthrowing their Aztec lords. Cortés captured Montezuma, who was then killed. (*See* SOUTH AMERICA.)

The eastern half of North America was made up of the eastern woodlands, occupied by descendants of the big game hunters who migrated from Canada. The Middle Ages coincided with the Temple Mound period, marked by plant cultivation and the development of villages into towns. Most lived in giant log cabins that housed as many as 2,000. The Iroquois nation in what is now upstate New York had a strong and sophisticated central government; a confederacy of tribes successfully defended itself against outsiders.

During the Middle Ages, the Central Plains were dominated by the Plains Village culture, a society where farming provided half the daily diet. In the Great Basin, the Shoshoni and Paiute did not have the large dwellings of eastern and western tribes, and thus carried their belongings on their backs when traveling.

Pre-Columbian Exploration. Europeans made several early excursions to the American continent during the Middle Ages, even before Columbus's trip in

1492. Explorer Bjarni Herjlfsson was traveling from NORWAY to GREENLAND at the end of the tenth century when his boat veered off course. His men spotted a land not mountainous like Greenland, but Herjlfsson refused to dock there. (*See* GREENLAND; ICELAND.)

In 1000, VIKING explorer Leif Ericsson landed on the northern edge of what is now Newfoundland. He established three countries on the land—Helluland (what is now Baffin Island), Markland (now Labrador) and Vinland (Newfoundland)—after discovering grapes and grapevines. His men built several homes, which were eventually unearthed by Norwegian archaeologists in the 1960s.

Ericsson's brother made a follow-up trip but was killed by Indians. His widow married an Icelandic shipowner, Thorfinn Karlsefni, who made an excursion to North America with three ships in 1003. They had a son, Snorri, who was the first European child born in North America. For at least the next two centuries, the Norse made trips to Newfoundland. Historians claim that, for no apparent reason, these excursions ended no later than 1347.

A century later, in 1470, two Germans in the Danish service—Didrick Pining and Hans Pothorst—undertook a voyage to ICELAND. Pining was named governor of Iceland from 1478 to 1490; some historians maintain that he also traveled to North America.

The native American population has been estimated at being between 5 to 15 million at the time Columbus arrived in 1492. Within 400 years the number fell to 200,000, from slaughter and disease. Yet modern historians credit the indigenous Americans with contributing innovations in farming and medicine vital to the Western world. (*See* EXPLORATION.)

NORWAY

In the Middle Ages, Norway was defined by its trading and colonizing ventures and its relations to its Scandinavian neighbors.

Before the VIKING age (800–1100) Norway was ruled by petty kings, with most of the political power in the hands of Norwegians in three different parts of the country—Oslofjord in the south, Bergen and the fjords in the west, and Trondheim in the north.

Independence. The unification of Norway began when Harald I Fairhair of the Scilfing clan, which claimed direct descent from an old Norse god, defeated a coalition of kings at the Battle of Havsfjord in about 890. Although Harald also conquered the Shetlands and Orkneys, he failed to establish a lasting unity. Harald drove many noble clans from Norway to settle in ICELAND and FRANCE. During the Viking age, as Norsemen conducted raids throughout western Europe, their settlements in France led to the establishment of the Norse duchy of Normandy.

Before Harald's death about 935, he divided his kingdom between his sons. One of the them, Haakon I, subsequently defeated his brothers and temporarily reunited the kingdom. Except for periods of military clashes between the king and local chieftains, and periods when Norway was ruled by one of its neighbors, Norway was, more or less, united and independent.

During the Middle Ages Norway was a highly agricultural society with few villages and barely any towns. The people lived on farms and grew crops, hunted, fished, and cut timber. Since the most settled areas were on or near Norway's long coastline, fish was not only a major source of food, but also the country's main export (80–90 percent of the total). Demand for Norwegian stockfish (dried, unsalted fish) increased after the population in Europe rose markedly after 1000 and the Church instituted fasting rules that banned the eating of meat on certain days. With the money derived from exporting stockfish, Norwegians imported grain and malt. The western port of Bergen became the hub of Norway's international trade, especially with ENGLAND and GERMANY.

Exploration. During the Viking age, Norwegian sailors, traders, and settlers set up permanent settlements on the islands around Britain and in IRELAND. They also ventured westward across the Atlantic to establish colonies on the Faroes, ICELAND, and GREENLAND and explored the coast of NORTH AMERICA.

Overpopulation of Norway's coasts was one of the leading causes of Viking expansion. As the population increased, settlement also expanded into the interior and into the thinly settled northern part of the country. Even with the Viking emigration, the population increased, reaching between 300,000 and 500,000 in the 1300s until the BLACK DEATH (1349–1350) and subsequent epidemics sharply reduced the figure.

Religion. CHRISTIANITY brought by missionaries from England gained a foothold in Norway in the late 900s and under Olaf I, who reigned from 1015 to 1028; it was established as Norway's official religion. King Cnut of England and DENMARK, with the help of unhappy Norwegian nobles, drove Olaf II out of the country. In 1035 Olaf's son, Magnus, returned to the Norwegian throne. After Magnus's successor, Harald III, died while invading northern England in 1066, Norway experienced a period of civil violence.

In the 1100s, Christianity gained a stronger foothold as a result of the mission of Nicholas Breakspear (later Pope ADRIAN IV). The establishment of the archbishopric at Trondheim brought Norway into the European community of Christian states.

Sverre (1184–1202) created a new nobility based on trade and consolidated his royal authority with the help of the popular party, the Birkebeiner. During his reign, a bitter quarrel broke out between church and state over the right to choose the Church's bishops. In 1217, the Birkebeiner put Sverre's grandson, Haakon IV (1343–1380), on the throne. Under Haakon and Magnus VI, who reigned from 1263 to 1280, medieval Norway reached its greatest power, peace, and prosperity. During these years, both Iceland and Greenland submitted to Norwegian rule, although the crown's hold on the Scottish islands weakened, with the southern group transferred to the rule of the Scottish king.

Foreign Rule. The separate development of Norway came to an end in 1319 when Magnus VII (1319–1343), who was also king of SWEDEN, came to the throne. Unpopular in Norway, Magnus was forced to cede power to his son, Haakon VI, husband of MARGARET of Denmark. Olaf IV, son of Norway's King Haakon VI and Margaret, became king of Denmark even before he assumed his father's Norwegian throne. Olaf's reign solidified the Norwegian-Danish union, and in 1397 Margaret united the rule of all three Scandinavian kingdoms—Norway, Sweden, and Denmark—under the terms of the Kalmar Union, according to which the Scandinavian kingdoms were to be "united forever." From that point, Norway virtually ceased to exist as a separate kingdom.

In the late Middle Ages, Norway declined as its political life was dictated by Denmark, and its trade was controlled by the HANSEATIC LEAGUE, which maintained its chief northern office in Bergen, creating concern in Norway about the wealth and influence of German merchants. Sweden soon expressed dissatisfaction with the Kalmar Union and finally left it in 1523. But Norway remained subordinate to Denmark, which negotiated the transfer of Orkney and Shetland to the Scots in the late 1460s. (*See* DENMARK; MARGARET OF DENMARK; NORMANS; VIKINGS.)

NOTRE DAME DE PARIS, CATHEDRAL OF

T he magnificent Cathedral of Notre Dame de Paris is one of the most important examples of French GOTHIC ARCHITECTURE. The foundation stone was laid by Pope ALEXANDER III in 1163, and the building took nearly 200 years to complete. It has for centuries provided artistic and literary inspiration—most notably in Victor Hugo's classic tale *The Hunchback of Notre Dame*. The cathedral is located on the Île de la Cité, in the River Seine.

Origins. Construction of Notre Dame began under the direction of Maurice de Sully, bishop of PARIS. The cathedral's high altar was consecrated in

1189, and the nave was probably finished around 1196. The west facade of Notre Dame, which includes the three famous "rose windows," was completed between 1225 and 1230. (*See* STAINED GLASS.)

The towers topping the west facade were completed around 1250 (although the spires that were supposed to crown them were never added). Other additions such as porches and chapels were added gradually over the next 100 years.

The cathedral's interior measures 427 by 157 feet, and the roof is 115 feet high. The doors of the western facade feature early Gothic carvings. The central spire was actually not added until the nineteenth century. (*See* CHURCHES AND CATHEDRALS.)

Later History. The cathedral was allowed to deteriorate somewhat over the next few centuries but remained a symbol of French history. In 1804, Napoleon brought renewed significance to Notre Dame de Paris when he crowned himself emperor there. A major restoration effort launched in the mid-nineteenth century helped bring back much of the cathedral's former glory. (*See* ARCHITECTURE.)

The Cathedral de Notre-Dame, Paris, as it appeared in the 13th century before the restoration of the façade.

NOVGORD

N ovgorod's location on the northwestern plain of European Russia made it one of the leading commercial and cultural centers in medieval RUSSIA. Founded in ancient times by the Slovenes on the Volkhov River, close to where it leaves Lake Ilmen, Novgorod attracted VIKING merchants who settled there in the early 800s. The close proximity of Novgorod to the Baltic Sea and to the headwaters of Russian rivers that flowed south to the Black and Caspian Seas made it the hub of the new kingdom of the Rus under the leadership of RURIK, who founded the Russian state in 862. (*See* RUSSIA.)

Novgorod's political preeminence was short-lived, however. After Rurik's successor Oleg captured Kiev in 882, he moved the capital south to Kiev, which thereafter became the center of Viking-Slavonic political power. While Novgorod accepted the rule of the Kievan princes, it became more Slavonic in its population, language, and cultural life, remaining a chief center of foreign trade and achieving self-government in 997. As the power of Kiev waned, the princes of Novgorod expanded their political and commercial influence. When the city achieved complete independence from Kiev in 1136, it became the capital of a republic that ruled northern Russia east to the Urals.

Under the inspired leadership of ALEXANDER NEVSKY, Novgorod defeated the Swedish army on the Neva in 1240. Two years later, Nevsky won the great battle on the ice at Lake Peipus against the TEUTONIC KNIGHTS. During the years of attacks by Mongol warriors from east-central Asia called Tartars, Novgorod paid tribute to the MONGOLS, but the city suffered less than the other Russian states. (*See* MONGOLS.)

Novgorod's location provided it with easy access to BYZANTIUM via the Dnieper, Volkhov, and Lovat Rivers and to the Caspian Sea via the Volga. The city became one of the main bridges of east-west trade, exchanging FURS, hides, honey, flax, tar, and slaves for cloth, corn, grain, silver, and silks. It established links with the lucrative spice trade and became one of the four chief trading centers of the HANSEATIC LEAGUE, along with London, Bruges, and Bergen. At the height of its commercial success in the 1300s, the city's population rose to 400,000, and German merchants maintained a thriving enclave there. The colorful splendor of the city during that period was marked by its hundreds of churches, shops, FAIRS, and markets, providing rich themes for later Russian art and folktales.

The 1300s also saw an increase in internal conflicts and in the city's long struggle with its rival principality, Moscow. Moscow launched military attacks against Novgorod in 1456 and 1470, and annexed it in 1478, ending its golden age—and its independence.

ODOACER

Odoacer (b. c. 433–d. 493) was a German chieftan of either Sciri or Rugian origin. He was also a soldier who, like other German chieftains, joined the Roman army. However, he revolted against his general, Orestes, and defeated him in 476. After this victory, Odoacer ended the formal existence of the western Roman Empire when he dethroned the last Roman emperor. Although he acknowledged the rule of the eastern emperor at CONSTANTINOPLE, Odoacer claimed ITALY for himself.

Odoacer ruled with moderation, not altering the underlying character of Roman rule. He conquered Sicily and Dalmatia, on the western coast of the Balkans, and feuded with Zeno, the emperor of the eastern half of the Roman Empire. In 488, Odoacer's downfall began when Zeno authorized the Germanic tribe of the OSTROGOTHS to invade Italy. Odoacer was defeated a number of times and was forced to retreat to his capital of RAVENNA. He withstood a three-year siege and eventually signed a treaty whereby he and THEODORIC, the Ostrogothic king, would rule jointly. However, Theodoric thought little of the treaty; he slaughtered Odoacer and his entire family at a banquet called to celebrate the agreement.

OMAR KHAYYAM

The man believed to have written some of the best-known works of Arabic poetry in history, Omar Khayyám (c. 1044–c. 1132), was better known for centuries as an accomplished physicist, mathematician, and astronomer, and was one of the leading intellects in medieval Turkey.

He was born in Nishapur, Persia (what is now Iran) as Ghiyath al-Din Abul Fateh Omar ibn Ibrahim al-Khayyám; *Khayyám* means "tentmaker," his family's occupation. He is known to have been well-educated for his time. He studied at Bukhara, Balkh, and Isphahan, under Hasan ibn Sabbah, member of the order of Assassins, and with the vizir Nizam al-Mulk.

Science. SELJUK Turkish sultan Malik Shah is known to have commissioned Omar in 1074 to work out a more correct solar calendar. He went to work at his observatory in Ray, and after five years emerged with his *Al-Tarikh-al-Jalali;* this calendar is accurate to within one day in 3,770 years, and anticipated the Gregorian reform He calculated the length of a solar year to an accuracy of one part in 100 billion. Given the technical limitations of the era in which he did his work, it is astonishing how accurate his work remains to this day.

Among Khayyám's other scientific achievements were two books on metaphysics, research into the specific weights of silver and gold, and a method for determining specific gravity. Khayyám also made major advances in the study of algebra. He wrote a textbook on algebra in Arabic, which would be translated into English in 1851. It is still considered a classic of the subject. Using equation techniques first developed by Euclid (whom Khayyám competently critiqued), he came up with a geometric method to solve cubic equations, and recognized 13 different cubic equations. He also expanded knowledge of parallel lines and the multiplication of ratios.

Malik offered Omar a place in the Seljuk court, but all Omar asked for was a pension to read and study in private. Malik granted this, and Omar spent a total of 18 years in Malik Shah's service. Omar made extensive plans for the construction of a major observatory at Isphahan, but the sultan died in 1092 before the plans were completed.

Poetry. Omar also pursued a nonscientific interest—the writing of poetry. In particular, he became interested in quatrains, a popular form of four-lined poetry where the first, second, and fourth lines rhyme. Quatrains were popular in medieval Persia, and Khayyám is reputed to have written over 1,391 quatrains before dying in Nishapur.

Over seven hundred years after Khayyám's death, in 1859, the British historian and translator Edward FitzGerald published the first Khayyám quatrains, or *Rubáiyát* (in Arabic), translated into English. Eight years later, FitzGerald published Khayyám's poetry in book form. The *Rubáiyát* caused a sensation. Beyond the initial surprise that such a well-known mathematician had also written poetry was the fact that Khayyám's poetry celebrated the earthly pleasures of love and wine over mystical understandings of God and life. His famous lines:

> *A Book of Verses underneath the Bough,*
> *A Jug of Wine, a Loaf of Bread—and Thou*
>   *Beside me singing in the Wilderness—*
> *Oh, Wilderness were Paradise enow!*

invoked bread and wine, used in the Church's eucharist, and placed them alongside poetry and sexual desire, concluding that a wilderness of these ingredients was sufficient Paradise. This sensibility shocked the Victorian world, and it made the *Rubáiyát* among the best-known poetic works of all time.

But more discoveries would surface in the twentieth century. Debates would rage over whether Khayyám was in fact the author of the *Rubáiyát*. Several historians alleged that many of the quatrains appeared before Khayyám's lifetime. It was also charged that FitzGerald distorted the original poems, recklessly lifting lines from one poem into another poem. Furthermore, while there was considerable contemporary evidence of Khayyám's scientific work, none of his peers ever wrote of his poetic skill; this facet of Khayyám's life remained unknown until 1859. In 1932, one scholar, H. H. Schaeder, came to the conclusion that "Omar Khayyám" was only a pseudonym for another poet or group of Persian poets and that the real Khayyám never wrote any poetry.

Disagreements rage to this day. While the authorship of the *Rubáiyát* is in doubt, few would question the eloquence of such lines as:

> *The Moving Finger writes; and, having writ,*
> *Moves on: nor all your Piety nor Wit*
> > *Shall lure it back to cancel half a Line,*
> *Nor all thy Tears wash out a Word of it.*

And none would deny the scientific brilliance Khayyám brought to medieval Turkey and the world. (*See* ARABIC LANGUAGE AND LITERATURE.)

ORESME, NICHOLAS

Nicholas Oresme (1325–1382) was a philosopher, economist, and scientist whose work laid the foundation for and anticipated the discoveries and astronomical theories of Galileo and Copernicus. Born in FRANCE, Oresme was educated at the University of PARIS and joined JEAN BURIDAN, rector of the university, in carefully examining Aristotelian SCIENCE. He came to the conclusion that Aristotle was incorrect in many aspects of ASTRONOMY, especially in claiming the heavens must be revolving around a stationary earth. His works on the subject became the starting point for the scientific revolution of the sixteenth century.

He was appointed dean of Rouen in 1364 and became chaplain to King Charles V the Wise in 1370. Charles commissioned Oresme to translate several important works by ARISTOTLE (from Latin into French); these translations were an important contribution to the development of the FRENCH LANGUAGE. In 1377, Oresme was made bishop of Lisieux, where he served until his death on July 11, 1382.

Oresme was also an important economic theorist. He argued that the monarchy did not have the authority to debase or devalue coinage. His work on coinage, *De moneta* (*On coinage*), written in 1360 but not printed until 1484, prevailed well into the seventeenth century. He is considered by many the greatest medieval economist. (*See* ASTRONOMY; MONEY AND CURRENCY; SCIENCE IN THE MIDDLE AGES.)

OSMAN I

Osman I (1259–1324) was the founder of the OTTOMAN Empire. He was the son of a SELJUK noble and military commander, and he inherited a small Turkish principality. Osman drew discontented Turkish workers who had been constantly attacked by the MONGOLS, and organized a scattered population into a strong land force. In 1290, he named himself sultan of the Turks and the Turkish state became known as the Osman realm. In 1304, Osman attempted to conquer Gallipoli, but the Catalan Company thwarted his attempt. He then returned to ANATOLIA where he would increase his territories at the expense of the weakening BYZANTINE Empire.

The Ottomans became the strongest force in the region, making Yenisehir their capital. By 1453, even Christians supported them. While Ottoman lore alleged that they stopped paying the Seljuks tribute in 1299, new research has concluded that they continued to do so after Osman's death in 1324.

Osman created the Ottoman dynasty, but did not set down law. His son and heir, Orkhan, would codify Ottoman rule during his reign (1324–1360).

OSTROGOTHS

The branch of the great Gothic nation that settled in modern Ukraine in the third century. In the fourth century, the Ostrogoths under the legendary king Ermanarich created a vast empire stretching from the Black to the Baltic Sea. In 372, the empire was destroyed by the Asian Huns, who made the Ostrogoths and other Germans into vassals. After the death of ATTILA THE HUN, the German tribes revolted and overthrew the Huns in 454. In the late 400s, the Ostrogoths grew in size and stature and began to pose a serious threat to the eastern Roman Empire. In response to this threat, Emperor Zeno approved the Ostrogoth invasion of the Italian domains of King ODOACER. The invasion was successful, and Odoacer was murdered by THEODORIC in 493 (at a meeting arranged under a truce).

Theodoric died in 526, and the Ostrogoths were soon in a state of disarray, mainly because of their religious conflict (they were Arians) with Catholic kingdoms. The Byzantine Emperor JUSTINIAN I sought to take advantage of this and in 534 attempted to reestablish control of Italy. After a long and brutal struggle, the Ostrogoths were finally defeated in 561. They were dispersed or assimilated into the Italians or other Germanic tribes, leaving little impact on the culture of Italy. (*See* BARBARIAN INVASIONS; ODOACER.)

OTTO I THE GREAT

Otto I the Great (912–973), Holy Roman Emperor from 962 to 973, was the founder of the German medieval kingdom; thanks to his rule, GERMANY became the dominant state in Europe in the tenth and eleventh centuries.

Early Years. He was born to King Henry I and his second wife Matilda, and was entrusted with the duchy of Saxony as a youth. After his father died in 936, he was elected king by a council of German dukes. Immediately after his election, he was faced with serious internal challenges from the dukes of the five chief "stems"—the tribal divisions—of medieval Germany: Saxony, Franconia, Swabia, BAVARIA, and Lorraine. Threatened by imminent foreign attacks, these dukes had submitted to the lordship of Otto's grandfather, Conrad I, and then to the rule of his father, Henry. However, Henry had served as little more than a military chieftain, and the dukes were left to rule independently within their own duchies. Otto, on the other hand, was determined to consolidate German power completely in his own hands and to limit the power of the dukes. At his CORONATION, held at CHARLEMAGNE's old capital of Aachen, he demonstrated these designs by having himself anointed by the bishop of Mainz, thereby declaring himself superior to the other dukes, and revealing his intent to forge a CAROLINGIAN theocracy across Europe.

His Administration. The coronation ceremony also demonstrated Otto's close association with the powerful German bishops. Otto relied on the bishops, generally the most literate and educated members of the kingdom (Otto only learned to read late in life), to serve as administrators and as allies against the German dukes; he rewarded them with large grants of land, governmental privileges, and secular offices. Since the episcopal office was not hereditary and relied solely on the prerogatives of the German king, Otto was also able to appoint members of his own family to important ecclesiastic positions; for example, he appointed his brother and trusted aide Bruno the archbishop of Cologne. His relationship with the Church helped supply Otto with valuable military support to check the aggression of the dukes, as well as to defend the realm against invasions from hostile neighboring countries. The alliance was largely responsible for the stability and prosperity that was Germany's blessing for much of Otto's reign.

Otto's program of consolidation brought him into direct conflict with the ducal powers; but with the financial and military support of the Church, he was able to withstand their challenges. From 936 to 941, he put down several rebellions, the first of which was led by Otto's half-brother Thankmar, with the support of the dukes of Franconia and Bavaria. In 939, Otto's younger brother Henry, assisted by Franconian and Lotharingian nobles and the French king Louis IV, rose up against him; but once again, Otto was victorious. Though fraternal tensions persisted, after Henry was caught in another conspiracy against Otto, the king pardoned his brother, and in 947 granted him the dukedom of Bavaria, securing his faithful service.

Military Career. In another attempt to secure his rule in Germany, Otto abolished the duchy of Franconia and incorporated it into his own territories in Saxony. He left the other duchies intact, but abolished most of the tribal dynasties and appointed his own kinsman and allies as their rulers. Rival dukes, however, threatened the security of his rule by frequently forming alliances with foreign powers. Thus, throughout his early reign, Otto was constantly engaged in WARFARE with his neighbors; victory on one front merely provided the opportunity for an invasion on another while the king was absent. However, through his military skill and his support from the Church, Otto was able to repel all invasions. He first achieved victory on the western front of his empire, establishing German dominance in the Lorraine and the western Frankish frontier with a successful campaign in 939–940. Otto also intervened in FRANCE to preserve a balance of power between rival claimants to the throne. At the same time, Otto managed to assert influence over much of the kingdom of BURGUNDY. When the Burgundian princess Adelaide, the widowed queen of Italy, was taken prisoner by Berengar II of Ivrea, a Roman noble, Otto invaded ITALY in 951. He defeated Berengar, making him his vassal, and freed the princess. He then married Adelaide and assumed the title king of the LOMBARDS.

Otto soon had to leave Italy to return to Germany, where another son, Liudolf, had risen up against him. At the same time, the perennially menacing Hungarians invaded, though Otto was able to defeat both forces, achieving a decisive victory against the Hungarians at Lechfeld in 955, neutralizing them as a foreign threat. As if to confirm his imperial designs, Otto was raised up on the shields of his nobles after the battle and paraded around the battlefield, as were the emperors of old. Otto then contin-

Otto I the Great.

ued his eastern expansion; he had won lands from the SLAVS in 937 and 948, gaining BOHEMIA as a German suzerainty. Now he again went on the offensive, threatening POLAND in 966, and eventually settling on the establishment of an archbishopric at Magdeburg in 968, which became a center for German missionary work in eastern Europe.

Later Years. Much of the final 12 years of Otto's life were spent below the Alps, fighting for control of Italy. After securing the German crown for his son, Otto II, in 962 Otto was called upon by Pope John XII to protect the PAPACY against the reestablished Berengar and was offered the imperial crown in exchange for his support. Otto was crowned in Rome at St. Peter's on February 2, 962, the first of several German Holy Roman Emperors. The coronation established a tradition of German rulers seeking recognition and imperial affirmation from the papacy. Eleven days later, Otto signed a treaty with the pope detailing imperial-papal relations. He quickly defeated Berengar and exiled him to Germany; however, in 963 John revoked his oath of loyalty and deposed Otto when he realized that the emperor planned to achieve complete imperial dominance over Rome, making all of northern Italy dependent on his rule. In response, Otto drove John from the papacy and installed Pope Leo VIII in his place, securing a promise that no future pope would be elected without the emperor's consent. However, the Romans soon tired of Leo, and allowed John to return; Otto went back to Rome and reinstalled Leo, suppressing the opposition. When Leo died in 965, the emperor replaced him with John XIII, but he too was rejected by the Romans. Otto headed once again to an unruly Italy, and he spent his final years (966–972) there, subduing the population. He even marched southward into Byzantine territory, and arranged for the marriage of his son Otto II to the princess THEOPHANO in 972. He returned to Germany in 973, where, several weeks later, he died.

Otto's reign was marked by great prosperity. He was a patron of the arts, and his support encouraged a cultural flowering known as the "Ottonian Renaissance." Some scholars dispute the extent to which Otto truly wished to replicate Charlemagne's total theocratic dominance over Europe, pointing out that Otto never made any attempt to rescue the papacy from the menacing Roman nobility and spent little time in Rome itself. They suggest that Otto was interested less in grand imperial ideology than in the pursuit of territory. He was also blamed by historians for involving Germany in the turbulent morass of Italian affairs. However, his power, military prowess, and diplomatic skill were indisputable and were recognized by his contemporaries. (*See* HOLY ROMAN EMPIRE; GERMANY; PAPACY; LOMBARDS; ITALY.)

OTTO III

O tto III (980–1002) was the grandson and son of the Holy Roman Emperors OTTO I and Otto II. He was elected German king when he was three years old, and was crowned in Aachen on December 25, 983, after his father died. Otto's closest male relative, the deposed duke of BAVARIA Henry II, attempted to control the regency. However, in 984 Henry was forced to turn the child over to his Byzantine mother, THEOPHANO, who supervised his upbringing until her death in 991. His grandmother Adelaide then took over until Otto reached his majority in 994 at age 16. Under Otto's administration, GERMANY enjoyed a period of relative peace, but the imperial power in ITALY declined as local princes asserted their independence and whittled away at the emperor's power base. Thus, during Otto's brief seven-year reign, he was rarely in Germany, devoting himself largely to consolidating and securing an empire based in ROME.

Papal Conflict. In 996, at the request of Pope John XV, Otto traveled to Rome to suppress a rebellion led by the Roman noble Crescentius. He crossed the Alps, defeated Crescentius, whom he then pardoned, and was crowned king of Lombardy. The pope in the meantime had died. Otto replaced him with his 23-year-old cousin Bruno of Carinthia, who became Gregory V, the first German pope. He also appointed Gerbert, his old friend and mentor, archbishop of RAVENNA. Soon after, on May 21, 996, Gregory invested Otto with the imperial crown. However, after Otto returned to Germany, Crescentius drove Gregory from Rome and replaced him with John XVI. Otto then returned to Italy in late 997, and defeated and executed Crescentius and the twelve other leaders of the uprising. He deposed John XVI—gouging out his eyes, cutting off his tongue and nose, and parading him through the streets of Rome on an ass, face to the tail—and reinstated Gregory. Otto made Rome the capital and the administrative center of his empire, building a magnificent palace on the Aventine, clearly hoping to renew the Roman Empire in which the pope would be subordinate to the emperor in religious and secular affairs. For the remaining months of his life, Pope Gregory opposed Otto's project. Gregory died in 999, and Otto replaced him with his admired teacher and ideological partner, the brilliant scholar, mathematician, and inventor GERBERT OF AURILLAC, who would become Pope Sylvester II.

Gerbert had introduced Otto to the possibility of his becoming a second CONSTANTINE, uniting all of Christendom under one glorious theocratic rule. Otto took for himself the titles "emperor of the world" and "the servant of Jesus Christ," and revived ancient

Otto III, depicted in illumination in his copy of the Gospels.

Roman and Byzantine court rituals. This highly developed imperial ideology was not immediately embraced by the Roman and LOMBARD aristocracy, who ignored the emperor's high-minded rhetoric and suspected instead simply a plot to secure German-Byzantine rule over Italy. Additionally, Saxon nobles were angered that Otto's policies neglected Germany, and were engaged continuously in damaging rebellions during the final years of Otto's reign.

In addition to Gerbert, Otto was also greatly influenced by Archbishop Adelbert of PRAGUE, who convinced him of his responsibility to incorporate pagan eastern Europe into his Christian empire. In 1000, Otto made a pilgrimage to Gniezno, POLAND. As a gesture of good faith, he granted the Christian Polish ruler, Boleslaw the Brave, an honorary title, making him an ally of the empire. He also established the archbishopric of Esztergom the following year, and supported the election of a sympathetic Christian duke, Stephen, as king of HUNGARY. If he had lived longer, Otto might have created a civilized, stable Christian kingdom out of the great mass of east central Europe.

Later Years. In his final years, Otto's attention was turned back to Italy. In 1001, rebels in Tibur rebelled against his rule and laid siege to the town. Otto was able to suppress the uprising but pardoned Tibur, which offended the Romans, who wished to see the rival city punished. The Romans, mistrustful of Otto from the start, rebelled against him and laid siege to his palace. Otto escaped to the monastery of St. Apollinaris near Ravenna and requested military support from his cousin Henry of BAVARIA. While waiting for the Bavarian forces to arrive, he died suddenly on January 23, 1002, at the age of 22. There is an unsubstantiated legend that both Otto and Gerbert (who died a year later) were poisoned by Crescentius's widow Stephania, who had become Otto's mistress. Henry's Bavarian troops arrived at Otto's castle soon after his death, and Henry succeeded Otto as emperor. He abandoned many of Otto's policies, and concentrated more extensively on Germany. Thus, the possibility of a restored Roman empire, so promising during Otto's short reign, withered with his untimely death. (*See* GERMANY; ITALY; ROME; PAPACY.)

OTTOMAN TURKS

D erived from the name of the founder of the dynasty, OSMAN I, the Ottomans were only one of several Asian tribes that came out of the cow-herding plains and settled in ANATOLIA. What distinguished them, however, was the delicate balances they struck—between their commitment to the spread of ISLAM and their tolerance toward other peoples and faiths; between the uncompromising authority of the sultan, the monarch, and the authority extended to functionaries at every level of government and administration; between the clan loyalty of the Ottoman aristocracy and the easy assimilation of the nobility of conquered peoples into the power structure. These precarious tensions created an empire that covered vast territories around the Mediterranean and a continuous imperial state that lasted from the early fourteenth century until 1922, just after the First World War.

Establishing Rule. Osman established a base inside the SELJUK empire with the help of the ghazis, Muslim extremists who sought ways of fulfilling the Islamic precept of JIHAD, waging war against the infidel. A brotherhood was formed between this herder people and mounted Islamic warriors, with which Osman was able to depose the Seljuks and stand poised against the Byzantine Empire, all in the first quarter of the fourteenth century. (*See* OSMAN I; SELJUK TURKS.)

Later in the century, Sultan Murad I, using the famed Janissaries—young recruits actually abducted from Christian homes, converted to Islam, and indoctrinated and trained to serve the sultan—extended Ottoman rule to all of Asia Minor, thereby ending Byzantine presence there, and into the Balkans.

Warfare. At the invitation of John VI Cantacuzenus, the Ottomans crossed the Bosporus in 1352 and invaded Europe, taking Adrianople in 1357. The Ottomans next turned their attention to SERBIA (mindful of the MONGOL threat from the east), and defeated the Serbs at the first Battle of KOSOVO in 1389,

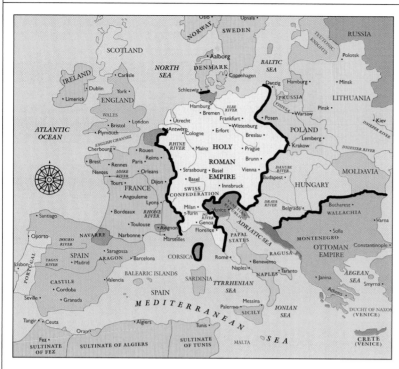

The Political Division of Europe in 1500. As the Middle Ages draw to a close, the map of Europe begins to take recognizable shape. England has been expelled from France (except for a single fortress); Constantinople has been taken by the Ottoman Turks, making them a threat to Europe for the next 200 years; and Maximilian I has solidified the Holy Roman Empire through the shrewd combination of military conquest and marital consolidation.

the sultan and his military bureaucracy, but the government was also receptive to the petitions of many groups in conquered lands. However, nearly every transition following the death of the sultan came about only through a fratricidal civil war, during which foreign enemies could nip at the outer territories and the military and nobility could consolidate their power. (*See* ANATOLIA.)

under the leadership of BEYEZID I. The fourteenth century ended with a massive Ottoman blockade of CONSTANTINOPLE and a crushing defeat of the Christian Crusade to lift it at Nicopolis in 1396.

Ottoman fortunes were temporarily set back when Beyezid was captured by the Mongol TAMERLANE at the Battle of Ankara in 1402. A struggle for succession fragmented the empire until control was reestablished by Muhammad I in 1413. Muhammad and his successor, MURAD II, reorganized the ghazis and resumed the conquest-engine that was the jihad.

The Ottomans quickly recognized that the political battles of the next century would be fought in the shipping lanes of the Mediterranean. They thus embarked on the long-term development of a navy, based at Gallipoli, that could challenge the Venetians on the high seas. VENICE attempted to forestall the Ottoman program, unsuccessfully attacking Gallipoli three times in the early 1400s.

In 1453, under Sultan Mehmed II the Conqueror, Constantinople, the Byzantine jewel, was captured by the Ottomans. Mehmed rebuilt the city into an even more splendid capital, renaming it Istanbul.

Meanwhile, the Ottoman push into Serbia had continued with a second Battle of Kosovo in 1446 in which Serbia fell. At mid-century, the Ottomans reigned over nearly all of Asia Minor and all of the Balkan states of Serbia and Bosnia. Now the sheer size of the empire made it unwieldy and further conquest impractical. (*See* ISLAM; CONSTANTINOPLE.)

The Ottoman state was highly centralized with

OXFORD PROVISIONS

T he document known as the Provisions of Oxford contained a series of limitations on royal power that the BARONS forced King HENRY III to accept at the Oxford PARLIAMENT of 1258. The barons, led by SIMON DE MONTFORT, earl of Leicester, were responding to Henry's governmental mismanagement and the heavy taxes he imposed to finance implementation of his son Edward's claim to the Sicilian crown. The barons made their money grants to him contingent on his acceptance of the provisions.

The provisions called for a council of 15 to advise the king and to meet three times a year with representatives of the realm, as well as for committees appointed to monitor various branches of government. The council would control the chancellor and treasury, and Henry could not act without its consent. The provisions also called for regular parliaments and the punishment of inept officials.

Henry was forced to accept the provisions because he needed to finance his Sicilian adventure. For several years the provisions kept the king's power in check, but baronial division allowed Henry to repudiate the provisions with papal approval in 1261. The civil war that followed, known as the Barons' War, ended with the king victorious. But the principle of constitutional limits on the power of the king had been established.

PAINTING

Compared to many other media in which artists worked in the Middle Ages, paint was inexpensive and readily available. Thus, all medieval cultures made use of painted decoration, from the seventh century Celtic manuscripts of Britain, such as the Lindisfarne Gospels and the BOOK OF KELLS, to the painted stucco reliefs of twelfth century Iran. While paint could be used for life-like depictions, it could also be used to mimic precious materials such as MOSAIC, marble, textiles, and metal.

Materials. Not all pigments were cheap, however. Particularly exquisite and lasting colors could be very costly and difficult to obtain, such as blue pigment made from lapis lazuli, purple murex dye made from shellfish, and gold ink, which required actual gold powder. These pigments, and the craftsmanship needed to prepare and apply them skillfully, could raise the value of painted objects, as was the case with manuscripts and European altarpieces. Like other luxury items such as spices and silks, rare pigments and dyes were widely traded in the medieval period.

The most commonly used binding agent to make pigments adhere to a surface was clarified egg-white, although plant gums, glues, and sizing of various kinds were also employed, especially for gilding. The encaustic technique, which used wax as a binding medium and which goes back as far as the late antique Egyptian mummy portraits, continued to be used as late as the sixth century in Byzantine icons. Oil as a binding medium appeared in the fifteenth century.

It was common in most types of painting and gilding to prepare the surface with one or more coats of gesso, a water-based paint made of glue and plaster, chalk, or gypsum. This substance provided a smooth, white support on any surface, to which the paint or gold foil could easily adhere. On porous wooden panels, many layers of gesso would be applied to create the desired smooth painting surface.

Forms. By the Middle Ages, painting was considered a highly skilled craft, and by the late Middle Ages, painters were organized into city-based GUILDS. The major forms of painting during the medieval period were MANU-SCRIPT ILLUMINATION, or book painting, wall painting,

and painting on wooden panels, although paint was also applied to cloth and three-dimensional objects. Particularly in the GOTHIC period (1150–1500), with the reduction of wall surface due to arches and colonnades, polychrome was applied to any available surface, such as capitals, ornamental details, and statues. Only traces of this work remain.

Book painting has a long history, starting as far back as the first century B.C.E., with the earliest recorded evidence of a codex, or book as we know it, with separate pages bound together and a cover. The first documented illustrated codex is from the fourth century, but actual surviving fragments date only from the sixth century. These early illustrations drew heavily on the traditions of Roman wall paintings, but gradually, medieval book illustrators developed their own distinctive regional styles. In the West, up until the thirteenth century, manuscript illumination was the exclusive province of ecclesiastics laboring in the scriptoria of monasteries, but by the fourteenth century in France, a culmination of book illustration had been reached by secular artists. In these manuscripts, such as the *Très Riches Heures* commissioned by the Duc de Berry, the vivid color rivals STAINED GLASS, while delicate, naturalistic drawings indicate a high refinement in the painter's expertise. (*See* STAINED GLASS; MANU-SCRIPT ILLUMINATION; MOSAICS. *Also* SCULPTURE.)

Wall painting on plaster walls involved two different techniques. One is called fresco ("fresh" in Italian), where the artist paints on wet plaster. The other

"The Dream of Life," from a fresco painting by Orcagna, in the cloister of Campo Santo, Pisa, 14th century.

is secco ("dry" in Italian) where the artist paints on dry plaster. Frescoes tend to survive better, as the paint bonds with the wet plaster. Like most other art forms in the Middle Ages, most wall paintings were done in places of worship, to decorate the House of God and to tell stories from the Scriptures. There were wall paintings as far back as the early Christian period, in the Catacombs, even before they decorated churches.

In BYZANTIUM, many of the medieval painted churches have been destroyed. Some surviving examples, such as the interiors of the eleventh-century rock-cut churches of Cappadocia in modern Turkey and the twelfth-century church paintings in Nerezi, Macedonia, are impressive reminders of the talents of Byzantine wall painters.

The Islamic world's restrictions on the use of figural art led to a distinctive painting style, dependent on geometric shapes and plant life for subject matter. The universal Islamic motif, the arabesque, is the most characteristic example of this style. One of the few remaining examples of Islamic wall painting is the dome painted with the constellations, at the eighth century desert palace of Qusayr Amrah in Syria.

Romanesque. Painting on wooden panels had a long pre-medieval history, especially around the Mediterranean. This tradition continued in the Byzantine territories in the form of ICONS, or portable religious portraits. In Europe, in the ROMANESQUE period (500–1150), wooden panel paintings were used to decorate the fronts of altars, commonly depicting a central tableau flanked by figures of saints. It is probably from these altar frontals that the earliest altarpiece developed in the eleventh and twelfth centuries. The importation of Byzantine icons to the West in the thirteenth century had a great influence on the shape and style of altarpieces, especially in ITALY. By the fourteenth century, these altarpieces had expanded into huge panels with numerous accessory scenes, although in northern Europe, they remained simpler. Byzantine influence can also be seen in the increasing numbers of small panels produced for private devotion in the fifteenth century and in the proliferation of the iconostasis, a tall screen of icons, in the Russian churches. Small panels were also used for portraits in the Gothic period, and larger panels decorated furniture and wainscoting. (*See* ROMANESQUE; GOTHIC ART.)

Painted textile decorations, like banners, shrouds, and wall hangings, were quick and inexpensive to make, and were decorative replacements for precious embroidery and tapestries. They were used for festivals and temporary displays and then disposed of, which is why so few examples survive in spite of ample documentary evidence indicating that painted cloth was commonly used. The use of stretched canvas as a support for painting began only in the fifteenth century.

PAPACY

The papacy is the bishopric of ROME, which claims to be the father (*papa*) of the Church. This claim is based on the Petrine doctrine, which has two components: first, that Jesus, as recounted in Chapter 16 of the Gospel of Matthew, made one of his twelve disciples, Simon Peter, the Vicar of Christ on Earth, the rock (Peter) upon which the Church was built with the power of the keys for opening and closing the gates of the Kingdom of Heaven; and second, that Peter (as well as St. Paul) ended up in Rome, was its first bishop, and thereby established the papal office and religious authority in which all of Peter's successors in Rome participated. Whether Jesus so designated Peter is plausible but uncertain. Whether Peter ended up in Rome (Paul did) is much less certain, since Peter opposed Paul's policy of opening up the Church to Gentiles; as one who wanted the Church to be a Jewish community, he was not likely to settle in Rome. This Petrine doctrine cannot be authenticated earlier than the second century C.E.; it was made fashionable by Pope Leo the Great in the fifth century. In 1953, the bones of St. Peter were purportedly found under a papal building in Rome and this claim is widely believed by Roman Catholics today. (The bones have been dated to the first century.)

Down to the ascension of the first Christian emperor CONSTANTINE I THE GREAT in 312, the pope had a great deal of prestige in and around Rome, perhaps generally in Italy, and possibly elsewhere in the West, but among the majority of Greek-speaking Christians in the eastern Mediterranean, he was not recognized as supreme to the four Greek patriarchs. In the fourth century, the pope was overshadowed by Constantine and his Christian imperial successors. In Church matters, in fact, Constantine relied upon the advice of a Palestinian Greek bishop and a Spanish Latin bishop, not the pope.

Ascension. The papacy rose to prominence in the fifth century with the downfall of the western Roman Empire. The pope in effect replaced the emperor as the chief official in Rome, responsible for importing grain and feeding the rapidly declining population, as well as negotiating with the German invaders and the Byzantine emperors. This was still the precarious position of the papacy in the 590s when GREGORY I THE GREAT became pope. His activism, missionary commitments, administrative competence, and political skill raised papal visibility in the West. Still, historians have pointed out that a history of the Church in FRANCE until the early eighth century could be written without any mention of the pope. The big change occurred in the 740s when the ambitious CAROLINGIAN family needed papal blessing to replace the old MEROVINGIAN dynasty as rulers of the Frankish empire. But under CHARLEMAGNE and his immediate successors in the eighth and ninth centuries, the frustrated pope again took a subsidiary position compared to the Carolingian leadership in both Church and state. The only accomplishment of the papacy in the Carolingian era was gaining imperial recognition of the PAPAL STATES, the Patrimony of St. Peter, in central Italy—which remained in existence until 1871 and of which the few square miles of Vatican City today are a remnant.

Reform. The same marginality of the papacy occurred under the Ottonian and Salian rulers of the first German empire in the tenth and first half of the eleventh century. Because of civil war in GERMANY in the 1060s and 1070s the papacy under cardinal Hildebrand (later pope GREGORY VII) was able to assert its independence from the German emperor and greatly expand and strengthen papal government in Rome. The College of Cardinals in Rome became the center of an international administrative system.

The Gregorian reform movement had a deep impact on family life, the discipline and literacy of the clergy, the codification of canon law, and the general advancement of learning and piety. But the high medieval papacy of the twelfth and thirteenth centuries remained in an almost constant tension with and conflict against European rulers to keep its independence in Italy and to guide and influence the national churches north of the Alps. These incessant struggles further transformed the papacy into a vast international bureaucracy and legal and TAXATION system centered on Rome, and by the mid-thirteenth century, the papacy showed more political power and administrative skill than spiritual leadership.

The Great Schism. Growing popular resentment and criticism from many intellectuals put the papacy in a weak position when confronted by the power and ruthless cynicism of the French monarchy in the first decade of the fourteenth century. The papacy became a puppet of the French monarchy and took up residence in AVIGNON, just across the French border. An effort to return the papacy to Rome resulted in the GREAT SCHISM of 1378 to 1418, when there were scandalously two, and even at one point, three competing popes.

Return to Rome. Under the aegis of Church reformers—who thought that the ultimate decision-making power in the Church should reside in periodic universal Church councils—and with the help of the German emperor, the papacy was restored to Rome. But the pope repudiated the conciliar movement and in the fifteenth century tried again to rule in the absolutist manner of the thirteenth century. The pope contributed to the rebuilding and beautification of Rome, now again a metropolis; he now became an important patron of the arts. In Italy, he was a political power. However, north of the Alps, his role in Church life was diminished in the fifteenth century in the face of royal power and the autonomous inclination of the great bishops. When a small group of German princes chose to support the revolt against Rome led by Martin Luther around 1520, the pope was powerless to stop this fragmenting of the Church, which spread rapidly until it embraced 40 percent of Europe's population during the sixteenth century

See CHRISTIANITY; GREAT SCHISM; PAPAL STATES; ROME; *and* AVIGNON. *A list of popes, indicating which have entries, appears in the Index. See also* CRUSADES; EASTERN ORTHODOX CHURCH; GREGORY I THE GREAT.

Pope Urban II presiding over the Council of Clermont in 1095, issuing a call for a crusade to free the Holy Land from Arab rule. From a 15th-century illumination.

PAPAL STATES

T he Papal States comprised a band of medieval territory centering on ROME and running across the peninsula about 200 miles north and south of the Eternal City. The popes also held large private estates in SICILY and from the fourteenth century in AVIGNON in southern FRANCE, but strictly speaking these were not part of the Papal States, whose official title was the Patrimony of St. Peter. The Papal States, much shrunken in size, had a post-medieval history and endured until the unification of the modern Italian Republic in 1871, and in a sense even until today; the few square miles of Vatican City in the heart of Rome technically constitute an independent country. This is recognized by the Italian government and other governments like the United States, which sends a special ambassador to the Vatican. It was not so recognized by the Germans in World War II, making it difficult for Pope Pius XII to provide refuge to Jews in the Vatican.

The Patrimony of Saint Peter did not officially come into existence until the middle of the eighth century, although the PAPACY had effectively been ruling Rome and its environs since the disappearance of the Roman emperor in ITALY around 450 C.E. In the eighth century, the papacy aimed to legalize its territory as an independent state and hopefully increase its size by producing a forged legal document called the Donation of Constantine. In this document, CONSTANTINE I THE GREAT comes down with dreaded LEPROSY in the second decade of the fourth century, and is cured by Pope Sylvester I. In gratitude, Constantine, in the Donation document, withdraws from Rome to found a new capital in the East at BYZANTIUM and cedes all of Italy (in some versions all of western Europe) to the papacy. After the Roman scribe John the Mangled-Fingers forged the Donation of Constantine, the papacy tried to sell its genuineness to the powerful CAROLINGIAN rulers, who held a loose control over northern Italy as well as ruling France and parts of western GERMANY. The resulting compromise, the Donation of PÉPIN (named after the Carolingian ruler) was formal recognition of the Patrimony of Saint Peter, the territorial belt centering on Rome.

From about 1160 to 1250, the papacy spent much of its time and money forming alliances and raising armies to keep the Holy Roman (German) emperors from swallowing up the Papal States, thus—so the popes feared—eroding papal authority. In 1500, there still existed a (reduced) Patrimony of Saint Peter, despite the fact that in the late fifteenth century the Donation of Constantine was proven to be a forgery by the Italian humanist Lorenzo Valla. Valla was by no means the first medieval scholar to suspect the authenticity of the Donation. Others, like Dante, recognized its existence but cursed it, causing the papacy to become entangled in political, military, and material affairs. (*See* PAPACY; HOLY ROMAN EMPIRE; CAROLINGIAN DYNASTY; CONSTANTINE I; ITALY; ROME; AVIGNON.)

PARIS

M edieval Paris was simultaneously the political capital of FRANCE, its commercial center, and the greatest intellectual and artistic city in northern Europe.

Beginnings. Paris began as a small Roman settlement on the Seine River. Saint Denis introduced CHRISTIANITY there in the late 200s, and legend has it that a threatened attack by ATTILA THE HUN was averted by a combination of the Roman general AETIUS and the fervent prayers of St. Geneviève, later designated the city's patron saint. The MEROVINGIAN king CLOVIS I captured Paris and made it his capital in 508. However, after Chilperic moved the capital in 567, Paris lapsed into obscurity. The VIKINGS sailed up the Seine and sacked Paris several times in the 800s.

The history of Paris changed dramatically in 987 when HUGH CAPET, duke of Paris, became king and made Paris the permanent capital of France. Under the CAPETIAN DYNASTY, the size and prosperity of Paris increased greatly as settlements around the Île de la Cité grew in size and linked together. In the eleventh century, the city spread out on the right bank of the Seine where merchant GUILDS formed and stimulated the growth of COMMERCE AND TRADE. Construction in the city continued in the twelfth century with the rebuilding of NOTRE DAME that began in 1163. Cathedral schools on the left bank of the Seine made that part of Paris the center of the city's intellectual life. The UNIVERSITY, which was to give Paris its distinct character, grew out of those cathedral schools. Recognized by PHILIP II AUGUSTUS in 1200, the University of Paris became a great European center of theology, attracting great theologians such as PETER ABELARD.

During the reign of Philip II Augustus, Paris began to greatly surpass the other cities of northern France. Philip built a wall around the expanded city, paved the streets, and constructed the Louvre palace. He also concentrated the city's markets at Les Halles and constructed buildings for them there. SAINT LOUIS IX built the impressive Sainte-Chapelle to house his collection of sacred relics. His chaplain, Robert de Sorbon, founded the city's first university college, which was opened in 1253 and was named the Sorbonne in his honor. During the thirteenth and fourteenth centuries, the University of Paris won intellectual distinction throughout Europe with outstanding teachers and scholars such as ALBERTUS MAGNUS and THOMAS AQUINAS.

Beginning in the second half of the fourteenth century, Paris suffered a reversal in its fortunes. THE HUNDRED YEARS' WAR, the conflict between the city's Burgundian and Armagnac factions, and the disruption and decline of commerce reduced the population and reversed the prosperity of the city. The English attacked the city regularly and occupied it from 1419 to 1436. Popular resistance to English rule allowed CHARLES VII of France to regain Paris in April 1436. However, it was not until the reign of Francis I (1515–1547) that the city's decline was stemmed and its restoration as a center of politics, commerce, arts, and letters began. (*See* FRANCE; UNIVERSITIES; HUGH CAPET; LOUIS IX; NOTRE-DAME; CHARLES VII.)

Paris as portrayed in the Beauvais Tapestry, 15th century. (Notre Dame Cathedral, top, center, stands not yet completed.)

PARIS, MATTHEW

The historic chronicles of Matthew Paris (died 1259), *Chronica majora,* provide a roughly accurate and colorful (if not slanted) account of medieval history in the twelfth and thirteenth centuries. Their rich detail makes them one of the most important historical records of the Middle Ages.

Matthew Paris was probably born in the late twelfth century, and he was admitted as a Benedictine monk at the Abbey of St. Albans, ENGLAND, in 1217. He spent the rest of his life there, but he often traveled. In 1248, he ventured to NORWAY to reform the monastery St. Benet Holm.

Sometime around 1235, Paris began work on the *Chronica majora,* which picks up where the earlier *Flowers of History* by Roger Wendover had left off, at the mid-eleventh century. Paris incorporated the observations he made during his travels, and used a variety of historical documents, some of which appear in an appendix. He knew King Henry III, the Earl of Cornwall, and several important figures, and his works include information obtained directly from them.

Paris wrote several abridged versions of *Chronica majora.* His very frank and opinionated style made these works very popular. Kings and nobles wanted to be remembered well in the history books, and gave Paris access to important places with the hopes of being written about in a favorable and memorable light. Paris also was a fine artist who illuminated his manuscripts with magnificently detailed drawings and sketches.

In addition to his chronicles, Paris wrote biographies on such individuals as Saint Alban, THOMAS BECKET, Edmund Rich, and EDWARD THE CONFESSOR. He also wrote a history of his monastery. Paris's works are noted for their rich detail, as well as for their author's unvarnished opinions on the Church and the nobility. Paris continued to work on his histories until he died at St. Albans in 1259. (*See* CHRONICLES; LITERATURE OF THE MIDDLE AGES.)

PARLIAMENT

During the late Middle Ages, the English Parliament (a "parleying" or meeting of the king with his ministers and assorted nobles and Church prelates to discuss matters of state) emerged as an assembly with considerable political power. The term was first used in the 1230s to describe the king's *Curia Regis,* a convocation of nobles and prelates summoned to advise the king; by 1350 it had developed into the House of Lords. Three times in the 1250s and 1260s county representatives were also summoned, as were burgesses in 1265. These county and town representatives who met separately from the nobles and prelates were the embryo of what developed by 1350 into the House of Commons. During the reign of King EDWARD I, Parliament took more definite shape. Edward's Parliament of 1295 included nobles, prelates, two knights from each county, two burgesses from each town, and representatives of the lower clergy. Around 1330, the lower clergy among the MPs (Members of Parliament) met in their own assembly. In Edward I's view, Parliament had three functions—judicial, fiscal (approving new taxes), and as a sounding board for royal policy and propaganda.

In the 1300s, Parliament increased its leverage over the king by withholding support for royal taxes until the king acted on certain petitions. Beginning with the reign of EDWARD II, consent of Parliament became a prerequisite for the formal enactment of statutes. When Edward was deposed in 1327, Parliament declared the action legal. The Good Parliament of 1376 conducted the first impeachment proceeding (against Lord Latimer and Richard Lyons for corruption) and also produced the first speaker of the Commons, Sir Peter de la Mare. By the end of the Middle Ages, the considerable influence and power of Parliament made it a formidable force in English politics.

Representative estate assemblies like the English Parliament were common in the thirteenth and fourteenth centuries. By 1500, only the estate of ARAGON in Spain and the English Parliament survived. The Aragon assembly was suppressed in the early sixteenth century, while the English Parliament flourished because King Henry VIII needed it to provide judicial legitimacy for the Reformation. (*See* ENGLAND; ARAGON; EDWARD I; EDWARD II.)

PASTON FAMILY

A prosperous eastern Norfolk family of the fifteenth century that left the largest known collection of English correspondence from their time. Discovered in 1735, the collection contains private letters, legal records, wills, and petitions and is now preserved in the British Museum.

The author of the earliest letter (from 1425) is William Paston I (1378–1444), a successful lawyer and a justice of the Court of Common Pleas. His son, John I (1421–1466), was also a lawyer and produced (or received) the bulk of the letters in the collection, many of which were to or from his wife, Margaret Mautby. The correspondence also includes the documents of John's two eldest sons, John II (1442–1479) and John III (1444–1504). Many of these letters concern Sir John Fastolf, a nobleman for whom both John I and John II

served as legal executors and for whose property both were involved in a number of nasty disputes over. The letters show a wealthy gentry family trying to survive during the volatile conditions of the era of the WARS OF THE ROSES.

Besides revealing much about domestic life and about regional and even national events during the reigns of HENRY VI, EDWARD IV, and RICHARD III, the letters hold great importance for philologists, and afford a glimpse at a crucial state in the development of the ENGLISH LANGUAGE. The letters were originally published in 1787, 1798, and 1823. They were republished in a more complete edition by James Gardiner in 1872–1875. (*See* CHRONICLES.)

PATRICK, ST.

E nough historical evidence co-exists with the legends that surround the life of St. Patrick (c. 385–c. 461) to construct the main outlines of his life and confirm the major contribution he made to the Christianization of IRELAND.

Patrick was born sometime between 385 and 390 in Britain at a place called Bannavem Taberniae, whose location today remains unknown, to a Christian family that possessed Roman citizenship. His father was an urban official, and his grandfather was a priest. When Patrick was about 16 years old, raiders captured him and took him to Ireland where they sold him into slavery. Patrick spent the next six years in Ireland forced to work as a herdsman. He escaped and returned home to his family briefly before he continued to Europe.

His Travels. Patrick traveled through Gaul, where he probably visited the monastery of St. Martin at Marmoutier. He entered the monastery at Lerins and stayed there long enough to receive his tonsure. About 413, he left the monastery and returned to Britain where he lived for several years with his relatives. During that time, Patrick had a vision and heard a divine voice telling him to return to Ireland and Christianize its people. To prepare himself for his mission, Patrick returned to Europe and spent twelve years studying and training at Auxerre.

In 431, Pope Celestine I chose Palladius to be the first missionary bishop to Ireland, but Palladius died shortly after he arrived. Germanus of Auxerre quickly consecrated Patrick a bishop and the Church sent him to Ireland as Palladius's replacement. Patrick landed in Ireland near Saul and remained there through the winter until spring when he went to Tara. At Tara, Patrick achieved success by gaining his first converts, who became the nucleus of his missionary team. He boldly challenged the local pagan priests by lighting an Easter fire on a nearby hill, an action which the court of the king of Tara reacted to at first with indignation, but then with respect and interest.

Spreading Christianity. After the king accepted CHRISTIANITY, Patrick made Tara the base of his operations and converted Meath, Leitrim, Cavan, and much of western Ireland. About 445, Patrick won the backing of Pope Leo I to establish an archbishopric at Armagh. Patrick, who spent more than 30 years preaching Christianity to the Irish, understood the social structure of the people and used it to his advantage to convert them tribe by tribe.

Patrick's organization of the Church according to tribal units helped establish the Celtic abbot-bishop system of Church government. Patrick succeeded in having the traditional tribal laws of Ireland codified according to Christian values, mollifying the harsher ones, especially those having to do with slaves and taxing the poor. Patrick is also believed to have introduced the Roman alphabet to Ireland.

In 457 Patrick retired to Saul, where he had first set foot on the island, and lived his last years there. His burial place at Downpatrick was a famous European shrine until 1539 when the English government, finding its popularity worrisome, had it destroyed.

Much of what we know about Patrick's life and career come from the writings he left behind. The primary source of information about his life is to be found in his *Confessio*. It is alleged that Patrick was prompted to write it to defend himself against an accusation which originated when he told a friend about a sin he had committed in his youth. When the friend told others and it raised a question about Patrick's fitness, Patrick wrote his apologia in which he expressed his disappointment over the accusations calling into question all the good work he had done in Ireland. In his *Confessio* Patrick wrote simply and movingly about his personal belief that God had called him to his mission, to which he gladly and faithfully devoted his life.

In addition to *Confessio*, Patrick wrote *Lorica* (*Breastplate*), a mystical, devotional poem written in Irish and Latin, a work sometimes called *The Cry of the Deer*. He also wrote *Letter to the Soldiers of Coroticus*, an angry attack against British slave traders and the clergy who did little to stop the trade. (*See* IRELAND.)

PEACE OF GOD; TRUCE OF GOD

The medieval Catholic Church was not above using WARFARE to further its aims. But it also appreciated the destructiveness of war. The Peace of God (*Pax Ecclesiae*) and the Truce of God (*Treuga Dei*) were created to limit the damage of war.

A 14th-century miniature of a legend associated with St. Patrick, "The Purgatory of St. Patrick," in which Jesus leads Patrick to a cave that is the entrance to hell.

The Peace of God dates from the tenth century. It was discussed at three Church synods in the French towns of Charroux, Narbonne, and Puy; with the support of Duke William V of AQUITAINE, it was adopted at the councils of Limoges in 994 and Poitiers in 999.

Essentially, the Peace of God prohibited acts of war or violence against any property owned by the Church and against members of the clergy and pilgrims. Merchants, peasants, and women of all ranks were also protected under the Peace of God. Farm equipment (including livestock) was covered as well.

To ensure that people followed the Peace of God, all men were required to take an oath stating that they would observe and enforce the decree. In 1038, the archbishop of Bourges decreed during the council held there that all Christian men aged 15 and above should take the oath, and then enlist in the diocesan forces.

The Truce of God dates back to the early eleventh century. The Synod of Elne, held in 1027, prohibited all warfare from Saturday night until Monday; this was extended to cover the period between Wednesday evening to Monday morning in 1042. Battle was also forbidden during Lent, Advent, the vigils and feasts of the Virgin Mary, and many other religious feast days.

The concept was adopted in FLANDERS at the Synod of Therouanne in 1063, and in Germany by the bishop of Liège in 1082. In 1085 a synod in Mainz established the concept over the entire HOLY ROMAN EMPIRE, and in 1089 southern Italy adopted the Truce of God as well. The COUNCIL OF CLERMONT decreed in 1095 that all adult males must take an oath accepting the truce. (*See* WARFARE; CHIVALRY; PAPACY.)

PEASANTS' REVOLTS

The Peasants' Revolts were occasional outbreaks of violent rebellion by the medieval peasant class. Though such revolts were relatively rare, the ruling kings and nobles lived in fear that the overwhelming majority of the population, the peasantry, would rise up. Free peasants and SERFS lived lives of oppression and drudgery, laboring from morning to night for barely a subsistence living. The Peasants' Revolts tended to break out during times of economic distress or when the nobility curtailed the liberties or privileges of the peasantry. Important revolts included the JACQUERIE in FRANCE (1358) and the British uprising in ENGLAND led by WAT TYLER in 1381.

The Jacquerie was fueled by the economic problems caused by the BLACK DEATH and the turmoil following the capture of the French King John II by the English. The ensuing wave of peasant violence, under the leadership of Guillaume Cale, led to a number of victories. The uprising was eventually crushed by the nobles of Picardy, led by the king of NAVARRE, Charles II the Bald. In the carnage that resulted, great masses of peasants were indiscriminantly slaughtered.

PEPIN III THE SHORT

Pépin III (714–768), known as Pépin the Short, was the son of CHARLES MARTEL, the father of CHARLEMAGNE, and the first CAROLINGIAN king of the FRANKS (751–768). He expanded the borders of the Frankish domain and formed an alliance with the popes in ROME that shaped the future of both the Frankish kingdom and the PAPACY.

Rise to Power. In 741, Pépin and his older brother Carloman succeeded and inherited the title of "mayor of the palace" from their father, Charles Martel, who had defeated the Muslim invaders from SPAIN. Soon, however, Pépin, who ruled Neustria, BURGUNDY, and Provence, and his brother, who ruled

Austrasia and what later became Thuringia, were also calling themselves "dukes and princes of the Franks." To ease the concern of other Frankish leaders worried about the brothers' growing power, in 743 the brothers had the MEROVINGIAN Childeric III named as nominal king of the Franks while they continued to exercise the real power.

His Reign. In 747, Carloman withdrew from politics and retired to the monastery of Monte Carlo to live a religious life. Deciding to declare himself king of the Franks, Pépin sent two Frankish Church leaders, a bishop and an abbot, to Rome to win the support of Pope Zacharias I. With the full backing of the Church and PAPACY, Pépin forced Childeric, the last titular Merovingian king and heir of CLOVIS I, to retire to a monastery. In November 751, at an assembly of Franks in Soissons, Pépin had himself proclaimed king. At the coronation ceremony, the ANGLO-SAXON monk Boniface, acting as the pope's representative, anointed Pépin in what was to be the first papal anointing of a Frankish king. (*See* CORONATION.)

Soon the new pope, Stephen II, who wished to be independent of the Byzantine Empire and the LOMBARDS, who were expanding their rule in ITALY, called on Pépin for help. In the winter of 753–754 after the Lombards forced Pope Stephen II to leave Rome, the

French fresco of the coronation of Pépin III the Short in 751, conducted by Boniface, who was acting as the pope's representative.

pope visited Pépin. That summer in a ceremony in the abbey church of SAINT-DENIS near Paris he anointed Pépin and also his two sons Charles (later Charlemagne) and Carloman. The pope formally declared that from that day forward the Franks were never to elect a king who was not of the sacred lineage of Pépin. He also bestowed on Pépin and his sons the ancient title of "patrician of the Romans."

In return for Pope Stephen's support, Pépin took his army to Italy to do battle against the Lombards. After he liberated the exarchate of RAVENNA and other Lombard cities, he presented their keys to Pope Stephen. Pépin's gift of a wide strip of land in central Italy to the pope became known as the "Donation of Pépin." The land, called the PAPAL STATES, remained under the rule of the popes until the unification of Italy in the nineteenth century. (*See* FRANKS; CHARLEMAGNE; CAROLINGIAN DYNASTY.)

PETER DAMIAN, ST.

eter Damian (1007–1072) was a key figure in the Church reform movement of the eleventh century. He was a doctor of the Church, an honorary title given to him by Pope Leo XII, reserved for those who are considered particularly adept at expressing Church doctrine.

He was born in RAVENNA, Italy, and educated there, as well as at Faenza and Parma. In 1035, after a brief career as a teacher, he became a member of the hermitage of Fonte Avellana, in the Apennines; he remained there for the rest of his life. He was named prior of the hermitage in 1043, and became a cardinal in 1057. Over the next 15 years, he served three popes.

He proved a tireless reformer, promoting poverty for clerics and celibacy for the clergy. He was a staunch opponent of the practice of buying and selling Church office, known as simony. He expressed his views often and earned a reputation for candor, yet he could be a skilled diplomat; he negotiated a reconciliation between the town of Ravenna and Pope Alexander II, who had excommunicated the town's archbishop.

PETER III THE GREAT

eter III (1239–1285) was the king of ARAGON, count of BARCELONA from 1276 until his death, and king of SICILY from 1282.

Son and successor of the Aragonese king James I, Peter aided his father in the Christian reconquest of SPAIN. However, his marriage in 1262 to Constance, daughter and heir of Manfred HOHENSTAUFEN, king of Sicily, drew him eastward and laid the foundation for Aragonese claims to Sicily and southern Italy. CHARLES OF ANJOU, a supporter of the pope, replaced Manfred as king of Sicily, but Charles ruled the kingdom with such a heavy hand that discontented islanders looking for outside help encouraged Peter to pursue his claim to the throne through his wife. Peter supported the rebels in their uprising against Charles, and after the insurrection of the SICILIAN VESPERS against Charles's rule in 1282, Peter took possession of the island and expelled the ANGEVINS over papal objections.

Pope Martin IV excommunicated Peter and declared that he was deprived of his states on the basis of the declaration of vassalage to the Holy See made by his grandfather, Peter II. The pope then granted the Sicilian throne to the son of the French king and helped organize a crusade against Aragon with the help of King Philip III of FRANCE. The French invaded Catalonia, but the crusade was stopped by Peter on land and defeated at sea by ROGER OF LORIA. An epidemic and the deaths of both Philip III and Charles of Anjou also contributed to the crusade's failure.

Peter's adventures in Sicily were unpopular with the Aragonese; to appease them, Peter was compelled to grant extensive privileges to the nobility and townspeople. One of Peter's greatest achievements was his founding of the first university in Aragon at Huesca.

Peter died in 1285 with his kingdoms secure. His oldest son, Alfonso III, succeeded him in Aragon, while in Sicily he was succeeded by his second son, James (later James II of Aragon).

PETER THE HERMIT

eter the Hermit (c. 1050–1115) was a French preacher and the leader of the so-called Peasants' Crusade of 1096. Following Pope URBAN II's call for a CRUSADE, Peter left his life of solitude and preached the crusade to the lower classes. Peter's skills as an orator allowed him to quickly inspire the peasants who joined the crusade to the Holy Land en masse. After gathering peasant forces in FRANCE and GERMANY, he led them through HUNGARY and BULGARIA into CONSTANTINOPLE. From there, they crossed to Asia Minor where Peter lost control of the throng. When he returned to Constantinople to ask for assistance from the emperor, the peasant crusaders were ambushed and slaughtered by the Turks, ending the Peasants' Crusade. The few survivors, along with Peter, joined the crusading army of GODFREY DE BOUILLON in 1097. (*See* CRUSADES.)

In early 1098, during the siege of Antioch, Peter attempted to desert the Crusade and return to France but was caught and brought back to the army in dis-

Peter the Hermit (far left) reports to Pope Urban II.

grace. He redeemed himself somewhat when he became an envoy to the Muslim army later in 1098. His preaching and support before the final assault on Jerusalem inspired the crusaders and Peter finally entered the Holy Land with the victorious crusaders in 1099. A year after the capture of Jerusalem, Peter returned to Europe where he established an Augustinian monastery in Belgium, becoming its first prior. He remained in that position until his death in 1115.

PETER LOMBARD

Peter Lombard (c. 1095–1160) is the author of *Sententiarum libri IV* (*Four Books of Sentences*), which became the standard theological text in colleges and UNIVERSITIES from the twelfth century well into the Renaissance.

Born in Lombardy, he was taught at Bologna, Reims, and PARIS. He taught theology at the school at NOTRE DAME in Paris and was ordained in 1144.

He attended the Council of Reims in 1148 and shortly thereafter began work on *Sententiarum*. Upon its completion in 1151, it was so well received that Lombard was thereafter known as *magister sententiarum* (master of the sentences). Among the subjects covered in the text are the Ten Commandments, sin and redemption, and the sacraments. Lombard's work is particularly noted for the way in which he clarified the sacraments and what they mean.

Lombard continued his theological studies, and in 1159 he was named Bishop of Paris.

PETER THE VENERABLE

Peter the Venerable (c. 1092–1156), also called Peter of Montboissier, was a noted twelfth–century theologian who, as abbot of the monastery at Cluny established himself as a strong leader and a powerful intellect.

Born in the French town of Montboissier, he was elected abbot of the Cluny monastery in 1122. Cluny had been one of the most important religious sites in Europe, but by the time Peter became abbot it had lost some of its influence. Under Peter's tenure, Cluny's reputation rose to new heights.

Peter was known for his keen administrative and diplomatic skills, his kind demeanor, and his gifts as a writer. Because of his talents, Cluny became the most influential of the over 2,000 MONASTERIES throughout Europe. Peter befriended PETER ABELARD after he had been condemned at the Council of Sens in 1140 and arranged a reconciliation of sorts between Abelard and two of his strongest foes, Pope Innocent II and ST. BERNARD OF CLAIRVAUX. He worked to transform the CRUSADES; instead of fighting to spread CHRISTIANITY, he believed, it would be more effective for Christians to travel as missionaries and convert the Muslims. He commissioned a Latin translation of the KORAN, which he studied carefully, hoping an understanding of ISLAM would help him and other Christians convince Muslims to convert. Peter was thereby the founder of Islamic studies in the Latin Christian world.

A prolific writer, he penned numerous treatises, sermons, hymns, and poems. Some 200 of his letters also survive.

PETRARCH

Although Petrarch (1304–1374) wrote during the late Middle Ages, this scholarly, well-traveled, prolific writer composed works that influenced learning and LITERATURE long after his death. In addition to poetry, Petrarch wrote hundreds of letters that provide a vivid picture of late medieval life as seen through the eyes of a scholar and traveler. His love of classical literature had an enormous impact on the study of the humanities. (*See* LITERATURE.)

Early Life. Petrarch, whose real name was Francesco Petrarca, was born in the central Italian town of Arezzo. His father, a minor civic official, was a friend of DANTE ALIGHIERI. The family moved to AVIGNON (which had recently become the seat of the Roman Catholic Church), where Petrarch's father hoped to procure a position in the papal court. Petrarch was sent to Montpellier, FRANCE, to study law in 1316. He went to ITALY to continue his studies at the University of Bologna, but gave them up to return to Avignon upon the death of his father in 1326.

Petrarch and his brother had been left a comfortable inheritance, and they spent the next few years living well. But although he enjoyed good living, he was not a squanderer. He replaced his law studies with writing and literary studies. He traveled widely, making the acquaintance of other writers.

Inspiration. On Good Friday, 1327, Petrarch spotted a beautiful woman in church who would become the inspiration for much of his poetry. The true identify of the woman, whom he called Laura, is unknown—nor is it known what, if any, relationship he had with her. (He did father several illegitimate children, one of whom cared for him in his old age.) But Laura served as the theme for much of his poetic output. Many of his poems celebrate her beauty and goodness; others profess his total devotion to her.

Partly to satisfy his thirst for knowledge (and perhaps to help take his mind off Laura), Petrarch spent the years 1330 to 1340 engaged in intense study and frequent travel. He studied classical Latin, and visited France, FLANDERS, and the Rhineland, where he met many scholars, adding to his growing collection of old manuscripts. He first visited ROME in 1337.

By now Petrarch's reputation as a scholar had spread throughout Europe, and he was invited in 1340 to become poet laureate of Rome. He continued to rely heavily on classical writers for inspiration, but also sought out more contemporary inspiration. In the ensuing years he would be molded by his own spiritual crises, the discovery of more antique manuscripts, his continued travel, and the effects of the Black Death, which some scholars believe may have claimed the life of Laura in 1348. He wrote prolifically, continued his scholarship, and went on several diplomatic missions for Rome. The writer BOCCACCIO became one of his closest friends.

Petrarch was an avid collector of scholarly manuscripts and he amassed a library of classical literature that included a number of Greek manuscripts, particularly of Plato's writings, though he never learned to read Greek.

Joos van Wassenhove's portrait of the Italian writer Petrarch hangs in the Palazzo Ducale in Urbano, Italy.

Later Years. Petrarch continued to write and to study as he grew older, though his health failed somewhat. He remained active until his death at his country home in Arqua, near Padua. An apocryphal account has it that he was found dead in his study with his head resting on a manuscript of the works of Virgil.

His Work. Petrarch is best known for his *Rime Sparse,* the collection of poetry that extols the virtues of Laura. Although much of Petrarch's work was written in Latin, the *Rime Sparse* is written in Italian. Works such as the *Secretum* (written as a dialogue between himself and ST. AUGUSTINE) outline his struggles with spirituality. *De vita solitaria* (*The Solitary Life*) celebrates the life of a poet, surrounded by scholarly writings and engaged in quiet contemplation. *Africa* is an epic poem about the wars between ancient Rome and Carthage. His interest in classical literature, which earned Petrarch the title of "Father of Humanism," inspired renewed study of ancient writings, which helped pave the way for the Renaissance.

PHILIP II AUGUSTUS

P hilip (1165–1223), reigned as king of FRANCE for more than four decades (1180–1223). He greatly solidified the power of the crown at the expense of the aristocratic elite and feudal lords and more than doubled the area of the royal lands.

Philip's birth to Louis VII of the royal CAPETIAN family and Adèle of Champagne was an occasion of great rejoicing since his father's first three marriages had produced only daughters. In 1179, after Louis suffered a stroke, in keeping with the French royal custom he had his son crowned. Shortly before the coronation, however, 14-year-old Philip became seriously ill. Louis left his sickbed to journey to Canterbury in ENGLAND to pray for his son's recovery at the tomb of his martyred friend, THOMAS BECKET. Philip recovered and was crowned king of France in the cathedral at Rheims on November 1, 1179.

His Reign. Early in his reign, Philip defeated the combined forces of FLANDERS, BURGUNDY, and Champagne, securing possession of Amiens, Artois, and part of Vermandois from the count of FLANDERS. In 1187, he attacked the English territories in France, and the following year joined forces with Richard, the rebellious son of King HENRY II of England, and forced Henry to cede several ANGEVIN territories to him.

After news of the Muslim capture of Jerusalem reached Europe, the pope called for a new crusade. RICHARD I LION-HEART, the new king of England, responded to the papal call immediately, but Philip delayed, waiting for his son's birth. In July 1190, the two kings finally departed on the Third Crusade.

Crusades. They laid siege to the key port of Acre, which surrendered in 1191. The kings quarreled, and Philip returned to France shortly after the fall of Acre. When Richard also left the crusade, he returned by way of Austria where he was captured by Leopold V of AUSTRIA (who turned him over to the German emperor, Philip's ally). During Richard's captivity (1192–1194), Philip joined forces against him with Richard's brother, John. After Richard gained his release by paying the German emperor a large ransom, he waged war against Philip, forcing him to surrender most of the Angevin territories he had won earlier.

War with England. When Richard died and John became the new king of England, Philip took up the cause of Arthur I of Brittany against the English and invaded John's French possessions. As a result of his decisive defeat of John in 1204, Philip captured Normandy, Brittany, Anjou, Maine, and Touraine, driving the English south of the Loire River. Philip later conquered Poitou as well. Philip's European supremacy was dramatically established on July 27, 1214, at the BATTLE OF BOUVINES, where Philip defeated the combined forces of John, the German emperor Otto IV, and the count of FLANDERS. When the English BARONS revolted against John the following year, they invited Philip's son, Louis VIII, to invade England and take the throne, but the plan never materialized.

Philip did not personally join the papal crusade against the ALBIGENSES in southern France, but he allowed his vassals to take part. Their victories paved the way for the crown's annexation of southern France during the reign of King LOUIS IX.

Philip strengthened the structure of the centralized French monarchy by creating a class of salaried officials—baillis in the north and seneschals in the south—who supervised the administration of the kingdom. Philip expanded the French court system, set up a central office in Paris for the permanent storage of royal records, and organized the collection of customs, tolls, fines, and fees due the royal treasury.

Centralization. Philip and his ministers made Paris and the Île-de-France the center of their system of centralized government, utilizing the resources of the newly created University of Paris. He was the first European king to employ law school graduates extensively as administrators. Philip paved the main streets of Paris, built a city wall, built the Louvre, and fiscally supported the construction of the great cathedral, NOTRE DAME de Paris.

Philip was not physically attractive (he had a hunchback), nor was he possessed of great charm. He was, however, a brilliant administrator, a wily diplomat, and a ruler driven to increase the power, wealth, and efficiency of the French monarchy.

PHILIP IV THE FAIR

During his 30-year reign, Philip IV the Fair (1268–1314) aimed to establish France as the "most Christian kingdom" of Christendom and himself as the "most Christian" of Christian kings. A series of strong ministers implemented flamboyant and aggressive policies, whose remarkable consistency reveals the king's guiding hand behind them. Philip was inspired by his grandfather SAINT LOUIS IX (r. 1226–1270), who died two years after Philip's birth and who, largely through Philip's efforts, was canonized in 1297. Philip established ecclesiastical foundations dedicated to Louis, and imitated many of his policies. However, Philip's unscrupulousness, rigidity, and suspiciousness rendered his efforts to become another "Saint Louis" strained and unrealistic.

Philip was the second son of PHILIP III THE BOLD (1270–1285), and his first wife, Isabelle of ARAGON. He succeeded his father in 1285 when his older brother Louis died prematurely in 1276, the rumored victim (by poisoning) of Philip III's second wife, Marie of Brabant. A year earlier, Philip married Jeanne, heiress of the county of Champagne and the kingdom of NAVARRE, which on her death in 1305 passed to their eldest son, Louis (after Philip's grandfather).

Church Relations. Louis had honored God and the Church but had carefully maintained France's independence from papal and episcopal control. Lacking his grandfather's genuine piety and having endured a particularly troubling childhood, Philip was tormented with worries about his soul's salvation, and stood in awe of the Church's power and authority. Philip presented himself as the premier champion of orthodoxy, rebuffed all slights against his authority, and declared that "he held the kingdom only from God."

He attacked the pugnacious and ambitious Pope BONIFACE VIII (r. 1294–1303), who sought to elevate the PAPACY and establish the pope as arbiter of Christendom. Irate at Boniface's interference with his taxation of the French Church and the pope's pointed criticism, fearful of being excommunicated, Philip charged Boniface with HERESY and flagrant immorality. He pressed Boniface to submit to conciliar judgment, and sent French agents to confront him at Anagni in September 1303. His next ecclesiastical victim was the military order of the KNIGHTS TEMPLARS, who had been the realm's chief financial agents. Convinced of their moral turpitude (and well aware of their wealth), Philip had them seized in September 1307 and, with the connivance of Pope CLEMENT V (r. 1305–1314), pursued the order to its destruction. This gained him a substantial financial profit—although not as much as he would have received had Clement not assigned the Templars' assets to the KNIGHTS HOSPITALLERS.

Military Career. Philip's desire to assert his superiority over his cousin EDWARD I of England (1239–1307), almost 30 years his senior and an experienced crusader, provoked a war with England in 1294, which did not officially end until 1303. As a result of the treaties terminating the conflict, Edward married Philip's half-sister Marguerite in 1299, and Edward's son and namesake wed Philip's daughter Isabelle in 1308 (a union that eventually resulted in their son claiming the throne of France). As a result of Edward's alliance with Philip's subjects the Flemings, the French were routed at Courtrai in 1302. In 1305, the French crushed the Flemings at Mons-en-Pévèle, and Philip imposed the harsh peace of Athis-sur-Orge.

Philip's military enterprises were expensive, as were other ventures, including the construction of an imposing royal palace on the Île-de-la-Cité in Paris. Philip manipulated the realm's coinage, and imposed harsh taxes on the kingdom, although he had great difficulty justifying these taxes during the period of peace from 1305 to 1313. During most of his reign, however, the reforming legislation he issued, his frequent consultation with his subjects, and the glory that he won for the kingdom ensured his popularity. Encouraging belief in the supernatural powers of the king, he vitalized and popularized the ceremony of royal healing in which he touched those afflicted with scrofula (known as "the king's evil") and purported to heal them. He promoted a reinterpretation of France's history, claiming CAPETIAN descent from earlier dynasties.

Expulsion of the Jews. Although he had relied on them for income since his accession, in the summer of 1306 Philip the Fair expelled the Jews from France. Until then they had lived in France on sufferance, like the Italian merchants (popularly called LOMBARDS). Both groups were skilled and wealthy financiers, and Philip taxed and exploited them, occasionally enforcing Saint Louis's prohibitions against usury to seize their profits. In banishing the Jews, Philip the Fair may have hoped to demonstrate that his piety exceeded Louis IX's, who had abhorred the Jews but tolerated their presence in France. At the same time as he was planning the expulsion, Philip followed Louis's example in forbidding private warfare against the expelled. Doubtless because of the economic crisis caused by the Jews' departure, in July 1311, Philip issued an extraor-dinary *ordonnance* instituting permissible interest rates, which he continued to sanction despite the prohibition against usury decreed by the general council of the Church convoked by Pope Clement V at Vienne in 1311.

Philip the Fair and his family, a contemporaneous illumination from the Book of Dina and Kalila, *France, 1313.*

Later Years. The troubles of the last year of Philip the Fair's reign seemed an eerie fulfillment of predictions of "great misfortunes and dangers" by the departing Jews and the dying threats attributed to the grand master of the Templars (who was burned in Paris in March 1314). Following grand festivities in Paris in June 1313, which celebrated the knighting of the king's three sons, domestic and fiscal crises followed, the former resulting from the public prosecution of the confessed lovers of his daughters-in-law and the latter from the resumption of conflict with the Flemings.

Shortly before Philip's death at 46 on November 29, 1314, regional alliances of the king's subjects, led by the barons of Champagne, protested royal fiscal and administrative policies, particularly Philip's failure to restore money levied from his subjects for the abortive campaign against Flanders in 1314 (as he had done in 1313). The allies forced Philip's short-lived heir and successor, Louis X the Quarrelsome (reigned 1314–1316), to sacrifice his father's chief ministers, reduce demands for taxes (leading him to exploit the Lombards and recall the Jews), issue numerous regional charters of privilege and promises of reform, and confirm his father's *grande ordonnance* of reform of 1303 and other pledges to improve the government and discipline royal officials.

(*See* FRANCE; PHILIP THE BOLD; BONIFACE VIII; JEWS, EXPULSIONS OF; EDWARD I.)

PHILOSOPHY IN THE MIDDLE AGES

Three communities produced philosophy in western Europe during the Middle Ages: the Jewish, the Islamic, and the the Latin Christian. In the East, thanks to the Greek Fathers of the Church and to the relative stability of the Byzantine Empire, Greek-speaking Oriental Christians preserved a philosophical tradition, unbroken since antiquity, throughout the Middle Ages. When CONSTANTINOPLE fell in 1453, Byzantine fugitives were ready to supply Western scholars with the texts of Greek philosophy as well as with instruction in their language. This long-delayed intervention and the excitement with which it was received bear witness to how little Byzantine philosophy had affected medieval Latins. Latin philosophy was much more deeply indebted to both Jewish and Islamic philosophers.

Forefathers. Three writers produced works that survived the downfall of the Roman Empire and provided a foundation for medieval Latin philosophy. They were AUGUSTINE OF HIPPO (North Africa), BOETHIUS (Rome), and Pseudo-Dionysius (Syria). The philosopher who would make a creative synthesis from these three thinkers and from the Greek Fathers of the Church was JOHN SCOT ERIGENA, the Irish philosopher who taught at the court of Charles the Bald in the ninth century. His creative synthesis of the "survivals" of ancient philosophy set out a new philosophy that was a combination of the Aristotelian, Stoic, and Platonic. It was also a philosophy in which mythology and rational discourse were combined in an original interpretation. Basic Greek philosophical terms such as physis, logos, theophania, and nous were interpreted in Latin. Physis, for instance, was translated by the Latin word *natura*. As interpreted by Eringena, natura did retain the original Greek sense of birth, "coming into being." Indeed, in a manner typical of Greek philosophy, Eringena managed to impart a truly Greek sense of philosophy to the Middle Ages. (*See* ARISTOTLE, STUDY OF.)

Latin Background. There was, of course, a great knowledge of the Latin classics; later, the Renaissance hunters of manuscripts would be indebted to those Irish monks who helped preserve the Latin civilization of the West. Here, the influence of Cicero and Seneca stand out. Through these writers, and through the Latin works of Augustine and Boethius, western Euro-

peans got a good sense of the riches of Stoic and Platonic philosophy. The Latin writers, especially Augustine, opened up new vistas in philosophy. It would, perhaps, be no exaggeration to claim that Augustine opened up the very modern existentialist themes and the deep analysis of the individual human psyche. This concern with the "archaeology of the self" was something new and original, not found in Greek philosophy. Augustine's writings would map out the mentality of the Latin Middle Ages. The *Confessiones* would present an intense analysis of the self in its search for truth and goodness in a very flawed and contingent world. *De doctrina Christiana* would take over the whole classical education program of the liberal arts and adapt it to Christian needs. *De civitate Dei* would present a very deep analysis of the mind outlining the fundamental role of memory in knowledge. *De Trinitate* would enable medieval thinkers to avoid the worst pitfalls of fundamentalism in reading and interpreting Scripture. The influence of Augustine on Latin medieval philosophy was immense and ongoing.

Philosophy class, as conducted at the University of Paris, from the Grandes Chroniques de France, *14th century.*

The one outstanding philosopher between Erigena and PETER ABELARD was undoubtedly ST. ANSELM of Canterbury. Following Augustine, he argued that a Christian has a duty to understand the content of faith by means of the "necessary reasons" of philosophy. The hermeneutical principle of *Credo ut intelligam* (I believe in order that I may understand) is made a fundamental basis of philosophical reasoning. Anselm is well known for his famous "ontological" proof for the existence of God, which has exercised philosophical minds up to Hegel and beyond. But Anselm's is not the so-called ontological proof of, say, Descartes, who would not accept Anselm's hermeneutical principle of belief and understanding. Anselm was a master-logician, and his work *De grammatica (On Grammar)* is a very powerful witness to his awareness of the possibilities of reason in the explication of belief.

The New Masters. By the mid-twelfth century, a new kind of philosopher had appeared: Peter Abelard. The product of the new urban life; he was the very paradigm of the philosopher within a school. Abelard's colorful life aside, his work as a philosopher in the field of logic and semantics, characterized as nominalist, is basic. Above all, Abelard drew attention to the difficulties with all absolute or extreme realisms. Convinced of the individuality of things, he also emphasizes the need for the mediation of human reason. His greatest contribution in ethics is his remarkable treatise *Scito te ipsum (Know Yourself)* with its very fine analysis of consent and intention in moral action. His work *Sic et non (Yes and No)* set out the methodology of school discourse in philosophy for the Latin Middle Ages. Issues would be argued looking at contradictory positions; problems would have to be rationally resolved. His other remarkable work is the treatise known as *Dialogus inter philosophum, Judaeum et Christianum* (Dialogue between a philosopher, a Jew, and a Christian).

Jewish and Islamic Influence. Between 1140 and 1280, the Western world would gain access to much of the Greek and Islamic textual deposit in science and philosophy. This work of translation introduced a fundamentally new element to the medieval Latin West: the influences of Jewish and Islamic philosophies. Much of the work of medieval Latin philosophers between 1200 and 1453 would involve an intensive dialogue between medieval Latin philosophers and their Jewish and Islamic counterparts.

The impact of MAIMONIDES on medieval Latin philosophers, especially in the doctrine of God, was very great. His works became a source of intense Jewish and Christian dialogue as is evident from the study circle at Naples that involved Master Peter of Ireland, the teacher of THOMAS AQUINAS. Indeed, Aquinas's theology is deeply indebted to Maimonides's doctrine of language about God. Notwithstanding the fact that Aquinas formulates a "positive" account of language about God, he draws greatly upon Maimonides. This positive dialogue was not appreciated by some, as evidenced by the *Condemned Propositions* at Paris in 1277. It would be the great MEISTER ECKHART who, in the late fourteenth century, would build whole sections of Maimonides into his symbolic-parabolic interpretation of Scripture.

Yet, Jewish philosophy was not just important in relation to medieval Latin philosophers; it was valuable in and of itself. Very much in the spirit of Anselm, Maimonides, in his major work, *The Guide for the Perplexed,* covers the issues concerning the relationship of faith and philosophical reasoning. Another significant Jewish philosopher was Saadiah Gaon, author of the *Book of Doctrines and Beliefs* and *Commentary on the Book of Creation.* Saadiah set out the basic discussion of the attributes and unity of God in ways that would be at the center of later Jewish philosophy. Next to Maimonides, the Jewish philosopher who had the greatest direct influence on the medieval Latin tradition was the author of *Fons vitae (Fountain of Life)*, Solomon ibn Gabirol. Gabirol's account of a neoplatonic universe influenced the very terminology (with such terms as "matter" and "form") used by Latin philosophers like ALBERTUS MAGNUS and ROGER BACON.

Gersonides (1288–1344) stands out as possibly the greatest Jewish philosopher after Maimonides. A philosopher, scientist, and a Talmudist, Gersonides' work on astronomy is of very great importance. In it, he attacked some of Ptolemy's theories, and proposed his own observations and experiments. His main philosophical work, the *Milhamot Adonai (Wars of the Lord)* covers the whole range of topics in medieval philosophy: the beatitude of the soul, future knowledge, the nature of God's knowledge and foreknowledge, providence, the motion of the heavens, and whether the world was eternal or created in time.

However, many Jewish philosophers, especially Maimonides, did much of their philosophical writing in Arabic. The impact of Arabic philosophy on the Latin medieval West was no less impressive. The first great influence came through the scientific texts translated into Latin in the twelfth century. This work had great influence, especially on English philosophers such as ROBERT GROSSETESTE. The second great influence was from AVICENNA (980–1037), who, between 1150 and 1300, counted such thinkers as Roger Bacon, Albertus Magnus, William of Auvergne, and Thomas Aquinas as his disciples. His doctrine on the Agent Intellect, his account of metaphysics, and in particular the distinctions of essence and existence, of necessary and contingent being, became fundamental.

The other major Islamic influence is that of AVERROES (1126–1198). His works appeared in the 1230s in translations by Michael Scot. His commentaries on the difficult texts of ARISTOTLE became the hermeneutical tool by which Latin readers could grapple with the Greek philosopher. Thus, Aristotle was read in the Latin West through the lens of Avicenna and AVERROES, leading to a crisis in 1277, when certain of their theses as interpreted by the Latin Averroists were condemned by the bishop of Paris, Etienne Tempier.

Yet there were other influences, especially AL-GHAZALI (1058–1111) in metaphysics, AL-FARABI (875–950) in political thought and theory of language, and al-Kindi (d. c. 870) in optics and science.

Christian Influence. Among medieval Christian philosophers, Thomas Aquinas, Albertus Magnus, and BONAVENTURA are major figures. Unlike the early thinkers, they lived in a new world, one in which non-Latin and non-Greek influences were important. The profound metaphysical thought of thirteenth-century Latin philosophers took up the traditions of the early medieval thinkers such as Eringena and later ones such as Abelard and Anselm. They combined ideas from these thinkers with a vastly expanded range of knowledge received from Persian, Arabic, and Jewish sources. They produced Questions, Summae, and Commentaries. In general, they interpreted Greek traditions in philosophy for their own schools. The traditions of Platonism, Aristotelianism, Stoicism, and even Epicureanism were taught. This time, however, they were combined with themes from Jewish, Persian, and Islamic philosophy into a profound synthesis. Contrary to what is commonly asserted, this was no mere baptizing of Aristotle. This was an intense philosophical dialogue of major proportions between Latin Western thinkers and Jewish, Islamic, and Persian thought.

With the end of the CRUSADES in 1292, so too ended this very fruitful dialogue. Medieval Latin thought developed into modern Western thought in the work of DUNS SCOTUS, Meister Eckhart, WILLIAM OF OCKHAM, Gregory of Rimini, and NICHOLAS OF CUSA. Duns Scotus developed a very rich philosophical reflection. Meister Eckhart developed a distinctive German philosophy out of the resources of Latin and German. New methods were developed: the English logicians developed embryonic calculus; William of Ockham ushered in a more precise linguistic philosophy; Gregory of Rimini recovered the doctrine of Augustine with new interpretive linguistic tools; and Nicholas of Cusa would take up the neglected works of Neoplatonism and fashion a new cosmology and a radical anthropology. In time, especially after the Byzantine-Greek influence in 1453, Renaissance philosophy would turn to Greek and Latin classics. Persian, Jewish, and Islamic work would be supplanted by a Western Renaissance attitude. The world of medieval philosophy would live on only in future histories.

See ARISTOTLE, STUDY OF; CHRISTIANITY; JUDAISM; *and* ISLAM, RELIGIOUS PHILOSOPHY OF, *for background. See also* PETER ABELARD; THOMAS AQUINAS; AUGUSTINE OF HIPPO; ROGER BACON; BOETHIUS; AND ALBERTUS MAGNUS. *Also* AVERROËS; *and* MAIMONIDES.

PICTS

The Picts were a Celtic tribe who inhabited Scotland. Although their origin is unclear, it may trace back as far as the third century of the common era. Never conquered by the Romans, the political history of the Picts was dominated by their relationship with the other inhabitants of SCOTLAND, the Scots. (*See* SCOTLAND.)

The Picts were divided into two kingdoms in the sixth century, but by the seventh century, they had become a single kingdom, pursuant to a military stalemate with the Scots. Later in the seventh century, Irish monks began to spread the Christian faith in Scotland while at the same time, Scottish tribes from IRELAND began to infiltrate the southwestern part of the Pictish kingdom. (*See* MISSIONS AND MISSIONARIES.)

In the eighth century, the Pictish royal family began to intermarry with western Irish royalty. The result was a line of kings with claims to both thrones, creating problems of succession. Eventually, the two kingdoms were unified. This unification contributed greatly to the formation of the kingdom of Scotland. (*See* CELTIC CHURCHES.)

PISA

Pisa is located in western Tuscany on the alluvial plains of the Arno River. Little is known about Pisa in the early Middle Ages. By the tenth century, however, the city became one of the wealthiest in Italy thanks to its location on the Via Aemilia, the coastal road to ROME, and through the development of its maritime trade within the western Mediterranean region. Around this time, Pisa also asserted itself militarily; with the help of the Genoan fleet, the city's naval forces drove the menacing SARACENS from Sardinia in 1016. In 1063 the Pisan fleet sacked Muslim Palermo. By the time of the First Crusade (1096), Pisans could contribute a significant naval force to the effort. As a result of their participation in the crusade, Pisa also began trading in the eastern Mediterranean; with the establishment of the Latin Kingdom of Jerusalem, Venetian merchants formed profitable ties with Syria, Acre, and other coastal cities. Thus, in the late eleventh century, Pisa became a flourishing commercial center. (*See* ITALY; COMMERCE.)

City on the Rise. The twelfth century brought even more prosperity to Pisa as it became an entrepôt for Tuscan exports and exploited the rich forest land to the north, producing timber and charcoal, leather, and furs. The city also thrived through the trade of iron and wheat. At the same time, Pisa's dominance in the western Mediterranean was challenged by its other prominent neighbors, FLORENCE and GENOA. The rivalry established was both commercial (especially with Genoa over trade with North Africa and Sardinia) and martial, resulting in several land and sea battles. The city was thus forced to maintain a strong army that was a growing financial burden on its populace.

In the thirteenth century, Pisa reached the peak of its power, prospering greatly by increased trade with North Africa, SICILY, the Mediterranean, and the Latin Kingdom of Jerusalem and by developing its emerging silk and WOOL industries. Its prosperity was evident in the construction of several impressive buildings, including the baptistery (1153–1265), the camposanto (1277–1283), and the famous leaning tower. The population of the city also grew, from an estimated 11,000 in 1164 to 38,000 in 1293. The Pisan nobles allied themselves with the GHIBELLINES, and enjoyed the support of the German emperors in naval battles with Genoa and land battles with Lucca and Florence.

However, Pisan growth also encouraged uprisings from the city's lower classes, who favored the GUELPHS over the mercantile government. These disturbances weakened Pisa, and helped bring about its defeat by Genoan ships in 1284 at the Battle of Meloria, after which Pisa's navy never recovered, though the city remained an important Tuscan commercial center until the end of the thirteenth century.

Decline. The city began to decline in the fourteenth century as infighting among noble factions led to the consolidation of power in the hands of a *signore*, often members of powerful families, such as the Donoraticos, who ruled in this manner from 1317 to 1347. Afterward, the city fell into the hands of a number of despots and military leaders, the first and most prominent of which being Pietro Gambacorta, who ruled from 1369 to 1392. Devastated by internecine fighting and by the raging plague, Pisa fell under Florentine control in 1406. Although it regained its independence briefly in the late fifteenth century, it was reconquered by Florence in 1509. The city remained a dominant commercial center until the silt deposited by the Arno made navigation up the river impossible in the mid-fifteenth century; afterward, it declined in importance as a provincial Tuscan town, best known for its fine art and architecture.

PISA, COUNCIL OF

A council convoked on March 25, 1409, with the aim of bringing the GREAT SCHISM to an end. Since it was not convened by a pope, it was never recognized as an ecumenical council. It failed, although it set the stage for the COUNCIL OF CONSTANCE, at which the Great Schism was ended.

The Council of Pisa first dealt with the position known as conciliarism—the theory that ultimate ecclesiastical authority lay with general councils of the Church rather than with the pope. Although the Italian cardinals under the Roman pope Gregory XII and the Curia of his Avignonese opponent, Benedict XIII, joined forces to convene the council, neither pope consented to attend, each bent on convening his own council. Despite the absence of the principals in the dispute, the council was supported by much of the Church hierarchy, most theologians, the UNIVERSITIES, the monastic orders, and the Western secular powers.

When the rival pontiffs persisted in refusing to appear, the council sanctioned the withdrawal of obedience from both pontiffs, and, on June 5, 1409, deposed both Gregory and Benedict. On June 26 Peter of Candia, a chief organizer of the council, was elected pope to replace them. As Alexander V, he presided over the later sessions of the council, which he dissolved on August 7, having called for another council for 1412 to take up reform. (*See* PAPACY.)

Although much of the Western Church adhered to the acts of the council and accepted Alexander V, Gregory and Benedict both declined to step down. Had Alexander V not died suddenly in 1410, their contempt of the council's decrees might not have prevailed, but Alexander's successor, the antipope John XXIII, proved unequal to the challenge. Hence the Council of Pisa yielded three pontiffs instead of one, only deepening the crisis in the short term, but ultimately forcing its resolution. (*See* GREAT SCHISM.)

PLANTAGENET

P lantagenet is the family name of the royal house that ruled England from 1154 to 1485. The name is believed to derive from the nickname of Geoffrey the Fair, count of Anjou, who used to wear a sprig of broom (*planta genista*) in his hat.

Geoffrey's son, HENRY II, who became king of ENGLAND in 1154, and his descendants—RICHARD I, John, HENRY III, Edward I, EDWARD II, EDWARD III, and RICHARD II—ruled through the male line until 1399 when Henry Bolingbroke (Henry IV) deposed Richard II. There is no evidence that any of these descendants of Geoffrey used the name Plantagenet.

After Richard was deposed, the Plantagenet line split into two branches—the houses of Lancaster and York. The Lancastrian branch of the Plantagenet line produced HENRY IV, HENRY V, and HENRY VI, while the Yorkist branch produced EDWARD IV, Edward V, and RICHARD III. Richard, the third duke of York and father of Edward IV, the first Yorkist king of England, only adopted Plantagenet as his family's surname in the late 1440s to help emphasize the superiority of the family's claim to the throne against the House of Lancaster before and during the WARS OF THE ROSES.

Shakespeare and many later writers and historians used the name as the surname of all the male lines beginning with Geoffrey of Anjou, both the direct male lines culminating with Richard II and the two branches of Lancaster and York that followed.

The Plantagenet dynasty came to an end with the death of Richard III in 1485, when Henry Tudor took the throne as Henry VII. However, even Henry owed his claim to the throne in part to his Plantagenet ancestry through the female line since his mother, Margaret Beaufort, was the great-granddaughter of JOHN OF GAUNT, the duke of Lancaster, who began the Lancastrian branch of the Plantagenet line. In 1486, when Henry married Elizabeth of York, Edward IV's daughter, both Plantagenet branches were reunited in the Tudor dynasty.

After 1485, the Plantagenet name lingered at the fringes of English political life. Viscount Lisle, the illegitimate son of Edward IV, bore the name Plantagenet. The name was also used by Richard, a stonemason in Kent, who died in 1550 and was believed to be the natural son of Richard III.

See KINGSHIP; ENGLAND; *and* WARS OF THE ROSES *for background. Also see entries on the lives of* EDWARD II; EDWARD III; HENRY II PLANTAGENET; HENRY III; RICHARD I; *and* RICHARD II.

POLAND

The medieval history of Poland is checkered with periods of prosperity and stability, mixed with periods of internal unrest, political fragmentation, and anarchical conditions.

Settlement. Before the tenth century, Poland lay outside the awareness of medieval Christendom. Archeological remains and historical reports indicate that in the early Middle Ages, Poland was settled by a number of migrating German tribes; by the ninth cen-

A 15th-century depiction of John Plantagenet, duke of Bedford, leading British forces in battle against the French.

tury, the military leaders of these tribes began to consolidate power and wealth, and their tribes developed aristocratic structures with basic territorial organization. By the tenth century, two tribes became predominant: the Polanie tribe, centered around Gniezno, and the Wislanie tribe, centered around Kraków.

Expansion. The Polanie ultimately conquered the Wislanies, and became the dominant power in the region; as they expanded their territories in the tenth century, the region they controlled became known as Polania. Medieval legend considers the original founder of the kingdom to be Piast, a pagan wheelwright who established a Polanie duchy in the late ninth century. The first ruler to make significant contact with the West was Mieszko (c. 930–992), a descendant of Piast, who was first mentioned by medieval chroniclers in 963. Mieszko benefited from his relationships with the German Holy Roman Emperors and became a vassal to OTTO I. He recognized the importance of CHRISTIANITY for the development of his kingdom, and converted to Roman Catholicism in 966. With the support of Bohemian missionaries, Mieszko worked to convert his pagan countrymen; the first Polish bishopric was founded at Gniezno, Mieszko's capital. Strengthening his relationship with the papacy, in 991 Mieszko subordinated his state to its authority. With the blessing of the pope, Mieszko was able to extend his own borders to the northwest and to the south. The last four years of his life were spent engaged in a war with BOHEMIA from which Poland secured parts of Silesia and Little Poland.

Mieszko was succeeded by his oldest son, Boleslaw I the Brave (992–1025), who continued the expansion of Polish domains begun by his father. Commanding a large military force and enjoying a strong relationship with the Emperor OTTO III, Boleslaw won imperial recognition of his independence as a duke of Poland. However, after the death of Otto and the accession of HENRY II, the relationship between Poland and the empire began to deteriorate. Boleslaw conquered Pomerania, Silesia, Slovakia, and Ruthenia for Poland; he had taken Bohemia, Moravia, and Lustatia as well, but was forced to relinquish control of the latter territories by Henry II. Eventually, a treaty was reached between Poland and the emperor in 1018, by which Henry recognized Boleslaw's independence and allowed him to continue his conquest south and southwest. In 1025, Boleslaw crowned himself king of Poland, now a major European kingdom.

Instability. When Boleslaw died a few months later, the kingdom quickly dissolved into a morass of regional factions. The eleventh century also witnessed widespread peasant uprisings against the king, the nobility, and the Church, which led to a reversion to paganism in much of the countryside. Boleslaw's successor thus abandoned thoughts of territorial expansion and concentrated on resolving internal issues. Neighboring states were able to take advantage of the unrest and recover land they had lost to Poland in the previous century. In the twelfth century, GERMANY recovered much of the lands east of the Elbe and continued to whittle away at the Polish borders well into the next century, as large numbers of German merchants settled in Polish cities and gained prominence there.

Poland saw the return of some stability and central authority with the rule of Boleslaw III the Wrymouthed (1102–1139), who promoted Christianity, repelled an invasion by Emperor Henry V, and gained control over western Pomerania. Boleslaw attempted to avoid the chaotic decentralization that had plagued Poland in the past by dividing his kingdom into duchies and portioning them out to his sons. But after his death, his heirs engaged in a violent struggle for supremacy, and Poland again fell into a period of disruptive infighting that was to last for 200 years.

Economics. Poland's economy prospered in the thirteenth century through advancements in agriculture and Poland's participation in the thriving European trade network. Additionally, new towns were founded and old ones rebuilt; these towns functioned much like the cities in Germany under the Magdeburg Law, as autonomous, self-governing bodies. The nobility and the Church also prospered in the thirteenth century, so that they could intensify their opposition to the king's power; by mid-century, the king's authority was limited to the city of Kraków, the new royal seat. The nature of the peasantry also changed, with many becoming increasingly more dependent on local lords.

The thirteenth century also brought with it serious foreign threats to Polish stability, the most severe coming from the north. In 1226, Conrad of Mazovia had called for the assistance of the German crusaders, the TEUTONIC KNIGHTS, in conquering PRUSSIA; after the conquest, however, the knights settled in the newly won territories and began eyeing Polish lands. They initiated a long-standing campaign to conquer and "civilize" its inhabitants. Another serious threat came in 1241 from the MONGOL invasion led by Batu Khan.

Casimir. By the late thirteenth century, Poland had fallen into the hands of Bohemian rulers. In 1320, Wladyslaw I, a Polish duke, assisted by the king of Hungary, successfully opposed the Teutonic knights, Bohemia, and rival Polish dukes; he seized the crown and reigned as king for thirteen years. His son, CASIMIR III, was even more successful and led Poland to an age of stability and prosperity. During his reign (1330–1370), Casimir reorganized the constitution, produced the first law code, and founded the University of Kraków in 1364.

He encouraged economic growth by opening Polish towns up to German and Jewish merchants and greatly improved the condition of the peasantry. Casimir was also able to achieve peace with Bohemia and the Teutonic Order, and recovered some of the territories Poland had lost from them. He increased Poland's overall size by more than a third during his reign, incorporating much of Halicz and Ruthenia into the kingdom. Poland's international reputation grew during Casimir's reign; when he died at the age of sixty in 1370, all of the country mourned—his reign was perhaps the most significant in Polish history.

Poland in the Late Middle Ages. Pressure from Bohemia in the west made Poland and Lithuania natural allies.

Succession. Casimir had no direct male heirs, and so, following a familiar pattern in medieval Polish history, the succession to his reign was marked by conflict and violence. Eventually, Louis I of Anjou, king of HUNGARY and Casimir's nephew, came to the throne. Louis relinquished much of his authority to the nobility. Louis was succeeded by his daughter Jadwiga in 1384, who married the grand duke of Lithuania, Jagiello. Jagiello converted to CHRISTIANITY; together, they worked toward the conversion of their people, both in Poland and in LITHUANIA. When Jadwiga died in 1399, Jagiello ruled Poland and Lithuania as Wladyslaw II, founding a new dynasty that ruled both states until 1572. Unimpressed with Wladyslaw's proselytizing efforts and greedy for Polish territory, the Teutonic knights intensified their missionizing and crusading in Poland and LITHUANIA during Wladyslaw's reign, but the combined power of the two states defeated the order at the Battle of Tannenberg in 1410, permanently crippling the order. But Wladyslaw could not recover much territory in the disappointing treaty of 1411. (*See* LITHUANIA; TEUTONIC ORDER.)

Childless with Jadwiga, Wladyslaw was forced to make further concessions to the nobility, and even to the *szlachta* (petty nobility), in order to arrange for the succession of his son by his fourth wife, Wladyslaw III, who ruled from 1434 to 1444, assuming the throne of Hungary when his brother Casimir IV was elected grand prince of Lithuania. After Wladyslaw III's death, Casimir came to the Polish throne, reaffirming the confederation between Lithuania and Poland, but again recognizing each other's sovereignty.

Late Middle Ages. During his long reign (1447–1492), Casimir rescinded the immunities and privileges previously granted to the upper nobility, strengthening the power of the central authority. He was forced, however, to grant privileges to the lesser nobility, which ultimately led to the weakening of royal power in the modern period. Casimir waged a thirteen-year war against the weakened Teutonic Order, recovering many of the lost territories (Gdansk, Pomerania, and western Prussia). During these years, the economy and the cultural life of Poland blossomed, and by the end of Casimir's reign, Poland had become a widely respected European power. (*See* HUNGARY; PRUSSIA; AND RUSSIA.)

PORTUGAL

Portugal—a small, narrow country on the Atlantic coast of the Iberian peninsula which it shares with SPAIN—was created during the Christian reconquest of the peninsula from the Moors. Unlike other lands that eventually became Spain, Portugal asserted and maintained its independence, emerging at the end of the Middle Ages as a formidable maritime power. (*See* SPAIN.)

Early Middle Ages. In the 400s, Germanic tribes overran the Iberian peninsula. The VANDALS and the Suevi were the first tribes to enter western Iberia, but soon the VISIGOTHS established their rule over most of the peninsula, although the Suevi were able to set up a kingdom that lasted until the late 500s.(*See* BARBARIAN INVASIONS.)

In 711, Islamic armies from Morocco invaded Iberia and conquered the peninsula except for a small area in the north which became the Christian kingdom of Asturias. When the tide turned and the Christians embarked on their reconquest of lost territories, Portuguese lands were incorporated into the Spanish kingdoms of Asturias and Castile and León. By the mid-800s the northern part of the region had its own governor; for the first time it was referred to as Portuguese territory. In the early 1000s, Ferdinand I of Castile and León took control of the land. The division of his kingdom among his children after his death (1065) led to the creation of the kingdom of Portugal.

Battle for Independence. In the early 1100s dynastic feuds set the heirs to the Portuguese territory against each other. In 1128, Alfonso Henriques seized the throne from his mother after he defeated her forces at the Battle of São Mamede. Defeating the Moors in 1139, he began calling himself king of Portugal. During his long reign Portugal established its independence from Castile and León and won recognition as an independent kingdom. Spain recognized Portugal's independence in 1143, as did the PAPACY in 1179.

Alfonso built a strong monarchy during his long reign. He also assisted in the creation of a strong church independent of the Spanish church, but it became a fierce rival to the crown, creating bitter Church-state struggles throughout the rest of the medieval period. Toward the end of Alfonso's reign, he ruled with his son and heir, Sancho I, who succeeded his father in 1185. Sancho encouraged settlement of the areas captured from the Moors. He also captured the Moorish capital of Silves but could not hold it.

The kings who succeeded Sancho I consolidated the crown's authority and made further advances against the Moors. Alfonso II, who reigned from 1211 to 1223, issued the first body of Portuguese law and summoned the first *Cortes*, a group of nobles and clergy chosen to advise the king. Alfonso also sent troops to aid Castile in its struggle against the Moors. The Christian victory over the Moors at the Battle of Las Navas de Tolosa in 1212 was regarded as the greatest victory of the reconquest. (*See* RECONQUEST.)

Sancho II, who ruled from 1223 to 1248, continued the Portuguese military advance against the

Moors, but when he could not control the forces that were bringing Portugal to the brink of civil war, the nobility deposed him and turned the government over to his brother, Alfonso III. Alfonso won back southern Portugal, the Algarve, from the Muslims, so that by the time Alfonso's son Dinis took the throne in 1279, Portugal was finally freed from the Muslim threat.

Expansion. Under the leadership of Dinis I, who reigned until 1325, Portugal entered a period of new growth and achievement. Dinis improved farming, reclaimed swamps and marshes, and planted forests. He extended his authority over border areas where he promoted resettlement, fortifying and building castles and strongholds on the frontier. He tried to bring under his control various orders of knights, such as the Templars and Hospitallers, who had settled in Portugal centuries earlier to battle the Moors. He built a navy to defend the coast and protect Portuguese shipping.

Following Dinis I's death, Portugal suffered from internal strife, conflicts with the kingdom of Castile, and devastation caused by the BLACK DEATH. A brief succession struggle ended in 1385 when the Portuguese cortes elected João I of Aviz as the new king. Castile, taking advantage of Portugal's turmoil, attacked, but was driven back that summer in two decisive battles: at Trancoso and at Aljubarrota.

Exploration. Much of Portugal's history in the 1400s—marked by discovery and conquest in Africa and the Atlantic—centered around the children of João I and their successors. In the early 1400s, Portugal set out on voyages of EXPLORATION into the Atlantic Ocean. They discovered the Azores in 1439 and sailed down the northwestern coast of Africa, where they rounded the previously impassable Cape Bojador.

After Portugal attacked but failed to take Tangier where the king's brother was held captive by the Moors, the kingdom shifted from military expeditions to maritime exploration under the leadership of João's son, Prince HENRY THE NAVIGATOR (1394–1460).

Exploration was given fresh impetus after Henry's death by João II, who sought to bypass the long land routes to the Asian spice trade and to make contact with the legendary Prester John in order to attack the Muslims from the rear. After Bartolomeu Dias rounded the Cape of Good Hope in 1487, the Portuguese sailed up the east coast of Africa. The Treaty of Tordesillas in 1494 divided the world beyond Europe into Spanish and Portuguese spheres of influence, which left the soon-to-be-discovered New World to the Spanish, except for the land on the Portuguese side of the line that became Brazil. (*See* EXPLORATION.)

Vasco da Gama's voyage to India at the end of the 1400s paved the way for what would soon become Portugal's worldwide empire, and placed Portugal at the forefront of European exploration and discovery.

PRAGUE, UNIVERSITY OF

T he University of Prague (also known as Charles IV University) is the oldest university in central Europe. It was founded in 1348 as part of the Holy Roman Emperor CHARLES IV'S push to making Prague a center of culture and learning.

Prague was established as a city on the banks of the Vltava River, in what was then BOHEMIA. In the ninth century, it quickly became a trading center. Germans, Slavs, Russians, and Turks traded there, as did Jews and Muslims. When Charles IV became king of Bohemia in 1346, he decided to expand the city. He built new churches and MONASTERIES and a bridge across the Vltava River. He invited scholars, artists, and architects to become a part of his court, perhaps the most notable of whom was the writer PETRARCH. He also built a university, which he named after himself.

The university was established with four faculties: theology, law, medicine, and the arts. It flourished during Charles's reign, which lasted until 1378. In the early fifteenth century, Prague entered a period of unrest engendered by the reforming activities of JAN HUS. The university aligned itself with the Hussite movement primarily because Hus supported greater Czech influence (at the expense of the German faculty) within the university. Throughout its history, the university has often found itself at the center of the conflicts that have characterized central European history.

PRISONS AND PUNISHMENT

T he medieval prison was really a holding place for those accused of crimes. Moreover, "imprisonment" included everything from having one's hands and feet chained to being confined to a particular town. Although criminals did not serve sentences for their wrongdoing, they were often severely punished. Many crimes were punishable by death; others by branding or mutilation, which would identify individuals as criminals for life. (*See* LAW, SCHOOLS OF.)

Early Medieval Punishment. Since criminals were executed or branded, early medieval society saw little reason to maintain prisons. Until the thirteenth century, people accused of crimes were often put through a trial by ordeal. In the belief that the innocent would come away unharmed or would quickly heal, the accused would be forced to do something injurious to themselves, such as immersing their hands into boiling water. (*See* TRIALS BY ORDEAL.)

Important prisoners, such as members of the nobility, were sometimes held for ransom. Often, they were placed in a castle's dungeon. Important political prisoners—for example, those who rebelled against the current ruler—were often sentenced to forced service in a monastery instead of being executed; for many, this confinement was just short of a full pardon.

A lord oversees a disobedient serf's punishment by the wheel, which maimed the victim and intimidated others.

Later Developments. Since prisoners in the late Middle Ages were often required to pay for their food and maintenance, prisons became sources of income as well as places of confinement. By the late thirteenth century, prisoners could buy their freedom by paying a fine. Religious orders collected money to help secure the release or ease the suffering of those imprisoned.

MONASTERIES were also used to incarcerate clerical wrongdoers and heretics. As HERESY became a more common charge, the number of individuals held rose significantly. The punishment for heretics usually involved TORTURE and execution, unless the heretic was willing to admit his or her crime and plead for forgiveness. As the Middle Ages progressed, the definition of heresy became more broadly based; for instance, people who made and used herbal remedies were frequently labeled practitioners of WITCHCRAFT. Heretics rarely languished long in prison; they were either soon tortured and executed, or they paid a ransom for their release. Buildings, such as the Tower of London and the Bastille in Paris, became celebrated as prisons, often for high-profile prisoners. (*See* TORTURE.)

PRUSSIA

P russia during the Middle Ages was a central-eastern European region on the southeast shore of the Baltic Sea, alternately under Germans and Polish rule. Prussia was later ruled by the German HOHENZOLLERN DYNASTY, which fell in 1918, leaving Prussia a German state until the political reorganization of Germany after the Second World War.

The original inhabitants of Prussia, closely related to the Latvians and Lithuanians, were tribal hunters or livestock breeders. They lived deep in the forests, and remained pagans until nearly the end of the Middle Ages. Although several attempts to convert the Prussians had failed, the TEUTONIC KNIGHTS, who had fought in the CRUSADES, conquered the region in the thirteenth century. Prussia at that time was a Polish territory, but the Teutonic knights had been awarded land in Prussia by the Polish duke Conrad of Mazovia as a reward for stifling an insurrection.

The Teutonic knights changed the landscape of Prussia dramatically. Forests were thinned out, replaced by the castles of German nobles who built them there. German farmers migrated to the area to work the land. Although still nominally a Polish territory, the Teutonic influence was overwhelming. The old Prussian language gradually gave way to German, although the old tongue did not die out completely until the seventeenth century.

When Poland and LITHUANIA united in the late fourteenth century, they were better able to meet the threat of the Teutonic knights. It was not until 1466, however, that the knights were defeated. Under the Treaty of Tornu, reached in 1466, the Polish crown acquired sovereignty of the former Teutonic holdings west of the lower Vistula River. Prussian lands that were east of the river were left in Teutonic hands, but as a fief of the Polish crown. (*See* GERMANY; POLAND.)

Eventually, the lands along the Vistula became known as Royal Prussia. Its people spoke primarily Polish even though it was located directly between Germany and East Prussia (almost all of whose inhabitants by then spoke German). In 1525, Albert of Hohenzollern, the last Teutonic grand master of East Prussia, transformed it into a duchy, thereafter known as Ducal Prussia. It was not until 1660 that Poland gave up its claim to the region under the Treaty of Oliva, which was signed that year and which made Prussia a sovereign state ruled by the Hohenzollerns.

PSELLUS, MICHAEL

M ichael Constantine Psellus (1018–1078) was an influential intellectual and political figure of the Byzantine Empire, a favorite of Empress THEODORA I and Emperor Constantine IX. Psellus gained a well-earned reputation as an amoral political schemer, surviving a number of emperors through flattery and manipulation. In 1071, Psellus engineered the replacement of Emperor Romanus IV Diogenes by his student, Michael VII, while Romanus was held prisoner by the SELJUK TURKS after his defeat at the BATTLE OF MANZIKERT.

RASHI

R abbi Shlomo Yitzhaqi (1040–1105), known as Rashi (an acronym of his Hebrew name), was the preeminent Jewish commentator on the Bible and the Talmud during the Middle Ages. He remains revered in Jewish rabbinic scholarship to the present day. Standard rabbinic editions of the Bible and the Talmud are still published with Rashi's commentary as a matter of course. (*See* JUDAISM.)

Rashi was born to a family of vintners in Troyes, located in northern France; one tradition has him belonging to a family of Jewish vintners known to have operated in the region at that time. Rashi's father died when Rashi was still a young man, requiring him to attend to the family business instead of attending the great rabbinic seminaries in Worms or Mayence. Instead, he attended these academies for only two months a year, keeping lecture notes (when study was usually exclusively transmitted orally). The destruction of the academy of Mayence during the First Crusade in 1096 suddenly made those notes very valuable as the only surviving record of centuries of Jewish learning. Rashi used these notes as the basis for his commentary, a work remarkable for its delicate terseness. He also pioneered the use of non-Hebrew vernacular terms to explain difficult words and passages. Rashi served as the rabbinic leader of Troyes, making it a center of Jewish learning in the post-Crusade medieval period. His grandchildren, among whom was JACOB BEN MEIR, were known as Tosaphists, a term denoting their continuing Rashi's teachings and methods.

RAVENNA

S trategically located on the Po River in the northeast of Italy, Ravenna served as the capital of the declining Roman Empire in the early part of the fifth century. (*See* ITALY.)

Ravenna was an unimportant Roman city until the emperor Honorius (384–423) fled there in 404 when the Germanic VISIGOTHS threatened ROME. Honorius's choice of Ravenna reflects the empire's loss of power insofar as the royal court needed not only the protection of the army but also Ravenna's impregnable location inside marshy plains and canals.

After the final collapse of the Western Roman Empire, the German ODOACER deposed the last puppet emperor (476) and made Ravenna the capital of his short-lived kingdom. Odoacer retreated to Ravenna during his war with the OSTROGOTHS and withstood a three-year siege (489–492). The war ended when the Ostrogothic king THEODORIC THE GREAT killed Odoacer. Theodoric then made Ravenna the capital of his Ostrogothic kingdom. During the long and successful rule of Theodoric (493–526), Ravenna attained its medieval apogee.

After Theodoric's death, the Ostrogoths fought a long war with the Byzantine Empire (the successor state to the eastern Roman Empire) and made Ravenna their last stand in the first stage of the war. In 539, the Byzantine general BELISARIUS finally captured Ravenna and the city became the capital of the Exarchate of Ravenna, the center of Byzantine power in Italy. The Byzantine hold on Ravenna lasted until 751 when it was captured by the LOMBARDS.

A few years later, in 754, Ravenna changed hands again when it was conquered by the FRANKS. The Frankish king PÉPIN III THE SHORT donated Ravenna to the PAPAL STATES. In the twelfth and thirteenth centuries Ravenna became an independent commune before losing its independence to VENICE in 1438.

The most lasting impression on Ravenna was left by the Byzantines and, to a lesser extent, the Italian GOTHS. Their artistic influence was the key contributor to its many CHURCHES and spectacular MOSAICS.

RAYMOND IV

R aymond IV of Toulouse (c. 1042–1105) is also known as Raymond I of Tripoli, which he conquered in 1102. He was also count of Toulouse, in which capacity he joined the First Crusade; he was the first Western ruler to join the CRUSADES. He was also one of the most successful fighters of the Crusades, in the minds of many of its true military leaders, above even GODFREY DE BOUILLON.

Born in Toulouse around 1041, he was active in the reform movement organized by Pope URBAN II. It was Urban who encouraged Raymond to participate in the crusade. Despite his personal dislike for the Byzantine emperor ALEXIUS I COMNENUS, Raymond proved to be a loyal and relentless fighter who helped capture Jerusalem for the West. While there, he repelled an attack on the city by the FATIMID DYNASTY of Egypt.

Despite his heroism, Raymond never sought land or title for himself. He did build the castle of Mons Peregrinus near Tripoli, and his heirs established the Latin countship of Tripoli. But Raymond refused to accept any principalities, turning down even the crown of Jerusalem. Raymond continued to live in Tripoli at his castle after he conquered the city. He was living at Mons Peregrinus at the time of his death in 1105.

RECCARED I

Reccared I (c. 560–c. 601), son and successor of Leovigild, was ruler of the German Visigothic kingdom of SPAIN (586–601). In the first years of his reign, he converted the VISIGOTHS from Arianism to orthodox CHRISTIANITY. Since the Visigoths had been Arian for over two centuries, Reccared had to crush a number of rebellions. After the Visigothic conversion, only the LOMBARDS in ITALY remained Arian. The conversion removed a barrier between the occupying Visigoths and the native population; hitherto the Visigoths had been an alien group living among the diverse Iberian population. Reccared, however, never brought complete unity to the Spanish population of Basque separatists, Germanic Suevi, Arians, and Jews.

Reccared undertook a number of reforms that strengthened the Visigothic kingdom and the church. He made the kingdom into an orthodox Christian monarchy that lasted until the Arab conquest of Spain in 730. Through a number of measures, he tied the KINGSHIP to the sanctity of the Church. He increased cooperation between the bishops and the monarchy in great councils, and also adopted the practice of having bishops anoint the king at the time of ascension. Working closely with Pope GREGORY I, the Catholic Reccared engaged in massive repression of religious minorities despite his former tolerance as an Arian.

RECONQUEST

The Reconquest (*Reconquista*) is the term used to describe the recapture of SPAIN from the Muslims by the Christian states of the north.

After the breakup of the Islamic empire of the UMAYYAD DYNASTY in the early 1000s, a number of emirates emerged, the most important of which was that of the ABBADIDS of Córdoba. To defend themselves against ALFONSO VI of Castile they called in the Berber ALMORAVIDS from North Africa for help. The Almoravids proceeded to take over Muslim Spain but were themselves replaced by another BERBER dynasty, the ALMOHADS. In the decisive Battle of Las Navas de Tolosa in 1212, ALFONSO VIII of Castile defeated the Almohads, and his successors went on to conquer most of Andalusia. (*See* SPAIN; PORTUGAL.)

Although the recovery of the lands lost to the Moors in the 700s had opened with the capture of Toledo in 1085, the establishment of the Kingdom of PORTUGAL, and the capture of Lisbon in 1148, the reconquest began in earnest only after the Battle of Las Navas de Tolosa in 1212.

JAMES I THE CONQUEROR of ARAGON and Catalonia raided Valencia in 1225, seized the island of Majorca in 1229, and then conquered the Valencian lands from 1232 to 1245. In the meantime, Ferdinand III and his son ALFONSO X THE WISE of Castile and León captured Córdoba in 1236, Jaen in 1246, Seville in 1248, and Cadiz in 1262. By the end of the 1200s only the kingdom of Granada was still in Muslim hands.

As the Christians advanced south through Muslim Spain, they allowed conquered communities to continue as independent enclaves, a Muslim policy that the Spanish Christians emulated. The policy allowed the conquered Muslims, called Mudéjars, to retain their religious, judicial, and political institutions.

The Muslim political state that lasted the longest was Granada. Its protected position behind mountains allowed it to survive the reconquest until it was finally forced to surrender in 1492.

RHETORIC

Rhetoric, the art of persuasive speaking and writing, has been a valued skill since ancient times. During the Middle Ages, rhetoric exerted an influence on everything from sermons to speeches to government form letters. Although rhetoric developed somewhat differently among Europeans, Arabs, and Jews, the goals were the same: concise speech and writing that communicated clearly. With more trade being conducted, with populations rising, and with LITERACY increasing, how people expressed themselves, both in speech and in writing, took on considerable importance.

European Rhetoric. Early medieval rhetoric took its form from the rhetoric of the Romans, particularly Cicero, who wrote extensively on the art of persuasive oration. These principles were applied not only to speeches, but to poetry and religious works as well.

Rhetoric was considered so important that it was taught as one of the seven liberal arts comprised of the trivium (rhetoric, grammar, and logic) and the quadrivium (geometry, astronomy, arithmetic, and music). It was eventually broadened to encompass poetry, preaching, and letter writing. The latter became increasingly important as literacy rates rose and as more legal and civil matters necessitated written records. Not surprisingly, letter-writing studies flourished in Bologna, home of the premier medieval law school. Rhetoric was also important to the Byzantines, who favored formally structured speeches and letters.

Islamic Rhetoric. Religion played a more significant role in the Muslim approach to rhetoric. Scholars studied rhetoric to help them better understand passages from the KORAN. As of the ninth century, however, Arabic books on rhetoric do show other examples of literary rhetoric, such as poetry. The Muslims also innovated the use of sample drafts—the form letter—of various official documents in manuals for government clerks. (*See* LITERATURE.)

Hebrew Rhetoric. Rhetoric was an important art in the Jewish community, though the only medieval book on Jewish rhetoric that survives is the twelfth century *Book of Discussion and Conversation* by Moses ibn Ezra. The book, written in Arabic, closely follows the tenets of Arabic rhetoric. But Jews took guidance from the older Latin tradition as well. In the fifteenth century, the Jewish scholar Judah ben Jehiel produced a comprehensive book on rhetoric and the BIBLE.

RHODES

R hodes is a large island in the Aegean Sea, ten miles south of Asia Minor. In the Middle Ages, Rhodes was usually securely part of the Byzantine Empire. During the late Middle Ages, Rhodes became the arena of a long struggle between crusaders, Italian traders, the decaying Byzantine Empire, and the emerging power of the OTTOMAN TURKS. In the fourteenth century, Rhodes was considered a bulwark against the Ottomans. The Turkish conquest of Rhodes in 1522 was symbolic of the dominance of the Turks over eastern Christian states.

The surface of Rhodes is covered by mountains, the highest of which is Mount Attairo at almost 4,000 feet. The rest of the island is marked by ranges of modest size that in ancient times were thickly covered by trees. Rhodes has an agreeable climate and fertile soil, which in earlier times, produced a variety of wines.

Rhodes became a territory of the Byzantine Empire, the successor state of the eastern half of the Roman Empire, and remained Byzantine until the eleventh century, except for brief periods of occupation by the Arab caliphate from 653 to 658 and from 717 to 718.

After 1018, the island came under the influence of the emerging trading powers of VENICE. By the thirteenth century, Rhodes was controlled by Italian adventurers, although they periodically had to seek the protection of the emperor of NICAEA (the strongest successor state of the Byzantine Empire) when Rhodes was threatened by the Ottoman Turk sultans.

In 1310, the crusading military order of the KNIGHTS (HOSPITALLERS) OF ST. JOHN of Jerusalem, looking for new fields for activity after the Arab reconquest of Palestine, took over Rhodes under the sponsorship of GENOA (Venice's archenemy) and the PAPACY, in the hope that Rhodes would impede the growing naval power of the Turks. Trade by Greeks and Italians flourished in Rhodes during the reign of

15th-century plan of the island of Rhodes, from the Saintes Pérégrinations de Hiérusalem *by Breydenbach.*

the knights. Rhodes was also a center of piracy sponsored by the knights and others. The knights became quite wealthy and spent lavishly, rebuilding the city of Rhodes and constructing a large fleet. Under the crusader king Peter I of CYPRUS (1349–1369), the knights gained Adalia and Corycus in Asia Minor. Peter conducted raids on Syria and launched a serious but ultimately unsuccessful invasion of Alexandria in Egypt. For a time, Rhodes succeeded as a well-fortified obstacle to Turkish expansion. Rhodes repelled Turkish assaults in 1440, 1444, and an epic siege in 1448. However, the strategic location of Rhodes made its conquest inevitable; in 1522, the Ottomans under SULEYMAN I the Magnificent finally captured the island.

RICHARD I LION-HEART

R ichard I Lion-Heart (also called Richard the Lion-Hearted, and *Coeur de Lion* in French; 1157–1199), king of ENGLAND (1189–1199), renowned for his courage in battle and exploits during the Third Crusade (1189–1192) and the personification of chivalric KNIGHTHOOD. A formidable soldier, strategist, and fortification builder, he nevertheless failed to retake Jerusalem from the Muslims. Modern commentators regard his glory as tarnished by a streak of ruthlessness and arrogance in his character.

Early Years. Richard was born in Oxford, England, the third child of the ANGEVIN king HENRY II of England, first of the PLANTAGENET dynasty, and of ELEANOR OF AQUITAINE. Control of Normandy, Anjou, and Maine, as well as his claim to the English throne, had been bequeathed to Henry by his parents, Geoffrey Plantagenet and Mathilda, granddaughter of WILLIAM I THE CONQUEROR. He enlarged these holdings substantially, adding BRITTANY, the Vexin, and other domains by military, diplomatic, and other expedient means. Eleanor herself controlled both AQUITAINE and Poitou, where Richard was raised at

Eleanor's splendid court at Poitiers. He was given an exceptionally good education in addition to being taught mastery of arms. Eleanor ensured his recognition as duke of Aquitaine in 1172. Angered by their father's humiliating refusal to accord them power they thought their due, Richard and his older brothers, Henry and Geoffrey, unsuccessfully rebelled against their father in 1173 and 1174. Geoffrey even obtained the support of Eleanor, the king of SCOTLAND, and King Louis VII of France, but to no avail.

Richard I Lion-Heart mortally wounded by an arrow shot by Bertrand de Gordon at the siege of the Castle of Chalus in Limousin, France, 1199. From a 15th-century manuscript, Chroniques de Normandie.

Knighted by Louis during this rebellion, Richard nevertheless secured his father's forgiveness. He became heir to the throne of England on the death of the younger Henry, who died of dysentery in 1183 in the midst of a bloody attempt (with the support of Geoffrey and the Aquitainian nobility) to assert precedence over Richard in Aquitaine. Henry II's later attempts to circumscribe Richard's authority and to make his youngest son John his agent in Aquitaine motivated Richard to ally himself against his father with the new French king, PHILIP II AUGUSTUS. (That Richard had been betrothed most of his life to Philip's sister Alice was a matter of indifference to him.) After a series of maneuvers and eventually open warfare, Richard and Philip forced Henry to cede his authority—and much of his treasury—to them. Henry II died shortly thereafter, in July 1189.

His Reign. Richard was crowned king of England at WESTMINSTER ABBEY in September, during the first of only two visits to England he is known to have made during his reign. Immersed in preparations for launching a crusade to retake Jerusalem, which had fallen to the Muslims under SALADIN, the sultan of EGYPT and Syria, in 1187, Richard was content to delegate the governance of England to others; he took little interest in England other than as a source of funds for his military ventures. (In fact, he never became sufficiently conversant with the English language to speak it.)

Richard joined the French under Philip at Messina in Sicily. Tensions quickly surfaced between Richard and King Tancred over the dowry of Richard's sister Joan, the dowager queen. When fighting erupted among the crusader troops and the citizens of Messina, Richard quickly took advantage of the situation to seize control of the city. Among the other terms of the ensuing Treaty of Messina, he acknowledged his young nephew Arthur of Brittany, the son of his brother Geoffrey, as heir to the crown, thus denying his younger brother John the succession in England (although not John's expectations of the Angevin possessions in France). Hostility simmered between Richard and Philip—always rivals, if sometimes allies. Philip drove a hard bargain when Richard repudiated his betrothal to Alice in order to marry Berengaria of NAVARRE, a step Richard evidently thought politically expedient.

The wedding took place in CYPRUS in May 1191, after Richard had overwhelmed Isaac Comnenus, the self-styled king of Cyprus, when Comnenus tried to detain Berengaria and Joan, her chaperone. Unexpectedly, Richard's relatively small army had been reinforced by the arrival of GUY OF LUSIGNAN, king of Jerusalem, whose claim to the throne from which he had already been evicted by Saladin had evaporated with the death of his wife in an epidemic. In this crisis, Philip II Augustus had elected to support the rival candidate, CONRAD OF MONTFERRAT, and Guy's appeal to Richard for his backing presaged the power struggles that were to vitiate much of what Richard achieved by force of arms during the Crusades. The KNIGHTS OF THE TEMPLE allied with Richard, making inevitable the alignment of their rivals (the Hospitallers) with Philip.

The Crusader. Richard proceeded to Acre. Arriving in June, after having been refused a landing at Tyre by Conrad, he was met with the acclaim and pageantry he craved. Although the Holy Roman Emperor, FREDERICK I BARBAROSSA, had mounted the largest crusading army ever, the Germans had arrived at Acre in tatters following the accidental drowning of the emperor in Cilicia. Philip, too, had preceded Richard, and like him had brought sophisticated siege equipment as well as fresh forces. Yet as a leader, Richard (and his generous bounties) appealed more to the fractious crusaders than did Philip, allowing him to lead a successful assault on Acre, which had been under siege since August 1189. The city fell in July 1191.

Richard was left to command the Crusade alone after the August withdrawal of Philip, who had little appetite for battle and was again pursuing his perennial interest in the Angevin possessions in France, joining with John against Richard as he had done before with Richard against Henry II. After Acre's surrender, Richard had his forces massacre some 2,600 Muslim prisoners—women and children as well as defenders. The repercussions of this brutal act were felt throughout the eastern Mediterranean, leading to many Christian prisoners being accorded the same treatment and stiffening Muslim resistance to Richard's advance. Yet he defeated Saladin's Muslim forces at Arsuf in September, giving him control of the city of Jaffa.

Richard moved on Jerusalem. But fierce dissension among the crusaders and fundamental differences in policy with the rulers of the Christian feudal principalities in the region undercut the military effort. Moreover, Richard was receiving dire reports about Philip and John's activities. Richard alternately launched military forays and pursued negotiations with Saladin, even advancing the proposal that his sister Joan marry Saladin's brother to attain peace. Twice Richard was on the verge of storming Jerusalem but was dissuaded by his counselors. Aware of the necessity of confronting John and Philip at home, in September 1192, he arranged a five-year truce with Saladin that left Jerusalem in Muslim control, but permitted Christian pilgrims access to the city.

Captive. Attempting to make his way to his realms by land after being shipwrecked in the Adriatic, Richard—disguised as a Templar—was seized in AUSTRIA by its duke, Leopold, who had been humiliated by Richard's troops at Acre. Leopold turned Richard over to the Holy Roman Emperor, Henry VI. Henry only freed his captive after he received the pledge of a huge ransom and the surrender of Richard's lands, which were returned to Richard as a fief. Richard arrived in England in March and was crowned a second time in order to reassert his royal right, forcing the treasonous supporters of John to submit. Again raising money by taxation and the shameless selling of offices and privileges, Richard campaigned against Philip in France for five years before concluding a peace. Shortly thereafter, Richard received an arrow wound during a siege of a defiant vassal's castle in Chalus, France. He died ten days later, on April 6, 1199.

Despite later legend, Richard spent only about six months in England; what advances were made in politics and economics during his reign can be ascribed to the efforts of his officials, WILLIAM MARSHAL, William Longchamp, and Hubert Walter, the Archbishop of Canterbury. Moreover, he failed to provide an heir: his only child was an illegitimate son, Philip of Cognac. At his death, he bequeathed his throne and his French territories to John, who soon squandered the fruits of his continental military successes. (*See* ENGLAND; CRUSADES; PLANTAGENET.)

RICHARD II

Richard II (1367–1400) became king of ENGLAND at the age of ten after the death of his grandfather, King EDWARD III, in 1377. His own father, EDWARD THE BLACK PRINCE, had died the previous year. A council of barons advised the boy but in the 1380s, by the time he was a teenager, Richard was already taking a more active role as head of state.

In 1381, during the PEASANTS' REVOLT, the 14-year-old king bravely met with the rebels, although the concessions he made were later nullified, and the rebellion was ruthlessly crushed. Two years after his wife, Anne of Bohemia, died, Richard married the eight-year-old daughter of the French king, CHARLES VII, in order to strengthen his truce with FRANCE. However,

Scene from a manuscript describing Richard II's campaign in Ireland, which proved to be a disaster.

Richard's homosexual inclinations contributed to his unpopularity among the nobility.

Richard was constantly faced with powerful opponents. He captured the duke of Gloucester and exiled the duke of Norfolk and Henry Bolingbroke, his cousin and heir to the enormous duchy of Lancaster.

In 1399, when Henry returned from exile and Richard, distracted by an ill-advised expedition to IRELAND, could not rally sufficient support to oppose him, Richard was forced to surrender his crown. Not content with an abdication, Bolingbroke called on PARLIAMENT to depose Richard on grounds of tyranny. Not long after Bolingbroke assumed the throne as King HENRY IV in 1399, Richard was murdered in prison.

RICHARD III

Richard III (1452–1485) was briefly king of ENGLAND following the death of his older brother, EDWARD IV, whom he served faithfully throughout Edward's reign (1461–1483).

At Edward's CORONATION, Richard was made duke of Gloucester at the age of nine. Afterward, he helped his brother in every way possible, fighting for him at Barnet and Tewkesbury and leading an invasion force against the Scots. When Edward died in April 1483, his oldest son, then only 12 years old, was proclaimed king as Edward V. Richard wrested custody of the young king from Edward's widow, Elizabeth Woodville, and her family, then proclaimed himself protector of the realm. Sensing a conspiracy brewing against him, Richard arrested Lord Hastings, a leading member of the council, and had him executed. He then had Parliament declare his brother's children illegitimate, imprisoned them in the Tower of London, and arranged to have them murdered.

Shortly after Richard had himself crowned in the summer of 1483, a rebellion broke out led by Richard's former ally, Henry Stafford, duke of Buckingham, who supported Henry Tudor (later Henry VII). After the revolt collapsed and Stafford was executed, Henry landed in WALES in 1485. He defeated and killed Richard during the Battle of Bosworth Field and went on to be crowned king of England.

Despite his usurpation of the throne, Richard was not the evil figure as portrayed by tradition and Shakespeare. His reputation as a villain was shaped by Tudor propaganda hoping to divert attention from Henry Tudor's own usurpation of the crown. Richard III was the last of the Yorkist kings. With his death, the WARS OF THE ROSES came to an end.

ROBERT D'ARBISSEL

Robert D'Arbissel (1047–1117) was a French preacher who established a religious order at Fontevrault, near Poitiers, at the beginning of the twelfth century. The order was especially noteworthy for the prominent role it gave to women.

Born in Arbissel, a small village in Brittany, Robert went to Paris to study LITERATURE and PHILOSOPHY. The bishop of Rennes asked him in 1089 to join the Church reform movement in BRITTANY. Robert campaigned strongly against simony (the buying and selling of Church offices) and endorsed celibacy for the clergy. Increasingly strict about his own practices, he became a hermit in a French forest in 1095.

Despite his hermitage, Robert continued to preach vigorously. He attracted many followers who, with his guidance, founded monasteries. In 1098, Robert decided he would devote the rest of his life to public preaching. He was a powerful speaker, and his sermons inspired individuals from all walks of life. In 1101, when Robert established his religious order at Fontevrault, he built separate facilities for men and women. Almost immediately Fontevrault established itself as a place where women had a greater say in religious matters. ELEANOR OF AQUITAINE, the French queen, retired there after she was widowed.

Refusing to accept the position of abbot (although he remained the order's spiritual director), Robert chose an abbess to head Fontevrault in 1115. He continued to travel and preach until his death two years later. (*See* MONASTERIES; WOMEN.)

ROBERT I THE BRUCE

Robert I (1274–1329) the Bruce holds an honored place in Scottish history as the king (1306–1329) who resisted the English and freed SCOTLAND from their rule. He hailed from the Bruce family, one of several who vied for the Scottish throne in the 1200s. His grandfather, also named Robert the Bruce, had been an unsuccessful claimant to the Scottish throne in 1290. Robert I Bruce became earl of Carrick in 1292 at the age of 18, later becoming lord of Annandale and of the Bruce territories in England when his father died in 1304.

Defiance. In 1296, Robert pledged his loyalty to King Edward I of ENGLAND, but the following year he joined the struggle for national independence. He fought at his father's side when the latter tried to depose the Scottish king, John Baliol. Baliol's fall opened the way for fierce political infighting. In 1306, Robert quarreled with and eventually murdered the Scottish patriot John Comyn, lord of Badenoch, in their struggle for leadership. Robert claimed the throne and traveled to Scone where he was crowned king on March 27, 1306, in open defiance of King Edward.

A few months later the English defeated Robert's forces at Methven. Robert fled to the west, taking refuge on the island of Rathlin off the coast of Ireland. Edward then confiscated Bruce property, punished

Robert the Bruce and his first wife, the daughter of the earl of Marr, 1306. The body of Robert the Bruce was laid to rest in Dunferline Abbey. His heart, however, was taken out of his body by Sir James Douglas when he was making a pilgrimage to the Holy Land. It was purportedly buried in Melrose Abbey in Scotland after Douglas's death in 1330.

Robert's followers, and executed his three brothers. A legend has Robert learning courage and perseverance from a determined spider he watched during his exile.

Robert returned to Scotland in 1307 and won a victory at Loudon Hill. Edward I launched a campaign against the Scottish rebels, but he died on his way north. He was succeeded by his son, EDWARD II, who was unable to continue his father's campaign. Robert launched his own campaign to regain control of Scotland, beginning in the north and advancing south, seizing one region after another and recapturing lands and castles from the English. In 1313, he captured Perth; a year later at Bannockburn, he inflicted a crushing defeat on a large English force under the command of Edward II. As the war continued, the Scots recaptured Berwick in 1318. When the English refused to make peace or acknowledge Robert as king of Scotland, Robert raided northern England as well.

Independence. In 1327, yet another English king, EDWARD III, tried to crush the Scottish rebellion. When he failed, the English crown finally agreed to the Treaty of Northampton (1328) that recognized the independence of Scotland and Robert's right to the throne. The treaty also provided for the marriage of Robert's son David to King Edward's sister. Robert spent the brief remaining years of his life in his castle in Cardross, where he died in 1329.

Robert solidified Scotland's status as an independent kingdom by securing an orderly succession for his son, who became King David II. He was followed by his son, Robert's grandson, Robert II.

ROBERT GUISCARD

R obert Guiscard (c. 1015–1085), the son of TANCRED DE HAUTEVILLE, was the NORMAN conqueror of southern ITALY. During his long and eventful career, he helped establish the Norman family of Hauteville as an important ruling dynasty on the political stage of medieval Europe. In the 1040s, Robert joined his brothers and other Norman adventurers in southern Italy and fought with them to expel the Byzantines. In 1057, he succeeded his brother Humphrey as count of Apulia. By the end of the decade, he emerged as the defender of papal interests in the south. In 1059, Pope NICHOLAS II invested him with Calabria and SICILY, most of which remained to be conquered, as well as Apulia. With the help of his younger brother Roger, who wrested Sicily from the Arabs, Robert asserted his control over the lands he was granted, defeating the Byzantines and fighting on behalf of Pope GREGORY VII against the Holy Roman Emperor HENRY IV. (*See* NORMANS; ITALY; SICILY.)

ROBIN HOOD

G iven modern perceptions, it may be easier to say what Robin Hood as portrayed in surviving medieval ballads was not: he was not the dispossessed earl of Huntingdon; he was not an ANGLO-SAXON freedom fighter against NORMAN oppression; and he did not live in the time of RICHARD I, but rather during the reign of an unspecified King Edward. Associated with Barnsdale in Yorkshire and with Sherwood forest in Nottinghamshire, his devotion was to the Virgin Mary rather than to Maid Marion.

Origins. Debates about the ballads of Robin Hood have focused on when they were written and their social appeal. The first reference to them is in the B-text (c. 1377) of LANGLAND's *Piers Plowman*, although the earliest surviving text, *Robin Hood and the Monk*, survives only in a manuscript of c. 1450. The major medieval source is the *Gestes of Robin Hood*, which appeared in five printed editions in the late fifteenth and sixteenth centuries, although it was based on a manuscript, now lost, of perhaps a century earlier.

The Real Outlaw. Other stories of medieval outlaws, such as those of Hereward the Wake, featured actual historical individuals. Inevitably, efforts have been made to identify real-life models for the characters of the Robin Hood ballads. Robert Hood, a porter in the household of EDWARD II in 1323–1324 has been a particularly popular candidate for the role of the outlaw hero himself. More recently, the existence of "Robynhood" surnames, of which the earliest known example dates from 1262, has been seen as evidence that ballads were in existence long before the 1320s. In that case, a Yorkshireman of 1226, the only known medieval Robert Hood who was actually an outlaw, becomes a more attractive candidate for the role of the original Robin Hood.

However, given the extent to which the Robin Hood ballads reproduce the conventions found in many other medieval outlaw stories, discussions of their social appeal may be more significant than a search for their historical origins. For some scholars, the emphasis of the Gestes on Robin's yeomanly status identifies him as a free peasant. His plundering of wealthy landowners, such as the abbot of St. Mary's in York, shows him to be a plebeian hero whose exploits should be seen in the context of the agrarian class struggles of the thirteenth and fourteenth centuries.

Wide Appeal. For others, Robin's yeomanry places him amongst the households of the landed classes, like the knight's yeoman described by CHAUCER. His hostility to the treacherous sheriff of Nottingham and his sympathy with a knightly victim of ecclesiastical usury point to a more upper-class popularity. In fact, by the time of the Gestes, the ballads were the product of perhaps 250 years of evolution. Popular at the royal court, in gentry households, including that of the PASTON FAMILY, and amongst the local communities, the ballads owed their enduring charm to the fact that they were flexible enough to appeal to a wide range of groups, rather than being the exclusive property of any one SOCIAL CLASS.

ROGER LORIA

Roger Loria (also Ruggiero di Lauria; c. 1245–1304) was born in ITALY but grew up in the Aragonese court of PETER III THE GREAT, who named him grand admiral in 1283. He was an active participant in the revolt against CHARLES I OF ANJOU's rule of SICILY, known as the SICILIAN VESPERS, and distinguished himself in the ensuing struggles between the French ANGEVINS and the Sicilian-Aragonese. He achieved several notable naval victories, including a defeat of the French at the Bay of Naples in 1284 and a successful defense of Catalonia against the invading forces of King Philip III in 1285.

Loria also supported Frederick III's efforts to take the Sicilian crown from his elder brother, James II, king of Sicily and ARAGON and son of Peter III; but ultimately he switched his allegiance to the Angevin and Aragonese side in order to protect his Valencian property. In 1299 and again in 1300, Loria defeated the Sicilian fleets that he had once commanded. He retired to his estates in Catalonia after the war ended in 1302.

ROGER OF SALISBURY

Roger (died 1139) was a Norman priest who HENRY I brought to ENGLAND when he became king. Besides being bishop of Salisbury, Roger was a brilliant and powerful member of Henry's court and one of England's greatest statesmen. He ruled England in Henry's absence; later, he helped Stephen of Blois succeed Henry on the English throne, but fell when Stephen turned against him.

His Career. Roger was serving as a clerk at Avranches in Normandy when he came to the attention of the future king of England. Upon his accession to the throne Henry quickly put Roger's administrative skills to work. In 1101, Henry made Roger royal chancellor, but Roger resigned when he became bishop of Salisbury in 1102. He remained the king's chief adviser and administrator throughout Henry's long reign (1100–1135) and governed England during the king's long absences in Normandy. Roger's only official title, proto-justiciar of England, stemmed from his position as ruler of the kingdom during the king's absence. On behalf of the king, Roger streamlined royal government and introduced a new level of sophistication into the administration of the royal finances and courts. Perhaps his most lasting contribution was the creation and organization of the EXCHEQUER, the department of government that administers royal finances, which became the first effective fiscal system in Europe. He also sent royal justices out into the country to hear pleas and complaints from the people. (*See* MONEY AND CURRENCY; EXCHEQUER.)

As bishop of Salisbury, Roger rebuilt on a grand scale the cathedral at Old Sarum, the ancient fortress town located near Salisbury; he built many new churches, MONASTERIES, and CASTLES as well. Roger's control of both the Chancery and Exchequer increased as younger members of his family moved into positions of power. His son, Roger le Poer, became chancellor, and his nephew Nigel, bishop of Ely, was treasurer.

Downfall. The power and prestige of Roger and his family did not long outlive his service to King Henry. Roger was largely responsible for Stephen of Blois's ascension to the throne, and he was the dominant figure in the new king's government. However, Roger's power earned him the enmity of Waleran, the count of Meulan, who turned the new king against Roger. In 1139, King Stephen summoned Roger to Oxford and imprisoned him in the royal castle in Wiltshire, accusing him of treachery. According to Henry of Huntingdon, Henry starved Roger and tortured his son until Roger agreed to turn over his family's possessions. Roger died in poverty and disgrace on December 11, 1139, but the high-handed seizure of Roger's wealth lost the king many supporters.

ROLAND

Roland (d. 778) was a historical figure who was immortalized as a chivalrous hero in the 4,000-line epic poem *La Chanson de Roland* (*The Song of Roland*) The actual Roland was the prefect of the Breton March, or frontier, for the Frankish king CHARLEMAGNE. Roland was killed by the Basques when Charlemagne was forced to return to FRANCE to deal with a Saxon uprising. Roland and the rear guard of the army were ambushed by Basques in the Pyrenees mountains. Roland and his Frankish forces, which included many of the aristocracy, were trapped and killed at Roncesvalles. The stand of the FRANKS and Roland was remembered in a chronicle attributed to Turpin, archbishop of Reims. The retelling of his story in *La Chanson de Roland* is the first known example of the popular medieval artistic genre, CHANSONS DE GESTES (songs of heroic deeds) that upheld the ideal of the noble-warrior and the superiority of CHRISTIANITY. *La Chanson de Roland* is considered one of the great works of Western LITERATURE.

Since *La Chanson de Roland* is a vindication of Christian medieval civilization, the enemy of the poetic Roland becomes the Muslim SARACENS instead of the Christian Basques of the historical Roland. The poem also exaggerates the danger faced by Roland and the significance of his defeat. In the poem, Roland is betrayed by his evil stepfather, Ganelon, who makes an alliance with the Muslim chief Marsile. Marsile arranges a peace with Charlemagne, but treacherously attacks the Franks from the rear. Roland and his friend Oliver stand against the heathen army in a mountain pass. Oliver requests that Roland blow a horn calling for help but Roland, out of aristocratic pride, refuses until death is inevitable. Charlemagne returns too late; Roland has been killed fighting for king and Cross.

The anonymous poem was written in the late eleventh century. It has remained popular due to its straightforward narrative, exciting story, and the unambiguous moral symbolism of the characters. The poem presents a picture of heroic Christendom, infused with the values of the feudal order: the loyalty owed to one's superiors and the hierarchical system.

The CHANSONS DE GESTE were common to northern France in the High Middle Ages. These epic poems usually began as an oral tale that circulated before being written down in the eleventh and twelfth centuries. Meant to entertain royal courts, they therefore praised the social function of the lords. Kings in these poems are weak secondary figures, and the clergy merely assistants to aristocratic warriors. Peasants are absent, except as field workers and victims of feudal wars. Personal loyalty remains at the moral heart of the stories; vassalage is the only legitimate relationship.

ROLLO

Rollo (c. 860–c. 932), leader of VIKING pirates who raided the French coast and settled at the mouth of Seine, was the first ruler of Normandy. According to Icelandic SAGAS he was of noble Norwegian ancestry. His name, Rolf Gangr, was later gallicized to Rollo. His years of raiding in FRANCE included sailing up the Seine and sacking PARIS in 910. In 911, after the FRANKS defeated his army outside Chartres, Rollo was forced by the Treaty of Saint-Clair-sur-Epte to pay homage to Charles III the Simple, king of the West Franks. The Franks gave Rollo land along the Seine as a fief that he and his men already occupied on condition that he defend it against attack and be baptized. In 912, Rollo, baptized as Robert, became the first duke of Normandy. The land he was granted marked the beginning of the history of medieval Normandy. (*See* VIKINGS.)

ROMANESQUE

The architectural and artistic style that flourished in western Europe between c. 950 and 1150. Characterized by the use of antique Roman architecture as a model, it featured a return to monumental artwork, such as frescoes and relief sculpture. Such permanent art signaled a new sense of security throughout Europe after several centuries of upheaval caused by successive barbarian invasions. The influence of the NORMANS on the growth of towns was one of the strongest factors contributing to the mood; thus, the Romanesque is also called the Norman style.

Church Influence. After the passing of the millennium, which some had predicted would mark the end of the world, and with the growth of wealth and population, there was a surge in building construction and sponsorship of the decorative arts under the aegis of the expanding Roman Catholic Church, especially from the Benedictines of the order of Cluny. The establishment of a series of monasteries and churches replete with saints' relics along the pilgrim's route from St. Martin of Tour in FRANCE to SANTIAGO DE COMPOSTELA in SPAIN spread this movement.

The cruciform basilica plan of BYZANTINE and CAROLINGIAN origin, consisting of a central nave, transept crossing, and semicircular apse, was improved upon by the addition of side aisles, galleries, and radiating chapels to house the requisite relics, the viewing of which was the main objective for making the pilgrimage. Massive stone walls now supported masonry barrel vaults, thereby raising the height of the ceiling and allowing for a clerestory—a high windowed wall.

The façade of Notre Dame la Grande in Poitiers, France. The design of the portals are characteristic of the style.

Another legacy of the Carolingian period was the "westwork" or western facade of the church with flanking symmetrical towers, multiple stories, and upper chapels for dignitaries.

European Influence. Different areas of Europe developed variations based on their distance from the creative center in France. After 1066, the Norman influence reached ENGLAND, and the innovations of Cluniac France were refined even further. At Durham Cathedral (begun 1093—completed 1104), for instance, rib vaulting (thin, diagonal arches capable of supporting lighter walls) was introduced.

Northern SPAIN, where CHRISTIANITY engaged in an ongoing struggle against the Muslim south, was tied politically and economically to southern France and northern Italy. In the early eleventh century, Sancho the Great of NAVARRE encouraged the influx of Cluniac monks, with their zeal for building monasteries, into Spain. The French style of massive walls, round arches, and barrel vaults combined in some areas with a more conservative Italian LOMBARD style that retained timber ceilings or rafters.

The Romanesque architectural style influenced the other arts, as with the reliquary, above.

Stylized figures were carved on columns and capitals. Dormant since the Fall of Rome, relief sculpture—a form of building decoration found primarily around the outer doors—was revived. Sculptural art was almost always religious in nature, with favorite themes being the majesty of Christ, the Last Judgment, and the torments of Hell. After the First Crusade (1095–1099), depictions of fantastic, imagined exotic peoples and creatures became common. Inside the churches, frescoes adorned the walls and vaults, their vivid colors brightening the somber stone interiors.

MANUSCRIPT ILLUMINATIONS, highly developed in the monasteries, often drew on the imagery of the Apocalypse. Ornate initial letters incorporated human figures, dragons, and floral motifs; the figures sometimes assumed the shape of the letter. Romanesque sculptures and manuscript illuminations are characterized by an impressionistic style aimed at stimulating an emotional response in the viewer. The best surviving example of this Romanesque impressionism are the sculptures over the doorway to the church at Vézélay in southern France.

In the later twelfth century, the more naturalistic GOTHIC Style began to supplant the Romanesque.

Milestones in Romanesque Architecture	
1000	Romanesque churches begin to appear throughout Europe.
955-1010	Abbey church of Cluny, France.
1024-1084	Mont-Saint-Michel, Normandy.
1030-1061	Cathedral of Speyer, Germany.
1063	Construction begins on cathedral of Pisa, Italy.
1088-1130	Abbey church of Cluny is reconstructed.
1093-1133	Durham Cathedral is built in England.
1149	Additions are made to the Holy Sepulcher church in Jerusalem.
1152-1174	Cathedral erected in Zamora, Spain.

See ARCHITECTURE; CHURCHES AND CATHEDRALS; NORMANS; CAROLINGIAN RENAISSANCE; ROME *and* GOTHIC ART AND ARCHITECTURE. *Related material may be found in* MANUSCRIPT ILLUMINATION; PAINTING; *and in* BYZANTINE ART AND ARCHITECTURE.

ROME

The Germanic invasions of the 400s and 500s hastened the fall of the Roman empire, leaving the city of Rome a shadow of its former glorious self. During the Middle Ages, the city became the arena of a long power struggle between popes, German emperors, city nobles, and foreign invaders. Although the city had little commercial importance, it remained the principal city of medieval Europe on the strength of its classical past and the prestige derived from being the seat of the bishop of Rome, or pope.

City Under Siege. The sack of the city by ALARIC I the VISIGOTH in 410 and by the VANDALS in 455 caused political power to shift to RAVENNA, which the GOTHS made their capital and from which they ruled ITALY. The PAPACY stayed in Rome where the prestige of popes as St. Peter's successors made them the main source of power and influence in the city. The diplomatic efforts of Pope Leo I (440–461) helped keep ATTILA THE HUN away from the city. The last Roman emperor, Romulus Augustulus, was deposed in 476. THEODORIC THE GREAT ruled Rome from Ravenna for 30 years in the early 500s. (*See* PAPACY; ITALY.)

The city suffered greatly from the wars between the Goths and the Byzantines. In 552, the Byzantines under Narses captured Rome from the OSTROGOTHS, finding it depleted and in disarray. (The population of Rome remained less than 50,000 for the rest of the Middle Ages.) Narses became the first of the Byzantine exarchs (viceroys) to rule Italy from Ravenna. Rome's decline became worse 20 years later when another German group, the LOMBARDS, invaded Italy and isolated Rome from contacts with the Byzantines, who at the time controlled southern Italy.

By the late 500s, much of Rome's civic and social organization was in a state of collapse. Civic offices responsible for maintaining the city's aqueducts, walls, and imperial palaces were gone or bankrupt. Even the consuls and Senate—the city institutions from the early years of the republic—ceased to function.

Gregory I. Pope GREGORY I THE GREAT (590–604) attended to the problem of the disrepair of the aqueduct system and ancient buildings. He also helped free the city from the control of the exarchs. He used Church land and resources to supply the city with food and services, and gave care and protection to homeless refugees. (*See* GREGORY I.)

Gregory's assertion of Rome's primacy in Christendom had a great influence on the fortunes of the city. Roman missionary work in ENGLAND and GERMANY increased the city's importance as it increasingly became a pilgrimage destination. Gregory's skill managing Church lands set the stage for the PAPAL STATES.

Outside Assistance. As ties to BYZANTIUM loosened in the 700s, the Lombard threat intensified. When the Lombards seized towns in the Tiber River valley north of Rome and threatened to attack Rome itself, Pope Zacharias I appealed to the FRANKS for help. In 756, the Lombards sacked Rome, but soon the Franks under PÉPIN III THE SHORT came to the rescue. When the Lombards attacked again in 773, CHARLEMAGNE intervened. His arrival in Rome marked the beginning of a long period of Frankish protection of the city and the designation of Frankish rulers as *patricius Romanorum*—protectors of Rome. Pope LEO III crowned Charlemagne the new Roman emperor on Christmas Day, 800. (*See* CORONATION.)

The interests of the city's noble families and the papacy often clashed in the following centuries. When local nobles took control of the papacy, the German king OTTO I entered the city in 962 to restore imperial control and protect the pope from unruly Romans. The grateful pope crowned Otto emperor, thus laying the foundation for the HOLY ROMAN EMPIRE. The German emperors tried to keep order in Rome, but the constantly feuding nobles were the real rulers of the city, choosing popes who suited them best.

Power Struggles. By the 1000s, the papacy and the college of cardinals became stronger. At the end of the century, the German king Henry IV and Pope GREGORY VII became locked in a bitter struggle over who had the right to choose Italian bishops. In 1084, Henry entered the city and chose a new pope, Clement III, to replace Gregory; Clement in turn crowned Henry emperor. The NORMANS, who supported Gregory, arrived in the city several weeks later and defeated the Germans, but they also went on to sack and burn parts of the city. (*See* GERMANY; GREGORY VII.)

After the German emperors reestablished their control of the city, they gave the Romans the right to choose their own magistrates and senators. Tensions arose between the papacy and the Roman commune, the government which managed the city. Tensions between GUELPHS AND GHIBELLINES plagued the city and erupted into civil strife under Pope INNOCENT III until Emperor FREDERICK II restored peace.

During the "Babylonian captivity" between 1304 and 1377, when the papacy was relocated from Rome to AVIGNON in southern France, Rome suffered a sharp decline of pilgrims, leaving it desolate and in turmoil. After the papacy returned to Rome in the late 1300s, Pope Boniface IX forced the commune to recognize his right to appoint city officials and supersede city law. In the early 1400s, the papacy succeeded in establishing itself as the unofficial fiscal administrator of the city.

The papacy of Martin V (1417–1431) marked the beginning of a strong papacy, with Rome poised to enter the Renaissance as the financial and administrative center of the Catholic Church.

ROYAL TOUCH

A quality attributed to French and English kings in the late Middle Ages where monarchs were able to cure sick people by mere touch. This Christ-like ability stemmed from the medieval doctrine that kings ruled through divine sanction. According to this belief, kings were the representatives of God on earth, and therefore secular rule was informed by religious meaning. The Royal Touch was a vivid symbol of the attempt to combine religious and secular authority. Monarchs gained the Royal Touch in the CORONATION ceremony through the ritual of anointment on the head by oil that had been blessed by the Church. In ENGLAND and FRANCE, this oil was also applied to the shoulders and hands, endowing the new ruler with the power to cure. The most common ailment purportedly cured by the Royal Touch was scrofula—enlarged lymph glands—jaundice, LEPROSY, and other disorders. (*See* KINGSHIP; MAGIC AND FOLKLORE.)

King EDWARD THE CONFESSOR of England reportedly cured a woman's infected throat glands. King Robert II the Pious of France healed lepers and other sick people, both through touch and the sign of the cross. In 1124, an abbot recounted that King Louis VI of France cured numerous people of scrofula. Louis's father, Philip I, could also heal the ill until he forfeited this ability because of his sinful behavior. This belief continued until the late eighteenth century.

RURIK

The VIKING leader (d. 879) who is traditionally credited with founding the Russian state. Rurik was born in Friesland, a region in present-day Holland, which his father controlled. After leading raids in FRANCE, ENGLAND, and GERMANY, Rurik gained control of a large tract of land in Jutland. However, he soon abandoned his claim under pressure from rival chieftains. (*See* VIKINGS.)

In the 850s, Rurik and his two brothers led a band of Vikings into northwestern RUSSIA where they established a settlement near Lake Ladoga. Rurik soon moved part of the settlement to nearby NOVGOROD, according to legend, at the invitation of the local SLAVS. There he established the seat of his power and built a fortress from which he could rule the Russian lands. His rule extended as far south as Kiev where his successors founded the powerful Kievan state, which lasted until the 1200s.

Rurik left Russia in 873 to rule over the inheritance left him by his father in Friesland; he left his

Russian domain to his kinsman, Oleg. Thereafter, Russian princes in both Kiev and Moscow claimed descent from Rurik, as did the grand princes and czars who ruled the grand duchy of Moscow and later all of Russia until the death of Feodor in 1598. (*See* RUSSIA.)

RUSSIA

At the beginning of the Middle Ages, what is now called Russia was an East Slavic land made up of several city-states. They were primarily agricultural societies that domesticated cattle. Slavic merchants in the trading centers soon realized they needed protection. A band of Viking merchant-adventurers, the Varangians, passed through en route to CONSTANTINOPLE in 860, and occupied Kiev.

A New Dynasty. The Vikings were ousted by the Varangian Oleg from the northern city-state of NOVGOROD, and a new dynasty began. By the end of the tenth century, there were equal populations of SLAVS and Varangians in the new land, which became known as Kievan Rus, after the major principality of Kiev (located in the central, southern portion of the state).

Kievan Rus was eventually strong enough to challenge the Byzantine Empire, starting with Oleg's attack in 907. The two states made treaties during the tenth century to establish trade; Kievan Rus sent fur and honey to the empire. Oleg's successor, Igor, was

Russia in the late Middle Ages. *Russia had more in common with the Europe of half a millennium earlier—small feudal states under the threat of large powers.*

killed in 945 during a winter trade expedition.

Igor's son Svyatoslav grew up to lead Kievan Rus's military conquest of the Bulgars, responding to attacks by the Khazar tribe. He in turn was ambushed and killed in 972 by Byzantines from Pecheneg in the south, who, according to legend, turned Svyatoslav's skull into a drinking cup.

His son Vladimir (died 1015) succeeded him, and fortified the southern districts to withstand Pecheneg assaults. He converted from paganism to Orthodox CHRISTIANITY and convinced his people to do the same—one of the many ways Byzantium influenced Kievan culture. However, the Rus resisted the Greek influence, which had changed Byzantine culture.

Instability. Under the reign of Vladimir's successor, YAROSLAV THE WISE, Russian culture became more integrated with European life. Russian-born princesses married into the royal families of NORWAY, HUNGARY, and FRANCE. He also turned back Pecheneg takeovers, forcing them to retreat to the Balkans. After Yaroslav's death, while different tribes banded together to form the *Chernye Klobuki* or the "Black Hoods" to guard Kievan princes, Turkish invaders started to make gains. Yaroslav's successors had little effectiveness in halting them and encountered difficulties in simply keeping Kievan provinces together. Sometimes, Rus principalities in the southern steppes joined foreign states, including the Cuman-Kipchack tribes, in fighting the Rus. (*See* YAROSLAV.)

The Holy Wars in the twelfth century moved Russia as well as POLAND further inland. Germany's expansion hindered Russia's expansion into Europe and Russia became more rural as a result. By the time the crusaders overthrew CONSTANTINOPLE in the early thirteenth century, Kiev was no longer Kievan Rus's major city, as changes in trade routes pushed the eastern city of Vladimir-Suzdal to the forefront. As Russia was shut off from the West economically and culturally, the Church's influence on daily life grew.

Mongol Invasions. The disunity among Russian tribes paved the way for Mongolian armies to overrun Rus in 1237, leveling Kiev. The MONGOLS also reorganized the Tatars and created the GOLDEN HORDE at the Volga that ruled Rus for the next two centuries. The Mongols enslaved and killed Russians, forcing al-

Icon of Our Lady of Vladimir. Vladimir marked the beginning of Russia's intense involvement with Christianity.

legiance to the Khan. Eventually the Tatars were successful in Turkicizing the Horde.

Nevsky. Because ALEXANDER NEVSKY, leader of Novgorod, made certain to cooperate with the Horde, Novgorod became a major Kievan Rus city. Nevsky was a strong military leader. He led victories against the Swedes and, at the Battle On the Ice in 1242, against the TEUTONIC KNIGHTS. A decade later the Tatars named Nevsky a grand prince. During his reign, the chief cleric of Rus abandoned Kiev for Vladimir. Nevsky's son, Daniel, having become the prince of Moscow, annexed the surrounding territories. Within a century, Moscow was the center of Russia. Moscow's first prince was David; his son Ivan I, its first grand prince, moved the capital from Vladimir to Moscow in 1328.

Fall of the Horde. Slowly, LITHUANIA started controlling Russian principalities; it took over Kiev in 1361, and unsuccessfully attacked Moscow twice. Moscow's grand prince DIMITRI DONSKOI joined forces with the Lithuanians, and led victories over the Tatars at the Battle of Kulikuvo in 1380, after the Russians had refused to pay tribute to the Golden Horde. After the Russian victory, the Horde relented on the issue of tribute, and Dimitri's son Vasili I kept the Tatars and Lithuanians from taking over. Vasili II's reign saw the crumbling of the Horde; by the 1450s Moscow was free of Horde influence.

Vasili's son, Ivan III, expanded Moscow, incorporating most Russian principalities, an area covering 15,000 square miles. After centuries of isolation, Ivan III attempted to reintroduce Russia to Europe. He attempted to reclaim Russia's Byzantine heritage. His second wife was Zoe Palaeologa, the niece of Byzantine emperor Constantine XI. Their son, Vasili III, called Moscow the "third Rome" and resumed relations with the HOLY ROMAN EMPIRE.

Russia developed a European-style feudalism that was to stifle its development and keep it in somber bondage for the rest of the Middle Ages. (*See* NEVSKY; NOVGOROD; GOLDEN HORDE.)

SAGAS, NORDIC AND ICELANDIC

Sagas are long narratives that appeared in NORWAY, ICELAND, and other parts of Scandinavia during the Middle Ages. The word "saga" is old Norse for "story," and these stories, originally unwritten, were passed down orally for generations before they were transcribed beginning in the thirteenth century.

Origins. Sagas were originally a means of preserving history. Informal histories have existed among people for thousands of years, but sagas (like the ancient Greek epics) presented a consistent set of events with a fairly definite chronology. Since these stories were at first passed down orally, certain details were lost or transformed; it is not uncommon for several versions of the same saga to exist.

Sagas can be divided into three primary groups. The family sagas were probably the most common; they dealt with the histories of individual families and were passed down through the generations. Kings' sagas focused on the various kings of Norway and the events of their reigns. The heroic saga, probably the best known type, chronicled the deeds and adventures of legendary Scandinavian heroes.

Many sagas were written in a detached, objective style, which many scholars mistakenly believed meant they were historically accurate. Later research has revealed that the sagas often made use of fictitious situations that were grounded in a remote historical reality.

Sagas often include accounts of supernatural events or references to Norse mythology; some make references to CHRISTIANITY (which was not introduced into Scandinavia until the ninth century). Such sagas as the *Volsungasaga* tell of mythical beings, such as the race of dwarfs known as the Nibelung. These sagas were adapted in GERMAN LITERATURE as the *Nibelungenlied* (*Tales of the Nibelung*).

Famous Sagas. Surviving saga manuscripts reveal richness of detail and subtle characterization. In addition to their value as literary works, they have been instrumental in giving scholars a picture of medieval Scandinavian life.

The *Njala* saga is one of the most famous of the family sagas. It tells the story of Gunnar and his close friend Njall. Gunnar marries a beautiful but treacher-

A 14th-century manuscript of Snorri Sturluson's Prose (Younger) Edda, *a collection of ancient skaldic epic poetry compiled around 1222.*

ous woman, who is ultimately responsible for his death and the destruction of his family and community. Its description of important events is enriched by its treatment of human emotions.

Other famous family sagas include the *Eyrbybgja*, which includes a number of supernatural events, and the *Laxdaela*, which chronicles events against the backdrop of a love triangle. The Icelandic historian Sturla Thordsson wrote the *Sturlungasaga* in the thirteenth century; it is notable for its inclusion of many of the author's contemporaries.

It was during the Middle Ages that the VIKINGS sailed from Norway and discovered the islands of Iceland and GREENLAND. The written accounts of these voyages are of particular interest to scholars because they describe not only the exploration of Greenland and Iceland, but also the earliest known European explorations of NORTH AMERICA. Among the most important of these sagas are the *Greenlanders' Saga* and the *Saga of Erik the Red*.

Well-known kings' sagas include the *Heimskringla*, written in the thirteenth century by Snorri Sturluson. This saga—actually a series of short sagas—chronicles the kings of Norway. One of the best known heroic sagas is the *Grettis*, which follows the adventures of Grettir, an Icelandic outlaw. Grettir fights with a monster called Glamr and later with a troll woman—not unlike the English story of BEOWULF. (*See* MAGIC AND FOLKLORE.)

Icelandic Sagas. The literature of the Norsemen survives mainly in the sagas and legends of Iceland because very little of the Scandinavian medieval vernacular literature remains. The Norwegians settled Iceland in the late 800s and brought with them a body of oral mythological poetry that flourished on the island, protected from the warlike atmosphere in Norway.

The best literature that has survived from the period before 1100 are the Eddic poems, which are condensations of ancient plays in alliterative verse about old Scandinavian heroes and gods.

The title *Edda* applies to two distinct works in Old Icelandic. *Elder Edda*, or the *Poetic*, is a collection of 34 heroic poems or poetic sagas, composed between 800 and 1200, but not compiled until the late 1200s. The manuscript of the *Poetic Edda* called the *Codex Regius* is regarded as one of the most valuable collections of Old Norse legend, myth, and poetry. *The Younger Edda*, or *Prose*, is a handbook of skaldic (ancient Scandinavian) poetry compiled by the Icelander Snorri Sturluson about 1222.

The Eddic sagas are long narratives describing the exploits of notable Norsemen. Although the sagas are concerned mostly with events in the 900s or 1000s or even earlier, they were not committed to writing until the 1200s and 1300s. The Eddas are invaluable sources on pre-Christian Scandinavian culture. (*See* ICELAND; GREENLAND; NORWAY; LITERATURE.)

SAINT-DENIS, ABBEY OF

Located some ten kilometers north of NOTRE DAME and the center of PARIS, the abbey church of Saint-Denis (now a cathedral) stands above the site where Denis, first bishop of Paris, martyr, and patron saint of France, was buried. According to GREGORY OF TOURS (died 594), Denis was one of seven bishops sent from Rome to Gaul, where he was martyred during the first great persecution of Christians under the emperor Decius (r. 249–251). More than 300 years later, Geneviève (who would become patron saint of Paris) inspired the erection of a small church to honor Denis. Numerous sarcophagi, some containing princely accouterments and one containing the remains of Queen Aregonde (d. c. 565), witness the importance attributed to the site and its surrounding shrines by the faithful, who wished to be interred nearby. (*See* CHURCHES.)

Establishment. Dagobert (608 –639), the powerful king of the united FRANKS, established the foundations of the church's future greatness by enlarging Geneviève's sanctuary, adding impressive marble columns and commissioning a shrine and other ornaments from the goldsmith Eloi (Eligius). Dagobert granted lands and privileges to the abbey, and instituted the perpetual chanting of psalms. Most important, he made the abbey a royal necropolis by having himself interred there. His wife Nanthild and their son Clovis II (r. 637–657) were also buried there. Clovis II's wife Bathild instituted monastic observance at Saint-Denis and other important churches of the realm.

Carolingian Support. The abbey was fortunate in acquiring the favor and support of CHARLES MARTEL, mayor of the palace and the founder of the CAROLINGIAN DYNASTY. Charles sent his sons to the abbey to be educated, and he himself was buried there. His son Pépin, who became mayor after his father, installed Fulrad as abbot of Saint-Denis. In 751, through Fulrad's agency, he received papal approval for the deposition of the last MEROVINGIAN ruler and his own accession as king of the Franks. In 754, Pépin, his wife Bertha, and his sons Carloman and Charles (the future CHARLEMAGNE) were anointed and blessed by the exiled Pope Stephen at Saint-Denis; subsequently Pépin and Bertha were both buried at the abbey. By 775, Fulrad and the Carolingian kings had created a glorious new church, its crypt sheltering the tomb of Saint Denis. Charlemagne attended the consecration of the church, which he claimed to have constructed and decorated. The Carolingians showered favors on the abbey; Charles II the Bald (823–877) was its special patron, ordering his burial there, enriching it with relics that included the crown, a nail of the Passion, and the arm of Saint Simeon.

Writings. Abbot Hilduin (died 840) was one of the abbey's great leaders. He enlarged the church, adding a chapel at the eastern end of Fulrad's apse. But most important were the texts produced by him and his disciple HINCMAR (made archbishop of Reims in 845), which elevated Saint-Denis's status by recording the miracles which had made Dagobert the abbey's earliest royal patron. Legends had already begun to accumulate about the saint. By the early sixth century, Pope Clement was said to have sent Denis to Gaul; by the end of the century, two companions in martyrdom, Eleutherius and Rusticus, had been

The Tomb of Dagobert, constructed by St. Louis in the abbey church of Saint-Denis. Dagobert is depicted being carried away by demons after his death and then rescued by angels.

assigned to him. But Hilduin and Hincmar also confirmed and popularized the identification of Denis with Dionysius the Areopagite, one of Saint Paul's most important converts, bishop of Athens, who was apostle of all Gaul, and credited with philosophical and visionary Greek writings that were actually composed in the sixth century. The Byzantine Emperor Michael the Stammerer sent a copy of these texts to Saint-Denis in 827. Hilduin did a rough translation, but his version was soon superseded by the more polished rendition by JOHN SCOTUS ERIGENA for Charles the Bald. The writings of Hilduin and Hincmar confirmed the tradition associating Denis's martyrdom with Montmartre ("mount of the martyrs"). Some skeptics raised doubts about these stories, but PETER ABELARD's observation in 1121 that BEDE identified Dionysius the Areopagite as the bishop of Corinth caused more problems for him than for the abbey, which, in 1216, received relics of Denis of Corinth from Pope INNOCENT III. A special Greek mass composed for Saint Denis's feast day in the late twelfth century reveals the endurance of Hilduin's and Hincmar's work.

Fulrad's and Hilduin's efforts ensured that the fame and status of Saint-Denis would survive the Norman incursions and the political uncertainties of the tenth century. HUGH CAPET and his descendants, who replaced the Carolingians as rulers of France, formed a close alliance with Saint-Denis; all but three of the kings of the CAPETIAN DYNASTY were buried there.

Redesign. Abbot SUGER radically transformed the church of Saint-Denis between 1135 and 1144. Constructing an impressive westwork, a new chevet and crypt, he linked the western addition to the Carolingian nave. Unable to rebuild the entire church as he planned, he took great pains to harmonize the antique remains with the new additions. The architectural innovations—the lightened walls and enlarged windows—were accompanied by carefully designed and crafted STAINED-GLASS windows on Old and New Testament themes. Suger also enriched the treasury with precious liturgical objects. He increased the wealth of the abbey, in all likelihood resorting to forgery to gain control of the priory of Argenteuil. His successor Odo of Deuil increased the prestige of Argenteuil by associating with it the relic of the seamless tunic of Christ, a gift, he claimed, of Charlemagne's daughter, Theodrade. BERNARD OF CLAIRVAUX praised Suger for the reforms he instituted, although SUGER is known to have retained the elaborate plainchant long practiced at Saint-Denis. Under Suger the ornate service for the anniversary of King Dagobert (established in 1108) was regularly performed, and the monthly celebration endowed by Charles the Bald to commemorate his anniversary was revived and embellished, preparing the way for many such royal anniversary services.

SALADIN

S aladin (Salah al-Din Yusuf ibn Ayyub; c. 1137–1193), founder of the AYYUBID dynasty of EGYPT and Syria who restored Jerusalem to Muslim control in 1187 and subsequently defended it from Christian crusaders under RICHARD I LION-HEART during the Third Crusade. (*See* CRUSADES.)

Early Career. Born in the castle of Takrit in Mesopotamia, Saladin was of Kurdish descent. His father, al-Ayyub, and uncle, Shirkuh, rose in the service of Nureddin, in Aleppo, Syria. Most notably, they delivered control of DAMASCUS to Nureddin (1154) in the aftermath of the death (1146) of its ruler, Zangi. They also established Syrian rule over Egypt by 1168. Saladin's own military career began in Aleppo in 1152, after which he was appointed head of the security forces in Damascus in 1156, and thereafter Nureddin's chief liaison officer. In a series of campaigns Saladin took a prominent part in suppressing the heterodox FATIMID caliphate there (personally killing its vizier, Shawah, in 1169) and preventing it from falling into the hands of the Latin Christian crusaders (collectively known as the FRANKS), who he had already driven back at Alexandria in 1174. (*See* FATIMID DYNASTY; EGYPT.)

Rise to Power. In March 1169, Saladin succeeded his uncle as vizier and commander of the Syrian troops. At the insistence of Nureddin, he restored orthodox Sunni ISLAM (1171). Although Saladin shared Nureddin's animus toward the FRANKS, he evidently chafed somewhat under Nureddin's control, probably because the latter wished to divert Egyptian resources to the Holy War against the Franks in Syria, while Saladin was more preoccupied by internal security. When Nureddin died in 1174, his power base in Egypt consolidated, Saladin began to assert his own domination over the Syrian sphere, taking Damascus in 1174, Aleppo in 1183, and Mosul in 1186 from the descendants of Zangi and Nureddin. The economic, administrative, and military reforms he had undertaken in Egypt now put its resources at his command.

The Crusades. Thus strengthened and presented with provocation by Frankish violations of the tenuous existing peace, he moved against the Franks, routing them at HITTIN in northern Palestine in July 1187. In a swift and devastating campaign, he went on to capture almost all of the Frankish territory in the Levant south of Tripoli, leaving only the ports of Tyre and Ascalon and a few northern castles in Frankish hands. Jerusalem surrendered in early October on generous terms; characteristically, Saladin did not exact retribution for the slaughter that had followed the crusaders' capture of the city some 88 years before. Fresh campaigns after the fall of Jerusalem completed the Muslim sweep of the region, with the exception of Antioch

Saladin in an early 13th-century portrait.

and Tripoli. Ascalon surrendered to Saladin (1187) in order to secure the release of GUY OF LUSIGNAN, king of the Latin Kingdom of Jerusalem. Yet Saladin did not pursue the city of Tyre, allowing the Franks to regroup there. On their own, they were too weak to reengage Saladin; but in 1191, they were aided by the European forces of the Third Crusade, notably the French under King PHILIP II AUGUSTUS, the English under RICHARD I, and contingents from ITALY. Almost unaccountably, given their strength and tactical position, the crusaders under Guy had decided in August 1189 to besiege Acre, which might have held out successfully were it not for the arrival of these reinforcements. Richard's and Philip's new weapons broke Acre's resistance, despite Saladin's efforts to relieve the city, and the formidable Egyptian fleet was destroyed by Italian naval forces. After a year of frustrating encounters with Richard's forces, punctuated by equally frustrating negotiations, Saladin managed to keep Jerusalem out of the hands of the Christians but by no means to expel them. In September 1192, he and Richard agreed to a truce that left Saladin in control of Jerusalem but permitted Christian pilgrims access to the city. It also reestablished (with its seat in Acre) the Latin Kingdom of Jerusalem, which had been nearly extinguished. Exhausted by his campaigns, Saladin succumbed to illness in Damascus on March 4, 1193.

A Legend. Like his rival Richard, Saladin's military prowess and his character became the stuff of legend, celebrated and embellished after his death to inspire emulation as well as admiration. Unlike Richard, who slaughtered the defenders of Acre, Saladin was generally generous toward his defeated enemies, although he was a fierce and harsh enough commander until they were defeated. Like Richard—to whom he reportedly once supplied a fresh horse in the midst of combat against him—he led his troops personally, although he does not seem to have shared Richard's utter recklessness as a fighter. Saladin's

Ayyubid descendants were soon displaced by those of his brother al-Adil Saif-ad-Din, but Saladin remained the model prince. (*See* RICHARD I LION-HEART.)

SANTIAGO, KNIGHTS OF

The order of the Knights of Santiago was one of a number of knightly military orders that played a central role in the Christian RECONQUEST of Iberia. In 711, the Muslim armies invaded the Iberian peninsula and by 716, they had destroyed the Spanish Visigothic kingdom. Founded to protect Christians and further the reconquest of SPAIN, the orders themselves were small feudal powers governing lands they had conquered or those bequeathed by the various Christian kings of Spain. Like other European crusading orders, these knights combined military zeal with the religious fervor and rules of a monkish order.

Establishment. The Knights of Santiago were one of the first orders established and given the all-important papal recognition. The order was created in the twelfth century to protect Christian pilgrims traveling to the tomb of Saint James at Compostella from Moorish bandits. Thirteen knights began the order by dedicating themselves to the monastery of Sant' Eloa at Luho in Galicia and adopting the Augustinian rules. The monks, in return for the considerable wealth dedicated to the new order by the knights, agreed to provide hospital services. In 1173, this agreement was finalized between the monks and D. Pedro-Fernando de Fuentes Encalada, the head of the knights. On July 3, 1175, Fuentes went to ROME where the pope approved the new order in the bull *Benedictus Deus*.

The military members of the knighthood were governed by a Council of Thirteen, with a "master" as the ultimate authority. The religious members of the orders submitted to a figure called the grand commander. The knights ruled as feudal lords. In their territory, the order built defensible enclaves or, in larger towns, fortresses. The local peasants were responsible for supplying the garrison with food and were given protection in return. In its earliest history, the knights successfully expanded their territory. However, in 1195, the knights, along with the crusading Orders of CALATRAVA and ALCÁNTARA suffered a great defeat at the hands of the Moors at Alarcos. Despite this defeat, the Moors were pushed consistently southward, with the order of Santiago gaining more and more land.

Division. In 1203, the order experienced a major schism when rival masters were elected, each one supported by different Christian kingdoms. A major chapter in the history of the order began in 1226 when the order made an alliance with the king of Castile. However, the Castilian King Alfonso IV was concerned about the loyalty of this powerful organization and sought to control it by making his son grand master. Conflict between the order and the monarchy ensued on the death of Alfonso when his successor and half brother, Pedro the Cruel, ordered the execution of Alfonso's mistress (also mother of the then-current master). Pedro invited the master to a meeting and promptly had him murdered.

This schism ended only at the end of the century with the election of the infant Henry of ARAGON as master. Further schisms took place in 1445 and 1543. The internal struggles of the order diminished as its importance lessened with the successful conclusion of the RECONQUEST. In 1493, after the death of the grand master, King Ferdinand V of Aragon gained control of the Order when Pope Alexander VI pronounced him mastery of the order. (See ARAGON; RECONQUEST; ALCÁNTARA; CALATRAVA; and KNIGHTHOOD.)

SARACENS

Term used by Christian writers to denote all Arabs and Muslims. Derived from the name of a Bedouin tribe of the Sinai, the Banu Sara, known to the missionaries of St. Catherine's monastery, the name came to have militaristic connotations. The term was also applied to the SELJUK TURKS during the CRUSADES. (See ARABS; CRUSADES.)

SASANIANS

Dynasty that ruled Persia from 226 to 651, the year of the Arab conquest. The last native rulers of Persia were named after Sassan (hence they were also known as the Sassanids), an ancestor of the kingdom's founder, Ardashir I. Bitter enemies of the Romans and the Byzantines, the empire withstood pressures from both until the last Sasanian king, Yazdegird III, was deposed by the Arabs.

SAXONS

The Saxons were a Germanic people who inhabited northern Germany along the Baltic coast and the North Sea. In the declining years of the Roman Empire, the Saxons were notorious for their North Sea piracy. Beginning in the fifth century, the Saxons spread from their home base of Saxony to other parts of northern GERMANY, as well as Gaul (modern-day FRANCE) and the British Isles.

Along with two other peoples, the Angles and the Jutes, the Saxons invaded Britain and settled in the regions known today as Essex, Sussex, and WESSEX. The Saxons were allies of the Frisians who occupied the northern part of the Low Countries, but they became enemies of the FRANKS as their expansion threatened Frankish holdings. CHARLEMAGNE launched an assault on the Saxons in 772, battling them sporadically for some 32 years, before the Saxons finally capitulated and Saxony became part of the Frankish empire.

In the tenth century, the Saxons rose to prominence when Henry I of Saxony was crowned king of Germany (and later Holy Roman Emperor); the House of Saxony would hold sway for another century. It was his son, OTTO I, who began the tradition in 962 of being crowned emperor by the pope, a practice that would last nearly 500 years until the reign of MAXIMILIAN I. In all, five Saxon kings served. The last Saxon king, Henry II, tried unsuccessfully to annex POLAND. Upon his death in 1024, his son, Conrad II, became king of Germany and founded the Salian dynasty. (See BARBARIAN INVASION; ANGLO-SAXONS; ENGLAND.)

SCHOLASTICISM

As the concept of university education took hold in western Europe, scholars began to question whether knowledge could be combined into one unified discipline. What they sought was a body of knowledge that included religious teachings, classical teachings, and worldly understanding. This desire led to the development of Scholasticism. The Scholastics, as its proponents were called, tried to reconcile conflicting ideas in Church and classic texts, and to make those ideas compatible with worldly knowledge; their goal was to create a unified belief system that accommodated both piety and scholarship.

Scholasticism held influence for several hundred years and was the subject of debate among generations of scholars. Some clerics feared it because they felt it encouraged the questioning of religion, which would ultimately drive people away from the Church. But Scholasticism was an all-encompassing theory that, at its best, gave individuals a more logical picture of religion and its meaning without detracting from its importance. It is no accident that most of the great Scholastic philosophers had close ties to the Church.

Origins. Before the Scholastic movement began, scholars who examined the BIBLE were often perplexed when they found different passages that seemed to contradict one another. More troubling to many was how to reconcile the theories of the great philosophers, particularly ARISTOTLE, with biblical teachings. Aristotle, who lived during the third century B.C.E., asked questions about many of the issues of concern to theologians. What was the relation of the natural world to humankind? Who is God, and what is His role? Aristotle tried to answer his questions through careful analysis and observation.

Aristotle suggests in his *Metaphysics* that there is a "first mover" who initially set the world into motion; he also expresses his belief in a "supreme intellect." Medieval writers believed that Aristotle was describing God. In works such as *On the Soul*, he posits that the human soul exists, but that it is not made of matter. These beliefs were examined by scholars to determine their connection to religion. The sixth-century scholar BOETHIUS, a founder of Scholasticism, was greatly influenced by Aristotle in his work, *The Consolation of Philosophy*. PETER ABELARD agreed with Boethius's conclusion that reason was the key to understanding.

As schools and colleges organized into universities, the study of Aristotle became more common and more popular. In the twelfth century, Peter Abelard became famous for his explorations of Aristotle's teachings. A brilliant but arrogant man, Abelard made many enemies, and was eventually tried for HERESY. The more temperate (and likable) philosopher ALBERTUS MAGNUS helped popularize Scholasticism; his most famous pupil, THOMAS AQUINAS, wrote important works that gave Scholasticism more momentum.

Later Developments. Aquinas's argument to prove the existence of God offers a good example of how the Scholastics tried to balance PHILOSOPHY with religion. Aristotle had argued about the process of motion; based on analysis and experience, for something to move it had to have a "mover" (as with his "first mover"). Aquinas takes Aristotle a step further and claims that God was the "original mover."

By the time of Albertus Magnus and Aquinas, Scholasticism was a strong presence in academic communities throughout Europe. Religious scholars spent much of their time trying to apply Scholastic principles not only to contradictions between religion and philosophy, but within CHRISTIANITY itself. Often, they would find biblical passages that contradicted one another or Church writings and decrees that conflicted with Scripture. By applying logic, as Aquinas had done, they were able to find acceptable reasons for any discrepancies. Scholars presented their views in writing primarily through commentary, question (debate), and *summa* (summary).

By the late thirteenth century, the Church was beginning to react against Scholasticism. The study of Aristotle and the doctrines of the Church, many leaders believed, were simply not compatible. In 1277, the bishop of Paris decreed that Aristotle could no longer be taught or read at the university. The Scholastic movement continued unabated for some time in ENGLAND, however, where there was no ban.

The succession of philosophers who followed Aquinas changed the direction of the Scholastic movement. Two of the best known were the Scottish theologian JOHN DUNS SCOTUS and WILLIAM OF OCKHAM of England. Duns Scotus admired the teachings of Aristotle, but questioned whether religion and philosophy could truly be combined. He died while still a young man, but Ockham continued his work. Ockham introduced the philosophy later called nominalism, which held that only objects actually seen were real, and that some scientific principles could be proven only by actual experience rather than by plain reason.

He also held, however, that God's power was absolute; there was no reason to explain it in rational terms. The power of God was a matter of faith, he added, and faith was not an abstract concept. By stating that it was not necessary to look for rational concepts in religion, Ockham was actually setting the stage for the end of the Scholastic movement.

Eventually, scholars began to agree with Ockham that there was no real need to find ways to combine religion, philosophy, and worldly thought. Scholasticism began to fade away in the fifteenth century, as the scholars of the Renaissance were seeking the answers to very different questions and examining new concepts.

See PHILOSOPHY; SCIENCE; ARISTOTLE, STUDY OF; UNIVERSITIES; *and* CHRISTIANITY. *See also* PETER ABELARD, AVERROES; BOETHIUS; JOHN DUNS SCOTUS; THOMAS AQUINAS; MAIMONIDES; *and* WILLIAM OF OCKHAM.

SCIENCE

The phrase "science in the Middle Ages" may seem a contradiction in terms. The popular view of the medieval period as an era of ignorance and superstition, in which religious authority stifled all critical and creative intellectual activity, allows no room for anything that could be called scientific achievement. On closer scrutiny, however, the popular view turns out to be a caricature. Opportunities for scientific activity varied over time and from place to place throughout the medieval period. From humble beginnings in the early Middle Ages, education grew into a thriving industry, with the natural sciences as one of the centerpieces of the educational enterprise. Out of this activity emerged scientific achievements of considerable significance.

Origins. Medieval science traces its roots to Greek antiquity, with the writings on natural philosophy and cosmology by the philosophers Plato and ARISTOTLE; on mathematics and mathematical science by the mathematicians Euclid and Archimedes and the astronomer Ptolemy; and on MEDICINE and biological subjects by the physicians Hippocrates and Galen and the field biologist (and multitalented) Aristotle. Their writings (and others like them) constitute the "classical tradition" in the natural sciences.

The classical tradition had a complicated fate. Beginning late in the fourth century B.C.E. with the Asian conquests of Alexander the Great, Greek culture (including the classical tradition) was diffused eastward into regions conquered much later by Islamic armies. Ultimately, a taste for Greek learning was transmitted to Muslim elites, who arranged for the translation of major scientific works of the classical tradition into Arabic. Out of these translations grew a flourishing Arabic scientific tradition, which spread throughout the Islamic world as far west as Spain. In the twelfth century, after the Christian conquest of Spain gave Western Christendom access to libraries of Arabic books, this material was translated once again, now into Latin. By this circuitous route, a relatively full version of the classical tradition in the natural sciences reached western Europe by the the thirteenth century.

Early Medieval Science. Early medieval Europe, having no access to this full collection of classical scientific writings, was dependent on a much thinner version of the classical tradition that had come through the writings of educated Romans, such as Cicero (106–43 B.C.E.) and Pliny (23–79 C.E.), who excerpted, epitomized, explained, or quoted classical Greek sources. This version of the classical tradition was the only body of scientific knowledge available in the early Middle Ages, surviving in the monasteries, where it was put to limited use as the handmaiden of theology and religion. The Northumbrian monk BEDE (d. 735), for example, wrote several textbooks for his fellow monks, including two on timekeeping and the CALENDAR (an astronomical subject during the Middle Ages), designed to regulate the daily routine of monastic communities and determine the religious calendar for the year.

In the eleventh and twelfth centuries, Europe experienced a political, social, economic, and intellectual rebirth. Two developments critical for the growth of scientific activity were the arrival (by about 1200) of the fuller version of the classical tradition in Latin translation and the emergence of universities where the classical natural sciences at last found a secure institutional home. Bologna was founded about 1150, followed by Paris and Oxford 50 to 70 years later.

The High Middle Ages. The early defenders of the newly translated learning felt anything but secure as the challenge that dominated the intellectual life of the thirteenth century was to assess the legitimacy and utility of the new learning, pagan in origin and frequently at odds with Christian belief. Study of the clas-

sical tradition had been justified during the early Middle Ages as the handmaiden of religion. But now, with a fuller version of the classical tradition in hand, the tradition appeared a bit more menacing. Would it be possible to discipline a servant who denied the creation of the world by an omnipotent God, who disbelieved in divine providence, who was skeptical of miracles, and who proclaimed that reason and sense experience were the only sources of truth? And was it worth the trouble?

There was considerable skirmishing over these questions. Teaching of Aristotle's "books on nature" was forbidden at the University of Paris early in the thirteenth century. Toward the end of the century, 219 propositions allegedly being taught in the faculty of arts at Paris were condemned by the local bishop. For those less extreme, there was still much reason for concern. ROGER BACON (c. 1220–1292), for example, a Franciscan friar and one of the first medieval Europeans to assimilate the classical tradition in its full breadth, feared that the religious authorities would repudiate the classical natural sciences, banning them from the universities and religious orders, thereby depriving Christendom of an inestimable treasure. He appreciated the theological objections to the classical tradition, but he believed that these tensions could be eliminated by suitable clarification, correction, reinterpretation, and (on occasion) retranslation. He was convinced that the newly available knowledge, especially mathematics and what he called "experimental" science, could serve vital Christian purposes.

Eventually, the moderate view of Bacon and others prevailed. By the end of the thirteenth century, the classical tradition, with its natural sciences, had become one of the centerpieces of university education throughout Europe. The Church, through its support of and authority over the universities (especially in northern Europe), had become the major patron of scientific learning.

Whether religious patronage resulted in religious control over the content of scientific learning is a difficult question, since conditions varied from discipline to discipline and from time to time, as well as with local circumstances and particulars. It is safe to conclude, however, that except for a handful of theologically sensitive topics, scientific investigation was pursued without close Church supervision. The university professor could pursue his scientific quarry wherever it led and defend whatever conclusions he arrived at, without interference. There were occasions, of course, when theological doctrine necessitated a particular conclusion (for example, on the origin of the cosmos and the nature of the soul). But there were also cases in which theological influence directed scientific investigations into channels that led toward what we now judge to be important scientific truths. For example, the idea of a universe containing infinite void space grew from investigations inspired by the Christian doctrine that the are no limitations (other than the laws of logic) on the kind of universe that an omnipotent God could have created.

Achievements in the Sciences. Although many medieval scholars were determined to apply themselves to the whole range of classical natural sciences, they worked within a tradition (classical) and a context (Christian) that identified certain problems as critical ones, demanding attention. Because Aristotle's works were central to the curriculum of the universities, practically every subject he addressed attracted scholarly interest. The natural sciences included cosmology, matter, motion, meteorology, sense perception and other cognitive faculties, botany, and zoology, to name but a few. Aristotle's scientific ideas were not beyond criticism (contrary to widespread mythology). His theories about the fundamental nature of things certainly provided a framework within which almost all scholars worked, but there was scarcely a claim within that framework that was not closely scrutinized by scholars eager to establish a reputation for critical acumen.

Cosmology, besides being prominent in Aristotle's works, was also relevant to theological concerns and became a major topic of investigation. The educated accepted the sphericity of the cosmos as a whole and of the earth at its center; no known medieval scholar believed in a flat earth, despite the several biblical passages that seemed to suggest such a view. Mathematical ASTRONOMY was practiced by a small number of expert mathematicians, who regulated the calendar, made planetary observations required for horoscopic astrology, and criticized the details of the inherited Greek astronomical models. Theories of light (which had metaphysical significance) and vision (the chief sense for the acquisition of knowledge) were developed to a high degree of refinement. The kinematics of motion, developed in the course of the fourteenth century at Paris and Oxford, provided the conceptual framework for Galileo's analysis of freely falling bodies 300 years later. Finally, medicine and as-

"God creating the world by compass," after a miniature from the 15th-century work Trésor, *by Brunetto Latini.*

sociated biological knowledge were vigorously cultivated.

But does such activity really deserve to be called "science?" Medieval scholars of the high and late Middle Ages, still working under the powerful influence of the classical tradition and within the context of Christian belief, had ideas about nature, with languages for talking about it, methods for exploring it, and criteria for judging the theories thus developed. The tests of logical consistency and empirical adequacy were commonly applied to theoretical claims. Some of the results (notably in astronomy and optics) were, in their methods and substantial portions of their content, identical with what practitioners of those disciplines would now call science. Other aspects of the medieval achievement differed widely from their modern counterparts—but we find in the Middle Ages the ancestors and precursors of many modern scientific disciplines, which, although not identical to their offspring, share with them a family resemblance, and are thus entitled to claim the family name—and be considered scientific.

See ASTRONOMY; ARCHITECTURE; ALCHEMY; CALENDAR; MAGIC AND FOLKLORE; MEDICINE AND CARE OF THE SICK; MINING. *See also* ARISTOTLE; ARABIC; BACON, ROGER; FIBONACCI, LEONARDO; NICHOLAS OF CUSA; ORESME, NICHOLAS.

SCONE, STONE OF

The Stone of Scone in Scotland was brought to Old Scone (west of the modern village of New Scone) by Kenneth MacAlpin after he seized the throne of the PICTS in 843. He placed the stone, a symbol of his ancestry, in a hilltop church. For the next four and a half centuries, Scottish kings from Kenneth I to Charles II went to the site for their CORONATION, up until 1296 when it suddenly disappeared; it was probably hidden to keep it from falling into the hands of the English king Edward I who was trying to bring Scotland under his rule. (*See* SCOTLAND.)

SCOTLAND

During the Middle Ages in the northernmost part of the British Isles, Scotland emerged as an independent kingdom. In the early medieval period, Scotland had been a patchwork of small kingdoms and tribal units. But in the eleventh century, these small states united to become the kingdom of Scotland. For the most part, Scotland retained its independence for the remainder of the Middle Ages, but it was never completely free from the dominating influence of its powerful English neighbor to the south.

During the early Middle Ages several distinct groups—PICTS, Irish, Britons, Angles, and beginning at the end of the 700s, Scandinavians (VIKINGS)—populated Scotland. The Picts in the north and east were the strongest of the groups before the arrival of the Vikings. The Irish (called Scots), who lived in the west, maintained ties with northern IRELAND, while Britons lived in the south and Angles (English) had settlements on the east coast. After Irish and Pictish families began intermarrying in the 700s, their kingdoms were often ruled by the same king. The monarchy of Scotland evolved from this union and the patrilineal succession it established; it borrowed its traditions from both peoples. In the late 800s, the kingdom of Scotland began absorbing the British and English kingdoms in southern and eastern Scotland.

The Norman Conquest of ENGLAND in 1066 made a deep and lasting impression on Scottish history. The kings of Scotland looked with favor on the NORMAN noblemen, prelates, and settlers who came north to live in Scotland, since these Norman newcomers strengthened the Scottish monarchy. The Scottish kings gave the new Norman settlers land and titles in return for which the settlers became loyal followers who helped the Crown quell uprisings and control rebellious Scottish lords. The Anglo-French influence that the Norman settlers brought to Scotland also enlarged the horizons of Scottish culture and strengthened the ties between England and Scotland.

Saxon, and then Norman-ANGEVIN monarchs in the south, constantly put pressure on Scottish kings. The Scottish king Malcolm III MacDuncan married Margaret, a member of the West Saxon dynasty, and their sons ruled Scotland for more than 50 years. The Scottish kings who followed established feudal ties to the English Crown. Inside Scotland, the Crown consolidated its authority and expanded its territorial control. In 1263, the king of Scotland seized the Western Isles after defeating the Norwegian king in battle.

Relations between Scotland and England became critical following the death in 1290 of Queen Margaret, the last of the line of direct descendants of Malcolm MacDuncan. When 13 Scottish nobles claimed the vacant throne, King Edward I of England was asked to intercede. He chose Baliol, but with his Welsh successes in mind he took advantage of the disorder to try to establish his overlordship over Scotland.

Scottish resistance to Edward's plan to bring Scotland into the English fold found its first leader in WILLIAM WALLACE, a knight who enjoyed the support of the growing middle class of small landowners, merchants, and townspeople. After the English defeated Wallace and his supporters in 1298 at the Battle of Falkirk, the leadership of the resistance passed to ROBERT I BRUCE, who had been one of the 13 claimants to the throne in 1290. Bruce seized the crown for himself in 1306 and continued to lead the Scottish resistance against England. In 1307, King Edward I died, having failed to bring Scotland under English rule. Seven years later, Bruce led the Scots to a decisive victory over the forces of EDWARD II at BANNOCKBURN, upholding Scotland's independence. Bruce continued to resist the English successfully until his death in 1329. (*See* ROBERT I THE BRUCE.)

The conflict resumed in 1341 when EDWARD III invaded Scotland. However, this new threat to Scottish independence ended when Edward turned his attention to fighting the French on the continent in what proved to be the opening phase of the HUNDRED YEARS' WAR. Scotland's alliance with FRANCE against England strengthened Scottish independence.

During the late Middle Ages, the kings of Scotland were determined to make their country an important European kingdom. In the late 1300s, the landowners in southern Scotland drove the last of the English from their border lands. Even though Scotland remained a poor country with limited arable farmland and natural resources, it was able to establish a high level of culture. (*See* SCONE, STONE OF.)

In 1371, Robert II, grandson of King Robert I through his daughter Marjory, became the first member of the House of Stuart to assume the throne. Robert and the Stuart kings who followed him built castles and courts that rivaled those of France. Thanks to the increased levels of culture and prosperity and the French successes against England in the finale of the Hundred Years' War, the end of the 1400s was something of a golden age in Scottish history. Literature and the arts flourished; Scottish musicians went to the continent to study, returning to train others. The poetry of Robert Henryson and William Dunbar became widely acclaimed and did much to enhance the cultural reputation of the nation. Universities founded in Scotland in the 1400s—St. Andrews (1414), Glasgow (1451), and Aberdeen (1495)—established levels of learning and scholarship that won the newly formed country greater respect throughout Europe. (*See* PICTS; ENGLAND; WILLIAM WALLACE; BANNOCKBURN.)

SCULPTURE

The art of sculpture declined after the dissolution of the Roman Empire, and freestanding sculpture as a major art form would not become widespread again until the Renaissance. But the art of sculpture became an important element of religious ARCHITECTURE, especially in Europe, between the eleventh and the fifteenth centuries.

Romanesque Influence. During the early Middle Ages, sculptors modeled figures after earlier Roman and Greek statues, but the quality was not of the same caliber. In Europe, small relief sculptures (in which the figures project from the surface) were often found on small crosses and chests. No one was sculpting large-scale works matching the ambition and skill of Greek and Roman civilizations.

Beginning around the eleventh century, when the ROMANESQUE style of ARCHITECTURE began to take hold, artists began to design large-scale sculptures. Most of these were done in relief, and created for cathedrals and churches. Most Romanesque sculpture was created in FRANCE and ITALY. French Romanesque sculpture was most prevalent in BURGUNDY, Languedoc, Toulouse, and Provence. The themes were religious, and the sculpture evoked religious fervor, but it did not have the classical lines of ancient Roman sculpture. Romanesque sculptures in Italy had more of a classical appearance. The figures were usually religious, but relief sculptures in the cathedral of Modena depict Aesop's fables and the legend of KING ARTHUR.

Gothic Style. In the mid-twelfth century, the Gothic style that was already supplanting Romanesque architecture in cathedrals began to exert influence on sculpture as well. Gothic sculptures were more like the classical models—lifelike and refined. But as with Romanesque sculptures, they primarily appeared on houses of worship.

Gothic sculpture included detailed leaves, flowers, and intricate patterns along with religious scenes and figures. Common religious themes were the life of Christ and the Last Judgment.

The Gothic style originated in France and soon spread to other parts of Europe, particularly GERMANY, Italy, and northern SPAIN. Many sculptors used limestone, but Italian sculptors worked with marble, which allowed for more refinement. The style in Italy, called Italian Gothic,

produced some of the most impressively detailed pieces of the period.

Gothic sculpture was popular until the fifteenth century, when the number of cathedrals being built began to decline. By then, some of the great Renaissance sculptors, such as Michelangelo, had begun to produce a very different type of work.

Sculpture in Britain was less prominent than in the rest of Europe. The most noteworthy surviving examples are statues on tombs, such as the statues of knights atop their tombs in WESTMINSTER ABBEY.

Outside Europe. Byzantine sculpture consisted mainly of bas-relief images on church facades. Secular sculptures from early Islamic palaces include statues of dancers and nobles, both freestanding and in relief. By and large, however, those cultures focused much more of their artistic attention on painting and ceramic tiles for decorating buildings. (*See* ARCHITECTURE; GOTHIC ART; BYZANTINE ART; PAINTING; ROMANESQUE.)

SELJUK TURKS

The Seljuk Turks, a Turkish family of nomadic origin, established dynasties in Asia, as well as minor dynasty lines in Iraq, Syria, and Anatolia. They were one of many nomadic tribes that adopted ISLAM in the 900s, and they entered the service of Muslim princes in Khorasan. As devout Muslims, the Seljuk Turks not only threatened CONSTANTINOPLE before the First Crusade, but also were a constant threat to all pilgrims to the Holy Land. Though they were eventually overthrown, they played a significant role in world history. Historian Philip K. Hitti wrote: "It was the Seljuks who held back the Byzantines, dealt the first blows to the Crusaders, and paved the way for their Ottoman kinsmen."

The Seljuks got their name from their founder, Seljuk (known as the Iron Bow), a tenth-century Turkish sultan. In 985, he broke up with his Oghuz overlord and fled from Transoxiania to Jand, where he converted to the Sunni sect of the Muslim faith. He compelled his family and retainers to practice a more orthodox form of Islam as

The statues of the south porch of the Bourges Cathedral were sculpted in the 12th century. For much of the Middle Ages, sculpture was an art in service to architectural needs.

opposed to the then-popular folk Islam that stressed mysticism and magic. The Seljuks became warriors in military service for Muslim princes; they served the Samanids and Ghaznivids. In 1035, Toghrïl Beg (c. 990–1063), one of Seljuk's grandsons, fled with his brothers from military service in central Asia to the Khwarizmian service. The new Oghuz leader there expelled them. Toghrïl migrated to Khorasan, where the leader had officially denied access to the Seljuks.

Rise to Power. The Seljuks came to prominence under the leadership of Toghrïl Beg. He conquered Khorasan in 1037 and took control of the whole Persian plateau by 1040, defeating the Ghaznivid army at Dandanqan in May of that year. Many Seljuks worked their way as far west as Iraq in their quest for riches. Toghrïl established his headquarters at Rayy, where he masterminded attacks on Iraq and ANATOLIA.

In 1055, the Seljuks overtook BAGHDAD, deposed the Buyid dynasty and rescued Caliph al-Qaim from the local chieftain. In gratitude, the caliph gave Toghrïl the title of "sultan" and "king of kings." With Persia in decline at this time, Toghrïl was looked to as the one to restore order; many saw him as the legitimate heir to the ARABS. However, there was dissent within his own ranks; members of his tribe plotted to overthrow him. Toghrïl was able to quash these uprisings; his later successors would not be as fortunate.

Some historians allege that Toghrïl wanted his nephew SULEYMAN to succeed him, but that after Toghrïl's death, ALP ARSLAN maneuvered himself into position to succeed. Regardless, Arslan continued his uncle's dominance, this time by working east, with the advice and help of his vizir, Nizam al-Mulk. Arslan also faced internal conflict; he went to war against his kinsman Qutlumush in 1064, just after taking over. Three years later, he fought against his own brother Qavurd. Known as the Brave Lion, Arslan completed the subjection of Persia and Armenia and founded the sultanate of Rum. In August 1071, the Turks soundly defeated the Byzantine army and captured their leader, Emperor Romanus IV Diogenes, at the BATTLE OF MANZIKERT. The Turks succeeded largely by shattering the Byzantine system of communication. This victory was the beginning of the end of the Byzantine Empire, strengthening Turkish dominance in the Middle East. After the battle, the Seljuks poured across Asia Minor and dominated Anatolia, conquering Byzantine provinces one by one; the Turks control this section of Asia to this day. Arslan's army turned Anatolia into the sultanate of Rum. (*See* ANATOLIA; ALP ARSLAN.)

Expansion. Alp's son and successor Malik Shah extended and developed the Seljuks. His empire reached from Afghanistan to the Byzantine borders, from the Mediterranean to central Asia; most historians consider him the greatest member of the family line. During this period, the Seljuks in Anatolia became more independent from central authority. Under his leadership the Turks conquered Jerusalem in 1072, Syria in 1080, and Antioch in 1085. His brother, Suleyman, captured Konya with a band of Turks from Anatolia in 1075, and conquered Iznik. Two years later, the Great Seljuk named him sultan of Anatolia.

The Seljuk's conquest of Jerusalem, combined with their threat to Christians making pilgrimages to the Holy Land, angered Romanus's successors. They petitioned the Vatican for aid and support. Pope URBAN II denounced the Seljuks' seizing of holy places in Palestine and vowed attack. His audience replied, "*Dieu le veut!*" ("God wills it!"). This was the start of the Crusades. (*See* CRUSADES; SULEYMAN.)

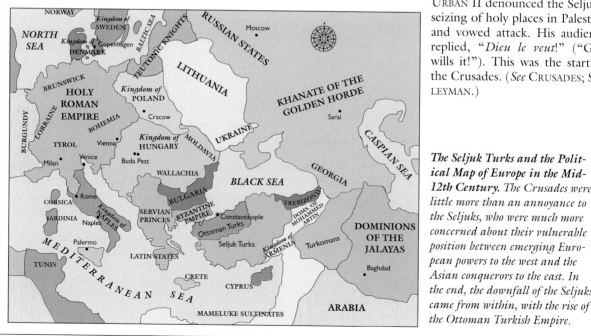

The Seljuk Turks and the Political Map of Europe in the Mid-12th Century. The Crusades were little more than an annoyance to the Seljuks, who were much more concerned about their vulnerable position between emerging European powers to the west and the Asian conquerors to the east. In the end, the downfall of the Seljuks came from within, with the rise of the Ottoman Turkish Empire.

SERBIA

U ntil the sixth century, the Byzantine Empire dominated the area that would become Serbia. In the middle of the sixth century, SLAVS migrating from the north settled into its central and eastern parts. By the beginning of the seventh century, they had overrun the Byzantines, and occupied nearly the entire region. In the seventh century, another tribe, the Serbians (considered to be of either Slavic or Iranian descent) migrated into the region, and settled between the Danube River and Macedonia. The Serbians organized themselves into numerous small principalities, called *zhupas*, under the leadership of *zhupans*, or princes, and conquered the Slavs. However, they assimilated almost entirely into the Slavic communities, and the term "Serbian" came to describe the conquered Slavic people. (*See* SLAVS.)

In the ninth and tenth centuries, the zhupans fought amongst themselves, and a few managed to consolidate power and increase their territorial holdings. The threat of a Bulgarian invasion from the east unified the princes momentarily, but after peace was established, they continued their feuding. In the late ninth century, Peter, son of Gojnik, emerged as the dominant zhupan. With Bulgarian support, he expanded his domain westward to the Bosnia River valley. It was at this time, perhaps at Peter's command, that the Serbs were converted to CHRISTIANITY.

Leadership. In 917, the Bulgarians broke the peace, invaded Serbia, and took Peter prisoner. The Bulgarians tried to install loyal zhupans on the Serbian throne, but for the most part the zhupans supported Byzantium, which was farther away from Serbia and thus able to grant it more independence. Eventually, no longer able to tolerate the unruly princes, Bulgaria annexed Serbia in 924, ravaging much of the land. Serbia was able to regain its independence later in the century and, for the time being, remained neutral during the ensuing conflicts between BULGARIA and BYZANTIUM. Around this time, the zhupa of Duklja became prominent, and began to extend its control over much of Serbia. Led by Stephen Vojislav in the 1030s, Duklja was involved in a guerrilla campaign against Byzantium and achieved full independence in the 1040s, after turning back a Byzantine invasion. In the following years, Duklja annexed other surrounding zhupas and became the leading Serbian state. After a brief truce with Byzantium, a renewed attack against Duklja in 1089 devastated the state, allowing many of the annexed states, such as Raska, Bosnia, and Zahumlje, to assert their independence. Duklja never fully recovered from the attack, and leadership of Serbia in the following century passed on to the zhupa of Raska.

In 1090, Vukan of Raska took the title grand zhupan and submitted to Byzantine overlordship, though he continued to push southward into Macedonia and Byzantine territory. But by the mid-twelfth century, the Serbians had begun another unsuccessful revolt against Byzantine rule. After a period of instability and revolts against the Byzantine-appointed rulers, in 1166, a new dynasty appeared in Raska, the Nemanjic, which would rule Serbia until 1371. Stephen Nemanja emerged as the dominant ruler after subduing his brothers, who began to consolidate their power in other zhupas. Stephen was forced to swear his allegiance to the Byzantine Empire, but as the empire declined in the late twelfth century, he was able to extend his power south into northern Macedonia and Kosovo, and to acquire Duklja (later called Zeta). When he attempted to form a coalition with the HOLY ROMAN EMPIRE, the Byzantines invaded Serbia and defeated Nemanja in 1190. However, they granted Serbian independence and allowed Nemanja to retain much of his territorial holdings. In 1195, Nemanja abdicated and became a monk (which would become something of a family tradition), and the title grand zhupan was passed on to his younger son Stephen I.

Quest for Power. Stephen I fought with his older brother Vukan, who had established an independent kingdom in Zeta. But with Byzantine backing, Stephen was able to conquer Zeta and incorporate it into his kingdom. After successfully repelling a Bulgarian invasion, Stephen was offered the royal crown by Pope Honorius III in 1216, but Stephen's brother Sava intervened and insisted on an Orthodox coronation, receiving recognition from the deposed Byzantine emperor. Sava was also able to establish an autocephalous (independent) Serbian bishopric, and contributed to Serbian centralization by establishing many bishoprics under his leadership.

Under Stephen I's son, Stephan IV Uros, Serbia rose in power, enjoying significant economic development, annexing large territories in Macedonia and northern Epirus. With Hungarian backing, in 1276 Uros's son, Dragutin, overthrew his father, but was challenged by his brother Milutin. The rivalry between the two brothers led to a war that lasted from 1301–1312. After Dragutin's death in 1316, Milutin absorbed all of his lands, but after Milutin's death in 1321, another civil war erupted, as multiple claimants vied for the throne. The unrest and dynastic disputes did not come to an end until the ascension of Stephen IX Dusan (1331–1355), who in September 1331 was crowned king of Serbia. At first, Dusan was considered something of a puppet of the Serbian nobles who helped secure his election. But he soon demonstrated his strong-willed and independent spirit. Under Dusan, Serbia's borders were extended to their greatest boundaries in the Middle Ages, almost doubling in size, made possible by the civil war ravaging the Byzantine Empire. Dusan was able to seize almost all of Macedonia, Epirus, Thessaly, and much of Albania, unchallenged. Allying himself with Venice and HUNGARY, Dusan dreamed of creating a Serbian empire that could challenge the power of the newly emergent Turks. He even dreamed of marching to CONSTANTINOPLE, but died before he could begin.

Decline. Though successful in his territorial acquisitions, Dusan was unable to promote centralization or subdue the Serbian nobles. After his death in 1355, many of them rebelled, and much of the newly acquired territory, including Thessaly, Epirus, and Albania, seceded. Separatist struggles among the nobility led to considerable unrest in the late fourteenth century, and Serbia's weakened condition made it ripe for invasion by the OTTOMAN TURKS, who annihilated the Serbians at Chernomen in 1371 and ended the Nemanjic dynasty later that year. Weakened by this infighting, the Serbs, led by King Lazarus, suffered another great loss at the BATTLE OF KOSOVO in June 1389. Though the bloody battle was something of a draw, the Turks could afford to lose more men and go on conquering Serbian lands. By 1441, all of Serbia was annexed to Turkey, and except for a brief window of independence from 1443 to 1459, Serbia remained under Turkish control until the nineteenth century.

SERFS AND SERFDOM

Serfdom was a condition of hereditary and involuntary servitude that afflicted much of the western European peasantry during the Middle Ages. The population of serfs had two origins. Many serfs were descendants of slaves of the early Middle Ages. Others were formerly free peasants who descended the social hierarchy into serfdom due to poverty or the need of protection from a lord. While serfdom is often identified as the defining feature of medieval social life, it was the dominant mode of exploitation in western Europe only from the ninth to thirteenth centuries. A number of economic, political, and social causes led to the demise of serfdom in the fourteenth century. But while serfdom disappeared in western Europe, it emerged in eastern Europe. It was a particularly important institution in RUSSIA, where it lasted until the nineteenth century. (*See* FEUDALISM.)

The Manor. Serfdom was an integral part of the dominant manorial or seignorial economic and political system. In the manorial system, the lord or feudal aristocrat owned huge expanses of land. Some of the manor was held in common by the peasant and other parts were parceled to individual families. The peasants, in exchange for the land, owed the lord a fixed rent in money or crops. Additionally, peasants were obliged to perform labor on "public" functions administered by the lord, such as work on roads, bridges, and dams. The lord was obliged by the code of the seignorial system to protect the peasants in his manor, although there was no authority to compel such protection. While some peasants were free, at least in name, many others were tied to their particular manor, hence serfs. (*See* AGRICULTURE.)

Serfdom and Slavery. Although the living conditions of serfs varied depending on location, generalizations about their plight are possible. Serfdom was like SLAVERY, although formally, serfs were not slaves, that is, they were not considered mere property, bereft of all rights, public and private. Serfs were part of the lord's estate, so they passed on to another generation of lordship as did the land itself. Serfs could be bought and sold and were exchangeable for material goods or other serfs. Serfs required a specific act of liberation or "manumission" to gain or regain a state of personal liberty. If one serf married another serf from a different manor, the two lords could decide whether or not the family could stay together, or if one lord would buy out the others.

Serfdom did have some clear advantages as opposed to slavery. Serfs could own property and sustain themselves through the gains of their own labor. Further, in theory, the lord was obliged to protect serfs from external threats, although this side of the social compact was rarely fulfilled. Whatever rights the serfs had were limited in practice by their complete lack of mobility and legal rights (they could not even testify). The lack of public protection meant that the power of the lords was practically unlimited. Lords, however, often restricted their exploitation according to custom in order to ensure a continuous work force in the fields. While serfdom was an improvement over slavery, the life of the serf was certainly a miserable one. Serfs were poorly fed because they were responsible for their own subsistence. Like slaves, serfs worked the entire day without rest, leading lives of unrelieved drudgery.

Slavery in Europe waxed and waned in the early Middle Ages. The number of slaves in Europe declined after the fifth century conquest of the western Empire by the Germanic tribes. The institution of slavery was limited by Christian criticism, a moral argument unknown in pagan times. The Church decreed that only the pagan east Europeans, particularly the SLAVS (the word "slavery" derives from their name), could be enslaved. The number of available non-Christians declined as CHRISTIANITY spread eastward. However, the slave trade increased in the eighth century with the triumph of the Muslims, who were a ready and eager market for Christian and non-Christian slaves.

Peasantry. Despite the durability of the slave trade, by the ninth century conditions of involuntary servitude changed in fundamental ways. The lords began to replace slave gangs with families of slaves settled on plots of land. These slaves were required to work the land of the master, but they could also work for themselves. Instead of receiving subsistence from the master, the serfs of the ninth century could grow their own crops. Out of these crops, the serfs paid the master a fee. While this was a meager improvement over mere slavery, the new condition of the peasants entailed greater economic independence.

Peasants who fell out of the free peasantry class became the second source of the serf class. In the ninth and tenth centuries, western and central Europe were continuously pillaged by VIKINGS, MAGYARS, and Muslims. Many peasants sought protection from these attacks in the manors of lords. While some peasants kept their free status, many others fell into the status of serfdom. Unlike the descendants of slaves, these peasants consented to the constraints of serfdom, even though this consent was limited by their vulnerable predicament.

Because of the general collapse of systems of public law, even more peasants entered into serfdom between the eleventh and twelfth centuries. One of the characteristics of medieval feudalism was that public matters like justice became the property of private individuals. Stripped of the protection of courts and the law, peasants had difficulty proving they were free, and free peasants were inexorably drawn into serfdom.

The development of serfdom often depended on the political situation of a nation. In the Germanic HOLY ROMAN EMPIRE, for example, there was no strong centralized power to control the local princes. With a general collapse of public authority, there was no countervailing force against the lords who appropriated public functions. The lands of the German aristocracy became private empires. Many peasants, who had been free and obligated only to pay an annual fee to their lord, were forced into hereditary servitude.

Decline of Serfdom. The decline of serfdom began in the thirteenth century. Serfdom was a pillar of

A harvest scene of the early 1500s. The lords took great pains to regulate the serfs through a combination of appeals to their religious fervor and intimidation through the threat of force.

the feudal system; the decline of the system and the rise of the enemies of feudalism marked the beginnings of the liberation of the serfs. In FRANCE, a general movement for emancipation eventually made serfs a minority of the peasant population. In SPAIN, land conquered from the Muslims was settled by free peasants. The leaders of the Italian city-states eliminated personal servitude as a way to dilute the power of the opponents in the aristocracy and increase the number of tax payers. The distinguishing characteristics of serfdom began to fade as western Europe entered the late medieval period. On the one hand, the miserable plight of the free peasantry made them indistinguishable from serfs. On the other hand, some serfs rose in the social network. Lords granted serfs some privileges, thereby making them authority figures in the villages.

Various events in the fourteenth century—military conquests, the BLACK DEATH, economic crisis—were instrumental in the demise of serfdom. Amid the chaos of that century, lords had difficulty retaining the servitude of their serfs. The Black Death played a particularly important role in ending serfdom. It killed between twenty-five to forty percent of the population, creating a tremendous labor shortage and a need for a more mobile work force. The fifteenth century saw the end of serfdom in western Europe, although remnants persisted in other parts of Europe. Only in 1781 was serfdom legally ended in AUSTRIA, and the French Revolution freed the last serfs. The end of serfdom in western Europe, however, did not lead to improvements in the living conditions of peasants.

While serfdom was dying out in western Europe, it became the central economic institution of the emerging Russian state. As aristocrats amassed vast lands as their private domains, peasants lost their independent properties and were forced into the service of the landowners. These landless peasants lost social status compared to other peasants, even though they were not legally bound to the lords. In the thirteenth century, many peasants fleeing the conquering MONGOLS sought the protection of the landowners. The number of peasants living purely within the power of lords increased in the sixteenth century during the reign of Ivan the Terrible. In the seventeenth century, Russia's peasants were made subjects of their lords, only as free as was permitted by their master.

 See AGRICULTURE; FEUDALISM; SLAVERY; COMMERCE AND TRADE; GUILDS; *and* TOWNS, VILLAGES, AND CITIES. *The interaction of serfs with other social groups is discussed in* FAMILY LIFE *and* SOCIAL CLASSES AND CLASS CONFLICT.

SHIRE

The term "shire" emerged in eighth century ENGLAND as the common name for local government units and remained dominant until the NORMAN Conquest of the eleventh century. Shires were a phenomenon of the rule of the ANGLO-SAXONS, the descendants of the Germanic Angles and Saxon tribes who conquered Britain after the collapse of Roman rule in the fifth century. The shape of particular shires evolved in various ways. In western England, shires were organized by local Anglo-Saxon chiefs. Elsewhere, shires emerged out of tribal groupings, small kingdoms, and other power formations. (*See* ANGLO-SAXONS; FEUDALISM.)

In the late eighth century, the Anglo-Saxon king, ALFRED THE GREAT standardized the shire system. Alfred created royal deputies or "ealdormen" (later aldermen) who governed the shires. The ealdormen, who were often relatives of the kings or members of powerful, landed families, had numerous political and military duties. They supplied warriors for the king's wars, adjudicated at judicial courts, and served on legislative assemblies. They were also responsible for the enforcement of royal decrees. Another reorganization of the shires took place in the middle of the ninth century, when they were divided into smaller districts, called hundreds or wapentakes. In 1066, the Normans from northern FRANCE conquered the Anglo-Saxon kingdom, after which "county," from the French word for regional districts, became the dominant term for local government in England. (*See* ENGLAND.)

SICILIAN VESPERS

The name given to the riot that broke out in Palermo on Easter Monday 1282, at the hour of vespers, and led to the fall of the ANGEVIN government in SICILY. The people of Sicily, with the memory of a more tolerable HOHENSTAUFEN rule fresh in their minds, had suffered under the reign of the Angevin king, CHARLES I OF ANJOU. Charles was forced to increase taxes to defray the costs of the Angevin conquest, and brought to the island insolent French nobility and soldiers. On that fateful Easter Monday, March 30, a French gendarme made rude advances toward a Sicilian bride, as she was heading to church with her groom. Spurred on by the indignity, the Sicilian population of Palermo rose up in anger, killing over 3,000 Frenchman in a day of terrible rioting. There were reports of crazed Sicilian men ripping open the wombs of Sicilian women impregnated by French soldiers and nobles. Not even the clergy were spared, as Sicilians burst into churches and convents, killing French ecclesiastics.

The rioting quickly spread throughout the island, though some aristocratic families and cities, notably Messina, supported the French. Charles of Anjou swore revenge, and Pope Martin IV excommunicated the rebels and declared a crusade against Sicily. Most historians believe that the Sicilian Vespers was not a spontaneous outburst, but had been prepared by an organized underground financed by the Byzantines.

The Sicilians turned to PETER III of Aragon, who had married the daughter of the pre-Angevin ruling family; he was able to take advantage of the chaos by quickly sending in his own ships. Though Charles was supported by the PAPACY and by his nephew, King Philip III of France, the Angevin government fell. At Palermo on December 4, 1282, Peter was pronounced king of Sicily by the island's parliament, on condition that he respect its own laws and statutes. However, the fighting over the island raged for a decade, and it would not cease until the Peace of Caltabellotta in 1302. Some historians trace the origins of the modern Sicilian mafia to the Sicilian Vespers. (*See* SICILY.)

SICILY

Sicily's strategic position at the crossroads of the Mediterranean most influenced its history during the Middle Ages. It was a valuable market for the exchange of goods from long-distance trade, a focus for the mingling of cultures, and a center of translation for Islamic and Greek texts into the Latin of the Western world.

In the Middle Ages, Sicily had water in abundance from many springs and rivers, and the volcanic ash in the soil made it agriculturally productive. Its extensive forests provided wood for shipbuilding and protected the soil from erosion. Its most important product was wheat, the staple of the medieval diet, which Sicily exported in quantity, along with wine, olives, and fruit.

Early Middle Ages. Sicily became a Roman province in the second century B.C.E., though Sicilians continued to use the Greek language as well as Latin.

In 468, Sicily fell to the VANDALS invading from North Africa, and eight years later it was conquered by the OSTROGOTHS. A late Roman legacy was the "patrimony of St. Peter," in which the PAPACY acquired much land in Sicily through imperial and private gifts giving the popes a claim on the island throughout the Middle Ages.

In 535, Sicily was captured by General BELISARIUS for the eastern emperor JUSTINIAN I. Sicily was thrust into the limelight only briefly in the Byzantine period, in 660, when Emperor Constans II decided to move the capital of his empire to Syracuse, Sicily's most important city. In 668, however, he was assassinated, and the capital returned to CONSTANTINOPLE.

In 827, the emperor attempted to arrest Euphemius, an admiral of the Byzantine fleet stationed in Sicily. Euphemius organized a local revolt and set himself up in Syracuse as emperor. When one of Euphemius's subordinates rebelled in turn, the admiral called for help from the Arab Aghlabid, emir of Tunisia, who took advantage of this invitation and sent a conquering force of 10,000 men.

Arab Attacks. The attempts by the Arabs to take Sicily lasted for half a century. After 878, the Arabs moved the capital of the island from Syracuse to Palermo, which quickly became a magnificent city, larger than any Christian city except for Constantinople. Local authorities were tolerant of CHRISTIANITY and JUDAISM, and the rulers did not insist on conversion to ISLAM, especially since non-Arabs paid higher taxes. Advances in agricultural techniques and irrigation were introduced, as were new crops, particularly lemons, oranges, and sugarcane, and the cultivation of silk and cotton began.

Early in the tenth century, the Aghlabid dynasty of Tunisia was overthrown by the FATIMIDS, who went on to conquer EGYPT and moved their capital to Cairo. While North Africa was being fragmented by the Fatimids, a local Muslim family, the Kalbids, established themselves as rulers of Sicily in the 960s. Subsequent civil wars allowed the NORMANS to conquer the island.

Normans. There had been Norman mercenaries in southern Italy fighting either for local LOMBARD rulers or for themselves since at least 1018. By 1060, Robert d'Hauteville, called Guiscard, and his brother Roger controlled most of southern Italy when they began to turn their attention to prosperous Sicily. Roger led the conquest of Sicily, which began in 1060 and ended with the fall of Palermo in 1071.

Roger's widow, Adelaide, a northern Italian, established the court in Palermo when she acted as regent for her son, Roger II. In 1127, Roger II succeeded to the duchy of Apulia when Robert GUISCARD's heir died. In 1130, he persuaded Pope Anacletus II to crown him king of "the Kingdom of Sicily,"

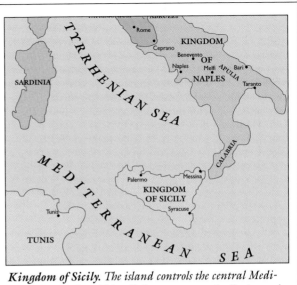

Kingdom of Sicily. *The island controls the central Mediterranean and could hardly be more strategically situated.*

which included most of southern Italy.

Unlike the ARABS, the NORMANS did not conquer Sicily to colonize it, but remained a minority ruling over a multilingual, multireligious population. The Normans made use of Arab craftsmen and builders and Arab and Greek administrators, and continued to use Arabic as an administrative language. Under Roger II this Arab-Norman culture reached its pinnacle; Roger himself spoke both Greek and Arabic.

Roger II's son, William I (r. 1154–1166), was not a strong ruler and left the administration of the empire to the people his father had brought in. A power struggle ensued between the barons of southern Italy and the Sicilian-based government, which led to religious riots and an end to the racial tolerance of Roger II.

William's death in 1166 left his queen, Margaret of NAVARRE, as the regent for their young son. To control the restive barons, the queen brought in French and Spanish kinsmen to administer the country. Another riot in 1168 caused many of the foreigners to flee. When William II came of age in 1172, he made some attempt to strengthen the central administration, but he died without an heir in 1189.

Hohenstaufens. Although the most direct heir to the throne was William II's aunt, Constance, the daughter of Roger II and wife of Henry IV, the HOHENSTAUFEN Holy Roman Emperor, the right of Henry to the throne of Sicily was contested by the Norman French barons. The barons supported William's nephew Tancred, who was already in Sicily. At Tancred's death in 1194, his son, still a minor, was crowned as William III; but Henry IV, with the help of the Pisan and Genoese fleets, easily captured the island.

Henry IV changed the fortunes of Sicily in a significant way—it was no longer an independent kingdom, but only a small part of a much larger empire, centered far to the north. Thus, whereas in the Norman period, no matter how much wealth the king and the barons accumulated, it was mostly spent within the kingdom. In the Hohenstaufen period the riches of Sicily began to be drained by a foreign power, for wars in which Sicily stood to gain nothing in return.

Henry died in Sicily in 1197, attempting to quell the first of a long string of local rebellions. He was succeeded by his son Frederick II, one of the most famous of the twelfth-century monarchs. He was only four years old when his mother died in 1198. Though she had appointed Pope Innocent III as the boy's guardian, a succession of German barons, who had been given fiefs in Sicily under Henry, occupied Palermo and kept Frederick there.

Frederick finally took over the government in 1208, but he preferred to live in southern Italy. Sicily gradually relinquished its central position and became a backwater of Italy. Burdensome taxes were imposed on Sicily's economy, which was also crippled by the exodus of a great part of the Arab population, who had been merchants, artisans, and agricultural workers. Ironically, Frederick himself was not anti-Arab; he had many Greek and Arab courtiers and promulgated laws protecting the rights of Muslim subjects.

On Frederick's death in 1250, the structure he had put in place fell apart, beginning a period of steady decline and civil war. The port cities, desiring the kind of independence enjoyed by the cities of Norman Italy, wanted to form a kind of federal republic under the banner of the pope. Against these attempts, the local barons backed Frederick's son, Manfred, as king.

French Rule. The popes offered the crown of Sicily to the son of the English king, Edmund of Lancaster, hoping England would have the resources to subdue the island, but a civil war in England made this unlikely. In 1261, the Crown was offered instead to CHARLES I OF ANJOU, brother of St. Louis, king of France. In 1265, Charles overthrew Manfred, and was crowned king of Sicily. Charles's capital was in NAPLES, and he imported Frenchmen as governors and justices, visiting the island of Sicily only once in his reign.

The SICILIAN VESPERS is a name given to a rebellion against the French that began in Palermo in 1282. It revived the push for urban self-rule, but internal disagreements kept the cities in turmoil. When the local barons offered the Crown of Sicily to Peter of Aragon, the husband of Manfred's daughter, Constance, the cities were powerless to resist.

The Aragonese held only Sicily; Naples was still under Angevin control. The Sicilian barons had exacted a promise from Peter that after his death Sicily would be inherited by one son and Aragon by another, so that they would have a king with Sicily's welfare at heart. But Peter's eldest son James insisted on retaining both kingdoms. He was advised by his Aragonese counselors to return Sicily to the ANGEVINS, but a younger brother, Frederick, who had grown up in Sicily and was the current viceroy, called a parliament of local barons, who elected him King Frederick III, rather than return to Angevin rule.

Late Middle Ages. After Frederick's death in 1337, the barons declared his son, Frederick IV, king of Sicily, and in 1372 Naples agreed to accept Sicilian independence. After Frederick IV's death, his daughter Maria was kidnapped in 1390 and married to Martin, the grandson of the king of ARAGON. In 1392, the Aragonese captured Sicily, and at Martin's death the kingdom was willed to his father, now king of Aragon.

ALFONSO V of Aragon, who ruled from 1416 to 1458, captured parts of southern Italy and again resided in Naples, which he used as a base for his wars against the cities of northern Italy. He was a generous patron of the arts and set up the first Sicilian university, in Catania. Alfonso's brother, John, inherited both Sicily and Aragon in 1458, while Naples was willed to Alfonso's illegitimate son. In 1479, John was succeeded by Ferdinand II, who married Isabella of Castile, uniting the two realms. (*See* NORMANS; HOHENSTAUFEN DYNASTY; PAPAL STATES; NAPLES; ITALY.)

SIGER OF BRABANT

Siger of Brabant (1235–1281) was a French philosopher whose interpretations of Aristotle's teachings led him to distinguish between theology and PHILOSOPHY. Other philosophers, such as THOMAS AQUINAS and his Scholastic followers, had tried to reconcile the teachings of ARISTOTLE with religion. But while Siger and his followers accepted the truth of the Catholic faith, they insisted that man had the right to follow reason; there was not one truth but two, that of traditional faith and that of science and reason. (*See* SCHOLASTICISM; PHILOSOPHY.)

Born in what is now Belgium, he became a professor at the University of Paris, where he studied philosophy. About this time Latin translations of Greek and Arabic works were becoming available to Western philosophers. Siger studied the philosophic works of AVICENNA and AVERROËS, from which he began to develop a new approach to Aristotle.

Siger maintained that humankind had an eternal, "intellectual" soul; individuals did not have their own souls and thus were not immortal. He set forth his views in a number of original works and commentaries on Aristotle. Siger was called before Church officials to answer charges of heterodoxy. The Church condemned more than 200 of Siger's propositions. He went to Italy to appeal, but was restricted to the custody of a cleric in the Tuscan town of Orvieto. The cleric went mad and stabbed Siger to death in 1281.

SIGISMUND OF LUXEMBOURG

Sigismund (1368–1437), the last HOLY ROMAN EMPEROR from the House of Luxembourg, sought to bring the empire back to the glory of the days of CHARLEMAGNE. He failed to meet most of his goals, but he did achieve a notable victory in helping settle the GREAT SCHISM that had divided the Western Church for nearly 40 years.

Born near Nuremberg, the younger son of Holy Roman Emperor CHARLES IV, Sigismund was ten years old when his father died. He was sent to HUNGARY, where he was to marry Maria, daughter of King Louis I the Great of Hungary and POLAND. Louis died in 1382, and Maria inherited the Hungarian crown (her sister, Jadwiga, inherited the crown of Poland). Sigismund was crowned king consort in 1387.

Badly in need of funds, Sigismund gave Brandenburg to his cousin Jobst, margrave of Moravia, in return for funds that he used to fend off challenges to his own crown from the rulers of NAPLES. A few years later, Turkish forces invaded Hungary, and Sigismund launched a crusade against them. Supported by the Church as well as the French, English, and Germans, his army advanced along the Danube River. But in 1396, Sigismund's troops were badly defeated at Nicopolis (in present-day Bulgaria); Sigismund barely escaped capture.

Meanwhile, Sigismund was also involved in a conflict with his half-brother, the Holy Roman Emperor Wenceslas, king of Germany and BOHEMIA. Wenceslas was not a popular ruler in Bohemia; he had the future St. John of Nepomuk (patron saint of Bohemia) drowned. Sigismund made a temporary peace with his half-brother in 1396. When Wenceslas was deposed in 1400, Sigismund tried to exploit the situation and take over Bohemia himself.

Over the next two decades, Sigismund tried unsuccessfully to end the HUNDRED YEARS' WAR, succeeded in ending the GREAT SCHISM at the COUNCIL OF CONSTANCE in 1414 but failed to protect JAN HUS from execution after promising his safety at the council; and sponsored a failed attempt at another crusade. Sigismund inherited the Bohemian crown in 1420 and spent the next 16 years putting down Hussite revolts. (See HUS, JAN; GREAT SCHISM.)

In 1431, Sigismund received the Lombard crown. In 1433 he was crowned Holy Roman Emperor. In 1436, he finally agreed to let the Hussites practice their religion and was received in Prague, reluctantly, as king of Bohemia. He died in Bohemia a year later.

SIMON DE MONTFORT

Simon de Montfort (c. 1208–1265) the Younger was a controversial political figure who led a revolt against ENGLAND's King Henry III and installed himself as ruler. He initially supported reform, but his excesses in wielding power turned many of his supporters against him.

Early Career. Born in FRANCE, Montfort came from a noble French family. His father, Simon de Montfort the Elder, was leader of the group that put down the ALBIGENSES (a religious group branded heretical). Simon the Younger also held claim to the earldom of Leicester through his father's mother. He gave up his share of the Montfort lands in France to his brother in return for the sole right to revive the now-lapsed claim. (See HERESY; ALBIGENSES.)

Montfort came to England in 1229 to reclaim his lands. He met HENRY III, and the two became friends. Henry arranged for Montfort to marry his sister, Eleanor. After a brief quarrel, the two men reconciled and the king gave Kenilworth Castle to Simon.

Montfort was known as a masterly administrator, but his detractors claimed that he was arrogant and power-hungry. Asked by Henry to help govern the French duchy of Gascony, then held by England,

A celebrated episode in the life of Simon de Montfort the Elder: the Siege of Toulouse in which Simon (top right) lost his life fighting the heretical Albigenses on June 25, 1218.

Montfort agreed, but only in return for a full regency and an unlimited expense account. Gascon nobles who had hated Henry, now hated Montfort instead.

Rise to Power. Once again a rift developed and once again the two were reconciled. But in the late 1250s, Montfort joined those English barons who sought government reform. The reforms known as the PROVISIONS OF OXFORD were written and presented to Henry in 1258. Henry at first accepted, but then rescinded them. Montfort, convinced that Henry was unfit to rule, raised a small army and captured and imprisoned Henry and his son.

Montfort ruled England as a military dictator. While he did attempt government reform—calling for two separate parliaments: one composed of four knights from each county to serve as representatives; the other of two representatives (burgesses) from each borough—his ultimate aim was to keep power in the hands of a few barons, whom he could control.

Montfort was so loath to share power that some barons began to realize that they had less power under Montfort than under Henry. Henry's son Edward had escaped captivity and had won the support of the royal army. The barons now supported Edward, who attacked Montfort and his followers at Evesham in August 1265. Montfort was killed and then beheaded.

SLAVERY

Slavery, common in one form or another since the beginning of history, was practiced in the medieval world. But by the end of the Middle Ages, slavery had all but disappeared in many places. Even where it still existed, it had become far less harsh; some households placed great trust in their slaves and treated them almost like extended family. But slaves still had no rights as individuals. The growth of CHRISTIANITY and ISLAM, both of which frowned on slavery, helped change people's attitudes, and many slaves were ultimately freed. Nonetheless, the slave trade contin-

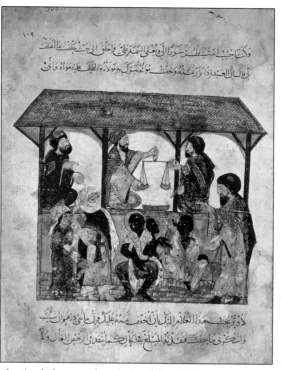

An Arab slave market, depicted in a 13th-century Islamic religious text. In Islam, slaves were protected because they were seen as likely future converts to Islam.

ued in some regions, notably along the Mediterranean coast and around the Black Sea.

Early Slaves. Germanic tribes in northern Europe invaded parts of ITALY in the fifth and sixth centuries as the Roman Empire declined. They enslaved many of their captives, and were known for their indifferent cruelty toward them. A slave's life was worth little; slaves could be executed for the most insignificant reason. In southern Europe, non-Christians were often sold as slaves to Muslims in SPAIN and North Africa. Muslims also enslaved prisoners of war.

The Muslims generally made their slave purchases from Europe because under their law, no one living under Islamic rule could be enslaved. The KORAN states that slaves should be treated with kindness and compassion; freeing slaves is an act of charity.

The Byzantines usually enslaved prisoners of war. Slavery gradually died off in the Byzantine Empire, primarily because the Byzantines were less and less victorious in war, and thus had fewer prisoners to enslave.

Changing Attitudes. Although slavery continued, and in some areas even flourished, it became less attractive in many segments of society. European rulers could not help suspecting that one reason for the Fall of ROME was that the ruling classes had relied too heavily on slave labor and could not maintain their economy when the slave population began to diminish after the second century. Gradually, rural slavery in Europe was transformed into FEUDALISM, in which SERFS worked the land on which they lived for the benefit of its owners. In return, they were granted a small wage and part of their harvest. Urban slaves tended to have different types of work, so their roles were often more that of servants or even administrators.

Religion also helped shape views on slavery. Neither Christianity, Islam, nor JUDAISM condoned slavery among people of the same race or religion. In some areas, slavery declined when many of the inhabitants converted to either Christianity or Islam. European slavery declined after the tenth century because the SLAVS (who were not Christian and thus often captured and enslaved) were gradually converted to Christianity. Countries such as Croatia, SERBIA, and POLAND were no longer attractive sources of slaves. Thus, slave traders set their sights on AFRICA, the Caucasus region, the Crimea, Turkey, and Mongolia.

Slaves who worked in large households were often treated quite well and given a remarkable amount of trust. In Islamic countries, slaves might provide housekeeping services: cooking, cleaning, and caring for children. But they might manage the household, and even take charge of the financial records.

In the Ottoman Empire, a special class of slaves made up the Janissaries, the regular infantry troops who actually became the military elite. These men would be captured when they were as young as eight. They would be given a Muslim education and taught to speak Turkish. Although they were converted to Islam, they were kept separate from other Muslims. Thus, they became extremely dependent on the reigning sultan. The sultan, in turn, was dependent on the Janissaries; they were his bodyguards, both at home and in battle. They occupied a place of honor in the Ottoman court.

Islamic slaves, in fact, were usually given training in respectable professions. They might go into business or science; they might even become scholars. They were also given Islamic instruction. As a result, most slaves were given their freedom while they were young. Some masters freed their slaves outright, while others allowed their slaves to earn money and then purchase their freedom. Usually, the freed slave would continue to work with the master. Muslims integrated former slaves into the fabric of the community, rather than treating them as outcasts.

In European households, slaves were often mistreated early on, but were given great leeway once they had become acclimated to the family they were serving. Medieval Europeans often regarded a particular slave as a trusted servant, but there was no attempt to integrate slaves into European society. This often created tension, even with trusted slaves. Slaves might not master the language or customs of the household, which could be frustrating for them as well as for their masters. Sometimes the addition of a young female slave into a household could create domestic difficulties. Often these young women would have children out of wedlock by their master.

Later Developments. By the end of the Middle Ages, slavery had disappeared in certain regions—Britain, FRANCE, Scandinavia, and GERMANY no longer dealt in the slave trade. As countries became more clearly defined, and as society's needs shifted, the need for slavery was greatly reduced in Europe—although many continued to profit from slave trade to other countries. (*See* SOCIAL CLASSES; FEUDALISM; SERFS.)

SLAVS

Europe's population during the Middle Ages consisted, in one way or another, largely of Slavs. They were the largest single ethnic group in Europe. At first, they were located primarily in eastern and southeastern Europe. The South Slavs comprised what are now the Serbs and Croats; the West Slavs were the ancestors of the Poles and Czechs; and the East Slavs—who became Eastern Orthodox— were the forerunners of the Russians and Ukranians. (*See* BARBARIAN INVASIONS; YUGOSLAVIA.)

This schism would help define the differences between Eastern and Western Slavs. Eastern Slavs were controlled by the violent Byzantine Empire, while Western Slavs were influenced by more progressive elements. (Some historians believe that the iron-tight control imposed on Eastern Slavic countries in the Middle Ages led inevitably to modern socialism.)

Early Middle Ages. During the fifth and sixth centuries, the Slavs lived west of the Dnieper River near the Carpathian Mountains. Their primary industries were knitting and weaving, and farming using a plow to which humans were yoked. During this time, the Slavs considered their land to be communal—there are no records or surviving Slav legislation regarding individual land ownership. Only movable items had the legal status of personal property. Slavs had a distinct belief in protecting forests, but there is nothing to show that they cared about borders. (As the Middle Ages progressed, monarchs began rewarding supporters with estates, and Slavic law belatedly recognized property rights.) Because all Slavs worked at the same profession and because there was no private ownership of land, there were no social strata—but neither was there any economic development.

Overrun by the AVARS in the sixth and seventh centuries, the Slavs began migrating westward into BOHEMIA, HUNGARY, and the Balkans. While the Western Slavs eventually assimilated into the European culture, the Eastern Slavs, who would migrate north into southern Ukraine, remained independent. The Eastern Slavs withstood onslaughts by the Byzantine Empire and led successful assaults on the Byzantines in alliance with proto-Bulgarians in 576 and again in 746, after which CONSTANTINOPLE signed a treaty recognizing BULGARIA as an independent state.

CHARLEMAGNE annihilated the Avars during the eighth century, which led to the creation of a Moravian kingdom, encompassing Bohemia, Poland, and Hungary. The kingdom ended in the early tenth century when it was conquered by the Magyars.

Integration. The Slavs started assimilating into the European population by intermarrying with members of other cultures, including violent societies such as the Huns and VIKINGS, whose warlike behavior they adopted. Slav households, previously matriarchal, gradually became patriarchal. The Slavs also developed stratified SOCIAL CLASSES, and their benign Slav folk and religious imagery grew more bellicose.

Conversion. The introduction of religion, therefore, came as a pacifying influence. The Slavs began converting to CHRISTIANITY during the seventh century, as missionaries entered Croatian lands. In the latter ninth century, Cyril and Methodius, missionaries sent to Moravia by the Byzantine Empire, received papal authority to translate Scripture into Slavic languages (for which they invented the Cyrillic alphabet). Western and northwestern Slavs fell under the Roman Church. (*See* AVARS; CHRISTIANITY.)

By the end of the Middle Ages, many of the independent Slav states had either collapsed or merged with larger entities, such as Bohemia (into Germany).

The Slavs had a major impact on medieval eastern European culture. No longer would eastern Europe rely on the landowner-slave economic relationship; instead, an early form of FEUDALISM, with free peasants on communes, supplied most of the labor. Once in Europe, Slavs proved to be adept at both work and war.

SOCIAL CLASSES AND CLASS CONFLICT

When writers of the medieval period came to describe the structure of their own society, they frequently did so in terms of the three classic "estates" or "orders": the clergy, the nobles, and the laborers—those who pray (*oratores*), those who fight (*bellatores*), and those who work (*laboratores*). Each of these estates was defined by its specific social function, and each was ranked hierarchically in terms of its status, of the value ascribed to its particular function. Thus the clergy, who showed men the way to eternal salvation, was the estate with the highest status, while the workers, whose manual labor supported the other groups, were the lowest in the social order, although they had reassurance that their patient endurance of the sufferings in this life made bliss in the next life all the more probable. Similar to limbs of a body, each order was expected to perform its own specific duties, not seeking to usurp the functions of the others. Social conflict was not inherent in the social order, which was seen as ordained by God, but rather arose from individual sin, from avarice and pride. The essentials of this view of society as an organic hierarchy were set out as early as the ninth century and continued to be produced into the late Middle Ages by writers such as John Gower and Thomas of Wimbledon.

Social Theory. Yet, the social practice of the Middle Ages was often at variance with this familiar social theory. When describing the precedence enjoyed by the different ranks of society, John Russell, the marshal to Humphrey, duke of Gloucester, did not place the clergy as an entire order above all other men. Despite the theory of the three orders, he was able to equate social ranks across the different orders: archbishops with dukes, bishops with marquises, earls, and viscounts; knights with unmitred abbots; worshipful merchants and gentlemen with parish clergy; and so on. In practice, social precedence was based on a pragmatic mix of birth, economic means, power, and dignity.

Despite the dominant social theory of the age, medieval people were, in their actual social practice, perfectly capable of seeing other people and of acting towards them in what we would regard as class, rather than estate, terms. For instance, the wage freeze introduced by the English Ordinance of Labourers of 1349, in response to the labor shortage created by the BLACK DEATH, sought to control those "servants" who would not work unless they received "excessive" wages from their "lords"; gave those lords first call on the labor of their own "bondsmen and tenants"; and prohibited artisans such as saddlers, tailors, and bankers from charging excessively for their goods. Here there was no need to distinguish between orders or estates. Landlords as a class, whether clerical or noble, were given identical powers over their tenants and employees. In this perspective, people were classified as landlords, wage-laborers, tenants, artisans, or merchants and were assumed to act according to their economic interests, forms of income, and property rights.

Class Structure. Medieval society was not, therefore, a society of orders in contrast with a modern society of classes. Rather, medieval men and women were classified at the time in different ways for different purposes. The individual was located at the meeting point of a number of different axes of social inequality and was a member of a variety of overlapping social groups according to estate, legal status, gender, class, status-group, and so on. One or the other would be emphasized in a particular context. In the context of manorial policies of the medieval English landlords, such as the shift from the leasing out of demesnes to direct management in the period between 1180 and 1220, the similarities between lay and ecclesiastical landowners are dominant. In the context of describing how individuals obtained access to such property and its mode of transmission, differences between the laity, who inherited their wealth, and the clergy, who acquired it through office, will be critical.

Conflict. As individuals, the members of any particular social group tend to confront each other as competitors: workers are in competition with each other for employment, peasants for land, nobles for royal patronage, clerics for promotion, and so on. One of the main ways in which the competing members of such groups come to feel a subjective sense of shared identity is through carrying on a common battle against another social group. Certainly, unlike those historians who have seen conciliation as more common than conflict in medieval social relations, the scholars who have emphasized the importance of class within the social hierarchy have tended to do so because of its tendency to generate class struggle. Class struggle is often thought of as "popular" in nature, made up of the revolts of peasants or the strikes of workers. In fact the actions taken by landlords in pursuit of higher rents and increased powers over their tenants were also instances of class conflict. The attempts by the abbots of Battle to undermine the particularly privileged tenure enjoyed by the customary tenants of the abbey's *leuga* (the land within a league of the abbey's altar) in the years after 1298, when they asserted their tenants' indentured status, their obligation to pay the manorial death duty (or "heriot"), and their inability to buy and sell the customary land by charter, were just as much examples of class conflict as were the resistance to them and the maintenance of the abbey's tenants' personal freedom.

Taking Sides. Nor was such conflict confined to individual landlords. Rather, in particular periods, we can see the landlords as a class going on the offensive over the twin issues that created friction between lord and tenants: the level of rents, tallages (taxes), and other impositions levied on the peasants and the degree of manorial control exercised by the lords over their tenants. Indeed, the period after the Black Death has been seen as one of general "seigneurial reaction," in which English landlords attempted to defend their interests, not only by the labor legislation noted above, but also by enforcing their local manorial rights, as when the bishop of Durham required individuals, groups of peasants, or village communities to maintain and work unoccupied properties in an attempt to

"Fortune and Poverty," an illuminated miniature from a 15th-century edition of Boccaccio's Decameron.

counter the effects of falling population. For many, this clash of a landlord offensive with the rising expectations of peasants and laborers that their newfound scarcity would result in high wages, low rents, and freedom that led to the PEASANTS' REVOLT of 1381, when the rebels from Kent, Essex, and the Home Counties marched on LONDON and demanded an end to serfdom. Similarly, in late medieval Catalonia, attempts by the propertied elite to limit peasant freedom provoked a violent response from their tenants. There, class conflict took the form of armed warfare, which eventually resulted in peasant victory and the granting of freedom and security of tenure. By contrast, in eastern Europe, from the Elbe to the Volga, the landlords gained the upper hand and the fifteenth century saw the beginning of a long-term trend towards serfdom.

Violent Reactions. Of course, peasant uprisings, like that of 1381 or the French JACQUERIE of 1358, were never simply economic in origin or merely the product of lord-peasant antagonisms. In 1381, failure in the HUNDRED YEARS' WAR, TAXATION, the state of national government, and growing central interference in the village were all sources of discontent within English society. Furthermore, armed uprisings were hardly the main form of popular social resistance in the Middle Ages. The choice facing the peasant was not one of open revolt or total acquiescence. Typically, conflict was local and piecemeal, centering on particular manorial obligations rather than seeking the abolition of all lordship. Thus, while the Peasants' Revolt was a failure in the short term, the English peasantry did go on to win its freedom in the later Middle Ages, securing an end to a mass of manorial services and obligations and obtaining new forms of land tenure called free copyhold and leasehold. In the pre-plague period, tenants had appealed to custom or to the privileges of the tenants of the royal Ancient Demesne in an effort to resist their landlords' attempts to take advantage of the surplus of tenants to raise their rents. Now villagers used the scarcity of tenants to secure wholesale concessions from their own particular lords.

Local Disputes. Similarly, in the TOWNS, the social structure had the inherent potential for conflict between merchants and artisans on the one hand and between masters and journeymen on the other. In the thirteenth century towns such as Leicester and Winchester, merchants sought to restrict the artisans' access to the market. In turn, masters keen to prevent journeymen from working up raw materials themselves, controlled wage levels by preventing their employees from forming their own GUILDS. Such conflict was particularly violent in fourteenth-century FLORENCE, most notably in the *Tumulto dei Ciompi* (1378). Nevertheless, in the towns, where social distinctions tended to be gradated on the basis of wealth rather than polarized around the possession of property, conflict often centered on political issues, on elections, and on the relative influence in town government of the *potentiores, mediocres,* and *inferiores* of urban society. (*See* GUILDS.)

For some historians, medieval society was a deferent society in which conciliation and consensus were more typical than conflict; for others, medieval social relations inevitably generated class conflict. Medieval class relations certainly had the potential to produce class struggle, whether initiated from above or from below, but perhaps more important are the ways in which such potential was realized and in which struggles varied in their form, intensity, and outcomes in different places and periods. More significant still is not just the existence of such conflicts, but rather their long-term effects in opening up or closing off particular paths of economic and social development. (*See* PEASANTS' REVOLTS; FEUDALISM; TOWNS.)

SOUTH AMERICA

The Middle Ages brought to South America the rise of a dominant empire stretching across most of its western coast, and the close of the Middle Ages coincided with its conquest by foreign explorers. (*See* EXPLORATION.)

Early Middle Ages. Three primary cultures dominated South America at the beginning of the Middle Ages. The Nazca culture in southern Peru was marked by its polychrome pottery. The elaborate artwork on its multicolored pottery depicted both scenes of typical life (farming, as well as the occasional beheading) and more fanciful scenes including monsters.

The Moche culture, located on the northern coast of Peru, developed fine-line drawing and sculpture. Anthropological evidence now suggests that there was greater economic stratification in the Moche culture than in the Nazca, as some Moche people were ostentatiously buried with their possessions.

Meanwhile, the Tihuanaku culture, located in southeastern Peru near Lake Titicaca, developed into a religious force, with many temples being built by the sixth century. The Tihuanaku spread its influence across Peru through culture, not by military force. Its god, Viracachu (the creator god of Peruvian mythology), was adopted by peoples throughout the region. Its influence spread to the Huari and Pacheco tribes.

By the end of the first millennium, the Tihuanaku influence began to wane as smaller cultures flourished along the Peruvian coast. Most of the surviving historical evidence indicates that the northern Peruvian coast had the greater amount of activity. One dynasty in particular, the Chimu dynasty of local nobles, eventually ruled an area over 1,200 miles long. Its capital was fenced in by a giant enclosure with walls 30 feet high. The Chimu were socially divided between royalty and commoners; strictly enforced the law, often burning criminals alive. However, women were granted equal status to men.

The Chimu had very detailed age rules within its society: adulthood began at age 25 and lasted until age 50, when people were classified as "half-old." At age 60 people were no longer forced to pay tribute or serve in the military. The Chimu also observed elaborate mourning rituals; widows of Chimu rulers were frequently sacrificed and buried next to their dead husbands. (*See* WOMEN.)

The Incas. The ultimate ruling dynasty of medieval South America was the Incas. Inca genealogical history begins in 1200 C.E. According to legend, they migrated to the Cuzco valley of southeastern Peru from the highlands under the leadership of their first ruler, Manco Capac. In the fourteenth century, under their fourth emperor, Mayta Capac, the Incas began to conquer neighboring villages, demanding expensive tributes from the vanquished. Mayta's successor expanded beyond Cuzco and built garrisons in conquered territories.

The Inca dynasty began in earnest under Pachacuti Inca Yupanqui in 1438. Pachacuti was effective both militarily and as an administrator. His reign marked the beginning of Inca expansionism as the Incas won territories in the north and south. The Incas controlled a region from what is now Quito to the Titicaca basin. Under the rule of Pachacuti and his son Topa Inca Yupanqui (who built the fortress surrounding Incas' capital city, Cuzco), the Incas developed a fierce army, capable of fighting throughout all of South America's vast and varied terrain, from the rain forests to the mountains. At their height, the Incas controlled most of South America, including parts of what are today Argentina, Bolivia, Chile, Colombia, Ecuador, and Peru.

The Incas were distinguished by their trained and

efficient central administration. They were patterned after such earlier cultures as the Chimu, but were decidedly more merciful. The Incas had no monetary system; commoners would pay taxes by working for the government and giving part of their produce to the Inca nobles. In exchange for this, the Incas protected their population during hardship, storing food and goods to use during famine and wartime.

The Incas did not kill their captives, but instead sent them to work. Inca society defined minute details of their subjects' lives—what types of work they would do, where they would live, even what types of clothes they could wear. However, the Incas practiced religious tolerance; other dynasties experienced internal unrest whenever a single ethnic group of vanquished people rose up in rebellion. Wisely, the Incas mixed together different ethnic groups of conquered people, so that one dominant rebel group could not develop. The Incas also quelled rebellions by incorporating the political structures of the people they conquered.

The Incas were one of the most highly developed indigenous groups in the Americas. They developed two paved, arterial roads running 2,250 miles north to south. They built an irrigation system in the desert and cut terraces into hillsides. They made bricks so finely that buildings could be constructed without mortar—the bricks fit perfectly together. The Incas were essentially a farming society; during their heyday they domesticated over 40 different types of plants. Their chief products were pottery, cotton, and wool.

Religion played a major role in Incan culture. Throughout the year, Inca ministers held public celebrations to mark special events in the religious life of the community. The emperor was believed to be a direct descendant of Infi, the sun god, and ruled the Incas by divine right. Group prayer focused on petitions against famine. The emperor traditionally married his sister. Villagers married one another rather than members of other tribes.

Even though the Incas did not write, they had an elaborate communication system. They communicated by smoke signals, as well as with the *quipu*, a cord with knotted strings. The quipu served as a sort of abacus; different sizes and positions of knots stood for numbers. The quipu was sent by relay 150 miles a day. By the end of the empire, a message could travel 1,200 miles in as little as five days.

By the time of Yupanqui's death in 1493, the Incas had stretched their empire as far south as Chile. Following a battle for succession, Huayna Capac led the Incas north to the Ancasmayo River. He died from a plague, possibly smallpox caught from a tribe that had in turn caught it from a band of Spanish soldiers. His death in 1525 left the Incas without solid leadership. One of his sons was named heir, while another son came forward and alleged that Huayna had given him control of the northern part of the empire. Civil war ensued.

Gradually, the Spanish inched closer to Peru. By 1535, the Incas were history, their roads destroyed, their homes vanquished. (*See* EXPLORATION; SPAIN.)

Above, mural from the temple of Chichén Itza, in Yucatan, showing a Mayan River settlement. Such thriving communities were typical throughout the Mayan and Incan empires of Central and South America during the late Middle Ages. Left, a pre-Columbian Incan figure. Incan culture was highly developed in the Middle Ages, rivaled only by China.

SPAIN

The Iberian Peninsula, which today is composed of the countries of Spain and PORTUGAL, was in the Middle Ages made up of an unruly assortment of disparate duchies and kingdoms, which were not united until 1469.

Roman Influence. The conquest of the agrarian natives of ancient Hispania by ROME in the third century B.C.E. ultimately benefited both sides. The Romans acquired proprietorship over large landed estates—the *latifundia* system—and rich tin mines, while the newly capitalistic tribal chieftains profited in the wine, olive oil, and grain trade with Rome. During this period of imperial occupation, cities developed, with the resultant bourgeois class of urbanites, and

Roman governmental administration and law were put into place. In the Iberian Peninsula, Roman cultural dominance was to last for seven centuries, long after the decline of imperial Rome.

The latifundia system of estate agriculture was the basis for the development of a privileged class of wealthy landowners, the eventual aristocrats, or *seniores*. Their privileged status was built upon the labor of the masses of slave or semifree peasants who worked the estates, the *humiliores*.

The Visigoths. The first major blow to the Roman system was the invasion in 409 of the Germanic VISIGOTHS from their "federated" army base in Toulouse, north of the Pyrenees. There had been previous forays into the peninsula by other Teutonics—FRANKS, Alans, Suevis, and VANDALS—but their toeholds were tenuous and their tactics terroristic. The Visigoths respected the Romanized majority, and their intention was to conquer and settle. They established a capital at Toledo, in the central plateau. During their 300 years of relatively untrammeled rule, they remained in the minority, but because of their previous status as federated soldiers of the now-moribund empire, they designated themselves the legitimate successors to Rome.

In the south, an area called Byzantine Spain, many Hispanics, with the aid of the eastern empire, threw off the GOTHIC domination and reestablished the unalloyed Hispano-Roman culture. One of the principal elements of this culture was its Catholicism and its ties to the Latin Church. The Visigoths were Arian Christians, and this elemental conflict exacerbated all others. In 587, RECCARED, the successor to one of the greatest Visigothic kings, Leovigild (568–586), converted to Catholicism. Leovigild had already succumbed to the Hispanic mentality; no longer just a military chieftain, but also a powerful landowner, he considered his reign an imperial legacy. Now, with the conversion of the Gothic monarch, the Hispanic majority, with the support of the Church, became allied with the conquerors. In 654, King Recceswinth promulgated *Liber Iudiciorum*, a legal compilation that combined Germanic customary law and Roman law.

Visigothic sovereignty remained a fragile construct, and in 711, it collapsed. The last Gothic king, Roderic, according to legend, violated the daughter of one of his nobles, Count Julian. The count then called in the Moors to avenge this insult. On July 19, 711, General Tariq and a BERBER army landed on the rock that bears his name "Gebel Tariq" (Mount Tariq), or Gibraltar. He quickly routed Roderic, who was killed trying to escape, and proceeded to conquer all of southern Spain.

Much of the surviving Visigothic ruling class found refuge in the Cantabrian and Galician (Asturias)

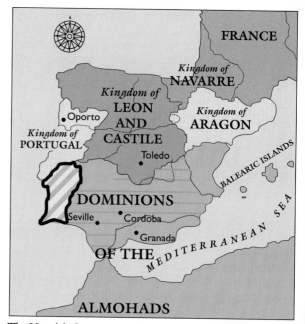

The Moorish Conquest and Christian Reconquest of Spain. Southern Iberia, fought over by the Christian North and Islamic North Africa, was a prized region in Europe.

north, but they had lost control of their territory. Still, the Gothic nobility left their mark on medieval Spain by creating a fusion of a somewhat degenerate classical culture and vigorous barbarian influences, evident in the administration, laws, and art, all of which combined elements of sophisticated Rome with rough but rational barbaric traditions.

Islamic Influence. The Islamic conquerors' initial aim was not to change the Hispanic-Christian value system, but to acquire as much land as possible. This laissez-faire attitude changed with the arrival, in 756, of a deposed Damascene UMAYYAD prince, Abd al-Rahman, who organized the regime in Spain under stringent Islamic rules. Severing the political ties with the eastern Arab governors (emirs), Abd al-Rahman created a unified state that persevered for 250 years.

This Muslim state, Andalusia, bordered on all sides by strongly Catholic kingdoms, zealously preserved its Muslim foundation and attempted unceasingly to suppress the indigenous Christian faith, with varying success. An ongoing factor in this struggle was the emergence of the Mozarabs—urban Hispanic-Romans, who remained Christian, but learned to speak Arabic and adopted much of the Islamic culture. In later centuries, the Mozarabic influence on Vulgar Latin, art, and poetry would spread northward into the kingdoms of Asturias, León, Castile, and ARAGON.

During the Caliphate of Abd al-Rahman III (912–961), his capital of Córdoba was recognized as the most culturally advanced city west of CONSTAN-

TINOPLE, and remained so for the following century. But in 1031, the declining caliphate broke into 23 petty kingdoms—the *reinos de Taifa*, from the Arabic word for faction. These separatist states, at war with one another and with their Christian neighbors, were united once more in 1086, under the ALMORAVID dynasty of North Africa. The Almoravids were succeeded in 1147 by another Berber group, the ALMOHADS, who were defeated in 1212 by Christian forces from Castile, NAVARRE, and Aragon at the decisive Battle of Las Navas de Toloso. After that, the only Moorish state to survive intact was that of Granada, until 1492.

The Franks. The Christian states had begun the long task of reconquering the peninsula from the Moors in the northwest province of Galicia, which had retained its independence, and which evolved into the kingdoms of Asturias, León, and Castile. The first loss of Moorish-held territory was to CHARLEMAGNE, whose armies penetrated through the Pyrenees and created the Spanish March north of the Ebro River. Here, in what was to become Catalonia, the predominant culture acquired a Frankish character.

But in the tough mountainous kingdom of Asturias-Galicia, where the remnants of Visigothic nobility had taken refuge, there were claims of direct Hispanic inheritance. During the reign of Alfonso II (791–842), the tomb of St. James (Santiago) was discovered at Compostela (his body having been transported to Galicia by angels), and the resultant cathedral shrine became the terminus on the Pilgrimage Road for pilgrims from all over Europe.

From Castile, Ferdinand I extended his authority over Aragon and León, and began the intensive push against the "infidel," forcing them south of the Tagus River. His son, ALFONSO VI, captured Valencia and Toledo in 1085, with the help of the legendary Roderigo Díaz de Vivar, "EL CID."

The twelfth century witnessed the political events which led to the development of three distinct Spanish kingdoms—Castile, Portugal, and the Crown of Aragon (the union of Catalonia and Aragon).

Portugal achieved independence in 1143 by declaring the former duchy a fief of the PAPACY, thus distancing itself from neo-Gothic movements in Castile.

Aragon. The rise of Aragon began with Alfonso the Warrior (1104–1134) when he acquired the powerful allies needed to expand into the plains south of the Pyrenees—French nobles and knights of the Palestinian crusading orders. With these allies, Aragon subjugated Saragossa and, sensing the fervent interest of Castile in Aragon's newly acquired lands, agreed to ally with its eastern neighbor, Catalonia. The first ruler of the Crown of Aragon and the founder of the house of BARCELONA was Ramón Berenguer IV, Count of Barcelona (Catalonia), who married Petronilla, the niece of Alfonso the Warrior, in 1150. With this union of Catalonia with Aragon and their combined conquest of the outlying Muslim areas, access was opened to the Mediterranean, and French dominance of the southern Pyrenees was ended. Between 1235 and 1238, the Crown of Aragon achieved sovereignty over the Balearic Islands, and captured Valencia from the Moors. In 1282, Pedro III married the granddaughter of Emperor FREDERICK II, thereby obtaining the HOHENSTAUFEN inheritance to SICILY.

Castile. Castile, which for a time in the twelfth century extended its influence over Aragon and Barcelona, suffered from prolonged wars with Portugal and Aragon and an unfortunate meddling in the HUNDRED YEARS' WAR in the thirteenth and fourteenth centuries. Repeated concessions to the feudal aristocracy weakened the monarchy almost to extinction; it was only the backing of the urban brotherhoods, the *hermandades*, that kept it alive. The lowest point of the Castilian monarchy came in 1369, when the ruler, Peter the Cruel, was murdered by his bastard half-brother, Henry of Trastámara (both the sons of ALFONSO X, a contender for the crown of Holy Roman Emperor during the Great Interregnum). The establishment of the House of Trastámara ended Peter the Cruel's attempt to curb the power of the nobility.

In spite of its political and economic woes, Castile managed to incorporate the contemporary European movements in Gothic art and humanism. The great cathedrals of Burgos, Toledo, and León were built, and the renowned School of Translators in Toledo, where Arabic texts were translated into Latin and Spanish, flourished in the thirteenth century.

During the course of the fourteenth century, contact between Castile and the Crown of Aragon was accentuated in the form of border wars, commercial interchange, and dynastic marriages. All of Spain, starting in 1391, conspired enthusiastically in the Jewish pogroms, which led to the creation of a nebulous social caste, the *conversos*—Jews who converted to Catholicism. Hostility toward the CONVERSOS would lead to the Spanish INQUISITION in 1478 and the expulsion of the Jews from Spain in 1492.

In 1469, the Kingdoms of Castile and Aragon were united with the marriage of Ferdinand II of Aragon and Isabella of Castile. As joint rulers, these "Catholic kings" (so designated by the pope) curbed the excesses of the feudal aristocracy, conquered the last Moorish possession, Granada, and sent Columbus to discover the New World. (*See* EXPLORATION.)

See BARBARIAN INVASIONS; BERBERS; VISIGOTHS; FRANKS. *See also* ARAGON; PORTUGAL; UMAYYAD DYNASTY; ABBASID DYNASTY; ALMOHADS; ALMORAVIDS; BARCELONA; RECONQUEST. *Also see* INQUISITION; SPANISH ART.

SPANISH ART AND ARCHITECTURE

The art and architecture of medieval SPAIN reflected the region's cultural and ethnic diversity—one of richest of the medieval world. Muslim, Jewish, and Christian cultures all played a role in shaping Spain's artistic development; influences from the Arab world, North Africa, and the rest of Europe left their mark as well.

Islamic Influence. The Muslims, who controlled much of Spain during most of the Middle Ages, had the most influence on art and architecture. (Islamic-Spanish art was known as Hispano-Moresque). Muslim rulers built magnificent palaces, such as Madinat al-Zahra, and elaborate mosques, such as the Great Mosque of Córdoba. The most famous Muslim palace, the ALHAMBRA, was built by North African Muslims who ruled Spain in the later Middle Ages.

The Muslims were responsible for the growth of the ceramics industry in Spain; they used ceramic tiles to decorate their palaces and mosques. Under the reign of the austere ALMOHAD Muslims from North Africa, which lasted from 1130 to 1269, there was noticeably less decoration, but the basic architectural styles remained the same. Even after the Christians took over the last Muslim Spanish stronghold of Granada in 1492, the ARCHITECTURE of the region retained a strong Islamic flavor for generations.

Jewish Influence. The Jews had lived in Spain since the fifth century, initially under the rule of the VISIGOTHS (who maintained control until the begin-

The Alcázar (Fortress) of Segovia, residence of the kings of Castile during the later Middle Ages. The word "alcázar" was also given to any fortified portion of a town or castle.

ning of the eighth century). They fared much better under Muslim rule because Muslim rulers were tolerant of Jews through much of their reign. Jews were able to develop their own rich artistic identity, and Jewish culture expanded and ultimately flourished. Some Jews, such as Hasdai ibn Shaprut in the tenth century and Samuel ibn-Nagrela in the eleventh century, held prominent positions in the royal Muslim court and encouraged the development of the arts in Spain. The Spanish Jews created illuminated manuscripts, including Bibles and copies of the Haggadah (the book of ritual for the Passover Seder). They also built a number of synagogues; two, one dating from the thirteenth century, survive in Toledo (both are now churches). Jewish influence waned as less tolerant Muslims took over Spain; when the Christians took over, they expelled the Jews from Spain in 1492.

Christian Influence. Most Christians who lived in Islamic Spain were Mozarabs, who adopted Islamic social customs but retained their religion. But the Christians controlled northern Spain during the Middle Ages. The primary artistic contributions from the Christians include illuminated manuscripts, the most famous of which is the *Commentary on the Apocalypse* (which many Christians claimed was actually a prediction of the CRUSADES).

Christian Spain adopted European architectural styles beginning in the eleventh century, particularly the ROMANESQUE, whose buildings were characterized by thick walls and small windows. The most famous example of Romanesque architecture in Spain is the cathedral in SANTIAGO DE COMPOSTELA.

Although the Christians gradually conquered the Muslims in Spain, region by region, over a period of nearly 400 years, they allowed the defeated Muslims to govern themselves in small independent enclaves, which is one reason Islamic influence on Spanish arts lasted long after Spain became a Christian country.

See ALHAMBRA; CASTLES AND FORTIFICATIONS; CHURCHES AND CATHEDRALS; JEWISH ART; ROMANESQUE ART AND ARCHITECTURE; SPAIN; *and* PORTUGAL. *Also* ARCHITECTURE; PAINTING; *and* MANUSCRIPT ILLUMINATION.

STAINED GLASS

The stained-glass windows created for medieval churches were revered for their great beauty and inspirational quality, but they also served the practical purpose of allowing light into cavernous GOTHIC edifices whose precursors had often been dark and forbidding. (*See* CHURCHES AND CATHEDRALS.)

Origins. Although "stained glass" is the common term for the colored glass that appears in windows, glass can be colored by several means besides "staining." Colored glass was known from ancient Egyptian times, but the manufacture of stained-glass in mass quantities began in Europe in the ninth century. The most common means of making stained-glass involved fusing metallic oxides (pigments obtained from metal ores) to glass in a melting pot. Different oxides produced different colors: cobalt produced blue, manganese produced purple, iron produced yellow. The exact shading of the colors varied with the proportion of materials and the melting time. Often the process was an exercise of trial and error, even for experienced glassmakers. (*See* GLASSMAKING.)

Enameled glass of varying colors was also sometimes used in stained-glass windows, as was glass colored by "flashing", in which a thin layer of colored glass is fused onto a clear piece of glass. A brownish paint made from iron oxide, known as grisaille, was often used to accentuate detail (such as folds in clothing) in stained-glass designs.

The oldest surviving stained-glass windows, dating from about 1065, can be found in the cathedral at Augsburg, GERMANY. Popular designs depicted stories or scenes from the BIBLE, as well as lives of the saints. Many also featured scenes from everyday life; the windows in the CHARTRES CATHEDRAL showing artisans at work are good examples. Often, panels of windows would lay out an entire story.

The advent of GOTHIC ARCHITECTURE popularized stained-glass windows for cathedrals. The earlier Romanesque-style cathedrals had thick walls and small windows that provided poor light. But large Gothic windows invited light into the massive cathedrals and inspired architects to explore new ideas on how best to channel that light. When stained-glass windows first began appearing in churches, some conservative members of the clergy questioned whether so much light should be let into the church. But light was also seen as symbolizing God; as light came through through colored glass, it often gave churchgoers a feeling of intense spirituality—the light that illuminated the church also illuminated them. On a less emotional level, since few people could read or write, the windows served an additional role as a source of religious instruction.

Creating a Window. Constructing a stained-glass window was in some ways similar to putting together a jigsaw puzzle. First, the artist would create a sketch, called a cartoon, of the design. Working from the cartoon, the artist would cut pieces of glass to fit the design. The glass was cut with a hot iron and trimmed with a pincer-like tool called a grozing iron. The pieces would be fitted into a lead framework, soldered together, and fitted into an iron armature.

The most skilled and talented glaziers were able not only to create effective designs, but also to combine the colors to create dramatic effects. Their talent extended beyond designing; they also had to be able to visualize how the various colors would filter the light.

The stained-glass window in the Church of St. Gudule, Brussels (in modern Belgium), depicting King Francis I and Eleanora at their devotions.

Stained-glass art was at its peak from the twelfth to the fourteenth century. Among the best-known examples, in addition to the Chartres windows, are those in the Le Mans cathedral, NOTRE DAME de Paris, and the Sainte-Chapelle in Paris. FRANCE, Germany, and FLANDERS were home to many stained-glass artists; ENGLAND often imported artists from the Continent to design windows for its churches and cathedrals.

Stained-glass windows were an especially revered art form. Often, when a cathedral was damaged by fire, one of the first tasks was to salvage as many windows as possible and install them in other buildings.

As the art of stained-glass evolved, artists experimented with new colors and techniques; some, for example, would layer two pieces glass, each of a different color, with portions of the upper layer carefully removed to create a unique effect. By the sixteenth century, artists were using larger pieces of glass in their windows, but the basic construction techniques remained essentially the same. Later, artists painted with enamels directly onto the glass—which did not produce the same splendid illumination as traditional stained-glass. The art of making stained-glass windows declined until the nineteenth century, when Victorian artists returned to the medieval techniques.

SUGER

Suger (1098–1151) was an important churchman, royal counselor, historian, and patron of the arts. Surmounting his humble origins as the son of a farmer, he rose to be one of the most influential men in twelfth-century FRANCE.

He was given as an oblate to the abbey church of SAINT-DENIS, near PARIS, at the age of ten, where his schoolmate was the future Louis VI. In 1122, he was made abbot, and sought to enhance the stature of the adjoining Church of SaintDenis, which housed the relics of the patron saint of France and was where all the French kings since HUGH CAPET were buried. (*See* SAINT-DENIS, ABBEY OF.)

Under his guidance, the church was renovated so drastically that it became the first example of the radical new GOTHIC style of architecture. In Suger's vision, light was the primary source of faith and divine inspiration, so his architecture opened up the dark, cramped church with its many aisles, columns, and walls, and flooded it with bright light from the innovative, jewel-like windows of STAINED-GLASS in the clerestory. Suger encouraged a vast array of master craftsmen to work at Saint-Denis—stained–glass makers, stone carvers, metalworkers, and goldsmiths. His efficient management of the monastery's holdings provided funds for his ambitious building program.

He wrote several books about the construction of the church as well as a biography of King Louis VI. During the Second Crusade (1147–1149), he served as regent of France in the absence of Louis VII. Historians credit Suger with significant improvement in the bureaucratic system of the Capetian monarchy.

SULEYMAN I

Suleyman I (also Suleiman; 1494–1566), known as the Magnificent, was sultan of the OTTOMAN Empire from 1520 to 1566. He enlarged the Ottoman empire through massive military campaigns, and oversaw a flowering of culture including literature, architecture, and art, funded by the acquired wealth of his conquests.

His first major military campaign resulted in the capture of Belgrade in 1521 and the death of the Hungarian king, Louis II, in 1526 in the Battle at Mohács.

Suleyman the Magnificent in battle (on the black horse), from the 15th-century work History of the Emperors.

The next campaign was an incursion into HABSBURG lands in 1532, which ended in a truce with Archduke Ferdinand. Suleyman was then able to turn his attentions to the problems in Anatolia to the east, which had begun during the reign of his father, Selim I. Popular and military revolts were quashed by the advancement of Suleyman's forces into Anatolia, from which they proceeded through Azerbaijan to BAGHDAD, conquering Iraq in 1535. Later campaigns into the area of Lake Van and Safavid Persia ended with a peace in 1555 between the Ottomans and the Safavids, but the basic disaffection of the eastern provinces remained.

Ottoman naval power increased in strength under Suleyman, whose admiral, Barbarossa, won battles against SPAIN, VENICE, GENOA, and Greece. The Ottomans captured Tripoli in 1551. The only areas that the Ottomans failed to capture were Malta in 1565 and India, where they fought the Portuguese in 1538.

By the end of Suleyman's reign, his empire covered three continents. He valued education and the arts, surrounding himself with talented statesmen, poets, and architects who left a legacy of great mosques in Mecca, Baghdad, and DAMASCUS. The question of Suleyman's successor resulted in mortal conflict with two of his sons, Mustafa and BEYEZID, both of whom he executed in favor of his son Selim.

SUTTON HOO

Sutton Hoo is an archaeological site near the English town of Woodbridge in East Suffolk, about 70 miles northeast of LONDON. Excavations in its burial mounds uncovered the remains of a Saxon ship thought to have been buried around 660. Although the ship itself had all but disappeared, the gold and silver objects buried with it (now in the British Museum) made Sutton Hoo one of Europe's most important collections of early medieval treasures. Discovered in 1939, it was not extensively excavated until 1946.

The collection's artifacts include an iron sword, wooden shield, silver bowls and spoons, a bronze bowl, drinking horns, a lyre, a helmet, a gold buckle, shoulder clasps, and a gold-framed lid for a purse (long since rotted away) which contained 37 gold coins. The only coin capable of being dated comes from the time of Theodebert II, king of the FRANKS in the early 600s.

The absence of a body suggested that the owner of the buried treasures was a Christian whose corpse had been buried elsewhere. However, more recent chemical analysis of the soil of the mound indicates the mound once contained a body that has since disintegrated. Archaeologists conjecture that the decayed body in the Sutton Hoo mound may have been that of the East Anglian king Raedwald, who converted to CHRISTIANITY, but returned to his pagan roots before his death in about 625.

SWEDEN

A t the beginning of the Middle Ages, Sweden was virtually unknown to the rest of Europe. The Byzantine historian Procopius and Jordones, the historian of the GOTHS, referred to Scandinavian voyagers, traders, and military men who had served in the armies of BYZANTIUM and Gothic ITALY. According to them, Sweden was inhabited by three major tribes—Swedes, Goths, and OSTROGOTHS. Other smaller tribes in southern and western Sweden were under the rule of the Danes.

Emergence. The medieval Swedish state is believed to have taken shape around Lake Mälaren in the fourth century, but its continuous political life did not begin until the ninth century, when the chief Swedish political center was at Uppsala. At that time, German missionaries came to the Swedish kingdom to spread the Christian faith, and the southern part of what later became Sweden, Scäne, was conquered and annexed by DENMARK.

The impressive culture of the Swedes prior to the VIKING Age can be seen from the rich grave relics found in the noble cemeteries at Valsgarde and Vendel. The peoples of Sweden lived in small villages and survived by farming, herding, hunting, and fishing, but trading was as important to the economy as agriculture. Archaeological evidence shows that the early Swedes traded with Greeks and Romans and later with Franks, ANGLO-SAXONS, and Irish. Birka, the new town the Swedes built on an island in Lake Mälaren, became the center of Sweden's international trade and a temporary residence for Swedish kings.

The Swedes were a loose tribal confederation nominally under royal rule. After the Swedish tribes chose a king, the other Gothic tribes in Sweden decided if they wanted to accept the Swedish choice, and sometimes they didn't. The Swedish king had little actual power except in time of war, and often the Goths preferred to have their own king.

Since Sweden was linked primarily by water, the Swedes readily traveled by ship on lakes and rivers and along the coast. The Scandinavians' ships were light and swift, and their navigation skills linked the various Scandinavian peoples and made the Viking Age (800–1100) possible by allowing them to sail the open seas and up and down the rivers of Europe. During that era, the Swedes played a major role in the expansion of the Scandinavians not only to the south and east, but also overseas to the west. In the tenth century, the Swedes, known as Varangians in RUSSIA, extended their influence all the way south to the Black Sea.

For much of the medieval period, the Swedes were in a state of conflict with both Danes and Norwegians. The emergence of an independent feudal class further weakened the authority of the Swedish crown, and towns and cities in Sweden won rights for themselves, strongly influenced by the German merchants of the HANSEATIC LEAGUE.

The Swedes were slow to accept CHRISTIANITY, which St. Ansgar first introduced about 829. In the tenth century, missionaries from ENGLAND and elsewhere spread the Christian religion, but paganism continued to thrive and was not fully eliminated during the reign of Eric IX in the twelfth century. Swedish kings were Christian, but several of the early kings were expelled by their pagan enemies. Christianity took better root in Sweden in the eleventh century after a diocese was established in the new city of Skara.

Politics. In political affairs, Sweden remained subordinate to the more powerful Denmark and to the Hanseatic merchants, who in the thirteenth century firmly established themselves on the island of Gotland. In the fourteenth century civil strife between the Swedish kings and the nobles who opposed them increased. The conflict ended in 1397, when Queen Margaret of Denmark was recognized under the terms of the Kalmar Union as the ruler of all three Scandinavian kingdoms—Denmark, NORWAY, and Sweden. Her reign ushered in a period of uneasy unified rule over the Scandinavian kingdoms. However, the Swedes left the union after Margaret's successors, who lived in Denmark, were unable to control Sweden, where the real power remained in the hands of the regents chosen by the Swedish diet. In the early sixteenth century, Christian II asserted his claim by force of arms. His massacre of Swedish nobles in what became known as the "Stockholm Blood Bath" in 1520 incited the Swedes to new and greater resistance. In 1523, they chose Gustavus Vasa as their king at Strangnas and crowned him Gustavus I.

Although Eric IX conquered FINLAND, Swedish settlements there did not become permanent until the late fourteenth century, when the Swedes settled on both sides of the Gulf of Finland. From their settlements they controlled much of the trade in northern RUSSIA. In the late Middle Ages the Swedes colonized the sparsely populated parts of northern Sweden.

SWITZERLAND

A country in central Europe that took its name from the valley of Schwyz, a mountainous territory separating the lakes of Zurich and Lucerne, which was the first canton to join the Swiss Confederation in 1291. However, Switzerland—as a unified and independent realm with a distinct national identity—cannot be said to have existed before the fifteenth century.

Settlement. By 400, the land that came to be known as Switzerland had been colonized by two different Germanic tribes; the western territories were settled by the Burgundians, who were quickly assimilated into the pre-existing Gallo-Roman population. The eastern territories, on the banks of the Rhine and the upper Alpine valleys, were settled by the Alemanni, a people from southern GERMANY and Alsace. The Alemanni were more numerous than the Burgundians, and were able to impose their own culture on the pre-existing population in the Aare valley. In the following centuries, the Alemannians moved westward, settling in the areas between the Reuss and Sarine rivers, and pushing farther into the upper Rhine valley. By the late fifth and early sixth centuries, both the Burgundians and the Alemannians had come under the control of the FRANKS, and were incorporated into the CAROLINGIAN kingdom in 746.

After CHARLEMAGNE'S death, his territories in the region of modern-day Switzerland were divided among his grandsons. By the year 1000, the region was divided into twelve bishoprics; territories had been granted to loyal favorites by kings and emperors, and new principalities were established. In the eleventh century, much of the region was united under the HOLY ROMAN EMPIRE. During this period, a number of feudal dynasties, such as the Zähringen, Savoy, Kyburg, and HABSBURG houses, were able to rise in power and increase their territorial possessions. The Zähringen dynasty founded several important towns in the twelfth century, including Fribourg, Bern, and Thun.

When the House of Lenzburg, another rival power in the region, disappeared in 1173, the Zähringens were able to extend their control over Zurich and the Uri valley. Thus, they were the first dynastic power whose territorial ambitions and possessions corresponded to the real boundaries of modern-day Switzerland. Under Duke Berchtold V, the family reached the height of its power, but when he died in 1218 with no heir, the family's influence waned. Many of their territories were incorporated back into the empire of FREDERICK II, the HOHENSTAUFEN ruler of the Holy Roman Empire; the House of Kyburg, whose family seat was in Zurich, inherited the Zähringen possessions south of the Rhine and became the dominant power in that region. Their decline and ultimate extinction in 1264 led to the rise of the Habsburg family.

Habsburgs. The Habsburgs took their name from the family's castle (Habichtsburg, or Hawk's Castle) overlooking the Aare River. They first became dominant in the region in the eleventh century, and by the beginning of the thirteenth were one of the most powerful families in southwestern Germany. Through faithful service to the Hohenstaufen emperor Frederick II, the Habsburg Rudolf received large grants of land, including Thurgau, Aargau, and Zurichgau.

In 1273, Rudolf was elected emperor. The imperial prerogative and the extinction of the Kyburg family, enabled him to extend his family's territories into the old Zähringen domains, acquiring Fribourg, Laufen, and Grasburg. Though Rudolf met some opposition from the local nobility, he was ultimately able to consolidate Habsburg power in the Rhine and Aare valleys, and to win from the king of Bohemia the fiefdoms of Austria and Styria. Rudolf also came to control much of the Waldstatte, a mountainous forest region that included the communities of Uri, Schwyz, and Unterwalden. Though over the centuries these communities had developed commercial and administrative ties, they had also become habituated to the beneficial neglect of larger territorial powers. Thus, the Habsburgs' ambition to dominate the central valleys south of St. Gotthard greatly alarmed the three communities. Uri and Schwyz had obtained imperial recognition of their states in charters from the Hohenstaufen empire.

After the death of Rudolf in 1291 and the frenzied struggle for new territories by his heirs, the communities recognized the need to band together in self-defense. On August 1, 1291, representatives from Uri, Schwyz, and Unterwalden signed a defensive pact that pledged mutual assistance against all enemies. This was not the first pact made between these three communities, but it is generally considered the birth of the Swiss Confederation, the foundation of modern Switzerland.

Rise of the Swiss Confederation. The following years witnessed a series of skirmishes and minor battles (immortalized in the legend of William Tell) between the communities of the Waldstatte and the Habsburg emperor Albert of Austria. With Albert's death in 1308 and the ensuing struggle for the imperial throne, the confederation feared an impending invasion, and decided to engage in a preemptive offensive strike, struggling to recover the Reuss valley and the St. Gotthard pass. The confederation achieved a stunning and decisive victory against the imperial forces on November 15, 1315, at the Morgarten pass, where peasant foot soldiers were able to ambush and massacre the armored knights of Leopold of AUSTRIA. After the battle, which assured the independence of the Waldstatte, the confederation's pact was reaffirmed and strengthened. This revised contract became the legal basis for relations between the Swiss cantons until the French Revolution. Encouraged by its victory, the confederation attempted to drive the Habsburgs completely out of the region, and the conflict between the two powers continued for the next 150 years. (*See* HABSBURGS.)

In the fourteenth century, the confederation, experiencing major population growth, began to expand its territories and incorporate new cities and communities. Lucerne joined the Swiss Confederation in 1332, Zurich in 1351, and Bern in 1353. The addition of these urban communities changed the character of the confederation, providing it with much-needed financial and military support, but compromising its original homogeneity and communality. However, the threat of the Habsburgs and other foreign nations presented the members of the confederation with a common enemy that preserved their cohesion and ensured their mutual cooperation. Aggression by Zurich and Lucerne led to further conflicts with the Habsburgs in the late fourteenth century, in which the confederates once again triumphed. Impressed by the Swiss Confederation's power and growing influence in the region, Zug (1364) and Glarus (1388) soon joined. (In the fifteenth century, the banner or seal of Zug became a symbol of Swiss independence.)

Expansion. In the following years, the lack of any major foreign threat allowed the individual constituents of the confederation to pursue their own interests and territorial ambitions; the cities increased their rural domains, and the mountainous cantons expanded significantly. The people of Uri pushed as far south as Italy before they were turned back by the duke of MILAN. In 1415, Bern led the confederation in the conquest of the last Austrian outpost south of the Rhine, Aargau. The confederation was victorious and much of the territory gained became the common domain of the confederation (*Gemeinen Herrschaften*). The fifteenth century brought more of these arrangements, and the shared administrative duties seemed to presage the beginning of a permanent communal organization stronger than a confederation. However, despite this cooperation, the fifteenth century also witnessed serious conflicts within the confederation. When Zurich attempted to expand to the east and south, the confederation felt itself threatened and fought with the city from 1439 to 1450. A treaty (1442) between the city and the Habsburgs further soured relations, but when the long and violent war finally ended, Zurich was readmitted into the confederation; any expansion it might have planned was blocked by the territorial acquisitions of Schwyz. After the war, many of the communities and cities on the left bank of the Rhine switched their allegiance from the Austrians to the Swiss. Thus, the cities of St. Gall and Schaffhausen and the region of Appenzell joined the confederation in the second half of the fifteenth century. With the Swiss occupation of Thurgau in 1460 and the purchase of Winterthur in 1467, the Austrians were completely driven out of the region.

The house of BURGUNDY, led by CHARLES THE BOLD, soon replaced the Austrians as the greatest threat to the Swiss. The Austrians had promised Alsace to the Burgundians, and their alliance presented the confederation with its next major challenge. Led by Bern, which had entered into a pact with the king of France, the confederation began the reconquest of Alsace in 1475. The Austrians soon allied themselves with the confederation when they realized that Charles's ambitious expansionist plans represented a greater threat, and together they achieved two crushing victories over Charles's powerful army in 1476. Afterwards, Fribourg and Soleure, having assisted the confederation against the Burgundians, joined in 1481. (*See* CHARLES THE BOLD; BURGUNDY.)

The confederation's unity was reaffirmed as Swiss (as the confederation was called) military power continued to draw hostile attention from its neighbors. As Bern defended itself on the east, Zurich did the same on the western front, engaged against Austrian forces. Tension between the Habsburg emperor MAXIMILIAN I and the confederation led to another war in 1499 in which the Austrian and the German Swabian League battled the Swiss force, now allied with Graubünden, a small confederation of communities that lay to the southeast. The Swabian War, as the conflict came to be called, was the final war of Swiss independence, and ended with the Peace of Basel on September 22, 1499. Confronted with Swiss military superiority, Maximilian abandoned his claims, implicitly recognizing Swiss independence. Two years later, in 1501, Basel and Schaffhausen joined the Swiss Confederation, bringing the number of members to thirteen. The confederation remained unchanged until the late eighteenth century. (*See* HOLY ROMAN EMPIRE; HABSBURG DYNASTY; HOHENSTAUFEN DYNASTY.)

TAMERLANE

Tamerlane (also Tamberlaine; 1336–1405) was a fiery, charismatic, brutal Mongol ruler who attempted to reclaim GENGHIS KHAN'S empire in the fourteenth century. His bloody reign inspired poetry from such later writers as Christopher Marlowe, Lord Byron, and Edgar Allan Poe.

Early Years. He was born Timur Leng in 1336 in Shahr-i-Sabz, south of Samarkand, the son of a Turk commander. As a young man, he injured himself in a sheep-raiding accident, and was unable to bend his right knee or raise his right arm ever again. This earned him the nickname Timur the Lame, which became Tamerlane. MONGOL power in Transoxiana had been significantly reduced from the days of GENGHIS KHAN, as various factions sought to assert leadership. Tamerlane claimed he was Genghis's descendant, but there is no evidence to support this, although apparently two of his four wives were related to Genghis. In 1361, Tamerlane became chieftain of the Timurid tribe. With Amir Husayn, his brother-in-law, Tamerlane began defending the Timurids against the dominating Chingisid tribe. Within a decade he defeated the Chingsids, and later Husayn's army itself. Tamerlane named himself sole ruler of Transoxiana in 1369. He saw himself as having been selected by God to lead, having been born during the conjunction of Saturn, Jupiter, and Mars. (*See* GENGHIS KHAN.)

Unknown artist's portrait of Tamerlane the Conqueror.

Military Career. After seizing power in central Asia, Tamerlane assaulted western Iran and eastern ANATOLIA for the next three decades, leading armies of upwards of 300,000. He began attacking Persia in the 1380s, burying 2,000 Persians alive during a raid in Isfizar, an assault he would later blame on his associates.

From 1392 to 1397 his armies engaged in the Five Years' Campaign against the GOLDEN HORDE in RUSSIA. In 1395, his armies finally crossed the Caucasus and devastated the Horde's forces, conquering Sarai and forcing merchant caravans to alter their routes in order to pay tolls to Tamerlane's army.

In 1398–1399, Tamerlane attacked India, and swiftly conquered Delhi after 100,000 captives were slaughtered. In battle on the banks of the Indus River against an army on elephants, his soldiers placed straw on their camels' backs, then set the straw on fire. The camels ran in alarm, and the elephants retreated, trampling many Indian soldiers in the process.

Tamerlane turned west and conquered DAMASCUS in 1400–1401, moving toward an assault on the Byzantine Empire. In 1402, Turkish Anatolia fell to Tamerlane. He forced many of the Anatolian soldiers to join his army, ultimately capturing the Anatolian leader BEYEZID, who died after eight months of torture. (*See* MONGOLS; BYZANTIUM; CHINA.)

Later Years. In his old age, Tamerlane began plans for an invasion of CHINA. He became sick after excessive eating and drinking at a celebration before the incursion; after three days of heavy drinking, he died from a fever on February 18, 1405.

Despite his physical handicaps (or perhaps because of them), Tamerlane was an exceptional field leader, governing from horseback. Though his armies numbered in the hundreds of thousands, he kept his soliders in units of 10. As a political leader, he did not establish government in the lands he conquered, though he would make Samarkand his capital. During his reign, Tamerlane beautified Samarkand, importing captured artisans from Syria and India to design buildings. He would generously reward good workers, but on one occasion, Tamerlane had two artisans hanged for building a mosque porch he did not like.

Tamerlane's bravado was legendary. Before assaulting Damascus, he announced, "I am the scourge of God appointed to chastise you, since no one knows the remedy for your iniquity except me. You are wicked, but I am more wicked than you, so be silent!"

TANCRED DE HAUTEVILLE

Tancred (d. 1112) was a NORMAN BARON from near Coutances whose many sons from his two marriages went to southern ITALY in 1016 to seek adventure and fortune. With his first wife, Tancred had five sons, the oldest three of whom—William, Drogo, and Humphrey—became, each successively in his turn, count of Apulia. (*See* NORMANS.)

Tancred's second wife, Fredesendis, bore him seven sons. The oldest, ROBERT GUISCARD, and the youngest, Roger, had outstanding political careers. Both were involved in the conquest of SICILY from the ARABS and in laying the foundation for the later kingdom of NAPLES and SICILY. After the pope recognized Robert Guiscard as lord of Apulia and future ruler of Sicily, then still in Muslim hands, by the Treaty of Melfi in 1059, Robert played a leading role in papal and Byzantine politics in Italy. Meanwhile, Robert supported his brother Roger's conquest of Sicily, which he ruled as count; the conquest was completed in 1091. A memorial to Tancred and his family, the great cathedral of Mount Royal near Palermo, with its Byzantine MOSAICS, remains standing today.

TAPESTRIES

apestries are decorative fabrics in which a design is woven directly into a piece of cloth. The method of manufacture makes them heavier and more durable than dyed or painted cloth or embroidery. Tapestries are also more difficult to execute, however, and during the Middle Ages it was a privilege to possess one.

Beginnings. Decorative woven wall hangings existed not only in Europe but in the East as well as the Far East. At the beginning of the Middle Ages, embroidery was popular, as were dyed and painted cloth designs. But true tapestries did not become popular in Europe until after the thirteenth century. (The famed BAYEUX TAPESTRY is not a true tapestry but an embroidery.)

Before the CRUSADES, silk weavers from CONSTANTINOPLE had begun to settle in Greece, CYPRUS, and ITALY; by the twelfth century SICILY had established itself as the center of the decorative weaving industry for both Europe and the Islamic world. Knights returning from the Crusades brought with them a fondness for the luxuries they had enjoyed in the Middle East.

Most of the scenes depicted on tapestries focused on the lives of saints or heroes, but many also chronicled everyday life. They were thus not only ornamental, but entertaining. Tapestries had a practical purpose, too—the thick material insulated cold stone castle walls. But they were unmistakably a luxury item, and only the nobility or the most well-to-do of the upper middle classes could afford them. Because they were transportable, nobles could easily take them from one castle to another, and tapestries became treasured family heirlooms. (*See* CASTLES; FURNITURE.)

Creating a Tapestry. Weaving tapestries was a complex procedure that required great skill and talent; this made them highly prized and costly. First, an artist would create a sketch, or cartoon, from which a tapestry could be woven. Another artist would enlarge and color the sketch to a full-scale pattern for the weaver to follow. The weaver would then work from this pattern, often embellishing it to suit his taste.

As tapestry weaving became more widespread, it fell under the regulation of guilds, which ensured the quality of both the weavers and the materials used. WOOL was the most common material, English wool being considered the most durable. High-quality dyes were used to guarantee rich colors that would not fade or run. (*See* WOOL TRADE.)

By the middle of the fourteenth century, the major tapestry centers were in PARIS and Arras (in FLANDERS). Arras became the chief center in the fifteenth century, but in 1477, Louis XI of FRANCE destroyed Arras, leaving tapestry weavers to take up their trade in other Flemish cities. Eventually, many settled in SPAIN, ITALY, and England.

Tapestries sometimes had the status of an official document. Below, the Beauvais Tapestry *contains a plan of Paris, including the newly built Cathedral de Notre-Dame.*

Tapestries lost much of their popularity as the Middle Ages came to an end; Renaissance society favored paintings. The nineteenth century saw some renewed interest in the art form, and artists including Picasso and Matisse explored the art of tapestry making in the twentieth century. Splendid collections of late medieval tapestries are on display at the Cloisters Museum in New York City and the Cluny Museum in Paris. (*See* FURNITURE; BAYEUX TAPESTRY.)

TASSILO III

In 757, Tassilo (742–794), the 15-year-old duke of Bavaria, became the vassal of the Frankish king PÉPIN III THE SHORT after a Frankish conquest. At the ceremony he submitted to Pépin by swearing an oath of allegiance *per manus* ("by his hands") that involved kneeling before Pépin and having his raised hands clasped by his new lord. It is the first recorded evidence of a feudal ceremony in the Middle Ages. During the reign of Pépin's son, CHARLEMAGNE, Tassilo broke his oath and tried to withhold his tribute. When Charlemagne threatened to attack his duchy, however, Tassilo submitted again and was forced to offer his son as a hostage. A Frankish assembly sentenced Tassilo to death for his insubordination, but Charlemagne commuted the sentence to life imprisonment, allowing Tassilo to live out his life in a monastery. In 794, the year of Tassilo's death, Charlemagne terminated Tassilo's legal claim to the duchy of BAVARIA and added it to his kingdom.

TAXATION

The people of the medieval world were subject to a wide variety of taxation. In western Europe, local lords and monarchs taxed their subjects heavily. In the early Middle Ages, payment was made in crops or services, such as a term in the royal army, or by providing special labor. Monetary taxation would not be imposed until the middle of the eleventh century in most areas of western Europe.

The Norman Conquest of 1066 paved the way for the forms of taxation that would eventually be adopted throughout western Europe in the twelfth and thirteenth centuries. The NORMANS maintained virtually all taxes in force before the invasion and imposed several of their own. Taxes were paid to the monarch for the import and export of goods, for domestic trade, and on movable wealth. Every member of the realm (save the clergy) was also required to pay a tax on income. (*See* NORMANS; MONEY AND CURRENCY.)

As if these taxes were not enough, the average Eu-

ropean worker in the Middle Ages also had to pay taxes to the Church. The most common tax imposed by the Church was the tithe. Everyone, royalty included, was required to pay this tribute to the PAPACY in return for its favor and protection. Even the clergy itself could not escape the taxation of the Church—monks, bishops, and other high members of the clergy were all required to make payments to the papacy.

The financing of the Crusades demanded an income tax on all the clergy by the papacy. Monarchs taxed the clergy further, with the pope's permission, and special taxes were levied in many countries (France especially) in an effort to help finance the CRUSADES.

All of this taxation led to friction among all those involved in the taxation process. The kings' inability to tax the clergy without papal permission was a constant source of dispute; the clergy resented the taxation imposed on them by the monarchs as well as by the papacy; the papacy was furious that either faction would even question papal supremacy on any matter. The people, of course, were reluctant to accept any taxation and were not at all shy about revolting, as they did in France in the JACQUERIE (1358), and in ENGLAND in the PEASANTS' REVOLT of 1381.

In the Byzantine Empire, landowners had to pay taxes on the land they farmed; those who merely worked the land were assessed other forms of taxation. Taxes for road building, the farming of state-owned land, and the upkeep of the army were imposed when needed. Special tax exemptions were often made to religious groups, large landowners, and foreign merchants as an incentive both to keep those individuals in the empire, as an enticement to increase their importing and exporting—activities that led to taxation of the general population later in the process.

Taxation in the Islamic world was also based on agriculture. There was a division in the types of taxation imposed on landowners. Lands owned by Muslims were taxed significantly less than lands captured from non-Muslims in battle. Beyond this distinction, Muslim leaders taxed land according to its productivity. The standards for applying these taxes changed constantly, varying with a particular crop's harvest.

LEGEND AND LORE

Lady Godiva

In England, one eleventh-century protest against taxes became the stuff of legend. Lady Godiva, wife of Leofric, earl of Mercia, in protest of burdensome taxes imposed by her husband, threatened to ride naked through Coventry unless the taxes were rescinded. Leofric did not attempt to interfere with the protest, but issued a decree that any townsperson caught looking at his naked wife would be put to death. The story first appears in the chronicles of Roger of Wendover, who wrote in the thirteenth century. Roger writes of a "Peeping Tom" who looked out the window to catch a glimpse of Lady Godiva as she passed, and was struck blind (or dead) after his furtive glance.

TEUTONIC KNIGHTS

A chivalric order founded in Acre to run a field hospital in 1198 during the Third Crusade. It was probably established independently of a German hospice in Jerusalem dating from the 1140s. The order was international with possessions throughout Europe—its local houses, or commanderies, made up of knights, clerics, and brothers, and numerous supporting staff (from squires to women domestics). The Teutonic Knights nevertheless had a stronger ethnic identity than did the Templars and Hospitallers, larger military orders with an international structure. Committed, as were the larger orders, to the defense of the Holy Land, the Teutonic Knights at the same time aggressively served German territorial ambitions. Eventually they realized the organizational model of the *Ordenstaat* (an independent sovereign entity) to a greater degree than any other military order, establishing (after failed attempts elsewhere) an independent state on the shores of the Baltic, in PRUSSIA.

Establishment. Ongoing relations between the crusaders of the HOLY ROMAN EMPIRE and the numerically far superior French and English ones created the need for a German hospital, and the presence of German crusaders in Palestine fostered the establishment there of a military order on what had become a familiar model; the Teutonic Knights evidently adopted the rule of the Templars in military matters and that of the Hospitallers in their nonmilitary and charitable endeavors. The order was approved by Clement III in 1191, granted further privileges by Celestine III in 1196, and approved as a full military order by INNOCENT III in 1198–1199. A generation later the Knights' grand master claimed the possessions of the earlier German hospice and thenceforward operated from Jerusalem. Like the Templars and Hospitallers, the Knights held castles in Palestine, notably Montfort near Acre, construction on which began in 1226. Most of these were purchased by the order, which remained smaller and less wealthy than the other international orders. Although as involved as the others in military and political affairs, it was not steeped in political intrigue like its Frankish counterparts.

Expansion. In 1226, Grand Master Hermann von Salza (r. c. 1210–1239) accepted the lordship of southern Prussia in exchange for the order's defense of Christian Polish realms against pagan Prussian tribes. Eleven years later, the order gained Livonia (Latvia, Estonia, and LITHUANIA) on absorbing the Order of the Sword-Brethren, another military order active in the Baltic region, which had been nearly annihilated by the Lithuanians. The order was, however, subjected to heavy criticism from within and from without for pressing its Baltic expansion. In 1242, the Knights invaded Orthodox Christian RUSSIA but were repulsed in a battle on Lake Peipus by Russian armies under ALEXANDER NEVSKY. Despite subsequent rebellions in both their northern and southern territories, the order's control of these regions had been consolidated by the end of the thirteenth century. After the fall of the Latin kingdom of Jerusalem in 1291, the order had moved its headquarters to VENICE; feeling itself vulnerable to the pressures that had destroyed the Templars, the order then moved to Marienburg in its Prussian stronghold in 1309. Thus the order chose a Baltic destiny that by the 1330s set it on the path toward the *Ordenstaat,* gradually selling or losing its possessions elsewhere in Europe and narrowing recruitment to southern GERMANY, its traditional source of recruits and patronage. The Knights colonized Prussia, establishing thousands of towns. (*See* POLAND; RUSSIA.)

Decline. By this time the order had occupied Danzig (modern Gdansk), alienating its former ally, POLAND, now a formidable opponent. In 1386, the grand duke of Lithuania, Jagiello, converted to Christianity, taking the name Wladyslaw II; hostilities between the Lithuanians and the Teutonic Knights did not cease, however, and Wladyslaw forged alliances with the Knights' enemies. In 1410, a combined force of Livonians, Poles, Hungarians, Cossacks, Tatars, and others inflicted a crushing defeat on the Knights at Tannenberg. Although drastically weakened, the order held on in Prussia until 1467, when it was compelled to relinquish its territory in western and then eastern Prussia; it was left holding eastern Prussia and Konigsberg as a vassal of the king of Poland, its powers and revenues much curtailed. To the north the Livonian brethren pursued a somewhat independent course; during the fifteenth century, they again engaged the Russians to the east. In 1502, they checked the advance of Ivan III of Moscow, but by the time Ivan the Terrible invaded in 1558, they could no longer resist, and their control of Livonia came to an end.

In 1525, the conversion to Lutheranism of the grand master Albrecht von Brandenburg had again altered the order's status. Albrecht secularized the order in Prussia and was invested as duke of Prussia. The order, however, undertook military duties only intermittently. The Livonian brethren likewise chose secularization in 1561–1562. After the nationalization of its remaining possessions in France following the French Revolution and its dissolution throughout the Napoleonic empire in 1809, it survived only in AUSTRIA, and there only covertly. It was reconstituted in Austria in 1839 as the Order of the Teutonic Knights with purely charitable functions, returning to its original purpose. Now headquartered in Vienna, the order has survived to the present day with this mission.

THEODORA

Theodora I (500–548), wife of the Byzantine emperor JUSTINIAN I, was a significant political figure in her time and one of the most powerful women in Byzantine history. She was famous for her physical beauty, intelligence, and political shrewdness. Theodora had considerable influence on her husband and on public matters; she is credited with preserving his rule during the Nika riot. Though ruthless against her enemies and in protecting the position of Justinian, Theodora was generous, actively promoting the position of women in the Byzantine Empire. The details of her life are unclear, the main source being Procopius, an enemy of both Theodora and her husband.

Early Life. Theodora was probably born in CONSTANTINOPLE. Her father was an animal trainer for the circus and a member of the Green party (a political faction opposed by the Blue party). Her mother was a performer in the circus. On her husband's death, Theodora's mother remarried and tried to get her second husband hired in the same job. Because the Greens ignored her pleas and the Blues gave employment to her new husband, Theodora and her mother became adherents of the Blue party. According to Procopius, Theodora became a performer and a prostitute. He recounts extravagant tales of her sexual exploits, stories that historians have attributed to his antipathy. After perhaps giving birth to an illegitimate child, Theodora moved to North Africa with a civil servant with whom she had become involved, but she soon returned alone to Constantinople. On the ship back she is said to have converted to the heretical Monophysite sect, a fact that would have important political implications for the empire later in her life.

Justinian. Her first meeting with Justinian probably occurred while he was endeavoring to win the allegiance of the Blues. Justinian fell in love with Theodora. After they became lovers, he made her a patrician. Their hopes of getting married were at first opposed by the emperor's aunt, the empress Euphemia, and by a law that forbade marriage of the nobility to performers. The empress, however, died in 523, and the emperor Justin, Justinian's uncle, was persuaded to repeal the troublesome law. In 525, Theodora and Justinian married; after Justin's death in 527, they were crowned co-rulers. Despite Theodora's ascension, much of the Byzantine elite continued to hate her because of her "low" birth.

Most imperial spouses tended to stay in the background, but Theodora's prominence in internal and

Bust purported to be that of Byzantine Empress Theodora.

foreign matters is beyond dispute. Theodora's name was cited in state documents and oaths of allegiance and engraved on churches. The papacy addressed letters to both the emperor and empress, and diplomats made official state visits to her. (*See* JUSTINIAN.)

The Riot. In 532, Theodora's most notable political intervention occurred during the Nika riot. This event was triggered by the unusual union of the Blue and Green parties in opposition to Justinian. The riot spread throughout the city to the point where Justinian's counselors advised the royal court to abandon the capital. Theodora, however, broke ranks with the advisers and declared that it was better to die ruling than live well as fugitives. Procopius quotes her: "For an emperor to become a fugitive is a thing not to be endured; the purple [of royalty] makes a fine winding sheet [shroud]." Justinian took heart and entrusted the crushing of the rebellion to his general BELISARIUS. The rioters were forced into the Hippodrome, where over forty thousand of them were butchered, including the nephew of a former emperor who supported the rebellion.

Despite her support of such brutality, Theodora supported important liberal internal reforms. She was a devoted adherent of Monophysitism and protected some Monophysites despite the orthodoxy of her husband. Theodora set up a Monophysite monastery in Constantinople that protected refugee bishops; she played a central role in deposing Pope Sylverius and replacing him with the gentler Vigilius. Theodora's influence on her husband, however, was not without limits. It took her ten years to get Justinian to remove the famous praetorian prefect in the East, John of Cappadocia. (*See* NESTORIAN CONTROVERSY.)

Theodora was financially generous in her support of churches, orphanages, and other public works. It was she who had laws passed prohibiting the sale of young girls. She also used her influence to change the divorce law in order to protect women after the end of their marriages. In 548, Theodora died of cancer.

THEODORIC THE GREAT

Theodoric the Great (c. 455–526) was king of both the OSTROGOTHS and ITALY. He is considered the greatest of the German princes during the period of the Wandering of the Peoples and the Fall of the Roman Empire. Although beginning and ending in murder, his reign in Italy was prosperous and successful. Theodoric, however, could not overcome the political and religious obstacles to the establishment of a permanent Ostrogothic kingdom.

Early Years. Theodoric was born in an Ostrogothic settlement in Pannonia, about the time his uncle Walamir defeated the sons of ATTILA THE HUN. Theodoric spent his teenage years in CONSTANTINOPLE, where he gained a deep appreciation of Roman civilization. After the death of a rival in 481, Theodoric became king.

His early career was tied to the eastern empire and its emperor Zeno. Theodoric aided Zeno, and was rewarded with imperial titles; he also pillaged eastern provinces, including Macedonia and Thessaly. In 488, Zeno persuaded Theodoric to invade Italy in order to oust the German king ODOACER, who had become independent of the eastern empire. Theodoric defeated Odoacer at Sonius and Verona in 489. The defeated Odoacer retreated to RAVENNA, where he survived three more years with the help of defecting OSTROGOTHS and the Burgundians. Finally, in 493, Odoacer agreed to a truce whereby he would rule Italy jointly with Theodoric. The agreement, however, was a ruse, and Theodoric killed Odoacer with his own hands at a banquet at which the truce was to be confirmed.

The New Ruler. Theodoric settled in at Ravenna as the eastern empire's designated ruler of Italy. Although Theodoric respected Roman civilization, he gradually sought complete independence from Constantinople, in part through the development of a system of alliances based on marriage ties between Germanic kingdoms. Theodoric sought to gain the allegiance of the Italian people and the Catholic Church while tying together the Frankish kingdom in Gaul with the two Gothic kingdoms in Italy and SPAIN.

Theodoric's domestic goal was the restoration of Roman culture and political organization. He retained the Roman bureaucracy and placed Romans in top positions. The Roman aristocrat Cassiodorus became Theodoric's idealogue, writing the *History of the Goths*. Cassiodorus developed the term *civilitas* to describe the merging of the Roman and Gothic ways of life.

Theodoric sought to improve the living conditions of Italians to win them over to his new regime. He initiated a program of public works, including the draining of marshes and building of harbors, and supported the arts. His economic reforms, such as the reduction of taxes, fostered the development of AGRICULTURE. Theodoric also brought a measure of safety to the countryside by allowing Italians to follow Roman law while Ostrogoths followed German law.

Nevertheless, Theodoric alienated the Italians for two reasons: he confiscated one-third of all private Italian land and gave it to his soldiers. This was necessary for his continued rule, since providing for soldiers was the first demand placed on tribal leaders. Secondly, while Theodoric allowed complete religious freedom, Italians resented his continued adherence to Arianism.

Later Years. Despite his successes, the two fundamental challenges to the Ostrogothic kingdom were apparent during Theodoric's lifetime: the developing alliance between the FRANKS and the Byzantines; and the new imperialism of the Justinian dynasty in Constantinople. Justinian put aside religious differences with the pope and entered into a secret agreement with ROME that attracted a number of Roman aristocrats who had once been allied with Theodoric. Among these aristocrats was the philosopher BOETHIUS, who was one of Theodoric's chief advisers. When Boethius's dealings with the emperor's enemies were made public, Boethius and his father-in-law, Symmachus, were imprisoned and murdered by Theodoric. Theodoric's own death in 526 was rumored to have been hastened by his remorse over the murder of Symmachus. Theodoric was succeeded by his ten-year-old son Athalaric, under the regency of his daughter Amalasuntha. (*See* OSTROGOTHS; ITALY.)

Theodoric was a popular ruler, though he created the conditions that led inevitably to the destruction of the Ostrogothic people. He never won the allegiance of the Italians and kept the Ostrogoths an alien people. He fostered fear of the Ostrogoths in Constantinople, but failed to create a counterpower of German nations. Shortly after his death, the Byzantine Empire invaded Italy. By 544, after Italy had been laid to waste, the kingdom that Theodoric had founded was conquered, and the Ostrogothic people ceased to exist.

THEODOSIAN CODE

The Theodosian Code was created in 438 by Theodosius II, ruler of the eastern Roman Empire. The code was a comprehensive listing of imperial decrees and laws issued by the Christian Roman emperors from CONSTANTINE I THE GREAT to Theodosius. Theodosius modeled his code on two earlier codifications written in the reigns of Diocletian and his immediate successors, neither of which has survived. The code resulted from eight years of labor by a commission appointed by the emperor. The finished work filled 16 books, which are further divided by titles relating to specific fields. Among the governmental topics covered in the code are political offices, military affairs, and religious affairs. The decrees and laws are recorded in chronological order. Decrees made after the publication of the code were called "novels." (*See* LAW, SCHOOLS OF; JUSTINIAN CODE.)

The code is significant for a number of reasons. First, it supplies the best insight available into the working of Roman government in the fourth and fifth centuries. Second, the code illuminates the impact of CHRISTIANITY on Roman law and tradition. Third, the code supplied a base of information for the JUSTINIAN CODE of the sixth century. Fourth, the Theodosian Code was eventually introduced into the western empire, where it had an important influence on the Germanic tribes that established kingdoms in the former provinces of the western empire. The Germanic VISIGOTHS, for example, enforced a "Roman Law of the Visigoths" for Roman subjects of their kingdom that was a simple abridgement of the Theodosian Code.

THEODULF

heodulf (c. 750–821), a Spaniard of Visigothic descent, bishop of Orléans, was a noted scholar and envoy in CHARLEMAGNE'S court. He was active in southern FRANCE and in 800 took part in the trial of Pope LEO III in ROME. He wrote poems, Church statutes, a theological treatise, and an edition of the BIBLE in Latin that included variant readings. His poems, some of them satirical, provide a look at some of the more lively features of CAROLINGIAN court life. Late in his life, Theodulf was implicated in the revolt of Bernard of Italy against LOUIS I THE PIOUS, Charlemagne's successor. He was removed from his bishopric and exiled to Angers, where he died.

THEOPHANO

heophano is the name of two women, mother and daughter, who were important in European politics. The first Theophano, born about 936, was empress to three Byzantine rulers: Constantine VII, Romanos II, and Nicephorus II Phocas. She is believed to have murdered all of them.

The second Theophano was a far more important—and far less unsavory—character. Born in 956, she was married at 16 to the German king Otto, son of the Holy Roman Emperor OTTO I. This marriage helped unify the Byzantine and German (or Holy Roman) empires. A year later, Otto I died; Otto II was accepted without opposition as his successor. During his reign, Otto managed to expand and solidify the empire. But when he died suddenly in 983, his son (and ostensible successor) was only three years old.

He was crowned OTTO III, king of GERMANY, with Theophano serving as co-regent (with her mother-in-law, Adelaide). Theophano's regency was not without its problems. Many Germans were dis-

trustful of her Greek Byzantine heritage, and the military felt that a man should be in charge of the regency. (*See* KINGSHIP; WOMEN.)

One of Theophano's greatest personal ordeals occurred when Otto III was kidnapped by the duke of BAVARIA, Henry the Quarreler, who demanded that the kingdom and the throne be turned over to him. There was an uproar among other German nobles, and Henry returned the young king, unharmed.

Theophano died in 991 in the NETHERLANDS. After her death, Adelaide served alone as regent.

THIERRY OF CHARTRES

hierry of Chartres (c. 1100–1156) was one of the most important theologians and thinkers of the twelfth century. He was known as a gifted teacher (the scholar JOHN OF SALISBURY was among his pupils) and a progressive scholar.

Born in FRANCE, he taught for many years at CHARTRES, where his brother, Bernard of Chartres, served as chancellor. After teaching in PARIS for five years, he returned to Chartres, where he replaced his brother as chancellor and also served as archdeacon. He remained there for several more years before retiring to a monastery, where he stayed until his death.

During his years of teaching he impressed many of the leading thinkers of his day, including such theologians as PETER ABELARD. He was part of the Scholastic movement, in which spirituality, knowledge, and PHILOSOPHY are considered interrelated, not mutually exclusive. His *Heptateuchon* (*Book in Seven Volumes*) was not published during his lifetime, but it includes many classic works from ancient authors expounding on the classical seven liberal arts. He translated a number of Arabic texts into Latin, which helped popularize the sciences—an Arab forte during the Middle Ages—among Europeans.

TOLEDO, COUNCILS OF

he councils of Toledo were a series of 18 Church councils in the Spanish city of Toledo, beginning in the fourth century and ending shortly before the Muslims conquered SPAIN in 711. While the councils were convening, Toledo was usually under the control of the VISIGOTHS; in fact, it became their capital in the sixth century. The Visigoths were converted to CHRISTIANITY at the end of the sixth century, but Toledo was a Christian city during virtually the entire period of Visigothic rule.

The first council of Toledo was held about 400; the second was not held until more than 100 years later. The third council, held in 589, had particular importance because it was at this council that RECCARED, the Visigothic king, announced his conversion to Catholicism. The Visigoths had long been Arian Christians, and his father, Leovigild, had tried to impose that belief on his subjects. Reccared, who came to the throne in 586, realized that, with most of his subjects Catholics, tolerance and acceptance would be far more effective in unifying the country against possible invaders. (*See* RECCARED.)

Among the attendees at the Councils were bishops, abbots, and other clergy, but nobles were also in frequent attendance. Most of the councils were held during the seventh century. The last one was held in 702, less than a decade before the Muslim conquest.

TORTURE

Torture is the intentional use of physical or psychological pain to gain advantage over an individual. By punishing people with extreme pain, torturers hope to extract confessions, obtain information about their enemies, or intimidate others into cooperating or confessing their crimes. An apparently common element of ancient civilizations (ARISTOTLE defended the practice), torture reached its medieval peak in the twelfth century, being used in capital cases as well as against suspected heretics.

Origins. The ancient Greeks used torture against slaves as a means of extracting information, and the Romans adopted the practice. Judicial torture was even included in the emperor JUSTINIAN I's famous legal code. It was believed that torture would spur those giving testimony—particularly slaves and free citizens of low rank—into telling the truth.

As the Roman Empire declined, so did adherence to the Justinian Code—and so, too, did the use of torture. It was replaced in many areas by methods that were not always less cruel—combat or TRIAL BY ORDEAL, for example—but torture as outlined under Roman law became less frequent. Germanic legal practice, along with English common law, developed doctrines different from the absolutist JUSTINIAN CODE. The recognition of circumstantial evidence, for example, made the need for confession less critical.

Revival of Roman Law. Germanic law, like English law, made no provision for the use of torture against free citizens; in time, the practice virtually disappeared. But by the twelfth century, governments throughout Europe had begun to reexamine the Justinian Code. Eventually, every country except ENGLAND returned to Roman practices, which meant that torture once again became a valid legal tool. In most of Europe, suspects could be convicted on the basis of

confession, but not circumstantial evidence. Eyewitness accounts were acceptable for conviction, but for many crimes, at least two accounts were needed. Torture was reintroduced as an an effective (and, to many, a necessary) means of obtaining information. Torture was supposed to be legal only if there was a large body of evidence against the accused, but that was often a theoretical rather than a practical point.

Except in England and the Scandinavian countries (where trial by jury was practiced), torture reappeared. As the INQUISITION gained more power and Inquisitors gained more influence, torture became increasingly viewed as an important weapon against HERESY. The antiWITCHCRAFT mania that took hold during the Middle Ages and lasted for several centuries led to the torture of many women who were suspected of consorting with demons. Inquisitors hoped that, by using torture, they could gain not only confessions from heretics, but information to be used against others. Often, victims of torture confessed to whatever crimes of which they were accused. Innocent people confessed to such crimes as sorcery and witchcraft, and provided names of other "wrongdoers," who would be summarily rounded up and tortured until they, too, confessed their crimes and informed on others.

Types of Torture. The methods of torture involved cruel devices that were designed to inflict not only extreme pain, but often permanent disability as well. As a rule, however, most of those being tortured were put to death after undergoing torture.

Among the elaborate torture devices was the rack, which stretched the limbs; the strappado, which hoisted the victim (to whom weights were attached) into the air by a rope tied to the hands; and the thumbscrew, which gradually crushed the thumb in a vicelike grip lined with metal studs. One common means of torture was to tie a victim's hands behind his back, raise him up several feet by his hands, then drop him in small increments. Some victims would be placed first in very hot and then very cold water. Others would have their heads bound so tightly their skulls would crack .

Many argued against torture, even in antiquity. ST. AUGUSTINE denounced it in the early Middle Ages, noting that it afforded "certain punishment" even in the face of "uncertain crime." Even among Inquisitors, there was a realization that confessions extracted under torture were worthless. But the practice continued and remained widespread until the Enlightenment in the eighteenth century.

See HERESY; INQUISITION; PRISONS AND PUNISHMENT; WITCHCRAFT AND SORCERY; WARFARE; *and for more on the legal ramifications, see* JUSTINIAN CODE; LAW, SCHOOLS OF; *and* TRIAL BY ORDEAL.

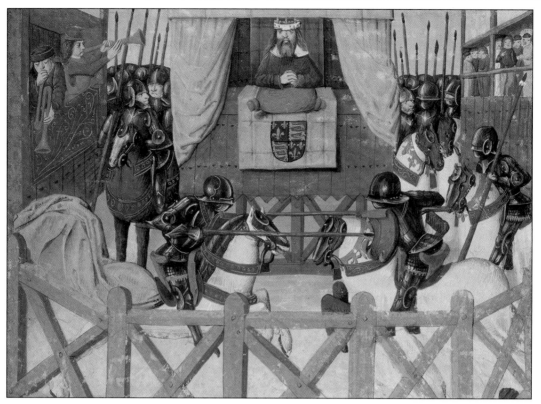

Tournaments were presided over by royalty as a ceremonial show of fealty and power. Above, a 15th-century Flemish miniature showing King Richard II presiding over a tournament held at Lambeth Palace.

TOURNAMENTS IN THE MIDDLE AGES

Perhaps no other image so embodies our concept of the Middle Ages as that of the tourneying knight in shining armor. A vision of magnificence portraying the very spirit of CHIVALRY, he wields his lance in a gallant display of prowess and valor. The medieval tournament was not always the regulated sport and exhibition of pomp and splendor it later became. Like many other chivalric institutions, the tournament is believed to have had its origins in FRANCE, which the later description of tournaments as *conflictus gallicus* by English writers seems to confirm. It is not certain when tournaments first emerged as a distinct form of martial sport. In the late eleventh century, the practice of charging as a coordinated unit with couched lances (tucked lightly under the arm rather than used as a spear or thrown overarm) developed as a new military tactic. This new tactic demanded team practice and training, and tournaments may have developed in response to this demand.

The *mêlée* tournaments of this early period were very hazardous and bloody affairs, hardly distinguish-

able from actual battle. The boundaries were usually unmarked (the field specified was only in reference to the space between two towns), and although the principal weapons were the sword and lance, there were no regulations on WEAPONRY. The only sporting compromises allowed in this contest were the provision of refuges, enclosed areas where participants could safely rest or rearm. The general understanding was that the object of the tournament was to capture and ransom one's opponents, not to kill them.

Of course, fatalities were inevitable and these, combined with the cost and the damage done to local property, were no doubt the grounds of the Church's disapproval of these events. The COUNCIL OF CLERMONT in 1130 declared that "we firmly prohibit those detestable markets or FAIRS at which knights are accustomed to meet to show off their strength and their boldness." Secular authorities also disapproved, recognizing that tournaments could create a serious breach of the peace or be used as a disguise for baronial revolt. Despite consistent ecclesiastical condemnation and prohibition over two centuries, and intermittent secular prohibition, tourneying flourished and spread. In the first half of the twelfth century, the tournament was encouraged and glorified in chivalric literature. By the end of the century its popularity had spread throughout western Europe.

In the thirteenth century, the tournament became more regulated and more ceremonious. "Lists," or enclosed areas, became standard. Blunted weapons were more frequently used, and the martial sport that previously focused on participants began to cater to the spectator. This century saw the growth in popularity of the joust. Jousts were specifically single combats, although the combatant might be part of a team. Opponents charged at one another with lances from opposite ends of the lists. The increased importance of heralds and HERALDRY points to the presence of an attentive audience who wished to know who the individual knight contestants were.

Tournaments became much more theatrical from the thirteenth century onward. For example, the participants assumed the roles of the knights of Arthur's Round Table at the tournament at Hem in 1279. At Cheapside in 1362, seven knights jousted as the Seven Deadly Sins against all comers. A distinctive form of the sport called the *pas d'armes* became popular in the fifteenth century. In this form, an individual or a team would declare the intention of defending a given area against challengers. It usually involved staging, acting, and a plot based on a chivalric romance. Tournaments became occasions of great festivity and were often an integral part of the celebrations held in honor of victorious campaigns, diplomatic meetings, coronations, knightings, christenings, and weddings.

The original *mêlée* form of tournament became rare and was replaced by the very lavish, expensive, exclusive, carefully planned spectacles of the later Middle Ages. The invention of the tilt, a barrier running the length of the lists and separating the opponents, and the development of special armor (heavier and more expensive than armor for war) further decreased the risks of the sport. The dangerous and chaotic mock warfare of the eleventh and twelfth centuries had been transformed gradually into a highly formal and ritualized pageantry with little emphasis on martial skill by the sixteenth century.

In ENGLAND, tournaments were outlawed for much of the Middle Ages until King RICHARD I decreed that they might take place, but confined them to specific areas in the counties of Sussex, Wiltshire, Warwickshire, Northamptonshire, and Nottinghamshire.

Changes in warfare led to a decline in the sport. By the seventeenth century, the tournament was a sentimental memory of the past.

See ARMS AND ARMOR *and* WEAPONRY *for the tournaments tools; See* GAMES AND PASTIMES *and* WARFARE *for more on tournament practices. See* CHIVALRY; COURTLY LOVE; HERALDRY; *and* KNIGHTHOOD *for more on values.*

TOWNS, VILLAGES, AND CITIES

Of the three successor civilizations to the ancient Roman Empire—Byzantium, the Islamic Arab world, and Catholic western Europe—the first two, BYZANTIUM and ISLAM, perpetuated the focus of ROME on urban living. The Roman (Latin) word for city, *civitas*, also meant civilization, and the medieval Byzantine and Islamic societies and cultures were constructed around urban centers. From CONSTANTINOPLE in the east, with its three-quarters of a million or more people, to Arabic Córdoba in SPAIN, with a population of 200,000, the Mediterranean world ruled by the Greeks and Arabs offered the pleasures of urban life: open-air markets; food stalls and restaurants; comfortable villas; centers of spirituality, entertainment, and learning. The capability of providing well-constructed places and fresh water, and removing garbage and human and animal waste, all of which the Romans had made hallmarks of their civilization, was perpetuated in the Byzantine and Islamic cities. (*See* BYZANTIUM; ISLAM.)

Western Europe was different. Its focus was on the country village (500 or fewer inhabitants) and the small town (comprising 1,000 or 2,000 people). Cities were rare and much marveled at, and their size in Catholic Europe was severely restricted. In the year 1000 C.E., in contrast to the metropolises of Constantinople and Córdoba, ROME had only 25,000 people living amid the ruins and vacant buildings of a city that once had housed a million people in 150 C.E., and Rome was the largest city in the Latin Catholic world. Even in 1300, PARIS had only 100,000 people, LONDON and FLORENCE perhaps 75,000, and Rome had barely managed to grow to 100,000 inhabitants.

But by 1300, urban enclaves had come to loom large in certain parts of Latin Europe—the southern half of ENGLAND, northern FRANCE, southeast and southwest France, the Rhine Valley, and northern Italy. Medieval people would consider any site embracing at least 5,000 people a city and any location encompassing between 1,000 and 5,000 people a town. By 1300, 10 to 15 percent of Europe's population lived in such urban environments.

European Cities. The cities were all walled to protect them from war and marauders. If an urban center had a bishop's cathedral, it was officially a "city"; otherwise it was a "borough" or "burg" (the word that originally meant "fortress"). The borough had grown up under the protecting walls of a lord's fortress. Afterward, the bourgeoisie or burghers had built a wall around their own streets, and the urban enclave itself became a fortress, with the lord's castle—or in the case

Above, an aerial view of the famed walled town of Carcasson in southern France. At right, a typical medieval town scene: Apothecary Street, where the meeting hall of the apothecary guild was located. Shown are the shops of a tanner, furrier, barber, and tailor.

of an episcopal city, the cathedral—standing on a hill in the center of the burghers' shops and domiciles. In time, all space was used up in the urban enclave, and people began to build houses and shops in the suburbs, nestling outside the walls of the old borough or city. After a few decades a new wall was built enclosing the suburbs, and then new suburbs under the second set of walls developed. Thus, medieval cities grew in concentric circles marked by the periodic building of new walls until the early fourteenth century, when famine and pandemics stopped the growth of urban populations until about 1500. By then, artillery had made its appearance in siege WARFARE; the big guns could fire cannon balls and frequently breach the old medieval walls, so urban wall-building slowly disappeared.

Here or there an affluent town might throw up a wall around itself, but most towns lay open to the countryside. Their inhabitants were closely involved in the surrounding rural economy, with many towns-people owning land worked by peasant SERFS or, as serfdom waned in the later Middle Ages, by wage laborers. The towns' economies were focused on providing markets for the country population as well as their own inhabitants. The towns also served as organized centers where wool was woven in peasant houses in the surrounding countryside—the so-called putting-out, or domestic, system of industry.

Guilds. In both towns and cities, industrial craftsmen were organized into GUILDS whose masters set product standards and wages for the journeymen workers and conditions of apprenticeship for the young novice craftsmen. In the cities and boroughs, the masters of the craft guilds were often rich and visible personages. They supervised public entertainments, ran burial societies, established their own chapels, and often played a role in town governments.

In the larger urban enclaves, however, it was the masters of the merchant, not the craft, guilds who dominated the autocratic town councils. These were scions of wealthy families engaged in international or at least long-distance trade, who invested their capital in BANKING and credit operations and became billionaire capitalists with fine houses. They engaged in assiduous patronage of the arts and churches. When the larger boroughs and cities found themselves within the centralized monarchies after 1150, the high bourgeoisie from the merchant guilds, who controlled the town councils, negotiated for rights of self-government with the royal officials, with varying degrees of success. Cities and boroughs that were independent came to be called communes, a term originally meaning a sworn association.

Urban Concerns. Aside from the threat of war, marauding barons and mercenaries, and ambitious, tax-hungry royal officials, the urban societies of the later Middle Ages faced three great threats: fire, pandemics of plague, and the need for adequate water and sewage facilities. With more than half the urban houses constructed of wooden timbers, nothing could be done about fire except to rebuild the frequently burned-down structures. Plague was sometimes alleviated by strict quarantine regulations, but the favorite response of the wealthy burghers was to flee to the countryside when the pandemic occurred. Getting pure water into the city from external sources—the Romans had accomplished it—was always a problem in medieval times; the bourgeoisie relied heavily on digging wells, which were easily polluted, within the city walls. Their greatest challenge was getting rid of garbage and human and animal waste. Every night, carts piled high with such perilous stuff would wend their way from a large city into the countryside for dumping purposes. It was the public health menace that more than anything else kept medieval cities small, and made them carefully regulate the entry of more inhabitants. After a plague had decimated a particular urban population, immigrants—especially those with skills and money—were welcome, but normally immigration into cities was severely restricted or all but prohibited. (*See* BLACK DEATH; MEDICINE.)

In spite of these problems with infrastructure, the medieval European societies shared with those in BYZANTIUM and ISLAM the cultural and intellectual amenities of civilized living. The Latin world also offered urban centers of learning, art, and spirituality that were the focal points for long-range COMMERCE within Europe and beyond. The staples of this trade were textiles, grain, weapons, furs, spices, jewels, art works, and slaves. The upper social strata of medieval cities were fiercely proud of their urban amenities and quick to compare themselves to the admirable Romans. Perhaps what would seem most remarkable to us in medieval cities were the number of churches and chapels—London in 1400 had some 300 places for communal prayer.

Villages. In spite of all this, the great majority of medieval European people lived in rural villages. There were of two kinds: the nucleated and, less commonly, the extended. In nucleated villages the inhabitants' houses were congregated very close together at a crossroads where the necessary amenities of a parish church, a grain-grinding mill, and possibly a handful of tiny shops were also located. Nearby were a common pasturage for cattle and sheep and, surrounding the village, the strips and blocks of farmland to which the peasants went out daily (except for attending church on Sunday morning) to labor. The extended village featured the inhabitants' houses strung out at length over the roads leading to the middle of the village. Behind each house was a plot of land used for a garden.

There was a time before 1200 when three-quarters of medieval villages were governed and taxed by manorial lords through managerial and judicial stewards. The peasants had mandatory labor obligations of so many days per month for work on the lord's nearby private estates. As serfdom slowly dissipated after 1200, the villages came to be institutionalized in a myriad of ways. By 1500, some were completely au-

tonomous. In others, there were loose vestiges of medieval manorial lordship. In still others, there was a middle way by which the peasants owed rents or even some of the old labor obligations, but they still largely governed themselves through a village council. The villagers varied in income almost as much as the inhabitants of the class-ridden towns and cities. Some were affluent and had an eye to moving up into the neighboring gentry. Others were in effect peons who barely subsisted as day laborers.

In times of war or civil war, unless a lord, abbot, or bishop exerted himself to send in his soldiers to protect the peasants, the open villages could suffer cruel depredation from armies and freebooting brigands. The peasant casualties would be numerous. The dispersed villagers would hide out in the forests and hills until the threat had passed, returning only to find their crops and domesticated beasts stolen, their houses pillaged and burned down, and the imminent threat of starvation facing them. On the other hand, late medieval artists never seemed to tire of painting pictures of fat, happy peasants drinking and dancing on the common greensward, from which it may be surmised that there must have been such people.

See BANKING; COMMERCE AND TRADE; GUILDS; FAMILY LIFE; ENGLAND; FRANCE; *and* GERMANY *for material on urban development. See* NOBLES AND NOBILITY *and* SERFS AND SERFDOM *for more on town culture.*

TRAVEL AND TRANSPORTATION

The Middle Ages is commonly described as a time of localism, when people had limited opportunities or desire to venture beyond their villages and regions. Despite this, travel and transportation were still important elements in the medieval social structure. The medieval population had commercial, religious, and political reasons for travel. Kings and their courts toured constantly in order to promote and affirm the power of the monarchy throughout the kingdom. This was an essential function, due to the decentralized political systems of the Middle Ages. Church officials also traveled in order to reinforce the authority of the Church. For the peasantry, travel meant pilgrimages to ROME and other sacred places. In the early Middle Ages, primitive transportation technologies and unsafe conditions limited travel. As time passed, conditions improved, leading to increased confidence and the ability to travel.

Dangers. Travel was common in the classical

(Greek and Roman) period, aided by the elaborate and famous system of Roman roads that linked the European and Mediterranean parts of the Roman Empire. The fall of the Roman Empire, however, severely, limited travel. The physical infrastructure of Europe declined with the collapse of centralized authority. The early medieval period was a time of localism, when consciousness of and interest in distant lands evaporated. This period was also fraught with danger for travelers. For the most part, public order was enforced by local lords rather than national monarchs. These lords had neither an interest in controlling thieves outside their locality, nor the ability to do so. Travelers could be robbed, killed, or kidnapped, with those kidnapped liable to be sold into slavery. The emergent feudal social order also militated against travel. The new class of SERFS were legally tied to the land and therefore prohibited from going elsewhere.

Despite these limitations, travel was still central to certain aspects of medieval life. Kings often spent much of their lives on campaigns either to enforce their tenuous hold on feudal possessions or, more com-

Wagon technology as described and depicted in 1028 in the encyclopedic work De Universo, *by Hrabanus Maurus.*

monly, to present themselves to their subjects. Much of the royal household—with riches, advisers, and family—would journey with the monarch. The traveling king heard complaints about royal officials, adjudicated disputes, and in some countries, enacted his quasi-divine status in such acts as the "ROYAL TOUCH." Monarchs also moved about the country as a form of leisure officiating at TOURNAMENTS and enjoying feasts and hunts while staying at the estates of their vassals.

Pilgrimages. The Middle Ages was a intensely religious civilization, and hence much travel was linked to the Christian faith. For the peasants allowed to travel, pilgrimages were a central event in their oppressed and tedious existence. Pilgrimages served a number of functions. For some, a pilgrimage was the only way to see the world beyond their village. Pilgrimages were also a way to atone for sin and gain absolution. Pilgrimages were often made to sacred locations where the relics of saints were kept. Rome and Jerusalem were the most popular places among them, although there were hundreds of other such locations. Other religious travelers were high Church officials going to Rome for councils and lesser officials moving through Europe to take up positions or supervise subordinate clergy.

Trade. Throughout the Middle Ages, the capability for travel waxed and waned depending on political and economic conditions. The CAROLINGIAN age of the late seventh and eighth centuries saw increased political authority and growing wealth. Trade therefore increased, with cargo boats traveling on rivers in FRANCE and GERMANY. Italian traders, particularly in France, went to the East, bringing back spices, silks, and other exotic goods to Europe. Starting in the middle of the eighth century, however, the progress of the Carolingian era was reversed by the devastating raids of VIKINGS, Muslims, and MAGYARS (an Asiatic tribe that settled in central Europe). The raids made travel and trade impossible and reinforced localism.

Starting in the tenth century, the ability to travel rebounded. Wealth and trade increased, and merchants employed sophisticated measures to transport their goods, such as hiring middlemen to do their traveling for them. Important new destinations of travel were FAIRS, where merchants gathered to trade. Fairs were a source of revenue for local lords, who endeavored to enforce safe passage for both purveyors and customers. Religious travel also intensified with the development of touring of relics. When a church or monastery needed funds, the institution would put its relics on tour and charge a fee for viewing or praying before them. With increasing safety, pilgrimages became more popular—so popular that in the thirteenth century the French council forbade pilgrimages to Rome because of fears of temporary depopulation. Late medieval pilgrimages inspired the first hints of a tourist industry with the advent of tour books, ferries, and inns. (*See* COMMERCE; TOWNS; CHRISTIANITY.)

TRES RICHES HEURES

Among the most outstanding BOOKS OF HOURS produced during the Middle Ages. *Les Très Riches Heures* (actually created as two volumes) was prepared in Bourges by the three Limbourg brothers, Dutch manuscript illuminators in the late fourteenth century for John, duke of Berry, the uncle of King Charles VI of France. One volume, *Les Belles Heures,* contains miniatures by Jacquemart of Hesdin.

The work, created in the style known as International GOTHIC, is housed in the Condé Museum.

TREBIZOND EMPIRE

The empire of Trebizond was one of three Greek successor states formed after CONSTANTINOPLE was occupied by the Fourth Crusade in 1204. The empire actually came into existence days before the capture of Constantinople when ALEXIUS I COMNENUS and David Comnenus took Trebizond. After the fall of Constantinople, the Comneni brothers conquered Paphlagonia in Asia Minor with the aid of Georgian mercenaries, although over time much of this territory was lost. Eventually, the empire was located on a strip of land between the Pontic Mountains and the Black Sea. Alexius Comnenus became its ruler and took the title of Grand Comnenus.

Unlike the other two successor states, the empire of NICAEA and the despotate of Epirus, Trebizond was not involved in the death struggle with the Latin Kingdom and the attempt to recapture Constantinople to reestablish the Byzantine Empire. The empire of Trebizond remained politically independent and relatively disengaged in the turbulent affairs of the times—a result in large measure, of its inaccessibility between mountains and the sea. The empire survived until 1461, and was thus the last outpost of Byzantine civilization. (*See* BYZANTIUM.)

The isolation of Trebizond allowed it to resist many threats: the SELJUK and OTTOMAN TURKS; the Latin Kingdom; and the Greek empire of Nicaea. The Trebizond empire was successful economically because of its strategic trading position—it controlled the routes between Asia, Persia, and central Europe. Through the support of the ruling line of the Grand Comneni, Trebizond became a center of learning and attracted many scholars. The empire was also known for its libraries, and visitors were impressed by the beauty of its churches, monasteries, and gardens.

Politically, the empire intermittently fought with and paid tributes to the great political forces of its time: the Seljuk sultan of Iconium; TAMERLANE; the Turkoman chieftains; and the Ottoman sultan. In 1240, Trebizond made an alliance with the Sultanate of Iconium and Nicaea against the MONGOLS. The alliance was defeated and the emperor of Trebizond

"June: Haymaking," from the Trés Riches Heures. *In the background is Sainte-Chapelle of Paris.*

wisely chose to become a Mongol vassal. The Comneni family managed to survive during the fourteenth century while creating several religious foundations that still exist today, the most famous being the church of St. Sophia.

The Fall of Constantinople in 1453 spelled the beginning of the end for the Trebizond empire as gradually it and its surrounding allies began to crumble. Inevitably, the empire fell to the Ottomans and Muhammad II in 1463. (*See* OTTOMAN TURKS.)

TRIAL BY ORDEAL

The medieval practice of trial by ordeal had as its basis the Christian belief that God protected the good and punished the wicked. Yet the ordeals themselves were hardly better than TORTURE, and the outcome of such a trial was often the result more of luck than of guilt or innocence.

Beginnings. Ordeals have existed in various cultures at different times, but the medieval ordeals stemmed from Germanic law. The Germans believed that the victims of crime (or, in the case of murder, their families) should be compensated. Accused criminals could do this by paying a *wergild* (literally, "man money") to make up for the lost or injured victim. If the accused refused to accept responsibility, or claimed innocence, another means was needed.

Wealthy or prominent citizens could choose trial by oath, or compurgation, in which they swore their innocence and produced "oath-helpers" who attested to the oath's truthfulness. For others, the common method was trial by ordeal.

The ordeal was seen as a means of allowing divine intervention in a case. It was believed that innocent individuals would not suffer ill effects from the ordeals; guilty ones, however, would be marked as such by their adverse reactions.

Types of Ordeals. Ordeals were supposed to be neither punishment nor TORTURE, although in reality they included many elements of both. Those who failed an ordeal were usually executed; frequently, those who did not fail nevertheless often died as a result.

In the "Judgment of the Glowing Iron," the accused was forced to carry a red-hot piece of iron or stone a specified distance. His hands would then be bandaged. If after three days the burn caused by the hot iron was infected, he was guilty. The "Test of Boiling Water" required the accused to take a stone out of a pot of scalding water. As with the hot iron, the accused's hands would be examined after three days. In the "Ordeal of the Bier," reserved for murder cases, the accused would stand near the victim's body. It was believed that the victim's blood would flow if the murderer was near.

One of the most commonly used ordeals was the "Test of the Cold Water." The accused would be tied up and then thrown into a body of water. If he was guilty, he would float—the common belief being that water, as a divine element, would not accept an impure individual. If he was innocent, he would sink to the bottom—which may have exonerated him but did little for his chances of escaping death by drowning.

The "Trial by Combat" ordeal required accused and accuser to fight. The innocent party would emerge the winner. If the loser was still alive, he would also be charged with making a false claim. Individuals could hire "champions" to battle for them—which obviously put wealthy or powerful individuals at an advantage (they could hire the strongest man in the village to serve as replacements). Mindful of this, ruling monarchs placed strict limitations on how and when trial by combat could be employed.

Role of the Church. Proponents of trial by ordeal defended the painful and often fatal tests on the grounds that those who were defendants were usually already reputed criminals. The Church thus reluctantly accepted ordeals as a method of proof and a means of thinning the criminal population.

The Church, uneasy about claims that ordeals offered a divine judgement, tried at first to modify the process. It gave defendants an opportunity to confess to a crime before having to undergo an ordeal. It also allowed those convicted by ordeal to be punished by amputation rather than execution.

Eventually the Church withdrew its support for trial by ordeal. The Fourth LATERAN COUNCIL, which convened early in the thirteenth century, decreed in 1215 that priests would henceforth be forbidden from taking part in ordeals.

As legal systems changed throughout Europe, reforms eliminated trial by ordeal until it all but disappeared by the beginning of the fourteenth century. Ironically, trial by combat was not technically abolished in ENGLAND—where common law and trial by jury had first flourished—until 1819. (*See* PRISONS AND PUNISHMENT.)

A 15th-century depiction (by Bouts) of an offer made by the widow of a murdered man to undergo trial by ordeal.

TRISTAN AND ISOLDE

The Celtic legend of Tristan has inspired numerous stories and poems over the centuries, but it is GOTTFRIED VON STRASSBURG'S version, written about 1210, that is most highly regarded.

The Story. The tale of Tristan and Isolde (also known as Tristram and Iseut) has taken many forms, but the basic plot remains the same: Tristan is the nephew of King Mark of Cornwall, who wishes to marry Isolde of IRELAND. He sends Tristan to escort her back to Cornwall. During the journey back, Tristan and Isolde accidentally consume a love potion that had been meant for her and Mark; the two fall hopelessly in love. The betrayed King Mark banishes the young lovers to a forest where they eventually die.

A miniature from a 15th-century manuscript shows King Mark stabbing Tristan as he is serenading Isolde.

In some versions, Tristan dies, but not Isolde; in others, Tristan and Isolde are separated but are reunited—and then they die; in still others, Tristan falls in love with a false Isolde until the real Isolde returns.

Gottfried's version, of which the ending has been lost, focuses strongly on the CHIVALRY and COURTLY LOVE aspect of the story. Tristan is depicted as a loyal and devoted lover, willing to sacrifice his own well-being for Isolde's happiness. Nothing is known of Gottfried's life, but he is known to have based his retelling of the story on a version written by Thomas of Brittany. (*See* COURTLY LOVE; LITERATURE.)

TROUBADOURS

Music and poetry were two of the most popular forms of entertainment in medieval Europe, and both the writers and the performers (often one and the same) were held in high esteem. The best known of the poet-composers were the troubadours of southern FRANCE. They flourished in the twelfth and thirteenth centuries, and helped popularize composing in the vernacular rather than in Latin.

The troubadours' counterparts in northern France were known as *trouvères*; in GERMANY they were known as *minnesingers*. Today the terms *troubadour* and *minstrel* are often used interchangeably, but there were differences. In general, troubadours composed music and wrote poems, but did not usually perform; minstrels were professional performers who may or may not have written or composed their own material. (Minstrels who traveled from town to town were known as *jongleurs*.) Most troubadours composed for the upper classes; many, in fact, were themselves of noble lineage. (*See* MUSIC IN THE MIDDLE AGES.)

Most troubadour poems were short, with several eight-line rhyming stanzas and one or two shorter stanzas. Rarely was a troubadour poem more than 60 lines long (although many troubadours did compose longer poetic works as well). The subject matter of troubadour works was secular rather than religious, a point made perhaps more strongly by the fact that they were written in vernacular French. By far the most popular theme was COURTLY LOVE—the poet would celebrate the beauty and virtue of the woman he loved, and tell of his success (or lack thereof) in winning her heart. Courtly love was a highly idealized form of romance, in which the lover would offer his complete devotion to the object of his affection. (Often, poets would compare this devotion and loyalty to a vassal's loyalty to his lord). In addition to describing the poet's love for his lady, the composition would also describe the lady's control over the poet's life and happiness.

Romance was not the only subject covered by the troubadours. Many of their songs dealt with political and moral themes. Furthermore, not all performances consisted of song; dance was common as well.

Troubadours received the patronage of nobles, not only in France, but in Italy and Spain; ELEANOR OF AQUITANE was a noted patron. Not surprisingly, many troubadours wrote songs of praise to these nobles.

The trouvères of northern France covered many of the same topics as the troubadours in their poetry. They wrote in the northern French dialect, or *langue d'oil*, while the troubadours wrote in the southern French dialect, or *langue d'oc*. Both spread their themes and ideas of courtly love to the rest of Europe. (*See* CHIVALRY; ELEANOR OF AQUITANE.)

TWELFTH-CENTURY RENAISSANCE

Although the European Renaissance began toward the end of the fifteenth century, the Middle Ages experienced a cultural rebirth at the the end of the eleventh century that lasted until the end of the thirteenth, known to historians as the twelfth-century renaissance. New ideas sprang forth in PHILOSOPHY, LITERATURE, ARCHITECTURE, and SCIENCE. The feudal system was gradually replaced by more permanent systems of government. The balance of economic and political power began to shift from the powerful Byzantine Empire to western Europe. Many historians believe that it was this twelfth-century renaissance that made the later Renaissance possible.

Beginnings of Change. Toward the end of the eleventh century, western Europe began to shake off its pessimism and torpor. Scholars began to show a marked interest in the works of the ancient Greeks and Romans, and education assumed a more prominent role. Trade with other countries increased, and cities began to grow. Cities such as ROME, GENOA, and BARCELONA became centers of international trade. Large cities saw the construction of impressive and intricate Gothic cathedrals.

Cities also became centers of learning. The law school at the University of Bologna, the Sorbonne in Paris, and Oxford in ENGLAND attracted students from throughout Europe. Studies of the ancients led to a renewed interest in philosophy; such philosophers as ST. ANSELM and ALBERTUS MAGNUS helped open the doors to new intellectual inquiry.

The greatest achievement of twelfth century European culture was the creation of the UNIVERSITY—a teaching center that granted degrees and was at the center of intellectual creativity, typified by PETER ABELARD, JOHN OF SALISBURY, and many others.

As the cities grew in size and offered more economic opportunity, more people migrated to them. Gradually, Europe was moving away from being an exclusively agricultural society. As governments were established in England, France, and other countries, local lords became less powerful. The well-trained scholars produced by the universities provided ideal administrators for the emerging royal governments.

The twelfth-century renaissance was driven by an intense study of Latin literature and of Greek philosophy and science in translation. It represents a transition deeply affected by the memory of the past and shaped in many directions by critical intelligence.

The rise of vernacular tongues, such as French, English, and Italian, allowed writers to experiment. By the twelfth century, many individuals were writing complex and impressive works in these new languages—paving the way for later authors such as CHAUCER and PETRARCH.

The late twelfth- and early thirteenth-century poetry of CHRÉTIEN DE TROYES and WOLFRAM VON ESCHENBACH exemplified a heightened interest in individual human personality. The psychological facets of human love received close scrutiny.

Religious Changes. The twelfth century was not, however, only an age of secular renaissance. It was also a time of a great change in religious feeling. There was a shift from concentration on the judging and wrathful deity of the Old Testament to the loving and self-sacrificing Jesus of the New Testament. The adoration of the Virgin Mary became a central part of Latin Christian thought and behavior. St. Anselm and St. Bernard of Clairvaux were leading exponents of the Marian devotion. This more emotional kind of piety received joyful expression in liturgy, painting, and architecture.

In the late eleventh century, western Europe entered a 200-year period of warmer weather than it had experienced in the previous 500 years. This benign climate produced a greater agricultural yield and thereby contributed to substantial population growth. In the twelfth century Europe's population doubled, and in the thirteenth century it tripled. These positive environmental changes fostered the optimism and creativity that marked the culture and religion of that era.

TYLER, WAT

Wat Tyler (d. 1381) was the leader of the English PEASANTS' REVOLT of 1381, one of several peasant uprisings in the late Middle Ages. With the scarcity of labor created by the BLACK DEATH (1349), peasants demanded the abolition of serfdom and the repeal of laws that fixed maximum wages. The revolt's immediate cause was the poll tax of 1381, which imposed a tax of a shilling per person.

The revolt started in June of 1381 in Essex and Kent. Tyler became the leader of the revolt in Kent. He and his followers occupied Canterbury, captured the sheriff of Kent, and destroyed property records. The Essex and Kent factions united and marched to London, where they occupied London Bridge and the Tower of London. They executed the Archbishop of Canterbury and destroyed the castle of the King's uncle, the hated JOHN OF GAUNT. The young King RICHARD II bowed to pressure and agreed to abolish serfdom and wage restrictions in Essex and Kent. Later, at another meeting with the king, Tyler made a number of radical demands. Tyler was murdered on the spot by the lord mayor of London. The rebels dispersed, and the king's promises were rescinded.

UMAYYAD DYNASTY

The Umayyads (also Omayyads) began as a clan of merchants based in Mecca. From their ranks emerged a Muslim dynasty that ruled a vast empire based in Syria from 561 to 750. When supplanted by the ABBASIDS there, they established a lesser caliphate in SPAIN that lasted to 1031.

Following the death of MUHAMMAD, several civil wars erupted for control of the burgeoning Islamic empire. Following the murder of Uthman, the third caliph, in 656, Mu'awiyah, governor of Syria and the son of the clan's founder, Abu Sufyan, emerged victorious over Ali, Muhammad's son-in-law, becoming the first Umayyad caliph. The Umayyads then divided into two branches: the descendants of Abu Sufyan—the Sufyanids—who reigned out of DAMASCUS; and the Marwanids, descendants of Marwan I, who rose to power in 684 after a civil war ended Sufyanid rule. The legacy of the Sufyanids was the expansionist policies of the Umayyads and other Islamic dynasties; under Abd al-Malik (r. 685–705), successor to Marwan I, the Umayyads reached their peak, establishing control (if not actual rule) over an area stretching from Spain, across North Africa and the Middle East, and as far east as India.

The Khorasan. With a limited population of Muslims in Syria, the Umayyads relied on garrisoned cities, called *khorasans*, to support their rule; local administration was turned over to the native power structure. This allowed the caliphs to maintain control at a distance and keep tax revenues flowing to Damascus. While the caliphs used this wealth to create and support a glorious Islamic culture, the authority given to non-Muslims in the administration of the empire did not sit well with the religious community.

The decline of the Umayyads began with a military defeat in 717 at the hands of LEO III THE ISAURIAN, the Byzantine emperor who began the recapture of ANATOLIA, completed in 740. Two talented caliphs—Umar II (reigned 717–720) and Hisham (reigned 724–743)—introduced reforms calculated to solidify Umayyad control over its widespread empire and focus military power against the Christians in Europe and the Byzantines in southwest Asia. But the tide had already turned and the Umayyads were barely able to maintain a stalemate against three forces: the North African BERBERS and central Asian Turks, who exploited their military vulnerability; and internal factions, generally from the religious right, for whom the empire was never authentically Islamic. The defeat of the Umayyads at Poitiers meant the end of any hope of maintaining the full extent of the empire.

The Hashimiyah. Dissatisfaction with the Umayyad's secularism, fueled by misgivings about their legitimacy, erupted into a civil war when Abu Hashim died in 716 leaving no male heirs. The religio-political sect, known as the Hashimiyah, began in the city of Kufah in the early 700s. Loyal to the House of Ali, they proclaimed Muhammad ibn Ali as imam (religious leader); in 749, Abu al-'Abbas was named as Saffah, the first Abbasid caliph. The Abbasid dynasty was to rule the Islamic world for some 400 years, while the Umayyads established the lesser caliphate of Córdoba in SPAIN. (*See* ISLAM.)

The last Umayyad caliph, Marwan II (r. 744–750), was defeated decisively by the Abbasids at the Battle of the Great Zab River in 750. Members of the royal family were hunted down and killed. One lone member, Abd al-Rahman, survived and established the Córdoba caliphate in 756. There, the Umayyads revived their support of Islamic culture and flourished until the RECONQUEST of Spain in the eleventh to the fourteenth centuries. (*See* ABBASID.)

UNIVERSITIES

The concept of the university had its origins in the Middle Ages. Schools had existed for centuries, as had academies of higher learning. But formalized, structured organizations created for the express purpose of educating a group of scholars in selected disciplines—as distinguished from religious schools and colleges—did not come into being until the thirteenth century.

The university was actually a legally recognized entity—a group of individuals organized in much the same way a modern corporation would be structured. The university was separate from other institutions; it stood on its own. Religious schools offered higher learning in theology and religious law, although they also taught other subjects. Islamic schools, for examples, prepared students for careers as clerical scholars, but ISLAM from the eighth to the eleventh centuries was renowned for scientific scholarship as well. Still, such schools, whether in Arab lands or in Europe, were controlled by a church or a religious body. They might boast excellent teachers and well-stocked libraries, but they were not separate, independent institutions.

Colleges, which appeared some time before universities, first emerged not as schools but as residences for scholars and students, often funded by outside sources. Gradually, they developed courses of study as well, but they were never as all-encompassing as the university. As a result, the modern university is still often composed of several colleges.

Early Universities. The first bona fide university was established in PARIS in 1221. It grew out of the efforts of Parisian scholars to organize. Following the model of town governments, and also of local GUILDS (the precursors of our modern unions and professional associations), this group created a legally recognized entity specifically licensed to teach prescribed courses of study. The University of Paris was licensed to offer degrees in theology, canon law, MEDICINE, and the arts. It eventually became known by the name of one of its early benefactors— Robert de Sorbonne.

The Church was still powerful and could still influence what was taught in the University of Paris; for example, in 1277 the bishop of Paris decreed that the study of ARISTOTLE was prohibited. But the university's legal status gave it more power. For all its power, the Church could not summarily disband the university. The university concept was also open to more students than Church schools, which were generally reserved for those planning a career in theology and the clergy.

Student-Sponsored Universities. Meanwhile, in ITALY, the University of Bologna was being organized by students in that city. It soon earned a reputation as the most prestigious law school in Europe. Bologna differed from the Sorbonne in several respects. There was more emphasis on practical studies; in addition to law, students could take courses such as composition in preparation for careers in the civil service. The University of Bologna was run entirely by students who elected their own administration, and thus had more influence over their teachers than was common in other schools. (They could, for example, vote to withhold the fees of teachers they found unsatisfactory.)

In Britain, the university concept soon took hold as well. Oxford, which was modeled after Paris, was established in the mid-twelfth century. Over the next two centuries, universities sprang up all across Europe. Many of these institutions are still in existence.

Below, a professor lecturing at the University of Paris, from Les Grandes Chroniques, *c. 1400. Top, the seal of the University of Paris, from a 14th-century die.*

University Life. University study was quite different in medieval Europe from what it is in the modern period. Students entered the university by the age of 14. They would first be schooled in studies based on the liberal arts, which were divided into two parts: the *trivium* ("three ways," from which the word *trivia* is derived), consisting of grammar, dialectic, and RHETORIC; and the *quadrivium* ("four ways"), which included arithmetic, geometry, ASTRONOMY, and MUSIC.

The typical course of study was six years of lectures, followed by two years of debate, or disputations, in which students would show what they had learned by putting forth specific theses and defending them with logic and argument. There were also examinations. Students who had successfully completed the requirements would be awarded a bachelor of arts degree. By then they would be about 22. Those who wished an advanced degree—a master's—were required to continue in their studies. The master's degree usually required a year of study. From there, the master of arts could go on to study such disciplines as law, medicine, or theology. Depending on one's course of study, this could mean up to a dozen more years of education.

Universities were originally housed in makeshift homes—classes might be taught in churches or monasteries. Eventually, they acquired their own separate buildings and would buy more of the surrounding land and buildings as they grew. Eventually, the university became a self-contained educational and residential structure, much like the modern college campus.

See ENGLAND; ITALY; PARIS; PRAGUE, UNIVERSITY OF; *and* LAW, SCHOOLS OF. *Also* ARISTOTLE, STUDY OF; ASTRONOMY; BOOKS IN MANUSCRIPT; GLOSSATORS; LATIN LANGUAGE AND LITERATURE; LIBRARIES; *and* SCIENCE.

URBAN II

Urban II (c. 1035–1099) was pope at one of the most turbulent times in the Church's history. Upon his election, he was unable to assume his papal seat for five years because Clement III was claiming the PAPACY. Later, he launched the first CRUSADE against the Muslim Arabs (called SARACENS) to liberate the Holy City of Jerusalem. But he was also a reformer, working to improve relations between the Roman and Byzantine churches.

Early Years. Originally named Odo of Lagery, he was born into a noble family at Châtillon-sur-Marne in the Champagne region of FRANCE about 1035. He was educated in theology at Soissons and Reims, and in 1055 he was named archdeacon of Reims. He remained there until 1067, when he became a monk at the abbey of Cluny—then the most influential center of monastic reform in Europe. He was named prior (superior) at Cluny in 1070.

Years at Cluny. Odo's years at Cluny gave him a chance to work closely with reforming clerics, who believed in service to Church and community. He also had an opportunity to hone his administrative skills. In 1079, he was sent by the abbot of Cluny on a mission to ROME. There, Pope GREGORY VII named him cardinal and bishop of the seaport city of Ostia.

In 1084, Odo was sent to GERMANY as a papal legate. Upon Gregory's death in exile in 1085, Odo continued to serve the new pope, Victor III. Victor died in September 1087, and there immediately ensued a struggle. Guibert of RAVENNA had been named Pope Clement III by HENRY IV in 1080 and had been serving in that capacity in Rome. Odo was elected pope on March 12, 1088, and took the name Urban II. But it would be another five years before he had gained enough widespread support to regain control of Rome.

Papal Reign. As pope, Urban continued many of the ecclesiastical reforms begun by Gregory. He also made attempts to establish diplomatic relations with the Byzantine emperor, ALEXIUS I COMNENUS. His efforts did not succeed, however, nor was he able to improve strained relations between Rome and the Church in Britain. He did, however, earn support from France and Spain and from Norman Christians.

In 1095, Urban preached that the Holy City of Jerusalem should be liberated from Muslim control. Soon after, at the COUNCIL OF CLERMONT, he called for the First Crusade. That crusade, launched in 1098, heralded a nearly 200-year series of battles between Christians and Muslims in a struggle to liberate the Holy Land, safeguard Christian religious sites, and bring Christianity to Arab lands.

Also important were Urban's reorganization of the Church and administrative improvements that centralized power in Rome. It was Urban who created the *Curia*, the administrative body of the papacy, and his actions began the process that ultimately led to the creation of the college of cardinals.

Urban died in July 1099. He was beatified by Pope Leo XIII in 1881. (*See* COUNCIL OF CLERMONT; CRUSADES; MISSIONS AND MISSIONARIES PAPACY; GREGORY VII.)

Miniature illumination from Le Miroir Historial, *a 15th-century French work, depicting Pope Urban II at the Council of Clermont excommunicating King Philip.*

URBAN VI

Urban VI (c. 1318–1389), pope from April 8, 1378 until October 15, 1389, the first pope to be elected in ROME after the seventy-year "Babylonian captivity" in AVIGNON. The atmosphere of violence in which he was elected, with unruly crowds demanding an Italian—if not a Roman—pope was soon surpassed by a tumult that eventually spread throughout all of Christendom, proved to be a truly disastrous choice for Urban. Whether because of his vigorous opposition to corruption or (as some suggested) because he was mentally unbalanced, he so alienated the cardinals who had elected him that they repudiated him after less than four months and chose a new pope, Clement VII (known as an antipope). Urban's defiant refusal to step aside created the crisis of papal legitimacy known as the GREAT SCHISM.

Born Bartolomeo Prignano in NAPLES, he showed ability as a canonist and administrator and was known for his personal austerity and rectitude. He had distinguished ecclesiastical tenures as archbishop of Acerenza (from 1363) and then Bari (from 1377), an influential member of the Curia, and finally as chief chancery official under Pope Gregory XI, showing no signs of the severe instability and violent temper that he displayed later. Urban was enthroned on April 18, 1378, but on August 2, the cardinals declared that they had chosen him under duress and that his election was consequently invalid. On September 20, they elected Robert of Geneva (Clement VII) in his stead.

When most cardinals defected to Clement, Urban simply named new cardinals to replace them. Urban and Clement, each with his court and Curia and each having excommunicated the other, contended for the allegiance of the rulers of Europe. Urban rejected any compromise; apart from his military and diplomatic confrontations with Clement (whom Urban forced to retreat to Avignon), he occupied himself chiefly with often bloody maneuvers intended to deliver control of the Kingdom of Naples (which had supported Clement) to his nephew. He also resorted to TORTURE against cardinals who supported Clement as his behavior became increasingly deranged toward the end of his reign. At Urban's death, the Church was in disarray, the pope's territories in anarchy, and the papal treasury empty. (*See* PAPACY; GREAT SCHISM.)

URSULA, ST.

Doubts about whether St. Ursula (believed to have flourished in the fourth century) actually existed have caused the Catholic Church

Engraving based on a painting on the supposed reliquary of St. Ursula at Bruges. Ursula is depicted disembarking from a ship in Cologne. In some versions of the tale, the barbarians who massacred Ursula were sent by Emperor Gratian because she had paid a large sum to the emperor's rival Maximus for the use of his fleet for the pilgrimage.

to eliminate her feast day in the reforms of 1969, but her story has become a well-known part of medieval lore. According to the *Legenda aurea* (Golden Legend), a thirteenth-century work by Jacobus de Voragine (c. 1230–1298), Ursula was an English princess who led an undetermined number of virgins on a pilgrimage to ROME. On the group's return trip, they were attacked by Huns near Cologne and massacred. The number of women killed varies from 11 to 11,000 according to the teller. The higher figure was accepted after a Roman burial ground was discovered in 1155 near Cologne that was purported to contain the remains of St. Ursula and her martyred companions.

A church was established in Cologne in the fifth century to commemorate the martyrdom of Ursula and her followers. The Order of St. Ursula (the Ursulines) was created in the sixth century for nuns dedicated to the education of young women. (*See* WOMEN IN THE MIDDLE AGES.)

VANDALS

The Vandals were one of a number of Germanic tribes that invaded the Roman Empire in the fifth and sixth centuries. The Vandals played an important role in the destruction of the western empire by their conquest of the North African provinces in 439. AFRICA provided much of the grain for the empire, and its loss was a devastating blow. The Vandal African kingdom itself was conquered by the Byzantine Empire in 534, after which the Vandals vanished from history. (*See* BARBARIAN INVASIONS.)

The Vandals, like other German tribes, were pushed into the Roman Empire when the Huns invaded central Europe. The Vandals moved into Gaul from their home near the Tisza River in eastern HUNGARY. In 409 they were defeated by the Franks, and the Vandal king Gosregisel was killed. Their new king, Gosregisel's son Gunderic, led the Vandals into Spain, where they split into two branches, the Asdingi and the Silingi. In 416, the Visigoths battled the Vandals on behalf of the Romans. The Silingi and their allies, the Alans, were destroyed. The Asdingi and another German tribe, the Suevi, were preserved because the Romans feared the growing Visigothic strength.

After their terrible defeat by the VISIGOTHS, the Vandals moved into Africa under the leadership of King GAISERIC. Historians conjecture how the Vandals managed to pass over sea into Africa, but in a matter of months the entire Vandal people had arrived in the Roman African province in 428. The Vandals quickly conquered much of the province and in 435 made a pact with the Roman emperor Valeninian II, leaving Carthage to Rome. In 439, Gaiseric abrogated the treaty and occupied the entire province

Gaiseric understood the tactical advantages of Africa, and built a fleet that made the Vandals the greatest power of the western Mediterranean. While not particularly tyrannical, the rule of the Arian Vandals was characterized by persecution of the Orthodox Church. The Vandals transformed themselves into fearsome pirates; in 455, they became the second German people to sack Rome. In a two-week pillage, the Vandals made off with much of the city's wealth.

In 523, when King Gelimer had sent much of the Vandal army to Sardinia to repress a revolt, the Byzantine emperor JUSTINIAN I authorized his great general BELISARIUS to regain North Africa. Justinian had been planning to aid the Sardinian revolt, but now chose instead to strike at Africa itself. The war in North Africa was characterized by mistakes on both sides. Gelimer missed a number of opportunities to sweep away the Byzantine forces, composed predominantly of untrustworthy Germanic and Hunnic troops, as when he paused to mourn the death of his brother Ammatas rather than follow up a victory. When the Vandals had lost the war, Gelimer fled to Moorish areas before finally surrendering—according to legend, laughing as he surrendered, recognizing his changed fortunes. After the Byzantine victory, the Vandal kingdom and the Vandal people left the stage of history.

VENICE

The most serene republic of Venice (*la Serenissima*) was unique in the Middle Ages among the cities of Europe, in several ways. First, it retained its independent, autonomous status for an incredible one thousand years, from its legendary founding in 726 until its takeover by Napoleon Bonaparte in 1797. Second, it never identified completely with the kingdoms of the West, but tended culturally and politically more toward the Byzantine East. Third, by zealously avoiding the cult of personality that so influenced other communities, particularly in ITALY, Venice ensured that no one person or family would ever be able to reign as dictator. Venice developed primarily as an urban, mercantile society; COMMERCE ruled, in the midst of a feudal culture, where land was wealth and churchmen and warriors dominated. This unusual orientation toward commerce and away from land accumulation eventually made Venice into the most prosperous state in the civilized world and the crossroads between East and West. (*See* ITALY.)

Establishment. The area that was to become Venice—islands in the northeastern Adriatic which created salt marshes and lagoons—was first inhabited by peoples traditionally said to have come from ANATOLIA and Illyria. These settlers had by 400 C.E. created several prosperous towns such as Padua and Altino along the edges of the lagoons. It was the Germanic and Hunnic invasions in the fifth century that drove many of these Romanized city dwellers in desperation onto the previously inhospitable islands of the lagoon. But now this very inaccessibility became an advantage, and their maritime communities prospered.

As early as 466, the first representative assembly of island dwellers met in Grado to develop a system of self-government. By 523, THEODORIC THE GREAT addressed a letter to the "maritime tribunes" of the Veneto, asking for the use of their "flat-bottomed barges" to transport wine and oil from Istria to the Roman provinces. The *Altino Chronicle*, written in the

Above, the overall view of a prosperous Venice, from the Peregrinatio, *a work printed in 1486. At right, woodcut of a Venetian merchant.*

twelfth century, which is the principal source for these early years, records a formal trade agreement in 565 between the Venetian island traders (primarily in salt) and the Byzantine Empire.

The LOMBARD invasions of the sixth century effectively eliminated the Roman provincial towns ringing the lagoon, sending the remnants of Roman government scurrying onto the island settlement of Heraclea. A single military official of the eastern empire, called a *dux*, wielded only nominal power among the tribunes of each lagoon locality, and advent of the ICONOCLASTIC CONTROVERSY of 726 caused even this tenuous hold to loosen. The decree of the Byzantine emperor LEO III outlawing the use of ICONS was disputed by these tribunes. In defiance, they elected their own *dux* (*doge* in the Venetian dialect), Ursus, or Orso. This first stirring of independence against their Byzantine overlords marked the beginning of the thousand-year Venetian republic and an unbroken line of 117 doges.

Playing Both Sides. The rise to dominance of the CAROLINGIANS in the West and their power struggle with the Byzantine Empire also involved the Venetians. Pro-Carolingian and pro-Byzantine factions created a crisis when Doge Giovanni Galbaio murdered the pro-Carolingian patriarch of Grado, Giovanni, the foremost ecclesiastic in the area. His nephew and successor, Fortunatus, was ultimately forced to flee to CHARLEMAGNE'S court, where he lobbied for an invasion of the lagoon.

In 810, Charlemagne's son Pépin attacked the area with initial success, but the inhabitants fled to the Rialto Islands in the center of the lagoon, and Pépin was unable to follow. After a six-month stalemate, Pépin withdrew; the Venetians had again succeeded.

By the *Pax Nicephori* of 811, the Byzantine Empire retained Venice as an eastern satellite, but the nascent republic was granted trading rights within the Carolingian west. This generous compromise separated Venice from the political upheavals in Italy, sparing it the excesses of the feudal system.

Another consequence was the establishment of the Rialto as the center of government of the Venetian communities. Under the first doge of Rialtine Venice, Agnello Participazio, a great building program began with draining, buttressing against the sea, and the driving of countless wooden piles as foundations.

The defining moment for Venetian identity occurred in 828, when two Venetian merchants arrived from Alexandria with the purported body of St. Mark the Evangelist, blatantly stolen from its Alexandrian crypt. A legend justified the theft by claiming that while he was still alive an angel had appeared to St. Mark in the lagoon saying, Peace be to you, Mark (*Pax tibi, Marce . . .*) ; in this place will your body lie. A basilica was promptly built next to the doge's palace to house the relics, and thereafter St. Mark and his lion became the symbols of Venice. Symbolically, the very fact that the apostle rested in Venice for all time implied a spiritual superiority, separating the Church in Venice from the conflicts that developed elsewhere in Europe.

Commercial Dominance. Venice now proceeded to consolidate its position as a commercial power, taking advantage of the weakening hold of the eastern empire in the West. The key to this trading expansion was control over the Adriatic Sea, which also meant eliminating the threat posed by the pirate hordes of the eastern coastline. As of 948, in a series of military ventures and judicious marriage alliances under Doge Pietro III Candiano, Venice started by taking control of the north Adriatic peninsula of Istria. Eventually the pirate menace in the mid-Adriatic was overcome. These successes in penetrating and dominating the mid-Adriatic were solidified by the famous statesman and soldier Doge Pietro II Orseolo in 1000, when he proclaimed himself duke of Dalmatia.

Extending the sway of the Venetian fleets to the eastern Mediterranean was achieved as a reward for military aid to the Byzantine emperors, in 992, against the Muslims, and again in 1082 against the NORMANS. Concessions were given allowing Venetian merchants not only to trade duty-free in the empire, but also to set up autonomous districts in each city. These concessions highlighted Venice's great importance in the trading and transport of lumber, metal, furs, and Slavic slaves from Europe in exchange for luxurious goods like spices, dyes, and gemstones from the East.

Domestic Struggles. A growing rift emerged between the conservative older families, who clung to the dogeship to protect their status and wealth, and the aggressive "nouveau riche" elite, who wanted to continue to develop trade abroad and at home. The newer group saw unrestricted trade as crucial to growth and wanted to limit the influence of the entrenched families such as the Participazio, Candiani, and Orseoli. Meanwhile the older families were beginning to ally themselves with feudal interests, and were investing in land. These groups' opposing goals eventually led to the first check on the doge's autonomy—the establishment of a regular group of councillors. However, since the doge and the councillors were nominated by a select number of wealthy merchant families, the continued emphasis on commercial expansion was ensured. (*See* COMMERCE AND TRADE.)

An obvious corollary to the prosperity that this commerce brought was population growth. It has been estimated that by 1200, Venice was already one of the largest cities in the West, with 70,000 residents, and that almost the entire area that constitutes the present-day city had been built.

Venice's prodigious wealth and dominance of Mediterranean commerce stemmed from the government sponsorship of trading fleets and the restriction of financing to Venetian citizens only. They alone took the risks and they alone kept the profits. About 1100, to ensure that Venice would take the lead in shipbuilding, the massive state-operated Arsenale shipyards were established. By 1150, it employed some 16,000 workers.

Crusades. One of their most important shipbuilding contracts came in 1202, during the Fourth Crusade, to provide 200 ships to carry approximately 33,000 crusaders to the Holy Land. Until then, Venice had remained relatively aloof from the CRUSADES. When only half the promised number of crusaders arrived (with half the money), Doge Enrico Dandolo offered to defer the debt if the crusaders would help in retaking the mid-Adriatic city of Zara, which had recently revolted. This was agreed to (and accomplished) as was an arrangement to repay the debt with booty from the coming Crusade. This arrangement thus benefited the Venetians greatly when the crusaders changed course and sacked Constantinople rather than Jerusalem. Venice was awarded three-eighths of the empire and many treasures, including the four bronze horses that decorate the Church of San Marco.

Internal Administration. Once again, new sources of wealth raised more families into the elite ranks, causing tension between them and the old guard. The dogeship of Giacomo Tiepolo, elected in 1229 with the strong support of the artisan GUILDS, was seen as a victory for these newcomer families and for the powerless artisan guilds. A long series of wars throughout the thirteenth century with Venice's archrival, GENOA, added to the social and political tensions, coming to a head in 1310 with the Querini conspiracy. The Querini family, in concert with a Tiepolo heir, Baiamonte, attempted to overthrow the doge, Pietro Gradenigo. The attempt failed, but it led to important governmental innovations.

One was the creation of the Council of Ten, a secret committee, meant to be temporary, which evolved into a permanent intelligence-gathering body with powers of summary justice in cases of treason or sedition. Even this secret committee, however, was obliged to work under the scrutiny of the doge and the six councillors.

The Querini-Tiepolo conspiracy also led to a legal clarification of noble status. Only those who had the right to sit on the Major Council, a hereditary group of about 1,000 important merchants, qualified. Thus, political status equaled social status, and the nobility's shared commercial zeal guaranteed continued prosperity, even in the turbulent fourteenth century, a time of wars, plagues, and shrinking markets.

In the fifteenth century, Venice shrewdly took advantage of the city-state wars on the Italian mainland, carving out a large portion of northeastern Italy to add to its territory; thereby consolidating its vast commercial empire with a rich land-based state, and ensuring its importance during the Renaissance.

VERDUN, TREATY OF

The treaty drawn up and sworn to at Verdun in August 843 shaped the political future of Europe by dividing the Frankish empire into three parts. Designed to end the dynastic struggle that had broken out among CHARLEMAGNE's grandsons, the treaty gave Charles the Bald the western part of the empire, which stretched from the Atlantic south to SPAIN, with its eastern border roughly along the Schildt, Saône, and Rhône Rivers. This primarily Romance-speaking territory later became the kingdom of FRANCE. Louis received the part of the empire that lay east of the Rhine, as well as the counties of Speyer, Worms, and Mainz west of the river, consisting mostly of Franconia, Saxony, BAVARIA, and Swabia—what would later become GERMANY. The treaty granted the oldest grandson, Lothair, the title of emperor and the central part of the empire. Known as the Middle Kingdom, his portion was a long stretch of land that extended from the North Sea southward through Lorraine and BURGUNDY into Provence and Italy and included the empire's two capitals—AIX-LA-CHAPELLE (Aachen) and ROME. (*See* CAROLINGIAN DYNASTY.)

VIKINGS

Vikings were Scandinavian groups from NORWAY, SWEDEN, and DENMARK who in the ninth century moved as marauding bands in two directions. Some penetrated Slavic RUSSIA and played a role in the murky politics there in the next two centuries, one that culminated in the creation of the Kievian state by a Slavic prince, Vladimir, in 980 with help of Norse Vikings called Varangians. The majority of the Scandinavian immigrant warriors moved westward. They took to their longboats, propelled mainly by oars, with usually one square mainsail, and containing 30 or 40 warriors and their armaments. The draft of the Viking boats was sufficiently shallow to allow them to sail far up the rivers of western Europe.

Invaders. Vikings invaded ENGLAND, IRELAND, and various places in northern FRANCE, and occasionally a Viking expedition turned up on the coast of ITALY. The Vikings were heathens, but even after the conversion of Norway and Denmark to CHRISTIANITY was under way in the eleventh and twelfth centuries, another overseas Viking migration occurred—this time to ICELAND and GREENLAND. Perhaps they made their way to an American coastal territory called VINLAND, which has been identified

with various landfalls from Newfoundland to Cape Cod, Massachusetts.

In a long-range perspective, the Viking migrations and conquests that began in the ninth century were the second stage of Scandinavian immigration into western Europe. The first phase began about 1000 B.C.E. and involved crossing the Baltic into Germany and slowly moving up the Rhine-Danube frontier of the Roman Empire by 300 C.E. These Germanic peoples involved in these BARBARIAN INVASIONS of the Roman Empire—namely the GOTHS and FRANKS, along with the obscure Varangians of old RUSSIA and the Vikings who attacked western Europe in the ninth and tenth centuries—settled Iceland after 1100, and reached the coastline of North America. All these groups were ethnically the same people pouring out of Scandinavia in stages and in various directions. (*See* BARBARIAN INVASIONS.)

Reasons for Expansion. What caused the Scandinavian—and in particular the Viking—migrations is not altogether known. Until their conversion to Christianity, the Scandinavians were illiterate. What is known about them comes from fragmentary archaeological evidence and what the peoples they invaded said about them, which was extremely hostile. As far as the Latin writers of ninth-century and tenth-century western Europe were concerned—all of them clerics—the Vikings were a scourge of the worst order. They were heathen robbers bent on pillaging churches and homes, looting monasteries and cathedrals, raping nuns, and in some cases seizing agricultural land from peaceful farmers.

Historians speculate that the Scandinavians were impelled to move southward by overpopulation, deteriorating climate and food supply, political squabbles in which the losers were driven overseas, or a combination of all these factors.

Some historians take a more positive view of the Vikings. They were as interested in trade as in war and looting. It is believed

12th-century Norwegian wood carving from a church portal, depicting a scene—Sigurd killing the treacherous Regin—from the Saga of Sigurd Favnesbane.

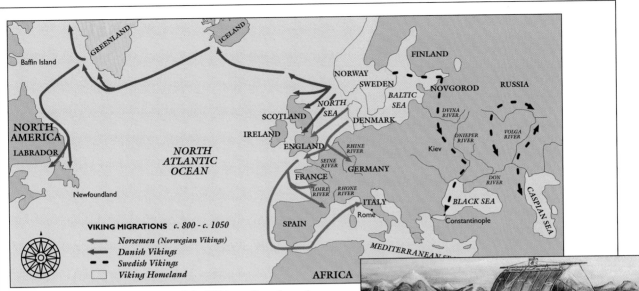

The Explorations and Conquests of the Vikings. *Forced to rely on the sea for sustenance, the Vikings built fleets of swift and powerful ships (right, depicted near Dawn Ladir Cliffs in Norway) with bows shallow enough to navigate up European rivers to mount assaults on European lands, thus combining trade, exploration, and conquest in one nautical instrument.*

they were trying to integrate themselves into the economies of the countries they invaded; eventually they did so. They were attracted by the wealth and trading opportunities of CONSTANTINOPLE, which drew them to attempt to traverse the river systems of Russia. The Vikings stood in awe of the rich farmlands of northern France and southern England and sought access to the markets created by the abbeys and towns.

In Latin writings, the Vikings appear as fierce heathen warriors and ruthless pillagers from about 850 to about 1000. Finally they did settle down, especially in eastern England and the part of northern France originally called Neustria and later (and still) Normandy. In time the Vikings became Christian lords, farmers, and merchants, just like everyone else.

Settlements. Both the English kings and the French emperors in the ninth century found it very difficult to withstand the Vikings in battle, although the latter's numbers must have been small compared to the indigenous population. Rulers in both England and France tried to buy off the Viking invaders, with little success. A better stratagem was adopted about 900 by allowing them to settle large contiguous tracts of land and farming principalities and live peacefully with their neighbors. By 1000, this settlement policy was working in both the Danelaw (eastern England, where the Danish law ran) and in the new French Duchy of Normandy. In the latter region, Vikings led by a Danish duke Rollo settled in, as was already the case in England. They converted to Christianity and accommo-

dated themselves to the prevailing political and economic system. They were known for heavy drinking and violence, but this was not unusual behavior among the warrior class of Europe at that time. In England they became known for their massive consumption of mead, a high-proof beer made from fermented honey. In Normandy—with the help of Benedictine monks—they invented a brandy made from applejack and named after a bishopric, called Calvados (the brown lightning of the medieval world, still drunk by some today). The Viking invaders in their long boats were all males. As they settled in, they sent home for women, but many must have married locally.

England underwent the peculiar experience of yet another Scandinavian invasion in the 1020s and was incorporated into the great northern empire of the Danish ruler Cnut. He was a skillful ruler and a friend of the Church; he made a pilgrimage to Rome. After Cnut's death in 1035 his sons, in familiar Viking fashion, fell to feuding over the thrones of England and Denmark. The English nobility finally ejected the Danish dynasty from their island and restored the native ANGLO-SAXON ruling family.

Meanwhile in Normandy, the descendants of ROLLO had improved their government with the help of Benedictine monks imported from northern Italy and the Rhineland. Under ducal patronage, the monks created elegant abbeys that were centers of learning, piety, and art. They also served the dukes as secretaries and advisers. In the 1050s, Duke William the Bastard drew upon this background to create the most centralized feudal state in Europe. As the Norman nobility multiplied their numbers, he looked around for a place to make use of his surplus military capacity. He had a vague claim to the English throne through an obscure aunt and a promise made to him by EDWARD THE CONFESSOR. William slyly got the blessing of the pope for an invasion of England and landed on its southern coast in the fall of 1066. He defeated and killed the English king and took over the rich country, which had a population of one million people, probably four times that of Normandy. He ruled as WILLIAM I THE CONQUEROR until his death in 1087. His direct descendants still rule England.

Before Duke William appeared on the scene and took advantage of the burgeoning warrior class of Normandy, a prominent Norman family, the Hautevilles, had reasserted their Viking heritage and begun an invasion of SICILY, a rich granary with wealthy cities, that was politically divided between the Byzantines and the Arabs. After much hard fighting and wily negotiating, the Hauteville lineage emerged as dukes of Sicily and of a part of southern Italy by 1100. Again exhibiting the Viking wanderlust and intrepitude BOHEMUND, a Hauteville, played a key role in the First Crusade of 1096 and became prince of Antioch in Syria. Today in the hills above Palermo, Sicily, the Norman Sicilian church of Mount Royal, built in the Arabic style, with its blazing MOSAICS installed by Greek craftsmen can be seen in its pristine grandeur—a splendid monument to Viking travels and conquests. (See NORWAY; EXPLORATION; SAGAS.)

Sagas. An intimate portrait of Viking society and behavior is provided by a half-dozen Icelandic SAGAS written in the thirteenth century. These narratives describe life in twelfth-century Norway and Iceland. The world depicted here is much like Germanic society of the fifth and sixth centuries: much fighting, drinking, and promiscuous sex—but many disputes are resolved peacefully around the campfire over a keg of beer. There was a strong consensual element in this Icelandic political structure. Kings and great lords were not autocrats. Women were frequently abused, but some women, as in sixth-century France, played an influential role in decision-making. Women, whose advice was often listened to, were outspoken and often listened to. A large colony of Icelanders settled in central Manitoba about 1910. They came down directly from their homeland through Hudson Bay via perilous and frigid seas like their forefathers a millennium earlier crossing the Baltic and North Seas. Here the Viking migrations at last reached a final destination.

VILLON, FRANÇOIS

François Villon (1431–c. 1463) was one of the best-known medieval poets in FRANCE. His poems are still admired for their passion and sincerity. (See FRENCH LANGUAGE; LITERATURE.)

Born in PARIS to a poor family, Villon was brought up by a priest. He studied at the University of Paris, where he received a master's degree in 1452. He barely supported himself—yet he found the time to write.

In 1455, he was accused of murdering a man and sentenced to death, but commuted to a 10-year exile from Paris. He lived an itinerant, apparently aimless life, although he continued to write. Among his works are numerous ballads and poems, as well as two mock wills: *Lais* (1456) and *Testament* (1461). Two of his most highly regarded poems are the "Debate Between Villon and His Heart" and the "Ballad of Hanged Men."

In 1463 Villon was arrested for theft; this time he was sentenced to death. He was released on appeal, but exiled from Paris. Where he went, how he died, or whether he continued to write remain a mystery.

VINCENT OF BEAUVAIS

Vincent of Beauvais (1190–1264), a thirteenth-century French Dominican scholar, compiled possibly the most ambitious work of the Middle Ages—an encyclopedia of all existing knowledge called the *Speculum majus* (*Great Mirror*), a definitive reference work for over five centuries.

Born in the French town of Beauvais, he became a Dominican friar and went to Paris about 1220. While there, he came up with the idea of a single, universal source summarizing all the knowledge known to humankind up until then. He began collecting material from a number of sources, and continued to do so after his transfer to a new monastery in his home town. By the 1240s, he had made considerable progress, and received the support of King LOUIS IX.

The *Speculum majus* consists of three sections: *Speculum naturale*, on the sciences; *Speculum historiale*, on the history of the world as of Adam and Eve; and *Speculum doctrinale*, on such topics as economics, mathematics, and language. A fourth section, *Speculum morale*, on morality, was added by an unknown source some years after Vincent's death. Of particular importance is Vincent's inclusion of ancient Greek and Roman material, which had fallen out of favor earlier in the Middle Ages but was given new importance after the TWELFTH-CENTURY RENAISSANCE.

Upon completion, the *Speculum majus* contained over 80 volumes and some three million words.

VINLAND

Vinland is the land in the Western Hemisphere discovered and explored by Leif Ericsson, son of Eric the Red. According to the Icelandic SAGA entitled *Saga of Eric the Red*, in the collection of tales known as the *Hauksbok*, it was on a return trip from NORWAY to GREENLAND in 1000 that Leif Ericsson was blown off course and came upon lands not previously known to the VIKINGS. He explored the new land and found grapes, self-sown wheat, and a type of tree called mausur. After he collected specimens, he returned to Greenland. (*See* EXPLORATION.)

In another version of the story, contained in the *Saga of Olaf Tryggvason* in the *Flateyjarbok*, Ericsson completed his journey from Norway to Greenland and then set out from there about 1002 on a voyage to western lands where he discovered several new places and settled in Vinland for the winter. (*See* NORWAY.)

Neither Ericsson's expedition nor later Viking voyages, particularly that of Thorfinn Karlsefni, succeeded in establishing a settlement. The hostility of the natives of Vinland toward the intruders may have been a major factor, but another reason might have been that maintaining settlements on Greenland was already pressing Viking resources to the limit. (*See* VIKINGS.)

Most scholars believe Leif Ericsson landed somewhere on the coast of NORTH AMERICA, but there has been a great deal of debate about the location of Vinland. Various places from Newfoundland to Virginia have been advanced, with Nova Scotia and New England the most popular choices.

Many experts believe that the name Vinland itself gives some clue as to its location. The reference to wine in its name, combined with several references to grapes and wine in Norse sagas would lead to the conclusion that Vinland must be located below the northern limit for grape growing; hence the New England speculation. However, in 1960, an area called L'Anse aux Meadows was discovered in northern Newfoundland. The archaeologist who discovered the area believes that the *Vin* in Vinland had nothing at all to do with wine. Instead, he maintains it referred to the old Norse syllable meaning "pasture." Carbon-14 dating confirms that the site is indeed Norse and pre-Columbian, possibly from about the year 1000.

VISIGOTHS

The Visigoths represented half of the great GOTHIC nation who emigrated from Scandinavia and played a central role in the fall of the Roman Empire. By the third century C.E., the Visigoths had settled by the Danube in central Europe. For a time, the Visigoths and Romans coexisted and engaged in peaceful trade. But in the fourth century, the balance of power changed when the Huns invaded Europe, destroying the vast empire of the OSTROGOTHS, forcing the Visigoths into Roman territory.

In 378, the Visigoth cavalry destroyed the Roman army at Adrianople, killing the emperor and ending the supremacy of the Roman legions once and for all. The Romans were compelled to settle the Visigoths within the empire, in the Balkans. The Visigoths, however, revolted and a long struggle ensued, which included the famous first sacking of ROME by the Visigothic king ALARIC I in 410.

By the end of the fifth century, the Visigoths had settled in southwest FRANCE but in 507, their French kingdom was shattered by CLOVIS, king of the FRANKS, and they were forced southward into SPAIN. By 585, the Visigoths, under Leovigild, had annihilated the Suevi kingdom in northern Spain; by 621, they had successfully expelled the Byzantine Empire from the south of Spain. In 589, the Visigothic king RECCARED violently converted the Arian Visigoths to Catholicism. The Visigothic Spanish kingdom survived until the Muslim conquest of 711, after which the Visigoths disappeared from history. (*See* GOTHS; OSTROGOTHS.)

VLAD III THE IMPALER

Vlad the Impaler was a staunch fighter for freedom and independence. But his reputation, the most grisly portrayal of which is in Bram Stoker's 1897 novel *Dracula*, was also that of a bloodthirsty ruler who cruelly killed thousands.

Vlad Tsepesch (the Impaler).

In 1448, Vlad III Dracul returned from exile to claim the throne of his father, Vlad II Dracul, prince of Walachia, who had been overthrown. He was repelled and went into exile for eight years. He returned to the throne when he swore allegiance to the Hungarian king. Over the next six years, he brutalized the inhabitants of the region, killing his enemies by impaling them. He was deposed and exiled to HUNGARY. He returned in 1476, but was soon killed in battle.

WACE

Robert Wace (c. 1100–1175) was a Norman-French poet and chronicler whose known works include three works of hagiography and two histories in verse.

King HENRY II, ruler of ENGLAND and Normandy, appointed Wace canon of Bayeux. In 1160 he asked him to write a chronicle of the dukes of Normandy. Written in Norman French and based mostly on Latin sources, the *Roman de Rou* contains a famous description of the Norman victory at the Battle of HASTINGS.

Wace also composed *Roman de Brut,* a long, unfinished chronicle in verse based on GEOFFREY OF MONMOUTH'S *Historia regum Britanniae.* It chronicles English history from the time of Brutus the Trojan, the mythical founder of England, up to Wace's own time. The work, in which the legend of King Arthur's Round Table makes its first appearance, helped popularize the Arthurian legend on the Continent.

WALDEMAR I THE GREAT

Waldemar I the Great (1132–1182), the king of DENMARK whose reign lasted for a quarter of a century (1157–1182), brought his country's civil wars to an end and established Denmark as the leading power of Scandinavia.

For 60 years, following the death of Sweyn II Estridsen, nephew of Cnut I the Great and Denmark's first king, Denmark had been ruled by Sweyn's five sons, each elected king in succession, but after the last son died in 1134, family members fought for power. In 1147, the Danish throne was claimed by three men—Waldemar, Canute, and Sweyn III. After fierce fighting, Waldemar received Jutland as his share of Danish territory. Canute was assassinated, most likely on orders from Sweyn, who seized the crown. Waldemar waged war against him and in 1157, defeated him in a decisive battle near Viborg. Waldemar was now uncontested ruler of Denmark, but faced a major problem when his country was overrun by the WENDS.

Waldemar joined forces with HENRY THE LION of Saxony and Albert the Bear of Brandenburg to defeat and subjugate the Wends, forcing them to accept CHRISTIANITY. To win German support, Waldemar became a vassal of the Holy Roman Emperor FREDERICK I BARBAROSSA. Later, however, he was strong enough to assert his independence. Waldemar codified the laws of Denmark and expanded the size of his kingdom by seizing Norwegian territory. He increased his international prestige and influence by marrying one of his daughters to a son of Frederick I. His half brother Absalon, archbishop of Lund and his closest adviser, helped him establish his dynasty on the Danish throne. Waldemar's son, Canute VI, succeeded his father and ruled Denmark for the next 20 years (1182–1202). (*See* DENMARK; FREDERICK I BARBAROSSA.)

WALDENSIANS

The Waldensians (also Waldenses) were a heretical sect comprising followers of Peter Waldo (d. 1216). Waldo had been a wealthy merchant in Lyons who, after a deeply religious experience, gave away all his wealth to the poor and became a mendicant preacher ministering to the poor and needy. In 1179, Waldo and his followers were granted permission (reluctantly) by Pope ALEXANDER III to preach publicly and tend the needy, but the criticisms the Waldensians leveled at the Church itself led to their being condemned as heretics in 1184. (*See* HERESY.)

The Waldensians impugned the validity of sacraments administered by unworthy priests and decried the veneration of saints and relics. They objected to all forms of killing, whether in war or as criminal punishment. The movement spread to southern France, Spain, Germany, and northern Italy, but after the harsh repressions of the sect by Pope INNOCENT III, most members capitulated and rejoined the Church. Only in the remote mountain enclaves in southern FRANCE did some Waldensians survive to the seventeenth century.

WALES

Medieval Wales arose out of the confusion caused by the withdrawal of the occupying Roman legions from the British Isles in the early fifth century and the resultant raids and settlement of the invading Germanic tribes from the Continent. The original Celtic inhabitants of Britain were now scattered to the more remote areas, where they retained much of their ancient culture. Regarded as "foreign" by the ANGLO-SAXON settlers, one such isolated group of Celts became the Welsh.

Early History. Traditional lore, collected in the *Historia Brittonum,* attributed to Nennius, places the origin of the powerful dynasty of GWYNEDD in the lowlands of Scotland, while place-names on the island of

Anglesey and in the southwest attest also to an Irish influence. The earliest history of Wales revolves around several distinct kingdoms. By the early sixth century, these were Gwent in the southeast, Dyfed in the southwest, Powys in the eastern midlands, and the most important, Gwynedd, in the northwest. From these separate petty kingdoms, strong leaders occasionally appeared who would subjugate or unite adjacent areas; eventually, over centuries, a unified Welsh identity developed. (*See* GWYNEDD.)

The kingdom of Gwynedd proved to be dominant and ultimately the most influential. From the fortified island of Anglesey, bulwarked by the massif of Snowdonia and the Menai Strait, the rulers of Gwynedd preserved their territory and expanded.

By the late eighth century, the land area of Wales had acquired a loose border, and the adjacent ANGLO-SAXON kingdoms suffered from Welsh raids. This led to the construction of an eastern barricade, stretching southward 120 miles from the Dee estuary, commissioned by the Mercian king Offa, and thus called Offa's Dyke. (*See* ENGLAND.)

Religion and Politics. The early Welsh and English were separated by another national divide: the Welsh were Christians, with a monastic tradition already well established by the early sixth century, while the Anglo-Saxons retained pagan rites until much later. Although mostly monastic in structure, the Church in Wales also established several bishoprics, the most important being St. Davids in Dyfed. Later ecclesiastical conflicts would arise because the Welsh church considered itself separate from the Church of England, retained St. David's as its archbishopric, and would not submit to the authority of Canterbury.

Politically, the Welsh system came to resemble the English in that the ruler presided over a clan, and clan members vowed allegiance on the basis of the personal strength of the chosen ruler. However, because Welsh law required that a kingdom be divided among royal heirs, retention of power in one family was made difficult, unlike the law of primogeniture in England (according to which the inheritance is the eldest son's alone). The poor economy in Wales, the lack of town development, and the absence of a feudal system, precluded the development of an administrative hierarchy, which would have aided royal expansion. Still, in spite of the obstacles, some rulers did manage to bring a form of unity to the disparate Welsh kingdoms.

The first such was Rhodri Mawr (the great) in the ninth century. This king of Gwynedd acquired Powys in 855. By 877, he had subjugated Ceredigion, thereby achieving lordship over most of Wales. His fabled military skill did not save him from being killed by the English in 878, but his sons continued his efforts and pushed farther south, even inciting the intervention of ALFRED I THE GREAT, the Anglo-Saxon king.

Hywel Dda (the good), Rhodri's grandson, acquired the kingdom of Dyfed through marriage, earning the title of "king of the Britons" from the English. In the 40 years before his death in 950, Hywel's accomplishments included issuing the first "royal" coinage, sponsoring a compilation of Welsh law, which bears his name, disseminating the cult of St. David, and making St. Davids in Dyfed the ecclesiastical center of Wales.

Disorder reigned after Hywel's death, with Viking raids and English incursions spreading havoc, which the rivalries of competing petty lords did nothing to mitigate. No fewer than 35 violent deaths of rulers are recorded in the *Brut y Tywsogion* (*Chronicle of the Princes*) between 950 and the Norman Conquest.

For a brief period, from 1039 to 1063, one ruler did impose a sort of unity. This was Gruffydd ap Llywelyn, who during this time became ruler of Gwynedd, Powys, and finally all of the south. His power and wealth, and his raids into England, finally caused EDWARD THE CONFESSOR, king of England, to travel to the border of Wales to come to terms. But Gruffyd lacked the support and the administration necessary to retain power. He was finally undone by his own Welsh neighbors, who killed him and then sent his head to Edward the Confessor as appeasement.

The Normans. This indication of Welsh disunity was soon seized upon by the NORMANS who invaded England in 1066. The Normans, under WILLIAM I THE CONQUEROR, were an accomplished military force, with long experience in border conflicts in their native Normandy. William's strategy was to establish strong subordinates in newly built castles along the borders, or marches, of Wales, and from there push ever farther into Welsh territory. The marcher lords thus created—such as Hugh Avranche, earl of Chester; Roger of Montgomery, earl of Shrewsbury; and William Fitz Osbern, earl of Hereford—attracted Norman and French settlers to establish boroughs around the new castles, and thereby extended Norman influence and the spread of towns into Wales. (*See* NORMANS.)

With the Normans also came Benedictine and CISTERCIAN monks, with strong ties to ROME and to Canterbury as the archbishopric. Inevitably, the new ecclesiastical practices of the Roman Church overwhelmed the traditional Welsh church, and St. Davids became subordinate to Canterbury.

By 1090, much of Wales was in Norman hands and at least nominally under the control of the king of England. Only in the north, in perpetually feisty Gwynedd, were there strong Welsh rulers. The first was Gruffyd ap Cynan, who regained Gwynedd in the time of HENRY I. He was succeeded by his son, Owain Fawr (the Fair).

Owain (died 1170) proved to be an impressive ruler, who tested the might of Henry II and his troops in a revolutionary alliance with Powys and other Welsh kingdoms, and won. He maintained the independence of Gwynedd, styled himself "prince" rather than "lord," and even sent an ambassador to the court of Louis VII of France. (*See* OWAIN GWYNEDD.)

Rebirth. The successes of OWAIN GWYNEDD led to a resurgence in Welsh pride and traditions, opening the way for a literary and cultural revival. Owain's grandson, LLYWELYN AP IORWERTH, afterwards known as Llywelyn the Great, aspired to a united Wales, with himself at the head as the prince of Wales, doing homage for all the other lords to the king of England, and securing this position for his son and heirs by instituting a law of primogeniture. In both these goals he succeeded, even increasing his stature by marrying a daughter of King John in 1204. By his death in 1240, after some setbacks with HENRY III, he had managed to create a centralized government, with trained civil servants and a privy seal, as in England. A monetary economy began and trade flourished. Codified law texts had begun to stress the importance of the individual, giving less authority to the clan. His daughters were married to important marcher lords such as William de Lacy and Ralph Mortimer, bringing his principality ever closer to England as an ally.

His son David succeeded him and maintained Llywelyn's achievements, giving himself the title "Prince of Wales," but his death in 1246 without an heir gave the advantage back to Henry III. In the Treaty of Woodstock of 1247, David's nephews ceded the homage of the Welsh lords to the king of England.

England. The year 1254 signaled a new era in the relations between Wales and England. Henry III bestowed on his son Edward the earldom of Chester, which in 1237 had reverted to the Crown, and thus placed a determined aggressor on the border of Wales.

The following decades, until 1283, were years of conflict between the new Prince of Wales, Llywelyn ap Gruffyd, his brother David, who coveted Llywelyn's position, and EDWARD I. When civil war broke out in England in 1263 between the Crown and the BARONS headed by SIMON DE MONTFORT, Llywelyn chose the side of the barons, betrothing himself to de Montfort's daughter, Eleanor. His successes in battles led in 1267 to the Treaty of Montgomery with Henry III, which formally recognized the principality of Wales.

Thereafter, threats to Llywelyn's sovereignty came from his own three brothers, especially David, and from uneasy marcher lords such as Gilbert Clare and Roger Mortimer. Clare built the formidable castle of Caerphilly as a symbol of his opposition.

Llywelyn himself caused his eventual downfall by seriously offending the ambitious new king, Edward I.

He refused to attend the CORONATION in 1274, resisted five summonses to travel to England to do homage to Edward, and castigated Edward for harboring his rebellious brother David. In 1277, Edward attacked Anglesey, defeating Llywelyn and humiliating him with the harsh terms of the Treaty of Conway.

In 1282, David once again rebelled, but now against England, and soon enlisted the leadership of Llywelyn. The defeat of the rebellion signaled the end of Welsh independence, with the brothers' heads displayed at the Tower of London as traitors.

Now Edward began the systematic annexation of Wales, starting with a costly program of castle-building to dampen any thoughts of Welsh rebellion. These castles, such as Caernarvon and Harlech, were garrisoned by English soldiers, attracting English colonists. With the inauguration of the future EDWARD II as Prince of Wales in 1303, the annexation was complete. Despite periodic resistance by Welsh patriots, such as OWAIN GLYN DWR in 1400, England retained its hold. During the HUNDRED YEARS' WAR, Welsh longbowmen were part of the English armies. A new Welsh gentry developed, preserving Welsh language and culture but supporting England. Finally, the Tudor royal dynasty of England, which supplanted the PLANTAGENETS in 1485, originated in Wales.

WALLACE, WILLIAM

W illiam Wallace (c. 1270–1305) was a Scottish soldier whose role in leading resistance to English rule made him a national hero. In 1297, he led a small force that burned Lanark and killed the English sheriff whom King EDWARD I had installed to enforce his claim to overlordship of SCOTLAND. Wallace then mobilized a much larger force, which routed the English at the Forth River and raided several counties in northern England. For a short time, he served as guardian of the kingdom for the imprisoned King John Baliol, but King Edward I defeated his army at Falkirk in 1298, forcing him to retreat northward. After going to FRANCE to seek help from the French king, he returned to Scotland to continue to lead the resistance against English rule. The English captured him in 1305 and brought him to London, where he was found guilty of treason and executed.

WALSINGHAM, THOMAS

T homas Walsingham (c. 1360–1422), a Benedictine monk, is best known for his chronicles of the abbey of St. Albans in Hertfordshire.

Little is known about Walsingham except that he took up the task of continuing the *Chronica majora*, the chronicle that had last been kept by MATTHEW PARIS (d. 1259). The chronicle had been started when St. Albans was first founded, and it was Walsingham's desire to create and maintain a continuous, unbroken history. (Paris had taken up the work from the chronicler Roger of Wendover, who died in 1236.)

Walsingham's work, the *Historia anglicana*, covers the years from 1272 to 1422, shortly before his death. It provides important historical information not only about St. Albans, but also about the rulers RICHARD II, HENRY IV, and HENRY V, and their reigns.

WALTER THE PENNILESS

W alter (d. 1097) was the leader of a "Peasants' Crusade" organized in the summer of 1096. The band of just a few thousand pillaged the Balkan countryside on their way to Asia Minor to join up with (or wait for) PETER THE HERMIT. Walter himself was an impoverished French knight from Cologne who grew impatient waiting for the First Crusade to begin. He was killed, and his group was decimated by the Turks at Civetot on October 21, 1097.

WALTHER VON DER VOGELWEIDE

W alther von der Vogelweide (c. 1170–c. 1230) was perhaps the most famous singer and composer in medieval GERMANY. Although his melodies no longer exist, his surviving lyrics are noted for their beauty and directness. Walther became a professional musician at about the end of the twelfth century and composed for more than 30 years. Not only were his melodies and lyrics popular, he was also in possession of a beautiful singing voice.

Much of Walther's work, like that of all court musicians in Europe, reflects the patronage of one or another noble (he had many during his career). His biting lyrics and outspoken views did not allow him to remain in any one patron's service for long. He would often write songs praising one potential ruler, wear out his welcome, then write songs in praise of a new patron, often a bitter rival of the former employer.

Many of his lyrics also celebrate courtly and physical love. One of his most famous love songs is "*Unter der Linden*" ("Under the Linden"). He also composed religious songs, many of which were sung by pilgrims as they journeyed to religious sites. (*See* MUSIC.)

WARFARE

T he western empire was replaced at the end of the fifth century by a number of Germanic kingdoms. These settler states could not afford to maintain the Roman bureaucracy or its huge military organization. Instead, they used their own military system based on land tenure, in which lands were awarded to nobles and warriors in lieu of cash payments. The original Germanic armies were quite familiar with Roman practices. For many years, Germans had served in Roman armies as officers, soldiers, and with their chiefs as part of allied or auxiliary contingents. The FRANKS remained an infantry force for some time. The OSTROGOTHS, VISIGOTHS, and VANDALS were all acquainted with both Roman and Asiatic horsemanship; the HORSE subsequently played an important role in their military activity.

Birth of the Cavalry. This system of service evolved into FEUDALISM. CAROLINGIAN France was the birthplace of this way of life. The realm established by CHARLEMAGNE stretched from the Danemark in the north and the Saxon Marches in the east to the Catalan March in the south. The most prominent feature of this kingdom was the mounted warrior. The army had to be mobile and quickly marshalled to fight an enemy after traveling a great distance. The horsemen offered an advantage over the infantry as they could reach a threatened province by using existing Roman roads. The local lords could be summoned to appear with their contingents as the royal army arrived. This force had to be prepared to fight ARABS, Norsemen, MAGYARS, and Saxon rebels.

The great age of feudal cavalry covers the period between 1060 and 1300. There are many problems for historians trying to write about the development of the cavalry and its equipment. The first problem is the stirrup: there is little solid evidence of exactly when and how the stirrup arrived in Europe. The origins of this very important piece of cavalry equipment lie in central Asia, and scholars believe it arrived during the Carolingian period. The Byzantines may have possessed it a few years before that. In antiquity, heavy cavalry troops had used saddle pads and were able to strike with a lance, spear, or sword from horseback, using a downward overhand stroke. There is some debate about whether or not such cavalry could break the aligned front of an infantry formation.

The stirrup probably arrived with the AVAR invasions of central Europe. A saddle with stirrups afforded the rider a firmer seat when attacking. A weapon could be cradled in an underarm position, and the horseman could strike a target more firmly. This technical innovation aided the training of the warrior and his ability to control his horse.

The horseman was required to constantly maintain a warhorse. In FRANCE or ENGLAND, this might require the expenditure of a year's income. A knight might travel on a campaign with at least three horses. Besides the warhorse, he needed a saddle horse and a packhorse as well. Originally, neither the knight nor his men were compensated for the loss of animals during their term of service. As armor became heavier, it became necessary to breed larger horses for military purposes.

The Feudal Army. In time, the association between military service and land tenure denoted noble status. The words for cavalry soldier and gentleman became synonymous—*chevalier* (French), *cavaliere* (Italian), *caballero* (Spanish), *ritter* (German). The English "knight" comes from the ANGLO-SAXON *cnicht*, a household retainer or servant.

The expertise of feudal armies has been debated through the years. The sources used as evidence about military practices—CHANSONS DE GESTE, chronicles, and ordinances—are notoriously unreliable. But it seems certain that the monarch and the lords kept a number of knights and horsemen at their residences. These men were employed in a number of prestigious positions, and as a result, they were well practiced in the use of arms. They could fight on foot or on horseback; they were the nucleus of any host that would assemble in the time of war.

During the actual fighting, these more or less permanent soldiers would be in the first of the three cavalry formations that usually made up a feudal army. The traditional method was to deploy three banners—two for the attacking force and a third in reserve. The more experienced men would lead the charge; contrary to popular belief, they tried not to run chaotically all about the field. The formation would advance at a walk, then start to trot a few hundred yards from the enemy formation, and then charge the last 75 yards. (No doubt there were always, however, some individuals who ignored their orders.)

Another problem faced by feudal armies was one of command and control. The nature of feudal society dictated that the prominent lords and knights step into the first rank during the battle, making command difficult if not impossible. The war commanders thus had to be proficient warriors, which quality did not always make them suitable for command.

The Norman Conquest. The Norman Conquest affords an example of how well a feudal army could function. During this period, infantry had been replaced by horsemen as the premiere combatant. Anglo-Saxon England still relied on a Germanic infantry host. When the NORMANS threatened the king-

The charge of the horsemen of Faramouz. As late as the 14th century, cavalry assault from Saracens and from eastern invaders was still feared thoughout Europe.

dom, HAROLD II GODWINSON, the last Anglo-Saxon king of England, gathered up his army and went to fight the first of his enemies. He fought and defeated a Viking host that had landed in the north at Stamfordbridge. After this battle, the Anglo-Saxons had to make a forced march to the south to meet the Normans at Hastings. (*See* ANGLO-SAXONS; NORMANS.)

The BATTLE OF HASTINGS is thus a clear case of a well-armed infantry on good ground being attacked by a cavalry-based feudal army. The Anglo-Saxons only used horses as transportation. Harold arrived with his housecarls (bodyguards), the notables and their troops, and called out the militia. The Norman army consisted of William's vassals; volunteers from France, BRITTANY, and FLANDERS; and a contingent of archers and spearmen. The Norman army attacked the Anglo-Saxon position on a hill. The battle was very difficult, with the Normans mounting successive attacks on the Anglo-Saxon formation. Despite a number of repulses, the Norman horse units reformed on a number of occasions to resume the attack, an indication that tactical leadership was good and the horses well exercised.

The Normans used their infantry to inflict casualties on the Anglo-Saxons by shooting arrows into their formation. The fighting continued amidst rumors that William had been killed or wounded. He took off his helmet and showed himself to silence the rumors of his demise. It was, in fact, Harold who had been slain. With their leader killed, the Anglo-Saxon army was broken—with no commander, there was no control.

After Hastings, infantry as a combatant force was eclipsed, but it had not disappeared altogether. Viable infantry still existed in SCOTLAND, SWITZERLAND, and northern ITALY. The age of the mounted warrior would last until the end of the fourteenth century.

Fortification. The feudal system brought to England by the Normans was built around the stone castle. These castles were places of political, military, and religious authority. The castle extended Norman rule throughout England and into WALES and IRELAND. The kings of France and England held hundreds of castles in an effort to maintain and extend their authority. The English kings held extensive lands in France, while the French kings were attempting to consolidate their authority and lands at the expense of the local magnates, including the English kings.

Castle-building led to the second most important aspect of warfare in the Middle Ages—siege warfare. In areas such as the Low Countries, great chains of barrier fortresses were constructed. Wars were fought between the armies of the HOLY ROMAN EMPIRE, France, England, and local magnates for the possession of the wealthy cities in that region. Sieges were the predominant method of warfare and were conducted on a regular basis. The siege required the employment of pioneers, artificers, and engineers. The preferred method was to persuade the castle or city to surrender by offering terms. When all else failed, the walls had to be breached and the castle taken by storm. Artillery pieces called the onager and trebuchet were used to hurl large stones, some weighing half a ton, into the fortress. Dead and diseased animals were also hurled in order to create panic and start an epidemic. Saps and movable towers were used to infiltrate the castle walls, and tunnels were dug to undermine them. Siege warfare was made easier with the introduction of gunpowder. Artillery pieces utilizing gunpowder were in use by the late fourteenth century.

The Church. The role of the Church in medieval warfare is significant. Through this period the PAPACY and local Church authorities attempted to set limits on when and how conflicts could be conducted. An important issue was the just or moral war. Parties involved in wars tried to give acceptable reasons for their conduct. The Church tried, through the Truce of God, to arrange that Christmas, Easter, and "days sacred to the Virgin" would be times of truce. The Church also tried to enforce periodic bans on the carrying of weapons.

Siege of a town defended by Burgundians, led by Charles VI, from the Chroniques de Monstrelet, *c. 1500. In the late Middle Ages, the attention of military planners focused on methods of breaking through castles and fortifications.*

During this era, efforts were made to determine who were combatants in a war and who were not. Church authorities tried to exclude women, the very young, and the elderly as harmless noncombatants. They tried to lessen violence in the society as a whole. The knightly TOURNAMENT was a specific target. In the days of John the Marshal, these were bloody exercises using existing weaponry, although later blunted swords and breakaway lances became the norm. The accidents that occurred still made tournaments extremely dangerous. (*See* TOURNAMENTS.)

None of these principles applied to infidels, however. The beginning of the CRUSADES was marked by horrific communal massacres. The Jewish populations of the Rhineland and of England were slaughtered. When Jerusalem was taken by storm during the First Crusade, the population was similarly treated, and when RICHARD I LION-HEART broke his word to the Muslim garrison at Acre, they too were butchered. Medieval warfare had a dark side—the code of CHIVALRY and good manners did not always prevail.

By the end of the fourteenth century, the feudal system was undergoing change. When the king assem-

bled his army, he and his officials often had difficulty filling the ranks. As the wars got further away from where the lords and their vassals lived, they became less likely to serve. The English kings dealt with this growing problem by using a system known as scutage. The system originated from a Norman custom of giving payment to employ a mercenary in lieu of service. Custom and law dictated that service range from 40 to 60 days at the knight's expense. Knights and their men-at-arms were not compensated for the loss of their horses or equipment; if they were taken prisoner, the ransom had to be paid by their friends and family.

In northern Italy, the wealthier classes liable for service paid for soldiers to be hired in their stead. The local nobility and the municipal authorities preferred this arrangement—there was a reluctance to see the lower social classes armed in any numbers. In France and England, the aristocracy was not overly enthusiastic about doing more than looking for volunteers. In the highlands and mountains of SWITZERLAND and the Rhineland, men were forced by poverty and underemployment to become hired soldiers.

The HUNDRED YEARS' WAR changed the nature of warfare in the Middle Ages. The English generally used volunteers, paid troops, and local allies. The French used both the feudal levies and a smaller number of regular soldiers. The French feudal army lacked the experience and skill to defeat the English in the field. Gradually, the kings of France—Charles VI and his successors—turned to paid regulars. They recruited in the provinces and in Switzerland; the English were eventually driven out of France except for Calais, which they retained. Firearms and cannons became a feature of the standing army of France.

The Italian city-states employed great bands of mercenaries. The great rivals of the French monarchy, the dukes of BURGUNDY, created a standing army. The feudal knight was no longer the major force behind military activity.

 See AGINCOURT, BATTLE OF; ARMS AND ARMOR; ARTILLERY; CASTLES AND FORTIFICATIONS; CHIVALRY; CRUSADES; HASTINGS, BATTLE OF; HORSES; HUNDRED YEARS' WAR; KNIGHTHOOD; PEACE OF GOD; WEAPONRY.

WARS OF THE ROSES

For a 30-year period, English history was dominated by a dynastic struggle between the Houses of York and Lancaster, both of whom claimed legitimacy as descendants of King EDWARD III. The name of the conflict was taken from the emblems of the two houses: red rose for Lancaster; white rose

for York. The civil war involved the aristocratic followers of both sides.

Seeds of Conflict. When HENRY V died in 1422, his son Henry VI was only nine months old. HENRY VI was crowned that year and reached his majority at age 15. Shortly after that he married Margaret of Anjou, in 1444. The court and government of Henry VI were dominated by his two principal advisers—Henry Beaufort, duke of Somerset, and William de la Pole, duke of Suffolk. The queen quickly allied herself with this faction, regarded as corrupt by most of the social classes. Another important factor was the humiliation felt by the aristocracy by the defeats suffered by English armies in France. (*See* SOCIAL CLASSES.)

The unpopular Suffolk was impeached and banished—and murdered on his way to FLANDERS. Somerset remained in control, but JACK CADE'S rebellion of 1450 demonstrated the negative feelings of the public toward him. The rebellion was put down by the authorities, and Richard, duke of York, emerged as the head of the opposition. An able soldier and a lieutenant of France, he was banished to IRELAND and ordered never again to set foot on English soil.

York returned to England to impeach Somerset. He enjoyed the support of the powerful northern magnates the Nevilles, but his attempt to drive Somerset from power failed; he was arrested in 1452 and later released when he rallied his supporters to reconquer Guienne. The effort ended in defeat at Castillon, the last great battle of the HUNDRED YEARS' WAR, after which only Calais remained in English hands.

Prelude to War. The two rival factions were in essence fighting for control of the council and PARLIAMENT. Both accepted the unity of the kingdom and its existing form of government. The crisis began to escalate in August 1453, when fighting erupted at Stamford Bridge between the Percys and the Nevilles. At this time Henry VI became deranged for a period of 16 months. Margaret of Anjou gave birth to a son, which ensured the succession of the Lancastrian line. Somerset was attacked in the Parliament of 1453–1454, and since the king's insanity could no longer be hidden, York was declared protector of the realm. This put York in a commanding position that he did not enjoy. The king recovered in late 1454, and York had to relinquish his position and allow Somerset to control the king. York retired to Ludlow castle, summoned his retainers, and was joined by the Nevilles and their retainers. The stage was set for what came to be known as the Wars of the Roses.

The Battles. The wars are divided into three periods: 1455–1464; 1469–1471; and 1483–1487. The first major battle took place at St. Albans, May 22, 1455. The Yorkists won the day, and the king, the duke of Buckingham, and the earls of Devon and

Dorset were captured. Clifford, Somerset, Stafford, Percy, and Harington were killed. York was made protector in October, and Warwick was made captain of Calais. York lost the protectorship early in 1456 and returned to Ireland. Margaret gained control of the court and the government, but Warwick refused to surrender Calais, and it became a refuge for Yorkists. In the summer of 1459, both sides started to rearm and raise troops.

October of 1459 saw the Yorkists defeated at Ludford. York was forced to flee back to Ireland and his army was dispersed. In June 1460, Warwick landed at Sandwich with 2,000 men of the Calais garrison. He was accompanied by the earl of Salisbury and York's son Edward, earl of March. The king and queen were at Coventry when they received the news of Warwick's landing, and they immediately gathered an army. Warwick entered LONDON on July 2. The king halted at Northampton to gather reinforcements.

The Battle of Northampton on July 10 ended in a Yorkist victory. The king was captured and many prominent Lancastrians lay dead on the field of battle. York came over from Ireland in mid-September, while the queen and her son fled to WALES and then north to raise another army. They then began their march south. York sent his son Edward, earl of March, to the Welsh border. Warwick remained in London to keep the capital loyal and to guard the king. On December 9, York left London with his younger son Edmund, taking with him all the artillery from the Tower. His objective was to prevent the concentration of the Lancastrian armies. A battle took place on December 16, when the Yorkist army clashed with Lancastrian forces on their way to join Margaret.

York arrived at Sandal Castle on December 21 and found that his army was severely outnumbered. He remained in the castle waiting for Warwick and his son Edward to join him. On December 30, York reconsidered his situation, believing the Lancastrian army to be smaller in number than he was originally informed. The Yorkists assaulted the troops deployed in front of them, but it proved to be a trap. York, his son Edmund, his two uncles Sir John and Sir Hugh Mortimer, and Sir Thomas Neville were all killed. The earl of Salisbury was captured and executed.

Trouble for the Yorkists. The death of Richard of York was a huge blow to the Yorkists. However, both Warwick and Edward, now the duke of York, were raising new armies and continued the fight. After defeating the Yorkists at Wakefield (Sandal Castle), Margaret's army marched to London to rescue the king, and her unpaid troops started to pillage the countryside on the way. The situation looked bleak for the Yorkists, but Edward's victory at Mortimer's Cross on February 2, 1461, saved the day. The second Battle of St. Albans was fought on February 17, 1461. The Lancastrians started off with the advantage, but were unable to defeat Warwick. The queen waited nine days for London to fall. It would not. The Yorkists relieved London when they proclaimed Edward king on March 4. Margaret, along with the rescued Henry, fled to Scotland. By this time, the remaining Lancastrian army was based in Wales. Edward's early reign was spent consolidating his power. The Battle of Hexham, fought on May 15, 1464, and the subsequent executions ended the Lancastrian resistance. The queen fled to Anjou, and Henry was discovered hiding in a monastery and was taken to the Tower.

Warwick. Edward IV was truly king in his own right. During this time, Warwick was trying to assume dictatorial powers. He opposed the king's marriage to Elizabeth Woodville—he was trying to arrange a French marriage. Warwick found himself eclipsed by the new queen's family, the Woodvilles and the Greys. In 1467, the king openly broke with Warwick and repudiated the French treaty of alliance, favoring an alliance with Burgundy. Warwick then engineered a revolt among the Nevilles in the north. He also enlisted the support of the king's brother Clarence. Warwick landed at Kent with a force from Calais. The royal army was defeated and Edward was taken prisoner and handed over to Warwick, who executed many of Edward's leading supporters. But Edward managed to reverse the situation. The unsuccessful Lancastrian revolt in Lincolnshire in 1470 was attributed to Warwick, who was charged with trying to place Clarence on the throne. Warwick and Clarence fled to France and allied themselves with the Lancastrian cause.

In September, Warwick and Clarence landed at Devon, and many of Warwick's supporters rallied to his cause. Edward was forced to flee to the Low Countries, and Henry was released from the Tower and restored to the throne. Margaret refused to come to London and kept prince Edward with her. Clarence made peace with his brother, and Edward returned to fight in the Battle of Barnet on April 14. The Lancastrians were defeated, and Warwick and his brother Montagu were among those killed. On that same day, Margaret and prince Edward returned from France.

On May 4, 1471, Edward IV defeated the Lancastrians at Tewkesbury. He captured Henry VI, the queen, prince Edward, and many Lancastrian nobles. The prince was killed after the battle, along with the captured noblemen, and Henry was murdered in the Tower. Queen Margaret was also put in the Tower, where she remained until she was ransomed by her father. The lands of the defeated parties were given to his brothers Clarence and Richard. By 1477, Clarence's many plots caused the king to put him in the Tower, where he died six months later.

The last stage of the Wars of the Roses was the period between 1483 and 1487. Edward IV died in April, 1487. The events that followed his death are unclear, as his will did not survive. Richard, duke of Gloucester, was the intended regent, but he was not on the best of terms with the queen and her allies, many of whom had titles and important positions in the government. Unfortunately, a great deal of our knowledge of these events is clouded by Tudor propagandists, the chief among them being William Shakespeare. Having seen the consequences of the minority of Henry VI, Richard decided to take the throne for himself. His power base was in the north, as he had married Ann Neville, one of Warwick's daughters.

End of the Wars. RICHARD III ruled England for 26 months while the uncrowned Edward V and his younger brother languished in the Tower. The exact circumstances of their death remain obscure. The new king had to deal with a series of local rebellions led by Henry Tudor, earl of Richmond. On August 22, 1485, the armies of Richard III and Henry Tudor met at Bosworth Field. The royal army was defeated and Richard was killed. Henry Tudor was proclaimed Henry VII. The newly crowned king had to deal with his predecessor's supporters, which he did, surviving the plots and rebellion of Perkin Warbeck and Edward of Clarence. He further strengthened his hold on the crown with his marriage to Elizabeth of York. As king, Henry gave England a well-ordered central government and a regular system of TAXATION, and the nobility became reconciled to Tudor rule. (*See* ENGLAND; CADE, JACK; RICHARD III.)

Wars of the Roses Milestones

1422	Death of Henry V.
August 1453	Skirmish at Stamford Bridge between Percys and Nevilles.
May 22, 1455	Battle of St. Albans—first battle is won by the Yorkists.
July 10, 1460	Yorkist victory at Northhampton.
December 21, 1460	Major Lancastrian victory at Battle of Wakefield (Sandal Castle)
March 29, 1461	Yorkist Edward IV defeats Lancastrians at Towton.
May 4, 1471	Edward IV defeats Lancastrians at Tewkesbury; captures Henry VI.
1483	Death of Edward IV.
August 22, 1485	Decisive victory of Lancastrian Henry VII at Bosworth Field.

WEAPONRY

S oldiers in the Middle Ages employed a diverse array of weaponry, from expensive, rare swords to commonly available daggers. The use of weapons depended on whether the warrior was mounted or fought on foot, as well as on his SOCIAL CLASS. The cost of military technology meant that WARFARE was, in large measure, reserved for the wealthy—a fact that may explain why pitched battles between organized armies were such rare events. Successful campaigns had more to do with the construction and conquest of fortifications than with defeating the enemy on the field of battle. Consequently, siege tactics and artillery were central features of war during the Middle Ages. In the late fifteenth and sixteenth centuries, the main types of medieval weaponry—swords, lances, arrows, stone projectiles—became obsolete with the development of guns and gunpowder, much more efficient methods for the creation of mayhem.

Cavalry was the dominant, but not exclusive, type of soldiery in the Middle Ages. The efficiency of the cavalry charge was dependent on the organization of the charge; a well-timed charge could crush anything before it. The expense of the apparatus of knightly warfare—sword, lance, knightly armor—was too great except for the wealthiest landlord. While in mythic portrayals of medieval warfare the lance is pictured as the primary cavalry weapon, in fact, the sword was the most important weapon wielded by horsemen in battle. While the lance increased the force of the cavalry charges, it clearly took second place to the sword.

The Sword. Swords were the grandest weapons in the Middle Ages. Their virtues were sung in epics, and some accorded the sword magical powers. Unlike other weapons, which emerged from HUNTING, the sword developed solely as a killing instrument in combat between humans. Swords were very expensive and therefore a killing tool solely of the elite. The high cost of swords sprang in part from the difficulty of their construction. Blacksmiths hammered and welded together thin strips of steel and iron in the center, then added sharp edges of hard steel.

Swords were often constructed on the specific instructions of individuals, and consequently one finds a wide variety of them in the Middle Ages. Nevertheless, some patterns in sword design can be discerned. From the eleventh to the thirteenth century, double-edged swords were made for maximum killing efficiency in a slashing movement. From the mid-fourteenth to the sixteenth century, swords were made with a sharp point that was functional for a thrusting strike. This latter development corresponded with the increased use of plate armor that was harder to penetrate than the older chain mail.

The early lance was a simple wood pole, 10 to 12 feet long, with a steel point. Longer and lighter lances were used by the armies of the Byzantine Empire and the Muslims. From the end of the fourteenth century, the lance grew heavier, thicker, and broader. In the full body plate armor that developed in the fifteenth century, a resting place for the lance was made part of the breastplate. Although mostly an offensive weapon used in the charge of the mounted knights, the lance may sometimes have been used in a defensive manner by knights who had been dismounted. Despite its reputation as the knightly weapon par excellence, the lance had limitations. It was easily broken and, amid the whirlwind of battle, was difficult to replace.

Infantry. Although cavalry was the central weapon in the Middle Ages, the infantry played an important role. The infantry was used as a shield for the cavalry in siege warfare and as an additional striking force in pitched battles. The weapons of the infantry were particularly varied. Spears, about nine feet long, were common weapons. Spear-bearers were often grouped together, forming a hedge of spears, in order to stop fearsome cavalry charges. Two-handed swords were used by the infantry. Daggers were popular tools for killing knights through openings in armor as well as for mercy killing of the wounded. A variety of axes were employed in the Middle Ages, often as thrown weapons but sometimes as hand weapons. The most famous axe-bearers were the ANGLO-SAXONS, who wielded a two-headed axe. Other weapons included the flail, a threshing instrument, altered by the attachment of balls and chains; spiked clubs encased in iron; and mallets.

In the fourteenth century, the Swiss cantons created the most efficient infantry force in the history of the Middle Ages with their feared weapons of the halberd and the pike. The halberd had an ax-shaped head with a hammer or spike on the other side, and the pike was a spear about 15 to 18 feet long. Whereas the pike had previously been a defensive weapon, the Swiss transformed it into a devastating offensive instrument. Swiss soldiery was organized into moving blocks of pikemen that were almost invincible when competently commanded. The halberd was used as part of the block of pikemen, and sometimes halberd bearers formed their own blocked formations.

Bows and Arrows. Projectile warfare was common in the Middle Ages. At the start of this period, slings were still used but were eventually made obsolete by the growing use of the bow and arrow. The place of arrows in medieval warfare has been the sub-

Miniature from late medieval work Coquetes de Charlemagne *bears the caption "Single combat to be decided by the judgment of God." In spite of weapons, shields, and armor, the outcome was believed to be divinely ordained.*

ject of a vigorous debate among historians. One view is that archery became central on the battlefield in the fourteenth century. The successes of the British during the HUNDRED YEARS' WAR are explained by the revolutionary efficiency of the Welsh "longbow." Another view rejects the theory of a fourteenth-century "revolution" in archery. According to this historical interpretation, military leaders recognized the importance of archers as early as the ninth century. The English, from this perspective, did not make a better bow and arrow, but simply used archers in greater numbers.

Two types of bows were used in the West: self-bows and crossbows. Self-bows were constructed out of wood. In general, the elementary nature of self-bows meant that little technical improvement was possible, although the weapon did become more powerful if the arms were lengthened. Different types of arrowheads were utilized in the Middle Ages. Broadhead arrows were useful against unarmored people or horses, while narrow, square heads were needed to penetrate armor.

The development of the crossbow was a central event in the history of medieval warfare. Though the crossbow existed in antiquity, it only came to be employed widely in the late eleventh century. The devastating power of the crossbow was widely recognized, so much so that a religious council banned its use against Christians while recommending its use against heathens. In a crossbow, the bow was set horizontally on a stock or tiller and fired much like a rifle. The crossbow had a number of advantages. It carried weighted arrows that ripped through most armor. Smaller men were able to fire the crossbow across long

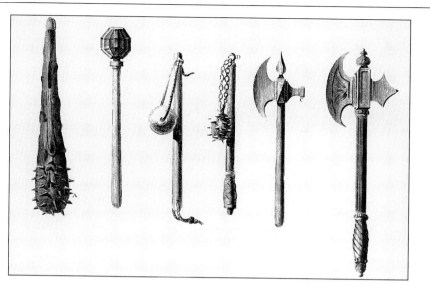

Medieval weapons were designed for fighting at close quarters. From left, a spiked club; a hammer club; two versions of the ball-and-chain; and two axes—a poleax, which combines the features of a hammer, ax, and dagger; and a halberd, which could be used as a dagger or as an ax. All required strength and skill.

distances. Finally, the crossbow could keep an arrow in place; thus it could be preloaded. The main disadvantage of crossbows is that they took a long time to reload. The crossbowman sometimes required the help of an assistant to help with the loading process. Even with an assistant, loading took so long that crossbowmen required the protection of pavises, large shields, lest they be decimated by archers who reloaded with far greater speed.

Gunpowder. Cannons and gunpowder also helped to revolutionize warfare in the Middle Ages. Before the cannon, stone projectiles were hurled at castles by various instruments. Ballistas were like huge crossbows, inherited from Roman times, that hurled stones through a torsion effect. The mangonel, also activated by torsion, used a slingshot motion. The most useful precannon artillery device was the trebuchet, which worked like a spring or seesaw. The short end of the device was weighted by a large object; a spring on the long end held the projectile. When it was fired, the long end was compressed and released. The trebuchet could hurl objects 200 to 400 yards.

Early uses of gunpowder included "sapping"; that is, the placing of explosives at the base of a castle wall. The fundamental change in warfare took place in the fourteenth and fifteenth centuries with the invention and increasing use of cannon. In its primitive stage, the cannon often backfired and recoiled. Quickly, however, the cannon became an essential tool of siege tactics and changed the face of medieval warfare. The use of cannon by the French brought a quick end to the long Hundred Years' War and helped the OTTOMAN TURKS occupy CONSTANTINOPLE. The efficiency of cannons against castles and over distances led to the use of artillery by both the besieged and the besiegers.

See ARMS AND ARMOR; ARTILLERY; CASTLES AND FORTIFICATIONS; CHIVALRY; CRUSADES; HERALDRY; HUNTING AND FOWLING; KNIGHTHOOD; KNIGHTS OF ST. JOHN; KNIGHTS OF THE TEMPLE; TOURNAMENTS; *and* WARFARE.

WENDS

The Wends were a collection of Slavonic tribes who settled in the region east of the Elbe and Saale Rivers. They defeated the AVARS to the south in 623 and, eight years later, the FRANKS at Wogastisburg. By the ninth century, the Wends were organized in federations with a tribal and clan structure whose pagan practices invited conversion attempts by neighboring Christian states. These missionary efforts at converting the pagan tribes had no effect until the tenth century, when the Saxon emperors of GERMANY instituted a new policy of Christianization by the sword. In 929, HENRY I's army put down a Wend revolt at Elbe, and the Wends were forced to accept CHRISTIANITY. The HOLY ROMAN EMPIRE defeated the Wends at Mecklenberg in 955. In 983, the Wends revolted against the Germans and reinstated paganism; they also instituted FEUDALISM. In 1147, they sacked Lübeck and defeated the Danes, but HENRY THE LION, the duke of Saxony, quickly annexed the Wends' territory. In 1162, the Wends surrendered to the Germans and Danes after their defeat at Demmin. (*See* SLAVS.)

WESSEX

Wessex was one of the ANGLO-SAXON kingdoms in ENGLAND during the early Middle Ages. According to West Saxon legend, Cerdic led the Saxons, who landed in Hampshire about 500. His grandson Ceawlin unified the Saxon settlements in the area and drove the Celts out of the land between the upper Thames valley and the lower Severn. In the 600s and 700s, the West Saxon region was overshadowed by a succession of stronger Saxon states: Kent, Northumbria, and Mercia. Egbert, king of Wessex (802–839), established himself as overlord of England, but his successors were forced to give up many of his gains and defend Wessex against Danish invaders.

The reign of King ALFRED THE GREAT (871–899) and the defeat of the Danes put Wessex at the center of the English political stage. In the 900s, the West Saxon kings—Edward the Elder, Athelstan, Edmund, and Edred—succeeded in establishing their control over virtually all of England, including the Danish enclave of the Danelaw. However, the unity collapsed when King ETHELRED (978–1016) was unable to resist the new wave of Danish invaders and their leader Cnut, who established his rule over England in 1016. The end of of Danish rule led to the reign of King EDWARD THE CONFESSOR (1042–1066), the last of the Wessex kings descended from Alfred the Great.

WESTMINSTER ABBEY

Westminster Abbey is best known as the church in which English monarchs are crowned. Located in LONDON, the imposing structure is also one of the most famous examples of GOTHIC architecture in Britain. Built in the English Gothic style but with noteworthy French touches, it has been called "the most French of all English Gothic churches."

The site where Westminster Abbey now stands was originally the home of a small monastery (*minster* originally meant "monastery"), which was enlarged by St. Dunstan about the tenth century. In the middle of the eleventh century, EDWARD THE CONFESSOR built a

Late medieval engraving of interior of Westminster Abbey.

new church on the site, which was consecrated in 1065. He died the following year and is buried there. WILLIAM I THE CONQUEROR was crowned at Westminster Abbey; since then, every English monarch except for Edward V and Edward VII (who were never actually crowned) has been crowned there.

In 1245, HENRY III tore down everything but the nave of the church and built the present structure. Henry admired the French cathedrals, and his first architect, Henry of Reims, was French. Although the abbey is English in character, its height and additions, such as flying buttresses, unquestionably indicate French influence. Later the old nave was replaced—a job that began in 1376, but was not completed until the next century. (*See* GOTHIC ART.)

Many kings and queens are buried at Westminster Abbey, although none have been buried there since George II in 1760. Many famous Britons, from Oliver Cromwell to T. S. Eliot, are also buried there, as is the Unknown Warrior from the First World War.

WILLIAM I THE CONQUEROR

William I (1028–1087), known as William the Conqueror, was the duke of Normandy. He conquered ENGLAND and became its king in 1066. He was a remarkably talented man whose political and military skills earned him a leading position in the European affairs of his day. His conquest of England forever changed the course of English history.

Early Years. He was born the illegitimate son of Robert I, duke of Normandy, and Herleve, daughter of Fulbert of Falaise, a tanner, in 1028. William was only six years old when the Norman lords named him heir to the duchy at the insistence of his father, who was about to leave on a pilgrimage to the Holy Land. Robert died in Asia Minor while returning from Jerusalem; his death ignited a power struggle in the duchy, from which William barely escaped with his life. Four of his guardians were murdered, one of them killed in the very room where the boy was sleeping.

William survived thanks in large part to assistance from the king of France, HENRY I. In 1046–1047 William's cousin, Guy of Burgundy, tried to seize control of the duchy with the help of some other rebellious Norman lords, but Henry's intervention helped William defeat them at Val-es-Dunes in 1047. His position remained vulnerable, however, because of continued internal dissent, hostile Anjou to the south, and a change in French royal policy. Only after he had successfully defended his duchy against invasions by the count of Anjou and by FRANCE was William secure.

His Reign. William strengthened his authority

over the Norman nobility, consolidated his control over the Church, and enlarged his domain. Between 1054 and 1064, William extended his influence to Ponthieu, the Norman Vexin, BRITTANY, and Maine and achieved a Flemish alliance with his marriage to Matilda, the daughter of Baldwin V, count of FLANDERS. William also made an alliance with the counts of Boulogne. His establishment of feudal ties and alliances with the nobles of the region solidified his position in northern France.

By 1065, William had unified Normandy, expanded his domain, established his superiority in northern France, and developed a solid working relationship with the Church. When King EDWARD THE CONFESSOR of England died childless in 1066, William was in a strong position to claim the throne. In 1051, King Edward, who was William's uncle, had invited William to England and, as William claimed later, promised that William should succeed him as his heir. In 1064, Harold, the English earl of WESSEX, visited William at Normandy. Harold was also a potential heir to the throne, but William claimed Harold's visit to Normandy was in deference to William as future king.

Battle of Hastings. When William learned that King Edward died and Harold had taken the throne, William secured the blessing of the pope, raised an army, gathered a fleet, and sailed for England. On October 14, 1066, William defeated Harold (who died in the battle) at Hastings. After overcoming resistance in southeastern England, William marched his army to LONDON, which surrendered to him peacefully. On Christmas Day, 1066—ten weeks after the Battle of Hastings—the Archbishop of Canterbury crowned William king of England in WESTMINSTER ABBEY.

William lost no time building and garrisoning castles around the country, but at the outset he allowed the English nobles who survived the Battle of Hastings to keep their lands. He harshly suppressed the rebellions that broke out in various parts of the country. He also called in the titles of the lands of the nobility and redistributed them to his Norman followers as part of his feudal restructuring of the country. The military portion of the Norman Conquest ended in 1072, when the NORMANS defeated the followers of Edgar Atheling and their Scottish and Danish allies.

William instituted reforms and changes that influenced the future course of the English church. He appointed LANFRANC OF BEC Archbishop of Canterbury, substituted European prelates for many English bishops, and took personal charge of church affairs. In 1076, he established a system of separate church courts. He ordered a survey of England, which was made in 1085–1086 and whose results were recorded in the DOMESDAY BOOK. In 1086, William instituted the Oath of Salisbury, which established the important

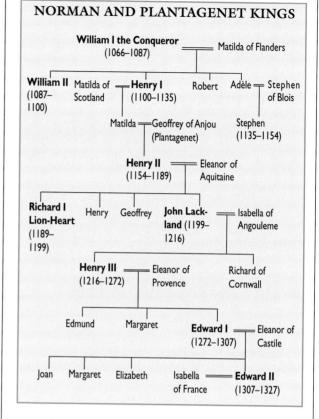

NORMAN AND PLANTAGENET KINGS

- William I the Conqueror (1066–1087) = Matilda of Flanders
  - William II (1087–1100)
  - Matilda of Scotland = Henry I (1100–1135)
    - Matilda = Geoffrey of Anjou (Plantagenet)
      - Henry II (1154–1189) = Eleanor of Aquitaine
        - Richard I Lion-Heart (1189–1199)
        - Henry
        - Geoffrey
        - John Lackland (1199–1216) = Isabella of Angouleme
          - Henry III (1216–1272) = Eleanor of Provence
            - Edmund
            - Margaret
            - Edward I (1272–1307) = Eleanor of Castile
              - Joan
              - Margaret
              - Elizabeth
              - Isabella of France = Edward II (1307–1327)
          - Richard of Cornwall
  - Robert
  - Adèle = Stephen of Blois
    - Stephen (1135–1154)

precedent that loyalty to the king supersedes loyalty to any subordinate feudal lord within the kingdom.

Two Domains. William spent the last two decades of his life traveling back and forth between his two domains—Normandy and England. In England he waged military campaigns against WALES and SCOTLAND, which strengthened English control over both regions. While in France, he seized more territory and successfully defended Normandy against the French king. William's formidable leadership skills were evident in his control over the Norman colonization of England and his ability to adapt English and Norman institutions to his rule. The close relationship that William established between England and France influenced the course of events in both countries.

William was fatally injured in a riding accident during a military campaign in France. He died in Rouen and was buried in a Norman abbey in the northern French town of Caen. He arranged for his two sons, Robert II and William II, to succeed him in Normandy and England respectively.

See HAROLD II GODWINSON; HASTINGS, BATTLE OF; NORMANS; DOMESDAY BOOK; *and* ENGLAND. *Also* BAYEUX TAPESTRY; ENGLISH LANGUAGE AND LITERATURE; FRANCE; LANFRANC OF BEC; LONDON; WARFARE; WESSEX.

WILLIAM I THE LION

During most of his long reign, William, king of SCOTLAND (1143–1214), had little choice but to be a vassal of English kings. He struggled to win and maintain his independence, but his successes were intermittent and short lived.

William was the son of Henry, sixth earl of Northumberland, and grandson of the Scottish king, David I. In 1165, at the age of 22, he succeeded his brother Malcolm IV as king of Scotland. Early in his reign he set out to recover Northumberland, his father's domain, seized by the English in 1157. Three years after he became king, William joined forces with King Louis VII of FRANCE against ENGLAND in what was the beginning of a long alliance with France.

In 1173, William supported the rebellion of the elder sons of HENRY II of England against their father in hopes of winning their backing for the restoration of his family's control of Northumberland. The sons—Henry, Richard, and Geoffrey—who received encouragement from Henry's wife, ELEANOR OF AQUITAINE, were allied with Louis VII of France; Philip, the count of FLANDERS; and an assortment of rebels in England and Normandy. The alliance directed against Henry launched a series of raids and revolts, but it was poorly coordinated. With the support of key barons, Henry was able to prevail against his enemies.

During the rebellion against Henry, William led his forces south into Northumberland. He was defeated and captured by Ranulf Glanvill, one of Henry's chief ministers, and was forced to sign the Treaty of Falaise (1174), which turned Scotland into an English fief. After his release, William asked the PAPACY in ROME to declare the Scottish church independent of English control. However, a quarrel with the papacy delayed the decision until 1188, when Pope Clement III declared the Scottish church subject only to Rome.

The following year, William took another step to win his independence from English control when he paid RICHARD I of England 10,000 marks to annul the Treaty of Falaise. In 1199, after John became the new English king, William resumed his efforts to win back Northumberland. He abandoned his claim in 1209, when John threatened armed attack and forced a harsh treaty on him.

William strengthened Scottish royal power by expanding the feudalization of his realm. He established feudal ties with local leaders in northern Scotland and suppressed several revolts. He also centralized and improved the administration of his kingdom. Although William never did succeed in freeing himself from his vassalage to the Crown, he was able to maintain that his ties of vassalage were based on his rule of land claimed by the English, not on his position as king of Scotland. Nonetheless, although he tried his best to fend off the territorial ambitions of the kings of England, he was forced to become a vassal of both Henry II and John. (*See* SCOTLAND; HENRY II.)

WILLIAM IX OF AQUITAINE

William IX (1071–1126), ninth duke of AQUITAINE and seventh count of Poitiers, was also one of the first TROUBADOURS. His poems are among the earliest existing examples of the troubadour's art, and he may have been the first poet to compose verse about COURTLY LOVE.

William was an active member of the aristocracy who went on two separate and lengthy crusades for the Church. But along with his sense of duty to his Church came a belief that life must not be taken too seriously. His poems reflect this; of eleven existing works, five are serious, focusing on love or CHIVALRY. But the other six are burlesques that mocked royalty, the Church, and even his own soul. One such poem was considered so offensive that later translators often refused to render the work into English. (*See* CHIVALRY; COURTLY LOVE; LITERATURE; MUSIC; TROUBADOURS.)

WILLIAM OF MALMESBURY

William of Malmesbury (c. 1090–1143), a Benedictine monk, was a historian whose chronicles of life in ENGLAND were known for their freshness and innovative style. His works served as the model for historical narratives through the late Middle Ages and beyond.

Born in England, William was educated at the MONASTERY at Malmesbury. Fascinated with history since childhood, but disappointed by the quality of historical works available to him, he decided to write his own histories. His best-known works are his *Gesta regum Anglorum* (a history of Anglo–Saxon England), *Gesta pontificum* (an ecclesiastical history) and *Historia novella* (a history of his contemporary England). William made effective use of stories and anecdotes in his works to help hold the reader's interest. He also was among the first historians to use nonwritten records (he might use local architecture, for example) on which to base his observations.

William spent many years as librarian of Malmesbury Abbey, turning down the chance to serve as its abbot. He died there in 1143.

WILLIAM OF OCKHAM

Like many great thinkers, the medieval philosopher William of Ockham (also Occam; c. 1285–1349) suffers the curse of being known overwhelmingly for one principle. But it is an important one: "Ockham's razor" states that the simplest explanation for any problem is the best explanation. Ockham developed this principle in reaction to philosophers who tried to explain abstract problems by adding more and more steps to their theories to make them appear more valid. He believed that adding these additional steps subverted the truth and only served to force unworkable ideas. Ockham's razor has long been considered one of the most valuable rules of science.

Early Life. William of Ockham was born in Ockham (near Surrey), ENGLAND. Like the philosopher DUNS SCOTUS, he became a FRANCISCAN FRIAR and studied at Oxford. During Ockham's lifetime, the philosophy of SCHOLASTICISM, which tried to combine worldly, philosophical, and religious ideas into one unified belief system, had become quite popular. But Ockham's views did not mesh with those of the Scholastics at the University of Paris. To begin with, he believed that God's power was an absolute that could not and need not be explained by reason. Nor was it an abstract notion. God's power was simply a matter of faith. Moreover, as long as God existed, nothing else was truly necessary. Ockham thus struck a blow against the Scholastics by claiming that there was no need to assign rational ideas to religion.

His Work. Ockham's PHILOSOPHY is often called nominalism (although in reality it was only a part of his belief system). Abstract terms, said Ockham, were merely "names" that did not exist in reality, but only in the mind. Only objects that were actually perceived were real. He also believed that some scientific principles could only be known through actual experience instead of reason. Therefore it was possible to create a world of nature based on scientific reason, but the way to God came only from revelation and personal religious experience. By proffering this philosophy, Ockham was the great antagonist of THOMAS AQUINAS.

Scholasticism was not Ockham's only target. He had strong opinions about theology as well. One of his most controversial beliefs was that transubstantiation—the belief that the bread and wine used during the sacrament of Communion actually become the body and blood of Christ—was incorrect as stated. Instead, he argued, the body and blood of Christ occupied the space that was previously occupied by the bread and wine. In other words, there was no conversion of one material to another.

But the belief that generated the most controversy was Ockham's stand against papal supremacy. When Ockham was summoned to AVIGNON (then the papal seat) in 1324 on charges of HERESY, he began to study the writings of Pope John XXII. Soon, Ockham became convinced not only that papal supremacy was wrong, but that John himself was a heretic. In 1328, he fled Avignon and settled in BAVARIA, where he came under the protection of the Holy Roman Emperor Louis IV (a political opponent of the pope). Although he eventually made a halting peace with Avignon, he remained in Bavaria, where he spent the remainder of his life working on his writings and in conversations with MARSILIUS OF PADUA. He died in Munich about 1349, probably during the BLACK DEATH.

His Legacy. In the period 1350–1500, Ockham's ideas came to dominate universities in England and GERMANY and also challenged theories in Italy. Martin Luther said that he was a follower of Ockham. In important ways Ockham anticipated the ideas of the late eighteenth-century German philosopher Immanuel Kant. In the late twentieth century Ockham came to be regarded as possibly medieval Europe's greatest philosopher. (*See* PHILOSOPHY; SCHOLASTICISM.)

WILLIAM OF RUBRUQUIS

William of Rubruquis (also known as Willem van Ruysbroeck; c. 1215–c. 1295) was a French Franciscan friar who traveled to the Mongol empire for King LOUIS IX in the mid-thirteenth century. His report to the king is one of the most valuable medieval European accounts of Far Eastern culture and government.

Born in the French village of Rubrouck about 1215, William became a FRANCISCAN as a young man. He was in CONSTANTINOPLE in 1253 when Louis IX asked him to embark on an informal mission to Mongolia. William and his party traveled more than 5,000 miles by oxcart to the palace of the great khan at Karakorum, in central Mongolia. Received graciously by the khan, William and his party remained for nearly a year before setting forth on the journey back. Upon his return, he wrote a thorough, observant, and impartial account for the king. He died in 1295, not long after MARCO POLO returned from his travels.

WILLIAM OF WYKEHAM

William of Wykeham (1324–1404) was bishop of Winchester from 1367 to his death. He entered royal service in 1349 and rose to become a royal chancellor in 1367. In 1371, he was accused of malversation (misconduct) but was acquitted of the charge and returned to the chancellorship, serving until 1391. His great contribution to English life was the founding of New College of Oxford University (1380) and Winchester College (1382), originally a school built to provide housing for 70 poor scholars.

WITCHCRAFT AND SORCERY

A type of supernatural control over anything from illness to the weather that some human beings were believed to possess. As this power became increasingly suspect in the eyes of the Church, its practitioners, often called witches, were believed to be in concert with demonic forces. During the Middle Ages, hundreds of people, mostly women, were executed as heretics because they were thought to be witches. Saint JOAN OF ARC was burned as a witch in 1431. (*See* HERESY.)

Origins. Medieval witchcraft and sorcery evolved from ancient folk MEDICINE and healing practices. Before the time of Hippocrates, women were primarily in charge of healing and medicine. Many had a strong knowledge of botany, which enabled them to formulate herbal "cures" or palliatives. (*See* ALCHEMY; HERBALS; MEDICINE AND CARE OF THE SICK.)

By the fourth century C.E., science had gained a strong hold on the medical profession. Women were allowed a much smaller role in medical practice (although they continued to serve an important function in childbirth as midwives). Many continued to work with herbs and folk remedies; in time an element of MAGIC was introduced. So-called sorcerers would use not only herbs, but incantations that were designed to call forth spiritual powers. With the establishment of CHRISTIANITY, many of these incantations borrowed from Christian prayers and even the BIBLE itself. Sorcery became a mix of paganism, common folklore, and even normative religion.

Accusations of Heresy. As Christianity spread throughout Europe, the Church took an increasingly negative view of sorcery. When the influential ST. AUGUSTINE declared in the fifth century that magic was the work of evil spirits, the Church concluded that sorcerers were much worse than pagans—they were, in fact, it was alleged, actual worshippers of the Devil.

Witches, it was believed, consorted with evil spirits and through them followed the Devil's commands. Though they might claim to have the power to heal, they actually used their powers to inflict illness or death on their enemies. The use of midwives remained popular throughout the Middle Ages, but when a baby was stillborn or died shortly after birth (not at all an unusual occurrence), witchcraft—and hence the midwife—was often thought to be the culprit.

By the twelfth century, the Church had determined that witchcraft was HERESY, and embarked on a mission to eradicate all witchcraft and all witches. Heresy at that time was a crime punishable by death, usually by burning at the stake. By the time of the INQUISITION, suspected witches were routinely put on trial—always with the presumption that they were guilty. These individuals, after their arrest, would be excommunicated, tortured, and ultimately executed. It was hoped that through TORTURE the accused heretics would not only confess their crimes but also name other witches; many did, hoping to escape further pain, only to be put through more torture.

The image of the witch persisted well past the Middle Ages. Above, an engraving after Holbein of a witch, from a 16th-century German translation of Boethius's Consolations of Philosophy.

The antiwitch mania gained momentum with the publication of the Dominican friar Heinrich Institoris's *Malleus maleficarum* (*Hammer Against Witchcraft*) in 1486. Witchcraft trials continued for more than two centuries afterward.

Was it malicious persecution of innocent people that lay behind the witchcraft craze, particularly hostility towards aging women who were considered a burden to their families and could be judicially and conveniently removed as heretical witches? Or was there an actual increase in the practice of witchcraft by would-be witches and practitioners of the occult during this era, one serving as a release from the economic and psychological stresses in late medieval society? Historians have been able to discern both forces at work. (*See* MAGIC AND FOLKLORE; MEDICINE; *and* WOMEN.)

WOLFRAM VON ESCHENBACH

The medieval poet Wolfram von Eschenbach (c. 1170–c. 1220) is best known for his epic poems *Parzifal* and *Willehalm*, but in a lifespan of less than 50 years he managed to compose some 40,000 verses.

Despite his prolific output, most of the details of his life remain unknown. Probably born in BAVARIA, he is believed to have been a Rhineland knight who worked under the patronage of a German noble. He may also have been a minnesinger—the German equivalent of a TROUBADOUR. *Parzifal* is based on the Arthurian legend of the knight Percival and the Holy Grail; it contains a great deal of religious symbolism. The Grail symbolizes redemption, the Grail Kingdom symbolizes heaven, and so on. Parzifal's adventures can may also be viewed as symbolic of human suffering. But Wolfram may have meant the poem to convey a political message. Its detailed account of the exploits, successes, and setbacks of the young Parzifal would have had a strong impact on young knights and nobles of the HOLY ROMAN EMPIRE trying to find the path to leadership. The nineteenth-century composer Richard Wagner set the story to music in the opera *Parsifal*, in which von Eschenbach appears as one of the characters. (*See* ARTHUR, KING; LITERATURE.)

Wolfram also began the poem *Titurel*, which he never completed. Also based on Arthurian legend, it tells the story of Titurel, Parzifal's great-grandfather, and his efforts to safeguard the Holy Grail.

WOMEN

Medieval women's lives were as diverse as men's. It is only in the past few decades that scholars have come to recognize the importance of medieval women's contributions and added women to the general histories of the age.

Women contributed to all the major movements that spelled success for an emerging European civilization. These areas included economy, politics, religion, and literature. Undoubtedly, the achievements of some particular women have been lost to historical memory. But a significant number of women gained recognition for their individual dedication and accomplishments, and the impression they left upon culture and society.

Early Middle Ages. In the early Middle Ages, that is, in the age of conversion and settlement in Europe, monastic women participated in establishing the Christian religion anew. In the age after the breakup of the CAROLINGIAN empire, in the tenth and eleventh centuries, women played even more significant roles. The tenth century was so filled with war it has often been called the age of iron. A few forceful women with land and inheritance rights (strong family backing) achieved impressive gains. They were rulers over property and castles and exercised rights of justice and military command. They were the proprietors of churches, and participated in important assemblies of leaders of Church and state. Women's monastic houses, particularly those on the Iberian Peninsula and in what is today GERMANY, were led by a series of able women administrators. Matilda, daughter of the Holy Roman Emperor OTTO I, ruled vast lands from her monastic house at Quedlinburg and won the title of metropolitana (ruler over bishops) from her clerical biographer. Great houses such as Matilda's made significant contributions to the pacification that helped usher in the prosperity of the late eleventh and twelfth centuries in Europe. Women contributed as well in agricultural production; as alemakers, glassmakers, and textile workers; in sales as fishwives; or as associates of their husbands in the heavier industries of coopering, smithing, tanning, and salt panning. A flexible division of labor between men and women produced industrious families that lent their skills and labor to the development of agricultural surplus and the growth of TOWNS.

Religion. This earlier age differed from the age that would follow. While misogynous arguments had been present within the inherited corpus of Christian writings, they had seldom been trotted out while women were sources of patronage and livings for clerical scribes, who were the influential writers of the age. In the Gregorian reform, an effort to reform the PAPACY of the late eleventh and twelfth centuries, much control was removed from the hands of secular rulers, women and men alike, in the appointment of priests and bishops. Devout women, like the Abbess Matilda of Quedlinburg of an earlier day, were deprived of their power and influence. In an attempt to end clerical marriage, authorities attacked women as corrupting influences. Religious women tended to turn toward mysticism; the last nonmystical literary composition attributed to a nun in the Middle Ages is the *Hortus deliciarum*, written in prose and poetry in part by Herrad of Landsberg between 1160 and 1170. Secular women lost authority to the more complex institutional bureaucracies of Church and state.

The twelfth century, in spite of these pressures and changing social contexts, was the great age of women's contributions to medieval religion, literature, and music. Abbess HILDEGARD OF BINGEN (d. 1178) in western Germany published devotional literature that won the approval of the papacy. Her writings also demonstrate a quiet but persistent claim to women's equality (or more) with men as servants of Christ. (Her songs, combining liturgical and popular strains, have become very well known in recent decades.)

Aristocratic women such as ELEANOR OF AQUITANE, queen of ENGLAND, and her daughter, Countess Marie of Champagne, were major patrons of vernacular writers, including at least one accomplished woman poet, MARIE DE FRANCE. The sensitivity in this romance poetry to the relationships between men and women, and the psychological aspects of human love, directly reflects the attitudes and interests of the great literary patronesses.

Defining Gender. In the revival of learning of the twelfth and thirteenth centuries, the ideas of ARISTOTLE took on new importance. As a result, notions of gender increased in circulation and consequence, becoming more authoritative over time when they provided a rationale for new actualities. Thomas Aquinas adopted Aristotle's polar scheme for defining "woman" (note the singular). A set of qualities associated with male—limit, odd, one, right, square, at rest, straight, light, and good—were opposed to a parallel alignment of traits associated with female—unlimited, even, plurality, left, oblong, moving, curved, darkness, and evil. In the *Summa Theologica*, Question 92, Aquinas defined man as the image of God in being active, formative, and tending toward perfection. Woman, on the other hand, was defined as opposite, or passive, material, and deprived of the tendency toward perfection. This set of assumptions, when applied to women's rights in law, to their participation in ruling assemblies, or GUILDS, or institutions of learning, meant that women could be excluded on the grounds of their incapacity. Flexible assumptions about gender that had prevailed in the earlier Middle Ages were being replaced by more rigid assumptions about woman's nature and natural subordination.

Women saw their inheritance rights curtailed as well as their participation in the emerging institutions of the increasingly complex European civilization that they had helped to build. They did not, however, cease making significant contributions to medieval life. Since polar notions of gender were applied in only a sporadic and arbitrary manner to everyday life, women could often continue to make contributions to society

and produce for the economy even while they were being shut out of positions of authority. In some instances they continued to write, as was the case with CHRISTINE OF PISAN (1364–c. 1430) who stoutly defended women, in all their variety, as equals to men.

Power and Discrimination. In the barbarian society of the Germanic kingdoms in the early Middle Ages, women of the nobility had a greater freedom of action and share of power than in the organized state and family-driven world after 1150. Yet the cult of the Virgin Mary, central to devotional life in the later centuries of the Middle Ages, propagated a feminized piety at the very time that the legal and scholastic structures were placing women's behavior under restraint. The rise of the UNIVERSITIES as centers of learn-

The Three Virtues—Reason, Uprightness, and Justice—urge Christine de Pisan (in bed, presumably in a dream) to write a book of ethics for women to be used for instruction, right. Miniature from the 1405 work Livre des Vertus.

ing in the period after 1150, with their strictly male population, was decisive in reducing women's role in the shaping of late medieval culture. There was some alleviation of this categorical marginalism of women during the Italian classical Renaissance of the fifteenth century, but even there women suffered from the male educational privileges. The key schools in the Renaissance were of secondary not higher education, but the classical humanist schools refused women access to learning almost as severely as the universities had done. There was enormous gender discrimination, therefore, in the cultural and intellectual areas of medieval life after 1150.

In all centuries among the peasant and artisan classes, women's labor was channeled in rough equality with men. Women did a large share of farm work, and in the cities common industries like brewing were dominated by women's productivity. In the thirteenth and fourteenth centuries as women's access to learned culture deteriorated in the face of universities and the classical humanist schools, women came to play a greater role in elementary education and in health and counseling services, especially in urban areas. The second woman's order of the Franciscans, the order of Claire, and the lay women's communal associations called the BEGUINES, were prime avenues for this role.

See FAMILY LIFE; MEDICINE AND CARE OF THE SICK; SOCIAL CLASSES AND CLASS CONFLICT; FEUDALISM; SERFS AND SERFDOM. *Also see articles on the lives of women, such as* JOAN OF ARC; HILDEGARD OF BINGEN; THEODORA.

WOOL TRADE

The principal region supplying raw wool in the Middle Ages was ENGLAND, because of its ideal climate—cool and damp—for raising thick-coated sheep. GERMANY, SPAIN, and FLANDERS also exported wool, but on a smaller scale and of lesser quality. (*See* CLOTHING AND COSTUME; FUR TRADE.)

Raw wool was combed, cleaned, woven into cloth, and then dyed. In the early thirteenth century, only two major dyes were used: woad, a deep blue, and madder, a bright red. *Grain*, or *kermes*, a scarlet dye that was both rare and valuable, was used to produce garments for royalty and the wealthy. As more dyes became available through trade with the East, and the cloth-making industry became more organized and well developed, more dye colors became available.

FRANCE and ITALY emerged as secondary producers of cloth in the late Middle Ages. Italian cloth merchants had an advantage in the production of cloth because of their status as papal tax collectors in England, where they were free to trade for the highest-quality raw wool. Several European FAIRS, most notably the one at CHAMPAGNE, developed where wool from England was traded for goods from all over Europe and beyond. The first commodity that members of the HANSEATIC LEAGUE traded in and regulated was wool and wool products. (*See* HANSEATIC LEAGUE.)

GUILDS of cloth producers formed to control the quality of the wool, the dyes, and the finishing; arrange for the transport of raw wool; and negotiate increased wages and reduced tariffs for the industry. Members of these guilds were financially and politically powerful and often enjoyed special status from the crown.

Two advances in production revolutionized the production of cloth from wool: the spinning wheel and the fulling MILL. The running water necessary to oper-

A 14th-century miniature from a work by Boccaccio depicting the character Tanaquil (also known as Gaia Caecilia) at a loom with other women spinning wool. A large percentage of wool cloth was created from thread spun on thousands of looms in homes throughout England and the Low Countries.

ate these mechanisms required the cloth-making industry to move from urban to rural areas. As a result, the primary areas of wool production by the fifteenth century became the Cotswolds and East Anglia, where landowners became powerful and wealthy.

Wool also created political ties that monarchs found difficult to counter: Flanders and European countries dependent on English raw wool for their textile industry openly supported England in its various wars with France and the NORMANS.

WORMS, CONCORDAT OF

The Concordat of Worms was a compromise reached between the Church and the HOLY ROMAN EMPIRE. It was signed by Pope Calixtus II and Holy Roman Emperor Henry V in 1122.

A debate that had been ongoing through the Middle Ages (and has lasted into modern times) developed into a heated power struggle between HENRY IV and Pope GREGORY VII at the end of the eleventh century. The debate concerned who was to dispose of Church offices. Were abbots and bishops to be chosen by the Church? Or, since the abbots and bishops were subjects of the crown, were they to be chosen by the emperor or kings, and invested with the symbols of ecclesiastical office by them?

The debate, called the INVESTITURE CONTROVERSY, lasted for a number of years, with no resolution in sight. But a similar problem between the Church and the English kings had been settled in 1107; drawing from that model, the two sides spent the next 15 years working toward a similar settlement.

Under the Concordat of Worms, the power to elect bishops and abbots would rest with the Church, but the emperor would be allowed to decide any election that was contested. In addition, any bishop or abbot was to be invested first with the powers and privileges of a vassal to the emperor, known as the *regalia,* and second with the parallel privileges of the Church, or the *spiritualia.* The Church thereby gained recognition of its spiritual autonomy, but in practice the crown continued to control the selection of bishops and abbots. (*See* INVESTITURE CONTROVERSY.)

WULFILA

ulfila (also Ulfilas; c. 311–c. 383), the Arian bishop to the VISIGOTHS, instrumental in the development of a written GERMAN LANGUAGE. Wulfila created a GOTHIC alphabet through a combination of Greek and Latin letters in order to translate scripture. His written works were essential in the transmission of aspects of Roman civilization to the Germanic peoples.

Wulfila was born in Visigothic territory west of the Danube. He converted to the heretical Christian Arian sect as a young man when living in CONSTANTINOPLE. The Arian clergy anointed him bishop and commissioned him to convert the Visigoths. After Wulfila gained an Arian following among the Visigoths, he and his small flock were compelled to flee to the south of the Danube because of persecution by a pagan Visigothic king. Although exiled, Wulfila continued his vocation by sending missionaries to the trans-Danubian Visigoths. The Visigoths were eventually converted to Arianism under their Christian chief, Frithigern. Wulfila died in Constantinople, where he had gone to settle a dispute among the city's Arians.

WULFSTAN OF YORK

ulfstan of York (also known by his Latin name, "Lupus"; d. 1023) was a religious leader and political adviser in ENGLAND in the early part of the eleventh century. He possessed a talent for both writing and politics; in addition to penning numerous religious pieces, he helped draft many English laws and provided political advice to both kings ETHELRED II the Unready and Cnut.

Religious Career. Where and when Wulfstan was born is unknown; he may have been a Benedictine monk, but this too is unclear. What is known about him with certainty is that he became bishop of LONDON in 996 and remained in that position until 1002.

At that point, he was named bishop of both Worcester and York. He held the Worcester position until 1016 and the York position until his death seven years later.

During his service as bishop, Wulfstan wrote several pastoral pieces, including the *Canons of Edgar.* His writing style is so distinctive that it has been easy for scholars to recognize and document it. He is also considered one of the most original writers in England up to the time of the Norman Conquest of 1066.

Wulfstan also enlisted the help of the renowned writer and theologian AELFRIC, who wrote two pastoral letters for him. Wulfstan's best-known work is his homily *Sermo Lupi ad Anglos* ("Wulfstan's Sermon to the English"), which he wrote about 1014. It is a passionate call to Englishmen to reclaim what he saw as lost morality and reform their lives. Wulfstan was concerned about the state of religious affairs in England; his writings advocated Church reform, particularly in determining the relationship of Church and state.

Political Career. Wulfstan's interests did not rest solely with religious matters. Extremely interested in society and politics, he became an influential political adviser in the last two decades of his life. One of his best works about social justice is his *Institutes of Polity,* which, in addition to again defining Church versus state powers, discusses the responsibilities of all individuals and classes, from king to peasant.

His other writings include drafts of legal codes (civil as well as ecclesiastical) and laws for the men who served as king of England during his service as bishop. His role as adviser to Ethelred and Cnut was timely, as England was then in a period of upheaval.

Ethelred II ruled from 978 to 1013 and again from 1014 to 1016. A weak ruler who was suspected of murdering his half brother to succeed to the throne, Ethelred has been blamed for the successful Danish invasions of England beginning in 980 and lasting beyond his death 36 years later. Ethelred was briefly ousted as king in 1014 when Sweyn I Forkbeard (Cnut's son) was accepted as king in his place. The events surrounding Ethelred's ouster and Sweyn's installation as king served in part to influence Wulfstan to write *Sermo Lupi ad Anglos.* But Sweyn soon died and Ethelred was invited back to the throne, which he held until his death in April 1016. Wulfstan advised the king, beginning in 1008, and helped draft his laws, but was unable to keep Ethelred from making many of the mistakes he made.

Cnut proved to be a better pupil and a far more able ruler. When he first became king of England in 1016, he was not friendly toward the English. He confiscated a number of English estates and gave them to Danish supporters; he also installed several VIKINGS in administrative positions. As for his advisers, he surrounded himself with other Danes. But gradually Cnut warmed to the English. Eventually, he invited Wulfstan and others to serve as advisers. Wulfstan is credited with convincing Cnut to rule England as a benevolent ruler, not as a conqueror. Drafts of laws from the period display Wulfstan's distinctive style.

Cnut proved to be an effective king. Under his reign, England enjoyed peace and prosperity. He also became an important ally of the Church, visiting ROME and making many generous donations, again indicative of Wulfstan's influence at work.

Wulfstan worked on behalf of the Church and England for the rest of his life; he died in May 1023.

WYCLIFFE, JOHN

The controversial English theologian John Wycliffe (c. 1330–1384, also Wyclif) is best known today as the scholar who initiated the first full English translation of the BIBLE (known as the Wycliffe Bible). During his lifetime, he earned a reputation as a stalwart advocate of Church reform. His views on Church doctrine and the role of the clergy made him a hero to many and provided him with a large following. But the Church saw him as a heretic, spending many years trying to silence him. Ultimately, Wycliffe's ideas influenced the religious hierarchy in Europe; many scholars say he was instrumental in events leading to the Protestant Reformation.

Early Life. Wycliffe was born in a small village in Yorkshire about 1330 and was educated at Oxford, where he later taught for nearly 30 years. He was a follower of SCHOLASTICISM, the philosophy that tried to reconcile the teachings of respected philosophers with the teachings of the Church. Over the course of his teaching career he wrote several philosophical and theological texts, and served as a rector in several parishes.

Beginnings as a Reformer. Wycliffe was trained in theology and PHILOSOPHY, and many of his writings deal with those subjects. But ultimately, he made his name in matters that were decidedly practical in scope. During a meeting of PARLIAMENT in 1371, he expressed his agreement with those who believed Church property could be seized in times of emergency by whoever ruled the country. This was the beginning of Wycliffe's trouble with the Church establishment.

Soon, Wycliffe was attacking the clergy and Church doctrine itself. He differentiated between what he called the "actual Church" and the "true Church." The actual Church, he explained, was the hierarchical structure created by the clergy. The true Church, however, consisted of those who truly believed in the Church's teachings. Wycliffe condemned what he saw as the hypocrisy of the clergy, many of whom lived amid great wealth. The Bible, which he considered the sole authority on matters religious, did not sanction opulent lives for servants of the Church. But he also condemned the monastic life. The Bible did not teach, he claimed, that individuals should be separated from others—and monks could not associate even with other churchgoers.

If the Bible was the sole source of Church doctrine, Wycliffe further reasoned, members of the clergy could only exercise the authority of their office as laid out by Scripture. Not even the pope, he said, had unquestionable authority; true authority came only from the Bible.

Church Response. The Church was furious with Wycliffe over his pronouncements. Pope Gregory XI called for his arrest in 1377. Wycliffe was fortunate enough to have influential friends able to protect him from the Church's wrath (the royal family had not forgotten his stand on Church property). But in 1380, Wycliffe crossed yet another line with his contention that transubstantiation (the belief that the bread and wine of Holy Communion actually become the body and blood of Christ during the Mass) was not supported by the Bible. Now Wycliffe had disparaged one of the sacraments. A commission at Oxford condemned his teachings as heretical. Although he was not punished, he was forced to leave Oxford. He spent the last few years of his life in the town of Lutterworth, where he continued to write and speak out against the clergy until his death on the last day of 1384.

Continued Influence. Wycliffe's influence went beyond his teachings. Although scholars doubt that he actually worked on what would become known as the Wycliffe Bible, (Nicholas Hereford is believed to have done much of the work), it was at his instigation that the Bible was translated from Latin into English. For the first time, individuals who could read English but not Latin would be able to read their own Bible.

Wycliffe attracted a large following during his lifetime; after his death, many of his followers (known as LOLLARDS) took up the task of reforming the Church. They encouraged people to read the Bible, and they preached against the excesses of the Church. HERESY was made a capital crime in England in 1401, and the Lollards were branded heretics soon afterward; many were executed for their activities. Wycliffe's teachings spread beyond the British Isles, however. In Bohemia, JAN HUS, rector of the UNIVERSITY OF PRAGUE, formed a movement based on Wycliffe's philosophy; its followers were known as Hussites. The Hussites were to be an important reforming religious and social force in BOHEMIA during the fifteenth century, as the Lollards had been in England a century earlier. (*See* HUS, JOHN; BIBLE; PHILOSOPHY.)

YAROSLAV THE WISE

Yaroslav (d. 1054) ruled a united Russian nation during the eleventh century. His drafting of a law code for the young nation earned him the name Yaroslav "the Wise." His reign is seen as the high point of the Kievan Rus civilization.

He was the son of Vladimir I, who gave him the city of Rostov in 988. From 1010 to 1019, Yaroslav ruled NOVGOROD. He granted the city a charter, thus marshaling support when he was named grand prince of Kiev in 1019. Vladimir's death sparked a brutal civil war, and Yaroslav fought his brother Mstislav for control of the land. In 1036, Mstislav died, and Yaroslav gained control of the entire country.

Yaroslav extended Russian territory to the south and west, leading armies against the Poles, the Baltic realms, and the Byzantine Empire. Though Yaroslav had been lame since he was a boy, he proved brave in battle. He made Kiev a major trade center and extended Russia into Europe through marriage: his daughter Anne married King Henry I of France in 1044, and his sisters and daughters married into the royal families of HUNGARY, NORWAY, and POLAND.

During Yaroslav's reign, Kiev saw an upsurge in learning and art. In 1030, he began the first school in Novgorod. Scholars who emigrated to Kiev translated Greek and Latin texts into the native Slavic language. Cathedrals named for the Wisdom of God were built in Novgorod and Kiev; Kiev alone had some 400 churches.

Early in his reign, Yaroslav also built new city walls for Kiev. The "Golden Gate" (Russian legend claimed that tolls were paid in gold) fortified Kiev against enemy attack.

Near the end of his life, Yarolsav helped to draft the *Ruskais Pravda,* the first codified law in Russia, which served as a model for similar codes elsewhere.

Yaroslav's death in 1054 precipitated tension within Kiev. Smaller city-states broke away from their confederation and Yaroslav's heirs were incapable of asserting leadership. By 1240, Kiev was so weakened that it proved an easy target for a band of Asiatic MONGOLS, who invaded and sacked Kiev. (*See* RUSSIA.)

YUGOSLAVIA

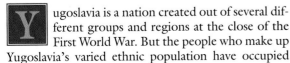

Yugoslavia is a nation created out of several different groups and regions at the close of the First World War. But the people who make up Yugoslavia's varied ethnic population have occupied that region of Europe for hundreds of years.

The basic makeup of the population occupying the region during the Middle Ages was Slavic, Serbian, and Croatian. The Slavs were first in the region, and the southern Slavs ("yugoslavs") constitute part of the ancestry of today's Serbians, Croatians, and Slovenes. Originally a nomadic people, they eventually became farmers, but all land was held communally. Not until the late Middle Ages, when nobles gave away land to those they favored, would Slavic law reflect the need to recognize private land ownership. (*See* SLAVS.)

By about the sixth century, groups from the East—it is believed most likely from Iran—began to settle in the Balkan region. The two main groups were the Serbs and the Croats. They assimilated into Slavic culture quickly.

Croatia, which borders the Adriatic Sea, had the benefit of sea trade, though the major cities were under Byzantine control. Later, the key port of Dubrovnik would become a seat of Croatian culture, but as a Byzantine protectorate rather than a Croatian city.

Both the Serbs and the Croats had to contend with attacks from their neighbors—Bulgarians and MAGYARS in particular. In the tenth century, the various lands that made up Croatia (including Dalmatia and Pannonia) were united under the leader Tomislav, who was the first to be called king by his people. For the next 200 years Croatia flourished. It became a leader in trade and spent lavishly on culture and the arts. Serbia, meanwhile, found itself disintegrating until a new, strong dynasty was formed in the eleventh century. The Serbian king Vukan, who reigned at the end of the twelfth century, tried to expand Serbia's holdings by annexing regions such as Macedonia, which were under Byzantine control.

Byzantine CHRISTIANITY had been introduced into the region around the sixth century; by the end of the Middle Ages most of the population was EASTERN ORTHODOX. (*See* EASTERN ORTHODOX CHURCH.)

As the Middle Ages drew to a close, so did independence for Serbia and Croatia. Serbia managed to remain independent until the OTTOMANS conquered the Byzantines in 1453. Afterward, Serbia became a part of the Ottoman Empire. Croatia, too, eventually fell into Ottoman hands, but it had been conquered by HUNGARY nearly 300 years earlier. From 1107 until the Ottoman conquest, the king of Hungary was also the king of Croatia. Even as a part of the Ottoman Empire, however, the Serbs and Croats maintained both their cultural and religious identity (although some did convert to ISLAM). The region remained part of the Ottoman Empire until it was officially dismantled at the close of the First World War.

INDEX

Article titles appear in **bold**. Image locations are indicated in *italic*. Major articles and general surveys are indicated in **red bold**.

Credits: The editors gratefully acknowledge the expert assistance and kind permission of Art Resource and Corbis-Bettmann for use of the following images: (All images listed are copyright © 1999 by the grantor.) Art Resource, NY: 12, 48, 212, 215, 257, 317, 363, 388, 448; Art Resource, NY/Alinari: 199; Art Resource, NY/Werner Forman: 89, 186, 315, 370, 426; Art Resource, NY/Giraudon: 15, 19, 27, 61, 69, 94, 118, 141, 160, 165, 170, 178, 216, 222, 251, 259, 289, 299, 303, 347, 348, 352, 366, 391, 415, 420, 434; Art Resource, NY/Image Select: 116; Art Resource, NY/Erich Lessing: 20, 82, 118,138, 153, 154, 208, 211, 230, 297, 424, 429; Art Resource, NY/The Pierpont Morgan Library: 35, 73, 80, 144, 180, 208; Art Resource, NY/Scala: 25, 37, 42, 47, 76, 75, 81, 84,87, 92, 110, 133, 147, 149, 163, 168, 194, 195, 239, 240, 269, 305, 316, 320, 322, 345, 398, 406, 414, 416; Art Resource, NY/SEF: 11, 373, 402; Art Resource, NY/Vanni: 211; Art Resource, NY/The Victoria & Albert Museum: 151, 220; Art Resource, NY/Visual Arts Library: 410; Corbis/Paul Almasy: 235; Corbis/Dave Bartruff: 46, 105; Corbis-Bettmann: 37, 39, 40, 48, 64, 74, 130, 131, 135, 137, 143, 146, 163, 164, 177, 204, 207, 213, 226, 236, 246, 249, 263, 271, 273, 276, 288, 293, 301, 312 331, 333, 356, 361, 383, 393, 396, 412, 424, 427, 440, 441; Corbis/David Lees: 143; Corbis/National Gallery Collection; By kind permission of the Trustees of the National Gallery: 235; Corbis/Gianni Dagli Orti: 22, 24, 50, 73, 127, 175, 226, 232, 342; Corbis/Philadelphia Museum of Art: 256.